International Dictionary of
LIBRARY HISTORIES

International Dictionary of
LIBRARY HISTORIES

VOLUME 1

Introductory Surveys

Libraries:
Ambrosiana Library
to
National Library of Brazil

Editor
DAVID H. STAM
University Librarian Emeritus
Syracuse University

FITZROY DEARBORN PUBLISHERS
CHICAGO · LONDON

Copyright © 2001
FITZROY DEARBORN PUBLISHERS

All rights reserved including the right of reproduction in whole or
in part in any form. For information, write to:

FITZROY DEARBORN PUBLISHERS
919 North Michigan Avenue, Suite 760
Chicago, IL 60611
USA

or

FITZROY DEARBORN PUBLISHERS
310 Regent Street
London W1R 5AJ
UK

British Library and Library of Congress Cataloguing in Publication Data are available.

ISBN 1-57958-244-3

First published in the USA and UK 2001

Typeset by City Desktop Productions, Franksville, Wisconsin
Printed by Edwards Brothers, Ann Arbor, Michigan
Cover design by Peter Aristedes, Chicago Advertising and Design, Chicago, Illinois

Cover illustration: The New York Public Library; copyright © New York Public Library; photo: Don Pollard

Dedicated
To the Memory of

Gladys Krieble Delmas (1913–1991)

And to my own colleagues and mentors who believed, with her, in the sharing of knowledge, its preservation and dissemination:

Robert Allen	Joseph C. Mitchell
Patricia Battin	Paul Mosher
Timothy H. Breen	Alice Prochaska
Richard W. Couper	Thomas Ragle
Arthur Curley	Robert Shackleton
David V. Erdman	Lacey Baldwin Smith
Vartan Gregorian	Deirdre C. Stam
Warren J. Haas	W. Lawrence Towner
Donald W. Krummel	James M. Wells
Patricia H. Labalme	Walter Muir Whitehill
Antje B. Lemke	Alexander Wilson
Richard Macksey	

CONTENTS

Editor's Note	*page* ix
Introduction	xi
Advisers and Contributors	xviii
List of Entries	xxi
Abbreviations	xxv
Introductory Surveys	3
Libraries: Ambrosiana Library to National Library of Brazil	185

EDITOR'S NOTE

Our purpose in preparing an *International Dictionary of Library Histories* is to provide a broad selection of institutional histories for many of the world's principal libraries and of other libraries having globally or regionally notable collections, innovative traditions, and distinctive and interesting histories. The work is organized into two sections of essays. The first is a series of 34 essays on various types of libraries ranging alphabetically from African American libraries to workers' libraries, together with 13 geographical essays on library development in regions of the world sporadically represented elsewhere in these volumes. The second and far larger section consists of a diverse selection of individual institutional histories of 224 libraries from throughout the world, from the Ambrosiana Library in Milan to the Zürich Central Library. All of the libraries included are functioning and open for business as we go to press, although a few may be closed for renovation (e.g., the Polish Library of Paris). Excluded are libraries, now extinct, such as those from Sumeria to late Roman times, and many other remarkable collections that no longer exist or have merged beyond recognition. Neither the long-lost Alexandrian Library nor the not quite established Alexandrina Library finds its place here. Also excluded are those remarkable libraries of the imagination so skillfully created by Jorge Luis Borges, Richard Brautigan, Elias Canetti, Umberto Eco, Arturo Pérez-Reverte, and other creative writers.

The process of selection was complex and not without difficulty. Initially the Board of Advisers reviewed a list prepared by the editor of more than 500 potential libraries to be considered for inclusion. The advisers in turn responded with their own lists of additions and deletions from the original list, yielding a slightly pruned list still too unwieldy for the planned scope of the project. Further consultation with the advisers resulted in the editor's final selections based on criteria of historical importance, size, quality, uniqueness, accessibility (although Mount Athos is surely an exception), and other more subjective factors. A few topics and libraries are not present because of difficulty in finding appropriate contributors. Although the resulting coverage clearly has an Anglo-American bias, recognizing our primarily English-speaking audience, it covers much territory and many institutions whose library histories are inaccessible or unfamiliar, at least in English.

Each of the historical essays on individual institutions includes a headnote giving the library's English name, its official name if different, address information (including the 2001 Web address if available), the year of founding, statistics of holdings, and selective listings of special collections. Within the last section of "Special Collections" we have tried to give an overview of the general strengths of the collection under the heading of "Areas of Concentration," although this has sometimes been omitted when the library tends toward fairly comprehensive collecting over all fields. Further selective listings of "Individual Collections" and of "Papers" of prominent individuals or institutions illustrate the institution's particularly important special collections.

The compilation of reliable statistics has been a vexing task, mainly because of the incomparability of much of the data. To avoid any impression of precision we have rounded all figures, except for incunabula, to the nearest thousand (see the editor's "Introduction"). All of the essays conclude with a section of "Further Reading" related to the specific topic or institution discussed.

Acknowledgments

My primary debts are to my commissioning editors in Chicago, first Carol Burwash and then Robert M. Salkin. To our distinguished Board of Advisers I am indebted for help in resolving many of the difficult issues of selection and in finding appropriate contributors for individual articles. The ultimate responsibility for both is mine. A remarkable group of contributors has made the work possible, and they have endured our editorial importunities with invariable good grace. Other staff at Fitzroy Dearborn—Beth Wittbrodt as editorial assistant, Anne-Marie Bogdan as bibliographer, and Ellen Brink as indexer—have been unfailingly helpful and a pleasure to work with. The dedication page conveys my continuing debt to a remarkable group of people whom I've been privileged to work with over the past 40 years.

DAVID H. STAM
Syracuse, New York
August 2001

INTRODUCTION

When Paul Schellinger, editorial director of Fitzroy Dearborn Publishers in Chicago, approached me in late 1997 with a proposal to prepare a compendium of library histories, I was just completing a lengthy library career, on the verge of retirement, and vulnerable to his request to take on a new project. Little did I know when accepting the assignment that the work would occupy the majority of my time for almost four years, involve me in a global email network, and provide enormous stimulation en route to the publication now in hand. The intent was to take advantage of the burgeoning field of library history in creating a major reference work of a scope without apparent precedent. In the English-speaking world the subject of library history has seen the development of two successful scholarly journals (*Library History* in Britain [1967–] and *Libraries and Culture* in the United States [1988–], superceding the *Journal of Library History* [1966–87]), the international growth of the Society for the History of Authorship, Reading, and Publishing (SHARP) and its annual volume of *Book History* (1998– ; also available electronically), and the initiation of several projects dealing with the history of the book in a number of English-speaking countries, for example, *The Cambridge History of the Book in Britain* (1999–), and similar works in Australia, Canada, Ireland, Scotland, the United States, and elsewhere, all linked in various ways to library history. The late-20th-century focus on book history has developed concurrently with a growing scholarly dependence on digital resources, a change that is profoundly affecting contemporary libraries and therefore their recent history. The proliferation of library history studies in western European countries can also be gauged by the activities of the International Federation of Library Associations (IFLA) Round Table on Library History and similar national organizations in France, Germany, Great Britain, and the United States.

There are a number of models on which this book relies, especially the broad-ranging but relatively brief entries in *Encyclopedia of Library History* (1994), edited by Wayne A. Wiegand and Donald G. Davis, and the magnificent German compendium edited by Bernhard Fabian, *Handbuch der historischen Buchbestände in Deutschland* (28 vols., 1992–2000), together with its Austrian (4 vols., 1994–97) and European (10 vols., 1998–2000) companions. Wiegand and Davis give capsule histories for approximately 60 specific libraries, chiefly national, but their book is more broadly concerned with general library issues than with individual histories. Fabian and his team have produced a monumental enumeration of German libraries by region and city, including brief essays on regional and urban library development, analytical sections of history, description, special collections, catalogs, archival sources, and publications, together with some statistics. Both are extremely valuable compilations. Colin Steele's *Major Libraries of the World: A Selective Guide* (1976) was an invaluable aid in our own selection of subjects. Most of the 32 libraries included in Anthony Hobson's *Great Libraries* (1970) are covered in our *International Dictionary of Library Histories*. Yet we have discovered no major reference work, certainly none in English, presenting narrative historical essays on the major libraries of the world. However selective we have had to be in meeting the constraints of cost and space, we believe this work to be the first of its kind.

Many of the institutions covered here have substantial published accounts noted in the sections of "Further Reading." Others have none. In fact the general search for recent material on research and scholarly libraries seems to reveal more speculation about their future than analysis of their historical past. Part of our intent is to redress that imbalance.

If not comprehensively global, this book does provide a wide sampling of the kinds of work now being pursued in library history from a variety of perspectives. The approaches of our contributors are almost as diverse as the libraries they describe. Some have concentrated on collection growth and loss, others on leadership and organizational change, some on problems, others on solutions. Some essays emphasize the current situation, especially for libraries of more recent foundation, including many of the more recent national libraries. We have tried to take a light editorial hand to these varying approaches while imposing some degree of consistency. Particularly compelling to the editor are those that relate a library's history to the social, political, and intellectual context in which the library developed.

From the great variety of these library histories, a number of common themes emerge clearly, and most of the entries reflect these common elements of library history. In simplistic terms it is fairly obvious what all libraries do, whether for the private collection of an individual, or a national library for an international audience. For library history purposes it is convenient to map these processes by "following the book," that is, to analyze all the things that can happen to a book (or to other media) in its library life: selection, acquisition, cataloging, classification or arrangement, physical processing (binding, marking, repair), shelving and storage, use and circulation, physical decay and subsequent repair or replacement by a surrogate, and on occasion withdrawal. Additional factors that make these processes more or less effective include administration, policy, staffing, reference services, facilities, security, finances, external relations, and technology. Taken together these themes cover the common ground of library history. What remains is the intellectual construct on which the whole is based, what constitutes the sometimes unique and often imitative nature of the library. It may be useful for some readers if we expand briefly on some of these themes.

Collections

At the heart of any library's history is the development of its collections, though it is possible to have an interesting history without significant extant collections. For some libraries major acquisitions become their defining moment, determining future directions. Part of the interest lies in the provenance of such collections, their sources in spoils of war, monastic confiscation, gift and exchange, temporary deposit or "permanent loan," but their primary interest lies in their contents.

Many of the libraries discussed here were intended at the outset as comprehensive, universal, encyclopedic, complete collections either of the entire universe of knowledge or particular segments of it. That was the idea behind the Alexandrian Library, the motivation of omnivorous private collectors such as John Dee (who built his private library for public use) and Sir Thomas Phillips (who wished to have one copy of every book ever printed), and for many of the great research libraries of modern Europe and North America. Representative was the position of the New York Public Library (NYPL) in the 1940s: "The ideal object of such a library is a complete record of human thought, emotion, and action. Its collections should be developed without distinction as to language, date, and place of publication. In short it should have everything."[1] Such aspirations have invariably included the caveat, "as resources permit" (as did the NYPL statement), and reality has seldom matched the ideal. A long cycle of price escalation, diminished purchasing power, expanded book production, changing patterns of funding, and collaborative attempts to overcome shortfalls had effectively buried the idea of comprehensive collections by the later 20th century.

Equally problematical is the demand that since libraries cannot have everything they must at least save everything they do have. The history of libraries no more supports that principle than its corollary desideratum of collecting everything. The issue reached flash point in the United States in early 2001 with the publication of Nicholson Baker's *Double Fold: Libraries and the Assault on Paper,* a polemic against the widespread library practice of discarding newspapers after microfilming. Although drawing attention to some important and often neglected issues of library preservation, Baker's argument largely ignored the exigencies of library funding "as resources permit" and deprecates the almost universal materials of libraries about space problems (so amply demonstrated in the following pages). Issues of library reformatting,[2] weeding, withdrawal, exchange, deaccessioning, and disposal are extremely problematical and often hazardous to the librarian, but it does seem foolish to argue, as some have, that the original selection decisions are any more infallible than the retention decisions that eventually must follow.[3] All such judgments are ultimately subjective.

Scholarly libraries today still covet and treasure the physical artifacts they have collected for millennia, but technology has diverted many librarians away from those primary materials to the development of electronic resources. For all the advantages that such resources bring to scholarship, their acquisition has tended to have an homogenizing, leveling effect among all scholarly collections, diverting from the pursuit of the unique and distinctive. Since many of these electronic resources are "acquired" on lease rather than by purchase, the library is left with no tangible asset at the end of the lease period, other than invoices for renewal. University and other research libraries at the beginning of the new century are beginning to recognize their responsibility for the electronic scholarship produced in their own institutions and are searching feverishly for a solution to the problem of long-term preservation of these information sources. Ironically, these very developments have inadvertently revived the idea of comprehensiveness in the idle and facile talk of computer mavens, administrators, and entrepreneurs who promise potential completeness for the digital world, often called "the Library of Congress in a shoebox." It remains to be seen whether these blandishments will lead to an information utopia or a dystopian Tower of Babel.

Cataloging and Classification

The history of cataloging is an essential sub-field of the history of libraries: a library without organization is no library, not even a warehouse.[4] The term denotes the orderly description of books and other materials according to national and international cataloging standards to assure the differentiation of any one book from any other. Modern technical jargon has renamed cataloging information *metadata*, that is, information about the data or material (author, title, subjects, place, publisher, date, etc.), information that traditionally appeared on catalog cards, in large printed books, or even in manuscript volumes.

Catalogers and librarians have been creating such metadata from time immemorial, from the cuneiform lists of Sumerian religious texts, through the bookish Renaissance, to the retrieval of today's favorite internet bookmarks. The development of these tools of access is not a neutral activity: their structures can say a great deal about the history, assumptions, purposes, biases, and fundamental worldview of any library, or even of the library's ignorance of them. A fairly simple example is the selection of terminology describing minority groups: Negroes or blacks, Indians or Native Americans, Eskimo or Inuit, aborigines or savages. The changing fashions of the politically correct often can be tracked by the selection of such headings in relation to date of publication or the period when cataloged.

Classification, in contrast to cataloging, deals with the organization of materials for location and retrieval according to some code of access, whether on physical shelves or by hypothetical arrangement in a database. In 1545 Konrad von Gesner, a Swiss naturalist whose previous work had been in the classification of fishes and quadrapeds, published the first volume of his *Bibliotheca universalis*, the first international and comprehensive bibliographical dictionary.[5] The first edition consisted of one volume of alphabetical entries by author's Christian name for all the books Gesner could locate by Latin, Hebrew, and Greek authors; a second volume covered the same material rearranged in 21 subject categories; the third dealt with theology; and a supplemental fourth volume appeared in 1555. The books themselves would be organized by size. Modern practice is a combination of Gesner's two contributions, subject arrangement with a few size subdivisions, according to various organizational schemes such as the Dewey Decimal Classification or that of the Library of Congress. Accustomed as we are to finding books organized by subject on library shelves, that system varies from Gesner's preference. Even today, size remains the primary criterion of shelving organization in many European and some North American scholarly libraries. Its advantages in optimum use of space, greater security, improved physical support of adjacent volumes, ease of maintenance, and lower cost of preparation have to be weighed against the disadvantages of inaccessibility in closed stacks, staff costs of retrieval, and limitations on unfettered browsing. Again, the history of classification theory and technique forms an integral part of library history, relating to the often-insoluble questions of access versus security, use versus survival, and the contrast between public needs and the librarian's convenience. Cost lies at the heart of these issues, mainly because the processes are so labor intensive.

Staffing

Sufficient labor has never been characteristic of libraries, and it is often surprising to read of the minimal staffing of some of the venerable early libraries. When Cambridge University Library in 1721 added to its staff of one librarian an additional proto-librarian, it was said that "the former's job was 'to lay books on the shelf' and the latter's 'to brush the dust of[f] them.'"[6] As libraries have grown in complexity, so have their personnel grown in expertise and sophistication as well as cost. It is fair to say that librarians have been at the forefront of development of standardized large-scale databases of unique materials and in the sharing of that information nationally and internationally. Many of those accomplishments are recorded in these volumes. Nonetheless, the librarian's image and status has troubled the profession for at least a century.[7] Numerically dominated by women who were generally absent from the roles of management, only in the last third of the 20th century have women achieved proportionate leadership in the field.[8] Salaries for librarians have also traditionally lagged behind other intellectual occupations, and it is often the social utility of libraries rather than monetary compensation that motivates library staff.

Security

The history of library theft has its own fascination,[9] constituting a sad litany of library loss. Tracing that history can be very difficult because institutions have traditionally preferred to cover up such losses, thinking they reflect badly on their stewardship of valuable materials. My own institution of Syracuse University experienced some major losses in the 1960s, typically an inside job (as has happened in recent years in other institutions such as the Chester Beatty Library, Boston College, and the University of Pennsylvania), yet the first public acknowledgment of the Syracuse thefts appears in these pages. Fortunately, librarians have come to realize that secrecy impedes the search for and retrieval of stolen books, and more recent practice is for full disclosure of such losses.

Preservation

In the stewardship of the patrimony that their collections represent, librarians face a paradoxical conflict between preservation and access; in pursuing their respective missions librarians inhabit an ambiguous area of concern between the welfare of their users and the welfare of their collections, the demands of the present and the expectations of posterity, if one may speak of the unknown. Sometimes these perspectives are not in conflict, but usually the competent librarian will have to forge some healthy balance between the two concerns. Librarians in scholarly research libraries will tend toward the conservative, arguing that relatively restrictive policies for collection use are in the best interests of their users, that care and protection are beneficial for both present and future users.

In any case, the issues of library preservation have become a worldwide preoccupation of research libraries during the past 30 years, often led by national libraries and corsortial efforts toward training, rationalization of potential duplicative activities, and research. Examples are the European Register of Microform Masters (EROMM) in Europe, and the activities of the Council on Libraries and Information Resources (CLIR) in the United States. The concern for the book and preservation of print continues, but inevitably the focus has shifted to concerns about other and more threatened media such as film, recorded sound, and digital collections. Much of the present impetus toward digitization of special collections lies in the preservation impulse to protect fragile materials from use and abuse, while making the content of those materials more widely available through their digital surrogates.

More general academic libraries tend to be hybrids of research collections and collections for wide and heavy use, close cousins to public libraries that, in the extreme, consume their resources and discard them when overused or when not used sufficiently. The balance is difficult to achieve; few institutions would support a library with perfectly preserved collections and no readers. That situation must be the province of the private collector, and even few of those want no readers at all. For all other libraries, the problems remain and grow as acquisitions come in faster than most libraries' ability to deal with their preservation requirements.

Statistics

Caveat lector: All library statistics should be regarded as impressionistic and flawed. The data sources for these volumes are the best available, including the *World Guide to Libraries* (15th ed., 2000);[10] the "Annual Library Statistics, 1998–99" of the Standing Conference of National and University Libraries (2000); *The World of Learning* (51st ed., 2001); for U.S. university libraries, *ARL Statis-*

tics, 1999–2000 (2001); reports made directly to the publisher from the libraries themselves; and occasionally library websites.

All these sources are dependent on the self-reporting of individual libraries and are not subject to independent assessment, other than by some common-sense comparisons. The problems lie not only in the natural inflation that comes with self-promotion or the political pressures (both in academia and government) to win preferment, but also in the varying ways in which materials are counted. Joseph Green Cogswell, the first librarian of New York's Astor Library, when asked how many books would be in the new library, demurred, finding it too difficult to count what should be called books—20 bound pamphlets in one volume, a periodical run in 20 volumes, ephemera, art objects. His facetious suggestion in 1848 was to measure holdings by weight (even the absorbent qualities of paper obviates that answer in different climates).[11]

Extensive duplication also skews library statistics and the ability to evaluate collections by numerical size. Stolen and missing volumes are seldom accounted for, nor are the books still on shelves but mutilated beyond use, or effectively lost through misshelving. Careful inventories and counts are expensive and seldom performed, except by very small libraries. There are at least four different ways of counting manuscripts and archives: by linear feet (itself an ambiguous measure); by individual item number, often yielding counts in the millions; by discrete collections; and variations of these three, separating autographs, medieval manuscripts, and literary and other archives into different categories. A good example of the problem is the practice of some Russian libraries to count medieval manuscripts as those produced through the early 18th century and the end of Old Church Slavic, a far different measure from other western practices. Such discrepancies can easily be spotted throughout these volumes.

Most problematic are the Soviet-era libraries where regulations promulgated in the 1920s required that periodical issues normally be counted as separate volumes, thus giving some apparently astronomical figures for what would otherwise seem modest collections (e.g., the Scientific and Technical Library of Kazakhstan claims more than 23 million volumes and 17 million microforms, figures to be regarded with some skepticism). Incentives to improve rankings and to meet hypothetical quantitative targets of planning bodies are open inducements to statistical manipulation resulting in further inaccuracies, even in the most respectable of institutions. Nor are definitions uniform: does the National Library of Thailand's claim, for example, of 10,000 incunabula (see *World Guide to Libraries,* which also lists 11,500 incunabula for the National Library of Armenia) meet some definition other than complete pre-1500 printed books? By contrast, what should we make of the Parliamentary Library of Tuvalu in Funafuti, which lists all of 600 volumes and 12 periodicals? Another problem is the difficulty of coordinated counting of the collections of extremely decentralized libraries with their branches and institute libraries. Many of these units are autonomous from their umbrella institutions and find no compulsion toward statistical responsibility.

Few library statistics convey any sense of quality in the collections they purport to analyze. Even the figures for incunabula, for which we have presented fairly precise counts, are misleading as to quality, given the variables of uniqueness, rarity, parchment copies, condition, illustration, and completeness. Some of the smallest libraries described in the *International Dictionary of Library Histories* have the highest density of extraordinary materials (e.g., the Chester Beatty Library or the Folger Shakespeare Library). An opposite problem was faced by many post-Soviet libraries in carrying out widescale projects to cull large accumulations of publications of government propaganda, an interesting conundrum of censoring the censored for practical non-ideological reasons. The lesson is that these numbers should always be regarded as approximations, estimates of size but certainly not quality. What counts in the end is not how much enters a library but what emerges from it: the increase in learning, the growth of knowledge, the dissemination of scholarship; the inspiration of the inquiring mind; the mundane and the profound reflections of any library user.

Growth and Space

Whatever their flaws, library statistics do reflect a certain reality. For all libraries that share aspirations to conserve the records of the past, the reality of constant growth is matched by the inexorable need for additional space to house the growing collections. It is axiomatic that any library will outgrow its available space, and that more space or reduced holdings must follow. The rapidity of growth in the second half of the 20th century in both the United States and the Soviet Union reflected their race for scientific superiority, and the rapidly expanding collections in both spheres. Symbolic of this growth has been a major Library of Congress project over the last 20 years to catalog its massive "arrearages," including large numbers of books in unidentified languages.

Various strategies have been used over a long period of time to deal with the problem: size classification was intended as a space saver, as were compact storage and remote storage approaches. Miniaturization to reduce materials to film or digital form has been effective but criticized in some cases for failing to retain originals (to do so would mean losing the space advantage). Redefinition of scope and narrowing of collecting scope to concentrate on specific fields, often accompanied by severe weeding of out-of-scope materials, has mitigated the problem for some institutions, as has the proliferation of branch libraries, spreading resources more widely, and in the extreme, zero-growth policies in which libraries allow no additions without corresponding withdrawals. Coordinated collection development within regions, countries, or among comparable libraries has also helped spread the burden, with increasing use of collaborative remote storage facilities. Essays throughout these volumes amply document the problem of building facilities commensurate to the growing collections. Promises of miniaturization, or even downsizing, allow administrators to hold out temporarily against the forces of new construction, but eventually a case will be made that inexorable growth must be accommodated.

Loss and Decay

Time the destroyer is time the preserver.
—T.S. Eliot, "The Dry Salvages," *Four Quartets*

Paradoxically, all of this growth continues despite the draconian Malthusian ways of bibliographic population control noted throughout these essays: war and the spoils of war, earthquakes, book burnings, censorship, monastic suppressions, vermin, ideological and ethnic warfare, iconoclasm, intentional disposal and unintentional neglect, and sheer indifference. All have played a role in the reduction and destruction of libraries throughout history. Some revive after total destruction: the libraries of the Benedictine Abbey of Monte Casino, a major force in Middle Age book production and its survival into the Renaissance, were destroyed no fewer than five times, most recently during World War II. Appropriately enough the abbey's symbol is the phoenix and the library continues, although never the same. Similarly, the National Library of Bosnia and Herzegovina at Sarajevo was virtually destroyed in 1992, a victim of war and conflicting ideologies, but it is now building new collections with international assistance.

The litany of library destruction is indeed dismal: beginning before Alexandria the devastation is continuous. A few examples may seem invidious since the phenomenon is so widespread, but here are some at random. In Iberia there were fewer books at the end of the Middle Ages than there had been in the 1200s. The 17th-century library of the Cathedral in Seville had 20,000 volumes, burned by the French in 1808. The Royal Library of Sweden burned twice in the 17th century; the Escorial in 1671; the University of Copenhagen in 1718; Moscow University in 1812. Slovenian libraries were hit by earthquake in 1855 and by German bombers in 1944. The Bavarian State Library lost a quarter of its collection in 1943, while the University in Leipzig lost most of its buildings and much of its collection at the same time. The Catholic University of Louvain has its own particularly sad but courageous story. Among North American libraries, Harvard (1764), the Library of Congress (1815 and 1851), and the University of Toronto (1890) can be cited for major fires. Stanford University has suffered fire, flood, and earthquake during the last quarter century: the list goes on—these are not isolated examples.

These libraries still exist in some form. They are far outnumbered by those that have disappeared altogether, from Ancient Mesopotamia, from Ninevah to Caesarea, from Anglo-Saxon England, from medieval Europe, from early Egypt to Nazi confiscations and Stalinist seizures. Much as we might deplore recent cultural destruction by the Afghan Taliban, it is wrong to think of such iconoclasm as a recent phenomenon. Or that the decay of the works of Osymandius was an aberration.

Conclusion

It would be easy to take the optimistic view that, despite the magnitude of loss over time, there are sufficient shards of the past to reconstruct the essentials of that past, that the evidence that survives is in constant reevaluation in any case, and we can be thankful for what we have. Against that view we have to end with a strong caution. The migration of evidence of the past into electronic form is still a gradual process, and for the most part libraries attempt to retain the original sources (paper manuscripts and archives). But as new forms of the records of civilization come into existence only in electronic form, and as the uncertain longevity of that evidence continues, we face the very real possibility, even probability, of the outright loss of ever-greater parts of the human record. My fear is that, as it has with our natural environment, the need for instant gratification and profit will lead to long-term impoverishment, however useful the new resources are.

In the final analysis, libraries appear to be many things to many people. Part of their role is symbolic, to represent the power and prestige of their nation, their university, their municipality.[12] Renaissance princes saw their collections as symbols of power just as their industrial counterparts in the early 20th century saw their accretions as symbols of temporal cultural power. University library rankings are thought to indicate their status in the academic world. Public libraries throughout the world were and continue to be symbols of open society and are therefore judged according to their accessibility. All of these symbols shine more or less brightly as governments, administrations, financial resources, and popular mores fluctuate and heighten or lessen the concern for library access. Despite their dismaying history of loss, libraries have shown an enduring quality that will continue if we learn the lessons offered by library histories such as these.

DAVID H. STAM
Syracuse, New York
August 2001

Notes and References

1. Roland A. Sawyer, "Selection of Books in the Reference Department of the New York Public Library," *College and Research Libraries* 16 (1944): 20.

2. For an extensive discussion of this issue see *The Evidence in Hand: The Report of the Task Force on the Artifact in Library Collections* (Washington, D.C.: Council on Library and Information Resources, 2001).

3. David H. Stam, "'Prove All Things: Hold Fast That Which Is Good': Deaccessioning and Research Libraries," *College and Research Libraries* 43 (January 1982): 5–13.

4. But see Richard Brautigan's *The Abortion: An Historical Romance, 1966* (New York: Simon and Schuster, 1972), an imaginary work that features a "library" in which authors are invited to place their works in any location of their choosing.

5. Donald W. Krummel, "Gesner, Conrad," in *ALA World Encyclopedia of Library and Information Services*, ed. Robert Wedgeworth (Chicago: American Library Association, 1980), 218–19.

6. David McKitterick, *Cambridge University Library: A History* (Cambridge: Cambridge University Press, 1986), 169–70.

7. Christopher Hitchens provides a timely example in his review of *The Intellectual Life of the British Working Classes*, by Jonathan Rose, *The Times* (London), 25 July 2001: "The current scene would depress the old disputatious artisans as much as it would discountenance Matthew Arnold; is it possible to think of an occupation in our present culture that carries less prestige than that of librarian?"

8. One curious by-product of this work is a long list of librarians, famous for far different reasons from their roles as librarians. It is presented here for the amusement of the idle reader, including the library where the person served: Pope Pius XI (Vatican Library); August Strindberg (Royal Library of Sweden); philosophers Gotthold Ephraim Lessing and Gottfried Leibnitz (Herzog August Library), David Hume (Advocates' Library, Edinburgh), George Berkeley (Trinity College Library, Dublin), and Johann Herder (Bibliotheca Regensis in Weimar); Argentinean author Jorge Luis Borges (National Library of Argentina); novelist Angus Wilson (British Museum Library); poets Philip Larkin (University of Hull) and Archibald MacLeish (U.S. Library of Congress); the brothers Grimm (University of Göttingen); Marcel Duchamp (Sainte Geneviève Library); Yale University president Ezra Stiles (Redwood Library); University of California Berkeley and Johns Hopkins University president Daniel Coit Gilman (Yale University Library); Casanova de Seingalt (for the Count of Waldstein, Bohemia); Chairman Mao Zedong (Peking University Library); and Whitaker Chambers (New York Public Library).

9. Nicholas Basbanes, *A Gentle Madness* (New York: Holt, 1995).

10. The *World Guide* lists over 42,000 libraries and understandably disclaims any liability for errors or omissions in their brief entries. We should do the same.

11. Joseph Green Cogswell, *Life of Joseph Green Cogswell As Sketched in His Letters* (Cambridge: Riverside Press, 1874.)

12. See Thomas Richards, *The Imperial Archive: Knowledge and the Fantasy of Empire* (London and New York: Verso, 1993).

ADVISERS

Basbanes, Nicholas A.
Carpenter, Kenneth E.
Cole, John Y.
Dain, Phyllis
Fabian, Bernhard
Haeger, John W.
Jakubs, Deborah L.
Joyce, William L.
Kasinec, Edward

Krummel, D.W.
Mosher, Paul H.
Prochaska, Alice
Rütimann, Hans
Vaisey, David
Wiegand, Wayne A.
Willison, Ian R.
Zorzi, Marino

CONTRIBUTORS

Allworth, Edward A
Anghelescu, Hermina G.B.
Ashby, Anna Lou
Ashton, Jean W.
Aubertin-Potter, Norma A.
Awcock, Frances H.
Balazic, Dare
Basbanes, Nicholas A.
Baur, Siegfried
Beam, Kathryn L.
Bell, Alan
Bodmer, Jean-Pierre
Boone, Jennifer
Bradley, Bruce
Browar, Lisa M.
Brown, Iain Gordon
Bürger, Thomas
Bussi, Angela Dillon
Calff, Josje S.
Calvert, Philip J.
Carpenter, Kenneth E.
Carroll, Carol Anne
Chase, Lynne C.
Cho, Chansik

Chou, Yu-Lan
Coates, Peter Ralph
Cole, John Y.
Cook, J. Frank
Coop, Bronwyn V.
Cossard, Patricia Kosco
Crandall, Ralph J.
Cronenwett, Philip N.
Crowe, William J.
Cubbage, Charlotte A.
Dain, Phyllis
Dalbello, Marija J.
Damen, Jos
Davidson, Russ T.
Davies, Martin
Davis, Donald G., Jr.
Davis, Robert H.
De Vos, Wim
Donlon, Patricia
Duggan, Mary Kay
Eaton, Nancy L.
Ebeling-Koning, Blanche T.
Edelman, Hendrik
Eide, Elisabeth S.

Elliott, Vic
Engel, Ryan T.
Engst, Elaine D.
Ermel, Malle
Evans, Gwynneth
Fiering, Norman
Freeman, Robert S.
Freshwater, Peter B.
Fullerton, Jan
Gabel, Gernot U.
Galli, Christof
Garrett, Jeffrey
Gaynor, Edward
Go, Susan
Grealish, William
Green, James N.
Grendler, Marcella
Groebli, Fredy H.
Grossman, Sarah
Gruys, J.A.
Gwinn, Nancy E.
Häkli, Esko E.
Haller, Bertram
Hallewell, Laurence
Harris, Ian
Harris, Philip R.
Hayes, Helen
Hazen, Dan C.
Heaney, Henry
Heilbrun, Margaret
Heinzer, Felix
Helenese-Paul, Kathleen
Hench, John B.
Henchy, Judith
Herkovic, Andrew C.
Hoare, Peter
Holmes, Fontayne
Holzenberg, Eric J.
Horstbøll, Henrik
Huemer, Christina
Imnadze, Eter
Jackson, William Vernon
Joel, Jonathan
Jones, Peter M.
Jónsson, Steingrímur
Joseph, Jennifer M.
Joyce, William L.
Kasinec, Edward
Kawasaki, Yoshitaka
Khvedeliani, Nana
King, Cornelia S.
Kingsley, Nicholas
Kishi, Miyuki
Kloosterman, Jaap
Kolbet, Richard M.

Kreslins, Janis A., Sr.
Kreslins, Janis, Jr.
Krummel, D.W.
Kuhta, Richard J.
Lajeunesse, Marcel
Landon, Richard
Lara, Elmelinda
Larsgaard, Mary L.
Lee, Hwa-Wei
Lemke, Antje Bultmann
Lewis, Nancy R.
Li, Guoqing
Line, Maurice B.
Lotman, Piret
Loup, Jean L.
Luck, Rätus
Luft, Eric v.d.
Lüthi, Christian
Lynden, Frederick C.
Macksey, Richard
Madden, Lionel
Malone, Cheryl Knott
Manning, Martin J., Jr.
Marcum, Deanna B.
Mark, Niels
Massil, Stephen W.
Matthews, Linda M.
Maylone, R. Russell
McCarthy, Muriel
McCrank, Lawrence J.
McCurdy, Linda
McKitterick, David J.
McNally, Peter F.
McNiven, Peter
Mehr, Kahlile B.
Meredith, Michael
Meyer, Daniel
Miller, Sara F.
Mills, William J.
Molz, Kathleen
Monnier, Philippe M.
Morris, Nancy
Morrish, Peter S.
Mosher, Paul H.
Navickiene, Aušra
Naylor, Bernard
Nelles, Paul
Nikolaev, Nikolaj I.
Nonack, Stephen Z.
Olson, Michael P.
Parks, Margaret E.
Pearson, David
Peltier-Davis, Cheryl Ann
Penney, Christine L.
Pennington, Kenneth

Peterson, Lorna
Poon, Paul W.T.
Powell, Michael
Prietto, Carole A.
Raffelt, Albert
Reidy, Denis V.
Reidy, Susan
Reimo, Tiiu
Reinitzer, Sigrid
Reiter, Manuela M.
Riedinger, Edward A.
Robillard, Sylvain
Rodriguez, Ketty
Rogan, Mary Ellen W.
Rose, Jonathan
Saunders, E. Stewart
Schiff, Judith A.
Schlechter, Armin
Schmidt-Glintzer, Helwig R.H.
Seissl, Maria
Seymour, Chaim
Shefrin, Jill
Sherry Rich, Margaret M.
Shih, Virginia Jing-yi
Shipp, John
Shpilevaia, Lyudmila
Shuler, John A.
Siemaszkiewicz, Wojciech
Simpson, Donald B.
Singh, Gurnek
Singh, Jagtar
Smith, Dennis

Stam, Deirdre C.
Steele, Colin R.
Stewart, David R.
Stollberg, Jochen
Stout, Leon J.
Streit, Samuel
Sullivan, Larry E.
Taglienti, Paolina
Taher, Mohamed
Taitt, Glenroy R.P.
Torres, Victor F.
Traister, Daniel H.
Tucker, John Mark
Vaisey, David
Van Peteghem, Sylvia
Walker, Paula M.
Walsh, Anne T.
Walsh, Morag
Warburton, Eileen H.
Waterman, Sue
Wenzel, Sarah G.
Werner, Gloria S.
Whittaker, David J.
Wiegand, Wayne A.
Wiese, Hermann
Wilson, Myoung Chung
Winkler, Kevin B.
Wroble, Lisa A.
Yocum, Patricia B.
Zeng, Marcia Lei
Zorzi, Marino

LIST OF ENTRIES

INTRODUCTORY SURVEYS

African American Libraries
African Libraries South of the Sahara
Archives
Art and Architecture Libraries
Balkan Libraries
Bibliophile Society Libraries
Buddhist Libraries
Caribbean Libraries
Central American National Libraries
Central and Eastern European Libraries
Central Asian Libraries
Christian Libraries
Circulating Libraries and Reading Rooms
Digital Libraries
English School Libraries
Genealogical Society Libraries
Government Libraries
Historical Society Libraries in the United States
Iberian Libraries
Icelandic Libraries
Islamic Libraries
Jewish Collections and Jewish Libraries
Land-Grant University Libraries
Latin American National Libraries

Law and Legislative Research Libraries
Map Libraries
Medical Libraries
Medieval Libraries
Membership/Social/Subscription Libraries
Middle Eastern Libraries
National Libraries
Online Catalogs
Pacific Islands Libraries
Performing Arts Libraries
Polar Libraries
Prison Libraries
Private Libraries
Public Libraries
Renaissance Libraries
Royal Libraries
School Libraries and Media Centers
Science, Technology, and Engineering Libraries
South Asian Libraries
Southeast Asian Libraries
Special Libraries
Women's Libraries
Workers' Libraries

LIBRARIES

Ambrosiana Library (Biblioteca Ambrosiana)
American Academy in Rome Library
American Antiquarian Society
Archbishop Marsh's Library
Australian National University Library
Austrian National Library (Österreichische Nationalbibliothek)
Bavarian State Library (Bayerische Staatsbibliothek)

Birmingham Central Library
Bolton Library at Cashel
Boston Athenaeum
Boston Public Library
Brigham Young University Library
British Library
Brown University Library
Canada Institute for Scientific and Technical Information

Capitular Library of Verona (Biblioteca Capitolare di Verona)
Catholic University of Louvain Library (Katholieke Universiteit te Leuven/ Université Catholique de Louvain)
Center for Research Libraries
Charles University Libraries (Univerzita Karlova Knihovny v Praze)
Chester Beatty Library
Chetham's Library
Chicago Public Library
Chinese University of Hong Kong Library System
City and University Library of Bern (Stadt- und Universitätsbibliothek Bern)
City and University Library of Frankfurt am Main (Stadt- und Universitätsbibliothek Frankfurt am Main)
City University of Hong Kong Library
Columbia University Libraries
Complutensian University Library and Madrid's Academic Libraries (Biblioteca de la Universidad Complutense de Madrid)
Cornell University Library
Dartmouth College Library
Documentation and Information Center of the Chinese Academy of Sciences
Duke University Libraries
Durham Dean and Chapter Library
Durham University Library
Edinburgh University Library
Emory University Libraries
Enoch Pratt Free Library
Estense University Library, Modena (Biblioteca Estense e Universitaria, Modena)
Estonian Academic Library (Eesti Akadeemiline Raamatukogu)
Eton College Library
Family History Library
Folger Shakespeare Library
Free Library of Philadelphia
Free University of Amsterdam Library (Universiteitsbibliotheek Vrije Universiteit Amsterdam)
Fudan University Library (Fudan Daxue Tushu Guan)
Georgian State Public Library
German National Library (Die Deutsche Bibliothek/Deutsche Bibliothek Frankfurt am Main/Deutsche Musikarchiv Berlin)
Glasgow University Library
Göttingen State and University Library, Lower Saxony (Niedersächsische Staats- und Universitätsbibliothek Göttingen)
Grolier Club Library
Harvard University Library
Helsinki University Library/National Library of Finland (Helsingin Yliopiston Kirjasto/Helsingfors Universitetsbibliotek)
Herzog August Library Wolfenbüttel (Herzog August Bibliothek Wolfenbüttel)

Historical Society of Pennsylvania
Howard University Libraries
Huntington Library, Art Collections, and Botanical Gardens
Indiana University Libraries
International Institute of Social History (Internationaal Instituut voor Sociale Geschiedenis)
Jagiellonian Library (Biblioteka Jagiellońska)
Jewish National and University Library (Bet Ha-Sefarim Ha-Leummi Weha-Universitai)
John Carter Brown Library
John Rylands University Library of Manchester
Johns Hopkins University Libraries (Including the George Peabody Library)
Kyoto University Library (Kyoto Daigaku Toshokan)
Latvian Academic Library (Latvijas Akadēmiskā bibliotēka)
Laurentian Library of the Medici (Biblioteca Medicea Laurenziana)
Leeds University Library
Library Company of Philadelphia
Library of Congress of the United States
Library of the Royal Palace, Spain (Real Biblioteca)
London Library
Los Angeles Public Library
Luis Angel Arango Library (Biblioteca Luis Angel Arango)
Lund University Library (Lunds Universitetsbibliotek)
Malatestiana Library, Cesena (Biblioteca Comunale Malatestiana, Cesena)
Manchester Public Libraries
Mazarine Library (Bibliothèque Mazarine)
McGill University Libraries
Mitchell Library
Moscow M.V. Lomonosov State University A.M. Gor'kii Scientific Library (Nauchnaia biblioteka im. A.M. Gor'kogo Moskovskogo gosudarstvennogo universiteta im. M.V. Lomonosova)
Mount Athos Monasteries Libraries
Municipal Library of Lyons (Bibliothèque municipale de Lyon)
National Agricultural Library of the United States
National and University Library of Bosnia and Hercegovina (Nacionalna i univerzitetska biblioteka Bosne i Hercegovine)
National and University Library of Croatia (Nacionalna i sveučilišna knjižnica)
National and University Library of Strasbourg (Bibliothèque Nationale et Universitaire de Strasbourg)
National Art Library, Victoria and Albert Museum
National Central Library (Republic of China; Kuo-li chung-yang t'u-shu-kuan)
National Diet Library of Japan (Kokuritsu Kokkai Toshokam)
National Libraries of Italy
National Libraries of Korea (Gungnip Jungang Doseogwan/Gukhoe Doseogwan)
National Library of Australia
National Library of Brazil (Biblioteca Nacional)

National Library of Canada
National Library of Chile (Biblioteca Nacional de Chile)
National Library of China (Zhongguo Guojia Tushu Guan)
National Library of Cuba, José Martí (Biblioteca Nacional José Martí)
National Library of Estonia (Eesti Rahvusraamatukogu)
National Library of France (Bibliothèque nationale de France)
National Library of India
National Library of Indonesia (Perpustakaan Nasional Republik Indonesia)
National Library of Ireland
National Library of Latvia (Latvijas Nacionālā bibliotēka)
National Library of Lithuania, Martynas Mazvydas (Lietuvos nacionalinė Martyno Mažvydo Biblioteka)
National Library of Mexico (Biblioteca Nacional de México)
National Library of New Zealand
National Library of Norway (Nasjonalbiblioteket)
National Library of Pakistan
National Library of Poland (Biblioteka Narodowa)
National Library of Portugal (Biblioteca Nacional)
National Library of Quebec (Bibliothèque nationale du Québec)
National Library of Romania (Biblioteca Națională a României)
National Library of Russia (Rossiiskaia natsional'naia biblioteka)
National Library of Saints Cyril and Methodius (Bulgaria; Narodna Biblioteka Sv. sv. Kiril i Metodii)
National Library of Scotland
National Library of South Africa
National Library of Spain (Biblioteca Nacional)
National Library of Thailand (Hosamut Hang Cha)
National Library of the Czech Republic (Národní knihovna České republiky)
National Library of the Philippines
National Library of the Republic of Argentina (Biblioteca Nacional de la República Argentina)
National Library of Ukraine, V.I. Vernads'kyi (Natsional'na biblioteka Ukrainy im. V.I. Vernads'koho)
National Library of Venezuela (Biblioteca Nacional Venezuela)
National Library of Vietnam (Thu Vien Quoc Gia/Thu Vien Khoa Hoc Tong Hop)
National Library of Wales (Llyfrgell Genedlaethol Cymru)
Newberry Library
New-York Historical Society Library
New York Public Library
New York State Library
Northwestern University Libraries
Ohio State University Libraries
Peking University Library (Beijing Daxue Tushuguan)
Pennsylvania State University Libraries
Pierpont Morgan Library
Polish Library of Paris (Bibliothèque Polonaise de Paris/Biblioteka Polska w Paryżu)

Princeton University Library
Public and University Library of Geneva (Bibliothèque publique et universitaire de Genève)
Public Library of the University of Basel (Öffentliche Bibliothek der Universität Basel)
Redwood Library and Athenaeum
Royal Library/National Library of Sweden (Kungliga Biblioteket, Sveriges Nationalbibliotek)
Royal Library of Belgium/Royal Library Albert I (Koninklijke Bibliotheek van België/Bibliothèque royale de Belgique/Koninklijke Bibliotheek Albert I/Bibliothèque Royale Albert Ier)
Royal Library of Denmark (Det Kongelige Bibliotek)
Royal Library of the Netherlands (Koninklijke Bibliotheek)
Royal Monastery of El Escorial Library (Real Biblioteca del Monasterio de El Escorial)
Russian Academy of Sciences Library (Biblioteka Rossiiskoi Akademii nauk)
Russian State Library, Moscow (Rossiiskaia gosudarstvennaia biblioteka)
St. Andrews University Library
St. Gall Abbey Library (Stiftsbibliothek St. Gallen)
St. Petersburg State University Scientific Library (Sankt-Peterburgskii Gosudarstvennyi Universitet Nauchnaia Biblioteka)
Saxon State Library/State and University Library of Dresden (Sächsische Landesbibliothek—Staats- und Universitätsbibliothek Dresden)
Shanghai Library
Skokloster Castle Library (Skoklosters Slott)
Slovenian National and University Library (Narodna in Univerzitetna Knjižnica)
Smithsonian Institution Libraries
Stanford University Libraries
State and University Library (Århus, Denmark, Statsbiblioteket)
State Library of Berlin—Prussian Cultural Foundation (Staatsbibliothek zu Berlin)
State Library of New South Wales
State Library of Victoria
Swiss National Library (Schweizerische Landesbibliothek/Bibliothèque nationale suisse/Biblioteca nazionale svizzera/Biblioteca naziunala svizra)
Syracuse University Library
Tartu University Library (Tartu Ülikool)
Tbilisi State University Grigol Tsereteli Academic Library
Toronto Public Library
Trinity College Library Dublin
United States National Library of Medicine
University and City Library of Cologne (Universitäts- und Stadtbibliothek Köln)
University and State Library of Münster (Universitäts- und Landesbibliothek Münster)
University Library in Bratislava (Univerzitná knižnica v Bratislave)

University Library of Amsterdam (Bibliotheek van de Universiteit van Amsterdam)
University Library of Freiburg in Breisgau (Universitätsbibliothek Freiburg im Breisgau)
University Library of Ghent (Universiteitsbibliotheek Gent)
University Library of Graz (Universitätsbibliothek Graz)
University Library of Heidelberg (Universitätsbibliothek Heidelberg)
University Library of Leiden (Universiteitsbibliotheek Leiden)
University Library of Leipzig (Universitätsbibliothek Leipzig)
University Library of Munich (Universitätsbibliothek München)
University Library of Tübingen (Universitätsbibliothek Tübingen)
University Library of Utrecht (Universiteitsbibliotheek Utrecht)
University Library of Vienna (Universitätsbibliothek Wien)
University Library of Wrocław (Breslau) (Biblioteka Uniwersytecka we Wrocławiu/Biblioteka "Na Piasku")
University of Birmingham Library
University of British Columbia Library
University of California Berkeley Libraries
University of California Los Angeles Library
University of Cambridge Libraries: Cambridge University Library
University of Cambridge Libraries: Libraries outside CUL
University of Cambridge Libraries: King's College Library
University of Cambridge Libraries: Trinity College Library
University of Chicago Library
University of Coimbra Library (Biblioteca Geral da Universidade de Coimbra)
University of Florida George A. Smathers Libraries
University of Hawai'i at Manoa Library
University of Illinois Library
University of Iowa Libraries
University of Kansas Libraries
University of London Libraries
University of Melbourne Library
University of Michigan Libraries
University of North Carolina Libraries
University of Nottingham Library
University of Oxford Libraries: Bodleian Library
University of Oxford Libraries: Libraries outside the Bodleian
University of Oxford Libraries: All Souls Library
University of Paris Libraries: Sainte Geneviève Library (Bibliothèque Sainte Geneviève)
University of Paris Libraries: Sorbonne Library (Bibliothèque de la Sorbonne)
University of Pennsylvania Libraries
University of São Paulo Library (Universidade de São Paulo Sistema Integrado de Bibliotecas)
University of Sydney Library
University of Texas Libraries
University of Tokyo Library System (Tokyo Daigaku Toshokan)
University of Toronto Libraries
University of Virginia Library
University of Washington Libraries
University of Wisconsin Libraries
Uppsala University Library (Uppsala universitetsbibliotek)
Vatican Apostolic Library (Biblioteca Apostolica Vaticana)
Vilnius University Library (Vilniaus Universiteto Biblioteka)
Warsaw University Library (Biblioteka Uniwersytecka w Warszawie)
Washington University Libraries
Wellcome Library for the History and Understanding of Medicine
Württemberg State Library (Württembergische Landesbibliothek)
Yale University Library
Zürich Central Library (Zentralbibliothek Zürich, Kantons-, Stadt- und Universitätsbibliothek)

ABBREVIATIONS

Note: Many entries below are not truly acronyms or abbreviations;
there are no full names to which they correspond.

AALL	American Association of Law Libraries
AALS	Association of American Law Schools
ABI/INFORM	ProQuest Direct ABI/INFORM Global Text Retrieval System
ABINIA	Asociación de Bibliotecas Nacionales de Iberoamérica (Association of Ibero-American National Libraries)
ABN	Australian Bibliographic Network
ACIS	academic computing and information services
ACLIS	Australian Council of Libraries and Information Services
ACLS	American Council of Learned Societies
ACRII	*Anglo American Cataloging Rules,* 2nd edition (revised 1998)
ACRL	Association of College and Research Libraries (North America)
ACURIL	Association of Caribbean University, Research, and Institutional Libraries
AFML	Armed Forces Medical Library (USA)
AGRIS	Agricultural Research Information Service
AIM-TWX	Abridged Index Medicus Teletypewriter Exchange Network (NLM)
ALA	American Library Association
ALEPH	Automated Library Expandable Program (integrated library system marketed by ExLibris, Israel)
ALIA	Australian Library and Information Association (formerly the Library Association of Australia)
AMC	Archive and Manuscript Control (archival descriptions standards developed by RLG)
AML	Army Medical Library (USA)
ANZTLA	Australian and New Zealand Theological Library Association
APLA	Association of Parliamentary Libraries of Australasia
APLAP	Association of Parliamentary Librarians of Asia and the Pacific
APLIC/ABPAC	Association of Parliamentary Librarians in Canada/L'Association des Bibliothecaires Parlementaires au Canada
ARL	Association of Research Libraries (North America)
ARLIS	Art Libraries Society (UK)
ARLIS/NA	Art Libraries Society of North America
ARSC	Association for Recorded Sound Collections
ARTFL	Project for American and French Research on the Treasury of the French Language (University of Chicago)
ASLIB	Association for Information Management (London; originally Association of Special Libraries and Information Bureaux)
ATLA	American Theological Library Association
ATLAS	ATLA serials project
AVLINE	MEDLARS database (citations to post-1974 medical audiovisuals, NLM)

BALLOTS	Bibliographic Automation of Large Library Operations using a Time-sharing System (Stanford University)
Best-Seller	library management software program marketed by Best-Seller and used at the National Library of Quebec
BIALL	British and Irish Association of Law Libraries
BIAS	Bibliotheks-Ausleih-System (Siemens Library Circulation System)
BIS	bibliographic information system
BITNET	electronic networking system launched by CREN in 1986 for worldwide educational communication
BL	British Library (prior to 1973, the British Museum Library, or BML)
BML	British Museum Library
BN	Bibliothèque nationale (precursor of present-day BNF)
BNF	Bibliothèque nationale de France
BUILDER	Birmingham University Integrated Library Development and Electronic Resource project
CADIST	Centre d'Acquisitions et de Diffusion de l'Information Scientifique et Technique
CAGRIS	Caribbean Agricultural Information System
CANCERLIT	MEDLARS database (citations to post-1963 articles about cancer)
CAN/SDI	Canadian Selective Dissemination of Information
CARIS	Current Agricultural Research Information Service (India)
CARISPLAN	Caribbean Information System for Socio-Economic Planning
CASL	Council of Australian State Libraries
CASLIN	Czech and Slovak Library and Information Network
CATLINE	MEDLARS database (NLM)
CATNYP	New York Public Library OPAC
CDNL	Conference of Directors of National Libraries
CDNLAO	Conference of Directors of National Libraries in Asia and Oceania
CDS/ISIS	UNESCO database management system
CEN	Catalogus Epistularum Neerlandicarum
CENL	Conference of European National Libraries
CERL	Consortium of European Research Libraries
CERNET	China Education and Research Network
CIC	Committee on Institutional Cooperation (USA)
CIDC	Cornell Institute for Digital Collections
CIP	Cataloging in Publication
CISTI	Canada Institute for Scientific and Technical Information
CLAC	Centers for Reading and Cultural Activity (Côte d'Ivoire)
CLIO	Columbia Libraries Information OPAC
CLIR	Council on Library and Information Resources (Washington, D.C.)
CLR	Council on Library Resources (Washington, D.C.; predecessor of CLIR)
CLSI	circulation system marketed in the 1970s by Computer Library Systems, Inc.
CMLA	Cleveland Medical Library Association
CN MARC	Chinese MARC
CoBRA	computer and bibliographic record actions
COM	computer-output microfilm
COMLA	Commonwealth Library Association (Kingston, Jamaica)
COPAR	Cooperative Preservation of Architectural Records
CPA	Commission on Preservation and Access (Washington, D.C.; merged with CLR to form CLIR in 1994)
CREN	Corporation for Research and Educational Networking
CRL	Center for Research Libraries (Chicago)
Crolist	integrated library system in Croatia
CSIC	Consejo Superior de Investigaciones Científicas
CSTNet	China Science and Technology Network
CUNet	Caribbean Universities Network Project
CURL	Consortium of University Research Libraries (Great Britain)

CWIS	campus-wide information system
DDC	Dewey Decimal Classification
DEP	Division of Extramural Programs (NLM)
DFG	Deutsche Forschungsgemeinschaft (German Research Foundation, a federal German funding agency)
DHEW	Department of Health, Education, and Welfare (USA)
DIRLINE	Directory of Information Resources Online (NLM)
DLF	Digital Library Federation (USA)
DLO	Division of Library Operations (NLM)
DOBIS	an IBM integrated information system that flourished briefly c. 1985–95
DOCLINE	NLM document delivery database
DOS	disk operating system
DRA	Data Retrieval Associates (vendor of library automation systems, acquired by SIRSI 2001)
EAD	Encoded Archival Description
EARL	Consortium of Public Library Networking (UK)
EARN	European Academic and Research Library Network
ECRL	Eastern Caribbean Regional Library Association
ELHILL	MEDLARS online retrieval system
ELIS	*Encyclopedia of Library and Information Science* (edited by Allen Kent et al., 67 vols., including supplements, 1968–2000)
ELNET Consortium	Estonian Library Network Consortium
ENSSIB	École nationale supérieure des sciences de l'information et des bibliothèques (France)
ENVIS	Environment Information System (India)
ERNB	Estonian Retrospective National Bibliography
ESTC	*English Short Title Catalogue* (computer file, describes English or English-language imprints, 1473–1800, available through RLIN)
ETCL	Electronic Text Centre Leiden
ExLibris	Israeli vendor of ALEPH and ALEPH 500
FAUL	Five Associated University Libraries (New York)
FIAF	Fédération Internationale des Archives du Film (International Federation of Film Archives)
FOIA	Freedom of Information Act (USA)
FTP	file transfer protocol
FUNRES	Fundación para el Rescate del Acervo Documental Venezolano (Foundation for the Rescue of Venezuelan Documentary Materials)
Gabriel	European gateway to European national libraries online
Geac	Canadian library system vendor
GIS	geographic information system
GK II	*General Catalogue of Printed Books* (British Library)
GLADIS	University of California Berkeley Library OPAC
HABS	Historic American Buildings Survey
HARNET	Hong Kong Academic and Research Network
HEIDI	Heidelberger Bibliothecks-Informationssystem
HISTLINE	History of Medicine Online (NLM)
HKInChiP	Index to Chinese Periodicals of Hong Kong
HMD	History of Medicine Division (NLM)
HRAF	Human Relations Area Files
HTML	hypertext markup language
IALL	International Association of Law Libraries
IAML	International Association of Music Libraries
IBERMARC	Iberian MARC standards
ICA	International Council on Archives
ICT	information and computer technology (university computing organizations)
IFD	International Federation for Documentation

IFLA	International Federation of Library Associations and Institutions
IGI	International Genealogical Index
IGM	Internet Grateful Med (NLM)
ILL	interlibrary loan
ILS	integrated library system
INNOPAC	online library computer system of Innovative Interfaces, Inc.
INSDOC	Indian National Scientific Documentation Centre
IRLA	Independent Research Library Association (USA)
ISBD	International Standard Bibliographic Description
ISBD (ER)	International Standard Bibliographic Description (Electronic Resources)
ISBN	International Standard Bibliographic Number
ISO	International Standards Organization
ISP	Internet service provider
ISSN	International Standard Serial Number
ITI	International Theater Institute (UNESCO)
JLS	Jamaica Library Service
JSTOR	Journal Storage (online full-text database of scholarly journals)
KUINS	Kyoto University Integrated Information Network System
LAB	Library Association of Barbados
LACAP	Latin American Cooperative Acquisition Program
LAN	local area network
LATT	Library Association of Trinidad and Tobago
LC	Library of Congress (Washington, D.C.)
LCSH	Library of Congress Subject Headings
LDMS	library data management system
LEXIS/NEXIS	online information service for legal and other disciplines
LHNCBC	Lister Hill National Center for Biomedical Communications (NLM)
LIAJA	Library and Information Association of Jamaica (formerly the Jamaica Library Association, JLA)
LIAS	Library Integrated Access System (Pennsylvania State University)
LOCATORplus	NLM OPAC and bibliographic retrieval system
LSCA	Library Services and Construction Act (USA)
LSTRC	Literature Selection Technical Review Committee (MEDLINE)
MadCat	University of Wisconsin-Madison Libraries OPAC
MARBI	Machine-Readable Bibliographic Information (interdivisional committee of ALA that reviews and recommends standards for machine-readable forms of bibliographic information)
MARC	MAchine-Readable Cataloging (basic format of Anglo-American and other cataloging conventions adopted in other countries)
MEDCARIB	Caribbean database for medical libraries
MEDLARS	Medical Literature Analysis and Retrieval System (NLM)
MEDLINE	MEDLARS Online
MELVYL	University of California Berkeley Library System online database
MeSH	Medical Subject Headings (NLM)
MIRLYN	Michigan Records Library Network
MLA	Music Library Association (USA)
NACSIS	National Center for Science Information Systems (Japan)
NAIP	North American Imprint Project
NALDOC	National Agricultural Library and Documentation Centre (Hungary)
NARA	National Archives and Records Administration (USA)
NARESA	National Resources, Energy, and Science Authority (Sri Lanka)
NASK	Polish Research and Academic Network
NATIS	National Information Systems
NBINet	National Books and Information Network (Republic of China)
NCBI	National Center for Biotechnology Information (NLM)

NCFC	National Computing and Networking Facility of China
NDL	National Diet Library of Japan
NEH	National Endowment for the Humanities (USA)
NEHA	Netherlands Economic History Archive
NEHGS	New England Historic Genealogical Society (Boston)
NELINET	New England Library Network (regional consortium providing OCLC access and other services)
NICHSR	National Information Center on Health Services Research (NLM)
NIH	National Institutes of Health (USA)
NISO	National Information Standards Organization (USA)
NISSAT	National Information System in Science and Technology (India)
NLM	National Library of Medicine (USA)
NN/LM	National Network of Libraries of Medicine (NLM)
NNO	National Network Office (NLM)
NOTIS	Northwestern Online Totally Integrated System (originally developed by Northwestern University, NOTIS became an independent company in 1987 and was acquired by Ameritech in 1991; it now uses the system name Horizon)
NPAC	National Program for Acquisitions and Cataloging (LC)
NRC	National Research Council (Canada)
NRLF	Northern Regional Library Facility (University of California)
NSA	National Sound Archive (BL)
NSF	National Science Foundation (U.S. federal funding agency)
nTitle	new Technology in the Learning Environment (University of Iowa)
NYPL	New York Public Library
NZBN	New Zealand Bibliographic Network
NZLA	New Zealand Library Association
OASIS	Online Archival Search Information System (Harvard University)
OCCS	Office of Computer and Communications Systems (NLM)
OCLC	Online Computer Library Center, Inc. (the Ohio College Library Center, founded 1967, became OCLC, Inc., in 1977, then the OCLC Online Computer Library Center, Inc., in 1981; it acquired WLN in 1999)
OLIS	Oxford Libraries Information System
OPAC	online public access catalog
OSALL	Organization of South African Law Libraries
OVID	OVID Biomedical and Health Care Collections (Chinese University of Hong Kong)
PAC	Program of Preservation and Conservation (IFLA)
PDF	portable data format
Pica	Netherlands Center for Library Automation (commercial library information service in Leiden, acquired by OCLC, Inc., in 1999 and currently expanding its services in Europe, particularly in Germany)
PLC	Polar Library Colloquy
PORBASE	Base Nacional de Dados Bibliográficos (Integrated National Library/Union Catalog of Portugal)
PRO	Public Record Office (London)
PsycLIT	database of psychological literature
RLG	Research Libraries Group (international consortium of research libraries with primary programs dealing with shared resources, archives and manuscripts, cultural materials, and digital preservation)
RLIN	Research Libraries Information Network (the bibliographic utility of RLG)
RLIN AMC	Research Libraries Information Network Archives and Manuscripts Control System
SAA	Society of American Archivists
SAIBIN	Sistema Automatizado de Información de la Biblioteca Nacional (Venezuelan database)
SALALM	Seminar on the Acquisition of Latin American Library Materials
SATIS	Scientific and Technical Information Service (UK)
SBN	Servizio Bibliotecario Nazionale (National Library Service, Italy)

SCAUL	Standing Conference of African University Libraries
SCECSAL	Standing Conference of Eastern, Central, and Southern African Librarians
SCIPIO	RLIN database of art and rare book sales catalogs
SCOLCAP	Scottish Libraries Co-operative Automation Project
SCONUL	Standing Conference of National and University Libraries (UK)
SCURL	Scottish Confederation of University and Research Libraries
SDC	SAARC (South Asian Association for Regional Cooperation) Documentation Center
SDI	selective dissemination of information (current awareness services to inform users of new publications in their fields of interest)
SDRC	Scholarly Digital Resources Center (University of Iowa)
SEB	Sistema Español de Bibliotecas
SERLINE	MEDLARS serials database
SFX	library management program created at Ghent University, Belgium, now marketed by ExLibris
SGML	standard generalized markup language
SIAS	Siemens/SISIS Informations- und Ausleihsystem
SIBI/USP	Universidade de São Paulo Sistema Integrado de Bibliotecas
SIBMAS	Societè Internationale des Bibliothèques et Musèes des Arts du Spectacle (International Association of Libraries and Museums of the Performing Arts)
SIRSI	integrated library system marketed by SIRSI Corporation (acquired DRA 2001)
SIS	Division of Specialized Information Services (NLM)
SLA	Special Libraries Association
SLIC	Scottish Library and Information Council
SOCRATES	Stanford University online catalog
SOLINET	Southeastern Library and Information Network (regional cooperative providing access to OCLC and other services)
STC	*Short-Title Catalogue of Books Printed in English . . . and of English Books Printed Abroad 1475–1640* (edited by A.W. Pollard and G.R. Redgrave, et al., 1926; revised 1976–91)
STCN	*Short-Title Catalogue, Netherlands* (pre-1800 Dutch national bibliography, in progress)
SuDoc	Superintendent of Documents (USA) classification system
TLA	Theatre Library Association (New York)
TOFT	Theater on Film and Tape (New York)
TOXLINE	MEDLARS database (post-1977 citations of toxicological studies)
TRLN	Triangle Research Library Network (North Carolina)
TWIST	Teaching with Innovative Style and Technology (University of Iowa)
UDC	Universal Decimal Classification
UGL	undergraduate library
UMI	University Microfilms, Inc.
UNESCO	United Nations Educational, Scientific, and Cultural Organization
UNISYST	a world science information system developed by UNESCO
URBS	Unione Romana Biblioteche Scientifiche (Rome)
URL	Uniform Reference Locator (the address for Web home pages)
UTLAS	University of Toronto Library Automation Systems
VIA	Visual Information Access (Harvard University)
Voyager	Web-based library automation system marketed by Endeavor Information Systems, Inc.
VTLS	corporate name of the Virginia Tech Library System, a library system developed at Virginia Polytechnic and State University and now an independent company
WAIS	wide area information server
WALA	West African Library Association
WCTOP	World Confederation of the Teaching Profession Assemblies
WESTLAW	West Publishing Company online legal research system
WGL	*World Guide to Libraries* (15th ed., 2000)
WLN	Washington Library Network (now part of OCLC)

INTRODUCTORY SURVEYS

African American Libraries

The phrase *African American libraries* can be used to denote two different categories of institutions. It can refer historically to the libraries designed for use solely by African Americans during the era of legal racial segregation. Included were public libraries such as the Western Colored Branch of the Free Public Library Louisville (Kentucky) and the independent Durham Colored Library (North Carolina), which provided alternatives to the central public libraries that refused service to African Americans. Also included were academic libraries such as those at Tuskegee Normal and Industrial Institute (now Tuskegee University; Tuskegee, Alabama) and Fisk University (Nashville, Tennessee), institutions founded to help educate African American students after the Civil War.

The phrase also can refer to research libraries documenting African American life and culture with materials by and about blacks. The two categories overlap because some libraries founded in response to or as a result of segregation laws and traditions fought against racist stereotypes by amassing collections recording the richness of black experiences and expression. Those holdings now constitute some of the most significant collections of African Americana in existence.

In general, public libraries created to serve only African Americans began to desegregate during the civil rights era in the mid-20th century. As the demographics of city neighborhoods shifted and so-called urban renewal reconfigured the terrain, some of the buildings were sold or demolished and the collections and records dispersed or destroyed. One exception is Louisville's Western Branch, which remains in its original Carnegie building and still maintains its own archives and related holdings.

Other public library systems have developed significant collections for the study of black culture and life. The Detroit Public Library (DPL) in Michigan holds the Burton Historical Collection, an extensive local history collection donated in 1914 by attorney Clarence Monroe Burton. The collection includes material documenting African American life in Detroit as far back as 1795. Also at DPL is the E. Azalia Hackley Memorial Collection of Negro Music, Dance, and Drama. The Detroit Musicians Association established the collection, named after a local musician, in 1943 with a gift of original materials. The collection has since grown to include rare books, recordings, photographs, and substantive vertical files. Individual manuscript collections, including the papers of several prominent African American women, are also housed at DPL. Similarly, Illinois' Chicago Public Library (CPL) houses the Vivian G. Harsh Research Collection of Afro-American History and Literature at its Carter G. Woodson Regional Library. The collection was started by Harsh in 1932 when she became the first African American to head a branch of the CPL. The collection now totals more than 70,000 books, 500 periodical titles, and manuscript materials.

For the most part, the academic libraries founded during the age of segregation have survived, and their collections continue to nourish the literature of black studies. Among them are the holdings at Clark Atlanta, Fisk, Hampton, and Tuskegee Universities. In 1946 Atlanta University (which later merged with Clark College to form Clark Atlanta University) purchased the Henry P. Slaughter collection, which formed the basis for its special collection of Africana. From its earliest days, the library at Fisk acquired materials documenting African American experiences before 1865. In 1936 the university bought the complementary Southern YMCA College library in Nashville, Tennessee, with collection strength in the post-1865 period. From the 1940s through the 1960s, Fisk added a number of literary collections, including materials by Langston Hughes, Charles Waddell Chesnutt, and Jean Toomer. At Hampton Institute (now Hampton University) in Hampton, Virginia, George Foster Peabody donated more than 1,000 items by and about blacks to the library in 1908. Six years later the university purchased the Phil B. Brooks collection, totaling 10,000 items on slavery and Reconstruction. The library also collected papers documenting the lives of individuals involved in the institution, including Samuel C. Armstrong and Hollis Burke Frissell. The Peabody collection now includes more than 30,000 items by and about African Americans. At Tuskegee, the Hollis Burke Frissell Library, constructed in 1932, houses the Washington collection of rare books, first editions, and other materials by and about blacks, as well as the Tuskegee Institute archives. In 1968 the massive newspaper clipping files and other materials compiled at Tuskegee's Department of Records and Research were transferred to the Washington collection and archives. Manuscript collections of individuals associated with the institution include the papers of Robert Russa Moton and George Washington Carver.

Another important gathering place for African Americana is the Library of Congress in Washington, D.C., which houses the archives of the American Colonization Society, the National Urban League, the National Association for the Advancement of Colored People (NAACP), the papers of Booker T. Washington and other influential African Americans, and transcripts of slave narratives.

The most significant libraries grew not only out of institutional efforts but also out of the individual initiative of collectors who searched for and invested in the recorded cultural production and related materials of people of African descent. Scholars and others have used materials in these collections to produce thousands of books, articles, exhibitions, and films, attesting to the libraries' essential role in knowledge generation and cultural production. The following profiles briefly trace the histories of one public, one academic, and one independent research library as examples of the interplay of institutions and individuals in founding and maintaining libraries dedicated to collecting materials related to African American history, culture, and experience.

Schomburg Center for Research in Black Culture

Perhaps the best-known collection is that housed at the Schomburg Center for Research in Black Culture in New York City, with print and nonprint holdings documenting not only African American life but the African diaspora. The library is named for bibliophile Arthur Alfonso Schomburg, who was born in Puerto Rico in 1874 and moved to New York in 1891. Interested in black history, Schomburg began building his collection with purchases from used and antiquarian bookshops, auction houses, and other venues. At a time when works by black writers and artists were undervalued, Schomburg leveraged his clerk's pay to create a major collection documenting the African diaspora.

With the Harlem Renaissance of the 1920s, appreciation for African American literature and art increased. In 1925 the New York Public Library's (NYPL) 135th Street Branch in Harlem established a Division of Negro History, Literature, and Prints. The next year the library secured a $10,000 gift from the Carnegie Corporation for the purchase of Schomburg's collection of almost 3,000 volumes, more than 1,000 pamphlets, and numerous manuscripts and prints. Schomburg continued adding to the collection and served as its curator in the 1930s. After Schomburg's death in 1938, Lawrence D. Reddick served as curator until 1948, followed by Dorothy Williams' brief administration. Williams advocated positioning the Arthur A. Schomburg collection, as it was then called, more firmly in the research community. Jean Blackwell Hutson, who began working at the Schomburg in 1948 and served as its chief from 1972 to 1980, realized that goal during her tenure. Hutson capitalized on the resurgence of interest in black studies in the 1960s and involved individuals, organizations, and foundations in financially supporting the collection. In 1972 the NYPL transferred the collection from the Branch Libraries administrative division to the Research Libraries and renamed it the Schomburg Center for Research in Black Culture. In 1980 the center moved from the old 135th Street Branch into an adjacent new building it still occupies on Malcolm X Boulevard in Harlem. The research library now holds more than 5 million items in all formats, including art and artifacts.

Under the direction of Howard Dodson (1984–), the center has continued to collect materials by and about people of African descent. In addition to rare books and pamphlets, the center's holdings include such ephemera as antiapartheid posters, antislavery medallions, and photographs and music from the United States, the Caribbean, and South America. In keeping with Arthur Schomburg's desire to make his collection more widely available by housing it at the public library, the "Digital Schomburg" now makes images, texts, and exhibitions accessible on the Internet (www.nypl.org/research/sc/sc.html).

Moorland-Spingarn Research Center

Another major collection is housed at Howard University in Washington, D.C. In 1914 Howard alumnus and trustee Jesse E. Moorland donated to the university his collection of approximately 3,000 books, pamphlets, and other materials related to African and African American culture. In 1930 Howard graduate Dorothy Burnett Porter (later Dorothy Burnett Porter Wesley) became curator of what was then called "The Moorland Foundation, a Library of Negro Life," a post she held until her retirement in 1973. She envisioned the collection not only as a service to scholars researching black experiences but also as a means to inform and inspire African American students. Under Porter's direction, the library acquired activist attorney Arthur B. Spingarn's private collection of approximately 5,000 volumes in 1946. She subsequently augmented the Spingarn Collection of Negro Authors with the acquisition of the Spingarn Negro Music Collection in 1958, the largest such collection in existence at the time.

In addition to building the collections, Porter worked to provide greater intellectual access through various cataloging, indexing, and bibliography projects. Among the resources she compiled or helped to create were *A Catalogue of the African Collection at Howard University* (1958), *Journal of Negro Education: Index to Volumes 1–31, 1932–1962* (1963), *Negro Protest Pamphlets: A Compendium* (1969), and *The Negro in the United States: A Selected Bibliography* (1970).

In 1973 the university reorganized the Moorland and Spingarn collections, the Ralph J. Bunche Oral History Collection, the Black Press Archives, and the university museum and archives into a single administrative entity called the Moorland-Spingarn Research Center, with Michael Winston as director. To emphasize the research aspects of the collections, Winston created the Manuscript Division, later subdivided into manuscript, music, oral history, and prints and photographs units, where the papers of actor Paul Robeson, historian Rayford Logan, attorney Charles H. Houston, and other accomplished leaders reside. During the current administration of Thomas C. Battle, who joined the center in 1974 and became director in 1986, the archival and manuscript materials have grown to total more than 17,000 linear feet. Additionally, the center holds some 175,000 bound volumes as well as periodicals, newspapers, artifacts, photographs, maps, and audiotapes. In 1996 the center created a philanthropic organization called the Friends of the Moorland-Spingarn Research Center to encourage financial support beyond that provided by the university.

Amistad Research Center

An independent library, the Amistad Research Center (ARC) is located on the campus of Tulane University in New Orleans. Founded in 1966, it is the newest of the institutions described here but has in common with them an aggressive collecting stance. The American Missionary Association (which a century earlier had founded Fisk, Atlanta, Hampton, and other institutions of higher learning for African Americans) deposited its archives at Fisk University in 1947. The archives, now numbering more than 100,000 letters and numerous other records, formed the core of the ARC collection at Fisk, where history professor Clifton H. Johnson served as founding director. The ARC moved to the campus of Dillard University in New Orleans in 1969, and in 1987 to the Tulane campus.

The focus of the ARC collection is primary source material documenting the history of African Americans and other ethnic groups, particularly Native Americans, Latinos, and Asian Americans. The ARC also holds African and African American art, including the Aaron Douglas collection, featuring original works by Douglas, Hale Woodruff, Richmond Barthe, and Elizabeth Catlett, among others. The papers of Woodruff, Barthe, and Catlett are among the center's 450 manuscript collections, as are the papers of other important figures, such as civil rights activists Fannie Lou Hamer and Benjamin Hooks and writers Countee Cullen and Chester Himes.

Frederick L. Stielow, who served as the ARC's executive director in the mid-1990s, encouraged the use of electronic communication, and during his tenure the library launched its website (www.arc.tulane.edu). Donald E. DeVore, executive director from 1996 to 2000, oversaw a collection of more than 10 million documents, periodicals, newspaper clippings, and photographs.

In 1999 the center received a $186,000 grant from the federal Institute of Museum and Library Services to digitize 5,000 rare documents and images relating to the Amistad event and the American Missionary Association. Archival guides and teaching materials are also being created as part of this project, which is a collaboration between the center and the Louisiana State University Digital Library.

CHERYL KNOTT MALONE

See also Howard University Libraries; New York Public Library

Further Reading

Battle, Thomas C., "Moorland-Spingarn Research Center, Howard University," *Library Quarterly* 58 (April 1988)

Britton, Helen H., "Dorothy Porter Wesley: A Bibliographer, Curator, and Scholar," in *Reclaiming the American Library Past: Writing the Women In,* edited by Suzanne Hildenbrand, Norwood, New Jersey: Ablex, 1996

Johnson-Cooper, Glendora, "African-American Historical Continuity: Jean Blackwell Hutson and the Schomburg Center for Research in Black Culture," in *Reclaiming the American Library Past: Writing the Women In,* edited by Suzanne Hildenbrand, Norwood, New Jersey: Ablex, 1996

Josey, E.J., and Ann Allen Shockley, editors, *Handbook of Black Librarianship,* Littleton, Colorado: Libraries Unlimited, 1977

Malone, Cheryl Knott, "Accommodating Access: 'Colored' Carnegie Libraries, 1905–1925," Ph.D. diss., University of Texas at Austin, 1996

Sinnette, Elinor Des Verney, *Arthur Alfonso Schomburg, Black Bibliophile and Collector: A Biography,* Detroit, Michigan: The New York Public Library and Wayne State University Press, 1989

Wilkins, K.G., "At Age 32, the Amistad Center Is Poised for Attention," *American Libraries* 29 (January 1998)

African Libraries South of the Sahara

Many libraries existed in sub-Saharan African countries from the first quarter of the 19th century. Private and institutional libraries existed as early as the 16th century, particularly in Mali and Ethiopia, but planned development of libraries was rare until after the 1920s, with major growth occurring between 1960 and 1975. With some exceptions, the development of libraries in former British colonies seems to have been more rapid than in the former French, Belgian, Portuguese, and Spanish colonies, owing to historical differences in colonial policies and settlement patterns.

As of 1988 all but perhaps four or five of the sub-Saharan African countries had libraries of some kind. Approximately half of the countries in this region had established library networks, and several had very active and modern national library services.

Examples of Early Library Development by Europeans and Americans in Africa

In 1761 Joachim Von Dessin bequeathed his 4,000-volume private library to the Dutch Reformed Church to create a public library for the benefit of the community. In 1818 Charles Somerset, then governor of the Cape, set aside tax money to create the South African Public Library, which still houses Von Dessin's library. Subscription libraries existed in South Africa as early as 1838 and were later developed into a public library system.

Colonel Ralph B. and Ailsa Turner were instrumental in establishing rural circulating libraries for the Kenyan British colony in the early 1930s, with funding from the Carnegie Corporation and the American Library Association (ALA). Black and Indian Kenyans were excluded from this service until 1958, when the McMillan Library in Nairobi removed racial requirements for membership. The rural service ceased in 1963 with Kenya's independence. The Kenya National Library Service was founded in 1965 on the foundations of the East African Literature Bureau's Kenya presence, with funding from the British government.

In 1950 the South African Library Association asked Douglas H. Varley, librarian of the South Africa Library in Cape Town, to report on library service in the Rhodesias and in Nyasaland. The Varley report recommended a planned national free library system for the three territories, with a national council at government level, coordination between all libraries, and the creation of a union catalog. Backing for these ventures was not found immediately, although in the following decade coordination of research materials increased, and a union list of periodicals for the Federation of Rhodesia and Nyasaland was published in 1962.

Alan Burns, Ethel S. Fegan, and Kate Ferguson were some of the major figures in library development in Nigeria in the 1930s and 1940s. Libraries in Lagos were founded and supported by the Colonial Office and funded by the Carnegie Corporation; these were not racially exclusive by policy. Carl M. White, a specialist in library development for the Ford Foundation, was sent to Nigeria in 1962 to manage the founding of the National Library of Nigeria, which was established to serve government information needs, act as a national bibliographic center, and promote the development of libraries in Nigeria. One of White's early recommendations was the removal of the subscription charge instituted by Kate Ferguson at the Lagos public library. White was followed by two other advisors in succession, owing to the delay in appointing a library director. The position was finally filled by Deputy Director S.B. Aje after the Nigerian civil war. Under the 1970 National Library decree, branches were established in the states of Nigeria. By the mid-1970s the library employed 30 professional librarians and held 150,000 volumes and 2,500 journal subscriptions.

Public and School Libraries

The first national public library service established by statute in sub-Saharan Africa was the Ghana Library Service. It was provided for by the Ghana Library Board Act of 1948 and continues to set a standard of achievement for public libraries in Africa. Public library development escalated in the 1960s and 1970s, with local librarians trained abroad taking over management positions in the mid-1970s. But a decline followed in the 1980s and 1990s owing to economic problems and the removal of libraries as governmental priorities.

Students are often the greatest users of public libraries in sub-Saharan Africa, as elsewhere. If they exist at all, school libraries are often grossly inadequate in collections, facilities, and staff. Class textbooks may be the only reading material, and in many schools a few copies must be shared among a number of students. Many early founders of public libraries were opposed to the collection of textbooks, not wanting to see their reading rooms packed with local students. These attitudes have shifted in recent years. Very popular textbook libraries have been created in Zimbabwe and other countries, and collaborations between public and school libraries has begun.

In general, public libraries have started to invest in services that address the real information needs of their communities, including the needs of the illiterate or newly literate. These issues are currently the subject of lively and complex debates on the nature of African librarianship and libraries.

Literacy, Oral Culture, and Libraries

Prior to colonization, writing systems existed in various parts of sub-Saharan Africa but were limited in use and almost always took a secondary position to the dominant oral culture. African libraries were often founded to serve urban educated populations, not those of oral traditions, and in most cases were unsympathetic to the information needs of these populations.

Rural information and cultural centers are being created to find new approaches to reaching the general public with library service. These libraries or centers may lend books and other educational materials, provide reference services, screen films, and support many cultural activities. The most successful have significantly increased library use; good examples are the Centers for Reading and Cultural Activity (CLAC) in the Ivory Coast, the Public Library and Rural Audio Libraries in Mali, and the Culture Houses in Zimbabwe.

Rural audio libraries have been founded to address the preservation and transmission of oral culture. Mali began such a project in 1981. Librarians tape-record the local oral tradition, including history, tales, myths, riddles, traditional technologies, and pharmacology, making the recordings available through collective listening sessions. The recordings may also be transcribed and published. Other programs have included the Swaziland Oral History project established in 1985 (which is based in the National Archives of Lobamba), the Oral Traditions Association of Zimbabwe, the Oral Traditions Association of Southern Africa, and the East African Center for Research on Oral Traditions and African National Languages (which is based in Tanzania). Recording, storage, and bibliographic control of oral records can be expensive. Although such projects have been recommended for public libraries, it is possible that academic or national libraries may be better able to support this work.

Academic and Research Libraries

Academic libraries in the sub-Saharan region were mostly founded after World War II, although many colleges existed as early as the 1820s and may have had academic libraries early in their histories. One of these is Fourah Bay College in Sierra Leone, which was established in 1827 and affiliated with Durham University (England) in 1876. Another such library is the Albert Cook Medical Library at Makarere University in Uganda. One of the most important medical libraries in Africa, it is known internationally for its collection on tropical medicine. The Cook library suffered setbacks under the government of Idi Amin, but as of the late 1980s it had approximately 50,000 volumes and received more than 1,234 periodical titles. Good research collections are most likely to be available in the oldest, most established academic libraries, such as those in Ethiopia, Kenya, Liberia, Mauritius, Nigeria, Senegal, Sierra Leone, and South Africa.

Academic libraries in Africa have generally been modeled on European university libraries and are administered in similar ways. To fill staff needs, academic libraries may train graduates of their parent university and then send them to library schools for professional degrees. Occasionally, librarians hold full academic status, although this is less common now than in the past, and subject specialists are rare.

Collection development is often done with an eye toward acquiring material of national interest as well as serving the needs of the university community. As much as 90 percent of materials may be purchased from publishers outside Africa, under the constraints of limited availability of foreign currencies. Maintaining subscriptions to foreign journals can be problematic, and many university libraries have devised creative arrangements with foreign agents to handle payments, claims, and delivery of issues.

Library instruction is offered at most university libraries through tours and orientations and by encouraging students to seek assistance from librarians. This limited level of instruction has been criticized as particularly inadequate for the many students who have almost no experience with libraries. Occasionally, students are taught to use reference materials and given exams on this knowledge. Library services are often limited owing to a shortage of staff and materials.

Academic libraries in Africa seem more likely to cooperate with libraries in Europe than with those in other nations within Africa, which may be partly owing to the poor communications infrastructure within Africa. However, there is a well-established interlibrary loan network in southern Africa.

Research Station Libraries

Many of the earliest scientific libraries in Africa were government research libraries, founded to serve agricultural and natural resources departments. Agricultural libraries in research stations may be the only libraries in rural areas and can play a vital role in government extension services. Large proportions of Africans are employed in agriculture, and the development and extension of agricultural information services is a subject of interest and experiments, including functional literacy instruction.

Archives

In the early 1970s two centers of archival education were set up in Senegal and Ghana to serve the francophone and anglophone African nations, respectively. These programs were established on the recommendation of the International Council on Archives, with funding from the United Nations Development Program. The curriculum originally focused on records management and archives administration, but the Ghana program has since geared its program toward the study of records and information as a strategic resource.

Cultural Libraries

Cultural libraries are maintained in host countries by foreign nations to represent the latter's culture and civilization. These nations have included the United States, the Soviet Union, Great Britain, France, and Germany. Their services can include reading rooms, language classes, and audiovisual materials. These libraries seem to be appreciated as a resource by their users but are also viewed with suspicion by some citizens who associate them with colonial promotion of foreign cultural values and norms.

Mobile Libraries

The use of mobile libraries has been another way to address the information needs of rural areas. A lending service provided out of a van or truck may serve towns and villages that cannot support a library building or librarian. Many countries, including Kenya, Ghana, Tanzania, and Sierra Leone, instituted mobile library services to rural areas in the 1960s and 1970s. Often these met with initial success but failed within a few years owing to financial, staffing, and management problems, as well as poor rural roads. The Bendel State Library in Nigeria was still operating its service in 1996. As of 1999, the Bulawayo Library in Zimbabwe was providing successful bookmobile service to 37 schools, reaching approximately 37,000 children with only two bookmobiles.

African Publishing and Collection Development Issues

The problems of the publishing industry in Africa are also the problems of libraries. Without a strong local publishing industry, libraries must import expensive materials from abroad, and in general 70 to 90 percent of library materials are imported. The African publishing industry is hampered by the fact that African markets for books are still relatively small compared with those in more developed nations. Literacy, publishing, and libraries are interdependent in their development.

Collection development in sub-Saharan African libraries may be largely or wholly dependent on foreign donations, which can be of variable use and quality. The American Association for the Advancement of Science (AAAS) is a major donor of research journal titles. A principal donor of new and used books is Book Aid International, which includes librarians on its staff. Book Aid has teamed with the African Books Collective to promote African titles abroad and to ease their distribution internationally within Africa.

A noted early supporter of African authors and publishing was the East African Literature Bureau. In 1945 Elspeth Huxley (later the author of *The Flame Trees of Thika: Memories of an African Childhood*) was invited to evaluate and report on the availability of reading materials in eastern Africa. Huxley suggested the formation of a central library system to which existing and new libraries would be loosely linked. She also recommended the creation of an East African Literature Bureau to publish affordable publications without a primary focus on profit. The bureau was established in 1948 under the direction of Charles Richards, previous manager of the Christian Missionary Society bookshop in Nairobi and author of several titles in Kiswahili. Richards, who had a deep interest in aiding the development of African literacy, authorship, and publishing, remained in this position until 1963, making the bureau unique at the time in its real efforts to reach the general public. Some of the senior Kenyan staff of the bureau went on to significant careers in Kenyan librarianship.

In 1963 President Kwame Nkrumah convinced the Macmillan publishing company to form a joint venture with the government of Ghana to publish Ghanaian school textbooks. The result was the Ghanaian Publishing Corporation. Macmillan went on to form similar textbook publishing partnerships with Tanzania, Uganda, and Zambia.

Professional Organizations

At least 25 countries have professional library and information science associations, and as of 1988 Nigeria, Senegal, Sierra Leone, and Uganda have had two or more national associations. The first regional library association in sub-Saharan Africa was the West African Library Association (WALA), which was established in 1954. No national library associations existed in sub-Saharan Africa until 1962, when WALA was dissolved. The Ghana Library Association and the Nigerian Library Association were then formed by previous members of WALA. International organizations include the Standing Conference of African University Libraries and the Standing Conference of Eastern, Central, and Southern African Librarians.

Library Education and Literature

No library education program existed until 1950. In the 30 years that followed, the rate of development in library education and professional organizations was extraordinary. The first library education program for nonprofessionals was begun in 1950 at the University of Ibadan in Nigeria, and in 1960 the first professional library education program in sub-Saharan Africa, the Institute of Librarianship at Ibadan, was initiated. In 1962 the University of Ghana opened a Department of Library Studies, and a library school for francophone Africa was established at the University of Dakar in Senegal. Development of library education increased at a steady rate, and the first international meeting of the Standing Conference of African Library Schools was held in Dakar in 1973.

By the mid-1970s African authors were responsible for more than half of the publications on African libraries. African journals of library and information science appear to have been relatively numerous in the 1980s, but many have since ceased or suspended publication. Librarians often lack access to current professional journals and time for research. African library journals currently include the *African Journal of Library, Archives and Information Science,* and the *South African Journal of Library and Information Science.*

Technology

Telecommunication infrastructures vary widely among African nations. Replacement parts and skilled repair technicians for technical equipment are often scarce. Donations of computer information systems are increasingly common, but even if they are paid for entirely by foreign donors, internal funds may not be available for maintenance and updates.

E-mail is increasingly available, especially through universities. The greatest success story of Internet technology implementation is in Zambia, the first nation north of the Limpopo and south of the Sahara to introduce e-mail, via ESANET in 1991. In 1995, with a one-year grant from the World Bank, the University of Zambia established ZAMNET, a for-profit Internet service provider making full commercial Internet service available to the entire country, with fees well below the average for sub-Saharan Africa.

CD-ROM projects are multiplying and seem promising, especially for research libraries. In the early 1990s AAAS conducted a three-year CD-ROM pilot project in seven African universities to determine how document delivery could supplement journal subscriptions. The participants were Addis Ababa University and the Universities of Dar es Salaam, Ghana, Ibadan, Malawi, Zambia, and Zimbabwe. The Universities of Dar es Salaam and Ghana experienced the most success, partly owing to the strong support and involvement of faculty.

Funding and Resources

Since their creation, libraries in sub-Saharan Africa generally have continued to suffer from a lack of books and current journals, as well as a scarcity of funding for basic repairs, salaries, equipment, and programming. Government support for libraries is often limited to paying staff salaries. Kwame Nkrumah in

Ghana and Julius Nyerere in Tanzania were two national leaders who supported library development, but many governments increasingly view libraries as a luxury. Foreign financial support for African libraries, particularly from the Carnegie Corporation and the Ford Foundation, has been of great benefit, but strong local government support is necessary for development of new programs and support of existing services.

Economic conditions in the region are improving, and it is the general economic climate that has the most vital influence on the development and maintenance of libraries. However, the constraints on African libraries are still centered on lack of funds and therefore lack of facilities, materials, and staff salaries. The disruptions of political and social conflicts, poverty, war, and disease in many countries have often eroded or completely undone the hard work and achievements of librarians and libraries. Despite these constraints, creative innovations in services, progress in collaborative programs, and continuing development of library services and librarianship are evident throughout the region.

SARA F. MILLER

See also National Library of South Africa

Further Reading

Abegaz, Berhanu M., and Lisbeth A. Levey, *What Price Information? Priority Setting in African Libraries,* Washington, D.C.: American Association for the Advancement of Science, 1996

Alemna, A.A., "Towards a New Emphasis on Oral Tradition as an Information Source in African Libraries," *Journal of Documentation* 48, no. 4 (December 1992)

Alemna, A.A., "An Overview of the Library and Information Research Scene in West Africa," *African Journal of Libraries, Archives, and Information Science* 8, no. 1 (April 1998)

Banjo, Gboyega, "Libraries and Cultural Heritage in Africa," *IFLA Journal* 24, no. 8 (July 1998)

Cobley, Alan G., "Literacy, Libraries, and Consciousness: The Provision of Library Services for Blacks in South Africa in the Pre-Apartheid Era," *Libraries and Culture* 32, no. 1 (Winter 1997)

Mambo, Henry L., "Public Libraries in Africa: A Critical Assessment," *African Journal of Libraries, Archives, and Information Science* 8, no. 2 (October 1998)

McIlwaine, John, *Writings on African Archives,* London and New Providence, New Jersey: Zell, 1996

Olden, Anthony, *Libraries in Africa: Pioneers, Policies, Problems,* Lanham, Maryland, and London: Scarecrow Press, 1995

Raseroka, H.K., "Changes in Public Libraries during the Last Twenty Years: An African Perspective," *Libri* 44, no. 2 (June 1994)

Sitzman, Glenn L., *African Libraries,* Metuchen, New Jersey, and London: Scarecrow Press, 1988

Taylor, Loree Elizabeth, *South African Libraries,* London: Bingley, and Hamden, Connecticut: Archon Books, 1967

Wise, Michael, editor, *Aspects of African Librarianship: A Collection of Writings,* London and New York: Mansell, 1985

Archives

Nature, Goals, and Principles

As the modern research library began to take shape in the second half of the 19th century, these institutions, more often than not, contained archives and manuscript material, sometimes in copious quantity. Collectors such as Reuben Gold Thwaites gathered such material for the State Historical Society of Wisconsin, for example, or Hubert Howe Bancroft for the University of California, both of whom, as with so many others, turned over to these emergent institutions the fruits of their energetic effort. The institutions were remarkably successful in amassing this source material, and both archival and manuscript material was very extensively represented in research libraries by the opening decade of the 20th century. It took a considerably longer time, however, for the institutions to develop an understanding of this material and how and why it was created in the first place, and to develop policies and procedures for its effective management and use.

Through a concerted effort, the policies and understanding necessary to organize this material has evolved to a point where there is a broad consensus on what these materials are, what they represent, and how critical they are for sustaining historical scholarship, not only for the field of history, but for any academic discipline for which an historical approach to research is central or useful. To this end, the Society of American Archivists (SAA) publication *A Glossary for Archivists, Manuscript Curators, and Records Managers* (1992) has defined *archives* as documentation "created or received and accumulated by a person or organization in the course of conduct of affairs, and preserved because of their continuing value." The term is also used to designate a building storing such material, as well as the program authorized to manage the records. More recently, the term *archive* has also come to mean the act of storing material permanently via electronic means.

The term *archives* has generally referred to the permanently valuable noncurrent records of an institution or organization, whereas the term *manuscripts* has traditionally been used primarily to describe the records formed by an individual or family. In recent years, the functions and activities performed by archivists and manuscript librarians have converged (especially as personal and family papers have acquired the attributes of archives, specifically the serial institutional affiliations of individuals), and the terms are increasingly being used interchangeably. Nonetheless, the tradition associated with institutional records has in the main guided archivists, as does that of personal papers for those working with manuscripts. Whether these historical records are part of one tradition or the other, however, documentation is an essential element in the maintenance of the memory of individuals and communities alike, both in sustaining historical awareness and in validating claims to individual rights and group identity. In the last 20 years or so, both the archival and manuscript traditions have fallen under the growing influence of library procedures, particularly as technology has directed cataloging and created standardization and uniform rules for arranging and describing archival and manuscript material, for cataloging finding aids, and for mounting complete finding aids online.

Physically, archives in particular have included a wide range of media upon which information is recorded. These media have included cuneiform tablets and papyrus in ancient times, parchment and paper beginning in the early Common Era, and, more recently, a plethora of media, including maps, still photographs, motion pictures, videotapes, sound recordings, magnetic tapes, and now electronic records. Archivists identify permanently valuable institutional documents, regardless of media, and arrange their transfer to archival custody. Whether records are from the parent institution or acquired from outside institutions, organizations, and/or individuals, they are saved for preservation and use by those affiliated with the records-creating agency, by private citizens and groups concerned with preserving rights, and by scholarly researchers. These records are found in a wide array of repositories ranging from governmental agencies and offices at all levels to historical societies, religious organizations, businesses, labor organizations, and museums. Some of these repositories have received the records of their parent organizations or collected them from others for decades, indeed centuries, whereas others have been gathering historical records for a comparatively short time.

Institutions have performed archival functions for as long as documents have been created, starting in the Ancient Near East with the earliest forms of libraries, small collections of institutional records, predating by centuries the presence of archives in modern research libraries. By the 17th century the concept of archives was acquiring substance through works of jurisprudence and philology. Indeed, the development of the techniques of forgeries was entangled in the evolution of the scholarly method, as each side learned from and tried to prevail over the other. This dynamic was central to the evolution of managing early records via epigraphy, papyrology, study of seals (sigillography), paleography, and diplomatics in governmental and church archives. In the later Middle Ages and early modern periods, church and state bureaucracies elaborated and generated more complex documents in support of the work of the parent organization. The outbreak of the French Revolution led to affirmation of the public importance of state records, and an independent national system of archives administration was established for the first time. The state became responsible for preserving and maintaining records, to which public access was provided. Over the last two centuries the concept has spread, if in an uneven manner, to most other governments and many organizations.

Once in custody, archives are organized, described, and then made available for administrative and/or research use. They may be consulted in their original format or, more recently, via microforms, photocopies, publication, or, more recently still, digitized surrogates of documents. Archivists and records managers have gravitated more closely together to facilitate the more efficient transfer of records, to devise optimal ways of creating records (to reduce their bulk and simplify their disposition), to arrange for their temporary storage, and to determine their appropriate final disposition (i.e., retention in an archives or temporary storage in a records center before destruction).

By the late 19th century, archival work began to take shape around two principles very different from the principles of library cataloging and classification emerging at about the same time. Insofar as archives were not collected but rather created and received as an outgrowth of the conduct of business, they were not individually produced and identified. Instead, they were part of a succession of documents with similar characteristics and functions. This was expressed through the fundamental principle of *respect des fonds,* by which records were grouped according to the nature of the office or organization that generated or received them. Similarly, their original arrangement reflected the purposes for which the documents had been created, so that their original internal structure and organization was preserved to maintain those interrelationships. This is the heart of archival organization of materials. French and European *fonds* are broadly comparable to English record groups and subgroups reflecting the subordinate offices of an administrative hierarchy. Such records tend to exist in file units, folders, dossiers, or case files, which are in turn grouped into series (a body of file units linked together by filing scheme, function, activity, or subject, or a particular physical characteristic or relationship stemming from the creation, accumulation, or use of records).

As governmental documentation acquired public importance, such documents were thought to be inalienable and thereby part of a continuing custodial file. The chain of custody became important to archivists, and the maintenance of the collective memory was generally seen as a consequence of this custodial responsibility. Similarly, a "document" could be destroyed only after legislative authorization officially discharged it from its rightful place in the patrimony. The elements of legislation regulating public records came to include a definition of public archives and designated responsibility for preserving the documents containing legal, administrative, evidential, and research values. The legislation ideally also contained a definition of public archives and conferred responsibility to inspect public archives, establish standards of records management, and manage noncurrent records. The archives were given sole responsibility for appraising records for disposition (either destruction or retention), as well as authority governing destruction of noncurrent public records and transfer of permanently valuable records to archival custody. Authorization for arrangement and description of records, creation of standards for access to public records, definition of duties of records managers, and provision for protection of private archives with historical value were also specified in such legislation. By contrast, private manuscripts were treated by law primarily in terms of their copyright status or because they were part of a national cultural patrimony, rather than as evidence of governmental activity or guaranteeing the rights of individuals. Even today, manuscripts are treated principally in terms of their copyright status and issues pertaining to privacy, as the celebrated case of reclusive American author J.D. Salinger demonstrates.

Archives and libraries share a common purpose of acquiring, preserving, and promoting the research use of materials, although they differ in the nature of the materials they preserve and also in the principles and techniques they employ in managing their respective holdings. Libraries are collecting agencies, whereas archives are receiving agencies. Archives function by maintaining the integrity and original order (where possible) of unique and interrelated documents that are created in the course of conducting transactions, whether for an institution, an organization, or individuals. These principles are, of course, very different from the manner by which published library materials came to be grouped together or classified by subject and then cataloged as individual, but not unique, cultural records containing common elements such as author, title, publisher, place and date of publication, and other information such as controlled subject headings.

The advent of electronic records poses a daunting threat to the very theoretical foundations of archival work. Because of the dynamic nature of the hardware and software used in creating electronic records, archivists can no longer wait until records become inactive to appraise them for retention purposes. Archivists and records managers alike must be involved in the creation of electronic records in order to capture the attributes of the originals and to ensure that those will be preserved, even as systems are modified and replaced. Electronic digital objects must be preserved for future access, but provision to do so will be in the design of current systems, not in later appraisal. Moreover, the very rapidity with which systems are redesigned and improved introduces a serious problem of obsolescence in maintaining software for accessing electronic records, and the systems themselves seem to degrade quickly, thereby compounding the preservation problem. Beyond that, electronic records are themselves susceptible to degradation by exposure to electromagnetic fields, power outages, fluctuations in voltage, and by that infrequent but capricious scourge of "system failure," causing a general lack of proven durability for electronic records. Proposals to "refresh" or "regenerate" records periodically or to provide for their maintenance in systems with interoperable platforms that can migrate records are being discussed, although little consensus has yet emerged.

Archival Selection and Records Management

Whereas records from the ancient and early modern periods were characterized by scarcity and were perforce retained when discovered, the profusion of modern records, beginning in the second half of the 19th century, led archivists to select records (the archival term is *appraisal*) for permanent retention and disposal. This is not a document-by-document selection process but rather a process of judging what record series best documents the essential functions and services of the parent organization, or which files contain historically important information. There has been a burgeoning body of literature devoted to appraisal, beginning with the 1898 manual *Handleiding voor het ordenen en beschrijven van archieven* of the Dutch archivists Samuel Muller, Johan Adriaan Feith, and Robert Fruin. Somewhat earlier, in the last third of the 19th century, Prussian archivists emphasized regulations concerning arrangement of records, *Provenienzprinzip,* or the principle of provenance by which records should not be mixed with those of a different origin, and, where possible, the original order of documents should be maintained. By the early decades of the 20th century, British archivist Hilary Jenkinson spoke of the importance of uninterrupted custody to ensure the retention of legal and evidential values in records. Jenkinson wanted to separate archives from records management and thought that archivists should accept only those materials that administrators offered them. The U.S. archivist Theodore R. Schellenberg wrote extensively on a related subject, the "life cycle of records" (*Modern Archives: Principles and Techniques*, 1956).

U.S. archivists have long placed a premium on information values in records as a criterion for selection, as opposed to evidential values in records that seemed more subjective and less responsive to research interests. (Evidential values show the origin and organization of agencies, their policies, and programs; how authority was delegated and regulatory information was implemented; how resources were allocated; and how policies and procedures were developed.) Following Schellenberg's writings, American archivists gravitated to information values as unique data that could be tied to broad research concerns based on knowledge of research trends and needs. As most appraisal decisions were executed at the aggregate level, record series present their own patterns of decision making: large subject-classified files are easier to purge of housekeeping records, whereas case files represent specific problems and often contain unique information that was not easily resolved by sampling the records.

The advent of electronic records complicates the appraisal process, especially because of the ease in altering electronic records, the difficulty of tracing where an electronic record originated, and the ease in manipulating data contained in such records. The principle of retaining documents with information and evidential values still holds, although application of these concepts to electronic records is considerably more difficult.

Archival Processing: Arrangement and Description

Archival processing (the arrangement and description of records) differs from the bibliographic description traditionally accorded to library materials. A bibliographic description of a published work usually represents an individual entity for which there is a one-to-one correspondence between the description and the item described and deriving directly from the physical item. Archival description represents groups of documents, often in different physical formats but sharing a common provenance. The description briefly surveys the entity collectively and then describes its subunits, emphasizing intellectual structure and analyzing both its content and the context of its creation, not its physical characteristics. A practical consequence of these differences is that bibliographical descriptions of library materials are relatively brief, whereas finding aids can run to hundreds of pages.

The theory and practice of arranging and describing archives is of relatively recent origin, as individual and organizational records became bulky. Prior to that, the quantity of archival material posed no particular problem for custodians or researchers, and cataloging procedures dating from the late 19th century used calendars and lists in recording individual items chronologically or by some other scheme. Older documents, such as charters or treaties, could be readily listed as well, as could correspondence and accounts. Before the 1930s, processing of archival material was limited essentially to systems for describing correspondence. There were methods for classifying central files of institutions and organizations, but there was little concern (in government, business, or elsewhere) about systematic descriptive media for records.

The retirement of files in Europe was limited to the transfer of very old records to archives, as little if any thought was given to organizing or disposing of the mass of more contemporary records. By the middle of the 19th century, however, inconsequential records began to be haphazardly weeded out. During World War I waste paper was important in manufacturing bullets, so papers, sometimes including important government records, were used to meet war production needs. Despite this, there was still no real concern for the survival of records. One exception was Poland in the 1930s, where modern records remained of great interest, as its older records were in Russia, Austria, and Germany after partition in the late 18th century. Poland therefore was among the leaders in developing policies and programs for appraising and disposing of records. No other European country did so until after World War II.

In the United States, private businesses (such as the railroads for which the Interstate Commerce Commission issued regulations) tried to rationalize record keeping in the last third of the 19th century. Banks and insurance companies did likewise, and separate archives were also beginning to appear elsewhere, including universities. Archival holdings were frequently subjected to reorganizations thought to be improvements, but often with little regard for organic relationships or functional structures. Archives came to be seen as arsenals of history, and the arrangement of their holdings by date, geography, and subject was often implemented in the service of history (as in the state archives of New Hampshire and Massachusetts in the first half of the 19th century). Dossiers and individual documents were frequently removed from series and placed in other arrangements, often influenced by historical importance and/or library classification. Such changes often obscured or compromised the official and legal character of the records and destroyed the context necessary to evaluate historical source materials. Such rearrangement also often rendered finding aids useless, and new and detailed arrangements and classifications had to be made.

By the late 19th century, however, the two essential principles—those of provenance and respect for original order (the registry principle)—were formulated, and archival processing work began to advance, if slowly, toward codification. After some years of lobbying by the professional historical organizations, the National Archives of the United States was created in the mid-1930s, and contemporary archival practices slowly began to take hold there and in other American repositories. As archival procedures developed in the first half of the 20th century, the practice of arrangement followed the principles of provenance and original order, permitting physical and administrative control and basic identification of total holdings of an archival repository. The practice entailed packing materials by series in containers and in folders within containers, along with the appropriate labeling of folders. Such arrangement can proceed from the largest unit within a parent organization down to the individual document. Record groups were formed by provenance according to the existence of parent units and modified by administrative history, complexity, and the volume of records. A series in the archival sense consisted of documents in file units that were already structured by the office that originated, maintained, and used them, in accordance with its filing system or because they related to a particular function or subject, resulted from the same activity, had a particular form, or because of some other unifying relationship arising from their creation, receipt, or use.

Description is the process of establishing a context in which the contents and significance of holdings can be demonstrated through the preparation of finding aids, which can include guides and catalogs, inventories and registers, special lists, calendars, indexes, accession and location registers, box, and shelf lists. Appraisals, reports, and software documentation (for electronic records) also serve incidentally as finding aids. In recent years, there has been a trend toward producing specific descriptive documents.

Inventories (or registers) have emerged as the basic finding aid in establishing intellectual control of archival materials, the ability to retain and retrieve the subject content of these materials.

Finding aids are prepared at the record group or subgroup level, in which the unit of entry is the series. An institutional history, or in the case of personal papers, a biographical sketch, defines the group or subgroup and provides a general description of the structure and function of the agencies and offices whose records are being described, or the career and accomplishments of an individual. The characteristics and general contents of the records themselves are recorded in a scope and content note. The body of the inventory or register contains individual series entries organized within the framework of the subgroups. A paragraph describes the arrangement of the documents, gaps in the series, details on the functions and activities, the subjects covered in the series, and restrictions on access and use. Lists, indexes, and file titles are often attached to series descriptions to further assist the researcher, when their inclusion is warranted.

The structure and function of the creating agency remains the basis of all descriptions of holdings, thereby preserving the integrity of the archives and their legal and official character as well. Knowledge of the structure and functions of the originating agency remains the best guide to the widely varied subject matter of archives.

Beginning in the 1960s, automated systems were developed to facilitate control of archival material. These early efforts were initially batch-processed off-line on mainframe computers, and it was not until the advent of the MAchine-Readable Cataloging (MARC) Archives and Manuscripts Control (AMC) format in the early 1980s that automated systems for cataloging archival descriptive media achieved widespread adoption. Since then, their use has spread rapidly, being implemented for academic research libraries through large bibliographical organizations such as the Research Libraries Group (RLG) and for smaller repositories through use of microcomputer systems using compatible and exportable versions of the AMC format. Standardization of the format of finding aids as well as issues of authority control and subject access have obliged archival repositories to refine notoriously idiosyncratic policies and procedures for processing archival materials, for coordinating descriptive work, and even for standardizing appraisal decisions and developing cooperative approaches to the acquisition of archival material.

More recently, the U.S. and Canadian archival community has taken the lead in developing Encoded Archival Description (EAD) as a means of mounting standardized finding aids on the Web, where they may be accessed by archival professionals, researchers, and a wider public. The EAD format allows repositories to enter descriptive information containing standardized categories of descriptive information for formatting and display in Standard Generalized Markup Language (SGML), a hardware- and software-independent standard for encoding textual material across a variety of online platforms, preserving the organization and appearance of the information as originally input. This information includes the title, span dates, creator, and physical extent of the records, the name of the holding repository, and a scope and content note on the materials, as well as a brief biography or history of the creator. In addition, there is information on access restrictions (if any), more detailed information by box or folder of material and related material, as well as direct access to digital surrogates of the manuscripts, audiovisual material, audio recordings, maps, and the like.

Reference and Access

As in libraries, the basic purposes of archival work are to identify and preserve important records and to make them accessible for research use. Beyond that, however, libraries and archives differ not only in terms of the nature of the material they manage but also in those whom they serve. Internet access is rapidly changing and expanding the user communities of both libraries and archives. The broad constituency of libraries has been a more general public, whereas research libraries primarily serve those in the educational and scholarly communities. Moreover, archival repositories serve as the collective memory for institutions, organizations, and agencies, as well as individuals and families. These entities often have legal requirements for the records they must preserve and, in some cases, for access to them.

Recent legislation has created contradictory impulses: One is to promote "freedom of information" to public records, mandating public access to records except in certain categories relating to national security, trade secrets, and the like; the other is to protect privacy of individuals by restricting the release of personally identifying information. Nonetheless, archives serve as a historical memory, preserving a cultural patrimony constituted in artifacts whose authenticity and record of custody promotes confidence in the very integrity of those artifacts. These materials take on the quality of evidence in both its legal and historical dimensions.

Regardless of the constituency served, the provision of access to records constitutes archival reference work, including providing records to researchers in search rooms, providing information that describes records and their attributes, copying records for research use, lending records to researchers, and exhibiting records. In addition to these direct services, there is the production of documentary publications, books, and articles based on archival holdings, as well as interpretive programs that seek to explicate and interpret records for specialized communities and the general public.

Archival records serve a variety of purposes: They are made available to their agency creators and successors for administrative and/or legal purposes and to document fiscal accountability; to individual citizens to support their rights or personal curiosity; to researchers and historians for information relevant to topics in any number of academic disciplines; to genealogists, local history practitioners, and community activists; to those advocating project development; and to a great many others. Most archives maintain statistical records of the volume of reference use to protect the records and to document broad use of such records. They also try to protect the confidentiality of such use. As repositories are seen increasingly as cultural facilities, the widening appreciation of their cultural role tends to expand the constituencies to which they are responsible as well as accountable.

Policies governing service to researchers show a trend in recent years toward democratizing access by eliminating privileged access to records—making restrictions to archival material more uniform and time-certain rather than open-ended and unclear. In the same way, archivists discourage deposits of collections that might later be withdrawn, as this practice is burdensome to scholars trying to track down cited documentation. Equally, government records are closed for shorter periods, and there is an effort to reduce the volume of records that are classified for security purposes. In the United States there have been efforts to promote access through the Freedom of Information Act (FOIA), although there have been countervailing efforts to protect individual privacy. FOIA promotes access to agency records except in a range of topics for which access is restricted, such as national security and foreign policy issues, commercial and financial data, investigation, and personal information. Privacy legislation limits access to information about individuals (e.g., medical records, criminal justice investigations, and social security numbers), usually for a period of approximately 75 years in the United States and for approximately 90 years in Canada.

Photocopying has dramatically increased the availability of records to researchers, often obviating the need for researchers to copy passages or even take notes. Electrostatic and photographic copies often bring together records relevant to a particular subject from disparate holdings, while micrographic copies can be helpful where there are long runs of related records. Copies are also available for sound recordings, moving images, and electronic records. Repositories are taking special precautions in copying records under copyright protection, being careful to note the status of copyrightable material where possible, warning researchers not to violate copyrights, and trying to extend the concept of fair use by which one reproduction of a copyrighted item may be made by a researcher for study purposes only. Scanning is seen increasingly in search rooms, although its status, particularly with regard to information in copyright, remains unclear.

Indeed, the advent of technology, the ease of reproducing copyrighted material, and recent trends in court decisions cast a worrisome aura over the research use of such materials. Digitized files, printed or archival, are often governed by licensing agreements and contract law rather than by the constitutional provisions of copyright. Provisions for use of archival materials is further restricted by limitations on fair use of previously unpublished material. Court decisions involving J.D. Salinger and Richard Wright correspondence indicate that copyright holders may be entitled to first publication, eclipsing even the fair use doctrine in the limited first publication of archival material. Additionally, separate efforts are underway to extend even further the copyright protection of databases and their use. These various developments raise the issue of the nature and quality of access to cultural and historical records at a time when the very theoretical constitutional foundations of copyright are also being called into question.

Archival records usually are limited to on-site use at the archives but are sometimes loaned to the creating agency if it needs them for administrative or legal purposes. Records in fragile condition may be copied rather than subjected to such use. Archival records are lent to nongovernmental repositories for exhibition only under the most stringent of criteria. Members of institutional consortia sometimes lend records to other members for the convenience of researchers. Subpoenaed records are usually supplied in copy format.

Exhibitions provide another form of access, generally in the form of an outreach program. Such programs promote the popular understanding of historical records and their appreciation as cultural artifacts. Exhibitions are typically now produced at all types of archival repositories, as a means of interpreting holdings concerning specific subjects on anniversaries or when public attention might be focused on a particular subject.

Documentary publication is an extension of reference service and very often enables researchers to use edited, published documents rather than originals. In addition to letterpress, microfilm publication of entire collections is a way of mitigating the problem of selection. Many archives publish such materials, such as the letters of the Continental Congress in the United States or a long run of historical papers at the Public Records Office in the United Kingdom.

Archival materials come in a wide variety of formats and present a broad array of information of value not only to the generating institution or individual, but also for its broader value in cultivating the historical memory and the subsequent formation of historical knowledge. It is an essential source material found in research libraries, as in other repositories, and its cultivation and preservation is a vital attribute in fulfilling the very purposes of such institutions.

Professional Literature

Archival literature has been slow to develop, has been characteristically fugitive in nature (that is, it has been widely scattered and difficult to locate), and has appeared, until recently, primarily in article form. In recent years, however, it has experienced a remarkable expansion and a growing scholarly sophistication. Doubtless, this has been the result of the growing number of graduate archival educational programs and the demonstrated importance of archival materials to research in the humanities and social sciences.

Perhaps the single most comprehensive source for publishing and distributing archival publications is the Society of American Archivists (SAA), which maintains an active archival publications program, including reprinting of classics and collaborating in recent years with various publishers. The SAA series *Archival Fundamentals*, of which James M. O'Toole's *Understanding Archives and Manuscripts* (1990) and Lewis J. and Lynn Lady Bellardo's *A Glossary for Archivists, Manuscript Curators, and Records Managers* (1992) are part, provides comparatively recent commentary on archival theory and practice. SAA also publishes a variety of titles on electronic records and the challenges that they pose.

WILLIAM L. JOYCE

Further Reading

Bellardo, Lewis J., and Lynn Lady Bellardo, compilers, *A Glossary for Archivists, Manuscript Curators, and Records Managers,* Chicago: Society of American Archivists, 1992

Brooks, Philip Coolidge, *Research in Archives: The Use of Unpublished Primary Sources,* Chicago: University of Chicago Press, 1969

Daniels, Maygene F., and Timothy Walch, editors, *A Modern Archives Reader: Basic Readings on Archival Theory and Practice,* Washington, D.C.: National Archives and Records Service, 1984

Jenkinson, Hilary, *A Manual of Archive Administration Including the Problems of War Archives and Archive Making,* London and New York: Milford, 1922; revised 2nd edition, London: Lund Humphries, 1965

Jimerson, Randall C., editor, *American Archival Studies: Readings in Theory and Practice,* Chicago: Society of American Archivists, 2000

Muller, Samuel, Johan Adriaan Feith, and Robert Fruin, *Handleiding voor het ordenen en beschrijven van archieven,* Groningen, The Netherlands: Van der Kamp, 1898; 2nd edition, 1920; as *Manual for the Arrangement and Description of Archives,* translated by Arthur H. Leavitt, New York: Wilson, 1940

Nesmith, Tom, editor, *Canadian Archival Studies and the Rediscovery of Provenance,* Metuchen, New Jersey: Scarecrow Press, 1993

O'Toole, James M., *Understanding Archives and Manuscripts,* Chicago: Society of American Archivists, 1990

Samuels, Helen Willa, *Varsity Letters: Documenting Modern Colleges and Universities,* Chicago: Society of American Archivists, and Metuchen, New Jersey: Scarecrow Press, 1992

Schellenberg, Theodore R., *Modern Archives: Principles and Techniques,* Chicago: University of Chicago Press, 1956

Schellenberg, Theodore R., *The Management of Archives,* New York: Columbia University Press, 1965

Art and Architecture Libraries

What Is an Art Library?

The seeker of information on art and architecture typically looks in a variety of institutions for material. Most frequently, researchers find printed materials in museum libraries, art-oriented collections in academic libraries, and art materials in public libraries. Less frequently visited, owing in part to more limited access policies, are libraries held by private companies (including auction houses, dealers, and architectural firms) or art-oriented collections in research institutes devoted to the arts specifically or to overlapping subjects (such as botany, medicine, printing, and engineering). Art librarianship has been ambivalent as to whether visual resource libraries (e.g., photograph and slide collections) and graphic collections constitute art libraries. There has also been some question about whether archival materials, including some works on paper, belong under the rubric of art libraries. These questions of scope are being answered on a practical if not a theoretical level by the cohesive influence of new technologies that integrate text and image. The term *art library* has traditionally referred to a physical building with a collection; art librarianship is now seeing the growth of virtual libraries made up of collections of art works and related information in digital representation. Although this digital information lacks the physicality of a traditional library, its management involves many of the same issues: selection, organization, intermediary equipment, distribution, preservation, copyright, and service practices.

As most art resources are housed in institutions with broader missions (such as public libraries, museums, universities, art schools, or research institutes) where art collections tend to be integrated with collections on other subjects, this article will focus on art library collections rather than libraries per se. Despite diversity in institutional settings, the concept of "art and architecture collections" gains its considerable cohesion from three factors: linkage to the formal, integrated, academic tradition of art and architectural history; reliance upon a few centralizing reference works and services; and strong, interlinked professional societies of art and architectural librarians.

The Literature of Art and Architecture

The traditional categories of art and architecture literature include biographies, technical textbooks for practitioners and conservators, handbooks and guidebooks for connoisseurs, treatises on criticism and aesthetics, and materials for education and appreciation. These categories of material were found in art library collections from the first flourishing of art literature in the Western classical world and were firmly established as a typology in the Italian Renaissance. A review of the development of fundamental texts in the integrated field of art and architectural history sheds light, however indirectly, on the nature and chronology of institutional collecting in this field.

Outstanding works from antiquity that saw renewed interest in the Italian Renaissance begin with Vitruvius' *Ten Books on*

Architecture, a textbook on classical orders, acoustics, city planning, and the social status of the architect. Also included from antiquity are the biographies of artists as recounted by Pliny the Elder in his *Natural History.* Pliny popularized the idea of flowering and decay in the arts that has persisted for centuries. Although Plato considered the visual arts merely as "sensory deception," his concept of the ideal was brought to bear on art criticism in the Renaissance. Classical guidebooks are epitomized in Pausanias' guide to Greece, which dates from the second century.

Medieval art literature often emphasized technical instructions (for example, the mixing of colors and alloys). Advice on rendering sacred legends appeared in the *Mt. Athos Painters' Guide* of Dionysios of Furna (born c. 1670 and died after 1744), and Villard de Honnecourt's sketchbook from the 13th century represents French Gothic solutions to artistic problems. Although little biography or philosophy of art has survived from the Middle Ages, the memoir of Abbot Suger concerning the renovation of the cathedral of St. Denis in 12th-century France provides insight into motivation and method.

Fifteenth-century Florence, Italy, can be considered the birthplace of modern art literature in which scientific naturalism sought theoretical foundation. Outstanding works include Leon Battista Alberti's *On Architecture* (c. 1450) and *On Painting* (1435), which sought a scientific foundation for artistic practice; Lorenzo Ghiberti's *Commentaries* with his autobiographical and critical musings; Piero della Francesca's treatise on perspective; and Leonardo da Vinci's 16th-century observations later compiled into his *Treatise on Painting.* The Neoplatonic theory of "divine ecstasy" found its way into the emerging concept of art theory. Other outstanding examples of the period are Albrecht Dürer's *Manual of Measurement* (1515) and his *Four Books on Human Proportion* (1528). Late Renaissance and mannerist emphasis upon classical learning can be found in the architectural and model books of Giacomo Vignola, written in 1562, and Andrea Palladio's in 1570. Guidebooks to the picturesque flourished at the time, exemplified by Jacopo Tatti Sansovino's 1556 book on the sights of Venice and Bocchi's *Beauties of Florence* (1581). Artists' biographies in the early Renaissance turn up in more general works by Dante and Boccaccio, culminating in Giorgio Vasari's highly influential *Lives* (1550). Benvenuto Cellini's 16th-century autobiography of an artist in the decline of the Renaissance was not published until the late 18th century.

Art literature of the baroque and neoclassical periods saw some innovations, although it largely followed the patterns set by the Renaissance. Beyond 17th-century Italy, Karel van Mander's *The Painter's Book* (1604), while drawing upon Pliny and Vasari, adds significant material on masters from the Netherlands. In Germany, Joachim von Sandrart's *German Academy of the Notable Arts of Architecture, Sculpture, and Painting* (1675) contributed information on German artists and others whom the author met on his travels. England contributed Nicholas Hillyard's 1658 work on the technique of miniature painting, and France saw a contribution in 1667 from Charles Le Brun on the portrayal of effects and facial expressions.

Eighteenth-century Western art literature was greatly enriched by the work of three English theorists: William Hogarth's *The Analysis of Beauty* (1753), Joshua Reynolds' *Discourses* (1771), and Edmund Burke's *A Philosophical Enquiry into the Origin of Our Ideas of the Sublime and the Beautiful* (1756). German theory was dominated by Johann Winckelmann, who approached art history as a scholarly and scientific study in his *History of Ancient Art* (1764). Systematic reference works made their appearance, the first most likely being Johann Rudolf Füssli's *Universal Dictionary of Artists* (1763).

The 19th century saw the continuation and systematization of older forms, such as Adam von Bartsch's *Le peintre-graveur* (1830). It also witnessed, in England, the appearance of an enthusiastic literature expressing Romantic taste for neo-Gothic architecture exemplified by the work of the architect Augustus Pugin and the vast output of John Ruskin. Advocacy of a return to the imagined, idyllic world of medieval craftsmen is exemplified in the writings of the Pre-Raphaelite painter and literateur William Morris and also in theories of the German Werkbund and Bauhaus. France witnessed debates on the nature of art in the work of the creative writers Charles-Pierre Baudelaire, Émile Zola, and Joris K. Huysmans.

Architects and painters who contributed to contemporary theory include Frank Lloyd Wright, Le Corbusier, Wasily Kandinsky, and James M. Whistler. With the symbolist and cubist movements that spanned the centuries, the nature of art and literature continued to preoccupy writers, most notably Paul Valéry, Guillaume Apollinaire, and André Breton. In the 20th century the dominant names were Ernst Gombrich, whose *Art and Illusion* (1960) explored perception and the psychology of interpreting images; Heinrich Wölfflin, whose *Principles of Art History* (1932) sought basic approaches to the visual character of artwork; and Erwin Panofsky, whose learned and graceful prose addressing iconographic concerns attracted a generation of followers. The 20th century gave rise to the critic as celebrity; the importance of Clement Greenberg's role in the mid-century popularity of abstract expressionism cannot be overlooked. It is too early to identify the dominant names and works in the more recent movements in art historical theory grounded in semiotics, deconstruction, postmodernism, and new art history, but one can find ample evidence of interest in these theoretical approaches in modern-day art library collections.

The Nature of Art and Architecture Collections Today

Collections in art libraries today, as distinct from architectural libraries, include the full range of traditional types of printed materials relating to art. In some cases these traditional forms have become further refined into clearly defined subcategories. Current art library collections would describe their categories of materials as encyclopedias and dictionaries; serials; catalogues raisonnés that attempt to organize a cohesive body of work, usually of a single artist, by theme and chronology; monographs dealing with artists' lives and work; iconographic handbooks and emblem books; corpora that draw together art objects of a particular place or type; auction catalogs; exhibition catalogs; monographs dealing with themes, styles, or media; Festschriften made up of essays honoring scholars or other dignitaries in the field; historical guidebooks and maps; archaeological reports; ethnographic studies; technical information on materials and methods; price guides; and, increasingly, conservation information. Information on career opportunities and health and safety issues also is available for artists. Many of these categories of information exist today in digital form. Some libraries maintain extensive picture collections and clipping files on artists and their work. The interdisciplinary nature of many topics, such as women's art or film studies, is causing a broadening of user expectations and a widening of collection scope.

Most architectural library collections are located in schools of architecture or architecture and engineering. Collections also exist in the few research institutes covering this area and in architectural firms (seldom available to the public). Like art collections, the holdings of architectural libraries have reflected the changing nature of their literature over time. In addition to printed publications constituting the cornerstone of art and architectural history, architectural libraries collect many other forms of specialized information, including current handbooks and manuals of practice, folios of drawings and illustrations, architectural surveys, trade catalogs, building code documents, preservation information, and books on mathematics and geometry. Some architectural collections include three-dimensional models, a form popular since the Renaissance. Modern libraries have become repositories of archival material generated by architects and firms; the program of Cooperative Preservation of Architectural Records encourages preservation of these ephemeral records and assists users in gaining access to them. Contemporary architectural libraries strive to keep up with information on new materials and techniques and to incorporate digital information related to design and construction. Increasingly, there is also an interest in geography in its broadest sense, including human use of structures, landscape, topography, climate, ecology, and conservation issues.

It is difficult to generalize about the role of visual images in art and architecture collections, but they have always been at the vital core of the disciplines of art and architecture. Visual resource collections—clippings, slides, and graphic reproductions of various kinds—can be variously administered as integral parts of an art or architectural library within a single institution or quite separately from a print-oriented library in the same institution. Documentary photographic collections that are relatively freestanding include the Alinari Photo Archive in Florence (begun in 1854); Bildarchiv Foto at the Phillipps University in Marburg, Germany (1929), publisher of the Marburger Index and producer of ICONCLASS, a system for classifying iconographic imagery; and the Census of Antique Works of Art Known to the Renaissance, housed at the Warburg Institute in London. Other extensive collections include the Frick Art Reference Library's picture files in New York; the Index of Ancient Art and Architecture in the Deutsches Archaologisches Institut in Rome; the Index of Christian Art at Princeton University (New Jersey); the Photographic Archives of the Caisse Nationale des Monuments Historiques et des Sites in Paris (also known as Art in France: the French State Photographic Archives); the Witt Library Photograph Collection in the Courtauld Institute of Art, centered on European and American artists from 1200 to the present and located at the University of London; the Getty Center for the History of Art and Humanities Resource Collections (Los Angeles, California); and several university slide and image collections such as that located at the Fogg Museum at Harvard University (Cambridge, Massachusetts). Many of these collections are represented at least in part in microform and in digital form.

Computer technology is currently drawing visual resource collections and traditional art and architectural libraries more closely together, and both print-oriented and visual libraries are using the same technologies and facing the same issues in developing digitally based services. Curators of visual resource collections have had mixed professional identities, defining themselves variously as art historians, curators, or librarians. Today they are drawn together in a number of allied professional organizations and activities, and further moves toward cooperative endeavors can reasonably be anticipated. Neither the visual resource collection nor the print-oriented art/architecture library can exist today meaningfully without the other. Given the strong aesthetic appeal of printed books for the traditional art librarian, the move to digitization for textual information sometimes has been a reluctant one. Nevertheless, enthusiasm for digitized images is quite high despite the preference of some users for photo-offset illustration and slides rather than the digital format technologies now available.

Many art and architectural libraries oversee archival collections. These collections may document the history of the parent museum, for example, or may have archives of artists or architects of interest to the library, including works of art on paper (such as drawings or photographs). These collections present formidable conservation needs as well as access issues. Many libraries with archival collections are affiliated with the Research Libraries Group (RLG) and have described their collection in RLG's Research Libraries Information Network (RLIN) Archival Resources program. Descriptions of these holdings are thus available internationally online.

The central core of the bibliography of art and architecture is organized by a few dominant indexes and reference works, many in digital form or published in both hard copy and electronic versions. The basic tools include *BHA: Bibliographie d'histoire de l'art/Bibliography of the History of Art* (1990–), representing a merger of the French *Répertoire d'art et d'archáologie* (1910–89) and the U.S. *RILA: International Repertory of the Literature of Art* (1975–89). Other reference tools constituting the backbone of the discipline are *The Art Index* (1929–), *ARTbibliographies MODERN* (1969–), *The Art and Architecture Thesaurus* (1990–), *Allgemeines Lexikon der bildenden Künstler von der Antike bis zur Gegenwart* (known as Thieme/Becker and now being updated as the *Allgemeines Künstler Lexikon*) (1907–50; 1983–), McGraw-Hill's *Encyclopedia of World Art* (1958), and

Grove's *Dictionary of Art* (1996). The online bibliographic utility OCLC has made available information on bibliography and locations; RLG has greatly enhanced art reference work through its art-oriented programs and services; and Sales Catalog Index Project Input Online (SCIPIO) is available on RLIN. For architecture, ubiquitous modern reference tools include the *Avery Index to Architectural Periodicals* (1973–), *The Architectural Periodicals Index* from the Royal Institute of British Architects (1973–), *The Catalog of the Avery Memorial Architectural Library* (2nd edition, 1963, with supplements), *Catalogue of the Royal Institute of British Architects Library*, published since 1984 in *Architecture Database* (1937–), and the *Avery Obituary Index to Architects and Artists* (2nd edition, 1980). Many of these tools are also available on RLIN.

Major Art and Architectural Libraries

Some 50 years ago, when art and architectural history focused mainly on "high art" in Western Europe, it was possible to speak confidently of the "best" library collections and research centers supporting this discipline. In recent decades the identification of outstanding libraries is more difficult and probably less useful, as the art canon has expanded to include non-mainstream art institutions and traditions (including art variously described as local, naive, primitive, and folk), crafts, industrial arts, "material culture," art of the non-Western world, and art of the Americas. Many of the traditionally renowned institutions retain their eminence, but there are some conspicuous newcomers to the scene with different subject emphases. The judgment of excellence is made even more difficult by the current interest in the social context of works of art; local historical societies are often as helpful as art collections for such investigations. The situation is further complicated by factors related to politics. Many fine libraries in the traditional Western-oriented mode of the early part of the century have been badly damaged by war, and others have been unable to continue their earlier commitments because of financial problems.

Given the European origin of much early art historical publication, it is not surprising that many of the oldest and most extensive art library collections are still to be found there. German art libraries often had their origins in small book collections in art academies first founded in the late 17th century. Court and royal libraries also developed into collections with wider accessibility. Specialized art libraries developed in the 19th century, some associated with research institutes. Museum and university collections flourished in the 20th century. Outstanding German collections are the comprehensive Kunstbibliothek of the Staatliche Museen zu Berlin preussischer Kulturbesitz (founded in 1867); the Bibliothek des germanischen Nationalmuseums (1852) in Nuremberg; the Kunst- und museumsbibliothek und rheinisches Bildarchiv in Cologne (1957), which includes older and modern art; the Zentralinstitut für Kunstgeschichte in Munich (1946), with its origin in Nazi libraries of confiscated books; and the Sächsische Landesbibliothek in Dresden (1956), where several art history reference works have been developed.

Austria's most important art collections are located in institutions with larger missions: the Kunsthistorisches Museum and the Österreichisches Museum für angewandte Kunst; the Museum des 20. Jahrhunderts (1962), which houses the collections for the Museum moderner Kunst; the Bundesdenkmalamt, which supports monument restoration; and the Akademie der bildenden Künste, the oldest architectural library in the country.

The Netherlands is rich in art libraries. Prominent among them are the libraries of the Rijksmuseum and the Kunsthistorisch Instituut, both in Amsterdam, and the Rijksbureau voor kunsthistorische Documentatie in The Hague.

Art library collections in France are many and rich, although specialized art libraries are a fairly recent phenomenon. Important collections are held in general repositories such as the Bibliothèque nationale and the Archives Nationales (both in Paris). More specialized Parisian libraries include the library of the École Nationale des Beaux-Arts (formerly the Académie Royale de Peinture and de Sculpture); the Bibliothèque Centrale des Musées Nationaux at the Louvre Museum; the Bibliothèque d'Art et d'Archéology (Fondation Jacques Doucet), given to the University of Paris in 1917; the Bibliothèque des Arts Décoratifs; and the Documentation du Musée National d'Art Moderne, founded in 1955 and now housed in the Centre Georges Pompidou.

Italy has long had specialized art libraries, although the concept and term *art library* became common only in the 20th century. Older centers for the study of art exist in regional capitals (for example, the Biblioteca Marucelliana in Florence). The Biblioteca dell'Istituto Nazionale d'Archeologia e Storia dell'Arte (founded in 1922 and located in the Palazzo Venezia in Rome) serves in a sense as the national art library. Among libraries with extensive and important original print collections are the Castello Sforzesco in Milan, housing the Biblioteca d'Arte and the Achille Bertarelli collections. Manuscripts can be found in the famed Biblioteca Medicea-Laurenziana (1571), a Florentine structure designed by Michelangelo. Museum libraries are particularly rich in resources; outstanding among them are the civic museum libraries of Venice, Padua, Verona, Reggio nell'Emilia, Bolzano, Trieste, Piacenza, and Bologna. Among specialized libraries are the Istituto Centrale per il Restauro in Rome and the Archivio storico delle arti contemporanee in Venice, which deals with contemporary art, theater, and film. Several major libraries were established by foreign institutions and individuals, among them the rich collections of the Bibliotheca Herziana (1913) in Rome and the Kunsthistorisches Institut (1988–97) in Florence, the Biblioteca Berenson at I Tatti in Florence (now owned by Harvard University), and the libraries of the British School in Rome, the American Academy in Rome, and the German Archeological Institute. More recent is the Fondazione Giorgio Cini in Venice. And although it is not specifically an art library, the Vatican Library is indispensable for historical research in art and architecture.

In Russia, the Russian State Library serves as the national art library. The library of the Hermitage in St. Petersburg is a leading art library for nations of the former Union of Soviet Socialist Republics (USSR); more local collections are housed in universities, museums, and public and art school libraries. (This mixture of institutional settings for art collections is characteristic of many Eastern European nations.) Literature on Russian decorative arts can be found in the City of Westminster public library in London.

Nordic art libraries follow a pattern that is seen in the Swedish situation. Outstanding Swedish art libraries include the Kungliga Akademi för de Fria Konsterna (Stockholm), founded by King Gustav III in 1775, and the Konstbibliothek (Stockholm), a 19th-century library with the largest art collection in the country. Sweden's most important architectural libraries include the Konsthögskolans Arkitekturskola (Stockholm) and libraries that serve technical institutes and universities in Stockholm, Lund, and Göteborg. Crafts and design collections exist in many small local institutions.

Spanish libraries specializing in art begin with the Instituto Diego Velásquez at the Consejo Superior de Investigaciones Científicas in Madrid and the Laboratorio de Arte Francisco Murillo Herrara, founded in 1907 at the University of Seville. Also significant are the Biblioteca Nacional in Madrid, the Instituto Amattler de Arte Hispanico in Barcelona, the Real Academia de Bellas Artes de S. Fernando in Madrid, the Real Academia de Bellas Artes de S. Carlos in Valencia, and the Real Academia de Bellas Artes de S. Isabel de Hongría in Seville. The art literature of Spain's Moorish period is well represented in the libraries of the Patronato de la Alhambra in Granada and the Museo Arqueólogico in Córdova.

Major Portuguese art library collections are held by the Academia de Belas-Artes, which includes photographic inventories of the national heritage, and the Museo Nacional de Arte Antiga, both in Lisbon. In 1957 the Serviço de Belas-Artes of the Fundaçao Calouste Gulbenkian began acquiring photographic and archival materials for the new Centro de Investigação e Pesquisa in Lisbon.

Early English art collections were usually developed by royalty or wealthy commoners; royal collections still exist at Windsor Castle. In the second half of the 18th century, art libraries were established in the Royal Academy and at the British Museum, both in London. In the 19th century libraries relating to art education were developed at the Victoria and Albert Museum in London (now the National Art Library) and in several schools of design. Significant collections exist today at the British Library (London) and at the universities of Oxford and Cambridge. The Tate Gallery collection (London) in modern art library materials is particularly strong. Important collections are held at research institutes such as the University of London's Conway Library of the Courtauld Institute and the Warburg Institute Library, which specializes in the influence of classical antiquity on European civilization. Many important collections, especially of architectural material, are located in schools of design. The strongest architectural library is at the Royal Academy of British Architects in London. Scotland's most charming example of the art library genre is the library of the Glasgow School of Art, designed and furnished by Charles Rennie MacIntosh and still in use today.

Art library collections in the United States began to appear in 19th-century museums such as the Boston (Massachusetts) Museum of Fine Arts (1879); in public libraries such as the Boston Public Library (1854) and the New York Public Library (1895); in the Washington, D.C., Library of Congress (1800), with its Prints and Photographs Division begun in 1896; and in universities. The early 20th century saw the establishment of significant and relatively independent collections. Among these were the Art Institute of Chicago's Ryerson Library (1901); the Pierpont Morgan Library (1906) in New York; the Marquand Library of Princeton University (1908); Princeton's Index of Christian Art (1917); Harvard University's Fine Arts Library (1927); New York's Museum of Modern Art Library (1932); the National Gallery of Art (1941) in Washington, D.C.; and the Getty Center for the History of Art and the Humanities Resource Collections (1982) in Los Angeles, California.

Significant fine arts material exists in Yale University's Beinecke Library (New Haven, Connecticut) and the Yale Center for British Art; the Institute of Fine Arts at New York University; the University of California at Los Angeles, with its Elmer Belt Library of Vinciana; the Smithsonian Institution's combined library for the National Museum of American Art and the National Portrait Gallery (both in Washington, D.C.); the Frick Art Reference Library (New York), and the Metropolitan Museum of Art (also in New York). More specialized collections are the Dumbarton Oaks Research Library in Washington, D.C. (Byzantine civilization); the Winterthur Museum in Winterthur, Delaware (American decorative arts); the Cooper-Hewitt Museum library in New York (decorative arts); the Huntington Library, Art Collections, and Botanical Gardens in San Marino, California (British art); and the Cleveland (Ohio) Museum of Art (Oriental). Not to be overlooked are the Archives of American Art housed in the Smithsonian Institution in Washington, D.C., and other locations. Additional printed material and image archives can also be found in many larger museums, institutions of higher education, and historical societies both large and small.

In recent decades, programs of OCLC and RLIN have enabled researchers to learn about the resources of many collections throughout the United States and elsewhere via the data contributed to these cooperative online catalogs. Through a tiered system of referral and cooperative arrangements, users in the United States can generally gain access to highly specialized research collections if their needs cannot be met locally. The objective of user service has been identified as a goal of U.S. librarianship for many years, perhaps best described by Erwin Panofsky in *Meaning in the Visual Arts* (1955). Concerning his research foray to the New York Public Library shortly after his immigration to the United States in the 1930s, he wrote,

> In the New York of the early 1930's . . . the European art historian was at once bewildered, electrified, and elated. He feasted on the treasures assembled in museums, libraries, private

collections, and dealers' galleries.... He was amazed that he could order a book at the New York Public Library without being introduced by an embassy... and that everybody seemed actually eager to make material accessible to him.

Most Canadian art collections today are found in public museums, universities, or public libraries. An exception is the privately funded Centre Canadien d'Architecture (1979) in Montreal (Quebec), the place of origin of the Canadian Architectural Records Survey. Among outstanding academic libraries with art collections are those at McGill University (Montreal) and the University of Toronto (Ontario), both institutions dating from the 1890s. Strong holdings are also found at the Metro Toronto Library and the Canadian Conservation Institute in Ottawa (Ontario). Important museum collections include the National Gallery of Canada Library in Ottawa, the Royal Ontario Museum and the Art Gallery of Ontario (both in Toronto), and the Montreal Museum of Fine Arts. Inuit art and craft are represented in collections of the Winnipeg (Manitoba) Art Gallery and the records of the Hudson Bay Company, held by the Provincial Archives of Manitoba.

Australian art libraries first emerged from 1820 to 1840 as small collections in mechanics' institutes and schools of art. The 1850s saw the founding of state libraries and galleries with small collections. The State Library of Victoria was the first to staff a separate art library serving the National Gallery of Victoria and its art school, which shared the same building until 1968. Holdings on Australian art can be found at the Mitchell Library in Sydney and the National Library of Australia in Canberra. The Museum of Contemporary Art in Sydney and the National Gallery of Australia (Canberra), both founded in the 1980s, have growing collections of library materials.

Until the 19th century, South America had few libraries and little tradition of conserving written or visual records. Monastery libraries, dating from the 16th century and later, were among the exceptions. Printing first came to Brazil in 1808, and the Biblioteca Real founded in Rio de Janeiro in 1810 became the national library in 1878. This library holds the most comprehensive collection of art materials in the country. The colonial and imperial periods are represented in Brazil's museums. Significant Brazilian holdings are found also in the Escola de Belas Artes of the Universidade Federal do Rio de Janeiro, the Secretario do Patrimônio Histórico e Artístico Nacional in Rio, the Fundação Pró-Memória in Brasília, and the Instituto Histórica e Geográphico Brasileiro (based in Rio). Other significant Latin-oriented art library materials can be found at the Universidad Nacional Autonoma in Mexico City, Mexico.

The development of art libraries in the Muslim world follows a different pattern from those in Europe and the Americas. Until printing began in the Muslim regions in the 18th century, all printed books were imported from Europe. The written word had a privileged role in Islamic thought, and the adoption of print was therefore accepted with some reluctance. Additionally, printed material from abroad was seen as inconsistent with the established order. Printing of the Qur'an and sacred texts was initially forbidden. Arabic printing in Egypt came with the French occupation of 1798 to 1801, and after an initial period of copying of European types, Arabic types took firm hold by the mid-19th century.

Even before the introduction of printing, libraries were extremely important in the Islamic world. Many began as private collections and were soon incorporated into mosques and *madrasas* (study centers), although some independent libraries did exist. Because calligraphy is a major art form in Islam, most Islamic libraries can be considered art libraries. Specialized art libraries are fairly rare. Notable collections are located in the Istanbul University Library and at the American University in Cairo in its Creswell Library of Islamic Art and Architecture. The art of countries that are traditionally considered at the center of the Islamic world can be studied in the institutions of those countries and in some foreign libraries including the British Library, the library of the Louvre, and the Wilbour Library of Egyptology at the Brooklyn Museum in New York.

The study of African art is rooted in cultural anthropology and has drawn traditionally upon ethnography, history, and archaeology. Many of the libraries with pertinent collections in these fields are found in Europe and the United States. They include the Museum für Völkerkunde in Berlin, the British Museum in London, the Pitt Rivers Museum in Oxford, the Koninklijk Museum voor Midden-Afrika in Tervuren, Belgium, and the Musée de l'Homme in Paris. A number of U.S. institutions have significant photo archives of African materials, such as the Peabody Museum of Archaeology and Ethnology at Harvard University, the American Museum of Natural History (New York), and the Field Museum of Natural History (Chicago, Illinois). Colonial libraries that documented early European contact with Africa include the Biblioteca Apostolica Vaticana in Rome, the Bibliothèque Africaine in Brussels (Belgium), and various missionary society archives, such as the archives of the American Methodist Church at Drew University in Madison, New Jersey, or records of Roman Catholic activity now in the Vatican Library. From the 1960s on, major libraries on African material were developed in the United States, specifically in universities, including Yale, Northwestern (Evanston, Illinois), Columbia (New York), Iowa (Iowa City), Indiana (Bloomington), and the University of California at Los Angeles. In museums, there has been a shift in emphasis recently from ethnographical interpretation to art historical presentation. Pertinent museum libraries reflecting this shift include the Musée National des Arts Africains et Océaniens in Paris, the Robert Goldwater Library of the Metropolitan Museum of Art in New York, and the Smithsonian Institution's National Museum of African Art in Washington, D.C. In Africa itself there are relatively few libraries dealing with African art. Collections can be found in Guinea-Bissau, Senegal, and Nigeria. Art libraries in Zimbabwe and South Africa are relatively well developed in this area, with museums (e.g., the South African National Gallery Library in Cape Town), public libraries (e.g.,

Johannesburg Public Library), and schools of art holding the majority of art materials.

Libraries in Japan have a long history, beginning before the eighth century with aristocratic and warrior families who collected clan records, religious texts, and literary works in *bunko,* or storehouses. Buddhist temples included areas for storing *sutras,* temple records, and other written materials. As calligraphy is a major Japanese art form, these historical libraries are by nature of art history significance. Printing in Japan flourished after 1600 with the rise of cities and a moneyed economy, supplemented by a high level of importation of foreign books—art materials among them. Specialized art and architectural collections, however, are a fairly recent development. Most are in universities (e.g., the Tokyo University Library and the Library of the Department of Architecture in the Faculty of Engineering in Kyoto University), or museums (e.g., the Tokyo National Museum). Important to art research is the recently established Japan Art Documentation Society and its influential bulletin.

Libraries also have long been part of civic life in China, as evidenced in the Han period (206 B.C. to A.D. 221) and flourishing as early as the Ming Dynasty (1368–1644). By the early 20th century, Chinese scholars had produced a very large body of writing on art, including biographies of artists, critical works, and inventories. The concept of art centered on calligraphy and painting, including Buddhist cave painting, with sculpture and ceramics receiving far less emphasis. The study of Chinese art in recent times (specifically since the death of Mao Tse-tung in 1976) has been aided by an active program of systematic archeology and by contact with worldwide approaches to art history. Special collections relating to Chinese art of all regions exist in the National Palace Museum in Taiwan, where the Qing palace collection was deposited in 1949; the University of California at Los Angeles (e.g., the Chinese Palace Archives); the Arthur M. Sackler Gallery Library in the Freer Gallery of Art Library in Washington, D.C.; the library of the Boston Museum of Fine Arts; and the Cleveland Museum of Art. In China itself, alternate periods of growth and destruction through war and ideology have severely affected collection growth in all libraries. Statistics on Chinese libraries are still meager, but evidence suggests that specialized art collections are not considered a national priority.

Outstanding architectural collections of Chinese materials can be found in several U.S. institutions: the Avery Architectural and Fine Arts Library of Columbia University, the Ryerson and Burnham Libraries of the Art Institute of Chicago, and the American Institute of Architects Library in New York City. Significant collections also reside in the Oriental and India Office of the British Library, the Library of the Royal Asiatic Society in London, the Percival David Foundation of Chinese Art at the University of London, and the Musée Guimet in Paris, where Indo-Chinese material can also be found in abundance.

The art and architecture of India can be studied at the Indira Gandhi National Center for the Arts in New Delhi, at the National Art Library in London (reflecting the largest Indian art holdings outside of India), and at the Musée Guimet in Paris. The art library collections of other Asian nations are still insufficiently known beyond their borders. This situation should change in response to efforts of the International Federation of Library Associations and Institutions (IFLA) and other agencies and with the aid of new technologies.

Art and Architecture Librarianship

During the past 30 years, scholars in the fields of art and architecture have shown growing interest in the social context, meaning, and function of art objects and activities. Reflecting this interest, part of the "new art history," art librarians have indicated in their literature that they, too, are attuned not only to objects and artifacts themselves but also to the social implications of art activity and the social meaning of art works. In art librarianship, this awareness has been evident most obviously in the expansion of collections to include humanities and social science material useful to the interpretation of art. Interest in the social aspects of art activity can also be seen in the stated commitment of professionals in this field to art librarianship as a social endeavor, one that has the potential to lead to positive social change. This sensitivity to library service in the context of a broader social mission is evident in a spirit of cooperation in the professional activities of the discipline that has led to greatly improved services for users and to considerable professional gratification for art librarians themselves. Ideas are not without progenitors. Among the strongest voices in the social advocacy movement have been Philip Pacey, Trevor Fawcett, Clive Phillpot, and Jan van der Wateran of the United Kingdom; William Dane, Antje B. Lemke, Betty Jo Irvine, and Toni Petersen of the United States; Murray Waddington and Mary F. Williamson of Canada; and Margaret Shaw of Australia.

Professional organizations for art and architecture librarians and for visual arts curators have proliferated in recent years. The largest organization is the loose affiliation of art library societies of various regions. The Art Libraries Society of North America (ARLIS/NA), founded in 1972, is the largest of these entities, with several chapters throughout the United States and Canada. The Art Libraries Societies for the United Kingdom and Ireland (1969) was the first of the ARLIS organizations. Other ARLIS organizations are found in Australia and New Zealand (1975), the Scandinavian countries (1983), and Norway (1986). Other organizations, sometimes overlapping ARLIS, include the Scottish Visual Arts Group, the Netherlandish Overleg kunsthistorischen Bibliotheken, and the Association for the Visual Arts in Ireland. Significant for image librarians/curators is the Visual Resources Association, based largely in the United States. Architectural librarians may belong to the Society of Architectural Historians and the American Association of Architectural Bibliographers, in addition to organizations for practitioners in a number of countries. International cooperation for art and architecture collections has been strengthened by the Art Libraries Section (1977) of IFLA. Major professional publications include *Art Libraries Journal,* published in Great Britain, and *Art Documentation,* the official journal of ARLIS/NA. Both journals provide generous documentation on the history of art libraries.

DEIRDRE C. STAM

Further Reading

Art Libraries Journal (1976–)
Freitag, Wolfgang M., "Art Libraries," in *Encyclopedia of Library and Information Science,* edited by Allen Kent et al., vol. 1, New York: Dekker, 1968
Gombrich, E.H., "The Literature of Art," *Art Documentation* 11 (1992)
Jones, Lois Swan, *Art: Research Methods and Resources: A Guide to Finding Art Information,* Dubuque, Iowa: Kendall/Hunt, 1978; 3rd edition, as *Art Information: Research Methods and Resources,* 1990
Jones, Lois Swan, "Art Libraries," in *Encyclopedia of Library History,* edited by Wayne A. Wiegand and Donald G. Davis, New York: Garland, 1994
Jones, Lois Swan, and Sarah Scott Gibson, *Art Libraries and Information Services: Development, Organization, and Management,* Orlando, Florida: Academic Press, 1986
Pettengill, George, "Architecture Libraries and Collections," in *Encyclopedia of Library and Information Science,* edited by Allen Kent et al., vol. 1, New York: Dekker, 1968
Potts, Kenneth, "Architectural Libraries," in *Encyclopedia of Library History,* edited by Wayne A. Wiegand and Donald G. Davis, New York: Garland, 1994
Viaux, Jacqueline, compiler, *IFLA Directory of Art Libraries; Répertoire de bibliothèques d'art de l'IFLA; Addressbuch der Kunstbibliotheken von IFLA; Directorio de bibliotecas de arte de la IFLA* (multilingual English-French-German-Spanish edition), New York: Garland, 1985

Balkan Libraries

General Background

The Balkan peninsula consists of a group of countries that are heterogeneous from political, cultural, ethnological, linguistic, and religious perspectives. The Roman Empire's conquest of parts of the Balkan region left influences that have survived until the present time, either in the language (Romanian is a Romance language) or in the religion practiced in certain countries (Croatia, Bosnia-Herzegovina, Macedonia, Montenegro, Romania, and Albania have large Roman Catholic populations). The Eastern Roman (Byzantine) Empire's control of the Balkans, which began during Emperor Constantine's reign in the fourth century, ended in the seventh century when migratory peoples of Slavic origin captured most of the Balkans. Bulgaria, Serbia, Slovenia, and Bosnia-Herzegovina have preserved the most long-lasting Slavic influence from ethnic and linguistic standpoints. Some Slavic languages are written in the Cyrillic alphabet, others in the Roman. The religion of the Slavic zone is preponderantly Eastern Orthodox, and Greeks and most Romanians are also Orthodox Catholics.

The countries in this geographical area share a few commonalities, among which is the domination of the Ottoman Empire over the entire Balkan Peninsula, domination that in certain regions began during the late 1300s and ended during the 1870s. Five centuries of Turkish rule introduced Islam to the region, and some of the Balkan countries (Bosnia-Herzegovina, Albania, Montenegro, and Macedonia) have preserved a significant Muslim component in their population. During the rise of the Hapsburg Empire and later the Austro-Hungarian Empire, parts of the Balkan Peninsula (Serbia, Slovenia, Bosnia-Herzegovina, Croatia, and Transylvania) were annexed and placed under the domination of Austria-Hungary until World War I.

The interwar period witnessed the consolidation of the Balkan states into independent kingdoms. One of the outcomes of World War II was that, in most Balkan states—Albania, Bulgaria, Romania, and Yugoslavia—the monarchy was abolished and these countries developed into "people's democracies," becoming subservient (to various degrees) Communist allies of the Soviet Union. Unlike the rest of the Balkan states ruled by authoritarian regimes, Greece followed a different path and became a presidential democratic republic in 1973; in 1981 it joined the European Community. In the Soviet satellite states, Communist-type authoritarian regimes seized power, with isolation from the West, centralization of the political and economic systems, and ideological social and cultural life becoming the norm during the Cold War period.

The fall of the Berlin Wall in 1989 led to the collapse of Communism throughout Central and Eastern Europe. The new political parties that replaced the Communist parties and took control of the emerging democracies faced huge difficulties in trying to transform the old centralized state-run economies into economies based on the unfamiliar concepts and practices of private enterprise. More than a decade after the end of the Communist era, the transition to democratic forms of government and the movement toward market economies has proven more difficult and painful than anticipated. All of the former Communist countries have experienced soaring inflation, rampant unemployment, and increasing degradation of social and cultural life.

From a territorial perspective, Albania, Bulgaria, Romania, and Greece have remained within their post–World War II boundaries, whereas the Yugoslav federation broke up into the six independent states of Serbia, Slovenia, Bosnia-Herzegovina, Croatia, Macedonia, and Montenegro, some of which are still experiencing violent outcomes that culminated with the wars in Bosnia and Kosovo in the 1990s.

Development of Libraries

Over the centuries each of the Balkan states developed its own ethnic, linguistic, and cultural identity. Despite the heterogeneity of their national characteristics, the countries of the Balkan peninsula underwent similar cultural and educational developments. The constant struggle of the Balkan countries to preserve their national identities during five centuries of Ottoman rule resulted in late development of their national cultures.

The flourishing civilization of ancient Greece produced manuscripts on papyrus and vellum belonging to political leaders, playwrights, poets, philosophers, and scientists of the time. The fate of many ancient Greek libraries remained uncertain, with some transferred to Rome after the conquest of Athens by the Roman Empire. The early history of libraries in the rest of the Balkan region followed a pattern similar to that of libraries in Western Europe. The first Byzantine libraries were established during the fourth century in connection with monasteries and cloisters that acquired and preserved primarily Christian literature. The manuscript collection of the Holy Mountain (Athos), which totaled 14,000 documents, was one of the earliest and most significant in Greece, and part of it is now held by the National Library of Greece in Athens. Unlike religious establishments in Western Europe, where scriptoria developed into productive copying centers, Byzantine libraries developed into translation centers where religious texts were translated into the vernacular languages spoken in the region. In addition, with the advent of printing these religious establishments became the first centers to foster printing efforts in the Balkans. The first works of Serbia, Bulgaria, and Romania were printed in Cyrillic and in Church Slavonic in their respective territories at the beginning of the 16th century.

The Ottomans were not supportive of cultural developments among their subjects. In fact, they actively opposed the ideological and technological changes taking place throughout most of the rest of Europe. Owing to the Ottoman ban on printing, there was no printing activity in Greece until 1821, and Greek books were printed in Italy, Germany, and the Romanian principalities. As in Western Europe, the existence of ecclesiastic libraries was paralleled by that of libraries owned by distinguished scholars who collected important ancient works.

During the medieval period, a few local princes established court libraries and supported scholars who compiled historical chronicles, but the 500-year Ottoman oppression delayed national cultural development in the Balkans. Countries in the region experienced a prolonged Middle Age period melding into a late Enlightenment period, with only muted Renaissance accents. Printing centers became more numerous during the 17th century despite Ottoman efforts to keep them under control, and the period was characterized by the presence of significant ecclesiastic and private libraries. In the part of the Balkans incorporated into the Austro-Hungarian Empire (Slovenia, Croatia, and Transylvania), German-type education was supported by the establishment of libraries for teachers and students in high schools (lyceums), which became mandatory during the 18th century.

The echo of the 1848 European revolution reached the Balkans, bringing about social unrest and attempts to change the status quo, which contributed to the weakening and eventually the collapse of the Ottoman Empire. The national awakening following the Turks' loss of supremacy in the region led to the creation of independent states in the Balkans and the revival of national identities.

Most public libraries emerged in the mid-19th century, either from school libraries that opened their collections to the public or from subscription-operated reading rooms and book clubs. The establishment of public libraries was an integral part of the national emancipation movement in the Balkan states, facilitating access to the written word for a wider segment of the literate population. Public libraries also played an important role in assisting with the consolidation of the Balkan national states and the promotion of national cultural values. The first public library opened in 1828 in Greece, followed by the first public libraries in Romania (1836), Croatia (1838), Bulgaria (1856), and finally Albania (1912). The collections of these public libraries consisted of works donated by local patriots such as teachers and politicians, whose goal was to contribute to the cultural revival of their countries and to raise the consciousness of the ordinary people, making them aware that they were the heirs of fine medieval civilizations and that preserving national cultural identity was a patriotic duty.

The mid-1800s also saw the establishment of national cultural and educational institutions and associations such as museums, theaters, academies, universities, and libraries. Literary societies and the first academies of science, art, and learning were founded in 1864 in Romania and Serbia, in 1868 in Croatia, and in 1869 in Bulgaria. The first universities organized following Western principles and endowed with libraries were established in Romania (1860: Iasi, 1872: Cluj, and 1891: Bucharest), in Greece (1837: Athens and 1926: Thessaloniki), in Croatia (1874: Zagreb), in Serbia (1905: Belgrade), and in Bulgaria (1909: Sofia).

The post–World War I era represented a period of growth in the library field in the Balkans. The establishment of public, school, and academic libraries became an intrinsic feature of the process of urbanization. This period was also characterized by ambitious collection development efforts through acquisitions from local publishers and through purchases of mostly French, British, and German books and periodicals. In addition to acquiring new items, attempts were made at organizing library collections through the development of various classification schemes that proved more or less successful until the Universal Decimal Classification system was adopted. The post–World War I period can be considered the era of retrospective bibliographic work in the Balkans, characterized by significant efforts to produce inventory lists, catalogs, and bibliographies of first imprints in each country. During the interwar period, the number of school, public, and academic libraries in the Balkan countries increased owing to government support and private initiative, thus ensuring wider access to the printed word. World War II disrupted the activity of libraries of all kinds. In the aftermath of the war, the Communist takeover of the Balkan states (with the exception of Greece) fostered a revision of the goals and mission of libraries in this region.

During the post–World War II period, the Communist states began large-scale programs to change their library systems, based on the Soviet model. During this period, libraries served as political propaganda tools for mass indoctrination with the dogmas of the Marxist-Leninist ideology. Their primary mission was to build strong holdings of political literature and to preserve the national cultural heritage rather than to provide access to the intellectual content of their collections. The user-centered approach to services, so widely practiced in the Western world, continued to remain an elusive desideratum in Balkan libraries. Libraries in Communist countries were government-subsidized and heavily centralized, with decisions made at the top level imposed downward through the hierarchy.

Post-1990 attempts to automate library services in the Balkans have been affected by poor infrastructures (inadequate telecommunication networks, the paucity of appropriate equipment, and the absence of national standards and trained personnel) throughout the region. Other challenges have been rampant inflation that diminishes the libraries' ability to purchase hardware and software capable of supporting the implementation of integrated systems and an acute lack of the cooperation needed to create local, national, and regional information networks and policies. The need for library staff with information technology skills has also been a significant issue affecting the implementation of integrated library systems. International efforts made possible assessments of the state of librarianship in the Balkan region, and such efforts also facilitated exchanges of librarians. This has enabled library staff from Balkan countries to participate in training sessions in Western Europe and North America. Continuing education seminars have been organized in which library and information science professionals from Western Europe and North America conducted workshops and lectured on contemporary issues in library and information science. Technical support and expertise from technologically advanced countries continues to be greatly needed in the Balkan region.

The first meeting of librarians from all the Balkan states took place in 2000 in Ankara. Participants presented assessments of the state of librarianship and library education in their countries, shared common concerns, and discussed venues for cooperation at the regional level. The second meeting is scheduled for the end of 2001 and will be hosted by Romania.

National Libraries and Their Responsibilities

Bulgaria and Greece established their national libraries immediately after liberation from Turkish domination. The National Library of Bulgaria was founded in 1878 and the National Library of Greece in 1821, whereas national libraries in Albania and Romania were creations of the 20th century (1922 and 1955, respectively). Each of the six republics of the former Yugoslav federation established a national library: the Slovene National and University Library (1919), the National and University Library of Croatia (1945), the National Library of Serbia (1947), the National Library of Macedonia (1944), the National Library of Bosnia-Herzegovina (1945), and the National Library of Montenegro (1946). The two autonomous provinces of Kosovo and Vojvodina also established national libraries: the National and University Library of Kosovo (1970) and the National Library of Vojvodina (1948).

The compilation of national bibliographies with several series covering different formats and media, based on the legal deposit copy, has been one of the many functions specific to national libraries. In the former Yugoslavia, the Yugoslav Bibliographical Institute was responsible for the development of the country's national bibliography, *Bibliografija Jugoslavije*. The breakup of Yugoslavia made the future of the national bibliographies of the region uncertain. After Yugoslavia's dissolution, each national library assumed the role of national bibliographic agency.

Library Education and Professional Associations

Communist rule discontinued all forms of library education in the Balkan states. No librarians were graduated from any university, and all library directors were political appointees—faithful followers of the Marxist-Leninist doctrine. Under these circumstances, during the last decades of the Communist period it was the responsibility of national libraries and other major academic libraries to offer on-the-job training and continuing education courses to university graduates interested in becoming librarians. The courses focused on traditional librarianship and included collection organization, cataloging, and classification.

Service-oriented reference librarianship, as practiced in the Western world, has never been adopted in the Eastern bloc. Even today, there are librarians in this part of the world who continue the old practices of protecting their collections and perceiving their institutions as guardians of national cultural treasures rather than information centers aimed at serving all segments of the population. After 1990 library schools were restored within major universities, but they lack faculty adequately trained to teach the latest advances in the library and information science field. The curricula carry a heavy component of history and foreign language classes. The U.S. Information Agency has sponsored library professionals under the Fulbright program to teach library and information science courses during one or two semesters in Balkan library schools.

Post-1990 political pluralism allowed the creation of library associations in the Balkan countries; some countries had more powerful professional associations than others. In the former Yugoslavia, librarians were members of the Union of Librarians Associations of Yugoslavia, which relocated its headquarters to a different capital every two years. In Romania the library association was discontinued in the 1970s along with the school of library science. In 1990 library associations were established in Romania and Bulgaria and became active at the national level. After the demise of Communism, Balkan libraries rejoined the International Federation of Library Associations (IFLA), and each year an ever-increasing number of librarians from the Eastern bloc find the necessary resources to attend IFLA conferences and make their voices heard.

Collections

During the Communist regime, libraries served as propaganda tools for mass indoctrination, and library collections in pre-1990 nondemocratic societies of the Balkans reflected the political orientation of the governments in power. The publications of the leading Communist parties were abundantly represented on library shelves in the Eastern bloc, whereas anti-Communist literature, writings of local authors living in exile, and historical works focusing on the traditional parties and monarchic periods were consistently banned from library collections. Major libraries followed specific guidelines in order to purge their collections of works deemed harmful to the building of the Communist society. Party and state regulations stipulated that blacklisted materials be removed from shelves and incorporated into a distinct collection, often called "the secret collection" or "the forbidden collection." Only researchers granted special permission by Communist Party authorities were allowed access to banned works. In other instances censorship was so drastic as to result in the physical destruction of documents. Except for limited collections in local branches of public libraries, all libraries in the Soviet bloc were organized with closed access. In reading rooms, patrons were only allowed free access to small collections of reference materials and current periodicals.

The lack of hard currency prevented libraries in Eastern Europe from purchasing books and periodicals published in the West. Their collection development relied heavily on exchange programs with other Communist countries, among which the Soviet Union was the primary partner. After the demise of Communism, the extensive holdings of Soviet literature were the first to be discarded. In the early 1990s substantial donations of books and periodicals from Western European and North American countries attempted to fill the gap, especially in the fields of business, management, new technologies, and social sciences.

During the collapse of Communism, Eastern European libraries were also confronted with the overwhelming effects of freedom of the press. Formerly all publishing activities were state funded and controlled. The demise of Communism led to the decentralization and privatization of publishing houses and the proliferation of private publishers, who issued primarily reprints or translations of formerly banned books and types of literature (such as erotic and astrological books) not allowed during the Communist regime. The explosion of privately owned newspapers and magazines and the lack of reinforced legal deposit laws caused chaos in bibliographic control activities, and the national bibliographies were not able to reflect accurately the editorial output of the 1990s.

The Balkan states have recognized the need for national information policies and legislation to protect intellectual property and to regulate publishing and library activities. Drafts of library laws await discussion in the parliaments of several countries. Unfortunately, libraries and their specific issues have never represented a priority on any post-Soviet Balkan political party's agenda. Balkan legislators do not seem to perceive the library as a component of the democratization process or an institution that contributes to national empowerment and the development of an informed citizenry.

During the Communist period, major systems of workplace/enterprise libraries existed, generally funded and run by the trade unions and separate from public, academic, school, and special libraries. Their collections contained Marxist-Leninist literature and translations of Russian and Soviet classic works into vernacular languages. After 1990 the trade union libraries underwent thorough culling and were later either disbanded or incorporated into school and public library collections, as their parent institutions had ceased to exist. Owing to a severe shortage of funds, some workplace libraries, inadequate as they were, became the seed libraries of private universities founded after 1990.

Under Communist rule, Eastern European libraries were government subsidized through ministries of culture and education. In the 1990s, a significant number of libraries of all types closed because of budget cuts and inflationary economies. Despite this loss, the number of readers increased significantly owing to several factors, including the availability of previously banned materials that attracted journalists and researchers, the emergence of private universities with a growing number of students, and a substantial increase in book prices that made it difficult for individuals to buy books for their private collections.

Several libraries in the Balkans were victims of the fight against Communism. The Central University Library in Bucharest was engulfed by the flames of the December 1989 popular revolt. The United Nations Educational, Scientific, and Cultural Organization (UNESCO) and private foreign support turned this library into the premier library in Romania, equipped with state-of-the-art technology enabling it to become the first library in the country to make its catalog searchable online via the Internet. The National and University Library of Bosnia-Herzegovina in Sarajevo was destroyed in 1992 during the civil war following the country's decision to declare its independence from Yugoslavia. The fire ignited by grenades completely destroyed the historical library building and 90 percent of its collections. UNESCO adopted a resolution to support the reconstruction of the library and its endowment with new collections. Croatian libraries were ruthlessly attacked by Serbian troops in their attempt to devastate cultural and historical monuments associated with Croatian national pride. At the beginning of the 21st century, all of these libraries are in the process of healing from war wounds. In their recovery efforts, they are raising funds to reconstruct buildings and collections.

Automation of Library Services

Basic equipment vital to facilitating the research process and taken for granted in the West (such as copy machines) were luxuries in Balkan libraries during the Communist regime, when photocopying any library material meant obtaining special authorizations, signatures, and stamps before a single copy was made. All duplication methods were severely limited and strictly kept under surveillance. Even today copiers are a rarity in Eastern bloc libraries. Microfilm and microfiche readers are not regarded as a necessity because there has been no concerted effort to microfilm collections. Entire collections of old periodicals are stored in basements, which are often cold and damp. A few microfilming projects sponsored by international firms have begun to salvage old periodicals to make them accessible for research. At this stage, digitization projects seem to be in the distant future.

In terms of automation, Balkan libraries lag behind their Western counterparts, which began to automate their activities in the 1970s. In addition to outdated collections, inadequate buildings, and poor infrastructures, one of the most striking effects of Communism on libraries has been the lack of awareness that interaction, cooperation, and coordination are crucial in this domain. The outcome is that every Balkan library that has begun automation efforts has done so independently rather than with the goal of joining local, regional, national, and international networks. Shared cataloging is extremely rare and, when it does exist, it is limited to a restricted number of participating libraries.

Automation efforts are taking place disparately. Some libraries are at an incipient stage of retrospective conversion of their collections, whereas the staff of others can only dream of one day having the means to implement and gain access to networked computerized services. Owing to slow progress in the automation of their services, only a few Balkan libraries have been able to link to international information networks and make parts of their catalogs available through the Internet. One reason for the lack of cooperation among libraries in the Balkans is the difficulty of creating a shared cataloging system capable of ensuring access and retrieval in the differing languages and alphabets (Roman, Cyrillic, and Greek) used in the region. In the early 1990s, when international organizations began funding automation projects in formerly Communist countries, they gave priority to libraries in Central Europe. More than ten years after the collapse of Communism, Eastern European libraries that have relied only on government funding are behind those of Central Europe.

International Support

The collapse of Communism in Eastern Europe drew the attention of the international library community to this part of the world. As noted previously, numerous teams of library and information science professionals from the United States, Canada, and Western Europe went to Balkan countries in the 1990s to assess library conditions and needs, consult with local librarians, and conduct workshops and seminars. Other programs assisted Balkan libraries with significant shipments of books, periodicals, and equipment, and Balkan librarians shared their experiences under the aegis of various library institutions and associations. A number of librarians from the Balkan region were sponsored to earn master's degrees in library and information science at universities in the United Kingdom and the United States. In addition, international conferences were dedicated entirely to the subject of libraries in formerly Communist countries.

At the beginning of the 21st century, Balkan libraries continue to face financial hardships that prevent them from smoothly overcoming the transition period toward complete automation of their services and from effectively joining the international library network. They remain in great need of support from their national governments and from the international library community in order to regenerate and become compatible with their counterparts in technologically advanced countries.

HERMINA G.B. ANGHELESCU

See also National and University Library of Bosnia and Herzegovina; National and University Library of Croatia; National Library of Romania; National Library of Saints Cyril and Methodius (Bulgaria); Slovenia National and University Library

Further Reading

Keller, Dean H., editor, *Academic Libraries in Greece: The Present Situation and Future Prospects*, Binghamton, New York: Haworth Press, 1993

Lass, Andrew, and Richard E. Quandt, editors, *Library Automation in Transitional Societies: Lessons from Eastern Europe*, New York and Oxford: Oxford University Press, 2000

Libraries and Culture 36, no. 1 (2001) (special issue edited by Hermina G.B. Anghelescu and Martine Poulain entitled "Books, Libraries, Reading, and Publishing in the Cold War")

Turfan, Barbara, Kathleen Ladizesky, and Inese A. Smith, editors, *Emerging Democracies and Freedom of Information*, London: The Library Association, 1995

Bibliophile Society Libraries

It is natural to suppose that all bibliophile societies maintain libraries, but in fact such collections are the exception rather than the rule. (The phrase *bibliophile society* is used in this essay in preference to *book club*, because the latter term today embraces literary societies, casual reading groups, and subscription programs such as the Book-of-the-Month Club.) None of the English or European societies maintain any library other than an archival run of their own publications. They are without exception "moveable feasts" on the pattern established by their common ancestor, the English Roxburghe Club (founded 1813), and consist of occasional dinners and lectures held at restaurants or social clubs, with no fixed abode. Where there is no permanent clubhouse, there can be no library.

Most U.S. bibliophile societies follow the European model, with a few important exceptions. The majority of U.S. societies were established between 1884 and 1895, and their founders were all influenced, to a greater or lesser degree, by the social and cultural uplift movements prevalent in the United States during the final decades of the 19th century. Like their European cousins, the primary aim of U.S. bibliophile societies was (and is) to celebrate and promote fine book production. Indeed, in the preface to his *American Book Clubs* (1987), author Adolf Growoll defines his subject strictly as "an association of two or more persons whose exclusive purpose it is to publish either original matter or reprints of scarce or curious books." But whereas that exclusivity of purpose holds true for European bibliophile societies, which tend to focus on fine printing produced by book lovers for book lovers, the constitutions of the major U.S. clubs all reflect a desire to educate the public in the art and history of the book. Publication programs were an important means to that end, but where local resources permitted, a number of U.S. societies took the unusual step of establishing clubhouses in which exhibitions could be held and library collections maintained. These groups include the Grolier Club of New York (1884), the Rowfant Club of Cleveland (1892), the Book Club of California (1912), and Boston's Club of Odd Volumes (1887). The Caxton Club of Chicago (1895) and California's Zamorano Club (1927) once maintained libraries but no longer do so.

Second only to the Grolier Club Library (described in detail elsewhere in this volume), the Rowfant Club boasts the largest U.S. bibliophile society library. Books are collected in accordance with the object of the club, noted in David Alan Novak's centenary volume as the "critical study of books in their various capacities to please the mind of man." The 7,500-volume collection includes Boswell and Johnson material, examples of the work of woodcut artist John De Pol and papermaker Dard Hunter, topographical works on London and Edinburgh, Rowfant Club publications, Stevensoniana, books about books, and bookplates and other ephemera. Smaller in size, but of perhaps more scholarly importance, is the 2,500-volume Albert Sperisen Library of the Book Club of California. As described on the club's website, the collection consists chiefly of examples of fine printing, graphic arts, and bookbinding; landmarks and firsts in the history of bookmaking; bibliography; and books about books. The library is available during business hours for consultation by members and the public and has been professionally cataloged to exacting standards, with all titles listed in an international database available online, increasing its accessibility and usefulness. Most of the holdings are 20th-century publications; one-fifth concern paper or binding or are special examples thereof; approximately one-quarter are reference works on the history and technique of printing; and at least another one-quarter are fine press products issued largely but not exclusively from California.

Boston's Club of Odd Volumes library has approximately 2,200 titles. It was established as a bibliographical reference collection but now includes works by members on bookish subjects and miscellaneous titles of bibliophile interest. The collection is open only to members.

ERIC J. HOLZENBERG

See also Grolier Club Library

Further Reading

Growoll, Adolf, *American Book Clubs*, New York: Dodd Mead, 1897; reprint, New York: Franklin, 1964

Little, David B., *The Centennial Book: The Club of Odd Volumes, 1877, Number 77 Mount Vernon Street, Boston, Massachusetts*, Lunenberg, Vermont: Meriden-Stinehour Press, 1987

North, Ernest Dressel, "Some Notes on American Book Clubs," *Bibliographica* 2, no. 7 (1986)

Novak, David Alan, editor, *The First One Hundred Years, 1892–1992: A Keepsake Volume for the Centenary of the Rowfant Club*, Cleveland, Ohio: Rowfant Club, 1992

Piehl, Frank J., *The Caxton Club, 1895–1995*, Chicago: Caxton Club, 1995

Buddhist Libraries

Buddhism forms a major cultural link between the people of Asia from India to the Pacific, and its libraries have a long history of textual preservation. The historical Buddha, known as Sakyamuni, lived around 500 B.C. in northern India. Around the first century B.C., Buddhism began to develop a sacred literature, originally written in two related Indo-European languages, Pali and Sanskrit. The Buddhist scriptures are known as the Tripitaka or Tipitaka (literally meaning three baskets), consisting of the disciplines for monastic life, the major teachings, and scholarly commentaries on the teachings. The Tripitaka comprises the complete canon of Buddhist texts written between 500 B.C. and the beginning of the Christian era.

The Buddhism of China, Japan, and Korea differs considerably from that of Sri Lanka, Burma, and Thailand, which remains closer to the early teachings. The form of Buddhism that is perhaps best known in the West is Zen. This school arose in China but then flourished, particularly in Japan. Zen, with its emphasis on meditation, had a considerable influence in 20th-century Europe, North America, and Australia. This influence was largely owing to the Japanese scholar Daisetz Teitaro Suzuki.

JAGTAR SINGH

History

According to the seventh-century Chinese pilgrim Xuanzang, the great northern Indian monastery complex at Nalanda possessed three multistory libraries in the early seventh century A.D. Although this may have been exceptional, substantial libraries certainly existed in many early Buddhist centers, but none of these are extant, and their holdings and organization are a matter of conjecture.

More is known about historical Buddhist libraries of eastern Asia. The Annals of the Sui Dynasty recount that in 518, the last year of the dynasty, Emperor Wu "made a large collection of 5,400 Buddhist canonical books and placed them in the Hualin Garden." A catalog was compiled at the time, although this was certainly not the first Chinese collection of Buddhist literature.

Copies of sacred texts donated to temples by wealthy Chinese laity were stored in sutra repositories. One standard design, apparently invented by the sixth-century lay master Fu Tashi, consisted of a tall, octagonal, revolving cabinet (*chuan lun cang*) containing banks of drawers, hinged around a central pillar. It was easy to use and had the added advantage that illiterate persons, although unable to read the sacred writings, could touch and spin the cabinet as a merit-making act. The magnificent revolving cabinet of the Nan chansi in Suzhou is said to have cost 10,000 strings of cash, with another 3,600 strings spent on its more than 5,000 manuscript scrolls. Completed in 863, it had 64 seats arranged around a central repository whose turning could be stopped only with the aid of a sturdy brake. Another celebrated repository at the Jin gesi on Mount Wutai contained the Tripitaka in more than 6,000 fascicles written in gold and silver ink on dark blue paper. Catalogs of the seventh to eighth century suggest that each drawer of a typical repository contained approximately ten scrolls.

From 972, printed sacred texts in China began to assume a new stitched book shape, and different forms of library housing, usually large wooden closets, evolved. Libraries were generally located on the upper floor of one of the major halls of a monastery complex, often somewhere near the entrance to the precincts. Typically it consisted of cases containing the Tripitaka, a central altar containing a variety of images (the bodhisattva Guanyin was often represented among these), and tables and chairs, including some arranged in an adjoining room for the use of visitors. The library usually also provided storage for wooden printing blocks as well as living quarters for the librarian and his assistant. It was not uncommon for such libraries to double as One Thousand Buddha Halls (*Qian fodian*). A Platform for Drying Sutras in the Sun (*shai jingtai*) was positioned just in front of the library. Here, on the sixth day of the sixth month, books were spread in the sunshine and cleaned. Although this task was performed by monks, laypeople also attended the event as a merit-making exercise.

The oldest Japanese Buddhist sutra repository (*kyozo*) appears to have been Prince Shotoku's private study, the Yumedono (Dream Hall) at the Horyuji on the outskirts of Nara, dating from the early seventh century. The Yumedono is supposed to have housed Shotoku's manuscript copy of a treatise on three sutras (*Sangyo gisho*), the first scholarly work by a native Japanese. However, the *kyozo* of most early Japanese Buddhist temples, such as the Todaiji, Genkoji, and Kofukuji, housed Chinese classics as well as Buddhist literature. Another early temple, the Enryakuji, established by Saicho in 788 as the headquarters of the Tendai school, housed a collection of 230 writings in 460 volumes imported from China. Today this library is maintained in the city of Otsu near Mount Hiei.

In line with the ordinances of the Taiho Code of 701, the Zushoryo, the first archival library in Japanese history, was founded to store Buddhist images, scriptures, and other writings. Five copies of every book written or copied in temples were supposed to be lodged there. At its inception the Zushoryo provided some degree of general access, but after 728 entrance to those below high court rank was prohibited.

Written texts have been the object of extreme devotion in Japan, leading to a highly protective attitude toward their custodianship. Indeed, sacred writings must be carefully handled in all parts of the Buddhist world. They are placed on specially constructed stands for reading purposes, and it is forbidden for women to rest them on their laps. Some Buddhist libraries, such as the Shugei Shuchiin, established by Kukai in 828, did allow limited access to commoners, but the traditional position was that "the people must be made to obey and not to learn." Nevertheless, a prominent eighth-century convert to Buddhism,

Isonokami no Yakatsugu (a Japanese ambassador to China), is renowned as the founder of Japan's first public library, the Untei, which consisted of a pavilion on the grounds of his family temple.

The ruling clan of eighth-century Japan encouraged the copying of Buddhist sutras as a means of ensuring the prosperity of the state and the welfare of the people. Because the presence of sacred writings was essential to the establishment of a temple, many new temples were established around this time. By the Kamakura period (1192–1333), sutra copying was conducted mainly within the monastic libraries themselves, and by the 15th century many temples had a book room (*shoin*) that, apart from its function as a repository, was used for reading and writing and also for literary gatherings.

The history of Buddhist libraries in Southeast Asia is somewhat opaque. In Burma a Buddhist library is said to have been established in Pagan as early as the 11th century by King Anawrahta. This eventually evolved into the Pitaka Taik. In 1795 a British envoy to Burma described the royal library of Amarapura as the largest royal library between the Danube and China. In neighboring Thailand in the 17th century, King Narai appears to have ordered his royal scribes to gather all known religious and legislative writings, thus establishing the Royal Library at Ayutthaya, which was subsequently destroyed by the Burmese invasion of 1767. However, the tradition of Southeast Asian royal libraries continued into the Chakri dynasty, when Rama I had the Mondira Dhamma library of Buddhist scriptures built on the grounds of his new palace in Bangkok in 1783.

IAN HARRIS

Some Modern Buddhist Libraries

For the purpose of illustration, this essay discusses three examples of contemporary Buddhist collections: the Australian Buddhist Library in the National Library of Australia, Canberra; the Central Institute of Higher Tibetan Studies Shantarakshita Library in Sarnath, India; and the Buddhist Library in Singapore. Finally, the essay discusses a growing virtual library of Buddhist studies now available on the Internet.

Australian Buddhist Library, National Library of Australia

This library, formerly situated in central Sydney, donated its entire 3,000-volume collection in 1987 to the National Library of Australia in Canberra. At the request of the donor, the books have been kept together as a separate collection and retain the name Australian Buddhist Library. In Sydney, the library was assembled between 1984 and 1987 through the generosity of the Liao family and other benefactors. According to its founder and director, Eric Liao, the library was established in 1984 to meet a growing public need for readily available reference materials on Buddhism. It was soon decided to transfer the library to a large, established institution with the resources necessary to maintain the collection over the long term and an active policy of acquiring Buddhist materials. Hence the National Library was chosen. The donation constituted a major addition to the National Library's already substantial collections on Buddhism.

The move to Canberra involved careful packing of 3,000 books, including editions of the scriptures in Chinese, English, Pali, Burmese, and Thai. For the Liao family, the motivation for donating the collection to the library rather than to a temple was that it would be more easily accessible to scholars and readers interested in Buddhist philosophy and religion. Books from the Australian Buddhist Library may be borrowed by interlibrary loan. For the benefit of researchers, the library offers a useful catalog of the collection, available in the Asian Collections Reading Room.

The Asian and English language holdings of the Australian Buddhist Library cover many aspects of Zen, from philosophy and psychology to literature, the arts, gardening, and the Japanese tea ceremony. One of the most eye-catching artifacts displayed in the National Library is a life-size replica of a Thai seated golden Buddha, characteristic of representations found in India, Sri Lanka, Burma, and Thailand, a gift that accompanied the library donation.

The collection consists mainly of Chinese- and English-language works on Buddhism as well as items in other Asian languages. There are reference works, monographs, periodicals, audiotapes, and a Tripitaka section, including editions in Chinese, English, Pali, Burmese, Sinhalese, and Thai. The Khmer-language Tripitaka is the rarest edition of the Buddhist scriptures held by the library. It is believed to be one of only a handful remaining after the wholesale destruction of books during the Khmer Rouge regime in Cambodia (1975–79). The library's set had been purchased in 1970 as part of the Coedes collection on Indochina. Professor Georges Coedes, director of l'École Française d'Extreme Orient, had collected widely during his long career in former French Indochina. Another historic Buddhist treasure is preserved in the library's storage vault. This is the Korean Tripitaka—the Koryo Taejang Gyong, 1,340 volumes of a Korean edition of the Chinese Buddhist canon that was brought, according to popular legend, to China from India by an itinerant monk. Its delicate pages, held together in the ancient Chinese manner with waxed orange thread, are enclosed between heavier waxed paper covers. Researchers who wish to view the Korean Tripitaka must give 24 hours notice to Asian Collections staff. It is worth the wait to view the volumes, as these were produced from woodblocks dating from 1251, blocks still used by monks of the Haeinsa Temple in southeastern Korea. The Tripitaka contains 1,524 texts in 6,558 chapters, first published in 1011. The library's copy is one of only eight copies made from the original woodblocks and bound in the same size as the original. Probably the most beautiful Buddhist text produced more recently is the Nyingma edition of the Tibetan Tripitaka; the library's set is from a limited edition of 100 numbered copies. These books with flame-orange bindings were produced by Tibetan Buddhist monks, who took refuge first in India and later in California after being exiled following the Chinese takeover of Tibet in 1949.

The library also houses materials relating to Buddhism's social and political dimensions. From Thailand, an overwhelmingly Buddhist country, the library has a major set of cremation volumes. These uniquely Thai publications are produced in limited numbers to honor a deceased person and are distributed at his or her funeral. Each contains a short biography, tributes from family and friends, and perhaps extracts from the subject's own writings, a favorite piece of literature, or material concerning a topic that was of special interest. Cremation volumes are particularly valuable as they often contain information about important people that is not found elsewhere, and for historians they provide a rare and personal insight into the subject's life and times.

The Burmese-Pali Tripitaka in the Australian Buddhist Library collection deserves special mention. Its original was taken from a series of marble engravings ordered in 1856 by King Mindon, founder of Burma's royal city of Mandalay and governor of the Fifth Buddhist Synod. The library's copy was made by means of ink and stone rubbings—a lengthy and painstaking task, as the original engravings filled some 729 marble tablets that still occupy a 13-acre site in Mandalay. The collection also includes editions of the well-loved Jataka Tales. These Buddhist folk stories have endured throughout the Buddhist countries of North and Southeast Asia for centuries. They are cautionary tales with a moral, such as "The Dog Who Wanted to Be a Lion," "The Greedy Crow," and "The Tortoise Who Talked too Much."

For art lovers, the library holds *Ten Lives of the Buddha: Siamese Temple Paintings and Jataka Tales* (1972) by Elizabeth Wray, Joe D. Wray, Clare Rosenfield, and Dorothy Bailey, a book of elegantly executed color photographs of Thai temple paintings. These are in striking contrast to the Ghandara-style wall mural paintings and sandstone carvings of northern India, as depicted in Jeannine Auboyer's *Buddha: A Pictorial History of His Life and Legacy* (1983). Klaus Wenk's *Wandmarlereien in Thailand* (Mural Paintings in Thailand, 1975) is held in the rare book collection. The Asian collections also contain many lavishly illustrated publications on Chinese, Japanese, Korean, Tibetan, and Southeast Asian Buddhist arts. Also of interest to English speakers is the library's collection of Buddhist journals and newsletters from Australia and elsewhere, such as *Bodhi Leaf* (1979–), published by the Wat Buddha Dhamma at Wisemans Ferry, New South Wales; the *Middle Way* (1943–), from the London Buddhist Society; and the *Newsletter* (1993–) of the Tibetan Buddhist Society of Victoria.

Access to the materials is facilitated by an Australian Buddhist Library catalog listing its collections by language and by subject (in each language), according to the U.S. Library of Congress classification scheme. The materials are housed in the Asian collections section of the National Library, where they are available for use in the Asian Collections Reading Room by users who may consult copies of the catalog there and request them. They may also be borrowed via interlibrary loan, subject to the usual requirements.

Central Institute of Higher Tibetan Studies, Shantarakshita Library

The Shantarakshita Library was named after the great Saint Shantarakshita, who explored Buddhism in Tibet in the eighth century. Sarnath, where the library is located, is said to be the site of the Buddha's first sermon. The institute was an outcome of dialogue between the Dalai Lama and Pandit Jawaharlal Nehru, the prime minister of India, in 1967. It was granted independent status in 1978 under the Indian Department of Culture, Ministry of Human Resource Development. In 1998 it obtained the status "Deemed to be University" under the University Grants Commission. The library has a wide range of books on Buddhology, Tibetology, Himalayan studies, comparative religion, Sanskrit, philosophy, literature, and the history and culture of Tibet, as well as a rich collection of nonbook materials. The audiovisual section is well equipped with computers and advanced facilities for microfilming, printing, and photocopying.

At present, the library database covers approximately 55,000 books, 12,000 journal articles, and some 25,000 other items accessible from every computer station of the library. A comprehensive database includes all Devanagri, Tibetan, and Roman documents, including books, journal articles, videocassettes, and microfilms. Data entry of complicated Tibetan *pothis* and other documents is still in progress. As the library is a member of the Information and Library Network (INFLIBNET), it has become a core information resource center for scholars of Buddhology, Tibetology, and Himalayan studies. The library uses Colon Classification and AACRII (*Anglo American Cataloging Rules*, 2nd edition) for processing the documents.

In India, other Buddhist collections of repute can be found at the Library of Tibetan Works and Archives, Dharmsala; Tibet House, New Delhi; the Central Institute of Buddhist Studies, Leh; the Sikkim Institute of Tibetology, Gangtok; the Asiatic Buddhist Society, Calcutta; Namgyal Institute, Dharmsala; the Punjabi University, Patiala, Guru Gobind Singh Department of Religious Studies; and the University of Delhi.

Buddhist Library of Singapore

Singapore's Buddhist Library was established in 1981 in the Geylang area of Singapore with the aim of providing and promoting Buddhist education. In addition to collecting resource material on Buddhism and related topics, it also sponsors courses, talks, and meditation retreats on a regular basis. The library has published several books on Buddhist studies by renowned Buddhist scholars. One recent innovation is the production of an animated video on the life of the Buddha. As a nonsectarian organization, the library serves as a platform for members of various Buddhist schools to learn, discuss, and teach Buddhism. Over the years, membership has grown from 300 to more than 3,000. Having established close links with

Buddhist organizations in Singapore, the library now seeks to reach out to Buddhists overseas, including via electronic media.

The Buddhist Research Society manages the library, and membership is open to all. The reading room is open to the general public; however, book loans are restricted to library members. Members are also given priority when registering for courses and other activities conducted by the library.

The library's collection includes approximately 15,000 books in English and Chinese on most areas of Buddhism, including scriptural texts, doctrine and philosophy, ethics, meditation, devotion, and the arts. Also available is a sizable collection of books on related fields, such as the major world religions, Eastern and Western philosophy, comparative religion, language studies, psychology, and ecology. The children's section is a separate collection catering to junior library users.

The Buddhist Library has developed its own catalog and classification system, designed specifically for Buddhist subjects. The electronic automated catalog allows for efficient literature search and information retrieval. The library subscribes to local and international Buddhist periodicals to keep its users updated on current topics of interest and news in the Buddhist world. The catalog is not yet available through the library's website.

Over the years, many talks have been delivered at the library by eminent Buddhist teachers and recorded on audiotapes, available for listening in the library. Copies may also be purchased at a nominal price. There is a collection of videotaped talks, discussions, and documentaries of interest to Buddhists. These are screened at meetings or classes organized by the library. Despite very limited financial resources, the Buddhist Library in Singapore serves an important regional role in the organization and dissemination of Buddhist thought.

Buddhist Studies WWW Virtual Library (www.ciolek.com/WWWVL-Buddhism.html)

This Internet-based site keeps track of leading information facilities in the fields of Buddhism and Buddhist studies. Currently this and related documents provide direct World Wide Web links to more than 600 specialist information facilities worldwide. All links are inspected and evaluated before being added to this virtual library. The major categories on the site are pure land Buddhism; Tibetan studies; Zen Buddhism; Buddhism internet resources: metaregister; major Buddhism World Wide Web sites; electronic resources for the study of Buddhist texts; and Buddhism Gopher, File Transfer Protocol, mailing lists, and chat rooms. Linked resources available through the site include Buddhist InfoWeb; Theravada Buddhist InfoWeb; Zen Buddhist InfoWeb; and Buddhist Art.

JAGTAR SINGH

Further Reading

"Central Institute of Higher Tibetan Studies Shantarakshita Library: A Profile," *INFLIBNET Newsletter* 6, no. 1 (January–March 2000)

Croucher, Paul, *Buddhism in Australia, 1848–1988,* Kensington: New South Wales University Press, 1989

Faulk, Tina, and Andrew Gosling, "Collecting Karma," *National Library of Australia News* 9, no. 7 (April 1999)

Gosling, Andrew, "A Journey to Asia," in *The People's Treasures: Collections in the National Library of Australia,* edited by John Thompson, Canberra: National Library of Australia, 1993

Welch, Theodore F., *Toshokan: Libraries in Japanese Society,* London: Bingley, and Chicago: American Library Association, 1976

Caribbean Libraries

The term *Caribbean,* if applied in its widest geographic context, describes all the lands washed by the Caribbean Sea. As would be expected in an area so geographically dispersed, library development patterns are varied, and it would be very difficult, if not impossible, to provide a concise overview of all libraries in the region. This essay is limited to discussion of the English-speaking Caribbean islands.

The English-speaking or British Caribbean is defined as all of those countries that were formerly colonies of Great Britain. This grouping includes the islands of Anguilla, Antigua/Barbuda, Barbados, the Bahamas, the British Virgin Islands, the Cayman Islands, Dominica, Grenada, Jamaica, Montserrat, St. Kitts/Nevis, St. Lucia, St. Vincent and the Grenadines, Trinidad and Tobago, the Turks and Caicos Islands, and the mainland territories of Belize and Guyana. Many of these countries have now become full-fledged independent states or have attained some form of limited self-government with continued colonial affiliations to Great Britain.

The independent territories have formed themselves into an economic grouping referred to as the Caribbean Community (CARICOM). Some of the members of CARICOM also belong to a smaller regional body, the Organization of Eastern Caribbean States (OECS). Since library and information services have been relatively well developed in the larger territories of

Barbados, Belize, Guyana, Jamaica, and Trinidad and Tobago, the major focus will be on services in these countries. Library development in the smaller countries (the grouping identified above as the OECS countries) will be discussed to a lesser extent, as growth has been hampered by limited financial and human resources. This essay will focus on public libraries, national and school libraries, special libraries, and academic libraries. Mention will also be made of national and regional library associations and library education and training in the English-speaking Caribbean.

Public Libraries

Organized public library systems in the English-speaking Caribbean were not created until well into the 19th century, when governments in the various territories enacted public library legislation. Prior to this action, most islands benefited from what can be described as subscription services, including Antigua (1830), Barbados (1847), Trinidad and Tobago (1851), Jamaica (1879), and St. Vincent and the Grenadines (1893).

In tracing the historical development of public libraries, two reports—Ernest Savage's *The Libraries of Bermuda, the Bahamas, the British West Indies, British Guiana, British Honduras, Puerto Rico, and the American Virgin Islands: A Report to the Carnegie Corporation of New York* (1934) and Nora Bateson's *Library Plan for Jamaica* (1945)—are regarded as influencing the foundation and growth of modern public libraries as they exist today. Savage's report in particular, resulting from a survey conducted on the condition of libraries in the Caribbean in 1933, pointed to the rudimentary state of existing institutions: a dearth of trained librarians, poor book stock, and almost no cooperative ventures among libraries. Recommendations emanating from both reports led to much needed financial assistance from two international funding agencies: the Carnegie Corporation and the British Council.

The Jamaica Library Service, established in 1948, benefited from one such allocation, a grant of £70,000 from the British Council. This service has progressively advanced over the years and is now viewed as one of the leading public library services in the region.

Similarly, with assistance initially from the Carnegie Corporation and later the British Council, the Eastern Caribbean Regional Library (ECRL) was set up in Trinidad and Tobago. Operating from 1941 to 1958, the ECRL established a library service first for Trinidad and Tobago and subsequently for all of the islands in the Eastern Caribbean. The Eastern Caribbean Regional Library was very influential in assisting island libraries in developing legislation to facilitate the provision of free library services. Additionally, the ECRL was, in effect, the main coordinating body for professional training, cooperation, union cataloging, and interlibrary lending.

At the present time, public libraries in the Caribbean region are at various stages of development. In countries such as Barbados, Belize, Guyana, Jamaica, and Trinidad and Tobago, growth can best be described as steady, benefiting largely from government subventions and the support of a cadre of dedicated professionals. These countries have been able to develop comprehensive services at a national level, which are administered through a major library, usually headquartered in the capital and offering a service through branch and mobile libraries. Public library services in both the large and small islands have the same basic elements of public libraries elsewhere: they are free; organized into adult, children's, and reference departments; and offer outreach activities.

In the smaller islands (those belonging to the grouping defined as the OECS), natural disasters such as hurricanes (Antigua), volcanic eruptions (Montserrat), fires, and earthquakes have played a major part in disrupting the provision of library services. Here the rate of development of public libraries has been slower, and in some instances it has been hampered by the lack of resources (financial, human, and infrastructure) required to improve library services.

At the Antigua Public Library, for example, more than 170 years since its formation in 1830, the vision of constructing a permanent library building has not yet been realized. Nevertheless, the library still services a population of approximately 70,000. Currently the library administration is actively pursuing a five-year strategic plan aimed at formulating a collection development policy, increasing physical access for all members of the community, extending outreach services, and investing in the modern information technology required to meet current and future online information needs.

In the absence of traditional national libraries in all islands, excluding Jamaica, many public libraries have had to combine both national and public library functions. This has been achieved with some measure of success in territories such as Belize, Guyana, and Trinidad and Tobago. In Belize, the National Library Service through its public library system provides creative and innovative outreach programs, interlibrary lending, bibliographic searching, Internet, and audiovisual services. As a de facto national library it seeks to collect, preserve, and make available the nation's printed heritage.

Public and National Library Systems in Jamaica

Jamaica Library Service

The Jamaica Library Service (JLS), established in Kingston in 1948 through the cooperative efforts of the government of Jamaica and the British Council, provides a comprehensive service throughout the island via 13 main public libraries. Functioning as a statutory body under the portfolio of the Minister of Education and Culture, the Jamaica Library Service administers two major programs: a free public library service operated through an intricate network of 615 service points (including bookmobile stops) servicing both urban and rural areas, and a school library service covering 918 government-assisted schools. JLS offers services including reference, loans, research, book request/reservation, interlibrary loans, referrals, professional/technical assistance, current awareness and community information service, Internet services, outreach programs, services for the visually impaired. It operates a website at the address www.jamlib.org.jm.

The National Library of Jamaica

Jamaica has the distinction of being the only country in the English-speaking Caribbean with a traditional national library as defined by K.W. Humphreys in his 1966 article "National Library Functions." The National Library of Jamaica (NLJ), founded in Kingston in 1979, was based on the former collections and staff of the West India Reference Library of the Institute of Jamaica. The NLJ's main responsibility is to collect, preserve, and make available all material published in Jamaica, by Jamaicans, and about Jamaica. The library has an extensive collection of material on Jamaica and the Caribbean dating back to the 16th century. The collection is varied, consisting of books, pamphlets, periodicals, newspapers, programs of events and activities, clippings files, maps, manuscripts, historic prints, photographic prints, slides, phonograph records, compact discs, audiotapes, films, and videocassettes.

As of 1999 the NLJ held 46,000 volumes, 1,000 current serials, 3,000 manuscripts, 5,000 maps, and 20,000 microforms. Services offered include reference; research; compilation of bibliographies; assistance to libraries attached to the public and private sectors; photocopying and photographic reproduction; online search services; assignment of International Standard Book Numbers (ISBNs) to Jamaican publication (assignment of ISBNs for other Caribbean countries is provided by the CARICOM secretariat); registration of publications in the absence of modern copyright legislation; provision of Cataloging-in-Publication (CIP) data to publishers; the building of a national bibliographic database; distribution of CDS/ISIS, the database management system designed by United Nations Educational, Scientific, and Cultural Organization (UNESCO); and current awareness services. The NLJ operates a website at the address www.nlj.org.jm.

Public and National Library Systems in Trinidad and Tobago

Trinidad and Tobago holds the unusual position of being the only territory in the English-speaking Caribbean that maintains three separate public library services. The Trinidad Public Library (the original subscription library) dates back to 1851. The Carnegie Library (the islands' first free library) opened in 1919, and the Central Library of Trinidad and Tobago was established in 1941. All three institutions have now been integrated in accordance with a government decision of 1993 that created the National Library and Information System (NALIS).

NALIS was established specifically to provide for the development and coordination of all library and information services in Trinidad and Tobago. Operating out of the capital city, Port of Spain, its Public Library Division has specific responsibility for administering and coordinating a network of 19 branch libraries and mobile units in urban and rural areas. The National Heritage Library Division performs some of the functions of a national library. This division is a valuable reference resource for Caribbean heritage material, as it seeks to collect, organize, and disseminate information about all of Trinidad and Tobago's diverse ethnic groups and cultures. A new National Library building is currently under construction and is scheduled for completion in September 2002.

As of 1999 NALIS held 442,000 volumes and 500 current serials. It offers services including lending, reference, Internet access, literacy support, research, photocopying, outreach activities, consultancy and management services to the public and private sectors, creation of the national bibliographic record, national referral service, national depository, international document supply service, national information service for the physically disadvantaged, and research in library and information science. NALIS operates a website at the address www.nalis.gov.tt.

School Libraries

School libraries in the Caribbean are found in both primary and secondary schools. Administration of these libraries varies from country to country. In some territories the Ministry of Education and/or the public library administers an island-wide service. In Trinidad and Tobago, for example, school libraries are coordinated by the Ministry of Education, whereas in Jamaica they are part of the public library system.

Historically, libraries were developed mainly in secondary schools. These schools were provided with trained librarians who were expected to build collections to support the school's curriculum. The construction of a number of primary schools in Trinidad and Tobago led to the establishment of primary school libraries offering a very basic service, often supplemented by the services of bookmobile units and public library branches. Most of the primary school libraries are staffed by paraprofessionals.

Special Libraries

Although library development in the 1940s and 1950s was concentrated in the public library area, the growth of special libraries really began in the 1960s. Two key factors influenced the growth of special libraries: the movement toward independence for many of the Caribbean countries and the subsequent development of specialized institutions within the public sector to facilitate economic and social development policy.

Special libraries in the Caribbean are therefore found mainly in government ministries and departments, quasi-governmental institutions, and scientific and technological research bodies, as well as in regional and international organizations. In the larger territories, particularly Jamaica and Trinidad and Tobago, there are well-established libraries serving the information needs of the judiciary, the central banks, and the major government ministries such as Finance, Planning and Development, Energy, and

Social Development. In Trinidad and Tobago the library of the Ministry of Finance, Planning, and Development is the repository of a large collection of unique historical documents, studies, and reports, which have informed national economic and social planning. Services offered by these libraries include selective dissemination of information, reference, research, the compilation of subject bibliographies, and online search services. Many of these special libraries are now staffed by professionals.

Although there was rapid growth of special libraries in the larger countries of the Caribbean, many of the smaller territories were unable to develop similar services owing to a lack of financial resources and a shortage of trained personnel. Regional cooperation in information services was and still remains essential but elusive for the smaller territories.

From the late 1970s to the early 1990s, cooperation among special libraries in the Caribbean was facilitated through the United Nations Economic Commission for Latin America and the Caribbean, which undertook the establishment of several specialized information databases/networks on behalf of Caribbean governments. The first network to be established in the late 1970s was the Caribbean Information System for Economic and Social Planning, through which the libraries of the various national planning institutes contributed abstracts of key economic documents and other publications. In addition, Caribbean databases were developed for agricultural information: the Caribbean Agricultural Information System (CAGRIS); for the energy sector: the Caribbean Energy Information System (CEIS); and for the health sector: the Medical Caribbean Database (MEDCARIB). The staff of the national focal points were provided with specialized training in techniques for indexing and abstracting and in the use of the designated software package Mini/Micro CDS/ISIS, which facilitates database creation and, more recently, permits interactivity through hyperlinking; it was distributed free of charge by UNESCO, which has influenced its widespread use in Caribbean libraries. As a result of the development of the information networks, special libraries have been at the forefront of library automation in the Caribbean.

Academic Libraries

The establishment of academic libraries in the English-speaking Caribbean is closely linked to the establishment of the University of the West Indies (UWI) and the University of Guyana (UG). The first academic library was established at Mona, Jamaica, in 1948 at the inception of the University College of the West Indies. Subsequently, campuses and libraries were established at St. Augustine in Trinidad and Tobago (1960) and Cave Hill in Barbados (1963). The library of the St. Augustine campus inherited the collection of the former Imperial College of Tropical Agriculture (ICTA), which was merged with the university in 1960; this collection served as the nucleus of the new library. Likewise, the University of Guyana Library was established in 1963, the same year as the university.

All three main campus libraries have experienced growth and development in accommodation, stock, services, and technology. From unsuitable accommodation, all the libraries now occupy purpose-built facilities. Both the Mona Campus Library and the St. Augustine Campus Library have been extended more than once. In addition, two branch libraries—the Medical Library and Science Library—were erected at Mona in the 1970s. At St. Augustine, the Faculty of Medical Sciences Library, a branch of the Main Library, was established in 1989. At Cave Hill, the Law Library is maintained as a separate library from the Main Library and is an integral part of the Faculty of Law.

Collections: Content and Scope

The collections of the main libraries on the three UWI campuses and at UG support the teaching and research activities of their respective faculties and specialized schools. All three campuses offer degrees in natural sciences, social sciences, and the humanities, and the collections reflect these general areas. In addition, each campus has specialized faculties: medicine and library science at Mona; agriculture, engineering, and medical sciences at St. Augustine; and law at Cave Hill. Correspondingly, the basic and largest collections in the specialized disciplines reside on the relevant campuses.

The libraries of UWI and UG are organized into subject divisions corresponding to the faculties on the campuses. All of the libraries maintain a West Indian collection containing material by West Indians and about West Indians and the West Indies/Caribbean area. All of these libraries aggressively seek to acquire special collections of national and regional significance. For example, the library at the St. Augustine Campus holds two collections, the Eric Williams Memorial Collection and the Derek Walcott Collection, which have been named to the UNESCO Memory of the World Register, recognizing their international significance and the need to protect them for posterity.

Each library is also a partial depository for the publications of the United Nations and some of its specialized agencies. In the absence of national libraries in Trinidad and Tobago, Barbados, and Guyana, the main libraries on these campuses act as the deposit library for national imprints. Holdings for each campus library include monographs, serials, maps, manuscripts, pamphlets, audiocassettes and videocassettes, slides, computer files, microforms, and CD-ROMS.

Services and Technology

The libraries offer a wide range of services to their users. These include loan facilities, reference services, computer-based and CD-ROM literature searching, Internet access, interlibrary loans, ordering of photocopies, current awareness, and accessions lists.

Automation is a feature common to all three UWI campus libraries. All of the libraries have kept pace with technological advances in the library and information field, although some are more advanced than others in the utilization of such technologies. The Virginia Tech Library System (VTLS) supports cataloging, the public access catalog, circulation, acquisitions, and serials control.

The three main libraries of the University of the West Indies have automated cataloging systems and membership in the online bibliographic service OCLC. The libraries also have access to a variety of electronic resources, including EBSCOhost and OCLC FirstSearch, and several online databases are available to its users. The University of Guyana Library is a beneficiary of the Caribbean Universities Network Project (CUNet) and enjoys the interchange of electronic mail and files among CUNet members.

The main library at St. Augustine already operates a Local Area Network (LAN) that delivers Internet services and productivity applications to staff desktops and computers for library users. The library LAN is now being linked with other LANs across the campus to become part of the Campus Wide Information System. A media laboratory is currently being developed to help create materials for teaching and presentation. Users will have access to equipment and software for authoring, desktop publishing, graphic design, and animation.

Other Campus Libraries

Specialized research libraries and documentation centers, which are independent of the main libraries, have developed on all three campuses. Most of these libraries serve the departments, faculties, or institutes in which they are located and may also be accessed by the wider university community. Libraries and/or documentation centers are attached to the following campus institutions: Sir Arthur Lewis Institute of Social and Economic Research; School of Education; Institute of International Relations; Seismic Research Unit; Caribbean Agricultural Research and Development Institute; Caribbean Food and Nutrition Institute; Caribbean Industrial Research Institute Technical Information Service; Hugh Wooding Law School Library; and the Seminary of St. John Vianney Library.

Library Associations

Library associations in the region have been instrumental in strengthening libraries and advancing librarianship as a profession. The larger islands, by virtue of more qualified librarians and other library personnel, have been able to establish and maintain active associations. Such is the case of the Library and Information Association of Jamaica (formerly the Jamaica Library Association), the Library Association of Trinidad and Tobago, and the Library Association of Barbados. These organizations are persistent in their efforts to unite persons engaged or interested in the field of library and information science. All three associations hold regular professional meetings and produce official publications.

In the smaller territories there are very few active library associations. As a result, library and information professionals tend to become active in regional associations. At the regional level, three associations whose sphere of influence includes the wider Caribbean can be identified: the Association of Caribbean University, Research, and Institutional Libraries (ACURIL), whose annual conference attracts delegates from the English-, Dutch-, French-, and Spanish-speaking territories; the Seminar on the Acquisition of Latin American Library Materials (SALALM); and the Commonwealth Library Associations (COMLA). Library associations in the Caribbean (local and regional) have been very successful in their attempts at strengthening libraries, providing continuing education opportunities for information professionals, and promoting cooperative activities between libraries.

Library Education and Training

Library education and training in the region began in 1948 with the establishment of the Eastern Caribbean Regional Library School in Trinidad and Tobago. The school's program was officially endorsed by the British Library Association and consisted of a correspondence course followed by three months of lectures and in-service training. Formal education and training of library and information professionals in the English-speaking Caribbean is currently being undertaken by the Department of Library and Information Studies, located at the Mona Campus.

Established in 1971 through a grant from UNESCO, the library school offers a three-year undergraduate degree program (library studies major) and a fifteen-month postgraduate program leading to the Master of Library Studies. As part of its outreach program to the wider Caribbean, over the years the school has offered continuing education courses for library and information professionals.

CHERYL ANN PELTIER-DAVIS, KATHLEEN HELENESE-PAUL,
JENNIFER M. JOSEPH, ELMELINDA LARA, AND
GLENROY R.P. TAITT

Further Reading

Bateson, Nora, *Library Plan for Jamaica*, Kingston, Jamaica: Government Printer, 1945

Douglas, Daphne, "British Caribbean," in *Contemporary Developments in Librarianship: An International Handbook*, edited by Miles M. Jackson, London: The Library Association, 1981

Ferguson, Stephney, "Jamaica," in *ALA World Encyclopedia of Library and Information Services*, edited by Robert Wedgeworth, Chicago: American Library Association, 1980

Humphreys, Kenneth W., "National Library Functions," *UNESCO Bulletin for Libraries* 20 (1966)

Jordan, Alma Theodora, *The Development of Library Service in the West Indies through Interlibrary Cooperation*, Metuchen, New Jersey: Scarecrow Press, 1970

Peltier-Davis, Cheryl, "Meeting the Challenge: Public Libraries as National Libraries: The Caribbean Experience," Master's thesis, The University of the West Indies, 1995

Savage, Ernest, *The Libraries of Bermuda, the Bahamas, the British West Indies, British Guiana, British Honduras, Puerto Rico, and The American Virgin Islands: A Report to the Carnegie Corporation of New York*, London: Library Association, 1934

Central American National Libraries

Stretching from Mexico in the north to Panama in the south, the five Central American republics became independent when the Central American federation broke up in 1838. Costa Rica, El Salvador, Guatemala, Honduras, and Nicaragua remain linked by geography, climate, and similar economies (their primary exports still consist mainly of agricultural commodities, chiefly coffee). Guatemala, Honduras, and El Salvador were once part of the pre-Columbian Mayan empire. Individual populations, still increasing at a rapid rate, ranged in 1999 from approximately 4 million (Costa Rica) to more than 12 million (Guatemala); population density is highest in El Salvador.

The latter part of the 20th century was not kind to the region, bringing political strife (including a 12-year civil war in El Salvador) and natural disasters such as earthquakes and hurricanes. Except in Costa Rica, damage to the economies and social fabric was severe. Although recoveries in the 1990s were encouraging, much remains to be done. Funding for most cultural activities, including all types of libraries, remains scarce, and radical improvement is not likely in the near future. Overall, there are more similarities than differences in the five national libraries, including some of the problems they face in the new millennium.

Costa Rica

The 1880s saw the establishment of a number of important educational and cultural institutions in Costa Rica, including the national archives, the national museum, and the national theater. The national library's creation also took place during that decade; it was created by decree on 31 October 1888, although it did not open its doors (in San José, the capital city) until 1890. Miguel Obregón Lizano, who headed the General Directorate of Libraries (Dirección General de Bibliotecas) and was former librarian of the University of Santo Tomás, played an important role in this act, and when the university closed, its collection passed to the national library.

The Miguel Obregón Lizano National Library (Biblioteca Nacional Miguel Obregón Lizano, or BNCR) has always operated as a unit of the Ministry of Culture. Its first director, Bernarbé Quirós Pacheco, served from 1890 to 1899. Two of his successors enjoyed especially long tenures: Joaquin García Monge (1920–36) and Julián Marchena Villa Riestra (1938–67).

As there were no library schools, finding adequately trained staff was difficult until a university-level program was begun in 1968 at the University of Costa Rica. However, the library association (Asociación Costarricense de Bibliotecarios, founded in 1949) actively sponsored workshops, lectures, and other types of in-service training, with some assistance from the Organization of American States (OAS). More recently, the availability of library school graduates from the University of Costa Rica and the National University (a program opened in 1977) has made it much easier to recruit qualified staff.

The BNCR's collections (numbering approximately 4,000 volumes when it opened in 1890) have grown steadily, as the following figures indicate: 100,000 volumes in the 1930s; 130,000 in the 1960s; 175,000 in the 1980s; and more than 270,000 in 1999. Approximately 3,500 current and previously published serials are also held. (Although Costa Rica's is the largest national library in Central America, the library of the University of Costa Rica is larger, with more than 450,000 volumes.)

Legal deposit (requiring two copies of all Costa Rican publications be given to the library) brings in most national items, both monographic and serial, to the BNCR. On the basis of these receipts, the library prepares the national bibliography. Purchase funds are used mainly for foreign items, although the BNCR does have some exchange partners. Over the years the library has received gifts from both individuals and organizations; for example, in 1934 the government of Spain presented 1,500 volumes of works by Spanish authors, originally kept in a special room but later integrated into the general collection. Since the 1950s the United States has contributed some titles, both in English and in translation, on U.S. politics, economics, literature, and culture.

Of its present holdings, approximately 70,000 volumes form the national collection, which was organized as a separate unit in 1945. Files of the country's newspapers and serials are extensive (probably the most complete in Costa Rica). The Reference Department holds more than 6,000 volumes of dictionaries, encyclopedias, almanacs, and bibliographies.

The library's first quarters were modest (several rooms), but by 1907 it had moved to its own building. As collections and services grew it became insufficient, but the many requests for a new building did not bear fruit until a purpose-designed, modern facility was constructed from 1969 to 1971. Like all of the national libraries in the region, the BNCR serves both the general public and the scholarly community. There are approximately 2,000 users each month, mostly secondary school students who come to study as well as to use library materials for assignments. As universities have improved their collections and services, the number of post-secondary students who frequent the library may have decreased.

El Salvador

The National Library of El Salvador (Biblioteca Nacional de El Salvador, or BNES) was established by presidential decree in the capital city of San Salvador on 5 July 1870 but almost immediately put under the Consejo Superior de Instrucción Pública (Public Instruction) to operate as a part of the National University of El Salvador. Separated administratively from the university in 1887, it remained in the same building until 1934, when it was moved to the national theater. In 1938 the Círculo Militar building was bought for the library, and it remained there for 26 years. The government then constructed (from 1959 to 1963) a nine-floor building for the national library and the national archives, but it suffered damage in the 1965 earthquake. The Ministry of Education took over most of the building to house its offices in 1968, leaving only the north tower for the library. The 1986 earthquake and floods completely destroyed this building as well as important parts of the collection. For the next seven years, the library's resources and services functioned in several temporary sites.

Finally, the large building that formerly housed the national mortgage bank was assigned to the library and officially opened in January 1994. Adaptation of this structure for library purposes was only partially successful; it proved expensive to operate (especially in utility costs), was poorly maintained, and provided poor working conditions for staff. In the spring of 2000 the library administration proposed bringing in outside consultants to determine whether the building should be abandoned. Fortunately, no serious damage was caused by the earthquake in 2001.

Up to 1995 the BNES had 27 directors (five women and 22 men), of whom only two had training in librarianship. Baudilio Torres had the longest tenure (1945–62). The director currently reports to the National Cultural Council. Since the introduction of automation, training courses have been given for staff; several also spent a year (1995–96) at the library school of the University of Puerto Rico, a project funded by the Agency for International Development.

At the opening of the library in 1890 there were approximately 6,000 volumes. The collections grew to 70,000 volumes in the 1960s, 95,000 in the 1980s, and approximately 150,000 volumes in 1999. Losses over the years have, however, been significant, although there are no precise figures. In addition, many damaged books required conservation. The library established a Salvadoran Room (Sala Salvadoreña) in 1994 to house publications received by legal deposit, as well as old and valuable Salvadoran imprints. There are also a special Argentine Collection including that country's history and literature since 1800 and a fiction collection that contains not only contemporary Latin American novels but also Spanish translations of well-known British, French, and U.S. novels up to the contemporary period. Another room contains publications of the United Nations Educational, Scientific, and Cultural Organization (UNESCO), OAS, and other international organizations.

The operating budget provides no funds for purchases, but several foreign governments have donated money to purchase books. In the mid 1990s a grant from the government of Spain was used for reference works and for books for cultural centers outside the capital, and $60,000 came from the government of Sweden. The library has been trying to establish a nonprofit foundation as a way of securing additional private funding, but enabling legislation has not yet been passed.

The situation in El Salvador is unique because there is an independent research library (founded in 1948) in Santa Tecla, one of the capital's suburbs. It contains the collection of Manuel Gallardo and was named after his grandfather, a well-known doctor of the same name. The library's general support comes from the Fundación Dr. Manuel Gallardo and varies with the income from coffee produced on its plantation. The holdings (80,000 volumes in 1999) consist of general materials, reflecting the founder's personal interests in literature and the arts, to which reference material has been added. More important are the Salvadoran and Central American items, including early imprints, serial runs, and government publications that Gallardo collected. These resources survived the civil war and the 1986 earthquake undamaged and probably exceed those of the BNES in both quantity and quality. The 2001 earthquake left the building severely damaged, and books had to be placed in temporary storage; plans are being made for reconstruction. For this reason the Gallardo Library has taken on a special importance in the country's cultural patrimony. It seemed to be the best place to prepare a retrospective national bibliography, and such a project was launched in 1992, drawing on the experience in Nicaragua (discussed below). It was hoped that this compilation would list Salvadoran publications up to a given date (1990, for example) and that henceforth the BNES would issue a current national bibliography. The staff has prepared data sheets for approximately 18,000 titles, two Fulbright grantees have worked on the project, and the French and U.S. embassies have provided additional assistance, but considerable work remains before the bibliography can go to press.

Guatemala

To understand the National Library of Guatemala (Biblioteca Nacional de Guatemala, or BNG), it is necessary to remember that in the colonial period (which began c. 1810) the capital of the General Captaincy of Central America was located in Guatemala in what is now the national capital, Guatemala City. The many convents and monasteries of the era often had libraries containing books brought from Spain and other European countries. When the BNG was established by decree on 18 October 1879, its earliest collections included volumes from such religious establishments that had been closed.

The library had approximately 42,000 volumes in the 1930s; in 1999 its resources exceeded 200,000 volumes. Although the BNG is the designated recipient of Guatemalan publications via legal deposit, the requirement is difficult to enforce and fails to bring in many current publications. To increase input of these items, the library has established a special unit, the Sección de Bibliografía Nacional, that compiles data on new publications and encourages authors and publishers to supply copies. The library attempts to keep its holdings current by purchase of other needed items, both domestic and foreign. Probably the most important of the library's resources are found in the rare books section, which by 1995 contained approximately 18,000 works published from the 15th through the 19th centuries.

The library's building, an impressive structure facing the main plaza, was opened in September 1957. The BNG is a unit within the Ministry of Culture and Sport. It also maintains branches in several other cities. Two important services for readers are reference (most collections are in closed stacks) and services for children and students that assist them with school assignments and promote reading. Like many other national libraries in Latin America, the BNG functions as both a research library and a public library for Guatemala City.

Honduras

The National Library of Honduras (Biblioteca Nacional de Honduras, or BNH) was established in 1880 in the capital city of Tegucigalpa. A year later it held 2,000 volumes; by 1911 there were 7,000, and in 1914, 14,000. The Pan American Union's 1963 directory (*Guía de bibliotecas de América Latina*) reports only 37,515 volumes; if correct, this would mean that in that period the library was adding only approximately 500 volumes per year. By the 1980s the book stock had increased to 55,000 volumes, and it had grown to 70,000 by 1999. This makes it the smallest collection of the Central American national libraries. By a 1993 decree, authors are required to provide one copy of their works to each of six national institutions, including the BNH. The size of the acquisition budget is presumably small, or, as in El Salvador, it may be nonexistent.

The library has moved several times, first in 1906 and again in 1963. By the 1980s its present quarters were considered inadequate, and the government's plans for a civic center in the Miraflores district of Tegucigalpa included a new building for the BNH. Unfortunately, appropriate funding was not available, and the devastation caused by the 1998 hurricane and the subsequent need for extensive reconstruction and rebuilding left little grounds for optimism about capital budgets for cultural programs, except perhaps through external assistance from foreign aid programs or foundation grants.

From 1975 until recently, the BNH was a unit of the Secretariat of Culture and Tourism, but the Secretariat of Culture and Arts set up five institutes, and the BNH was placed in the Honduran Institute for Books and Documents (Instituto Hondureño del Libro y el Documento). Given the library's pressing need for space, serial holdings were transferred to a new institution, the Ramón Rosa Serial Library (Hemeroteca Nacional Ramón Rosa).

Since its founding the BNH has had 23 directors; the longest tenure was that of Miguel Angel Ramos (1937–52). As there is no library school in Honduras, it continues to be difficult to secure professional staff. Nevertheless, the present administration hopes to modernize the library and provide additional services, such as automation of technical processes, the opening of 53 public libraries in cooperation with cities and towns, the promotion of reading, and the increase of exchanges with foreign institutions. For the first of these, assistance has come from the Swedish International Development Authority (ASDI) and through the cooperation of the National Library of Nicaragua. ASDI has also extended its relationship to other Central American national libraries.

Nicaragua

The Ruben Darío National Library of Nicaragua (Biblioteca Nacional Ruben Darío/Nicaragua, or BNN) opened in Managua, the capital city, in 1882, although the government decree for creating the institution was issued in 1871. The first collection consisted of 2,106 titles in the social sciences, science and mathematics, and humanities. In the early years Ruben Darío, Latin America's most famous poet and the founder of modernism, worked in the library that now bears his name. By 1899 the BNN had grown to 7,353 volumes and 250 pamphlets. In 1952 the library received 8,000 volumes from the United States when the American Libraries closed. The library's collection numbered approximately 70,000 volumes when the 1972 earthquake struck; all but some 8,000 were lost. Enormous efforts to rebuild the library have taken place, and the collection had returned to approximately 70,000 volumes by the 1980s and to approximately 150,000 by the late 1990s.

Present resources are divided among the general collection, the national collection, the Ruben Darío room, the Julio Cortázar collection, and the holdings of UNESCO and other international organization documents. The Ruben Darío room holds various editions of the poet's translations, biographical and critical studies, and deluxe printings.

The BNN was first housed in the national government's main building (Palacio Nacional) but was forced to become an itinerant library after the 1931 and 1972 earthquakes. In 1981 it moved into adequate quarters in the Edward Contreras complex. Adaptation of this building resulted in the creation of a children's room, a reference room with open shelves, a periodicals room, and stack and staff areas. At the end of the 1990s the library returned to renovated quarters in the Palacio Nacional.

The library is a unit of the Ministry of Culture. In 1989 the Hemeroteca Nacional (serials collection) and the Public Library Network (Red de Bibliotecas Públicas) were combined administratively with the library, as were the national archives somewhat later. The library's bibliographical work in recent years has been impressive. Most notable was the preparation of the national bibliography, a joint undertaking with the Latin American Bibliographical Foundation in California, with funding from the U.S. National Endowment for the Humanities. After several years' work, the retrospective portion, *Nicaraguan National Bibliography/Bibliografía nacional Nicaragüense, 1800–1978*, appeared in 1986 (three volumes). The BNN then prepared a supplement covering 1979 to 1989 and has continued the series. In addition, it produced a periodical listing in two parts, *Catálogo de periódicos y revistas*, covering 1830 to 1930 and 1931 to 1978. The library also maintains an extensive bibliography on Ruben Darío.

In the past 20 years the library has modernized its processes and procedures. With advice from UNESCO beginning in 1980, the BNN started to apply information technology to its operations. In 1984 a cooperative program with the Royal Library of Sweden, financed by ASDI, began. It included staff exchanges, creation of a bibliographical database, and short courses. By 1989 UNESCO's MICROISIS was serving as the basis of a national information system. The collaboration with ASDI is ongoing; it operates without a permanent Swedish staff in Managua, but rather with experts and advisers sent for varying periods as needed.

Regional Cooperation and Interlibrary Relations

For many years the five Central American national libraries had little interaction with each other. Their contacts with other libraries were, for the most part, with institutions in their own cities. With regard to foreign libraries, the relations were almost exclusively bilateral; for example, they dealt with cultural and development assistance agencies of such countries as Spain, the United States, France, and Japan. Projects with the large foundations were less frequent, given such foundations' reluctance to deal with government bodies. The same applied to contacts with international organizations such as UNESCO and OAS. Although it is true that directors of national libraries often went to meetings and seminars convened by OAS (for example, the 1972 Inter-American Seminar on Libraries, Archives, and Centers of Documentation in Washington, D.C.), there was little or no certainty that all would be in attendance.

Two recent developments brought extensive changes and enhanced the contact between these national libraries. The first was the creation of the Association of Ibero-American National Libraries (Asociación de Bibliotecas Nacionales de Iberoamérica, or ABINIA), to which all belong. Annual meetings take place in different cities each year and most, if not all, directors attend. This development was related to a second: In 1991 the five Central American national library directors met in San José and the next year in Managua. With support from ASDI, these annual sessions now discuss the problems and prospects of these institutions. After several meetings, Belize and Panama were asked to join the group, so that the meeting now takes place in one of the seven capital cities.

A review of the history and present situation of the five Central American national libraries shows many similarities, whereas their differences are often more of degree than substance. All of their collections are relatively small, even in comparison to sister institutions in South American countries. The chief source of acquisitions, legal deposit, has often been less effective than it should be. Budgets for acquisitions have been small or even nonexistent. Gift and exchanges have been spasmodic, often doing little to enhance the collections. Nevertheless, in each republic the national library is regarded as the repository for the national patrimony of printed material. It is not possible to judge how adequate their resources are for the demands placed upon them, demands that come not only from scholars but from secondary and university students; each national library is, de facto, the public library for that nation's capital city. To cite one example, the national central banks generally have far better collections in the fields of economics, fiscal policy, and related subjects, even though they, too, are subject to the vagaries of government funding. As universities in the region have greatly improved the collections and services in their libraries, the national library no longer remains the only research collection. In fact, one or more universities in each country may have more important resources—especially those in foreign languages—than those of the national libraries.

Another similarity is the lack of a retrospective national bibliography, except in the case of Nicaragua. Each library is aware of its responsibility to produce a current national bibliography but often is unable to prepare it in a timely fashion. Automation of cataloging provides some hope for improvement.

Information technology has, however, proven to be a double-edged sword in these institutions. It offers much promise but at present often diverts limited funds and staff. Beyond the initial capital expenditure, systems must be kept current with new versions of software. When there is no money to acquire new books and serials, converting a card catalog to an online catalog may not be a high priority for the use of limited funds.

It may appear that the lack of adequate funding is the only problem these libraries have faced and thus generous budgets would solve their problems. This is not necessarily so; beset by inadequate buildings, collections needing preservation, staff with inadequate training, and large numbers of students crowding out scholars in the reading rooms, there is a great need to develop long-range plans and to establish clearly the institutions' priorities.

WILLIAM VERNON JACKSON

Further Reading

Granados, Teresa, and Birgitta Bergdahl, editors, *El progreso de la biblioteconomía . . . : Memorias del seminaro en Managua, Nicaragua, 5–8 Marzo, 1995*, Uppsala, Sweden: Uppsala University Library, 1995

Historia de las bibliotecas nacionales de Iberoamérica: Pasado y presente, 2nd edition, Mexico City: Universidad Nacional Autónoma de México, 1995

Central and Eastern European Libraries

The most restrictive definition of this geographical area covers approximately the modern-day nation states of Austria, Croatia, the Czech Republic, Estonia, Germany (especially the former eastern territories), Hungary, Latvia, Lithuania, Poland, Slovakia, and Slovenia. The present-day population of these territories numbers approximately 189 million people, and their histories and book cultures are often closely intertwined, highlighting notable similarities (as well as differences) in their historical development over more than a millennium.

In spite of the political, religious, cultural, economic, and social diversities of this vast and populous region, as well as the provisional nature of any historical periodization, one can identify at least eight chronological periods in the library history of Eastern and Central Europe: the Early and High Middle Ages (eighth to 14th centuries); the 15th and 16th centuries; the 17th century; the 18th, 19th, and early 20th (to 1918) centuries; the interwar period; World War II; the Communist/Socialist era (1945–89); and the post-Communist era (since 1989–91), which has witnessed the revival of independent states in much of this region.

Chronological Development

Eighth to 14th Centuries

During much of the medieval period, libraries and scriptoria developed in the monasteries of the Catholic religious orders—principally the male houses of the Cistercians, Bernadines, Premonstratensians, Augustinians, Benedictines, and later the Jesuits—that proliferated in Eastern and Central Europe, as well as being attached to bishoprics and the courts of the royal and feudal elite.

15th and 16th Centuries

With the coming of the printed book to much of the area in the 15th century, libraries began to flourish at royal and feudal courts, cities, guilds, and institutions of higher learning. Through the 16th century, libraries that developed in these territories reflected the shared social, political, and cultural values of the age, reinforced by a common system of education.

17th Century

During the 17th century, the rise of the first modern nation states began, with the attendant breakdown of supraterritorial uniformity that had characterized the medieval and early modern periods. This process had a profound impact on libraries and their contents, leading to greater heterogeneity than previously.

18th, 19th, and Early 20th Centuries to 1918

This process of development was carried through and sharpened during the 19th century and included the growth of learned societies and institutions in the Baltics during the first half of the century, as well as national revivals in the Polish, Hungarian, Bohemian, and Moravian (Czech) lands. During the second half of the 19th century, comparable national revivals took place among the Slovaks, Slovenes, Croats, Galicians, and Serbs. Also notable during this period was the growth in the number of specialized libraries for research in the physical and applied sciences and the humanities, as well as the creation of the great libraries of Eastern and Central European academies of sciences. Social and reading libraries, regional collections, and (in some lands) collections for the use of parliamentary, administrative, and other governmental bodies developed. By the outbreak of World War I in 1914, national libraries had become active participants in the bibliothecal world of most countries in Central and Eastern Europe, a role maintained and enhanced into the 21st century.

Interwar Period

The period between the world wars (1919 to 1939) saw significant achievements in the maturation of independent national book cultures throughout much of Eastern and Central Europe, reflecting the newly found political independence of the peoples of the former Hapsburg and Russian Imperial lands.

World War II

The years 1939 through 1945 were devastating for the book cultures of the entire region, witnessing the destruction or displacement of entire libraries of important historical book collections, as well as the demolition of the cultural achievements of the previous two decades of independence.

Communist/Socialist Era, 1945 to 1989

The postwar period saw the imposition of Communist regimes in all areas of the region except Western Germany and Austria. In practical terms this meant the imposition of Soviet library policies and practices throughout Eastern Europe. These remained in force, with varying degrees of administrative conformity to the Soviet model, until the success of liberating movements such as the Solidarity Movement in Poland, the Velvet Revolution in Czechoslovakia, and the Singing Revolution in the Baltics, culminating in the implosion of the Soviet Union. The reunification of East and West Germany and the dissolution of Czechoslovakia and Yugoslavia are only two of the major political events of the last decade that have had important consequences for library structures in this region. One consequence has been the infusion of significant funding for automation and infrastructure upgrade from organizations such as the Andrew W. Mellon Foundation (for the Baltics), the George Soros Foundation (for Eastern Europe and beyond), and the Council of Europe (for the libraries of Poland, Hungary, the Czech and Slovak Republics, and, to a lesser degree, the former Yugoslav Republics).

The German language and Germanophone culture has, since the High Middle Ages, been one of the principal influences throughout this region; it was especially strong in the regions of the Baltic coastal region and in the south Slavic lands. Whereas the Roman Catholic faith and its sacral language of Latin remained potent forces in the book cultures of Eastern and Central Europe until the 16th century, by the beginning of the modern period other religious movements were growing, especially Protestantism and, to a much lesser degree, Eastern-rite Catholicism and Orthodoxy. These movements encouraged the development and use of vernacular Baltic, Slavic, Finno-Ugric, and Germanic languages, which continued to expand vigorously.

Expatriate book culture (and libraries) also played an important role in countries such as Poland, Czechoslovakia, and the Baltic countries of Latvia and Lithuania before World War I and particularly after World War II. Poles, Bohemians, Estonians, Lithuanians, and Latvians living abroad created libraries (and publishing enterprises) in such far-flung cities as New York, Chicago, Stockholm, Paris, and Toronto, in part because of the political restraints placed on publishers and libraries in these countries in the 19th century and periodically during the 20th century.

Geographic Overview

The Germanies

Along with the neighboring crown lands of the Hapsburgs, the book and bibliothecal culture of the Germanies has had a significant influence on Eastern and Central Europe for more than a millennium. These cultures have set models for library techniques and theory in the modern-day Baltics, Hungary, and the Bohemian and Moravian areas of the Czech Republic. Scriptoria and monastic libraries developed in the Germanies in the Early Middle Ages. The beginnings of the modern research library in the Germanies, however, may be traced to a later period, with the 14th-century founding of university libraries in Cologne (Westphalia) in 1388, Heidelberg (Baden-Württemberg) in 1385, and Erfurt (Thüringia) in 1392. In subsequent centuries, many court and princely libraries developed, along with notable collections belonging to the burghers and the wealthy cities of Bavaria, such as Augsburg and Nuremberg. By the age of the printed book and the Reformation, municipal public libraries were founded in Magdeburg (1525), Strasbourg (1531), Augsburg (1537), and Konigsburg/Królewiec/Kaliningrad (1541) in East Prussia. The founding of the important Bäyerische Staatsbibliothek (Bavarian State Library) in Munich can be traced to the mid–16th century, the great German archival library in Leipzig to 1812, and that in Frankfurt-am-Main to 1846. A small but important collection for the Slavic Sorbian minority was created in Saxon Bautzen (Sorb Budiscyn/Budyšin).

Today, important state, city, and university libraries (combining several functions) survive in Hamburg, Göttingen, Cologne, and Frankfurt-am-Main. Major university libraries exist in Freiburg, Tübingen, Munich, Erlangen, Marburg, Heidelberg, Kiel, Bonn, and Münster. Specialized research libraries also exist, such as the Universitätsbibliothek Hannover und Technische Informationsbibliothek (Library of Technical Information in Hanover) and the Deutsche Zentralbibliothek für Wirtschafts-Wissenschaften (Library of World Economy) in Kiel.

Austria

Today's Österreichische Nationalbibliotek (Austrian National Library) traces its origins to the 14th century, with the establishment of princely libraries during the early Hapsburg era. Considerable consolidation of formerly scattered aristocratic collections occurred initially during the latter half of the 15th century, during the reign of Frederick II, and in the 16th century under the reign of his son. The resulting collection eventually began to be considered the court library and, in 1624, by imperial decree, became a legal deposit library for all publications issued throughout the empire. From 1723 to 1726 it moved into its present facility on the Josefsplatz in Vienna. In subsequent decades this collection grew through the incorporation of the libraries of several Hapsburg emperors, the court library of Graz (1752), the Universitätsbibliothek Wien (University of Vienna Library, 1756), and the municipal library of the same city. During the tenure of the Orientalist Josef von Karabacek, the library attained the rank of one of the major scholarly research libraries in Europe.

The reigns of Maria Theresa and her son Joseph II had a profound impact on library history for the nationalization, consolidation, and incorporation of monastic—(principally Jesuit)—collections in the Universitätsbibliothek Graz (University Library in Graz, founded 1573) and the new University of Vienna Library (1775). The Bibliothek der Österreichischen Akademie der Wissenschaften (Library of the Austrian Academy of Sciences) was founded in 1847.

As with other states succeeding to highly bureaucratic imperial powers, the Austrian government inherited significant libraries, such as the Bibliothek und Österreichische (Administrative-Legal Library) within the structure of the federal chancellor's office and the Rechtsdokumentation im Bundeskanzleramt (Austrian Patent Agency Library) in Vienna. In the administrative centers of regional government, there are scholarly libraries of a regional character.

Hungary

One of the earliest important manuscript collections in the entire region, the Corvin library of Renaissance illuminated manuscripts was assembled by Mátyás Hunyadi (King Matthias I) and included the work of Italian and Ragusan (from Dubrovnik) artists, as well as that of local illuminators. In the 16th century, school libraries began in present-day Hungary, and social libraries of Hungarian reading clubs developed in the first half of the 19th century. In 1802 Count Ferenc Széchényi gave his personal library to the state, forming the basis of the present-day national library, the Országos Széchényi Könyvtár (National Széchényi Library), now housed in the Buda Palace complex. The Magyar Tudományos Akadémia Könyvtára (Library of the Academy of Sciences) was founded in 1826, the Országgyülési Könyvtár (Parliament Library) in 1870 (reorganized during the Communist era in 1958), and the specialized Juhász Gyula Tanárképzö Föiskola (Library of Pedagogy) and Országos Müszaki Információs Központ és Könyvtár (Library of Technology) in 1873 and 1883, respectively. Major city libraries emerged in the southern city of Szeged (Somogyi- Könyvtár) in 1881 and in Budapest in 1904 (now the Fövárosi Szabó Ervin Könyvtár, or Erwin Szabo Municipal Library).

Czech Republic

The earliest libraries in the territory of the Czech Republic arose in the tenth century and were associated with the court of the bishop of Prague (Praha) and the Library of the Benedictine Fathers in Brzhenova. Univerzita Karlova Knihovny v Praze (Charles University Library) was founded in 1348. What was to become (in 1935) the national library was founded, in 1777, on the basis of several earlier collections: the Old Carolinum Library of the Charles University, the St. Clementinum College Library (1556), the New Carolinum Library (1638), and various Jesuit academic libraries and private collections. In the late 18th to early 19th centuries, university libraries began to develop in other cities as well. By the first half of the following century, city libraries began to develop in Prague and other cities. The 19th century saw the establishment of the Knihovna Akademie věd České republiky (Library of the Academy of Sciences) and the Knihovna Národního muzea (National Museum), all in Prague. In the 1830s and 1840s, readers' society libraries and the first public libraries began to flourish.

The interwar period of the First Republic (1919–39) saw the unification of Bohemia, Moravia, Slovakia, and sub-Carpathian Ruthenia (since 1945 a part of the Soviet Union, now independent Ukraine), as well as significant achievements in education, scholarship, and libraries, some aspects of which were vitiated by the war, Nazi occupation, and subsequent years of severe Communist rule. In the years after World War II, attempts were made to unify and regularize the Czech (and subsequently, Slovak) libraries on the model and with the practices of other Eastern European regimes.

Slovakia

The first public libraries appeared in the 16th century, when Slovakia was part of the Kingdom of Hungary. As evidence of the revival of Slovak (and Rusyn) national sentiment, the Matica slovenská and its library (today the Slovak National Library) were founded in 1863 in the small northern town of Martin. During the Communist era in 1954, it was officially designated the Slovak National Library. A 1959 law created two national systems of library organizations, one for Bohemia and Moravia, and another for Slovakia. Among the largest of the research libraries are those of the Ústredná knižnica Slovenskej akadémie vied (Central Library of the Slovak Academy of Sciences) and the Univerzitná knižnica v Bratislave (University Library of Bratislava), both in Bratislava, the Štátna vedecká knižnica (State Scientific Library in Kosice) in Eastern Slovakia, as well as the libraries of specialized educational institutions. Public libraries are currently organized according to administrative-territorial divisions; that is, by region, district, city, and town.

Croatia and Slovenia

Both Croatia and Slovenia were heavily under the influence of Hapsburg cultural models for centuries, and in the post–World War II period they were part of the Socialist Republic of Yugoslavia. The earliest notable libraries in Croatia developed at the coastal Dominican monastic community in Dubrovnik (founded in 1230), Split (1243), and the Franciscan Monastery in Zagreb (1250). In 1387 the monastic order of the Little Brothers established a library in Dubrovnik. The role of a national library is played by the Nacionalna i sveučilišna knjižnica (National and University Library) in Zagreb, based on a Jesuit collection of the 17th century. A university library was established in the coastal town of Rijeka (Sveučilišna knjižnica Rijeka) in 1627, and a scholarly library was founded in Zadar (Znanstvena knjižnica) in 1856.

The Narodna in Univerzitetna knjižnica (National and University Library) of Slovenia in Ljubljana was founded in 1774 and contains significant collections of Latin printed books, incunabula, and illuminated manuscripts. Other notable Slovene libraries include those of the Knjižnica Narodnega muzeja (National Museum, founded 1827), the Biblioteka Slovenske akademije znanosti in umetnosti (Academy of Arts and Sciences, founded 1938), and the Centralna tehniška knjižnica univerze v Ljubljani(Central Technical Library, founded (1949).

Poland and Lithuania

As in much of Eastern and Central Europe, the earliest libraries in present-day Polish territory were attached to monasteries and the courts of feudal rulers. The first significant research library was founded at the Uniwersytet Jagielloński (Jagiellonian University) in Kraków (1364). The first public library collection was established in Warsaw in 1747 through the benefaction of wealthy monks, bishops, donors, and collectors Andryej Stanisław and Josef Andrzej Załuski. One of the major research libraries, the Ossolineum library and research center, was founded in Lwow/Lviv/Lemberg in 1827. After 1945 it became the Biblioteka Zakładu Narodowego im. Ossolińskich (Ossolineum Library) in Wrocław, and, despite depredations to its collections during World War II, it continues as one of the major research and book studies centers in Poland. After the third partition of Poland in the late 18th century, Wrocław became part of Prussia and later the Russian Empire. In 1817 the Biblioteka Uniwersytecka w Warszawie (Warsaw University Library) was established. After Polish independence in the 20th century, the Biblioteka Narodowa (National Library) was established in Warsaw in 1928.

Book studies—especially in the areas of descriptive bibliography, history of book culture, and library science—have been widely cultivated in Polish libraries for more than a century; hence, a wide number of books, periodicals, and electronic publications in these disciplines have been issued by Polish libraries.

Closely related politically and culturally to Poland during much of late medieval and early modern times was the Rzezpospolita (Polish-Lithuanian Commonwealth), where 14th- and 15th-century libraries in Lithuania were formed by princes and nobility. The first private libraries appeared during the reign of Sigismund II Augustus. The library of the Vilnius (Wilno/Vilna) Jesuit College was founded in 1570 and later provided the basis for the Vilniaus universiteto biblioteka (Vilnius University Library). By the 19th and early 20th centuries, school, public, social, and cultural libraries were created. In addition to having considerable significance for the book cultures of a number of Slavic (Polish, Belarusian, Church Slavic) and other Baltic book traditions, Vilnius was an important center for Yiddish and Hebrew books. The Strashun collection of Yiddish and Hebrew manuscripts and printed books was founded in 1892.

Twentieth-century developments in Lithuania followed the broad patterns of development outlined above. After Lithuanian independence from the Russian Empire in 1920, the role of the Lietuvos nacionalinė Martyno Mažvydo Biblioteka (Martynas Mažvydas National Library of Lithuania, founded in 1919 and named after the 16th-century printer Martynas Mažvydas) in Vilnius became increasingly important in the bibliographical and political life of the country. Retaining their importance are the historic Vilniaus universiteto biblioteka (Vilnius University Library), the Lietuvos mokslų akademijos biblioteka (Library of the Lithuanian Academy of Sciences, founded 1941), the Lietuvos technikos biblioteka (Lithuanian Technical Library in Vilnius, founded 1957), and the public library in the important regional cultural center of Kaunas (Kauno apskrities viešoji biblioteka).

Latvia and Estonia

The earliest libraries in present-day Latvia first developed in the 13th century in monasteries established by German missionaries, who were associated with the Livonian Knights. In 1524 the influential municipality of Riga founded the first city library, now the Latvijas Akadēmiskās bibliotēkas (Latvian Academic Library) in Riga. In the same century, the Bibliotheca ducis Curlandiae (Library of the Dukes of Courland/Kurzeme) was founded in Kuldiga and later relocated to Jelgava/Mitau/Mitava. With the incorporation of Courland into the Russian Empire during the reign of Peter I, this rich collection of books and manuscripts was moved again to St. Petersburg, where today it is among the most important collections held by the Biblioteka Rossiiskoi Akademii nauk (Russian Academy of Sciences Library). Another important Latvian collection founded during the 16th century was that of the Jesuit order in Riga, which in the 17th century found its way to the Uppsala universitetsbibliotek (Uppsala University Library) in Sweden. The year 1775 marked the establishment of the library of the Academia Petrina (Peter Academy) in Mitau, as well as the city library in Liepaja/Libau/Libava.

After the establishment of Latvian independence, a central (later state and national) library began its operations in Riga. (Of the Baltic States, Latvia will be the last to construct a new building for its collections.) At least one of the identifiable achievements of the bibliothecal work of the postwar years of Soviet occupation was the opening of large subject collections in the field of medicine (1945) and technology (1950).

Among the oldest libraries in Estonia, the library attached to the church of St. Olaia was founded by 1552, and constitutes one of the more important collections of the Eesti Akadeemiline Raamatukogu (Estonian Academic Library, founded 1947). By the end of the 18th century, pay (or subscription) libraries were opened in both Tallinn/Reval and Tartu/Dorpat/Iurev. In 1802 the Tartu Ülikool (Tartu University Library) was established by the Russian Imperial government, with scholarly collections established in other towns as well. By century's end, Enlightenment societies began to create collections that, during the period of interwar independence, were often reorganized into public libraries. With the coming of Estonian independence, a national library (Eesti Rahvusraamatukogu), formerly a state library, was founded in 1918. It now occupies a large modern building opened in 1993.

EDWARD KASINEC AND ROBERT H. DAVIS JR.

See also Austrian National Library; Bavarian State Library; Charles University Library; City and University Library of Frankfurt am Main; Estonian Academic Library; German National Library; Göttingen State and University Library, Lower Saxony; Herzog August Library Wolfenbüttel; Jagiellonian Library; Latvian Academic Library; National and University Library of Bosnia and Hercegovina; National and University Library of Croatia; National and University Library of Strasbourg; National Library of Estonia; National Library of Latvia; National Library of Lithuania, Martynas Mažvydas; National Library of Poland; National Library of Romania; National Library of Saints Cyril and Methodius (Bulgaria); National Library of the Czech Republic; Saxon State Library/State and University Library of Dresden; Slovenia National and University Library; State Library of Berlin—Prussian Cultural Foundation; Tartu University Library; University and City Library of Cologne; University and State Library of Münster; University Library in Bratislava; University Library of Freiburg in Breisgau; University Library of Graz; University Library of Heidelberg; University Library of Leipzig; University Library of Munich; University Library of Tübingen; University Library of Vienna; University Library of Wrocław (Breslau); Vilnius University Library; Warsaw University Library; Württemberg State Library

Further Reading

Historical Atlases

Hupchick, Dennis P., and Harold E. Cox, *A Concise Historical Atlas of Eastern Europe*, New York: St. Martin's Press, and London: Macmillan Press, 1996

Magocsi, Paul Robert, *Historical Atlas of East Central Europe*, Seattle and London: University of Washington Press, and Toronto, Ontario: University of Toronto Press, 1993

Sellier, André, and Jean Sellier, *Atlas des peuples d'Europe Centrale*, Paris: La Découverte, 1991

Overviews

Al'bina, Larissa, et al., *Histoires de bibliothèques*, Paris: Ministère des Affaires Étrangères, Secrétariat d'Etat à la Francophonie et aux Relations Culturelles Extérieures, 1992

Fabian, Bernhard, editor, *Handbuch deutscher historischer Buchbestände in Europa*, 10 vols., Hildesheim, Germany, and New York: Olms-Weidmann, 1998–2000

Zharkov, V.M., editor, *Kniga: Entsiklopediia* (The Book: An Encyclopedia), Moscow: Bol'shaia Rossiiskaia Entsiklopediia, 1999

Germany

Buzás, Ladislaus, *German Library History, 800–1945*, translated by William D. Boyd, Jefferson, North Carolina: McFarland, 1986

Fabian, Bernhard, and Karen Kloth, editors, *Handbuch der historischen Buchbestände in Deutschland*, 27 vols., Hildesheim, Germany, and New York: Olms-Weidmann, 1992–2000

Jochum, Uwe, *Bibliotheken und Bibliothekare, 1800–1900*, Würzburg, Germany: Königshausen and Neumann, 1991

Kunoff, Hugo, *The Foundations of the German Academic Library*, Chicago: American Library Association, 1982

Olson, Michael P., *The Odyssey of a German National Library: A Short History of the Bayerische Staatsbibliothek, the Staatsbibliothek zu Berlin, the Deutsche Bücherei, and the Deutsche Bibliothek*, Wiesbaden, Germany: Harrassowitz, 1996

Ruppelt, Georg, editor, *Bibliothekspolitik in Ost und West: Geschichte und Gegenwart des Deutschen Bibliotheksverbandes*, Frankfurt: Vittorio Klostermann, 1998

Schmitz, Wolfgang, *Deutsche Bibliotheksgeschichte*, Bern, Switzerland, and New York: Peter Lang, 1984

Austria

Unterkircher, Franz, Rudolf Fiedler, and Michael Stickler, *Die Bibliotheken Österreichs in Vergangenheit und Gegenwart*, Wiesbaden, Germany: Reichert, 1980

Hungary

Foldesi, Ferenc, editor, *Bibliotheca Corviniana, 1490–1990*, Budapest: Helikon, 1990; as *Bibliotheca Corviniana, 1490–1990: International Corvina Exhibition on the 500th Anniversary of the Death of King Matthias, National Széchényi Library, 6 April–6 October 1990*, Budapest: National Széchényi Library, 1990

Kovács, Máté, editor, *A könyv és könyvtár a Magyar társadalom életben, az államalapítástól 1849-ig.* (The Book and Library in Hungarian Cultural Life, from the Beginnings to 1849), Budapest: Gondolat Kladó, 1963

László, Péter, *A Somogyi-Könyvtár száz éve: Könyvtártörténeti tanulmányok* (The Somogyi Library at 100: Historical Studies), Szeged, Hungary: Somogyi-Könyvtár, 1984

Mazal, Otto, *Königliche Bücherliebe: Die Bibliothek des Matthias Corvinus*, Graz, Austria: Akademische Druck- und Verlagsanstalt, 1990

Németh, Mária, *The National Széchényi Library*, 3rd revised edition edited by Ilona Kovács, Budapest: Országos Széchényi Könyvtár, 1985

Slovakia

Ecker, Juraj, *Dejiny Univerzitnej knižnice v Bratislave, 1919–1985* (History of the University Library in Bratislava, 1919–1985), Bratislava: Univerzitná Knižnica v Bratislave, 1994

Kimlička, Štefan, *Katalóg slovenských knižníc: Fondy, služby, špecialisti; Catalogue of Slovak Libraries: Holdings, Services, Specialists* (bilingual English-Slovak edition), Bratislava: Stimul, 1992

Pasiar, Štefan, *Dejiny knižníc na Slovensku* (A History of the Libraries in Slovakia), Bratislava: Slovenské Pedagogické Nakladatelstvo, 1977

Ryznar, Eliska, "Czech Libraries and Archives," and "Slovak Libraries and Archives," in *Books in Czechoslovakia: Past and Present*, by Ryznar and Murlin Croucher, Wiesbaden, Germany: Harrassowitz, 1989

Czech Republic

Cejpek, Jiří, Ivan Hlavácek, and Pravoslav Kneidl, *Dějiny knihoven a knihovnictví v českých zemích a vybrané kapitoly z obecných dějin* (A History of Libraries and Books in the Czech Lands and Selected Chapters from General History), Prague: Karolinum, 1995

Kneidl, Pravoslav, Anna Rollová, and Pavel Preiss, *Strahovská knihovna Památníku národního písemnictví: Historické sály, dějiny a růst fondů* (The Strahov Library Monument of National Literature: Historical Rooms, History, and Development of Collections), Prague: Památník Národního Písemnictví, 1985

Libraries of the Czech Republic; Bibliotheken der Tschechischen Republik, Prague: Ministry of Culture of the Czech Republic, 1996

Croatia

Dobric, Bruno, editor, *Čitaonički i knjižnični pokret u Hrvatskoj u 19. i 20. Stoljeću* (The Reading Room and Library Movement in Croatia during the 19th and 20th Centuries), Pula, Croatia: Sveučilišna Knjižnica, 1996

Morovic, Hrvoje, *Povijest biblioteka u gradu Splitu* (A Sketch of the Split Library), Zagreb: Društvo Bibliotekara Hrvatske, 1971

Stipcevic, Aleksandar, editor, *Libraries in Croatia*, translated by Aleksandra Horvat and Danica Ladan, Zagreb: Croatian Library Association, 1975

Tibor, Klaniczay, editor, *A Bibliotheca Zriniana története és allománya; History and Stock of the Bibliotheca Zriniana*, Budapest: Argumentum Kiadó, 1991 (with summaries in English and Serbo-Croatian)

Poland

Bieńkowska, Barbara, and Halina Chamerska, *Tysiąc lat książki i bibliotek w Polsce* (A Thousand Years of Books and Libraries in Poland), Wrocław, Poland: Zakład Narodowy im. Ossolińskich, 1992

The Baltic States

Kocere, Venta, *Latvian Academic Library,* translated by L. Secenova, Riga: Latvian Academic Library, 1994

Sinkevičius, Klemensas, *Lietuvos TSR biblioteku istorija, 1940–1980* (A History of the Lithuanian Academy of Sciences Library, 1940–1980), Vilnius, Lithuania: "Mokslas," 1983

Vikšraitienė, Sigita, Emilija Banionytė, and Birutė Butkevičienė, *Lietuvos didžiosios bibliotekos; Biggest Libraries in Lithuania* (bilingual Lithuanian-English edition), Vilnius, Lithuania: Lietuvos Biblioteknikŋ Draugija, 1997

Central Asian Libraries

Today's political boundaries of Central Asia—roughly similar to those of medieval times—place this grand area of more than 1.5 million square miles between the Azerbaijan Republic on the west and the People's Republic of China on the east. On the south it reaches to the Islamic State of Afghanistan and on the north to the Russian Federation. As late as 1926 there was only a 3.8 percent literacy rate among the mostly rural inhabitants. Since late 1991, when the Union of Soviet Socialist Republics (USSR) dissolved, five independent republics have emerged. Their combined population in 2000 reached 57 million, including non-Central Asians. Later Soviet sources calculated nearly 100 percent literacy by omitting those more than 50 years of age from the figures.

Early Beginnings

The introduction of the Islamic faith into the area by the armies of Arabia, starting in the seventh century A.D., quickly wiped out existing libraries. The famed Central Asian historian, Muhammad ibn Ahmad Biruni, reported that the Arab Muslim governor of Sogdia and Khwarazm, in the heart of southern Central Asia, destroyed manuscripts and their indigenous custodians in his domain as early as the eighth century A.D.

Muslim rulers and magnates then built up their own royal libraries and private holdings of manuscripts acceptable under Muslim law. In the tenth century A.D., a young student, Ibn Sina (Avicenna), later a world-renowned Central Asian philosopher and physician, wrote in Arabic in his autobiography that he had asked Nuh ibn Mansur, the Samanid Amir of Bukhara, to permit him to go into his library. Because Ibn Sina had previously helped to treat the Amir for an ailment, the potentate granted this non-noble access to the many rooms of the Samanid court library. Each room held a special category of manuscripts stored in chests. One room held manuscripts about Arabic language and poetry, another held manuscripts concerning jurisprudence, and other rooms were devoted to different fields of knowledge.

Bukhara's Farajak seminary, one of the oldest Muslim *madrassahs* (seminaries) in the entire region, had collected numerous rare writings by the tenth century A.D. Farther south in Merv, a great cultural center of that era, the holdings of the Aziziye Library reached 12,000 volumes. The Islamic philanthropic system of *waqf* (endowment) substantially aided some libraries.

During the pillaging of Merv by nomadic Seljuk forces, the invaders turned public and private libraries into plunder or dust. Rashid ad-Din, in Khwarazm, accused of stealing books from Merv in A.D. 1141–42, wrote a sharp rejoinder to governor Hasan Qattan, who had complained about him:

> Behold, God hath placed me by lawful means in the way of a thousand volumes of choice books and noble treatises, and I have bequeathed them all to the libraries that have been founded in the countries of Islam, that the Muslims might profit by them.

The Mongol invasion beginning at Khwarazm in A.D. 1219, led by the non-Muslims, Genghis Khan, and his sons and generals, ravaged the great Aziziye Library in Merv and many others. The Mongols placed little value on Muslim books and writings. Under Timur Leng (Tamerlane), ruler from 1370 to 1405, who claimed genealogical links to the Mongols, great collections of manuscripts were assembled in Kesh (now Shahr-i Sabz) and later in Samarkand, his splendid capital. Another Timurid sultan, famous later in India as Babur Padishah—founder of the Mogul Dynasty—fought a rearguard action against the Uzbek nomads who were menacing Timurids as he fled with his forces from Central Asia into Afghanistan. The sultan's court librarians (*kitabdar*, in Tajik), Abdullah Kitabdar and Khwaja Muhammad Ali (presumably keepers of the sultan's books and papers), joined in the retreat. In his famous memoirs, the diarist Babur never specifies the librarians' bookish duties; rather, he relates in various entries that his doughty librarians often performed military service and, in the case of Abdullah Kitabdar, repeatedly joined Babur Padishah in bouts of drinking and versifying. He rewarded them handsomely.

The Timurid's Uzbek rivals entered lower Central Asia as nomads, but they proved less likely than preceding invaders to destroy cultural institutions. The new rulers, Shaybaniy Khan (1500–10) and his pious nephew, Ubaydullah Khan (1534–39), implanted an orthodox religious fervor in the regime and offered models of literacy. Both wrote poetry and religious tracts. This emphasis subsequently slanted the content of library collections toward theology and religion and somewhat away from the previous Timurid emphasis upon art, literature, history, and science. Pious works made up a large share of Qul Baba Kukeldash's library, considered one of the very best collections in Bukhara during the first half of the 16th century.

The Russian Conquest

Like earlier marauders, the Russian military commanders and accompanying area specialists who invaded the region initially plundered those libraries that still existed at court. In 1873 the administrative papers and the royal manuscript collection were taken from the archives of the Khan of Khiva (earlier Khwarazm) and found their way mainly to St. Petersburg, the Czarist Russian capital, thus denying them to Central Asian users.

Until 1920, when Russian troops terminated the two remaining semi-independent states—the Amirate of Bukhara and the Khanate of Khiva—small, old-style collections of religious manuscripts continued to exist in seminaries and at court. During the first two decades of the 20th century, Central Asian reformists (*Jadids*) created libraries and reading rooms and published books for their students and followers. The prominent reformist, Mahmud Khoja Behbudiy, a moderate Islamic legal authority, organized a notable library and bookstore. He made it the largest and best reformist institution of its kind in Samarkand's old city. His collection became more widely known in the region as the Behbudiy Library after the archconservative Bukharan Amir had him assassinated in 1919.

The large, supraethnic Turkistan Autonomous Socialist Soviet Republic (TASSR), established in 1918, reached from the Caspian Sea to China and from the 45th parallel to Afghanistan. Its Council of People's Commissars (CPC) on 14 April 1919 made all previously public, city, institutional, and private libraries the property of the TASSR. The CPC transferred them to the control of the People's Commissariat for Education, with its special library department.

Ethnic Partition of the Library System

In 1923 and 1924, the USSR's leadership in Moscow abruptly dismantled the earlier Kyrgyzstan Autonomous Socialist Soviet Republic and the TASSR's broad cultural and political structure. Five newly constituted but dependent administrative units, each named for a principal nationality (see below), began managing and developing their own library networks with constant tutelage from Moscow. Each unit's libraries focused largely upon a single nationality and its namesake language to an extent not seen during the tenure of any previous government.

Recognizing the anomaly of large-scale library expansion in the presence of a disastrously illiterate populace, the new managers initially concentrated on creating low-level literacy centers, clubs, and simple reading rooms. These adopted two aims: to provide space where thousands of scarcely competent instructors endeavored to teach adults and children to read and write and to supply a platform for incessant Marxist political indoctrination. Officials applied like measures universally across the five main administrative units of the region—Kazakhstan, Kyrgyzstan, Tajikistan, Turkmenistan, and Uzbekistan.

Kazakhstan

By 1910 Russian conquerors of Kazak territory set up a small central library in their headquarters at Vernyi, and by 1913 they had established some 80 small libraries in various places, with 50,000 books in total. Approximately 95 village reading rooms held another 48,000 volumes. These served primarily the Slavic immigrants, floods of whom immigrated to Central Asia starting in the late 19th century.

Kazakhstan is enormous by comparison with the remaining administrative units of Central Asia. In the pre-Soviet period of Russian colonization, hordes of immigrants with special economic privileges and land grants in Kazakhstan overwhelmed the nomadic Kazaks, the most numerous indigenous nationality of the region (fewer than 4 million as late as 1926).

In 1931 the Kazakhstan Autonomous Soviet Socialist Republic (KASSR) began to build up the Pushkin National Library (named the National Library since independence) based on the initial contributions of the Slavic library in Vernyi (now Almaty). The second largest library in the country, it claims more than 5 million volumes. Its chief librarians have visited Western institutions and established book exchanges with a number of those institutions in the United States and elsewhere. The Director of the National Library has stated that it will not move to the town of Astana with the national capital, despite the shift of most government agencies there.

Two other principal libraries in the 1990s—the Central Library of the Kazak Academy of Sciences and its 16 branches in Almaty and the Central Library of the Al-Farabi Kazak State University in Almaty (Kazakhstan's largest academic library)— held 6.7 million and 1.5 million volumes, respectively. An interlibrary council under the Kazakhstan Republic's Ministry of Culture formulates and directs library policies for the nine major libraries in Almaty and the 19 regional public libraries around the country.

Kyrgyzstan

Like Kazakhstan, Kyrgyzstan continues to use mainly the Russian language in its library network as well as in everyday urban speech, communications, the educational system, and publishing. Kyrgyzstan's libraries stock largely Russian-language books and periodicals. The State Public Library established in 1934 in the republic capital Bishkek (then Frunze) holds some 3.5 million volumes, making it the largest in Kyrgyzstan. Two other important libraries, the Kyrgyzstan State University Library and the

Kyrgyzstan Academy of Sciences Library (also in Bishkek) together report collections numbering approximately 1.7 million volumes. All of the republic's main libraries were established in the 1940s or later. In the 1990s and early 2000s, economic constraints drastically limited the funding of every library in Kyrgyzstan.

Tajikistan

Comparable limitations and conditions apply even more severely to Tajikistan's library system, owing to the catastrophic effects of the violent civil war in the country during the 1990s. Tajikistan's libraries, unlike those in more nomadic republics of the region, benefited from a tradition of awareness, among intellectuals, of the country's deep layers of settled civilization and medieval rule by cultured dynasties.

The Firdausi Tajik National Library in the capital, Dushanbe (officially called Stalinabad from 1929 to 1961), claims some 3 million volumes, many manuscripts, and current periodicals. Until Soviet authorities severed Tajikistan from Uzbekistan in 1929, Uzbekistan's library system in Bukhara, Khojand, and Samarkand served the local Tajik population to some extent. The Tajikistan Academy of Sciences Library, along with the Tajikistan University Library (both located in Dushanbe) report some 1.3 million volumes. The Tajikistan State University Library, founded in 1948 (the largest academic collection in the country), grew to one million volumes by the 1990s.

Like other Central Asian republics, Tajikistan supports several specialized small urban libraries, none founded earlier than 1933: the State Archives, the Library of the Institute of History, the Library of the Institute of Language and Literature, and the Library of the Oriental Institute.

Turkmenistan

Libraries in the large territory of Turkmenistan (188,500 square miles), the least-populated (4.5 million people) independent republic in Central Asia, today remain considerably disabled by several factors. They suffer from population dispersion and from a shortage of resources and up-to-date electronic systems and automation. Except for dispersion, those same drawbacks retard library development in two similarly poor but much smaller countries in the area: Kyrgyzstan and Tajikistan.

Before 1920 Turkmenistan's capital, Ashgabat, served as headquarters of the Czarist Transcaspian Oblast' (Province) and its military governor and possessed a Russian library. That collection provided the basis for the Soviet-era Turkmen Oblast' Public Library, founded in 1921. Three years later it changed into the State Library of the Turkmenistan Soviet Socialist Republic (Turkmenistan SSR). By 1993—with a new, specialized building and a change of name from State Library to National Library—it possessed 4.5 million volumes.

The small Central Scientific Library of the Academy of Science, founded in 1941 in the Turkmenistan SSR, grew to 1.2 million volumes in the 1990s. The library of the Turkmenistan University (established in 1950) holds 410,000 volumes, and the library of the Turkmenistan Medical Institute (started in 1932) contains 278,000 volumes. Both institutions are in the city of Ashgabat and are smaller than comparable institutions in other republics of the region. In January 2001 the Turkmen president, Saparmirat Turkmenbashi, ordered the State Library "liquidated" to close what he saw as a center for subversive thought.

Uzbekistan

Circa 1925 Uzbekistan's political authorities converted Tashkent's ethnically neutral Turkistan State Public Library into the State Public Library of the Uzbekistan Soviet Socialist Republic (Uzbekistan SSR). To support literacy programs and to reach the semiliterate and literate citizens, the republic, by far the most urbanized in the region, had opened 162 of what it termed mass libraries as early as 1928.

Emulating the Library Campaign (*Bibliotechnyi Pokhod*) begun in Moscow, Tashkent officials in late 1929 pursued a program of discarding books "not answering contemporary needs"—according to Communist Party (CP) phraseology—and training new librarians while filling their ranks with promoted workers from the CP and Komsomol (Communist Youth League) members. This high-pressure approach to library work failed to realize the gains expected from it.

A library census conducted throughout the USSR in the fall of 1934 made this failure apparent. In the Uzbekistan SSR as of 1 October 1934, 2,555 libraries held an aggregate book fund of 5.2 million volumes. Among them, 1,397 functioned in rural localities, where each library averaged approximately 500 volumes, compared with urban libraries, each averaging 4,700 volumes. The census also showed that most libraries in the 20 subregions and 12 towns of the Uzbekistan SSR held predominantly Russian language materials, despite the fact that literacy in Russian remained quite low among Central Asians. Only approximately one-third of collections in Uzbekistan consisted of books in the Uzbek language. Many of those published in Uzbek after 1924 had been translated from Russian. In rural areas, numbers of books in public libraries per 100 persons by the end of the 1930s averaged approximately 15, whereas in urban settings they averaged 99 for each 100 persons.

Uzbekistan's libraries developed slowly until World War II but paradoxically made a great leap ahead between 1941 and 1945. The leadership of the USSR, for security during the conflict, hurriedly transferred numbers of research institutes, universities, scholars, and librarians from Moscow and other western cities southeastward into Central Asia's settlements. Publishing of books and periodicals increased accordingly, which led to greater library capacity, better services, and more efficient cataloging.

Uzbekistan's readers enjoyed wide choice. Mass libraries grew in number steadily in the 1970s, from 5,745 to 6,700. By 1979 the overall quantity of volumes in those libraries had reached 55.8 million (perhaps by counting journal issues separately). In the larger central institutions, listed holdings were as follows: the Alisher Navoi State Public Library of

Uzbekistan, 4.2 million volumes; the Fundamental Library of the Uzbekistan SSR Academy of Sciences (founded in 1933), 1.6 million; the Fundamental Library of Tashkent University, 2.5 million; the Fundamental Library of Samarkand University (established in 1927), 1.3 million; and the Republic Library for Science and Technology, 2 million.

Pervasive Library Censorship

In the 1960s and 1970s politicians employed several methods to restrict choices of reading material. They centralized library administration and tightened controls over mass libraries; librarians and teachers strongly urged readers to adhere to recommended reading lists; Communist Party ideologists censored books and periodicals at the source of publication and published many works themselves; and librarians actively purged library collections of works offering what they considered dangerous ideas from foreign authors or from politically discredited Central Asian writers.

As library resources have shrunk since 1990, tendencies toward ideological control have intensified. Almost to the end of the Soviet Union's existence late in 1991, censorship remained prevalent in all institutional libraries, where librarians (supervised by CP ideologists) segregated from approved readings most noncommunist foreign political and social literature and a great majority of creative writing. The libraries kept those indexed publications in locked stack sections accessible only to certified readers who carried special passes.

After 1991 the libraries of Tajikistan, Turkmenistan, and Uzbekistan continued to function under arbitrary political systems and a censored press. The governments of Kazakhstan and Kyrgyzstan, undemocratic in many respects, allowed some latitude for criticism and competition of ideas but continued to dominate and manipulate the media and communications, as well as library budgets, in Central Asia. Thus all five Central Asian republics persistently restrict freedom of expression, press, and education and thereby undermine open political and public life in society and damage the most important and revealing mirror of that life—the library system.

EDWARD A. ALLWORTH

Further Reading

Allworth, Edward A., *Central Asian Publishing and the Rise of Nationalism: An Essay and a List of Publications in the New York Public Library,* New York: New York Public Library, 1965

Aman, M.M., "Education for Library and Information Science in the Soviet Autonomous Republics," *Journal of Information Science* (1992)

Curtis, Glenn E., *Kazakstan, Kyrgyzstan, Tajikistan, Turkmenistan, and Uzbekistan: Country Studies,* Washington, D.C.: Division Headquarters, Department of the Army, 1997

Francis, Simon, *Libraries and Information in the Near East and Central Asia,* London: British Library, 1995

Grimsted, Patricia Kennedy, *A Handbook for Archival Research in the USSR,* Washington, D.C.: Kennan Institute for Advanced Russian Studies, 1989

Kasymova, A.G., *Istoriia bibliotechnogo dela v Uzbekistane* (A History of Library Development in Uzbekistan), Tashkent, Uzbekistan: "Uqituvchi," 1981

Poletaeva, L., *Qazaqstannyng ulttyq kitapkhauasy; National'naia biblioteka Kazakhstana; The National Library of Kazakhstan, 1931–1991* (trilingual Kazakh-Russian-English edition), Almaty, Kazakhstan: "Oner," 1991

Sikorskii, Nikolai Mikhailovich, editor, *Knigovedenie: Entsiklopedicheskii slovar* (Book Study: Encyclopedic Dictionary), Moscow: Sovetskaia Entsiklopediia, 1982

Christian Libraries

All the glory of the world would be buried in oblivion, unless God had provided mortals with the remedy of books.
—Richard de Bury,
14th-century bishop of Durham, *Philobiblion*

The integral relationship between Christianity and its texts has from the earliest times secured a central place for books, for learning, and for libraries. The passing of two millennia has witnessed an ebb and flow in the intensity of Christian scholarship, yet it has always been the case that theological learning is impossible without libraries collecting the wisdom of the past and anticipating future theological discussion.

Earliest Christian Libraries

The establishment of the Christian canon has classically been a subject of interest chiefly to theologians and textual critics. It also has a direct bearing on the origins of Christian libraries. It is certain that as such an accord was reached, early Christian communities would entrust a member of the community with the task of providing care and security for those documents that authentically encompassed the soul, identity, and cohesion of this upstart, frequently embattled religion.

The impulse to keep valued texts safe but accessible shaped the patterns of early collections, and in fact the first recorded mention of early Christian library activity survives from a context of hostility. Under the Roman Emperor Diocletian in the third century, a series of edicts against the Christians included orders that Christian books be seized and destroyed. From this it can be inferred that it was typical for a congregation to possess a valued trove of texts of one kind or another, and that the authorities considered the destruction of such materials to be an effective means of suppressing the Christian faith.

Bishop Alexander of Jerusalem established a library during his tenure in the first half of the third century, as is evidenced by the records of an actual user, Bishop Eusebius of Caesarea in Palestine (third and fourth century), who cites some of the works he found (for example, in Eusebius' *On the Martyrs of Palestine*, of which a Syriac translation is still extant). There is an intriguing possibility that Alexander's library had as its model the legendary classical collection of Alexandria: It may be that while still in the Egyptian city, Origen encouraged Alexander as a student to initiate a center for study in Jerusalem. Origen also had a hand in the establishment of the early Christian library of greatest renown, that at Caesarea, which initially consisted principally of his own private collection. The great Jerome was later associated with this library, though most of the specific library work appears to have been done by Pamphilus, who, according to Jerome, "searched throughout the world for examples that were true and eternal monuments of gifted writers." (Only a fragment survives of the *Life of Pamphilus*, often referred to by Eusebius, describing Pamphilus' liberality to poor students, quoted by St. Jerome.)

Through the efforts of Pamphilus and Jerome, the library grew to include thousands of volumes, a staggering accomplishment when the labor involved in copying by hand is considered. The breadth and quality of this collection is attested to by the range of sources cited by Eusebius, who relied on this library in research for his works. Primary collections included all the works of Origen, as well as contemporaries such as Clement of Alexandria, Appolinaris, Justin, Irenaeus, and virtually all the important ecclesiastical writers of the period. As the library performed the critical functions of copying, revising, and gathering texts into usable selections, scriptural texts were present in abundance.

Caesarea's was, in almost every modern sense, principally a research rather than a congregational/liturgical library. In this setting ambitious, critical works were housed, and ever more ambitious and critical works were likely written. Regrettably, it is not certain what became of the collection, except that it is lost almost without a trace. It was some time before any Christian library again rose to the standard set in Caesarea.

Less is known of a specifically Christian library in Alexandria, as distinct from the renowned classical library of earlier centuries. Given the prominence of the city within the Greek world of letters, it is quite possible that authoritative teaching figures such as Pantaeus and Clement put their personal libraries at the disposal of students and that over time a Christian library took shape. It was not until the fourth and fifth centuries, when political conditions permitted, that Episcopal libraries (with official materials collected at the behest of bishops) took shape in Rome, situated in the Lateran Palace. Here were housed not only theological works but, in keeping with the administrative function, archives as well.

Of all the Christian libraries in the West in the first six centuries, the most is known about the library at Hippo, home of Augustine (A.D. 354–430), the greatest theologian of the age. No distinction is made in the contemporary accounts between Augustine's personal library and that of the church, so it is probable that the two were housed together. The librarian recorded more than 1,000 items under Augustine's personal authorship, and the collection is certain to have included scriptural books, the works of other Latin and Greek Christian writers, and a rich selection of secular works. The collection was fully cataloged (perhaps Augustine himself had a hand in this), but along with the rest of the collection, this index is lost.

When it was safe to do so, Christianity made the most of the accomplishments of Roman civilization with respect to books and libraries. If the possession of a well-stocked library was considered an enviable adornment in a Roman home, it is probable that a similar element of prestige was conferred on those Christian gathering places that possessed the premier collections of letters and texts. Jerome (third and fourth centuries), for example, was able to assume that wherever there was a congregation, books would be found. In the course of things, those churches that became regional administrative centers tended to develop the best collections.

Of early Christian libraries in the East, far less is known. The Imperial Library of Constantinople encompassed at its peak more than 100,000 items, but in no sense was it a theological library.

Libraries in the Monastic Setting

The earliest examples of monastic libraries were in Egypt. Monasteries under the direction of Pachomius (fourth century) and Shenute (fifth century) required that members learn to read, and it was further expected that they would borrow and study texts from the community's collection. Twentieth-century archeological discoveries at sites such as Phobaimmon and Nag Hammadi, for example, indicate that there was extensive activity in writing and copying texts, and one library catalog from the period lists 80 titles. Collections were comprised of biblical texts, lectionaries, church canons, hagiography/biography, and the like.

In Eastern Christendom, monastic libraries developed on a similar pattern from the third century. Catalogs were simply inventories of items held by the community. On those rare occasions when a community's benefactor donated a personal collection, the tendency was not to dispose of questionable or even heretical works: Given the short supply of texts, almost any item would be considered a rare book. The common practice in monastic life was for the abbot (or equivalent) to be charged with the responsibility of securing and caring for the collection.

The most enduring image of early Christian (and monastic) libraries and librarianship comes from southern Italy in the person of Cassiodorus. Like no one else of his time, he left a compendious work of bibliography, the *Institutiones divinarum et saecularum litterarum,* which surveys first Christian and then secular texts, providing notes and commentary along the way. An earlier attempt at Rome to establish a theological school had been frustrated, and so on his family's estate at Calabria he established the Vivarium, a setting in which systematic theological study could be fully integrated into monastic life. With this in view he assembled a large library of both Christian and classical texts and designed a curriculum of study. He undertook his monastic and bibliographic work only after a long and well-rewarded career in the service of the Goths, and hence the essence of his work was combating the growing chaos of the world. The *Institutiones* note how he had these sub-collections housed, what they included, and how they were obtained.

The Late Middle Ages

Cassiodorus may have been aware of the inception of the library at Monte Cassino under the influence of St. Benedict. In any event, with the Imperial City increasingly under attack, the locus of library activity shifted increasingly to rural monastic houses. Benedict supported and energized the place of the library in the community by delegating senior brothers to patrol at a set hour to ensure that no one was engaged in idle chatter, rather than being diligent in his reading.

During succeeding centuries, such libraries played an increasingly strategic role in defending the tradition of learning from decay, pillage, and even disappearance. By the standards of the later Middle Ages, a monastery collection numbering more than 1,000 would have been considered very large. Quality and utility (rather than mass) were most desired. Catalogs varied in complexity and size, and chained books were common enough to indicate that security was a concern.

We know a little about the physical design of some libraries of the period from extant documents. Typically a large, pillared hall would serve as a reading room, with built-in cupboards to store the books. Carrels for study were often set around the perimeter to exploit available light. An additional floor might house a scriptorium.

The same period saw the flowering of monastic libraries in Britain. Once the Roman occupation ended in the mid-fifth century, Columba founded the meditation and copying center at Iona off the coast of Scotland. A century later Augustine arrived, sent to England by Gregory the Great, setting in motion efforts to assure greater conformity to the will of Rome on the part of the English church. A side-effect of this harmony was a marked increase in monastic library development in England, and a key figure in this maturing was Benedict Biscop of Wearmouth on the North Sea Coast. In the tradition of Pamphilus and Cassiodorus, Biscop traveled far to get the works he required. He sought out the best sources of supply for books among the desolate remains of ancient civilization in Italy. Most importantly, what he retrieved from the continent contained everything that was necessary for understanding the main outlines of the Christian learning of the ancient world. The perfect testimony to the value of his diligent endeavors is that they supported the scholarship of Bede, the greatest example of Benedictine scholarship and of the use to which a Benedictine library can be put.

The rise of universities and their libraries was energized greatly by bequests such as those of Bishop Robert Grosseteste to the monastic institutions that eventually developed as Oxford University, England; Duke Humphrey of Gloucester to the colleges at Cambridge; and Robert de Sorbonne to the University of Paris. The emerging university libraries, small though they may have been at first, rapidly assumed a different function from that of monastic libraries. Research activity, rather than copying and preservation, predominated. And it is fair to say that the advent of a new technology—the printing press—in the mid-15th century helped to take this distinction (the beginnings of a demand model) still further.

In France prior to 1200, all of the major theological schools emerged in the environs of cathedrals, among them the schools of St. Victor at Notre-Dame (founded 1108) and Sainte-Geneviève (Monts-le-Paris). This association of the cathedral and academy proved to have a decisive influence on determining both where and how theological research and education were to be carried out for centuries to come.

By 1500 there were between 75 and 85 universities in Western Europe. Most began without formal libraries, but over the course of time the use of private tutors' collections in faculties of theology and elsewhere gave way to more methodical and sustainable collection schemes.

The Renaissance and Reformation

If the later Middle Ages were characterized by the rescue and preservation of Christian texts by monastics on the fringes of the world, the Renaissance was an era of recovery. It is doubtful whether the history of Western civilization has ever seen, before or since, such a hunger for ancient texts and their contents. Admittedly, this appetite was more for Greek and Latin classical texts than for Christian theological works, but the effect was a positive one for libraries of every kind.

The advent of the printing press had a direct and rapid effect on libraries, for it offered not only the prospect of more copies of more volumes on the market but also made the unprecedented range of available editions a consideration. The desired classics were appearing in versions more reliable than their predecessors because of Humanist scholarship. With new, bound formats and with the capacity to produce multiple copies, the prospect of a work of scholarship disappearing became much less likely.

This shift of focus showed itself first in Italy. During the 14th century, Petrarch, Boccaccio, Salutati, and others rediscovered, aggressively collected, and copied manuscripts from all-but-lost collections. Significantly, when this appetite turned into something of a gold rush, it was almost invariably to places such as the Benedictine library of Monte Cassino that text hunters turned. For economic and other reasons, Florence became the center of such activity. Across Europe the focus for library expansion and activity became the royal or princely libraries. Aggressive activity in collecting, gathering, and protecting texts from their scattered locations was chiefly the role of individuals rather than churches or even universities.

The greatest of these book hunters were personal agents of wealthy noblemen. Perhaps this is why the greatest legacy for theological librarianship of this essentially humanist cultural movement was the effect it had on the Vatican Library. Its earlier collection had been dispersed during the interval at Avignon, so that on his accession in 1447 Pope Nicholas V found only 350 volumes extant. The library of the Vatican was brought back to health essentially as an accumulation of personal library collections, such as that of the Duke of Urbino, whose 1,120 volumes were added to the Vatican Library after his death in 1519.

In the Low Countries and in England the effect of the Renaissance was somewhat different. Erasmus of Rotterdam was a fine and aggressive collector in his own right who, with great erudition, brought together the best of the specifically Christian tradition with the emergent humanism of the continent. The benefits of such efforts on the Reformation period and beyond are impossible to calculate.

The turmoil generated by the English monarchy's break with Rome in the 16th century had a devastating effect on theological library collections. In Yorkshire alone there were more than 50 abbeys and priories, each having at least a modest library. And yet within the space of little more than a generation, this whole structure was crudely dismantled. State-authorized visitations during the reigns of Henry VIII and Edward VI meant the breakup of collections, not only in the monasteries but at the universities as well. Insofar as this process was guided by any principle, it was to suppress that which was medieval and to elevate that which was classical and humanist in character. In large measure this had the desired effects of cutting libraries in the British Isles loose from the literary tradition associated with Rome and turning interest toward the English and Celtic traditions within the church. There is some evidence that the abrupt change of fashion in theological literature and learning brought in by the Henrician Reformation had the curious effect of extracting significant portions of monastic collections from purely religious surroundings. So quickly did materials intrinsic to the Roman Catholic tradition become devalued (the monarchy was aggressive and quite ruthless in moving the church in the direction of Protestant humanism) that it was not uncommon for displaced monks, friars, and abbots to be able to take with them, gratis, books from monastic libraries.

Additionally, some private collectors (including John Leland, Matthew Parker, William Cecil, and Robert Cotton) spared some of the monastic holdings from destruction. It was the spirit of such generosity and efforts to overturn the Reformation's more destructive impulses that moved Thomas Bodley to help reestablish the Bodleian Library at Oxford in 1602.

Similar currents can be observed in the Continental Reformation, with some books taken from the monasteries and moved to Lutheran churches. A more enduring effect was the shift of surviving monastic collections to the universities. Many universities that were founded in the 16th century had their libraries enriched by works taken from Dominican and Jesuit libraries, among others. The University of Leipzig, for example, received 1,500 manuscripts and 4,000 printed books in this manner. The University of Basel received the contents of both the city's cathedral library and a nearby Dominican library. This can hardly have been what the monks and scribes had in mind during their earlier toil, but at least the works lived on in active use. Many libraries suffered damage or disruption during the Thirty Years' War in the 17th century, but in general the 17th and 18th centuries were a period of remarkable growth in theological collections of Continental Europe. Again, the uniform trend was away from the cloisters and into the academies.

The Enlightenment: Different Faces of Change

Religious dissent in England had the effect of prompting some dissenters to leave for the New World, where their views on church, state, and education found expression in new colleges. Many of those who remained in England found themselves denied access to the universities by the Acts of Uniformity (1549 and after). Their response was to found their own academies, 35 of which were established between 1680 and 1780. Library resources for these schools were chiefly supplied by the private collections of the academies' benefactors. During the same time period, endowed libraries for the use of parishioners were also established, where it appears that literature was made available to keep readers from lapsing into the easy moral ways thought to be characteristic of the Restoration era.

The labors of the English clergyman-philanthropist Reverend Thomas Bray (1656–1730) demonstrate how far a philanthropic vision for Christian libraries could sometimes extend. It came to Bray's attention that many British and colonial ministers, both Anglican and dissenting, simply lacked the means to procure theological books and were effectively consigned to rural parishes where they were not within reasonable distance of books to borrow. The result was Bray's formulation of parochial and lending libraries. He drafted a six-page list of titles to be included, with the aim of setting up such collections for every deanery in England, and appealed to the aristocracy for donations of books and money. Eventually the Society for Promoting Christian Knowledge, which he helped to found late in the 17th century, thought well enough of the enterprise to undertake its sponsorship.

The new idea of a regional or even a lending library of theological literature was taken further by a nonconformist Scot, James Kirkwood, who proposed the support of such ventures with a property tax. Kirkwood won the support of the scientist

Robert Boyle for the translation and distribution of Gaelic Bible translations in the north of Scotland. In this formerly deprived region he also helped to establish 77 lending libraries in the early decades of the 18th century.

By contrast, the paroxysm that rocked France at the end of the 18th century was felt by its libraries, initially by those of the Jesuits. Whether this disruption was impelled by the jealousy of other orders or whether anticlerical sentiment was simply an explosion looking for a place to occur, the Jesuits took the brunt. A series of edicts meant to rein in their influence and holdings culminated with the actual dissolution of the order in 1773. Most French universities, having close ties with the church, did not survive the Revolution. The idea was to confiscate collections and redistribute them for the benefit of the public. One contemporary estimate put the number of books seized at 12 million. The urge to protect personal literary property had its effect once again, however, and many of the items made their way into clandestine or private collections.

The Genesis and Development of the Seminary Library

Theological collections had almost always been a component part, often indeed the central part, of cathedral or university libraries. But the adoption of the seminary or divinity school as an adjunct of a college presented a new model for theological libraries.

The idea of an independent seminary had occasional antecedents in Europe, but the model that emerged in the U.S. colonies was in almost every respect unique. Harvard College (Cambridge, Massachusetts), Yale College (New Haven, Connecticut), and other institutions were established for the training of clergy, but at the time this was not considered to be a specialized or professional education. The lines of demarcation between secular and theological learning were not clear. Of the 400 books donated by John Harvard shortly after the founding of the college, approximately two-thirds were theological, and as the collection's growth depended largely on donations from clergy, this proportion did not change rapidly. The Harvard shelf-list was compared with another recommended list of the time, Richard Baxter's *Christian Directory* (1673), which showed the Harvard collection to be meager, at best. Baxter's *Directory*, together with Samuel Willard's *Brief Directions to a Young Scholar* (1735), Cotton Mather's *Manductio ad Ministerium, Directions for a Candidate of the Ministry* (1726), and Jonathan Edwards' *The Preacher, As Discourse . . . To Which Is Added a Catalogue of Some Authors* (1705) were some of the conspectuses for theological literature used at the time.

In the 18th-century U.S. colonies, consensus on theology and theological training came under considerable strain. Traditionally, it was thought that theological training was best carried out through a rigorous program in academic subjects. But revivalist trends outside the academies and theological ferment within led to increasing distrust of this largely intellectual approach.

The option of personal apprenticeship in the home of a respected clergyman—what came to be called the "Schools of the Prophets"—grew in popularity in the aftermath of the Second Great Awakening (c. 1740). Joseph Bellamy of Bethlehem, Connecticut, was probably the best example. His personal library consisted of approximately 100 books and at least 350 pamphlets (an essential medium for broadcasting sermons at the time). There is some irony in the fact that, although it removed many of the best divinity students from academies, this unorthodox approach produced more than its share of highly learned pastors, on the strength of the erudition of the "Prophets," their power of example, and perhaps the quality of their personal libraries.

This unorthodox trend in the training of Protestant ministers helped to prepare the ground for another development in theological libraries: the institution of freestanding schools of theology. Some divinity schools (Harvard, Yale) remained affiliated with their original colleges, whereas others (Andover Theological School, Princeton Theological Seminary, Pittsburgh Theological Seminary) became independent entities. But what is of signal importance in all cases is that here were assembled collections for theology and divinity and nothing else. Again, donations and purchases of private theological collections provided the foundation for seminary libraries (most notably the Van Ess collection by the Burke Library of Union Theological Seminary, New York City). Several were formed on this basis by the end of the 18th century, including New Brunswick Theological Seminary (New Jersey), and St. Mary's Seminary (Baltimore, Maryland). The first part of the 19th century saw excellent theological collections gathered at Union Theological Seminary, Andover Theological School (later merged with the Harvard Divinity Collection), Hartford Theological Seminary (sold much later to Candler School of Theology at Emory University), Yale Divinity School, Colgate-Rochester (and subsequent mergers from Bexley Hall and Crozer Theological Seminary, also in Rochester, New York), General Theological Seminary (New York City), Drew Theological Seminary (Madison, New Jersey), Princeton Theological Seminary, Gettysburg Theological Seminary, St. Charles Borromeo Seminary (Philadelphia, Pennsylvania) and others. In the Midwest, the St. Mary of the Lake Seminary (Mundelein, Illinois) was founded in 1844, and on the west coast what is now the Pacific School of Religion (Berkeley, California) came into existence in 1866.

The 20th Century and Beyond: Growth, Retrenchment, Redefinition

Depending upon the perspective, trends during the last century can be seen as evidence of a bright or an uncertain future for Christian theological libraries. In Europe by the end of the 19th century, theological education and training for the ministry had come almost universally under the auspices of the universities. Among other things this usually meant the demise of discrete theological collections within separate facilities, although this did not necessarily mean the devaluation of such collections. Indeed, it is fair to say that as the 20th century opened, not only the finest theological collections but the most erudite and distinguished centers of theological research were in Germany and Britain (at the German universities of Heidelberg, Tübingen, Göttingen, and Berlin, as well as at universities in the United Kingdom such as Oxford, Cambridge, and Edinburgh, to name only a few).

What could not have been predicted was the devastation brought by wars, from the beginning to the end of the century. In France, the University of Nancy lost its library in 1914, as did the University of Louvain in the same year. Great libraries of theology at Monte Cassino (Italy), Dresden (Germany), and Caen (France) were destroyed in 1944. As recently as 1992, the state library at Sarajevo (Bosnia) fell victim to a rocket attack. The numerical losses here and elsewhere were unthinkable. In Germany, the universities of Hamburg and Frankfurt lost 600,000 volumes and the University of Würzburg 350,000.

Political as well as military upheavals have had an adverse effect on European theological library collections and activity. Libraries in Eastern Europe illustrate this vividly: Collection priorities in places such as Jena (Friedrich Schiller University), Rostock (University of Rostock), and Leipzig (University of Leipzig) could hardly be said to have been favorable to theological research during the years 1945 to 1990. Moreover, since the reunification of the two Germanies, the massive amounts of money and personnel that it would take to restore theological collections back to acceptable standards has not been easy to come by.

Of all continental theological collections, few managed to navigate the various catastrophes of the last century better than the Vatican Library. Steadily enriched by a sequence of outstanding gifts over several centuries, even the French Revolution and the Napoleonic Era did little lasting harm. By the end of the 19th century the library encompassed close to a half-million books and tens of thousands of manuscripts. Several of the popes (for instance, Leo XIII and Pius XI) have taken a keen and active interest in the library, and great effort and expense have been taken to ensure that the collections not only continue to grow but are also well cared for. Like many of Europe's great theological libraries, the Vatican provides bibliographic searching, now enabled globally via the World Wide Web. Increasingly, well-financed libraries such as the Vatican Library are working aggressively to develop plans for mounting digital versions of some of their resources (most often archival materials) on Web servers.

In the United States, both denominational and nondenominational schools of theology saw remarkable proliferation by the middle of the 19th century. When in 1924 the first comprehensive study of ministerial education was undertaken, 161 Protestant schools were listed in the United States and Canada. This number increased to 224 a decade later. In his important survey of theological libraries in 1930 (in volume III of *The Education of American Ministers*), Yale Divinity School's librarian, Raymond Morris, indicated that theological libraries ranged in size from a few hundred volumes up to almost 200,000 (131 libraries were surveyed in the late 1920s). This was impressive numerical growth, but he found that libraries were almost always under-supported financially, with repercussions being felt in collections, facilities, and staffing.

Within the Catholic communion in North America, growth patterns had also been phenomenal. An overview in October 1960 by John H. Harrington entitled "Catholic Theological Seminaries and Their Libraries" in *Library Trends* listed 93 diocesan seminaries (50 considered major), as well as 294 "houses of study," with a total of almost 20,000 students in preparation. Although at that time none of the Catholic collections were on the same scale as the largest Protestant libraries, many contained more than 100,000 items.

It is clear now that by the time the surveys by Robert Beach and John Harrington were carried out (1960) a watershed had been crossed, and that demographics of theological education and of church attendance were in the process of rapid change. Among Catholic seminaries, the number of candidates for the priesthood has fallen drastically in the past 30 years (by two-thirds, according to some estimates). On the Protestant side, whereas enrollment was still fairly strong, the proportion of graduates selecting parish ministry as a vocation declined. The second half of the 20th century contrasted sharply with the first: The number of theological colleges and libraries had grown too quickly and too broadly to correspond with trends in the last three decades of the century. This has posed enormous, complex challenges for seminaries and their librarians. These include the pressure to amalgamate theological schools and libraries (each with their own distinct traditions and policy) as well as an uneven geographic distribution of schools and libraries.

The Character of North American Theological Collections

The magnificent wealth of resources now in evidence is the result of a complex and lengthy development process. There have been various routes taken to attain the caliber of many collections today. Some libraries have relied principally on rapid denominational growth that generated demand for clergy and brought in the funding required from denominations and benefactors; some have prospered from the skill and vision of exceptional library leadership; some have built their reputations on exquisite collections purchased and donated by private individuals; and still others have excelled in cultivating niche collections or services.

It is fair to say that in the 21st century the legacy remains strong, but the superstructure that supports it shows signs of strain. Examples of such difficulties include the decline in church membership within many denominations; the number of seminarians and the tuition revenue they contribute; steadily increasing costs of adding to collections, as well as of housing and preserving them, that make it difficult for all but a few libraries to maintain adequate budgets; rapid incursion of communications technology and electronic resources that call into question the continued need for physical library collections; and the growing demand for distance-learning programs, forcing seminaries to reconfigure the way they offer access to course materials.

It cannot be predicted what effect these developments may have on theological libraries in the 21st century. In cases where the parent institutions have found it impossible to remain in operation, libraries have been sold intact or dispersed. Where there are a number of reasonably compatible schools in a specific area, libraries have been merged outright or retained as separate libraries within a consortial arrangement. In the latter case, efficiencies result from reciprocal borrowing privileges and from avoiding duplicate acquisitions when possible.

It seems a foregone conclusion that there will be further retrenchments in the coming years, quite likely on a more widespread basis. With trends such as these emerging in recent years, the role of the American Theological Library Association (ATLA), founded in 1947, has been of vital importance. The primary function of ATLA has been to offer coordination and support of theological library activity in the United States and Canada. ATLA's other notable contributions have been the development and production of *Religion Indexes* (1949–) in print and more recently in electronic versions, and its preservation initiatives in assembling core theological collections in microform, beginning in 1973.

The most recent initiative from ATLA has been its serials project, ATLAS, which will bring 50 major theological periodicals to market in an alternative, electronic format. ATLA has ongoing relationships with sister agencies such as the International Council of Theological Library Associations and the Australia New Zealand Theological Library Association.

Summary

The role and function of theological libraries have always been characterized by continuity amid turmoil, resourcefulness with frequently inadequate resources, and advocacy of that which is of lasting value within a setting of constant ecclesiastical, societal, and political change. In the words of Cassiodorus, "Our aim is both to preserve what is old and to build something new; we desire to raise up things that are modern without diminishing the works of our ancestors."

Only on rare occasions have the legacy and contributions of theological libraries been noted, and then usually long after the fact (Thomas Cahill's *How the Irish Saved Civilization* [1995] provides a pleasant exception). But lasting acclaim is quite beside the point; from Pamphilus of Caesarea onward, theological libraries have most often been energized by the efforts of those who savor a degree of anonymity.

The information age is often considered either a dire threat or a plausible alternative to the perpetuity of printed texts and paper-based library collections. Of course, it also holds out the promise of unprecedented collaboration between the excellent collections and the astute librarians who work in them. Hence there is reason for hope that the best days for theological libraries lie not in the past but in the future.

DAVID R. STEWART

See also Malatestiana Library, Cesena; Mount Athos Monasteries Libraries; St. Gall Abbey Library; Vatican Apostolic Library

Further Reading

Allison, W.H., "Theological Libraries," in *The New Schaff-Herzog Encyclopedia of Religious Knowledge,* edited by Johann Jakol Herzog et al., vol. 11, New York and London: Funk and Wagnalls, 1908

Beach, Robert F., "Protestant Theological Seminaries and Their Libraries," *Library Trends* 9, no. 2 (October 1960)

Clement, Richard W., "Renaissance Libraries," in *The Encyclopedia of Library History,* edited by Wayne A. Wiegand and Donald M. Davis, New York: Garland, 1994

Cross, Claire, "Monastic Learning and Libraries in Sixteenth-Century Yorkshire," in *Humanism and Reform: The Church in Europe, England, and Scotland, 1400–1643,* edited by James Kirk, Oxford and Cambridge, Massachusetts: Blackwell, 1991

Dare, Philip N., "Theological Libraries," in *The Encyclopedia of Library History,* edited by Wayne A. Wiegand and Donald M. Davis, New York: Garland, 1994

Gamble, Harry Y., *Books and Readers in the Early Church: A History of Early Christian Texts,* New Haven, Connecticut: Yale University Press, 1995

Gambrell, Mary Latimer, *Ministerial Training in Eighteenth-Century New England,* New York: Columbia University Press, 1937

Gapp, Kenneth S., "Theological Libraries," in *Twentieth-Century Encyclopedia of Religious Knowledge,* edited by Lefferts A. Loetscher, vol. 2, Grand Rapids, Michigan: Baker, 1955; 2nd edition, 1991

Hadidian, Dikran Y., "Seminary Libraries," in *The Encyclopedia of Library and Information Science,* edited by Allen Kent et al., vol. 36, New York: Dekker, 1983

Harrington, John H., "Catholic Theological Seminaries and Their Libraries," *Library Trends* 9, no. 2 (October 1960)

Henry, Patrick, editor, *Schools of Thought in the Christian Tradition,* Philadelphia, Pennsylvania: Fortress Press, 1984

Jackson, Sidney L., *Libraries and Librarianship in the West: A Brief History,* New York: McGraw-Hill, 1974

LeJay, Joseph, and Otten, Paul, "Cassiodorus," in *The Catholic Encyclopedia,* edited by Charles B. Herbermann et al., vol. 3, New York: Appleton, 1908

Morris, Raymond, "The Libraries of Theological Seminaries," in *The Education of American Ministers,* vol. 3, New York: Institute of Social and Religious Research, 1934

Rockwell, William Walker, "Theological Libraries in the United States," *Religion in Life* 13, no. 4 (September 1944)

Sharpe, John L., III, and Kimberly Van Kampen, *The Bible as Book: The Manuscript Tradition,* London: British Library, 1997; New Castle, Deleware: Oak Knoll Press, 1998

Southern, Richard, "A Benedictine Library in a Disordered World," *Downside Review* 94 (July 1976)

Stewart, David R., "Libraries, Western Christian," in *Encyclopedia of Monasticism,* 2 vols., edited by William J. Johnston, Chicago and London: Fitzroy Dearborn, 1999

Thurston, Herbert, "Libraries," in *The Catholic Encyclopedia,* edited by Charles B. Herbermann et al., vol. 9, New York: Appleton, 1910

Circulating Libraries and Reading Rooms

Booksellers have been making part of their stock available to customers on a rental basis from as early as the 14th century, when local statutes in various European university towns required them to lend manuscripts to students. With the rise of general reading interest in the 17th and 18th centuries, booksellers throughout Europe formally began to establish circulating libraries, later also known as rental, lending, or commercial libraries, as annexes to their sales activities. Parallel to this development was the establishment of reading rooms, often in coffeehouses initially, where readers could consult newspapers and magazines for a small fee.

It was the sharp increase and the spread of popular literature—books, newspapers, and magazines—in the latter part of the 18th and the 19th centuries that made the circulating library an established and important part of the book trade. During the same era, subscription libraries were being created in many towns as private, charitable institutions. With financial support from well-to-do citizens, these libraries mostly served the growing merchant and trade class. The content of these libraries was generally educational and scholarly and was intended mainly for the upper classes. In contrast, the proprietary circulating libraries catered to the more common men and women, whose reading tastes rapidly influenced the publishing world. Social libraries, on the other hand, were often much more conservative in their selection of materials for use.

For a nominal fee, either for a set period of time or per transaction, readers in a circulating library could gain access to a wide selection of popular books. With this increased market, retail booksellers could purchase larger inventories and sell off the used copies when interest declined. Printed catalogs as well as newspaper ads often served as marketing tools.

At the beginning of the 19th century, such libraries and reading rooms were present in most large cities and increasingly in smaller communities as well. Some were very large, such as Allen Lane's Minerva Press Circulating Library in London and Hocquet Caritat's Circulating Library in New York. The latter contained more than 30,000 volumes. Both Lane and Caritat offered to supply aspiring booksellers elsewhere with an inventory and catalog wholesale. Many such libraries were much smaller. A notable number were operated by women, undoubtedly in response to the increasing women's reading market. Not all circulating libraries were operated by booksellers, however. They could also be found in stationary, tobacco, and confectionery stores and even barber shops. Most of them were relatively small neighborhood operations.

Other reading rooms operated on a larger scale. Some were opulent in design, with a wide selection of domestic and foreign newspapers and magazines, such as Eastburn, Kirk and Co. in New York, which opened in 1814. It was the emergence of the novel as the most popular reading genre that propelled circulating libraries to become a major market force, especially in Great Britain. Mudie's Select Library in London operated from 1842 until the 1930s and soon became a dominating force with a stock of millions of books, reaching the British reading market through innovative marketing and distribution techniques, including home delivery. In time Mudie's became the single largest customer for popular fiction. Their main competitor, W.H. Smith, had a substantial market penetration as well, in part through their railway station stores. Although not on such a scale, similar libraries were operating in all major cities of Europe and the United States.

The decline of circulating libraries began in the early part of the 20th century. After many years of professional debate as to the social appropriateness of reading novels, public libraries slowly began to increase their stock of popular books and provided services free of charge. Increased public funding after World War II allowed for the opening of many new public libraries and their branches.

The emergence of the paperback book, as well as book clubs, offered readers inexpensive alternatives. Although home delivery of portfolios of magazines remained popular into the 20th century, ultimately that market declined as well.

W.H. Smith closed its library operation in the 1960s, and by that time circulating libraries had all but disappeared. Popular literature, of course, still thrives, but its distribution now takes place through mass-market merchandising as well as through public libraries.

HENDRIK EDELMAN

Further Reading

Altick, Richard D., *The English Common Reader: A Social History of the Mass Reading Public, 1800–1900*, Chicago: University of Chicago Press, 1957; 2nd edition, Columbus: Ohio State University Press, 1998

Eliot, Simon, "Bookselling by the Back Door: Circulating Libraries, Booksellers, and Book Clubs, 1870–1960," in *A Genius for Letters: Booksellers and Bookselling from the 16th to the 20th Century*, edited by Robin Myers and Michael Harris, Winchester, Hampshire: St. Paul's Bibliographies, and New Castle, Delaware: Oak Knoll Press, 1995

Griest, Guinevere L., *Mudie's Circulating Library and the Victorian Novel*, Bloomington: Indiana University Press, and Newton Abbot, Devon: David and Charles, 1970

Kaser, David, *A Book for a Sixpence: The Circulating Library in America*, Pittsburgh, Pennsylvania: Beta Phi Mu, 1980

Shera, Jesse, *Foundations of the Public Library: The Origins of the Public Library Movement in New England, 1692–1855*, Chicago: University of Chicago Press, 1949

Digital Libraries

The very phrase *digital library* seems inherently contradictory. Digital information is represented by a series of ones and zeros and cannot be read without being submitted to a computer program. A library, on the other hand, is an organized collection of books and other materials easily read by humans. Despite the contradictory nature of the phrase, it is rapidly becoming a well-known, if not well-understood, concept in librarianship.

The great advantage of digital libraries is that collections in electronic form can be viewed by anyone with a computer located anywhere in the world. The compelling ideal of universal collections has motivated much of the work in digital library development.

Defining the Digital Library

Although the phrase *digital library* has been used for only a few years, computer scientists and engineers have been imagining the concept for a long time. Those who originally described the idea generally meant a virtual library—a vast and universal collection of information instantaneously accessible to anyone, anywhere.

As early as 1945, Vannevar Bush, in his landmark *Atlantic Monthly* article "As We May Think," described the Memex machine, in which microfilmed texts were stored in associative memory trails. Bush is credited with the first description of the concept of hypermedia; he conceived of a knowledge management system in which library materials would be linked to one another in much the same way that the human mind makes conceptual connections.

In 1965 J.C.R. Licklider published *Libraries of the Future* as the product of a study sponsored by the Council on Library Resources. Licklider, best known for his research on computer time sharing, was the first to think that more than one person could share a computer at the same time. He described a future library in which a computer-based system might create a new "thinking center." When imagining the computerized library, however, he did not go so far as to assume that every person would have a computer. Instead he described a configuration, the technical details of which he left to the future, by which different people could simultaneously use remote extensions of one central computer at the same time.

Ted Nelson began the Xanadu project in 1965, which included storing texts electronically and linking them horizontally (through related concepts) and hierarchically, creating a system of both hypertext and hypermedia. The ability to go from one text to another gave librarians the idea of building libraries in electronic form that allow readers to move seamlessly from one source to another.

The dream of a comprehensive library that features instantaneous access has a very long tradition. James O'Donnell reminds us that this "fantasy is almost coterminous with the history of the book itself" in "The Virtual Library: An Idea Whose Time Has Passed" (*Avatars of the Word: From Papyrus to Cyberspace*). The founding of the Library at Alexandria was based on Ptolemy's dream of gathering copies of all of the books of the world into a single collection, with a system of pigeonholes designed to hold papyrus scrolls so that users had easy and convenient access to available information.

The dream of the virtual library was incorporated into a larger, more technical vision of a digital library. Although it is impossible to pinpoint the first use of the term, it is easy to find numerous references to digital libraries in the popular press by the late 1980s. A more technical definition was developed when the National Science Foundation (NSF) announced its Digital Library Initiative in the early 1990s. It became readily apparent that the NSF wanted to stimulate research, especially among computer scientists, to produce a better understanding of the requirements for making electronic information universally accessible. But its emphasis was more on experimentation with retrieval systems, indexing methods, and search engines than on assembling any kind of collection resembling a library.

Libraries Become Digital

For most large research libraries, the lure of external funding stimulated a strong interest in digital libraries. The U.S. Library of Congress (LC) announced plans in mid-1994 to create the National Digital Library, building on its efforts to establish a series of electronic collections that constitute the "American Memory." Congress agreed to support a $15 million effort, provided that matching funds of $45 million could be secured from the private sector. Then the LC unveiled its ambitious program of creating 5 million images of its special collections by the year 2000 and was successful in raising the full $60 million required for the effort, including special staffing devoted exclusively to digital library work. The goal was met by collaborating with other research libraries.

Simultaneously, the directors of a group of research libraries (with funding from the Commission on Preservation and Access to explore the implications of digital technology for preservation) suggested to Patricia Battin, then president of that commission, that it was impossible to limit the implications of digital technology to considerations of preservation. They argued that the far-reaching influence of digital technology on the very nature of the research library warranted consideration of a more important issue: the ways in which digital technology would transform libraries. A dozen U.S. libraries constituted themselves as the Digital Preservation Consortium to learn more, collectively, about digital technology. When the consortium learned of the LC's plans for a digital library, they proposed that the Library of Congress and the National Archives join together with their group of research libraries for greater collaborative purposes.

In 1995 the national Digital Library Federation (DLF) was established as a charter group and identified its primary mission: to establish the necessary conditions for creating, maintaining, expanding, and preserving a distributed collection of digital materials accessible to scholars and a wider public. Participants in the federation committed themselves to shared investment in developing the infrastructure needed for libraries of digital works, an infrastructure intended to enable digital libraries to bring together, or federate, the works each manages for its readers.

Donald Waters, the first director of the federation, recognized that it would be difficult to proceed without a shared definition of a digital library, and he proposed the following in 1995:

> Digital libraries are organizations that provide the resources, including the specialized staff, to select, organize, provide intellectual access to, interpret, distribute, preserve the integrity of, and ensure the persistence over time of collections of digital works so that they are readily and economically available for use by a defined community or set of communities.

This definition is notable for its inclusiveness. Members of the federation recognized that the concept of a digital library had many different connotations. The comprehensive definition was developed to suggest that there is a set of attributes that gives coherence to the concept of digital libraries. It includes the functions of collection, organization, preservation, access, and economy.

In its early stages the Digital Library Federation set itself apart from the many scanning projects going on in various libraries by adopting the following four goals for successful digital libraries: (1) organizing, providing access to, and preserving knowledge that is born digitally; (2) leveraging digital library facilities for managing intellectual works in support of efforts to redesign the scholarly communication process; (3) providing an accessible and durable knowledge base that helps to improve the quality and lower the costs of education; (4) extending the reach of research and higher education to new segments of the citizenry.

From these four goals, the DLF adopted four organizing themes for action, themes that serve to develop federated digital libraries and advance the separate institutional goals:

To focus attention on libraries of digitally born materials. Although many in the library community have a preoccupation with conversion of special collections materials to digital form, the DLF deliberately chose to concentrate on organizing, providing access to, and preserving original materials born digitally, especially the substantial electronic resources that it licenses for use. A high priority has been the development of the archival rights and technical mechanisms for preserving the integrity and ensuring the persistence of these digital works over the long term.

To help with the integratation of digital materials into the fabric of academic life. A critical focus for such integration is defining the circumstances under which conversion to digital form is justified. Conversion projects that facilitate the extension of higher education and promise to improve the quality and lower the cost of research and education deserve special attention. For such projects, DLF focuses on measures of quality in conversion and on the methods for storing and providing persistent access to converted works.

To stimulate the development of a core digital library infrastructure. The network and systems requirements for digital libraries and their means of authentication and authorization are DLF's highest priorities. Other key priorities include the development of metadata structures and systems of archiving for digital works of knowledge.

To help with the definition and development of the organizational support needed for effective management of digital libraries. Organization is an essential part of the general infrastructure for digital libraries, but it is often overlooked in the preoccupation with technical infrastructure. Organizational issues that need attention include identifying institutional values and strategies for managing intellectual property in digital form and defining the technical skills necessary for the operation and management of digital libraries, as well as identifying means for developing them.

Other Initiatives

Several initiatives launched by universities and nonprofit organizations have deepened the general understanding of digital libraries. The appearance of electronic journals, both from commercial publishers and scholarly societies, has forced virtually all libraries to come to terms with what it means to integrate electronic content into traditional collections. Questions of ownership versus access have been highlighted as libraries begin to consider how long-term access will be provided for electronic journals.

As users have become more familiar with electronic journals and have come to value the electronic search capabilities that are now available, projects to convert long runs of journal files into electronic form have become popular. Journal Storage (JSTOR), supported initially by the Andrew W. Mellon Foundation, identifies commonly held titles in the humanities and social sciences that could be converted in full text to digital form and made accessible to scholars and students in universities and colleges of all sizes and types. The original impetus was to free up shelf space in overcrowded libraries, but as JSTOR has grown, users are especially pleased with the features of easy access and convenient searching across titles, although most libraries have been reluctant to dispose of physical volumes now represented in JSTOR. Similarly, Project Muse has converted the files of periodical titles published by the Johns Hopkins University Press to digital form and made them available as a package subscription to colleges and universities.

Nearly all of the Digital Library Initiative grants made by the National Science Foundation have produced tools for information retrieval, searching, or digital archiving of electronic content, but many questions remain. First, there is currently no sure method of guaranteeing the long-term availability of electronic materials. Digital archiving has become a high-priority research area. Groups such as the Council on Library and Information Resources, the Coalition for Networked Information, and the

Research Libraries Group are all working on different aspects of the problem. Second, although the Digital Library Federation has made considerable progress on the infrastructure for digital libraries, there is still no unified plan for digital content. Extensive work lies ahead if the digital content that is now being managed heterogeneously by a wide variety of libraries is to form something resembling a comprehensive library that students and scholars can use easily.

DEANNA B. MARCUM

Further Reading

Bush, Vannevar, "As We May Think," *Atlantic Monthly* 176, no. 1 (July 1945)

Ekman, Richard, and Richard E. Quandt, editors, *Technology and Scholarly Communication,* Berkeley: University of California Press, 1999

Garrett, John, and Donald J. Waters, *Preserving Digital Information: Draft Report of the Task Force on Archiving of Digital Information,* Washington, D.C.: Commission on Preservation and Access, 1995

Graubard, Stephen R., and Paul LeClerc, editors, *Books, Bricks, and Bytes: Libraries in the Twenty-First Century,* New Brunswick, New Jersey, and London: Transaction, 1997

Hawkins, Brian L., and Patricia Battin, editors, *The Mirage of Continuity: Reconfiguring Academic Information Resources for the 21st Century,* Washington, D.C.: Council on Library and Information Resources and Association of American Universities, 1998

Lesk, Michael, *Practical Digital Libraries: Books, Bytes, and Bucks,* San Francisco: Kaufmann, 1997

Licklider, J.C.R., *Libraries of the Future,* Cambridge, Massachusetts: MIT Press, 1965

O'Donnell, James, *Avatars of the Word: From Papyrus to Cyberspace,* Cambridge, Massachusetts: Harvard University Press, 1998

Waters, Donald J., "What Are Digital Libraries?" *CLIR Issues* 4 (July/August 1998)

English School Libraries

The history of English school libraries inextricably weaves itself through the history of education in England. Historical references may be found to school libraries from as early as the eighth century, but until the 19th century most of the evidence lies in accounts of individual schools. Detailed, systematic statistics do not appear until the late 20th century. Even today the English school library is difficult to categorize because it remains caught between the disciplines of education and librarianship. The school librarians organizations for professional development in England reflect this uncertain status. The School Library Association represents teachers who run school libraries, and the Library Association's (LA) School Libraries Section supports chartered (professional) librarians in schools. Unlike Scotland and Northern Ireland, England has never passed a statutory requirement mandating school libraries. Consequently, a broad spectrum of practices characterizes English school libraries both historically and today.

Laurel Clyde compiled the most detailed description available of the history of English school libraries through the 19th century in her article "The Schole Lybrarie: Images From our Past." She points out the dearth of scholarship on this subject, which she ascribes to the gray disciplinary area into which school libraries fall. As Clyde and other researchers illustrate, school libraries occupy a very small niche in general library histories and frequently are ignored in histories of education.

The earliest accounts of school libraries that Clyde found referred to the eighth-century church schools at York and Hexham. The collection at York supported a general medieval school curriculum that included Latin, Greek, and theology. Between the eighth and 16th centuries, the few references to school libraries emphasized the precious nature of books before paper and printing became commonplace. Collections were very small, were used mainly on school premises, and were sometimes chained to desks. During the 12th century at St. Paul's school in London, the penalty for failing to return a book was excommunication.

As educational emphasis changed so did the nature and number of school libraries; members of the growing middle class needed to educate their sons to prepare them for a suitable vocation. The 16th and 17th centuries saw tremendous growth in grammar schools. Annals concerning individual schools mentioned libraries, though never librarians. Birmingham, Shrewsbury, and Westminster built separate libraries for their schools. The library built at Shrewsbury included space for study as well as storage for materials. While relying to some extent on donations to build the collection, the school also dictated that funds should be set aside to purchase library books. A handwritten parchment catalog was written for the collection in 1603. A 17th-century survey of grammar schools included a question about the existence of libraries, and responses indicated that in certain instances rooms had been set aside specifically to house books. Besides books, which continued to be chained to desks in some schools, these rooms might also contain scientific instruments, maps, and globes. No uniformity in use or procedures existed among school libraries, but the idea that they had a place in education was becoming more widespread. A 17th-century treatise on education, Charles Hoole's *A New Discovery of the Old Art of Teaching Schoole* (1660), highly recommended libraries as pedagogical tools. Not until the 18th century did the library at Shrewsbury unchain its books and allow students to take them out of the building. Shrewsbury's collection had grown from 132 volumes in 1607 to 1,500 volumes in the 1730s, and the greater availability of books undoubtedly influenced the decision to circulate materials. By the 19th century the libraries of some public schools, such as Birmingham, Easter Ross, Hawkeshead, and Shrewsbury, had become sources of reading materials for their communities. However, the fortunes of public school libraries took a downturn at the same time, according to the Public Schools Commission Clarendon Report of 1864. While the well-known public schools (Eton, Harrow, Rugby, Shrewsbury, St. Paul's, Westminster, and Winchester) had circulating collections, the data suggests that the students rarely used the libraries. Laurel Clyde theorizes that public schools in general suffered from anti-intellectual attitudes during much of the century.

Alec Ellis illustrates that 19th-century sources provided more detail about school libraries in his article "School Libraries and the Cross Commission." Organization records show that the Society for Promoting Christian Knowledge helped to fund more than 2,400 school lending libraries, and the Religious Tract Society provided library grants to more than 3,000 schools. Many of these school libraries also circulated materials to their local communities, echoing the practices of some public schools.

The English government began to gather educational data in a more systematic way, partly in response to the numerous reform groups that sprang up in the 19th century. A statistical compilation that included school libraries made up part of the lengthy Schools Inquiry Commission *Report of the Commissioners* (commonly called the Taunton Report) of 1868. Clyde's analysis of the results shows that 40 percent of all Victorian grammar schools had libraries and that the majority of these were open to the entire school population.

With the Education Act of 1870, the English government began the slow move toward free, compulsory education (fully realized with the Education Act of 1944) and also began to establish the machinery for regulating and recording educational progress. Beginning in 1880 the annual reports of the Committee of Council on Education had to include the number of extant school libraries. Ellis used these reports to calculate that from 1880 to 1901 the number of elementary schools increased from 17,614 to 20,116, while the libraries in them increased from 2,092 to 8,272.

Accompanying statutory educational reform were changes in educational philosophies that sparked some interest in school libraries. The Cross Commission, set up in 1888 to inquire into the workings of the Elementary Education Act, recommended that libraries be established in schools. The London school board instituted rotating library collections, with 40,000 books shared between its 350 school libraries in the 1880s. Despite these advances, Ellis' research indicates that most school libraries of the late Victorian era disseminated recreational literature and had little to do with actual school curricula.

In the beginning of the 20th century little improvement was made in the status of school libraries. Some cooperation existed between public libraries and school libraries, and library categories began to be less defined (for example, at Leeds public libraries were placed in schools and staffed by teachers). During the 1920s public libraries began to object to supporting school libraries without extra funding. In response, some local education authorities provided funds to public libraries specifically to set up loan collections for the schools, creating the precedents for today's School Library Services (SLS).

After World War II the School Library Services emerged as very successful support mechanisms. Run by public libraries and funded by local education authorities, SLS provided central collections of books and other media as well as professional advice on library administration. There was still no set of standards applied to school libraries and no uniformity to the services of the SLS. However, by 1964 a committee on public library standards reported that all county and many metropolitan library services provided education-authority-funded books for schools.

The 1930s to the 1960s saw the first national promotion of school libraries through the School Library Association (SLA), an organization founded in 1937 to support teacher-librarians, and through the School Libraries Section of the LA, also established in 1937 but for chartered school librarians. Unfortunately, the two associations reflected, and perhaps exacerbated, the uncertain status of school libraries. Both organizations viewed school libraries as integral to the mission of supporting curricula. However, the SLA viewed school libraries as the province of educators and stressed library training for teachers, whereas the School Library Section felt that schools should employ professional librarians.

The 1960s and 1970s saw few new developments in school libraries. Both the LA and the SLA issued school library standards guidelines in 1970; however, the guidelines presented differing viewpoints, had no force of law behind them, and added fuel to the disagreement over chartered librarians versus teachers trained to staff libraries. Thanks to advances made in the previous three decades it did become standard to include libraries in newly built schools. Some valuable initiatives also issued from local authorities. Several School Library Services, most notably that of the Inner London Educational Authority, demonstrated that high quality school library service could be achieved in collaboration with public libraries.

The recent history of English school libraries bears out Rebecca Knuth's assertion that they suffer the same recurrent cycles as educational reform, a highly politicized issue in contemporary England. In 1984 the Library and Information Services Council published a report that focused on the role of the school library as a pedagogic tool. *School Libraries: The Foundations of the Curriculum* stirred discussion throughout the educational community about the inadequacies of English school libraries. Detailing the woefully underfunded and understaffed state of school libraries, the report went on to make 40 recommendations that would create dynamic libraries where students could learn the intricacies of information science. Closely following the report, the SLA and the LA formed a joint standing committee to unify lobbying efforts on behalf of school libraries, and the two organizations have continued to cooperate.

In 1988 the Education Reform Act mandated sweeping changes in the basic structure of the school system. Before 1988 local education authorities made many independent decisions about their curricular requirements. The 1988 act established a national curriculum with required subjects, national testing, and distinct phases for educational progress up to the age of 16. Margaret Kinnell has detailed the many parts of this act, which emphasized the teaching of information acquisition and manipulation, which should require substantial participation from school libraries. Ironically, the sections of the act dealing with school administration may have weakened the effectiveness of school libraries. The act took much of the school budget control away from the local education authorities and vested it in individual schools. No provisions were made for school libraries in the new "local management of schools" system that bypassed the local education authorities, nor in the budgetary requirements of the local education authorities. Many education authorities shifted funding responsibility to SLS by requiring them to sell their services to schools. Several studies show that this has worked in districts that already had strong School Library Services but has caused other Services to close, leaving nothing to take their places.

The 1990s were the first period during which any extensive gathering of school library statistics was done. In the latter part of the decade the LA commissioned a survey of secondary school library provisions throughout the United Kingdom, and the Library and Uniform Statistics Units (LISU) at Loughborough University conducted both a survey of library provision in independent schools and a survey of secondary school library users. Until then library school statistics were generally folded into surveys of education.

The statistical data show that English school libraries entered the 1990s with the same lack of status and uniformity that has plagued them throughout the century. In almost every category of the LA's 1997 survey of secondary school libraries the lack of consistency in practices stands out. The executive summary of the survey reveals that in 1997 most schools had libraries; most libraries had at least one computer workstation and a majority employed an automated management system, although only 30 percent had Internet access. The survey went on to reveal that a majority of schools used their library staff to teach information skills; a majority of schools used SLS, but 15 percent had no SLS; almost 24 percent of the libraries had a full-time chartered librarian, 30 percent had full-time teachers in charge, and almost 15 percent had either a part-time teacher or librarian as staff. The types of materials supplied by school libraries, as well as the amount spent per student on stock, varied wildly.

The 1998 LISU Survey of Independent School Libraries showed results similar to the LA's research on secondary school libraries, with the exceptions that overall funding and library stock was slightly better per number of students and library automation more widespread. The annual (since 1989) LISU Survey of Library Services to Schools and Children in the United Kingdom tracks staffing, service provision, expenditures, and use of SLS. The 1997–98 statistics provide evidence of the changes SLS has undergone since the 1988 Education Reform Act. While the majority of funding for School Library Services still comes from local education authorities, 40 percent of their income is earned directly from schools. Staffing levels of SLS have fallen gradually during the past five years. Although School Library Services do possess materials across a broad range of media, 96 percent of their stock is books. As was indicated in other surveys, a great deal of variation exists within the practices of local authorities.

The last decade of the 20th century offered English school librarians a new national curriculum, new funding and management paradigms, and, with the rising importance of information technologies, potential for the exploitation of their research expertise. Recent developments indicate that English school libraries are benefiting from public awareness that school resources, including libraries, have been underfunded. In 1999 the government provided an extra £60 million to buy books for school libraries. However, it seems likely that the fortunes of the English school libraries will continue to rise and fall with those of the English education system in general.

CHARLOTTE A. CUBBAGE

Further Reading

Clyde, Laurel, "The Schole Lybrarie: Images from Our Past," *School Libraries Worldwide* 5 (1999)

Ellis, Alec, *Library Services for Young People in England and Wales, 1830–1970*, Oxford and New York: Pergamon Press, 1971

Ellis, Alec, "School Libraries and the Cross Commission," *Library Association Record* 90 (1988)

Fea, Valerie, "United Kingdom," in *School Libraries: International Developments*, edited by Jean E. Lowrie and Mieko Nagakura, 2nd edition, Metuchen, New Jersey: Scarecrow Press, 1991

Kinnell, Margaret, "Supporting the National Curriculum: English Secondary School Libraries during a Period of Transition," *The International Information and Library Review* 26 (1994)

Kinnell, Margaret, "Policy for Secondary School Library Provision in England and Wales: An Historical Perspective," *Journal of Librarianship and Information Science* 27 (1995)

Knuth, Rebecca, "Factors in the Development of School Libraries in Great Britain and the United States: A Comparative Study," *The International Information and Library Review* 27 (1995)

Lawson, John, and Harold Silver, *A Social History of Education in England*, London: Methuen, 1973

Small, Graham, "Secondary School Libraries in the UK: Staffing, Provision, and Scope," *The School Librarian* 46 (1998)

Stott, C.A., "The School Library Movement in England and Wales," *Library Trends* 1 (1953)

Genealogical Society Libraries

Genealogists, historians, biographers, sociologists, anthropologists, and other researchers who need genealogical materials customarily use public and historical society libraries as well as the collections of major genealogical organizations. In Europe, where genealogical societies are mostly of 20th-century vintage, the great national and university libraries—many of which have been collecting material for several centuries—may be preferred. Of the 14 or so largest genealogical collections in the United States, nearly half are housed in the Boston (Massachusetts), New York, Detroit (Michigan), Fort Wayne (Indiana), Dallas (Texas), Houston (Texas), and Los Angeles public libraries. The balance are held at the Library of Congress (LC); the Daughters of the American Revolution (DAR) Library in Washington, D.C. (the only hereditary society library on this list); the Historical Society of Pennsylvania (Philadelphia); the Western Reserve Historical Society (Cleveland, Ohio); the State Historical Society of Wisconsin (Madison); the American Antiquarian Society in Worcester, Massachusetts; and the Newberry Library in Chicago (apart from LC, all private facilities best known for other collections but with large genealogical holdings).

Genealogists and historians also frequently use university libraries, which often have large collections in U.S., British, and European local history. Research in this field is nonetheless often centered in the libraries of several genealogical societies. The largest collections are those of the New England Historic Genealogical Society in Boston (NEHGS); the New York Genealogical and Biographical Society (NYGBS); the National Genealogical Society (NGS) in Arlington, Virginia; and the Family History Library (FHL), the large facility in Salt Lake City, Utah, belonging to the Church of Jesus Christ of Latter-day Saints. Each of these four societies also sponsors scholarly publications (journals, magazines, or newsletters) and a wide variety of educational programs, including national or regional conferences, courses, seminars, individual lectures, and tours, frequently abroad.

Many smaller genealogical societies have been incorporated in the last several decades; their library holdings are often housed in local public libraries or historical societies. A few societies own or rent buildings and have small professional or volunteer staffs. These smaller collections usually contain items of local, state, or regional interest, as well as standard reference material and some compiled genealogies in print. The four largest libraries mentioned above (NEHGS, NYGBS, NGS, and FHL) own a sizable percentage of the 10,000 or more published compiled genealogies. NEHGS has almost all such works for New England, plus many more on non–New England families. FHL has, in addition, most 20th-century volumes for the whole country, plus many foreign works. These libraries also house almost all local history materials, such as mugbooks (county histories with pictures of citizens treated therein), town histories (frequently with genealogical registers covering all residents through a certain date), centennial publications, and all printed state, county, or town source records (vital data, wills, deeds, court papers, church and cemetery data, censuses, military lists, and even extracts from family Bibles).

Compiled genealogies of the 19th century often contain erroneous European origins, irrelevant coats of arms, and garbled accounts of colonial generations. A large body of 20th-century periodical literature and several hundred multiancestor works (often commissioned from professional genealogists and covering several dozen families in the patron's ancestry) correct many of these errors and cover much of the population (for New England especially) not covered in compiled genealogies. The multiancestor works generally cover the male line descendants plus daughters (but usually not the offspring of daughters) of Great Migration immigrants to New England or early settlers in Dutch New York, Quaker Pennsylvania, and the Tidewater South. Especially since the U.S. bicentennial (1976) and the publication of Alex Haley's *Roots* (1977), many genealogies have treated 18th-century German or Scots-Irish families, plus later immigrant families (often post-1840), who are frequently Irish, Italian, French-Canadian, or Jewish. Several African American genealogies and regional collective studies have appeared as well, but only a handful of such works cover recent Hispanic or Asian American families (a situation likely to change soon).

The four major genealogical society libraries also contain significant material on microfilm and microfiche. NEHGS has sizable holdings for New England and eastern Canada. FHL has filmed and partially extracted a sizable percentage of existing primary documents (again, mostly vital data and the other types of sources listed above) from throughout the world. More than 2 million reels have been collected to date and over 600 million birth and marriage records have been extracted onto the International Genealogical Index (IGI). The IGI and other parts of the Mormon Family Search program, plus the NEHGS *Register* index (1847–1994, with 1.3 million entries) are available online. Genealogical society libraries often have websites, some with extensive databases.

The New England Historic Genealogical Society

In 1845, when the New England Historic Genealogical Society in Boston was founded by a handful of local antiquarians and book dealers, no institution devoted specifically to the study of genealogy existed anywhere in the Western world. The Society's founders were inspired in part by John Farmer's publication of the first New England genealogical dictionary in 1829. The Society's journal, long called the *Register,* began in 1847 and has been published every quarter for 155 years. One of its founders, Lemuel Shattuck, was a public health pioneer who designed the new forms used for post-1840 Massachusetts vital records and the 1850 federal census forms. The Society's library, which was started almost immediately after its founding, rented space in Boston until 1870, when it acquired the first of three buildings (on Somerset, Ashburton, and Newbury streets) that have housed it since. Monthly meetings, a Committee on Heraldry, register form (a standardized style for compiled genealogy), pioneer English origin studies by Henry F. Waters, and an index to the first 50 volumes of the *Register* were major 19th-century achievements. Women were admitted to the Society in 1898.

In the first decades of the 20th century, 75 volumes of alphabetized vital records of Massachusetts towns were published. Under Librarian William Prescott Greenlaw (assistant librarian, 1894–1902; librarian, 1902–29; assistant treasurer, 1929–45) and with many donations from leading genealogists of their day, the collections were expanded to cover the entire United States and much of Europe. Greatly expanded since the early 1980s, membership is now 19,000, and the collection of books and microforms exceeds 200,000. NEHGS holds manuscript collections that include the genealogical papers of many of the major scholars in this field, plus numerous unpublished genealogies and town genealogical registers (especially for New England), notes for various classic genealogies and town histories, and many account books, diaries, Bible records, cemetery inscriptions, and other items. Duplicates of 30,000 frequently used genealogies, local histories, and reference works form a circulating library.

NEHGS now publishes a magazine, at least one newsletter, and numerous books per year, including several volumes of the Great Migration Study Project (on New England immigrants to 1641), eight volumes of transcriptions of 19th-century Irish immigrant "missing friends" advertisements, a new series of vital records, various compiled genealogies, several guidebooks, and an index to the *Register*, volumes 51–148. Education programs include lectures, weekend seminars throughout the country, week-long seminars and courses in Boston, and research or heritage tours to Salt Lake City, Washington, D.C., Canada, England, and elsewhere. In the past two decades, the staff has expanded from 15 to 70 and includes both genealogical scholars and professionals in related areas. In the last decade the Newbury Street facility, including the research library, has been fully renovated and a second site established for the circulating library and sales department. Responding to the Internet revolution that makes genealogical data instantaneously accessible to thousands of researchers, NEHGS recently established its own website (www.newenglandancestors.org).

The New York Genealogical and Biographical Society

Through the U.S. Civil War, the existence of NEHGS was precarious. Following the tentative first quarter-century of NEHGS, postwar Gilded Age prosperity, the growth of urbanization, and a concurrent nostalgia for seemingly lost village life led to the flowering of antiquarianism, and historical and genealogical societies were founded throughout the country. NYGBS began in 1869; its scholarly journal, *The New York Genealogical and Biographical Record*, began that same year and has now reached 130 volumes. Although the NYGBS library contains a significant amount of New England, mid-Atlantic, and other material, it specializes in material on the genealogical history of New York State, especially the early settlements by the Dutch in the Hudson Valley and the English on Long Island. Membership in NYGBS has reached 3,000. Its newsletter lists many "hidden" sources for New York families. The Society now owns a large building on 58th Street in mid-town Manhattan. The nearby New York Public Library owns copies of most genealogical books in print, but it does not sponsor genealogical research.

The National Genealogical Society

The National Genealogical Society was founded in 1903 in Washington, D.C. (but is currently in Arlington, Virginia), and its journal, *The National Genealogical Society Quarterly*, began soon after. Its library includes many books sent for review, much on surrounding mid-Atlantic and southern states, and sizable collections for other areas. Its near neighbor, the Library of Congress, owns all genealogical works copyrighted in the United States. Another neighbor, the DAR Library, holds all material generated by Daughters of the American Revolution members and owns many genealogies and town histories as well. NGS has chosen in recent years to focus its efforts on annual educational conferences. The library has received several large book donations, and an expansion of its facility is planned. Membership in NGS exceeds 17,000, and its journal is a major forum for advanced methodology. The annual national conference of NGS, held in conjunction with local genealogical societies throughout the country, is the major professional gathering in the field.

The Family History Library

The Family History Library of the Church of Jesus Christ of Latter-day Saints is discussed elsewhere in this volume. Begun in 1894, the great Mormon genealogical effort of the last century was geared around finding the single source that revealed the greatest number of names in any given culture and microfilming all such records for which permission could be obtained. Since for the modern British Isles and much of the European continent over the last several centuries that format was the parish register or an ecclesiastical substitute, a sizeable percentage of FHL microfilm is of such records. Complementing this parish material is a large quantity of censuses, wills, deeds, and other records of special importance to American genealogists. Since the church now undertakes more microfilming in Asia and Latin America, this emphasis on the parish register may well change.

Together, these genealogical society libraries, historical societies, and public libraries with genealogical collections considerably augment university or academic libraries by documenting the lives of millions of individuals of the modern era.

RALPH J. CRANDALL

See also Family History Library

Further Reading

Beard, Timothy Field, and Denise Demong, *How to Find Your Family Roots*, New York: McGraw-Hill, 1977

Filby, P. William, compiler, *Directory of American Libraries with Genealogy or Local History Collections,* Wilmington, Delaware: Scholarly Resources, 1988

Parker, J. Carlyle, *Going to Salt Lake City to Do Family History Research,* Turlock, California: Marietta, 1989; 3rd edition, revised and expanded, 1996

Schutz, John A., *A Noble Pursuit: The Sesquicentennial History of the New England Historic Genealogical Society, 1845–1995,* Boston: New England Historic Genealogical Society, 1995

Government Libraries

The state is not a natural unity in the sense that some people think, and that what has been alleged to be the greatest good in states does in fact make for their dissolution; whereas that which is the "good" of a thing makes for its preservation.
—Aristotle, *Politics, Book II* (c. 334–323 B.C.)

The only way to erect such a common power, as may be able to defend [men] from the invasion of foreigners, and the inquiries of one another . . . is to confer all their power and strength upon one man, or upon one assembly of men.
—Thomas Hobbes, *Leviathan* (1651)

Government is a contrivance of human wisdom to provide for human wants. Men have a right that these wants should be provided for by this wisdom.
—Edmund Burke, *Reflections on the Revolution in France* (1790)

Archival Origins

Governments and organized structures of knowledge have coexisted as long as humans have been able to communicate complex thoughts. In fact, the ability to communicate above an instinctual level assumes the capability of storing memories of previous understanding or knowledge for later use. Civilization also assumes the ability to use these stores of knowledge and to modify, add to, or delete from them according to current circumstances or demands. For many early human societies, the foundations for this complex organized transmission of communication remained primarily oral for millennia, as evidenced by the historic and sociological qualities of numerous creation myths that began as spoken traditions and were only written down many centuries later. As governments grew into complex social organizations dependent on technology as well as tradition, it became possible to manage these structures of knowledge and shared memories over increasingly longer spans of time and place. From this perspective, the more a government knew about what might motivate a burgeoning population of unrelated people, the more effective it might be in achieving the necessary support from (if not the complete obedience of) the masses.

Six thousand years ago this internal governing motivation could be found throughout the expanding cultures of the Americas, Asia, the Indian subcontinent, and the Middle East. It drew upon the accumulated store of a society's collective customs, rules, regulations, religious beliefs, and sanctions, tying this vital social knowledge to more immediate information and understanding of other cultures and local phenomena such as tides, floods, and astronomy (for the measurement of time). Libraries in these early city-state civilizations were often little more than oral traditions and customs written down through evolving systems of writing. Written records were kept close to the seat of government and religious activity. For example, Sumerian libraries (around 3,000 B.C.) have been described as organized collections of laws, bylaws, and important events, recorded on clay tablets and stored in rooms that were part of carefully designed and centralized government/temple complexes. As these physical spaces became increasingly regulated by successive generations of ruling authorities, certain individuals skilled in the arts and crafts of record keeping (scribes, archive keepers, and the technicians who prepared the clay tablets) were trained by the rulers to care for the collections. Early classification systems, judging from archaeological records, were lists of tablets organized not by title, but by the first lines of each record.

A good deal of this early organized knowledge remained intimately linked to three other social motivations. The first was the need to serve predominant religious beliefs by spreading the faith and training new leaders in the religious hierarchy. Second was the necessity of assuring success in military campaigns and conquests via training and provisions for large standing armed forces, accompanied by essential intelligence and strategic knowledge of an enemy's capability and terrain. The third social motivation was the need to support an evolving network of regional and continental economies that replaced the earlier informal exchange of goods (barter) with the systematic and regulated use of coin and symbolic currency (gold, silver, amber, gems).

This intricate weaving of civic, military, economic, and religious missions is clearly evident throughout the centuries of

Egyptian civilization. Egyptian libraries, often associated with temples and ruling elites, were among the first to exploit the possibilities of a new medium: papyrus. As the civilization spread its influence beyond the Nile River valley, the portability of paper and the expressiveness of Egyptian hieroglyphics divided writing into three categories: religious (hieroglyphic); hieratic (read by the priests); and epistolographic or demotic (for everyday uses). Obviously this expanded the demands of classification and storage, and the complexity of the libraries' physical structure reflected these changing needs. Egyptian civilization, from the evidence of archaeological findings, also appears to be one of the first to foster a true mass reading culture.

As early civilizations and their cities grew in size, complexity, and geographic influence, the government library concept shifted, with an evolution in writing, record keeping, and methods of communication over space and time. As experiments with different recording mediums (plants, clay, animal tissue, wood, stone) continued, the scope and depth of a library grew to depend on the medium's durability, ease of storage, and transportability. Through the centuries, these preclassical civilizations developed more complex writing systems. Scribes and governors began to use certain types of material for permanent records and other types for more immediate commercial or military needs. The final element in these early libraries depended on the ability to copy. Obviously, the mechanical arts of early civilizations, though marvelous in many ways in advancing the understanding and spread of the written record, largely depended on scarce resources and the ability of individuals who were trained to copy records by hand. This inability to reproduce copies easily severely limited a ruling government's ability to expand a system of libraries beyond a central location and a few regional centers.

As the concept of government evolved from the roughly hierarchical command and control structures of agrarian civilizations, the relationship between writing, reading, and cultural knowledge began to change as well. A few centuries before the Western world's Christian era began (many ancient civilizations on the Asian and Indian subcontinents had been keeping organized written records for far longer periods of time), the spread of writing evolved from simple record keeping for commercial, military, or religious purposes to more general artistic and economic uses that appealed to other elements of a culture's population. As generations of scribes trained in the centralized institutions of the Middle East traveled and established commercial operations in regions of various empires, the knowledge of writing and organization of collections of written material also spread.

As the variety of written products expanded to include more stable writing media and many languages, the challenge of early library collections was to keep everything in order. Expansion of trade among these empires meant the greater possibility of migration among the people, and when people traveled they would often take with them written texts and records, along with their own languages and oral traditions. Surviving records, along with archaeological evidence, from the classical periods of Greece and Rome clearly indicate specific architectual changes in library areas. Government record centers were transformed from simple storage rooms to areas with elaborate alterations to reflect an expanding list of "subjects," as well as more efficient use of physical space to store different "mediums" (among them maps, scrolls, early papyrus "books," and tablets).

Written material, books, scrolls, maps, and astronomical charts were no longer the sole province of the ruling class and its bureaucracy. A healthy commercial trade in books thrived throughout the civilized ports of Europe, the Middle East, Africa, and Asia, as improvements in transportation expanded the ancient trade routes further east, west, north, and south. For the first time, libraries and publishing were established by private individuals or new organizations not directly associated with the ruling classes. Government libraries began to collect material produced through private centers of knowledge and research. Philosophers and scientists came to shape knowledge structures and ways of organizing schools of thought based on the exchange of written records that challenged and complemented the traditional structures fostered by the ruling and religious classes.

The Alexandrian Model

The Alexandrian Library, along with other ancient Greek and Roman institutions, is a prime example of how the concepts of a popular and government library began to emerge, separate, and influence one another in their mutual development. The library and museum complex at Alexandria (extant from approximately 320 B.C. through A.D. 646) remains the most potent metaphor for this framework of global cultural literacy. Linked forever with Alexander the Great's dreams of uniting the known world under a common culture (i.e., government), this Hellenic academic complex, built by Alexander's successors, is the first powerful model that binds a government's public information obligations to the cultural sense to preserve and distribute knowledge beyond the immediate needs of a state's day-to-day survival. It was also one of the first instances in which the reputation and name of a benevolent ruler depended on the ability to preserve and promote information among and between different cultures. Surviving descriptions of the library include many elements now associated with national libraries and other government-supported cultural institutions. It was a vast eclectic collection, gathered through a combination of compulsion (ships sheltered in Alexandria's harbor were often boarded by library workers who confiscated all manuscripts and other written material) and assimilation (many of its holdings originated in other cultures—and languages—conquered by the Hellenic empire). The academics associated with the library before its destruction clearly felt that the institution was a gift to the world, one with which a growing class of writers and scholars wished to be associated.

Even after its slow destruction during the last centuries of the Roman Empire, Alexandria's cultural icon, as a model of civil authority actively supporting the collection and diffusion of public knowledge, continued to evolve. The various governors of Rome and its provinces directly supported the creation of libraries and even encouraged the location of popular libraries in the major public baths of Rome. This exchange of written material, in turn, supported an active private book trade, along with technological innovations in the types and qualities of material used for written records. The practice of organizing categories of knowledge with specific canons and subject areas developed from the elements established by Greek culture. Although private libraries were evident, the concept of a government library was still largely bound to the ruling class (sometimes hereditary, sometimes religious, sometimes both). The spread of popular literacy through a robust private market in books and reading was further reinforced by the notion of public education for children of the ruling classes. Certainly the expansion of trade and the conquest of northern Europe encouraged the spread of geographic and astronomical knowledge in the Hellenic period, as the indigenous cultural and technical knowledge of conquered civilizations were absorbed and recorded by Roman scholars. The expansion in knowledge worked in tandem with the evolution of a common form in writing and language and copying technology, along with innovations in transportation and communications, to span the vast geographical distances of the Roman Empire.

Medieval Development

From around A.D. 500 to A.D. 1300, the dominant influences over the Western civilizations (and to a lesser degree those of Asia and the Pacific) revolved around two critical developments: the global expansion of organized religion and the concurrent development of global trade routes and commercialization. The ebb and flow of public authority from secular to spiritual purposes, as an increasingly centralized Christian church assumed the reigns of international government from the Roman empire; the rise of Islam as a counterfaith throughout the Middle East and Asia; and eventually the internal reformations of Protestant beliefs channeled and changed the definition of a government library. The written text became focused on the needs of spirit and church first, and the problems and opportunities of the world second. Ancient texts of science and art were often discarded or forgotten because they did not resolve the immediate problem of personal salvation introduced by Martin Luther's revolutionary faith. The new religious authorities encouraged libraries, but they were much more limited in their purpose and scope than previously.

For the organized church (whether Christian or Islamic), the struggle to sustain a sanctioned set of rituals and holy texts, interpreted by an official bureaucracy of priests and religious officials, became paramount. Libraries and collections of books, as keepers of the true faith, developed into essential battlegrounds. Unsanctioned texts were kept as a matter of course within these official libraries, but the distribution to the masses of this profane knowledge was greatly limited. Islam, in its own state of passionate conversion and advocacy, accepted many ancient texts rejected by the Christian church, thus preserving and transmitting much of Hellenic and Roman science. For the new faith championed by Luther and the other reformers, the concept of personal salvation supported the idea that if people were able to read holy texts for themselves their relationship to God would be more effective and immediate. So the proliferation of information and the expansion of the book trade to spread Bible translations into other cultures was one of the principal influences in recreating libraries as open institutions of learning.

Each of these events pushed the ability to speak and write into a new realm of importance. It was no longer enough for rulers to demonstrate that only a chosen few could understand the sacred texts. The economic transformation of the traditional religious hereditary ruling classes into early nation-states was based less on the immediate bonds of blood and ancient tribal relations and more on a symbolic political, economic, and military hegemony. With this devolution and evolution of public authority, the combination of religious and secular power that supported the creation of libraries as representations of a society's ruling class fell apart and came together in surprising new ways. The expansion of trading markets, the compulsion for organized personal salvation, and the ability to control diverse cultures within the vast new geography of a nation-state demanded that nonreligious authorities encourage and promote literacy in other elements of society. The Islamic and Christian churches accomplished this task through surprisingly similar approaches (if, indeed, creating entirely different results). Through a succession of military and cultural conversions, each faith established churches and trained generations of religious leaders who would guide the spiritual well-being of the populace through local churches. Governors and merchant classes trained whole segments of the population to understand and grasp the symbols of commerce and trade. As a result of this secular training, institutions of learning and technological knowledge were established outside the reformation turmoil of Christian and Islamic churches. For the first time in eight centuries, Western civilization rediscovered the independent worldviews and theoretical thinking of the ancient world, and the initial tenets of the scientific method were outlined. Along with the new way of thinking, which sought replication and sharing of information, the growing nation-states became natural depositories for this secular information. This led, over the next 700 years, to a succession of scientific and technical revolutions. As the written record of the ancients and the accumulating knowledge of the expanding European region met other cultures around the world in the Americas, Asia, and Africa, so too came the demand for a written record of the physical world (i.e., science.)

Nation-States and Libraries

From 1300 to 1800, the new global culture developed from several improvements in technology, primarily the printing press and improvements in transportation. As a result, the ideas and foundations of the modern nation-state were formed during this period, the last 25 years of which culminated in democratic revolutions in both Europe and the Americas. The idea of government became defined less by tradition, local custom, or practice, and more by abstract theories and principles. The rise of nation-states around the world during this period refashioned the relationship between government and the individual. New foundations in economic and social relationships among people were further shaped with the spread of literacy and commercial opportunity that led to new demands from citizens of nation-states to insist that government become less a dictator of individual fate and more a collective caretaker that fosters the fortunes of its citizens. The printing press and expanding global book cultures contributed to this diffusion. Many modern-day national government libraries began during this period, building on libraries founded by royal families. In addition, many associations and societies (mutually supported by the ruling classes) began to gather books and materials to support specific commercial or scientific projects.

It could be argued that there were two great influences on the creation of government libraries within early modern nation-states: global economic competition and armed conflict. The democratic revolutions of the late 1700s transformed the image of government libraries from bastions of national pride and culture to institutions for the service of citizens bound together by economic and political ties. Here again, the complex interplay among the revolutionary developments in scientific knowledge, transportation, and communication contributed to the creation of many government collections. Often these collections were much more specialized than those found just 100 years earlier.

For instance, military authorities focused on acquiring the latest weather and geographic information and built specialized collections of scientific and cartographic information about other parts of the world where the national interest might need defense or expansion. National and local governments made successive improvements in public works, roads, rivers (to control seasonal flooding), sanitation, and public communication (postal networks), as citizens migrated from farms to cities to work in the factories opened during the Industrial Revolution. Much of this civic improvement developed out of better statistics gathering, record keeping, and standardization, as public authorities worked to assure that they knew where and how the people were living, as well as ensuring that the economic system functioned in an effective fashion. Government divisions primarily involved in commercial or economic matters built libraries of statistics and financial information. Increased specialization moved government libraries from their ancient function as large general collections (usually the most complete in a society) to a new status as related, but independent, institutions that concentrated their collections on selected topics or special purposes.

The U.S. Example

The development of civil institutions in the United States is fairly typical of this type of modern government library. From the foundation of the Library of Congress in the early 1800s, through the growth of national libraries associated with different cabinet-level departments (e.g., agriculture and medicine), to the National Archives in the last half of the 20th century, a definitive link has existed between U.S. scientific and cultural progress and the development of government collections of information. Much of the framework for national information organization and collection (from records of congressional proceedings, to patents and trademarks, to freedom of the press) is embedded within the Constitution. Although the early congressional library was huge by most library standards of the time, there were many pre-1800 libraries in the United States larger than any U.S. government collection. However, even this early in its bureaucratic development there were already specialized collections found in several military offices, the Patent Office, and judicial offices.

This ratio of size between government and public collections remained relatively stable through the Civil War. However, by the last quarter of the 19th century, an explosion of technological, scientific, and commercial activity had swelled the size and number of government collections. Dramatic improvements in printing and paper technologies facilitated this increase in available material. Between 1850 and 1920, the federal government created major collections through the work of the Smithsonian Institution, the Patent Office, the Coast and Geodetic Survey, the Army Corps of Engineers, the Army Medical Office, and the United States Geological Survey. In addition, the function of the Library of Congress was enhanced as a national bibliographic center and recipient of copyrighted material.

As the flow of material into collections increased, the techniques and procedures fashioned to organize and describe the material were improved. By the early 20th century, government libraries were setting the standards for other libraries throughout the country. The concepts of public library and government library began to merge, both in reality and through bibliographic practice. Much of this standardization was fostered through the growth of regional and national library associations. When such professional influence was matched with the financial patronage and influence of the first generation of industrial and commercial leaders, the library concept and its profound influence on society achieved its first stage of universal acceptance. For the first time a government and the well-being of a discrete, visible library collection became important, not so much through physical custodial responsibility but through the encouragement and creation of standards and protocols and rational enforcement of citizens' access to broadly available library services.

International Development

Comparable developments of national bibliography building and enforcement of standards can be found in many other governments and their libraries around the globe. Much of the political and social upheaval of the last 100 years pushed the idea (and limits) of a nation-state, transformed through a renewed sense of global culture and governance. Much of this internationalism has become embodied in institutions fashioned in the wake of World War II (such as the United Nations, the International Court of Justice, and the International Monetary Fund) as well as in the integration of global markets forged through improvements in communication and transportation. At the same time, the idea of a nation-state, with its comparable belief in the national state of information, is developing into a sense of public information that is not strictly linked to a national purpose but framed through the exchange of commercial and intellectual property rights. The institutions created during the Middle Ages and Renaissance—universities, labor guilds, commercial organizations, and national governments—no longer hold the same geographic and administrative influence on the production and distribution of public information. As the third millennium begins, governments and their libraries are no longer the sole keepers of either the technology or the bureaucracy that govern the public diffusion of knowledge. The rapid rise of the global information infrastructure through telecommunications and computers enables individuals and non-traditional cultural institutions to share information and knowledge more rapidly without the traditional permission or mediation of public authorities.

Governments of all types face a host of issues that focus on service and response to specific citizen needs. Information and libraries have become, in some ways, byproducts of this process. Exceptions are instances where a government still serves as the primary mediating force between users and information (such as national institutes of medicine) or a major regulatory agency governs processes or events that transcend purely commercial or individual economic interests. Indeed, the regulations that govern the electronic exchange of knowledge over the next century shift the traditional roles of governments and their libraries from those of collectors to those of standard bearers. They assure that the public information transmitted through global networks will enjoy some degree of authenticity, if not accuracy. The mutual purposes of global market commercial mechanisms, married to government protection of the public sphere, will build the next iteration of the original "government" libraries of Sumeria and Alexandria.

JOHN A. SHULER

Further Reading

Adkinson, Burton W., *Two Centuries of Federal Information*, Stroudsburg, Pennsylvania: Dowden Hutchinson and Ross, 1978

Conway, James, *America's Library: The Story of the Library of Congress, 1800–2000*, New Haven, Connecticut: Yale University Press, 2000

Eisenstein, Elizabeth L., *The Printing Press As an Agent of Change: Communications and Cultural Transformations in Early-Modern Europe*, 2 vols., Cambridge and New York: Cambridge University Press, 1979

Johnson, Elmer D., *History of Libraries in the Western World*, New York: Scarecrow Press, 1965

Parsons, Edward Alexander, *The Alexandrian Library, Glory of the Hellenic World: Its Rise, Antiquities, and Destructions*, New York: American Elsevier Press, and London: Cleaver-Hume Press, 1952

Rosenberg, Jane Aikin, *The Nation's Great Library: Herbert Putnam and the Library of Congress, 1899–1939*, Urbana: University of Illinois Press, 1993

Williams, Patrick, *The American Public Library and the Problem of Purpose*, New York: Greenwood Press, 1988

Historical Society Libraries in the United States

The term *historical society* commonly refers to an organization devoted to the history of a particular geographical area (be that a nation, state, county, or municipality), but there are many groups focused on specific interests or identities as well. Some religious denominations have historical societies, such as the Congregational Historical Society. Numerous railroads and other forms of transportation are the subject of interest and are represented by groups such as the Western Pacific Historical Society and the American Truck Historical Society. There are ethnic historical societies such as the Chinese Historical Society of America, the National Japanese American Historical Society, the American Historical Society of Germans from Russia, the American Irish Historical Society, and the American Jewish Historical Society. There is the Gay and Lesbian Historical Society, the Historical Harp Society, the *Titanic* Historical Society, and the Great Lakes Shipwreck Historical Society. In short, there exist historical societies devoted to an exceedingly diverse range of subjects.

Some of these societies maintain museums as their primary function; others exist primarily to bring together like-minded individuals in meetings where they present, hear, and discuss papers. Many, even those without libraries, hold relevant manuscripts or printed materials. Others collect historical materials and make them accessible, in part through publication, as did the very first historical society in the United States, the Massachusetts Historical Society. Until after World War II, few U.S.

university libraries were collecting for research as opposed to instructional needs. Thus the collection and preservation of the source material for U.S. history has been primarily the work of other types of libraries, especially historical society libraries.

The Massachusetts Historical Society, established in 1791 immediately following the formation of the new republic, was founded in Boston by Jeremy Belknap, whose work during the 1770s and 1780s on a history of New Hampshire had made clear to him that there was no repository for historical materials and that much information was being lost. Belknap's advocacy of the collecting of historical materials in the colonies went back to at least 1774, but he initially hoped that Harvard College in Cambridge would do the collecting. Despite favorable votes on different occasions by the Harvard board of overseers, nothing developed. Even in 1787, when Belknap, himself an overseer, was asked to head a project to collect historical materials, the college did not follow through, failing to appropriate funds for the purchase of an extensive collection of U.S. newspapers formed by Ebenezer Hazard. It is not surprising that Harvard failed to act. Its resources were small, and educational institutions were not then the locus of learned culture. Learned culture was civic culture, and it was to the community that Belknap turned, to gentlemen of like interests.

In establishing the Massachusetts Historical Society, Belknap and his associates could have formed a society of broader range, but they realized that the chances of success would be increased by limiting their purposes. Rather than forming a learned society of scientific and literary scope, they explicitly concentrated on the historical. Although natural history was included, the emphasis was on human history, particularly on sources that might convey the spirit of the age. Belknap and his successors in other institutions emphasized the need to collect what seemed to be only of passing interest: "Political pamphlets, Newspapers, Letters, funeral and Election Sermons and many other papers which are now regarded only as beings of a day may if preserved give posterity a better idea of the Genius and Temper of the present age (and of our most material Transactions) than can be derived from any other source," as Belknap put it in a draft letter of 1774. Subsequently, Christopher Columbus Baldwin of the American Antiquarian Society (1835), Edward De Peyster of the New-York Historical Society (1866), and Charles H. Bell of the New Hampshire Historical Society (1873) all argued for collecting the least product of the press or pen, as did John Langdon Sibley of the Harvard College Library in 1856. At times statements of this comprehensive view of history are coupled with a clear emphasis on a democratic history that would encompass the ordinary people on whom democracy rested.

This desire for universal representation was not always manifested in practice, but societies did collect printed and manuscript materials from all segments of the population. To be sure, Belknap and others felt that historical societies should search for and solicit materials rather than merely wait for donations, but everyone lives in a certain milieu, and it was to people of their own typically upper-class circles that early historical societies turned. Since to a very large extent early historical societies collected by distributing circular letters soliciting material, these seldom reached those who occupied marginal positions in society.

One can see the soliciting of gifts for a society as a way of extending the influence of individuals. In state after state, it was an individual collector or a small number of collectors of autographs and manuscripts who sought to extend their reach and to provide for the preservation of their own collections through the founding of historical societies.

These efforts led to the formation of historical societies in all of the eastern states except Delaware before the U.S. Civil War, particularly in the last two decades before the war. Figures on the formation of historical societies (broadly defined so as to include, for example, the American Statistical Association) show that between 1790 and 1819, nine societies were formed. The number jumped between 1820 and 1829 to 15 new societies for the decade, staying at roughly the same level in the 1830s, with 17 new societies. Another jump during the 1840s brought the total to an additional 27 new societies, with continued growth between 1850 and 1859, during which time 35 more were formed.

Urbanization and the concentration of wealth it entailed were clearly crucial, for the societies were overwhelmingly in urban areas. A large number were, however, short-lived, as in the South and West, where they failed to obtain the endowments that would make continuation possible. An element behind the failure of societies in the West was also the transience of the population.

Although these societies were basically independently financed, some had support from local governments in the form of subsidies for publication or the provision of space in public buildings. In the Midwest, however, starting in the 1850s with the Wisconsin Historical Society, a new pattern of support developed: ongoing annual subsidies from state governments. Minnesota, Iowa, Kansas, and Ohio all chartered societies in the 1850s, and the publicly supported historical society became the standard throughout the country, except along the Atlantic seaboard.

Historical societies have served differing purposes throughout their existence. To Lyman Draper, the builder of the Wisconsin Historical Society in Madison from 1854 to 1886, the society was a means of making the state and its potentialities known. The existence of a society was generally seen to confer prestige, to promote a state as a place for settlement. Societies also served more direct governmental functions. The functions of the state library and the historical society overlapped, and some societies assumed care for the state archives. In 1957 the responsibility for state archives lay with state historical societies in ten states. Although boosterism is not currently as overt a motive as earlier, cultural institutions do affect the perception of a locality, and awareness of this is no doubt behind the ongoing formation of local historical societies (and often the impetus for municipal support as well).

In the 19th century publishing collections of documents was, next to collecting material and housing it, the primary function of historical societies. Editing and publication of manuscripts has continued to be a crucial purpose of some historical societies, and although print publication still plays a role, historical societies have also used modern media to disseminate their holdings. The Massachusetts Historical Society, notable for its print publications, has also published large quantities of material on microfilm; the American Antiquarian Society played a crucial role in publishing early American imprints in microform, and its rich cataloging records, available electronically, can be considered another means of publication. For some historical societies, publishing was once an area in which they competed. At the present time the competition is much more focused on exhibitions: the American Association for State and Local History, headquarterd in Nashville, Tennessee (an outgrowth of the Conference of State and Local Historical Societies that first met in Chicago in 1904), gives awards for exhibitions that are announced in its quarterly *History News*.

Today's historical societies generally seek to create public programming, to educate the community, and some, such as the American Antiquarian Society, try to multiply their usefulness through programs for those who will teach elsewhere or make use of their historical resources. Historical societies especially emphasize the education of children, with exhibitions that appeal to a wide audience, particularly young people, often with objects other than books and manuscripts.

Whereas the three earliest historical societies—the Massachusetts Historical Society, the New-York Historical Society, and the American Antiquarian Society—had initially all collected objects of various sorts, two of them ceased to do so early on, putting all of their resources into the library. Only the New-York Historical Society continued broader collecting, and it is using those materials in a new exhibition area intended to attract the general public. The Wisconsin Historical Society pioneered public outreach at the end of the 19th and the start of the 20th century; it even appointed a museum chief in 1908. What Wisconsin had done earlier and what the New-York Historical Society is doing now are typical of the activities of smaller local societies around the country that emphasize collections other than paper. Moreover, those institutions that were basically only libraries are joining with local museums, thereby enabling both to carry out their role in community education more effectively. An example is the Center for Maine History in Portland, a merging of the Maine Historical Society and the Longfellow House.

In the meantime, the collections of printed and manuscript materials have become ever more valuable to historians. No one today sees national history as resulting from the history of localities as was once the case, but the holdings of historical societies have new importance. Those materials gathered with a comprehensive view of history and an awareness of the need for documenting the lives of people earlier overlooked do make it possible to study previously marginalized segments of the population, which is precisely what so many historians are now seeking to do. Old publications as well as unpublished resources have new life, and it is likely that their utility will be enhanced by the computer and by new approaches of historians.

KENNETH E. CARPENTER

See also Genealogical Society Libraries; Historical Society of Pennsylvania; New-York Historical Society Library

Further Reading

Dunlap, Leslie W., *American Historical Societies, 1790–1860*, Madison, Wisconsin: s.n., 1944

Jones, H.G., editor, *Historical Consciousness in the Early Republic*, Chapel Hill: North Carolinian Society and North Carolina Collection, 1995

Tucker, Louis Leonard, *Clio's Consort: Jeremy Belknap and the Founding of the Massachusetts Historical Society*, Boston: Massachusetts Historical Society, 1990

Tucker, Louis Leonard, *The Massachusetts Historical Society: A Bicentennial History, 1791–1991*, Boston: Massachusetts Historical Society, 1995

Van Tassel, David D., *Recording America's Past: An Interpretation of the Development of Historical Societies in America, 1607–1884*, Chicago: University of Chicago Press, 1960

Whitehill, Walter Muir, *Independent Historical Societies: An Enquiry into Their Research and Publication Functions and Their Financial Future*, Boston: Boston Athenaeum, 1962

Iberian Libraries

Spain's Libraries

The library system in Spain consists of the national library, archives, archeological museum, and art gallery in Madrid, and seven regional libraries in provincial capital cities such as Barcelona, Zaragoza, Valencia, and Seville. These libraries contain more than 8 million volumes and 7 million manuscripts, with major archives for Castile-Leon in Simancas, the Crown of Aragon in Barcelona, and the Indies in Seville. There are also 67 university library systems with more than 200 academic, discipline-based libraries holding more than 28 million volumes, 115 academy and special libraries with more than 2 million volumes, 95 institutes in the national research council, 24 major museum libraries, and 71 public library systems.

Holdings

Libraries in Spain hold more than 40 million volumes, in excess of 30 major manuscript and incunabula collections, and special collections dating to late antiquity. Collection strengths are in local, regional, and national history; Hispano-Arabic culture; classics; the Mediterranean area; Spanish culture, language, and literature; theology and church history; the history of science and medicine; and overseas exploration and empire, especially in Latin America. There are large regional collections from Basque, Catalan, Gallego, Valencian, and Andalusian publishers.

Portugal's Libraries

The library system in Portugal is composed of the national library, archives (Torre do Tumbo), and museum in Lisbon; 13 university, 20 college, 43 academic, and 30 institute and special research libraries; and 350 public libraries.

Holdings

Portugal's libraries hold more than 6 million volumes and 5 million manuscripts, with special collections dating to late antiquity. Collection strengths are in local and regional history; cartography; age of discovery and economic history; overseas exploration and colonialism in Africa; and Portuguese culture, language, and literature, including that of Brazil.

Classical Heritage

The Luso-Hispanic historiographic tradition of libraries is thoroughly classicist. It implicitly assumes continuity in library development from the ancient to the modern world, but the thread of continuity between the Middle Ages and classical antiquity is often stretched thin. Nevertheless, Iberian library historiography appears to have begun with the Palatine Library in Rome, when Augustus Caesar placed a Hispano-Roman from Valencia, Caius Julius Higinius, in charge of this venerable institution. This historiographic tradition forms a *mentalité* linking classical culture and formal education with literacy and libraries, but hard evidence of government-sponsored libraries reliant on texts and widespread literacy is lacking in the Hispanic provinces until the late empire. Such centers as Tarraco (Tarragona), capital of the Tarraconensis, or Hispalis (Seville), two of the largest Roman cities in the western Mediterranean, were thought to have had temple libraries on the acropolis and in the forum, but their government character may be considered closer to archives than Roman public libraries. The isolated and fragmentary survival of papyri and parchments attests to centers of literacy and documentation practices, but not necessarily anything more than household libraries. Christianity changed that, however, with whole working collections in major episcopal sees, as evidenced by the earliest conciliar *acta* and more consistent references to a literary core, and, by the sixth century, extant codices and increased documentary remains. However critical, these are not plentiful.

Despite assumptions about the durability of libraries, library history in Spain, as elsewhere, is more a story of paucity than plenty, alternating destruction and revival, and insecure continuity at best, but certainly not a record of continual progress. The Pirenne thesis seems more applicable to Iberian library history than the Gibbonesque interpretation based on what happened in Italy with the barbarian invasions. The Visigothic overlay in Hispania, mainly on the central highland, allowed Romano-Christian culture to continue. The Vandal scourge was destructive, but short-lived, along a narrow path, and with no major permanent immigration. The Suevi intrusion into Lusitania also left many Christian monastic centers and episcopal sees intact. Thus Iberian local and regional government and culture continued in Christian form, but decreased population, fewer and smaller urban centers, and a decline in cross-country and overseas commerce resulted in localization and parochialism, and thereby an isolation of learning in select centers, with sporadic library development. Christian alternation between benign neglect and purges of the ancient inheritance to selective preservation and expansion upon classic foundations meant chance survivals and spotty continuity at best.

Church-related libraries can be identified at major metropolitan sites throughout the peninsula as small-scale affairs in the Middle Ages. Manuscripts illustrate monastic libraries as fitting into a single *armarius*, or book closet, that held perhaps 30 codices at most. Codices traveled across the Mediterranean, as in the case of the illustrated Byzantine Codex of Skylitz (sixth century), which came to Spain via Sicily, but these are isolated exemplars that hardly point to a flourishing East-West book trade. Cultural life was largely oral, aural, and visual (dramatic and liturgical arts). Ecclesiastical *acta* of the Visigothic Hispanic Church suggest that emissaries carried letters between sees, and packets of excerpts and treatises, such as encyclicals, made the rounds so that letter and charter books and codices of compiled excerpts, abstracts, and records were more plentiful than full classical texts copied completely in scriptoria. Scribal production served both archives and libraries, and apart from the latter were separate collections in treasuries and official church books (bibles, gospels, missals, lectionaries, etc.) and were often kept adjacent to sanctuaries just as hymnals were kept in choirs. The greatest scion of the Romano-Visigothic Church, St. Isidore of Seville, worked with a corpus of only 154 Latin titles, mostly Patristic and heavily theological, which has been considered a good sample of what survived. He did not use the encyclopedic work of Cassiodorus and never really accomplished command of Greek for the few original sources available to him. Judging from his writings, Archbishop Martin of Bracaria (Braga, Portugal) had access to a library that included Greek texts, probably at the monastery of Dumio.

Bishops Eugenius and Julian of Toledo obviously had a growing library at their see in the Visigothic capital, and some kinds of libraries were thought to have operated in the sees of Mérida, Barcelona, Zaragoza, Cartagena, Toledo, and Seville. The archbishop of Tarragona and two of his deacons, when fleeing their see for the Italian Ligurian coast as the city prepared for the Muslim onslaught, took what ceremonial books they could carry onto their boats. At the same time, Visigothic manuscripts traveled with exiles following Bishop Theodulf of Zaragoza to the Carolingian monastery of Ile d'Barbe near Lyon. These examples are slim traces to build a case for continuity with Roman imperial foundations or any of the great libraries of antiquity. Only 240 codices are extant from the Visigothic period, priceless survivals over the centuries, attesting to what must have been a rare, ghetto-like literate culture inside monastic enclosures and episcopal sees, but not a pervasive literate culture with a plentitude of libraries.

Medieval Libraries

The Muslim invasion of Romano-Visigothic Hispania and Lusitania (711–18) was different from the Germanic barbarian invasions because of the destruction of the Romano-Christian establishment. These conquerors were a sophisticated lot, and through successive waves of Arab and Berber immigration Muslims achieved a two-thirds majority in most of the peninsula (the whole population is estimated at only 5 million inhabitants at the time). Muslim religious, Arabic language, and North African cultural differences meant this was more than a military and political subordination, as in the case of the Visigoths, but an alien domination of indigenous culture. The Iberian peninsula entered into a prolonged period of almost constant warfare alternating between *jihad* and *reconquista*—more than seven centuries, and even longer considering post-medieval Luso-Hispanic expansion into Africa, across the Atlantic, overseas into Asia, and into northern Europe.

Muslim Libraries of al-Andalus

The historiography of Arabic-Muslim libraries is also wedded to classical continuity, since medieval Hispano-Muslim libraries are always linked from the old Persian Empire to predecessors in the old caliphate in Bagdad (where three dozen different libraries are known) and through al-Hakim's 12th-century "house of wisdom" in Cairo. Late medieval tales exaggerated the greatness and volume of these libraries—inaccurate quantitatively but correct metaphorically in contrasting these great Arab-Muslim foundations to the relatively modest ventures in the Christian West. Imitations were developed by the Umayyad western caliphate at Córdoba, without indebtedness to the Romano-Visigothic peoples they subdued or the Jewish and Mozarabic (minority Arabic-speaking Christian) communities in their midst. Muslim libraries were transported implants that brought both Qur'anic theological corpora and "New Learning"; this was unknown in the West, based on lost Greek works, including Aristotle, as well as new math (i.e., algebra), science, and applied engineering (such as sophisticated hydraulics), plus a refined cosmopolitan culture.

Córdoba grew to more than 200,000 households, making it the largest city in the West, a focal point for the revived Mediterranean book trade, and home to the largest of 70 known Hispano-Muslim libraries. Founded by 'Abd al-Raḥmān III's son, al-Ḥakam II, who worked in the Alcázar library and its large scriptorium, this complex expanded to an estimated 400,000-plus volumes. Its catalog took up 40 to 50 folio volumes. Other lesser libraries, but major by Christian standards, developed at Almeria, Granada, Seville, Toledo, and Valencia. School and religious libraries flourished in Córdoba with state-mosque patronage, and copyists, including an estimated 170 women Qur'anic scribes and artisans, produced an estimated 8,000 codices annually. Private libraries such as that of Ab al-Mūtrif, known because of its yearlong liquidation sale that brought in a fortune of 40,000 dinars, far exceeded anything in the Christian West. The philosopher Averroës tells of the rich bibliophile, Aixa, whose library was distributed as a gift to the inhabitants of the city. The library of Ibn Tufas is described as a high-walled enclosure adjacent to the house: Its stacks had decorated wood trim and armaria with lattice-work doors; reading areas were decorated with grillwork, green curtains, and painted walls; patio gardens with fountains cooled the interior; and it included a scriptorium, where six copyists labored. Under the direction of a *ṣāḥib*, the arrangement was by subject: religion and theology with subdivisions for the Qur'an, commentaries, law, and mysticism; letters on the seven liberal arts; and philosophy and science, including mathematics, medicine, physics, metaphysics, and music.

Luso-Hispanic Christian Libraries

Although Mozarabic communities may have maintained some remnant of Christian libraries in their churches, the transition to Arabic as the dominant spoken language so criticized by Abbot Esperaindeo in ninth-century Córdoba, perhaps more than pressure from above, militated against the survival of centers of Christian learning under Muslim occupation. Northern centers beyond Muslim reach in Pamplona, the capital of Navarre, Oviedo of Asturias, and León had early libraries where works not extant elsewhere miraculously survived, including some classics, such as Juvenal's satiric verses, Virgil's *Aeneid*, Porphory's treatises, fables, and Visigothic codices carried north from Seville and Toledo. Exiled Mozarabes founded the monastery of Samos in Lugo, St. Cosmos in León, Sahagún, San Cebrian de Mazote, San Miguel de Escalada, San Pedro de Eslonza, and others, which had small libraries that included remnants from the south and active scriptoria that revived old traditions of copying, compiling, and bookmaking. Catalan monasteries such as Ripoll, where the scholar Gerbert and future pope (Sylvester II) scavenged for manuscripts along the piedmont, and Canigo and Cuixa, high in the Pyrenees, kept rare treatises in math, science, and philosophy in addition to the

Christian classics and staples of monastic life. Ninth-century scribes at Urgel in the north country tried to memorialize some oral history in the most rudimentary of chronicles. In Vic, where churchmen kept some contact with Rome (as evidenced by its rare papal papyri), scribes began a formal documentation system of record keeping and archives. Sant Cugat above Barcelona was insulated enough to have a small library, but coastal towns were raided repeatedly, and the Mediterranean remained a Muslim sea until the late 12th century. Monasteries closer to the militarized zone or Hispanic March were not part of the Carolingian revival of letters with the clerical reforms of Alcuin and his school. Indeed, Catalonia's ecclesiastic and monastic medieval archives were developed far better than its libraries, even those attached to episcopal schools. Notable late medieval collections, such as those assembled with royal patronage at the Cistercian monasteries of Poblet and Santes Creus, have not survived, but the former's vaulted library is physically intact as a testament to medieval transitional (Romanesque to Gothic) library architecture. These establishments were huge in contrast to more common, smaller libraries. Northern Christian Spain was primarily rural; villages that expanded to 10,000 were considered cities, and Spain's largest towns, such as Barcelona, in their medieval heyday stood at 30,000, in stark contrast to metropolitan Córdoba. Libraries on frontiers, where mobility was necessary for survival, were and are still uncommon phenomena. Scale must be understood; only in myth did great libraries exist in small places.

What is surprising is not the relative absence of Christian libraries or their diminutive size, but that they existed at all and grew in number, accompanied by the stubborn persistence of the classical heritage in education in any form. Monastic foundations by the early dynasty of Castile-León such as San Pedro de Arlanza, Cardena, Valeranica, Silos, Ona, and in the Rioja region of San Millan de Cogolla and San Martin de Albelda were therefore important. The trans-Pyrenean Benedictine networks established first by Moissac Abbey and then, more far-flung, by the monastic family of Cluny from Burgundy, extended during the tenth century through Castile-León into Portugal. Finally, in the 12th century the Cistercians connected peninsular houses with those of ultra-Pyrenean Europe, just as the growing network of papal legates, couriers, and diplomats after the Gregorian Reform linked Iberian episcopal sees to all others and to the Holy See.

In Portugal the earliest medieval libraries are documented at Guimaräes, then Porto, and later at the Cistercian abbey of Alcobaça and in Lisbon. Manuscripts traveled with couriers along established routes between commercial centers, with layovers for copying at episcopal and monastic scriptoria, leading to scattered libraries and more secure survival of multiple copies than lone, chance survivors. Archives, libraries, and scriptoria blended organizationally, as when loose parchments were converted into charter books in 12th-century record keeping. Like liturgical works, law codification and territorial government increased the need for libraries that were pragmatic, working collections, more pervasive, active, and influential than the esoteric historic collections lauded by the classicists as the most important feature of medieval library development.

Although rural monastic libraries remained important, many were absorbed into episcopal libraries. Those libraries in urban centers of government, ecclesiastical and secular, became the dominant forces in cultural development during the high Middle Ages in Spain and Portugal as elsewhere. This was especially true as cathedral schools for the *studium generale* developed into universities in the late 12th and early 13th centuries. Cathedral libraries existed at Santiago de Compostela, Oviedo, León, Burgos, Pamplona, Urgel, Vich, Gerona, and Barcelona in the northern kingdoms, and others were developed soon after as the frontier moved southward at Tarragona, Lérida and Tortosa, Zaragoza, Segovia, Avila, and Lisbon. In Toledo, Archbishop Raimundo (1125–51) and his successors as the primates of Spain developed one of the principal libraries and translation centers of the peninsula. It was the destination for many scholars from the north eager to secure texts for their fledgling libraries in France, Germany, and England. Reconquered cities such as Valencia, Mérida, Córdoba, Seville, and Granada would also develop cathedral libraries. Santiago, Palencia, Zaragoza, Barcelona, and Valencia witnessed such developments, but in Castille-León, the most famous were at Valladolid and Salamanca (1215–60), the models for five royal foundations in the late medieval and early modern period. Alfonso X established the University of Seville in 1254; in Portugal the medieval University of Coimbra, founded in 1291 first in Lisbon, was the most important. Private scholars libraries, such as that of Juan de Segovia at Salamanca in 1457, fed into these corporate libraries, but they were in the 200-volume range, hardly comparable with the nearly 2,000 volumes already assembled at the Sorbonne. The growth of the major peninsular libraries was an early modern phenomenon, their rare content linking Christian Europe with Jewish and Muslim learning.

Alfonso X *el sabio* (the Wise) in the 13th century, known for his law compilations, chronicles, and scientific treatises, displayed a wide range of knowledge from sources thought to be very rare, such as Josephus, Ptolemy, surviving Latin classics, Arab chroniclers, and medieval encyclopedists such as Peter Lombard and Vincent of Beauvais. Acquisitions were not all historical; many were contemporary, including music, stories, and romance-language commentaries. Many sources were known through Arabic intermediary texts translated into Latin and old Castilian. The vernacular had become the language of scholarly discourse, with works in Catalan, Castilian, and Portuguese appearing regularly in texts and official documents.

Crusading mentalities were hardly conducive to preserving the culture of the enemy in languages no longer read. Rather than seize Muslim libraries as spoils of war to augment late medieval libraries of the new regime, numerous collections were destroyed in siege warfare, random pillage, and lamentable public book burnings demonstrating the arrival of a new cultural regime. When salvage efforts began in earnest, following the expulsion of the Jews and conquest of Granada, and when Christians were no longer threatened by minority status, the remnant of

Arabic libraries in Spain was minuscule. Even so, during their sack of Tunis in 1536, when many volumes from al-Andalus had been rescued, the armies of Charles V delivered a last crippling blow to Muslim culture by burning Arabic books *en masse*. Fez suffered the same fate. Imperial troops in 1527 treated Christian libraries little better during their sack of Rome. Felipe II tried to preserve Arabic works in the Escorial, some of which arrived there totally by chance, as in the case of the capture of a Moroccan galley full of books. But a tragic fire in 1671 destroyed 8,000 of them, leaving only 2,000 for posterity from the more than 500,000 believed to have existed on the peninsula at one time. Sadly, the holdings of all libraries in Spain and Portugal at the end of the Middle Ages were fewer than held there during the 1200s. Even printing could not immediately replace this loss of manuscript codices.

Early Modern Libraries

In the aftermath of the Reconquista and European internecine war between Hapsburg imperial interests and France, general instability meant the dispersal of many older libraries, and new ones were constantly being created by salvaging the old. This was especially true of manuscripts as commodities of trade and the spoils of war, while new books were being acquired mainly in print. In some cases, libraries such as those of the Catalan-Aragonese kings and nobles in the kingdom of Naples fell prey to the French; remnants ultimately worked their way to Fontainebleau and the Bibliothèque nacionale. Others simply disappeared piecemeal, as in the case of the 14th-century royal libraries of Pere IV, Martin "the Humane," and Alfonso V, from which remnants survived in monastic libraries until the mass upheavals of 1835. The Escorial epitomizes the Spanish Renaissance library built retrospectively by the amalgamation of other libraries and through print acquisitions for current coverage. It also signaled royal patronage in a way not previously characteristic before the peripatetic courts of Portugal, Castile-León, and the Crown of Aragon settled down in Lisbon, Madrid, and Barcelona, respectively. Some noble libraries, such as those of Enrique de Villena, the marquess de Santillana, or of the counts of Benavente by the mid-14th century, were better developed than any libraries of the Crown. The Count of Haro, in retirement, built a hospital library at Veracruz de Medina de Pomar, and the Mendoza family, with powerful connections throughout Spain, including the famous cardinal, acquired 632 volumes inventoried in 1523. Royal families had books more as exemplars and treasury pieces, sometimes keepsakes and diplomatic gifts, but not really useable libraries. Avid readers such as Juan II could, of course, avail themselves of any library at will. Isabela la Católica enjoyed a library scattered along her itinerary from Segovia to Toledo, Arevalo, and Granada and traveled with a book chest as part of her entourage. Likewise the Portuguese court carried libraries about, from João I onward until the 15th century, when these tended to stay in Lisbon, where Dom Afonso created a permanent royal library. Most of these noble and royal collections ranged from 150 to 250 volumes, and other private libraries were not very large. Their importance lies in how they fed into institutional libraries, making the rich historical research collections of modern Spain and Portugal.

One of the exceptional private libraries of the peninsula was the Biblioteca Fernandina or Colombina in Seville, the bibliographic legacy of Hernando Colón, son of Admiral Cristobal Colón (Christopher Columbus) and Beatriz Henriques de Arana. He consolidated the books of his father and uncle Bartolomeo for a core collection of more than 300 volumes, augmented during extensive diplomatic travels throughout Europe (1513–26). His collection, housed in a magnificent estate library along the Rio Guadalquivir in 1525, was subsidized by the emperor after 1536 with book buying trips to the capitals of Europe. The will of Hernando's son, Luís Colón, devoted 100,000 *maravedis* annually for a perpetual endowment of the library, but after his death the personal connection between the collection and the family waned. After a prolonged court battle, it passed in 1552 to the Cathedral of Seville, where it was installed in a side nave redecorated by Luís de Vargas. Juan de Loaisa's 1684 inventory describes more than 2,000 volumes and some of the finest bindings anywhere. It was an international collection that grew to exceed 20,000 volumes; partial inventories indicate that 4,160 were in Latin, 850 in Greek, 500 in French, but only 64 in Castilian. Neglected during the 18th century, it was salvaged by the Mercedarians for the Collegio de San Laurenceano, which was burned by the French in 1808. Little survives today except remnants scattered in Spain's main libraries.

Despite such tragedies, libraries developed throughout the peninsula and were increasingly public. Private libraries often fed into larger institutions. Among the most distinguished of private libraries was that of Diego Sarmiento de Acuña, count of Gondomar. At its home in Valladolid with deposits in Madrid, according to inventories in 1623, this library grew to 15,000 volumes largely by collecting during diplomatic missions, for example, to the court of James I in England. Some books were later removed because English was not a common foreign language among educated Spaniards. After 1785, under pressure from Carlos III, most of this library passed to royal libraries, mainly the Biblioteca del Palacio Real, while portions went to the Academia de la Historia and the nascent Biblioteca Nacional. Also exceptional was the library of the count-duke de Olivares, don Gaspar de Guzmán, strongman for Felipe IV, who likewise began collecting in 1621 when in royal service. Among others, he acquired the library of the noted Aragonese historian Jerónimo de Zurita, which grew so large it was deposited in several places. It ultimately went in bulk to the Escorial. Likewise the library of don Juan Francisco Pacheco Téllez de Girón, count of Uceda, also built in government service, ended up mostly in Madrid. It is from inventories of such libraries that the bibliographer Nicolas Antonio was able to compile his famous *Biblioteca Hispana Nova* in two volumes, documenting Spanish authors who lived before 1500.

Perhaps the most famous university library in Spain was at Salamanca, which by 1504 bulged beyond its original quarters and one expansion. A new Gothic library was built in 1509 and enhanced throughout the 16th century by several scholars' libraries of Greek and Latin classics. This century of growth was followed by one of stagnation, however, and the University of Salamanca library did not really achieve a renaissance until the mid-18th century, as attested to by the three-volume catalog of José Ortiz de la Pena (1777). In Portugal, notable collections were assembled by the Jesuits in the Colegio de Santo Antão after 1553.

Modern Libraries

After a dismal hiatus in library development following the War of the Spanish Succession and political fiascoes of the 18th century, Iberian libraries took on a more public character, first by opening to the public for four hours daily. Then, as exemplified by the transition of the Biblioteca Real into the Biblioteca Nacional, support was transferred from sporadic royal largess and noble patronage to more constant, if frugal, city and state financing. The Cortes, regional councils of representative government, became primary movers in local library development, as in the case of Bartolomé José Gallardo in Cádiz, where a library, initially of 2,000 volumes, grew into 10,000 volumes in just a few years. The reforms of Carlos III had far-reaching effects on libraries and education, including the formation of the Biblioteca de la Universidad Complutense de Madrid. In addition to the idealism of private, royal, and ecclesiastic research libraries becoming public, academic libraries also expanded use by memberships and guest scholars. All of Spain's libraries benefited from the massive destruction of libraries in France during the Revolution of 1789 and its aftermath but were subjected to problems of their own during the Joseph Bonaparte regime in Spain and later during the turmoil of intermittent civil war and experimental, unstable republics. Indigenous libraries were often destroyed, dispersed, and recollected. Madrid's institutions benefited most from the recovery: for example, the new Spanish academies of fine arts, language and culture, and history, which fostered research libraries of 20,000, 80,000, and 200,000 volumes, respectively.

University libraries benefited from the dispersion of Jesuit collections; major deposits went to Oviedo, Santiago, and Valladolid; 12,000 volumes enriched Salamanca; and more went to Granada and Seville. The empress Doña Maria had influenced the conversion in 1603 of the motherhouse and its Colegio de la Compania in Madrid (1560–) into the Colegio Imperial. Its Jesuit collections subsequently (1770–) supported the revival of theological studies in the Reales Estudios de San Isidro. When the Jesuits returned from 1815 to 1820 and 1823 to 1834, they resupplied their confiscated libraries with new holdings, only to lose them again, including some 34,000 volumes to the Universidad Complutense de Madrid. Cardinal Francisco Antonio de Lorenzana built a major library in Toledo in 1771. He held positions, such as inquisitor general to the combined sees of Toledo and Mexico City, plus a role in the Roman curia which allowed him to acquire books from multiple sources and disperse them as well. The final dispersion of his main library in 1881 distributed some 70,000 volumes, dating back to the earliest printing in Europe and the New World, to the Universities of Salamanca, Madrid, and Barcelona, plus the Biblioteca Nacional. Remnants of this rich library remained in Toledo, however, to be transferred first in 1919 to the Hospital de Santa Cruz and in 1966 to a new facility.

King João V of Portugal was a major patron of the library at Coimbra, which had a new library built from 1717 to 1725. The Portuguese crown also installed a magnificent library in its palace at Mafra, but Lisbon's libraries, including the castle keep of archives and books—the famous Torre do Tumbo—suffered major damage in the earthquake of 1755. The Crown thereafter reassembled its holdings in the outlying castle of Ajuda, where the 19th-century historian-librarian Alexandre Herculano synthesized the country's history. The royal collection grew to 100,000 books and 30,000 manuscripts.

While new research libraries were created from amalgamations of old ones, genuinely new but modest popular libraries were founded in more than 50 cities throughout the peninsula in the 19th century. The largest in Barcelona, Valencia, Seville, and Madrid held approximately 10,000 volumes each. These were often supported by friends, groups, and organized local philanthropy, as in the early involvement of Gaspar Melchor de Jovellanos in Seville's libraries before his rise in the civil service to chief minister of Spain. Largely under his leadership and largess, the library of the Sociedad Económica de Amigos del País grew in stature and size and was ultimately converted into a public library, which in 1858 fell under the administration of the Biblioteca Nacional.

After the popular revolution of 1868, "la Gloriosa," during the leadership of Generals Prim and Serrano, libraries of all types were secularized and brought under local government rule. At the same time in Portugal, the Real Biblioteca Publica da Corte, which had been founded in 1796, was transformed into the Biblioteca Nacional de Lisboa. Both countries moved under the same liberal influences, but these actually endangered libraries as mobs rioted and looted landlord establishments. Several major monastic libraries were lost in New Catalonia during a wave of violence in 1835 when even the royal tombs were desecrated, and the vast medieval Cistercian archives, now in the Archivo Histórico Nacional, had to be salvaged from the floors of abandoned monasteries. On the other hand, inspired by Manuel Ruiz Zorilla's rhetoric and series of decrees, Spain experienced a mass movement toward popular libraries as the means to eradicate ignorance and empower the common man. The universities were brought into an initiative to create public and school libraries, mostly from donations, one or two for each educational district. Between 1869 and 1870, 93 public libraries were founded, mainly from confiscated and redistributed books. By 1882 some 746 such libraries had been founded with a total of 171,083 volumes, mostly duplicated titles covering a range of 300 works, but they remained closed most of the time for lack of staff and proper facilities. As in the case of the transition of Spain's Biblioteca Real to the Biblioteca Nacional, Portugal's Real Biblioteca Publica da Corte was converted by royal decree into a royal library accessible by the public. It was augmented by the Real Mesa Censoria, where confiscated collections of religious institutions were reassembled. These were integrated into the national library of Portugal in 1836 when it took over the Convento de São Francisco in the center of Lisbon.

Intermittent civil war and political instability thwarted the best intentions of liberal reform governments. Throughout the 19th century, libraries of the old establishment were lost, from burning by the invading French in 1809 of rabinic and Arabic libraries in Zaragoza salvaged after the Reconquista to destruction of notable libraries in Bilboa by civil war in 1874. Attempts in educational innovation as a national system and the turn-of-the-century popularization of public libraries came to be associated in Spain with *"menéndezpelayismo"* after Marcelino Menéndez Pelayo's intellectual leadership and service as director of the Biblioteca Nacional. Other intellectuals, such as the historian Rafael Altamiro, who influenced the liberal government of Jose Canalejas, led the creation of a university extension service for community-based education. This in turn promoted the need for school and public libraries, as well as university libraries known for their undergraduate services rather than historic collections. Small libraries of 4,000 to 5,000 volumes were fostered throughout the peninsula, with local literary societies sponsoring reading programs and serving as book clubs. The popular libraries founded in 1911 in Madrid and Barcelona were to serve as models for cities in the provinces.

In Catalonia, the Institut d'Estudis Catalans was instrumental in spreading popular libraries and fostering public research for the study of regional culture in northeastern Spain. Elsewhere in Catalonia networks of community libraries were developed.

In Portugal, after the republic was founded in 1910, popular libraries and reading rooms spread to every town, and the new University of Lisbon (1911) became a center of library science and professionalization of librarians. Antonio Paz y Melia wrote about this movement before World War I as crucial to the diffusion of culture. It was not the European war that brought such developments to a standstill in Spain during the Second Republic, but the country's own bitter and highly destructive civil war (1936–39).

The Fascist government of Antonio Salazar, during Portugal's Estado Novo after the fall of the republic in 1926, can hardly receive credit for what little Portuguese library development took place. The Franco government's consolidation of power in Spain included a standardization of culture, such as educational reforms imposing Castilian as the national language for Spaniards and replacing regional languages and dialects. Such reforms had both positive and negative effects. A short-lived Junta de Cultura was replaced in 1938 by the Servicio de Defensa del Patrimonio Artístico, which enforced the ban of 1936 against the publication of pornography as well as socialist, communist, and libertarian literature, and completed a nationalization of libraries begun in 1937. A more centrally controlled ministry of national education replaced the servicio for public instruction. All such moves in censorship, central government control, and the overlay of a standardized national culture were in the name of "nuestra gran Cruzada Nacional" for the unity of the motherland, "la Patria," and the Catholic religion.

Such an ethos and thorough centralist nationalism from Madrid resulted in a genuine system—publicly funded—with an almost military-like hierarchy in an enlarged bureaucracy for what had hitherto been a rather chaotic development of different kinds of libraries dependent on unstable funding, local philanthropy, and charismatic leadership. Perhaps most indicative of such developments was the foundation, inspired by Ibañez Martín, of the Consejo Superior de Investigaciones Científicas on 24 November 1939. It operated research libraries in Madrid, which together acquired 700,000 volumes from the amalgamation of suppressed and disbanded libraries throughout Spain. A third creation in 1941 was the Biblioteca Central Militar, which grew to more than 250,000 volumes in three decades. In the provinces the budding public library movement was almost halted, with a reduction of municipal libraries from 152 to only 70 viable institutions. In regions where the fighting had been particularly heavy, such as Teruel and Valencia, two-thirds of the libraries disappeared. It was not until the 1940s that this lost infrastructure began to be rebuilt under the direction of leading educator-librarians such as Miguel Artegas (from Santander).

The Franco government began to relax its tight grip after the Pacts of Madrid with the Vatican and the United States for normalized international relations were signed in 1953. After 1951 a group in the Ministeria de Educación under Joaquín Ruíz Jiménez began to bring about significant changes. Thereafter progress was sporadic, interrupted by student rebellions, political terrorism, and seemingly senseless bombings (one of the worst in February 1956, continuing through the trial of the Basque Seven in 1971) that triggered police reprisals, crackdowns, and an unusually edgy Guardia Civil, followed by periods of normalcy. The Servico Nacional de Lectura after 1952 revitalized the popular programming associated with the previous public library movement. In 1956 legislation reorganized Spain's libraries under the leadership of the Biblioteca Nacional and its Cuerpo Facultativo (faculty of library science), which undertook widespread reforms and professional training. The 1960s therefore witnessed a general revival of community-based and regional libraries and a growing acceptance that not everything had to be centered in Madrid. Symbolic of this change of heart was the return in 1954 of 1,000 manuscripts, hoarded in the palace library in Madrid, to their rightful home in Salamanca on the 700th anniversary of the University of Salamanca. The government fostered regional Casas de Culturas everywhere. Into the 1970s, Spain had 1,300 public libraries in operation, with 5 million volumes serving more than 10 million users annually.

National Patrimonies and Information Organizations: Archives, Libraries, and Museums

One of the remarkable achievements of the Franco era was Spain's unified approach to library, archive, and museum development as different aspects of a common cause—the preservation of Spain's heritage and promotion of culture. Such a national organization had much earlier beginnings, however, in the professionalization of librarians, archivists, and curators and the pervasive sense of a national patrimony that deserved preservation and continuous development. Even when religious communities were suppressed in the sweeping social reforms in Spain of Juan Alvaréz Mendizabal during 1835 and in the appropriation of noble estates thereafter, there was the profound sense that the state, for the public good, had to take charge of this rich patrimony. In 1837 and 1844, commissions were established to inventory the historical sites, monuments, and works of art in the country. In 1869 under Ruíz Zorilla the government expanded such protection to libraries and archives, fearing their loss owing to fire, transfer, and a system of theft that fed illicit traffic in books through Europe and to the United States. Most cultural institutions were dependent upon provincial governments, but state aid became increasingly common even though the political turmoil of the 19th century meant that it was sporadic. The major libraries all undertook significant bibliographic compilations that served as inventories as well. More than treasuries, however, these institutions took on a new role in reforming the society they documented, in keeping with the famous laws passed in 1857 under Minister Claudio Mayano for Instrucción Publica outside the classroom, in libraries, archives, and museums, and with field trips to historical sites. Articles 163 and 166 called for augmenting these institutions to meet this challenge of public education, including better pay for employees engaged in cultural and information work, and created a professional association of archivists and librarians led by the administrations of the Archivo Histórico Nacional and Biblioteca Nacional. From this movement came the Junta Superior Directiva de Archivos y Bibliotecas del Reino, led by the historian Modesto Lafuente, director of the Escuela de Diplomática for professional studies in documentation. Curators and archeologists were added to the group a decade later with the establishment in 1867 of the Museo Arqueológico Nacional. Consequently, when Spain entered the 20th century, organizations were in place to build a strong national system of cultural institutions including libraries, archives, and museums.

The public library movement, as defined in Spain by the 1901 *reglamento* for public library services, meant that all institutions with which libraries collaborated adopted a service orientation toward the public. In 1902 legislation directed a massive effort in cataloging and indexing collections throughout the country, and the cultural renaissance associated with Menendez Pelayo meant not only access to holdings for scholars but for the public at large through reading libraries, popular editions, lectures, and exhibits. The new academically respectable and professional journal *Revista de archivos, bibliotecas y museos* fostered this multi-type cooperation and cross-disciplinary approach to cultural and information resource management. (The journal was suspended in 1931, but resurrected from 1947 to 1974.) Support was always forthcoming from faculty who moved freely back and forth between these institutions and their universities. When Elias Tormo, a *catedratico* (university professor) in art history, became the minister of public education in Spain, the Patronato de la Biblioteca Nacional was founded as a center for the Cuerpo Facultativo. The national library's center for bibliographic research was dedicated on 15 June 1942 as the Instituto Nicolas Antonio de Bibliografía associated with the CSIC. Under the influence of Minister Sintes in the 1950s, this institute was transformed into a network for bibliographic control, the Servicio Nacional de Información Documental y Bibliográfica, which in 1970 became the Instituto Bibliográfico Hispanico, with oversight of legal deposit, copyright, and uniform cataloging.

The organization of archives, libraries, and museums also became more centralized and hierarchical along Franco lines under a high commission with regional coordinators who worked with the ministry of education and new military guards and urban regimes. In 1947 the myriad organizations involved in libraries and public education, archives and government, and museums and historical preservation were merged into one large professional organization, the Asociacion Nacional de Archiveros, Bibliotecarios y Arqueológos (ANABA), which assembled in Madrid for the first time in 1950. ANABA fostered collaborative work for bibliographic control and access across all institutions and for all Spanish-language materials and, after 1981, professional education through the Centro de Estudio Bibliográficos y Documentarios. Outreach was promoted by the Comisari de Estension Cultural under the minister of education, leading to the creation of 9,000 municipal and village centers for adult and continuing education, all connected with public libraries and backed by the academic and research library system. The government leadership position was still associated with the Ministerio de Cultura and, as the Franco government prepared to give way to a constitutional monarchy, a series of influential leaders in the Dirección General (Miguel Bordonau, Eleutero González Zaptero, and Luís Sánchez Belda of the Archivo Histórico Nacional) oversaw major growth in collections; improvement of facilities; better access to catalogs, early automation, and networks; and preservation microfilming and restoration work (at the Centro Nacional de Conservación y Microfilmación Documental y Bibliográfica, founded in 1981).

The proliferation and growth of Iberian libraries after the 1970s has been phenomenal. It was the wealthy Fundação Calouste Gulbenkian that, following the model of Carnegie philanthropy in the United States, established 235 libraries in Portugal to stimulate recovery from the centuries of neglect libraries suffered from World War I until the ousting of Salazar in 1974. Thereafter Portugal began to imitate Spain's approaches to library organization as part of the national cultural patrimony. Both countries have been spectacular in rapid modernization of their libraries, turning to automation and networking on a grand scale commensurate with Spain's joining the European Community and the advent of the Internet and Web-based digital technology. In Spain, 24 museums with their libraries report to the Direccion General de Bellas Artes y Bienes Culturales under the protection of the Patrimonio Historico within the ministry of culture and education. Under this same secretariat falls the Direccion General del Libro, Archivos y Bibliotecas, which is responsible for coordinating libraries in Spain through a system of autonomous communities; the Biblioteca Nacional; and the Institute for Cinematography and Audiovisual Arts. The latter is separate from the Institute for Fine Arts and Music and the Teatro Real. Each of these government directorates maintains a documentation center to assess the holdings of their institutions, design acquisition and preservation programs, and create large interdisciplinary databases, websites, and networks linking all of the country's cultural and information resources. In Portugal PORBASE has provided access since 1987 to a national union catalog. In Spain RedIRIS serves a network of 50 university libraries; the library school at Salamanca maintains even more inclusive sites, including *Bibliotecas universiades Españolas,* which is integrated with special and public libraries into a directory for all *Bibliotecas españolas.* This website points to 67 university library sites and 130 library catalogs. Such sites also maintain links to major national libraries of the world and nearly 100 national and international library directories in what José Antonio Merlo Vega calls a global "ring of libraries" (http://exlibris.usal.es/bibesp). In addition to Spain's university libraries, there are seven regional cooperatives or networks, seven special (medical networks), 90 discipline-specific libraries, 71 public systems, eight "scholars" libraries, and a host of school libraries. The Web-based organization of Spain's libraries and Internet access to them is state of the art.

LAWRENCE J. McCRANK

See also Library of the Royal Palace, Spain; National Library of Portugal; National Library of Spain; Royal Monastery of El Escorial Library; University of Coimbra Library

Further Reading

Buller, Nell L., *Libraries and Library Services in Portugal,* Halifax, Nova Scotia: Dalhousie University, School of Library and Information Science, 1988

Cano, V., "Bibliometric Overview of Library and Information Science Research in Spain," *Journal of the American Society for Information Science* 50, no. 8 (June 1999)

Domingos, Manuela D., *Subsidios para a historia da Biblioteca nacional,* Lisbon: Instituto da Biblioteca Nacional do Livro, 1995

Escolar, Hipolito, *Historia de las bibliotecas,* Madrid: Fundacion German Sánchez Ruiperez and Ediciones Piramide, 1985; 3rd edition, 1990

Faulhaber, Charles B., *Libros y bibliotecas en la España medieval: Una bibliografía de fuentes impresas,* London: Grant and Cutler, 1987

Hanson, Carl A., "Were There Libraries in Roman Spain?" *Libraries and Culture* 24 (Spring 1989)

Jiménez, Miguel, and Alice Keefer, "Library Automation in Spain: An Overview," *Program* 26, no. 3 (1992)

Jiménez, Miguel, and Alice Keefer, "Networking in Spain," *Libri* 43, no. 3 (July 1993)

Lasperas, Jean-Michel, "Inventaires de bibliotheques et documents de librairie dans le monde hispanique aux XVe, XVIe et XVIIe siècles," *Revue française d'histoire du livre* 28 (1980)

Mayol, Carmé, and Angels Massisimo, "Libraries and Librarianship in Spain," *IFLA Journal* 19, no. 2 (1993)

Ortega y Gasset, José, "Mission del bibliotecario," *Revista de occidente* 47–48 (1935); as *Mission of the Librarian,* Boston: G.K. Hall, 1961

Padover, S.K., "Muslim Libraries," in *The Medieval Library,* edited by James Westfall Thompson, Chicago: University of Chicago Press, 1939

Icelandic Libraries

Origins

The relationship between Icelanders and books is a special one. According to the *Statistical Yearbook* of the United Nations Educational, Scientific, and Cultural Organization (UNESCO), more books are published per capita in Iceland than in any other country. A rumor claims that there are more writers than there are readers in Iceland.

The *Íslendingabók* (Book of Icelanders), the first Icelandic history, written circa 1125 by Ari the Wise, states that when the first settlers came from Norway by the end of the ninth century, there were some Christian men in Iceland who did not want to stay on among the heathens. According to Ari, they left behind some Irish books, bells, and croziers. In other words, books have existed in Iceland longer than Icelanders!

Handwritten-book production started in Iceland in the 12th century; during the 13th and 14th centuries most of the famous saga manuscripts were written. Approximately 700 volumes of medieval manuscripts (1150–1550) have survived to the present. Although the first printing press was established as early as the 1530s, it remained the only press in Iceland for almost 350 years. It was run by the bishops and in the 19th century by government authorities, printing mostly religious books, two to three per year on average, slightly increasing by the beginning of the 19th century as some types of secular books became more frequent. However, the authorities were cautious and did not want all sorts of books printed. Therefore, handwritten-book production of secular texts of all kinds survived in addition to printed texts throughout the 19th century, until many new printing presses were started in the last quarter of that century.

Although books have always played an important role in Icelandic society, very little is known about Icelandic libraries in the late Middle Ages. An effort has been made to reconstruct the libraries of the saga writers by trying to trace the sources they used. There is evidence of libraries in a number of monasteries before the Reformation of 1550, as well as at the two bishoprics of Skálholt and Hólar through 1800. The fate of these libraries is not clear, although the 17th-century Scandinavian interest in old sagas and histories led to the transfer of nearly all medieval manuscripts to Sweden and Denmark, either as originals or as new copies of the worn originals.

In the late 18th century, efforts were made to establish reading societies, both in the southern and the northern parts of the country. These were not successful among a largely rural population. Reykjavík, the only urban area, had only 300 citizens in 1800, whereas the country as a whole had only 50,000 inhabitants.

The National Library of Iceland

In 1818 Carl Christian Rafn joined Copenhagen's three-year-old Icelandic Literature Society. He suggested that the society should nominate candidates for a committee to work toward establishment of a public library and donated some 22 books to start the process. This was the beginning of Islands Stiftsbibliotek, the county library of Iceland, which later developed into Landsbókasafn Íslands, the National Library of Iceland (NLI). Although the year 1818 is considered the founding year, the library did not operate until at least 1825, when the books were placed in the tower of the Reykjavík Cathedral; the library remained there for more than half a century. NLI got its first governing board in 1826, and in a report of that same year, acquisitions (mainly donations) had reached 1,545 volumes, more than half of them given or collected by Rafn.

By the mid-19th century Reykjavík had grown to a city of 1,100 inhabitants. The ancient parliament, Althingi (originally founded at Thingvellir in 930 where it operated until 1800), was reestablished in Reykjavík in 1845 in addition to a learned secondary school and a seminar for clerical education. The cathedral was renovated and enlarged, and Jón Árnason was hired as librarian in 1848 to supervise temporary moves of the library books. By that time the library had grown to approximately 5,700 volumes, including some 450 volumes of duplicates. Despite a low salary, Árnason stayed until 1887, and as he left, the collections numbered approximately 20,000 volumes. He compiled a printed catalog of Icelandic books and manuscripts in 1874. Árnason had earlier complied a 232-page catalog of the secondary school library; printed in 1862, it was the first major library catalog to be printed in Iceland, making Árnason the first professional bibliographer in the country.

In 1845 Bishop Steingrímur Jónsson (a member of the NLI board) died, leaving his huge private archives to become the core of the NLI's Manuscript Department. During the decades to come the Manuscript Department grew, mostly through donations and acquisitions, including the archives of the leading Icelandic 19th-century politician Jón Sigurdsson, bequeathed to the library on his death in 1879. The manuscript holdings of the NLI consist primarily of private archives of prominent Icelanders of the 19th and 20th centuries.

In the beginning of the 1880s the NLI moved from the Cathedral tower into the new building of the Althingi. This move solved the library's housing problems for a short time, but the increase in book stock made it necessary to start planning a new building. That was achieved in 1908 with a new building in the center of Reykjavík that housed, in addition to the library, the National Archives, the National Historical Museum, and the National Museum of Zoology. In the decades to come the museums were moved to other locations and NLI took over their sections of the building. However, the housing problem continued as both stock and personnel increased.

Earlier the NLI was given the right of legal deposit of all Icelandic imprints (1887). Prior to that only the Royal Library in Copenhagen and the University Library in Copenhagen had received deposit copies. Árnason's successor, Hallgrímur Melsted, started compiling an annual accession catalog in 1887, *Ritaukaskrá,* which was published without interruption through 1944 when it was replaced by a new yearbook, *Árbók,* containing the annual national bibliography as well as articles on book history in the broadest sense. In 1975 the national bibliography was separated from the annual yearbook and has been published annually as *Íslensk bókaskrá,* with five-year cumulations.

Around the turn of the century, the NLI hired editor, poet, and politician Jón Ólafsson as a cataloger. During his years as an immigrant in the United States and Canada, Ólafsson had become acquainted with U.S. libraries. Ólafsson rearranged the library and instituted the Dewey Decimal Classification system, which has dominated Icelandic libraries since that time.

University of Iceland Library

The NLI has always been Iceland's main research library, offering services to academic researchers as well as the public. Háskólabókasafn, the university library, was not founded until 1940, when the new central building for Háskóli Íslands, the University of Iceland, was inaugurated at the university campus. Although the university library was formally founded at this late date, its roots go back to the library of the clerical seminar in the mid-1840s. That collection became the core of the institutional library collections of the university's School of Theology when the University of Iceland was founded in 1911. Similarly, the collections of the Medical School (founded in 1876) and the

Law School (founded in 1908) were inaugurated in the respective faculty libraries of the university. The faculty library for arts and humanities benefited from generous donations in the 1930s, such as those from Copenhagen University professor Finnur Jónsson (7,500 volumes in 1934) and from businessman Benedikt S. Thórarinsson (8,000 volumes in 1940), including many old and rare Icelandic imprints.

In the beginning of the 1970s, the book stock of the university library had grown to 165,000 volumes through foreign acquisitions, donations, and legal deposit copies. By that time the housing problem had become intolerable. Short-term solutions such as deposit libraries and institutional libraries within the university were expensive and inconvenient for everyone. A permanent, radical solution was necessary.

The Merger

In the 1950s the idea of uniting the NLI and the University of Iceland Library was launched. In this small country, many things supported the merging of these two relatively large research libraries in Reykjavík into one, not least of which was the housing problem plaguing both libraries. Although a good idea without any opponents or active resistance, it took some 20 years to start planning a new library building and another 20 to complete it. Opened on 1 December 1994, the united Landsbókasafn Íslands–Háskólabókasafn is by far the largest library in Iceland, housed in a building of 15,600 square yards (more than 3 acres), with 100 staff members and a stock of more than 900,000 volumes. It is the pride of the 260,000 Icelanders.

The new building has been a success and has opened up many new possibilities. Automation that had started in the two libraries some years earlier has developed, and a library system named Gegnir (run as a national union catalog in cooperation with several other research libraries) has modernized library work fundamentally. Furthermore, digitization projects have been started: 250 old maps have been scanned and published on the Web; a major project scanning saga manuscripts and related literature, in cooperation with Cornell University, is ongoing; and an 18th- and 19th-century newspaper scanning project is being planned. These projects can be reached through the library's website at www.bok.hi.is. Yet it appears clear that an addition to the new building will be necessary in the near future.

Other Icelandic Libraries

Other research libraries in Iceland are rather small, most of them either college libraries or special libraries in Reykjavík or in the country. A special library worth mentioning here is the medieval manuscript collection in the University Institute Stofnun Árna Magnússonar in Reykjavík, which contains the old Icelandic saga manuscripts. Originally collected in Iceland by the end of the 17th and the first decades of the 18th centuries by the Icelandic scholar Árni Magnússon in Copenhagen, the manuscript collection was by his death in 1730 donated to Copenhagen University and since 1760 kept under the Danish Arnamagnæn Foundation. After complicated discussions between Icelanders and Danes spanning approximately half a century, the Danish parliament in 1965 passed a law that made possible the return of a major part of the collection; 1,666 medieval and younger manuscripts concerning Icelandic matters, and from the collections of the Royal Library 141 Icelandic manuscripts, including the Codex Regius (a 13th-century manuscript of the poetic *Edda*) and *Flateyjarbók* (a 14th-century collection of histories of Norse kings). After restoration and microfilming, the manuscripts were gradually transferred to Iceland from 1971 to 1997.

As the Islands Stiftsbibliotek, founded in 1818, was located in Reykjavík in the southern part of the country, an interest of founding libraries in other quarters of the country arose. The first of these quarter libraries were founded circa 1830 and grew over the years into regional public libraries that, by the end of the century, had received the right of legal deposit for Icelandic imprints. The biggest of these is the Amtsbókasafn, the quarter library in Akureyri in the northern part of Iceland.

Around the mid–19th century, some reading societies that evolved into public libraries were established in the rural areas of the country. There are now some 25 public libraries throughout the country. The largest is the Borgarbókasafn Reykjavíkur (Reykjavík Public Library), founded in 1923 with roots in the People's Reading Society of 1901. The strength of the Reykjavík Public Library was owing in large measure to its first librarian, Sigurgeir Fridriksson, who studied librarianship at the newly founded Danish school of librarianship in Copenhagen. Fridriksson had also taken a study tour of Swedish libraries, and later he traveled to North America, where he took courses at the New York Public Library and visited other libraries in the United States and Canada. Owing to Fridriksson's Danish education in librarianship, the classification system he chose for the Reykjavík Public Library was a Danish version of the Dewey Decimal Classification system, which the library still uses. Besides its central library, the Reykjavík Public Library has six branch libraries in the suburbs of the city and also runs mobile libraries. It is the second largest library in Iceland, in both personnel and book stock.

In the last two or three decades, school libraries have developed in all parts of the country. Outside of Reykjavík some of the public libraries have functioned as school libraries as well as small research libraries. Private libraries, of both individuals and families, have been common for some time. It is not unusual for people to borrow books from friends rather than going to official libraries. In 19th-century Icelandic newspapers, announcements can be found requesting that a loaned book be returned to a book owner who has forgotten to whom it was loaned.

It should be mentioned that two libraries abroad have extensive collections of Icelandic imprints; some books in these collections are unique, being the only existing copies known to have survived to the present. These are the Royal Library in

Copenhagen, which acted as the island's national library in past centuries when Iceland was under Danish rule, and Cornell University Library, which has by far the largest collection of Icelandic books in the United States, originally bequeathed by Daniel Willard Fiske circa 1900. Both of these libraries received legal deposit copies from Iceland until 1976.

STEINGRÍMUR JÓNSSON

Further Reading

"Iceland, Libraries In," in *Encyclopedia of Library and Information Science*, edited by Allen Kent et al., vol. 11, New York: Dekker, 1969

Sigurdsson, Einar, "The Next Ten Years in National Libraries: The National and University Library of Iceland," *Alexandria* 12, no. 2 (2000)

Islamic Libraries

Introduction

In the seventh century at Mecca came the first Qur'ānic revelation that ordained reading. Amazingly, this revelation soon led to a sea of books, translations, interpretations, and reproductions. To facilitate easy access for Muslims to this sea of books, librarians evolved the art of librarianship in the Islamic world. Their infrastructure embraced such diverse characteristics as Islamic values; scholarly librarians; knowledge acquisition, assimilation and transfer, classification, preservation, and dissemination; reference tools; the institution of *waqf* (pious endowment); book bazaars; binding arts; calligraphy; and classical Islam's scientific achievements.

The term *Islamic libraries* refers to information handling by or about Muslims and/or management of Islamic resources anywhere in the world. This essay presents the marriage of Islam and librarianship.

In *Islamic Librarianship* (1997), the scholar Mohamed Taher conceptualized Islamic librarianship as follows:

(1) The Islamic worldview is based on the Qur'ān and the Prophet Muhammad's traditions. The spread of this worldview through *madrasa* (school or college) for boys and instruction of girls at home resulted in an expansion of literacy in a predominantly oral culture. Gradually, several African and Asian languages adopted the Arabic alphabet and Arabic numerals. Free access to knowledge and transfer of books emerged in this process, emphasizing that "books are for use."

(2) Islam facilitated paths to develop ideas by way of analogy and consensus and promoted inquiry in natural and physical sciences, leading to advances in all branches of learning, a precursor of the Renaissance. Islam also ordained a holistic approach to life, synthesizing the spiritual and mundane. With a strong desire for a different lifestyle and the need to apply revealed knowledge to geopolitical issues, additional information became a sociocultural necessity, and libraries facilitated access to it. In other words, Islamic authorities saw to it that "every reader finds his or her book."

(3) Muslims imported and shaped ancient sciences into an innovatively new worldview and finally exported this thought to the information haves and have-nots. Mechanisms were evolved to assure "every book its reader."

(4) In Islam the seeking and dissemination of knowledge is worship. Based on the Prophet Muhammad's emphasis on seeking knowledge, even from as distant a land as China, education and training gained momentum early in the history of Islam, perhaps a precursor of the information age. The classical period of Islam (eighth to 13th century) helped to save ancient learning from extinction and to disseminate that knowledge in an enlarged and enriched form. Although the glory soon diminished, dissemination continued as a service "to save the time of the reader."

The appearance of paper industries in Samarkand (750), Baghdad (794), Damascus and Cairo (950), and eventually Spain (1151) helped lead to the Gutenberg era of printing. Prior to that time, Muslims used papyrus, parchment, and bark to form books bound into codices. The transfer from manuscript to paper resulted in the emergence of books fashioned as we know them today. With paper (*warāq*) came the profession of the *warraq* (paper dealers), writers, translators, copiers, booksellers, librarians, illuminators, and in fact all those involved in book production.

The abundance of books created additional jobs for copyists, proofreaders, collators, binders, calligraphers, book decorators, and book illuminators. The book bazaars that eventually grew in every city soon became arsenals of a lively literary culture, supplementing the already growing libraries. Proscription of graven images, and imagery in general, directed the arts in Islam away from painting, drawing, engraving, and sculpture and toward architecture and calligraphy. Hence bookbinding, calligraphy, and other artistic achievements gave Islamic civilization a distinct place in the world of art and aesthetics.

So influential was this Islamic spirit that within three centuries public libraries in urban areas became widespread. What happened in the early period of this civilization left many spellbound. Ziauddin Sardar notes in his 1999 essay, "The Civilization of the Book," that in fewer than 100 years the book had been established as a basic tool for the dissemination of knowledge. This was accomplished through the framework of Islam, the basic tenets of which touched the individual, society, and civilization, enabling the society to produce a significant information infrastructure.

The major historians of the Islamic library world include Sa'd, the first sāhib al-masāhif, curator of books (c. 710 C.E.); ibn al-Nadīm (10 A.C.), the first bibliographer and cataloger and author of *Kitāb al-Fihrist;* Ibn Sīnā (or Avicenna, 10 A.C.), the first librarian designate in the Middle East; Amīr Khusro (11 A.C.), the first librarian designate in South Asia; Ibn Khaldūn (14 A.C.), the foremost Islamic historian; Yusuf I. Sarkis, an historian on Arabic publishing; and many others.

Library Scenario

Libraries have been attached to mosques, *madrasa* (universities), *Jāmi'a* (academies), *dargah* (shrine), *qanqah* (tomb), and *bayt al-hikma* (research center) from their beginnings. Historically, mosques and *madrasa* first appeared followed by *bayt al-hikma,* the royal collections, and private libraries. Although *kitāb* in Arabic and the Qur'ān refers to "book," modern Arabic has a generic word, *maktaba,* for library (root k-t-b). Interestingly, the Qur'ān refers to ink, pen, papyrus, parchment, and an excess of books as a "donkey laden with books." Library names had a prefix by location (*bayt* or *dār* [domain], *khizāna* [treasure]) or by activity (*hikma* [wisdom], *'ilm* [knowledge]), and these prefixes were at times interchanged. In Persian-influenced South Asian libraries, use of the term *kutub khana* (bookstore) is common. The titles of library staff also varied. Islamic libraries evolved uniquely, without much imitation of their contemporaries in Rome or Byzantium.

Mosque Libraries

Mosques are unique social institutions performing multiple tasks, including facilitation and dissemination of learning. Interestingly, mosque libraries became the first public libraries in Islam, used by students, teachers, worshipers, and anyone who sought a particular book. Although the first book to enter was the Qur'ān, donation, duplication, and acquisition were also common. Mosque libraries systematically appeared in the time of the Abbāsids (750–1258). Although the majority of mosques had a few copies of the Qur'ān in small libraries, a few large mosques had several large libraries. Cordoba, Spain, conquered by Muslims in 750, became one of the most cultured cities in Europe within the next three centuries under the later Umayyad dynasty.

Dargah libraries are adjacent to mosques and hence rarely classified as distinct or separate from their mosques. Such *dargah* libraries are frequent in South and Central Asia.

Bayt al-Hikma

As compared to mosques and *madrasa,* the *bayt al-hikma* had more secular than spiritual material. In Baghdad the Abbāsid Al-Ma'mūn founded the *bayt al-hikma* (library and astronomical laboratory) to promote research in scientific and technological areas. Its collection was a magnet for scholars of the age and grew from war bounty, a generous donation of Armenian books by Emperor Leo V, and especially from exorbitant purchases in distant lands.

People from all countries came to Baghdad in order to study various sciences in libraries where the books were completely at the disposal of all users: "The library was known in the whole world and attracted students in such manner that the astronomer Abū Mashat, coming from Khorasān with the intention of going to Mecca to perform the pilgrimage, decided to go and see it. He was so enthusiastic about it that he remained there and did not continue his journey" (quoted in Elayyan, 1990).

In Cairo the palace had an internal library called Khazā'in al-Dākhila and a state library called Dār al-Hikma, founded by the Fātimids' ruler al-Hākim. The Egyptian historian Maqrizi in his Khitat states that the library was opened on the tenth day of Jumai II of the year 395 (1004 C.E.) in the building called Dār al-Hikma:

> Books were brought from the book-chests of the palaces (residences of the Fātimid Caliphs), and the public was permitted to enter. Anyone was at liberty to copy the book he wished, and whoever wanted to read a certain book found in the library could do so. Men of learning studied the Qur'ān, astronomy, grammar, lexicography and medicine. Moreover, the building was adorned by carpets and all doors and hallways had curtains. Managers, servants, porters, and other menials were appointed to maintain the building. From the library of the Caliph al-Hakim, books which he had donated were brought (to Dār al-Hikma). (They were) in all sciences and literatures and of superb calligraphy such as no other potentate had even been able to collect. Al- Hākim permitted admittance to everyone, without distinction of rank, who wished to read or consult any of the books. (Sibai, 1984)

For research institutions as such, there has been much continuity. Early translation bureaus in Baghdad were copied in Hyderabad, India, under the Nizām in the 19th century. Contemporary agencies promoting research and dissemination exist, such as the International Institute of Islamic Thought, Herndon, Virginia; the Faisal Foundation, Riyadh, Saudi Arabia; the Islamic Foundation in Leicestershire, England; Islamic universities in Islamabad (Pakistan) and Malaysia; the Islamic Development Bank in Jeddah, Saudi Arabia; and the Khan Program for Islamic Architecture at Harvard University (Cambridge, Massachusetts). Islam, as studied in the West, came to be known as oriental studies. Major examples can be found at the School of Oriental and African Studies at the University of London and in the Oriental Institute at the University of Chicago.

Madrasa Libraries

Every mosque had a *madrasa*—a school, college, and learning academy—and no city or town lacked this educational resource. A single instance suffices to show how the rulers and the ruled built these edifices. The wazir of the Saldjuk, Sultan Malik Shah, Nizām al-Mulk, revolutionized educational patterns, both in curriculum and content, in Nishapur and Baghdad and set a model for all later institutions. The resulting academies accordingly prioritized book collecting to deal with the sciences taught there. To this day, Islamic religious sciences follow the Nizamiah pattern. Although *madrasa* libraries are common in Muslim countries, there are also many in India and other countries in which Muslims are in the minority. Jāmi'a Azhar in Cairo (founded in the tenth century) is the greatest such center today and has been modernized in every sense. Its library ranks as the second largest in Egypt after the Egyptian National Library.

In Fez, Morocco, the impact of scholarly interaction and reading also had its impact.

> The Sultan of Morocco, Abu Yusuf, having concluded peace with Don Sancho, demanded back the beautiful books which fell into his hands during his campaign in Muslim countries. The Spanish prince complied with his request, and sent to him a large number of books, which the Sultan deposited in a college which he had built at Fez. The books, thus, were placed at the disposal of the literary men who might require their use. (Khuda Bakhsh, 1902)

Private Libraries

Scholars throughout the area had private collections for their own use, built not only by elite scholars but by bibliophiles who regarded their treasures as worthy of preservation and then donated them to mosques, shrines or schools where they could be cared for and consulted by scholars. On his death in 1229, Yakūt, author of celebrated geographical and biographical dictionaries, left his books as *waqf* to the Zaidi shrine (a mosque) in Baghdad.

Bibliophiles prospered despite the strain and stress in obtaining their desired books. The historian al-Birūni, who mastered Sanskrit, Persian, and Arabic, spent 40 years seeking a copy of Mani's Sifr al-Asrar. The philosopher and physician Ibn Rushd (Averroës) was unable to consult a monograph dealing with the Mutazilah. Firishta, another historian, visited the royal library of the Farūqi Sultans at Khandesh, India, in 1604 and from one of the books in this library he copied the history of Farūqi. The 13th-century Spanish historian Ibn hayyan did not buy many books because the libraries he used owned all that he needed.

The 19th and 20th century's Khuda Bakhsh Oriental Public Library in Patna, India; the Raza Library in Rampur, India; and the Salar Jung Museum and Library in Hyderabad, India, are good examples of individual aspirations to build unique collections. An automobile mechanic, Samad Khan in Hyderabad, built a single collection of more than 25,000 volumes, which was recently purchased by the Center for Research Libraries (Chicago, Illinois).

Palace Libraries

Sultan Nūh Ibn Mansūr invited Ibn Sīnā (Avicenna) to the Samanids' capital of Bukhāra between 976 and 977, and Ibn Sīnā's narrative about the sultan's library makes interesting reading:

> Having requested and obtained permission (from Sultan Nūh) to visit the library, I went there where I found many rooms filled with books which were packed up in cases (or trunks) row upon row. One room was allotted to works on poetry and Arabic philology; another to jurisprudence, and so forth, the books on each discipline being kept in a separate room. I then read the catalog of ancient authors and requested the books I needed. I saw in this collection books the very titles of which were unknown to most people, and which I myself have never seen either before or since. (Sibai, 1984)

In India the 800-year Muslim rule brought academic pursuits and individual scholarship to India among both the upper classes and the masses. Abul Fazl's Ain-i-Akbari, for example, reports about the reading tastes of the supposedly illiterate bibliophile, Mogul Emperor Akbar.

> His majesty's library is divided into several parts; some of the books are kept within, and some without, the Harem. Each part of the library is sub-divided according to the value of the books. Prose books, poetical works, Hindi, Persian, Greek, Kashmiri, and Arabic are all separately placed. In this order they are also inspected. Experienced people bring them daily and read before His majesty, who hears every book from the beginning to the end. (Taher, 1994)

Other Developments

When the Abbāsids became politically weak, the cultural life of the people as a whole did not diminish as a result. Each principality developed its own lifestyle. The Umayyad of Spain, the Fātimid of Egypt, the Hamdanid of Aleppo, the Buwayhid of Persia, the Samanid of Bukhara, and the Ghaznavid rulers all established libraries. Between the fall of Baghdad in 1258 and World War II, independent principalities developed in Istanbul, Timbuktu, Samarkand, Chittagong, Jakarta, Delhi, Gujarat, Bijapur, and Gulbarga. Book burning did occur (even among the ruling classes), but these excesses did not equal those of Europe. During the last two centuries European influence helped facilitate standards of modern librarianship in the Islamic world.

Today all Muslim countries have library systems, though standardization and services are at different levels in each country. Administration and management of libraries had its own pattern under respective governments and authorities. Larger libraries had among their staffs librarians, library assistants, copyists, writers, translators, binders, and many others. At the library of Banū Ammar in Tripoli, 180 copyists worked in shifts around the clock. Khan-I-Khanan, an Indian noble, had 95 library employees and invented a tracing paper of seven colors and variegated paper. Financial support for mosque and other religious libraries was a result of *waqf* and supported, among other services, dissemination, visitor accommodation, and salaries. The *waqf* stipulated that each document be registered, resulting in at least a shelf list, if not a user-friendly index. Bibliographic description included the title, author, size, calligraphic style, and collation (expressed in volumes). Books were arranged in subject order in a *madrasa* library, for example, according to courses offered. The Imperial Library of Moguls was arranged in a locally devised subject order. The designated librarian was usually a scholar. Circulation rules varied, depending on restricted or unrestricted endowments. The collections were stored in wooden cabinets with ornamented calligraphy or with glass doors.

Professional Development

Research areas in Islamic librarianship can be explored in three broad perspectives: technical, professional, and historical. Although some attempts to automate Islamic libraries do exist, much systematization is needed. In this technical area, the field is yet to come to terms with a variety of issues. The debate continues on almost every aspect of cataloging, classification, indexing, automation, data entry formats for bibliographic description, MAchine-Readable Cataloging (MARC), and the application of Arabization standards.

Many libraries use Dewey Decimal Classification and the Library of Congress or adaptations thereof for their classification systems. Ziauddin Sardar's *Islam: Outline of a Classification Scheme* (1979) for Islamic studies is based on the facet analysis of Indian library science pioneer S.R. Ranganathan. Organizations such as ALESCO, Gulfnet, ARABSAT, and ARIS-NET have reduced some networking hurdles, but wider attitudinal changes and professional commitment are needed from all those involved. Many significant issues need consideration, such as terminology, chronological sources, primary resource and nonbook electronic resources and their identification and location, the place of the book in Islam and the place of Islam in books, and the institutional roles in developing Islamic librarianship.

The chief professional organizations in the field are Malaysia's Congress of Muslim Librarians and Information Scientists; the Middle East Studies Association, which includes both academics and professionals; and the Islamic Library Association in Hyderabad, India. Meho's recent bibliography indexes 1,000 documents in the field. Periodical indexes in print include the *Muslim World Book Review*, *Periodica Islamica*, and a Website for *Index Islamicus*.

Summary

The history of libraries in Islamic civilization and its patterns of book trade, collection development, and the art and craft of book manufacture all show "that the infrastructure for dissemination of information evolved naturally during the classical Muslim period" (Sardar, 1999). What developed later is the support system, which continues to evolve. Authorities, institutions, leaders, and professionals must now recognize the importance of these historical developments as they adapt to the modern requirements of a new library infrastructure.

MOHAMED TAHER

See also Iberian Libraries; Middle Eastern Libraries

Further Reading

Elayyan, Ribhi Mustafa, "The History of the Arabic-Islamic Libraries: 7th to 14th Centuries," *International Library Review* 22 (1990)

Ferahian, Salwa, S. Thibaudeau, and J.E. Leide, "Teaching Library Skills to Graduate Students from the Islamic Countries: Cooperation between Librarians and Second-Language Specialists," *Middle Eastern Library Association Notes* 62 (1995)

Hamadeh, Mohammed M., "Islamic Libraries during the Middle Ages," Ph.D. diss., University of Chicago, 1962

Imamuddin, Sayyid Muhammad, *Hispano-Arab Libraries*, Karachi: Pakistan Historical Society, 1961

Khuda Bakhsh, Salahuddin, "The Islamic Libraries," *The Nineteenth Century and After* 52 (July 1902)

Lerner, Frederick Andrew, "Libraries of the Islamic World," in *The Story of Libraries: From the Invention of Writing to the Computer Age*, by Lerner, New York: Continuum, 1998

Mackensen, R.S., "Four Great Libraries of Medieval Baghdad," *Library Quarterly* 2, no. 3 (1932)

Meho, Lokman I., and Mona A. Nsouli, compilers, *Libraries and Information in the Arab World: An Annotated Bibliography*, Westport, Connecticut, and London: Greenwood Press, 1999

Sardar, Ziauddin, *Islam: Outline of a Classification Scheme*, London: Bingley, and New York: Saur, 1979

Sardar, Ziauddin, "The Civilization of the Book," in *Ilm and the Revival of Knowledge*, http://msanews.mynet.net/books/ilm, 1999

Sibai, Mohamed Makki, "An Historical Investigation of Mosque Libraries in Islamic Life and Culture," Ph.D. diss., Indiana University, 1984

Taher, Mohamed, *Studies in Librarianship*, 3 vols., New Delhi: Anmol, 1997; see especially vol. 3, *Islamic Librarianship*

Taher, Mohamed, and Donald Gordon Davis, *Librarianship and Library Science in India: An Outline of Historical Perspectives*, New Delhi: Concept, 1994

Jewish Collections and Jewish Libraries

Introduction

The literature that forms the nucleus of a Jewish collection was written over a period of more than 4,000 years. In 1947 the caves of Qumran yielded up the Dead Sea Scrolls, a 1,900-year-old library, which was most certainly not the first Jewish collection.

The Jews are known as "the people of the book" and have always been characterized by a high degree of literacy, even in those periods and places when the majority of their non-Jewish neighbors were illiterate. The aim of this article is to discuss a selection of major Jewish collections, past and present. The bibliography refers the reader to more comprehensive discussions.

Judaic Literature

The center of any collection of Jewish religious literature is, of course, the Pentateuch (the first five books of the Bible) together with its many commentaries. The Babylonian Talmud (which was edited and closed circa 500 C.E.) Tractate Baba Batra (leaves 14 and 15) discusses the canonization of the Jewish Bible (the Christian Old Testament), although the canon was probably established some time before. The Bible is complemented by the so-called oral law, basically a redaction of rabbinical discussions that includes the Mishnah, the Babylonian Talmud, and the Talmud of Jerusalem. There is additional exegetical literature. Jewish law and religious practice were later codified by Maimonides (1135–1204) and by Rabbi Joseph Caro (1448–1575). There are also rabbinical responsa, novellae on the Talmud, and ethical, philosophical, and mystical works. A minimum useful Jewish collection would number approximately 400 books.

Reverence and Aridity

Two major events in the last two centuries have influenced any academic consideration of Jewish collections. Religious Jews do not throw away sacred texts but either bury them or store them in a *genizah* in a synagogue. The *genizah* in the synagogue in Fustat (Cairo) yielded 210,000 fragments of parchment and printed material, including both sacred texts and everyday material of sociological significance, some of which date back to the 11th century C.E. In 1897 Solomon Schechter succeeded in transferring some 140,000 items to Cambridge University Library. The rest of the material is distributed among other major libraries.

In 1947 a Bedouin discovered an ancient library in a series of caves in the Qumran area near the Dead Sea. The 1947–48 period yielded 70 documents, including seven well-preserved scrolls. The last of the caves (Cave XI) was discovered in 1956. The main library was found to have been in Cave IV, which yielded approximately 589 manuscripts, of which 120 were Biblical manuscripts. An almost complete scroll of the Book of Isaiah dated to the second century B.C.E. was found in Cave I. It is believed that the library belonged to a sect, possibly the Essenes, that lived in the era between 125 B.C.E. and 68 C.E. Both collections survived because of Jewish reverence for the written word and the dry climate in the two areas.

The Invention of Printing

The first Hebrew books were printed within 35 years of the invention of printing, the first dated one being Rashi's commentary on the Pentateuch and Jacob ben Asher's Arba'ah Turim omf 1475. The first recorded printed edition of the Babylonian Talmud was in 1482 in Spain. The major edition was printed by Daniel Bomberg in Venice in 1520. This edition includes commentaries, and its layout was retained for most succeeding editions. Most editions of the Babylonian Talmud comprise 20 printed volumes and thousands of leaves. The most valuable parts of contemporary Jewish collections are manuscripts and incunabula, works printed before 1501.

Private Collections

Private collections are usually ephemeral. Most collectors tend to have more than one heir and the collection is often divided after death. In many cases, the heirs lack the collector's interest and dispose of the collections. Sometimes the collector prefers to sell or donate the collection to a major library to prevent it from being dispersed.

There are, however, extant catalogs of private collections. In her 1993 work on Italian Jews in the Renaissance, Shifra Baruchson analyzes 430 catalogs of private libraries prepared in Mantua in 1595 for submission to a censor appointed by the Catholic Church. She found printed books on a variety of subjects, including liturgy, the Bible, Jewish law, ethics, grammar, oral law, philosophy, literature, mysticism, and science.

The largest known private collection was built by Samuel Oppenheimer in the late 17th century and numbered approximately 7,000 printed volumes and 1,000 manuscripts, almost entirely Hebraica. It was acquired by the Bodleian Library (Oxford, United Kingdom) in 1829. Among important collections of the 20th century were the Sassoon library in England, which was broken up and sold, and the Weiner library on the history of anti-Semitism, which found its way to Tel-Aviv University in Israel. Professor Gershom Scholem bequeathed his 25,000 volumes on Jewish mysticism to the Jewish National and University Library (Jerusalem), where it is located in a separate reading room. The Chabad-Lubavich library in New York City ceased to be a private library in an interesting manner. The library belonged to the rebbe, or leader, of a Hassidic sect and was passed down from father to son. The sixth rebbe, Rabbi Yosef Yizhak Schneersohn, emigrated from the Soviet Union via Poland to the United States. Part of his library was confiscated by the Soviet authorities, but when he died in 1950 he left a very large collection. His son-in-law succeeded him as the head of the Chabad organization, but his brother was his personal heir and laid claim to the library. A New York court resolved the dispute, ruling that the library belonged to the Chabad organization and not to the rebbe personally.

Synagogues and Talmudical Seminaries

Many synagogues throughout the world have built up libraries for the use of their congregants. Most of these collections are relatively small, but one exception to this rule is the Yeshurun Synagogue in Jerusalem, which has an important library.

The *yeshivah* (talmudic seminary) is the center of traditional higher Jewish learning. Many orthodox Jewish youth spend some time in such an institution. Others devote their life to Jewish learning. A library is an essential part of any Yeshivah, but its collection tends to be limited to relevant material. In his work on *yeshivah*, Y. Aronson surveyed six of the major institutions in Israel. Ponevezh, a major ultra-orthodox *yeshivah* founded in 1944, had a collection of more than 40,000 volumes for a student body of some 950. Merkaz Harav, a modern orthodox *yeshivah* with a student body of 500, had some 20,000 volumes.

United States

The Hebraic Section of the Library of Congress (LC) was established in 1914 as part of the Division of Semitica and Oriental Literature. Its beginnings can be traced to Jacob H. Schiff's gift in 1912 of nearly 10,000 books and pamphlets from the private collection of Ephraim Deinard, a well-known bibliographer and bookseller.

In the years that followed this initial gift, the library has developed and expanded its Hebraic holdings to include all materials of research value in Hebrew and related languages. Today the section houses works in Hebrew, Yiddish, Ladino, Judeo-Persian, Judeo-Arabic, Aramaic, Syriac, Coptic, and Amharic. Holdings are especially strong in the areas of the Bible and rabbinics, liturgy, Hebrew language and literature, responsa, and Jewish history. Extensive collections of printed editions of Passover Haggadot have been assembled, as well as a comprehensive collection of Holocaust memorial volumes.

The Hebraic Section received a second major boost as a result of the enactment of Public Law 480 (PL-480) in 1958, through which 25 U.S. research libraries (including the LC) were supplied with a copy of virtually every book and journal of research value published in Israel. The PL-480 program for Israeli imprints, coordinated by the LC, lasted nine years, from 1964 to 1973, and provided each of the participating institutions with an average of 65,000 items over the course of the program.

Almost 150,000 items are housed in a stack area adjacent to the section and are available for examination by researchers and scholars. Housed among the 2,000 rarities in the special collections of the Hebraic section are cuneiform tablets, manuscripts, incunabula, *kettubot* (marriage contracts), micrographics, miniature books, and amulets. There are more than 200 Hebrew manuscripts and 39 incunabula in the library's collection. The general catalog can be found on the Internet at http://lcweb.loc.gov.

The Dorot Jewish Division of the New York Public Library (NYPL) is one of the greatest collections of Judaica in the world. The division was established as a distinct collection with funding contributed by Jacob Schiff in 1897, just two years after the formation of the NYPL. Abraham S. Freidus, cataloger of the Astor Library's rich collection of Judaica, was appointed the division's first chief and presided over its rapid growth for 25 years. The library's foundation for collections on Jewish subjects in Hebrew and other languages was provided by holdings from the Astor and Lenox libraries. This existing nucleus was quickly expanded by the acquisition of the private libraries of Leon Mandelstamm, Meyer Lehren, and Isaac Meyer, as well as some holdings of the Aguilar Free Library, a small public library operated by a group of philanthropic Jews in the 19th century, which merged with the NYPL in 1903.

Today the Dorot Jewish Division contains a comprehensive and balanced chronicle of the religious and secular history of the Jewish people in more than 250,000 books, microforms, manuscripts, newspapers, periodicals, and ephemera from all over the world. Approximately 40 percent of the division's holdings are in Hebrew characters and the remainder are in other languages, primarily English, German, Russian, and French. The collection has very few manuscripts but does include 40 incunabula. The basic catalog of the collection was published by G.K. Hall in 1960, with supplements in 1975 and 1981. Records of material cataloged after 1971 are available online through the Research Libraries Information Network (RLIN), WorldCat of the online bibliographic service OCLC, and CATNYP (NYPL's local system).

The Harvard University Library (Cambridge, Massachusetts) is the oldest library in the United States and the largest university library in the world. It acquired Ephraim Deinard's library in 1929, including 29 manuscripts and 15 incunabula. Widener Library, Harvard's main library building, contains one of the finest Middle East research collections in the world, the largest research collection of Israeli publications and Israel-related materials outside the state of Israel. Many of these publications are Hebrew materials issued in Israel (some 70,000 titles). Of special interest is a collection of modern Israeli ephemera, including most of the election propaganda issued by Israeli political parties. Widener Library collects materials in all languages published worldwide that relate to Israel. These collections cover all aspects of the Middle East and include printed materials, microforms, audiovisual materials, and electronic databases. The Harvard University Library *Catalog of Hebrew Books* was published in 1968 in 6 volumes. Today, the general university library catalog is available via the Web at http://hollis.harvard.edu.

The Jewish Theological Seminary of America (New York City) has a very rich collection. The manuscript collection includes more than 11,000 codices and 30,000 *genizah* fragments. There are more than 400 Pinkassim (record books) from Jewish communities and organizations throughout Europe, Africa, Asia, and North America, dating from the 16th to the 20th centuries. The scope of the collection of 20,000 early printed books includes practically the entire output of various

Hebrew presses in the 15th and 16th centuries. The library broadside collection comprises approximately 4,000 rare, fragile, and significant pieces spanning five centuries (the 16th century through the 20th) from many communities in Europe, Israel, and America. The library's online catalog may be found at www.jtsa.edu.

The Hebrew Union College (HUC), located in Cincinnati, Ohio, is the oldest Jewish seminary in the United States. The collection holds 5,000 manuscripts and 140 incunabula, as well as a special collection of liturgical music. The Birnbaum collection contains unique copies of liturgical scores created before 1840. Cities represented include the German cities of Hamburg, Braunschweig, Hanover, Magdeburg, Breslau, Stettin (now Szczecin, Poland) and Koenigsberg (now Kaliningrad, Russia). In addition, approximately 300 folio volumes give a nearly complete picture of liturgical as well as musical developments in central Europe during these years. The Birnbaum collection was acquired by HUC in 1918 during Librarian Adolph S. Oko's trip through Europe to buy Judaica for the expanding HUC library in Cincinnati. The library has a printed catalog, *Dictionary Catalog of the Klau Library, Cincinnati,* published in 1964 and available online at www.huc.edu.

The Mendel Gottesman Library of Hebraica/Judaica of Yeshiva University (New York City) houses one of the world's great Judaic research collections. The collection consists of more than 200,000 volumes in a variety of languages, dating from the 15th century to the present day and including 600 manuscripts and 41 incunabula. The library maintains more than 700 current journal and newspaper subscriptions and includes 20,000 retrospective periodical volumes. The catalog is available online at www.yu.edu.

The YIVO Library of the YIVO Institute for Jewish Research (New York City) is a special library collecting material in or about Yiddish. It contains more than 350,000 volumes. The YIVO archives hold more than 22 million documents, photographs, recordings, posters, films, videotapes, and other artifacts. Together they comprise the world's largest collection of materials related to the history and culture of East European and American Jewry. YIVO has the foremost collection of books and documents written in Yiddish. The archives and library's holdings, however, also include many works in English, French, German, Hebrew, Ladino, Polish, and Russian. Its online catalog is available at www.yivoinstitute.org/archlib/archlib_fr.htm.

Other U.S. libraries with significant Jewish collections include Brandeis University (Waltham, Massachusetts), the University of California in Los Angeles, and Columbia (New York), Stanford (California), and Yale (New Haven, Connecticut) Universities.

United Kingdom

The British Library (BL) collection (formerly the British Museum Library), in addition to a substantial collection of Hebrew books, has approximately 3,000 Hebrew manuscripts and some 150 incunabula. The collection was originally based on a gift of books by Salomon da Costa in 1759. Items of special interest include autographed responsa by Maimonides and a rich Karaite collection. The library's catalog of Hebrew books was prepared by Joseph Zedner in 1867 (*Catalogue of the Hebrew Books in the Library of the British Museum*). The general catalog of the BL is accessible via the Internet at www.bl.uk.

The Bodleian Library at Oxford University includes among its Hebrew collection some 3,000 Hebrew manuscripts and 67 Hebrew incunabula. Almost 50 percent of its Hebrew language holdings (including some 1,600 manuscripts) originated in two private collections, that of Rabbi David Oppenheimer (purchased in 1829) and the collection of Heiman Michael of Hamburg (purchased in 1849). The latter collection includes *The Elephantine Papyri* discovered at the end of the 19th century and some 10,000 genizah documents. The manuscripts were first cataloged by Adolf Neubauer and Arthur Cowley in *Catalogue of the Hebrew Manuscripts in the Bodleian Library,* which was republished in 1994 with a supplement by Malachi Beit-Arie. Cowley published a catalog of the books in the library in 1929, which was followed in 1931 by a second catalog by Steinschneider, the famous bibliographer.

The Jewish collection at Cambridge University is of special interest because it includes some 140,000 fragments from the Cairo Genizah. It has approximately 1,000 other Hebrew manuscripts, and its catalog, *The Hebrew Manuscripts at Cambridge University: a Description and Introduction,* by Stefan C. Reif, appeared only in 1997.

Jews' College in London received the private library of Moses Montefiore (initially on loan) in 1898, which included 586 manuscripts. Its collection today includes 700 manuscripts and 8 incunabula. Other libraries of interest in the United Kingdom include the university library of Leeds and the University of Manchester, John Rylands Library.

Israel

The World of Learning, 1999 lists seven libraries in Israel with more than 250,000 volumes. These libraries have the following volumes and current serials holdings, respectively: the Weizmann Institute (Rehovot), 250,000 and 1,450; Ben-Gurion University (Beer Sheva), 720,000 and 5,000; the University of Haifa, 780,00 and 8,000; Bar-Ilan University (Ramat Gan), 850,000 and 4,500; Tel-Aviv University, 880,000 and 4,800; Technion (Haifa), 900,000 and 5,000; National Library/Hebrew University (Jerusalem), 4 million and 15,000. (Note that all the major libraries serve as university libraries. The central Internet site for these libraries is libnet.ac.il.)

Of the university libraries, the Jewish National and University Library and the Wurzweiler Library of Bar-Ilan University specialize in Judaica. The Maimonides Library, affiliated with the Tel-Aviv municipal library, also has an important Judaica collection. Other prominent libraries include the library affiliated with the Chief Rabbinate, the Kook Institute Library, the Ben-Zvi Institute Library (specializing in the history of the land of Israel) and the Yad Vashem Library (specializing in the Holocaust), which are all located in Jerusalem.

Other Countries

Among the libraries with Judaica collections, the National Library of Russia, St. Petersburg, is known for its great collection of Hebrew manuscripts and has the richest collection of Karaite material in the world. The manuscripts were photographed, and the microfilms are available in the Jewish National and University Library in Israel. Denmark's Royal Library (Copenhagen) includes the Bibliotheca Simonseniana. The Bibliothèque nationale de France (Paris) has an important Jewish collection, as does the Vatican Library in Rome. The Bibliotheca Rosenthaliana (whose nucleus was donated by the heirs of Leeser Rosenthal of Hannover) at the University of Amsterdam was described in the *Catalog der Hebraica und Judaica*, compiled by Mayer Roest (1875; reprint 1966).

CHAIM SEYMOUR

See also Jewish National and University Library

Catalogs of Hebrew Collections

Beit-Arié, Malachi, compiler, *Catalogue of the Hebrew Manuscripts in the Bodleian Library: Supplement of Addenda and Corrigenda to Vol. 1 (A. Neubauer's Catalogue)*, edited by R.A. May, Oxford: Clarendon Press, 1994

Cowley, Arthur E., compiler, *A Concise Catalogue of the Hebrew Printed Books in the Bodleian Library*, Oxford: Clarendon Press, 1929

Dan, Yosef, et al., compilers, *The Gershom Scholem Library in Jewish Mysticism*, 2 vols., Jerusalem: The Hebrew University, 1999

Harvard University Library, *Catalogue of Hebrew Books*, 6 vols., Cambridge, Massachusetts: Harvard University Library, 1968

Hirschfeld, Hartwig, compiler, *Catalogue of the Hebrew MSS of the Montefiore Library and of the Hebrew Manuscripts in the Jews' College, London*, London: Gregg International, 1904; reprint, Farnborough, Hampshire: Gregg International, 1969

Klau Library, *Dictionary Catalog of the Klau Library, Cincinnati*, 32 vols., Boston: G.K. Hall, 1964

Neubauer, Adolf, and Arthur E. Cowley, compilers, *Catalogue of the Hebrew Manuscripts in the Bodleian Library and in the College Libraries of Oxford*, 3 vols., Oxford: Clarendon Press, 1886–1906; reprint, 1 vol., Oxford and New York: Clarendon Press, 1994

New York Public Library Reference Department, *Dictionary Catalog of the Jewish Collection*, 14 vols, Boston: G.K. Hall, 1960

Reif, Stefan C., et al., compilers, *Hebrew Manuscripts at Cambridge University Library: A Description and Introduction*, Cambridge: Cambridge University Press, 1997

Roest, M., compiler, *Catalog der Hebraica und Judaica aus der L. Rosenthal'schen Bibliothek*, 2 vols., Amsterdam: Clausen, 1875; reprint, Amsterdam: Israël, 1966

Steinschneider, M., compiler, *Catalogus Librorum Hebraeorum in Bibliotheca Bodleiana*, 2nd edition, 3 vols., Berlin: Welt-Verlag, 1931

Van Straalen, Samuel, compiler, *Catalogue of the Hebrew Books in the British Museum Acquired during the Years 1868–1892*, London: British Museum, 1894; reprint, Hildesheim, Germany, and New York: Olms, 1977

Zedner, Joseph, compiler, *Catalogue of the Hebrew Books in the Library of the British Museum*, London: Wertheimer Lea, 1867

Further Reading

Aronson, Y., "Yeshivah Libraries in Israel," *Judaica Librarianship* 6, nos. 1–2 (1991–92)

Baruchson, Shifra, *Sefarim ve-kor'im: Tarbut ha-keri'ah shel Yehude Italyah be-shilhe ha-Renesans* (Books and Readings: Reading Habits of Italian Jews in the Renaissance Period), Ramat-Gan, Israel: Bar-Ilan University Press, 1993

Faber, S., "Judaica Libraries and Literature," in *Encyclopedia of Library and Information Science*, edited by Allen Kent et al., vol. 13, New York: Dekker, 1968

Gaster, Theodor H., editor, *The Dead Sea Scriptures in English Translation*, Garden City, New York: Doubleday, 1956; 3rd edition, Garden City, New York: Anchor Press, 1976

Gold, Leonard Singer, editor, *A Sign and a Witness: 2,000 Years of Hebrew Books and Illuminated Manuscripts*, New York: The New York Public Library and Oxford University Press, 1988

Halivni, David Weiss, *The Book and the Sword: A Life of Learning in the Shadow of Destruction*, New York: Farrar Straus and Giroux, 1996

Posner, Raphael, and Israel Ta-Shema, editors, *The Hebrew Book: An Historical Survey*, Jerusalem: Keter, and New York: Amiel, 1975

Rabinowicz, Harry M., *The Jewish Literary Treasures of England and America*, New York: Yoseloff, 1962

Steinzaltz, Adin, *The Essential Talmud*, translated by Chaya Galai, Jerusalem: Edanim and New York: Basic Books, 1976

Vermès, Géza, *The Dead Sea Scrolls in English*, Baltimore: Penguin, 1962; 4th edition, Sheffield, South Yorkshire: Sheffield Academic Press, 1995

Land-Grant University Libraries

The democratic impulses that brought land-grant universities into existence in the mid-19th-century United States resulted in a new type of higher education in the country. Older colleges had grown out of mostly Protestant interests in educating clergy and in preparing men to become capable merchants, responsible citizens, and ambassadors for dominant national values. Professional emphases incorporated law, medicine, and theology. Except for the arrival of women's colleges and coeducation, the central functions of higher education remained relatively unchanged from their inception until the birth of land-grant colleges, seminar instruction, and graduate research programs in the latter part of the 19th century. Ivy league schools such as Harvard, Yale, Princeton, and Columbia Universities, along with scores of midwestern liberal arts colleges, had been defining higher education for decades. As an alternative, the land-grant universities—73 in number—initiated new programs in technology and agriculture and supplied fresh pedagogical perspectives in the context of expanding economic and social purposes.

The Land-Grant Act of 1862, known commonly as the Morrill Act after Representative (and later Senator) Justin Smith Morrill of Vermont, was the first of several laws that established and expanded programs of higher learning for students in agricultural, industrial, and technical fields. While the land-grants developed technical expertise for the Industrial Age, they did much more. By making higher education accessible to agricultural interests, they greatly expanded opportunities for the rising middle classes by merging the powerful symbols of the independent yeoman farmer and the self-made man. Frederick Rudolph, in his 1962 history of U.S. higher education, concluded that land-grant universities held a "romantic regard for the farm but a hard-headed regard for the factory" thus achieving "as perhaps no other institution, a symbolic value for a democratic society."

The states varied widely in taking advantage of the opportunities afforded by land-grant legislation. Some expanded the functions of existing private or public colleges by providing them with land while others created new institutions with or without private benefactors. Lack of structural uniformity among land-grant institutions resulted in a typology of schools still evident in the 21st century. Such distinctions are in some instances little more than minor bureaucratic details; in other instances they became major features of institutional culture with strong determinants for library development. Most historians of land-grant university libraries concur that structural variations, in combination with related factors, lie at the very heart of why land-grant university libraries tend to be, with notable exceptions, among the least well-funded of U.S. academic libraries.

Neither the compelling ideals nor the legislative mandates inaugurating land-grant institutions were intended to result in the exclusion of the arts, humanities, and basic sciences. While many land-grant colleges focused on applied science, industrial education, and agriculture, failing to develop broad course offerings for several years or even decades after they were founded, a small corps created strong humanities and social sciences programs from the beginning. These institutions adopted broad perspectives from their earliest days, thus creating local cultures that required strong library development. Such growth was characterized by the accumulation of rich retrospective collections, early implementation of organized reference services, a heightened professional consciousness among library workers, and budgetary commitments tied to departmental collections and graduate research interests. During the last quarter of the 19th century and the first quarter of the 20th, when the broad outlines of research libraries began to take shape, a small group of land-grant university libraries emerged as national leaders with overall collection size as the essential if not the sole criterion for significance. Even today such schools maintain preeminence. Table 1 identifies the top four land-grant libraries, identifying raw numbers and rankings from data compiled on the 100 university library members of the Association of Research Libraries (ARL).

The third-ranked research library by collection size, the University of Illinois at Urbana-Champaign, follows only Harvard and Yale. While the Universities of Illinois, California, Cornell, and Wisconsin along with others including Minnesota and Ohio State have risen to national prominence based on multiple criteria, such institutions are more exceptional than representative.

Twenty-one states adopted a different model, one that tailored curricula to more tightly defined objectives. These schools emphasized industrial and mechanical education, which expanded rapidly by the 1890s and was complemented by instruction, extension services, and laboratory research in such basic and applied disciplines as agronomy, animal husbandry, botany, chemistry, farm management, horticulture, plant pathol-

Table 1
Land-Grant Universities Arranged by Four ARL Criteria in 1997

University Library	Volumes (rank)	Current Serials (rank)	Total Expenditures (rank)	Total FTE Staff (rank)
Illinois, U-C	9,300,000 (3)	90,900 (3)	$26,700,000 (18)	514 (13)
California	8,900,000 (4)	79,440 (4)	$38,000,000 (6)	603 (6)
Cornell	6,448,000 (11)	62,075 (8)	$32,000,000 (10)	567 (9)
Wisconsin	5,962,000 (14)	40,000 (20)	$29,862,000 (15)	538 (11)

Source: "Rank Order Tables of University Libraries 1996–97" in *ARL Statistics 1998/99*, comp. by Martha Kyrillidou and Michael O'Conner (Washington, D.C.: ARL, 2000), pp. 24-39, 32-37, 40-44, 54-56. Parenthetical numbers refer to ARL rankings of university libraries.

ogy, and veterinary medicine. Most universities in this category did not substantially strengthen scientific curricula until the 20th century, and they did not dramatically expand the social sciences and humanities until the enrollment explosions of the 1950s and 1960s. These schools have in common the existence of another state university (with strong curricula in law, medicine, and the humanities) with which they compete for state-level support. The top three libraries in this category are presented in Table 2.

Still a third type of land-grant college was developed in 17 other institutions, Historically Black Colleges and Universities (HBCUs). They provide many of the same programs of instruction, research, and service as their better-funded counterparts. See Table 3 for the three largest according to collection size.

By virtually any standard, the University of Illinois at Urbana-Champaign has emerged as the premier land-grant university library. To have created the largest library at a public university is a signal achievement in its own right, but it heralds much more. It involves, either as determinants or as by-products of collection growth, strong development in a wide range of library services. Thus Illinois demonstrated leadership in automation, shared resources, archives management, faculty-librarian cooperation, scholarly production by professional staff, the development of support for library projects, and a number of other areas. The library has further benefited from synergy with a fine school of library and information science. In a unique way the library system at Illinois has become a major resource of the university, essential to faculty and student recruiting and a vital feature of the university's public image, facts fully understood by Illinois administrators as well as by university constituents throughout the nation.

The foundations for a strong library were put in place by three librarians, all of whom directed the library and the library school simultaneously: Katharine Lucinda Sharp (1897–1907), Phineas L. Windsor (1909–40), and Robert B. Downs (1943–71). Downs, in particular, became adept at obtaining specialized libraries from booksellers and private collectors and at expanding funds for continued acquisitions. Librarian-faculty collaboration resulted in strong retrospective holdings in classical languages and literature, 19th- and 20th-century English and American literature, economic history, the history of science, Latin American history, and Middle Eastern history in addition to specialized holdings pertaining to John Milton, William Shakespeare, and H.G. Wells.

Counterparts built rich collections as well. The University of California, Berkeley, distinguished itself for historical collections focusing on the United States West Coast and Latin America as well as China, Japan, and East Asia. Donald Coney served as director during the years of unprecedented growth, 1945 to 1968. At Cornell the first president, Andrew Dixon White, collaborated with the first librarian, Daniel Willard Fiske (1868–83), an accomplished linguist and former diplomat whose wide-ranging interests in the humanities formed the nucleus for the university's great collections. Special strengths include U.S. history, drama, German literature and history, languages and literature generally, and Scandinavian materials (including Icelandic). The University of Wisconsin, Madison, is equally distinguished, benefiting not only from a strong library school but also close proximity to the library of the Wisconsin State Historical Society, which developed rich complementary collections. Wisconsin has specialized in collecting ephemera from political and social radical and reform movements, collections that support curricular strengths at Madison. While all of these institutions developed holdings of rare depth in humanistic disciplines, they have not neglected the creation of extensive research collections in the sciences and social sciences.

National-level leadership for the land-grant libraries was provided by Charles Harvey Brown, library director at Iowa State University from 1922 to 1946. Brown was a forthright spokesman on behalf of the library's central purposes: to provide

Table 2
Land-Grant Universities with a Comprehensive Public University in the Same State Arranged by Four ARL Criteria in 1997

University Library	Volumes (rank)	Current Serials (rank)	Total Expenditures (rank)	Total FTE Staff (rank)
Michigan State	4,272,000 (26)	27,314 (43)	$18,184,000 (44)	304 (46)
North Carolina State	2,829,000 (54)	35,082 (27)	$19,631,000 (40)	316 (43)
Texas A&M	2,646,000 (60)	36,632 (26)	$19,800,000 (39)	412 (21)

Ibid, 52–55, 57, 63, 72.

Table 3
Three Historically Black Land-Grant Colleges and Universities Ranked by Library Collection Size

University Library	Volumes	Current Serials	Total Expenditures	Total FTE Staff
Southern University, Baton Rouge	1,396,602	1,967	NA	44
Florida A&M	551,271	5,501	$4,106,363	63
N. Carolina A&T	448,769	3,972	$3,726,787	52

Source: Compiled from *American Library Directory 1999–2000.* New York, R. R. Bowker, 1999.

the reading materials essential for research and instruction and to offer the aid necessary to ensure the effective use of such materials. Brown, like Robert B. Downs, contributed much to the professional literature, including the library portion of the *Survey of Land-Grant Colleges and Universities* (1930), a massive compilation assembled by Arthur J. Klein, chief of the Division of Higher Education in the United States Bureau of Education. Brown directed a committee that created a 70-page questionnaire that drew a response rate of 98 percent. He concluded that even though the separate land-grants (including Iowa State) focused on strong user services and current serial holdings, almost half of them held fewer than one-fourth of 21 basic science journals. He observed a wide gap between nine or ten leading land-grant libraries and the remainder, which lacked collections adequate to their needs.

Brown was well respected by the deans and presidents with whom he worked, and he enlarged his circle of influence to include librarians, educators, and higher education administrators throughout the nation. Downs credited Brown's influence with the University of Illinois faculty in helping secure his appointment as library director in 1943. Brown was active in creating the Association of College and Research Libraries, securing relative independence for it and keeping it under the umbrella of the American Library Association. He was a powerful voice for librarian-faculty partnerships and high standards for professional staff.

Following World War II, higher education underwent major expansion as returning veterans entered college in record numbers. They and their progeny 20 years later set colleges and universities on a period of extended growth that would not end until economic dislocations in the 1970s. During this time land-grant curricula across the nation became fully comprehensive and began to make ever higher demands on local library resources. The land-grant libraries embraced a wide range of responses that included user instruction in the 1970s, online searching in the 1980s, and strong consortial arrangements during the entire period. Economic recession hindered retrospective collection growth in both the early 1980s and the early 1990s.

By the last decade of the 20th century, personal computing had combined with Internet technology to offer research libraries the hope of vastly distributed resources. The concept of "just-in-time" rather than "just-in-case" began to take hold in the thinking of collection management librarians, and document delivery emerged as an attractive alternative to the building of prohibitively expensive retrospective collections. Echoing Charles Harvey Brown, land-grant librarians urged new criteria for measuring the quality of research libraries, criteria grounded as much in effectiveness of service as in overall collection size. The rise of digital libraries expanded access to intellectual content, further underscoring the special niche of land-grant institutions: reaching out to new constituencies in a technical environment that offers not necessarily the promise but certainly the possibility of educational and economic opportunity through the democratizing aspects of rapidly growing information technologies.

JOHN MARK TUCKER

Further Reading

Cross, Coy F., II, *Justin Smith Morrill: Father of the Land-Grant Colleges,* East Lansing: Michigan State University Press, 1999

Davis, Donald G., Jr., and John Mark Tucker, "Change and Tradition in Land-Grant University Libraries," in *For the Good of the Order: Essays in Honor of Edward G. Holley,* edited by Delmus E. Williams et al., Greenwich, Connecticut: Jai Press, 1994

Eddy, Edward Danforth, Jr., *Colleges for Our Land and Time: The Land-Grant Idea in American Education,* New York: Harper, 1957 (includes a list of land-grant university libraries)

Ernest, Douglas J., *Agricultural Frontier to Electronic Frontier: A History of Colorado State University Libraries, 1870–1995,* Fort Collins: Colorado State University, 1996

Ernest, Douglas J., "Historiography and the Land-Grant University Library," *Advances in Librarianship* 22 (1998)

Higley, Georgia Metos, "Women Librarians at the Western Land-Grant Colleges," in *Reclaiming the American Library Past: Writing the Women In,* edited by Suzanne Hildenbrand, Norwood, New Jersey: Ablex, 1996

Holley, Edward G., *The Land-Grant Movement and the Development of Academic Libraries: Some Tentative Explorations,* College Station: Texas A & M University Libraries, 1977

Rouse, Roscoe, Jr., *A History of the Oklahoma State University Library,* Stillwater: Oklahoma State University, 1992

Rudolph, Frederick, *The American College and University: A History,* New York: Knopf, 1962; reprint, with new introduction and supplemental bibliography, Athens: University of Georgia Press, 1990

Smith, Jessie Carney, "Patterns of Growth in Library Resources in Certain Land-Grant Universities," Ph.D. diss., University of Illinois, 1964

Unger, Harlow G., *Encyclopedia of American Education,* 3 vols., New York: Facts on File, 1996; see especially vol. 2 (includes a list of land-grant university libraries)

U.S. Dept. of the Interior, Office of Education, *Survey of Land-Grant Colleges and Universities,* 2 vols., Washington, D.C.: GPO, 1930

Wiegand, Wayne A., editor, *Leaders in American Academic Librarianship, 1925–1975,* Pittsburgh, Pennsylvania: Beta Phi Mu, 1983

Latin American National Libraries

Introduction

The first national libraries in Latin America (here defined as encompassing the entire Western Hemisphere south of the United States and Canada) were established in the early 19th century after the wars of independence from Spain (although those of Colombia and Ecuador trace their origins back to the 18th century) and thus will soon celebrate their bicentennials. The newest, in Jamaica, dates from 1979.

Although this dictionary contains separate accounts of the largest national libraries (Argentina, Brazil, Chile, Mexico, and Venezuela), as well as an essay discussing Cuba, one focusing on the Caribbean, and another dealing with five libraries in Central America, it is worthwhile to look at them as a group. Despite variations in history, operations, and place among national cultural institutions, they do share many common characteristics and face similar problems.

This entry is limited to 25 libraries, designated as or functioning as the national library in the following countries: Argentina, Barbados, Belize, Bolivia, Brazil, Chile, Colombia, Costa Rica, Cuba, the Dominican Republic, Ecuador, El Salvador, Guatemala, Guyana, Haiti, Honduras, Jamaica, Mexico, Nicaragua, Panama, Paraguay, Peru, Trinidad and Tobago, Uruguay, and Venezuela. The purpose of this article is not to present dates and statistics on individual institutions but rather to give the reader a general overview of all the national libraries in the region with emphasis on their similarities, which of course may vary in degree. To many of the general statements appearing below, one or more libraries may be exceptions. Space limitations permitted the selection of only a few aspects of their structure and operations: founding, place in the government, collections, personnel, finance, and information technology. Another section covers their new association, the Asociación de Bibliotecas Nacionales de Iberoamérica (ABINIA).

History and Place in Government

All but two of the 25 institutions in Latin America were founded as or became national libraries in the period between the Napoleonic Wars and World War II. Thus they belong to what has been called "the second generation," as they came after and differ from the 20 or so "first generation" national libraries, which came into being before 1801 in western Europe and the United States as outgrowths of royal libraries or private collections purchased for the nation.

With few exceptions, the concept of the national library in Latin America related to democratic ideals, and these libraries were often proposed and encouraged by intellectuals as national and public libraries open to all potential users. It is doubtful that these leaders realized that, in time, the chief users would not be "intelligent laypersons" but students from primary, secondary, and tertiary level institutions. Although the five libraries in English-speaking countries did not, in some cases, lose their public library function, they too stem from a philosophy of "open to all."

The founding dates of 25 Latin American national libraries can be outlined as follows: pre-1800: Colombia, Ecuador; 1810–50: Argentina, Barbados, Bolivia, Brazil, Chile, Mexico, Peru, Uruguay, Venezuela; 1851–1900: Costa Rica, El Salvador, Guatemala, Honduras, Nicaragua, Panama, Paraguay; 1901–50: Belize, Cuba, Guyana, Haiti; 1951–99: Dominican Republic, Jamaica; not available: Trinidad and Tobago.

Latin American national libraries have generally been placed in ministries or departments responsible for culture or education, and over the years some libraries have been transferred from one to the other more than once. A more recent trend has been to establish national cultural councils with greater autonomy for managing programs in the arts, museums, libraries, national heritage groups, and even sports. Two libraries, those of Brazil and Venezuela, have become independent agencies and fall outside of this structure. In Mexico the national library was attached to the national university in 1929 as a part of the Institute of Bibliographic Research. Another unique case is that of Trinidad and Tobago, where the National Heritage Library is a joint operation of the Central Library of Trinidad and Tobago and the Trinidad Public Library.

By tradition the director of a national library in Latin America is not a librarian or bibliographer but an important cultural figure—historian, writer, educator (for example, Jorge Luis Borges in Argentina). The deputy director, at least toward the end of the 20th century, was frequently a trained librarian, but in smaller countries it is no longer unusual to see a leading librarian in the post of director.

In most countries the staff consists of civil servants, who fall into such categories as professional, administrative, and custodial. Total staff may reach several hundred persons as in Brazil, Mexico, and Venezuela. Of 17 libraries for which statistics are available, eight have staffs of more than 100, whereas nine have fewer than 100. Salaries at all levels are often lower than in the private sector or even in government agencies. For professional librarians in almost every country, special and university libraries offer higher remuneration, leading to considerable turnover. There are many longtime employees with on-the-job training, often with good results.

Collections

National library collections vary greatly in size. Six institutions have more than one million volumes, whereas an equal number have fewer than 100,000. A middle group (half of the total) claim holdings between 100,000 and 1 million volumes. In most cases these are minimum figures, because newspapers and periodicals form separate departments (*hemeroteca*), with statistics giving holdings in number of titles rather than volumes or volume equivalents. Nearly all institutions have nonbook and audiovisual materials, as well as some in electronic form available through the Internet. Brazil now reports its total holdings as 8.5 million units in all formats.

In all countries, resources are overwhelmingly national in character, having come through legal deposit, which means that most items were published in the 19th and 20th centuries; some libraries (including Mexico) have extensive holdings of colonial imprints. Although only two countries lack a law of legal deposit, nearly all national librarians find that compliance leaves much to be desired; some believe as much as one-fourth to one-third of the national production fails to arrive. Remedial steps are both costly and time-consuming, but some success results from efforts to identify the library as custodian of "the national memory." Revisions in the law are bringing audiovisual and electronic materials into the scope of legal deposit.

As a result of the dependence on legal deposit of national publications, the number of foreign imprints forms a relatively low percentage of holdings, even for materials from neighboring countries. Gifts of current imprints from the cultural sections of foreign embassies (especially those of the United Kingdom, France, Spain, and the United States) partially compensate for the lack of purchases. These titles, however, are almost always in the humanities and social sciences, rarely in science and technology, and almost never include serials. Some gifts come from U.S. and European universities with programs of Latin American studies.

Every national library appears to have received bequests of several private libraries formed by writers, politicians, and bibliophiles. In most cases these volumes remain separate and are housed in a room with a portrait or bust of the donor. For such collections, a catalog or inventory is available, and the room is usually open a few hours a week to qualified researchers. Some of these libraries have a special emphasis or subject strength, but most are eclectic.

Exchange programs with both national and foreign libraries are common. A significant number of U.S. government publications have come through Smithsonian exchange, but in general the national libraries have failed to exploit this source, often owing to lack of staff, the miscellaneous nature of items they can utilize, and a lack of specific goals for the program.

Funds for acquisition of new materials are severely limited—a few libraries have no budget at all (the assumption being that everything needed will come through legal deposit). Priorities go to building up reference and bibliographical resources. Overall, it is difficult to determine the full nature and extent of these national collections because there are few guides, descriptions, and subject catalogs. Even in countries where the national library is not the largest collection (Argentina, Jamaica, Costa Rica), its holdings are the country's best for national history, literature, and culture. Current journals in science and technology are more commonly received by university and research institute libraries.

In recent years national libraries have become aware of the deterioration of some volumes, especially in 19th-century and later imprints. The larger institutions have succeeded in mounting conservation and preservation programs, and grants from international organizations such as the Organization of American States (OAS) and the United Nations Educational, Scientific, and Cultural Organization (UNESCO) have aided in setting up conservation laboratories and in training staff.

Finance

Although without exception these national libraries are financed almost entirely by public funds, it is almost impossible to make comparisons in the level of support owing to incomplete data, differences in purchasing power of the national currency and in the effects of inflation, variation in accounting systems, and failure to separate capital and operating expenditures. Nevertheless, there appears to be a general consensus among informed observers that these libraries are acutely underfunded. There is, however, little agreement on how budgets might be increased as prospects for more money from governments do not appear bright for several reasons. In some countries priority must go to reconstruction needed after natural disasters (as in El Salvador), while in others (for example, Argentina) the economy is stagnant. Where new buildings are needed (as in Bolivia and Honduras), capital expenditures may take priority over increased operating budgets.

Private sources may include the creation of friends groups, but their contributions would probably be modest in size. Setting up a foundation may provide a vehicle for obtaining gifts from both corporations and individuals. Campaigns for gifts in kind (i.e., books and computers) are sometimes suggested, but results have been disappointing as the materials donated are often outdated or unsuitable. As most private gifts are uncoordinated, their contribution to overall needs may not justify fund-raising efforts. Large-scale development plans made by outside experts (for example, the Master Plan for Argentina's national library), while appealing on a theoretical basis, may be too ambitious in the real world.

Gifts and grants from foreign overseas development agencies (such as the Agency for International Development and the Swedish International Development Agency), foundations, and other nongovernmental organizations usually support only specific projects, at present weighted heavily in favor of information technology and conservation. Nevertheless, the Lampadia Foundation and its subsidiaries in Argentina, Brazil, and Chile are aiding the national libraries in those three republics; the Mellon Foundation has made a substantial grant to the National Library of Chile and has helped in training some staff in four of the Central American countries; and the Council on Library and Information Resources has supported conservation work at the National Library of Venezuela. Grant-making agencies, however, sometimes fail to realize that large projects (such as creation of a complete online catalog) depend on a bibliographical infrastructure that may be inadequate; this is especially true of institutions in smaller, poorer, and technologically less-developed nations.

Other proposals to secure more money through required purchase of library cards and fee-for-service activities may not be compatible with government regulations prohibiting agencies from retaining revenue from services provided. Circumventing this through outside contractors has, in some cases, been quite unsatisfactory.

Information Technology

Information technology, over the past couple of decades, has proven to be a double-edged sword for most of the national libraries of Latin America. Although there have been some notable successes (including Chile and Venezuela), in many other cases the results have been disappointing. At the outset of the period, few libraries had staff capable of understanding the background for technology applications. This situation often left libraries at the mercy of commercial vendors and high-priced consultants that did not necessarily have the library's best interests at heart. The wheel was often reinvented.

One of the problems that arose was the failure to comprehend that computer systems, unlike earlier equipment, have a short life span. The costs of keeping current with the latest versions of operating systems has had unanticipated financial consequences, requiring cuts in other parts of a budget already stretched thin to cover basic expenditures. National libraries in smaller and poorer countries lack books, staff, space, and money. They must, at least to some extent, meet these requirements before plunging into projects requiring computer equipment and technicians in information science.

The result has been that failures outweigh successes, projects remain incomplete, cost overruns occur, and information technology staff have little or no comprehension of library functions. Unfinished projects abound, yet new proposals flood in. Outside experts, consultants, and foundations (especially those in the United States) fail to realize that the "bibliographical infrastructure" in some (but not all) countries remains insufficient for computerization without a larger investment in the overall institution.

Cooperation among the National Libraries

For many years contacts among the Latin American national libraries, even between neighboring countries, was limited and sporadic. In 1989 that changed dramatically with the founding of the Association of Ibero-American National Libraries (Asociación de Bibliotecas Nationales de Iberoamérica, or ABINIA) with the following objectives: (1) to make both public and governmental agencies aware of the importance of bibliographic and documentary treasures of the member countries; (2) to adopt policies, strategies, standards, and training programs for the preservation of national library collections; (3) to adopt compatible technical standards that would guarantee bibliographic control and facilitate exchange of material and information on automation and information systems; (4) to develop national and regional reference resources that would encourage research and exchange of information and to link national libraries with other libraries and information systems; (5) to disseminate information on collections via catalogs, publications, and exhibitions; (6) to support academic and other training programs for updating and improving human resources; and (7) to gather and keep up-to-date information about Ibero-American national libraries.

Membership has grown to include all 17 national libraries in the Spanish-speaking countries of the Western Hemisphere and Brazil, as well as the national libraries of Spain and Portugal; it does not include Haiti or any of the libraries in the English-speaking countries in the Caribbean.

In its first decade the association made important progress in reaching these goals, including publication of a volume of histories of the member libraries; collection of statistical data on the libraries' collections, finances, personnel; and compilation of a union catalog of more than 180,000 books published from the 16th century to 1850. Additional projects are in progress.

The association operates through an annual general assembly, a council of directors, and a secretariat located in one of the member libraries. ABINIA also maintains a website.

As the older Latin American national libraries approach their bicentennials, they (and their younger sisters) must balance the use of information technology with their roles as "repositories of the national memory."

Strategic plans for each library could be helpful, but they must be realistic and include prioritized goals with realistic time frames. They must cover development of print, audiovisual, and electronic resources while securing compliance with legal deposit laws and balance services to present users with preservation for the future; these plans will also require improvement in staffing. Equally, if not more, important will be overcoming the gap between budgets and fiscal needs through government and private income sources and balancing the desire to upgrade technology with a realistic assessment of the national ability to change.

In October 2000 the U.S. Library of Congress sponsored an important meeting in Washington, D.C. This symposium, "National Libraries of the World: Interpreting the Past, Shaping the Future," brought together more than 150 scholars and librarians to consider the significance, influence, and future of national libraries. Although few countries from Latin America were represented, the ramifications, particularly those concerning digital strategies, will undoubtedly influence library development in the region.

The national libraries of Latin America have, over time, accomplished a great deal with limited resources. With planning and diligence, progress can continue in the 21st century.

WILLIAM VERNON JACKSON

See also Caribbean Libraries; Central American National Libraries; Luis Angel Arango Library; National Library of Brazil; National Library of Chile; National Library of Cuba, José Martí; National Library of Mexico; National Library of the Republic of Argentina; National Library of Venezuela

Further Reading

Biblioteca Nacional de Venezuela, *Diagnóstico bibliotecas nacionales latinoamericanas afiliadas a ABINIA, año 1993*, Caracas: ABINIA, 1994

Cornish, Graham P., *The Role of National Libraries in the New Information Environment*, Paris: UNESCO, 1991

Ferguson, Stephney, "Defining a Role for a New National Library in a Developing Country: The National Library of Jamaica, 1980–1990," *Alexandria* 8, no. 1 (1996)

Gómez, Gonzalo Pérez, and Miguel Ángel Pérez Villaneuva, *Historia de las bibliotecas en Mexico*, Mexico City: SEP, Dirección General de Bibliotecas, 1986–

Historia de las bibliotecas nacionales de Iberoamérica: Pasado y presente, 2nd edition, Mexico City: Universidad Nacional Autónoma de México, 1995

Peltier-Davis, Cheryl, "Public Libraries as National Libraries—The Caribbean Experience," *Alexandria* 9, no. 3 (1997)

Zamora, Rosa Maria Fernandez de, and Clara Budnik, "Looking After the Bibliographic Heritage of Latin America," *Alexandria* 13, no. 1 (2001)

Law and Legislative Research Libraries

By definition, a *law library* is a specialized library defined by its subject matter—its functions, collections, and services are determined by the nature of legal information and research. *Legislative reference service* is assistance given by a library to government agencies and to a legislature, especially in problems of political administration and in connection with proposed or pending legislation. Within library functions at the state or national level, such assistance sometimes includes the drafting and indexing of bills.

Origins

The nature of law and the need of practitioners to have access to its written sources has supported the development of large legal collections throughout the ages, from Justinian's 600,000-volume Imperial Library in fifth-century Constantinople to the million-volume collections at the Library of Congress (Washington, D.C.) and the Harvard Law School Library (Cambridge, Massachusetts), which are still considered two of the largest law libraries in the world. During the 20th century, other important law libraries developed in most major or Western countries, including England, France, Germany, and most of the British Commonwealth. Some of these libraries, such as those at the four Inns of Court, founded in 16th-century England, and the Advocates Library, established in Scotland in 1653, have ancient roots, but the size of their collections, such as the 150,000 volumes at the Bodleian Law Library at Oxford, England, cannot compare to the collections of 500,000 or more volumes found in many contemporary academic, public, bar, and court law libraries of the United States.

The growth of law libraries in the 20th century was complemented by the formation of law library professional organizations. The American Association of Law Libraries (AALL), founded in 1906, became the profession's largest and most significant national organization, reaching a membership of approximately 5,000 by 1990. By comparison, the British and Irish Association of Law Libraries, founded in 1959, and the Canadian Association of Law Libraries and the German Association of Law Libraries, both founded in 1971, indicate the relative international strength of law libraries and the law library profession in the United States. By 1990 there were at least 11 separate national law library associations representing the law library profession in countries as diverse as Australia, the Netherlands, New Zealand, Nigeria, South Africa, West Germany, and the West Indies, but the major organization continues to be AALL. The creation of the International Association of Law Libraries (IALL) in 1969 emphasized the increased importance of foreign and international law to law libraries and their users, especially in the United States. By 2000 IALL had approximately 1,000 members representing nearly 50 countries, with a strong membership from the United States.

Importance of Printing

The history of law libraries is tied closely to the history of printing. Early societies had only a few basic legal documents (e.g., the Ten Commandments, Hammurabi's Code, and the Roman Twelve Tables). Although legal materials were written in stone and not easy to alter, copying by scribes led to errors in transcription, so the earlier, original documents were always preferred. By the fifth century A.D. the Roman Empire had accumulated a great body of law consisting of a complex mass of imperial constitutions, edicts of magistrates, and related materials. These materials served as the basis for the four works collectively known as the *Corpus Juris Civilis,* which profoundly influenced the development of European law and law libraries, which in turn developed with the introduction of printing in England (1476).

Printing guaranteed accuracy in the reproduction of case law, supported the transformation of the common-law legal system, encouraged the development of law libraries, and allowed for the publication of law books. In 1537 the first law reports were printed and became part of the common-law legal system exported to the British colonies, particularly those that are now part of the United States.

Colonial America

The law libraries of the original British colonies in the United States were private collections of English legal materials and English law with a mix of local ordinances. These private collections became the basis for the large institutional law libraries that followed. The ready availability of English law profoundly influenced the development of U.S. law and U.S. law libraries even after the Revolutionary War. In particular, William Blackstone's four-volume *Commentaries on the Laws of England* (1770), which restated basic principles found in English reported decisions, became essential to legal practice in America and was the first important law book to be reprinted there (1772). English law books continued to dominate U.S. law libraries until well after the Revolutionary War, with the publication of the British supporter and lawyer James Kent's *Commentaries on American Law* (1826–30).

Access to law books was essential to the study and practice of law in the United States, and large private collections were often used as the basis for offering courses in legal education. The most eminent of these law office schools was founded at Litchfield, Connecticut, in 1784; it promoted access to its private collection as an important offering at the school. Also, bar and membership libraries emerged in the early 19th century to provide a more economical means for providing access to the law. Such libraries included the Social Law Library in Boston, Massachusetts (1804) and the Library of the Association of the Bar of New York (1870).

Public Law Libraries

Public law libraries, often considered government libraries, began to appear in the early 19th century with the establishment of New York's Allegheny County Law Library (1806) and a system of county law libraries in Massachusetts (1815). These were created to serve the local legal community and public officials but were open to the public and supported by various sources of income. In 1842 Massachusetts began to use court filing fees to finance its Boston-area law libraries, a method that enabled the Los Angeles County Law Library to become one of the most significant of its kind in the United States.

State Libraries

The state libraries that also emerged during the 19th and early 20th century were often dominated by their law collections but were not separately designated as law libraries, although they identified with the law library community. The National Association of State Law Libraries met jointly with the AALL from its founding in 1906 until 1936. The separation of law materials from the rest of a state library's holdings usually occurred when space constraints demanded it. Typically a law collection would remain or be moved to a location convenient to its most frequent users, such as the state supreme court, and laws were introduced to keep these materials separate from the nonlegal community. State libraries, like most law libraries, also function as legislative research centers; many are separate functions and designated accordingly (e.g., the California Research Bureau in Library and Courts Building, Sacramento; the Maryland Department of Legislative Services, in Library and Legislative Services, Annapolis; and the Texas State Legislative Reference Library, Texas State Capitol Building, Austin).

Library of Congress

The Library of Congress in Washington, D.C., began primarily as a law library, based on the private collection built by Thomas Jefferson; however, as the library grew more diverse in its collections, the need for a separate law library became evident. In 1832 Congress enacted a bill to make the Law Library a separate department within the Library of Congress. The librarian of Congress retained the power to appoint all of the Law Library's employees. No separate national law library ever emerged in the United States, and even though the Library of Congress developed the largest collection of legal materials in the country, it never assumed a national leadership role in this area because its first priority was and is to serve members of Congress and their staffs. For this purpose, the Legislative Reference Service (now the Congressional Research Service) was created in 1946 for the analysis, appraisal, and evaluation of legislative proposals. In addition, each chamber of Congress maintains its own library, although these are primarily legislative in nature, supporting the bill-making functions of Congress: the Senate Library and the House Legislative Resource Center.

Other Federal Law Libraries

A number of other important federal law libraries were founded in the early 19th century, including those in the Treasury Department (1789) and in the library of the Department of Justice (1831). Today every cabinet department has its own law library and most federal agencies have their own basic legal reference collections, if not fully stocked law libraries. Legislation was passed in 1843 to create a separate law collection for the U.S. Supreme Court, and the first Supreme Court librarian was appointed in 1887. Minimal professional attention was typical of the management of law libraries throughout the 19th century, and the civil service system further hindered the staffing of federal law libraries by not recognizing legal training as credible experience for library positions.

University Law Libraries

University-affiliated law schools began with Harvard Law School (founded in 1817), which had a library that benefited from the donation of several strong private collections of law books. In 1871 Christopher Columbus Langdell was appointed dean of the Harvard Law School and transformed U.S. legal education and the role of academic law libraries with his idea of law as a science, the available materials for which are contained in books. The Langdell case method, which involved students reading edited versions of appellate decisions and discussing their application to similar, hypothetical situations, encouraged the establishment and growth of other university-affiliated law schools in which law libraries became very important, although many of the early institutions lacked professional guidance. Two world wars and the legal realist movement of the 1930s heightened a broader perspective in law library collections.

Legal Reporting Systems

An important innovation in legal research came with a unified system for reporting all federal and state court cases: the National Reporter System, which was launched by John West and the West Publishing Company in 1879. It was followed by the introduction of the West key-number digest scheme for indexing case law (1887), the development of selective case reporting systems with annotated reporters and annotated statutory codes to provide subject access to legislation and to link case law to legislation, and the evolution of Frank Shepard's case citation system (1873), which enabled researchers to locate all subsequent opinions that had cited any reported case or statute. These developments enhanced legal research and contributed to a separation of law librarians from other library professionals, an action that officially occurred at the 1906 meeting of the American Library Association, when law librarians formed the American Association of Law Libraries (AALL). Within two years, the new association had more than 75 members and was publishing *Index to Legal Periodicals* and *Law Library Journal*. In 1935 AALL voted to meet at the same time and place as the American Bar Association (ABA) rather than the American Library Association; its executive board approved a report maintaining that legal education was essential and library training desirable for a law librarian. In 1941 a special program in law librarianship was developed at the University of Washington (Seattle). Under the leadership of Marian Gould Gallagher (professor and law librarian, 1944–81) this program produced some of the nation's leading law librarians for nearly five decades. By 2000 courses in law librarianship, legal bibliography, and legislative searching were part of the curriculum established by the ABA and the Association of American Law Schools.

Online Searching

With the introduction of full-text computer-assisted legal research systems in the 1970s, law libraries moved into a new era of leadership. In 1973 Mead Data Central Corporation made the LEXIS legal and legislative research system commercially available. The LEXIS system was initially conceived by the Ohio Bar Association as a full-text computer-assisted retrieval system designed for direct use by lawyers doing their own research; backed by the giant Mead Corporation, it caught traditional legal publishers by surprise. Three years later West Publishing Company responded with its own online legal research system (WESTLAW), which initially utilized software developed for the Canadian-based Quick Law system to make West's headnote indexing system electronically searchable. Today the two systems are similar to one another in database coverage and both are among the largest online systems in the world, making online legal and legislative research possible. The full texts of federal and state laws and court decisions, texts and periodicals, and specialized materials can be retrieved via these systems.

For many years one of the most important online legislative search tools, in addition to LEXIS, was LEGISLATE, which could also produce full texts of Congressional testimony and government press briefings, especially the daily ones at the White House and the State and Defense Departments. In 1999 LEGISLATE was being replaced by GalleryWatch.com, an online subscription service that offers one-stop shopping for comprehensive federal legislation and agency information, including up-to-the-minute reports on House and Senate floor actions, Congressional voting records, and customized legislative bill tracking. More comprehensive is THOMAS, a search tool produced by Congress that makes it possible to access the pending status of legislation before Congress. It is a full-text database of legislation introduced into Congress before 1989 and summary information of legislation introduced before 1973, although this portion does not contain the full text of bills. In THOMAS it is possible to access the *Annals of Congress, 1789–1793*, early precursors to the *Congressional Record*.

The *United States Code* (the body of federal law in which new laws eventually find their place) is online from several sources, including GPO Access, the Government Printing Office homepage, and the House of Representatives Internet Law Library. These rapidly growing technologies also include major indexes and databases on CD-ROMS. At present there are no links available in Thomas or any other Internet site that map a given public law to its place in the *United States Code*.

In the 1970s law firms began to hire more librarians than ever before, many with both law and library degrees, changing the nature of the AALL from an organization dominated by law school librarians to one in which law firm librarians became a majority. The largest law collections are still at the U.S. Library of Congress and a score of U.S. academic and bar association libraries. They are particularly important for the access they provide to international materials, which is often better than that available in the countries of origin. There are notable collections in Canada—especially the Supreme Court of Canada Library, the Canadian government's major legal collection—and in Great Britain.

International Law Librarianship

In other countries, separate law libraries for the legal profession are not as prevalent as in the United States, and legislative research is handled mostly through parliamentary libraries. Non-Western countries with strong law libraries are usually those colonized by Western nations, especially those with a common-law legal tradition. In Africa the most significant law libraries are found in Nigeria and South Africa. Nigerian law libraries have a longer history than Nigerian public libraries and trace their history to 1900 with the establishment of a court library in Lagos serving the Lagos High Court (now the West African Court of Appeal) and the Federal Ministry of Justice. Today Nigeria has an extensive system of court, academic, and private law libraries and a Nigerian Association of Law Libraries (1975). In South Africa a network of law libraries emerged, and the Organization of South African Law Libraries was formed in 1980. In Asia colonization of the Philippines (first by Spain and then the United States) helped to encourage the development of law libraries in support of its legal system. In addition to government, court, and private law libraries, standards modeled after those in the United States required all Filipino law schools to maintain separate, professionally staffed law libraries, such as the law library at the University of the Philippines Law Center (Diliman, Quezon City).

Related to law librarianship in non-Western nations are strong national economies and an interest in international commerce. Noteworthy is Japan, where there is an important law library at the University of Tokyo's Center for Foreign Law. Other major Japanese law libraries support domestic bodies such as the Ministry of Justice Library (Homusho Toshokan) and the National Diet Library (Kokkai Toshokan), established to support the Diet, Japan's Parliament. In South Korea a major law library developed to support the national legislature, the National Assembly Library (Kukhoe Tosogwan). With the pressures to increase international trade during the late 20th century, other non-Western countries also began showing an interest in developing their law libraries, particularly the former East European Bloc countries and the People's Republic of China, where socialist law systems had earlier limited the development of separate law libraries.

Parliamentary Libraries

With the end of the Cold War and the introduction of democracy to countries that were previously dictatorships, there has been an increase in the development of parliamentary (also called congressional or legislative) libraries, mostly based on the U.S. model, to support the legislative bodies. The largest in the world, in terms of its depth of service and collections, is still the U.S. Library of Congress, but there are impressive collections in many European countries, such as those that support the British and French Parliaments. The parliamentary library in Ottawa has modeled many services to its Canadian parliamentarians on the Congressional Research Service at the Library of Congress. In April 1990 the Speaker of the U.S. House of Representatives appointed a special task force on the development of parliamentary institutions in Eastern Europe to recommend and implement initiatives to help in building strong institutions that can function independently in a multiparty democratic environment. One of the most important initiatives was the *Parliamentary Reference Library Bibliography of Core Materials,* prepared in 1991 by the Congressional Research Service and the United States Information Agency to provide library and research resources to the parliamentary libraries of Eastern Europe, although the list has become a guideline for other countries as well. For example, the Kenyan Parliament asked the Information Resource Center in the U.S. Embassy in Nairobi for assistance in setting up a resource center that would include a parliamentary hot line, long-term research support services, and Internet connections for research by parliamentarians.

Parliamentary librarians form the Section on Library and Research Services for Parliaments, part of the Division of General Research Libraries, in the International Federation of Library Associations (IFLA), established out of a need by legislators for up-to-date, reliable, adequate libraries and dissemination facilities. At the regional level, there are smaller associations of parliamentary libraries, such as the Association of Parliamentary Libraries of Australasia, Association of Parliamentary Librarians of Asia and the Pacific, Association of Parliamentary Librarians in Canada/L'Association des Bibliothecaires Parlementaires au Canada, Conference of Black Sea Countries, as well as groups for the Nordic countries, South Asia, and Latin America.

MARTIN J. MANNING JR.

Further Reading

American Association of Law Libraries, Task Force on the Value of Law Libraries, *Law Librarians: Making Information Work,* Chicago: American Association of Law Libraries, 1996

Blunt, Adrian, *Law Librarianship,* New York: Saur, 1980

Brock, Christine A., "Law Libraries and Librarians: A Revisionist History; or, More Than You Ever Wanted to Know," *Law Library Journal* 67 (1974)

Danner, Richard A., *Strategic Planning: A Law Library Management Tool for the 90's,* New York: Glanville, 1991; 2nd edition, as *Strategic Planning: A Law Library Management Tool for the 90's and Beyond,* 1997

Ellenberger, J.S., "History and Development of the Modern Law Library in the United States," in *Law Librarianship: A Handbook,* edited by Heinz Peter Mueller and Patrick E. Kehoe, vol. 1, Littleton, Colorado: Rothman, 1983

Garson, Marjorie A., et al., compilers, *Reflections on Law Librarianship: A Collection of Interviews,* Littleton, Colorado: Rothman, 1988

Gasaway, Laura N., and Michael G. Chiorazzi, editors, *Law Librarianship: Historical Perspectives,* Littleton, Colorado: Rothman, 1996

Jacobs, Roger F., "Law Libraries," in *World Encyclopedia of Library and Information Services,* 3rd revised edition, edited by Robert Wedgeworth, Chicago: American Library Association, 1993

Kehoe, Patrick E., Lovisa Lyman, and Gary Lee McCann, editors, *Law Librarianship: A Handbook for the Electronic Age,* Littleton, Colorado: Rothman, 1995

Kohl, Ernst, editor, *World Directory of Parliamentary Libraries of Federated States and Autonomous Territories,* Bonn: Deutscher Bundestag, 1993

Mersky, Roy M., and Richard A. Leiter, compilers, *The Spirit of Law Librarianship: A Reader,* Littleton, Colorado: Rothman, 1991

Reams, Bernard D., Jr., editor, *Reader in Law Librarianship,* Englewood, Colorado: Information Handling Services, Library and Education Division, 1976

Map Libraries

Although there are many articles on specific map libraries, there are very few published studies of map libraries as a group. The classic work on map libraries is John Wolter's 1973 ELIS article, in which he discusses both map and geographical libraries. Since that time, seekers of writings about map libraries have, in the main, had recourse to directories of map libraries—for the world as a whole, and for countries such as Australia, Canada, and the United States—and to publications of individual map libraries from annual reports, bibliographies, and brochures presented in hard copy and, increasingly over the last five years, on websites. This essay will focus on map collections of Europe (the earliest map collections in the Western world) and North America, with an emphasis post-1900 on the United States and Canada, which have the most numerous collections.

The somewhat misleading implication of the term *map library* is that such libraries contain maps and little or nothing else. In actuality there are few map libraries currently in existence that have only maps. Almost all have not only sheet maps, atlases, and globes, but also other forms of cartographic material (geospatial data), such as remote-sensing images (e.g., aerial photographs and satellite images), and often periodicals and monographs relating to cartographic materials. Map collections seldom exist in and of themselves; it is far more frequent for them to be part of some larger unit, usually a library or a government agency.

It is not known when map drawing began. A continuing thread in publications on the history of cartography is the periodic announcement of the discovery of a map even older than the oldest one previously found; currently, the oldest known maps date from around 2000 B.C. It is also unclear how long maps have been collected into libraries. There is, for example, no specific mention about maps as part of the holdings of the magnificent library of Alexandria, Egypt, nor have lists of only maps from the Middle Ages been found, although individual maps themselves are mentioned in library inventories. Judging from these listings, it was probably during the 14th century that maps began to be considered a legitimate item to be collected, with the first map collections being established in the 15th century.

The invention of printing in the 1450s meant that maps and atlases could be more readily produced. The excitement and perils of the voyages of discovery and exploration, especially from the 16th century on, not only produced maps but also prompted collection of those maps by private individuals and public libraries. As is the case today, some of these private collectors did present their collections to public libraries. At the end of the 16th century, the Hofbibliothek in Munich received the large map collection of the Fuggers of Augsburg, the Dresden map collection was based on a gift by Kurfurst August of Saxony, and the British Library's map collection received a magnificent gift of maps from George II in the mid–18th century.

But overall, from 1459 to 1790 very few map collections were established, in contrast to the time period from 1790 to the middle of the 19th century in Europe, when many important collections were developed. This period was particularly important because it coincided with the initiation of the topographic mapping of countries carried out by their respective national surveys and also because of the charting of the oceans and of coastlines, again by government-funded surveying. Both activities were a result of economic and military needs.

The founding and growth of geographical societies were also of considerable importance, as there were often close relationships between the societies, the early surveys, and the cartographers and surveyors involved in the mapping of the Earth. The time from the mid–19th century to World War I was a period of growth not only for exploration and discovery but also for collections. It is the period since World War II, however, that has seen the largest growth in map collections, both in number and size.

During World War II, the holdings of map libraries suddenly became of crucial importance to the military. In the United States, the Army Map Service sent out a plea to U.S. map libraries, including Harvard University Library (Cambridge, Massachusetts) and the New York Public Library, to loan maps to the armed forces. These acts of patriotism by map libraries, especially in the 15 years immediately following the war, contributed to the growth of public and university map collections in the United States. The U.S. Army Map Service set up a depository program in which it would place topographic and road maps of non-U.S. countries in a selected number of map libraries. This pattern of federal agencies depositing maps with public and university libraries was followed by the U.S. Geological Survey (USGS)—in spite of its name, its main product is topographic maps—as well as the U.S. Coast and Geodetic Survey/U.S. National Ocean Survey and the extensive U.S. government documents depository program administered by the Superintendent of Documents (SuDoc). In the mid-1960s the number of libraries that could receive depository status was increased, and many map libraries in the United States date their largest growth or their establishment from the time of this expansion.

In the early 1970s the most substantial number of collections in Europe were located mainly north of the Alps and west of the Poland-USSR border, and in nearly all cases in capital cities of countries and provinces.

In 1984 USGS, the U.S. Defense Mapping Agency (previously the Army Map Service and by the 1990s known as the U.S. National Imagery and Mapping Agency), and the then U.S. National Ocean Survey consolidated their depository programs with that of SuDoc. This is the most generous of the depository programs of the Western nations, but programs in other countries do exist. Canadian map libraries have a similar depository arrangement with Canada's national mapping agency, and a few selected British libraries receive a copy of each map published as a part of the copyright act. Some federal agencies did have depository programs for libraries outside their own countries (as did USGS in Canada), but these sadly ended in the 1990s. Although the number of maps received by a depository map library fluctuates from year to year, at its height (in the predigital-data days of the 1970s and 1980s) it was easily 4,000 to 5,000 sheets annually and remains at a few thousand per year.

A survey of U.S. map libraries in the late 1980s, sent out to approximately 3,000 U.S. map collections, revealed some startling totals of all cartographic holdings: 38 million maps, 25 million aerial photographs, 8 million satellite images, 2.5 million manuscripts, and 280,000 atlases. These holdings existed in 449 university libraries (46 percent of the total number of map collections); 180 public libraries (18 percent); 168 state/federal collections (17 percent); 105 private collections (11 percent); and 73 geoscience libraries (8 percent). Twenty of those libraries had more than 250,000 maps as of 1 January 1989, according to David Cobb's *Guide to U.S. Map Resources* (2nd edition; 1990).

An additional growth area for map libraries, most noticeably since the 1970s, has been that of remote-sensing imagery and, more specifically, aerial photographs and satellite images; those of the general area in which a map library is located, preferably for several different dates, have been acquired by many collections. These satellite images are obtained from the Unites States' Landsat satellites, first launched in 1972, and from satellites with similar sensors, most notably those of France (the Satellite Pour le Observation de la Terre, or SPOT) and the former Soviet Union.

The burgeoning of the Web in recent years necessitated the maintenance of two collections—one hard copy and one virtual—with links to online maps or to stable sites in the library's online catalog for websites. One of the best known of the websites that provide links to online maps is Odden's Bookmarks (oddens.geog.uu.nl/index.html). Map libraries are using their websites as an excellent method of outreach and information for users, thus leaving the printing of paper copies to individuals. Cartobibliographies and accessions lists are rather easily turned into hypertext markup language (HTML) or Adobe Acrobat Portable Data Format (PDF) files. It is complicated and expensive for a library to scan its maps and make them viewable on the Web—in effect putting the library's exhibits online—but many libraries have done so, with one of the most notable sites being the Library of Congress' Geography and Map Division (lcweb.loc.gov/rr/geogmap/).

The major types of map collections and examples of each are:

Map collections of national libraries (France's Bibliothèque nationale, Département des Cartes et Plans; the British Library's Map Library; the Alexander Turnbull Library at Wellington, England; the U.S. Library of Congress Geography and Map Division; the National Library of Australia Map Library; and the National Library of Finland Map Collection).

Government libraries or collections with a specific function (the British Public Records Office Library; Cartographic Archives of the National Archives of the United States; France's Institut Géographique National; and the Public Archives of Canada map collection).

University research libraries (England's Bodleian Library (Oxford) and Cambridge University Library; and the University of California map libraries, Harvard University Library, and the University of Illinois Library in the United States).

Public libraries (New York Public Library and the Free Library of Philadelphia, Pennsylvania).

Geographical society libraries (American Geographical Society Collection held at the University of Wisconsin–Milwaukee's Golda Meir Library and the Royal Geographical Society in London).

Historical and other learned society libraries (Minnesota Historical Society, the New-York Historical Society, and the State Historical Society of Wisconsin).

Libraries with distinguished collections usually include large collections of topographic maps, nautical charts, and remote-sensing images, with relatively smaller collections of pre-1900 maps (usually called "early maps"), notable for their rarity and financial value. The European national libraries in particular specialize in early maps, whereas university collections specialize in the large collections of maps, charts, and images; especially in U.S. university libraries, early maps are often kept in special collections rather than in the map library.

Conclusion

From its sparse beginnings in the 14th and 15th centuries, the map library as a type of collection has seen massive growth, mainly in the 20th century. Map librarians view the 21st century as a time that will see at least as much change as the last one, particularly in geospatial data collected digitally. In a world where the Web is always with us, it seems obvious that geospatial data will, in many cases, have a mainly digital life. But questions remain: How will map libraries quickly move their most heavily used holdings to Web form? How will this change the way a map library looks and more importantly how it works? At least here we see a marked similarity with the beginnings of map libraries, where no one knew all of the answers or even all of the questions. What we do know is that the future of map libraries is, like that of so many other types of libraries, firmly planted in the digital realm.

MARY L. LARSGAARD

Further Reading

Böhme, Rolf, compiler, *Inventory of World Topographic Mapping,* edited by Roger Anson, 3 vols., London and New York: Elsevier, 1989–93

Cobb, David A., compiler, *Guide to U.S. Map Resources,* Chicago: American Library Association, 1986; 2nd edition, 1990

Harley, J.B., and David Woodward, editors, *The History of Cartography,* Chicago: University of Chicago Press, 1987–

Langeraar, W., *Surveying and Charting of the Seas,* Amsterdam and New York: Elsevier, 1984

Larsgaard, Mary, *Map Librarianship: An Introduction,* Littleton, Colorado: Libraries Unlimited, 1978; 3rd edition, Englewood, Colorado: Libraries Unlimited, 1998

Ristow, Walter W., editor, *World Directory of Map Collections,* Munich: Verlag Dokumentation, 1976; 3rd edition, edited by Lorraine Dubreuil, Munich and New York: Saur, 1993

Ristow, Walter, "The Greening of Map Librarianship," *Bulletin* (Special Libraries Association, Geography and Map Division) 111, nos. 2–9 (1978)

Wolter, John A., "Geographical Libraries and Map Collections," in *Encyclopedia of Library and Information Science,* edited by Allen Kent et al., vol. 9, New York: Dekker, 1973

Medical Libraries

Ancient Medicine

Medical literature is nearly as old as medicine itself. The trial and error of prehistoric healers grew into a refined lore that was recorded as soon as the respective ancient cultures invented systems of writing. Many of the earliest surviving written artifacts, such as the Code of Hammurabi, have significant medical content. Several Egyptian papyri of the third and second millennia B.C. are detailed medical or surgical treatises that still exist. Among these are the Ebers Medical Papyrus at the University of Leipzig, the Edwin Smith Surgical Papyrus at the New York Academy of Medicine, the Kahun Gynecological Papyrus at University College of London, the Brugsch Medical Papyrus at the Egyptian Museum of Berlin, and the Chester Beatty Medical Papyrus at his eponymous library in Dublin.

The earliest extant writings in Ayurvedic medicine date from the second millennium B.C., but the standard Indian medical and surgical traditions are thought to have begun in the first millennium B.C. with the Sanskrit works of the legendary physician Charaka and the surgeon Susruta. By the eighth century B.C. the Chinese already had recorded advanced systems of medicine and surgery. Hundreds of Assyrian and Babylonian cuneiform medical and surgical writings survive from the seventh-century B.C. library of Ashurbanipal. Most other ancient literate cultures have similar examples. Many such documents from throughout the world have clinical relevance even today. All these writings pre-date Hippocrates, the "father of Western medicine." Besides Hippocrates, the major authors of ancient Greek medicine were Aristotle and Galen. All three were well represented in ancient Mediterranean libraries, but none of these libraries, as far as we know, was specifically dedicated to medicine.

Arabic Influences

In the tenth century the hospital and medical school at Gondeshapur, Persia, had the world's most extensive medical manuscript collection. The Academy of Gondeshapur, founded in pre-Islamic times by Nestorian Christians, was the pinnacle of the intellectual life of the Eastern Caliphate and served as the model for at least 70 libraries established by the Western Caliphate, mostly in Spain. Between the ninth and 12th centuries, the two caliphates produced such physicians as Rhazes, Haly Abbas, Abul Qasim, Avicenna, Avenzoar, Averroës, and Moses Maimonides. The Greek-Arabic tradition in medicine was introduced to the West by Constantinus Africanus at Salerno.

Medieval Europe

The Vatican, Salerno, and several medieval European monastery libraries, especially in France and Ireland, were rich in the medical literature of the Latin West from classical times through the Dark Ages, including the works of Isidore of Seville, Venerable Bede, Alcuin, Hrabanus Maurus, and Trotula of Salerno. This literature, however, has not been of much consequence in the development of medicine.

The story of the transmission of ancient Greek medical culture to medieval western Europe parallels the familiar account of ancient Greek culture in general coming to the West in the 11th to 13th centuries via new Latin translations of first-millennium Arabic translations of ancient Greek texts. In the 14th and 15th centuries, Byzantine medical manuscripts also began arriving in the West as Eastern Christian intellectuals fled the Turks.

Formal medical education in the West began at the six great medieval universities: Bologna, Padua, Paris, Montpellier, Oxford, and Cambridge. The libraries of each of these universities held significant medical manuscript collections before Gutenberg's press.

Private Collectors and Bibliographers

From antiquity until the mid-19th century, the greatest medical libraries were owned by private physicians. Among the most important of these collectors were Giovanni de Dondi, Amplonius Ratingk, Hermann Schedel, Ulrich Ellenbog, Hieronymus Muenzer, Hartmann Schedel, Nicholas Pol, William Harvey, Jean Riolan, Gabriel Naudé, Gui Patin, Vospiscus Fortunatus Plempius, Thomas Browne, Nathan Paget, Francis Bernard, John Locke, Hans Sloane, Richard Mead, Robert Erskine, Edward Worth, John Douglas, William Hunter, John Coakley Lettsom, John Crawford, Johann Friedrich Blumenbach, Caleb Hillier Parry, Matthew Baillie, G.F.B. Kloss, and Peter Mark Roget.

Extensive private collections have more recently been built by five generations of the Warren family of Boston, Thomas Radford, Hugh Lenox Hodge, Samuel David Gross, Oliver Wendell Holmes, Samuel Lewis, William Worrall Mayo, William Read, Jean Martin Charcot, Joseph Meredith Toner, Joseph Lister, Charles N. Hewitt, Joseph Frank Payne, William Osler, D'Arcy Power, Henry Barton Jacobs, Albert Moll, Harvey Cushing, Arnold Klebs, LeRoy Crummer, Axel Erik Waller, Hiram Winnett Orr, Frederick Charles Pybus, Logan Clendening, Davis Evan Bedford, John Farquhar Fulton, Arthur D. Ecker, Josiah Charles Trent, and Haskell F. Norman. By the end of the 20th century most of these collections belonged to institutional libraries.

Great libraries, public or private, cannot exist without great bibliographers. Western medicine has never lacked such scholars. Among the most noteworthy medical bibliographers are Symphorien Champier, Otto Brunfels, Conrad Gesner, Israel Spach, Pascal LeCoq, Johannes van der Linden, Martin Lipen, James Douglas, Albrecht von Haller, Wilhelm Gottfried Plouquet, Adolf Carl Peter Callisen, Ludwig Choulant, Robert Fletcher, John Shaw Billings, William Osler, Cushing, Klebs, Fielding Hudson Garrison, Francis Erich Sommer, S.A.J. Moorat, Walton Brooks McDaniel II, Hans Sallander, Dorothy May Schullian, Leslie T. Morton, Frederick Noel Lawrence Poynter, Francesco Cordasco, John B. Blake, Peter A. Krivatsy, Richard J. Durling, Jeremy M. Norman, Diana H. Hook, Robert B. Austin, Joan Stuart Emmerson, David T. Bird, Robin M. Price, and Larry J. Wygant.

The Modern Era

Until the 19th century, stand-alone institutional medical libraries were unusual. Most of the major university, public, societal, and proprietary libraries throughout the world had significant medical components by the 18th century, but medical literature was not yet so vast as to require separate repositories.

Today these separate libraries typically belong to medical schools, hospitals, medical professional clubs such as the College of Physicians of Philadelphia or the Royal Society of Medicine, geographically oriented medical societies (local, provincial, regional, national, or international), specialized medical organizations such as the March of Dimes or the American Hospital Association, group practices, or individual physicians. Each of these different entities has its own reasons for collecting.

The U.S. Medical Library Movement

A typical physician of 1820 would likely regard a 17th-century medical text as being of clinical importance, but a typical physician of 1880 would not. In 1820 medical libraries venerated medical tradition; in 1880 physicians saw little need to do so. Attracted by the discoveries of anesthesia (1846) and antisepsis (1867), the generation of physicians and surgeons who came of age during the U.S. Civil War or shortly thereafter were generally not interested in preserving the records of bygone medical eras. They believed that medical progress did not require libraries but only modern clinical and experimental results.

This antihistorical group dominated U.S. medical culture in the 1880s, but it was gradually supplanted in the 1890s by younger physicians such as James R. Chadwick, George Milbry Gould, William Osler, William Browning, Frank William Marlow, and Charles D. Spivak, who recognized the edifying value of the documents of medical history. They called their mostly successful crusade the Medical Library Movement. Their impetus was not only the veneration of tradition but the rediscovery in the 1890s that medical libraries offer excellent support for current clinical research.

The goals of the Medical Library Movement were to improve service, professionalize medical librarianship, establish standards, facilitate acquisitions, broaden holdings, and encourage the proliferation of significant medical collections in outlying areas. Toward these ends, a committee of physicians and librarians founded the Medical Library Association (MLA) on 2 May 1898 in Philadelphia. Throughout the 20th century, MLA principles guided medical library practice not only in North America but worldwide.

A survey in 1898 found that of 120 U.S. medical schools, only 24 had affiliated libraries. Directly addressing this perceived need, Gould, Osler, and a few others in the 1890s encouraged physicians to bequeath their personal collections of books to medical schools and other health care institutions, especially since these institutions had few other ways to acquire books. Gould devised an interlibrary exchange program for duplicates and other unwanted titles. North American medical libraries increased rapidly in both number and size. By the time of Abraham Flexner's critical evaluation of all medical schools in the United States and Canada (the "Flexner Report" of 1910), medical schools were expected to include strong perennial funding for their libraries within their regular budgets.

Representative American Medical Libraries

The oldest important medical library in the United States is that of the College of Physicians of Philadelphia (CPP), founded by a donation of books and manuscripts from John Morgan, the second surgeon general of the Continental Army, in 1788, just a year after CPP's own founding. Because CPP is a fellowship organization rather than an educational institution, its library collections generally reflect the interests of its fellows, among whom have been such eminent medical bibliophiles as Samuel D. Gross, S. Weir Mitchell, George William Norris, Edward Bell Krumbhaar, and Samuel X. Radbill. A major advance occurred in 1953 when W.B. McDaniel II divided the collection into historical and general collections and relinquished his position as CPP librarian, which he had held for 20 years. He became CPP's first curator of historical collections, a position he held for another 20 years and in which he achieved worldwide fame. In 2000 the library contained approximately 400,000 volumes, including roughly 300,000 in the Historical Services Division. Among the historical collections were approximately 440 incunabula; 12,000 pre-1801 imprints; unusually extensive 18th- and 19th-century journal holdings; more than one million manuscripts; more than 20,000 images, including the Samuel B. Sturgis collection of approximately 10,000 portraits; and thousands of pamphlets, trade catalogs, unbound theses, and ephemera. The Francis Clark Wood Institute for the History of Medicine was founded at CPP in 1976 to promote the use of historical resources in both the Historical Services Division and the Mütter Museum.

John Stearns, Valentine Mott, John Wakefield Francis, and Isaac Wood founded the New York Academy of Medicine in 1847 as an activist reform organization. Its mission involves promoting public health, ethical health care practice, professional standards, equitable heath care policy, and efficient delivery of health care services, especially in urban settings. Wood founded the library at the inaugural meeting with a gift of Martyn Paine's *Medical and Physiological Commentaries*. The collections were augmented substantially by Samuel Smith Purple and by the year 2000 included more than one million volumes.

Ward Nicholas Boylston, a lawyer, founded the medical library of Harvard College in 1800 by donating approximately 1,100 medical volumes that had belonged to his physician uncle, Zabdiel Boylston, one of the first smallpox inoculators in the United States. In 1816 several professors at the Harvard Medical School resolved to donate books to found that institution's library. The two Harvard medical libraries led parallel existences, the former tending toward older materials and the latter toward current clinical information. During the last quarter of the 19th century, the former, along with the collections of approximately half a dozen other Boston medical libraries, was transferred to the Boston Medical Library Association. The Francis A. Countway Library of Medicine was founded in 1960 as the merger of the Harvard Medical School Library and the Boston Medical Library. It also serves the Harvard School of Public Health, the Harvard School of Dental Medicine, and the Massachusetts Medical Society. In 2000 it held more than 630,000 volumes.

In 1805 James Jackson, John Collins Warren, and seven other Boston physicians established a weekly meeting to exchange medical ideas; their little society, the Boston Medical Library, subsequently began to acquire books and journals for its own use. By 1823 its collection numbered 1,311 volumes. The Boston Athenaeum acquired the collection in 1826. Access was only by subscription. In 1875 a group of physicians led by Henry Ingersoll Bowditch, Oliver Wendell Holmes, and James R. Chadwick—representing the Boston Society for Medical Observation and motivated by perceived needs for better cataloging, less restricted access to library materials, and a comfortable reading room stocked with current medical journals—wrested the medical department from the Athenaeum, reorganized it as the Boston Medical Library Association, and immediately started a concerted, ambitious, and mostly successful acquisitions policy.

The Cleveland Medical Library Association was founded in 1894 during the Medical Library Movement. Its first acquisition was a 1555 copy of *De humani corporis fabrica* by Andreas Vesalius, who had revolutionized the study of anatomy with its first edition in 1543. In 1966 it entered into an agreement with Case Western Reserve University to create the Cleveland Health Sciences Library (CHSL), consisting of the Allen Memorial

Medical Library, focused on the clinical sciences and including the Dittrick Medical History Center; and the Health Center Library, focused on the basic sciences and the various health professions. In 2000 CHSL held approximately 380,000 volumes, including 60,000 rare book titles in the Dittrick Center.

Many medical libraries separate clinical from historical materials, not only putting old, scarce, or rare items in vaults, but also putting the clinical and the historical items under different administrations. For example, at the Johns Hopkins University, two libraries have divided these duties since 1929, when both were established: the William H. Welch Medical Library, created as the merger of the Hopkins hospital and medical school libraries, and the Library of the Institute of the History of Medicine, founded by Welch. The Welch Library adheres to the traditional "three-legged stool" model of medical service (i.e., research, teaching, and patient care), but the "fourth leg," the historical dimension of medicine, belongs to the institute, now a division of the Johns Hopkins Department of the History of Science, Medicine, and Technology, which itself is jointly administered by the School of Medicine and the School of Arts and Sciences.

National Medical Libraries

It is increasingly common for developed countries to have national medical libraries, either de facto or de jure. Among the most prominent are the German National Library of Medicine (Deutsche Zentralbibliothek für Medizin) in Cologne, the Wellcome Trust Libraries in London, the Czech National Medical Library (Národní lékařska knihovna) in Prague, the Caroline Institute Library (Karolinska Institutets Bibliotek) in Stockholm, the Interuniversity Library of Medicine (Bibliothèque interuniversitaire de Médecine) in Paris, the National Library of Health Sciences (Terveystieteiden keskuskirjasto) in Helsinki, the State Medical Library (Biblioteca Medica Statale) in Rome, and the National Library of Medicine (NLM) of the United States in Bethesda, Maryland. The NLM is the largest medical library in the world.

Countries without separate national medical libraries typically have significant medical collections in their national libraries.

Standardized Collection Development

There are two basic tools that medical collection development librarians typically use to build core collections. The Brandon-Hill lists (i.e., "Selected List of Books and Journals for the Small Medical Library," "Selected List of Books and Journals in Allied Health," and "Selected List of Nursing Books and Journals" by Alfred N. Brandon and Dorothy R. Hill) have been published biennially in the *Bulletin of the Medical Library Association* since 1965 and also have been widely offprinted.

The Dawn of Automation

The clientele of medical libraries consists largely of clinical practitioners whose need for accurate and timely information is often literally a matter of life and death. Because the users of medical libraries typically need information more quickly than those of other kinds of libraries, medical libraries have been in the vanguard of technological innovations in data searching and document retrieval and delivery. A medical library became the site of the world's first interactive online bibliographic retrieval service when, in 1968, Irwin Pizer established the State University of New York Biomedical Communication Network (SUNY BCN) on the campus of the Upstate Medical Center in Syracuse, New York. By 1976 SUNY BCN had evolved into a commercial system, Bibliographic Retrieval Services, later called BRS Online. Ovid Technologies bought BRS in 1994 and Wolters Kluwer bought Ovid in 1998.

Late-20th-Century Medical Information Science and Ethics

Medical libraries serve six categories of users: (1) health care professionals and practitioners; (2) scholars and researchers; (3) teachers; (4) students; (5) patients; and (6) patients' friends and families. Each of these six groups has a different set of needs and expectations. Sometimes there is conflict between what physicians tell patients and what patients find in medical libraries. In such instances medical reference librarians must avoid even the appearance that they are dispensing medical advice to patients, yet at the same time they must provide these patients with the medical information they seek, while not alienating the physicians.

This ethical and political dilemma can be exacerbated by computerized medical information science systems. Practitioners can find full-text, up-to-date clinical studies and scientific data through such online services as MD Consult, the Cochrane Library, Evidence Based Medicine Reviews (EBMR), Micromedex, Cumulative Index to Nursing and Allied Health Literature (CINAHL), and Medical Literature Analysis and Retrieval System Online (MEDLINE). Free access to these professional-level online bioscience services is typically offered by larger medical libraries. Meanwhile, consumers easily find questionable medical information on the Internet. Medical reference librarians can be caught in the middle, especially if a physician is unwilling to discuss alternative treatments with a patient.

The IAIMS Initiative

NLM has always been in the forefront of medical information technology. Beginning in 1983 it promoted Integrated Advanced Information Management Systems (IAIMS), which are institution-specific computer networks intended to create seamless online point-of-care interfaces for practitioners among library databases, local information files, current medical literature, and computerized patient records without betraying patient confidentiality. IAIMS can use the Unified Medical Language System (UMLS) of machine-readable vocabulary and the National Research and Education Network (NREN) to integrate information retrieval systems with hospitals, medical schools, medical libraries, and other health care institutions. Success in IAIMS always involves a close working relationship among the library, computer services, and clinical departments of any medical institution. Two of the most successful IAIMS projects were implemented in the 1990s at the University of Rochester Medical Center and the Columbia-Presbyterian Medical Center. Also in the 1990s, medical curriculum, medical care, and medical research were all enhanced at the University of North Carolina, Chapel Hill, by a major enterprise-wide information technology innovation, the University of North Carolina Literature Exchange (UNCLE).

ERIC V.D. LUFT

See also United States National Library of Medicine; Wellcome Library for the History and Understanding of Medicine

Further Reading

Birchette, Kathleen P., "The History of Medical Libraries from 2000 B.C. to 1900 A.D.," *Bulletin of the Medical Library Association* 61, no. 3 (July 1973)

Brodman, Estelle, *The Development of Medical Bibliography*, Washington, D.C.: Medical Library Association, 1954

Bulletin of the Medical Library Association (1911–)

Bunch, Antonia Janette, *Hospital and Medical Libraries in Scotland: An Historical and Sociological Study*, Glasgow: Scottish Library Association, 1975

Fulton, John Farquhar, *The Great Medical Bibliographers: A Study in Humanism*, Philadelphia: University of Pennsylvania Press, 1951

Keys, Thomas Edward, *Applied Medical Library Practice*, Springfield, Illinois: Thomas, 1958

Osler, William, compiler, *Bibliotheca Osleriana: A Catalogue of Books Illustrating the History of Medicine and Science*, Oxford: Clarendon Press, 1929; reprint, Montreal, Quebec: McGill-Queen's University Press, 1969

Postell, William Dosite, *Applied Medical Bibliography for Students*, Springfield, Illinois: Thomas, 1955

Thornton, John Leonard, *Medical Books, Libraries, and Collectors: A Study of Bibliography and the Book Trade in Relation to the Medical Sciences*, London: Grafton, 1949; 3rd revised edition, edited by Alain Besson, Aldershot, Hampshire: Gower, 1990

Tunis, Elizabeth, compiler, *A Directory of History of Medicine Collections*, Bethesda, Maryland: National Library of Medicine, 1990; 10th edition, 2000

Van Ingen, Philip, *The New York Academy of Medicine: Its First Hundred Years*, New York: Columbia University Press, 1949

The Watermark: Newsletter of the Archivists and the Librarians in the History of the Health Sciences (1976–)

Medieval Libraries

For almost 1,000 years from the death of the famed politician and scholar Boethius in 524 (one conventional reckoning of the onset of the Middle Ages), libraries in the West were largely formed and sustained by the Christian church. Boethius himself evidently had a substantial collection of books—his unfinished project was to translate all of Plato and Aristotle into Latin for a world increasingly barbarian and ignorant of Greek—but the system of public libraries as it had existed in the Roman empire was by his time in a state of collapse. As a senator and consul of Rome, Boethius served Theodoric the Great, king of the Ostrogoths and, from 493, of Italy. Theodoric retained much of the administrative system of the Romans, but successive incursions of Huns, Goths, and Vandals had shattered much of their cultural heritage, of which Boethius was the last great representative. None of the rich imperial libraries of Rome seems to have actively survived into the sixth century.

The Dark Ages

Another high official under Theodoric, the senator Cassiodorus, took a different path, one which was to prove a model for the survival of learning over the next few, increasingly dark centuries. The relatively benign reign of Theodoric and the short-lived reconquest of Italy by the Byzantine emperor Justinian gave way to the catastrophic invasion of the Lombards in 568, which laid waste to much that remained of Roman culture in Italy. Other provinces of the old empire (Gaul under the Franks, Spain under the Visigoths, North Africa under the Vandals and then the Arabs) fared no better. Education and the provision of books had, for the most part, long passed into the hands of the church, and most Christians of the time were hostile to pagan literature. Consul of Rome in 514, Cassiodorus retired from the civil service to his estates in the far south of Italy some time around 550 and founded a monastery called Vivarium from its fishponds.

Cassiodorus was not so much concerned with preserving ancient literature as with educating Christian clerics. But he saw, as Augustine had seen, that a grounding in the traditional liberal arts was a necessary preliminary to the interpretation and understanding of the Bible. This program of study, set out in his treatise on divine and secular learning, *Institutiones divinarum et saecularium litterarum*, necessarily involved a supply of books and the foundation of a library. His monks were enjoined to copy manuscripts as an act of piety, paying close attention to the accuracy and presentation of their handiwork. Pagan works stood on the shelves as ancillary to Christian studies. The library of Cassiodorus, apparently arranged by subject in at least ten *armaria* (book cupboards), is the only sixth-century example of which there is definite knowledge.

The monastery of Vivarium and its library seem not to have long survived the death of Cassiodorus circa 580, but amid growing political disintegration and cultural decay it set an example that was widely followed elsewhere. Especially important were the Benedictine houses, above all the first foundation (circa 540) of Benedict himself at Monte Cassino, north of Naples. The writing of manuscripts was not an explicit part of the Benedictine rule, but common and private reading as a spiritual exercise were prescribed. That presupposed books, although in general they were not the sort of Christianized classics that Cassiodorus had encouraged. The founders of Western monasticism aimed rather at inculcating the core texts of Christianity, the Bible and Psalter in particular, and steering their brothers away from the corruptions of classical rhetoric and poetry.

The Irish missionary St. Columban, who founded the houses of Luxeuil in western France and Bobbio in northern Italy, took no interest in profane culture. The monastery at Bobbio grew to become one of the great early scriptoria. In the seventh century, however, the texts in its library were exclusively religious in character, many of them written on palimpsest manuscripts of ancient Latin authors. Benedictine scriptoria, and with them libraries, became active not in the time of St. Benedict himself but under the impulse of Irish (and later English) monks on the continent in the seventh and eighth centuries. The influence of the Anglo-Saxon missionaries, principally the Wessex-born Boniface and his allies and helpers, was especially strong in Germany, leading to the foundation of episcopal centers such as Mainz and Würzburg and of monasteries that were to become famous for their libraries, such as Fulda (744) and Hersfeld (770). The Anglo-Saxons brought with them a script and books from the well-stocked English libraries. In the course of time the preparation (and even sale) as well as consumption of books became a characteristic aspect of continental monastic life and the library a central part of the monastery.

Other accumulations of books were found in episcopal and metropolitan centers, although the slight evidence that exists suggests that there would be little more than Bibles and service books, plus the essential basic grammars and arithmetics, with perhaps a sprinkling of homiletic and pastoral literature. A larger collection, although still very modest by modern standards, was maintained in the Lateran Palace in Rome. Into this collection had come some of the books dispersed from the Vivarium library. By acts of successive popes, many of them were dispersed again, as in 597 when Gregory the Great gave books to St. Augustine of Canterbury to begin his work of converting the English, or again around 720, when the abbot of Monte Cassino received books from Rome during the reconstruction of the monastery after its sack by Lombards. As early as 649, Pope Martin I met a request for manuscripts from the bishop of Maastricht by complaining that book lovers had pillaged his Lateran library. The famous *Codex Amiatinus* of the Bible, the oldest manuscript of the Vulgate, was written late in the seventh century in a Northumbrian monastery (either Wearmouth or Jarrow in England). Its decoration, showing on the title page a cabinet with folding doors for book storage, was modeled on a lost Vivarium manuscript taken to Northumbria from Rome in 678 by the founder of the monasteries, Benedict Biscop. Benedict's protégé, Abbot Ceolfrid, was taking the *Amiatinus* to Rome as a present for the pope when Ceolfrid died at Langres in 716. Such long-distance cultural exchanges helped to build a library, even in the remote north, that could nourish the mind of a man who scarcely set foot outside his monastery but yet became the most learned scholar in the Europe of his day, the Jarrow monk known as the Venerable Bede. In Spain the cathedral library of Seville must have supplied the great bulk of the omnivorous reading of the first encyclopedist of the Middle Ages, Isidore, saint and bishop, who left a record of the collection in a poem, "Versus titulis bibliothecae." The church, with its enduring international structure of bishops and abbots, provided a vital conduit for the traffic in books at a time when political conditions were often chaotic and cultural levels generally depressed.

The Age of Charlemagne and Its Aftermath

For all its missionary energies, the Frankish Merovingian period, until 750, really was the Dark Ages as far as book learning was concerned. The great awakening came with the successors of the Merovingians, Pépin III and his famous son, Charlemagne, who gave his name to the Carolingian dynasty of the Franks. In alliance with the papacy, Charlemagne built an empire that embraced much of Europe, discovering a pressing need, as he himself stated, for educated administrators of his lands. By imperial decree, numerous schools attached to monasteries and cathedrals were set up. Charlemagne placed Alcuin of York, the leading European scholar of his day, at the head of the foremost European cultural center of the late eighth century, thus at the head of the educational system and indeed of literary culture as a whole.

Alcuin was dismayed by the low level of book provision that he found in Frankish Gaul (or Francia, as it had become) and energetically imported books from England and Rome. He spent his last years as abbot of St. Martin in Tours, where he presided over a great upsurge of copying of profane as well as religious texts, in the newly reformed calligraphic bookhand known as Carolingian minuscule. At the same time, and with imperial encouragement, there was a burst of scribal and literary activity in abbey and cathedral scriptoria throughout the empire, the example set by the court library of Charlemagne himself at Aachen. The titles of classical books jotted down in a Berlin manuscript circa 790 have been shown to be a partial list of the library at Aachen. It is remarkable for the range and rarity of the authors represented—Sallust, Martial, Lucan, and Cicero, for example—some of whose books had scarcely survived the Merovingian period. Indeed, it is characteristic of many textual traditions propagated in Carolingian times from old (fifth- or sixth-century) manuscripts, without an intermediate stage. Very little that was recopied in the crucial ninth century was subsequently lost, and the diligent collecting of these earlier representatives themselves ensured the survival of many ancient codices in capitals and uncials.

Many monastic libraries evidently relied upon copies taken from the palace library for their stock. Some, such as Corbie on the Somme or St. Martin at Tours, seem to have benefited spectacularly from their close connection to the court. Other books would be bequeathed by wealthy patrons or procured from outside by persistent begging for loans such as Lupus, Abbot of Ferrières (south of Paris) in the mid-ninth century, engaged in for much of his life. Monastic and cathedral libraries also freely exchanged copies of works as they were needed, along regular routes of circulation. France, especially in the north and central areas, had the lion's share of this general revival of learning in terms of numbers of books produced, but the old Irish monasteries in Germany—Fulda, Hersfeld, St. Gall—and more modern foundations such as the imperially favored abbey of Lorsch, south of Mainz, also housed and recopied large numbers of manuscripts old and new, some of them of great importance. Of the seven ancient Italian manuscripts on which the text of Virgil rests, at least four were preserved in Carolingian monasteries in France and Germany.

The evidence for the arrangement and contents of libraries in and before the ninth century is sparse. In the earliest times the numbers to be stored were small. As there was no pressing problem of storage or access, the need for elaborate finding aids did not arise. Between 300 and 400 manuscripts—most with two or more works within them—was a good-sized collection for a Carolingian monastery: St. Gall owned 395 codices in 835, and the Cologne cathedral had 108 in 833. From the most prolific scriptorium of that age, that of Tours, 350 manuscripts still survive. The oldest library catalogs, such as that of Fulda in the mid-eighth century, are no more than lists of titles, often imperfect and for the most part simple inventories of the books as they stood on the shelf. The order of the lists reflects the usual subject arrangement: Bibles first, followed by glosses, liturgies, patristic works, philosophy, law, grammar, sometimes with historical and medical works at the end, and classical works scattered among the relevant headings. The Lorsch catalogs of the earlier part of the ninth century are a good deal lengthier and more detailed, with 590 titles arranged in 63 classes. Since monasteries were places of education as well as worship, many of the classical texts and nearly all the grammatical works would have been used as school texts. Books were usually stored in cupboards, either in the church or in the cloister closest adjoining it, sometimes in the refectory (for communal reading) as well. The separate library room was, in general, a later development, but an early ninth-century plan, believed to be an idealized scheme of a monastery with a bibliotheca and scriptorium attached to the church, survives in St. Gall. Nearly 8,000 manuscripts from Carolingian scribes also survive. By the middle of the ninth century, books were ubiquitous and even laymen owned them. The private library of a scholar or cleric may have amounted to 30 volumes, with several texts in each.

The succeeding two centuries saw something of a decline from the *renovatio* in its full tide under Charlemagne and his immediate successors, as the empire started to fragment under the strain of incursions of Norsemen, Saracens, and Magyars. Of course, manuscripts continued to be copied and scholars to be formed, but monasteries (including their schools and libraries) were more subject to sacking and dislocation. New monastic orders such as the Cluniacs, Cistercians, and Carthusians at first contributed little to the preservation of literature. There were still brilliant high spots, such as the teaching at Rheims of the polymath Gerbert (as Sylvester II, pope in A.D. 1000) or the revival of intense activity on texts at Monte Cassino under Abbot Desiderius. Nonetheless, from the middle of the 11th century the vitality of intellectual life gradually but ineluctably began to pass to the cathedral and urban schools. Some of these—notably at Bologna (Italy), Paris, and Oxford (England)—became the first universities in the course of the 12th century.

The 12th-Century Renaissance and the Rise of the Universities

The so-called Renaissance of the 12th century was a compound of several new currents in intellectual life. Hand in hand with widespread growth in literacy went the rediscovery of the logic of Boethius and through him of Aristotle, a greatly enhanced access to philosophical commentaries and science transmitted by the Arabs, and the rise of scholastic logical methods as an aid to theological enquiry in urban schools. These factors, soon reinforced by the arrival of the new and disputatious mendicant orders, led to a considerable increase in the number of books in circulation. The nature of the books also changed, from large imposing tomes for use in the church or refectory to portable small-format volumes or working copies and scholar's texts in cramped and frequently highly abbreviated handwriting. The mendicants (Franciscans and Dominicans initially) moved around a good deal in pursuit of their studies and, not having scriptoria in their houses, tended to acquire books by purchase or exchange. A sign of the expansion of the book trade is the first record of a retailer of books in Paris in 1170.

The rise of the universities, their colleges, and the religious houses that soon clustered around them imposed great pressure on book production. This was met by extensive university regulation and by the development of the *pecia* system, most thoroughly at Paris. In this system, official, controlled copies of necessary school texts were supplied as unbound exemplars from which scribes could transcribe piece by piece (commonly a quire, or section of eight leaves), enabling rapid concurrent multiplication of texts. Exemplars were displayed at regular intervals so that students could see what was available for copying at prices fixed by the university authorities. Even so, manuscript books were generally too expensive for ordinary students to buy. From the 13th century it became common for them to borrow books from colleges and convents against pledges for their return. These loans would generally be from the small library or *bibliotheca minor*, with less valuable or important books, as distinct from the *bibliotheca communis*, the common library with its chained books for the sole use of the fellows or friars of the house.

The rapid increase in book stocks and the need to control them within and beyond the institution led to advances in cataloging. Books were often divided into works pertaining to the various faculties (theology, law, and so on). All treatises within a manuscript, instead of just the first, were listed, with a system of letters that enabled the book to be located quickly. Such was the system, imitated elsewhere, in use at the Sorbonne in Paris, which became the effective seat of the theological faculty of the university and whose library numbered 1,722 volumes in 1338. The high point of medieval library cataloging is found in the three-part catalog of Dover Priory in England, made in 1389. Here every volume is listed and every tract identified, the tract's position within a volume entered by leaf number, the opening words (the incipit) of each quoted, and the whole rendered accessible by a shelf list and an alphabetical index of all the works in the library. The 13th century also saw the first attempts at compiling interlibrary catalogs that enumerated all the works held at libraries within a particular province. This novel form of cataloging reached its greatest elaboration in the *Registrum Anglie* of the English Franciscans late in the century, embracing the collections of no fewer than 185 houses in England, Scotland, and Wales.

The range of subjects held in institutional libraries also greatly expanded in this period as theology and Aristotelian philosophy intensified their hold on academic life (more especially in the north, whereas scholastic approaches to law and medicine were more dominant south of the Alps and Pyrenees). It was no longer enough to have inherited codices of the church fathers, plus a sprinkling of grammars, classical works, and a book or two of natural science. Room had to be found for the 8 million words of Thomas Aquinas and many other scholastic authors almost equally prolific, besides the countless summaries, indexes, concordances, and commentaries that aided study.

On the other hand, academic libraries, including those of the friaries, were more single-mindedly professional in their scope; in general, these excluded the vernacular texts and works of classical imaginative literature that the old monastic libraries had preserved (or sometimes merely warehoused) for centuries. As late as 1424, in the first catalog of Cambridge University Library, 122 donated volumes are listed in nine subject divisions, but the one for poetry and chronicles is a heading and no more. Religion, theology, and canon law account for three-quarters of the collection. But the development of central university libraries, a *bibliotheca publica* for the general use of members, lagged well behind those of colleges, faculties, and religious houses, and they are seldom found before the 15th century. Merton College, Oxford, had approximately 500 manuscripts when its new library (still in use) was finished in 1378. At the same time the University of Oxford itself had no more than two or three boxes of books, the ownership of which was disputed by a college, and they were not chained and made accessible till 1412. Indeed the university as a corporation had no considerable number of books until Duke Humfrey of Gloucester gave it some 280 manuscripts in the years 1435 to 1444. In all medieval libraries, donations and bequests were the normal means of growth. It is rare to find sums of money set aside specifically for library purchases.

Once libraries had outgrown the cupboards or chests of earlier times, a separate library room became a common feature from the 12th century onward. The arrangement of a typical late medieval library is known from some surviving examples, although the fittings in all of them have been altered over the centuries. In general the room would be long and fairly narrow, built on the second floor to protect against damp and give adequate light. Ranged along the walls between the windows and projecting at right angles from them would be long lecterns for reading the books. The books themselves would lie flat on shelves underneath the lecterns, to which the reader (standing up) would bring them on chains. There was often a written shelf list affixed to the end of each lectern to show what books were on the shelves. This would be, in effect, an extract of the catalog, which continued to reflect the actual physical grouping of the codices. The common libraries of convents and colleges would usually be kept locked, the key in possession of the librarian, who could be variously called the *armarius, cantor* or *precentor, librarius, custos librorum,* or *bibliothecarius*. The position and duties of the *librarius* were laid down in some detail by Humbert of Romans, general of the Dominicans, in his *Instructiones officialium* from around 1260, and these were often adapted and expanded in later library regulations. Not all the books in an institution were chained: It was the custom in colleges and friaries, as it was earlier and continued to be in monasteries, to make an annual distribution of books to fellows, brothers, or monks for their learned or edifying reading. These loans could on occasion stretch out over many years, or even a lifetime.

From Private to Public Libraries

It is really only from the 13th century onward that substantial collections of books in private hands can be identified. Naturally there were small deposits, perhaps largely of vernacular romances and epics, in royal households from an early period. Some of these came eventually to form the nucleus of national collections, but the age of true book-loving royalty and nobility lay in the future, in the 15th and 16th centuries. The remarkable *Biblionomia* of Richard de Fournival, poet and chancellor of the cathedral of Rheims, sets out a radically new scheme of classification for a library: Starting from philosophy, it reached the queen of sciences, theology, by way of medicine and canon and civil law. Perhaps the earliest specific and organized system of book arrangement in a library, the scheme seems to have been based on de Fournival's own collection, which must have numbered more than 300 manuscripts; a large portion of them entered the Sorbonne and then ultimately the Bibliothèque nationale in Paris. The bishop of Durham, Richard de Bury, reached a wider audience with his famous *Philobiblion*, an extreme expression of bibliomania but full of fascinating detail on the care and preparation of books. Although only four of his manuscripts are known to survive, contemporaries noted that he possessed more books than any man alive.

One of those contemporaries was the Italian poet and scholar Petrarch, who as a young man met de Bury at Avignon. More discriminating than the bishop and imbued with a wholly different spirit of nascent humanism, Petrarch was a considerable collector of books, a copyist and book hunter, and an inveterate annotator. There is a note of his favorite reading, above all the classics and Augustine, but no list of the books he owned survives, although many of the books themselves do. Petrarch's importance in library history lies in his conception of a public library, which he desired to found at Venice by bequeathing his own books to the republic. He intended that it should be further built up with public funds for the edification and convenience of the citizens and grow to equal the libraries of antiquity. For unknown reasons the plan, though agreed to by the republic of Venice, fell through. But the idea, here put forward for the first time, remained alive and bore fruit in the next century with the bequests of the books of Niccolò de' Niccoli to Florence and of Cardinal Bessarion to Venice, both of which became public libraries in the sense of being open to all qualified scholars.

With the time of Petrarch and his successors we are verging on the Italian Renaissance. But different parts of Europe absorbed the Renaissance at different rates, and there was still plenty of medieval backwardness for Italian humanists such as Poggio Bracciolini to mock as they scoured the old monastic foundations of the north in search of ancient texts. Yet with the steady expansion of literacy throughout 15th-century Europe, the traditional means of ensuring the survival of books continued apace. These included the large and diverse collection of manuscripts assembled and given to his own foundation at the new university of Erfurt in northern Germany by Amplonius Ratingk, physician and bibliophile. The Collegium Amplonianum has long been defunct, but the Bibliotheca Amploniana survives nearly intact from the days when Amplonius himself drew up the detailed catalog and regulations for its use.

With the invention of printing around 1450, the scale and nature of libraries changed forever. The great Benedictine monastery of St. Emmeram at Regensburg in southern Germany had been assembling manuscripts for 500 years when print arrived. In 1500 a new catalog was made, one of the most developed of the hundreds of medieval library catalogs. Of its 700 volumes, some 250 were already printed books, separately listed and thus incidentally providing the first ever catalog of incunabula.

MARTIN DAVIES

Further Reading

Bischoff, Bernhard, "The Court Library of Charlemagne," in *Manuscripts and Libraries in the Age of Charlemagne,* translated and edited by Michael Gorman, Cambridge and New York: Cambridge University Press, 1993

Cavallo, Guglielmo, editor, *Le biblioteche nel mondo antico e medievale,* Rome: Laterza, 1988

Christ, Karl, "Das Mittelalter," in *Handbuch der Bibliothekswissenschaft,* vol. 3, *Geschichte der Bibliotheken,* edited by Fritz Milkau, Leipzig: Harrassowitz, 1940; as *The Handbook of Medieval Library History,* revised by Anton Kern, translated and edited by Theophil M. Otto, Metuchen, New Jersey, and London: Scarecrow Press, 1984

Humphreys, Kenneth William, *The Book Provisions of the Mediaeval Friars, 1215–1400,* Amsterdam: Erasmus Booksellers, 1964

McCrank, Lawrence J., "Libraries," in *Dictionary of the Middle Ages,* edited by Joseph R. Strayer, vol. 7, New York: Scribner, 1986

Reynolds, Leighton Durham, and Nigel Guy Wilson, *Scribes and Scholars: A Guide to the Transmission of Greek and Latin Literature,* London: Oxford University Press, 1968; 3rd edition, Oxford: Clarendon Press, and New York: Oxford University Press, 1991

Riché, Pierre, "Les bibliothèques et la formation de la culture médiévale," in *Le pouvoir des bibliothèques: La mémoire des livres en Occident,* edited by Marc Baratin and Christian Jacob, Paris: Albin Michel, 1996

Thompson, James Westfall, *The Medieval Library,* Chicago: The University of Chicago Press, 1939; reprint, with a supplement by Blanche B. Boyer, New York: Hafner, 1965

Wormald, Francis, and Cyril Ernest Wright, editors, *The English Library before 1700: Studies in Its History,* London: Athlone Press, 1958

Membership/Social/Subscription Libraries

Membership libraries is a term coined in the late 1990s by surviving examples of what had once been the dominant library form in the United States. These libraries chose to employ the term because *membership libraries* suggests to the modern ear libraries that have members, whereas *social libraries* no longer conveys meaning. However, the phrases are synonymous.

Membership libraries are (and were) voluntary associations the support for which comes from individuals. The libraries, nonetheless, consider themselves to be "public." That term has come to be associated with libraries supported by taxation, but these libraries are public in the sense of not being personal. They are owned and used by members of the public, and indeed, before the second half of the 19th century, often referred to themselves as public libraries.

Reliance on financial support by individuals is what all membership libraries have in common, but otherwise there were many different types. One way of distinguishing the various types is according to their primary mode of financing and their legal basis. According to this division, there were two main types: the proprietary library and the subscription library. In the proprietary form, the individual member was, as the name implies, a proprietor, and the proprietary form was a common-law partnership based on the joint stock principle. One purchased a share or, in some cases, shares in the library and received a share certificate. A share could be sold or given away, either during one's lifetime or by bequest. In the subscription library, members subscribed (i.e., paid annual fees), and a subscription library was a common-law corporation.

In practice these two types commonly blended for financial reasons. The proprietary library would need more funds for ongoing operations, including purchase of books and periodicals, than could be generated by investing revenue from the sale of shares, particularly as the share revenue went in part into the purchase of library materials. Thus a library that was at first solely a proprietary library might permit use of the collection by those who paid an annual fee. In some cases a proprietary library of the early 19th century might even permit borrowing on a book-by-book fee basis, thus serving in effect as a commercial circulating library as well as a membership library. Similarly, the subscription library, as well as needing current funds for ongoing purchases and services, required capital to provide stability and so would institute different classes of membership.

Subscription and *proprietary* were not part of the names of libraries, but a number of other terms were. Sometimes these reveal the nature of a library and its users, but not always, particularly in the 18th century. At that time, before there was any standardization of names, one finds the use of *library company* (Library Company of Philadelphia [Pennsylvania], established 1731), or *library society* (Charleston [North Carolina] Library Society, 1748; New York Society Library, 1754), or simply *library* (Redwood Library [Newport, Rhode Island], 1747, with *Athenaeum* later added to its name).

Toward the end of the 18th century and in the first decades of the 19th, the term *social library* was used in the name of many voluntary associations created to form libraries, although the term was supplanted toward mid-century by *library association*. Whether termed a *social library* or *library association*, these were general or strict social libraries, to use the terminology of library historian Haynes McMullen. These libraries had a general collection and, particularly in rural communities, were used by men and women of all occupations and classes, although sometimes a woman's access came only through a male family member.

The numbers of such libraries became extensive in the northeastern part of the United States starting in the 1790s, and later in the Midwest and West, as those areas were settled. There is a clear correlation between population density and the prevalence of libraries, which is certainly one of the reasons why there were fewer such libraries in the South. While there were 84 of these libraries before 1786, the number for the period between 1790 and 1876 is 2,463.

In the decades around the turn of the 19th century, these libraries, except for those in cities, tended to be very small, with the number of books being in the low hundreds and the number of members also very small. (Since each member may have represented a household, the actual number of readers of a library's books could have been much larger.) The pattern was for a leading citizen or citizens to announce a meeting to consider forming a library. Those in attendance would choose officers (president, vice-president, treasurer, librarian, and board members), and they would also set the price of a share. With the share payments in hand, a leading member, often a clergyman, would decide what books to buy. These generally would consist of a few theological works, some multivolume histories such as David Hume's *History of England* (1754–62) or William Robertson's *History of the Discovery and Settlement of America* (1777), perhaps a life of George Washington, a book or two of moral instruction for youth, and a collection of brief pieces published under a title that included the word *ladies*. One or two blank volumes would be purchased along with the printed books. One would be used to record the rules, the names of the members, and the accounts of annual meetings. The record of books borrowed would also be recorded in a volume, one or two pages per member. A catalog with brief entries would also be compiled (and perhaps even printed) occasionally, with a list of the members. Customarily, the books were kept in an individual's home and were accessible only a few hours per week.

Rarely was it expected that a library would grow to any significant degree once the initial purchase had been made. Those that did grow (and made provision for growth by assessing members sufficiently large annual fees) were the larger libraries in the cities—those that have survived to this day. It seems that only in locations where there were numerous publishers were members sufficiently conscious of new, desirable books to assess themselves annual payments in order to acquire them. Generally, in rural areas few regular additions were made to the collections. As a result, the more avid readers eventually would read all of the books in a library, which would mean they no longer had a reason to be associated with it. With diminished interest from the leaders, annual meetings would no longer be held to choose officers, amend rules, and enforce fines. The library would become moribund, and most of the books would disappear, or perhaps be incorporated at some point into a successor institution, even into a publicly financed library.

A few membership libraries for groups other than men (i.e., for young people or for women) did exist in rural areas, but it was primarily in the cities that a wide variety of specialized membership libraries were developed. The first kind to be established was the athenaeum, a term imported from Britain. It suggested an elite institution and one that existed primarily to make information accessible, often through newspapers, rather than books for reading at home. The first, the Boston Athenaeum, established in 1807, was a decidedly elite institution, with a share price of $300. (Others customarily set the share price at a sum of perhaps $25, which was still high.) Not only did a high share price guarantee an elite institution, it also brought in the financial resources that were needed to provide the newspapers and periodicals of the day, that is, the sources of information required by the business and cultural elite. Of course, an athenaeum also needed to provide the space in which books could be read. An elite membership meant substantial payments, and library benefits fostered institutional survival. Of the 19 libraries at the November 1998 Membership Libraries Conference, "athenaeum" was the most common appellation: the Athenaeum Music and Arts Library, La Jolla, California; the Athenaeum of Philadelphia; the Boston Athenaeum; the Minneapolis (Minnesota) Athenaeum; the Nantucket (Massachusetts) Athenaeum; the Portsmouth (New Hampshire) Athenaeum; the Providence (Rhode Island) Athenaeum; the Redwood Library and Athenaeum; and the Salem (Massachusetts) Athenaeum. Most were started before 1820.

In addition to athenaeums, a few other specialized membership libraries were formed in the first two decades of the 19th century, with a few (libraries for women or for young people) coming into existence earlier. These were uncommon, but in 1820 another type of specialized membership library began to be created in numerous locations. These were libraries formed for young men, some for specific categories of young men, such as apprentices, mechanics, and mercantile and law clerks. Some of these libraries were entirely or partially charitable undertakings, provided to foster self-improvement and to give young men a wholesome place in which to spend their leisure time. With growth in membership, these libraries often became broader cultural institutions, sponsoring public lectures and ongoing educational programs. For their membership they also provided opportunities for the exercise of political and managerial skills. The elections of officers were frequently hard fought, and the officers, along with making vital decisions about the institution, were also responsible for running meetings and writing annual reports.

These libraries, like athenaeums, created a community among their members, and those communities shaped their members' reading practices. They made of reading something other than an individual, private activity. This applied not only to young men's libraries but to other occupational groups with membership libraries, such as farmers, lawyers, and physicians. There were also religious libraries formed to acquire religious books. Immigrant groups had membership libraries, particularly German immigrants. After the Civil War, "ladies' libraries" became common, especially in the state of Michigan.

Membership libraries continued to be formed in significant numbers throughout the 19th century. In the period from 1871 to 1875, far more membership libraries were formed than tax-supported public libraries, except in New England. In the rest of the country, the number of membership libraries in existence in 1900 exceeded the number of public libraries. The philanthropy of Andrew Carnegie changed the ratio.

The interrelationship between membership libraries and public libraries was complex and varied greatly from one location to another. Sometimes the existence of a membership library did forestall the creation of a public library, for just as the athenaeums often became substantial institutions, so did many of the libraries serving various groups of young men. Thus in New York City the Mercantile Library came to be a highly successful institution, with 8,300 members in 1875, a collection of 160,000 volumes (the fourth largest in the country), and a circulation of 200,000, the highest in the country. It survives to this day. In Boston, by contrast, the Boston Public Library hastened the demise of that city's Mercantile Library.

Dependence on funds from members led many membership libraries to broaden their membership well beyond the initial group, most particularly to include women as well as men. With that broadening came new funds to purchase more of the popular output that publishers were increasingly producing. This created a spiral of success, with money translating into more books and more members, and hence more money for more books. No obstacles stood in the way of membership libraries' buying multiple copies or providing services such as personal delivery of books, provided the associated expenses could be managed. Such services paved the way for large circulations and large numbers of loyal members.

However, without significant endowment a downward spiral eventually resulted in the demise of most of these institutions. Public libraries required payments of fees at times in their early years, but public librarians learned that even small fees deterred large numbers of citizens from becoming library users. Starting in the second half of the 19th century, U.S. citizens generally came to believe that the provision of reading matter was a public good, although to this day it is not universally believed that libraries should be supported by taxes.

KENNETH E. CARPENTER

See also Bibliophile Society Libraries; Boston Athenaeum; Grolier Club Library; Library Company of Philadelphia; Redwood Library and Athenaeum

Further Reading

Allen, David, "Eighteenth-Century Private Subscription Libraries and Provincial Urban Culture: The Amicable Society of Lancaster, 1769–c.1820," *Library History* 17 (2001)

Augst, Thomas, "The Business of Reading in Nineteenth-Century America: The New York Mercantile Library," *American Quarterly* 50, no. 2 (1998)

King, Marion, *Books and People: Five Decades of New York's Oldest Library*, New York: Macmillan, 1954

McMullen, Haynes, "The Very Slow Decline of the American Social Library," *Library Quarterly* 55 (1985)

McMullen, Haynes, *American Libraries before 1876*, Westport, Connecticut: Greenwood Press, 2000

Shera, Jesse, *Foundations of the Public Library: The Origins of the Public Library Movement in New England,* *1629–1855,* Chicago: University of Chicago Press, 1949

Story, Ronald, *The Forging of an Aristocracy: Harvard and the Boston Upper Class, 1800–1870*, Middletown, Connecticut: Wesleyan University Press, 1980

Middle Eastern Libraries

The earliest archives (i.e., collections of unique documents of a legal, economic, or administrative nature, as well as letters) and libraries (i.e., collections of works fo1r which multiple copies exist at different locations and times) we know from the Middle East are those using a cuneiform script. Written mostly on clay tablets, these texts have been especially well preserved throughout the ancient Near East. The oldest true libraries date from between 1500 and 1000 B.C. Archaeological evidence attests to substantial collections in the Hittite cities of Ugarit, Emer, Hattusa, Sapinuwa, and Sarissa; in the Mitannian (in Alalakh and Akhetaten) area in northern Mesopotamia; in Nizi in Syria; and in central Mesopotamia in the Middle Assyrian city of Assur. Libraries have been discovered in Babylon and the Elamite city of Kabnak.

Thirty libraries from 1000 to 300 B.C. have been uncovered. There were 15 libraries from the Neo-Assyrian cities of Assur, Kalhu, Dur Sarrukin, Niniveh, and Huzirina and 15 libraries from the Neo-Babylonian cities of Babylon, Sippar (the collections of which are exceptionally well preserved), Ur, and Uruk. The most extensive collection from this period is that of King Ashurbanipal in Ninevah (668–627 B.C.), which numbered approximately 25,000 tablets. Libraries of cuneiform tablets have been found in both official buildings and private residences, but there is little difference between the two in terms of collections.

In the Levant and surrounding areas, archives and libraries date from the period 800 to 300 B.C., although no libraries have thus far been excavated, most likely owing to the perishable writing materials used (papyri, leather, and ostraca rather than clay tablets). There are only a few remains of archives from Aramean, Israelite, and Phoenician states in Samaria, Lachish, Arad, and Jerusalem.

Perhaps the most famous library in history, the library of Alexandria (known as the Museum of Alexandria) was built in the third century B.C. by Ptolemy I and II. It included not only an extensive collection but also facilities for scholars who lived and worked in the library. The museum was especially important in the development of the library as an institution in its size (several hundred thousand volumes) and scope. Its early founders sought to create a universal collection, although most of its texts were in Greek. The fate of the famous library has been the subject of much scholarly debate. The museum was destroyed in A.D. 272 and the collection moved to the Serapeum, which itself was destroyed in 391, although Hellenic studies continued in Alexandria until the eighth century.

The second century B.C. saw the rise of important libraries in Asia Minor, including the famous rival of the Museum of Alexandria, the Pergamon Library. In response to this challenge, Ptolemy V of Egypt stopped shipments of papyrus, an act that led Eumenes II of Pergamum in 192 B.C.E. to develop parchment (*pergamena*), a more durable material and hence an important technical advance in the history of libraries. Other libraries in the area included one at the temple of Aescalapius and the Celsus Library, built by Julius Aquila in A.D. 135.

The earliest recorded Christian library is that founded by Bishop Alexander in Jerusalem in A.D. 250. More significant, however, was that founded by Origen and Pamphilus at Caesarea in Palestine, which served as the first Christian university and was probably the most significant such institution until the founding of Constantinople. By the fourth century, however, that great city became the center for most library activity in the eastern Mediterranean. Under the early patriarchs, libraries were built through which the scholarship of Athens, Asia Minor, and Alexandria was preserved for another 1,000 years. Although many libraries were established between the founding of the Byzantine Empire by Constantine the Great and the conquest of Constantinople by Mehmet in 1453, most were destroyed in numerous rebellions and invasions, especially by the crusaders. Monasteries had libraries as well, many of which cataloged their holdings. Notable among them was the library of 20,000 volumes at the Aya Trioda Monastery at Heybeliada, founded in the tenth century. When the Ottomans conquered Constantinople, they did not destroy the libraries, and some ancient books have been preserved.

Libraries developed quite early in Islamic history, largely as a result of the commitment to literacy on the part of early Muslims. Collections of sacred texts were attached to early mosques, such as al-Aqsa (c. 634) in Jerusalem and the Great (Umayyad)

Mosque in Damascus (c. 721). Institutions called *bayt al-hikma* (the house of wisdom) were also established very early. These employed scholars to work, dispute, compose, translate, and pursue astrological studies within the institution. The first *bayt al-hikma*, founded in the late seventh century, is that of the Umayyad Caliph Mu'awiya. By the early eighth century, the regular position of *sahib al-masahif* (curator of books) had been established. Under the 'Abbasids, and especially the Caliph al-Ma'mun, the institution of *bayt al-hikma* expanded and developed to include all known branches of learning. Al-Ma'mun's institution thrived until the tenth century.

Eventually, *bayt al-hikma*, centers serving individual scholars, were replaced by *dar al-'ilm* (house of knowledge, sometimes called *dar al-kutub*, or house of books), which served as public academies. Their collections comprised a range of translated and Arab-Islamic sciences and included chairs for the teaching of both doctrine and the natural sciences. Recognizing the institution as a powerful influence on the development of religious and political thought of the day, the appointed 'Abbasids sought to control scholarship through large bequests and founded such institutions in the big cities of Mesopotamia, Syria, and Egypt.

Early in the history of *dar al-'ilm* (the eighth century), the Arabs began to use the Chinese method of making paper, which replaced parchment and papyrus as the primary writing surface and helped to advance the explosion of book production in the Islamic empire.

In addition to *bayt al-hikma* and *dar al-'ilm,* many important libraries developed in conjunction with mosques. Book collections in mosques typically originated as gifts and bequests (*awqaf* or *habus*) by caliphs, scholars, and notables. Only rarely were books purchased for mosque collections. More often, scholars copied or transcribed older works and donated these copies to the libraries of the mosque in which they taught or worked. Some of the best known are described below.

Al-Andalus

The Grand Mosque of Cordoba contained a large collection of books and masāhif. Founded in 786 by the Umayyad prince Abd al-Rahmān, this library was destroyed in 1236 by Ferdinand III of Castile and León.

Morocco

Built in 859 by Fatima la-Fihri, the Qarawiyyin Mosque in Fez contained three libraries, the most prestigious of which was that founded by al Mutawakkil Abu Inan in 1349. Another important collection of rare manuscripts existed in the Grand Mosque of Tétouan.

Tunisia

The two most important mosque libraries in Tunisia belong to the Qayrawan (Jamí 'Uqba, built between 670 and 680 by 'Uqba Ibn Nafi, an important center of learning and culture) and the Zaytuna mosques (founded in 699 by Hassan Ibn al-Numan and currently known as Zaytuna University). The Qayrawan Library, popularly known as the 'Atiqa (old) Maktaba, dates from the early ninth century. The books of the 'Atiqa Library were either destroyed or stolen when the Banu Hilāl, sent by the Fatimid caliph, al-Mustansir, ravaged the city. The Zaytuna Mosque had two libraries: the Abdaliya (or Sadiqiya) founded by the Hafside prince Abu Abd Allah Muhammad Ibn al-Husain and the Ahmadiya Library, which also dates to the Hafside period (1227–1574). Its collection was built with bequests, the most prominent of which came from Abu Faris Abd al-Azīz, whose 1394 bequest is said to have contained 36,000 volumes.

Egypt

One of the oldest and largest mosque libraries is that of al-Azhar Mosque in Cairo. Founded under the Fatimid caliph al-Muizz in 973 as the library of a Shiite *madrasa* (school), it gradually developed into one of the principal centers of higher education in the Muslim empire. Although built as a forum for advancing Fatimid ideology, it quickly accumulated books in a variety of subjects such as history, arithmetic, and astronomy. The original library was centrally located in a large chamber near the mosque's pulpit. In 1753 the compound was torn down and the collection broken up. In 1897 a central depository, officially called the Azhar Library, was established, and the books were brought together again and cataloged. The Azhar Library collection has steadily grown to contain several hundred thousand volumes, including numerous rare manuscripts.

Syria

The Umayyad Mosque in Damascus, originally built by al-Walīd Ibn Abd al-Malik in 714, housed collections of Sunni study circles. In addition, its holdings included privately donated collections as well as those established at the various schools, enclosures, and mausoleums attached to the mosque. The most renowned collection in this last category was the library of the Qubbat al-Māl, which, when first opened in 1899, is said to have included parchment codices and manuscripts in Aramaic, Greek, Hebrew, Coptic, Latin, and French. Most of the holdings were given to the German emperor William II and only a few pieces kept for the National Archives in Damascus.

The Arabian Peninsula

As one of Islam's early sponsors of public education, the Haram at Makka was one of the first mosques to have a book collection. Such collections were housed in various libraries, the earliest being the khizana in the Maliki enclosure, first mentioned in writing in 1095. Other libraries could be found in madrasas near the Haram. The Sharabiya Madrasa is said to have housed a valuable collection that, however, had been lost by the end of the 16th century. Another existed in the Qaytbay Madrasa founded in 1477. The best known and possibly the largest library founded at the Haram was the Sulaymaniya, established by the Ottoman sultan Abd al-Majīd and located behind the Well of Zamzam. Much of this collection was destroyed in a flood in 1861. Like the Haram, the Prophet Muhammad's mosque in Medina housed several book collections. The most famous is the Maktabat al-Haram al-Nabawi. Most of the mosque's collections were lost in a 1481 fire. In response, Sultan Qaytbay founded and endowed the collection of the Ashrafiya Madrasa in 1482. In the southern part of the peninsula, cities such as Taizz, Ibb, and Tarim in Yemen had mosque libraries. The oldest and largest, however, was the Mutawakiliya of the Grand Mosque of Sana. Its holdings included a rare manuscript that belonged to the Imām al-Mansūr Abd Allah.

Iraq

Baghdad was the center of learning and culture for the eastern half of the 'Abbāsid empire (750–1258) and as such was home to numerous mosques, madrasas, and libraries. One of the most prominent libraries was that of the mosque of Abu Hanifa Nu'man. Personalities such as the physician Yahya Ibn Jazla, the historian al-Zamakhshari, and Abd al-Salam Ibn Muhammad al-Qazwini, a prominent Mutazilite, bequeathed their book collections to this institution. Also important was the Haydariya Library of the Grand Mosque of al-Najaf, which was well established by the tenth century. It reportedly housed manuscripts dating to the first century of the Islamic era. Many of its valuable holdings were lost in a fire in 1354.

Palestine/Lebanon

Al-Aqsa Mosque in Jerusalem developed early into an important academy for religious and secular studies and had a large collection of books in its schools, including the Nasriya, Nahawiya, Farisiya, and Ashrafiya madrasas. Other important mosque libraries were located in the Jazzar Mosque in the ancient coastal city of Acre and in the Grand Mansuri Mosque in Tripoli. The latter received a large gift of books in 1677 from Mustafa Miqati, a renowned Tripoli scholar.

Iran

In Iran, too, libraries have a long and distinguished history. R. Homayoun Farokh, in his "History of Books and the Imperial Libraries of Iran," describes 459 libraries that existed in the area from ancient times to the Mongol invasions of the 13th century, including libraries in every major city, the most important being the collections in Nishapur, Isfahan, Ghazney, Shiraz, Merve, and Mosul. The 14th century saw the establishment of important libraries: one in Maragheh, which housed more than 400,000 works, many translated from Chinese, Mongolian, Sanskrit, Arabic, and Assyrian languages; a second, the Rashidi Library near Tabriz, also included an extensive international collection. The oldest library in existence in Iran, the Razavi Library in Meshhad, was also founded in the 14th century in connection with the shrine of the eighth Shiite imam, Reza. The Sheikh Safi Library, which also began at this time, lasted until the 19th century, when most of its books were transported to Russia. The Safavid period (1501–1736) also saw the founding of several important libraries, including the Royal Library in Isfahan and the Armenian Library in Jolfa, still in existence today. During the Qajar period (1794–1925), the Sepahsallar Library was built in Tehran in connection with a mosque; it gave rise to the Sepahsallar School, also known for a time as the College of Theology. The Royal Library was also established by Fath Ali Shah Qajar and located in the Golestan Palace in Tehran.

The Ottoman Period

The Ottoman period (1301–1914) also saw extensive library activity. Before the Ottomans, the Seljuks built *madreses* (schools) in Anatolia. In Konya, a Seljuk capital, the first library was established in the Iplikçi medrese on the order of Şemsüddün Altun Aba in 1201. Its surviving collection was moved to the Konya Yusuf Ağa Library at the end of the 19th century. Another noteworthy library was the Sadreddin-i Konevi Library, established in 1274. Set up during the reign of Giyaseddin Keyhusrev III, it developed into a well-known center of scientific learning. Some Seljuk libraries continued under the Ottomans. Other collections were taken either to the Konya Yusuf Ağa Library or the Hemdem Çelebi Library in the Mevlana convent. Some Anatolian chieftains, such as Ismail Bey of the Candaroğlu, had private libraries.

Once in power, the Ottomans further developed the Seljuk institutions. Sultan Mehmet the Conqueror was a major contributor. In 1451 he established a library in Cihannüma Kasrı at his palace in Edirne. Approximately 1,500 titles of this collection were lost in a fire, and the fate of the remaining books is not known. Mehmet set up a private library in Topkapı Saray where he also established the Ederun School. Remainders of the private library can now be found in the collections of Aya Sofya, Nuruosmaniye, and Hamidiye. The books of the Ederun School are at the Koğuşlar Kütüphanesi in Topkapı. Mehmet set up strict rules for administering the libraries he endowed. The *hafiz-i kütüp*, or librarian, had to be intimately familiar with the contents of the collection, and assistants had to keep accession records. In later years the administration of libraries became corrupt, and many manuscripts were sold. During the Tanzimat era (1839–76), Sultan Abdulmejid I reformed the laws. Ottoman scholars who had visited the West founded a learned society called the Camiyet-i Ilmiye-i Osmaniye, which in turn founded the first modern library in Turkey. Ten articles addressing its administration, accession, cataloging, lending, and preservation governed its administration. Although proposals for a national library were submitted, nothing came to pass until 1869, when the Ministry of Education was formed and a national library was established at Beyazıt Külliyesi. In addition, the government compiled a list with all the holdings of 63 libraries in Istanbul. When the last sultan, Abdül-Hamid II, was deposed in 1914, the holdings of his library at Yildiz Palace were transferred to Istanbul University.

The late Ottoman period saw important developments in Palestine. There were, for instance, large private collections in Jerusalem, some open to the public. The best known is the Ragib al-Khālidī in Jerusalem, containing 5,000 manuscripts and another 5,000 volumes in Arabic, Persian, Turkish, French, and English, which was open to the public as the Maktabat al-Khalidiya at the beginning of the 20th century. Another private library originating in the 18th century was the Khalili Library located near the Haram al-Sharif. It was said to contain some 7,000 volumes in Arabic.

Christian communities have long maintained libraries in monasteries, churches, and missions. Most, however, were collections rather than organized libraries. In the 19th century, some communities, such as the Greek Orthodox, centralized their collections. The Byzantine scholar Athanasios Kerameus compiled a four-volume catalog of a collection that contained 2,350 Greek manuscripts, mostly on theology and liturgy. Another remarkable library, reportedly established in the middle of the fifth century, is that of the Armenian patriarchate maintained at the St. James convent in Jerusalem, with more than 20,000 books and more than 3,800 manuscripts in Armenian, Syrian, Coptic, Ethiopian, Arabic, and Turkish. In the Franciscan St. Savior (San Salvatore) Monastery, which dates back to the establishment of the Order of the Franciscans in the Holy Land, a library was first installed on Mount Zion and then moved to Jerusalem and reorganized in 1558. Besides theological treatises, it contained texts of Roman authors such as Plutarch, Gaius, Titus Livius, Hippocrates, and Galenos. Other collections of importance in Jerusalem existed in the St. George Cathedral and College (founded 1892), Dormition Abbey (Benedictine), the Ratisbone Monastery (Catholic), the St. Mark Monastery (Syrian), and the Deir al-Sultan (Ethiopian).

At the end of the Ottoman rule in Palestine, Christian communities had established biblical and archaeological research and teaching institutions which housed libraries as well. Schools such as the Ecole Biblique Archéologique Française, the American School of Oriental Research, and the Deutsch-evangelische Institut für Altertumswissenschaft des heiligen Landes had important research libraries.

Other Regional Libraries

European consulates also established libraries that catered to their nationals. Two consular libraries, however, were particularly well known both in Europe and Palestine. The first Prussian consul, Ernst Gustav Schultz, established a research library for the use of German travelers in Jerusalem. Emil Roediger from Halle prepared a list of books called the "Königliche Bibliothek in Jerusalem," which served as the basis of the collection. Thus for the first time a European research library was systematically imported into Palestine, and books published in Palestine found their way into libraries in Europe. Also, the British consul James Finn founded the Jerusalem Literary Society, which in turn established an important library.

Waves of Zionist immigration to Palestine in the late 19th century significantly changed the nature of the Jewish communities in Palestine. The Jewish tradition of study and learning fostered the establishment of rabbinical libraries in synagogues, traditional schools, and *yeshivot* (academies of Talmudic learning), which were, by this time, supplemented by secular literature. Between 1883 and 1919, new Jewish libraries emerged in Jerusalem, Safed (present-day Zefat in Israel), and Jaffa as well as the new settlements founded during the waves of immigration. Toward the end of the Ottoman rule, many newly emerging public libraries set out to collect and preserve the heritage of the Jewish people. Other libraries were geared toward communities in agricultural settlements or toward teachers and students. Of the latter category, some developed into educational institutions and some into public libraries. Finally, there were the workers' libraries emerging from the socialist movement. Because the local Ottoman and Muslim cultures had no influence over Christian or Jewish communities, European, and especially German, ties were cultivated in the establishment of these institutions.

The colonial and postcolonial period has seen the establishment of national libraries in most, but not all, countries of the Middle East and North Africa. Some, such as those in Egypt and Algeria, have state-run libraries dating from the mid-19th century, although most are considerably more recent, with several established only within the last two decades. Generally speaking, the region suffers from the lack of professional training for staff and funding for equipment. Turkey has three library science programs and a few exist in the Arab world, notably in Egypt and Rabat, Morocco, but many important positions at these institutions are filled by non-librarians. The development of legislation in many Arab countries, especially with regard to the introduction of copyright and legal deposit laws, standards for bibliographic description, cataloging in publication, the publication of national bibliographies, and interlibrary loan regulations, has been encouraging.

National Libraries in Arab Countries

A description of a few representative national libraries from the Arab world will serve to exemplify the nature of the institution in the region.

In Iraq the National Library at Baghdad (Maktabat al-Wataniya) began as a public library called Maktabat al-Salam. In 1929, with a collection of some 4,000 books, it was moved to the al-Mansuria madrasa, where it was called Maktabat al-Amma. In 1961 the Iraqi government passed the National Library Act, establishing the National Library, renamed al-Maktaba al-Wataniya, as an independent governmental department. In 1970 a deposit law was instituted.

In nearby Syria the national library began in 1919 when the Arab Academy was charged with the supervision of the al-Zāhiriyya Library, founded in 1880. Its collection consisted at that time of the surviving manuscripts from different small libraries in Syria. In 1919 al-Jazā'irī published a catalog (*sijil*) of this collection. The academy increased the holdings of the manuscript collection and started acquiring books. As a result, the collection grew from 2,465 manuscripts to 22,000 volumes between 1919 and 1945. At that time, the al-Zāhiriyya was more a public than a national library because no obligation for a legal deposit had been introduced. The library also lacked a number of functions and services that typically characterize national libraries. With the beginning of independence in 1946, the need for a modern national library first emerged. In 1968 the Ministry of Culture officially issued a decision to establish a national library. But it was not until 1978 that construction began. The library, Al-Assad Library, was inaugurated in November 1984.

The idea for a national library in Lebanon began in 1885 as the project of Philippe de Tarazi, a Lebanese nobleman. It was not until 1921, however, that the institution came into being with Tarazi as its director. The collection at that time consisted of Tarazi's private library, but it has suffered from a lack of direction since then. The national deposit law was passed in 1941 and revised in 1952 and 1959 but was never fully enforced. The library sustained significant damage and loss during the Lebanese civil war.

The history of Jordan's national library begins in 1977, when the Directorate of Libraries and National Documents was established as part of the Ministry of Culture and Youth. The directorate was closed down in 1990 and replaced by three new units created within the Ministry of Culture and Youth: the National Library, the National Documentation Center, and the Royal Cultural Center. In 1992 a new copyright law, covering both printed and nonprint materials, designated the National Library as the country's legal deposit library. In addition to the development of national libraries, there have been other large library projects. Best known, perhaps, is the Bibliotheca Alexandrina, an ambitious international project to create a modern version of the classical Library of Alexandria. The project, which began in 1989, is planned for 8 million volumes as well as impressive research and technical facilities, but owing to budgetary problems, probably housed only 250,000 when it partially opened in spring 2000. Other new projects include the King Fahd National Library in Saudi Arabia, which will eventually house 500,000 publications, and the library services at King Abdul Aziz City for Science and Technology, founded in 1977. In Kuwait three university libraries were constructed in the late 1990s.

Non-Arab countries in the Middle East have also established national libraries. The Beyazıt State Library (Beyazıt Devlet Kütüphanesi), the first Turkish state-run library, was opened in 1884. After the establishment of the Turkish Republic, the Law of Education (1924) decreed that all private foundation libraries were to be given to the Ministry of National Education and managed by the Directorate of Libraries. Various proposals to establish a national library in Turkey were discussed (notably in 1862, 1917, and 1933), and the depository law was enacted in 1934, but it was not until 1948 that the national library was opened. In 1950 the National Library Law, stating the founding principles, functions, and duties of the library, was enacted. Five years later the Bibliography Institute was established. The institute took over the publication of the national bibliography. The library has been using the *Anglo-American Cataloguing Rules*, 2nd edition (AACR 2) since 1985, and in 1995 the holdings numbered 1.5 million volumes.

The National Library in Iran was founded in 1939, with the core of its collection coming from the earlier public library. Over the course of its history, the library has purchased several private libraries, including many of old Persian manuscripts. The library also received 600 books from the Iranian and Russian Bank and, in 1941, a substantial collection from the German government. In 1968 a legal depository law was enacted, although (as is the case for many such laws in the region) it has not extended to government publications. An ambitious plan for a new national library began in 1977 but was stalled by the Iranian revolution. Meanwhile the library continued to grow, absorbing the collection of both the Pahlavi Library and the Tehran Book Processing Center. In 1991 a program in library science was added to the National Library and the government resumed plans to build the new national library. By 1995 an architectural plan for the project had been selected, though no further progress is reported on its website.

Israel

In 1884 scholars in Jerusalem founded a collection that was incorporated in 1892 into the Beth ha-Sefarim Midrash Abrabanel founded by B-nai B'rith. By 1902 its holdings had reached 22,000 volumes. In 1920 the Abrabanel was taken over by the World Zionist Organization and was given the name of the National Jewish Library (Beth ha-Sefarim ha-Leumi). In 1924 it was attached to the Hebrew University and renamed Jewish National and University Library.

CHRISTOF GALLI

See also Islamic Libraries; Jewish Collections and Jewish Libraries; Jewish National and University Library

Further Reading

Heffening, Willi, and James Douglas Pearson, "Maktaba," in *Encyclopaedia of Islam, CD-ROM Edition*, Leiden, The Netherlands: Brill, 1999

'Ishsh, Yusuf, *Les bibliothèques arabes publiques et semi-publiques en Mésopotamie, en Syrie et en Égypte au Moyen Age*, Damascus, Syria: Institut Français de Damas, 1967

Pedersén, Olof, *Archives and Libraries in the Ancient Near East, 1500–300 B.C.*, Bethesda, Maryland: CDL Press, 1998

Schidorsky, Dov, "Libraries in Late Ottoman Palestine between the Orient and the Occident," *Libraries and Culture* 33, no. 3 (Summer 1998)

Sibai, Mohamed Makki, *Mosque Libraries: An Historical Study*, London and New York: Mansell, 1987

National Libraries

What is a National Library?

National libraries—libraries formally established by a country to perform national functions—are now an accepted fact of library life, but they are historically a relatively recent phenomenon. Many have a long ancestry, but they did not become "national" (that is, recognized as belonging to the nation) until the mid-18th century. Their main function, the collection of the nation's publications, was not formalized until the 19th century, although it dates back to the granting of legal deposit to the Bibliothèque royale of France in 1537. Another established function is the production of a current national bibliography. Conservation of the national collection did not become a major issue until the last 20 years.

Different Types of National Library

The term *national library* can refer to a variety of institutions. Some countries have de facto national libraries. In the United States the Library of Congress is primarily what its name says, but it is also recognized as the national library, as is the National Diet (Parliamentary) Library in Japan, which was modeled on it. Not until the last few years have the Royal Libraries of Denmark, the Netherlands, and Sweden been officially and formally recognized as the national libraries of their countries.

National subject libraries are not uncommon. Several countries have national science libraries, whether in name as in Denmark, which has a National Library of Science and Medicine and a National Technological Library in addition to the Royal Library, or de facto, like the Canada Institute for Scientific and Technical Information, which is government-funded but not recognized as a national library. The United States has, in addition to the Library of Congress, a National Library of Medicine and a National Agricultural Library. Several countries, especially in Asia, have separate national scientific and technological information centers, which include libraries; INSDOC, the Indian Scientific Documentation Centre, is an example. These were set up largely because governments believed that their national libraries had neither the systems nor the inclination to provide scientific information and dissemination services.

There are also libraries that serve particular relatively small sectors of the community at a national level and carry the title of "national," for example national libraries for the blind, though in one or two cases (as in the United States) these are part of the main national library. Divisions by format are common, but separate national collections of audiovisual media are often known as "archives" (e.g., the National Film Archive in the United Kingdom).

In smaller European countries national libraries may serve also as university libraries. In other continents it is much more common for national libraries to double as public libraries. Some African countries (e.g., Kenya, Malawi, and Botswana) have "National Library Services," which aim to serve the whole country. In several countries, especially in Africa, the national library and the national archives have been combined, for example Bolivia, Kampuchea, and Zambia.

Countries with More than One National Library

A few countries have two national libraries, apart from those that have separate science libraries. Denmark has, as well as the Royal Library in Copenhagen, a State and University Library in Århus, both with legal deposit. Italy has two Biblioteche Nazionali Centrali, in Rome and Florence, which divide national functions between them; there are also *biblioteche nazionale* in eight of the country's regions. Some "countries" consist of several "nations." In Czechoslovakia and Yugoslavia, until they broke up into separate countries; the component states already had national libraries. The main present examples are in the United Kingdom, Canada, the Russian Federation, and the Federal Republic of Yugoslavia. The Biblioteca de Catalunya in Barcelona, while not officially recognized as the national library of the province, is certainly thought of as such.

Political Connections

National libraries are inevitably subject to political influence. A change in government can lead to changes in funding, a change of director, and sometimes shifts in direction. In most countries the appointment of the director of the national library is a political one, made sometimes with little reference to relevant experience or expertise.

Functions

Before World War II the functions of national libraries were ill defined. Decolonization and the subsequent birth of newly independent states after the war changed this. A United Nations Educational, Scientific, and Cultural Organization (UNESCO) Symposium on National Libraries in 1958 was followed by several statements of functions, notably by K.W. Humphreys, in a 1966 article in *Unesco Bulletin for Libraries*. The fundamental functions he proposed—"The outstanding and central collection of a nation's literature, Depôt légal, Coverage of foreign literature, Publication of the national bibliography, National bibliographical information center, Publication of catalogues [and] Exhibitions"—have been modified and queried since, but no similar attempts have been made recently.

Collections

The most basic function, that of collecting the nation's published output, has been thrown into disarray by the growth first of non-book materials such as sound recordings, films and videotapes, then of "static" electronic media (CD-ROMs, DVDs), and finally of "immaterial" media such as radio and television broadcasts and material on the World Wide Web. The internationalization of publishing has added a further complication: Publications may be written in one country, printed in another, and published in several simultaneously. This has made nonsense of the legal deposit laws of some countries, especially in Eastern Europe, which make the printer responsible for deposit.

The whole concept of a comprehensive collection of national publications is also being disputed on both practical and economic grounds, as it involves not only questions concerning the necessity of collecting electronic publications but also issues concerning the advisability and feasibility of collecting all printed matter. The costs of storage, preservation, and recording amount to very high figures over the years. In any case, much locally produced material is not collected at all. Some countries, for example Norway, have introduced legislation that covers broadcast as well as electronic media, but except in countries with a small output such comprehensiveness is inconceivable.

Audiovisual media are collected by some national libraries. A few collect them comprehensively, as in Norway, but most (e.g., the Bibliothèque nationale de France) exclude films. Some (e.g., the British Library) collect audio media only. Where there are national collections of these materials at all, they are often called national film or sound archives.

Some national collections, mainly in smaller countries, acquire material relating to the country—published or written about it, written by authors born in or associated with it, and in the language of the country, wherever such material is published. Such aims are appropriate if the object is to have a collection relating to the nation. In the case of countries such as the United Kingdom and the United States, the sheer volume of material makes such a goal totally unattainable.

Bibliographic Control

Although current national bibliographies date back to 1790, and whereas now most national libraries produce them, only one or two did so before World War II. Even now this is not a universal function (the Library of Congress has never produced one). Large developed countries can make a profit from the sale of frequently issued bibliographies, but small published output in less developed countries and smaller nations makes frequent publication difficult. There are also difficulties in production, and backlogs of two or more years can result. With the ability to make up-to-date online bibliographies available and to produce outputs as desired, the need to print regular issues on paper is being questioned. Australia has already abandoned its printed bibliography.

Some major national libraries, notably those of the United States, France, and the United Kingdom, embarked upon complete catalogs of their holdings long before the advent of automation. The use of computers from 1960 made this much easier, although it was still necessary to convert old records into electronic form, whether by key-punching or (more recently) by scanning and optical character recognition. Libraries in a number of developed countries have followed suit.

Bibliographic Services

The years since World War II have seen an increase in services provided by national libraries to other libraries, prompted by need and enabled by information and communications technology. Since 1901 the Library of Congress has sold catalog records (as cards) to other libraries, an example followed at a long distance by the British National Bibliography after World War II. The production of national bibliographic records was greatly facilitated in the late 1960s with the large-scale automation of cataloguing and the advent of machine-readable cataloging and the MARC (MAchine-Readable Cataloging) format. The more efficient production and supply of cards were succeeded by the provision of computer-generated microfilm, then by CD-ROMs and online. It is now virtually routine for the national library to make records of their acquisitions available in these ways. National libraries have also worked toward harmonizing their records to make interchange and combined databases easier.

Communities Served

Most national libraries in the more developed countries are basically libraries for researchers. In less developed countries, they tend to double as public libraries and in small countries often include also archives. However, there is now pressure to make the research-oriented libraries more accessible to the general public. Electronic technology should make this easier, as digitized material can be made accessible to anyone with access to a computer.

Subject Focus

Very few national libraries have given the same priority to science and technology that they give to the humanities and social sciences. Although science and technology publications are acquired as part of legal deposit, the libraries have rarely aimed to collect foreign material in these areas, nor have they generally tried to exploit these parts of their collections. It is for this reason that several countries have established documentation centers.

There are exceptions. Two of the institutions that went to form the British Library were the National Lending Library for Science and Technology and the National Reference Library of Science and Invention. The National Library of Scotland set up a separate Scottish Science Library in 1989. The National Library of Australia is an example of other national libraries that have made efforts to utilize their non-humanities collections fully. Others, including the National Library of New Zealand, have followed the British Library's example by setting up Business Information Services.

Interlibrary Document Supply

Interlibrary document supply, although a major growth area for libraries in general since World War II, is not a significant function of most national libraries at present. Some do not lend original items under any circumstances, although they will supply paper or microfilm copies, while others will lend as a last resort. The British Library is unique in providing an interlibrary supply service as a major activity; any registered library can use it.

Conservation

Conservation became a major preoccupation in the 1980s, with the recognition that books were decaying faster than any amount of expenditure could remedy. Efforts were first directed to methods of mass paper conservation, but more recently at least equal attention has been given to digitization. Some national libraries have assumed leadership of national conservation activities and set up national preservation offices.

National Leadership

Leadership aspects have become more important as information and communications technology has opened up new opportunities for electronic interchange of bibliographic records at a national level. The national library, as the most authoritative creator of records, has been the natural protagonist. National Bibliographic Agencies are now virtually essential if the national output is to be controlled. They need not be, but usually are, located within national libraries. The national library is the channel through which the country contributes records to international databases and receives them from other countries. It has been argued that the main purpose of comprehensive national bibliographic control is an international one, to ensure comprehensive worldwide control.

Centers for the Book

A fairly recent trend has been the establishment of Centers for the Book, with the Library of Congress taking the lead in 1977, followed by the United Kingdom and South Africa. These vary in their functions, but they have in common a celebration of the printed book. Other countries may follow suit.

Management and Friends of the Library

With the increasing scale of operations, and with increased financial and performance pressure by government, management has been recognized as vital. As part of their response, many national libraries in developed countries have, voluntarily or at the behest of government, produced strategic plans, in some cases business plans. Another trend is to have bodies of Friends of the National Library, which constitute supporters' clubs, important because national libraries have no clearly defined clientele as do other types of library. These may also raise some income for national libraries.

Groupings

A notable feature of recent years has been the creation of regional groups. The initial urge toward cooperation was largely the result of the automation of catalog records and the subsequent ability to share creation of and access to them. To this has been added cooperation in preservation, and most recently in digitization. Other topics discussed have included legal deposit, especially in relation to electronic publishing.

The first group in the field, in 1974, was the Conference of Directors of National Libraries (CDNL), which has a worldwide membership. It was followed in 1979 by the Conference of Directors of National Libraries of Asia and Oceania (CDNLAO). With 18 members (ranging from China, Japan, India, and Australia to the Cook Islands and Kiribati), it covers all of southern and eastern Asia, but not western or central Asia. CDNLAO has been mostly concerned with development. The Conference of European National Librarians (CENL), founded in 1987, has 41 members from 39 countries, has undertaken several useful projects, notably CoBRA (Computer and Bibliographic Record Actions); which has removed several barriers to the interchange of bibliographic records between European countries. Finally, the Asociación de Bibliotecas Nacionales de Iberoamérica (ABINIA), established in 1989, is a linguistic rather than regional association, since although the original initiative came from South America, its membership consists of 21 national libraries of Spanish- and Portuguese-speaking states in Europe and Latin America, in addition to Puerto Rico.

Historical Overview

National libraries in the more or less modern sense began to appear in the 18th century; by 1800 there were more than 20, all of them in Europe except the Library of Congress (founded that year), none of them formally recognized. In the 19th century nearly all other countries in Europe established national libraries, as did most countries in South America. Many of them had prestigious buildings, but the collections were often very limited. The third wave started in the late 19th century with a trickle of new national libraries in Africa and Asia, followed by a flood after World War II and decolonization. During the period from 1900 to 1965 several developed countries also created national libraries, and other national libraries, including those of France, Germany, Japan, and the United Kingdom, have recently undergone major reorganizations. The trend over the centuries has been from collecting to control, and from control to services, with national coordination along the way. The national library as understood today is a creation of the last 50 years.

History by Continent

Europe

The earliest library that can be considered a "real" national library, as it was the first to benefit from legal deposit (1537) and as the country's boundaries were largely settled soon after 1500, is the Bibliothèque nationale of France. This began in the 14th century as the personal collection of King Charles V. Other royal or ducal libraries that turned into national libraries are those of Austria, Sweden, Denmark, the Netherlands, and Luxembourg.

It is extremely difficult to say when the various libraries became national. Legal deposit privileges were granted to some libraries before they were officially given national status, while a few (e.g., the Dutch Royal Library) still do not have it, and non-national libraries may also have deposit privileges. The date of opening to the public is another imperfect criterion. The French Bibliothèque royale was opened to the public in 1720, the British Museum Library in 1759, and the Danish Royal Library in 1793, but in many if not most cases there were restrictions on who could use the library. Official recognition as a national library is the best criterion. The renaming during the French Revolution of the French Bibliothèque royale as the Bibliothèque nationale—the first use of such a name—was a landmark.

The British Library's origins typify the devious path many libraries took to becoming national. Although a proposal for a national library had been made in 1707, it was not until 1752, when Sloane's collection of books, manuscripts, and natural history specimens formed the nucleus of the British Museum, that one came into being. In the mid-19th century the British Museum Library underwent massive changes; it was transformed under Antonio (later Sir Anthony) Panizzi, one of the greatest names in national librarianship, who advocated a "universal collection." Its name did not change until the British Library was set up in 1973, carrying out some basic national functions before others were added to it by its amalgamation with other national libraries and with the *British National Bibliography*. The British Library is probably unique in having the national collection of patents. Another major reorganization after World War II was in Germany, which in 1990 brought together the Deutsche Bücherei in Leipzig, the Deutsche Bibliothek in Frankfurt, and the Deutsches Musikarchiv in Berlin to form the new Deutsche Bibliothek.

The countries in Eastern Europe that were part of the Soviet bloc until 1989–90 had had national libraries for some years; the Czech State Library has its origins in a library of 1348. Others are more recent: Bulgaria's was established after liberation from Ottoman rule in 1878–79, and Poland's was not created until 1928. The national libraries of the Baltic republics all grew from public libraries in the capital cities in 1918–19. After 1945 they were all obliged to follow the Soviet model, in particular taking overall responsibility for the nation's library system, including the establishment of standards and library education. When the Soviet Union came to an end, the national libraries' control over other libraries was gradually relaxed. Their funding declined, as (much more dramatically) did that of the Russian State Library, and with it their ability to acquire foreign material.

Although most European national libraries are distinct institutions, in the Slavic Balkan states and the Nordic countries they are combined with university libraries, with the exception of Norway, whose national library split off from the University of Oslo Library in the last few years. Unusually in Europe, the national libraries of the Baltic republics, Armenia, Georgia, and Malta grew from public libraries.

There are several examples of national libraries in "nations within nations." As already noted, the countries that left Yugoslavia in 1990 already had their own national libraries, as did Slovakia. The current Federal Republic of Yugoslavia has, as well as a Yugoslav national library, national libraries for the republics of Serbia and Montenegro and the two provinces of Kosovo and Vojvodina. The United Kingdom has, as well as the British Library, a National Library of Wales and a National Library of Scotland. Other examples are the National Libraries of Greenland and the Faroe Islands, both semi-autonomous parts of Denmark. Russia has since 1991 had both a State Library in Moscow, founded in 1925 as the Lenin State Library but developed from a library established in 1862, for the whole Russian Federation, and the older Russian National Library (formerly the Saltykov-Shchedrin Library) in St. Petersburg for Russia alone. Every European nation now has a national library, even the tiny states of Andorra and Liechtenstein.

Anglo-America

Canada has, in addition to its National Library in Ottawa, the Bibliothèque nationale de Québec in Montréal. The United States, as already mentioned, has the Library of Congress, the largest library in the world by some distance, and also national libraries for medicine and agriculture. Among its librarians have been several of the great names in national librarianship: Ainsworth Rand Spofford (1865–97), who transformed it into an institution of real national importance; Herbert Putnam (1899–1939), a professional librarian, who was responsible for several major initiatives, such as a new classification scheme, a national union catalog, and the printing and sale of catalog cards; and L. Quincy Mumford (1954–75), who oversaw a revolution in librarianship enabled by information technology and a huge expansion in foreign acquisitions.

Latin America and the Caribbean

As one country after another in Latin America gained its independence, new national libraries were established, as an expression of nationhood and to maintain a record of the country's history and culture. Between 1810 and 1835 most South American states created them, sometimes based on existing public libraries, and usually serving as the public library of the capital city. Venezuela's (called Instituto Autónomo Biblioteca Nacional y de Servicios de Bibliotecas) has charge of all public libraries in the country. The national libraries of Colombia and Brazil grew from royal libraries.

Some were created much later: Mexico's had a slow birth in the mid-1800s and finally came into being in 1867. It is now part of the Instituto de Investigaciones Bibliográficas of Universidad Nacional de México, together with a separate newspaper and serials library (Hemeroteca Nacional). Paraguay's national library was not established until 1909. Some South American national libraries (Brazil, Chile, Mexico, and Venezuela) have several million volumes.

Most of the national libraries of Central America are much smaller. Dates of creation range from Haiti's, which opened in 1825 with 440 books, through El Salvador's in 1870 to Panama's in 1942 (40 years after independence). In the Caribbean, Cuba's Biblioteca Nacional "José Martí" (as it is now called) dates back to 1901; like Venezuela's, it heads the public library network.

The fact that many Latin American national libraries double as public libraries is partly due to their origins, but that they remain so is perhaps due more to a general neglect of public libraries. The result is that collections endure much wear and tear from use by the public, especially schoolchildren. Conservation is a matter of particular concern.

Africa

Most African countries did not become independent until after World War II, when they too began to establish national libraries. The former French colonies Tunisia and Algeria already had national libraries, established in 1845 and 1855, respectively. The only other pre-1900 national libraries in Africa are those of Egypt (1870) and South Africa. The South Africa Library was set up in Cape Town in 1818, followed by a State Library in Pretoria in 1887; the two, which performed complementary functions, have recently been amalgamated.

Few national libraries were established in colonial times. As national imprints were few while there were many documents to be collected and preserved, archives were often given priority. Gabon's National Archives, created in 1969, included a National Library; and in Congo a library, archives and documentation service was created in 1971, with a People's National Library as one part. Zambia and Zimbabwe have a National Archives, and there is also a Zambia Library Service. Botswana established a National Archives and Records Service in 1967. Morocco has a combined Bibliothèque Générale et Archives.

As financial resources were very short, the establishment of new national libraries usually took the form of giving national functions to an existing library. Nigeria, more populous than any other African country and richer than most, is an exception; it finally established a separate National Library in 1963. In common with National Library Services (see below), it has branches over the country.

A few countries (Democratic Republic of Congo, Cameroon, Kenya, Malawi, Angola) created national libraries in the 1960s, but the 1970s saw the greatest founding of national libraries in Africa. Although doubling as a public library is the common pattern in Africa, there are exceptions. The Swaziland National Library Service shares with the University of Swaziland the functions of a national library. In Sudan, which has no national library, the University of Khartoum Library performs national functions.

National Library Services exist in Botswana, Kenya, Swaziland, Tanzania, and Zambia. These emphasize the "leading public library" role, exercising leadership and coordination, and in some cases having branches in other towns.

Asia

No national libraries as such were created in Asia before 1900, although there were early precursors. Calcutta Public Library (1835) became the Imperial Library in 1903 before being renamed the National Library of India in 1948. Other early public library precursors were in Burma (Myanmar) and in the Philippines, where the National Library still serves as a public library, with nearly 500 branches throughout the country.

One of the few Asian national libraries established between 1900 and 1945 was the Jewish National and University Library, which grew from a 19th-century collection of the Jerusalem B'nai B'rith Lodge and was formally attached to the Hebrew University and given its present name in 1924; it serves as the library of the Hebrew University, as the national library of Israel, and as the national library of the Jewish people. The Cetnral Asian republics, while they formed part of the USSR, had their own national libraries, which developed from public libraries in the 1920s and 1930s, and they still have a role as such. They are large libraries, three of them claiming over 4 million items (Kazakhstan's claims over 6 million).

As in Africa, most national libraries in Asia came into being after World War II, nearly all of them evolving from public libraries. They range from that of the Maldives (1945) to that of Indonesia (1980). The two largest and most comprehensive national libraries in Asia are those of China and Japan. The Japanese National Diet Library was created in 1948 on the model of the U.S. Library of Congress by joining the Diet and Imperial libraries. A parallel library (known as the Kansai-kan), located some 300 miles from Tokyo in Kansai Science City, is due to open in 2002, designed to give a wide range of services using all possible electronic facilities. The National Library of China is one of the four or five biggest libraries in the world (holding about 15 million items); its predecessor was the Metropolitan Library of Peking (established 1910).

Australasia and Oceania

The National Library of Australia was established in 1901 as the Commonwealth Parliamentary Library, and it did not take its present title until 1961. Reductions in acquisitions in the early 1990s led to the concept of the "national distributed library," whereby all major libraries contribute to the national collection. The National Library of New Zealand had somewhat similar origins, coming into being in 1965 as a result of merging three libraries, one of them the General Assembly Library. It too has been enterprising but has had to manage on much smaller funds. Efforts in the mid-1990s to create a joint Australian–New Zealand bibliographic network foundered.

A few of the Pacific Island nations have their own national libraries or national library services, in all cases established since World War II; the smallest is probably that of Tuvalu (population 13,000). Kiribati (population 78,000) has a combined National Library and Archives, which also contains a public library. Other countries in Oceania that have national library services of some kind are the Cook Islands and the Solomon Islands.

The Future of National Libraries

Extensions of services and activities have been limited by two factors: a relative decline in government funding, and the ability of other bodies, including other libraries, to perform the same services equally well if not better. National libraries may be drawn back to their original basic functions of collection of national publications, maintenance and preservation, and recording. Ambitions to be universal libraries, as envisaged for the British Museum Library by Panizzi in the 19th century, have also been greatly constrained. Some national libraries, notably those of China, France, Japan, and the United Kingdom, still maintain a very broad collecting policy, but only the Library of Congress can now claim to be a universal library. Most national libraries, especially in countries other than those in Europe and developed English-speaking countries such as Australia, are fundamentally collections of national imprints, with supporting collections of reference materials and general works such as major histories.

The future of national libraries is threatened by various developments, in addition to the reduction in government funding. The biggest challenge comes from information and communications technology. This enables national libraries to carry out their functions far more effectively and efficiently, and even to add to those functions; however, it also enables other bodies to perform them. The OCLC bibliographic database in the United States is used far more by libraries for their own bibliographic purposes and for interlibrary document transactions than that of the Library of Congress. The reference function of national libraries too is eroded when more and more material can be consulted remotely online. Even the collection of national imprints can be shared, as it is in some countries.

It will, however, be a long time before online access supersedes consultation of the printed page for material in the humanities and in book form, and there will always be a need to conserve old and rare treasures. In any case, even if national functions are spread among various bodies, there still has to be national coordination and leadership. These could, in principle, be performed by a body with no collecting, preserving, or recording responsibilities, but this is unlikely to happen if only because national libraries are a potent symbol of national identity and culture; this is a main explanation of the quite numerous buildings that have risen up in recent years.

National libraries are shop windows on a major part of the national heritage. This function can now be enhanced, since other parts of the national heritage—for example, museum objects and paintings—can also be digitized. We may see a coming together of various national institutions; experiments are already taking place.

MAURICE B. LINE

Further Reading

Aje, Simeon B., "National Libraries in Developing Countries," *Advances in Librarianship* 7 (1977)

Alexandria: The Journal of National and International Library and Information Issues (1989–)

Al-Nahari, Abdulaziz Mohamed, *The Role of National Libraries in Developing Countries, with Special Reference to Saudi Arabia,* London and New York: Mansell, 1984

Esdaile, Arundell, *National Libraries of the World: Their History, Administration, and Public Services,* London: Grafton, 1934; 2nd edition, completely revised by R.J. Hill, London: The Library Association, 1957

Humphreys, K.W., "National Library Functions," *Unesco Bulletin for Libraries* 20, no.4 (July–August 1966); reprint, in *National Libraries,* edited by Maurice B. Line and Joyce Line, London: Aslib, 1979

Humphreys, K.W., *A National Library in Theory and Practice,* London: The British Library, 1988

Kent, Allen, et al., editors, *Encyclopedia of Library and Information Science,* New York: Dekker, 1968–

Line, Maurice B., "Changing Perspectives on National Libraries: A Personal View," *Alexandria* 13, no. 1 (2001)

Line, Maurice B., and Joyce Line, editors, *National Libraries,* London: Aslib, 1979

Line, Maurice B., and Joyce Line, editors, *National Libraries 2: 1977–1985,* London: Aslib, 1987

Line, Maurice B., and Joyce Line, editors, *National Libraries 3: A Selection of Articles on National Libraries, 1986–1994,* London: Aslib, 1995 (this volume and the two above contain many key articles on national libraries in general as well as on particular libraries)

Tyulina, N.I., "National Libraries," in *Encyclopedia of Library and Information Science,* edited by Allen Kent et al., vol. 19, New York: Dekker, 1976

UNESCO, *National Libraries: Their Problems and Prospects: Symposium on National Libraries in Europe, Vienna, 8–27 September 1958,* Paris: UNESCO, 1960

Wedgeworth, Robert, editor, *ALA World Encyclopedia of Library and Information Services,* Chicago: American Library Association, 1980; 3rd edition, 1993 (contains essays on national libraries in general and on numerous particular national libraries)

Wiegand, Wayne A., and Donald G. Davis, editors, *Encyclopedia of Library History,* New York: Garland, 1994 (contains essays on national libraries in general and on numerous particular national libraries)

Willison, Ian R., "The National Library in Historical Perspective," *Libraries and Culture* 24, no. 1 (Winter 1989)

Online Catalogs

Historical Perspective

Printed card catalogs (and, to a lesser extent, printed book catalogs and microform catalogs) were the primary tools for identifying titles held by a library until the mid-1970s. With libraries' increasing use of computers, online computer-based cataloging began to be used in the late 1960s. By the late 1990s online catalogs were the primary access tool for identifying materials in library collections. What card catalogs remained contained, for the most part, the residue of titles for which the card catalog record had not yet been converted to machine-readable format.

The adaptation of Online Public Access Catalogs (OPACs) in place of card catalogs, book catalogs, and microform catalogs resulted from five major trends affecting libraries: (1) increasing labor costs for creating catalog records and maintaining printed catalogs; (2) creation of the MAchine-Readable Cataloging (MARC) record format by the Library of Congress as a standardized way of describing publications in computer records; (3) emergence of computer networks that allowed libraries to share machine-readable catalog records, thus reducing local costs associated with cataloging; 4) enhanced ability to search computerized catalogs in ways not possible with printed card catalogs, book catalogs, or microform catalogs; and 5) the ability to use a centralized machine-readable catalog record in other related library computer systems, such as circulation systems and acquisitions systems.

These trends were accelerated by the emergence of library cooperatives such as the Ohio College Library Center, established in 1967 (later renamed the Online Computer Library Center, Inc., and now known simply by the acronym OCLC) and the Research Libraries Group (RLG), established in 1974. Library cooperatives provided shared technical capabilities and dedicated library networks to facilitate shared cataloging. Another important catalyst was the emergence of library automation vendors that specialized in automated library applications. Library cooperatives and library automation vendors provided cost savings to libraries as compared to manual systems and local development of automated library systems. Over time the cooperatives and vendors continued to develop their systems and offered many features in addition to online catalog capabilities.

With the emergence of the Internet and the World Wide Web in the 1990s, dedicated library networks began to give way to use of the Internet as the international communications highway. Dedicated networks such as that employed by OCLC tended to become specialized networks for which highly reliable production systems and special security were needed. The Web became the open system architecture of choice for the public to access library resources. This move facilitated international cooperation in ways that surface mail and print catalogs could not. The Web began to support the globalization of information access, and online catalogs continued to have a role in that process. They provided an important part of the infrastructure needed for global resource sharing and the emerging digital libraries.

The Library of Congress

The U.S. Library of Congress (LC) was an early adapter of library automation techniques partly because of its size and the need to find more efficient methods for its internal operations. Those operations included the printing of catalog cards that were purchased by other libraries worldwide to describe books they had acquired. Under the leadership of Henriette D. Avram, the Library of Congress established the MARC format for describing publications as a method for automating the printing of catalog cards and internal LC systems. It also then sold the machine-readable records to any library, bibliographic utility, or vendor. These purchased MARC records could be used in local library systems, consortia systems, or vendor systems, thus eliminating the need to create such records locally. MAchine-Readable Bibliographic Information (MARBI), an interdivisional committee of the American Library Association that reviews and recommends standards for machine-readable forms of bibliographic information, provides oversight for changes to the MARC format, thus providing a mechanism for keeping the format current with changes in cataloging practice.

The MARC format (and variations on it established in other countries) became the basis for exchanging catalog records between computer systems internationally. This early standardization for the description of publications and the availability of central suppliers of records greatly expedited the use of shared cataloging records nationally and internationally. Similarly, the Library of Congress later made its subject headings database available to libraries and vendors in machine-readable format, and the National Library of Medicine made its medical subject headings (MeSH) available to the library community for use in automated systems. Again, this expedited the use of subject headings and cross-references in online library catalogs and vendor products.

Library Cooperatives and Vendor Utilities

Beginning in the late 1960s, libraries joined in various computer-based cooperative activities. Some cooperatives or networks were state based, such as the Washington Library Network (WLN). Others were regional, such as the New England Library Network (NELINET) and the Southeastern Library and Information Network (SOLINET). Some state-based or specialized cooperatives became regional (WLN) or national (OCLC and RLG) over time as they enlarged their scope of activities. In many cases, regional networks became members of and distributors for OCLC, which had become a national cooperative by 1977. Some library automation vendors such as Data Research Associates in St. Louis loaded LC MARC records as a core database and added customer records that were then sold to other customers. In all cases, online cataloging was a key service that allowed libraries to reduce local cataloging costs and to use cataloging records to locate titles in other libraries for interlibrary loan purposes. Because serial (periodical) articles made up a high proportion of interlibrary loan requests, union lists of serials were a common by-product of these cataloging databases. This aided libraries in filling interlibrary loan requests for journal articles.

Local Library Catalogs and Integrated Library Systems

During the 1960s, libraries began automating specific functions, particularly circulation records and acquisitions functions for purchasing library materials. In each case, abbreviated bibliographic (cataloging) records had to be created as the basis for the transaction being conducted. As cataloging records became available from LC, library cooperatives, or commercial vendors, libraries began to make the bibliographic (cataloging) database the central file from which other subsystems pulled cataloging records to support other operations. These systems became known as integrated library systems, eliminating the need to create separate title records for each subsystem.

Typically, a library staff member would search a national database, whether mounted by a cooperative, a library vendor, or locally (e.g., MARC records mounted locally by a large research library). If a record was found for that publication, the catalog record would be downloaded into the local system. If no record was found, the staff member could create a record, add it to the central database for others to use, and download it into its local system as well. That record could then be used for multiple applications such as acquisitions (ordering and fund accounting), the OPAC, circulation, interlibrary loan, or media booking systems. Local automated library systems generally migrated from stand-alone functions to integrated systems with many functions operating from a central cataloging database that described the titles for that library's collection.

Retrospective Conversion

Libraries began by cataloging newly purchased materials in machine-readable format as they were added to collections. As more and more libraries accepted the operational and functional benefits of online catalogs, it became increasingly desirable to convert older titles into machine-readable format so that all titles could be available in their local OPACs. Library cooperatives and vendors developed specialized services for converting retrospective titles and adding them to online catalog databases. Because of the cost for this activity, it took large libraries many years to complete retrospective conversion so that all of their collections were represented in their online catalogs. Many large research libraries owning millions of titles were still doing retrospective conversion at the beginning of the 21st century.

The Z39.50 Search Protocol

Because the search software for OPACs often differed in their design, bibliographic utilities such as OCLC and RLG offered a way of searching efficiently, as the titles for most libraries resided in centralized databases, often called bibliographic utilities. The combination of using bibliographic utilities for searching, cataloging, and interlibrary loan, linked to local systems for local library operations, remained the norm until the early 1990s, when distributed processing and the use of smaller servers and client/server architecture began to replace large mainframe computers.

Client/server architecture allowed for an alternate design logic that would permit searching across local systems, but there was no standardized way to do so. The emergence of the Z39.50 search protocol was intended to format searches in a standardized way so that they could be applied across platforms that used different search engines. This new capability opened a debate (which continues into the 21st century) about centralized versus decentralized computing architecture for online catalogs.

International Issues

Libraries in countries other than the United States have had a number of concerns that go beyond those of U.S. libraries. First, because of different cataloging codes and practices, many countries made changes to the MARC format in their countries. Thus the MARC format had variations around the world that complicated sharing of machine-readable cataloging records between and among different countries. There has been an ongoing effort within the International Federation of Library Associations and Institutions (IFLA) to reconcile these practices and to create a uniform format called UNIMARC, but its acceptance has been slow. It is not currently clear whether UNIMARC will become widely accepted, even in Europe.

Because of the variety of languages and alphabets utilized in other countries, libraries outside the United States have put more effort into automated systems that can handle a variety of character sets and display those character sets in the original alphabets rather than as transliterated characters. This function is particularly important for languages such as Arabic, Chinese, Japanese, and Russian, which are widely used in addition to English. Transliteration of these alphabets or characters is not sufficient for scholars who need to understand the original text. A format called the "Unicode standard: worldwide character encoding" developed by the Unicode Consortium provides an enhanced character set that represents most alphabets and languages. However, Unicode was still not widely used at the end of the 20th century.

Online Catalogs Versus Indexing/Abstracting Databases

Online catalogs continue to describe publications only at the title level. For periodicals or scholarly journals, the individual articles contained within the title continue to be described in indexing and abstracting publications that are produced by publishers. The use of automation to create electronic versions of these indexing and abstracting publications paralleled the automation of library catalogs. Publishers and vendors began to mount these indexing/abstracting databases on networks and to charge libraries to search them. Alternately, they would sell the databases to libraries or consortia for use in local or consortia systems. Users first have to search the indexing/abstracting databases to identify pertinent journal articles then have to search online library catalogs to see which libraries own that journal title. Usually circulation systems show what specific volumes a library owns. This process is very cumbersome from the user's perspective.

Several projects were under way in the late 1990s to link citations in indexing/abstracting databases to online catalog entries automatically so that users could be guided from a specific journal citation to an owning institution and eventually to actual delivery of the article to the user. Libraries that loaded indexing/abstracting databases locally often developed "link to holdings" capabilities with their local OPACs. Publishers united around a unique article identifier as another approach. Herbert Van de Sompel, Head of Library Automation at the University of Ghent in Belgium (working with the National Information Standards Organization and the Digital Library Federation), proposed a technical protocol called the "SFX Framework for Context-Sensitive Reference Linking" to link journal article citations to full-text subscription databases. Refining these linking capabilities for seamless search to delivery is a key capability needed as digital libraries evolve.

Metadata

The rapid adaptation of the Internet for scholarly communication in the mid-1990s and its commercialization following the development of the World Wide Web resulted in unprecedented changes in library automation and networking, including effects on online catalogs. As the amount of information and full-text publications increased exponentially on the Internet, many computer scientists questioned whether traditional cataloging techniques could scale up to organizing the quantities of information being mounted on the Web. A new form of description called "metadata" began to evolve. Metadata is information about data. It describes certain features of data found on the Internet: what that Internet resource is, what it is about, where it is, and so on.

A second concern was that many forms of information require descriptors that go beyond traditional cataloging rules. Metadata evolved as an extended concept of description for such formats as spatial data, geographical data, statistical databases, and gene banks. OCLC defined a core set of data called the "Dublin Core" that was widely accepted as a minimum set of descriptors and a format for description for such material. Traditional cataloging elements made up a subset of metadata elements. However, the use of metadata and the definition of metadata elements for different types of information are still evolving.

The Future of Online Catalogs

As libraries took on an increasing role in locating publications, information, or data, whether or not owned by them, the role of OPACs was debated: Should they describe only titles that libraries actually owned, or should they also include materials that libraries subscribed to, licensed, or had access to through various consortial arrangements or via the Internet? The rapid growth of the Internet and the Web accelerated this debate. By the end of the 20th century, catalogers were becoming metadata specialists and were including entries in online catalogs for Internet resources not actually owned by the library. Whether the online catalog would migrate into the library portal for locating Internet resources or would be one tool among many for identifying Internet resources was still not clear as libraries entered the 21st century. Regardless, the inclusiveness and flexibility of the online catalogs were much greater than the printed card and book catalogs available when libraries entered the previous century.

NANCY L. EATON

Further Reading

Aveney, Brian, and Brett Butler, *Online Catalogs/Online Reference: Converging Trends,* Chicago: American Library Association, 1984

Avram, Henriette D., *The MARC II Format: A Communications Format for Bibliographic Data,* Washington, D.C.: Information Systems Office, Library of Congress, 1968

Crawford, Walt, *The Online Catalog Book: Essays and Examples,* New York: G.K. Hall, Toronto: Maxwell Macmillan Canada, and New York: Maxwell Macmillan International, 1992

Hudgins, Jean, Grace Agnew, and Elizabeth Brown, *Getting Mileage out of Metadata: Applications for the Library,* Chicago: American Library Association, 1999

Lange, Holley R., and B. Jean Winkler, "Taming the Internet: Metadata, a Work in Progress," *Advances in Librarianship* 21 (1997)

National Information Standards Organization (U.S.), *Information Retrieval (Z39.50): Applications Service Definition and Protocol Specification,* Bethesda, Maryland: NISO Press, 1995

Peters, Thomas A., *The Online Catalog: A Critical Examination of Public Use,* Jefferson, North Carolina, and London: McFarland, 1991

Taylor, Arlene G., *The Organization of Information,* Englewood, Colorado: Libraries Unlimited, 1999

Yee, Martha M., and Sara Shatford Layne, *Improving Online Public Access Catalogs,* Chicago and London: American Library Association, 1998

Pacific Islands Libraries

The scope of this article includes the islands of the Pacific, from Papua New Guinea in the west to French Polynesia in the east. The geographical range extends northward to Guam and Palau in the west, but not to Hawai'i in the east. Nor does it include the Philippines, Indonesia, Australia, or New Zealand. The region has no history of written languages, though there are strong traditions of using the spoken word to store and transmit necessary information such as land ownership, tribal histories, genealogy, and the skills of fishing and agriculture. This oral tradition has usually been supported by visual elements, including woven panels, carvings, and house decorations, that serve as memory aids for the speaker.

Into this region, European settlers of the 19th century brought their languages, books, printing presses, and the social constructs of literacy and libraries. Settlers commonly brought books with them, and as transportation improved, newspapers and magazines from their home countries were received regularly. Missionaries were at the forefront of translating local languages and developing orthographies, especially in Tonga, from which the knowledge of local languages flowed out around the southern Pacific in the early 19th century. By the middle of the century these were some of the most literate communities in the world.

Early Libraries

Possibly the first library in the region was established in Levuka, then the largest European settlement in Fiji, between 1858 and 1862 by William Thomas Pritchard, the British consul there. He had become tired of dealing with cases of drunkenness and riotous behavior among the British community, as Levuka offered little else in the way of entertainment, and he planned on providing a secluded room stocked with periodicals and books. He also anticipated that the Levuka reading room would be used for public meetings to discuss matters of communal concern. Although approximately four such meetings were held, Pritchard eventually abandoned his plan when he realized that a library would not have the same allure as the public house. By 1868 a more prominent reading room had opened again in Levuka. Despite the apparent lack of interest in actually using it, there is clear evidence of a collective aspiration for a more genteel and civilized status that could only be cultivated if civic institutions such as a library were a part of the town. It was not long, however, before the reading room was closed and its stock transferred to a new mechanics' institute founded in 1873. (Coincidentally, a mechanics' institute was the first lending library founded in Wellington, New Zealand, in 1841, perhaps illustrating that settler communities needed to associate literacy with practical endeavors before a library could survive.)

In 1904 the first library in Suva, the new capital of Fiji, was established and the first librarian appointed. The original site was the Queen Victoria Memorial Hall, where the books were transferred from the mechanics' institute. Major Henry Marks was a significant donor of materials, helping to build the collection into something useful in its early years. In 1907 U.S. philanthropist Andrew Carnegie offered the Suva Town Board £1,500 for construction of a public library building, an offer that was accepted with alacrity. Initial plans for a wooden building were changed when the government insisted upon a concrete structure in return for its allocation of a piece of land. The Carnegie building was opened in 1909 and still stands, with its pseudoclassic design looking somewhat incongruous in the middle of a bustling South Pacific city.

During World War II, the books were moved upstairs while the library area was used by a U.S. dental unit. It is said that visiting servicemen stole a considerable number of the library's books. When the prospect of air raids by Japanese aircraft was at its height, the books were removed completely to a tunnel under Gordon House, the residence of the British high commissioner. The cure was almost as bad as the complaint, for many books were damaged by mildew and dampness, although the surviving volumes were removed to the dry side of the island for a time before being returned to the Carnegie Library in 1944. Up to this point, the library was used almost exclusively by Europeans. However, a 1963 report by D.M.N. McFarlane and H.H. Madams insisted that the library be multiracial and seek to educate and advance all races, although it also stated that all books should be in English. Only two years later, a Fijiana section was established, and the Suva City Library now stocks materials in English, Fijian, and Hindi languages.

University of the South Pacific

Now hosting one of the premier libraries in the region, the University of the South Pacific (USP) was established in 1967 in Suva, Fiji, and its library opened the following year, initially in the former officer's mess of the Royal New Zealand Air Force base used for the new university. The university is a regional institution serving the Cook Islands, Fiji, Kiribati, Marshall Islands, Nauru, Niue, Samoa, Solomon Islands, Tokelau, Tonga, Tuvalu, and Vanuatu; it is funded by all member countries in proportion to their populations. It acts as the national library for Fiji and other island nations associated with the university, primarily by identifying and collecting publications, producing bibliographies, and acting as a deposit library.

Harold Holdsworth was appointed university librarian in 1969 and became one of the outstanding figures in the development of libraries in the South Pacific. He immediately created the Pacific Collection, and it is for this and its work in regional bibliography that the library is best known. Holdsworth became aware of the enormous amount of gray literature produced in the region—that is, reports by consultants, government officials, churches, and others that were printed in very small numbers and frequently left uncataloged by most libraries. The Pacific Information Centre was established with the intention of filling this bibliographical need, and its success is a tribute to Holdsworth and the librarians who followed him.

In recognition of its regional role, the library is the regional depository of numerous international and regional organizations, such as the United Nations; the United Nations Educational, Scientific, and Cultural Organization (UNESCO); the World Bank; the European Commission; the Food and Agriculture Organization; the Pacific Commission; and some U.S. and Canadian government bodies. There are legal deposit laws in Fiji and the Solomon Islands requiring publishers to provide at least one copy to USP, but the library still finds it hard to obtain material from other Pacific countries and often staff members must travel to acquire government and other materials. The use of staff time for this purpose is evidence of the importance placed upon the acquisition of regional materials.

For a number of years there has been an undeniable tension between the university in its regional role and the constituent countries wishing to see more local benefits resulting from their expenditure on higher education. In part USP has met these concerns by developing a separate campus in Alafua (Samoa) to serve the school of agriculture and the newer Emalus (Vanuatu) campus that serves the law school. The libraries of both these campuses are eminent within the region in their specialist fields. The presence of these institutions has not deterred other island countries from establishing their own universities or national libraries; Samoa, for example, created a new university (with a library) of its own in the early 1990s.

Papua New Guinea

The first libraries in Papua New Guinea were the public libraries opened shortly after the end of World War II. The most significant development came with the opening of the University of Papua New Guinea Library in Port Moresby (as the library of the University of Papua and New Guinea) in 1965. For several years the library was wholly funded by the Australian government, although that support has now ceased. The building was completed in 1969 and has been extended twice, in 1971 and 1976. The collection developed quickly and was soon comparable to other university libraries in the region. It now has approximately 400,000 items. The most important materials lie in the Papua New Guinea Collection (approximately 80,000 items), including legal deposit materials and important archive materials such as those of the Anglican and United Churches and the Planters' Association. Collecting government documents is very important, yet it is difficult because such documents tend to go out of print very quickly. Another important library holding is the Hugh Stevenson collection of Papua New Guinea artifacts, artwork, and sculpture.

The Papua New Guinea University of Technology in Lae appointed its first librarian in 1969 after trying to manage for several years without a library service. The Matheson Library has developed into a useful technological collection for the country and has its own Papua New Guinea collection. Recently, a third university opened in Goroka in the eastern highlands, with a collection focused on educational materials.

The National Library Service of Papua New Guinea was established in 1975, the same year the country became independent of Australian administration. The most recent legislation governing the service is the National Library and Archives Act (1993), which created an Office of Libraries and Archives with two sections: the National Library Service and the National Archives and Public Records Service. The main building in Waigani, a suburb of the capital, Port Moresby, was an independence gift from Australia to the new nation in 1975. In addition to the building, the National Library of Australia accepted the responsibility for developing initial collections using guidelines provided by John Yocklunn, the first national librarian of Papua New Guinea. Books, films, and maps, many of historic interest and not otherwise available, were collected from Australian government departments, including the former Department of External Territories Library, and transferred to the new National Library of Papua New Guinea. Most of these documents are now in the Papua New Guinea collection, an important national collection of some 30,000 items. Materials acquired through the legal deposit provisions of the act are held in this reference collection. One of the anomalies of library development in Papua New Guinea is the existence of two fine Papua New Guinea collections, one at the university and one at the National Library, which is only a mile away in the suburb of Waigani. Unfortunately, there is little access to libraries in much of the rest of the country.

Other Libraries of the South Pacific

The main library in Samoa is the Nelson Memorial Public Library in Apia, which contains a Samoa and Pacific collection of printed books, as well as a special Robert Louis Stevenson collection of materials about the writer, who lived in the islands for a number of years. The Solomon Islands National Library Service was established in 1979 and has a Solomon Islands collection that includes valuable archival materials from the country's colonial past and more recent materials deposited under legislation passed in 1972. There are also national libraries in the Cook Islands, Kiribati, Tuvalu, and Vanuatu. The South Pacific Commission, based in Noumea, New Caledonia, has a library with a collection related to economic development, fisheries, and other critical topics.

The North Pacific

The largest library in the northern Pacific is the Robert F. Kennedy Memorial Library of the University of Guam (Mangilao). Originally a land grant institution, the school was established in 1952 and became a university in 1968. The library occupies a two-story building renovated in 1993 that houses more than 85,000 volumes, 665,000 microforms, 2,900 serial titles, and 4,900 pieces of audiovisual software. Special collections include the Guam and Micronesia collection of approximately 40,000 volumes on Guam, Micronesia, and other Pacific islands, as well as unpublished dissertations, 16-mm film, videocassettes, news reprints, brochures, and other ephemera.

Francophone Libraries in the Pacific

Libraries in the French-speaking countries and territories are of more recent origin than institutions in the anglophone areas. The Bibliothèque Universitaire de la Nouvelle-Caledonie was established in 1985. It now houses a multidisciplinary collection of 22,000 volumes, 250 periodical titles, and dissertations on microfiche.

PHILIP J. CALVERT

Further Reading

Baker, Leigh R., *Development of University Libraries in Papua New Guinea,* Metuchen, New Jersey: Scarecrow Press, 1981

Borchardt, D.H., and J.I. Horacek, *Librarianship in Australia, New Zealand, and Oceania: A Brief Survey,* London: Pergamon Press, 1975

Calvert, Philip James, "The Levuka Reading Room: Fiji's First Library," *The Journal of Library History* 20 (1985)

Cohen, A., J.T. Crotts, and I. Lovas, "Developing Library and Information Services in Micronesia," in *Libraries: Global Reach, Local Touch,* edited by Kathleen de la Pena McCook, Barbara J. Ford, and Kate Lippincott, Chicago: American Library Association, 1998

Plumbe, W.J., *Libraries and Archives in Fiji: A Chronology,* Suva: Fiji Library Association, 1984

Wright, Stephen, "The University of Papua New Guinea: An Academic Library in a Developing Country," *Library Association Record* 92 (1990)

Performing Arts Libraries

The performing arts are defined as those activities in which humans recite words, produce music, or execute movement in front of other humans, either in person or through a recorded medium, for entertainment and enlightenment. Performing arts libraries in this context are those institutions that document theater, music, motion pictures, radio, television, dance, circus, vaudeville, Wild West shows, puppetry, and all varieties of public celebrations. Thespis stepping forth from the chorus to declaim the first solo lines by an actor, the premiere of Stravinsky's *The Rite of Spring,* Charlie Chaplin and Mickey Mouse on screen, and Gypsy Rose Lee's striptease onstage at Minsky's—all sit comfortably under that large umbrella called the performing arts.

Because of their broad and unique scope, performing arts libraries usually exist within museums and archives, where these subjects are documented not only in books but also in scripts and scores; ephemeral materials such as programs, clippings, and tickets; visual materials such as photographs, set and costume designs, posters, and blueprints; archival holdings of personal papers and organizational records; and new formats such as video, film, and recordings. Whether the institutions hold and collect materials related to all the performing arts or are narrow in scope and define their collections by a particular discipline within the performing arts, they are all performing arts libraries.

Beginnings through the 19th Century

The history and development of performing arts libraries is indivisible from the history and development of the performing arts themselves. Although the performing arts library is a creation of the 20th century, the organization, documentation, and collection of performing arts materials began in antiquity. Much of our knowledge of library activities in the Greek and Roman period is almost exclusively related to live theater. Production records, including lists of actors and winning plays, were kept for the City Dionysia Festivals dating from the fifth century B.C. Aristotle's library included his own plays and writings on theater, as well as his own records of the dramatic festivals compiled in book form as the *Didaskalia*. The Athenian theater led to what may have been the first public library when, as actors began altering the texts of plays by Aeschylus, Sophocles, Euripides, and others, official copies of these plays were ordered to be transcribed and made available for use as the standard of comparison for rewritten texts. These official texts were seized and moved to the library at Alexandria, Egypt, in the second century B.C., where they were copied and widely distributed.

During the medieval period, when the overwhelming majority of citizens could neither read nor write, liturgical ritual emphasized visual and aural performance over the written word, using religious pageants and choral music. From the early Christian era until the late 19th century, the collection and organization of music materials dominated the development of performing arts libraries. Monasteries became repositories for liturgical music texts. Cathedral schools later replaced monasteries as centers of education and included collections of music materials. As music became a part of university curricula and activities, music scores and books were included in library collections in European universities.

Library development accelerated in the 16th century with the arrival of new printing processes and the first library catalogs, which showed the extent of music holdings in royal libraries. When the first national library of Spain (the Royal Monastery de El Escorial Library in Madrid) opened, it included commissioned works of liturgical music among its holdings. This era also saw the rise of many prominent private collections of music, later to serve as foundations for academic and national libraries. For example, during the 18th century Napoleon's military victories brought library holdings as war prizes that enriched the already vast music collection of Paris' Bibliothèque du Roi, which later became France's Bibliothèque nationale.

The 19th century witnessed a flowering of music collecting activities in several types of repositories. The Bodleian Library opened at Oxford, England, in 1602 with music as a key part of its first printed catalog, but it did not undertake serious collecting efforts until the 19th century. Particularly strong in English music, the Bodleian saw its holdings increase owing to its status as a copyright depository library. Its music holdings were arranged and cataloged in 400 volumes midway through the century. The British Museum Library already held a sizable collection of music books and manuscripts when Antonio Panizzi arrived at mid-century as library director. Among his innovations was the introduction of systematic collection development, which he actively applied to the music collection through purchase, consolidation of music holdings, and solicitation of large music gifts from private collections. Concurrently, British public and municipal libraries began circulating music books and scores.

Europe saw the acquisition of music materials by national, academic, and conservatory libraries. In 1824 Berlin's Royal Library was the first to create an official music department, whereas the Herzog-August Bibliothek in Wolfenbüttel and the Preussische Staatsbibliothek in Berlin (later the Deutsche Staatsbibliothek) housed major music collections. In France, the Paris Royal Library was one of the largest libraries in the world, with a strong music presence. The Paris Opera collected music and other materials related to its performances, thus distinguishing itself as one of the first company, or in-house, libraries. Vienna's Nationalbibliothek contained one of the world's most important music collections, with more than 4,000 music manuscripts by 1900. The Gesellschaft der Musikfreunde (Friends of Music) in Vienna, founded in 1812, featured a large collection of Austrian music and acquired a significant portion of Johannes Brahms' private library. Hungary's first public institution devoted to the teaching of music was established in 1836 in Budapest. Later renamed the Béla Bartók Conservatory, much of its library holdings were destroyed during World War II. Nevertheless, it remained an invaluable music repository, with many autograph music manuscripts of Hungarian composers. The Bartók Conservatory later became part of Hungary's largest music library, the Franz Liszt Academy of Music, founded by the composer in 1875. The State Library of St. Petersburg, strong in Russian opera, benefited from the collection development policies of its librarian, Modest Andreevich Korf, during his tenure in the 1850s.

In the United States, public libraries opened around the country but were slow to acquire music materials. Nonetheless, the Boston (Massachusetts) Public Library actively acquired a number of important music collections, including a donation of Allen A. Brown's music library. The Brooklyn (New York) Public Library began circulating music on a trial basis in the 1880s. Author and critic George Upton was instrumental in the development of music materials in Chicago's Newberry Library. As music consultant to the Newberry's chief librarian, William Frederick Poole, he guided its music acquisitions, including the purchase of the library of Pio Reese in 1888, insuring the Newberry's rank as one of the foremost musicology collections in the United States. In the 1860s two music conservatories, the Peabody in Baltimore, Maryland, and the New England Conservatory in Boston, Massachusetts, established libraries to support their curriculum for use by their faculty and students.

The U.S. Library of Congress (LC) in Washington, D.C., founded in 1800 as a federal library, based much of its early collection development on the personal library of Thomas Jefferson, which included a number of music books. Its Music Division opened on the cusp of the 20th century, and its holdings increased rapidly owing to its status as a depository library under the federal copyright act. As a copyright depository, the LC also amassed a voluminous collection of published and unpublished American plays. In 1894 the library began collecting in the nascent medium of motion pictures with the deposit of the first copyrighted film, "The Edison Kinetoscopic Record of a Sneeze."

Elsewhere, the first theater library in the United States was formed from the books, personal papers, and business records of actor-manager Edwin Booth at New York City's Players Club in 1888. At first only available to the actors, playwrights, and other theater artists who made up the club's membership, it later opened its doors to the public and acquired important collections in the areas of magic and burlesque.

The LC, the national library of record, and the Players Club, a private repository founded on an individual collection, mark significant segues in the evolution of performing arts libraries as we know them today. In surveying the history of this type of library, a number of distinctive threads are revealed. First, the performing arts library is primarily a phenomenon of the 20th century. Though the foundations of many of the leading institutions in this field were laid in the previous century, it was not until the 1930s that classification and organizational schemes for documenting these materials and the establishment of performing arts library organizations brought a level of professionalism to these institutions. Second, many of the institutions that hold and collect materials related to the performing arts are narrow in scope and define their collections by a particular discipline or geographic area. Third, many of the great performing arts repositories are founded on the holdings of individual collectors who acquired manuscripts, broadsides, play scripts, designs, and ephemera over the course of a lifetime of collecting.

Fourth, the new direction of cross-disciplinary research in the latter part of the 20th century has infused performing arts libraries with a new group of scholars who use performing arts research to develop new inroads in their respective fields. Finally, the Internet has significantly increased access to performing arts materials.

Because the world of the performing arts is broad, analysis of these resources are arranged by subject focus and include highlights from the fields of music; theater; dance; film, radio, and television; and popular entertainment.

The 20th-Century Explosion

Music

It is impossible to enumerate all the libraries containing scores, manuscripts, music books, recordings, personal papers, archival records, and the ephemera related to music performance. Yet the history of the development of music holdings in libraries is marked by a number of significant events.

Through the generosity and vision of two donors, the LC established foundations to support collection development, commissions, and public performances. The Elizabeth Sprague Coolidge Foundation, created in 1925, supported chamber music commissions that in turn became part of the library's music collection. This example of collections studied and utilized in the creation of new art is one of the significant legacies of the performing arts library in the 20th century. The donation by Gertrude Clarke Whittall of Stradivari instruments in the 1930s served as the cornerstone for the library's collection of musical instruments, and her financial support enabled the LC to present performances, lectures, and other programming. These efforts were emulated by other philanthropists whose donations in dance, theater, film, and other areas have enhanced the LC's performing arts collections. At the same time, Oscar Sonneck, the first director of its Music Division, enhanced the systematic organization of music materials with his creation of a music classification schedule now used in music libraries throughout the United States.

Other developments served to increase activity in and demand for performing arts materials in U.S. libraries. The boom in music publishing in the early part of the century, as well as the inclusion of music in school curricula, created a demand for music materials in libraries. Public libraries benefited from generous endowments by the Carnegie Foundation and began circulating music scores and books, plays, recordings, and other performing arts materials.

The personal library of 19th-century musician and teacher Lowell Mason served as the foundation for the new music library at Yale University (New Haven, Connecticut) in 1917. Music libraries were established at Harvard University (Cambridge, Massachusetts) in 1898 to support its music department and at the University of Rochester (later moved to the Eastman School of Music in Rochester, New York). The San Francisco (California) Public Library, founded in 1878, opened a separate music department in 1917. Like many libraries throughout the world, one of its collecting strengths was materials indigenous to its region, such as a large collection of sheet music of the Gold Rush era in northern California and the archives of the San Francisco Opera. Similarly, the public library systems of Chicago (Illionois), Philadelphia (Pennsylvania), and Boston (Massachusetts) collected materials on the music and arts organizations of their cities.

The Drexel Collection served as the foundation for the new Music Division created at the New York Public Library (NYPL) in 1911. An important repository of materials relating to all forms of music, its many highlights include the American Music Collection, which features the first edition of "The Star-Spangled Banner," and nearly 500,000 sheets of music by U.S. composers. In 1965 the Music Division moved to its present Lincoln Center home and joined the library's dance, theater, and newly established sound recording divisions to form the New York Public Library for the Performing Arts. Large circulating collections of music, theater, film, and dance materials are located in the same building. An extensive restoration was completed in 2001.

The 1931 founding of the Music Library Association helped to define music librarianship as a distinct field of the information profession in the United States. An international organization, the International Association of Music Libraries, was formed in 1953.

Music holdings in European and British libraries demonstrate the treasured musical legacy of these countries. In London, the British Library's earliest music manuscripts date from the Middle Ages, with every historical period represented. The provenance of its 5,000-item Royal Music Library can be traced to King George III, and its development through successive reigns mark it as particularly noteworthy. Elsewhere in Europe, Madrid's Biblioteca National and the Deutsche Staatsbibliothek in Berlin are the national depository libraries for Spain and Germany, respectively. Both include collections of music manuscripts, scores, and recordings reflecting the musical heritage of their countries.

Throughout the world, orchestras and opera companies maintain records of their activities. Whether donated to public libraries or housed in company archives, they offer a rich record of their country's musical performances. Hamburg's Staats- und Universitätsbibliothek contains the holdings of the Hamburg (Germany) Opera since its beginnings in the 17th century and is also noteworthy for its wealth of material related to Georg Friedrich Händel and Brahms. Similarly, in Frankfurt's Stadt- und Universitätsbibliothek, productions of the Frankfurt (Germany) Opera House dating to the 18th century are documented through a variety of performance materials.

One of Italy's most bountiful music libraries is found in Giuseppe Verdi's Conservatory of Music in Milan. Among its many highlights are scores from operas performed at La Scala and other theaters in the city from 1816 to 1856. The performing arts in Russia are well documented in state-supported libraries and museums. The Rimsky-Korsakov Museum and the

Museum of the History of Russian Opera can be found in St. Petersburg's State Institute of Theatre, Music, and Cinematography. The State Academic Theatre of Opera and Ballet in Baku, capital city of the Azerbaijan Republic, contains perhaps the foremost collection of Russian manuscript music in its Central Music Library. New Zealand's national library, located in Wellington, houses the archives for both the New Zealand Opera Company and the National Opera of New Zealand. In Australia, the Sydney Opera House and Melbourne's Victoria State Opera serve not only as company archives but also as general research and reference libraries for music and the performing arts.

In Japan, laws passed after World War II guaranteed government funding for university and public libraries. Two dozen public libraries were organized as performing arts centers, featuring theaters and museum facilities. Government funding also allowed religious groups to maintain archives, frequently including historical music materials. The Nanki Music Library in Tokyo was founded by Marquis Yorisada Tokugawa in the early years of the century. The Marquis, who had studied music in the West, sought to create a music collection containing both Western music and the music of his country.

The idea of separate recorded sound archives or collections in libraries did not gain acceptance until well into the 1950s. Among the first of these was the British Library National Sound Archive, established in 1955 as a separate entity but now administered by the British Library, featuring both published and unpublished audio recordings in all musical genres. Its holdings include audio recordings of performances by the Royal Shakespeare Company, among other stage companies, and British Broadcasting Corporation (BBC) radio dramas from the 1930s to the present. The vast Deutsche Musikarchiv in Berlin was established as a separate section of the national Deutsche Bibliothek in the 1960s and is the depository library for sound recordings in Germany.

For many years U.S. copyright deposit laws did not include sound recordings. Nonetheless, the LC began acquisitions of sound recordings in the early 1920s, and in 1940 it established a recording laboratory to undertake preservation efforts and create recordings from and for the collections. Its Recorded Sound Division was formally established in the 1960s, and with the 1976 Copyright Act revision, recordings were routinely deposited. The LC consolidated its entire film, video, and audio holdings into a single unit in 1978 named the Motion Picture, Broadcasting, and Recorded Sound Division.

Originally part of the Music Division at the NYPL, the Rodgers and Hammerstein Archives of Recorded Sound achieved separate status and facilities in the New York Public Library for the Performing Arts in 1965. It is a unique public repository of recordings in all formats, comprising everything from commercial record label releases to ethnic and tribal music to radio broadcasts to readings by John Barrymore and Tennessee Williams. The collection has been an industry leader in the field of preservation of sound recordings, and its staff engineers have been recognized for their innovative work, such as the transfer and remastering of the Mapleson wax cylinder recordings of Metropolitan Opera performances from the 1900s.

The concerns of sound recording archives and their professional staffs were addressed with the founding of the Association for Recorded Sound Collections (ARSC) in 1966. A leader in the dissemination of new information in this field, ARSC has issued numerous publications, including a union catalog of the largest U.S. sound archives. Other substantial sound archives are found at Stanford (California), Syracuse (New York), and Yale universities.

Theater

Theater libraries exist throughout the world in a variety of places and forms. Some are part of larger performing arts institutions, some are solely research-level collections in academic settings, some are government-run, and others are privately held. Most commonly, theater resources are found buried away in archival collections and ephemera files. The reason for this diversity stems from a historical prejudice against theater. Those who made their living on the stage were at best considered suspect, part of the fringe, not quite acceptable, and as such, the collection and preservation of theater materials marginal. In Europe, however, the great theaters created museums and libraries from their stockpiled holdings, and the plays themselves became part of national libraries through copyright procedures. In the United States, copyright encouraged the registering and cataloging of plays as literary works, although a puritan tradition stifled the growth of national and regional theaters.

These prejudices, unlike the attitudes toward and traditions in the field of music, perpetuated a lack of knowledge about theater resources and theater repositories. The situation did not change until the 1920s, when theater began to be viewed as a visual art form through the influence of artists and designers such as Edward Gordon Craig and Robert Edmond Jones. This change generated the creation of new collections and renewed interest in old collections. For this reason, the American Library Association funded a worldwide survey of theater holdings in 1934, conducted by George Freedley, curator of NYPL's Theatre Collection. More recently, another survey was conducted through the joint cooperation of the National Center of Scientific Research in France and Ohio State University (Columbus), with the 1992 volume *Bibliothèques et musées des arts du spectacle dans le monde* and the 1996 edition of *SIBMAS International Directory of Performing Arts Collections*. (SIBMAS stands for *Société internationale des bibilothèques et musées des arts du spectacle* [International Association of Libraries and Museums of the Performing Arts].)

In Europe, repositories such as Austria's Nationalbibliothek contain manuscripts of plays from the 16th century, as well as programs and playbills, stage and theater models, engravings, and photographs. The Austrian Theater Museum holds materials on theater, opera, dance, film, and many forms of popular entertainment. The Royal Library (Kongelige Bibliotek) in Copenhagen, Denmark, houses a large collection of Scandinavian plays and the Nationalmuseet holds a fine collection on Asian theater. The Theaterhistorisk Museum of Copenhagen was opened in 1922 in the old building of the Court Theater, with materials dating from the mid–18th century.

France, with its long theater tradition, holds many theatrical treasures. The Bibliothèque nationale in Paris boasts a wide-ranging collection of performing arts materials, representing ballet, opera, music, theater, mime, puppetry, and film. Its Department des Arts du Spectacle, established in 1920 with a donation from Auguste Rondel, includes theatrical materials from around the world and throughout many historical periods. The Bibliothèque nationale's status as a depository library ensures that its collections of performing arts materials are preeminent, but it also boasts many large special collections of individuals and theater companies of France.

Berlin's Academy of the Arts (Akademie der Künste), founded in 1696 and reorganized in 1954, contains collections of many famous playwrights, directors, and actors of the German performing arts community. The Schiller National Museum of the German Literature Archive (Schiller-Nationalmuseum of the Deutsches Literaturarchiv) in Marbach collects materials on theater, opera, dance, film, radio, television, and cabaret. The German Theater Museum, founded in 1910 when German actress and playwright Clara Ziegler left her home and all personal belongings to the city of Munich, contains materials on all aspects of theater, including music and dance, and contains a large collection of scene and costume sketches. Universität Hamburg holds in its theater collection records and promptbooks from the Hamburger Stadttheater that date to the mid–18th century.

In Rome, the Burcado Library and Theater Collection houses a notable collection of Italian theater materials spanning the 16th century to the present. The library's roots stem from a 1929 donation of the Burckardt mansion in Rome that now houses the collection.

The British Library's theater holdings include all plays submitted to the Lord Chamberlain's Office for examination and licensing from 1824 to 1968. Plays submitted under the terms of the 1968 Theatres Act continue to be collected. The Theatre Museum of the Victoria and Albert Museum (London), considered to be the ranking theater collection in England, is especially rich in its scene and costume design. Its holdings document the history of all Britain's performing arts from the 16th century to the present. The National Video Archive of Stage Performance was established in 1992 through an agreement between the Theatre Museum and the theatrical unions to preserve live stage performances for research and study.

The Birmingham (England) Shakespeare Library, founded in 1864 as part of a Shakespeare tercentenary celebration, is part of the Birmingham Public Library and includes books and ephemeral materials on all aspects of Shakespeare's life and works. An aggressive collecting policy has made this collection the largest collection of Shakespeare materials in the United Kingdom.

In the United States, the first theater library established in the 20th century was Harvard University's Theatre Collection, founded in 1901 on a gift of portraits of actor David Garrick that was quickly followed by other notable individual collections, including that of Robert Gould Shaw, the Theatre Collection's first curator. The Folger Shakespeare Library of Washington, D.C., established in 1932 with a collection of materials owned by Henry Clay Folger, is a premier collection of materials by and about William Shakespeare and houses a replica of the Globe Theatre, which is used for performances.

Repositories in the city of New York include the Theatre Collection (renamed the Billy Rose Theatre Collection in 1979) of the NYPL for the Performing Arts and the Theater Collection of the Museum of the City of New York. The Museum contains materials on theater and theater architecture of the New York metropolitan area. The NYPL's Theatre Collection was established in 1931 as a provision of the estate of David Belasco. This donation, added to other previously donated theater materials, became the cornerstone of the collection. Its first curator, George Freedley, was a well-known member of the theater community who, with his collection development strategies, laid the foundation that made the collection one of the world's leading repositories of performing arts materials today. An innovative component of the collection is its Theatre on Film and Tape Archive (TOFT) founded in 1970 by Betty Corwin. The archive, which tapes live performances of New York and regional U.S. theater productions, has served as a model for other videotape archives such as that of the San Francisco Performing Arts Library and Museum.

In Asia, the Beijing University Library in China houses a collection of plays, posters, costumes, set models, films, and videos. In Russia, the A.A. Bakhrushin State Theater Museum and the Russian State Archives of Literature are examples of repositories documenting the theater arts of the former Soviet Union. Japan's National Theater in Tokyo includes a theater museum that enjoys national library status and holds materials on the country's traditional performing arts. Other Japanese collections of note include the Zenshin-za Theater Company and the Tsubouchi Memorial Theater Museum of Waseda University. In Australia the performing arts are documented in various states and cities throughout the country. Both the State Library of Victoria and the Victoria Arts Trust in Melbourne collect materials in all theater-related subjects.

Other major factors in the development of theater and performing arts collections include the 1937 founding of the Theatre Library Association in the United States. Its purpose was to promote the collection, preservation, and use of performing arts materials. Another organization, SIBMAS, is international in scope. Founded in 1954 as a section of the International Federation of Library Associations and Institutions, this organization has devoted much effort to making performing arts materials visible and accessible to the public throughout the world.

Sometimes collaborative efforts are begun that enhance the ability of a community to do research and preservation in its subject field. Collaborative projects not only aid the sharing of resources but also help in the creation of new projects and archival facilities for the performing arts field. Founded by the United Nations Educational, Scientific, and Cultural Organization in 1948, the International Theatre Institute promotes awareness and cooperation among performing arts organizations throughout the world. Located in approximately 90 countries, its facilities include libraries and archives open to the public documenting international theater through plays and periodicals. All of these efforts have shaped theater and performing arts repositories as we know them today.

Dance

Whereas performing arts libraries are 20th-century institutions, the systematic collection of dance materials is even newer and, to a large extent, has been defined by the technologies of the latter part of the century, most specifically film, video, and digital delivery.

Because of the ephemeral nature of dance, its representation in libraries has often been in tandem with theater and music materials. Many dance collections developed out of company records of theater and opera organizations (the Museum and Library of the Paris Opera being one such example). Today repositories attached to dance companies and schools are numerous, including London's Laban Centre for Movement and Dance. These collections include personal papers, scores, audio/video archives, and computer programs (such as Calaban and Laban Writer) that assist students and choreographers in computer-generated dance notation. Now part of London's Royal Academy of Dancing, the Benesh Institute is an international study center, with its core of 500 dance scores in Benesh Movement Notation, as well as materials on dance anthropology, ethnic dance forms, and dance therapy. In Russia, materials documenting the histories of that country's two most celebrated ballet companies can be found in Moscow's Bolshoi Theater Museum and in the Kirov Theater Museum in the St. Petersburg State Academy of Theater Arts.

The 1976 revision of the U.S. copyright law, allowing for copyright registration of choreographic works, has had significant impact on national libraries around the world; as copyright depositories, they have added videotaped dance holdings at a rapid rate. Among the first dance-related acquisitions of the Library of Congress were 18th- and 19th-century dance manuals offering instruction in social dance of the period. The LC's commission in 1944 of Aaron Copland and Martha Graham's *Appalachian Spring* added documentation of that important work to the library. The library benefited tremendously from the 1976 copyright revision, as choreographers deposited videotapes for posterity. In turn it has attracted important dance collections, notably the Martha Graham videotape collection.

Several state institutions in Germany document dance. The German Dance Archives in Cologne, founded just after World War II, is that country's largest dance collection and serves as a center for documentation, research, and information about dance. In Bremen the German Dance Film Institute was created solely to document dance through videotape.

The most noteworthy dance repository in the world is the Jerome Robbins Dance Division of the NYPL's Library for the Performing Arts. Established in 1944, this archive documents dance in all forms—theatrical, folk, social, and ethnic—and contains materials in a wide array of formats. Foremost among its holdings are more than 10,000 films and videotapes and an ongoing oral history project. Its holdings are documented in the *Dictionary Catalog of the New York Public Library Dance Collection,* first published in 1974, and its annual supplement on paper and CD-ROM.

The Dance Collection was one of the founding members in 1992 of the Dance Heritage Coalition. This group of major dance collections was formed to address issues of dance documentation and preservation and has aided institutions in preserving, publicizing, and promoting access to dance holdings. Through their efforts, a cooperative project involving search tools has been developed so that archival materials, including encoded archival descriptions, can be accessed more easily via the Internet.

Film, Radio, and Television

The new technologies in film, television, and radio in the 20th century expanded the scope of the performing arts, changed the complexion of entertainment, and made them perhaps the most popular entertainment media of all time, for now performances can be viewed by the public in their homes and neighborhoods. These media have also created new collecting areas for performing arts libraries. Although interest in these forms of entertainment has been widespread, recognition of the need for documentation did not move as swiftly, especially with television, once considered to be a more "common" form of entertainment and not initially of scholarly interest. Soon, however, the need to document and preserve the new entertainment phenomena became apparent when deterioration of film resulted in the loss of much early television and film history. Libraries, museums, and archives throughout the world recognized the need to preserve and document these materials.

An instrumental organization in the history of film preservation is the International Federation of Film Archives (La Fédération Internationale des Archives du Film), founded in 1938 to promote preservation of and access to the film medium in all its manifestations. Currently it includes members from more than 100 archives in more than 60 countries. Collections housed in national repositories, museums, and university archives have opened all over the world with the primary purpose of preserving national film and television resources. A recent list of worldwide film and television archives contains approximately 150 archives with repositories in North America, South America, Europe, Asia, Africa, and Australia. These include La Fundación Cinemateca Argentina; the National Film Archive of India; ScreenSound Australia (formerly the National Film and Sound Archive); and the Russian State Film and Photo Archive, which documents the history of Russian filmmaking from 1896.

In the United States, the motion picture collection of the George Eastman House in Rochester, New York, is one of the oldest film collections, with silent film holdings second to none. The Center for Motion Picture Study of the Academy of Motion Picture Arts and Sciences in Los Angeles, California, houses the Margaret Herrick Library, which was established in 1991 and collects materials on the history of the film industry and film personalities.

The Department of Film and Video at New York City's Museum of Modern Art (MoMA) was conceived in 1932 by Alfred Barr, the museum's first director. Barr instructed the film curator, Iris Barry, to visit Hollywood and solicit films from the major producing studios. This precipitated donations from Walt Disney, Mary Pickford and Douglas Fairbanks, Warner Bros., Harold Lloyd, and Paramount, among others. In addition, Barry traveled to Europe and the Soviet Union, collecting foreign films. Today these films are housed in Hamlin, Pennsylvania, at the museum's Celeste Bartos Film Preservation Center, a state-of-the-art preservation and research facility that opened in 1996.

The University of California at Los Angeles Film and Television Archives is the world's largest university collection of film and television programs, spanning 1890 to the present and including 30 million feet of newsreel footage. Another superior collection is the film and script holdings of the University of Southern California in Los Angeles. The Museum of Television and Radio, with archives and viewing facilities in both Los Angeles and New York, collects programs from network, cable, and local broadcasts. Canadian broadcasting materials can be found at the Public Archives in Ottawa, Ontario, and the Canadian Broadcasting Corporation Archives in Toronto, Ontario. Founded in 1933, the British Film Institute (BFI) in London serves as the United Kingdom's national film repository, and library services are only part of its total information, conservation, and distribution activities. The largest film archive in Europe, its collection of feature films, documentaries, newsreels, animation, and television programs in a variety of formats are available through its National Film and Television Archive; its library holds printed materials. The BFI also offers booking services for films in its collection, operates an archival footage licensing unit, and creates databases of indexes to film periodicals and other information.

Popular Entertainment

Popular entertainment has existed from the beginning of recorded time: from Circus Maximus to the Cirque du Soleil, from miracle plays to historical pageants of the 19th century, from court entertainment to burlesque and vaudeville. Documentation of popular entertainment, however, has only been of scholarly interest since the latter part of the 20th century, generated by cross-disciplinary research and, with it, new documentation of resources. Theater collections usually handle the bulk of these materials, as the field of theatrical performance is often given a broad scope. Materials on amusement parks, world's fairs, and aquacades, also within the scope of popular entertainment, are often linked to locale and are points of pride for historical societies and local collections.

In the United States, new cross-disciplinary subjects have generated interest in performing arts repositories where much popular entertainment material has been unobtrusively tucked away. Repositories such as Harvard's Theatre Collection and the Billy Rose Theatre Collection contain many types of popular entertainment materials relating to vaudeville, musical halls, burlesque, circus, puppetry, and magic.

In Europe, repositories such as the Archive and Museum of Flemish Culture in Antwerp and the International Carnival and Mask Museum in Binche hold materials on public celebrations, festivals, and puppet theater in Belgium. The Netherlands Theater Institute also collects materials on puppetry, circus, cabaret, and other forms of popular entertainment. Materials on puppetry are universally found in theater collections. However, the holdings of the National Bunraku Theater in Osaka, Japan, are primarily on the art of puppetry as it is employed in the traditional theatrical art of Bunraku. The Theater Museum of Japan's National Theater also includes materials on pantomime, circus, and music halls. Circus materials are generally found in theater repositories, although examples of circus subject collections include the John and Mabel Ringling Museum in Sarasota, Florida, and Circus World in Baraboo, Wisconsin.

The Wild West show is a U.S. phenomenon and part of a distinct cultural experience. Collections in the United States specializing in western lore and culture, such as the Buffalo Bill Historical Center in Cody, Wyoming; the Amon Carter Museum in Fort Worth, Texas; and the Research Center of the Gene Autry Museum of Western Heritage in Los Angeles, California, usually contain materials on this unique form of entertainment. It would be remiss not to mention the Popular Culture Library at Bowling Green State University in Bowling Green, Ohio. Founded in 1969, this collection is dedicated entirely to the subject of U. S. popular culture.

New Developments

With the introduction of the Internet, libraries have expanded their information base in ways never imagined in the past. Performing arts information, often difficult to locate, has become easier to find through these new technologies. The virtual library has indeed embraced the performing arts field as well as others. The performing arts, as visual and aural media, lend themselves well to resources on the Internet. Online exhibits and music and video clips can be found throughout cyberspace at the touch of a keystroke. The online catalogs of many large university and public libraries are fully searchable via the Internet. Libraries will also link outside their websites to others of subject interest. Researchers can now sit at home and find subject information on the performing arts as well as information on performing arts organizations.

KEVIN B. WINKLER AND MARY ELLEN W. ROGAN

Further Reading

Buck, Richard M, editor, *SIBMAS International Directory of Performing Arts Collections,* Haslemere, France: Emmett, 1996

Cohen, Selma Jeanne, editor, *International Encyclopedia of Dance,* New York: Oxford University Press, 1998

Darnay, Brigitte T., editor, *Subject Directory of Special Libraries and Information Centers,* vol. 4, Detroit, Michigan: Gale, 1988

Giteau, Cecile, editor, *Bibliothèques et musées des arts du spectacle dans le monde,* Paris, France: Centre National de la Recherche Scientifique, 1967; 4th edition, 1992

Jackson, Allan S., "Theater Libraries and Collections," in *Encyclopedia of Library and Information Science,* edited by Allen Kent et al., vol. 30, New York: Dekker, 1980

Marco, Guy A., "Music Libraries and Collections: Historical Survey," in *Encyclopedia of Library and Information Science,* edited by Allen Kent et al., vol. 18, New York: Dekker, 1976

Matlaw, Myron, editor, *American Popular Entertainment: Papers and Proceedings of the Conference on the History of American Popular Entertainment,* Westport, Connecticut: Greenwood Press, 1979

Performing Arts Resources (1974–)

Rachow, Louis A., editor, *Theatre and Performing Arts Collections,* New York: Haworth Press, 1981

Williams, Sam P., compiler, *Guide to the Research Collection of the New York Public Library,* Chicago: American Library Association, 1975

Polar Libraries

Polar libraries fall into two categories: libraries located geographically in the polar regions (chiefly the Arctic), and those located elsewhere but with collections devoted to these regions. The former category includes public libraries serving Arctic communities, scientific stations (Antarctic and Arctic), and shipborne expedition libraries. Such collections generally include publications of general interest as well as specifically polar material. With the exception of public libraries whose history is better studied within the context of their national library systems, this article covers both categories.

Shipborne Expedition Libraries

The origins of the polar library may be traced back to libraries carried aboard exploration vessels. Naval expeditions played a major role in the early exploration of both the Arctic and Antarctic. Ships were well provisioned to endure extended periods at sea. This was particularly necessary when they were required to winter in the ice and needed to be well stocked with books, as well as with other entertainment, to survive the tedium of the long dark period during which most sailing activities would necessarily be suspended.

Polar narratives often refer to books and reading. Thus French explorer Jean Baptiste Charcot took some 3,000 books with him on his second Antarctic expedition (1908–10). These were housed in two bookcases in the wardroom and on a shelf that ran around all the cabins. This collection was large but not exceptional. The libraries on Robert Falcon Scott's first and second Antarctic expeditions (1901–04, 1910–13) were similarly large, and for the first the catalog has survived. The books are classified under the following broad categories: biographical (93 titles), essays and philosophical (59), historical (46), travel (78), fiction (269), poetical (56), magazines, etc. (12), miscellaneous (2), reference (12), scientific (315), and expeditions (36). As these categories suggest, the library was markedly eclectic, with literature as well represented as science. Most of the scientific books were located in the cabins of the scientific staff, but these also housed books on other subjects. A complete set of Sir Walter Scott's *Waverley* novels was, for example, to be found in his namesake's cabin. The two largest collections, however, were kept in the wardroom (for officers) and mess deck (for the crew), with some division of function apparent, as the mess deck collection shows itself to have been selected for the crew's entertainment and edification. All magazines and much of the fiction (92 titles) were housed here, but so also were the only copy of William Shakespeare's works, Elizabeth Gaskell's *Life of Charlotte Brontë,* and John R. Green's *History of the English People.* Also predictably found here are Charles Dana's *Two Years before the Mast,* Frank T. Lomus Bullen's *Men of the Merchant Service,* and Edward Giffard's *Deeds of Naval Daring.*

From Charcot and his fellow-explorer Ernest Shackleton (1914–17) we learn that encyclopedias were particularly appreciated, especially for resolving arguments that might otherwise have become interminable. Shackleton found an unusual use for the *Encyclopaedia Britannica* while at Ocean Camp in the Weddell Sea, where his ship, the *Endurance,* had sunk and the expedition waited for the ice pack to carry them north toward the open sea. In *South,* his account of this expedition, he wrote,

"[O]ne genius having discovered that the paper used for its pages had been impregnated with saltpetre, we can now thoroughly recommend it as a very efficient pipe-lighter." Later in the same expedition, second-in-command Frank Wild described one of the smallest polar libraries located on Elephant Island, where 22 men wintered for 105 days under two upturned boats while awaiting Shackleton's return and rescue. The library consisted of two books of poetry, Nordenskjold's *Antarctica,* what remained of the *Encyclopaedia Britannica,* and a penny cookery book. The role of this tiny library in helping the stranded party to retain their sanity should not be underestimated.

The Pre-1939 Period

The earliest attempt to establish a publicly accessible polar library arose directly out of the Belgian Antarctic Expedition (1897–99). Belgian pride in this expedition was such that an Institut polaire international was founded at Brussels in 1907. Centrally involved was Georges Lecointe, second-in-command of the expedition and an enthusiast for Universal Decimal Classification (UDC), developed out of the Dewey Decimal Classification by two Belgians, Paul Otlet and Lafontaine. In 1906 at the Congrès international pour l'étude des régions polaires hosted in Brussels, Otlet advocated UDC as particularly suitable for the organization of polar materials. This advice was acted on by Lecointe, and the collections of the new polar institute were arranged accordingly. These Belgian initiatives were overwhelmed by World War I but were to have some influence across the English Channel when another polar institute was founded in Cambridge in 1920.

The origins of the Scott Polar Research Institute (SPRI) in Cambridge, England, go back to 1912, when two scientists of Scott's second Antarctic expedition were confined by a blizzard in a hut on the slopes of Mt. Erebus. In his retrospect of the institute, Frank Debenham notes that while he and Raymond Priestley were hunting for delicacies to eat, they found instead "some blue-lined foolscap [paper] . . . so heavy in quality and smooth of surface that it positively invited one to write. . . ." On this they wrote the germs of an idea for a polar institute. It is unclear to what extent they knew of the Brussels institute, but they too envisaged a central depository for expedition records and polar knowledge. Above all they wished future expeditions to be able to build on the knowledge gained by their predecessors rather than simply repeating earlier errors. In 1920 the Polar Institute was set up based on a promise of funds from the Captain Scott Memorial Mansion House Fund and this, with further assistance from the Pilgrim Trust, enabled construction of a fine building in 1934 with a well-equipped library at its heart.

Once established, the SPRI Library was soon to be the recipient of major private collections, the most outstanding being the Antarctic library of Hugh Robert Mill, former librarian of the Royal Geographical Society. Mill began collecting in 1902 when he started writing his book, *The Siege of the South Pole* (1905). By the time the collection came to SPRI, it consisted of more than 500 volumes but not, alas, a complete set of *Reports* from Fabien Gottlicke von Bellingshausen's expedition (1819–21), which Mill was reportedly unable to purchase from a Russian friend at any price. These *Reports,* the rarest of Antarctic rarities, have not been sighted since.

A few individuals have been particularly influential in the development of polar libraries. At SPRI the great shaping influence was that of Brian Roberts, a veteran explorer and professional diplomat. Roberts was head of the Polar Regions Section at the British Foreign and Commonwealth Office, but from 1944 to 1975 he also managed to work four days a week at SPRI as a polar authority and library expert. If his greatest achievement was his contribution to the drafting and negotiation of the Antarctic Treaty (1959), his greatest love was the SPRI Library, to which he bequeathed his own fine collection. Although not a trained librarian, Roberts had a detailed knowledge of all aspects of library organization that would have been the envy of most professionals. In *The Organization of Polar Information* (1960), he summarized his views, emphasizing the need for collaboration between polar libraries and urging, in particular, adoption of a common classification system similar to that of Otlet and Lecointe, advocating Universal Decimal Classification. At SPRI all collections, including archives and library correspondence, were to be organized by UDC, for which Roberts compiled three editions of a special schedule for use in polar libraries (1950, 1963, 1976). Although used by a number of other libraries, UDC was never adopted as universally as Roberts had wished, but his cooperative vision has since underlain the work of the Polar Libraries Colloquy (PLC; from 1971 to 1988, the Northern Libraries Colloquy).

SPRI was established as an international polar information center at a time when polar expertise elsewhere was primarily the realm of individuals, some of whom possessed fine personal libraries that later formed the nuclei of institutional libraries. The most notable example is the Icelandic/Canadian/U.S. explorer Vilhjalmur Stefansson. After making notable discoveries in the Canadian Arctic, Stefansson moved to Greenwich Village, New York, where his ever-expanding library was the center of his world. From the late 1930s the collection was housed in three adjoining four-room apartments in Greenwich Village. He and his staff of librarians welcomed anyone interested in polar research, as well as his many acquaintances from around the world. Books were everywhere, even under the kitchen sink and between spices and baking soda on his kitchen shelves.

This library and Stefansson's enabled him to act as Arctic consultant to government and commerce, a role in which he flourished, particularly during the 1940s and 1950s, when cold weather warfare became a matter of major national concern. Stefansson was to discover during the McCarthy era that acquiring a polar library was not entirely without risk because, in order to obtain publications, he had joined a number of organizations accused of being Communist fronts. He then was pressed to explain his membership in these. His U.S. Navy–funded work on an *Encyclopedia Acrtica* was halted by these suspicions. In 1951 his library was acquired by Dartmouth College.

Post-1945, the Cold War, the Antarctic Treaty, and Current Trends

Up to 1939 the history of polar libraries is essentially that of isolated government and private initiative amid general international neglect. This situation was changed by alarming revelations of deficiencies in cold weather warfare equipment and techniques during World War II, and by subsequent appreciation that the Arctic "Mediterranean" constituted a likely major military theater in any conflict between the United States and the Soviet Union. No longer politically and strategically peripheral, the Arctic attracted huge national investment, additionally supported by growing awareness of the region's resource potential. Existing research facilities grew and new institutes were established, few without libraries. Polar libraries also benefited from U.S. government concern about a distinct Soviet lead in cold-related expertise. Soviet polar literature was eagerly collected, major works translated, and two comprehensive bibliographies funded, *The Bibliography of Cold Regions Science and Technology* (1951–) and the *Arctic Bibliography* (1953–75), with works in Russian especially well represented. Coordination of these two bibliographies was undertaken by the Cold Regions Research and Engineering Laboratory (established in 1951) and the Arctic Institute of North America (established 1946) respectively, both of which built up extensive polar libraries, as did the Library of Congress (LC), where much of the work was done.

For Antarctica, the great stimuli were the International Geophysical Year (IGY, 1957–58)—during which the continent was subject to intense scientific scrutiny—and the Antarctic Treaty (1959). Both resulted in the establishment of scientific stations, many originally intended as temporary (for the IGY) but that became long-term following the signing of the treaty. National Antarctic institutes were set up in a number of countries, library provision being required for both these institutes and individual stations. Although the libraries of the national institutes tended to be purely scientific, those of the stations mixed science and leisure in a manner essentially similar to the earlier shipborne expedition libraries. Antarctic science benefited considerably from the generosity of the U.S. government in funding the comprehensive *Antarctic Bibliography* (1965–) compiled at the LC.

The 1990s have been a period of retrenchment for many polar libraries. In the Antarctic, the 50-year moratorium on mineral exploration as well as tighter controls over waste disposal agreed to in the Protocol on Environmental Protection (1991) have contributed to a downturn in interest among some countries as research has become more expensive and the prospect of financial return reduced. Libraries serving such national programs have inevitably been affected. In the Arctic the end of the Cold War has reduced available resources more generally, an effect only partially mitigated by initiatives fostering increased international collaboration in this region. Against these trends, growing awareness of the crucial role played by the polar regions in global systems and in world climate has secured continued funding in countries with major scientific programs.

Polar libraries are likely to continue to experience "boom and bust" cycles reflecting the characteristic nature of development in the polar regions. In consequence their libraries and librarians have become something of a breed apart. The biennial meetings of the Polar Libraries Colloquy are events to savor, with experiences exchanged not only on making the most of scant resources but also on how to enjoy the good times when they come. For a comprehensive list of Polar and Cold Region libraries and archives, see www.UROVA.FI/HOME/ARKTINEN/POLARWEB/POLAR/LIBD/NDER.HTM.

WILLIAM J. MILLS

Further Reading

Corley, Nora T., compiler, *Polar and Cold Regions Library Resources*, Ottawa, Ontario: Northern Libraries Colloquy, 1975; 3rd edition, compiled by Martha Andrews, Ann Brennan, and Liisa Kurppa, Boulder, Colorado: Polar Libraries Colloquy, 1994

Debenham, Frank, "Retrospect: The Scott Polar Research Institute, 1920–45," *Polar Record* 4, no. 29 (1945)

Hills, Gordon H., *Native Libraries: Cross-Cultural Conditions in the Circumpolar North*, Lanham, Maryland: Scarecrow Press, 1997

Hunt, William R., *Stef: A Biography of Vilhjalmur Stefansson, Canadian Arctic Explorer*, Vancouver: University of British Columbia Press, 1986

King, H.G.R., and A. Shirley, editors, *Polar Pundit: Reminiscences about Brian Birley Roberts*, Cambridge: Scott Polar Research Institute, 1995

Mills, William James, and Peter Speak, *Keyguide to Information Sources on the Polar and Cold Regions*, London and Washington, D.C.: Mansell, 1998

Polar Libraries Bulletin (1990–)

Polar Libraries Colloquy, biennial conference proceedings

Robert, Brian Birley, *The Organization of Polar Information*, Cambridge: Scott Polar Research Institute, 1960

Shackleton, Ernest, *South*, London: Heinemann, 1919; New York: Macmillan, 1920; reprint, London: Penguin, and New York: Signet, 1999

Prison Libraries

From the beginnings of the penitentiary in the late 18th century until the recent past, books and libraries in prisons have been seen as instruments of behavioral control, reformation, moral education, and coercion, rather than as a means of opening and enriching the life of the mind. It may be said that all libraries in their beginnings shared this goal of moral reformation. The great difference in the history of libraries is that the patrons of prison libraries had little choice in their composition. Books were placed there for a specific purpose: to impose and reinforce the cultural hegemony of the dominant class. And even with this purpose in mind, prisoners had no easy time in using the books within these libraries. Today it is not much better; in fact, in some ways it is worse. With the decline of the rehabilitative ideal, libraries in prison have little meaning by themselves. The uses of libraries are now seen as subversive to the legal system, a means by which convicts can create judicial traffic jams.

There is evidence of books in libraries early in the history of penitentiaries. For most of their history, penitentiaries were generally based on the utilitarian principle of the greatest good for the greatest number. Pure utility justified punishment—a teleological philosophy that believed the means will lead to a beneficial end. It focused on equitable and rehabilitative treatment for transgressors based on a formula incorporating the nature of crime and its circumstances. Education and reading played a natural part in the utilitarian scheme for the reformation of character. Ideally, reading materials would induce an ethical and moral change in the convicts. "Mental improvement" would teach convicts delayed gratification, a central tenet in the middle-class moral world that encompassed the universe of prison reform. This ideology existed in the earliest prison in Philadelphia, Pennsylvania (1790), founded on Quaker ideals, and in the Eastern State Penitentiary in Philadelphia and the prison in Auburn, New York, both founded in the 1820s.

The history of U.S. prison reform can be broken into four periods: the early era, from the beginning of the penitentiary as we know it to the 1820s; the 1820s to the beginning of progressive penology, in the 1870s; the treatment era, from the 1870s to the 1970s; and the age of retribution, from the late 1970s to the present. It is only in this last period that the prevailing ideology shifted to a nonconsequentialist neo-Kantianism that removed the former ideological basis for the utility of prison libraries and threw them into a search for acceptable political grounds for their existence.

Most, if not all, books in the earliest prisons were of a religious nature. These small collections cannot be called organized libraries, but reading material existed, books whose aim was to strengthen character. To cite one example among many, in 1825 officials of New York's House of Refuge mentioned "instruction of the mind" and "literary improvement" most often as the means of reforming their inmates.

Prior to the Civil War, most U.S. prisons had some type of library or book collection, primarily composed of religious books and tracts. Reformative ideology decreed reading to be a weapon in the never-ending battle to readjust the deviant to proper thinking. For short periods there was a flurry of library activity, such as that at Sing Sing Prison (New York) in the 1840s under Eliza Farnham, the activist matron of the women's department. But organized library programs that provided nonreligious books were lacking in most states. Evidence exists that in 1847 New York was the first state to support a penal book collection with direct appropriations of funds.

It was New York that took the lead in prison reform. Beginning with the work of the New York Prison Association in the mid-1840s and picking up speed after the Civil War, penology became more and more scientific. To the postwar generation, knowledge was the key to social order, and social science was the key to this knowledge. With the tools of social science, criminologists claimed to know the laws that governed criminal behavior.

The New York Prison Association in 1865 authorized two reformers to study prison conditions in the United States. Their study fueled the new reform movement that culminated in the National Prison Congress in Cincinnati, Ohio, in 1870. The congress delineated the basic principles of reform that would dominate the progressive period. These principles included a strong emphasis on education and called for the provision of well-stocked libraries. Thus began an age of active development of prison reading and the organization of libraries that only ended in the 1980s. Reformers praised the rehabilitative powers of good reading and enthusiastically crusaded for books for convicts. There is evidence that by 1873 most if not all of the state prisons in the northeast and Midwest had libraries for their convicts.

The reformative powers of reading were well stated by reformer Enoch C. Wines in *The State of Prisons and of Child-Saving Institutions on the Civilized World* (1880):

> The Warden of one prison says "All the prisoners who can read understandingly avail themselves of the privilege. The improvement from it is astonishing. Young men who two years ago were taught their first lesson here are now good readers; and it seems as if they had changed entirely in body and mind. They keep themselves now neat and clean, while they formerly were very filthy in their habits. They have better manners, and look more intelligent, more like human beings. Ignorance makes many convicts; education alone makes the man."

This was indeed a strong statement for the almost magical rehabilitative powers of the book—not only would reading modify one's behavior, but it would improve one's looks as well!

Beginning with the 1870 National Prison Congress and continuing through the early 20th century, more and more prisons printed catalogs for their libraries, and various organizations issued pronouncements and standards for prison libraries. In 1876 the New York Prison Association published its *Catalogue and Rules for Prison Libraries*. This catalog gives the first indication of officially approved reading material for convicts, with the books graded from "A" to "L" depending on "usefulness." Prison libraries followed suit in printing catalogs of their collections. For instance, the Illinois State Penitentiary in Joliet library catalog showed 4,000 volumes in 1877, the largest prison collection of its time. Elmira Reformatory in Elmira, New York, founded in 1876, claimed to embody the most progressive of reformative principles, aimed at "total reformation" of the criminal character, with education and reading playing a major part in the rehabilitative process. According to the reformatory's annual report of 1894, it had a 3,000-volume library, the aim of which was to educate the prisoner:

> In the purchase of these works [books for the library] great care was always exercised, particularly to increase the files for the lower classes with suitable and adequate literature. The management places faith in the modern version of the old proverb—"Tell me what you read: I will tell you what you are." The original purpose of the library was mainly to educate the prisoners to a taste for healthy literature, whether romance or history; and this purpose still prevails as an all-important factor in the addition of prospective editions.

During the Progressive Era of the late 19th and early 20th centuries, utilitarian concepts of the worthiness of reading and libraries penetrated even into the southern United States, long a backwater of prison discipline. The *Louisiana Penitentiary Report* of 1896 and 1897 stated that "We know of no agency more productive of good results than moral reading." The Maryland penitentiary boasted a library of 5,000 volumes in 1900.

Farther west, however, there is mixed evidence of the existence of prison libraries. In 1877 the Colorado penitentiary in Canon City began using visitors' fees to support a library. An 1896 law in Utah provided for a prison library in its Salt Lake City facility. But in Oklahoma it was not until 1929 that the prison system recommended setting up a book collection to approximate that found in the state's eighth-grade curriculum.

The southern and western United States notwithstanding, the first decades of the 20th century were busy ones for advocates of prison libraries and moral education. Florence Rising Curtis published her surveys of institutional libraries in 1912 and 1918. In *The Libraries of the American State and National Institutions* (1918), she stated:

> The standard moral viewpoint that the prisoner finds in prison, in spite of discipline, [is] an opportunity to learn of the records of more notorious criminals. . . . He needs books to turn his thoughts into other channels, tales of adventure, histories of pioneer days and trail making.
>
> The salacious novel, with its suggestive descriptions and false standards, is not good mental food for the man who needs to learn self-control.

Between 1907 and 1916 the American Library Association (ALA) made several reports on prison libraries, although there is little evidence of their application. In 1930 the Committee on Institutional Libraries of the American Correctional Association (ACA) issued a manual for prison libraries, and in 1931 Austin MacCormick published *The Education of Adult Prisoners, a Survey and a Program*. In his book MacCormick stated that "the possible values of directed reading are almost limitless, especially in the field of adult education." MacCormick's book was sent to the heads of all prisons and reformatories. It persuaded the ALA and the American Prison Association (APA) to issue the *Prison Library Handbook* in 1932.

MacCormick's book and the APA/ALA book represented the culmination of progressive library ideology, and they accurately state the prevailing purpose of permitting reading behind bars—the cultural hegemonic tactic of persuading and controlling. This view remained the same for many years and was illustrated once again in the APA's 1939 *1000 Books for Prison Libraries*. The American Correctional Association issued another manual in 1950, fundamentally the same as the 1932 handbook. *The Objectives and Standards for Libraries in Adult Prisons and Reformatories*, approved by the APA and the ALA in the 1940s, had little that was different in its approach, as did the ACA's 1962 *Objectives and Standards*.

From the early 19th century, society's thinking changed from the idea that suffering wipes away guilt from crime and sin to the progressive period ideology that only mental and behavioral reform can eradicate a person's moral/legal guilt. But beginning in the 1960s and 1970s, a change in attitudes toward prison reform manifested itself in prison library service. Convicts began asserting their rights just as reformers were beginning to abandon the old rehabilitative methods. Believing that only failure resulted from the major emphasis on treatment, more and more prison professionals emphasized punishment pure and simple. The "just deserts" model, loosely based on neo-Kantian deontological ethics, stated that criminals were culpable and responsible and that punishment was the primary end of prison. If convicts changed their behavior, so much the better, but that was not the goal of a prison. Convicts, for their part, believed that they had a right to read what they wished and, as autonomous moral agents, to reform themselves if they wished. Infused with ideologies from the civil rights movement, some prisoners' rights groups, especially in California, drew up library policies that demanded the same reading materials as those available in the free community. Litigation coming from this movement resulted in a federal court mandate to establish prison law libraries. Then in 1966 Title IV of the Library Services and Construction Act (LSCA) provided federal funding for institutional libraries. State library agencies, the vehicle for these funds, began to lobby for prison library services, and more librarians became aware of the convict's informational plight. In the 1970s prisons hired professional librarians for the first time. Book budgets increased, collections grew, and it seemed that finally prison libraries were coming of age and getting in step with the principles and practices of the outside, free world.

ALA went along and drew up new standards for prison libraries in the 1970s, revising them in the 1990s. A number of court decisions placed prisons under judicial watch and protection. In 1977 the U.S. Supreme Court ruled in *Bounds v. Smith* that state prisons must provide "meaningful access to the courts through people trained in the law or through law library collections." It is questionable how meaningful the collections were, but the states had to maintain law library materials. During the 1970s, however, the whole concept of rehabilitation and treatment for offenders was called into question, with severe consequences for prison educational programs, including the library. Beginning in the late 1970s penologists and public officials reacted to the political activism of the 1960s with a neo-Kantian revival of the "just deserts" model of confinement, a backward-looking philosophy that had severe consequences for prison libraries. Prison officials used *Bounds v. Smith* to provide funds for law materials (to the detriment of the general prison library collections), and many library collections depended solely on LSCA funds for their general holdings.

In 1982 the ALA for the first and only time called for support of prison libraries through its "Resolution on Prisoners' Right to Read," which was adopted by the ALA Council on 13 July. During the 1980s librarians as well as penologists turned away from rehabilitation and treatment models. The goal for prison libraries was simply to meet the reading interests and informational needs of convicts. In 1992 ALA issued its Library Standards for Adult Correctional Institutions, which called for "the inmates' right to read and their right to free access to information. Services shall encompass the same variety of material, formats and programs as available in the outside community." Then in 1995 the International Federation of Library Associations and Institutions (IFLA) issued its revised *Guidelines for Library Services to Prisoners,* stating that "prisoners are as entitled as other citizens to have access to information and therefore to proper library facilities."

But reaction had already set in. In the 1990s politicians were in no mood to accede to a prisoner's right to read. On the contrary, they called for no frills and restrictions on privileges for prisoners. If reading was not rehabilitative, why provide books? Is reading for entertainment and pleasure reason enough to spend taxpayers' dollars? The U.S. Congress passed laws restricting a prisoner's access to courts, and the Supreme Court in *Lewis v. Casey* (1996) declared that convicts did not necessarily have the right to a law library. State prisons declared open season on law library collections. Arizona shut down 34 prison libraries and then contracted for paralegal firms to give convicts access to courts. Idaho, Georgia, and other states removed law books from prison libraries and contracted for outside legal services. Other states also began moving in the same direction.

At the beginning of the 21st century the outlook is bleak for prison libraries. Whereas most libraries in the United States and the more advanced nations offer sophisticated electronic information resources, prison libraries have difficulty even getting books. The LSCA was replaced in 1997 with the Library Service and Technology Act, which did not specifically provide for institutional libraries, and state officials were not inclined to use their funds or any others to connect convicts to the Internet.

Prison library provisions outside the United States are harder to assess. Most Western nations have recognized the need for some type of formal or informal reading program in their prisons. England and its former colonies such as Australia and New Zealand introduced libraries into their prisons long ago. In the 19th century, for instance, Elizabeth Fry brought religious reading materials to convicts in English prisons. It is fair to say that almost all official prison reading programs in England in the 19th century revolved around the Bible. It was not until the 20th century that prisons allowed reading for entertainment.

There was an articulated educational philosophy for prisoners in Nazi Germany in the 1930s. According to the 1938 article on prison reading by Hans Löwe, reading was aimed at character transformation, with a strict educational regimen supervised by the librarian. German prisons of the period allowed only serious educational work in their libraries.

All educational programs in prisons reflect the character of the prison conditions. Scandinavian countries, for instance, have relatively well stocked libraries, whereas many of the emerging nations have very little in the way of training, reading, or other educational programs. In fact, they have few conveniences at all. What little evidence exists of prison libraries in developing nations in Africa and other parts of the world illustrates the woeful lack of reading material for their charges.

IFLA recognized the poor state of prison libraries decades ago and issued a set of guidelines, first in 1992 and then a revised edition in 1995. According to its *Guidelines for Library Services to Prisoners,* "The collection must provide materials for reference, leisure reading, study, personal development . . . and cater for all type of readers/users. . . . Censorship of any kind shall not be exercised." The IFLA guidelines listed a variety of standards and basically called for reading opportunities similar to those available in public libraries. It is doubtful that many countries today follow these guidelines.

We live in an information age, one that is becoming more and more dependent on the Internet, yet not one prisoner in the United States has direct access to the Internet. Corrections officials see online access as a security issue, but lack of access to online information limits a convict's opportunity for self-education and thus the ability to make a successful transition back to the street. The one compromise is for librarians to mediate online access. This mediation is done in very few prisons. Prison libraries are caught in this information bind. Traditional libraries as reformative tools have no place in this scheme of things. Our society is not ready to provide convicts free access to information as we do for most citizens in the free world, for the simple reason that prisoners are not free.

LARRY E. SULLIVAN

Further Reading

Australian Library and Information Association, *Australian Prison Libraries: Minimum Standard Guidelines,* Barton, Australian Capital Territory: Australian Library and Information Association, 1990

Council of Europe Committee of Ministers, *Education in Prison,* Strasbourg, France: Council of Europe, 1990

Haug, Turid, "Library Services in Norwegian Prisons," *Scandinavian Public Library Quarterly* 13 (1984)

Jones, Edith Kathleen, editor, *The Prison Library Handbook,* Chicago: American Library Association, 1932

Kaiser, Frances E., compiler and editor, *Guidelines for Library Services to Prisoners,* The Hague: IFLA Headquarters, 1992

Löwe, Hans, "Die Aufgaben einer Gefängnisbücherei," *Die Bücherei* 5 (1938)

MacCormick, Austin H., *The Education of Adult Prisoners, a Survey and a Program,* New York: National Society of Penal Information, 1931; reprint, New York: AMS Press, 1976

Sullivan, Larry E., "Between Empty Covers: Prison Libraries in Historical Perspective," *Wilson Library Bulletin* 64 (1989)

Sullivan, Larry E., *The Prison Reform Movement: Forlorn Hope,* Boston: Twayne, 1990

Sullivan, Larry E., "Reading in American Prisons: Structures and Strictures," *Libraries and Culture* 33, no. 1 (1998)

Sullivan, Larry E., "To the Least of Our Brethren: Library Service to Prisoners," *American Libraries* 31, no. 5 (2000)

Vogel, Brenda, *Down for the Count: A Prison Library Handbook,* Metuchen, New Jersey: Scarecrow Press, 1995

Private Libraries

The histories of both private libraries and book collecting are subsets of general library history. The history of the private library is almost the exact equivalent of the history of book collecting, and writers often intertwine both subjects. For but one example, Arthur Humphreys' *The Private Library* (not a study of this type of library) is a guide to book collecting with chapters covering such topics as "good editions," "fine copies," and "boudoir libraries."

The private library has long been a link between individual collectors and those publicly accessible collections at which their holdings may finally arrive. As a collector's books increase in number to become more than a mere accumulation, they become instead self-consciously a "library" by virtue of sheer numbers or of thematic or subject-oriented integrity and comprehensiveness. Their next metamorphosis takes place when, while the collector lives or after the collector's death, the library opens to public use. Even if its contents are dispersed, they may become parts of other private libraries that eventually become public.

Whatever the virtues of private libraries, they are, precisely, *not* public. Those who write about them almost always locate their justification, their *raison d'être,* in this transformation from conspicuous signifiers of individual economic, political, or cultural capital into culture-preserving, research-supporting public collections. Collections that either remain truly private or end in dispersal of their contents produce no obvious public good. Since the public good is the main ideological buttress on which the value of any library normally rests, the idea of the private library thus occupies contested ground and has done so for a long time. Lawrence Thompson's survey of private libraries, the last notable discussion in English, does not consider the tensions inherent in the idea. Private libraries offer a fruitful arena for reconsideration of the nature and history of libraries generally.

Book collecting itself occupies the same contested ground. When they are published—made public—books fulfill their destiny. But if they are kept from public use, either through restricted publication or circulation or by removal to the precincts of a private and inaccessible library, books cease to fill their obvious function. The more unusual and valuable such privatized books are perceived to be, the more they become symbols, not of letters and learning, but of pride and greed. Views of private libraries reflect a similar potential for ambiguous movement between these two poles.

Such doubts about private libraries do not always characterize thought about them, however. Leapfrogging strict chronology for a moment, consider two private libraries so exemplary that they have been represented in fiction. Philadelphia writer-physician S. Weir Mitchell depicts a scholar named Clayborne in two novels, *Characteristics* (1891) and its sequel, *Dr. North and His Friends* (1900). Mitchell's portrayal, modeled in large part on Shakespearian scholar Horace Howard Furness Sr., draws also on another of his contemporaries and associates, the medievalist Henry Charles Lea. Furness and Lea both created distinguished private libraries in their subject specialties, as does the fictional Clayborne. Located in his home, his imaginary library is a source of great pride. He may show visitors Sir Walter Raleigh's copy of Torquato Tasso's *Rime, et prose* (Ferrara, 1583), Robert Burns' copy of an edition of Pope, or James Howells' *Epistolae Ho-Elianae* (London, 1737). This last volume, once Horace Walpole's, was later William Makepeace Thackeray's (or so Mitchell makes Clayborne allege: describing what is actually his own copy of Howells, Mitchell locates his real book in a fictional private library; Hazen's bibliography of Walpole's library provides "no evidence" for the Thackeray provenance).

Very occasionally, Clayborne may permit a book to leave his premises. A friend vacationing at Bar Harbor reads his copy of Henry Wotton's *Reliquiae Wottonianae* once owned by "Susanna Hopton" and annotated by "Tho. Hopton, 1695" to indicate that it was given to her by Isaac Walton. Usually, however, his books remain in Clayborne's home and do not circulate. Clayborne is a productive historian who specializes in Islam. His library is the basis of much of his work. Several medieval Arabic manuscripts that he occasionally displays typify his collecting more accurately than association copies of English literary landmarks. Both are equally at home in his library because Clayborne need adhere to no collecting policy other than acquiring books that please him. And it is at home, and only at home, that they may most usually be seen.

Similarly, Lea and Furness' libraries emerged from a tradition of private study that appears to differentiate them from a partly distinct, though concurrent, tradition of collecting represented by such near contemporaries as John Carter Brown, James Lenox, or J. Pierpont Morgan. Normally considered builders of private libraries, these three collectors seem from early periods in their collecting lives to have envisioned eventual public functions for their libraries. But Lea and Furness' collections originated in a notion of the library serving the ends of private scholarship, their own work on medieval history or the Shakespearean text. The scholarship might be of public benefit. But the library need not, at its inception, envisage, even implicitly, any eventual public role. Only after Lea's death did his children transfer the medieval portions of his much larger library to institutional, and hence public, hands. Only toward the end of his own life did Furness' son, who continued the Shakespearean project begun by his father and also maintained the library, do likewise.

Although the line between "private" and "public" seems obvious to many historians, it is actually not easy to draw. Differences between libraries such as Lea or Furness', on the one hand, and Carter Brown's, Lenox's, or Morgan's, on the other, tend to evaporate the more closely they are examined. These libraries might be private and closed, yet the right person might nonetheless gain access to their resources with the collector's permission, making them, at least momentarily, "public."

These tensions were framed at least as long ago as the second century A.D. when Lucian of Samosata criticized the collecting of "an illiterate book-fancier":

> You think that by buying up all the best books you can lay your hands on, you will pass for a man of literary tastes: not a bit of it; you are merely exposing thereby your own ignorance of literature.... How are you to know the difference between genuine old books that are worth money, and trash whose only merit is that it is falling to pieces?

Lucian's argument seems to rest on intellectual merits—or, rather, want of merits—from its very outset (this passage comes from Lucian's opening). But another basis for Lucian's attack emerges as he reaches his conclusion. Ironically admonishing the collector he apostrophizes to "buy book upon book, shut them up safely, and reap the glory that comes of possession," he makes clear that the collector's stupid inability to use his books is made worse by his mere "possession" of them. "Shutting them up" is what is truly troublesome:

> You will go on buying books that you cannot use—to the amusement of educated men, who derive profit ... from the sense and sound of ... [a book's] contents. ... [Y]our books are good ... to lend to other people; you are quite incapable of using them yourself. Not that you have ever lent any one a single volume; true to your dog-in-the-manger principles, you neither eat the corn yourself, nor give the horse a chance.

Lucian perceives bibliolatry as a species of selfishness with objects originally promulgated, disseminated, or published so as to reach the broadest possible publics. Such selfishness elicited little sympathy in the second century—or the 17th. In this view, which used to be encountered more frequently than Mitchell's benign approbation, book collectors and private libraries remove these materials from circulation. Only when they return them to circulation, by making them publicly accessible, do private (now public) collections merit praise.

The history of private collecting is extensive, although it is written most often from a European and U.S. perspective. The practice of building private collections, however, characterizes other cultures as well. In China, alongside governmental and bureaucratic libraries, private libraries (including royal libraries) can be traced at least as far back as the Ming Period (A.D. 1368–1644). The T'ien i ko, formed by the Fan family in Ningpo, for example, remains in existence. In Japan, during the Heian Period (A.D. 794–1185), nobles established private educational institutions for their sons, and such institutions often had libraries attached to them. Whether these were private or public seems a quibble. During the later Edo Period, around A.D. 1603, the Shogun Tokugawa-Ieyasu established a private library that is now partly preserved in the Naikaku-Bunko branch of the National Diet Library. India also saw private libraries established during the medieval period.

In the western tradition, the private library is said to begin with Aristotle, who gathered a library apparently intended for the eventual use of members of his academy in Athens. Many complications delayed realization of this intention and make the story of Aristotle's collection intrinsically interesting. More significant than the story itself is that, as an originary myth, it valorizes the goal of eventual public use that such a private collection was intended to support rather than purely private collecting and use per se.

Records of other Greek and Roman private libraries survive, Cicero's being among the most notable. The libraries themselves do not survive (although one might note such partial exceptions as the portion of a household library excavated at Herculaneum, much of it identifiably Epicurean philosophy in subject). The impulse to collect that such libraries represented, however, persists into cultures and time periods that no Aristotle, Cicero, or Epicurean is likely to have imagined.

Thus, for instance, very early in the Christian era, Paul writes to ask Timothy to return both a "cloke" Paul had left "at Troas with Carpus" and "the books, but especially the parchments," evidently also left behind (II Timothy 4:13). Paul must have had at least a small collection of books, presumably religious texts. When, in the sixth century, Cassiodorus established the monastery at Vivarium, one major impetus was his conviction that collecting and preserving the Roman literary legacy merited serious effort by Christians. His own manuscript collection constituted a major portion of the monastery's library, and his *Institutiones divinarum et saecularium litterarum* functioned as a guide for scribes and copyists with respect not only to practice but also to attitude.

But Cassiodorus' collection and the library at Vivarium also illustrate several problems that discussions of private libraries face. In what sense was Cassiodorus' collecting practice "private?" If he had long intended his books to become the property of a monastery, then were his motives not always in an important sense "public?" Moreover, in such a context—not only of a monastery but also, and more generally, a monastery in a society where literacy is itself at a premium—what might "public" have meant in the first place? In addition, Vivarium did not survive; its library was dispersed. To what degree does a "private" library that fails in its "public" incarnation matter historically (even for historians who do not view history whiggishly)?

That many "private" collections have been formed by royal or other public figures with some eventual public function in mind, not only in non-western and pre-Christian milieus but also in the Christian west, makes the first of these problems especially difficult to resolve. Jean de France, duke of Berry, collected books, as did King Richard III of England. In what sense were their collections personal?

These difficulties by no means evaporate as we approach more recent periods. With the example behind him of the *studiolo* of Federigo da Montefeltro, duke of Urbino, Pope Julius II had built in the papal apartments an extremely elaborate library, the Stanza della Segnatura. Decorated by Raphael, it was furnished with at least 220 known books. Was this library Julius'—or was it part of the Vatican Library awaiting transfer? Similarly, were the royal libraries that eventually became constituent parts of the British Library or the Bibliothèque nationale "private" or "public?"

Even of some libraries established by individuals who were not royal persons, these and similar questions might be asked. It seems merely obvious, for instance, that the library of Baldassarre Castiglione was private. Yet it was also intergenerational, some of it having reached Castiglione and his brother from their father, Cristoforo. Private family libraries are, of course, common. Count Heinrich IV zu Castell tried to establish a family library. Centuries later, successive earls of Crawford and Balcarres (whose lives spanned the period from 1812 to 1913) created the Bibliotheca Lindesiana. But the public roles of the Castigliones in Florence and the Castells in the Germanies leave open to question both how their libraries functioned and by whom, in addition to themselves, they might have been used.

Similarly, the books beautifully bound for Jean Grolier often tell the person who looks at them that they are intended not only for Grolier but also for his friends; these very words appear on the bindings themselves ("et amicorum"). Are these books private or public? When bookbinders began to decorate books in a humanist fashion in Florence at the end of the 14th and early in the 15th centuries, they created an ethos that Grolier's bindings brought to one triumphant conclusion (and in the wake of which Count Heinrich IV zu Castell followed). Felice Feliciano, Bartolomeo Sanvito, and their peers developed the humanist style for private collectors. But is it conceivable that they worked without any public pedagogical or aesthetic aims in mind? It would seem far more likely they expected such aims to be advanced by the ways in which they knew the books they bound were likely to be used.

In England, three late Tudor–early Stuart private libraries, those of John Dee, Simon Forman, and Robert Cotton, again illustrate this difficulty. Dee was a geographer and magician, Forman a physician and occultist. Both formed libraries that were partly scientific in nature, although Dee's library was so big that its range was quite extensive for its own or any other era. During his lifetime, Dee's library was a place of public resort at a known location (Mortlake). In contrast, Forman's, housed in a building separate from his London home, was essentially kept secret from his family and all but a very few of his closest friends. These differences may reflect others that distinguish these two people. Public Dee participated in the culture, even in the print culture, of his time. Private Forman, after a tiny venture into print, relied on older traditions of manuscript culture, providing extended annotations to manuscripts in his possession or fair copies of his works with space for annotations by those into whose hands he would give them. However private, even his manuscripts nonetheless assume use by others. Occupying another intellectual and social arena altogether, Cotton built a collection that became one of the glories of the British Library. In its own time, however, it functioned in part to fill the lacuna left by the nonexistence of institutions like the Public Record Office or the British Library. It was a place for research, some of it politically motivated, much of it carried on by members of "the public," into England's national history. All "private libraries," not one is private in the ways that Clayborne's fictional library seems to have been.

By the end of the 18th century, new attitudes about privacy, property, and commodification had helped elevate the regard in which people held private book collecting, and hence private libraries. A small industry designed to accommodate these new attitudes came into existence, shaping the book trade in ways that remain recognizable to this day. Mechanisms for distributing books to collectors through auction and dealer catalogs and the establishment of a specialized network of dealers trading in used and rare books were two major elements of this new industry.

This industry served a more varied consumer community than had previously constituted the upper reaches of the book-collecting universe. Buyers might still be listed in the *Almanach de Gotha*;

even today, the list of members of the Roxburghe Club can improve the education of anyone who thinks the British aristocracy survives only in fiction. But collectors might also be brewers' bastards, like Thomas Phillipps. The astonishingly successful acquisitiveness of a collector like Phillipps—who hoped to have one copy of every book ever printed, came appallingly close to realizing this desire, and whose books were still being dispersed more than a century after his own death—may stand for the similar activities of a vast private collecting community that came of age in the wake of the cultural and economic disruptions of the French Revolution. Influenced by the bibliographical excitement of aficionados like Gabriel Peignot and the romantic effusions of writers like Thomas Frognall Dibdin, both of whom championed the joys and the rigors of private collecting, that generation essentially defined what is still the general perception of collectors and private libraries. The air of genial self-satisfaction with which a *fin-de-siècle* novelist like Mitchell might regard an imagined private library such as Clayborne's, or such real private libraries as those of Lea or Furness, could already have been predicted in the preceding century or the early part of his own. So too might have been the eroticized—indeed, the often homoeroticized—language associated with book collecting and the creation of private libraries: that is, the surprisingly frequent sexual fetishization of manuscripts and books as "objects of desire" whose joys are best experienced in private.

These attitudes took root in various colonial societies on Europe's fringes, as well as in Europe itself. In the American colonies, for instance, William Byrd of Westover and James Logan were among notable private collectors, although Logan seems to have worked toward the eventual transformation of his library into a public ("Loganian") one. Valorization of private libraries was to gain strength throughout the 19th and 20th centuries. Private libraries would come to form the basis of many extraordinarily distinguished public repositories in both the old and new worlds.

Not all private libraries achieved such transfiguration, and the failures often merit attention as well as the successes. A classic 20th-century example of a private library that did not attain the public transformation its builder sought is the vast collection in the history of science formed by Robert B. Honeyman. Many of the books in Honeyman's collection have now entered other libraries, and the collection itself has been dispersed. The only record it leaves behind is the seven-volume catalog of its contents published by the auctioneer. By contrast, the private libraries of Henry Clay Folger, A. Chester Beatty, and Martin Bodmer are among the last century's success stories.

The private library has a long and distinguished history. Yet that history is not unalloyed by controversy and tension, like the closely allied history of book collecting. These tensions emerge from a perception of the nature of books and their public function. That function seems to be occluded when large numbers of unusual or rare books are removed from public access to a private arena. Uncertainty about the merits of relocating books from public to private may be heightened at a time when questions about the boundary between public and private have been raised in many related areas. The present century, though young, is already characterized by increased efforts to privatize, and to prolong the privatization of, intellectual properties. These efforts arise because of possibilities opened up by digital technologies generally and the Internet and the World Wide Web specifically for unregulated and unremunerated information storage, transfer, and access. At the same time, society's willingness to provide free, publicly accessible libraries, long taken for granted, has come into question. These questions reflect the economic pressures felt by purveyors of what appear to be declining information technologies supported by funders possessed only of diminishing financial resources with which to meet the many competing needs they face. The ambiguities of attitude on which these controversies and questions are based will, in the nature of things, reopen the closely associated arena of private libraries to renewed scholarly and historical investigation from many new viewpoints in the years to come.

DANIEL H. TRAISTER

Further Reading

The bibliography of the private library is in many respects co-extensive with that of book collecting. What follows concentrates heavily on recent English-language materials. It tends to reflect work used in the article above.

Barker, Nicolas, *Bibliotheca Lindesiana: The Lives and Collections of Alexander William, 25th Earl of Crawford and 8th Earl of Balcarres, and James Ludovic, 26th Earl of Crawford and 9th Earl of Balcarres,* London: Quaritch, 1977

Beck, James H., *Raphael: The Stanza della Segnatura,* New York: Braziller, 1993

Birrell, Thomas Anthony, *English Monarchs and Their Books: From Henry VII to Charles II,* London: British Library, 1987

Breslauer, Bernard H., *Count Heinrich IV zu Castell: A German Renaissance Book Collector and the Bindings Made for Him during His Student Years at Orléans, Paris, and Bologna,* Austin, Texas: Taylor, and Poestenkill, New York: Kaldewey Press, 1987

Cannon, Carl Leslie, *American Book Collectors and Collecting from Colonial Times to the Present,* New York: Wilson, 1941

Dickinson, Donald C., *Dictionary of American Book Collectors,* New York: Greenwood Press, 1986

Dorez, Léon, "La bibliothèque privée du Pape Jules II," *Revue des Bibliothèques* 6 (1896)

Fehrenbach, R.J., and E.S. Leedham-Green, editors, *Private Libraries in Renaissance England: A Collection and Catalogue of Tudor and Early Stuart Book-Lists,* Binghamton, New York: Medieval and Renaissance Texts and Studies, and Marlborough, Wiltshire: Adam Matthew, 1998

Hayes, Kevin J., *The Library of William Byrd of Westover,* Madison, Wisconsin: Madison House, 1997

Hazen, Allen Tracy, and Wilmouth Sheldon Lewis, *A Catalogue of Horace Walpole's Library,* 3 vols., New Haven, Connecticut: Yale University Press, 1969

Hobson, Anthony R.A., *Humanists and Bookbinders: The Origins and Diffusion of the Humanistic Bookbinding, 1459–1559, with A Census of Historiated Plaquette and Medallion Bindings of the Renaissance*, Cambridge and New York: Cambridge University Press, 1989

Humphreys, Arthur Lee, *The Private Library: What We Do Know, What We Don't Know, What We Ought to Know about Our Books*, London: Strangeways, and New York: Bouton, 1897; 5th edition, London: Strangeways, 1903

Mitchell, Silas Weir, *Characteristics*, New York: Century, 1892; 9th edition, 1902

Mitchell, Silas Weir, *Dr. North and His Friends*, New York: Century, and London: Macmillan, 1900

Munby, Alan Noel Latimer, *Phillipps Studies*, 5 vols., Cambridge: Cambridge University Press, 1951–60; abridged edition, as *Portrait of an Obsession: The Life of Sir Thomas Phillipps, the World's Greatest Book Collector*, edited by Nicolas Barker, London: Constable, and New York: Putnam, 1967

Myers, Robin, and Michael Harris, editors, *Property of a Gentleman: The Formation, Organisation, and Dispersal of the Private Library, 1620–1920*, Winchester, Hampshire: St. Paul's Bibliographies, and New Castle, Delaware: Oak Knoll Press, 1991

Peters, Edward, "Henry Charles Lea and the Libraries within a Library," in *The Penn Library Collections at 250: From Franklin to the Web*, Philadelphia: University of Pennsylvania Library, 2000

The Private Library (1957–)

Rebecchini, Guido, "The Book Collection and Other Possessions of Baldassarre Castiglione," *Journal of the Warburg and Courtauld Institutes* 61 (1998)

Ricci, Seymour de, *English Collectors of Books and Manuscripts (1530–1930) and Their Marks of Ownership*, Cambridge: Cambridge University Press, 1930

Sharpe, Kevin M., *Sir Robert Cotton, 1586–1631: History and Politics in Early Modern England*, Oxford and New York: Oxford University Press, 1979

Shearman, John, "The Vatican Stanze: Functions and Decoration," *Proceedings of the British Academy* 57 (1971 [i.e., 1973])

Sherman, William Howard, *John Dee: The Politics of Reading and Writing in the English Renaissance*, Amherst: University of Massachusetts Press, 1995

Sutton, Anne F., and Livia Visser-Fuchs, *Richard III's Books: Ideals and Reality in the Life and Library of a Medieval Prince*, Phoenix Mill, Gloucestershire: Sutton, 1997

Taylor, Marvin J., "The Anatomy of Bibliography: Book Collecting, Bibliography, and Male Homosocial Discourse," in *Textual Practice* 15 (2001)

Thompson, Lawrence S., "Private Libraries," in *Encyclopedia of Library and Information Science*, edited by Allen Kent et al., vol. 25, New York: Dekker, 1978

Traister, Barbara Howard, *The Notorious Astrological Physician of London: Works and Days of Simon Forman*, Chicago: University of Chicago Press, 2001

Traister, Daniel, "The Furness Memorial Library," in *The Penn Library Collections at 250: From Franklin to the Web*, Philadelphia: University of Pennsylvania Library, 2000 Wolf, Edwin, II, *The Library of James Logan of Philadelphia: 1674–1751*, Philadelphia, Pennsylvania: Library Company of Philadelphia, 1974

Wolf, Edwin, II, *The Book Culture of a Colonial American City: Philadelphia Books, Bookmen, and Booksellers*, Oxford: Clarendon Press, 1988

Public Libraries

Although the world's public libraries have a common mission in contributing to the educational, cultural, and informational requirements of their various publics, their dimensions and scope are shaped by a number of variables: the level of support they have from their governing authorities; the demographics of their users; the relationship between their development and the presence of a publishing operation and viable book trade within their respective countries; and, perhaps most important, historical forces that either promote or denigrate their contributions. In mission and purpose the world's public libraries have much in common, but in the amount of resources available to them in executing that mission, public libraries have many differences.

Over time the definition of a public library has changed. In the English-speaking world, the older meaning of public library designated any collection of materials to which members of the public had access. This meaning was inherent in the 19th-century compilation made by the U.S. Bureau of Education in its 1876 publication, *Public Libraries in the United States of America: Their History, Condition, and Management,* which listed academic, mercantile, theological, law, medical, and subscription libraries throughout the nation. In the present essay, however, the term *public libraries* will be used in the restricted and technical sense defined by William F. Poole, an experienced 19th-century librarian who directed a number of important libraries, including the public libraries of Cincinnati and

Chicago. In his essay for the Bureau of Education compilation, "The Organization and Management of Public Libraries," Poole noted that free libraries and free town libraries had existed in Europe for three centuries, but he further indicated that these libraries were intended for scholars and not for the "masses of the people," nor were they supported by public taxation. Commenting that the concept of public libraries for popular use had originated in England and in New England at approximately the same time, he then defined the public library as one that "is established by state laws, is supported by local taxation or voluntary gifts, is managed as a public trust, and every citizen of the city or town which maintains it has an equal share in its privileges of reference and circulation."

The Public Library: An Anglo-American Phenomenon

Sometimes referred to as an Anglo-American phenomenon, the public library is largely the product of the industrial revolution both in Britain and the United States. With increasing industrialization, the workforce, no longer primarily employed in farm labor, became concentrated in factory towns and cities. The educability of this workforce beyond the minimal requirements of reading, writing, and arithmetic became a matter of increasing concern on both sides of the Atlantic. The drive toward the education of workingmen and their families resulted in the creation of a number of agencies of self-enlightenment, with the consequent proliferation of the popular press, mechanics' institutes, lyceums, chautauquas, and public libraries.

Under the British unitary constitutional system of governance, action concerning the public library movement arose at the national level in the British Parliament, which in 1850 passed the first Public Libraries Act, a relatively weak enactment granting permission for local cities and towns to establish public libraries. The passage of this enactment should not be viewed as emblematic of an overwhelming desire by British lawmakers to aid in the literary aspirations of the poor and the working class. Indeed, opponents of the bill argued the reverse: The new libraries would not only add to the already burdened taxpayer, they would also enhance the discontent of the lower classes, encouraging them to revolt against the establishment. Nonetheless, social reformers and members of the rising middle class supported the bill. The main weakness of the 1850 law was the limitation placed on the amount that could be collected for library support. Initially the rate was fixed at one-half pence on the pound of the ratable value of the district in which the library was situated, but amendments in 1855 raised that figure to one penny on the pound. As a result, income from the penny on the pound ranged from less than £10 for a library in a rural district to more than £25,000 for one in a large city.

Under the federal governmental system of the United States, initiatives toward the creation of public libraries began, not at the national level, but within local and state governments, which have customarily been given responsibility for matters relating to education. During the early years of the 19th century, several small New England communities took steps to establish collections of books that were made available to the public. Included among them were Salisbury, Connecticut; Lexington, Massachusetts; and Peterborough, New Hampshire. The pride of place for being the first major metropolis in the United States to provide tax support for a public library goes to Boston, Massachusetts, which opened its library in 1854, six years after the State of Massachusetts had passed legislation enabling Boston to tax itself for the provision of library service. Subsequent legislation enacted in 1851 allowed other Massachusetts cities and towns to establish public libraries.

Historically the origins of the public library were associated with the altruistic impulse that led to reforms in both England and the United States to abolish slavery, treat the insane more humanely, deter criminals, and educate the young. During the 1970s a rash of articles appeared in the professional press by librarians urging a revisionist view of the origins of the public library. These articles attributed to its founders elitist attitudes directed toward the social control of library users. Although there may be some truth in this view, it is highly likely that humanitarian impulses were also involved, as in the case of Joshua Bates, the New England merchant whose gift of $50,000 was intended to make possible the initial book collection of the Boston Public Library. Writing in 1852, Bates recollected that as a poor boy unable to pay for a fire in his lodgings, he was allowed to sit in a local bookstore, reading what its proprietors "kindly permitted me to." Such an experience convinced Bates of the great advantage of a public library and became the rationale for his gift.

It is interesting to note that some of the framers of the early public libraries regarded them as investments. A January 1877 article in the *American Library Journal* entitled "How to Start Libraries in Small Towns" urged readers to draw on their communities for the library's financial support. The author, A.M. Pendleton, advised that prospective donors, even if poor, should be told that their contributions were not a gift "but an investment which will yield a larger income than you can get in almost any other way." Such a statement was no doubt merely rhetorical, but it does suggest how some of the library's founders perceived literacy, education, and the reading of books as an intellectual capital that would increase in value over time.

Antecedents to the tax-supported public library of the middle and late 19th century include the circulating libraries in both Britain and the United States (which charged a small fee for the borrowing of popular reading matter) and the "social" libraries that were generally of two types: proprietary libraries open to those who held shares in the communal property of books, and subscription libraries supported by the fees of the subscribers. Among the most notable of the subscription libraries was the Library Company of Philadelphia, Pennsylvania, founded by Benjamin Franklin in 1731, which still exists today as an independent research library. With the onset of the public library movement, however, the collections of many of the social libraries either disappeared or were consolidated with the newer public libraries.

The initial operations of 19th-century public libraries were somewhat limited where patron needs were concerned. Library users did not have access to books on open shelves but instead consulted catalogs of the holdings, from which they identified the materials to be borrowed. As some of these libraries were built before the invention of electricity, illumination was supplied either by sunlight or gaslight. Although reading areas did exist, the principal public space in these libraries was often an area reserved for the circulation function, where books were checked out and returned. Since children were not included, patronage of these libraries was reserved solely for adults. Perhaps the greatest limitation of these libraries was endured by African American readers in the southern regions of the United States, where service for black residents, if offered at all, was limited to users in segregated library facilities.

New Services at the Turn of the 20th Century

Some of these restrictions were eased with the coming of the 20th century. During the 1890s William Howard Brett, librarian of the Cleveland Public Library in Ohio, forcefully argued in the United States and in England for an open-shelf collection affording library users opportunities for browsing at their leisure. Initially rejected because of potential damage to the books, the open-shelf concept was nevertheless increasingly adopted by public libraries. As newer library buildings were built, reading room space increased, with shelving given over to a considerable part of the collection. Brett, in company with other library leaders, was also an enthusiast for library service to children, which began as a national phenomenon at the turn of the century. Story hours and book talks for children were initiated, and separate rooms in library buildings housing furniture on a scale suited to children became commonplace.

Considerable impetus was given to the public library movement in the United States by Melvil Dewey, an entrepreneurial librarian best known for his development of the Dewey Decimal Classification system, among the most widely used classification systems in the world even today. His role in founding the American Library Association (ALA) in 1876, his assistance to his British colleagues in the establishment of the Library Association in 1877, and his contribution toward the publication of the first professional journal for librarians, the *American Library Journal* (the prototype for today's *Library Journal*), made him a pivotal figure in 19th-century librarianship. Although he was never the director of a municipal public library such as that of Boston or Chicago, Dewey nonetheless through his writings and speeches served as a spokesperson for the public library movement. Among his many accomplishments regarding the public library, one that was particularly influential was the installation of a model book collection for the small public library in the U.S. Government Building during the 1893 Chicago World's Fair. Dewey not only arranged for this installation, he also promoted the publication of a catalog of these books that was subsidized by federal funds.

The Carnegie Benefactions

Furthering the influence of the United States on an increasingly global acceptance of public libraries as a corollary of public education were the turn-of-the-century benefactions of Andrew Carnegie, the Scottish-born steel magnate who had emigrated to the United States as a boy. Limited to communities in parts of the English-speaking world, the Carnegie largesse (beginning in 1886 and ending in 1919) aided in the establishment of 2,509 library buildings, at a cost of more than $56 million. In addition to Canada and the United States, other countries receiving Carnegie grants were Australia, England, New Zealand, Scotland, South Africa, and some English-speaking overseas possessions. In the United States alone, the erection of 1,679 buildings in 1,412 communities cost $41 million. With few exceptions, Carnegie did not endow these libraries. Instead he required that the community requesting a library building donate space for its erection and tax itself annually for its operating expenses at a sum that was at least 10 percent of the cost of the building itself.

The canniness behind this arrangement no doubt bespoke the mercantile background of the libraries' donor, who regarded his benefaction as a means by which the community intelligence could be greatly enhanced. As many Carnegie library users have testified, the value of recreational and educative reading was very real indeed. It must be said, however, that one perhaps unexpected outcome of the Carnegie benefaction was the growth of small-town libraries, poorly supported by a very low tax base and increasingly staffed by local residents without professional training.

Where the Carnegie legacy was perhaps greatest was in the building of branches of already established public libraries, especially in the cities of the eastern United States. His single largest library benefaction of more than $5 million went to the city of New York, resulting in the opening of more than 60 branch libraries in all five boroughs. The Free Library of Philadelphia added 25 branches and the Enoch Pratt Free Library in Baltimore, Maryland, built 14. In a reprise of the original Carnegie benefaction, the Carnegie Corporation of New York in June 1999 awarded a total of $15 million to the New York Public Library, the Brooklyn Public Library, and the Queens Borough Public Library (all in the city of New York) and to libraries in 22 additional cities serving large, culturally diverse populations. The funds celebrated the centennial period of Carnegie's munificence in 1899 to the city of New York's three public library systems and served as a reminder of Carnegie's generosity throughout the United States at the turn of the 20th century.

The proliferation of too many small library jurisdictions with insufficient tax bases in both the United States and Britain, largely induced by the Carnegie benefactions, became a matter of public concern in both countries following the Depression. At a time when approximately 50 percent of U.S. public libraries serving populations of 2,000 and under survived with annual incomes of $1,000 or less, Carleton B. Joeckel of the University of Chicago's Graduate Library School postulated that a level of minimum library service could only be achieved with an annual expenditure of $1.00 per capita in areas with a population of 25,000 or more, a figure that was recommended in the *Post-war Standards for Public Libraries* issued by the American Library Association in 1943. (In subsequent years, this figure was raised to $1.50 per capita.) Joeckel, who chaired the ALA's Postwar Planning Committee, further committed himself to the principle of the larger unit of library service in the committee's major report, *A National Plan for Public Library Service*, published in 1948. As the report's principal author, Joeckel pointed to the advantages of regional cooperation among libraries in certain geographic areas, envisioning that carefully planned programs of coordinated library services would lead toward the later organization of larger service units. At the behest of the Library Association in Great Britain, Lionel R. McColvin, city librarian of Westminster, conducted a one-man survey of public libraries during wartime, issuing his 1942 report, *The Public Library System of Great Britain*, with the principal caveat that the majority of British public library authorities were simply too small to engender sufficient income for them to function efficiently.

The ALA-endorsed solution in the United States was a call for the consolidation or federation of library jurisdictions and an appeal to the federal government for a program of grants-in-aid to assist those residents in rural areas who were not served by any public library. The Library Services Act of 1956 provided federal grants for this purpose. Although mergers between the public libraries of a county and a municipality occurred rather infrequently in the United States, the development of cooperative or federated library systems proliferated. These latter types of library systems allow individual public libraries to retain their local autonomy and their local sources of funding while at the same time encouraging cooperative activities for specific benefits, such as public relations for the library system, shared acquisitions of books and materials, and shared cataloging. New York state legislation enacted in 1950 eventually led to the establishment of 22 public library systems comprising more than 700 local libraries situated in the state's 62 counties, and the 1965 Illinois legislative mandate promoted the merger of that state's more than 550 public libraries into 18 systems. Libraries that engage in this type of federated activity are usually referred to as member libraries of the system rather than as branches, a term commonly used for the satellite agencies of an autonomous public library. Thus the Yonkers Public Library is a member of the Westchester Library System in the state of New York, whereas the New York Public Library maintains more than 80 branch libraries under its jurisdiction. Federal funds under Title III, Interlibrary Cooperation (an amendment to the Library Services and Construction Act passed in 1966), also encouraged efforts at library federation and furthered cooperation between public libraries and those serving academic institutions and elementary and secondary schools.

In Britain, McColvin redrew the local governmental map, urging that the roughly 600 separate library authorities then in existence be reduced, a reduction that was initially achieved through the Local Government Act that passed in 1972 and was enforced two years later. This legislation reduced the number of library authorities in England and Wales from 385 to 121. In 1973 a corresponding bill, the Local Government (Scotland) Act, halved the number of library authorities in Scotland from 80 to 40. In Northern Ireland the number of authorities was reduced from 16 to five. Currently some 160 library authorities represent more than 4,700 libraries in the United Kingdom.

The prescience of Joeckel, McColvin, and several of their contemporaries has been realized at least in part in their respective countries. The fiscal year 1997 public library statistics prepared by the U.S. Department of Education reveal that, of the 8,967 U.S. public libraries (administrative entities that may include a central building and satellite branches, thus making the total number of stationary outlets 16,090), 73 percent were members of a library system, federation, or cooperative service through which an individual library can gain support beyond its own resources. Circulation of library materials in 1997 was more than 1.7 billion, or 6.6 per capita. Reference transactions amounted to 287 million, or 1.1 per capita. Total nationwide visits to public libraries totaled more than 1 billion, or 4.1 per capita. Nationwide, 79 percent of public libraries had access to the Internet and 66 percent provided access to electronic services.

Statistics for libraries in the United Kingdom, largely derived from the 1997 report, *New Library: The People's Network*, published by the Library and Information Commission under the aegis of the Department for Culture, Media and Sport, indicate that 58 percent of the population holds library membership: 33.8 million out of a total population of 58.4 million. In 1995–96 there were more than 370 million library visits. Ten million people use libraries on a regular basis (at least once every two weeks), and the fifth most popular pastime in the United Kingdom is visiting the local library. Ongoing developments in computer/communications technology are adding a new dimension to the conceptual frameworks of interlibrary cooperation; this is evident in the EARL Consortium of U.K. Public Library Networking, established in 1995 to develop the role of public libraries in the dissemination of electronic information services.

Although both Britain and the United States share in the development of the public library movement, the extension of that movement began to occur shortly after the turn of the century, when the countries of northern Europe began to modernize their popular libraries. Here the model was that of the United States, which (according to Wilhelm Munthe, a Norwegian visitor to U.S. shores during the l930s) brought about a certain uniformity and standardization in the libraries of Scandinavia.

Public Libraries in Europe

Information about the current state of public librarianship in Europe has been facilitated by the creation of the European Union and the European Commission, which are charged with ensuring that the union attains its goal of an ever-closer community among its various peoples. Activity in the library area has been the responsibility of the commission's Third and Fourth Framework Programmes for Research and Technological Development and, more specifically, the Telematics Programmes of which libraries have been a part. (Telematics is the coinage referring to advanced computer/telecommunications applications to societal and economic concerns.) Under the commission's aegis, a "Green Paper on the Role of Libraries in the Information Society" was issued on the Web in 1998 and provided links to background information on the libraries of 17 European countries: Austria, Belgium, Denmark, Finland, France, Germany, Greece, Iceland, Ireland, Italy, Luxembourg, the Netherlands, Norway, Portugal, Spain, Sweden, and the United Kingdom.

Nations in northern Europe were shown to have relatively higher percentages of the national population registered as borrowers from public libraries (e.g., the United Kingdom indicated 59 percent, Finland 49 percent, Iceland 38 percent, and the Netherlands 29 percent). In contrast, southern European countries revealed a lower percentage of the total population registered as library users (Spain indicated 7.4 percent, Portugal 6 percent, and Greece less than 1 percent). The differences between the northern and southern regions of Europe are even more marked in the development of public libraries having sites on the World Wide Web. A report issued in January 1999 noted that more than 1,000 public libraries in some 30 European countries are now on the Web, with Finland being the leader (247), followed by Sweden (132), the United Kingdom (112), Denmark (107), Germany (102), the Netherlands (72), Lithuania (51), Spain (56), Norway (45), and Portugal (3).

Russia has a list of 26 public reference libraries on the Web and the Czech Republic reports 29. The countries of the former Eastern Bloc had a developed public library infrastructure, but with the dissolution of the former Soviet Union, some of these libraries have been severely impaired. Nonetheless, in an optimistic account of Russian libraries prepared for the 1994 annual International Federation of Library Associations and Institutions (IFLA) conference, Evgeny Kuzmin, an official of the Russian Ministry of Culture, emphasized that Russian libraries, however straitened, were "islets of miraculous viability and stability in the stormy sea of the Russian economy."

Public Libraries Elsewhere in the World

In general, public library development outside of the United States, Britain, and the northern countries of Europe has not necessarily followed the Anglo-American model. There are some notable exceptions to this generalization, Canada being paramount in developing public libraries along Anglo-American lines. In 1988 the Canadian Library Association commissioned a study, in part to assist governmental authorities in connecting all public libraries to the information highway. During its post–World War II development period, Japan in 1950 enacted its Public Library Law on April 30, a date that is observed annually as "Library Day." Almost 2,000 public libraries (main libraries and branches) provide circulating books and audiovisual materials, answer reference questions, and maintain special services for children and the handicapped. China maintains approximately 2,500 public libraries, ranging in size from the provincial libraries and those in the larger cities to those in villages and smaller districts. The largest of the public libraries is that of Shanghai, whose size is exceeded only by the National Library of China in Beijing. In 1997 the Shanghai library entered into a collaborative program with the Queens Borough Public Library, which provides material in 49 languages to serve a multiethnic population in one of the five boroughs of the city of New York. These two very large metropolitan libraries exchange personnel, business, and technical information and provide access to their libraries' respective websites.

The Spanish- and Portuguese-speaking countries of the western hemisphere have as a rule followed the precedents of Spain and Portugal, where the public library movement has not been as well articulated as that of northern Europe. Brazil, a federal republic and the largest country in South America, administers its public libraries through the Brazilian states, except for the municipal library in São Paulo founded in 1925. Argentina, South America's second largest country, maintains some 1,600 public libraries, known to its citizens as "popular libraries," but most of these are supported by nongovernmental institutions, with additional financial aid from government sources. In recent years Mexico has aggressively pursued a campaign to further its public library movement, having established a National Program of Public Libraries in 1983 that totaled approximately 5,500 administrative units in 1995. Because school libraries have not been as central to the non-English-speaking countries of the western hemisphere as they have been in other countries of the world, most school children look to their public libraries for homework assistance, and Mexico has instituted a program to train children in the use of computers located in these agencies.

Public Libraries in Developing Countries

So far this account has emphasized the public libraries in the more developed nations of the world, especially in the largest cities, where the public library is a full-service institution offering a comprehensive range of materials and affording services to all ages and to persons living in institutions, the homebound, and the handicapped. It could be argued, however, that equal emphasis should be accorded to those countries where public libraries, if they exist at all, are severely underfunded by their government authorities and limited in what they can offer their local communities. The transformation to an information- or knowledge-based society places additional burdens on the public libraries of poorer countries, as indeed it also does on underfunded areas in developed nations. Ariane Iljon, at a 1996 workshop on public libraries and the information society, spoke of the important role of the public library. Her remarks were summarized as follows: Public libraries have a key role to play as a gateway into resources of interest to their users. The present position of the majority of public libraries—under budget pressure, ill prepared for networking, with a poor level of technological skills of staff, operating mostly without a supportive national policy framework or a professional vision and often in isolation—means that they have a bad starting position for a successful change.

Unfortunately, all too many public libraries (even in highly developed countries) fall into this category, but the statement is profoundly true in those countries of the world that emerged from their colonial regimes as independent nations during the 20th century. In Africa, for example, in countries where the colonizers spoke either French or Portuguese, the public library was slow to develop. In nations where English was the spoken language, however, public libraries were modeled on the English example. At the outset most were primarily used by the colonial population and not by the African nationals, a policy that has only recently been rescinded. Similarly the former crown colonies in the British Caribbean did not really gain control over their nascent public libraries until the colonies had achieved independence.

During the period following World War II, the United Nations Educational, Scientific, and Cultural Organization (UNESCO), founded in 1946, assumed the goal of assisting libraries in developing countries and of promoting the development of documentation, library, and archival services as part of a national information infrastructure. In the years between 1966 and 1974, UNESCO held four major conferences in four regions of the world: Latin America (Ecuador, 1966), Asia (Ceylon, 1967), Africa (Uganda, 1970), and the Arab countries (Egypt, 1974). In an attempt to coordinate the findings of these four regional assemblies, UNESCO sponsored an intergovernmental meeting in Paris in 1974 which is referred to as the National Information Systems (NATIS) conference. It resulted in recommendations for the integration of the information resources of developing nations to eliminate overlapping jurisdictions (such as those between academic and public libraries) and to put into place national information policies. However well intentioned, the NATIS concept was abandoned by UNESCO in 1977, some 11 years after it was promoted in Ecuador. Part of the reason for its dissolution was UNESCO's subsequent emphasis on the development of a world science information system known as UNISIST, which resulted in UNESCO's activities relating to UNISIST taking precedence over the NATIS initiative. Other reasons came from the developing countries themselves, where new governmental administrators and policy makers perceived information flow as a side effect of the ever-increasing computer industry rather than the accumulation of books and nonprint media.

National Policies and Public Libraries

Although a totally unified national information infrastructure, for any nation, of the type envisioned in the NATIS concept still eludes accomplishment in either the developed or undeveloped countries, two relatively recent phenomena have brought about a renewed interest by national policy makers in the work of public libraries. The first, obviously, is the advent of computer/communications technology that permits an international exchange of information in digital form. The second, less familiar than the first, is the governmental reform movement that has attempted to render governmental bureaucracies less unwieldy and more sensitive to the needs of citizen-consumers and citizen-customers. The 1993 report, *From Red Tape to Results: Creating a Government That Works Better and Costs Less*, prepared under the aegis of former Vice President of the United States Albert Gore Jr., devotes an entire section to the application of market mechanisms to governmental agencies for the ultimate benefit of the consumer. In the revised edition of *Guidelines for Public Libraries* issued in draft form by IFLA in August 2000, the inclusion of a sample "customer care policy" is but one instance of the influence on libraries of the governmental reform movement, which emphasizes that users of public services be referred to as "customers" rather than "patrons."

With regard to the emerging information age, computer purchase and usage among middle-income and upper-income people is universally acknowledged. At the same time, however, low-income populations, faced not only with the purchase of a computer but also the need to pay for an online service provider, are increasingly left out of the information loop. Studies conducted by the U.S. Department of Commerce document the so-called digital divide between the information rich and the information poor, noting that provision for low-income persons to use computer technology is afforded almost entirely by public libraries and community centers. Eradicating the digital divide has become a major topic of concern for national governments, private foundations, nongovernmental organizations, and the computer industry itself. In 1997 William H. Gates III (chief executive officer of the Microsoft Corporation) and his wife, Melinda, established the Gates Library Foundation, which is making available $400 million (half in cash and half in software) over a five-year period to facilitate the purchase of computers and the training of staff in both U.S. and Canadian public libraries. In 1996 the U.S. Congress passed legislation creating the E-rate program, a federally subsidized telecommunications discount program allowing public libraries and public schools affordable access to the Internet. Discounts allocated to the recipients range from 20 percent to 90 percent. The largest discounts are granted to institutions in isolated rural areas and those in urban communities where there is a high incidence of low-income residents. In 1997 the British Arts Minister announced a fund of £6 million to bring local public libraries to the forefront of the information technology revolution. Also in that year, at a seminar sponsored by the Panos Institute and the Pan African News Agency, participants representing the media, nongovernmental organizations, and educational institutions in 19 countries issued the Dakar Declaration on the Internet and the African Media. The Declaration called on the governments of Africa to aid in the rapid development of the Internet and to ensure that African content be available on it. All of this activity bespeaks the reality that the information poor are not centered in one location but find themselves in practically every nation in the world.

Governmental reform movements occurring in the Western world have affected such nations as Canada, New Zealand, the United Kingdom, and the United States. Primary among these reforms is the market model, in which citizens are perceived not only as taxpayers but also as consumers of government service. Allied to the new public management philosophy of governance, the market model assumes that management is management, whether in industry or government, and that mechanisms used to motivate personnel are equally applicable in both the public and private sectors. One way that the market model operates is through the development of competing providers of public services, thus expanding consumer choice. Government subsidies for educational vouchers permitting children to pay tuition at private schools are but one example of the means by which citizens can be afforded greater options, even at the expense of traditionally tax-supported public school systems.

In subtle ways the market model has affected some public libraries. The right to know was traditionally offered as the rationale for governmental support of public libraries; with increased acceptance by industry as well as some governments that information is a marketable commodity, the usefulness of such a rationale may have to be reconsidered. Libraries that have begun to charge fees for their reference services have in a sense adopted the market model, as have those libraries that have established their own foundations for additional financial support. Since the market model is still in use, it is simply too soon to comment on the influence of market mechanisms on public-service institutions such as the public library.

The historical development of public libraries throughout the world is of necessity intertwined with the governments that support them. International organizations have emphasized the necessity for strong governmental leadership and have repeatedly expressed the ideal of the community library as a vehicle for free expression and free access to information. The UNESCO *Public Library Manifesto*, first issued in 1949 and subsequently revised with the cooperation of IFLA, asserts the role of the public library "as an essential agent for the fostering of peace and spiritual welfare through the minds of men and women."

In some nations of the world, such as the Nordic countries with their extremely high rate of literacy, the centrality of the public library among government supported public services is not in dispute. But in countries beset by a low standard of living and a high rate of illiteracy, the public library struggles against a myriad of problems to accomplish its mission. In summary one can only say that where public librarianship is concerned, much has been accomplished throughout the world since the 19th century; at the same time, much remains to be achieved.

KATHLEEN MOLZ

See also Birmingham Central Library; Boston Public Library; Chicago Public Library; Los Angeles Public Library; Manchester Public Libraries; New York Public Library; Public and University Library of Geneva; Public Library of the University of Basel; Toronto Public Library; Zürich Central Library

Further Reading

Black, Alistair, *A New History of the English Public Library: Social and Intellectual Contexts, 1850–1914*, London: Leicester University Press, 1996

Black, Alistair, and Dave Muddiman, *Understanding Community Librarianship: The Public Library in Post-Modern Britain*, Aldershot, Hampshire, and Brookfield, Vermont: Ashgate, 1997

"Creating a European Library Space," <www.cordis.lu/libraries/en/intro.html> (provides information on the work carried out by the European Commission from 1990 to 1998; more recent Commission initiatives are issued on the website <www.echo.lu/digicult/>)

Harden, Sheila, and Robert Harden, "Public Libraries of Europe," <dspace.dial.pipex.com/town/square/ac940/eurolib.html>

International Federation of Library Associations and Institutions, "Revisions [Draft] of IFLA's Guidelines for Public Libraries, June 2000," <ifla.org/VII/s8/proj/gpl.htm>

Kuzmin, Evgeny, "Russian Libraries in the Context of Social, Economic, and Political Reforms," <www.ifla.org/IV/ifla60/60-kuze.htm>

Martin, Lowell A., *Enrichment: A History of the Public Library in the United States in the Twentieth Century*, Lanham, Maryland: Scarecrow Press, 1998

Molz, Redmond Kathleen, and Phyllis Dain, *Civic Space/Cyberspace: The American Public Library in the Information Age*, Cambridge, Massachusetts: MIT Press, 1999

PubliCA (Public Libraries Concerted Action) <www.croydon.gov.uk/publica>

Shera, Jesse H., *Foundations of the Public Library: The Origins of the Public Library Movement in New England, 1692–1855*, Chicago: University of Chicago Press, 1949

Sturges, Rodney Paul, and Richard Neill, *The Quiet Struggle: Libraries and Information for Africa*, London and New York: Mansell, 1990; 2nd edition, London and Washington, D.C.: Mansell, 1998

UNESCO, "UNESCO Public Library Manifesto," <www.ifla.org/VII/S8/unesco/eng.htm>

United States Bureau of Education, *Public Libraries in the United States of America: Their History, Condition, and Management*, Washington, D.C.: GPO, 1876

Wiegand, Wayne A., *Irrepressible Reformer: A Biography of Melvil Dewey*, Chicago: American Library Association, 1996

Renaissance Libraries

The library was central to the cultural and intellectual life of the Renaissance. It served at once as locus of discovery and investigation, as study and intellectual workshop, and as archive and storehouse of knowledge. Although libraries flourished and developed under the influence of Renaissance patrons and their humanist advisors, the Renaissance library was very much defined by the society into which it was born. In an age in which books were expensive and consequently collections were small, even the largest rarely exceeded 1,000 volumes. And in a society where literacy remained the privilege of educated elites, so too the library served the professional requirements and cultural purposes of these same elites. Collections were largely utilitarian in purpose, shaped around the fulfillment of specific professional obligations or intellectual goals. Private libraries of the period were rather sharply framed around a handful of related strands of interest and inquiry. Large institutional collections, which enjoyed much greater stability, saw such Renaissance intellectual programs evolve and develop from one generation to the next. Focus on the scope and purpose of Renaissance libraries provides a useful framework in which to survey the major developments of the period.

Italian Humanism

Within the context of the humanist discovery of classical and Christian antiquity, the library in the Renaissance served a dual function. Humanism undertook to revive ancient learning through the restoration of the textual legacy of the ancient world. Essential to this goal was the task of exploring libraries that held the textual treasures of antiquity. These were rich ecclesiastical holdings that had been built up during the long Middle Ages, such as the St. Gall abbey in Switzerland, where Poggio Bracciolini discovered the complete text of Quintilian. There were many others as well. From manuscripts in these libraries, copies would be made or sometimes the original itself purchased (or stolen).

The humanists were concerned not only with rediscovering and conserving a textual tradition but also with recovering the cultural tradition that lay behind it. Individual humanists established collections that served as the basis of their own scholarship and frequently that of a like-minded circle of scholars. In Florence, Coluccio Salutati and Niccolò de' Niccoli, both key figures of Florentine humanism, built up large collections of manuscripts, largely of Latin texts of classical and patristic authors. Niccoli was one of the most avid early collectors of old copies of texts, which he knew to be more accurate than later copies. Greek émigrés such as Manuel Chrysoloras (who instructed an entire generation of humanists in the Greek language) had important collections of Greek texts that were more or less unknown in Western libraries until the late 14th century. Also at Florence, Fra Ambrogio Traversari was another early collector of Greek works, mainly those of the church fathers. But the most magnificent Greek collection was that of Cardinal Bessarion. His library of some 1,000 volumes (and even more titles) held hitherto unknown riches of classical Greek science and philosophy and Greek-language texts from the early church. It would be mined by generations of scholars hungry for knowledge of such works.

One of the largest private humanist libraries was that of Giovanni Pico della Mirandola, author of *On the Dignity of Man*. In his short life Pico collected more than 1,000 books, including Greek and, more rarely, Hebrew texts. Private humanist libraries remained an important feature through the late Renaissance. Fulvio Orsini in Rome and Gian Vincenzo Pinelli in Padua were two other important figures in this era of Italian library history. Orsini actively sought out manuscripts formerly owned by earlier humanists.

The ideal of a public library was one treasured by humanists and their patrons. Yet the term *public library* meant something very different to Renaissance scholars than it does today: It did not designate a library open to all comers. First and oldest of the available meanings of the term *public library* was that of a common library. Many libraries and colleges of the late medieval period had public libraries in this sense, usually meaning a collection for the collective use of the institutional community. Second was the notion of a library that served the public utility or was used for the public benefit, largely in a political sense: an archive, for example, or a library meant to support the jurisdictional and diplomatic activities of the ecclesiastical or secular political body it served. Third, a library might be in a public building or within the public space of a house or palace.

Perhaps the best early expression of the modern concept of the public library is to be found in the establishment of the San Marco library, the first public library at Florence. The foundation of the library was Niccoli's collection. Niccoli's intentions were for his library to be brought "to the common good, to the public service, to a place open to all, so that all eager for education might be able to harvest from it as from a fertile field the rich fruit of learning." Eventually, the executors of Niccoli's estate permitted Cosimo de' Medici to place the books in the library of the Dominican convent of San Marco, which Cosimo was then on the verge of constructing. The library opened in 1444 and was the first public library in Florence, containing 400 volumes laid out across 64 benches. The San Marco library embodied three different Renaissance concepts of a public library: It was the common library of the Dominican convent in which it was housed, a collection made available to a circle of humanist investigators, and an institution supported by the public patronage of an eminent ruler. In a similar fashion, Cardinal Bessarion bequeathed his library "for the public utility of scholars" to the Venetian republic, where it served as the foundation collection of the Biblioteca Marciana. The first establishment of the Vatican library (c. 1450) by Pope Nicholas V (Tommaso Parentucelli) "for the common convenience of men of learning," was founded upon the pope's personal collection.

Law and Politics

Personal and institutional collections alike in the period had evolved out of the working cabinets and collections of papers of members of the professions. Domestic and professional space of the period frequently overlapped within shared walls, and many private libraries were but extensions of the professional commitments of their owners. From early on, many court libraries incorporated archives of dynastic papers, legal documents, ambassadorial reports, and other instruments of estate and political administration. Although some royal and princely libraries of the period were intended for the recreational or spiritual needs of rulers, others were intended to serve their courts, to be used by men of learning and court officials. Under these influences court libraries emerged at Ferrara, Pavia, Mantua, and Urbino in Italy; in Aragon and later the Escorial Library on the Iberian peninsula; in Burgundy; at the Royal Library at Fontainebleu in France; at Munich, Gottorp, and Wolfenbüttel in Germany; and at Vienna, Prague, and Buda (Hungary) in Central Europe. In the late 14th century at Ferrara, the court library of the ruling Este family held, among other documents, the collection of chronicles in which dynastic events worthy of note had long been recorded. Two centuries later, Maximilian I of Bavaria similarly used the Imperial Library at Munich as a repository for dynastic archives, maps, and chronicles. King Philip II of Spain did much the same at the Escorial Library near Madrid.

Members of the legal profession had some of the largest private collections of the period, consisting of collections of civil and canon law, legal commentaries, and related works. Legal humanism, which applied the historical and philological study of texts to Roman law, was a crucial movement of the period, and lawyers' libraries were among the best equipped in works of classical authors and humanist history writing. The richest of such libraries, such as that of Antonio Augustín at Tarragona, Spain, would also house collections of antiquities, ancient coins, and inscriptions. In 16th-century Paris, scholarship and politics frequently collided in the libraries of members of the parliament, such as those of Henri de Mesmes and Jacque-Auguste de Thou. These libraries were filled with manuscript copies and printed texts of treaties and speeches, royal edicts, and the pamphlets and works of polemic that marked the period.

Science and Medicine

Renaissance studies of natural science, mathematics, and medicine were as dependent on newly discovered classical texts as were the studies of ancient languages and ancient history. Physicians and apothecaries, like lawyers, possessed some of the largest personal libraries in the period. Court libraries also frequently possessed rich collections of medical and astrological texts. In the 15th century, the Visconti-Sforza library at Pavia and the Este library at Ferrara contained good collections of Greek and Arabic medical and scientific works in Latin translation.

It was in search of the classical roots of mathematics, science, and medicine that a vast body of Greek manuscripts was redis-covered in the period. It has been estimated that Cardinal Bessarion's library held every major Greek text necessary for the rediscovery of ancient mathematics. Another humanist library rich in Greek scientific texts was that of the physician Giorgio Valla, closely associated with the court at Pavia, who translated Euclid and Archimedes into Latin. At Ferrara, the physician Nicolò Leoniceno sought direct contact with Greek sources of scientific learning, particularly Galen and Aristotle. Many of the works he collected had been known only through translation; others were completely new to contemporary Western science. Of his library of 345 volumes, 117 were Greek. Leoniceno succeeded in collecting almost every Greek scientific text known today. Works on alchemy and the occult also found a natural home in court collections in Italy, France, and Spain, and in ecclesiastical libraries in England and Germany. Many inhabitants of the byways of Renaissance science—such as Johann Tritheim at Sponheim, Germany; Giambattista della Porta at Naples, Italy; and John Dee in London—collected works on magic and the occult. Many Renaissance libraries, particularly court libraries that also housed informal scientific academies, contained collections of scientific instruments.

Geography and Ethnography

Even before the discovery of the New World, many libraries contained ancient and modern geographical texts and travel literature describing other nations and cultures. Through the 16th century the importance of such texts grew considerably. Works on the Ottoman Empire, Africa, Asia, and the New World were all avidly collected. One of the most marvelous of these collections was the library of Hernando Colón, the natural son of Cristóbal Colón (Christopher Columbus), in Seville, Spain. By the time of his death in 1539, Colón had amassed some 15,000 titles from across Europe. The Bibliotheca Colombina not only possessed several books owned by Columbus himself but also held many other works on cosmography and geography. Globes were normal pieces of library furniture in large institutional collections, and maps would also be found in many others. Ethnographical curiosities would sometimes be encountered. The de Mesmes library in Paris, for example, contained an entire human skin, as well as headdresses and other feathered articles from the New World.

Religion

Religious books and ecclesiastical libraries were central to the period. In modest private libraries, books of spirituality, scripture, and the church fathers predominated. Many private libraries of the period were comprised of but a single book—a devotional book of hours. Scripture and devotional works likewise formed the nucleus and frequently the most substantial part of many other court libraries. And the monastic and other religious libraries of medieval foundation were still going concerns (if poorly run by humanist standards). Yet many humanists looked to the stability of ecclesiastical libraries when disposing of their own collections. Giovanni Boccaccio left his library to the Augustinian monastery at Santo Spirito in Florence, Italy, more or less as a public benefaction. The library of Niccolò de' Niccoli was first deeded to the Camaldulensian monastery of Santa Maria degli Angeli in Florence before it was moved to the convent of San Marco.

Through the 15th and 16th centuries, some of the largest individual libraries belonged to cardinals of the Roman Catholic Church. For the most part, these collections were composed of works of canon law and the church fathers. Of Cardinal Bessarion's 500 Greek manuscripts, 36 contained biblical texts and commentaries, and a further 165 were devoted to the church fathers, theology, church councils, and canon law. His Latin collection was similarly oriented.

With the rise of church reform movements during the course of the 16th century, cardinals' libraries such as those of Alessandro Farnese (later Pope Paul III), Gian Pietro Carafa (later Pope Paul IV), Giulemo Sirleto, and Camillo Borghese (later Pope Paul V) assumed new importance. In its attempts to define points of doctrine and defend orthodoxy, the church relied heavily on such libraries as storehouses of ecclesiastical tradition. The Vatican library was refounded in 1588 by Pope Sixtus V with an ambitious program of collecting, scholarship, and printing in view, and the Escorial Library also embodied many aspects of church reform. In Italy, southern Germany, and France, the libraries of religious houses were established or renewed in the late 16th and early 17th centuries. Two libraries traditionally regarded as among the first modern public libraries emerged within this context of reform: the Bibliotheca Angelica in Rome (1604) and the Bibliotheca Ambrosiana in Milan, Italy (1607).

In Protestant nations, the Reformation brought both great destruction and unprecedented opportunities of acquisition for libraries and collectors. In Germany, the town libraries founded in many cities in the 15th century were looked to by Martin Luther and others for intellectual and political support of the Reformation. The period also witnessed the foundation of several court libraries. Ecclesiastical holdings dispersed at the Reformation found their way into ducal court collections at Heidelburg, Gottorp, Wolfenbüttel, and elsewhere in what is now Germany.

England, by contrast, had no great libraries founded during the dissolution of its monasteries. Figures such as John Bale and John Leland partially inventoried and attempted (unsuccessfully) to salvage the nation's bibliographical heritage. Collectors such as Mathew Parker, John Dee, and Robert Coton actively sought manuscripts formerly in the libraries of religious houses, amassing impressive collections. Proposals to Queen Elizabeth I by Dee and others for a national library on the continental model fell on deaf ears. Apart from the college libraries of the universities of Cambridge and Oxford (many of which had suffered during the Reformation), Britain's only institutional foundation of any great stability was the comparatively late foundation of the Bodleian Library at Oxford in 1602. Founded as a public library, it was regarded by contemporaries as both a bulwark of Protestantism and a store-house of knowledge of the kind enthusiastically described by Francis Bacon.

Architecture and Decoration

Until the second half of the 16th century, books in institutional collections were kept on open pulpit-style lecterns, usually chained in place. They were read on the spot, often from a standing position. In other instances they were kept in cupboards or chests. The pulpit scheme, for example, was chosen by Michelozzo for the San Marco library in the 1450s and again a century later, on a much grander scale, by Michelangelo for the Laurenziana library, Florence. The first library to use wall shelves built specifically to hold books was the Columbina in Seville in the 1530s, followed by the Escorial library, which opened in 1575. This soon came to be the standard storage system and would be used to great effect in many baroque libraries of the 17th century. Books were no longer chained in place, and although in some instances grilles or other devices would be used to prevent theft, the norms of civility and sociability, as well as a vigilant and increasingly professional corps of library personnel, became responsible for theft prevention. With the new system, books were normally shelved with spines facing the interior of the shelf. The author or title of the volume might be inscribed upon the exposed fore-edge; gilded or fluted fore-edges could add further decorative touches immediately visible to the visitor of the library. Library users could sit and read at large tables built for that purpose.

Decorative schemes frequently graced the walls of Renaissance libraries. Decorative programs varied greatly, but most played in some way upon the relationship of learning, wisdom, and piety through reference to classical or patristic figures, allegories of learning, and portraits or busts of men of learning. Apart from their artistic merit, such decorative schemes furnish useful insights into the wider cultural significance of libraries in that period. In 15th-century Italy, decoration of the humanist *studiolo* (study), which normally contained a book collection, was usually composed of portraits of famous writers. The private study of Pope Nicholas V, for example, was decorated with portraits of both pagan and Christian authors. At Buda, astrological imagery was employed in the library of King Corvinus of Hungary as it was later at the Escorial. Titian, Sansovino, and Veronese were among the artists involved in the elaborate cycle of allegories of learning and civic virtue that adorned the public library at Venice. At Rome, the Roman Catholic reform message of Sixtus V was driven home through a tripartite cycle incorporating the history of libraries in biblical, classical, and apostolic times, the history of the letters of the alphabet, and the history of the church councils. The apotheosis of the cycle confirmed the Vatican library as the storehouse of letters, Christian learning, and religious orthodoxy.

Catalogs and Classification

Catalogs of the period were usually some combination of an inventory, a quasi-legal list of the library's holdings, and a repertory (a guide to finding books within the physical space of the library). Catalogs invariably listed the contents of a library volume by volume. The volumes that made up a library frequently contained more than one text, not always by the same author and not always of related subject matter, and so catalogs would normally (though not always, particularly in the case of a simple inventory) itemize the entire contents of the volume. Depending on the size of the collection and the technical requirements of its users, the location of the book within the library would be signaled to the catalog's user. In more sophisticated catalogs, systems of cross-reference would be used to allow the user to find works of related subject matter that appeared elsewhere in the catalog. This system partially compensated for the problem of works that appeared out of their subject sequence owing to vagaries of binding practice. Alphabetical author indices would sometimes be compiled to aid the reader in finding works by a specific author.

Classification systems varied a good deal according to the strengths and uses of a particular collection. Normally some kind of hierarchical system was employed, with subjects deemed most important at the head of the catalog and lesser or peripheral subjects at the bottom. With very few exceptions, subject catalogs represented the physical arrangement of the collection within the library room. The standard classification system accorded scripture pride of place, followed by works of the church fathers, theology, sermons, and other religious works. Canon and civil law followed, then medicine. Next came philosophy, history, poetry, rhetoric, and grammar (the latter subject encompassing dictionaries, encyclopedias, and many works now considered works of literature). In collections that contained specialized works (on natural history or liturgy, for example), additional subject rubrics would be apportioned. Further subject subdivisions were sometimes used, particularly in the case of larger collections and with increasing frequency toward the end of the period. Although most collections contained predominantly Latin books, works in different languages, whether Greek or the vernacular, would be cataloged distinctly.

Book Supply and Location Strategies

Finding and procuring books frequently posed considerable difficulties. For Medici collectors in Florence, Traversari visited many Italian libraries to systematically search for manuscripts, and Bracciolini voyaged beyond the Alps for the same purpose. Niccoli dispatched lists of *desiderata* with cardinals traveling outside Italy. Greek texts were sought out with the aid of travel to Greece and Byzantium and through contact with Byzantine scholars. In building up the private Medici library (later the Laurenziana, housed in San Lorenzo, Florence) Lorenzo the Magnifico sent two in-house humanists, Janus Lascaris and Angelo Poliziano, on bibliographical searches. Lascaris alone acquired no fewer than 200 Greek manuscripts for Lorenzo in the period from 1489 to 1492. More often, commercial and diplomatic networks were regularly exploited to find desired books.

The most traditional means of obtaining texts was to employ copyists. After the foundation of the San Marco library at Florence, Cosimo de' Medici established a private library of his own, restricted to a limited circle of friends and clients. Cosimo turned to the Florentine bookseller Vespasiano da Bisticci: Employing an army of 45 scribes, Vespasiano furnished Cosimo copies of 200 manuscripts in the space of two years. Cardinal Bessarion set up two scriptoria for copying manuscripts, one in Rome and another in Crete. Frequently, humanist secretaries or their assistants would make copies, or if abroad, commission copies from local scribes. Informal networks of scholars, communicating by exchange of letters, would aid one another in procuring books. Well-established scholars would frequently succeed in having rare manuscript books from major collectors lent to them.

In the age of print, many individuals and institutions kept accounts with major printers (the Aldine press in Venice, the Junta in Florence, Estienne in Paris). The usual practice was to visit local booksellers' shops and bookstalls, many of which posted lists of their stock. Eventually the practice of printing such lists was adopted, and they circulated widely. Many collectors would rely on agents, who would visit the annual Frankfurt book fair in Germany, where printers and booksellers from across Europe met to exchange books. Trade in manuscripts as well as printed books on the open market remained brisk throughout the 16th century, and a lively market in secondhand printed books also flourished.

Many humanists such as Pico made and exchanged inventories of their collections. Vespasiano, when visiting the Urbino library established by Federigo da Montefeltro in the late 15th century, was able to compare it with inventories of "all the libraries in Italy" including the Vatican, San Marco in Florence, and the Visconti library of Pavia. Vespasiano even had a catalog of the university library at Oxford. At the end of the 16th century, library catalogs would begin to be printed, although this was by no means a widespread practice. The Frankfurt fair regularly printed its own catalog in the later period as well.

The increasingly systematic book-finding techniques of the Renaissance contributed to the development of modern bibliographical tools. The most magnificent of such undertakings was the *Bibliotheca universalis* (1545) of Conrad Gesner. Gesner undertook a universal bibliography of all known works—whether in print or manuscript, and whether extant, known by title alone, or available in fragments passed down in other texts—in the three biblical languages of Hebrew, Greek, and Latin. Gesner himself was involved in establishing a public library at Zurich in Switzerland, and the purpose of the work, he stated, was to aid public libraries in finding books. A late, emphatic expression of the Renaissance ideal of the library is represented by the famous *Advis pour dresser une bibliothèque* (Advice for Establishing a Library) of Gabriel Naudé, which appeared in Paris in 1627. Naudé proposed a universal library that would endeavor to collect all known books in all known languages, would trace the history of learning in all subjects from antiquity down to modern times, and would be open to all.

Legacy

Although many texts that were new or newly rediscovered were avidly sought out for Renaissance collections, such libraries rarely present a radical break with the medieval past and were instead the locus for the long process of evaluation and redefinition of the medieval heritage. What was truly new with the Renaissance library was the relatively large number of collections in the secular domain, the great number and size of personal collections, and the emergence of a distinct, professional bibliographical literature. When studied as evidence of the society that shaped them, libraries are invaluable guides to the intellectual and cultural life of the Renaissance. Away from the dazzling collections of court and intellectual elites, libraries provide valuable indicators of the role and levels of literacy in the period. Few Renaissance libraries survived the death of their owners intact. And although even fewer have survived as institutions to the present time, the manuscripts and early books of modern libraries abound with the ghosts of Renaissance collectors. The history of the Renaissance holdings of most of the great national libraries can be told largely through study of the fortune of Renaissance collections.

PAUL NELLES

Further Reading

Bianca, Concetta, et al., editors, *Scrittura, biblioteche, e stampa a Roma nel quattrocento,* Vatican City: Scuola Vaticana di Paleografia, Diplomatica, e Archivistica, 1980

Grafton, Anthony, editor, *Rome Reborn: The Vatican Library and Renaissance Culture,* Washington, D.C.: Library of Congress, and New Haven, Connecticut: Yale University Press, 1993

Hobson, Anthony, *Great Libraries,* London: Weidenfeld and Nicolson, 1970

Kibre, Pearl, "The Intellectual Interests Reflected in Libraries of the Fourteenth and Fifteenth Centuries," *Journal of the History of Ideas* 7 (1946)

Nelles, Paul, "The Library As an Instrument of Discovery: Gabriel Naudé and the Uses of History," in *History and the Disciplines: The Reclassification of Knowledge in Early Modern Europe,* edited by Donald R. Kelley, Rochester, New York: University of Rochester Press, 1997

Nelles, Paul, "Libraries," in *Encyclopedia of the Renaissance,* edited by Paul F. Grendler, vol. 3, New York: Scribners, 1999

Petrucci, Armando, "Le biblioteche antiche," in *Letteratura italiana,* edited by Alberto Asor Rosa, vol. 2, Turin, Italy: Einaudi, 1983

Rose, Paul Lawrence, "Humanist Culture and Renaissance Mathematics: The Italian Libraries of the Quattrocento," *Studies in the Renaissance* 20 (1973)

Tolly, Claude, editor, *Histoire des bibliothèques françaises,* 4 vols., Paris: Promodis–Éditions du Cercle du Librairie, 1988–92; see especially vol. 2, *Les bibliothèques sous l'Ancien Régime, 1530–1789,* 1988

Ullman, Berthold L., and Philip A. Stadter, *The Public Library of Renaissance Florence: Niccolò Niccoli, Cosimo de' Medici, and the Library of San Marco,* Padua, Italy: Antenore, 1972

Zorzi, Marino, "La circolazione del libro a Venezia nel cinquecento: Biblioteche private e pubbliche," *Ateneo veneto* 177 (1990)

Royal Libraries

Earliest Times

From the beginning of recorded civilization, collections of written materials were used by princely rulers as a means of expressing their supreme power. For convenience, such collections were often housed within the royal residence. Palace locations also fulfilled an important symbolic function. Palace libraries testified to the culture and wisdom of rulers; the libraries paid homage, often in the guise of memorials, to the glory of reigns. Also, much attention was paid to their architectural treatment. They owed their existence to the wealth and influence of rulers; this influence translated into gifts from subjects and prizes from foreign conquest. Further, the enduring practical value of the palace library as an adjunct to efficient government is undeniable.

Early civilizations were characterized by a concentration of wealth, power, and social initiative in the hands of rulers and priestly elites. The collections of clay tablets that formed some of the first libraries were assembled by kings who needed them to administer their complex empires. Because of this function, libraries retained their importance: When Alexander the Great struck out on his Eastern conquests, his civil servants studied and collected the literary culture of subdued lands in order to govern them more effectively. The administrative function of royal collections was also to the fore in ancient China. The imperial library there was placed at the disposal of royal advisors who used classical texts to enhance their counsel to the emperor.

For much of recorded history, there was little distinction between libraries and state archives; when these were not housed within the precincts of temples, they were kept in royal palaces. In the case of the early Egyptian dynasties—where the king was also a god—temple, palace, and library were likely to occupy the same building. Examples of palace libraries from antiquity are manifold. Ashurbanipal, King of Assyria, maintained a collection of 25,000 clay tablets in his palace at Nineveh. Rameses II of Egypt presided over a library of 20,000 papyrus rolls (many of a religious and philosophical nature) in his palace at Thebes.

Greco-Roman Libraries

Unlike the Babylonians or ancient Egyptians, Greco-Roman civilizations began to differentiate the functions of a library from those of an archive while Hellenistic rulers and the Roman emperors continued to play the leading role in creating and maintaining libraries. Kings had traditionally won prestige through military prowess or massive building projects. The promotion of scholarship now became an equally important source of renown; some rulers were scholars themselves, and a number of the libraries they established and nourished were attached to their palaces.

After the collapse of the Greco-Roman world, the Catholic Church replaced secular government as the patron of learning and the custodian of libraries during the Middle Ages. In medieval times the libraries of monasteries were more important than those of palaces; monastic scriptoria maintained the lifeblood of literary culture in the West. One exception to the monastic library dominance was Charlemagne's palace at Aachen, a product of the emperor's own intellectual interests.

The Renaissance

Regal patronage of libraries was renewed on a large scale during the Renaissance, when many of the libraries were courtly libraries assembled to preserve the new body of vernacular literature that expanded, particularly in France under the patronage of Charles V and great noblemen—such as Jean, Duke of Berry, and Philip, Duke of Burgundy—and in England under the patronage of Edward IV. Other notable royal collections were established by King Alfonso the Magnanimous of Naples and King Matthias Corvinus of Hungary. The Italian princes set up libraries as a part of their policy of cultural renewal. In Spain a library was built in the formidable royal residence of the Escorial, near Madrid, that was at once a monastery, a cathedral, and a palace (1584); it was one of the first libraries to jettison alcoves and book bays in favor of the wall-lined bookshelves with which we are familiar today. The Vatican Library, created in the 15th century, best illustrates the era's spirit of cultural renovations. Despite the religious context in which it was established, the pontifical library was an expression of contemporary princely ambition rather than a continuation of the medieval monastic library tradition. Successive popes enlarged the collection (including incorporating other palatial libraries into it, such as those of the Duke of Urbino or of Queen Christina of Sweden) and provided additional space within the Vatican Palace for the growing collection.

During the Renaissance, princely libraries, unlike university libraries, were considered private possessions, and admission was granted only to favorites of the prince. Also, the books in princely libraries were more luxurious, and new standards of cataloging, with emphasis on description of decoration and script, were developed, in part to prevent theft. By the 17th century, many of the private libraries of the 14th and 15th centuries became possessions, through inheritance and purchase, of sovereign princes, who allowed consultation to the public. Other libraries started through the generosity of princes, such as Cosimo de Medici in the mid-15th century, who purchased volumes and donated them, along with selected items from his own collection, to the Dominican convent of San Marco to establish a public library for the citizens of Florence. His grandson, Lorenzo the Magnificent, started the Biblioteca Medicea-Laurentiana for the same purpose.

The Reformation

The Reformation contributed an additional impulse to the establishment of libraries, where Protestant and Catholic theologians could obtain the bibliographic spoils of spiritual and intellectual war. Religious conflict led many of the leading German princes to finance the creation of libraries. One of the most interesting was the library set up by Duke Julius of Brunswick-Wolfenbüttel. His successor, Augustus, a noted bibliophile, produced most of the highly detailed catalogs, and later the library was to boast the great philosopher, mathematician, and political advisor Gottfried Wilhelm Leibnitz among its librarians and later Gotthold Ephraim Lessing, German dramatist, poet, and critic.

Changing Trends

The palace collections established after the invention of printing were much larger than those of the ancient world. Many were to develop into the principal libraries in their nation or region, a process that went beyond Europe as imperial powers imposed, with a heavy hand, their own literary culture on the peoples of the Americas and the East. Royal collections were often underscored by the policy of comprehensive collection and the adoption of compulsory copyright deposit in pursuit of this objective (this legal obligation was first introduced by Francis I of France in the 16th century). Soon "state libraries," with their increasing demands for space and their heavy use by scholars from outside the royal household, could no longer be maintained within palaces. They were instead to be housed in separate buildings or transferred to the jurisdiction of another institution. This is what happened to the royal library of the Hanoverians in Britain in 1757 when much of it was absorbed into the newly formed British Museum collection. In Prussia the library of Frederick William (the Great Elector) was opened to the public (1661), paving the way for state control in the early 19th century; in 1687 the Elector's Library in Berlin was opened to readers in the afternoons; and in 1726 the imperial library in Vienna, acknowledged as the European leader because of its manuscript holdings, became "national" in one sense when Emperor Charles VI gave it a new building.

German Ducal Libraries

In addition to the Herzog August Bibliothek, Wolfenbüttel lies near to several other ducal libraries. During the 19th century, many rare book collections, particularly from monasteries, were transferred to the libraries of ruling nobility; these, in turn, became part of regional and state libraries, the central research libraries of the individual states of the German Empire. One of the most important is the Saxon State Library (Sächsische Landesbibliothek), an outstanding cultural institution founded in 1556 as the Saxon Library in Dresden when Prince Elector Augustus (1553–86) started to acquire scholarly books and literary works for what was his personal library.

During the first half of the 18th century, under the rulers Augustus the Strong (1694–1733) and his son Augustus II (1733–63), Saxony reached the pinnacle of its cultural influence, manifested in Dresden's spectacular baroque architecture. The city became a major European cultural center, whose monarchs fostered the arts and made significant additions to its art, museum, and library collections. The Royal Library became a true state library for Saxony, adding many manuscripts, maps, and books from distinguished private collections. In 1727 the library moved into two wings of the Zwinger Palace, where it was made accessible to the public; by the end of the 18th century, it required more space and ended up in the Japanese Palace (1786–88). In 1806 Elector Frederick Augustus III became Frederick Augustus I, King of Saxony, and his library became the Royal Public Library and a center of library science in the 19th century. After the proclamation of the Weimar Republic (1919), it officially became the Saxon State Library. During World War II, the most valuable holdings of the Saxon State Library were moved to 18 castles and offices in the vicinity of Dresden. Because of this transfer, the holdings largely survived the bombing raids of February and March 1945 by the U.S. and British air forces that virtually destroyed the old city of Dresden and approximately 200,000 volumes of 20th-century holdings. In 1996, 440 years after its founding, a sampling of these treasures was displayed in the U.S. Library of Congress.

Other Collections

As European monarchies declined in the 19th and 20th centuries, the transfer to state control grew ever more frequent as royal libraries evolved into national libraries. Yet some important palace collections, such as those of the Vatican, the Escorial in Spain, or the Royal Library at Windsor Castle in England, still remain in their original regal locations. Others still retain their royal designation.

Belgium

Koninklijke Bibliotheek Albert I or Bibliotheque Royale Albert 1er (now part of the Royal Library of Belgium), one of the most important European libraries, originated with the collection of illuminated manuscripts from the 15th-century library of the dukes of Burgundy (librarie de Bourgogne). This collection formed the core of the first Royal Library established by Philip II, king of Spain and ruler of the Netherlands (1559), who brought to the court in Brussels all the books from his many palaces, notably those in Lille and The Hague, and the collections he inherited from his aunt, Mary of Hungary. In 1773, under the governorship of Charles of Lorraine, the Royal Library was opened to the public, and the collections grew. After years of neglect and several jurisdictional changes, including one as the Brussels Public Library, the Belgian government created the Royal Library of Belgium in 1837. Two years later it was opened to the public. In 1842 the collections of the city of Brussels were handed over to the state and added to those of the Royal Library. In 1935, at the request of Queen Elisabeth and her son, Leopold III, the Belgian government built a new library in memory of King Albert I, who died the year before. World War II delayed construction, but in 1953 King Baudouin laid the cornerstone of the new building, which was officially inaugurated in 1969. It now performs the functions of a national library and a central research library. The Parliamentary Act of 1965 obligated each Belgian publisher to deposit one copy of every work in the Royal Library.

Denmark

The Royal Library of Denmark (Det Kongelige Bibliotek) in Copenhagen was founded by Frederik III (1648–70) in 1653 with the monarch's purchase of the original records of astronomer Tycho Brahe's manuscripts and observations and a gift of three Icelandic manuscripts from the Bishop of Iceland. Between 1661 and 1664, the king bought or inherited three large aristocratic libraries, comprising 16,000 volumes of works on subjects such as Romance literature, history, geography, and mathematics. These became the core of the Royal Library, for which Peder Schumacher was librarian from 1663. In 1665 plans were begun for a separate library building that was completed in 1673. From 1662 compulsory deposit was established for Icelandic books and from 1697 for Danish books as well. By 1730 the library's collection included 40,000 volumes. After a fire (1728) destroyed the collection of the University of Copenhagen library, the Royal Library emerged as the only great library in the country. In 1943 the Royal Library and the university library were placed under the common direction of a national librarian. In the 1980s this arrangement was altered when the sciences and medicine department of the university library became a second national library separate from the Royal Library that, with the university library, was separately administered. By the 1990s the Royal Library and the university library's first department served as the national library of Denmark, the major subject library of humanities and social sciences for the University of Copenhagen, the deposit library for international organizations, and the book museum for Denmark.

France

In France private libraries created by the king, princes, and other nobleman flourished during the Middle Ages. Since

Charlemagne, the kings of France have had private libraries; some princes (such as the Comte d'Angouleme) had rich libraries that were later partly transferred to the king's library. The first Royal Library, which later became the Bibliothèque nationale, dates back to the reign of Charles V (1364–80), a great bibliophile and scholar who placed the manuscript treasures he inherited from his royal ancestors in the Louvre and appointed a scholar, Gilles Malet, to catalog them; the first catalog of the Bibliothèque nationale has a manuscript dated 1380. Louis XII (1498–1515) set a precedent by treating the Royal Library as a permanent institution accessible to scholars rather than just the royal household. Successive monarchs expanded the royal collection, known as the King's Library; in 1789, at the outbreak of the French Revolution, the King's Library possessed 300,000 volumes. It was renamed the Bibliothèque nationale by the revolutionary government in 1795.

The system of legal deposit in France, and subsequently throughout Europe, originated with Francis I (1515–47); his Edict of Montpellier (1537) established the principle of *depot legal* (copyright deposit), requiring publishers and printers to provide copies of every book published in France for the Royal Library to qualify for the king's authorization.

Great Britain

The most impressive library in the world, matchless in its resources for research into every aspect of human development, is the British Library, created by the British Library Act (1972) and formed from the merger of the former British Museum Library, the National Central Library, the National Lending Library for Science and Technology, the Patent Office Library, the Science Reference Library, and the staff of the *British National Bibliography*. The British Museum Library was founded in 1753 with collections from Hans Sloane, manuscripts from the earls of Oxford and Robert Cotton, and books from the Old Royal Library. In 1757 George II presented it with the Royal Library of the kings of England, back to Edward IV, which brought with it the right of free deposit of all books published in the United Kingdom. The second royal library, that of George III, was purchased from George IV (1823) and includes charters of the Anglo-Saxon kings.

Netherlands

The Royal Library of the Netherlands (Koninklijke Bibliotheek) began in 1798, when representatives of the Batavian republic decided to make the confiscated library of William V of Orange, with its 3,000 volumes, into a national library housed in The Hague. In 1800 the public was given access after a parliamentary committee granted permission. Under Louis Bonaparte as king of Holland (1806–10), the library was often called the Royal Library, but after the House of Orange was restored (1813), the new king, William I, renounced all claims to the collection. In 1982 the library was officially designated by law as the national library and given responsibility, but without authority of legal depository status, for collecting all materials published in the Netherlands.

Spain

In Spain during the Middle Ages, the best libraries were found in universities, especially the University of Salamanca, where King Alfonso the Wise, who had established a large private library, provided library and research services. However, the National Library of Spain, founded by Felipe V (1712) as a public library, belonged to the crown until 1836, when it was nationalized and became a governmental unit. The most famous royal library remained the collection in the Escorial palace.

Sweden

The Royal Library in Stockholm, Sweden (Kungliga Biblioteket) had its origins in the private book collections of the Swedish kings. Such a library is mentioned as early as 1568, when 217 books owned by Erik XIV were registered in a catalog. The first librarian was appointed by Gustavus II Adolphus in 1611. After the Thirty Years' War, the library's holdings were greatly expanded with books taken as war booty. An ambitious acquisition policy was continued under Queen Christina, but when the queen abdicated, she went abroad and took the most valuable parts of the collection with her. In 1661 the royal library was given the status of a national library when the printers of the realm were ordered to deliver deposit copies, and by the last half of the 20th century it acquired other functions. In 1953 the newly established Bibliographical Institute centralized bibliographical and cataloging tasks on a national level; in 1980 it was given responsibility for LIBRIA, a computer-based system common to all Swedish research libraries; and in 1988 the government directed the Royal Library to coordinate several library functions in the country and formed a special office for national planning and coordination for this purpose. An exhibition of the library's materials opened in September 1984 in conjunction with the Stockholm 1984 colloquium of the Association Internationale de Bibliophilie.

Today, the royal libraries of Europe are, for the most part, the core collections of what became their national libraries, but their importance to bibliographical development is inestimable. Like Thomas Jefferson's collection, which formed the basis of the U.S. Library of Congress, the private collections of many an otherwise obscure royal personage, developed to reflect personal interests, contributed significantly to national collection development. Although some of these institutions remained provincial or local libraries rather than national institutions and the government built its own national library from scattered collections throughout the country, by the year 1800 more than 20 counties had national libraries, although not all had that status at the time.

MARTIN J. MANNING JR.

See also British Library; Herzog August Library Wolfenbüttel; Library of the Royal Palace, Spain; Royal Library/National Library of Sweden; Royal Library of Belgium, Albert I; Royal Library of Denmark; Royal Library of the Netherlands; Royal Monastery of El Escorial Library

Further Reading

Black, Alistair, and Christopher Murphy, "Palace Libraries," in *Encyclopedia of Library History,* edited by Wayne A. Wiegand and Donald G. Davis, New York: Garland, 1994

Hobson, Anthony, *Great Libraries,* New York: Putnam, and London: Weidenfeld and Nicolson, 1970

Jackson, Sidney L., *Libraries and Librarianship in the West: A Brief History,* New York: McGraw-Hill, 1974

Krewson, Margrit B., editor, *Dresden: Treasures from the Saxon State Library,* Washington, D.C.: Library of Congress, 1996

Ridderstad, Per S., editor, *A Royal Library,* Stockholm: Kungliga Biblioteket, 1984

Uitzinger, Marjolijn, editor, *The Royal Library,* The Hague: Ministry of Education and Science, 1982

Wedgeworth, Robert, editor, *ALA World Encyclopedia of Library and Information Services,* Chicago: American Library Association, 1980; 3rd edition, as *World Encyclopedia of Library and Information Services,* 1993

Wittek, Martin, "The Albert I Royal Library," in *Encyclopedia of Library and Information Science,* edited by Allen Kent et al., vol. 42, New York: Dekker, 1987

School Libraries and Media Centers

A history of school library media centers must consider the rise of self-governance and the weakening or ending of monarchy in the 18th and 19th centuries. A review must also consider the development of universal primary education; increased literacy; a communications and industrial revolution, resulting in cheaper and more efficient ways to mass produce and distribute reading material; and educational practices that moved from strict recitation to the encouragement of independent reading and discovery. The modern school library media center is a culmination of the 18th- and 19th-century shift of libraries from private, individual treasure troves to shared public collections within a community. Its evolution into the institution we currently understand it to be is essentially a post–World War II phenomenon. Additionally, modern school library media centers follow different models: either funded and administered by the school district, separate and distinct from the public library, or administratively and financially intertwined with the public library system. The term *school library and media center* also reflects its history and function—from school library to media center to school library media center.

School library media center development may be characterized in four stages: (1) 19th century, marked by increased literacy, the public schooling movement, the industrial revolution, and urbanism; (2) 1920 to 1940, marked by growth as an offshoot of 19th-century development; (3) 1945 to 1970, marked by rapid expansion after World War II; and (4) 1970s, marked by global acceptance of the importance of school libraries.

The history of school library media centers around the world is complicated by the profound differences between developed and developing countries as well as by the national philosophies regarding education and the provision of library services through government support. With 188 member countries in the United Nations (and a total of 192 nations worldwide), a nation-by-nation account cannot be adequately addressed in these pages.

The continents of Asia and Africa illustrate the diversity of development for the school library media center. In Asia, post–World War II Japan adopted many U.S. educational practices, including the approach to school libraries. In China, the Cultural Revolution of 1966 to 1976 destroyed many school libraries, and work with children was not revisited until the early 1980s. Two African examples, Egypt and Nigeria, show that modern school librarianship came to Egypt in the 1950s and was developing in Nigeria at that time, getting stronger through the 1960s and 1970s. Table 1 provides the dates for the earliest recorded mention of school libraries in several representative countries, constructed from *School Libraries: International Developments,* edited by Jean Lowrie (1972) and Lowrie's article "School Library and Media Centers" in the *Encyclopedia of Library History* (1994; modified from the 2nd edition of *School Libraries: International Developments,* edited by Lowrie and Mieko Nagakura [1991]).

Table 1 demonstrates the diversity that the history of colonization, industrialization, and governmental response causes in the establishment of schools, public libraries, and school libraries; generalizations cannot easily be drawn. For the most part school libraries are late-19th-century establishments, but, as stated above, what we would recognize as school libraries today—teaching and learning centers with professionals devoted to their collection management and instructional role—are post–World War II inventions. What the school

Table 1
Earliest recorded reference to school libraries

Nation	Date
Australia	19th century
Canada	1850
China, People's Republic	1884
Denmark	1919
Egypt	1950s
Finland	1724 (Royal Secondary School Decree)
	1983 (Comprehensive School Act)
Germany	no date (reform of school libraries mentioned in 1960s)
Hong Kong	1963
Iceland	1908
India	no date (greatest development in 1960s)
Israel	Arab: no date
	Jewish: 1950
Japan	1868–1912
	1948 (School Library Advisory Council)
	1950 (Japanese School Library Association)
Jordan	1926
Malaysia	1960s
New Zealand	no date (greatest development in the 1960s)
Nigeria	no date (Nigerian School Library Association founded 1977)
Norway	1836 (legislated 1935)
Singapore	1973
South Africa	1894
South Pacific Island Nations	1960s–80s
Cook Islands	no date
Fiji	1970s
Kiribati	1982
Nauru	no date
Papua New Guinea	1966
Solomon Islands	1970s
Tonga	no date
Tuvalu	no date
Vanuatu	
Anglophone	no date
Francophone	no date
Western Samoa	1985
Sweden	1870s
Tanzania	1920s
Thailand	1956
United Kingdom	1888
United States	late 1800s

Source: Lowrie (1994); Lowrie and Nagakura (1991).

library looks like, how it is used in instruction, what its support is, and how it developed differs between and within countries. The United States provides a good example. Despite progressive development, the U.S. school library experience has not been the same for all of its citizens. Racial segregation, reservations for indigenous populations, and the coexistence of public and private schooling are examples of historical problems that a brief general history can obscure. National differences emerge that chronology does not explain, such as the experience of industrial and intellectual France, where school libraries differ markedly from those of the Scandinavian nations and Great Britain. Germany's excellent educational system does not fit the Anglo-American and Scandinavian model of school library organization because school and public libraries are combined in that country. The former Soviet Union was very supportive of libraries and libraries could be found in most schools, but its subsequent school library history is difficult to analyze.

How do children have access to books and how are books used by teachers and librarians in the teaching and learning process? A history of school library media centers suggests that there are various ways to approach these issues. The United States and United Kingdom use education reproduction theory to show how schooling mirrors social stratification (Peterson, 1998), family literacy (Taylor and Dorsey-Gaines, 1988), emergent literacy (Chall, 1983), and summer learning (Heyns, 1978).

International Association of School Librarianship

An examination of international organizations, professional library associations, and governmental organizations can also illuminate the history of school library media centers, emphasizing how young the institution of the school library media center is. On 20 November 1959 the General Assembly of the United Nations unanimously adopted as Principle 7 of the United Nations Declaration of the Rights of the Child that "the child is entitled to receive education which shall be free and compulsory at least in the elementary stages." School librarians and teachers recognized the importance of the school library in this declaration and organized themselves to influence international policy. At the World Confederation of the Teaching Profession Assemblies (WCTOP) in the 1960s, delegates interested in school libraries met to discuss common concerns. By 1971 the International Association of School Librarianship was established as an International Associate Member of the WCTOP. Since that time, the association has grown to include individual members (librarians, school library specialists/teacher librarians, teachers, and publishers) and institutional members. Its publication program supports and disseminates books, conference proceedings, a newsletter, reviews, and bibliographies.

International Federation of Library Associations and Institutions School Libraries Section

Library services to children and youth involve both public libraries and school libraries and are often funded by the same governmental authority. Thus it would seem only natural for public and school libraries to work closely together. In the International Federation of Library Associations and Institutions (IFLA), school libraries were part of the Public Libraries Section, not a strong position from which to accomplish the advocacy work for school libraries needed at the international level. At the 1973 General Council meeting of IFLA in Grenoble, France, the Section of Public Libraries recommended that approval be given for the formation of a subsection of the Public Libraries Section to provide for the interests and needs of school libraries. Eventually that subsection became its own section; the Section for School Libraries and Resource Centres went on to champion the role of the school library media center in the education of the child. One activity of the IFLA School Libraries Section, in accord with the United Nations Educational, Scientific, and Cultural Organization (UNESCO) Public Library Manifesto, was to promote acceptance by UNESCO of the School Library Manifesto: "The school library provides information and ideas that are fundamental to functioning successfully in today's information- and knowledge-based society. The school library equips students with lifelong learning skills and develops the imagination, enabling them to live as responsible citizens." A mission statement, statements on funding legislation, networks, goals of the school library, staff, and operation and management make up the manifesto. During the 26 October to 17 November 1999 General Conference of the 30th Session of UNESCO in Paris, the School Library Manifesto was ratified. The section will concentrate on implementing and disseminating the content of the manifesto to the school library community and education policy makers and practitioners at local and national levels.

IFLA Survey on National Policy for School Libraries

In 1993 UNESCO sponsored a five-day IFLA seminar on school librarianship at Caldes de Montbui, Spain, resulting in a recommendation to assess school library policies of member IFLA countries and to conduct a survey of national policies for school libraries. The results of the 100 countries surveyed and the 51 nations responding showed that 25 countries have national school library policies, two were formulating policies, nine had no policy in place, and 13 had school library policy as a local (city, individual school) responsibility. The 25 countries that reported having school library policies are: Australia, Czech Republic, Chile, China, Denmark, El Salvador, Estonia, Germany, Hungary, Ireland, Israel, Jamaica, Kazakhstan, Peru, Poland, Qatar, Russia, South Africa, Sri Lanka, Spain, Switzerland, Thailand, Trinidad and Tobago, Turkey, and Wales. The results of the survey served to illustrate the diversity in school library organization worldwide.

The State of the World's Children/The State of the World's School Libraries

UNICEF publications on the state of the world's children tend to focus on social issues, and its 1999 report focused on education. It documents inadequate or nonexistent buildings, conditions of war and poverty, and statistics that show that 130 million children of primary school age in developing countries grow up without access to basic education. The report places in context the international development of school library media centers as a young movement dependent upon national values regarding children and education. Diljit Singh's 1993 Ph.D. dissertation, "An International Comparative Study of School Libraries," demonstrates a lack of clear purpose for school libraries in many countries, hindering their development. Low rates of literacy, lack of trained personnel, and national economic and political instability are just some of the conditions facing many of the world's nations, conditions which in turn affect the healthy development of school library media centers. Nonetheless, the desire to reach common global goals for children and their education, the diligent international efforts of librarians and teachers, and the 1999 UNESCO-approved program and budget for renewal of education systems for the information age suggest that the development of school libraries will continue to be advocated as integral to the educational process.

Library historians agree that theoretical and historical knowledge regarding school library media centers is still in its infancy.

But there is also consensus that an effective school library serves education by promoting the reading habit. As the school library media center matures globally, so will its history; critical, comparative studies are certain to be forthcoming.

LORNA PETERSON

Further Reading

Chall, Jeanne S., *Stages of Reading Development,* New York: McGraw-Hill, 1983; 2nd edition, Fort Worth, Texas: Harcourt Brace College Publishers, 1996

Galler, Anne M., "National School Library Policies: An International Survey," *IFLA Journal* 22, no. 4 (1996)

Heyns, Barbara, *Summer Learning and the Effects of Schooling,* New York: Academic Press, 1978

Knuth, Rebecca, "Factors in the Development of School Libraries in Great Britain and the United States: A Comparative Study," *International Information and Library Review* 27 (1995)

Knuth, Rebecca, "On a Spectrum: International Models of School Librarianship," *Library Quarterly* 69, no. 1 (1999)

Latrobe, Kathy Howard, editor, *The Emerging School Library Media Center: Historical Issues and Perspectives,* Englewood, Colorado: Libraries Unlimited, 1998

Lowrie, Jean E., "School Library and Media Centers," in *Encyclopedia of Library History,* edited by Wayne Wiegand and Donald G. Davis, New York: Garland, 1994

Lowrie, Jean E., editor, *School Libraries: International Developments,* Metuchen, New Jersey: Scarecrow Press, 1972; 2nd edition, edited by Lowrie and Mieko Nagakura, 1991

Peterson, Lorna, "From Literate to Scholar: Teaching Library Research Skills to Sixth Graders Using Primary Documents," *Urban Education* 32, no. 5 (January 1998)

Singh, Diljit, "An International Comparative Study of School Libraries," Ph.D. diss., Florida State University, 1993

Taylor, Denny, and Catherine Dorsey-Gaines, *Growing Up Literate: Learning from Inner-City Families,* Portsmouth, New Hampshire: Heinemann, 1988

Science, Technology, and Engineering Libraries

Scientific, engineering, and technical libraries exist to support basic research and its applications, and there are examples of special libraries providing this function as early as the 16th century. Although their mission is the same as that of any other library—to collect, organize, and provide access to a collection of literature—the literature of science, engineering, and technology is vast, international, and multilingual. It is expensive to acquire and difficult to index. In addition to current materials, older and out-of-date literature must be available in the library's collection or through other resources. Scientific and technical libraries are largely defined by the methods, skills, and systems employed for the acquisition, storage, preservation, retrieval, and use of a collection of scientific and technical literature. These skills must also include providing access to the greater body of scientific and technical information that is outside any one collection.

The literature of science and technology includes several types of original research records that are typically collected by scientific libraries. All of these, since the 1980s or even earlier, have increasingly been produced, stored, and retrieved electronically, a development of immense significance for these and other libraries.

Two large groups of technical and scientific literature are the proceedings of conferences and research monographs. Patents, engineering specifications and standards, and technical reports are other groups, as are dissertations, manufacturers' literature, and *Festschriften* (publications honoring an individual scientist or scientific society). The largest percentage of materials in most scientific and technical libraries, however, is made up of periodicals.

Scientific periodicals and other serial publications were always intended to rapidly communicate the results of research. The earliest examples originated in the 17th century with the publication of the *Philosophical Transactions* of the Royal Society of London and the *Journal des Sçavans* (Journal of Scientists, the first independent scientific periodical), both of which started in 1665. Current issues are typically the most in demand, so it has been essential for scientific and technical libraries to maintain current subscriptions for titles relevant to their constituent users, and sufficient funds are required to do so. Back files of periodicals represent a permanent record of scientific work and research. Although older volumes may be consulted less frequently, current research often originates in the study of earlier work. Preserving and providing access to older periodicals (and to all archival technical reports, records of proceedings, monographs, and other types of scientific literature) has been an equally essential service of such libraries.

Since the beginning of the 19th century, the indexing of periodical literature has been recognized as a method of providing access to both current and historical publications. The first volume of *Philosophical Transactions* was issued with an index, for example. In order for researchers to review a large body of literature, however, collective indexes were needed that provided access to a number of different periodicals. Scientific and technical libraries have thus emphasized the acquisition and creation of collective indexes to periodicals and other types of scientific and technical literature.

Jeremias David Reuss, librarian of the University of Göttingen beginning in 1803, created the first periodical index devoted to the proceedings and periodicals of scientific societies. His *Repertorium Commentationum a Societatibus Litterariis Editarum* (1801–21) is a classified subject index to the publications of scientific societies issued before 1800. Many other specialized indexes to scientific and technical literature have followed. During the 1880s, for example, the need for more organized access to the literature of engineering resulted in the creation of the *Engineering Index*, which began in 1884 as a feature of the *Journal of the Association of Engineering Societies*. It soon relied heavily on a cooperative partnership with the Engineering Societies Library (ESL) in New York, a tie that became even stronger after the *Engineering Index* was purchased by the American Society of Mechanical Engineers in 1919. Even though publications owned by the library were being indexed in the *Engineering Index*, the library began its own index in the 1920s. A more comprehensive index was necessary to serve its users, so ESL created a card index to periodical articles that was similar to the card catalog of books.

But a system such as ESL's was expensive and labor intensive. Most scientific and technical libraries acquired published indexes instead, such as the Royal Society of London's *Catalogue of Scientific Papers*, which continued the work of Reuss' *Repertorium* by indexing papers in scientific periodicals that were published in the period 1800 to 1900. From 1901 to 1914 it was published annually as the *International Catalogue of Scientific Literature*. In addition to the *Engineering Index*, other specialized indexes became available to libraries in the early 20th century, such as *Science Abstracts* (1898–) for physics, *Chemical Abstracts* (1907–), and *Biological Abstracts* (1926–). In the mid-20th century, the various sections of *Current Contents* began offering a method to review current literature by reproducing tables of contents from major periodicals before the articles were cited in indexing and abstracting publications. A new method of indexing periodicals appeared in the 1960s with the advent of online bibliographic databases. By 1974 almost 100 databases were available; ten years later there were almost 3,000 bibliographic databases available to libraries, the majority oriented to the pure and applied sciences. Scientific and technical libraries subscribed through vendors or search services and began to offer the specialized reference service of database searching. Reference librarians who were trained in techniques of database searching learned how to use vendors' services and acted as intermediaries for the end users of scientific and technical information. Producing a bibliography of relevant citations was possible without reference to printed indexes or abstracts.

Providing convenient access to a collection of scientific literature has always been one of the primary functions of a science library. The membership of scientific societies placed so much importance on having access to that literature that they often created a library as one of their first acts. The Royal Society of London created a library in 1660 when the organization was still loosely defined and even before it received an official charter of incorporation from King Charles II in 1662. By this time, the Royal College of Surgeons had a long-established library founded in 1518. In the United States, the American Academy of Arts and Sciences started a library in Boston, Massachusetts, in 1780, the same year the academy itself was founded.

Collecting the official publications of a society and its membership was an important function of these libraries, but members also wanted access to other relevant publications. Thus arrangements for exchanging publications among societies were commonly used as a method of acquisition. Equally important for many science libraries was the gift or purchase of a personal collection or collections that served as a foundation for the library. The 19th-century astronomical library of James Ludovic Lindsay, 26th Earl of Crawford, is illustrative. Its nucleus was the library of Charles Babbage, the 19th-century mathematician and founder of the British Association for the Advancement of Science, acquired in 1872 and considerably expanded until 1888, when it became by gift the Crawford Library of the Royal Observatory in Edinburgh, Scotland. The collection of the naturalist Hans Sloan is another famous example. His library of 50,000 volumes formed an instant collection, not for any one learned society but for a national library, when it was purchased for the British Museum Library in 1753.

Private libraries were probably the earliest collections specifically created to support special interests in pure and applied sciences. The Swiss naturalist Conrad Gesner had an extensive library in the 16th century to support his voluminous work in botany, zoology, and paleontology. His contemporary, the English astronomer and mathematician John Dee, boasted that his library had more than 3,000 printed books and 1,000 manuscripts. Few European libraries could have surpassed it for science and mathematics, but the users of both Gesner's and Dee's collection, as with any private library, would have been limited to the collector and the group of associates and students who may have had access to it. Many private libraries, such as those of Lindsay and Sloan noted above, have approached institutional size. Joseph Banks amassed 25,000 volumes in his library during the late 18th and early 19th centuries. Alexander von Humbolt's library, another 19th-century example, numbered 11,000 volumes.

Many of these special private collections found their way into university libraries, often forming the nucleus of a university's science library or collection. Asa Gray, the botanist known for his early support of Darwin's theory, presented his collection to Harvard in 1865. Julius Nieuwland, the chemist who helped the Du Pont Company synthesize Neoprene, used his wealth to purchase books and journals for a chemistry collection that is now part of the science library at the University of Notre Dame (Indiana). In 1914 Stanford University purchased the collection of its second president, the earth scientist John Branner, which became a foundation for its Branner Earth Sciences Library.

Special libraries that support corporate or commercially sponsored scientific or technological research trace their origins to the latter half of the 19th century. In the United States, although they were not numerous, there were several examples of chemical, pharmaceutical, consulting, and engineering firms with established libraries before 1900. These special libraries collected standard reference works and professional scientific and technical periodicals to support the specific interests of the company's business. During the 20th century, special libraries became an integral part of many businesses and corporations, supporting a company's research and development activities in a wide range of both basic and applied sciences.

The need for a comprehensive collection of science and technology on a regional level in the United States was expressed in 1895 with the opening of the John Crerar Library in Chicago. The purpose of this privately endowed library was specifically to support scientific and technical research and education. Similarly, the privately endowed Linda Hall Library of Science, Engineering, and Technology in Kansas City began offering regional library services in 1946 and quickly grew to a national and international resource for scientific research. Both libraries are interesting examples of the use of private philanthropy to create independent engineering and science research libraries of national and international significance. Linda Hall retains its independence to this day, but the Crerar Library became part of the University of Chicago Library in 1981, when it merged with the university's science collections.

National libraries, on the other hand, are publicly supported, and many trace their origins to the 16th and 17th centuries. Most national libraries strive for comprehensive collections to serve a general community of users, but they often provide special services for science and engineering. For example, during the 20th century the Library of Congress (Washington, D.C.) and the British Library (London) developed special departments and library services specifically devoted to the literature of science and technology. In Canada a national science library grew out of a central library established in the 1920s for the National Research Council. In 1974 it became the Canada Institute for Scientific and Technical Information (CISTI), with a mandate to promote scientific and technical research in Canada by providing access to its comprehensive special collection and information services.

All libraries, regardless of their type, engage in the costly but essential service of cataloging and classification of collections. In scientific and technical libraries, cataloging and classification often have been adapted from general library practices to assist users in gaining access to technical literature. Some libraries, for example, created classified catalogs that took advantage of the detailed subject analysis offered by the classification system used. The John Crerar Library's classified card catalog was viewed as an innovation in 1896. Cards were filed in the numerical sequence of the Universal Decimal Classification, and there were often many cross-references for one book. It was a system that permitted detailed searching by subject and did not require a search of the shelves to find books on a similar subject. Another advantage was that users of the library were already familiar with the subject classification scheme. The Department of Technology at the Carnegie Library of Pittsburgh (Pennsylvania) created this type of catalog in 1910, as did the Engineering Societies Library in 1919. Interestingly, many online public access catalogs continue this function with features that allow sophisticated searching by keyword and by classification number, as well as other options.

The electronic accessibility of scientific and technical library resources at the beginning of the 21st century has begun to change the concept of a library. Many scientists and engineers now expect to find their information resources, at least in part, in a digital library instead of a traditional library building or room. One example is PubMed Central, a National Institutes of Health initiative that began in 2000 to form a central repository of research in the life sciences. Traditional scientific or technical libraries are now shifting their focus to collecting and organizing information into a format easily accessible via a repository of network-based information resources.

BRUCE BRADLEY

See also Canada Institute for Scientific and Technical Information; Documentation and Information Center of the Chinese Academy of Sciences; Medical Libraries; Russian Academy of Sciences Library

Further Reading

Bay, Jens Christian, *The John Crerar Library, 1895–1944*, Chicago: Board of Directors of the John Crerar Library, 1945

Johnson, Elmer D., *History of Libraries in the Western World*, New York: Scarecrow Press, 1965; 4th edition, by Michael H. Harris, Metuchen, New Jersey: Scarecrow Press, 1995

Kronick, David A., *A History of Scientific and Technical Periodicals*, New York: Scarecrow Press, 1962

Krummel, D.W., *Fiat Lux, Fiat Laterbra: A Celebration of Historical Library Functions*, Urbana: University of Illinois at Urbana-Champaign, 1999

Mount, Ellis, *Ahead of Its Time: The Engineering Societies Library, 1913–80*, Hamden, Connecticut: Linnet Books, 1982

Mount, Ellis, editor, *One Hundred Years of Sci-Tech Libraries: A Brief History*, New York: Haworth Press, 1988

Thornton, John Leonard, and R.I.J. Tully, *Scientific Books, Libraries, and Collectors: A Study of Bibliography and the Book Trade in Relation to the History of Science*, London: Library Association, 1954; 4th edition, as *Thornton and Tully's Scientific Books, Libraries, and Collectors . . .* , edited by Andrew Hunter, Aldershot, Hampshire, and Brookfield, Vermont: Ashgate, 2000

South Asian Libraries

South Asia includes India, Pakistan, Bangladesh, Sri Lanka, Nepal, Bhutan, and the Maldives. It has a long and rich tradition of excellent libraries dating back to the fourth century B.C.

In India three types of libraries existed during the ancient period (3000 B.C. to A.D. 1206) These were attached to palaces/courts, centers of learning, and centers of worship. Libraries also flourished at the University of Taxila in Gandhara until the fourth century A.D. and the University of Nalanda in Bihar between the fifth and 12th centuries A.D. Nalanda University had the largest library in Asia during the ancient period. In medieval India (1206–1757) Muslims brought with them a strong literary and cultural tradition that influenced the growth and development of libraries. However, the ancient Indian library tradition remained unchanged for a long time. During the British period (1757–1947), the first contribution of the East India Company (the representative of British power) to the development of libraries was the establishment of academies, such as Calcutta Madrassa and Calcutta Sanskrit College, to which libraries were attached. Independent India (1947–) appointed various committees and commissions to improve the condition of libraries in the country. Shiyali R. Ranganathan, the father of library science in India, has played a pivotal role in the development of libraries and librarianship in this country.

Before the creation of Pakistan as a federal Islamic state (1947) out of the partition of the Indian subcontinent, Lahore (capital of Punjab at that time) served as a center of library activities because of the city's rich library resources and services. In 1915 the Punjab University started the first library course at the university level in the then British Empire, directed by Asa Don Dickinson from the United States, who had been a student of Melvil Dewey. The partition of 1947 created a major setback for the library movement in Pakistan. But the founding of the Karachi Library Association (1949) and the Pakistan Bibliographical Working Group (1950) led to noticeable changes in attitudes to library service in the mid-1950s.

Bangladesh was an area of East Pakistan prior to 1972. Before the partition of India in 1947, it was the province of East Bengal and the Sylhet district of Assam. Libraries suffered great losses during the Bangladesh war in 1971, and the young country, hindered by a lack of resources, is still struggling to rebuild its collections. A key factor in the development of libraries in Bangladesh is support from developed countries. The most sophisticated libraries in the country are those specialized collections financed partly by external sources. Modern technology is available to only a few libraries in Bangladesh. Dhaka houses the premier academic library, the National Library, and nearly all of the special libraries. Only 5 percent of the people in Bangladesh live in Dhaka, the capital, yet more than 75 percent of the library resources are there.

Libraries, research, and learning have been a part of Sri Lanka's heritage, with records that date back as far as the third century B.C. Several ancient kings encouraged the development of literature by providing royal patronage. Temple libraries contained both religious and secular works written, preserved, and maintained by the Buddhist monks. English-speaking readers during the period of British rule used subscription libraries such as the United Services Library, founded in 1813. The Colombo Library was founded in 1824. The Royal Asiatic Society of Sri Lanka Library was established in 1845. The Colombo Public Library was established in 1925 by the Colombo Municipal Council through a merger of the Colombo Library and the Pettah Library (1829).

Establishment of the Government Oriental Library in 1870 can be considered the first initiative at the national level. The Museum Library (1870), a principal state reference library with 600,000 volumes, including manuscripts, served as a legal deposit library from 1885. Sri Lanka became independent from British rule in 1948.

Nepal has also been a center of learning since ancient times, and Sanskrit education flourished in Nepal before the sixth century A.D. Nepal is believed to have been a repository of world treasures on Tantrism, philosophy, Sanskrit grammar, astrology, religion, medicine, and Vedic literature. Despite its library tradition, education and libraries could not flourish in Nepal under the autocratic Rana rule from 1846 to 1951. Books, magazines, newspapers, radio, and other media of communication and academic study were banned for the majority of people. Even expressing the need for a library was forbidden and could lead to punishment. In 1929 Laxmi Prasad Devkota (a great Nepali poet) and some of his friends were punished for their decision to establish a public library in Nepal.

Although Bhutan has been independent since time immemorial, it was considerably influenced by the British during their rule in India. The development of a comprehensive education system was initiated in 1961; prior to that only traditional monasteries had formal library collections. Today there is an extensive network of schools and other educational institutions.

Regional collaboration among these libraries is growing. The South Asian Association for Regional Co-operation (SAARC) was formed in December 1985. A regional institution, the SAARC Documentation Center (SDC) was established in New Delhi in June 1994 to serve as an effective information system, particularly in the fields of science, technology, industry, and development matters for the seven member states.

National Libraries

Separate articles on the National Library of India in Calcutta and the National Library of Pakistan in Islamabad appear elsewhere in this dictionary. In Bangladesh, the Directorate of Archives and Libraries established the Bangladesh National Library and the Bangladesh National Archives in 1972. The National Library receives books by legal deposit under the copyright ordinance of 1974. No circulation of materials is permitted. From 1973 the library published the annual *Bangladesh National Bibliography* in both English and Bangla. As the Archives of East Pakistan were housed in Lahore (in West Pakistan) after independence, the new country of Bangladesh began with virtually no official records. In the years after 1971, the Bangladesh National Archives surveyed materials from the divisional government offices around the country and trained archivists to prepare the archival materials that could be preserved.

The National Library of Sri Lanka was established in 1990 as a result of the efforts of the Sri Lanka National Library Services Board that was set up by an act of Parliament in 1970. The National Library functions as the central coordinating agency for all aspects of national and international library and information services. It has had legal deposit privileges since 1974 and is also responsible for publishing the *Sri Lanka National Bibliography*. The Department of National Archives is also a legal deposit library.

The Nepal National Library was established in 1955 after the royal government bought the private collection of the royal priest Pandit Hemraj Pandey. It is located at Pulchok, Patan, in the Kathmandu Valley. The Nepal National Archive has a long history. It began in the time of the Mala kings more than two centuries ago. The Bir Library was renamed the Nepal National Archive and has a rich collection of 65,750 manuscripts, 12,000 on palm leaves. These manuscripts were microfilmed under a joint Nepal-German manuscript preservation project.

The National Library of Bhutan was established in 1967 with the objective of collecting and preserving ancient Bhutanese and Tibetan literary and scriptural documents dealing with the religion, culture, traditions, and history of the country. It has a branch library at Kungrabten Dzong, Tongsa district, and a public library in the capital, Thimpu. The government is also making efforts to develop the National Museum at Paro, where a large collection of national archival materials is being organized.

The National Library of the Maldives was founded in 1945 and has a collection of approximately 15,000 volumes. It is located in the capital city of Male and has special collections in Dhivehi, English, Arabic, and Urdu. It also publishes the *Bibliography of Dhivehi Publications*. The library of the Institute of Islamic Studies, founded in 1985, is another significant library in the Maldives, also located in Male. It has approximately 5,000 volumes and specializes in Islamic studies and literature.

Academic Libraries

The university and college libraries are the chief academic libraries in South Asia. The real thrust in the development of academic libraries in India came after independence. The University Grants Commission (established in 1953) provides financial assistance for collections, equipment, and buildings. It also helps to formulate staffing norms and grants academic status to professional staff members. Pakistan's University Grants Commission funds libraries at all public universities.

The University of Punjab Library, Lahore (established 1906), has a rich collection of 769,000 volumes. During 1990 the 23 university libraries in Pakistan contained, together with 142 constituent libraries, 2.9 million volumes; 435 college libraries developed at a slower rate, possessing 3.6 million volumes. Six academic libraries serve Bangladesh's student community: Dhaka University (established 1921), 500,000 volumes; Rajshahi University (1953), 230,000 volumes; Bangladesh University of Engineering and Technology (1962), 87,800 volumes; Chittagong University (1966), 117,000 volumes; Mymensingh Agricultural University (1966), 123,700 volumes; and Jahangirnagar University (1970), 50,000 volumes. Most of the university libraries are laden with textbooks, and their circulation is limited to faculty and graduate students. The majority of materials are in English, with Bangla, Urdu, Arabic, and Persian comprising the remainder of these collections.

The oldest academic library in Sri Lanka, founded in 1921 as the University College Library, became the University of Ceylon Library in 1942 and was moved to Peradeniya in 1952. Currently it has one of the largest collections in the country, numbering more than 500,000 volumes. The other nine state university libraries also have significant collections, with special collections on Sri Lanka and Oriental subjects in the larger universities. Teacher training colleges, colleges of education, and technical colleges also support good libraries. There are libraries at technical institutes for medicine in Kathmandu, engineering in Patan, agriculture at Rampur, and forestry at Hetauda. Trichandra Multiple Campus Library, established in 1918, is the oldest academic library.

Nepal has two universities and two royal academies. Tribhuvan University Central Library in Kathmandu is the largest and most well organized library in the country. It was established in Kirtipur, and the whole collection of the Central Library was handed over to it in 1962. It has played a leading role in the library movement in Nepal since 1963. It functions as a national library, promoting library development at all levels, serves as a depository library for United Nations documents, and cooperates in other international activities. The library has published the *Nepalese National Bibliography* since 1981. It also issues occasional bibliographies on various topics of interest and is a member of the International Federation of Library Associations and Institutions (IFLA).

Public Libraries

Provisions for public library development in India have been included in its five-year plans since independence. The Delhi Public Library was established as a pilot project in 1951 in cooperation with the United Nations Educational, Scientific, and Cultural Organization (UNESCO). It has become a model public library for South Asian countries. To date only ten states have enacted public library laws. A fairly good infrastructure of city and district libraries exists in India, but public library services are available, by and large, to urban residents only. Nevertheless, the Raja Rammohun Roy Library Foundation (founded in 1972) and the National Literacy Mission are significant initiatives in extending public library services to the rural masses. In Pakistan, the Punjab Public Library, Lahore (founded in 1884), holds the country's third largest collection, including 215,000 volumes, with 1,200 manuscripts in Arabic, Gurmukhi, Persian, and Urdu. The Dayal Singh Trust Library (1908) houses 122,000 volumes.

There are other very good public libraries with rich collections. The oldest libraries in Pakistan are the Karachi Metropolitan City Library (1851), with 43,000 volumes and the Sandeman Public Library, Quetta (1856), with 16,700 volumes. The Bangladesh Central Public Library (BCPL), Dhaka, is the headquarters of the Public Library Department and administers the government-sponsored divisional and district public libraries. BCPL has a collection of 10,000 volumes and is the focal point of all public libraries in Bangladesh. Divisional public libraries of approximately 30,000 volumes each are located in Chittagong, Khulna, and Rajshahi. There are some 65 district libraries in Bangladesh, each with approximately 4,000 volumes. Public libraries often focus on textbooks because the majority of their patrons are students. These libraries do not allow books to circulate.

Public libraries in Sri Lanka developed from subscription libraries such as the United Services Library. As local governments are not required to maintain libraries, the quality of public library service varies greatly from region to region. The country had 580 public libraries in 1990.

In March 1966 a decision was made to open public libraries in five developing regions of Nepal and to initiate mobile service through them with the assistance of the Danish International Development Assistance Agency, UNESCO, and the Nepal National Library. The Pokhara Public Library was entrusted with the responsibility of running a mobile library in the Kaski district of Nepal as an experiment. Public libraries in Bhutan and the Maldives are virtually nonexistent.

School Libraries

In India, the states are responsible for primary and secondary schools, and the level of library facilities in these schools varies considerably. Private schools have good libraries, but government schools suffer from a paucity of required materials and trained staff. School libraries are the weakest link in the library and information infrastructure in India. The condition of school libraries in Pakistan is equally unsatisfactory. In Bangladesh, most primary schools do not have libraries, whereas some secondary schools have library facilities, with teachers serving as librarians. The school library collections range in size from 500 to 5,000 books, but most libraries are at the lower end of the scale. English, Bangla, and Urdu materials can be found in these libraries. Audiovisual materials are not available.

Despite the rapid growth of public education since independence, school libraries are less well developed than other educational facilities in Sri Lanka. There are approximately 3,700 school libraries at all levels, providing document support in Sinhala, Tamil, and English. In Nepal, most schools do not have libraries, and the few that exist cannot be called school libraries, although some foreign-aided schools have better developed library services. In Bhutan, almost all of the schools and educational institutions have modest libraries that collect materials depicting the history, culture, and religion of Bhutan and neighboring countries.

Special Libraries

Special libraries in South Asia are generally associated with scientific organizations, research institutes, and government departments and are staffed by professional librarians. Most are well organized and cover fields such as agriculture, banking, children, medicine, science and technology, and the social sciences. In India, special and research libraries received generous funds from their parent bodies. As such, a systematic network of special libraries emerged in the country. There are now approximately 1,000 special libraries in the field of science and technology. Organizations such as the Council of Scientific and Industrial Research, the Defence Research and Development Organization, the Indian Council of Medical Research, the Indian Council of Agricultural Research, the Indian Space Research Organization, the Electronics Commission, and the Atomic Energy Commission have developed good libraries. The Anthropological, Botanical, Geological, and Zoological Surveys of India (all located in Calcutta), the Tata Institute of Fundamental Research (Bombay), and the Indian Institute of Science (Bangalore) have also developed specialized libraries.

The Indian National Scientific Documentation Centre, New Delhi, was founded in 1952 with assistance from UNESCO and functions under the council of Scientific and Industrial Research with regional centers at Bangalore, Calcutta, and Chennai. Since 1977 the National Information System in Science and Technology has linked national information centers in various parts of the country and provided assistance to them. The Environment Information System, set up in 1982, has a network of ten centers in research areas such as pollution control, toxic chemicals, coastal and off-shore ecology, and occupational health. An estimated 600 social science libraries are attached to government departments, research institutes, and other organizations. The Indian Council of Social Science Research, established in the late 1960s in New Delhi as a funding agency, has helped to develop many libraries. Nearly all government ministries and departments have their own libraries. There are several large libraries specializing in various areas of the humanities.

There are more than 330 special libraries in Pakistan, holding some 2.5 million volumes, many attached to universities and colleges. Some were established in the 1800s, including the Punjab Civil Secretariat Library (1885: 60,000 volumes) and the Punjab Textbook Board Library (1892: 32,000 volumes), both in Lahore. The Hatim Alavi Memorial Braille Library in Karachi (1977) provides valuable library services for the blind. The Pakistan Scientific and Technological Centre in Islamabad was able to computerize its bibliographical services in the mid-1980s.

The libraries of the Bangladesh Agricultural Research Council (BARC) and the International Centre for Diarrheal

Disease Research are well-staffed libraries receiving resources from Western countries. BARC Library has created the National Agricultural Library and Documentation Centre, which serves as a center for the Agricultural Research Information Service and the Current Agricultural Research Information Service. Other special libraries of interest are the Bangladesh National Scientific and Technical Documentation Centre and the National Health Library and Documentation Centre.

The National Resources, Energy, and Science Authority of Sri Lanka (NARESA), chiefly responsible for science information services, operates a Science and Technology Information Centre and coordinates information networks among science and technology libraries. NARESA was established in 1981 and replaced the National Science Council of Sri Lanka.

In Nepal, there are more than 70 libraries and documentation centers in government departments, research centers, and other organizations. The library of the Agricultural Projects Services Centre serves as a National Agricultural Documentation Centre. Madan Puraskar Pustalalaya is well known for its collection on Nepali languages and literature, and Asha Saphukuth has a good collection on Newari literature.

JAGTAR SINGH

See also National Library of India; National Library of Pakistan

Further Reading

Datta, Bimal Kumar, *Libraries and Librarianship of Ancient and Medieval India,* Delhi: Atma Ram, 1970

Khurshid, Anis, "Libraries and Librarianship in Pakistan," *Libri* 21 (1971)

Khurshid, Anis, "Pakistan," in *World Encyclopedia of Library and Information Services,* edited by Robert Wedgeworth, 3rd edition, Chicago: American Library Association, 1993

Mangla, Pramod B., "India," in *World Encyclopedia of Library and Information Services,* edited by Robert Wedgeworth, 3rd edition, Chicago: American Library Association, 1993

Misra, Jogesh, *History of Libraries and Librarianship in Modern India since 1850,* Delhi: Atma Ram, 1979

Ohededara, Aditya K., *The Growth of the Library in Modern India,* Calcutta: World Press, 1966

Piyadasa, T.G., *Libraries in Sri Lanka: Their Origin and History from Ancient Times to the Present Time,* Delhi: Sri Satguru, 1985

Rahman, Afifa, "Library Development in Bangladesh," *Herald of Library Science* 36, nos. 1/2 (1997)

Singh, Jagtar, "South Asia," in *Librarianship and Information Work Worldwide,* edited by Maurice B. Line, London: Bowker Saur, 1998

Syed, Mohammad A., *Public Libraries in East Pakistan: Yesterday and Today,* Dacca: Green Book House, 1968

Taher, Mohamed, *Librarianship and Library Science in India: An Outline of Historical Perspectives,* New Delhi: Concept, 1994

Southeast Asian Libraries

Myanmar, Thailand, Malaysia, Laos, Cambodia, Vietnam, Indonesia, Singapore, Brunei Darussalam, and the Philippines fall in the region of Southeast Asia. In terms of economic growth, Malaysia is ranked highest in the region, followed by Thailand. These countries can be divided into two groups on the basis of literacy rate. The group with the higher literacy includes Thailand (93.8 percent), the Philippines (94.6 percent), Vietnam (93.7 percent), and Singapore (91.1 percent). The other group is composed Brunei Darussalam (88.2 percent), Indonesia (83.8 percent), Malaysia (83.5 percent), Myanmar (83 percent), Laos (57 percent), and Cambodia (35 percent). At present the Internet is accessible to the first group, but it is likely that other countries in this region will soon have such access as well.

These ten nations have joined together to form the Association of Southeast Asian Nations (ASEAN) for the purpose of working together to promote economic growth and cooperation in various areas, such as culture, education, technical assistance, and sports. In viewing the progress of librarianship in this region, the countries that have made the most economic progress are those that have enjoyed a long period of political stability and are actively developing their countries' information infrastructure. Malaysia, Thailand, and Singapore provide good examples. Singapore, with its IT2000 and Library 2000 policy initiatives, has been steadily forging ahead in establishing itself as an "intelligent island," but not all Southeast Asian nations are developing at the same pace. Progress in education, health, literacy, and the promotion of reading varies drastically, sometimes hampered by a nation's extensive land area, the lack of well-trained personnel, undereducated population, and/or lack of government support. Some libraries in the ASEAN region have made greater progress than other Southeast Asian countries in terms of collection development, library education, computerization, cooperative projects, manpower training, and service improvements. Newly developing countries such as Cambodia, Laos, Myanmar, and Vietnam are slowly making attempts to restore much of what was destroyed through years of war and neglect.

In line with the ASEAN concept, the library associations of Indonesia, Malaysia, the Philippines, Singapore, and Thailand, and their national libraries convened in 1970 to form the Congress of Southeast Asian Librarians (CONSAL). CONSAL holds a conference every three years in each member country by turn, promoting cooperation in the fields of librarianship, bibliography, documentation, and related activities. Library development in many of the Southeast Asian countries is hampered by lack of funds or trained personnel. Not all the countries have the same level of government backing and centralized responsibility for library development. The diversity of languages and dialects in these countries also makes communication difficult.

Historical Development

The history of Myanmar's libraries began with King Anawrahta's violent seizure of Buddhist texts from Thaton in the late 11th century. This act established Pegan as a center for Buddhism over many centuries, and monastery libraries grew around it. The collection of scriptures, in palm-leaf manuscript form, was housed in the Pitaka Taik. Libraries in Thailand can be traced back to Hor Luang during the reign of King Narai the Great of Ayuthya in the 16th century, which was an attempt to gather together all extant religious and legal works. After that there were libraries in monasteries for monks and laymen to study, especially for the study of Buddhist holy law. In 1905 the first national library was established in Thailand by royal decree under the name Vajirayana Library. This was the starting point of the National Library and other categories of libraries in the country.

The first library established in Malaysia under British rule was a small subscription library in Penang in 1817. Vietnam's earliest libraries appeared in the 11th century. They were religious in nature, including Buddhist manuscripts and Confucian prayer books. In Indonesia, Balai Pustaka, the office in charge of promoting reading among the people, began to operate mobile libraries in 1918. The libraries in other countries of the region were largely religious in nature during the ancient period.

National Libraries

There are separate entries in this dictionary for the national libraries of Thailand, Vietnam, Indonesia, and the Philippines, and thus they are not included here. The history of the National Library of Myanmar is rooted in the establishment of the Bernard Free Library on 21 February 1883, before the British annexation of Upper Myanmar. During World War II, the Bernard Free Library was severely damaged but reopened on 1 August 1948. In 1952 it was transferred to the Myanmar government and began operations as the National Library under the Ministry of Culture. It receives books and periodicals under the Press Registration Act of 1962 and has now collected more than 287,297 items, including a rich collection of 11,000 rare and valuable Myanmar manuscripts. Myanmar also has its national archives, whose holdings include the entire run of the *Burma Gazette* (1875–1925 on microfilms and 1957–67 as hard copy).

The National Library of Malaysia was established under the provisions of the National Library Act of 1972 and has been part of the Federal Department of Archives and National Library since 1966. In 1982 it was placed under the Ministry of Culture, Youth, and Sport. The National Library Act was amended in 1987 with particular reference to the objectives and functions of the National Library. The Deposit of Library Materials Act of 1986 repealed the Preservation of Books Act of 1966 and made the National Library the sole legal depository for the country. It has published the *Malaysian National Bibliography* (quarterly) since 1967, with annual cumulations.

The National Library of Laos was established in 1956 under the Ministry of Information and Culture and moved under the Ministry of Education in 1976. It functions both as the national library and a public library, with holdings of about 300,000 volumes in Lao, English, and French. Prior to the establishment of the people's republic in 1975, the National Library received aid from the French and U.S. governments, private foundations, and Western scholars. The National Library of Laos published the *Lao National Bibliography* in three volumes (1968–74).

The National Library of Cambodia opened on 24 December 1924 and was administered jointly with the National Archives of Cambodia until 1953. After independence, this joint library and archive service continued for 21 more years, first under the Kingdom of Cambodia from 1954 to 1970, and then under the Khmer Republic from 1970 to 1975. On 17 April 1975 it suffered considerable damage and loss from attacking Khmer Rouge troops and had to be closed. It reopened on 1 January 1980. It currently holds 103,635 books and 710 palm-leaf manuscripts, primarily Buddhist religious texts; these palm-leaf manuscripts also have been microfilmed.

The National Library of Singapore was established in 1958 following the passage of the Raffles Library Ordinance of 1957, under which the Raffles Library (a subscription library) became public and national. As such, it inherited the legal deposit functions that had been in force since 1886, as well as archival functions added in 1938, but the archives were separated from the library in 1967. The library is the central agency for the Singapore Integrated Library Automation Service (SILAS), a national bibliographic network with a union catalog for its participating libraries.

Dewan Bahasa dan Pustaka (Language and Literature Bureau Library) in Bandar seri Begawan was established in 1965 under the Ministry of Culture, Youth, and Sports to develop and propagate the use of Malay, the official language of Barunei Darussalam. The main objective of this library is to promote Malay language and literature.

Academic Libraries

In Myanmar, university and college libraries have developed gradually since the introduction of a new system of higher education in 1964. Although six departments under the Ministry of Education oversee these libraries, they depend upon the Department of Higher Education for support. There are 31 academic libraries under the Department of Higher Education. The most developed ones are the University Central Library (UCL) in Yangon and the university libraries in Yangon, Mandalay, Mawlamyine, Taunggyi, and Magway. UCL, which was opened in 1929 as the University of Rangoon Library, was totally destroyed during World War II. Reopened in 1952, it now has a collection of about 400,000 books and periodicals, including a research collection of rare and valuable Myanmar and English books and periodicals and 16,000 old Myanmar palm-leaf manuscripts. Myanmar's academic libraries are decentralized, and the college libraries in Bassain, Magwe, and Moulmein are somewhat smaller.

In Thailand, university libraries are major holders of documents, materials, and information in all areas. In 1975 the public, government-supported university libraries, with the support of the Ministry of University Affairs (Subcommittee on University Library Development), began formal cooperation in acquisition, processing, and interlibrary loan. Cooperation among private university and college libraries began in 1985. The Provincial University Library Network (PULINET) was set up in 1986 to share university library resources at the provincial level. This led to the creation in 1992 of THAILINET (M), or Thai Academic Library and Information Network (Metropolitan), a network of 12 university libraries in the Bangkok Metropolitan area. College libraries under the Ministry of Education have created a collaborative computerized information network for 36 college libraries throughout the country.

In Malaysia, academic libraries (particularly the university libraries) are among the most developed in terms of infrastructure and resources. There are now eight main and 14 branch university libraries and 63 institutes of higher learning libraries. The university libraries are better funded and staffed than other libraries in the country. University library collections vary considerably in size.

Before 1975 the Buddhist Institute in Vientiane was one of the most important centers of scholarship in Laos. It maintained a substantial collection of works, many in Pali and Sanskrit, for the use of its students and foreign scholars. Sisavangvong University in Vientiane is the only university in Laos. Library facilities for its faculties of medicine, law, and education were mainly provided by Western governments and foundations; these are not extensive collections for research purposes. The libraries of the university's ten institutes range in size from 800 to 4,200 volumes.

Vietnam's ancient National University Library was founded in 1078 and reorganized in 1483. It has a strong collection of monographs and textbooks produced by the wood-engraving method in Chinese and Vietnamese. Today, all universities and colleges have their own libraries. Hanoi University has a library containing about 80,000 volumes. The book collections in more than 30 university libraries and 200 research libraries total over 4 million volumes.

Most colleges and universities (and their libraries) in Indonesia are comparatively new, especially those outside Java. Only the faculty of medicine of the University of Indonesia in Jakarta and the Institute of Technology in Bandung existed before Indonesia gained its independence in 1945. Most of the nation's libraries are owned by the government. An integrated university library system is managed by the Directorate of Higher Education, which is part of the Department of Education and Culture. In September 1984 an open university system was established, promising additional responsibilities and dimensions to Indonesian academic libraries.

The University of Singapore was founded in 1949 as the University of Malaya, and Nanyang University was founded as the Chinese language institution in 1956. In 1980 the two universities merged to form the National University of Singapore. The university library has more than 2 million volumes and 20,000 current serials in six constituent libraries. Nanyang Technological University, founded as a technological institute in 1991, has more than 150,000 volumes and 2,000 serials in its library. Other academic institutions include Singapore Polytechnic, the Institute of Education, and the private Trinity Theological College. The University of the Philippines Library System, established in 1908, is the largest of the state-supported academic institutions and is the national center for the Agricultural Information System (AGRIS); the University of the Philippines Law Centre is the largest and most comprehensive law library in Southeast Asia. The University of Santo Tomas Library, founded in 1605, is the republic's oldest university library. It has one of the largest book collections in the region, consisting of 820,000 volumes and many other materials. Libraries of state colleges and universities are minimal because a large portion of their budgets is spent on wages and maintenance services.

Public Libraries

For many years after independence in 1948, public libraries in Myanmar were not fully developed owing to political instability, illiteracy, and poor economic growth. Three or four major state libraries now provide the bulk of library service to the general population in Myanmar. There are 317 public libraries under the Information and Public Relations Department, of which the Sarpay Beikman Public Library in Rangoon is the most significant, having its own publishing house and also administering the reading rooms in many villages. It has about 74,000 volumes, of which 17,670 are in English.

Public library services are being developed in Thailand. By 1990 there were 519 public libraries throughout the country. Most have small reading rooms with about 2,000 volumes belonging to the Department of Non-Formal Education in the Ministry of Education. But library budgets are too small to bring collections and services up to standard.

Public library development in Malaysia is the joint responsibility of state, federal, and local government authorities. The National Library of Malaysia plays an advisory and coordinating role in the development of public libraries in the country.

Public library service in Malaysia has improved considerably, with 13 central libraries, 127 branch libraries, 530 rural reading rooms, and 66 mobile libraries providing service throughout the country.

Prior to the Pathet Lao takeover in 1975, a number of foreign governments (including France, the United Kingdom, and the United States) operated libraries and reading rooms in Vientiane and other major towns in Laos. In Vietnam, a large network of public libraries from central to village levels was established after the eight-year (1946–54) war against the French. Of its provincial libraries, the largest are in Hanoi, Hue, and Ho Chi Minh City.

Indonesia's 27 provincial capitals have provincial libraries, and about 275 public district libraries were in operation by 1984, with more than 100 mobile libraries to serve remote areas. The provincial and public libraries are managed centrally by the Center for Library Development, in cooperation with local governments. In Singapore, the National Library operates the public library system, which includes a central library, eight full branches, six bookmobiles, and fully computerized loan services.

Public libraries in the Philippines rely almost entirely on the financial support of their respective local governments, whether city, municipal, or provincial. There were more than 500 public libraries in the mid-1980s, of which 493 were under the supervision and control of the National Library through its extension division. Bookmobiles are available in seven provinces as part of the countryside development program, but even today library services to urban and rural communities are still considered inadequate.

School Libraries

In Myanmar, every high school has its own library, and a few school libraries have collections of more than 20,000 volumes, including many textbooks. The government of Myanmar is gradually increasing financial support for high school libraries, and the condition of school libraries is apparently improving. Thailand also has libraries in every school, but their sizes vary according to the size and support of their parent bodies. Secondary school students often go to university libraries for specific information needs.

There are about 7,900 schools in Malaysia, many with their own libraries. School library collections are relatively small and do not exceed 3,000 volumes. Malaysian school libraries are managed by teacher-librarians with basic educational qualifications and some library training. National coordination and supervision is provided by the School Library Unit in the Schools Division of the Ministry of Education.

In Laos, school libraries can be found only in a few primary and secondary schools. The French lycées and the technical schools have relatively modest library facilities. The Ministry of Education supervises almost 45,000 school and college libraries. More than half of Vietnam's 10,000 secondary schools have libraries. In its primary schools, the proportion is probably lower. In Indonesia, development of the state school libraries is the responsibility of the Center for Library Development. Effective school library service is handicapped by the shortage of available teacher-librarians.

All primary and secondary schools in Singapore, including 14 junior colleges and two centralized institutes, have centralized libraries. Some also have classroom libraries. School libraries are also developing into resource centers with audiovisual resources and facilities in addition to printed materials. School library development is handicapped by a lack of trained staff. In the Philippines, school libraries and media centers, both at the secondary and elementary level, generally remain neglected despite government requirements that each school provide adequate library services to its students. Private school libraries have better resources.

Special Libraries

Special libraries in Southeast Asia are found in research institutes, government agencies, professional and trade associations, learned societies, and business firms. In Myanmar, a special library of significance is the Research Library of Buddhistic Studies, with holdings that are world renowned. The Library of the Scientific and Technological Research Department is the only up-to-date library on science and technology in the country. The Central Biomedical Library (CBL) is the most advanced automated library; it has access to MEDLINE (the U.S. National Library of Medicine's online database for medical professionals) under World Health Organization (WHO) sponsorship. CBL serves as the national focal point of WHO/SEAR (South East Asian Region) Health Literature.

In Thailand, among libraries with special resources in science and technology are those of the Division of Scientific and Technological Information; the Department of Science Service; and the Ministry of Science, Technology, and Energy. The Thai National Documentation Center supplies scientific and technical information and publishes Thai abstracts for scientific and technical research.

Special library development in Malaysia began in 1901 with the establishment of the Institute of Medical Research Library. Special libraries represent one of the faster growing library sectors in the country. There are more than 300 special libraries, although many are relatively small. About 65 percent of them have collections of fewer than 5,000 volumes. In Laos, the Directorate of Archaeology in the Ministry of Culture has developed a collection of old and historical manuscripts. Prior to 1973, the U.S. Agency for International Development also maintained collections of documents of foreign assistance to Laos.

The Vietnamese National Center for Scientific and Technological Information and Documentation was established in 1990 in Hanoi by merging the Central Institute for Scientific and Technological Information (established in 1972) and the Central Library for Science and Technology (established in 1960). The Institute for Information on the Social Sciences, founded in 1976 in Hanoi, holds about 1 million items, and the Central Institute for Medical Science Information (1979), part of the Ministry of Health, has a collection of more than 50,000 volumes and 450 periodical titles. The General Sciences Library in Ho Chi Minh City holds more than 700,000 books and 3,000 periodical titles. It can be considered the second national library of Vietnam.

In Indonesia, national documentation and information centers in biology and agriculture, science and technology, and health and medicine carry out national functions in their respective fields of specialization. Although 295 special libraries could be considered the principal innovators in and advocates of library and information services, the system still faces financial and other handicaps in making the services effective for distant users.

There are 34 special libraries attached to government departments in Singapore, primarily serving their agencies. The Department of Statistics Library is open to the general public. In addition, there are 21 libraries of statutory bodies, including the Institute of Southeast Asian Studies. Twenty-nine libraries are attached to foreign agencies such as the American Resource Center, the British Council, and the Goethe Institute.

Special libraries in the Philippines grew from 51 in 1961 to 500 by the first half of the 1980s. The National Scientific Clearinghouse and Documentation Service Division of the National Science and Technology Authority was established in 1906. Its resources consist of 26,000 books, 7,000 pamphlets, 5,000 periodical and serial titles, and 6,700 nonprint materials. The agency provides computerized information service to the science community through its National Information System for Science and Technology. Other special libraries have outstanding collections in banking, management, business, and industry, including those of the Asian Development Bank (Mandaluyong City) and the Asian Institute of Management (Makati City).

JAGTAR SINGH

See also National Library of Indonesia; National Library of Thailand; National Library of the Philippines; National Library of Vietnam

Further Reading

Chan, Thye Seng, editor, *Introduction to ASEAN Librarianship: Library Computerisation*, Singapore: ASEAN Committee on Culture and Information, 1993

Gould, Sara, and Judy Watkins, editors, *From Palm Leaves to PCs: Library Development in South East Asia*, Boston Spa, Yorkshire: International Federation of Library Associations and Institutions, Programme for Universal Availability of Publications, 1995

Hepworth, Mark, and Michael Cheng, "Librarianship and Information Work in Southeast Asia," in *Librarianship and Information Work Worldwide, 1996/97*, edited by Maurice B. Line, London and New Providence, New Jersey: Bowker-Saur, 1997

Jaafar, Shahar Banun, editor, *Introduction to ASEAN Librarianship: Special Libraries*, Kuala Lumpur: ASEAN Committee on Culture and Information, 1993

Nera, Corazon M., editor, *Introduction to ASEAN Librarianship: Academic Libraries*, Jakarta: ASEAN Committee on Culture and Information, 1993

Soekarman, and S.S. Wardaya, editors, *Introduction to ASEAN Librarianship: School Libraries*, Jakarta: ASEAN Committee on Culture and Information, 1992

Wedgeworth, Robert, editor, *ALA World Encyclopedia of Library and Information Services*, Chicago: Americal Library Association, 1980; 3rd edition, as *World Encyclopedia of Library and Information Services*, 1993

Special Libraries

Special libraries are generally defined as libraries that serve clientele with specialized information interests, united through a common purpose. Special libraries can be found in corporations, medical centers, law offices, government agencies, associations, newspaper and broadcast organizations, religious institutions, hospitals and health agencies, museums, and other entities with special information needs. Special librarians have the charge of collecting and disseminating information that will directly serve the immediate and future needs of a particular enterprise through the provision of customized information services. The mission of the special library has been and continues to be one of providing an information service with maximum convenience to the user.

In this environment, the special librarian provides the value-added information itself rather than access to that information. There is an emphasis on anticipating information needs. Acquiring and delivering information to the client in anticipation of the need is a hallmark of special library service. Typically, collection development activities focus on very specialized areas. Collection characteristics differ somewhat from public and academic collections. The library is required to collect whatever it is that the parent institution requires. These materials may include patents, training manuals, company newsletters, marketing materials, and other internal and external information. Collection formats differ significantly and may include maps, architectural drawings, videos, recordings, prototype tools, and photographs. The archiving of materials that record the history of the institution remains an important function.

Endeavors to collect in specialized areas go back hundreds of years. Long before the concept of the public library was widely accepted, the importance of collecting for particular parties in order to address specific information needs was recognized. Public libraries have maintained special collections for those employed in business and industry since the industrial revolution. Companies have collected materials for the entertainment and education of their employees. Academic libraries have designated particular collections as unique. However, in the early years of the 19th century, libraries were established to serve the employees of mercantile, factory, and mechanics establishments. By the middle of the 19th century there were approximately 1,000 special libraries in Europe and approximately 185 in North America.

The National Library of Medicine (originally known as the Armed Forces Medical Library), the world's largest repository of medical information, began as a small private collection in the early 1800s. However, the special library as we know it today did not emerge until the late 19th or early 20th century. A growing awareness of the need for information that would directly facilitate the conduct of business precipitated the formation of special libraries for business and industry. The need for librarians who could analyze, synthesize, and disseminate information became apparent.

John Cotton Dana, a librarian at the Newark (New Jersey) Public Library in the 1890s, envisioned a special library that would remove many of the constraints and restrictions mandated by tradition in the public and academic library setting. As the founder of the Special Libraries Association (SLA), he foresaw a group that would support all libraries devoted to special purposes and limited clientele. At the first meeting of the SLA Dana spoke of the special library as "the library of a modern man of affairs." Dana's efforts were driven by the perception that, owing to its unique mission and clientele, the special library was not receiving the support it needed from other library associations. The motto of SLA, "Putting knowledge to work," was based on the comment by John A. Lapp in 1916 that "Undoubtedly one of the greatest problems of the time is to put knowledge which we possess at work."

The first examples of modern special libraries in the United States may be found in legislative reference work. In the 1920s state legislatures were the benefactors of this service through provision of digests of legislation, analysis of arguments, and other services, such as access to collections of related resources. In the early decades of the 20th century, the philosophy in special libraries was generally one of acquiring resources in case they would be needed in the future. Of the 975 special libraries in the United States in 1924, many of them collected far beyond the immediate needs of their users.

In 1924 the British version of SLA was born as the Association of Special Libraries and Information Bureaux (ASLIB). As science and technology information proliferated through heightened research efforts during and after both world wars, the need for special libraries as a conduit to this new information increased. This perception, coupled with an awareness of government's increased role in the life of its citizens, motivated institutions to support resource centers. By the 1930s special libraries began to assume a proactive stance. Librarians no longer waited for clients to request information but rather acquired, analyzed, and presented information to their constituencies in anticipation of need.

In the 1940s special libraries grew at a rapid pace. The postwar years brought both opportunity and challenge. A growing awareness of the global environment led Walter Hausdorfer, librarian at the School of Business, Columbia University (New York), to assert that the citizens of the United States had become citizens of the world by virtue of World War II; thus it was the duty of special libraries to make serious attempts to facilitate the flow of information to and from libraries around the world. The issue of cost-benefit analysis arose in the context of expenses associated with information acquisition and delivery and the value of the information provided. The concept of information as a commodity was born during the postwar boom. The need to establish special libraries in small companies also led library professionals to discuss the role of the common man in the information environment.

By 1953 there were 2,489 special libraries in the United States and Canada. Scientific and technical libraries joined the cadre of business and industry, humanities, and social sciences special libraries. As the scientific and technical fields rapidly developed, a need arose for current information. In many special libraries, the collection development plan changed and budget allocations shifted. Whereas book acquisition had always received a major share of the resources budget, periodicals and journals came to be viewed as equally important to the special library client and enterprise.

In the 1960s and 1970s independent information providers known as information brokers became part of the information service environment. Although special librarians used the services of these brokers, the primary clientele for a broker was the small company that could not afford or chose not to establish a special library within its organization. Special libraries again focused on the concept of information as a commodity. There was considerable discussion about the proprietary nature of information, the role of the special librarian, and the notion that information has monetary value.

During the 1980s the concept of electronic networking and telecommunications network technology allowed special librarians to share resources with their off-site clientele, other libraries, and the world at large. In the early 1990s, as computer technology provided conduits for new information applications, special libraries seized the opportunity. Concepts such as managing knowledge, collecting information to facilitate robust competition, and providing networks of databases through intranets and extranets proliferated. Global competition necessitated acquiring information on the competitor, the regulatory environment, and the industry at large. The image of the special library as a service entity rather than as a place was born.

For example, medical library facilities serving patients, families, physicians, and medical staff could now provide remote access to information for their clients.

Special libraries in countries other than the United States and Canada have developed somewhat along the lines of special libraries in North America. Collections of materials for specialized interests in religion, law, and medicine have existed since the sixth century. Scientific societies formed during and after the 16th century accumulated collections of science-related materials in special libraries. Trade associations also developed collections of specialized materials. The Hamburg (Germany) Chamber of Commerce established the Hamburg Commercial Library in 1735 to enable scholars to access information dealing with trade and commerce, geography, and navigation. This practice also flourished during the 18th and 19th centuries and led to the creation of the Royal Astronomical Society (1825) and the Science Museum Library (1883).

Modern special libraries have proliferated in Europe since the 19th century. Patent offices acquired publications that allowed patent officials to investigate and authenticate submissions. From that beginning, the spread of special libraries across the globe has accelerated. Special libraries function in Argentina, Australia, Greece, Iceland, Macao, South Korea, the United Kingdom, Zambia, and many other countries. However, an estimate of the number of special libraries worldwide is difficult to ascertain.

The creation and maintenance of special libraries within the United States and in other countries has proceeded along similar lines. It was not uncommon for industrial libraries to develop in a rather haphazard fashion. They often were assembled from the collections of employees and departments. In many cases professional librarians were employed only when access to specific information resources within the collection became problematic owing to the lack of a standardized classification scheme and an acquisitions plan.

Special libraries around the world have organized scientific information in a comparable manner. However, some countries maintain more nationally supported special libraries, with each providing information services within a selected field. This industry-specific information may be supplied by regional information centers. It is not uncommon for European countries to support the industrial information needs of local and regional firms through centralized services supported by the public libraries within a particular geographic area.

Within the special libraries of the early 21st century, information professionals perform many roles. All efforts are directed toward support of the institutional mission. Special libraries have been in the forefront of technology advances. Among all library types they continue to lead in the adoption and utilization of emerging technologies. They create and maintain databases of internal documents and intranets that incorporate external information, compile competitive intelligence, provide Selective Dissemination of Information services, and participate on senior management teams dealing with strategic planning.

A survey of special libraries conducted by SLA in 1999 found that the number of organizations that have an intranet grew from 64 percent in 1998 to 74 percent in 1999. Intranet use allows the delivery of information to the desktop of the user. Although budgets for information products and services have actually increased, information professionals continue to struggle with the allocation of time and human resources given their new roles and responsibilities. Special libraries in the 21st century facilitate the management of knowledge and information for the clientele, the enterprise, and society.

LYNNE C. CHASE

Further Reading

Ashworth, Wilfred, editor, *Handbook of Special Librarianship and Information Work,* London: Aslib, 1955; 7th edition, edited by Alison Scammell, 1997

Jackson, Eugene B., *Special Librarianship: A New Reader,* Metuchen, New Jersey: Scarecrow Press, 1980

Kruzas, Anthony Thomas, *Business and Industrial Libraries in the United States, 1820–1940,* New York: Special Libraries Association, 1965

Lerner, Frederick, *The Story of Libraries: From the Invention of Writing to the Computer Age,* New York: Continuum, 1998

MacCormick, Austin Harbutt, *A Brief History of Libraries in American Correctional Institutions,* New York: Osborne Association, 1970

Mitchill, Alma C., editor, *Special Libraries Association: Its First Fifty Years, 1909–1959,* New York: Special Libraries Association, 1959

Sharp, Harold S., editor, *Readings in Special Librarianship,* New York: Scarecrow Press, 1963

Special Libraries 87, no. 4 (Fall 1996) (special retrospective issue)

Special Libraries Association, Information Service Panel Survey: Summary Results <www.sla.org/research/surveys.html>

Special Libraries Association, Roles and Responsibilities of Information Professionals <www.sla.org/research/isp99.html>

Women's Libraries

The topic of women's libraries is a broad one that can include libraries *about* women's issues, *for* women as patrons, consisting *of* women's writing, and developed *by* women for various clienteles. As yet, there is no consistent way to differentiate among these categories. Although traces of at least some of these institutions can be found from the beginning of libraries themselves, the general consciousness of these categories of collections and libraries relating to women's experience is a phenomenon largely of the 20th century.

Awareness of women's libraries in scholarship, at least in the United States, can be dated from two pioneering exhibits of the late 1930s that addressed women and libraries. The first was the Huntington Library's (San Marino, California) 1936 exhibit entitled "Learning for Ladies 1508–1895." This exhibit is credited with inspiring several donors to develop and donate women's collections to educational institutions; examples are the collection given to Scripps College (Claremont, California) by Ida Rust Macpherson in 1936 and the collection donated by Bertha Overbury to her alma mater, Barnard College (New York City), in 1950. The second exhibit was the New York Public Library's (NYPL) "Women in the Making of America" in 1941. Interest in this topic grew in intensity from the 1970s, coinciding with the burgeoning of the feminist movement and with the establishment of women's studies programs in academic institutions. In the United States, San Diego (California) State University's program from 1970 is sometimes cited as the first such program. A modestly produced but significant publication with an international scope from this period was Maryann Turner's *Biblioteca Femina: A Herstory of Book Collections concerning Women* (1978).

Women's Works

Libraries devoted exclusively to collecting material written by women are few in number. An early example is a private library formed by Francis John Stainforth and listed in a *Catalogue of the Extraordinary Library, Unique of Its Kind, Formed by the Late Reverend F.J. Stainforth, Consisting Entirely of Works by British and American Poetesses, and Female Dramatic Writers* (1867). Another example is the famous and influential 7,000-volume international collection of literature by women formed for the Chicago World's Exposition of 1893 and displayed in the Women's Building; it is now part of the Biblioteca Femina at Northwestern University Library (Evanston, Illinois). Also housed at Northwestern is a collection of 2,000 volumes gathered in 1933 by the International Conclave of Women Writers, which met in Chicago and exhibited the collection as a "Women's World Library." Some separate collections in larger libraries reflect an interest in women's literary output, such as the collection begun in 1938 at Randolph-Macon Women's College (Ashland, Virginia) consisting of writings by Virginia women. Access to material written by women has recently been increased through the development of Internet sites dedicated to women's writing (usually from periods no longer covered by copyright), several of which have substantial full-text offerings as well as links to full-text sites maintained elsewhere. An example is the Women Writers Project of Brown University (Providence, Rhode Island) at www.wwp.brown.edu/wwp_home.html.

Libraries Created by Women

The most complex subtopic of women's libraries is that of libraries created by women. Women took two major roles in developing libraries that served wider clienteles. First, women's social organizations founded many public libraries in the 19th century. Recent research reveals several examples, with a concentration in the state of Michigan in the United States. Second, women librarians dominated the library profession (except for major administrative posts) from the 1870s onward, especially in the United States, and these pioneering professionals largely developed the norms for libraries as we know them today. Although the feminization of the profession has been a topic of research for at least three decades, the understanding of just how the presence of women in library work affected the fundamental concepts of the institution is still in development.

One of the difficulties associated with research on women's libraries is that the language of its scholarship remains in flux. Existing catalogs often reflect a time when awareness of women's issues was undeveloped, and standard classification schema have even been characterized as frankly sexist. Ruth Dickstein, Victoria A. Mills, and Ellen J. Waite have attempted to redress this situation in their *Women in LC's Terms: A Thesaurus of Library of Congress Subject Headings Relating to Women* (1988), listing more than 3,500 terms. Many libraries using traditional cataloging and classification terminology provide advice locally to the researcher on translating older terms into newer, feminine-oriented concepts. A notable effort to establish an entirely new classification terminology is Mary Ellen S. Capek's monumental *A Women's Thesaurus: An Index of Language Used to Describe and Locate Information by and about Women* (1987).

Large Research Collections about Women

Major research libraries throughout the world hold vast amounts of material on women's issues. Access to information on their holdings can be found in their catalogs, both in print (for historical material) and online, as well as through usual library reference tools. Many of these libraries maintain research guides to material on women (e.g., the NYPL's "Women's Studies: A Research Guide," available at www.nypl.org/research/chss/grd/resguides/womint.html). In addition to the NYPL, the U.S. Library of Congress, the British Library, and the Bibliothèque nationale de France should be mentioned in this context. Many of these libraries hold extensive archival collections as well as printed resources. A useful online resource for locating archival material relating to women is the comprehensive international site maintained by the Association of College and Research Libraries Women's Studies Section: "WSSLINKS: Archival Sites for Women's Studies" (gwis2.circ.gwu.edu/˜mfpankin/archwss.htm). The researcher examining literature from the late 1930s will find reference to a World Center for Women's Archives. This project, under the direction of peace activist Rosika Schwimmer and Mary Ritter Beard among others, was aborted at the beginning of World War II owing largely to lack of funds. (Schwimmer's archive is held by the NYPL.)

A number of outstanding libraries are devoted exclusively to women's issues. The outstanding U.S. example is the Arthur and Elisabeth Schlesinger Library on the History of Women in America at Harvard University (Cambridge, Massachusetts), begun in 1943 as the Radcliffe Women's Archives when suffragist Maud Wood Park presented her Women's Rights Collection to her alma mater, Radcliffe College. The scope has since enlarged to include all phases of women's activity in the history of the United States. In 1967 it was renamed to honor the Schlesingers in recognition of their contributions to the collection and to the field of women's studies. Strengths are 19th- and 20th-century social justice activities and domestic life, including etiquette books, culinary material, and popular women's magazines. A ten-volume catalog was published in 1984, and the website is located at www.radcliffe.edu/schles.

The Sophia Smith Collection had its origins in a 1941 proposal by Herbert Davies, president of Smith College (Northampton, Massachusetts), to build a collection of the works of women writers. The collection expanded to reflect the college's goal of "giving women the best possible education" in order to enable them to function as teachers, writers, mothers, and members of society. Most material is from 1865 and after and reflects the full range of women's roles. A catalog was published in 1975, and the website at www.smith.edu/libraries/ssc/home.html includes newly acquired material.

The Gerritsen Collection of Women's History, 1543 to 1945, has an unsettled history. An outstanding source for international women's history and the feminist movement, it was begun in Europe in the late 19th century by Aletta Jacobs, the first woman physician in the Netherlands, and her husband, Carl Gerritsen, a Dutch political leader. In 1903 the cataloged collection was acquired by the John Crerar Library in Chicago, Illinois, and augmented over time, but the material was sold in 1954. Much of the collection made its way subsequently to the University of Kansas (Lawrence).

The Fawcett Library, recently renamed the National Library of Women and currently hosted by London's Guildhall University, had its origins in the decision of the Fawcett Society in 1926 to establish a library to "commemorate women's long struggle for emancipation" and to prepare women for citizenship. Several earlier collections were integrated to form this large one, including significant material on medieval religious writers. Its website is www.lgu.ac.uk/fawcett/main.htm.

An extensive Parisian library devoted to documentation on women and feminism is the Bibliothèque Marguerite Durand, begun in 1897 and bequeathed by Durand in 1931 to the city of Paris. The founder was a journalist and director of the feminist daily *La Fronde,* published from 1897 to 1902. In addition to the printed collections, there are archives of politicians, soroptimists (members of womens' civic service organizations), female clairvoyants, feminists, and many others; information is available at www.iway.fr/femmes/docs/biblioMD.html.

Amsterdam's International Information Centre and Archives for the Women's Movement, begun in 1935, is the national center of expertise in the Netherlands on women and women's studies. Especially useful for international information is its searchable database of women's information services. For the developing world, women's information centers are most often organizations that maintain pamphlet collections, publications for sale, lists of organizations, and Web-based information on current issues. These can be located via the center's website (www.iiav.nl) or through Internet search engines.

Laura X developed the Women's History Resource Center Library in 1969 as an independent agency addressing women's interests. The library was located in her home in Berkeley, California, and financed originally with a legacy from her grandfather. Beginning with a childhood collection of biographies, Laura X's wide-ranging holdings, including contributions from the first International Women's Day (which she helped to organize), increased rapidly to fill every corner of her house. Staffing and fund-raising were problematic throughout the library's short life. After a few years, the scope of collecting was reduced to hard-to-find materials such as leaflets and manifestos. The original collection was sold in the mid-1970s, after microfilming, to three separate institutions: women's serials to Northwestern University (Evanston, Illinois), health and law materials to the University of Wyoming at Laramie, and pamphlets to Princeton University (New Jersey).

Among smaller libraries and collections that document women's experience, a few stand out, largely owing to their unusual nature. Lest it be thought that all libraries on women are sympathetic to issues of women's equality, the private library of the Englishman Anthony M. Ludovici (1886–1971) must be mentioned. Collecting on women's history, sexology, natural childbirth, emancipation, and suffrage, Ludovici considered himself a staunch anti-feminist, maintaining that his views rendered him the true friend of women. His collection is now in the University of North Carolina in Greensboro.

Other specialized collections include the Bennett College collection begun in 1946, also in Greensboro, which focuses on material by and about African American women of the 18th through 20th centuries. Although many art libraries now have women's collections, the National Museum of Women in the Arts in Washington, D.C., stands out. Intending to represent the full contribution of women to the arts, the museum's library has amassed 16,000 files on women, primarily in the visual arts. Another women's library that is significant for its location, collections, and activities is the Women's Library and Information Center Foundation in Istanbul. Opened in 1990 as the first women's library and information center in Turkey, its objective is to serve as an information resource for women's studies, providing information to the press and media, and having "influence on the improvement of conditions of women in Turkey." The center hosted the first International Symposium of Women's Libraries in 1991. Its inclusion of materials supporting political activism is characteristic of the more recently established libraries-*cum*-resource centers that document women's issues, and it is a natural bridge to the next category of libraries developed principally for women's use.

Libraries Developed for Women

The results of basic research on libraries created specifically for women are just beginning to make their way into the literature of women's libraries. Scholarship exists from recent decades on women's reading tastes and practices, but the record is scant on the manner in which favored texts were stored and organized for common use. Also in short supply is research on institutions serving women who were more or less isolated from male society and whose records have survived in at least fragmentary form. Among such institutions were convents, educational institutions for women, women's reformatories and prisons, ladies' membership libraries, women's clubs, ladies' reading clubs, public libraries with ladies-only reading rooms, and libraries in women's hospitals. The literature is just beginning to include accounts of libraries for women in the non-Western world; an example of this genre are women's educational institutions in the Islamic world. Recently, gender-specific libraries and resource centers have begun to serve such loosely defined categories of female readers as teenage girls, rural women, feminists, battered women, elderly women, and lesbians. Many collections of material about women began as libraries specifically for women, but finances, legal considerations, historical developments, principles relating to gender exclusion, and changes in mission have broadened their original intended readership.

Given the paucity of historical records, some specific instances of libraries created for women offer the best information currently available on this subject. In many cases it seems reasonable to infer that more examples of each type existed, but such conjecture must be tempered by an understanding of patterns of female literacy in earlier periods. Scholars frequently surmise that male society deliberately discouraged women from learning to read for fear of their corruption, preoccupation with romance, desire for adventure and sexual excitement, wasted time on reading fiction and other light literature, and development of politically seditious attitudes. Yet there is much evidence that literature found a female audience from as early as the 15th century, albeit small and primarily among the upper classes. Books owned by male relatives were presumably available to women, with the exception of legal and professional resources that may have been kept apart from the domicile, and court documents indicate that women inherited and thus owned books even in the Middle Ages.

Among the earliest libraries for women to be mentioned in the literature are those in women's religious communities. In the seventh century, for example, St. Aldem, referring to the nuns of Barking, England, in his *Diarium Illogicum,* likened them to bees collecting everywhere material for study. As for the content of those literary hives, one can extrapolate from studies of reading that nuns collected more vernacular literature than their male counterparts, in part because nuns were less often trained in classical languages. In 1428 ten sisters from Alsace, France, arrived in St. Catherine's in Nuremberg, Germany, to introduce the reformed Dominican life. They soon began a library; records consist of two book lists from the 15th century. Some books were copied there, and some were lent to the nuns of St. Gall, Switzerland, for copying. Books were primarily donated by relatives of this upper-class order. The texts were mostly in German and consisted of prayers, sermons, meditations, and tracts. Provenance marks on books once owned by these and other convents indicate something of the nature of these collections, but this kind of evidence gathering is slow and inconclusive. The tradition of convent collecting has continued in modern times, but the libraries tend to be small and are frequently broken up or moved as their institutions change over time.

By 1750 literacy had advanced into the middle classes, and by the end of the 18th century many women were avid readers and even produced magazines dealing with women's issues, although evidence is almost absent on their more serious reading habits. The term *ladies' libraries* as used in this period referred to anthologies packaged for a female audience, sometimes serving as texts for girls schooled at home, a tradition that had its roots as least as far back as the 15th century in England. Toward the end of the 18th century, paralleling the popularity of subscription and circulating libraries for men, new libraries were created that specialized in renting books to women, with material often distributed by mail. Such libraries typically offered a narrow range of materials thought to be suitable for women, and thus women's reading was limited by de facto censorship. Women read novels voraciously during this period, even though they faced criticism for spending their time in such idle reading.

The dawn of the 19th century saw the development of many libraries for women readers. A chronology of the earliest examples from the United States indicates the rapidity of development: 1795, the Female Library of Candia, New Hampshire; 1799, the Ladies' Library of Dublin, New Hampshire; 1813, the Ladies Library of Abington, Connecticut; and in 1816, the Ladies' Literary Moral Society Library of Walpole, Massachusetts. Many others followed in rapid succession, with activity shifting from the northeastern United States to the Midwest, and Michigan in particular, by the latter part of the century.

Academic libraries for women also proliferated in the 19th century. At Oxford University (England), five women's colleges were established in the period from 1879 to 1893, and most soon developed libraries. The library of Somerville College, a women's college of Oxford, opened with great fanfare in 1904, and it set a pattern of undergraduate accommodation to be adopted only later by the university at large. Beginning from scratch, Somerville was fortunate to acquire John Stuart Mills' personal library. Girton College at Cambridge University (England), established in 1869, began collecting material for its library in 1882 and was gratified to receive copies of their works from Alfred, Lord Tennyson, John Ruskin, and George Eliot (Mary Ann Evans) and opened the Stanley Library circa 1884. During this period, the United States saw the founding of several women's colleges with high educational aspirations; early among them was Mt. Holyoke Seminary (South Hadley, Massachusetts) of 1837, which retains considerable material on the history of its library.

In 1841 the Great Falls Manufacturing Company of Somersworth, New Hampshire, developed a library primarily for the 1,500 women hired to work in cotton weaving and manufacture. Organized in a local Baptist church, the library was available to dues-paying members, of whom three-quarters were women. The factory contributed to the upkeep of the library. Sheffield, England, probably had the first women's reading room (1860) in a public library, possibly to protect women from the rough male clientele that made female readers feel uncomfortable or unsafe. In the 1880s Marianne Farningham established a library with evening meetings in Nottingham, England, for young women who worked in the shoe factory there. Many other women's libraries emerged in this period in England and the United States as well as in other Western countries. In the Netherlands, for example, the Damesleesmuseum was established in The Hague. This library and reading room, originally with 500 volumes, was established in 1894 by 12 young women from the upper circles of society and was intended to offer members the opportunity to read newspapers and books in peaceful repose.

The little evidence available on libraries serving imprisoned women suggests that these facilities have increased markedly in the last 150 years in both quality and size. In the 1840s, the matron of Sing Sing's women's section (New York) started a library stocked with history, geography, and popular works. This collection was augmented by feminist writer Margaret Fuller, who visited in 1844. In 1909 English suffragettes were denied access to prison libraries until they demanded treatment as political prisoners, and even then the materials available to them were of little interest and less use until their supporters made gifts to the prison library. Some evidence of early-20th-century libraries serving imprisoned women can be found in the archives of Anna Spicer Gladding, librarian at the Reformatory for Women for delinquent girls in Framingham, Massachusetts, from 1932 to 1974 (now at the Schlesinger Library). It is probably indicative of the inconsequential role of the library, and of Gladding's beliefs about the purpose of prisons, that she could also serve as organist and choir director, become involved in the mother-child program, serve as leader of literary and nature study clubs, and direct theatrical productions. In recent years, standards for prison libraries serving men and women have become fairly common in countries with strong library traditions; these concentrate on materials of interest to all prisoners, such as legal sources. Women prisoners, however, seem to want traditionally women's materials. At the Bedford Hills Correctional Facility in New York in the 1970s, for example, women readers showed interest in materials on diet, exercise, needlework, art, and popular reading.

Libraries serving women in the 20th and 21st centuries have tended to shape themselves to serve subgroups of women with specialized interests. In the early part of the 20th century, numerous social clubs devoted to a range of issues established or enlarged their libraries to support their own missions. Libraries that could be characterized as feminist in orientation began to appear following the social ferment of the 1960s and 1970s. English examples included the Feminist Archive in Bristol, England (1978), with a focus on international political material, and the struggling Feminist Library in London (1975), established as the Women's Research and Resources Centre. The Hypatia Library, currently on deposit at the University of Exeter, England, consists in part of the Hypatia Collection developed by collector and social historian Melissa Hardie and her husband Philip Budden. It focuses on the intellectual contributions of women in literary, artistic, and scientific spheres internationally and was intended to inspire women to emulate these notables. In Scotland the Glasgow Women's Library is a women's space that is "comfortable, welcoming and safe, where women can browse, meet for coffee and are inspired by thousands of examples of women's creative work and achievements," according to the description on its website (www.womens-library.org.uk). The Centre for Women's Health in Glasgow has developed its collections and services to focus on such women's health concerns as childbirth, domestic violence, eating disorders, lesbian health and lifestyle, menopause, all areas of emotional and mental health, menstruation, and sexual abuse. In the United States, the Catalyst Information Center (New York City), founded in 1962, houses one of the largest collections emphasizing women and work in the United States.

Medical libraries for women, an older genre with a new life, include institutions such as the Women's Hospital of Greensboro, North Carolina, which assists its intended users by offering child-care facilities for those consulting its materials. Such libraries typically provide information on medical issues of particular interest to women, such as pregnancy, childbirth, contraception, menopause, eating disorders, and osteoporosis. American public libraries, although certainly not limited to female clientele, are developing outreach collections aimed at women with medical and other special needs, such as spousal assault victims and inhabitants of retirement communities.

The literature and the Internet are just beginning to include evidence of women's libraries and resource centers addressing the needs of non-Western and developing nations, as evidenced by publications such as Helena R. Hassan's *A Small Library for the Rural Woman: A Manual* (1991). The situation in India is representative: In recent years, at least three women's organizations have established libraries and information centers for public consultation, including the Sanhita Gender Resource Center in Calcutta, the Akshara Women's Resource Center in Bombay, and the Center for Women's Development Studies in New Delhi.

Internet Sites

Internet sites of major repositories have been extensively developed for further research. Several smaller or more locally focused libraries also maintain websites of exceptional utility. Among these are the "Guide to Uncovering Women's History in Archival Collections" maintained by the University of Texas at San Antonio (www.lib.utsa.edu/Archives/links.htm), the Mable Smith Douglass Library site of Rutgers University (New Brunswick, New Jersey) (www.libraries.rutgers.edu/rul/libs/douglass_lib/douglass_lib.shtml), the site representing Duke University's (Durham, North Carolina) Sallie Bingham Center for Women's History and Culture (scriptorium.lib.duke.edu/women), and the University of Wisconsin (Madison) System's site maintained by the Women's Studies Librarian's Office (www.library.wisc.edu/libraries/WomensStudies/). One can expect to see more online journals such as *Feminist Collections: A Quarterly of Women's Studies Resources* (www.softlineweb.com/softlineweb/genderw.htm).

Virtual libraries that address women's issues, not necessarily associated with large physical collections, are proliferating on the Internet. Several represent activist organizations that maintain publishing programs; often the works cited are for sale rather than consultation through the site. Although these Internet sites are an important source of information about current initiatives on improving women's lives, very few could be considered libraries in a traditional sense. This situation may change as more full text becomes available through Internet technology. Links to these organizations can be found on many of the websites associated with women's studies programs and libraries devoted to women's issues.

DEIRDRE C. STAM

Further Reading

Capek, Mary Ellen S., *A Women's Thesaurus: An Index of Language Used to Describe and Locate Information by and about Women*, New York: Harper and Row, 1987

Carter, Sarah, and Maureen Ritchie, *Women's Studies: A Guide to Information Sources*, New York: Mansell, and Jefferson, North Carolina: McFarland, 1990

Catalogue of the Extraordinary Library, Unique of Its Kind, Formed by the Late Reverend F.J. Stainforth, Consisting Entirely of Works by British and American Poetesses, and Female Dramatic Writers, London: Davy, 1867

Dickstein, Ruth, Victoria A. Mills, and Ellen J. Waite, *Women in LC's Terms: A Thesaurus of Library of Congress Subject Headings Relating to Women*, Phoenix, Arizona: Oryx Press, 1988

Flint, Kate, *The Woman Reader, 1837–1914*, Oxford: Clarendon Press, and New York: Oxford University Press, 1993

The Gerritsen Collection of Women's History: Short Title List, Glen Rock, New Jersey: Microfilming Corporation of America, 1976

Hassan, Helena R., *A Small Library for the Rural Woman: A Manual*, Kaduna, Nigeria: Jel Publications, 1991

Jackson-Brown, Grace, *Libraries and Information Centers within Women's Studies Research Centers*, Washington, D.C.: Special Libraries Association, 1988

"Research Resources," in *W.I.S.H., the International Handbook of Women's Studies*, edited by Loulou Brown et al., New York: Harvester Wheatsheaf, 1993

Scott, Anne Firor, "Women and Libraries," *Journal of Library History* 13 (1978)

Smith, Lesley, and Jane H.M. Taylor, *Women and the Book: Assessing the Visual Evidence*, London: British Library, 1996; Toronto, Ontario, and Buffalo, New York: University of Toronto Press, 1997

Stafford, Beth, editor, *Directory of Women's Studies Programs and Library Resources*, Phoenix, Arizona: Oryx Press, 1990

Turner, Maryann, *Biblioteca Femina: A Herstory of Book Collections concerning Women*, Warrensburg, New York: Celebrating Women Productions, 1978

Women's Memory: Proceedings of the International Symposium of Women's Libraries, 8–10 October 1991, Istanbul: Metis Yayinlari, 1992

Workers' Libraries

Industrializing societies always have provided fertile ground for workers' libraries organized by employers, governments, philanthropists, radical intellectuals, or workers themselves. They first appeared in Lowlands Scotland, a region marked by early industrialization and exceptionally high literacy rates. Lead miners were served by the Leadhills Reading Society (founded in

1741 and in use until around 1940) and the Wanlockhead Miners' Library (founded in 1756). One historian has located 51 Scottish working-class libraries organized by 1822, all governed democratically and charging annual fees of six shillings or less. Informal reading societies (often based in weaving communities) were still more numerous: They were smaller and usually short-lived, but some built collections approaching 1,000 volumes.

In the 1820s mechanics' institutes began to spring up throughout the English-speaking world. They often evolved into public libraries, especially in anglophone Canada. By 1851 there were approximately 700 mechanics' institutes in Britain, though their collections averaged just under 1,000 volumes. Mechanics' institutes often alienated workingmen, who chafed at their dress codes and bans on controversial literature. They created alternative libraries such as the Lord Street Working Men's Reading Room in Carlisle, founded when 50 men collectively bought newspapers to read about the European revolutions of 1848. The Reading Room grew rapidly and moved into a new Elizabethan-style building in 1851, with congratulatory messages from Charles Dickens and Thomas Carlyle. But that grand physical plant was only constructed with middle-class assistance, and the taint of bourgeois patronage drove away readers. On their own, Carlisle workingmen organized more than 24 reading rooms between 1836 and 1854, with almost 1,400 members and a total stock of 4,000 books.

Those figures suggest that there were thousands of worker-run libraries in industrial Britain, though most were small and ephemeral. By 1878 the London Society of Compositors had a 7,000-volume collection used by a quarter of its members, who mainly read Dickens, Charles Lever, and Charles Kingsley. Of the 900 clubs belonging to the Working Men's Club and Institute Union in 1903, 500 maintained libraries with a total of 187,000 volumes. The Co-operative Movement, inspired by Robert Owen, supported libraries that outnumbered public libraries in Britain in the 1860s and 1870s. They faded away as the public library system expanded, but as late as the 1930s the Royal Arsenal branch in Woolwich had a collection of 10,000 volumes.

In South Wales, miners managed more than 100 coalfield libraries by 1934, with an average stock of 3,000 volumes. Though Marxist coal miners sometimes gained control of acquisitions, readers were mainly interested in light fiction and the English classics: The most commonly stocked novelists were Dickens, Sir Walter Scott, H. Rider Haggard, and Mrs. Henry Wood. The pride of the system was the Tredegar Workmen's Institute, which boasted an 800-seat cinema, an inexpensive concert series, and an annual circulation of 100,000 volumes.

Around 1820 the first U.S. libraries for mechanics and apprentices were established in New York City; Philadelphia, Pennsylvania; Boston, Massachusetts; Bristol, Connecticut; and Portland, Maine. Eventually most of them were superseded or swallowed up by public libraries. By the mid-1800s Massachusetts mill owners were establishing factory libraries. Later, railroads such as the Baltimore and Ohio (1884) and the New York Central (1890) began distributing traveling book boxes to their employees. Libraries were also set up by labor unions, including several branches of the Western Federation of Miners. For a time the Virginia City, Nevada, Miners' Union library was the only public library in that town and had the largest book stock in the state. In 1902 unions in Victor, Colorado, refused the "blood money" of Andrew Carnegie and maintained their own library, though it was open to the general public and partly funded by the municipal government.

Libraries were also created for immigrant laborers. The Workmen's Circle, a Jewish socialist organization, stocked Yiddish books at its branches. Polish socialists founded workers' libraries in Chicago, Illinois; Cleveland, Ohio; and Rochester, New York. In Chicago, libraries for German workers were set up by unions, socialist associations, debating groups, and *Turnverein* (gymnastic societies).

In the 1930s the library of Commonwealth College, an Arkansas residential school for workers, created one of the United States' best collections of labor literature. With an annual budget of only a few hundred dollars, it relied mainly on donations of books from individuals and institutions. During World War II the National Maritime Union circulated book boxes among merchant seamen. Their contents offered a frankly radical perspective on politics and economics, as well as fiction and mysteries.

Nineteenth-century France was far behind Britain and the United States in building a public library system. The bourgeoisie envied the relative social peace across the channel, concluding that mechanics' institutes had made British workingmen sober and respectable and that France needed something similar. From 1862 the Franklin Society (with only one workingman on its 66-member governing board) encouraged the formation of popular libraries of "instructive works." Dickens and books by Jules Verne were acceptable, but those by Honoré de Balzac and most other modern novelists were discouraged. The *Ligue de l'enseignement*, founded in 1866, persuaded some benevolent employers (largely Protestant and Alsatian) to set up factory libraries.

French authorities were suspicious of worker-run libraries, and much of what historians know about them comes from police records. In 1867 conservative Catholics tried to shut down two such libraries in St. Étienne that stocked works by Voltaire, Jean-Jacques Rousseau, Eugène Sue, François Rabelais, Joseph Ernest Renan, Louis Blanc, Charles Fourier, and Pierre-Joseph Proudhon. The controversy convulsed the Imperial Senate, where critic Charles-Augustin Sainte-Beuve defended the right to read and, for his pains, was challenged to a duel. By 1882 the *Société des amis de l'instruction* was managing 18 worker-controlled subscription libraries in and around Paris, albeit subject to the supervision of the Interior Ministry. Even the Paris library of the anarcho-syndicalist *Bourses de travail* (which stocked such subversive novelists as Balzac, Émile Zola, George Sand, and Gustave Flaubert) was subsidized and ultimately controlled by the government.

In Germany, workers' libraries first appeared during the 1848 revolution. They were subject to police harassment until the antisocialist laws lapsed in 1890. Libraries then began to multiply among local chapters of the Social Democratic Party and trade unions. In 1914, 1,147 workers' libraries throughout Germany were circulating 2.2 million volumes annually, but only six collections had more than 10,000 volumes and most had fewer than 1,000. Very few employed trained librarians, though the workers' library movement did produce its own professional journal, *Der Bibliothekar,* founded in 1909. Most of these libraries were liquidated by the Nazi regime.

At first German workers' libraries provided political and social scientific books for trade unionists and party cadres. Later they drew in average workers, but only by stocking popular fiction. Between 1891 and 1911, light fiction went from 14.6 percent to 70.4 percent of books borrowed from the Berlin Woodworkers' Association Library, and the number of social science books borrowed plummeted from 22.7 percent to 2.2 percent. The supply of socialist literature in these libraries always far exceeded reader demand. Even when *Das Kapital* was borrowed, only the first few pages appear to have been well-thumbed.

Late-19th-century Sweden had a broad national commitment to *folkbildning* (continuing education for the people). Employers, philanthropists, socialists, labor unions, evangelicals, and the temperance movement all founded workers' libraries, at least 54 of them by 1917. The Stockholm *Arbetarebibliotek,* founded in 1891, was the largest public library in the country by 1900, with approximately 20,000 loans annually from a 7,000-volume collection. Beginning in 1912, workers' study-circles received state subsidies for book purchases, and 5,500 of these circles had set up libraries by 1939. All of these institutions helped to create an educated and politically sophisticated working class. As Prime Minister Olof Palme proclaimed in 1969, "Sweden is fundamentally a study-circle democracy."

The first Russian underground workers' libraries were organized in the late 1870s. One of them scattered its collection among several workers' flats in St. Petersburg until the police shut it down. By the 1890s employers were setting up nonpolitical factory libraries. Marxists charged that the government was narcotizing the proletariat by stocking public libraries in factory districts with romances and religious tales. After the 1905 revolution, legal trade union libraries arose in which Bolsheviks tried to introduce their own propaganda and remove ideologically incorrect literature.

Vladimir I. Lenin was an admirer of the U.S. public library system, and his wife Nadezhda Krupskaya was the driving force behind the Soviet library movement. Soon after the 1917 Revolution, Bolsheviks began relocating public libraries to working-class districts and purging their contents. Mobile libraries distributed books from central repositories to factories, workplace cafeterias, and workers' housing. Krupskaya set up railway car libraries for railway workers and peasants living along the lines. By 1929 9,226 trade union libraries were serving 2.3 million registered readers, though most were white-collar employees. The manual laborers who used these libraries generally preferred the old Russian classics to the new literature of socialism.

In the 1880s radical libraries for Jewish workers began to emerge in Russia. At first they were mainly clandestine and stocked only Russian literature, but toward 1900 some of them had acquired legal status and growing Yiddish collections.

In late-19th-century Poland, libraries were established in factories, either legally by employers or illegally by socialists. After World War I, an independent Poland created an impressive network of workers' libraries, but their collections were almost entirely destroyed during the Nazi occupation: 98 percent losses at the Lodz Electric Power Plant Library, 88 percent at the Knurow Mine Library, 95 percent at the Union of Foresters in Siedlce, and 100 percent at the Poznan Town Employees Library.

Jewish workers' libraries proliferated in interwar Poland, many of them (264 by 1939) sponsored by the Bund, the General Jewish Workers Union. Bund libraries were usually small and managed by untrained part-timers. A 1930s survey found that they averaged 155 readers and collections of approximately 1,250 volumes. Their book stock was 61.2 percent Yiddish, 17.0 percent Polish, and 5.3 percent Hebrew. Other Jewish socialist parties, trade unions, and even the Palestine-based Histadrut labor federation sponsored competing libraries, a reflection of the intellectual vitality and political fractiousness of Poland's Jewish community. The Bund-managed Bronislaw Grosser Library was the largest Jewish library in Warsaw, with a total of 30,000 volumes and the city's finest social science collection. Led by the legendary Herman Kruk, it introduced the apparatus of modern librarianship, including a Jewish decimal catalog system, a readers' adviser, bibliographic guidance for borrowers, and reading promotion campaigns in the press.

After the conquest of Poland in September 1939, most of these libraries were shut down, looted, or destroyed by Nazis or Soviets during the occupation. A few remained open only after politically suspect literature had been purged from their collections, and a few others operated illegally. By 1942 the Vilna Ghetto Library, directed by Kruk, managed to set up branch libraries at fur factories and lumber camps, though their readers would soon be exterminated.

The first libraries for Jewish workers in Palestine were set up in Rehovot (1891) and Petah-Tikvah (c. 1904). Established by emerging socialist parties and unions, such libraries became important cultural centers for laborers in small and underdeveloped Jewish communities. By 1935 the Histadrut had a central library of more than 15,000 volumes, as well as 125 branch libraries in kibbutzim, agricultural settlements, and towns.

Anarchists, who believed that self-education would emancipate the working classes, maintained People's Libraries in Argentina. In 1902 they founded the *Ateneo enciclopédico popular* in Barcelona, which sponsored classes, lectures, athletic activities, and field trips as well as a library. The only public libraries in many small towns in Spain were anarchist libraries, until they were suppressed by the Franco regime. In 1906 Jewish anarchists opened the *Arbeter Fraint* Club and Institute in London's East End, with an 800-seat hall, a free library, adult courses, lectures, concerts, and theatricals, including a Yiddish version of Henrik Ibsen's *Ghosts.*

Employee libraries were set up in the United States by Ford, Goodyear, and the National Cash Register Company. In Britain some were opened by paternalist manufacturers such as Cadbury (cocoa) and Lever (soap). Workplace libraries were also common at smaller firms such as the Loveclough Printworks, where Dickens accounted for 10 percent of all loans in 1892 and 1893.

Though socialists denounced employer-sponsored libraries, they were often well used, and some were far superior to anything workers could organize on their own. One reader compared the Great Western Railway Mechanics' Institute Library in Swindon, England, which boasted more than 20,000 volumes in the late 1880s, to a luxurious London club. A library expert proclaimed that the vast Krupp steelworks in Essen maintained Germany's best free public library: In 1909 it had 61,500 volumes and was patronized by nearly half the work force, which borrowed approximately 519,000 books. In Australia the New South Wales Railway Institute Library was clearly designed to produce obedient employees who would study technical literature rather than engage in labor agitation. But it was also one of the finest libraries in the country, at one time operating on a larger budget than the University of Sydney Library. By 1929 it had 48 branches and 46 smaller workplace collections, with a total of nearly 920,000 loans annually, reportedly the largest circulation of any Australian library.

More recently, workers' libraries have fallen victim to the decline of smokestack industries, the implosion of Communism, the spread of competing public libraries, and the rise of mass entertainment. The last British co-operative library (in Barnsley) folded in 1971, and only two Welsh miners' libraries survived to the end of the 20th century. As late as 1985 there were 7,916 trade union and workplace libraries in Poland, but most succumbed to the economic and political crises of the late 1980s and the subsequent collapse of the Communist regime.

China offers a dramatic illustration of the rise and fall of workers' libraries. The first such collection was founded in 1921 at the Changxindian Workers' Club in Beijing. (In Chinese the term *worker* includes white-collar and blue-collar employees.) The Communist Party sponsored secret factory libraries during the war with Japan and the civil war that followed. After the proclamation of the People's Republic in 1949, trade unions created thousands of new libraries, but their collections were destroyed or expropriated during the Cultural Revolution of 1966 to 1976. After 1978 the more pragmatic regime of Deng Xiaoping, committed to modernization, realized that Chinese workers had to make up the educational losses suffered during the Cultural Revolution. It therefore promoted the rapid recovery of trade union libraries, which emphasized technical instruction over political indoctrination.

In 1988 China had 246,901 workers' libraries, but there were only 93,388 by 1997. In a sense they were victims of Deng's success and China's new free-market economy. Today, profit-oriented factory managers and party officials see such libraries as a financial loss, to be cut back or eliminated entirely. And many of their readers have abandoned them for new forms of entertainment, particularly cinemas, discos, videocassette recorders, and private bookstalls that stock pornography.

JONATHAN ROSE

Further Reading

Ellis, Richard D., "Trade Union Libraries in the People's Republic of China," *Library Quarterly* 69 (1999)

Everitt, Jean, "Co-operative Society Libraries," *Library History* 15 (May 1999)

Graham, Brian T., *Nineteenth-Century Self-Help in Education: Mutual Improvement Societies,* vol. 2, *Case Study: The Carlisle Working Men's Reading Rooms,* Nottingham: Department of Adult Education, University of Nottingham, 1983

Langewiesche, Dieter, and Klaus Schönhoven, "Arbeiterbibliotheken und Arbeiterlektüre im Wilhelminischen Deutschland," *Archiv für Sozialgeschichte* 16 (1976)

Lyons, Martyn, *Readers and Society in Nineteenth-Century France: Workers, Women, Peasants,* London and New York: Palgrave, 2001

Raymond, Boris, *Krupskaia and Soviet Russian Librarianship, 1917–1939,* Metuchen, New Jersey: Scarecrow, 1979

Rose, Jonathan, *The Intellectual Life of the British Working Classes,* New Haven, Connecticut: Yale University Press, 2001

Schidorsky, Dov, "The Origins of Jewish Workers' Libraries in Palestine, 1880–1920," *Libraries and Culture* 23 (1988)

Shavit, David, *Hunger for the Printed Word: Books and Libraries in the Jewish Ghettos of Nazi-Occupied Europe,* Jefferson, North Carolina: McFarland, 1997

Steinberg, Hans-Josef, "Workers' Libraries in Germany before 1914," *History Workshop* 1 (Spring 1976)

Torstennson, Magnus, "Expectations and a Worthy, Respectable Position in Society: Means and Aims of Library Work within the Early Labour Movement in Sweden," *Svensk biblioteksforskning/* (Swedish Library Research) 1 (1995)

LIBRARIES

Ambrosiana Library

Address: Biblioteca Ambrosiana
Piazza Pio XI, 2
00123 Milan
Italy
Telephone: 2-80692-1
Fax: 2-80692-210
www.ambrosiana.it

Founded: 1609

Holdings (1999): Volumes: 400,000. Current serials: 140; documents on parchment: 12,000; engravings: 30,000; films: 3,000; graphic materials: 10,000; incunabula: 2,300; manuscripts: 45,000; microfilms: 15,000.

Special Collections: *Areas of Concentration:* European history from the 16th century onward. *Individual Collections:* Arab collection; Bobbio and Penelli libraries; Leonardo collection. *Papers:* Lodovico Ariosto; Cesare Beccaria; Cesare Cantú; Galileo Galilei; Alessandro Manzoni; Giuseppe Parini; Torquato Tasso.

The Ambrosiana Library of Milan, an autonomous institution entrusted to the Roman Catholic Church, was among those saved from the Napoleonic suppressions of the late 1790s, assuring the survival of one of the great libraries of the 17th century. It was founded in 1609 by Cardinal Federigo Borromeo. Born in 1564, Borromeo belonged to a Milanese family of great lineage and was barely 23 when elected cardinal in 1587. His illustrious family included St. Carlo Borromeo, also a cardinal, who was Federigo's cousin. Of a vivacious intelligence and very widely read, Federigo Borromeo's interests extended to the cultures of Asia, Egypt, and Africa, and a lively curiosity pushed him to the study of natural phenomena and the most diverse types of humanity. In Rome he had the opportunity to learn from Cardinals Cesare Baronio and Agostino Valier and to realize that the papacy's defense against the attacks of the Reformation needed to be founded on a solid cultural base. Having returned to Milan in 1601 as archbishop, Borromeo conceived the idea of creating a new library as an active center of Catholic culture, as well as the pride and glory of his home city. This was during the period when Thomas Bodley was constructing his great library at Oxford, England, and clearly Borromeo imagined an analogous institution, though of opposing religions.

The building was constructed according to his plans. The reading room on the ground floor was illuminated by two huge windows placed more than 30 feet from the floor so as to leave ample space for the walnut bookshelves inspired by those of the library of the monastery of El Escorial near Madrid (built by King Philip II of Spain in 1563). This hall, heavily damaged by World War II, has recently been restored; it once contained the 15,000 manuscripts and 30,000 printed books that Borromeo procured (now they are kept in other rooms).

The collection was built by Borromeo according to a precise project. Above all, he wanted Greek codices. One of his emissaries, Antonio Salmazio, spent a year at Corfu in search of manuscripts; other volumes were acquired in Chios and in Venice. In all, the Greek codices amounted to 1,000. Borromeo also sought out Oriental codices and procured more than 300 of these in Arabic, Persian, and Turkish. A learned Hebrew convert, Domenico Gerolimitano, obtained manuscripts for him in Hebrew. His librarian, Antonio Olgiati, future first prefect of the Ambrosiana, was sent in search of works to purchase in France, Germany, and the Netherlands. Francesco Bernardino Ferrari, himself a later prefect of the Ambrosiana, went through Spain on the same mission.

The two most extraordinary discoveries were made in Italy, especially the acquisition of a good part of the library of the Bobbio Monastery near Piacenza in Lombardy. Founded by the Irish monk Colombanus in 612, Bobbio had been one of the great centers of culture before Charlemagne and still preserved many codices produced in those years. Borromeo obtained 76 of them, including two written in Ireland. Between 1811 and 1815, the young scholar Angelo Mai, admitted to the Ambrosiana as a writer with a modest stipend, made sensational discoveries about some of these works. The ancient monks had scratched (i.e., erased) the parchment surface of older codices in order to transcribe different works on the now-blank pages. Beneath the *Paschale Carmen* of Sedulius appeared unknown writings by Cicero; beneath the Acts of the Council of Calcedon lay works by Pliny, Fronton, and Symmachus, and a tract addressed to the Gothic followers of the heresy of Arius. Later, unknown fragments of the *Vidularia* of Plautus emerged, and in 1817 pages from the four Gospels translated into the Gothic language by the Arian Bishop Wulfila in the sixth century were discovered, a monument without parallel in the history of Germanic languages.

In order to expose the earlier writings, Mai was authorized to use chemical agents. Unfortunately, in some cases the effect was destructive and the damage irreparable. But the resonance of the discoveries was great, and it became even greater when the famous young poet Giacomo Leopardi in 1820 dedicated an ode to Mai. By this time Mai had been transferred to the Vatican Library, where he had discovered Cicero's *De republica*. He eventually became a cardinal.

The other great acquisition effected by Borromeo was the library of Gian Vincenzo Pinelli. A Genovese, Pinelli had established his residence in Padua; from there he corresponded with scholars around the world, collecting rare codices, mainly from the rich market of Venice. Upon his death in 1601, his nephew, Cosmo Pinelli, duke of Acerenza, then grand chancellor to the kingdom of Naples, became his heir. Before the library left for Naples, the republic of Venice kept in its own archives approximately 200 codices deemed of political interest; the rest were loaded upon three different ships in Venice, in order to lessen the risk of loss. It was a wise precaution, as one of the galleys was captured by Barbaresque pirates who threw part of the collection of manuscripts into the sea, considering them worthless; some pages were traced, having wound up in the nets of fishermen. The galley was shipwrecked a short while later near Ancona, and it was possible to recover only 22 of the 33 cases on the beach. The other two ships arrived in Naples unharmed.

In June of 1608, the widow of the heir of Gian Vincenzo Pinelli placed the entire library at auction. Through his emissary, Grazio Maria Grazi, Borromeo was able to buy this extraordinary collection for a good price. There were some 200 Greek codices, including the celebrated Ambrosian *Iliad* (51 folios with 58 miniatures from the fifth or sixth century). Even in its incomplete state, the manuscript, perhaps executed at Alexandria, is a rare testimony to the art of book production in the later Roman Age. Only four illustrated secular codices survive from that period: the two Vatican manuscripts of Virgil, Dioscorides' *De materia medica* now in Vienna, and, of course, the *Iliad* of Pinelli. Among the nearly 300 Latin codices are one Horace of the tenth century and one Plautus of the 12th century. (A celebrated Terence of the Ambrosiana, executed circa A.D. 900 at Reims and richly illustrated, is of unknown provenance.) In the collection are various manuscripts previously belonging to Pietro Bembo—Petrarchan poet, refined man of letters, great collector, and eventually a cardinal. Among these manuscripts were love letters between Bembo and an extremely uncommon lady, Lucrezia Borgia (daughter of Pope Alexander VI and sister of the famous Cesare), who was at the time the letters were written the wife of Marquis Alfonso d'Este of Ferrara (her third husband). At the end of the codex, a thin parchment, folded and closed by four ribbons, contains a lock of blond hair, romantic testimony of a secret love which moved Lord Byron to tears in 1816.

Another important acquisition is owed to Grazio Maria Grazi: the Virgil belonging to Petrarch, with the poet's handwritten commentary mentioning the death of Laura. The codex is illuminated by the great Sienese artist, Simone Martini.

In 1609 the library was solemnly inaugurated. Instead of giving it his name or that of his family, the cardinal wished to call it Ambrosiana after the patron saint of Milan, Bishop Ambrose, antagonist of Emperor Theodosius in the fourth century. The library has functioned continuously until the present day, always maintaining its essential characteristic of accessibility. Even in the 17th century, during which it was difficult and sometimes impossible to inspect or examine the manuscripts of the best libraries, one could enter and study there without difficulty. This was true even for foreigners, who tended to encounter great difficulty elsewhere in Italy and on the continent.

According to Gabriel Naudé, the celebrated author of the *Advis pour dresser une bibliothèque* (1627), the Bodleian of Oxford, the Angelica of Rome, and the Ambrosiana were the most accessible libraries in Europe. To the Ambrosiana he dedicated the greatest praise for the great comfort it offered in reading, studying, and copying and the assistance of a librarian and three attendants. Later scholars complained of obstacles that made study difficult: numerous holiday closings, limited hours, and lack of good catalogs. These defects were remedied in the 20th century.

By the will of the founder, the administration of the Ambrosiana was given to a congregation of six conservators, as well as a senior member of the Borromeo family. The scientific activity of the library was delegated to the college of doctors, composed of nine members, later reduced to five. These doctors were assigned to assist scholars, to keep the library in order, and within three years of appointment to publish works demonstrating their competence and application. The prefect was appointed to coordinate the whole. This structure is still in use. Formerly elected by the doctors, the prefect is now appointed by the archbishop of Milan, who must consult with the conservators and doctors about appointments. Among past doctors of the Ambrosiana are several distinguished figures: the historian Ludovico Antonio Muratori (active in Milan from 1695 to 1700); Angelo Mai; and in the 20th century Achille Ratti (who became Pope Pius XI) and Giovanni Mercati (who became a cardinal).

Adjacent to the library the generous Borromeo wished to have an academy where the young might study art and painting. Between 1611 and 1620 a suitable building was constructed and adorned by various works of art, among them some by Raphael. One of these is the cartoon of the famous painting, "The School of Athens." The academy closed in 1776, but the picture gallery remains, today holding masterworks by Leonardo da Vinci, Botticelli, Luini, and Caravaggio.

In 1751 the Ambrosiana Library received as a gift the scientific museum of medical doctor Manfredo Settala, which he had formed during the 17th century. Of the many other important collections at the Ambrosiana, two deserve note: the Leonardo collection and the Arab collection. The first consists of 12 manuscripts in the hand of Leonardo da Vinci, donated in 1637 by the Marquis Galeazzo Arconati. Among these is the Codex Atlanticus, containing 1,750 technical/scientific designs of consummate artistry. The Arab collection is, after that of the Vatican, the best in Italy. It contains 2,200 manuscripts (the Vatican has 3,000). The 1,600 manuscripts collected by Giuseppe Caprotti (a late–19th-century Italian merchant who lived in Yemen) were added to Borromeo's acquisitions in the 20th century. In 1920 the Arab scholar Eugenio Griffini left to the Ambrosiana 50 codices that he had collected in Tunisia and Algeria. Another 180 codices were given in 1914 by the famous architect Luca Beltrami. Some Ambrosiana pieces are extremely rare or unique, such as an apocryphal Gospel of St. John of 1342, a book of sermons of the ninth to tenth century, and various texts relative to the exact, natural, and occult sciences.

Today the library maintains an attractive website through which some of its catalogs are available, as well as a schedule of hours and closings. Since 1976 the Accademia di San Carlo, a network of scholars throughout the world, has been a part of the Ambrosiana. It covers many fields of research but concentrates on history from the 16th century onward. The Ambrosiana has published a collection of studies on the sources of Lombard history called "Fontes Ambrosiani" since 1929, and other publications as well.

MARINO ZORZI

Further Reading

Codex: I tesori della Biblioteca Ambrosiana *(exhib. cat.)*, *Milan: Rizzoli, 2000*

Hobson, Anthony, *Great Libraries,* London: Weidenfeld and Nicolson, and New York: Putnam, 1970

Paredi, Angelo, *Storia dell'Ambrosiana,* Vicenza, Italy: Neri Pozza, 1981; as *A History of the Ambrosiana,* translated by Constance McInerny and Ralph McInerny, Notre Dame, Indiana: University of Notre Dame Press, 1983

American Academy in Rome Library

Address:	American Academy in Rome Library Via Angelo Masina, 5 00153 Rome Italy Telephone: 6-58461 Fax: 6-5810788 www.aarome.org/library.htm
Founded:	1894
Holdings (1999):	Volumes: 125,000. Current serials: 600; music scores: 4,000; photographs: 60,000.
Special Collections:	*Areas of Concentration:* Ancient art and archaeology; Greek and Latin literature; history of art and architecture, especially Italian; medieval and modern Italian history; music. *Individual Photographic Collections:* Askew collection; Bini collection; fellows' work collection; Masson collection; Moscioni collection; Parker collection; Van Deman collection. *Papers:* Eugene Berman; Frank Brown; Lucy Shoe Meritt; Gisela Richter; Gorham P. Stevens; Oliver Strunk; Albert Van Buren; Esther Van Deman.

The American Academy in Rome (AAR) began in 1894 as the American School of Architecture. During the intense period of creativity and collaboration that created the World's Columbian Exposition (Chicago, 1893), architect Charles Follen McKim conceived the idea of sending young U.S. architects abroad to perfect their education and to maintain a high level of design in the beaux-arts tradition. The first director of the school was Austin Lord (1894–96), and its first home was in the Palazzo Torlonia near the Spanish steps, fitted out with makeshift drafting boards. "A hallway recess accommodated the Library," wrote student Harold Van Buren Magonigle, "which consisted of a single copy of Middleton." This was probably John Henry Middleton's *Remains of Ancient Rome* (1892), in keeping with McKim's intention that the young architects draw their inspiration from classical antiquity. By February 1895 Magonigle was able to say, "We have the beginnings of a good library and Mr. Lord is adding to it all the time, besides the best casts that we can find."

More significant for the future direction of the library was the founding of the American School of Classical Studies in Rome a year later (1895). For one year, the two schools shared joint quarters in the Villa Aurora on the Pincio and discussed a merger under the name "American Academy in Rome," but relations broke down and the classicists moved out, taking their library with them. They settled first in the Villa Cheremetoff (Via Gaeta, 2) and later, in 1901, in the Villa Bonghi (Via Vicenza, 5). The architectural school, now including painters and sculptors, changed its name to the American Academy in Rome in 1897 and moved to the Villa Mirafiori (on the Via Nomentana) in 1906.

The classicists' library, established with a gift of $3,000 from Edwin D. Morgan, grew rapidly. In 1904–05 it received an especially valuable deposit of books on art history from Edward G. Brandegee and his wife. By the time the two schools finally merged in 1913 and moved into a splendid new building designed by McKim, Mead and White on the Janiculum Hill, it was the classicists' library (more than 8,800 volumes) that was installed in the handsome new vaulted wood-paneled library. The architects' library was relegated to a smaller room off the library entrance. The southwest reading room was used for the collection of almost 6,000 photographs.

The merger of the two institutions took the form of two new divisions: the "School of Classical Studies" for the scholars and the "School of Fine Arts" for the creative artists. The subsequent history of the academy is very much a story of the creative dynamics between these two entities, whether in collaboration or in competition, but in the library, the needs of the scholars usually prevailed.

The librarian at the time of the merger was Albert van Buren (1908–25), an archaeologist and graduate of the School of Classical Studies. Stanley Lothrop, assistant librarian, was responsible for the collections of medieval and Renaissance art history. The two librarians devised a new decimal classification scheme, published as a pamphlet entitled "Classification of the Library" in 1915 and still in use today. In its introduction, the library's collection policy is stated optimistically as the collection of "everything that has to do with the history of human life in Italy from the earliest times, and also with the history of human life in other countries in so far as that may be expected to throw light on Italian civilization." In his annual "Report of the Librarian" for 1911–12, Van Buren had expounded his belief that "a library should be more than a depository of books. It should be a laboratory . . . the contents of which should become as familiar to the scholar as are the furniture and fittings of his own house." Indeed, the design of the new library, while drawing some features from the Piccolomini library in Siena, had more in common with the library of a typical gentlemen's club in the United States. Three separate entrances ensured easy accessibility, and open shelves, comfortable alcoves, and abundant light created an ideal environment for study.

By 1920 the book collections had already outgrown the main reading room and overflowed into the first of several underground stacks. The photograph room had become a periodical room, and the arrival of the first fellows in musical composition led to the founding of a music collection, beginning with a gift of scores by Kate Freeman Carter, widow of academy director Jesse Benedict Carter. Other benefactors to the collections in the library's first quarter-century included William Wetmore Story, J. Pierpont Morgan Jr., Thomas Spencer Jerome, Eleanor de Graff Cuyler, Elihu Vedder, and William H. Herriman.

The library entered a new phase in 1926 with the resignation of Albert Van Buren as librarian (although he continued to serve as professor of archaeology until his retirement in 1946 and to work in the library until his death in 1968). His successor in 1926 was Milton Lord, who remained until 1930. Lord brought technological innovation to the library: the use of Library of Congress (LC) catalog cards and subject entries (although not the LC classification system) and the adoption of standard printed forms for book orders and periodicals check-in. In his four years at the academy, Lord also introduced a simple system of reserving books on tables, established a reference desk, improved signage, and gave orientation tours to fellows. The new card catalog was used as an index for periodicals as well as books, and a new "purchase list" recorded the locations of copies of desiderata in other Roman libraries. A balcony was built in the periodical room to bring all the periodicals together for the first time. Lord carried out the first systematic evaluation of the book collections in comparison with published standards. Not satisfied with revolutionizing the American Academy Library, he also took part in the effort to modernize the Vatican Library's catalog under the auspices of the Carnegie Endowment for International Peace. (Lord later served as librarian of the Boston Public Library and returned to the academy in 1971 and 1975 as librarian in residence.)

The collections were enriched during the 1920s and 1930s by gifts of significant personal libraries, including those of Professor Moses Stephen Slaughter, Edwin Collins Frost, H. de Nancrède, Samuel A.B. Abbott, and Esther Van Deman. Two major grants from the Carnegie Corporation in the 1930s permitted the librarians to focus once again on the collections, with the aid of such eminent scholars as Michael Rostovtzeff and Lily Ross Taylor (in Roman history) and Charles Rufus Morey and John Walker III (in the fine arts). Back runs of periodicals and monographic series were filled in and new subscriptions added, and volumes of collected essays were acquired and indexed. The library participated in a collaborative bibliography of Roman studies, under the direction of the Istituto di Studi Romani.

The academy and its library were closed during World War II. When Italy declared war on the United States in 1941, AAR properties were placed under the protection of the Swiss Legation. Four academy staff members remained at their posts, including Albert Van Buren and the acting librarian, Peter de Daehn (1940–61). In his obituary of Van Buren, Frank Brown (director of the AAR) called him "an unforgettable symbol of quiet but unbending resistance to barbarism as he daily made his courteous way on foot across the city from Via Lombardia to the Janiculum."

The postwar years brought new fellowships, expanded activities, and longer hours for the library. In 1961 an association of Friends of the Library was founded in New York by Lily Ross Taylor and Josephine Dodge Kimball, to help offset the rising cost of books and periodicals. Despite their efforts, the library, like many of its counterparts in the United States, lost significant purchasing power in the late 1960s and 1970s. A section in Rome of the Friends of the Library was initiated in 1971–72.

Major gifts to the library in the late 20th century included books from the personal libraries of Gisela Richter, art historian and curator; Eugene Berman, painter and stage designer; Oliver Strunk, musicologist; Frank Brown, archaeologist; and Richard Krautheimer, art historian. In 1991 the library was renovated as part of the general renovation of the McKim, Mead and White building, a project completed for the academy's centennial in 1994. The main reading room, the traditional heart of the library, was rededicated as the Arthur Ross Reading Room.

From its earliest years, the library had extended reading privileges to Italian and foreign scholars resident in Rome, whereas the academy fellows had enjoyed similar privileges in Italian state libraries, the Vatican Library, and the libraries of other foreign academies and institutes. Under the auspices of the Unione Internazionale degli Istituti di Archeologia, Storia e Storia dell'Arte in Roma, a union list of periodicals was published in 1975 and revised in 1985. Only at the end of the 1980s, with the advent of the first computers in Roman libraries, did serious planning begin for a collaborative database on a larger scale. The result was the Unione Romana Biblioteche Scientifiche (URBS), a consortium formed by the academy and four other libraries in 1992. URBS now comprises 16 members and a database of approximately 900,000 records that is maintained at the Vatican Library. In the mid-1990s the academy converted almost its entire catalog, including back holdings, into the new URBS database. The academy also joined the Research Libraries Group as a special member in 1993.

The study collection of photographs, part of the library since the early 20th century, was enriched periodically over the years by the donation or purchase of special collections. These include photos taken by or for John Henry Parker (late 19th-century images of Roman antiquities), Romualdo Moscioni (Etruscan art and monuments), H. Ess Askew (Arch of Septimius Severus); Esther Van Deman (Roman architecture), and Georgina Masson (Italian gardens). In addition, the photographic record of fellows' works (individual and collaborative projects at the academy) became part of the library collections circa 1932. In 1956 the academy agreed to house the collection of more than 3,000 photographs of Roman topography and antiquities donated by Ernest Nash to the Unione Internazionale degli Istituti di Archeologia, Storia e Storia dell'Arte in Roma. This collection became known as the Fototeca Unione. Laurance Roberts, the academy's director at the time, wrote in his quinquennial report, "This collection has taken the place of the old commercial collections which are now out of date and are not being increased, and is already of great use to scholars, editors and authors of archaeology books." Under the leadership of Karin Einaudi (1974–96), who became its director after Nash's death, the Fototeca Unione grew to more than 30,000 photos and was published in microfiche form. In 1996 the Fototeca Unione and the various historical collections housed in the library were brought together in a new photographic archive, under the auspices of the library but with its own staff. New efforts were undertaken to preserve the older collections and to catalog them into the URBS database. In 2001 the photographic archive was installed in a new home, a former garden house redesigned by architects Cinzia Abbate and Carlo Vigevano.

The year 1996 marked the opening of the Barbara Goldsmith Rare Book Room, designed by Michael Graves. The new room provided an elegant solution to the long-standing problem of protecting rare and fragile volumes in an open-stack collection that had been chronically cramped for space. Thirty years earlier, with the donation of rare books on art and architecture from the collection of Lewis Einstein, as well as funds for housing them, a special cage had been constructed for the library's rarest volumes, but by the 1990s this area had itself become overcrowded and difficult to use. The Barbara Goldsmith Rare Book Room, in contrast, offers ideal climate-controlled storage conditions and ample reading space.

As the AAR faced the third millennium, a new space planning effort was begun in 1998, as the library had once again outgrown its quarters. For a quintessential humanities collection with a disproportionate number of large, illustrated volumes, the prospects of off-site storage and digitization (although not unwelcome) imply changes in research methods and in the basic nature of the library itself.

CHRISTINA HUEMER

Further Reading

Valentine, Lucia N., and Alan Chester Valentine, *The American Academy in Rome: 1894–1969*, Charlottesville: University Press of Virginia, 1973

American Antiquarian Society

Address: American Antiquarian Society
185 Salisbury Street
Worcester, Massachusetts 01609
USA
Telephone: 508-755-5221
Fax: 508-753-3311
www.americanantiquarian.org

Founded: 1812

Holdings (2001): Volumes: 690,000. Current serials: 7,000; manuscripts: 2,000 collections; maps: 10,000; sheet music: 70,000.

Special Collections: *Areas of Concentration:* Almanacs; bibliographies; broadsides; engravings; genealogy; lithographs; local, county, and state history; manuscripts; newspapers; pamphlets; periodicals; photographs; pre-1877 U.S., Canadian, and British West Indian books; printed ephemera; sheet music; U.S. history, literature, and culture. *Individual Collections:* American engravings; Paul Revere prints. *Papers:* Ruth Henshaw Bascom diaries; Reverend William Bentley diaries; James Fenimore Cooper; Mather family papers; Isaiah Thomas's business papers.

Origins to 1908

The American Antiquarian Society (AAS) was founded in 1812 by Isaiah Thomas and other men prominent in civic, religious, and business affairs in Worcester, Massachusetts, Thomas's home town, and Boston, his birthplace. From the beginning, AAS has been both a learned society and a research library. It is a charter member of the American Council of Learned Societies (ACLS), founded 1919, and the Independent Research Libraries Association (IRLA), founded 1972. The society's mission is to collect, preserve, and make available for use the antiquities of the New World. The means by which the mission has been achieved have changed considerably from generation to generation. The relationship between learned society and research library and the library's existence independent of a college or university has provided tensions and opportunities over the nearly two centuries of the society's existence. The history of AAS and its library is remarkably indicative of trends within the larger society in librarianship, scholarship, and academic life, and the expectations of the public for cultural enrichment.

Thomas's own background provides context essential for understanding the circumstances of the society's establishment and subsequent history. Born poor, Thomas became the leading printer, publisher, newspaper editor, and bookseller in the generation that came of age with the American Revolution, an event in which he was a significant player. Proprietor of one of the leading patriot newspapers in the colonies, the *Massachusetts Spy*, Thomas helped guide the post-Revolutionary War quest for a U.S. national identity in part through his pioneering publications, including Bibles, spellers, schoolbooks, children's books, almanacs, novels, and other imprints. He amassed a substantial personal library of European and American imprints, including newspapers and other ephemeral materials, that served as primary materials for his two-volume *History of Printing in America* (1810) and, two years later, as the core of the AAS library. Thomas was ambitious, vain, insecure about his status—and generous. He came to envision himself as heir to the tradition of the learned printers of Europe. Many of the European and British imprints in his collection were inspirations for his own work. In establishing AAS as a learned society and as the first historical organization in the country to be national in its membership and purpose, Thomas became what he sought to be.

The cultural world in which Thomas grew to maturity has been characterized by historian John Higham as one of "boundlessness." The organization that Thomas founded fit that mold by taking as its province the antiquities, printed and otherwise, of all of the Americas and by participating in the debate with the literati of Europe concerning the alleged inferiority of the New World to the Old. The members of the society, then as now elected, were drawn from the ranks of persons similar to the founders—men of affairs who were expected to support scholarly and literary pursuits.

Thomas served as president of the society until he died, and he did much to direct its affairs, with help from several librarians. He gave the society his collection of some 8,000 books and bound newspaper volumes plus $20,000, contributed 150,000 bricks and $2,000 toward the cost of constructing the first purpose-built edifice for the library in 1819–20 (the library was first housed in his home), and at the age of 79, he even could be found mowing the lawn around Antiquarian Hall. He set the society's acquisitions program on its aggressive course by purchasing (and cataloging) the largest remnant of the library and an important body of manuscripts of the influential family of New England clergymen, the Mathers, from Hannah Mather Crocker in 1814. At the same time, the society actively supported and published archaeological research in the Ohio valley and elsewhere.

Christopher Columbus Baldwin (1831–35) was the ideal person to lead the society following Thomas's death at the age of 82 in 1831, not least because he kept faith with the founder's own institutional goals. A thoroughly dogged acquisitor, Baldwin greatly expanded the library through such major coups as obtaining some 10,000 duplicate pamphlets from the Boston Athenaeum and two and one-quarter tons of books, pamphlets, and manuscripts cleaned out of a Boston attic. Baldwin's diary account of the exhilaration he felt in discovering and savoring such a cache of treasures despite the almost intolerable heat, dust, and stench in that garret should be required reading for any institutional or private collector. Unfortunately for the society, Baldwin's life was cut short by a fatal stagecoach accident in 1835 while he was in Ohio on an AAS expedition to the Indian mounds.

The 43-year tenure of the next librarian, Samuel Foster Haven (1835–78), was as long as Baldwin's had been brief. He adhered to the expansiveness of the society's activities as learned society, library, and museum. He was more of a scholar than his predecessors and emphasized the society's scholarly role, skillfully editing volumes of the *Transactions and Collections* and the *Proceedings*, writing *Archaeology of the United States*, which the Smithsonian Institution published in 1855, and helping to supervise preparation of the second edition of Thomas's *History of Printing in America* (1874). In addition, he presided over the construction of the second Antiquarian Hall (1854) and an addition to it (1876). He doubled the size of the collections within the first two decades of his tenure and continued to build the library and artifact collections, though rather indiscriminately, until the end. He was also witness to the growing trend in U.S. intellectual life toward professionalization and specialization and played a role in one episode in this movement, the founding of the American Library Association (ALA) in 1876.

The last hurrah for the society's archaeological activities came during the faithful, if not brilliant, stewardship of librarian Edmund Mills Barton (1878–1908) when President Stephen Salisbury III provided the impetus, through his keen interest and financial support, for the Yucatán expeditions of Augustus LePlongeon and Edward H. Thompson. Waldo Lincoln, who assumed the presidency in 1907, led the two-decades-old movement to abandon the museum function once and for all and to let AAS be a great research library. He should also be credited with the inspired choice of the next librarian, Clarence S. Brigham (1908–59), who accomplished precisely that during his long service to the society.

The Brigham Years

Brigham arrived from the Rhode Island Historical Society, and within a year had set the institution's agenda on the course that would consume his energies for the next half-century. He outlined his policy in his first annual report as librarian (October 1909), a document that his successor Clifford K. Shipton likened to "a trumpet of revolution which must have shaken the dust out of the folios on the most distant shelves." For the library, Brigham preached the modern mantra of specialization and building strength upon strength. This meant concentrating on acquiring all possible U.S. books, pamphlets, broadsides, newspapers, magazines, and ephemera printed through 1820 and, more selectively, in such genres as almanacs, bookplates, children's literature, U.S. fiction, and U.S. newspapers beyond 1820. It also meant deaccessioning the now out-of-scope material that his predecessors had acquired and completing the dismantling of the museum and offering most of the artifacts to such other, more appropriate (and suitably specialized) repositories as the Peabody Museum at Harvard and the Smithsonian Institution in Washington, D.C. He also swiftly spent a legacy provided by former president Salisbury by constructing the present Antiquarian Hall (opened in 1910), and later added two new stacks (1924 and 1950) to house the collections that he had been acquiring at an astonishing rate.

Brigham was a brilliant institutional collector. Thanks to his astute cultivation of dealers and collectors, he succeeded in reeling in thousands upon thousands of items. When he arrived at AAS in 1908, the society possessed about 5,000 pre-1821 U.S. imprints; when he retired 50 years later, that number had grown to 50,000. At the beginning of his tenure the library as a whole included some 99,000 volumes, and at its end there were nearly 600,000. He directed that the early imprints receive detailed card-cataloging treatment, with subsidiary files arranged by printer, publisher, and bookseller; by date of imprint; and by place, which greatly facilitated the work of visitors to the library. By the time of Brigham's tenure, the great research universities had been established and academia professionalized. During this time there was a distinct clubbishness to the culture of AAS. The society's scholarly clientele was still largely male, white, and of Anglo-Saxon stock, not unlike the membership of AAS itself. Brigham would occasionally mail the key to the front door of the library to one or another trusted member of his "old boy" network, so the colleague could let himself in to do some research on a Sunday.

Brigham was elevated to the newly created position of director in 1930. R.W.G. Vail served as librarian for ten years and was succeeded by Shipton in 1940. When Brigham retired in 1959, Shipton became director. The only director to have held a doctorate, Shipton had been trained in colonial history at Harvard, was the author of Volumes 4 to 17 of *Sibley's Harvard*

Graduates (1933–75), and worked one day per week in Cambridge as archivist of Harvard University. He brought to AAS a renewed dedication to academic scholarship. He helped revolutionize research in early American history by committing AAS to edit for publication by Readex Microprint Corporation one of the earliest and most comprehensive microform sets, the two series of *Early American Imprints*, covering 1630 to 1800 and 1801 to 1819 (produced 1955–68 and 1964–82, respectively), that have made it possible to carry on original research in the field in libraries around the nation and the world. Gaining admittance to the library was formidably difficult during the Shipton years for anyone, such as doctoral candidates, doing practice research. (One of Shipton's motives in undertaking the Readex project was to save wear and tear on the originals.)

Postwar Changes

But change was in the wind. The great upheavals in society after World War II could not help but affect AAS. The GI Bill and other phenomena helped to enlarge and diversify the college student population and, in time, the professoriat as well. Sputnik and the New Frontier and Great Society legislation of the 1960s propelled the growth of existing colleges and universities and the creation of new ones. A legislative legacy of the Cold War, the National Defense Education Act affected even AAS, for funding under it led for a few years to close ties between AAS and the doctoral program in early American history at Worcester's Clark University. Not only were these graduate students admitted to AAS, they were given stack privileges. The culture of the Vietnam War era discouraged the acceptance of received wisdom, historical or otherwise. The 1960s saw the rise of new emphases in research and writing about U.S. history—new forms of social, intellectual, and cultural history, including the history of women, African Americans, and the laboring classes. As access to higher education broadened, as disposable income rose and leisure time increased, the public's expectations for cultural enrichment grew as well.

When Shipton retired as director in 1967, Marcus A. McCorison (1967–92), who had come on board as librarian in 1960 (and continued to hold the title), succeeded him. No less a resourceful bookman than Brigham, McCorison took the library collections in several new directions and, moreover, greatly expanded the society's usefulness and visibility, nationally, even internationally. He shortly organized a "treasures" exhibition, called "A Society's Chief Joys," which was displayed at venues in New York City, Chicago, and Los Angeles in 1969–70. Not long after, in 1972, he instituted a fellowship program to bring talented scholars and doctoral candidates to Worcester for periods of one to three months. The program has assumed great importance in the intellectual life of the society. By establishing the fellowship program and fostering the development of regional academic seminars and the AAS Program in the History of the Book in American Culture, McCorison and his staff provided the mechanisms by which scholars could come to AAS to perform research and, with the staff and other readers, form a mutually supportive scholarly community.

By the time he retired from the society in 1992, he had added some 115,000 items, mostly 19th-century materials, effectively broadening the library's focus beyond Brigham's emphasis on the colonial, Revolutionary, and early national periods. He also deaccessioned materials he judged to be out of scope, including some European imprints not related to the United States, Latin American imprints and newspapers, and most post-1876 primary materials.

He sought to make the collections better known by making certain that AAS holdings were included in bibliographies in progress, securing a long succession of grants from the National Endowment for the Humanities (NEH) and other philanthropies to reduce the backlog of uncataloged or undercataloged materials, joining the Research Libraries Group (RLG), and helping to pioneer the computerized cataloging of rare and other specialized research materials. In the latter instance, McCorison worked through the Independent Research Libraries Association (IRLA) that he and others had founded in 1972 partly to solidify the standing of independents before governmental funding agencies and private foundations. Through IRLA he worked to create protocols to adapt the standard MAchine-Readable Cataloging (MARC) format to the special demands and opportunities of rare and other specialized research materials. He applied these protocols to a new Online Public Access Catalog (OPAC) system that he commissioned for AAS from Inforonics, Inc. At one level, the commitment to effective cataloging and a professional staff able to mediate between reader and collections was a means to offset the inconvenience of the closing of the stacks to all readers, which he carried out, much to the consternation of some local academics and others. McCorison greatly enlarged (mostly through grant funding) and professionalized the staff, created the first permanent development office, mounted several successful capital campaigns, and oversaw the construction of a new office wing and renovation of parts of Antiquarian Hall in 1972.

The deep collections of AAS, especially with McCorison's addition of so many 19th-century items, helped to drive many of the scholarly trends of the last third of the century, including the history of gender, race, and class, and the rehistoricizing of literary studies. The detail and up-to-dateness of AAS cataloging both reflected and contributed to the new trends. For example, the imprint and manuscript cataloging that AAS was able to carry out with NEH funding beginning in 1972 was intended to capture subject headings most useful for researchers on women, African Americans, and others whose presence in the archive would have been inadequately recorded at best in previous generations.

The Society Today

In preparing for McCorison's retirement, the society's council decided to separate the two positions he held—director (later changed to president) and librarian. Nancy Burkett, a long-time member of the staff, became librarian (the first woman to hold such a senior position) in 1991. A year later, Ellen S. Dunlap, director of the Rosenbach Museum and Library, succeeded McCorison as president. In seeking a new chief executive, the council determined that a commitment to increasing visibility and providing broader service to new and existing constituencies should be a high priority. Since the mid-1970s, AAS had enlarged its constituencies and usefulness by organizing an annual research seminar for local undergraduates and through public programs such as lectures, exhibitions, concerts, and adult education courses.

One of Dunlap's first tasks was to prepare, with senior staff, an application to the Lila Wallace-Reader's Digest Fund to support various outreach and constituency-building activities. The resulting grant permitted the society to increase its public programming; to work with teachers in grades K–12 on curricula utilizing the society's primary source materials and its scholarly expertise; and to add a program of fellowships for historical novelists, playwrights, documentary film makers, and other artists and writers to conduct research at AAS on projects intended for the general public rather than academics. As its audiences have broadened and expanded under Dunlap's leadership, the society has maintained its mission of putting a world-class research collection and the generous expertise of its staff at the service of its core constituency—academic scholars. Grants from the Andrew W. Mellon Foundation provided funds to create or increase endowments for the curatorial departments, to convert a large part of its card catalog to machine-readable form, to add several new long-term postdoctoral fellowships, and to upgrade its computer capabilities, including installing a new, more user-friendly interface on the OPAC. As acquisitions grow, the collections become better cataloged, information about holdings is disseminated electronically, and programs are expanded. The number of researchers using the library in person and from a distance continues to increase and the publications and teaching of those who have spent time in the reading room continue to shape and reshape the way U.S. citizens understand their past.

At the end of the 20th century, the main challenges facing Dunlap and the society's staff were to consolidate changes in administrative, finance, and personnel structures and to raise $12 million to add to endowments for the acquisition of books, for outreach and (most importantly) to construct a new, state-of-the-art book stack at the rear of the building. Although Isaiah Thomas would scarcely understand such innovations as the computers scattered throughout the library and the presence of women in the society's two highest posts, he would not, for the most part, feel alienated. On the shelves of the Palladian-style Antiquarian Hall built by his successors still stand the 8,000 volumes he donated to establish the library, now kept company by hundreds of thousands of other books with which he would also feel entirely at home.

JOHN B. HENCH

Further Reading

American Antiquarian Society, *A Society's Chief Joys*, Worcester, Massachusetts: American Antiquarian Society, 1969

Brigham, Clarence S., *Fifty Years of Collecting Americana for the Library of the American Antiquarian Society, 1908–1958*, Worcester, Massachusetts: s.n., 1958

Burkett, Nancy H., and John B. Hench, editors, *Under Its Generous Dome: The Collections and Programs of the American Antiquarian Society*, 2nd edition, revised, Worcester, Massachusetts: American Antiquarian Society, 1992

Hench, John B., editor, *Serendipity and Synergy: Collection Development, Access, and Research Opportunities at the American Antiquarian Society in the McCorison Era*, Worcester, Massachusetts: American Antiquarian Society, 1993

Joyce, William L., "The Manuscript Collections of the American Antiquarian Society," *Proceedings of the American Antiquarian Society* 89 (1979)

Joyce, William L., "Antiquarians and Archaeologists: The American Antiquarian Society, 1812–1912," *Proceedings of the American Antiquarian Society* 91 (1981)

Proceedings of the American Antiquarian Society (1812–)

A Quarter Century of Visiting Fellowships at the American Antiquarian Society, 1972–1997, Worcester, Massachusetts: AAS, 1998

Shipton, Clifford K., *Isaiah Thomas: Printer, Patriot, and Philanthropist, 1749–1831*, Rochester, New York: Hart, 1948

Shipton, Clifford K., "The Museum of the American Antiquarian Society," in *A Cabinet of Curiosities: Five Episodes in the Evolution of American Museums*, by Whitfield J. Bell, Jr., et al., Charlottesville: University Press of Virginia, 1967

Whitehill, Walter Muir, "The American Antiquarian Society," in *Independent Historical Societies*, Boston: The Boston Athenaeum, 1962

Archbishop Marsh's Library

Address: Archbishop Marsh's Library
St. Patrick's Close
Dublin 8
Ireland
Telephone: 1-454-3511
Fax: 1-454-3511
www.kst.dit.ie/marsh

Founded: 1701

Holdings (2001): Volumes: 25,000 (mainly 17th-century). Incunabula: 80; manuscripts: 300.

Special Collections: *Areas of Concentration:* Calvinism in 17th-century France; ecclesiastical studies; Irish history and music; mathematics. *Individual Collections:* Elias Bouhéreau; Narcissus Marsh; John Stearne; Edward Stillingfleet. *Papers:* Richard Caulfield; Emily Lawless; William Reeves; Abraham Tessereau; Charles Alexander Webster.

Origins

Archbishop Marsh's Library, the first public library in Ireland, was founded by Narcissus Marsh in 1701. Marsh was an Englishman born in Hannington, Wiltshire, in 1638. He was educated at Oxford University, where according to his diary he studied "Old Philosophy, Mathematics, and Oriental languages." He became a clergyman in the Church of England and was appointed principal of St. Alban Hall in Oxford University.

In 1679, on the advice of the Duke of Ormond, Marsh was appointed provost of Trinity College, Dublin. Shortly after his appointment, he discovered that there was no library available to the public in Dublin, the library in Trinity College being accessible only to students and staff. He decided to build a public library but did not get the opportunity to do so until he was appointed archbishop of Dublin in 1694. As archbishop, Marsh lived in the Palace of St. Sepulchre (now the Kevin Street police station), which had sufficient land attached to it to build a library.

The Building

The archbishop employed Surveyor General William Robinson to design the library, a two-story L-shaped building. The ground floor was designed as a residence for the librarian and the upper floor as the library. The upper floor consists of two galleries. The first gallery is 60 feet long and 22 feet wide, the second 75 feet long and 16 feet wide, with the old reading room intersecting the two galleries. At the end of the second gallery are three wired alcoves, the "cages" where readers are supposed to have been locked so they could not steal the books. The library is furnished with dark oak bookcases, each with a carved and lettered gable topped by an archbishop's miter.

The Act of Incorporation

The library was incorporated in an act of Parliament of 1707 entitled "An Act for Settling and Preserving a publick Library for ever." This act gave the house and books to the following dignitaries and officials (and their successors) as governors and guardians: the Church of Ireland archbishops of Armagh and Dublin, the deans of St. Patrick's and Christ Church Cathedrals, the provost of Trinity College, the lord chancellor of Ireland, and three other legal governors. The offices of the legal governors became extinct in 1922 upon the formation of the Irish state. In 1970 the chief justice was appointed a governor to replace the lord chancellor, and since 1997 there have been two government appointees to the board.

Rules of the Library

At the Annual Visitation of the Governors and Guardians of the Library, held 8 October 1713, the following rule was made: "Concerning Those Who shall be allowed to study in the said Library, We order and appoint that all Graduats and Gentlemen shall have free access to the said Library on the Dayes and Hours before determined, Provided They behave Themselves well, give place and pay due respect to their Betters, But in Case any person shall carry Himself otherwise (which We hope will not happen) We order Him to be excluded, if after being admonished He does not mend His manners."

Foundation Collections

There are four main collections, the most important being the library of Bishop Edward Stillingfleet that Archbishop Marsh purchased for £2,500 in 1705. It contains 10,000 books on a wide range of subjects, including the classics, Bibles, prayer books, history, law, medicine, theology, witchcraft, travel, and religious controversy.

Marsh donated his own library of more than 3,000 books. The subjects include religion, philosophy, science, mathematics, and travel. His collection also includes books in Arabic, Syriac, Coptic (Ethiopic), Persian, and Turkish, as well as books in Hebrew, Chaldaic, Aramaic, Greek, and Latin.

The third collection is that of the Huguenot refugee and first librarian, Elias Bouhéreau. Bouhéreau, who came from La Rochelle in France, where as a Huguenot doctor he was not allowed to practice medicine after the revocation of the Edict of Nantes. Archbishop Marsh appointed him first librarian in 1701; he also gave his books to the library at that time. His collection contains books on religious controversy, history, science, and the classics. It also covers aspects of the religious, political, and social life of the French Protestants from the period leading to the Edict of Nantes (1598) to that which followed its revocation (1685). The collection also illustrates Bouhéreau's interest in his own profession of medicine and how receptive he was to new medical ideas and developments.

John Stearne, bishop of Clogher and friend of Jonathan Swift, bequeathed his books in 1745; his books are similar to those of Stillingfleet and Marsh. Although the library is made up of four separate collections, they make a homogeneous collection because they were formed at the same time, during the latter half of the 17th century. The collectors were men of similar tastes, and their interests are reflected in their collections. Each man's individual preferences are also indicated, however, by some of the volumes included in the collections.

A fifth collection is that of Godfrey Everth, whose compilation of more than 1,000 books was presented to the library in 1918. It consists of 19th-century standard works on poetry, drama, history, and travel.

Collection Description

The total number of volumes in the library is 25,000, but many of these volumes contain several works. A rough estimate of the number of books in Marsh's that were printed before 1700 includes 7,000 published in England, 4,000 from France, 2,600 from The Netherlands (including the Spanish Netherlands), 2,500 from Germany, 1,000 from Italy, and 1,000 from Switzerland. Although there are also some 17th-century books by Irish writers in the main collections, the majority of books of Irish interest date from the 19th century and are kept in a special room. These books consist of histories of Ireland, including ecclesiastical histories, biographies, and journals of antiquarian and historical societies. There are 300 manuscripts relating mainly to Irish history, including ecclesiastical history and music manuscripts from the 16th and 17th centuries.

The 19th Century

Marsh's Library was the only public library in Ireland for nearly 150 years and was used extensively throughout the 18th century. In the 19th century, when other libraries began to open in Dublin, Marsh's became run-down and dilapidated, and scholars and readers turned elsewhere. The absence of a published catalog of its holdings was another factor that led to neglect of the library.

In 1833 a number of duplicates were sold by auction (although many of these were not in fact duplicates), and the library's act of incorporation made it illegal to either lend or sell a book. The auction was carried out with the agreement of the keeper, Thomas Russell William Cradock, who was one of the most inept keepers ever appointed to the library. Some years later Cradock and the governors and guardians agreed to the removal of all the books in the library to the new National Gallery of Painting, Sculpture, and the Fine Arts. They also agreed that the library should be sold. The proposed removal and sale was prevented through the intervention of Benjamin Lee Guinness, who restored the library in 1862, repairing the fabric, building a new entrance, and funding the repair of important books and manuscripts.

Recent Developments

From 1980 to 2000 an extensive renovation of the library took place and facilities were installed for readers and visitors. These include the restoration of the former caretaker's quarters as a seminar/reading room, funded by the American Ireland Fund (currently Ireland Funds). Another new facility is the Delmas conservation bindery donated by the late Jean Paul Delmas in 1987–88. The Delmas bindery carries out book restoration and conservation of books and manuscripts for the library itself and for outside institutions and private collectors. It also includes a section for the conservation of prints, drawings, archival material, and works on paper.

Marsh's library catalog has been computerized and made available on the Internet, and the library has expanded its hours. The books are still on the same shelves where they were placed by Archbishop Marsh and his first librarian nearly 300 years ago, enabling them to be quickly retrieved for readers. Scholars and students are welcome to carry out research on the collections. Since the computerization of the catalog (completed in 1998), the increase in these readers has been dramatic, fulfilling the archbishop's wishes that the library would, as expressed in the 1707 statute, be an instrument "for the encouragement of learning."

MURIEL MCCARTHY

Further Reading

Coudert, Allison P., et al., editors, *Judaeo-Christian Intellectual Culture in the Seventeenth Century: A Celebration of the Library of Narcissus Marsh (1638–1713)*, Dordrecht, The Netherlands, London, and Boston: Kluwer Academic, 1999

Mant, Richard, *History of the Church of Ireland*, 2 vols., London: Parker, 1840; 2nd edition, 1841

McCarthy, Muriel, "Swift and Marsh's Library," *Dublin Historical Record* 27, no. 3 (June 1974)

McCarthy, Muriel, *All Graduates and Gentlemen: Marsh's Library*, Dublin: O'Brien Press, 1980

Stokes, George Thomas, "Narcissus Marsh," in *Some Worthies of the Irish Church*, by Stokes, edited by Hugh Jackson Lawlor, London: Hodder and Stoughton, 1900

White, Newport John Davis, *Four Good Men: Luke Challoner, Jeremy Taylor, Narcissus Marsh, Elias Bouhereau*, Dublin: Hodges Figgis, 1927

Australian National University Library

Address: Australian National Univeristy Library
R.G. Menzies Building (2)
Fellows Road
Australian National University
Canberra, Australian Capital Territory 0200
Australia
Telephone: 2-6125-2003
Fax: 2-6125-5008
http://anulib.anu.edu.au

Founded: 1946

Holdings (2000): Volumes: 2 million. Archives and manuscripts: 36,000 linear feet; current serials: 11,000; films and videos: 30,000; microforms: 10,000 sets.

Special Collections: *Areas of Concentration:* Anthropology; Asian literature; demography; history and political science relating to Africa, Asia, and the Pacific; library science; military and naval science; non-Western religions. *Individual Collections:* Noel Butlin Archives Centre for business and labor activities in Australia.

Origins

The Australian National University (ANU) was founded by an Act of the Australian Parliament in 1946 and was located in the nation's capital, Canberra. The ANU was established to bring leading Australian scholars back home from overseas and to develop research centers of world excellence at a time when such facilities were extremely limited in Australia.

The library was considered to be a crucial part of the university, and its creation was addressed at the first meeting of the Interim Council on 13 September 1946. One of the early issues debated was whether the structure of the library was to be a service established in a central physical location or a decentralized branch library operation. The initial decision to set up a series of largely departmental library collections across the campus has had ramifications to the present day.

The 1940s to 1960s

A.L.G. McDonald was appointed the first librarian in 1948. He worked in both Melbourne and Canberra from 1948 to 1950, as the library was initially housed in Ormond College at the University of Melbourne. Early emphasis was placed on building the collections. By the time the library moved to Canberra in December 1950, the collection had grown to 40,000 volumes. Twenty-five thousand volumes of Chinese material were acquired in Hong Kong in 1950, forming the basis of an outstanding Asian collection.

Significant growth in the library occurred during the 1950s, but a decision made in 1960 regarding the structure of the university was again to have long-term repercussions for the organization of the library and the provision of services. The proposal to merge the Canberra University College (then a relatively small undergraduate college affiliated with the University of Melbourne) with the ANU was finally ratified by Prime Minister Robert Menzies in 1960. This merger led to a significant and occasionally acrimonious debate on the need for major central library buildings to serve the two halves of the university. Two libraries were ultimately built—the Research Library, now known as the R.G. Menzies Building, and the General Studies Library, now known as the J.B. Chifley Building—instead of one central library, as had been advised by key librarians.

For two decades the two libraries duplicated subject material, depending on which section of the university ordered the material. The Institute of Advanced Studies and the Faculties (as the two halves of the university are now termed) had then, as now, a number of departments with the same subject focus, such as engineering, anthropology, and history. Further complications arose owing to the university's decision to create separate research schools in widely separated parts of the campus, which led to duplication in these locations. In a university not characterized by high-use collections, the consequent duplication of facilities and services led to significant recurrent costs during the 1960s and 1970s in the provision of services and development of collections.

The second university librarian, J.J. Graneek, a traditional scholar-librarian, was appointed from Queens University in Belfast, Northern Ireland, in 1963. Graneek's librarianship was characterized by a growing appreciation of the need for a centralized infrastructure to support the decentralized system. The Graneek era also marked the tentative beginning of library automation, particularly in the area of cataloging.

The 1970s and Beyond

The focus on automation was the driving force behind the appointment in 1973 of the third librarian, Milton Simms from James Cook University, following the retirement of Graneek in 1972. The early attempts at developing stand-alone automation systems at ANU created both difficulties and achievements, as elsewhere in the library world. Early homegrown circulation and acquisition systems were introduced only to be superseded by newer systems. It was not until later in the 1970s and 1980s, when systems were purchased from two commercial firms, Libramatics and, later, Urica, that the automation infrastructure settled down and the campus began to be linked electronically by centralized cataloging and circulation services.

By the mid-1970s a separate life sciences library (now the W.G. Hancock Building) was established, occupying the first and second floors of a multipurpose five-story building. In 1977 the continued lack of rational space planning surfaced again when 200,000 volumes of library material were moved to a library store on campus and replaced by an Instructional Resources Unit established in the basement of the Chifley Building.

It was thought that the placement of material in the store would only be a temporary matter until a new library building extension was erected. The Australian federal government's freeze on capital building and budget cuts since 1977, however, has meant that no significant library building (except an extension to the law library) has taken place since that time. A major extension to the Hancock Building opened in February 2001 and allowed for a final consolidation of holdings on a subject basis in the main library buildings.

The first major achievement in the area of collection rationalization followed a comprehensive review of the library in 1983 that recommended *inter alia a* consolidation of the holdings in the Menzies, Chifley, and Hancock Buildings. This was undertaken by 1986 with a massive move of library material to bring dispersed subject collections together in the main buildings. Significant devaluations of the Australian dollar in the mid-1980s led to a rationalization of the collections in the science branch libraries but also foreshadowed vulnerability in the area of collection purchasing, with 90 percent of materials acquired by ANU coming from overseas.

The proximity of the ANU to the National Library of Australia (NLA) has allowed the ANU Library to focus its collections on print and electronic resources, with cartographic, manuscript, and other categories of material being held in the NLA. The ANU, with the NLA, has nearly 80 percent of the Asian/Pacific holdings in Australia, and both contain important collections in certain Asian geographical and subject areas. The ANU's collection policy has been dovetailed with those of the NLA, but the opportunity for future joint initiatives still remains.

Automation

Milton Simms retired in 1980 and was succeeded in that year by Deputy Librarian Colin Steele, who has become the longest-serving university librarian in the institution's history. A major goal achieved under his librarianship was the linking of the campus collections and resources in a networked environment. In the early 1990s the library replaced the Urica system with the Innovative Interfaces integrated library management system.

In the early 1990s, with changing modes of access to information, the ANU Library became one of the first providers of structured Internet gateways for users. ANU pioneered the first subject pages coordinated to web material in an Australian university library and, subsequently, electronic reserve operations. The library won the National Victorian Association for Library Automation (VALA) Award for Innovation in Information Technology in 1994–95. The library also launched major Internet services to provide access to Indonesian and Chinese material.

In the mid-1990s the ANU linked with the Institute of Arts to create an additional academic dimension to the university. By the end of 2000, the library contained just over 2 million volumes, with 11,000 current serials housed in three main library buildings and seven branch libraries focused largely on the sciences. The ANU Library also provides desktop access at home and on campus wherever possible for staff and students via authenticated subject portals. The provision of information via the library's website ensures direct delivery of hundreds of electronic journals, as well as access to information through coordinated Web portals. At the end of 2000, 42,000 hits per week (weekdays) were recorded.

The ANU Library is a relatively young one, but its short history reflects the changes that have occurred in scholarly communication and that have provided an essential component of the infrastructure to support research and teaching.

COLIN R. STEELE

Further Reading

Steele, Colin, editor, *Australian Tertiary Libraries: Issues for the 1990s*, Adelaide, South Australia: Auslib Press, 1992

Vidot, Peter, *The History of the Australian National University Library, 1946–1996*, Canberra: ANU Library, 1996

Austrian National Library

Address: Österreichische Nationalbibliothek
Josefsplatz 1
Postfach 308
1015 Wien
Austria
Telephone: 1-53-410
Fax: 1-53-410 or 1-53-280
www.onb.ac.at

Founded: 14th century

Holdings (2000): Volumes: 3 million. Audio recordings: 25,000; autographs: 280,000; current serials: 18,000; graphic materials: 1.5 million; incunabula: 7,984; manuscripts: 52,000; maps: 259,000; microforms: 13,000; music manuscripts: 50,000; papyri: 140,000; printed music: 120,000.

Special Collections: *Areas of Concentration:* Austriaca; globes and maps; incunabula; manuscripts; music; papyri; photographs; prints and portraits. *Individual Collections:* Austrian Folk Song Institute; Austrian literary archives; Globe Museum; International Esperanto Museum; music collection; papyrus collection; Portraits, Pictures and Fideicommis Library. *Papers:* Ingeborg Bachmann; Thomas Bernhard; Erich Fried; Karl Kraus; Robert Musil; Heimito von Doderer; Hugo von Hofmannsthal.

History

The beginning of the Court Library, the predecessor of today's Austrian National Library (ANL), dates back to the Middle Ages. Duke Albert III was instrumental in centralizing certain treasures of secular rulers; he also promoted the University of Vienna, instigated the translation of Latin works into German, and founded a court miniature studio in which valuable manuscripts were produced. Most important in the present context, the oldest documented book in the ANL originates from Albert's collection: a book of Gospels dated 1368.

The next step toward the formation of a true imperial or court library was taken in the 15th century under the rule of Emperor Frederick III. Frederick brought all art treasures from the Hapsburg inheritance under his sole control. Frederick's son, Maximilian I, championed books and, thanks in great part to his marriage to Mary of Burgundy, the collections expanded. The library grew somewhat more systematically when Maximilian authorized scholars such as Jakobs Mennel, Ladislaus Sunthaim, and Johannes Cuspinian to compose and acquire books. By the beginning of the 16th century, the Court Library had acquired significant European book art, represented best by Bohemian, French, and Italian book illumination.

In 1504 the great humanist Conrad Celtis spoke for the first time of a *Bibliotheca Regia,* organized and expanded through purchases at the request of the emperor. The collections grew significantly throughout the 16th century, and as a consequence Emperor Maximilian II appointed the Dutch scholar Hugo Blotius to be the first librarian at the Court Library. Blotius devised both a name index of the library's 9,000 books and manuscripts and a thematic catalog containing the so-called "Turcica," or works relating to the Ottoman Empire.

Book collections in the 16th and 17th centuries increased appreciably. Deposit legislation was already in place in 1624, when an imperial decree ordered the delivery of one copy of every printed book from the spring and autumn fairs in Frankfurt to the library. In 1654 the Court Library acquired the Fugger collection and in 1665 the library at Ambras Castle moved to the Court Library.

Perhaps the most significant moment in the history of the Court Library occurred in 1722, when Emperor Charles VI commissioned the building of a library on what today is the Josefsplatz, designed by Josef Emanuel Fischer von Erlach. From 1730 until the early years of the 19th century, the library hall and its adjacent galleries housed manuscripts, incunabula, maps, globes, and autographs. Among the most valuable of acquisitions during that period was the library of Prince Eugene of Savoy, numbering approximately 15,000 volumes, purchased in 1737. The Court Library of the 18th century was essentially a place visited by scholars and diplomats, a grand location for the emperor's official and social functions.

The Court Library sought to transform its function at the begining of the 19th century. After the profound political events that had just transpired—the French Revolution of 1789, the foundation of the Austrian Empire in 1804, the abdication of the crown of the Holy Roman Empire of the German Nation in 1806—it became clear that the former Court Library was now thought of as a national library in deed if not yet in name.

One of the library's major organizational developments since the 19th century has been the establishment of individual collections to ensure their more efficient administration. With the end of the Austro-Hungarian Empire in 1918, a crucial chapter of European history was complete. The Court Library was renamed the Austrian National Library in 1920. The search for a national identity, at least initially, focused not on what was "Austrian" but on what was "German." In the interwar period the library endeavored to concentrate on collecting German publications, thereby contradicting (nominally) its would-be status as a national library. The uncertain status of Austria under the auspices of Nazi Germany conditioned the ANL: The mindset of librarians in Vienna was supposed to be "coordinated" (a Nazi term) to be in line with that of Hitler's and Goebbels' view of culture.

Not until after World War II did the ANL really become a symbol of the nation-state of Austria. The contemporary library is noted for two significant improvements to its everyday work flow: the opening of a modern reading room in the 1960s and the establishment of underground space for book storage. Today, early in the 21st century, the ANL is a vital player among European national libraries. Its 6.5 million books, manuscripts, and other materials comprise an unexcelled cultural treasure for Austria.

The library has coordinated its policies with those of other academic libraries in Austria since 1920, and from 1981 on copies of all printed works published in Austria are sent to the ANL under a type of legal deposit. General responsibilities fall into three areas: the special collections, the academic library, and duties fulfilled on behalf of all academic libraries in Austria.

The ANL seeks to fulfill its cultural and educational mission by hosting exhibitions, symposia, literary events, readings, and other activities. It has 15 reading rooms, indicating its role as *the* academic library of Austria. The rooms attract some 400,000 users annually, of which two-thirds are students and academics. The library also publishes the Austrian National Bibliography. It maintains an automated library network and a corresponding central editorial office. Both the Austrian Newspaper and Magazine Database and the Book Documentation Center are based at the library.

MICHAEL P. OLSON

Further Reading

Grabovszki, Ernst, "Österreichische Bibliothek: Rohstofflager der Zukunft," *Anzeiger: Die Fachzeitschrift des Österreichischen Buchhandels* 135, no. 15 (2000)

Krug, Hansjörg, "Die Österreichische Nationalbibliothek," *Börsenblatt für den deutschen Buchhandel* (25 September 1998)

Die Österreichische Nationalbibliothek: Geschichte, Bestände, Aufgaben, Vienna: Brüder Hollinek, 1954; 5th edition, Vienna: Österreichische Nationalbibliothek, 1979

Stummvoll, Josef, *Geschichte der Österreichischen Nationalbibliothek,* Vienna: Pracher, 1968–

The Treasure Houses of Austria: The Austrian National Library, Vienna: Federal Press Service, 1995

Bavarian State Library

Address: Bayerische Staatsbibliothek
Ludwigstrasse 16
80539 Munich
Germany
Telephone: 89-28638-0
Fax: 89-28638-2976
www.bsb.badw-muenchen.de

Founded: 1558

Holdings (2001): Volumes: 7.7 million. Current serials: 42,000; graphic materials: 1.2 million; incunabula: 18,600; manuscripts: 79,000; maps: 373,000; music scores: 280,000.

Special Collections: *Areas of Concentration:* Antiquity, history, and music literature; east and southeast Europe; East Asia; Middle East. *Individual Collections:* Balkan and Eastern European nations; classical studies; incunabula; musicology; rare books. *Papers:* Alban Berg; Oskar Maria Graf; Leo von Klenze; Alfred Kubin; Orlando di Lasso; Justus von Liebig; Kings Ludwig I and Ludwig II; Richard Strauss; Richard Wagner.

Origins, 1558 to 1600

The origins of today's Bayerische Staatsbibliothek (BSB, or Bavarian State Library) reach back over 500 years and can be traced to the tradition of patronage of the book arts begun by Wittelsbach Duke Albrecht IV and his successor Wilhelm IV. These Renaissance rulers commissioned richly illuminated manuscript versions of the Arthurian and Grail legends, chivalric and knightly works, and prayer books and missals, but also acquired both manuscripts and printed books by purchase or as gifts. Typical of these early holdings is the breviary for Emperor Friedrich III, created circa 1475, probably a wedding gift from the imperial court in Vienna upon Albrecht IV's marriage to the Hapsburg imperial princess Kunigunde.

The need for a library to house the ducal collection was not felt until 1558, early in the reign of the most illustrious and extravagant of the Renaissance princes of the Wittelsbach dynasty, Albrecht V. Albrecht. Albrecht attracted prominent musicians, composers (Orlando di Lasso), and painters (Hans Mielich) to his court from all over Europe and, like other aristocratic collectors of the age, was drawn to books as objects of display and representation; Albrecht also increasingly viewed books as resources in the battle against his confessional adversary, the Lutheran heresy. When in 1557 the library of the humanist and Orientalist Johann Albrecht Widmannstetter, a scholar's collection of approximately 500 printed works and 330 manuscripts, became available, Albrecht first intended to purchase it for his new anti-Lutheran Jesuit bulwark in Ingolstadt. But when it became clear that this collection was coveted by other European rulers, especially Maximilian, king of Bohemia, Albrecht acted quickly to purchase it for himself.

The Widmannstetter library was of high scholarly and artistic value, containing, among other treasures, 140 manuscripts in Hebrew and 50 in Arabic, along with important works of literature, law, and theology. Since at the time there was neither a library at court nor a court librarian, it was housed together with the court archives and entrusted to the archivist Erasmus Fend. Fend, who lacked the philological qualifications to be custodian of a scholarly collection, was succeeded by Aegidius Oertel, whose appointment decree of 26 February 1561 set forth that he was both to preserve and add to the collection, especially in the disciplines of theology, history, and the arts. All loans and acquisitions had to be approved by the court chancellor.

The acquisition in 1571 of the extraordinary library of Johann Jakob Fugger, numbering more than 10,000 printed volumes and 1,500 manuscripts, instantly elevated the small ducal library in Munich to a collection of European stature. A cultivated and widely traveled member of the Augsburg merchant dynasty, Fugger had used the far-flung connections of his family's trade empire to acquire rare books from all over Europe, even supporting copyists in Venice to reproduce books in Greek and Hebrew he was unable to purchase. His passion for the arts and for books drove him and his entire family into bankruptcy in 1564, despite the aid of his friend and patron Duke Albrecht, who after enormous loans employed Fugger as his seneschal and arts adviser at court. Perhaps in anticipation of the imminent acquisition of Fugger's library and its relocation from Augsburg to Munich, Albrecht decided to build a library on the floor just above the Antiquarium, the grand hall being built to house his collection of antiquities and other rare objects in the new ducal residence.

Completed between 1568 and 1571, this space above the Antiquarium became the ducal library's first permanent home.

One of the jewels of the Fugger library was itself a collection, that of the Nuremberg doctor and humanist Hartmann Schedel, purchased by Fugger from a Schedel heir in 1552. Not just a collector, Schedel was also the compiler of the *Liber chronicarum,* popularly known as the *Nürnberger Weltchronik* (Nuremberg Chronicle, 1493), one of the most heavily illustrated and technically brilliant printed works of the incunabula period. Schedel's own copy of the *Weltchronik,* brilliantly hand-colored and enhanced with his own handwritten commentary, came in this way to the ducal library.

Albrecht V acquired individual rarities in addition to entire collections. Among his trophies were an early 13th-century manuscript of *Tristan und Isolde* by Gottfried von Strassburg, which is to this day the oldest extant copy of this unfinished courtly epic, and a copy of the *Nibelungenlied* with richly decorated initials, known today as "Version D." (The BSB also owns Version A, acquired by purchase in 1810, as described below.) Albrecht V was probably also responsible for the acquisition of the so-called "Munich Boccaccio," an exquisitely illuminated copy of the French translation of Boccaccio's *De casibus virorum illustrium,* with 90 miniatures by Jean Fouquet and his school, dating from 1458. It is documented to have been in the Residence library by 1582 at the latest and so may have also been acquired by Albrecht's son and successor Wilhelm V, who continued his father's tradition of bibliophily and bibliothecal patronage. Wilhelm added important private libraries such as those of the legal scholar Johann Heinrich Herwart in 1585 (1,500 volumes), whose music manuscripts and early prints provided the foundation for the BSB's distinguished music collection, and Johann Georg von Werdenstein in 1592 (4,000 volumes). Valuable individual works were added as well, including the prayer book of Charles the Bald, a work of the ninth century so valuable that it is now kept in the *Schatzkammer* of the Munich Residence (a separate space reserved for the most valuable works, including many with jewel-encrusted bindings). By 1600 the *Hofbibliothek* owned approximately 17,000 volumes and had become, in the space of a few decades, not only one of the richest but also the largest library of German-speaking Europe, even larger than the Imperial Library in Vienna.

The development of any library must also be measured in terms of its organization. The first librarian, Aegidius Oertel, was dismissed in 1573, probably owing to the loss of 341 books from the library and an otherwise undistinguished record. But the next librarian, Wolfgang Prommer, who came with the Fugger library to Munich, applied the system he had inherited from his predecessor, Samuel Quicchelberg, to introduce order to the collection. The collections were first divided into Latin works and works in other languages. Within the Latin books, ten subject divisions were used; all other books were arranged by language. Call numbers were assigned based on subject class (*regio*), range (*turris*), shelf (*statio*), and finally shelf position. Prommer also created a number of useful catalogs and location tools: a shelf list with an alphabetical index, alphabetically arranged catalogs for each class, and even a keyword index for the historical class.

Armory of the Faith, 1600 to 1745

As the confessional differences that ultimately led to the Thirty Years War became ever more aggravated, the Hofbibliothek was increasingly pulled into the service of the old faith under the leadership of the Jesuits. During the rule of Duke (Elector) Maximilian I, a strong supporter of the Jesuits, the pursuit of entire collections was given less emphasis, as targeted acquisitions in the areas of history, law, and religion (including the extensive pamphlet literature of the age) were needed to support legal and historical research and propagandistic activity on behalf of the Catholic cause. The library's status as intellectual armory of the Catholic side was validated repeatedly by the Vatican, a calculated largesse that permitted the library not only to own and to grant access to, but even to purchase books placed on the papal index. In keeping with its new instrumental status, the library was moved out of its lavish representational setting above the Antiquarium and returned to the old residence in 1599. Maximilian, a tireless and visionary promoter of the need for a more developed library infrastructure, tried periodically, beginning as early as 1595, to enlist support among clerics for his remarkably modern plan to create a union catalog of all library resources in the duchy—support that especially the numerous Bavarian monasteries were unwilling to provide for fear that their collections might later be culled to strengthen further the court library. (This fear was well-founded, as events a century and a half later would show.)

In 1623, during the Thirty Years War, Maximilian I let pass an enormous opportunity for the Hofbibliothek. Following his victory over Protestant forces defending Heidelberg, the immensely valuable library of 3,500 manuscripts and printed books belonging to the Lutheran Count Palatine Ottheinrich fell into his hands. Maximilian, however, chose not to remove this "mother of German libraries" to Munich, and presented it instead as spoils of war to the pope. The "Biblioteca Palatina" resides in Rome to this day. As in 1632 the tides of war shifted and Swedish troops advanced on Munich, Maximilian had the most valuable holdings of the Hofbibliothek taken to his fortress in Burghausen on the Inn, far to the east. During the occupation of Munich by the Swedes, approximately 2,000 (mainly printed) works were plundered, most of which were subsequently lost. Some of these losses were recouped, at least numerically, when Maximilian claimed the library of the (Lutheran) dukes of Württemberg at Hohentübingen and transported it to his capital in Munich.

It is remarkable that despite the turmoil of war and the fiscal disaster that followed in its wake, Maximilian and his successor Ferdinand Maria could still mobilize the energy and the funds to develop their library infrastructure. Ferdinand Maria issued a decree in 1663 that not only provided the Hofbibliothek a set annual collections budget, albeit a modest 300 gulden, but also introduced the first depository law in Europe not connected with censorial review (as in France) or the granting of the printing privilege (as in England).

After 120 years of aggressive expansion, the high Baroque period and the reigns of Max Emmanuel and Karl Albrecht brought stagnation to the court library. Few, if any, new publications were purchased, and only two private libraries were added, those of the court librarian himself, Johannes Kandler, in 1720 and of Franz Hannibal von Mörmann, the Bavarian envoy to the court in Vienna in 1739. Upon Karl Albrecht's death in 1745, the library was not significantly larger than it had been 100 years before.

Recovery and Revolution, 1745 to 1803

The recovery of the court library and a period of enormous growth and development were inaugurated by the accession of an enlightened and energetic ruler to the Bavarian throne in 1745, Duke Elector Maximilian III Joseph, and with the appointment a year later of Andreas Felix von Oefele as court librarian. Oefele opened the library again to a broader public of scholars and government officials, used a regular acquisitions budget to develop the collections through current and retrospective purchases, and undertook a complete re-cataloging of the library's 20,000 volumes, producing 28 heavy tomes without, however, completing the task. The establishment of the Bavarian Academy of Sciences in 1759 contributed to the expansion of the library's clientele and stimulated broader use, also creating a body of scholars that came to regard the administration and expansion of the library as their mission and responsibility. But perhaps the most significant event of these years was in the area of collection growth, brought about by the dissolution of the Jesuits by order of Pope Clemens XIV in 1773 and the devolution of their possessions, including their libraries, to secular rulers all over Europe. The *collegium* (college of the Jesuits) in Munich, a vast complex in the center of the city, possessed a sophisticated library roughly the same size as the court library. Its 23,000 volumes became the property of the Hofbibliothek but for lack of space remained in what had been the *Jesuitenkolleg*. Under Duke Elector Karl Theodor, relocations of the library in 1778 from the Old Residence to what had been the Fuggerhaus (shared with the academy) and in 1784 (again with the academy) to the former Jesuit college, where it was merged with the Jesuit library, provided temporary relief for this collection, which by 1800 numbered more than 70,000 volumes.

Theodor also oversaw the transition of the Hofbibliothek into a more democratically accessible institution: In a ceremony on 28 March 1790, it was officially opened to the public. Little appreciated is the importance of his chief minister, Count Maximilian Joseph von Montgelas, for the development of the library during the following decades. Montgelas was an experienced historian, an extensive and expert user of archives and printed works. For almost 30 years, until his dismissal by Ludwig I in 1817, Montgelas exercised a discrete but profound influence on developments at the Hofbibliothek, contributing to its growth into one of the two or three most important libraries in Europe, as well as into a site of experimentation and innovation whose example would radiate well into the 20th century.

This was the era of the French Revolution and the Napoleonic Wars in Europe, a period that had an influence on the Hofbibliothek far more profound than the usual back-and-forth capture of valuable materials by opposing armies. (The Hofbibliothek lost only 15 manuscripts and 50 printed books to the French, some of which were returned after Napoleon's defeat in 1815.) For much of this period an ally of France, but always under its strong political and cultural influence (French was then the language of the Munich court), Bavaria was more aggressive than any other European power in emulating French policies toward hitherto independent ecclesiastical territories existing within its borders. Beginning in 1799, the monasteries of mendicant orders were secularized and their libraries (approximately 37,000 volumes) transferred to the Hofbibliothek, a process completed by 1803.

Aretin and Schrettinger, 1803 to 1843

Johann Christoph von Aretin, an historian, a firebrand pamphleteer, as well as a bibliophilic member of the Bavarian Academy of Sciences with aspirations of becoming a librarian at court, spent three months in Paris in 1801, observing how the revolutionary government there channeled the nation's confiscated library resources through *dépôts littéraires* into the national library. In February 1802 Aretin drafted a petition, signed by then court librarian Kasimir von Haeffelin, urging the state to do the same with all Bavarian monastic libraries, since it seemed probable that even those monasteries enjoying constitutional protection as members of the Bavarian parliament (*Landtag*) or as estates in the imperial parliament (*Reichsstände*) were on the threshold of expropriation. Aretin's request was fulfilled beyond his dreams. The secularization and the *mise à la disposition de la nation* of monastic libraries that followed, beginning in 1803 and lasting until approximately 1817, was part of a vast and systematic expropriation and dissolution of virtually all Bavarian monasteries and other ecclesiastical domains. Some of these, such as Tegernsee, Benediktbeuern, Sankt Emmeram, Passau, and Freising, had had scriptoria and libraries for more than a thousand years. Not counting the books and manuscripts that Aretin declined for the Hofbibliothek and that ultimately went to Bavaria's university in Landshut or to secondary school libraries, a staggering 450,000 books came to the Hofbibliothek within a mere decade and a half. After taking duplicates into account, the increase in titles numbered 200,000 printed books and approximately 20,000 manuscripts. The Hofbibliothek also acquired in 1803 and 1804 the entire court library of the Mannheim branch of the Wittelsbachs, which included 100,000 well-selected, maintained, and cataloged volumes assembled by Karl Theodor before coming to Munich, completing the metamorphosis of the Hofbibliothek, virtually overnight, into the second most important library in Europe, after the Bibliothèque nationale in Paris.

But was the Hofbibliothek still a library at all? As Otto Hartig wrote in an article for the magazine *Bayerland* in 1932, the secularization of monastery libraries meant for Munich "both untold riches and an immeasurable chaos that put to shame all previous library experience." For almost 15 years after 1802, scholars in Munich had to navigate between mountains of monastery books stacked in provisional warehouses throughout Munich, with no catalog to guide them. Aretin's attempts to stem this chaos are described in an unpublished history of the library for the years between 1802 and 1826 compiled by Martin Schrettinger, an ex-Benedictine monk who came to the court library in 1802. Schrettinger recounts how Aretin enlisted the services of "an entire horde of moonlighting servants, copyists, handwork apprentices, failed students, and other vagabonds" to record title information and, without any formal training, assign a subject designation so the books could be integrated into the systematic standard that Aretin had identified, namely the *Jenaer Literatur-Repertorium*, a classification scheme based on the Göttingen model, the most respected of the age. The result was, in Schrettinger's words, an "artificial chaos" that exacerbated the natural one, so that "only a fortunate coincidence permitted a requested book to be found, even after a search of several days." Schrettinger also documents in his manuscript history the equally disastrous attempt of Aretin's successor, Julius Wilhelm Hamberger, to apply the respected Göttingen classification and shelving scheme directly to the incommensurate conditions of post-secularization Munich. Hamberger, an experienced librarian from Gotha, arrived in Munich in March 1808 and worked with great determination but failed nonetheless, dying miserably in a Bayreuth insane asylum in 1813.

With the discrete patronage of Count Montgelas, whose personal librarian he had become following Hamberger's slide into madness, and also the support of then acting director Joseph Scherer, Schrettinger was given the opportunity to undertake the third attempt at damming the *Bücherflut* (flood of books) of Munich. Schrettinger had become reasonably well known in library circles across Germany as the author of a self-published treatise on *Bibliothek-Wissenschaft* (library science—incidentally the first recorded use of the term in any Western language) in 1808. In this work, based on a careful reading of the philosophy of Immanuel Kant, Schrettinger broke with the age-old requirement that libraries be shelved in subject order, instead insisting that any shelf order will do provided that a system of catalogs can direct users to a desired book's location. This revolutionary separation of catalog and shelf order relieved librarians of the need to debate conflicting classification possibilities for a given book before assigning a shelf location. Suddenly their work—ordering the collection so that known items could be found—could proceed very rapidly on the basis of new conventions governing the creation of main entries (*Hauptaufnahmen*) that Schrettinger also elaborated. From the time Schrettinger had been given permission to proceed in 1814, it took just three years to place nearly 500,000 books, bibliographically accessible, on the shelves. By 1818 a shelf list (*Nummern-Repertorium*) was also complete. Schrettinger then spent the remaining years of his life on a catalog of subject headings (*Alphabetischer Realkatalog*) that by his death in 1851 encompassed 84,000 volumes. (It was discontinued five years after Schrettinger's death but is still accessible today in the catalog room of the BSB.)

Schrettinger's monumental achievement was not generally valued during his lifetime, although a number of important European libraries, including Eichstätt, Frankfurt, Karlsruhe, Vienna, Budapest, and even Athens (which had a Wittelsbach as king after achieving independence from Turkey), adopted what was called the "Munich shelving scheme." Schrettinger was widely disparaged in traditional German circles—his introductory "textbook" to library science was not even owned by the library of the University of Göttingen 100 years after it was published. This neglect continued until the rehabilitation of his theoretical work in three famous essays by Georg Leyh, published in the *Zentralblatt für Bibliothekswesen*.

According to historian Rupert Hacker, by 1818 what by then was called the *Hof- und Centralbibliothek*—a name emphasizing that the library had been recognized as having important national functions—possessed holdings approaching 420,000 volumes. These consisted of the historical (pre-1803) core collection of 70,000 volumes, another 200,000 printed and 20,000 manuscript works appropriated from ecclesiastical and other confiscated libraries during the secularization, 100,000 volumes from the incorporated court library of Mannheim, and 30,000 volumes acquired by purchase or exchange, either individually or as part of whole libraries, between 1803 and 1818. Facilitating exchange and a constant source of revenue were an additional 200,000 often highly valuable duplicates left over from the secularization. Aretin especially promoted the sale of these duplicates in the early years, although his methods sometimes appear to have benefited not only the library but also his business partners in Munich. In any event, by 1811 Aretin had spent 135,839 gulden on acquisitions, in addition to the 44,000 gulden appropriated to his budget by the library's oversight commission despite the huge fiscal pressures of wartime and the flood of books already coming to Munich from secularized libraries. Among these purchases were important ones such as the 1810 acquisition of Version A of the *Nibelungenlied*. Paul Ruf's characterization of Aretin as a "bibliomaniac" would appear to have some justification, but without a doubt it was Aretin's extraordinary appetite for new books that laid the foundation for the library's enduring importance and reputation.

In particular the library's 22,000 manuscripts and 24,000 incunabula (including multiple copies of approximately 9,000 different works) qualified it in those years as one of the richest collections in the world, a status it has never lost. Ludwig Hain cataloged the incunabula holdings in his *Repertorium Bibliographicum*, published between 1826 and 1838. The Germanist and librarian Johann Andreas Schmeller performed a similar function for the manuscript collection, in the process bringing to light remarkable historical documents, including the famous *Carmina burana,* the collection of over 300 often ribald medieval songs in Latin and Middle High German made world-famous by Carl Orff in 1937. Aretin had discovered this 13th-century collection during his confiscation of the Benediktbeuern library in 1803; Schmeller's first printed edition was published in 1847. Indeed, much of the most important German research in the humanities during the 19th century in the disciplines of European and world history, philology, music history, Oriental and Asian studies, and linguistics was made possible by the unprecedented concentration of library resources in Munich.

Gärtner's New Library Building on the Ludwigstrasse, 1843 to 1945

The critical space shortage that resulted from the dramatic growth of the library was not addressed until Crown Prince Ludwig became King Ludwig I in October 1825. Ludwig I had grandiose architectural plans for his capital and also recognized the need for a new library building commensurate with the institution's growing renown. In June 1826, just eight months after becoming king, Ludwig ordered construction of a new building. The original site was to be Königsplatz, facing the Glyptothek museum, on the western periphery of the city. For numerous reasons, among them the limited size of the available site, this plan was later changed to an undeveloped area on the east side of the grand north-south boulevard that Ludwig planned between Munich and Schwabing, just south of the Ludwigskirche. The king entrusted the design to the gifted architect Friedrich von Gärtner but (often to Gärtner's consternation) remained actively involved in developing the plans himself, envisioning for "his" library a larger version of the Palazzo Ruspoli in Florence. Further input was solicited from Martin Schrettinger and the director of the library (since 1826), Philipp Lichtenthaler. The usual court intrigues—especially the jealous scheming of fellow architect Leo von Klenze—as well as fiscally motivated parliamentary resistance delayed completion by many years, but on 8 March 1843, after 11 years of intermittent construction, the keys to the new structure were handed to Lichtenthaler. Just four months later, the library completed its relocation from its old quarters in the Jesuit collegium.

Gärtner's new building for the Hof-und Staatsbibliothek (the name of the library from 1829 to 1918), with its imposing 500-foot-long brick facade along Munich's decorous Ludwigstrasse, framing Schwanthaler's statues of Homer, Aristotle, Thucydides, and Hippocrates watching over the main entrance, was one of the first major architectural projects executed expressly to house a large and growing library. On the inside it combined anachronistic baroque touches—a huge staircase at the entrance reserved for the king alone and, more generally, a lavish use of open space—with perceptive bibliotechnical innovations. Among these was the separation of storage, administration, and public areas, as well as the far-sighted provision for adequate growth space for the next century.

Acquisitions during the rest of the 19th century were fueled by a regular and growing collections budget for current and retrospective purchases, a renewed and strengthened depository law imposed on all Bavarian publishers (especially important following the legislation of copyright protection in 1840 and 1865), and the exchange, sale, and auction from the supply of duplicates, which by 1859 had dwindled to approximately half its original size. Between 5,000 and 6,000 incunabula were also sold by the end of the 19th century. Two of the library's three copies of the 42-line Gutenberg Bible were sold in 1832 and 1858, respectively. Such transactions financed significant new purchases, such as the acquisition of the library of the French Orientalist Etienne Quatremère, numbering some 45,000 printed works and 1,200 manuscripts, mainly in Arabic, Persian, and Turkish. Another section of the library to benefit from targeted purchases was the music collection, which became a separate department in 1857. From the earliest days of Albrecht V, the cultivation of the music collection was a priority of Bavarian rulers. This tradition was continued through acquisitions such as the collection of Anton Friedrich Justus Thibaut, bringing the total number of music manuscripts to more than 5,000 by the end of the century. The worldwide importance of the Staatsbibliothek as a repository of manuscript and printed music today remains undiminished.

Although yearly acquisitions climbed from 3,000 in 1850 to 15,000 in 1900 and the total number of volumes reached 1 million by the turn of the century, the Hof-und Staatsbibliothek was surpassed in size by the Royal Library in Berlin by the early years of the 20th century. Perhaps more serious, Munich began to lag behind other libraries in Germany and the world in the areas of collection organization and access. Important reforms were carried out under the administration of Hans Schnorr von Carolsfeld. Among them was the introduction of accession order (*numerus currens*) for new acquisitions, achieving at last the complete separation of shelf order and book content, mediated by catalogs, that Schrettinger had argued for a century earlier. (The BSB is to this day, with the exception of its excellent general reading room collection of some 41,000 volumes as well as a large stock of current journals, a closed-stack library.)

During the two world wars and the two decades between them, the fate of the BSB was inevitably tied to that of the rest of Germany. Surprisingly, even during the great inflation of the early 1920s, the library continued to acquire between 30,000 and 50,000 volumes per year. During the Nazi regime, foreign acquisitions became increasingly problematic, and the works of proscribed writers, though not destroyed, were separated from the rest of the collection. The exhibit activity of the BSB also reflected the exploitation of the library for Nazi purposes. An exhibit in May and June 1939 entitled "Spain in Book and Image" carefully curried favor with the recently triumphant Franco regime, whereas other exhibits, such as "German Alsace" and "England Unmasked," both of 1941, transparently served the political purposes of Hitler's Reich at war.

On the night of 9 March 1943, the first large air attack by Allied bombers was launched on the city of Munich. An incendiary bomb penetrated the glass roof of the main reading room and set off a fire that ultimately incinerated half a million volumes, one-quarter of the entire library. Destroyed in the fire were whole collections in the humanities and natural sciences, including what had been the world's largest Bible collection which, ironically, had been assembled by the atheist Aretin. The losses would have been far greater had not the director of the manuscript collection, Paul Ruf, taken care to distribute 1,400 large wooden crates of books and other treasures to safe places all over Bavaria, including many buildings that had been or were once again monasteries. This distribution recreated, if but for a moment in time, a decentralization of library resources that the Bavarian state had sought with uncompromising singleness of purpose to overcome 140 years before. In later attacks, further collections were destroyed (though on a much smaller scale), and by war's end only approximately 15 percent of Gärtner's library building remained.

Looking Ahead, 1945 to the Present

Physical recovery from the losses and destruction of the war reached a provisional conclusion in 1970 with the completed reconstruction of the south wing of the Gärtner library. Although many of the collections lost in the war were irreplaceable, a concerted effort was made to replace them using title lists, the antiquarian market, and exchange. Sizeable gifts from abroad and bequests of private scholarly collections have also helped reconstruct decimated subject areas.

Today, as the principal beneficiary of 500 years of collecting ardor of the Wittelsbach family, of the 200 monastery libraries secularized in Bavaria and its possessions between 1802 and 1815, as well as of numerous exquisite private, scholarly, and aristocratic libraries, the Bavarian State Library in Munich possesses extraordinary riches, among them close to 19,000 incunabula, 68,500 pre-1900 maps (373,200 total), and 45,000 bound manuscripts—this not including 29,200 music manuscripts and other treasures (79,300 total). In 2001 the collection numbered close to 7.7 million volumes, including more than 706,000 volumes in Eastern and Southeastern European languages, 190,000 from the Near and Middle East, and 285,700 volumes from East Asia. Accessions totaled 213,212 media in all formats, and the BSB maintained 42,100 current journal subscriptions. The acquisitions budget for 2000 was close to DM 20.5 million and for the staff, numbering 467 full-time employees, more than DM 39 million.

JEFFREY GARRETT

Further Reading

Bachmann, Wolf, *Die Attribute der Bayerischen Akademie der Wissenschaften, 1807–1827*, Kallmünz, Germany: Lassleben, 1966

Buzás, Ladislaus, and Fridolin Dressler, *Bibliographie zur Geschichte der Bibliotheken in Bayern*, Munich: Generaldirektion der Bayerischen Staatlichen Bibliotheken, 1986

Dachs, Karl, and Elisabeth Klemm, editors, *Thesaurus Librorum: 425 Jahre Bayerische Staatsbibliothek* (exhib. cat.), Wiesbaden, Germany: Reichert, 1983

Garrett, Jeffrey, "Redefining Order in the German Library, 1775–1825," *Eighteenth-Century Studies* 33, no. 1 (1999)

Hacker, Rupert, "Die bayerischen Herrscher der Spätrenaissance und das schöne Buch," in *Das Gebetbuch Maximilians I. von Bayern: Bayerische Staatsbibliothek München, Clm 23640*, vol. 2, Frankfurt: Fischer, 1986

Hacker, Rupert, "Bayerische Staatsbibliothek: Bestandsgeschichte," in *Handbuch der historischen Buchbestände in Deutschland*, edited by Bernhard Fabian, vol. 10, *Bayern-München*, Hildesheim, Germany, and New York: Olms-Weidmann, 1996

Hacker, Rupert, editor, Beitrage zur Geschichte der Bayerischen Staatsbibliothek, Munich: Saur, 2000

Hartig, Otto, *Die Gründung der Münchner Hofbibliothek durch Albrecht V. und Johann Jakob Fugger*, Munich: Königlich Bayerische Akademie der Wissenschaften, 1917

Jahn, Cornelia, Hermann Leskien, and Ulrich Montag, editors, *Bayerische Staatsbibliothek: Ein Selbstporträt*, Munich: Bayerische Staatsbibliothek, 1997

Kaltwasser, Franz Georg, *Die Bibliothek als Museum: Von der Renaissance bis heute, dargestellt am Beispiel der Bayerischen Staatsbibliothek*, Wiesbaden, Germany: Harrassowitz, 1999

Olson, Michael P., *The Odyssey of a German National Library: A Short History of the Bayerische Staatsbibliothek, the Staatsbibliothek zu Berlin, the Deutsche Bücherei, and the Deutsche Bibliothek*, Wiesbaden, Germany: Harrassowitz, 1996

Ruf, Paul, *Säkularisation und Bayerische Staatsbibliothek*, vol. 1, *Die Bibliotheken der Mendikanten und Theatiner (1799–1802)*, Wiesbaden: Otto Harrassowitz, 1962

Schrepf, Eva, "Die Bayerische Hofbibliothek (Staatsbibliothek), 1803–1843: Versuch einer Skizze ihrer Geschichte," master's thesis, Ludwig-Maximilians-Universität, 1989

Birmingham Central Library

Address:	Birmingham Central Library Chamberlain Square Birmingham B3 3HQ England UK Telephone: 121-303-4511 Fax: 121-233-4458 www.birmingham.gov.uk/libraries
Founded:	1865
Holdings (1999):	Volumes: 1.2 million. Archives and manuscripts: 26,250 linear feet; graphic materials: 2 million; maps: 52,000; microforms: 431,000.
Special Collections:	*Areas of Concentration:* Archives (official, private, and public); bindings; early and fine printing; history; local government; photography; railways; rare and early editions; records of industry; urban landed estates. *Individual Collections:* John Baskerville; Boulton and Watt archives of the Industrial Revolution; Francis Frith photographic archive; John Hardman and Company stained glass and metalwork archive; Middlemore Child Emigration Homes archives; Shakespeare collection; war poetry collection; Warwickshire photographic survey. *Papers:* Matthew Boulton; Cadbury, Calthorpe, and Gough family papers; Charles Parker; Benjamin Stone; James Watt.

Origins

By 1860 it was clear that many leading provincial cities in Great Britain were adopting library services according to the Public Libraries Act of 1850 (which permitted local authorities to set up services with the consent of the majority of ratepayers), and Birmingham voted to do likewise. A site in Ratcliff Place was acquired for a central library, and the lending library and newsroom opened in September 1865; the reference library followed a year later, with an initial stock of 16,195 books and 2,030 patent specifications. An important component was a Shakespeare Memorial Library, to honor the memory of the England's greatest literary hero, the books for which were presented by a voluntary committee on the condition that a separate room be set aside for the collection. At its opening in 1868, the collection contained 1,239 books in five languages, including a copy of the Fourth Folio edition of the plays (1685).

The general reference collections grew rapidly after the opening of the library, and by the end of the decade it contained some 24,213 volumes. The books initially acquired were selected to represent all shades of opinion, be of lasting value, and include rare and expensive books that individuals could not afford. Approximately half the additions to the collection continued to come from donations, including an important collection of editions of the works of Miguel de Cervantes given by William Bragge in 1873. The great prize of these years, however, was the acquisition of the Staunton collection of Warwickshire antiquities, purchased for £2,285 (raised by public appeal) in 1875. The collection included more than 2,000 printed books and pamphlets from the 15th century onward; drawings and engravings of Warwickshire towns and buildings; and a collection of manuscripts, medals, and coins that included the illuminated Register of the Guild of St. Anne at Knowle (1412–1535) and the antiquarian collections of Simon Archer of Umberslade, Thomas Sharp of Coventry, and William Hamper of Birmingham.

To provide improved facilities, work on an expanded building began in 1878, but on 11 January 1879 a workman thawing a gas pipe set fire to the wooden partition erected as a temporary end wall of the reference library. The principal contents of the lending library were rescued, but the building and practically the whole contents of the reference library were lost, with only 1,000 out of nearly 50,000 items saved. Of the irreplaceable manuscripts in the Staunton collection, only the Guild Book of Knowle was saved, whereas the Cervantes and Shakespeare collections were almost totally destroyed. Within hours of the catastrophe, poignant letters of sympathy began to flow in to the chairman of the Free Libraries Committee. William Bickley, a local antiquarian, noted that "the burnt paper fell freely about Moseley . . . I have a fragment of a page found in Wilmot's Field." Howard Pearson, a major donor to the Reference Library, wrote, "It seems to me the greatest calamity which has ever befallen us. We have little that is ancient and little that is splendid—this thing was our just and honest pride." A more optimistic correspondent recorded that "the Birmingham Library stood almost alone among provincial libraries in containing what cannot be replaced; on the other hand there is no town as certain as Birmingham to restore whatever admits of restoration."

Within days an astonishingly successful public appeal had been launched to augment the insurance value of the building and its contents, which raised more than £14,000 by the end of the year. Donations of books also flooded in, including works from the Royal Library and donations from the trustees of the British Museum, the Bodleian Library at Oxford, and the library committees of Liverpool, Manchester, and Glasgow. A gift by David Malins of approximately 350 works relating to Birmingham laid the foundation for renewing the local history collection.

Plans for a new library were produced by the original architects of the firm Martin and Chamberlain and approved at a meeting of the council on 24 May 1879. The mood of the city was summed up by Sam Gamgee, a Birmingham doctor and prominent citizen, who wrote to the mayor on 16 January: "Architects and builders must not be stinted; the new library building should be an educational edifice worthy of, and capable of safely preserving, the treasures which we all hope to gather together again . . . Many books are grown more scarce and costly . . . We must not allow the Birmingham Libraries Committee to be outbid in the market, when they have the chance of buying books for the information and culture of this and succeeding generations of Birmingham men and women."

The Second Central Library

After three years in temporary accommodations, during which time the donations of well-wishers and the active acquisition policy of the council had once again built up the collections of the reference library to some 50,000 volumes, the new Birmingham Central Library was opened on 1 June 1882. The opening ceremony began in the town hall with a series of speeches. Samuel Timmins, chairman of the libraries committee, assured the gathering that "no effort has been spared or will be spared to make the library which we are about to enter an honour, a credit, and a glory to the town." At a formal dinner that evening, Joseph Chamberlain said, "I suppose there are still some persons . . . who would [say] 'What have aldermen and town councillors to do with art or with literature? They are matters above their comprehension—their duties are paving and lighting and the removal of nuisances. . . .' Well, Mr. Mayor, in Birmingham we entertain a very different idea of the functions of local government. . . . We claim also [as] a right, as well as a duty, the privilege of ministering to its intellectual wants, and of contributing . . . to its cultivation and its refinement."

From its earliest days, the library had collected manuscript and printed materials relevant to the history of Birmingham and the surrounding counties, but under the leadership of Walter Powell (chief librarian, 1912–28), and more particularly that of his successor, Herbert Cashmore (1928–47), a new enthusiasm for this aspect of the library's work was apparent. By far the most important collection to be offered at this time was the archive of Matthew Boulton and James Watt, the pioneering steam engine manufacturers. This donation laid the foundation of the library's collections in industrial history, which were described in a 1994 speech by Professor Eric Robinson (a leading British economic and literary historian) as making the library "the most important center in the world for the study of the Industrial Revolution."

The Cashmore Years

Cashmore was renowned for his meticulous attention to detail. His obituary in the *Journal of the Society of Archivists* in 1972 recorded that "every letter and parcel received in the building was opened by him personally, and every reference library catalogue entry for books or manuscripts was approved by him in detail." Certainly his distinctive handwriting is all over the records of the period. He could be blunt and stubborn in debate, frequently infuriating his colleagues on the council of the British Records Association, but he was a sociable man, and his very human and totally candid diaries are full of references to weekend cycling trips and drives with friends. He was, perhaps, the most successful as well as the most autocratic of Birmingham's chief librarians.

Under Cashmore's enthusiastic guidance, the research collections of the library were developed and promoted as never before. In particular, renewed attention was paid to enlarging the collection of manuscripts, and a separate manuscripts section of the library was formed in 1932, eventually becoming the city archives of today. Among the material received in these years were records from a number of landed estates in the vicinity of Birmingham and a delightful collection of 18th- and 19th-century prompt books from the Theatre Royal, Birmingham. Many of these are manuscript copies or heavily annotated, and they form a source of international importance for the early history of pantomime.

The printed special collections were not neglected either. A regular stream of small donations and purchases of modern fine printed works was punctuated by occasional coups such as the purchase of a copy of John James Audubon's *Birds of America* (1827–38) for £150 in 1934. One of the greatest benefactors was Alderman William Aldington Cadbury, who formed a remarkable collection of early printed atlases that he presented to the reference library rather than keeping them for his personal use. He was a careful and selective buyer, acquiring only fine copies, many of them in good contemporary bindings. His gifts included a copy of the 1482 edition of Ptolemy's *Cosmographia*. The library has striven to build on the foundations laid by the Cadbury collection and has bought fine atlases of all periods up to the present day. The result is a collection unmatched in the U.K. public library sector in its scope and quality.

In 1938 the city council approved a resolution of the Libraries Committee that "the Central Library, built 56 years ago for the needs of a population of 400,000, is now seriously overcrowded and can no longer supply the needs of the population of Greater Birmingham, or provide for any extension in the many departments which claim adequate representation in the first [i.e. foremost] municipal library in this country." It authorized the preparation of competitive plans for the erection of a new library, but with the advent of World War II in 1939, plans were shelved for another generation.

During the war, the government considered it important for civilian morale that information and recreational reading continue to be provided, and it was therefore determined to keep libraries open wherever possible. Staff hours of duty were increased to compensate for a shortage of personnel, first from 38 to 42 hours a week and later to 46 hours, and the weekday closing time was brought forward to 6:00 P.M. in winter, to save on fuel for lighting and heating. Mercifully, the research collections in the reference library were unscathed, although their continuing presence in the center of the city was a source of anxiety to the Libraries Committee during the Blitz.

Cashmore retired as city librarian in 1947 but remained as librarian emeritus until his death in 1972. The principal impact of his immediate successors, Frederick J. Patrick (1947–56) and Vincent H. Woods (1956–64), was to shift the emphasis of the library's work away from the research collections into funding and promoting the commercial and technical libraries (founded in 1919 and 1924 respectively and located in the Council House), the importance of which to postwar reconstruction was widely recognized. In 1955 and 1956 it became necessary to move 60,000 of the less-used books from the reference library to an off-site storage facility, the first of a series of such temporary expedients that eventually scattered the book stock around the city. But by such means, the total stock of the reference library was able to rise to 700,000 volumes by 1960. New services were also being provided to respond to new needs and new formats, most notably the opening of the first phonograph record loan service in 1965 and the commencement of Asian-language collections in 1968.

The Third Central Library

At the end of the 1950s, the Libraries Committee once more added a new library building to its capital program. A site was chosen in 1960, and detailed planning began in 1964 under the guidance of William Taylor, who was appointed city librarian in that year (his tenure ended in 1977). Meetings between the architects from the John Madin Design Group and librarians were held throughout the project, consultation between designers and clients being recognized as crucial to the success of the building. The library formed part of a larger complex, some elements of which were never completed according to the original designs. Building work started at the beginning of April 1969 and was completed early in 1973 after lengthy delays caused by strikes in the building industry. The move of books, equipment, and other materials from the old library and its various outposts began on 6 June 1973 and took a little more than three months to complete. The new library opened progressively from the bottom floors upward between June and October 1973, and work then commenced on the demolition of the old library building.

The new central library held some 970,000 books in the reference collections and 100,000 in the lending library, accommodated on 31 miles of shelving that gave a total capacity of 1.5 million books. With space for 1,200 readers, the building was four times the size of its predecessor. It is hard to recapture how impressive and revolutionary the design of the new library seemed at that time. The architects were told that the rapid pace of change in library activities and the variety of demands made by readers meant they should not approach their task as being merely to provide a larger building with modern amenities. The opportunity of opening a new building was taken to introduce open access to a significant portion of the stock and to adopt a wholly departmental structure for the library. The original divisions have since been reduced in number, but the subject specialization permitted by the departmental approach has been successfully maintained to date. By early 2000, Birmingham Central Library was the only major public library in Britain to be organized in this way.

In a pamphlet entitled "Birmingham Central Library," published for the Annual Conference of the Library Association in 1975, which described the approach taken to the design of the library, great importance was placed on the need for flexibility and variety. It was noted that readers should have a choice of surroundings and atmospheres for their work, and this was achieved by segregating the busy lending services from the reference library where "the very wide range of readers . . . wish to spend long periods . . . in an atmosphere conducive to study." It was envisaged that the opening of the new building would stimulate an increase in use of the library; to cater to this, escalators were provided to facilitate mass transit through the building. Budgetary provision was made for enhancing the library's book fund and for employing 30 percent more staff in the new building.

Another major innovation was the introduction of a computerized catalog in 1973. Unfortunately, for financial reasons the planned transfer of pre-1973 catalog records to the new system has never been systematically undertaken, so that card catalogs remain in daily use throughout the library. Finally, the floors were planned with flexibility to allow for future changes in patterns of use, although unfortunately the need for pervasive electric wiring and computer cabling was not foreseen.

The growth in use rapidly exceeded all expectations, and it was soon apparent that the building, which was already the biggest public library facility in Europe, was not big enough. Serious overcrowding was apparent at busy times, and many sections ran out of space for their growing holdings before 1980, when the original fixed-position shelving in the stacks was replaced by rolling presses to provide additional capacity. Yet further space was required a few years later, and a massive library stack with mobile shelving—planned to accommodate 500,000 volumes—was built beneath the central library in 1986. It was anticipated that this would contain the expansion of the library's collections for 25 years, but the rapid growth of the holdings, and especially of the city archives, has meant that this space is already fully occupied.

The availability of space in the new library, when for decades expansion had been constrained by the limitations of the old building, enabled the reference library to make a number of very important acquisitions during the 1970s and 1980s. These included the personal papers of Matthew Boulton, one of the city's industrial pioneers (lent in 1974); the Skett collection of printed maps (given in 1978); the audio tapes and papers of Charles Parker, a BBC radio producer and pioneer of the recording of popular culture (lent in 1984); the Francis Frith photographic archive (purchased in 1985); and the William Ridler collection of modern fine printing (lent in 1988).

Since the early 1990s, under the leadership of successive chief librarians, a new emphasis has been placed on the library working in partnership with other agencies to support the broader social objectives of local and central government. This has brought new services into the building, such as a Childcare Information Bureau, and has refocused the work of many others. The number of patrons served has risen, reaching a peak in 1996, when 2.2 million visits were made to the library (an average of approximately 7,000 per day). At the same time, there has been a degree of financial stringency not seen since the 1950s, with significant reductions in the number of staff and drastic curtailment of the purchasing power of the acquisitions budget. The advent of electronic resources has required a major investment in cabling and equipment as well as in product licenses and staff training, most of which has only been possible with assistance of grants from central government and elsewhere.

Increasingly, the library looks to external funding to support new initiatives. The most significant examples of this have been two major grants from the European Regional Development Fund for developing the library's services to business enterprises in the West Midlands, and assistance from the Heritage Lottery Fund and private donors for the cataloging and conservation of all the collections relating to Boulton and Watt (begun in 1998). These developments have been possible because of a new political awareness of the social value of libraries in the United Kingdom, and the government has frequently cited the Birmingham Central Library as a model of best practice. Birmingham Library Services, of which the Central Library is the flagship, also operates a branch library system of 40 community libraries and mobile units.

NICHOLAS KINGSLEY

Further Reading

Allen, Phillip, *Atlas of Atlases: The Map-maker's Vision of the World: Atlases from the Cadbury Collection, Birmingham Central Library,* London: Ebury, and New York: Abrams, 1992

The Central Central Library: A Case Study of Birmingham Central Library in the City Centre, Bournes Green: Comedia, 1993

Coming to Light: Birmingham's Photographic Collections, Birmingham: Birmingham Libraries and Birmingham Museums and Art Gallery, 1998

Harrop, Dorothy A., *Catalogue of the William Ridler Collection of Fine Printing,* Birmingham: Birmingham City Council, Public Libraries Department, 1989

Langford, John Alfred, *The Birmingham Free Libraries, the Shakespeare Memorial Library, and the Art Gallery,* Birmingham: Hall and English, 1871; reprint, 1983

Mason, Amy, editor, *The New Birmingham Central Libraries: Proceedings of the twenty-first annual study group, Worcester, April 6 to 9, 1973,* London: Library Association, 1975

Notes on the History of Birmingham Public Libraries, 1861–1961, Birmingham: Birmingham Public Libraries, 1962

Rathbone, Niky, *Mirth without Mischief: An Introduction to the Parker Collection of Early Children's Books and Games,* Birmingham: West Midlands Branch of the Library Association, 1982

A Shakespeare Bibliography: The Catalogue of the Birmingham Shakespeare Library, Birmingham Public Libraries, 7 vols., London: Mansell, 1971

Bolton Library at Cashel

Address: Bolton Library at Cashel
John Street, Cashel
County Tipperary
Ireland
Telephone: 62-62511
Fax: 62-62068

Founded: 1744

Holdings (1999): Volumes: 12,000. Incunabula: 20; manuscripts: 25.

Special Collections: *Areas of Concentration:* Architecture; astronomy; ecclesiastical works; heraldry; history; law; literature; mathematics; medicine; natural sciences; travel. *Individual Collections:* Irish printing.

Origins

The diocesan library in Cashel, County Tipperary, was named after its founder, Archbishop Theophilus Bolton, and is one of the great treasures of the Church of Ireland. Bolton was born during the last quarter of the 17th century and was educated at Trinity College, Dublin. When still a young man he became canon of St. Patrick's Cathedral in Dublin, where Jonathan Swift was dean. Bolton was appointed archbishop of Cashel in 1730 after a brief spell as bishop of Clonfert and, later, bishop of Elphin. In Cashel he built a large house and library for himself, the first floor of which was modeled on the Long Room in Trinity College, Dublin. He had acquired some 6,000 volumes from the collection of his friend William King, the late archbishop of Dublin—a celebrated scholar, bibliophile, and book collector—and these, together with his own books, formed the core of the library. Theophilus Bolton died in 1744 having bequeathed his library together with explicit directions on the future of his books:

> First I the said Theophilus Bolton Arch Bishop of Cashel do hereby leave all my Books in my Library and dwelling house at Cashel for the use of the Arch Bishop of Cashel for the time being and the Clergy of the Diocese . . . my Will and meaning being that the said Books shall remain and continue in the said Library forever for the use of my Successors in the said see and the Clergy of the said Diocese for the time being and that none of the said Books be removed from thence.

Collections

The collection is small, but select. It is the collection of two archbishops and also includes portions of the collections of Archbishop Narcissus Marsh and Bishops Michael Jephson and Samuel Foley. The library has some 12,000 titles and is probably one of the finest collections of antiquarian books in Ireland outside Dublin. The collection includes a small number of manuscripts, together with the printed collection of ecclesiastical works and works on mathematics, astronomy, architecture, the natural sciences, medicine, literature, travel, geography, history, heraldry, military matters, politics, and the law. A collection of more than 200 pamphlets is significant, particularly in relation to 17th-century printings from Dublin, Cork, Kilkenny, and Waterford. There are some 20 incunabula, a wealth of later liturgical printings, and examples of the works of the great Continental printers of the 16th and 17th centuries.

Organization

In common with many of the cathedral libraries of Ireland, Cashel has suffered from neglect and lack of money and appreciation for its importance. In the late 18th century Archbishop John Cox arranged to have the books cataloged. His catalog and the listings of William King's books are vital sources for estimating the original size and content of the library. When militia troops were billeted in the adjoining building during the 1798 rebellion, the books were plundered for fuel. This was the beginning of the woes that have beset this library to the present day. In 1822 Archbishop Richard Laurence brought with him to Cashel his son-in-law Henry Cotton, the former sublibrarian in the Bodleian Library at Oxford. Cotton examined the library and in the same year (1822) in a report to Laurence commented, "As the Archbishop [Bolton] left no funds for the enlargement or even the preservation of the Collection, not only has it received no increase since his death, except by a few accidental donations, but [it] has fallen into such great neglect, that many of the books have been lost, many utterly spoiled by damp, and very many more left in such a state as to be useless without previous repair."

During Cotton's term, a chapter house and library were erected on the grounds of the cathedral. Designed and built by William Tinsley, the library building also echoed the style of the Long Room at Trinity College. During this period Cotton reestablished the library as a lending library, bringing in new theology and forming a clerical readers' circle. It was not until 1873 that a catalog of the Cashel Library was published. This was the first printed catalog and remained an important reference tool for more than a hundred years.

The Irish Church Act of 1869 dissolved and disendowed the Church of Ireland, leaving the library without any financial support, and it began to be seen as a drain on resources rather than an asset. It was not until 1961 when Dean Charles Wolfe came to Cashel that it began to recover. Although he sought and secured generous outside assistance from the corporate sector, the dean was forced to sell some of the collection in order to maintain the rest. Advice was sought and a London book dealer concluded, incorrectly, that the collection was primarily ecclesiastical in content and decided that sciences, mathematics, maps, and even history were unnecessary. The result was that hundreds of books were sold, many of them going to the Folger Shakespeare Library in Washington, D.C. The library was open to the public on a daily basis, and there was some optimism that the library's problems had been solved, although this optimism proved to be unfounded. Ten years later, when Dean David Woodworth arrived in 1984, the library was damp, with cracked or broken windows, and the books were badly in need of attention. A significant number of important titles had been stolen. The new dean was vigorous and committed, and within three years, with the help of local enterprise, the library was restored and a program of book conservation was initiated. The dean had begun to look outside the Cashel region for support in securing the future of this important collection when he died suddenly in 1994.

The Future

Under the guidance of the present dean of Cashel, Philip Knowles, the Bolton Library has forged a formal link with the nearby University of Limerick, and a joint committee of management has been appointed. The University of Limerick agreed that although the library will always remain in Cashel, the university will provide technological, cataloging, and academic support for the collections. As an initial step, the printed catalog has been submitted to the *English Short Title Catalogue* project. Plans are well advanced to put the entire catalog online, making it available to scholars from the university and the scholarly community at large.

PATRICIA DONLON

Further Reading

Carson, Harry, "Cathedral Libraries in Ireland," *An Leabharlann: The Irish Library* 14 (1998)

Woodworth, David, *Cashel's Museum of Printing and Early Books: A Short History of the GPA-Bolton Library*, Tipperary: Tentmaker, 1994

Boston Athenaeum

Address: Boston Athenaeum
10½ Beacon Street
Boston, Massachusetts 02108-3777
USA
Telephone: 617-227-0270
Fax: 617-227-5266
www.bostonathenaeum.org

Founded: Incorporated 1807

Holdings (1999): Volumes: 500,000. Archives and manuscripts: 600 linear feet, including eight pre-1600 manuscripts; current serials: 500; incunabula: 68; microforms: 1,000 reels; newspapers: 7,000 linear feet; sound recordings: 200 books on tape.

Special Collections: *Areas of Concentration:* Biography; book arts; books in Native American languages; broadsides; Confederate States imprints; 18th- and 19th-century tracts and pamphlets; fine arts; history; literature; 19th- and 20th-century American prints and photographs. *Individual Collections:* Boston Athenaeum and Boston Library Society archives; first editions and related works by Lord Byron, T.S. Eliot, John Fowles, and John Masefield; Francis Hindes Groome Gypsy collection; Merrymount Press archive; Provident Institution for Savings records; 17th-century works from the King's Chapel (Boston) library; Henry Rowe Schoolcraft collection of books in Native American languages; works from the libraries of General Henry Knox, Jean Louis (Cardinal Cheverus), and George Washington. *Papers:* P.T. Barnum; Cecilia Beaux; Nathaniel Bradlee; Charles Bulfinch; Isaac Hull; Stewart Mitchell; Robert Morris; John Singer Sargent; Cephas Thompson.

Introduction

The Boston Athenaeum is an independent membership library that has both public and private aspects. It serves its membership though library programs and offers lectures, exhibitions, concerts, and other events throughout the year. At the same time, it maintains and augments significant research collections—books, manuscripts, and visual materials—and makes these freely available to a broad community of scholars. Although it is principally a library, the Athenaeum has a museum function as well. Its collection of paintings, sculpture, fine furniture, and oriental carpets enhance the historic building, and the Athenaeum maintains an art gallery open to the public. Although it is a proprietary institution, yearly memberships are open to all.

The Anthology Society

In 1805 a group of learned gentlemen led by William Emerson began meeting in rented rooms in order to edit the *Monthly Anthology and Boston Review,* which published the writing of both new and established American and English writers. A plan for establishing a public reading room to house a library of periodical publications rapidly grew in scope as books, maps, and other materials were deposited by members of the society. In 1806 a new institution called the Boston Athenaeum was created and the collections of the Anthology Society reading room transferred to it. Modeled after the Athenaeum in Liverpool, England, the Boston Athenaeum was established as a proprietary library. The first sale of shares followed incorporation in 1807.

A Gentleman's Library

Although the Boston Library Society had existed since 1792, the Athenaeum's mission was a markedly more scholarly one. Library collections grew in all directions—literature, sciences, the arts—as the first librarian, William Smith Shaw, scoured Boston, and Obadiah Rich (U.S. Consul in Spain and one of the Athenaeum's founders) searched western Europe and England for books. The library of the American Academy of Arts and Sciences, the King's Chapel Library, the Theological Library, and the libraries of the Boston Medical Society and the Massachusetts Scientific Association were placed with the Athenaeum during the next two decades. Quickly outgrowing rented space in Scollay's Building, the Athenaeum purchased the Rufus Amory house in 1809. By 1821, however, these quarters were wholly inadequate to contain a collection of more than 12,000 volumes, and the library moved on to occupy the mansion in Pearl Street donated by merchant James Perkins. In these early years the Athenaeum was in essence a gentleman's library dedicated to the education and self-improvement of its members, operating with the cozy ambience of a private club.

The Athenaeum in Pearl Street grew in wealth and popularity. A public art gallery was opened in 1827 to show the collection of original Old Masters paintings and copies, plaster casts of antique sculpture, and the work of emerging American and European artists. Annual exhibitions were advertised and reviewed in the papers and drew large crowds. Plans were floated for constructing a lecture hall. Toward the middle of the century the Athenaeum, with almost 50,000 books and the largest collection of paintings and sculpture in New England, played a central role in the flowering of U.S. culture. It served as the working library of Bronson Alcott, George Bancroft, Ralph Waldo Emerson, Charles Sumner, and others; women such as social reformers Lydia Maria Child and Elizabeth Palmer Peabody were granted access to the collections.

As the downtown waterfront sections of the city were given over to commerce and the wealthy merchants moved their families to quieter districts such as Beacon Hill, the Athenaeum and other such institutions followed suit. Designed by Edward Clarke Cabot, its new Beacon Street building consisted of three floors behind its neo-Palladian facade: a sculpture gallery on the first floor, a library on the second, and a painting gallery on the top floor. Opened in 1849, the Athenaeum was the prototype of the single great hall library in the 19th century. The effect of this prominent edifice on the Athenaeum's fortunes was twofold. Important collections of books (including the library of George Washington) and works of art flowed into the building. In 1853 the city of Boston waged a campaign to secure the Athenaeum as the new public library. It was with difficulty that this vigorous sortie was deflected, but the gentleman's library endured.

Athenaeum trustees, and in particular those serving on the library committee, had complete control over the institution's affairs, down to the selection of books for the collection. Beginning at mid-century, however, capable administrators were hired who looked well beyond the boardrooms and dining clubs of Brahmin Boston to begin the march toward modern library practice. William Frederick Poole, librarian from 1856 to 1868, succeeded Charles Folsom. Poole's work as a student at Yale University (New Haven, Connecticut) had resulted in the publication of an index to periodical literature that became a standard source. As librarian at the Athenaeum he was notable for hiring Annie B. Harnden, the first woman employed in a library in the United States. Perhaps his most lauded achievement on behalf of the Athenaeum was to bring together the largest collection of materials published in the Confederate States. At the close of the Civil War, Poole sent trustee Francis Parkman and proprietor Algernon Coolidge south with instructions to ship to Boston any printed material they felt would be of lasting value. Books, full runs of newspapers, official records, and ephemeral publications were bought for next to nothing from their cash-poor owners.

The first printed catalog of the library was produced in 1810 and revised and expanded sporadically over the decades. But by mid-century the catalog had become unwieldy and imprecise owing to the size of the collection. Charles Ammi Cutter, Poole's successor, labored during the course of twelve years to produce his *Catalogue of the Library of the Boston Athenaeum* (1874 to 1882; reprinted 1974) and his *Rules for a Printed Dictionary Catalogue* (1875). These were nationally regarded schemes for systemizing the organization of knowledge, and the Cutter Expansive Classification System was adopted for use by many mid-Atlantic and New England libraries. (Today the "cuttering" of books is a feature of standard cataloging practice.) By training his professional focus on the organization and development of the Athenaeum's book collections, Charles Ammi Cutter had set the institution off on a new course.

Cutter's tenure at the Athenaeum witnessed the loss of a major element of the institution's program when the Museum of Fine Arts, founded by a number of institutions but principally the Athenaeum, moved out of the Athenaeum in 1876. When the museum moved to a building designed for it in the fashionable Back Bay district, the bulk of the Athenaeum's fine art collection was taken with it on deposit.

The "Family Library"

Like Cutter, William Coolidge Lane (librarian, 1893–98) was well connected to the emerging library profession. After five years of service, Lane returned to Harvard as college librarian to be followed by Charles Knowles Bolton, who served for 35 years.

Although the Athenaeum had relinquished its role as an art museum and had begun to restrict book acquisition to certain fields, by 1900 space was once again at a premium. The half-century old building was cramped and worn. The trustees were also concerned about the movement of the city's population away from Beacon Hill and feared that the library was situated in an increasingly inconvenient location for most members. They went so far as to purchase land in Back Bay and commission designs for a new library, but a determined group of proprietors (led by Amy Lowell) forced the issue of removal to a vote. When the vote narrowly went against them, the trustees sold the Back Bay land for a profit some years later, enabling them to renovate and expand the Beacon Street building. In 1912 and 1913, the contents of the building (including 200,000 books) were removed and the wooden structure gutted and rebuilt with steel to make it fireproof, and two floors were added.

Under Bolton's leadership, the Athenaeum assumed the split character that distinguishes it among libraries today. It is both a family library for its members, catering to casual reading interests, and a research library with important special collections for scholars. Bolton strengthened both aspects of the library's services. He established a children's room, greatly increased the size of the fiction collection, and dropped a number of scholarly periodicals that could be found at Harvard or the Boston Public Library. But he also purchased the library of an authority on the Gypsies, welcomed the gift of books owned by the All Around [Charles] Dickens Club of Boston, bought heavily at the sale of Confederate newspapers from Benson J. Lossing's library in New York in 1912, and initiated the collecting of bookplates and posters. To further encourage serious use of the collections, he experimented with making a "public secretary" available to members for typewriting and research. To satisfy the hunger for murder mysteries, a book mailing service was initiated to reach members away from Boston for the summer. Despite the restrictions that made it impossible for the library to collect comprehensively in any area, Bolton aimed for balance in a largely successful effort to please both camps of users.

Quiescence

The newly renovated and expanded facility was proving costly to maintain, and in 1915 the annual assessment was increased. At this time there were less than 800 shares in use. Unlike his predecessors, Bolton was fairly open with the proprietors about the institution's financial position and aggressively moved to reclaim unused shares. Without seeming to appear ungrateful for the somewhat casual generosity of the proprietors, he began to make yearly appeals for unrestricted funds in order to keep the building operational. For example, he raised the specter of members consulting the books in cold, dark alcoves. Money was needed for other purposes as well, and Bolton's efforts to attract and keep qualified staff led to the establishment of a staff pension fund supported by gifts and bequests. But all of these efforts seemed doomed to failure by the early 1930s as the effects of the Depression began to be felt. In 1932 expenditures, including staff salaries, were drastically cut. In the following year, Charles Knowles Bolton retired.

When they named Elinor Gregory to the post of librarian, the trustees were not entirely comfortable with placing such responsibility in the hands of a woman, and so they appointed Mark Antony DeWolfe Howe to share in the administration of the Athenaeum. By 1937 Gregory had proved herself and Howe was allowed to resign from his position as director to concentrate on writing the library newsletter, *Athenaeum Items*. These were challenging years for the institution, as it struggled to improve service and keep expenses down while operating with a deficit. Staff salaries were reduced again, with a proportionate reduction of hours worked. Other institutions, however, were more desperate: In 1939 the Boston Library Society fell victim to the economy, its proprietors voting to merge with the Athenaeum.

The Whitehill Years

Walter Muir Whitehill, who took over as director and librarian in 1946, was a scholar of wide-ranging tastes, from Spanish Romanesque architecture to local history and genealogy. A prolific writer and lecturer on many subjects, he used the Athenaeum as his working library; his *Boston: A Topographical History* (1959; 2nd edition 1968) was largely based on the library's collections. The image of the library for a quarter century was that projected by Whitehill with his tweeds, George V–style beard, and vague Oxford accent—the Athenaeum was once again a scholar's retreat. During Whitehill's administration the Athenaeum published Assistant Librarian Marjorie Lyle Crandall's catalog of the Confederate imprints collection (1955).

In 1963 it built one of the first workshops for the conservation and restoration of library materials; this was headed by George Cunha, who later founded what is now the Northeast Document Conservation Center in Andover, Massachusetts. A rare book vault was fitted in 1967. In that same year, the first woman trustee, Susan Morse (Mrs. Frederick W.) Hilles, was named.

The Athenaeum Rebuilds

By the late 1960s the collection totaled more than 400,000 volumes and the endowment stood at almost $4 million. Operating costs had doubled during the Whitehill régime, and even though the building's decor had been enhanced, a neglect of the physical plant resulted in major problems for Whitehill's successor, Rodney Armstrong, who became director and librarian in 1973. Armstrong's first concern was the aging building and paying for needed repairs. He immediately set to work. The position of programs officer was created to seek foundation and corporate funding, and a campaign to raise $1 million was launched. Most of the Athenaeum's works of art that had been on deposit at the Museum of Fine Arts since 1876, including Gilbert Stuart's iconic portraits of George and Martha Washington, were finally sold.

An effort to increase readership commenced with the introduction of life memberships; in 1979 there were increases in annual membership fees and assessments on shares. Armstrong began to hire professional librarians and to increase staff salaries and benefits. The composition of the board of trustees changed dramatically during his tenure, becoming more diverse and representative. It became an activist board, with younger members and more women; all now took seriously their fiduciary responsibilities to the Athenaeum. An annual appeal commenced in 1979 and the endowment began to increase dramatically, led by a proliferation of restricted book funds that Armstrong was aggressive in soliciting. In 1978 the old Cutter card catalog was closed and the library joined the online bibliographic service OCLC, becoming increasingly computerized. For the storage and consultation of the Athenaeum's collection of historic prints and photographs, a special study center was opened in 1984. In the end, Armstrong had put the Athenaeum back on a firm foundation for his successor, Richard Wendorf.

Richard Wendorf, recruited from Harvard's Houghton Library in 1997, brought with him a distinguished background in academia. Wendorf has paid particular attention to the scholarly mission of the Athenaeum, increasing the budget for special collections acquisitions and strengthening the research fellowships program established in 1996. He moved quickly toward implementation of the library's online catalog, *Athena*, and its website. Taking advantage of the soaring economy and the institution's healthy finances, the trustees and Wendorf moved to accomplish what had long been deferred—a major renovation and expansion of the building. When completed, the new Athenaeum will have improved climate-controlled stacks, a larger state-of-the-art conservation lab, a proper reading room for the consultation of rare materials, new art galleries, and a new children's library.

A successful capital campaign raising more than $30 million for the endowment confirmed the Athenaeum's position as the largest and richest of the nation's membership libraries.

The history of the Boston Athenaeum had been characterized by its polarities, swinging back and forth from the scholarly retreat to the family library. Was the Athenaeum principally a museum or a library? Should the institution build the research collections or support casual reading interests? Its administrators alternately were those who served as able custodians, preserving the treasures of the past for a select few, and those who embraced new technologies and opened the library to new constituencies, moving the library into the future. In the 21st-century Athenaeum, all of the desirable characteristics of both library types seem to have been successfully combined.

STEPHEN Z. NONACK

Further Reading

The Athenaeum Centenary: The Influence and History of the Boston Athenaeum from 1807 to 1907 with a Record of Its Officers and Benefactors and a Complete List of Proprietors, Boston: The Boston Athenaeum, 1907

Athenaeum Items (1979–)

Fifty Books in the Collection of the Boston Athenaeum, Boston: The Boston Athenaeum, 1994

Howe, Mark Antony DeWolfe, editor, *Journal of the Proceedings of the Society, Which Conducts the Monthly Anthology and Boston Review, October 3, 1805, to July 2, 1811,* Boston: The Boston Athenaeum, 1910

Hoyle, Pamela, Jonathan P. Harding, and Rosemary Booth, *Climate for Art: The History of the Boston Athenaeum Gallery, 1827–1873,* Boston: The Boston Athenaeum, 1976

Miksa, Francis L., editor, *Charles Ammi Cutter, Library Systematizer,* Littleton, Colorado: Libraries Unlimited, 1977

Quincy, Josiah, *The History of the Boston Athenaeum, with Biographical Notices of Its Deceased Founders,* Cambridge, Massachusetts: Metcalf, 1851

Slautterback, Catharina, *Designing the Boston Athenaeum: 10½ at 150,* Boston: The Boston Athenaeum, 1999

Story, Ronald, "Class and Culture in the Boston Athenaeum, 1807–1860," *American Quarterly,* 27 (1975)

Whitehill, Walter Muir, *Museum of Fine Arts, Boston: A Centennial History,* Cambridge, Massachusetts: Belknap Press, 1970

Boston Public Library

Address: Boston Public Library
Copley Square
700 Boylston Street
Boston, Massachusetts 02116
USA
Telephone: 617-536-5400
Fax: 617-536-4306
www.bpl.org

Founded: 1848

Holdings (2000): Volumes: 6.9 million. Current serials: 29,000; films and videos: 27,000; graphic materials: 1 million; manuscripts: 1 million, including 200 pre-1500 manuscripts; maps: 350,000; microforms: 4.8 million; music scores: 120,000; sound recordings: 57,000; video and film: 27,000.

Special Collections: *Areas of Concentration:* Business and finance; children's literature; fine arts; government documents; humanities; music; rare books; science and technology; social sciences.
Individual Collections: Ball collection; Benton collection of common prayer; Allen A. Brown music collection; Goya; Handel and Haydn Society collection; Eilen Kneeland collection; Koussevitzky collection; Maginnis and Walsh architectural collection; Prince collection of Americana, Rowlandson, and Toulouse-Lautrec; Albert Wiggins prints collection. *Papers:* Fred Allen; Nathaniel Bowditch; Maria Weston Chapman; Charlotte S. Cushman; Emily Dickinson; William Addison Dwiggins; William Lloyd Garrison; Rufus Griswold; Harolk Kaese; Hugo Muensterberg; Sacco and Vanzetti.

That the Boston Public Library (BPL) was the first large urban library supported by taxation and that its founding signaled the inception of the public library movement in the United States are accepted and well-known facts. The story behind this landmark event and the library's subsequent history are perhaps less well known but no less significant.

Following the recommendations of a joint special committee on the public library of the bicameral Boston City Council on 6 December 1847 and the express wish of Mayor Josiah Quincy, articulated in his final inaugural address on 3 January 1848, the city council directed the mayor to approach the legislature of the Commonwealth of Massachusetts to secure the "power to enable the City to establish and maintain a public library." The enabling legislation, signed by Governor Briggs less than two months later on 18 March, would affect affairs far beyond the confines of the city of Boston. As Horace Wadlin indicates in his history of the library, "It was the first statute ever passed authorizing the establishment and maintenance of a public library as a municipal institution supported by taxation."

The events that brought the city council to such action warrant some mention. In the spring of 1841 (Nicholas Marie) Alexandre Vattemare, a native of France and an accomplished ventriloquist, arrived in Boston on a mission. Vattemare envisioned a great enterprise—an exchange of books among the civilized nations of the world. This system was, in the ventriloquist's own words, "designed to give the intellectual treasures of the cultivated world the same dissemination and equalization which commerce has already given to its material ones." Such an exchange would, he hoped, create the nuclei of libraries throughout the country. In Boston Vattemare wished to see a number of the existing libraries united in a single institution. Although this dream went unfulfilled, gifts from the city of Paris in 1843, 1847, and 1849 were received by the city of Boston. These gifts were reciprocated, but more importantly, as a result of the second gift the above-mentioned joint special committee on the library was formed. This committee recommended that the gifts from Paris and any others that might be received be deposited in a room on the third floor of the city hall. Thus, the first step in the founding of the Boston Public Library had been taken; and, whether or not one considers Vattemare a charlatan (as some have suggested), or a man with a splendid mission, there can be no doubt that, in the words of Justin Winsor (as quoted in Wadlin's history), "In the agitation that Vattemare incited we must look for the earliest movements which can be linked connectedly with the fruition [the establishment of the Boston Public Library] now enjoyed."

Four full years elapsed before substantial action would be taken on the organization of the public library. During this interim there was some movement toward uniting the incipient public library with the established Boston Athenaeum. This discussion came to naught, and as a result these institutions have instead complemented each other for more than 150 years.

It was during these same years that the city began to receive substantial gifts from private individuals, including the first gift of money in the amount of $1,000 from Mayor John Prescott Bigelow and a number of public documents from various donors. Edward Everett, a former professor of Greek literature, U.S. congressman, governor of Massachusetts, ambassador to the Court of St. James, and president of Harvard College (Cambridge, Massachusetts) was among these donors. Everett's collection included nearly all federal documents from the founding of the republic to 1825, and the collection from 1826 to 1840 was, in his own words, "tolerably complete." In a 7 August 1850 letter to Bigelow, Everett argued that, if the city would provide a suitable building, "it would be so amply supplied from time to time by donations, that only a moderate appropriation for books would be wanted." The library's subsequent history proved this to be false, but his thoughts on a proposed public library (expressed in letters to the mayor) impressed George Ticknor, a lawyer, author, and former professor of French and Spanish languages at Harvard College.

In July 1851 Ticknor addressed a letter to Everett in which he articulated his vision of a public library. Although both men viewed the library as the noble completion of the system of public education about which citizens of Boston (the site of the first public school in the original U.S. colonies) were understandably concerned, Ticknor envisioned the library as a circulating collection of new and popular books. This was a novel idea to Everett, who responded in a letter dated 26 July 1851, "My present impressions are in favour of making the amplest provision in the library for the use of books there." As it happened, the future library would encompass both a circulating library of popular titles and a noncirculating collection of reference and research titles for consultation within the building. This arrangement has been maintained to the present day at the BPL and to a lesser degree at most urban libraries throughout the country.

Less than seven months later Mayor Benjamin Seaver recommended to the city council that a librarian be appointed, that a proper location be found for the institution of the public library, and that five or six gentlemen be appointed to serve with the joint standing committee as a board of directors or trustees of the public library. In May 1852 the city council adopted the recommendations of the mayor. The council appointed a librarian, Edward Capen, who had recently become secretary of the Boston School Committee; the council elected a board of trustees 11 days later. The persons chosen from the "citizens at large" were Bigelow; Nathaniel Bradstreet Shurtleff, who would later serve three terms as mayor and would edit the colonial records of the Massachusetts Bay and Plymouth colonies; Thomas Gold Appleton, who would donate to the library the Cardinal Tosti collection of engravings in 1869; and, of course, Ticknor and Everett.

The board met for the first time on 31 May 1852, with Everett as its first president. Four of the trustees (Everett, Shurtleff, Ticknor, and Alderman Samson Reed) were appointed to consider and report on the object and the best means of establishing a public library. This report, largely the work of Ticknor, was a magisterial blueprint for the fledgling library movement. Dated 6 July 1852, the *Report of the Trustees of the Public Library of the City of Boston* was of such import that nearly a century later Jesse H. Shera reprinted it in full as an appendix to his *Foundations of the Public Library: The Origins of the Public Library Movement in New England, 1629–1855*.

Two points of the report demand attention. The first was that the city library should be "the crowning glory of our system of City Schools"; that is, the library should provide for the further education of its citizens (beyond formal schooling). Thus the public library would be a further assurance of the goal of universal education. Next, in the establishment of such a library there should be no "sharply defined or settled plan, so as to be governed by circumstances as they may arise." This dictum allowed for maximum flexibility not only in responding to the needs of the latter half of the 19th century but also in addressing changing needs up to the present time. It should be obvious that these precepts have guided not only BPL but the entire public library movement in the United States to the present day.

A very happy and unexpected incident occurred as a result of this report. At the time of its publication in 1852, the city government was attempting to negotiate a loan with the house of Baring Brothers and Company in London. Included in the documents submitted to London to demonstrate the fitness of the city for such a loan was a copy of the first report of the trustees. Fortuitously, the report was read by the senior partner of the banking house, Joshua Bates, who had been born in Weymouth, Massachusetts, and had suffered from the want of such an institution in his younger days in Boston. He offered the then princely sum of $50,000 for the purchase of books, provided that the city secure and furnish a building to house them. This donation was not the last Bates' benefaction, and it is not surprising that after his death the main reading hall of the Boylston Street building, and later of the Copley Square building, were named in his honor.

The city's first ordinance on the library was adopted on 14 October 1852. Based on a preliminary draft submitted by the subcommittee of the trustees that had prepared the above-mentioned report, it empowered them to make "regulations for their own government and for the administration of the library." It also required an annual report of the trustees to be submitted to the city council, the annual formation of an examining committee to report on the condition of the library, and the annual election of a librarian. The wisdom of this latter stipulation was to be reconsidered in less than a quarter of a century.

By the end of 1852, Ticknor's plan and the endowments of Bates and Jonathan Phillips ($10,000 for the purchase of books), among others, set the stage for the opening of the Boston Public Library. On 20 March 1854 two rooms in the Adams School on Mason Street were occupied by the BPL. In less than two months books were circulating. This noble experiment was an immediate success: In its first five and a half months of operation, 6,590 persons registered and 35,389 books circulated. These statistics are all the more remarkable given that each patron was permitted only one circulating book (for a period of 14 days).

To allow for the greatest access, the library was open every day (excluding Sundays and holidays) from 9:00 A.M. to 9:30 P.M. Although its accessions file, card catalog, and shelf list (for the use of library staff) and its book catalog (available to the public in the reading room) assured excellent service, it became apparent immediately that the temporary location in Mason Street was unsuitable.

To remedy the inadequacy of the Mason Street quarters, in November 1854 a commission headed by Robert C. Winthrop, a former member of Congress, was appointed to erect a library building. A suitable location having been found on Boylston Street facing the Boston Common, a public invitation for the submission of proposed designs was issued in January 1855, and on 17 September of the same year the cornerstone of the building, based on the plan submitted by Charles Kirk Kirby, was laid. The commission requirements for the new building included a reading hall to accommodate 150 readers, alcoves to accommodate 200,000 volumes, a delivery room to accommodate 200 persons, and an area sufficient to house 20,000 books "most constantly demanded for circulation." More importantly, the building should be absolutely fireproof and should depend upon its usefulness for its effect rather "than upon any ornamental architecture or costly materials."

Upon seeing the plans for the Boylston Street building, Bates wrote from London on 6 July 1855 that he would supply needed titles: "I see no other way but that the Committee should make a Catalogue of French, German and Italian Books, and such English works as are most needed, the whole not to exceed $20,000 or $30,000. I will supply what money your funds will not pay for." As the collections had been growing by gift and purchase during the occupancy of the space in the Adams School, additional space had been obtained in the Quincy School on Tyler Street. These two locations were already full, and to accommodate and organize the new acquisitions arriving, a building in Boylston Place was rented. Charles Coffin Jewett, who had served as a librarian and a teacher of modern languages at Brown University (Providence, Rhode Island) and later as librarian at the Smithsonian Institution (Washington, D.C.), was employed to prepare the collection for its move to the Boylston Street building.

Shortly before the dedication ceremonies for the new building on 1 January 1858, the trustees requested that the city council allow for the creation of the position of superintendent and that the filling of such a position be entirely in the hands of the trustees. The request was partially successful. An amended library ordinance creating the position was passed on 2 January 1858, but the annual appointment of the superintendent, upon recommendation of the trustees, remained in the hands of the city council.

Jewett was appointed the first superintendent and remained in that position until his death in 1868. Edward Capen, whose duties were largely confined to circulation services, maintained the title of librarian until 1874, when he became the librarian at Haverhill Public Library (Massachusetts). It was under Jewett that the new library on Boylston Street, which cost the city $364,000 including land, became operational. The Lower Hall (primarily circulating material) opened for service on 17 September 1858; the Upper Hall (renamed Bates Hall in 1866) opened for service in 1861. The library in 1858 had a collection of more than 70,000 volumes, a great increase from the 9,688 volumes just five years before. These books were arranged in an ingenious method devised by one of the trustees (Nathaniel B. Shurtleff) and employing a decimal system. The first element referred to the alcove, the second number to the range, and the final to the shelf on which the desired book might be found. In addition to overseeing the publication of catalogs for both the Lower and Upper Halls, Jewett devised an indicator to show which books were in use, thus obviating the need for unnecessary trips to the shelves. Likewise, the ledger format for recording books in circulation was replaced by a more efficient slip system. Jewett's ultimate contribution came, however, just three months before his death in October 1867: the publication of the *Bulletin* of new books, which continued under variant titles until 1960.

Winsor, an author appointed to the board of trustees in 1867 and chairman of the 1867 examining committee, succeeded Jewett as superintendent in 1868. The report of the 1867 examining committee provided a "complete and searching" analysis of the state of the library and placed Winsor in a very opportune position to assume the responsibilities of superintendent. He immediately sought communication with other libraries in the United States and abroad, believing that knowledge of the best methods and organization of libraries could and should be shared. Although BPL was among the ten largest library collections in the United States in 1868, ranking second only to the Library of Congress, and although it was the only library of the ten that was supported mainly by municipal funds, Winsor was not blinded by the institution's achievements. He immediately set about ameliorating its defects. He introduced a card catalog (1872), improved the lighting in the "Stygian alcoves" of Bates Hall by installing gas jets, added windows to the exterior walls, and initiated subject bibliographies of the library's holdings for the use of the public that, according to the 1877 trustees report, had given the library "a reputation and a following both in America and in Europe." Winsor also instituted a branch system, the first in the United States, during his tenure. The East Boston Branch opened in 1870, followed by branches in South Boston, Roxbury, Charlestown, Brighton, and Fields Corner (Dorchester) during the next four years. Again, the institution of the branches was a direct result of recommendations made in the report of the 1867 examining committee on which Winsor had served.

It is a blot on the history of the library that the "Winsor Decade" ended as unfortunately as it did. In the winter of 1876 to 1877 the city council determined that fiscal cuts were required in Boston and that the library was one department in which cuts could be made. Instead of simply reducing the total appropriation for the library, the council determined to regulate the actual salaries of a number of officers of the library. Although the superintendent's salary had always been in the hands of the city council, this unnecessary meddling in the internal affairs of the library and the haggling over Superintendent Winsor's salary prompted him to accept the post of librarian of Harvard University. He was also named the first president of the American Library Association (ALA) in 1876.

The examining committee, the local press, and the *American Library Journal* all decried this scandalous turn of events. Fortunately, when Henry L. Pierce returned to the mayor's office in early 1878, he proposed that legislation be enacted to avoid such problems in the future. The Act to Incorporate the Trustees of the Public Library of the City of Boston was approved by the Massachusetts legislature on 4 April 1878. It read in part: "The said board may appoint a superintendent or librarian with such assistants and subordinate officers as they may think necessary or expedient and may remove the same and fix their compensation."

This action—and a later amendment to the City Charter (1885) that made city council members ineligible for membership on the board and reduced the number of trustees from seven to five—ensured the independence of the trustees for a century. Unfortunately, the library had already lost Winsor. Whereas he ably served as librarian at Harvard until his death in 1897, the BPL was "in the doldrums" (according to Walter Muir Whitehill's assessment in his 1956 *Boston Public Library: A Centennial History*) for the better part of the next decade, thanks to committee management by the trustees.

It was during this period that the specter of censorship was raised. From 1880 to 1882 a former employee accused the library of selecting books poorly. Although his charges attacked a wide variety of selections, his criticism of the acquisition of the Barton Library adequately demonstrates his misplaced concerns. It was determined that the Shakespeare holdings at the BPL were the finest in the United States at the time, and when the tempest settled, the library had weathered its first encounter with attempted censorship.

Concurrent with the censorship episode, the collections continued to grow and the first steps toward a new building were made. The city of Boston petitioned the state legislature and was granted a lot of land at the corner of Dartmouth and Boylston Streets in Boston's recently reclaimed Back Bay. This act of 1880 granted the land upon the condition that construction of the new building begin within three years. It soon became apparent that the designated site required more land, and the state legislature empowered the city "to take the land if necessary" (to remove the dwellings that occupied the additional land needed). During the following seven years the additional land was acquired, a three-year extension for the beginning date of construction was granted by the legislature, and a plan for the new building by City Architect Arthur H. Vinal finally was approved in 1886. Although the first pile was driven on 21 April of that same year and construction on the foundations was contracted and begun by the following summer, several occurrences would alter the plans and history of the new building on Copley Square.

In March 1887, at the behest of some prominent citizens, the Massachusetts legislature granted the trustees full power and control over the construction of the new central library. Less than ten days later Samuel Appleton Brown Abbott, a trustee of the library, traveled to New York to consult with Charles Follen McKim, an esteemed architect of the firm of McKim, Mead and White, about the new building. Trustees William W. Greenough and Henry W. Haynes met with McKim on the following day and were so impressed that by 30 March McKim was under contract to design the new building.

Abbott, who assumed the presidency of the board of trustees in 1888, guided the McKim Building to completion. The "first outstanding example of Renaissance Beaux Arts academicism in the United States," in the words of Peter Arms Wick, it stands as a testament to the civic pride of Boston's citizenry in the latter half of the 19th century. Its beauty is lasting, and it was declared a national landmark in 1973. The McKim Building incorporated the finest architecture, sculpture, and painting available at the time: Its cost was approximately $2.5 million. And although there were some problems—the MacMonnies' *Bacchante and Infant Faun* scandal (in which some Bostonians objected to the representation of a nude Bacchante holding a naked child, leading to McKim's withdrawal of his intended gift from the library), an attempt to obliterate the nudity of the boys depicted on the seal of the library over the central entrance, and the scotching of the McKim, Mead, and White acrostic on the library's façade—the construction was completed in less than seven years.

When the McKim Building opened as the central library in February 1895, the institution had considerably more than 500,000 volumes, ten branches, and a number of delivery stations—a formidable director was required. Having realized the pressing need for such a position, the trustees wrote in their 1895 report that "the responsibility for the proper administration of the Library in all its various departments must rest practically upon the Librarian." Their choice was Herbert Putnam.

Putnam, a Harvard graduate and son of the New York publisher George Palmer Putnam, had served as the librarian of the Minneapolis public library and earlier of the Athenaeum in Minneapolis, Minnesota. Under Putnam, who was appointed Librarian of Congress four years later, evening hours were extended and Sunday service introduced, and the Children's Room (the first such in the country), the Newspaper Room, and the Department of Documents and Statistics were opened. In addition, Putnam initiated interlibrary loan service and inaugurated a system of graded personnel appointments based upon examination. His was a tenure during which the day-to-day operations of the institution were well-regulated and systematized.

After a brief interim during which James Lyman Whitney served as librarian and the Department of Manuscripts was created, Horace G. Wadlin succeeded Whitney in 1903, although Whitney remained in service in other capacities until 1910. Formerly an architect and chief of the Massachusetts Bureau of Labor Statistics, Wadlin had never worked as a librarian but was chosen because of his demonstrated ability as a businessman.

The maintenance of day-to-day operations, rather than the creation of innovative services, would be the hallmark of Wadlin's tenure. Nevertheless, Wadlin did recognize the changing demographics of the city; he realized that book selection must be aimed at a widely diverse group of readers, including many recent immigrants (an example of the concern for multicultural needs that has influenced BPL since its founding). It was also during this period and with the help of Josiah Henry Benton (president of the board of trustees from 1908 to 1917 and later a great benefactor to the library) that the unsatisfactory branch buildings began to be replaced.

Wadlin's years at the helm spanned a period during which the library celebrated its first half-century. The institution had served its citizens well, but by 1913 the McKim Building was overcrowded, and an annex was begun in 1916 and occupied in the autumn of 1918. While the annex was being constructed, Charles Francis Dorr Belden, former State Librarian of Massachusetts, assumed the office vacated by Horace Wadlin. His 14-year tenure would include major repairs on the structure of the McKim Building (such as the elevators and heating and ventilating systems), which was then more than a quarter-century old. In addition, the special libraries floor was redesigned to properly house the rare books collection (in the north gallery). Five new neighborhood branches were completed, four with the direct help of Mayor James Michael Curley, and a business branch located next to City Hall was opened in May 1930. More importantly, as a result of the recommendations of an independent committee composed of the public librarians of New York, St. Louis (Missouri), and Cleveland (Ohio), the library became more independent of the trustees in terms of individual expenditures and day-to-day operations (a development that would be strengthened under Belden's successor) and instituted courses in library training. In 1931, the year of Belden's death, the library's appropriation from the city was more than $1.5 million.

Milton Edward Lord, a graduate of Harvard and most notably librarian of the American Academy in Rome and a member of the team of librarians engaged in reorganizing the Vatican Library's cataloging and classification system, assumed the leadership of the Boston Public Library on 1 February 1932, in the midst of the Depression. At a time when the need for more books was acutely felt (as a result of the state of the economy), the book budget shrank. The average annual rate of growth during the first two decades of Lord's tenure was lower than that of Winsor's day. But the organization of the library became much clearer and well-defined under Lord. His 1933 plan called for the creation of a circulation division, a reference division, and a division of business operations. The heads of these divisions would be accountable to the director for their functioning. Recognizing the growing importance of the rare books collections, Lord created the position of keeper of rare books and, after the acquisition of the Albert H. Wiggin collection of prints, he also created the position of keeper of prints. When there was pressure in 1952 to remove all "communist" material from the library, Lord battled the censoring forces and triumphed.

Lord's greatest strength was his grasp of all aspects of the institution under his care. His own words, written in August 1933 at the time of the reorganization mentioned above, capture it best:

> The Boston Public Library is an unusual institution. It is not only a large active public library in the usual sense of the term; it is also a great scholarly reference and research library, possessing many of the marks of the university library. Both of these characteristics require recognition.

When Philip J. McNiff, a graduate of Boston College and future president of the Association of College and Research Libraries, assumed the duties of director and librarian in the mid-1960s, he continued the work of his predecessor while putting his own unique stamp on these projects. Greater state and federal aid (a cause dear to Lord) allowed McNiff to considerably increase the holdings of the library. Assuming the responsibilities of the library of last recourse for the commonwealth, BPL began to serve as the research library for the state. During McNiff's directorate, the library became the headquarters for the Eastern Regional Library System of Massachusetts, providing equal service for more than 200 libraries in the eastern third of the state; became a founding member of the Boston Library Consortium; and continued the replacement of unsatisfactory buildings of the branch system (then numbering more than 20).

The high point of McNiff's tenure was the 1972 opening of a new addition, the Johnson Building, on land that had been occupied by the annex of 1918 that had been part of Boston University. The central complex, now covering a full city block, allowed for a circulating collection of 750,000 volumes as well as much needed space for the research library collections. This addition, designed by Philip Johnson and made possible in part by the generosity of John Deferrari (a real estate and securities investor), fulfilled plans that had been fermenting even before the previous administration. McNiff faced yet another challenge during his tenure—the unionization of all but management staff.

Both McNiff and his successor, Arthur Curley (a graduate of Harvard and the fifth director of the library to be elected to the presidency of ALA), faced the problem of fluctuating budgets. Budget cuts required the reduction of hours of public service, temporary hiring freezes, and periods of uneven acquisition of materials. Two actions that occurred during Curley's term demand recognition. The first was his suggestion to the trustees that a consulting firm be contracted to determine the adequacy of salaries at the library. The trustees agreed, and the study found that salaries were indeed below those of comparable institutions; they were adjusted as a result. More obvious to the public was Curley's desire to undertake the restoration of the McKim Building. Nine decades old when the first plans for restorations were made, the building required structural work, restoration of art work, and general housekeeping. Curley, who died shortly after the completion of the first part of Phase II of the restoration, deserves commendation for both of these initiatives.

It may be said that BPL claims a place of preeminence in the history of the U.S. library movement. A center of great innovation during its first 50 years, it has continued to build on its strengths up to the present time. Thus it began the automation of its catalogs in the 1970s and has acquired electronic resources to help maintain the quality and currency of its collections since that time. Unfortunately, the bulk of the catalog of the research library has not yet been converted to an online format, a great drawback to public service and a great challenge for the current administration. However, the library has provided leaders in the local, national, and international library world throughout its history.

This progress has not been without obstacles; politics and censorship have sometimes dogged its steps. Indeed, it appears that the present municipal administration is attempting to curtail the library's formerly semi-independent status. The number of trustees has been increased to nine members, and the mayor wishes to have the library's business procedures more closely aligned to other city departments, whether or not this serves the ultimate goals and mission of the library.

It was into this state of affairs that the current chief executive, Bernard A. Margolis (formerly of the Pikes Peak Library District in Colorado Springs, Colorado), stepped in March 1997. The censorship of Internet access for children was his first challenge in Boston. Although President Margolis seemed adamantly opposed to any censorship, he compromised by allowing filters to be placed on the computers used by children. Time will tell whether such political interference—and the library administration's reaction to it—will be a hindrance or a help to this great institution.

WILLIAM GREALISH

Further Reading

Shera, Jesse H., *Foundations of the Public Library: The Origins of the Public Library Movement in New England, 1629–1855*, Chicago: University of Chicago Press, 1949

Wadlin, Horace G., *The Public Library of the City of Boston: A History*, Boston: Trustees of the Boston Public Library, 1911

Whitehill, Walter Muir, *Boston Public Library: A Centennial History*, Cambridge, Massachusetts: Harvard University Press, 1956

Wick, Peter Arms, *A Handbook to the Art and Architecture of the Boston Public Library: Visitors Guide to the McKim Building, Copley Square: Its Mural Decorations and its Collections*, Boston: Associates of the Boston Public Library, 1977

Winsor, Justin, "Libraries in Boston," in *The Memorial History of Boston Including Suffolk County, Massachusetts, 1630–1880*, edited by Winsor, vol. 4, Boston: Ticknor and Company, 1881

Brigham Young University Library

Address:	Harold B. Lee Library Provo, Utah 84602 USA Telephone: 801-378-2926 Fax: 801-378-6708 www.lib.byu.edu
Founded:	1875
Holdings (2001):	Volumes: 2.6 million. Current serials: 16,000; films and videos: 3,000; manuscripts: 17,000 linear feet; microforms: 2.5 million; maps: 238,000; oral histories: 1,900; photographs: 600,000; sound recordings: 53,000.
Special Collections:	*Areas of Concentration:* Arts and communications; film and video; folklore; history of printing; 19th- and 20th-century U.S. literature; 19th- and 20th-century Western and Mormon Americana; photography; politics. *Individual Collections:* Aldine collection; Walter Mason Camp; J. Reuben Clark; Merian C. Cooper; Cecil B. DeMille; Estienne collection; Froben collection; LeRoy Hafen Western Americana collection; Republic Pictures music archives; university archives. *Papers:* Gertrude Bonnin (Zitkala Sa); LeRoy R. Hafen; David M. Kennedy; Gustive O. Larson; L. John Nuttall; Vernon Romney; Reed Smoot; James E. Talmage; Arthur Watkins; Ernest L. Wilkinson.

History

Owned and operated by the Church of Jesus Christ of Latter-day Saints (commonly called the Mormons), Brigham Young University (BYU) in Provo, Utah, was founded in 1875 as one of several academies established under Brigham Young's direction. It was officially named Brigham Young University in 1903. From very modest beginnings the university has grown to become one of the largest private, church-owned-and-operated universities in the United States. From a student body of several hundred in the 1880s to 30,000 today, the growth of the library mirrors this progress. Its goal of providing a balanced secular and religious education has also been a major influence on the development of the library. The primary mission of the library is to support the broad liberal arts undergraduate programs of the university.

In its first eight years the library managed to obtain about 500 volumes and 2,082 issues of periodicals, but in 1884 a fire destroyed two-thirds of its holdings. Until the 1920s growth of the collections was slow, but after 1920, especially with the help of individuals such as Alice Louise Reynolds, the collections grew more rapidly. Especially valuable were the book collections donated by individuals who had gathered significant private libraries. The most important were the George H. Brimhall Theological Library, the John A. Widtsoe Library of Agriculture, the Charles W. Penrose Poetry collection, the James E. Talmage collection, and the Heber J. Grant collection. Thus, by 1929 the library contained 35,000 volumes housed in the Heber J. Grant Building, which had been dedicated in 1925.

By 1951 the library contained 170,000 volumes; 20 years later it reached its first million. Space to house and maintain this growing collection has always been limited. In 1961 the J. Reuben Clark Library building was dedicated, followed by two additions, one in 1976 and a second in 1999. The building was renamed the Harold B. Lee Library in 1974 when the newly established law school was named after Clark. The Provo campus, in addition to the main Lee Library, also has the extensive Howard W. Hunter Law Library in the J. Reuben Clark Law School. The Lee Library also coordinates with the Joseph F. Smith Library at BYU-Hawaii (Laie) and the David O. McKay Library at Ricks College in Rexburg, Idaho. It also supplies books to the libraries in the BYU Study Abroad Centers in London, England, and in Jerusalem, Israel. The church's own extensive historical department and library in Salt Lake City are managed separately as a corporate repository.

Major developments in the library occurred during the BYU presidency of Ernest L. Wilkinson (1951–71). A conservative but dynamic attorney, he worked hard to build and broaden BYU's infrastructure. The appointment of S. Lyman Tyler as the library director in 1954 was critical for the development of the library. His 12-year tenure brought better administrative organization and vision to the library. He worked to get the new Clark Library built, organized special collections, established the Friends of the Library, and encouraged the increased use of automation. His successors, Donald K. Nelson (1973–80) and

Sterling J. Albrecht (1980–), built on and expanded Tyler's vision. BYU Library was one of the early members of the Research Libraries Group (RLG). Special Collections was officially named the L. Tom Perry Special Collections in 2000.

Special Collections and Manuscripts

The collections represent a number of areas, and the book and imprint collections span the 15th century to the present. Especially valuable are the Aldine, Estienne, Colines, and Froben collections. A rich fine printing collection complements the history of printing. Renaissance and Reformation era printed works are well represented. Specific collections focusing on individual authors include collections on Robert Burns, William Wordsworth, Walt Whitman, Herman Melville, and Louisa May Alcott. The Victorian and Edwardian collections are also strong. The LeRoy Hafen collection is a particularly broad collection of Western Americana.

Mormon and Western Collections

From its earliest years, published and unpublished material relating to the history of the Mormon Church and its broader setting in the U.S. West found its way into the library, but a systematic gathering can be seen beginning only in the 1930s. BYU professor M. Wilford Poulson collected diaries of Utah Mormon pioneers (mostly copies) for the library, and these were placed in a manuscript room organized in the new Grant Library. Newburn I. Butt, an indefatigable librarian from 1922 to 1968, also gathered and indexed Mormon periodical literature.

In 1955 the Archival Department was organized under the guidance of Tyler, then director. First located in the Karl G. Maeser Building, the archives moved into the first level of the new Clark Library in 1961. By the 1970s the Department of Special Collections and Manuscripts had assumed the basic shape and direction it has today. The department employed several key individuals who worked to acquire Mormon and Western materials. Particularly valuable was the role of Fred Rosenstock, a Denver rare book dealer who helped to acquire both rare book and manuscript items for the library. Named the L. Tom Perry Special Collections Library in 1999, this library is a major research center for Western and Mormon studies.

In its broadest sense, the Western and Mormon collection seeks to document the Latter-day Saints' history and experiences in all their varied dimensions: personal and institutional, male and female, 19th and 20th centuries. Its major focus is on the North American Mormon experience, and its great strength is in the breadth and depth of its collections, which include print, manuscript, visual, and audio materials.

Printed items provide a solid research base for Mormon studies. Using the union catalog in the two-volume *A Mormon Bibliography, 1830–1930: Ten Year Supplement* (Chad J. Flake and Larry W. Draper, compilers; 1989, 1992) as a measure, the BYU library holds about 60 percent (about 7,000) of the pre-1930 items listed. Only the Latter-day Saints Church's own library and archives in Salt Lake City have more. Combined with the substantial post-1930 era and the equally rich holdings of Utah and Western Americana and U.S. religious history (much of it purchased through the Daniel Jackling Endowment), the library and its broader holdings provide a strong historical context for Mormon history researchers.

Adding to and complementing the printed sources are the extensive manuscript collections. There are about 17,000 linear feet of manuscripts. Most have been donated, but the library has managed to purchase collections over the years. In several cases both the papers and personal libraries of individuals have been acquired. These include those of LeRoy Hafen, J. Reuben Clark Jr., M. Wilford Poulsen, Dale Morgan, J. Earl Arrington, and Steven Christensen. The extensive collection of British working-class literature gathered by English social historian John Fletcher Clews Harrison was acquired in 1990.

Only a sampling of the numerous Mormon and Mormon-related manuscript collections can be given here. The most significant would include the Newell K. Whitney collection, which, in addition to containing the earliest holographic copies of some of Joseph Smith's earliest revelations, contains personal and institutional records of the first decades of the church's history as gathered by one of the first Mormon bishops. The diaries and papers of Joseph Smith's brother Hyrum and his son John are important collections, collections that help document the Missouri and Illinois phases of the Mormon experience. The collections get stronger and more diverse as the Mormons' westward move into the Great Basin is documented. Overland journals, missionary records, and various institutional records provide ample sources for studying the Mormon exploration and colonization of the western United States. Over 500 missionary collections allow the researcher to trace representatives of the church into the British Isles, Europe, the Middle East, South Africa, India, and the Pacific in the years since about 1850.

The female Mormon experience is also represented in a variety of holdings. The 46-volume diary of Emmeline B. Wells allows the researcher to follow the major contours of the church's history through the eyes of a teenager moving west in 1846 to her years as the general president of the Female Relief Society in the 1920s. Both personal and institutional records provide important documentation for the Mormon woman's experience, and these have continued to grow following the organization of the Women's Research Institute on the BYU campus.

DAVID J. WHITTAKER

Further Reading

Allen, James B., Ronald W. Walker, and David J. Whittaker, *Studies in Mormon History, 1830–1997: An Indexed Bibliography*, Urbana: University of Illinois Press, 2000

Bitton, Davis, *Guide to Mormon Diaries and Autobiographies*, Provo, Utah: Brigham Young University Press, 1977

Flake, Chad J., editor, *A Mormon Bibliography, 1830–1930: Books, Pamphlets, Periodicals, and Broadsides Relating to the First Century of Mormonism,* Salt Lake City: University of Utah Press, 1978

Flake, Chad J., and Larry W. Draper, compilers, *A Mormon Bibliography, 1830–1930: Ten Year Supplement,* Salt Lake City: University of Utah Press, 1989

Flake, Chad J., and Larry W. Draper, compilers, *A Mormon Bibliography, 1830–1930: Indexes to "A Mormon Bibliography" and "Ten Year Supplement,"* Salt Lake City: University of Utah Press, 1992

Flake, Chad J., and Larry W. Draper, "Printed Mormon Americana at Brigham Young University," in *Mormon Americana: A Guide to Sources and Collections in the United States,* edited by David J. Whittaker, Provo, Utah: Brigham Young University Studies, 1995

Knight, Hattie M., *Brigham Young University Library Centennial History, 1875–1975,* Provo, Utah: Brigham Young University, 1976

Whittaker, David J., "The Archives of the Mormon Experience at Brigham Young University," in *Mormon Americana: A Guide to Sources and Collections in the United States,* edited by Whittaker, Provo, Utah: Brigham Young University Studies, 1995

Wilkinson, Ernest L., editor, *Brigham Young University: The First One Hundred Years,* 4 vols., Provo, Utah: Brigham Young University Press, 1975–76

British Library

Address: British Library
96 Euston Road
London NW1 2DB
UK
Telephone: 20-7412-7676
Fax: 20-7412-7609
www.bl.uk

Founded: 1973 (but mainly based on the collections of the British Museum Library, founded 1753)

Holdings (2000): Volumes: 16 million. Audio recordings: 1.2 million; cartographic items: 4.2 million; graphic materials: 237,000; India Office records: 260,000; manuscripts: 300,000 items; microforms: 4.3 million; music scores: 1.5 million; newspaper volumes: 657,000; patent specifications: 44 million; philatelic items: 8.1 million; theses: 608,000; videotapes: 19,000.

Special Collections: *Individual Collections:* Ashley library of Thomas J. Wise; Sir Joseph Banks library; Chinese manuscripts from the Dunhuang caves; Sir Robert Cotton; Henry Davis collection of fine bindings; John F. Dexter collection of Dickens; French Revolution tracts; Richard Grenville, Duke of Buckingham, from Stowe House; Thomas Grenville library; Robert and Edward Harley, Earls of Oxford; Hirsch music library; illuminated manuscripts; incunabula; King's Library; Old Royal Library; Qur'an collection; William Petty, Marquess of Lansdowne; Syriac material from the Nitrian desert; Thomas Tapling philatelic collections. *Papers:* William Cecil, Lord Burghley; Gilbert K. Chesterton; John Churchill, Duke of Marlborough; William E. Gladstone; William Morris; Florence Nightingale; Laurence, Lord Olivier; the Paston family; Sir Robert Peel; George Bernard Shaw.

The 18th Century

Until the foundation of the British Library in 1973, England had no national library (although one was set up for Wales in 1909 and for Scotland in 1925). In practice, however, the library of the British Museum acted as the national library of the United Kingdom for much of the 19th and 20th centuries, and in 1973 it formed by far the most important element in the British Library. The British Museum was established in 1753 as a result of Sir Hans Sloane offering his collections to the nation at the bargain price of £20,000. To his collections of books, manuscripts, natural history specimens, antiquities, and prints and drawings were added the manuscripts collected by Sir Robert Cotton and those acquired by Robert and Edward Harley, Earls of Oxford, to form the new museum. A lottery provided the funds to set this up under a board of trustees in Montagu House (a 17th-century mansion in Bloomsbury), and in 1757 George II presented to the new institution the Royal Library (called the Old Royal Library after the gift of the King's Library of George III in 1823), which dated back to the 15th century.

Of the three original departments of the British Museum, the Department of Natural and Artificial Productions was the least important at first, although from it developed all the departments of antiquities in the museum as well as the Natural History Museum, which has been at South Kensington since the 1880s. In the early years of the British Museum, however, the collections of the Departments of Manuscripts and of Printed Books were of much greater significance. Even so, in the 18th century these departments achieved relatively little.

1800 to 1837

Matters began to improve when Joseph Planta became principal librarian (director) of the museum in 1799. That year the library received a very important gift—the collection bequeathed by Clayton Mordount Cracherode. In 1807 the Department of Manuscripts acquired the manuscripts of the first marquess of Lansdowne as a result of a special Parliamentary grant. Similar grants enabled the library to obtain the Francis Hargrave collection in 1813 and the Charles Burney collection in 1818. Planta also argued successfully for special grants from the treasury between 1812 and 1817 to improve the collections of books relating to Britain and its overseas possessions. Important gifts also augmented the library, including the collections of Sir Richard Colt Hoare (1825) and Sir Joseph Banks (1827), and above all the library collected by George III (known as the King's Library). The gift of the King's Library by George IV was announced in 1823, and the books were transferred to the museum in 1828 after the construction of a special building to house them, as they could not be fitted into Montagu House. This collection increased the stock of the Department of Printed Books from 120,000 to 190,000 volumes. The department was also augmented by books from British publishers acquired by legal deposit. The right to such books under the copyright act passed to the British Museum in 1757 when it received the Old Royal Library, but not until the passage of a new copyright act in 1814 did more than a trickle of legal deposit material reach the museum.

By 1818 the reading room was being used by 10 to 30 persons each day, and the number of holders of readers' tickets had risen to about 200. A new catalog of printed books was published between 1813 and 1819, which, despite its many faults, was a considerable improvement over its predecessor of 1787.

By the time that Henry Ellis succeeded Planta as principal librarian in 1827, the future of the British Museum library was more encouraging. About this time two men joined the staff who would eventually transform their respective departments: Frederic Madden of the Department of Manuscripts and Antonio Panizzi of the Department of Printed Books. They became keepers of their departments in 1837, but even before this date modernization had begun. Construction of a new building for the museum was started in 1823, with work continuing until the end of the 1840s. The first stage of construction was the east wing, which contained the gallery that held the King's Library.

Henry Baber, keeper of printed books from 1812 to 1837, began in the 1830s to plan a new edition of the catalog of printed books. He also improved the intake of legal deposit material and obtained permission from the trustees of the museum to make routine purchases without first asking their permission. The series sales of duplicates, which had begun in 1769 to raise money for new acquisitions, was ended in 1832 when the trustees at last accepted that this mistaken policy had resulted in the library's loss of many important items.

Josiah Forshall, keeper of manuscripts from 1828 until 1837 (as well as secretary of the museum from 1828 until 1850), calculated that the museum had bought no more than 50 manuscripts before 1782 and only about 500 between 1782 and 1828 (excluding large collections bought with special grants, such as the Lansdowne and Burney manuscripts). By contrast, 3,500 were purchased between 1828 and 1835.

More people were using the reading room. By 1835 about 250 visited it each day, resulting in very uncomfortable conditions. New accommodations were provided in the north wing, which was built between 1833 and 1837. By the time this new room was ready, the museum had been investigated by two select committees of the House of Commons (1835 and 1836). Because of the recommendations of these committees, Forshall gave up the keepership of the Department of Manuscripts to concentrate on his duties as secretary of the museum, and Baber retired. In consequence, Madden and Panizzi took charge of the two library departments and a new age began.

1837 to 1857

Panizzi's first task was to organize the move of the books from Montagu House to the north wing of the new museum building. He then turned his attention to the new catalog that the trustees required, superintending the preparation of a new code of cataloging rules. His 1845 survey of gaps in the collections persuaded the treasury to increase the grant for the purchase of books to £10,000 per annum. Even though the full sum could not be spent in the early 1850s because of lack of space in which to house the books acquired, this grant enabled the department to increase the size of its holdings enormously by the end of the 19th century. (In 1838 there were 250,000 volumes and in 1884, 1.3 million.)

Madden also pursued a vigorous acquisitions policy, even though he had much less money to spend than Panizzi. Between 1839 and 1846 he acquired 5,400 volumes of manuscripts and more than 7,000 charters. He also began the *Catalogues of Additions to the Manuscripts,* which have been characterized by very high scholarly standards ever since. He also did a great deal to conserve those Cotton manuscripts that had been damaged in a fire in 1731. This was achieved with a staff of only 12 in the manuscripts department, of whom seven were attendants who carried out routine duties. (At this time Panizzi had a staff of 57 in the printed books department, of whom 30 were attendants.)

A royal commission investigating the museum held meetings from 1847 until 1849 and fully supported Panizzi in his dispute with the trustees concerning the new version of the catalog of printed books. The trustees wanted the sections of this catalog to be sent to the printer as they were completed, but Panizzi argued that until the work was fully prepared in manuscript form it would be foolish to commit any part of it to print because the later sections would inevitably necessitate alterations to the parts prepared earlier.

The royal commission recommended that the post of secretary to the museum should be abolished because Forshall had in effect taken over the running of the institution from Ellis, the principal librarian, who was nominally in charge. When the secretary's post disappeared in 1850, the work of enforcing the legal deposit provisions of the copyright act, hitherto dealt with by the secretary's office, was handed over to Panizzi. He carried out this task with great vigor, much to the annoyance of some publishers. In the three years before he undertook this work, the average number of volumes received each year was 3,342; between 1850 and 1856 the average rose to 5,097, an increase of 52 percent. The number of periodical issues acquired by legal deposit rose by the same percentage. Madden was congratulated by the royal commission on his success in organizing the cataloging of the manuscripts, and it was recommended that he should be granted more staff, especially to deal with the Oriental manuscripts, many of which awaited cataloging.

The need for more space for the museum's collections was emphasized by the royal commission. The immediate problem was to provide accommodations for the rapidly growing collections of the Department of Printed Books. Thomas Grenville's bequest in 1847 of his collection of 20,000 volumes, largely because of his friendship with Panizzi, enormously strengthened the museum's collections of rare books. But the arrival of this material provided an accommodation problem that greatly embittered the already bad relations between Madden and Panizzi, because the former was deprived of one of his galleries so that the Grenville books could be suitably housed. The increased purchases as a result of the larger annual grant and the growth in the number of legal deposit items led to a crisis that caused Panizzi, in 1852, to put forward his plan for a new building in the central courtyard of the museum, to be constructed mainly of cast iron.

Work began in 1854, and by 1857 the new round main reading room, encircled by the four book stacks known as the Iron Library, was open for use. The move of books into the new stacks was greatly simplified because Thomas Watts had evolved what he described as his "elastic system" of placing in the late 1840s, eliminating the need for pressmarks to be changed when blocks of books were moved to new locations.

1857 to 1899

The desire of the trustees that one of the most senior members of the staff of the Department of Printed Books should be the superintendent of the new reading room led to Watts being instructed, much against his will, to take on this task. He was the first of a line of superintendents who were able to be of great assistance to those who used the main reading room because of their knowledge and seniority. Unfortunately, in 1975 this tradition of having a senior member of the staff available in the main reading room was abandoned.

A service to the general public, as distinct from the readers, was the commencement of a series of exhibitions of manuscript and printed material. The first of these was held at the time of the Great Exhibition in Hyde Park in 1851. From 1857 on, permanent exhibitions were a regular feature of the library's work. Temporary exhibitions also became popular in later years.

Panizzi became principal librarian of the museum in 1856 and was succeeded as keeper of printed books by John Winter Jones. As soon as space was available in the new Iron Library, Winter Jones successfully pressed for the restoration of the purchase grant to £10,000 per annum from the lower levels to which it had been cut in the early 1850s because of overcrowding in the stacks. Consequently the book stock grew very considerably in subsequent years. Winter Jones also made sure that the preparation of the new catalog of printed books went forward steadily, both when he was keeper and after he succeeded Panizzi as principal librarian in 1866. He persuaded the trustees to set up a separate Department of Maps in 1867 by combining the relevant material from the manuscripts and printed books departments. He also convinced them to appoint a keeper of Oriental manuscripts working within the administrative structure of the Department of Manuscripts. The separate Department of Maps only existed until 1880, when the responsibility for maps was handed back to the manuscripts and printed books departments, but the Oriental manuscripts were combined with the Oriental printed books in 1892 to form a new Department of Oriental Printed Books and Manuscripts.

When Winter Jones retired in 1878, his successor as principal librarian was Edward A. Bond, who had been keeper of manuscripts since 1866, when Madden had retired. Bond was a man of vision, and when Richard Garnett (one of the outstanding members of the staff in the history of the Department of Printed Books) recommended that the new catalog be printed to save space, Bond supported him. Bond did this despite the objections of George Bullen, the keeper of printed books, who was conditioned by Panizzi's objection to the printing of the catalog being started before it was completely revised. The production of the *General Catalogue of Printed Books* between 1881 and 1905 was one of the major achievements of the library. It was controlled by Garnett, who combined this work with being superintendent of the reading room until the trustees relieved him of the latter task in 1884.

Bullen's contribution to recording the collections was to print a *Catalogue of Books in the Library of the British Museum Printed in England . . . to the Year 1640*. This appeared in 1884 and was the forerunner of specialized catalogs of parts of the collections. Outstanding examples of these were the short title catalogs of French, Spanish, German, Italian, and other categories of books that the library published in the 20th century. Another of Bond's innovations was the introduction of electric light into the museum in 1879. This made it possible for the main reading room (and later the exhibition galleries of the museum) to be kept open after dark. Bond also supported Garnett's plan to introduce movable presses into the book stacks to increase their capacity.

The construction of the White Wing (at the southeast corner of the museum building) in the 1880s made it possible to provide a special room for the consultation of newspapers, and the first students' room for the Department of Manuscripts. Previously most manuscripts had been read in the main reading room, with those requiring the closest supervision being consulted in the Manuscripts Saloon, where some of the staff worked. It was at this time that the main reading room was at the height of its fame, partly because Garnett was its superintendent from 1875 to 1884. His wide range of knowledge and ready accessibility to readers were much appreciated. He also took steps to reduce the time taken to supply books from the stacks.

Acquisitions continued to arrive in large numbers, and much important antiquarian material was purchased. Among the important manuscripts acquired was the Stowe collection. The system of international exchange of official publications was also started at this time, which led to great quantities of such material being acquired in the 20th century. Since Panizzi's time the aim of the library with respect to printed material has been to obtain all material of research value from all over the world, as much as possible. In view of the vast increase in world publications, achieving this aim obviously became less possible in the latter part of the 20th century than it had been in the 19th century. With regard to British material, however, the library has tried to acquire as complete as possible a collection of the national printed archive by legal deposit and purchase.

A constant theme in the history of the library has been the need for extra space to house the ever-growing collections of an institution that had as one of its fundamental doctrines the belief that, to safeguard the interests of future generations of scholars, material should not be discarded. Less than 30 years after the Iron Library was built, it became necessary to construct the White Wing and then to install movable presses in the main book stacks. A few years later (in 1905) the growing mass of newspapers obliged the trustees to move the bulk of them to a repository at Hendon, eight miles northwest of the museum. The King Edward Building was erected to the north of the existing museum building between 1906 and 1914; it was linked to the main building by an enlarged rare books reading room called the North Library. In due course the King Edward Building provided accommodation for the music room, the map room, the Copyright Receipt (Legal Deposit) Office, and the collections of official publications, as well as for some of the museum's departments of antiquities.

1899 to 1939

George K. Fortescue, who was keeper of printed books from 1899 to 1912 and had earlier been Garnett's successor as superintendent of the reading room, had noted the need for subject access to the collections. In response to this need and as a piece of private enterprise, he devised a subject index in the early 1880s that was produced every five years thereafter. One of the major enterprises of the library, the catalog of incunabula, was started during his period as keeper. The catalog records one of the largest collections in the world after a period of intensive purchasing on the part of the museum in the late 19th and early 20th centuries. In preparation for such a catalog Robert Proctor had begun the process of arranging the incunabula on the shelves in order of country, town, and press. Notable scholars who worked on this catalog were Alfred F. Pollard, Henry Thomas, and Victor Scholderer.

The Department of Oriental Printed Books and Manuscripts had a fine scholar, Lionel D. Barnett, as its keeper from 1908 to 1936. He had a remarkable knowledge of the languages of India; in the course of his career, he completed a monumental series of ten catalogs of works in these languages. The Department of Manuscripts also had a great tradition of scholarship. Notable in this connection were Edward Maunde Thompson (keeper of manuscripts, 1878–88; principal librarian, 1888–1909) and Frederic Kenyon (deputy keeper, 1898–1909; principal librarian, 1909–30).

World War I interrupted the normal work of the museum. The exhibition galleries were closed for much of the time, but the reading room service continued, even though many members of the staff were serving with the armed forces or in government departments. The building and the collections suffered no serious damage, although some of the most valuable material was evacuated from London after air raids became more frequent in 1917.

After the war the lack of space became so serious that a royal commission was established in 1927 to examine the difficulties being experienced by the British Museum and other national museums. Its recommendations forced the government to provide funds to deal with these problems. As a result the Hendon Newspaper Repository was enlarged, provided with a reading room (which opened in 1932), and renamed the Colindale Newspaper Library. The book storage and staff accommodations in the north wing of the museum were enlarged by inserting mezzanines, and a start was made on rebuilding the stacks of the Iron Library. (Two of the four main stacks had been rebuilt before World War II halted the work.)

At the end of the 1920s it was decided to print a new edition of the *General Catalogue of Printed Books*, which had appeared between 1881 and 1905. Unfortunately, the calculations about the number of staff needed for this project were incorrect, and although extra staff were ultimately obtained, progress was far too slow. The Department of Manuscripts had problems with the quinquennial volumes of its *Catalogue of Additions*. During the interwar period they increasingly fell into arrears, largely because of the influx of large collections of modern political papers that created more work than the department had staff to handle.

Important manuscripts were acquired during this time. An outstanding example was the *Codex Sinaiticus*, a Greek Bible of the fourth century that was bought by the trustees from the Soviet government in 1933 for £100,000. The greatest acquisition of the Department of Printed Books in the interwar years was the Ashley Library, which was bought in 1937 from the widow of Thomas J. Wise, who only charged £66,000 for it.

1939 to 1967

World War II had devastating effects on the Department of Printed Books. Evacuation preserved the most valuable printed books, as it did the collections of manuscripts and of Oriental books and manuscripts. Fortunately, the bomb that exploded in the King's Library in September 1940 only resulted in the loss of about 400 volumes, but large numbers of newspapers were destroyed when the Colindale Newspaper Library was bombed in October. The real disaster came in May 1941 when one of the four stacks of the Iron Library was set on fire by incendiary bombs with the loss of up to 250,000 volumes. Attempts to replace these began at once and continued into the 1980s.

After 1945 war damage to the buildings was repaired, a microfilming service was developed, and intensive efforts were made to obtain foreign publications that the library had been unable to acquire while hostilities continued. Purchasing of antiquarian material on a considerable scale was also resumed.

The senior keeper of printed books (under Cecil B. Oldman, the principal keeper) was Frank C. Francis, who later became director of the museum. A man of great vigor and determination, Francis decided to deal with the problem of slow progress on the revised edition of the *General Catalogue of Printed Books,* known as GK II. Despite opposition from those members of the staff who felt that a completely revised catalog would be of great service to scholarship, he forced through a plan to produce a photolithographic reprint of the 1881 to 1905 catalog, with entries for acquisitions to 1955 added. The production of this version of the *General Catalogue* in 263 volumes between 1960 and 1966 was a major achievement, even though this catalog had its faults.

Francis also believed that the library should revive its 19th-century tradition of providing a service to science as well as to the humanities, and he waged a campaign from 1951 on for the creation of the National Reference Library of Science and Invention, which came into existence as part of the Department of Printed Books in 1966 when the former Patent Office Library was incorporated into the British Museum.

Regular increases in the grant for purchases, together with a massive growth in the intake of official foreign publications and many more legal deposit items, caused the stock of the Department of Printed Books to rise to approximately 8.5 million volumes by 1973. By this date the Department of Manuscripts had about 83,000 volumes. The Department of Oriental Printed Books and Manuscripts contained more than 400,000 printed volumes and about 37,000 volumes of manuscripts. This growth of the collection of printed books forced the trustees to move material to the former Woolwich Arsenal (about nine miles east of the museum) from 1964 on, while they waited in hope for progress on a completely new building for the library departments immediately south of the museum. This building had first been discussed during World War II.

In the meantime, attempts were made to improve conditions in the existing buildings. When the main reading room was redecorated in 1952, fluorescent lighting was installed, an inquiry desk was constructed to accommodate staff who would deal with queries, a typing room and a number of microfilm reading machines were provided, and in 1960 a rapid photocopy service was begun. The manuscripts students' room was doubled in size in 1957, and from 1960 the main reading room was opened in the evenings two or three times each week.

In the postwar period one of the great problems of the Department of Printed Books (and, to a lesser extent, the Department of Manuscripts) was the difficulty of keeping up with the cataloging of the large influx of material. So when the application of computer cataloging began to be discussed, Francis insisted that the matter should be investigated to see whether these new techniques could help to solve the library's problems. Before these investigations were completed, the whole future of the library was thrown into doubt by the decision of Harold Wilson's Labour government in 1967 to withdraw permission for the construction of a new building for the library south of the museum. The government set up a committee under the chairmanship of Frederick S. (later Lord) Dainton to study national library provision and to make recommendations for future developments, but this failed to prevent the storm of protest caused by the government's action in abandoning the plan to build to the south of the museum.

1967 to the Present

The National Libraries Committee recommended in 1969 that a national library should be formed by bringing together the British Museum library (including the National Reference Library of Science and Invention), the National Central Library, the National Lending Library for Science and Technology, and the British National Bibliography. It also recommended that the building to house the former library departments of the British Museum should be on the site immediately adjacent to the museum. In 1975 an alternative site in the Euston Road adjoining St. Pancras station (about three-quarters of a mile north of the museum) was accepted. Soon after the return to power of the Conservatives in 1970, the government issued a statement in January 1971 accepting the main recommendations of the Dainton Committee and announcing that the new library would be called the British Library. The official announcement stated that the objectives of the British Library should be to preserve and make available for reference at least one copy of every book and periodical of domestic origin and as many overseas publications as possible; to provide an efficient central lending and photocopying service; and to provide central cataloging and other bibliographical services. An Act of Parliament was passed in July 1972 to set up the new institution, and it came into existence on 1 April 1973, beginning operations on 1 July.

With regard to the bodies that came together to form the British Library, the history of the library departments of the British Museum (the Departments of Printed Books, including the National Reference Library of Science and Invention; Manuscripts; and Oriental Printed Books and Manuscripts) has been outlined above. The National Central Library originated in the Central Library for Students, which came into existence in 1916 to supply books to students in the adult education classes run by the Workers' Educational Association. It soon began lending books to public libraries, reflecting its readers' needs. Its role as the center for interlibrary lending in the United Kingdom was recognized in 1931 when it was granted a royal charter and renamed the National Central Library. It not only lent books from its own stock (which suffered severe losses during an air raid in April 1941), but also maintained the union catalogs necessary for locating books in libraries prepared to cooperate in the interlibrary loan scheme.

In the late 1940s the need for improved library facilities for those engaged in scientific and technical research was recognized, and the Standing Scientific and Technical Information Committee of the Advisory Council for Science Policy recommended that a national scientific lending library should be established. Planning for a library to provide a postal loan service of scientific and technical literature began in 1956, and Donald J. Urquhart (a dynamic figure) was put in charge of the project. Stock was built up by purchase and by transferring material from the library of the Science Museum. A 60-acre site for the new library was selected near Boston Spa in Yorkshire, from which mail could reach almost any part of the United Kingdom within 24 hours. Buildings on the site were converted; books and periodicals were moved in, beginning in 1961; and in November 1962 the formal opening of the National Lending Library for Science and Technology took place. It soon became very successful in satisfying photocopying and loan requests for scientific material.

A committee of the Library Association (on which Francis of the British Museum was very active) was set up in 1947 to consider the provision of centralized cataloging and bibliographical services. The result was the foundation of the British National Bibliography, which produced the first of its weekly lists (based on the legal deposit material received in the Copyright Receipt Office of the British Museum) in 1950. Until 1967 the British National Bibliography was housed in accommodation provided by the museum; then its need for more space forced it to move elsewhere. In August 1974 the British National Bibliography organization joined the British Library.

There were other additions to the new library. In April 1974 the Office for Scientific Information (established in 1965) was transferred from the Department of Education and Science to form the Research and Development Branch of the British Library. In 1999 its successor, the Research and Innovation Centre, was moved from the British Library to become part of the Library and Information Commission. In 1974 the Library Association's library was handed over to the British Library board. The India Office Library (set up in 1801) and Records (which date back to the foundation of the East India Company in 1600) came to the library in April 1982 from the Foreign and Commonwealth Office, which had received them when the India Office came to an end in 1947. In 1991 the India Office Library and Records were merged with the former British Museum Department of Oriental Printed Books and Manuscripts to form what were called the Oriental collections within the British Library. The British Institute of Recorded Sound was organized in 1955 as a result of the enthusiasm and enterprise of Patrick Saul, substantially helped by Alec H. King, superintendent of the British Museum music room. In 1983 the institute was absorbed into the British Library and renamed the National Sound Archive.

In its early years the British Library consisted of a Reference Division (based in London and composed of the former library departments of the British Museum) and a Lending Division at Boston Spa (formed from the National Lending Library for Science and Technology and the National Central Library). The accession of the British National Bibliography in 1974 led to the formation of the Bibliographical Services Division, which was given control of the Copyright Receipt (Legal Deposit) Office, formerly in the Department of Printed Books.

After long delays, work on the library's new building in the Euston Road (designed by Sir Colin St. John Wilson) began in 1984. In December 1996 the first books were moved in, and the first reading room was opened in 1997. By 1999 all the books had been moved and the 11 reading rooms were in operation.

There were major reorganizations of the library in 1985, 1988, and 1996. In 1999, under the chief executive, there was a deputy chief executive and a director-general of collections and services. Directors were in charge of the various elements of the library—collections management (acquisitions, processing, cataloging and conservation); information systems; estates (accommodation); public services (including document supply); reader services and collection development; and special collections (including manuscripts, Oriental material, maps, music and sound recordings, and philatelic collections). Reporting directly to the chief executive were two directors, one of whom was in charge of finance and the other of staff matters. After the appointment of a new chief executive officer in 2000, there was yet another reorganization of the senior management structure of the library. Ten of the 11 posts listed above were abolished, and five directorates were established under the chief executive to deal with the following areas: scholarship and collections; operations and services; electronic strategy and programs; strategic marketing and communications; and finance and corporate resources.

The British Library Act (1972) provides that the board that administers the library should consist of not fewer than nine or more than 14 members. In 1999 there were 14 members including the chief executive. In 1999–2000 there were 2,339 staff members (including 949 managerial and professional grades) and 358 miles of shelving in use out of a total of 400 miles of shelving in the library. There were 1,480 reader and catalog desks in the Euston Road building, 145 at the Colindale Newspaper Library, and 76 at Boston Spa. The library spent more than £113 million in the 1999–2000 financial year.

The library depends very heavily on computerized systems for catalogs, acquisitions records, and readers' book requests. It aims to extend access to a wider reader base and develop a digital future for its collections and services.

PHILIP R. HARRIS

Further Reading

Barker, Nicolas, *Treasures of the British Library*, London: British Library, 1988; New York: Abrams, 1989

Chaplin, Arthur Hugh, *GK: 150 Years of the General Catalogue of Printed Books in the British Museum*, Brookfield, Vermont: Scolar Press, 1987

Cowtan, Robert, *Memories of the British Museum*, London: Bentley, 1872

Day, Alan, *The British Library: A Guide to Its Structure, Publications, Collections, and Services*, London: Library Association, 1988

Day, Alan, *The New British Library*, London: Library Association, 1994

Day, Alan, *Inside the British Library,* London: Library Association, 1998

Esdaile, Arundell, *The British Museum Library: A Short History and Survey,* London: Allen and Unwin, 1946

Harris, Philip Rowland, *A History of the British Museum Library, 1753–1973,* London: British Library, 1998

Harris, Philip Rowland, editor, *The Library of the British Museum: Retrospective Essays on the Department of Printed Books,* London: British Library, 1991

McCrimmon, Barbara, *Power, Politics, and Print: The Publication of the British Museum Catalogue, 1881–1900,* Hamden, Connecticut: Linnet Books, 1981

Miller, Edward, *Prince of Librarians: The Life and Times of Antonio Panizzi of the British Museum,* London: Deutsch, and Athens: Ohio University Press, 1967

Miller, Edward, *That Noble Cabinet: A History of the British Museum,* London: Deutsch, and Athens: Ohio University Press, 1973

Brown University Library

Address: Main Library
Brown University
10 Prospect Street (Box A)
Providence, Rhode Island 02912
USA
Telephone: 401-863-2162
Fax: 401-863-1272
www.brown.edu/Facilities/University_Library

Founded: 1767

Holdings (2000): Volumes: 3.1 million. Archives and manuscripts: 16,000 linear feet; audio recordings: 65,000; current serials: 14,000; film and video: 4,000 reels; graphic materials: 910,000; incunabula: 940; manuscripts: 16,000 linear feet; maps: 140,000; microforms: 1.8 million.

Special Collections: *Areas of Concentration:* Book arts; history of mathematics, science, pseudoscience, and magic; incunabula; military history; philately; publishing history; 20th-century English and European literature; U.S. literature and music; U.S. political, social, cultural, and business history. *Individual Collections:* American Mathematical Society archives; American sheet music; Anne S.K. Brown military collection; Annmary Brown collection of incunabula; Ciaraldi comic book collection; Dickinson family papers and library; Gorham Silver Company archives; Hall-Hoag collection of extremist and dissenting literature; Harris collection of American poetry and plays; James Laughlin collection on Ezra Pound, Thomas Merton, Gertrude Stein, and William Carlos Williams; Kirk collection on alcoholism; Knight, Champlin, and Galkin stamp collections; Lownes history of science collection; McLellan Lincoln; Miller collection of wit and humor; St. Martin's Press archives; Small Press archives; Smith magic collection. *Author Collections:* Dante Alighieri; William Blake; John Buchan; Horace (Quintus Horatius Flaccus); T.E. Lawrence; H.P. Lovecraft; Niccolò Machiavelli; George Orwell; George Bernard Shaw; H.G. Wells; Émile Zola.

The 18th-Century Library

Brown University, the seventh institution of higher education to be established in the original American colonies, was founded as Rhode Island College in 1764 in Warren, Rhode Island. Although constituted by Baptists, the original charter stated that "Into this Liberal and Catholic Institution shall never be admitted any Religious Tests but on the Contrary all the Members hereof shall for ever enjoy full free Absolute and uninterrupted Liberty of Conscience." Despite this spirit of toleration, qualified students were in short supply, and the college struggled to survive. Its first president and sole faculty member, the Reverend James Manning, initially earned his livelihood by serving as the local Baptist minister and operating a Latin school.

The poverty of the early college was reflected in the fact that it possessed no books until 17 June 1767, when President Manning established the library through his gift of Valentin Schindler's *Lexicon Pentaglotton*, printed at Hanover, Germany, in 1612. The first recorded purchase of books took place in 1768, when the Reverend Morgan Edwards was dispatched to England and Ireland to raise funds and buy books. Even so, as late as 1772 President Manning was compelled to state, "At present we have about two hundred and fifty volumes, and these not well chosen being such as our friends could best spare."

Classes were suspended during the Revolutionary War, and the library was sent to rural Wrentham, Massachusetts, where it was safeguarded by the Reverend William Williams, a member of the college's first graduating class. The Reverend Williams later joked that the library was so small that he was able to hide it in his kitchen table. Though the story may be apocryphal, the table is quite authentic. Today, the table and some 500 surviving volumes of the colonial-era library, known as the Williams Table collection, presides over the principal reading room of the John Hay Library. Williams himself is commemorated through an award periodically presented by the Friends of the Library to individuals who have provided extraordinary support for the Brown Library.

The Brown Family and the University's Move to Providence

In 1770 the College's governing body voted in favor of transferring the fledgling college from Warren to Providence in consideration of a substantial gift of funds offered by leading citizens of the latter town who wished to establish an institution of higher learning in their burgeoning city. The Providence group was led by the four Brown brothers, wealthy merchants and philanthropists who, once the college relocated to Providence, began the family's long history of support for the library. In 1783 John Brown proposed a subscription fund for the purchase of books for the library, offering to match the amount pledged by all other subscribers. The resulting fund made possible the purchase, in London, of some 1,400 volumes. The Brown family's gifts to the college were of sufficient frequency and importance that in 1804, when Nicholas Brown II donated the particularly large sum of $5,000, the corporation was prompted to change the college's name from Rhode Island College to Brown University.

The library's first published catalog, printed by John Carter, appeared in 1793. At that time the library had grown to 2,200 volumes, including books purchased in support of the curriculum and gifts of a rather haphazard nature. Even so, the germ of the Brown Library's future importance as a research collection was evident from the inclusion of numerous 16th- and 17th-century editions of the classics; scientific, legal, and political treatises; and even a healthy proportion of belles lettres that served to balance the expected preponderance of religious texts. Interspersed were individual titles of note such as Roger Williams' copy of the Eliot Indian Bible, annotated in code by Williams, and Benjamin Franklin's *Experiments and Observations on Electricity*.

19th-Century Expansion

As Brown's library continued to grow, its small quarters in University Hall became ever more cramped, and President Francis Wayland set out to address both the issues of inadequate space and inadequate funding for acquisitions. Again it was Nicholas Brown II who came to the rescue, providing most of the funds for both efforts. Manning Hall, a temple-fronted Greek Revival building, was completed in 1835 and housed the library on its ground floor with a chapel above. Within a few years, Brown also donated more than half of the $25,000 principal of the library's first acquisitions endowment, known as the Library Fund, 1840.

It was during Wayland's presidency that Charles Coffin Jewett was appointed librarian at Brown. Jewett, who subsequently would gain renown as the first librarian of both the Smithsonian Institution and later the Boston Public Library, was responsible for the highly regarded 1841 printed catalog of the Brown Library. He also greatly strengthened the holdings of the library through the purchase, in Europe, of 7,000 books in French, German, and Italian, with funds supplied by John Carter Brown, who at this point was embarking upon his own collection of Americana that would one day form the nucleus of the John Carter Brown Library (the John Carter Brown Library, which opened its doors on the Brown campus in 1904, is an independently funded institution not administered by the University Library).

By 1850 the library contained approximately 30,000 volumes, and Manning Hall was rapidly being outgrown. It was not until 1879, however, that a new library was completed, again through the generosity of John Carter Brown and his widow. The new structure, which today houses the Department of Economics, had a capacity of 150,000 volumes and was as modern as the technology and architecture of the day permitted. Open-shelf alcoves radiated from the central three-story-high reading room, and no wood was employed in the structure with the exception of furniture and shelving. It was at this time that the card catalog was introduced, eventually replacing the outdated book catalog.

The new library building and card catalog were undertaken during the tenure of Reuben A. Guild, librarian from 1848 to 1893. Like Jewett, Guild was nationally prominent. He was one of the founders of the American Library Association (ALA) and its first secretary. In addition, he wrote *The Librarian's Manual: A Treatise on Bibliography* (1858), one of the earliest works on librarianship published in the United States. Locally, he published histories of both the university and the library.

The Emergence of Special Collections

It was during Guild's tenure that the Harris collection of American poetry and plays came to Brown in 1884. The first of Brown's special collections to be so denominated, the 6,000-volume collection had taken form decades earlier as the private library of Albert Gorton Greene. After Greene's death the collection was acquired and expanded, first by Caleb Fiske Harris and later by Senator Henry Bowen Anthony, who bequeathed it to Brown University (his alma mater). All three men had built the collection on the basis of inclusiveness rather than canonical approbation, a highly unusual intellectual construct for the time. With an endowment established by Samuel Coffin Eastman, Greene's son-in-law, the Harris collection has continued to grow over the years to become the world's largest collection of its kind. It also has attracted complementary collections in other formats, such as manuscripts and sheet music, and in other literary and cultural genres, from fine press printing to comic books.

The Koopman Years

The dramatic changes affecting U.S. higher education in the last quarter of the 19th century manifested themselves at Brown during the late 1880s with the establishment of graduate programs, expanding undergraduate enrollment, and the foundation of the Women's College. Rapid library growth accompanied these changes, as noted by President Elisha Benjamin Andrews in 1892: "Surprising as it may seem, our Library Building, new as it is, and inadequate as are our funds for the stocking of it with books, is, if not outgrown, on the point of becoming so." Although additional space would not be forthcoming for several years, the substantial growth of the collections resulted in the adoption in the early 1890s of the Cutter subject classification for books, replacing the fixed location system that had preceded it.

In the first three decades of the 20th century Brown benefited considerably from the energies of two major figures in the university's history, President William H.P. Faunce and Librarian Harry Lyman Koopman (1893–1930). Koopman, under whose aegis Brown implemented the Library of Congress (LC) classification system, also presided over the continuing expansion of the collections and the construction of a new building that accommodated most of the library's space needs until the early 1960s. Like several of his predecessors, Koopman was also a well-known figure in the library world. He was elected president of the ALA in 1928, from which office he took a strong stand against censorship. In answer to the Customs Department's efforts in 1929 to bar works by authors such as Jean Jacques Rousseau, Honoré de Balzac, and Giovanni Bocaccio, he stated: "Every college in the country will have to 'shut up shop' if this continues. . . . If these books are going to be banned, they ought to go through with it and ban the Old Testament."

Koopman considered the new building, the John Hay Library, to be one of the signal achievements of his 37-year career at the helm of Brown's library. Completed in 1910, half of the construction costs were donated by Andrew Carnegie, who suggested that the new building be named for his friend John Hay, a distinguished diplomat and an 1858 graduate of Brown. With its formal public spaces, closed stacks, and rooms devoted to specialized collections, the John Hay was a typical academic library of its time, a building that fostered learning and research through dignity and tranquility.

The John Hay Library rapidly began to fill, both with additions to the general collections and with rare book and manuscript holdings that supported the expanding graduate programs. Among the most significant special collections to arrive during Koopman's tenure were the Rider collection on Rhode Island history, the Church collection on Latin America, the Chambers Dante Collection, the Hoffman Napoleon collection, and—most important—the McLellan Lincoln collection. Purchased by alumnus John D. Rockefeller Jr., the McLellan collection was one of the four most important private Lincoln collections and was deemed of sufficient importance that upon its arrival at Brown, two handsomely appointed rooms in the John Hay were dedicated to it.

Depression, War, and Recovery

With Koopman's retirement in 1930, Henry Bartlett Van Hoesen was appointed librarian. Van Hoesen's tenure (1930–49) coincided with two national calamities that adversely affected all research libraries: the Depression and World War II. Reduced salaries and acquisition budgets plagued the library well into the 1930s, and the war disrupted all aspects of university life, including the library's ability to acquire foreign materials. Even so the library continued to grow both incrementally and through gifts of focused collections, so much so that space was at a premium throughout this period. By 1937 there were no fewer than 17 departmental libraries scattered about the campus, libraries that were established less for the convenience of faculty and students than because the John Hay Library was filled to capacity.

The library's fortunes improved once again when Henry M. Wriston became president in 1937. A large addition to the John Hay Library was completed in 1938, allowing for the consolidation of many collections and services, excluding only physical and biological sciences, which retained their status as departmental libraries. Regaining much of the momentum it had lost during the Depression and World War II, the library had larger postwar acquisitions and operating budgets, and the Friends of the Library was constituted as an organization that would attract both in-kind and monetary gifts. Thus, Van Hoesen was able to complete his years as librarian of Brown University on a much more positive note than when he began.

Among the significant activities of Van Hoesen's tenure was the university's acceptance, in 1948, of the Annmary Brown Memorial. Completed in 1907 as a mausoleum for General Rush Christopher Hawkins and his wife Annmary Brown, the memorial also contained the general's important library of incunabula and the Hawkins's collection of academic art. Privately incorporated and endowed, the memorial's financial resources were so diminished by 1948 that it was deeded to the university in order to preserve it intact. Along with the building, the collections, and the surrounding land that was adjacent to the university's expanding dormitory system, the library acquired the services of Margaret Bingham Stillwell, who had been librarian of the memorial since 1917. Stillwell, who remained at the memorial until her retirement in 1953, was a renowned figure in the world of scholarly librarianship, her many publications ranging from the magisterial census of incunabula in U.S. libraries to her popular *Librarians Are Human* (1973).

Brown celebrated the acquisition of its 1-millionth volume in 1954. The iconic title was Descartes' *De Homine Figuris . . .* (Leyden, 1662), given by Albert E. Lownes, an alumnus whose massive collection of rare scientific books would come to the university at his death in 1978. Other significant collections that added to the library's holdings in the postwar period included the Morse whaling collection and the Gardner collection of Chinese history and literature, which formed the nucleus for today's East Asian collection.

New Buildings and New Challenges

Rapid growth of the collections once again led to a critical shortage of space, and the 1960s witnessed the most significant construction of new library buildings that Brown had ever experienced. Under the leadership of University Librarian David A. Jonah (1949–74), the John D. Rockefeller Jr. Library was completed in 1964 and a new Sciences Library built in 1970–71. The renovation and restoration of the John Hay Library into a state-of-the-art facility for special collections was undertaken in 1979–80 under Jonah's successors, Charles D. Churchwell (1974–79) and C. James Schmidt (1979–82).

The 1970s began turbulently for the Brown Library. In May 1973 the library's support staff formed a unit of the Service

Employees International Union, and the first contract between the university and the union was signed in November 1973 following a ten-day strike. A little more than six months later Charles Churchwell became university librarian, and faced with university retrenchment, set about centralizing library services. A result of these changes, which were complicated by a contract clause permitting the reopening of wage negotiations one year into the contract, was a second three-month strike in 1976. Since 1976 the library has experienced only one other strike, lasting some six weeks in 1990, over the issue of health care copayments.

The 1970s and 1980s saw major developments in library automation. In 1974 the library became a member of OCLC and the library also installed its own automated circulation system. In 1979, under University Librarian C. James Schmidt, Brown joined the Research Libraries Group. With the arrival of Merrily E. Taylor as university librarian in 1982, the library embarked upon a major effort to update its electronic environment. In September 1984 the Pew Memorial Trust granted the library $1.5 million for the installation of an online catalog of library holdings, and by 1988 the library unveiled its online catalog, Josiah, named for Brown's mythical professor of psycho-ceramics, Josiah S. Carberry. With this infrastructure in place, the library proceeded to establish a retrospective conversion unit, and with grants from Laurance Rockefeller and David Rockefeller and numerous Higher Education Act (HEA) Title II-C grants, conversion began in earnest. As of late 1998, almost 95 percent of the library's bibliographic records had been converted.

Collection development forged ahead in the 1970s and 1980s as well. Among the major collections that have arrived since 1980 are the Anne S.K. Brown military collection, the archives of the Gorham Silver Company, the library of the Rhode Island Medical Society, the H. Adrian Smith collection of magic, and the Hall-Hoag collection of extremist and dissenting literature. In 1988 Brown acquired its 2-millionth volume, a rare first edition (in Russian) of Ivan Pavlov's *Lectures on the Functions of the Main Digestive Glands*. By 1989 the library had completed fund-raising for a National Endowment for the Humanities grant that raised more than $3 million in new acquisitions endowments.

The Recent Past and Future Directions

The 1990s saw the library's holdings reach 3 million volumes with the acquisition in 1997 of three major additions to the collections, all acquired through the generosity of alumnus Paul R. Dupee Jr.: the Chris Philip collection on fireworks, which complemented existing historical strengths in Special Collections; a group of online databases published by Chadwyck-Healy, which took note of the future of electronic research data; and a collection of materials on Mexican history, primarily 19th-century, which complemented existing Brown collection strengths and recognized the international nature of research and teaching at Brown.

Also acquired by gift or purchase during the 1990s were a variety of focused collections that significantly strengthened the library's research capabilities. Among these collections were the Martha Dickinson Bianchi Collection, which contains papers of the family of Emily Dickinson as well as the 3,000-volume Dickinson family library; the Miller collection of wit and humor; the archives of St. Martin's Press; and several major author collections devoted to John Buchan, George Orwell, and H.G. Wells.

The library forged ahead in automation during the 1990s with the acquisition of the Innovative Interfaces integrated catalog, circulation, and processing system. By 1993 retrospective conversion was largely completed with a grant from the Davis Foundation, and with funding from the Champlin Foundations the library created a new electronic reference and information center for the Rockefeller Library. Since the mid-1990s, the Center for Library Technology, a multi-media instructional laboratory, and a Center for Digital Initiatives have expanded the library's electronic capabilities.

Fund-raising, an increasingly common necessity among U.S. research libraries in recent decades, has been a hallmark of Taylor's tenure as university librarian. Funds for specific projects, especially those involving electronic access and services, have been received from corporate, foundation, and governmental grants as well as support from alumni and parents. The online catalog, retrospective conversion, state-of-the-art workstation facilities, and digital initiatives have all been supported primarily through fund-raising. Endowment principal, which has increased staffing levels and acquisitions budgets in particular, has increased greatly through the generosity of alumni and parents as well as through grant initiatives. In 2000 the market value of the Brown University Library's endowment approached $40 million.

Looking to the future, the library must continue building upon its historical collections, supporting the teaching and research of its primary community, and taking advantage of new opportunities such as recent membership in the Boston Library Consortium. Immediate needs include expanded storage space, renovation of the Rockefeller and Sciences Libraries, and increased funds for acquisitions.

SAMUEL STREIT AND FREDERICK C. LYNDEN

See also John Carter Brown Library

Further Reading

Brown University Library, *Special Collections at Brown University: A History and Guide*, Providence, Rhode Island: Friends of the Brown University Library, 1988

Guild, Reuben Aldridge, *Historical Sketch of the Library of Brown University, with Regulations*, New Haven, Connecticut: Tuttle Morehouse and Taylor, 1861

Guild, Reuben Aldridge, "History of the College Library, 1770–1866," in *History of Brown University, with Illustrative Documents*, by Guild, Providence, Rhode Island: Providence Press, 1867

Jonah, David, "Brown University Library," in *Encyclopedia of Library and Information Science,* edited by Allen Kent et al., vol. 3, New York: Dekker, 1969

Koopman, Harry Lyman, "A History of Brown University Library," in *Report of the Committee,* by Brown University Survey Committee, Providence, Rhode Island: Brown University, 1930

Mitchell, Martha, "Harry Lyman Koopman," in *Encyclopedia Brunoniana,* Providence, Rhode Island: Brown University Library, 1993

Mitchell, Martha, "The Library," in *Encyclopedia Brunoniana,* Providence, Rhode Island: Brown University Library, 1993

Preface to the Catalogue of the Library of Brown University, with the Laws of the Library, Providence, Rhode Island: Brown University Library, 1843

Van Hoesen, Henry Bartlett, *Brown University Library: The Library of the College or University in the English Colony of Rhode Island and Providence Plantations in New England in America, 1767–1782,* Providence, Rhode Island: s.n., 1938

Canada Institute for Scientific and Technical Information

Address: Canada Institute for Scientific and Technical Information
National Research Council Canada
Building M-55, Montreal Road
Ottawa, Ontario K1A 0S2
Canada
Telephone: 613-993-1600
Fax: 613-952-9112
www.nrc.ca/cisti

Founded: 1924

Holdings (1999): Volumes: 8 million. Computer files: 3,000; current serials: 13,000; films and videos: 400; manuscripts: 263,000 linear feet; microforms: 3.5 million.

Special Collections: *Areas of Concentration*: Engineering; physical and life sciences; technology and health sciences.

Origins

The history of the Canada Institute for Scientific and Technical Information (CISTI) goes back 75 years. The institute's mission, like its name, has undergone changes over the decades. Its foundation, however, is the symbiotic nature of the relationship of CISTI to the National Research Council Canada (NRC). NRC is a federal agency and a leader in the government of Canada in matters of science and engineering, research, and development. This agency includes more than 20 research institutes and has overseen CISTI since the beginning. Today NRC has more than 3,000 employees from coast to coast and manages a budget of approximately $500 million (all figures in Canadian dollars). Approximately 10 percent of the Canadian federal budget devoted to science and technology goes to NRC.

World War I became the driving force behind the creation of NRC. When it was founded in 1916, it was simply a council composed of nine volunteers who held quarterly meetings. According to J.J. Brown's *Ideas in Exile: A History of Canadian Invention* (1967),

It was not until World War I that public attitudes towards science and technology changed sufficiently for the government to take any direct action to encourage research. With the bombing of London by zeppelins, however, even the most ignorant citizen could understand at last the relationship between inventions and warfare.

Established as a national scientific agency, NRC was created using the British Department of Scientific and Industrial Research as its model. Its first budget was $50,374. The first librarian of NRC, Beatrice Walling, was hired in 1917. Two years later the budget of NRC included an item labeled "miscellaneous, library" that was allocated $3,000. The embryo of what is CISTI came into being.

Despite the hiring of a librarian and the reference in the budget, it is nevertheless difficult to place the founding of the NRC library precisely in time. In fact, until the opening of the NRC Laboratories on Sussex Drive in Ottawa in 1932, the library had no official address. A small NRC collection was initially housed in modest offices in the West Block of the Parliament Buildings, at about the same time that Walling was appointed in 1917.

If there appears to be a general tendency to fix the inauguration date of the NRC Library in 1924, it is because the president at the time, the newly arrived Henry Marshall Tory, announced that he intended "building up a library that would serve scientific workers everywhere in Canada." Also in that year, the Research Council Act was passed by Parliament, making it possible to finance the first NRC research project. With the success of this undertaking, Tory was subsequently able to find the support needed to realize his big dream: the Temple of Science.

Officially baptized the NRC Laboratories, this Temple of Science was built at a cost of 3 million dollars. More than 2,000 handpicked guests inaugurated the temple with great pomp and circumstance on 10 August 1932. Despite much media coverage, little was said about the library. The laboratories were in the limelight. There were two reasons for this. In the first place, the collection of a mere 12,000 volumes looked lost in stacks designed to hold almost 500,000 books. But above all, the Great Depression was in full swing. Tory's inaugural address illustrated well what the future would hold: the need to justify every penny invested in his temple by demonstrating the financial success industry was already having as a result of the efforts of his researchers.

Searching for a National Mandate

Hidden in the background of the rich Italian-Renaissance-style building and not mentioned on the long list of important persons and doctors attending the event, there was a pioneer who had much greater ambitions for the library: Margaret Gill. Hired as a librarian by NRC in 1928, Gill had to overcome many obstacles in her efforts to increase the collection and to fulfill her aspirations to make the NRC Library an institution with a national mandate.

First, despite Tory's remarks, the original true mission of the NRC Library was not to serve the community of scientific workers across Canada, but rather NRC researchers busy in the first laboratories. The result of the Great Depression was that the NRC Library came face to face with this hard reality. Second, the librarians of the period were primarily female and the profession enjoyed very little decision-making power. During this period the administrator of the Montreal diocese gave sermons about "the criminal negligence of mothers who wanted careers for their daughters." We were a long way from library managers as we know them today.

Nevertheless, under Gill's 30-year reign, the NRC collection grew by a factor of 350, covering, by the end of the 1950s, more than 12 miles of stacks. In CISTI annals, 1957 (the end of Gill's career) is acknowledged as the year when the NRC Library started to fulfill its role as a national scientific library.

The Collection

Even though growth in the collection was impressive, given the budgetary limitations of the time, the library's real boom was still to come. Two factors begun before Gill's departure contributed to the expansion: CISTI's more clearly defined mission to serve NRC and the birth of the National Library of Canada in 1953.

The researcher clientele of NRC had already influenced the collection's orientation, with acquisitions focused on scientific and technical areas. More particularly, two world wars put a premium on research into strategic technologies. The NRC Library acquisition policy supported this momentum. Today the collection of documents, monographs, and periodicals in the technical sectors is still CISTI's crowning glory.

NRC researchers themselves contributed to the development of the tools and the products that constitute the technological infrastructure of the NRC Library, thereby directly supporting its national mandate. In view of Canada's vast size and its sparse population, the NRC Library's clientele has always been scattered from one coast to the other. Technology has thus played a major role in enabling the NRC Library to assume a national role.

The other important factor in the development of a national mandate for the NRC Library collection was the birth of the National Library of Canada in 1953. It was immediately obvious that the best use of the National Library's resources would be achieved by building collections in the social sciences and humanities, thereby avoiding duplication with the NRC Library as much as possible. That decision left the field wide open for the NRC Library to expand its official national mandate as a National Science Library. Unofficially this status was assumed in 1957, but in 1959 the National Science Library and the National Library of Canada signed a formal agreement regarding subject areas of responsibility for each institution. The official seal of legitimacy was granted in 1966 by the NRC Act.

It is interesting to note that the National Library of Canada is considered to be the only Canadian institution with a mission to conserve at least one copy of every document produced in the country, both scientific and nonscientific. The primary function of the National Science Library is, by contrast, international—that of providing the best possible collection for Canadian scientists. The distinction is important, because even today Canada represents only 4 percent of the world's production of scientific literature. Canadians use a far greater volume of scientific and technical information than they produce, requiring the CISTI collection to be broadly international.

The fact that the National Science Library has never been required to obtain all Canadian scientific documents and the fact that NRC researchers contributed to the development of its infrastructure combined to create CISTI's image. Today, CISTI is considered to be much more than a conventional library but is now seen as a national agency for the dissemination of scientific and technical information.

The Jack Brown Era

The notion of a national agency for the dissemination of information became a real part of the library's mission in 1957, a pivotal year in which a new leader, Jack Brown, took charge of the institute's destiny. The first official reference to such a mission statement came from him, and he retains a reputation as the visionary who had the most positive impact on the library's development.

The day that Brown arrived in his offices on Sussex Drive, he found a collection of national importance squeezed into extremely cramped quarters. Plans for the construction of a building that measured up to Brown's ideals were immediately under way. The dozen years that it took to get this megaproject poured in concrete was the same period as the revolution in information science, and Brown took steps to ensure that his library would not miss the technological curve. Toward the end of the 1960s, the Institute created pan-Canadian services that were propelled to commercial success by means of computer technology. The institute acquired an avant-garde image and the official status of National Science Library (NSL) of Canada.

In 1968 the NSL developed the first national selective information dissemination service, a sophisticated system used as a model by several foreign countries. In 1969 the government gave NRC an official mandate to develop a national scientific and technical information system. In 1971 NSL gave the CAN/SDI services software to the United Nations Educational, Scientific, and Cultural Organization for distribution to interested countries. CAN/OLE was created in 1972 and was the first real-time information tracking and distribution system in Canada.

In February 1974, when a new ultramodern building was finally ready to welcome it, the NSL was no longer just a library. A new roof along with new thinking helped Jack Brown to make his dream come true: expansion of the tentacles of a national scientific information dissemination network. The Canada Institute for Scientific and Technical Information officially saw the light of day under its new designation. The move itself was a matter of considerable staff pride in that the National Science Library continued to provide services without interruption during the move, which took one weekend. At the time, there were approximately 1 million volumes, 132 employees, and a new name.

Recent Trends

Innovative systems for disseminating information designed and implemented by CISTI have been refined over the years and have given it a certain reputation at the international level. After Brown's departure in 1979, Elmer V. Smith and later Margot Montgomery, as CISTI heads, only reaffirmed this desire to abolish borders.

Under Smith during the 1980s, CISTI acquired the requisite internal information science capacity to sustain an expansion of operations. In an interview for the June 1999 issue of CISTI news with Bernard Dumouchel, current director general of CISTI and one of Smith's lieutenants at the time, he noted, "During the 80s, we expanded the CISTI mandate by putting in place electronic systems for delivering documents, thereby greatly increasing access to our services."

Margot Montgomery arrived in 1991 and gave CISTI the indispensable commercial weapons it needed to enter the international market, then coming to terms with globalization. Indeed, her marketing strategy for international distribution of services has, among other factors, ensured a CISTI presence throughout the world. The NRC Research Press, the scientific publishing team, added the international credibility of its publications to CISTI's assets in 1994.

But all did not go smoothly, as the years of government cutbacks squeezed CISTI budgets and forced it, to a considerable degree, to embark on this international tangent in order to broaden its revenue base by developing new markets. Management's more business-oriented philosophy and the creation of a new department entirely devoted to marketing were something of a shock to the cultural values of the institute. The business notion of integrated marketing, although key to CISTI's future, required a great deal of effort to initiate.

The Canadian government's research and development policies are also having an impact on CISTI's mandate. As it rationalizes spending, the government diminishes its direct support of innovation. The federal government is more inclined to manage and coordinate than fund and conduct research and development. It is high on new instruments and mechanisms to promote knowledge transfer and tries to facilitate the flow of knowledge throughout the system of innovation by providing information to firms and institutions and fostering cooperation among the participants. CISTI has thus become the agency of choice on which to base a national scientific knowledge network and currently devotes a substantial portion of its resources to consolidating its national mandate in an increasingly electronic environment.

SYLVAIN ROBILLARD

Further Reading

Brown, J.J., *Ideas in Exile: A History of Canadian Invention*, Toronto, Ontario: McClelland and Stewart, 1967

Canadian Library Association Bulletin 16 (1959) (special libraries issue)

CISTI News (March 1984) (10th anniversary issue)

CISTI News (June 1999) (25th anniversary issue)

Steeves, Brian, *Growth of NSL/CISTI Resources and Services*, Ottawa, Ontario: National Research Council, 1993

Steeves, Brian, *The History of CISTI; L'histoire de l'ICISTI*, Ottawa, Ontario: National Research Council, 1993

Capitular Library of Verona

Address: Biblioteca Capitolare di Verona
Piazza Duomo, 13
37121 Verona
Italy
Telephone: 45-596516
Fax: 45-596516
www.rcvr.org/cultura/artgaleo

Founded: 517

Holdings (1999): Volumes: 80,000. Current serials: 90; incunabula: 247; manuscripts: 10,000 parchments and 716 bound volumes; music scores: 150; 16th-century editions: 2,500.

Special Collections: *Areas of Concentration:* Ancient Roman and Christian manuscripts. *Individual Collections:* Pacificus; Rather; Ursicinus. *Papers:* Archive of the Chapter; papers of the Fumanelli, Giuliari, and Pellegrini families.

In the fourth-century Roman Empire there were many publicly owned libraries open to a more or less general public. Rome, for example, had a total of 28. The Christian community also kept collections of books. Bishops, at that time elected by the clergy and people of the dioceses, were often members of illustrious and cultured families who chose good books for their churches. In the sixth to seventh centuries, Italian cathedrals, with their libraries and cathedral schools open for use by the clergy, achieved growing importance, becoming major centers of culture over vast regions.

Verona was one of the great cities of the Roman world. At the end of the fifth century, Ostrogoth King Theodoric, after his conquest of Italy in 493, made Verona his favorite residence. At the time, Verona's cathedral had a library and a scriptorium. Some, if not all, of the fifth-century codices now found at the Capitular Library (Biblioteca Capitolare di Verona, or BCV) were probably written there and have thus remained for 1,600 years in the very place where they were produced. These include an *Evangeliarium* on purple parchment, written in letters of gold and silver uncial; a *De civitate Dei* by St. Augustine, coming from the first half of the fifth century; an *Expositio in Evangelia* by St. Maximus, bishop of Turin, in which Roger Gryson recently (1982) was able to read some glosses written in a Gothic hand and containing Arian propositions (the Christian Goths followed the heresy of Arius); the *Institutiones* by the great jurist Ulpian (only two folios); the tract *De Trinitate* by St. Hilary, bishop of Poitiers; and a list of the Roman consuls from 439 to 494, contained in a palimpsest codex of the eighth century. Perhaps the most ancient is another palimpsest containing works by Livy, Euclid, Virgil, and an unknown Greek philosopher.

In a manuscript on the life of St. Martin of Tours, the scribe signed himself as follows: "My name is Ursicinus, Lector of the church of Verona" (lector being a grade of the minor orders of the clergy), confirming that he finished the work on the first of August under the consulship of Agapitus (i.e., in 517). From that date the founding of the library is sometimes taken. Production of these manuscripts continued in the seventh and eighth centuries and further expanded in the ninth century, when the learned and genial Archdeacon Pacificus of Verona took over the work of the scriptorium.

The Carolingian period was propitious for learned studies, which Charlemagne favored for his court and empire, especially in the cathedrals, where regular courses were instituted. Pacificus, as it appears from his epitaph, was a man of a thousand talents. He worked well with metal, marble, and wood; invented a night clock; and was the author of many works, including a commentary on the Old and New Testaments, a manual about calculus, and a topographical guide to Verona. He was an indefatigable copier. According to his epitaph, the scriptorium produced 218 manuscripts under his direction between A.D. 801 and 844, of which one-third were partly in his hand. There remain 27 in the Capitular Library, many probably written by him.

The tenth century was dominated by the personality of the Flemish Rather (Raterius), nominated bishop in 931 by the king of Italy, Hugo of Provence. Rather gave new dimension to the library. Among other things, he commissioned two copies of an eighth-century manuscript of the works of Livy: One remained in the library, the other was given to Emperor Otto I of Germany, who sent it to the Cathedral of Worms where it was rediscovered in the 16th century by Beatus Renanus. Thanks to the intelligence of its prefects, the BCV thus continued to maintain a link with the classical world and to conserve the rarest works of antiquity.

For approximately two centuries after 1000, changes in cultural taste caused ancient works to be ignored and neglected on the library shelves. A renaissance of interest in ancient civilization began, timidly at first, at the end of the 13th century in Venetian territory. Men of letters, judges, notaries, and cultivated lovers of literature wrote historic and literary works that revealed direct knowledge of some rare and almost nonexistent ancient works known to very few scholars at the time. Their basis was the library of the Abbey of Pomposa near Ravenna, and above all, the Capitular Library. Lovatus Lovati of Padua, for example, showed his knowledge of Catullus, Lucretius, Tibullus, and Seneca. Giovanni de Matociis of Verona distinguished the previously confused Pliny the Elder and Pliny the Younger; he had read the Pliny in the BCV. Benvenuto Campesani of Vicenza knew the work of Catullus well, writing poetically of the return of Catullus to Verona, alluding perhaps to a return to BCV of an antique manuscript or copy of Catullus from some far-off library to which it had inexplicably been transferred.

Years later, around 1340, Pietro (the son of Dante Alighieri) came to Verona to see Geremia of Montagnone's comments on Dante's works. During the same years, Simone d'Arezzo consulted the Capitular Library's Livy, and in 1345 Petrarch copied the letters of Cicero preserved there. Later he commissioned a copy of the *De re rustica* of Varro and also copies of other works. Thus the BCV helped bring together the first humanist library, that of Petrarch, a model for all others that followed.

In the early 17th century and in the succeeding period, political uncertainty and disorder caused the loss of many BCV manuscripts, including some of the most famous. Catullus, Varro, Pliny, Cicero, and Livy disappeared, but already copies of these manuscripts and their relevant commentaries were circulating among scholars in Europe. The cathedral chapter then limited itself to conserving what was left, which was no small matter. In 1630, during the Thirty Years War, Canon Rezani hid the manuscripts in a secret place for fear of German mercenary soldiers advancing toward Mantua. A short time later he died of the plague, along with 11 other canons of the cathedral, and the church lost track of its manuscripts. When Bernard de Montfaucon visited Verona in 1698, he did not see the manuscripts; indeed, the canons denied their existence. In 1713 Marquis Scipione Maffei, an eminent student of history and literature, convinced that the manuscripts still existed somewhere, persuaded Canon Carlo Carinelli to search for them. Carinelli had the idea to explore a cabinet atop a wardrobe closet, covered with planks and rags, where the manuscripts were found. When Maffei was informed, he rushed over to the library and there found the marvelous ancient manuscripts he had dreamed of locating.

Upon the great wave of enthusiasm that followed, the citizens of Verona decided to build a new library, and both funds and gifts flooded in as the building grew. The noble Bevilacqua family gave a Livy manuscript from the library of King Matthias Corvinus, and the Marquis Maffei bequeathed his archives. In 1797 Napoleonic commissioners, who searched all over Europe for works of art and other precious pieces to claim for France, took away a number of manuscripts (they were restored in 1816). But the worst danger—suppression—was avoided. In the 19th century the library was visited by many great scholars, including Barthold Niebuhr, who in 1816 discovered in a palimpsest the *Institutiones* of Gaius, an introduction to Roman law written in the sixth century.

On 4 January 1945 a bomb destroyed the 18th-century building, but fortunately the manuscripts had been moved to safety. As soon as the war was over, a new center for the library was built. Today the BCV contains more than 1,000 manuscripts. The nucleus of the collection is still the manuscripts of Ursicinus, of Pacificus, and of Rather. This is an exceptional example of continuity that is repeated only in the library of the Cathedral of Lyon in France, which contained only religious texts, not the classical works so important in Verona.

MARINO ZORZI

Further Reading

Giuliari, G.B. Carlo, *La Capitolare biblioteca di Verona* (1888), edited by Gian Paolo Marchi, Verona, Italy: s.n., 1993

Hobson, Anthony, *Great Libraries,* London: Weidenfeld and Nicolson, and New York: Putnam, 1970

Lowe, Elias A., *Codices Lugdunenses Antiquissimi: Le Scriptorium de Lyon,* Lyon, France: Amis de la Bibliothèque de Lyon, 1924 (for the analogies between the two most ancient libraries)

Marchi, Gian Paolo, "Breve discorso storico sulla Biblioteca Capitolare di Verona," in *I manoscritti della Biblioteca Capitolare di Verona: Catalogo descrittivo redatto da don Antonio Spagnolo,* edited by Silvia Marchi, Verona: Mazziana, 1996

Piazzi, Alberto, editor, *Biblioteca Capitolare, Verona,* Florence: Nardini, 1994

Catholic University of Louvain Library

Katholieke Universiteit te Leuven (Flemish)
Address: Centrale Bibliotheek
Mgr. Ladeuzeplein 21
B-3000 Leuven
Belgium
Telephone: 16-32-46-60
Fax: 16-32-46-91
www.bib.kuleuven.ac.be

Founded: 1425; 1968

Holdings (2001): Volumes: 3.4 million. Current serials: 13,000; films and videos: 2,000; incunabula: 708; manuscripts: 1,000; maps: 14,000; music scores: 2,000.

Special Collections: *Areas of Concentration:* Fencing; Flemish student life; Jansenism; Louvain Jesuits; medieval and Aristotelian philosophy; metaphysics and philosophical anthropology; process philosophy; Reformation. *Individual Collections:* Husserl archives (modern phenomenology and psychology); Leuven authors; Justus Lipsius; Spoelberch Leuven brewing collection; university archives.

Université Catholique de Louvain (French)
Address: Bibliothèque Générale et de Sciences Humaines
Université Catholique de Louvain
Collège Érasme Place Cardinal Mercier
31 B-1348 Louvain-la-Neuve
Belgium
Telephone: 10-47-49-01
Fax: 10-47-28-91
www.ucl.ac.be

Founded: 1425; 1968

Holdings (2001): Volumes: 2.5 million. Current serials: 7,000; incunabula: 112; maps 3,000; microforms: 266,000.

Université Catholique de Louvain (French) (continued)
Special Collections: *Faculty Libraries:* Economic sciences; exact sciences; general and human sciences; law; philosophy; psychology.

Origins

The Catholic University in the Belgian city of Louvain (Leuven) was established by Pope Martin V in 1425 at the instigation of Duke Jan IV of Brabant. The earliest university statute, from 1429, included a provision for a university bookshop, and handcopied texts with accompanying commentary were available through local booksellers. Early university students needed very few books. The individual colleges that made up the university relied upon private book collections of professors and the libraries and scriptoria of nearby abbeys. No single location was designated to house collections or to make them available to students for the purpose of study; for more than 200 years after its founding, until 1636, the Catholic University of Louvain had no central library.

Medieval to Modern

The development of printing and university presses provided books, which were much less expensive than manuscripts and had more uniform texts. Insufficient funds for the purchase of books and the absence of experienced librarians led to a decline in collections into the early modern period. By the early 16th century, the Catholic University had become the center of humanist learning, providing a forum for passionate debate on church doctrines. In 1517 the Dutch scholar Desiderius Erasmus founded Louvain's Collegium Trilingue (Trilingual College), unique in Europe at the time, for the study of both ancient languages and the sciences.

In 1519 Louvain became the first university publicly to denounce Martin Luther's challenges to traditional Catholic doctrine. The century's religious upheaval sounded the death knell for many medieval libraries, but under the influence of the Reformation, new libraries were established in Germany and the Low Countries. The ideas of the Counter-Reformation, and the Catholics who were persecuted in Protestant countries, eventually found refuge within the city of Louvain and its university.

During the Renaissance, the renewed interest in classical ideas revived the library as a center of university scholarship. Humanism was assured a place in academic life, creating the need for new and varied texts. University professors were no longer necessarily members of the clergy, and thus monastic libraries were not readily available to them to fulfill their needs for sufficient texts. Still, a central library was not part of university life.

A Central Library

At the beginning of the 17th century, the university was comprised of 43 colleges supporting 3,000 students. As with other universities on the continent, Louvain had been deeply influenced by the Counter-Reformation, favoring more centralized universities as a way to maintain the unity of Catholic teachings. The scientific revolution fomented debate over the cosmological hypotheses of astronomers, mathematicians, and philosophers, drawing denunciation from the church and creating a constant flow of controversial academic publication.

The university's first central library was finally established in 1627, with 800 works on theology and history given by Laurens Beyerlinck, canon of the Cathedral of Antwerp. A bequest of 900 volumes on mathematics and medicine was made by Professor of Medicine Jacobus Romanus. These gifts inspired Rector Cornelius Jansenius to secure ongoing financial support. An existing auditorium above the medieval draper's hall was designated as the library and dedicated in 1636. Jurist, bibliographer, Hebraist, and historian Valerius Andreas was appointed the first university librarian. The drapers' hall was remodeled in 1676 into what is today University Hall, yet it would be more than 50 years before a purpose-built building would house the growing collections. Through a renewed cultural interest in the library as the foundation for a great university, a new library building (in fact, a wing of University Hall) was planned in 1720 at the instigation of the builder and bibliophile Rector Hendrik Jozef Rega and his librarian, Gaspar Magermans, to house a collection of nearly 8,000 volumes. The first stone was laid on 22 April 1723, and construction was completed in 1733.

In 1748 the Belgian government in Brussels began to modernize its political and financial infrastructure. A new royal commissioner for the university, Patrice François Neny, was appointed in 1754. Neny appointed Corneille François Nelis as librarian. Under Nelis' guidance a university press was founded, contributing to the advancement of science and reviving the neglected art of printing in the Low Countries.

Between 1780 and 1797 the region was in utter chaos, even as the library grew to 50,000 volumes. When Austrian Emperor Joseph II tried to impose total reform on the university, theologians and other academics opposing his reforms staged a rebellion. The reforms were suspended, but more than half of the professors in Louvain were expelled as a result of their opposition. The emperor moved the university and its entire library to Brussels, leaving the seminary and faculty of theology behind.

As part of the old guard, the university's system of education fell victim to the French Revolution, in the attempt to create a republican system of education through *déchristianisation*. The Catholic University was abolished in 1797 and its collections dispersed. In 1789 an improvised army drove Austrian troops and leaders out of Brussels, leading to the establishment of the United Belgian States in 1790. The university's library was returned from Brussels. Conflict erupted once again when, in 1792, the French Republic conquered the tiny country, imposing anticlerical measures. The Catholic University was abolished in 1797 during the French occupation and remained closed until 1817 when it reopened as a state university.

After the abolition of the university, the library's 50,000 volumes were requisitioned by Leuven for use as a municipal public library from 1806 to 1817. This served as the library of the state university from that date until 1835, when the state university was again abolished. The city of Leuven again presented the library to the newly founded Roman Catholic university. After the Revolution, which led to Belgian independence in 1830, it was reestablished as a French-language, Roman Catholic university.

The American College was established in 1857 to train young people for work as missionaries in the United States. The university was now dependent for survival upon the fees of its 500 students and offerings from the faithful. Latin was no longer the language of instruction; most classes were taught in French, a few in Flemish. The Catholic University of Louvain prepared the young Catholic elite, preserving the religion of the past while uniting traditional and modern ideas of theology, philosophy, and science. Meanwhile, the library grew from 60,000 to 150,000 volumes in the last half of the 19th century.

World War I, 1914 to 1918

When war began in Europe in August of 1914, many foreign observers, including U.S. citizens, expressed great sympathy for neutral Belgium, suddenly under German occupation. The German invaders met unexpected military opposition and claimed that Belgian snipers had fired on them, in spite of eyewitness accounts to the contrary. German troops resorted to terrorism in order to demoralize the Belgian army and to punish civilian defiance. On the night of 25 August, German soldiers set fire to Louvain, ruining much of the city and completely destroying the university's library.

It is impossible to establish the value of the loss. Estimates include more than 250,000 books, 800 incunabula, and 1,000 manuscripts, some dating to the 12th century. This attack on a nonmilitary target, which had long been a distinguished symbol of culture and learning, epitomized senseless destruction; the events of the last week of August 1914 made martyrs of both the city of Louvain and its university library. The attack on European cultural heritage was carried out in blatant disregard for the recently established rules of warfare; it aroused unprecedented outrage against German *Kultur* and militarism, inspiring comparisons to the destruction of the ancient library at Alexandria.

This single act drove a profound moral wedge between Western Europe and the German cultural and intellectual life that had been so prominent in the years before the war. The Germans continued to insist that they had been victims of a sniper attack and that their reprisal was justified. German propaganda worked to sway world opinion, but the sacking of Louvain, especially the destruction of the library, brought endless protests to German embassies throughout the world. Expressions of solidarity and every form of support flooded into Louvain. Although U.S. President Woodrow Wilson appeared neutral on the issue in public, the U.S. people were extremely moved and sympathetically rose to swift and energetic action. Before the end of the war, many voluntary committees had formed to collect money and books, beginning the arduous task of rebuilding Louvain's library.

An unknown person created the Latin inscription (translated as "Here ends German culture") temporarily affixed to the burned-out shell of the library. British academics and other European intellectuals soon began publishing their expressions of disgust, and U.S. newspapers did so as well. German intellectuals responded in October 1914 with a manifesto supporting the sniper hypothesis. It was signed by 93 prominent scientists, artists, and intellectuals who unequivocally endorsed the Germans' right to reprisal.

Interwar Years

An international committee for the *reconstitution de l'Université de Louvain,* active since 1914, moved to The Hague in 1918 to coordinate relief activities. The 1919 Treaty of Versailles required Germany to replace all books and manuscripts that had been destroyed in the fire of 1914. The Germans carried out this task admirably; scholarly collections in every field were greatly enriched by donations of single volumes, manuscripts, and entire libraries and private collections of German professors. By 1921 Louvain's library contained 450,000 volumes, 210,000 of which had come through Germany's regular monthly shipments of books. Remarkably, these shipments continued faithfully until 1943. A bookplate was placed in each item. Inscribed in Latin, translated as "The seat of wisdom shall not be overthrown," each bookplate also carried an acknowledgment of that volume's status as part of German reparations. Through these reparations and the generosity of many countries, the university was successful in rapidly making functional collections available to scholars.

U.S. architect Whitney Warren designed a new building that became known as the American Library. Constructed between 1922 and 1928 with aid from U.S. President Herbert Hoover, Columbia University (New York City) President Nicholas Murray Butler, and many others, it was intended to be a lasting war memorial. Warren insisted on a Latin inscription ("demolished by German fury, reconstructed with American gifts") that raised furious opposition from the university's administration. After a bitter lawsuit, the library remained without an inscription of any kind.

World War II, 1939 to 1945

The Catholic University's library and its contents were again the center of controversy during this period. By the time France and England went to war with Germany in September 1939, most of the library's collection had been moved to safety in anticipation of Belgium's inevitable involvement. On 10 May 1940 the library staff carried the remaining materials to the basement. On the night of 16 May, in spite of the new building's fireproof cellars, the entire library went up in flames. One million books were lost. The Germans blamed the British, further poisoning already hostile relations. There was speculation that the destruction of the library was an act of revenge; German officers may have mistakenly believed that the anti-German slogan remained on the U.S.-built library's balustrade.

From its founding in 1425 until its destruction in 1914, the library of the Catholic University of Louvain preserved 500 years of cultural history in the Low Countries and the surrounding region; in so doing, it had preserved the roots of a distinguished institution as well. The losses of 1940 were quite different. They included large collections in more recent history, philosophy, and theology, as well as science. Their eclectic nature and the manner in which they were acquired provided a unique picture of the late 19th and early 20th centuries.

The flames of Louvain had symbolic significance for intellectuals in war-torn countries. Learned societies and publishers donated copies of their works, and many individuals provided single volumes, large collections, and entire libraries to restore the decimated library. By 1948, 400,000 books and 7,500 foreign periodicals had been cataloged. American friendship, worldwide support, and the idealism embodied in the bookplate inscription helped to preserve academic life and to keep the university and its library open throughout the war.

Decentralization

From 1900 to 1936, university courses were taught in both Flemish and French. As a result of political turmoil in the late 1960s, a partially French university in an otherwise Dutch city was no longer desirable. A law was passed recognizing separate Flemish-speaking and French-speaking universities in November 1968; the Flemish university remained in Leuven, whereas the French university moved to a new location on the outskirts of Ottignies and became the town of Louvain-la-Neuve.

This split began the process of modernization and necessitated the Herculean task of dividing the burgeoning collections. Rules were established to ensure that donors still living could decide the fate of their donations; if two copies of a work existed, one went to each location. All remaining materials were to be divided equally, with odd shelf marks staying in Leuven and even numbers going to Louvain-la-Nueve. Between

1970 and 1979, each location received approximately 800,000 volumes.

The central library of the Flemish university in Louvain became the central reference facility of that campus; specialized materials in various disciplines were placed in faculty libraries. The scattered libraries of this university were partially consolidated in 1974 with a new building for the faculty libraries. A new library for the faculty of theology also moved into a new building containing open stacks in 1974. One of Europe's finest theological libraries, it houses more than one million volumes, 150,000 of which are pre-1800. The faculty of medicine and its library, located in Brussels, obtained a new facility in 1994, incorporating the LIBIS online system. All branches and many smaller regional libraries use the integrated online system, AMICUS, developed at the National Library of Canada.

Louvain-la-Neuve's first new faculties were created in 1972. Six separate facilities currently house the *faculté* collections in the French-speaking university at Louvain-la-Neuve; a new joint library is planned to unite these under one roof. Gifts, loans, and trades regularly provide new materials to these thriving libraries, which, having survived the unimaginable not once but twice, have embraced technology to maintain the treasures of scholarship and culture.

MARGARET E. PARKS

Further Reading

Boileau, David A., and John A. Dick, editors, *Tradition and Renewal: Philosophical Essays Commemorating the Centennial of Louvain's Institute of Philosophy*, 3 vols., Louvain: Leuven University Press, 1992–93

Coppens, Christian, editor, *Leuven in Books, Books in Leuven: The Oldest University of the Low Countries and Its Library*, Louvain: Universitaire Pers Leuven, 1999

Crozier, Emmet, *American Reporters on the Western Front: 1914–1918*, New York: Oxford University Press, 1959

Derez, Mark, "The Flames of Louvain: The War Experience of an Academic Community," in *Facing Armageddon: The First World War Experienced*, edited by Hugh P. Cecil and Peter H. Liddle, London: Cooper, 1996

Essen, Léon van der, *A Statement about the Destruction of Louvain and Neighborhood*, Chicago: s.n., 1915

"New Plans Please Louvain Officers: Design of Warren and Wetmore Reproduces the Spirit of Belgian Nation," *Columbia Spectator: Louvain Library Supplement* (5 April 1922)

Rudy, Willis, *Total War and Twentieth-Century Higher Learning: Universities of the Western World in the First and Second World Wars*, Rutherford, New Jersey: Fairleigh Dickinson University Press, and London and Cranbury, New Jersey: Associated University Presses, 1991

Tuchman, Barbara Wertheim, *The Guns of August*, New York: Macmillan, 1962; as *August 1914*, London: Constable, 1962

De Universiteit te Leuven: 1425–1985, Louvain: Universitaire Pers Leuven, 1986; new edition, 1988; as *Leuven University: 1425–1985*, Louvain: Leuven University Press, 1990

Ville, Jean Baptiste de, *Back from Belgium: A Secret History of Three Years within the German Lines*, New York: Fly, 1918; 2nd edition, Chicago: De Ville, 1919

Waples, Douglas, "Belgian Scholars and Their Libraries," *The Library Quarterly* 10 (1940)

Center for Research Libraries

Address: Center for Research Libraries
6050 South Kenwood Avenue
Chicago, Illinois 60637
USA
Telephone: 773-955-4545
Fax: 773-955-4339
wwwcrl.uchicago.edu

Founded: 1949

Holdings (1999): Volumes: 5 million. Dissertations: 750,000; microforms: 1.6 million.

Special Collections: *Areas of Concentration:* Area studies programs for Africa, Latin America, Middle East, Slavic and Eastern Europe, and South and Southeast Asia; church missionary studies; college catalogs; foreign doctoral dissertations; foreign documents; foreign official gazettes; international, U.S., and U.S. ethnic newspapers; U.S. state documents; war crimes trials documents.

The Center for Research Libraries (CRL) is an international not-for-profit consortium of colleges, universities, and libraries that makes available scholarly research resources to users worldwide. CRL is governed by its member research institutions in North America and is funded by fees, grants, and contributions.

Midwest Inter-Library Center and the Esterquest Years

CRL was founded in 1949 as the Midwest Inter-Library Center (MILC) and incorporated by a group of librarian and academic representatives from the Universities of Chicago, Illinois, Indiana, Kansas, Minnesota, Purdue, Northwestern, and Iowa State, as well as Michigan State College and the Illinois Institute of Technology. The initial idea of a depository library for ten Midwestern universities became the basis of CRL's international cooperative collection development program supporting a centralized library collection.

Studies, discussions, and plans for a deposit library in the Midwest began in the 1930s. In 1940 13 Midwest university presidents undertook research on the design, costs, collections, and administration of a cooperative deposit library. A survey, financed by the Carnegie Corporation, explored the possibility of establishing a storage and distribution center for rarely-used books from the collections of 13 major Midwestern university libraries—the ten listed above (excluding the Illinois Institute of Technology) plus Kentucky, Michigan, Wisconsin, and Ohio State Universities. The report covered the objectives of economical storage, preservation, and increased availability of infrequently used materials. The 1940 proposal concentrated on establishing a storage facility, with the understanding that the deposit library eventually would have cooperative purchase and preservation programs. Cooperative storage was intended to defer construction of library buildings, thus leaving more financial resources for other library services. In addition, removal of infrequently-used materials from library stacks would eliminate recurring expenses to maintain and reorganize these volumes. Finally, the cooperative storage facility included a new fireproof building that would protect the books from excessive temperature changes, light, and dust.

Based on these assumptions, librarians developed four main goals for the center: coordination of collection policies, cooperative acquisitions, centralized cataloging, and cooperative storage of little-used materials. Of these programs only the deposit of infrequently-used but important research materials from member libraries and the cooperative purchase and centralized storing and cataloging of materials expected to be infrequently used occupied the center in its first 30 years. Grants were obtained from the Rockefeller Foundation and the Carnegie Corporation to fund the construction and equipping of a storage facility and to launch a program of operations. The center opened for business in 1951 under the directorship of Ralph Esterquest, former assistant director of the University of Denver Library. During its first decade, more than 2 million volumes were acquired, primarily as deposits from member libraries. As the cooperative storage program moved forward, it became clear that the deposits were melding together into discrete collections responsive to the needs of scholars. Given the inevitable gaps in the collections, the cooperative acquisitions program began with subscriptions to 40 newspapers on microfilm. Other purchasing programs were instituted to complete specific collections, thus raising their value.

A National Periodicals Center and the Williams Years

Esterquest left MILC in 1958 to become the director of the Harvard Medical School Library. In 1959 he was replaced by

Gordon R. Williams, assistant librarian at the University of California-Los Angeles. During William's tenure, MILC changed from a small Midwestern organization of 20 institutions to an organization of nearly 200 institutions in the United States and Canada. The collections grew from approximately 2 million volumes to more than 3 million. In 1959 the center filled 1,629 interlibrary loan requests, and in 1979 it filled more than 50,000. The name change from Midwest Inter-library to the Center for Research Libraries (effective 1 January 1965) reflected the expanding scope of programs as well as its international membership.

The rapid growth of membership in the 1970s is attributed to a change in program direction begun in 1975. CRL, in response to member concerns about local journal subscription cancellations, initiated a program to add subscriptions for titles being cancelled by members. Not surprisingly, the nominated titles grew explosively, and CRL, unable to sustain the expanding subscription costs through its membership fee structure, turned to the newly established British Library Lending Division as a source of journal article photocopies in lieu of adding more subscriptions. This Journals Access Service provided delivery from the United Kingdom of photocopies of articles from more than 60,000 journals. Often this was faster and cheaper than delivery from neighboring libraries in the United States. By 1980, however, the CRL purchasing budget was overwhelmed by pass-through payments for photocopies; purchasing of collection items diminished, and collection quality and growth suffered.

Director Williams envisioned the implementation of the British Library model in the United States by recasting CRL as a national lending library. When this idea attracted little support, he limited it to making CRL the core of a National Periodicals Center (NPC) partially modeled on the BLLD. The National Commission on Libraries and Information Science and the Council on Library Resources actively lobbied for the NPC concept and produced several versions of an implementation plan. Drafts of the Higher Education Act of 1965 included a bill to establish a National Periodicals Center, and in 1979 legislation to establish an NPC passed the full house as part of Section D under Title II of the extended and amended Higher Education Act of 1965. The NPC was excluded from the final legislation, and no efforts were made to renew the concept after Williams retired in 1980.

Cooperative Collection Development and the Simpson Years

CRL's fourth decade began with the appointment of Director (and later President) Donald B. Simpson, who served until his retirement in 1999. Simpson began his tenure by emphasizing improvements in five areas: (1) facilities, (2) bibliographic control of the collection, (3) access to journal literature, (4) preservation of the collection, and (5) the cooperative collection development program. In 1982 the center opened a new facility at 6050 South Kenwood Avenue. It continued to use the old building on Cottage Grove Avenue until 1992, when an addition to the Kenwood Avenue building was opened and the Cottage Grove building sold. Cataloging policies and procedures were upgraded and an online public access catalog was added along with the online bibliographic tool OCLC to provide worldwide access to CRL holdings 24 hours a day, seven days a week. Simpson studied the Journals Access Service (JAS) and the NPC issues and concluded that neither was in the long-term interests of CRL or the major research libraries of North America. He severed CRL's involvement with the NPC and stopped the JAS once online connections to the BLLD were available through OCLC and the Research Libraries Information Network (RLIN).

On the preservation front, thorough analysis of the brittleness of CRL's paper collections was undertaken, showing that one-third of the collections was endangered. A greatly expanded preservation effort was mounted, resulting in the reformatting of large segments of the most at-risk collections. The last initiative focused on clarifying the CRL program as it relates to cooperative collection development, a means by which participating libraries pool resources to share in both the burden of and the access to collection development and management. Unlike earlier efforts such as the Farmington Plan, in which individual libraries took responsibility for decentralized collection building for shared materials, the CRL program employed a centralized collection open equally to all and not subject to shifting local priorities. A collection development policy was published, enabling member libraries to participate more actively in the collection management process.

Although the results of these objectives were widely enjoyed by members, the financial burdens of the building program created concerns among some members who were happy to receive the benefits of a cooperative but less willing or able to underwrite the costs. Also, the elimination of the JAS (following online connection of OCLC and RLIN to BLLD) was unpopular among smaller member libraries. The membership declined throughout the 1980s and mid-1990s, bottoming out at 124 in 1996.

Working to overcome the decline in membership, Simpson redefined the cooperative collection program into five components, with each taking on and carrying substantial international responsibility for coordinating and maintaining collections at CRL and individual libraries. The five program components are: global newspapers, scholarly journals, international doctoral dissertations, repository collections, and area studies.

CRL continues to operate a global cooperative collection development program that assists academic and research libraries in making otherwise inaccessible and important research materials permanently available to scholars and researchers. The cooperative collection development program fosters the collection and preservation of research materials in print, microform, and electronic formats. CRL's program is supported by a large centralized collection consisting of the aforementioned five major components that member libraries can evaluate in ranking their local collecting decisions. Academic institutions and their libraries can often reduce the costs of acquiring, processing, preserving, and using carefully selected library materials held in shared ownership by CRL. The components are expensive to collect in relation to their use at any one institution but are cost effective when held in common and made available through pooled resources. Thus the program reduces the rising costs of providing local access to resources that have limited ongoing local demand. This direction placed renewed emphasis on the original purpose of the center: to collect and house in one place materials of importance to research and scholarship and materials that are rarely held and/or rarely used. Each of the program components has gained strength as clear initiatives have emerged to provide new directions. The Global Newspapers project is based in the International Coalition of Newspapers (ICON), a CRL effort to bring workable solutions to the growing problem of newspaper preservation around the world. The first activity of ICON is to build a database of newspaper holdings. One of the most significant problems for foreign newspaper collections in the United States is a lack of centralized and comprehensive information on newspaper holdings. The database, based on the 12 largest newspaper collections in the world, will facilitate collection building and will assist in identifying the best candidates for enlarged reformatting activities to ensure the preservation of the materials.

The Center for Research Libraries claims the world's largest collection of foreign doctoral dissertations. More than 750,000 dissertations form the collection and more are added each year. By policy these materials are "shelf cataloged," that is, in order on the shelf by the author's name, without cataloging. The assumption was that member libraries knew of the center's collection and so inquired at the center for a specific dissertation before looking elsewhere. The center now is considering various options to get the collection under bibliographic control and to inform the academic library and research communities of the collection.

The foreign doctoral dissertation collection is one example of the historical role the center has played in cooperative collection development activities. Begun early in the center's history, many libraries deposited their collections of dissertations at the center wanting to ensure the preservation of the materials and believing that one major national collection was all that was required.

Other examples of cooperative collection development leading to major collections of national importance include the foreign official gazette collection, which is being developed by deposit from member libraries, and the collections developed by the six area studies programs of the center.

The area studies projects at CRL are active and productive in acquiring and preserving unusual and notable resources in support of area studies scholarship. The six programs are the Cooperative Africana Microform Project, which promotes the preservation of publications and archives concerning the nations of Sub-Saharan Africa; the Latin American Microform Project, which is completing a major digitizing project of Brazilian presidential papers; the Middle East Microform Project, which seeks to acquire microform copies of unique research materials pertaining to the field of Middle Eastern studies and to preserve deteriorating printed and manuscript materials of scholarly value; the South Asia Microform Project, with holdings in excess of 100,000 and now engaged in building the Digital South Asia Library, which seeks to make digitally available resources of all kinds and in all formats from locations throughout the world; the Southeast Asia Microform Project, which is a collection of materials related to the study of Southeast Asia; and the Slavic and East European Microform Project, which acquires and preserves materials pertaining to the field of Slavic and East European studies.

The Issues, Then and Now

Despite a few successes, all highly localized, librarians still aspire to decentralized cooperative collection development. The idea of sharing materials while building notable collections fulfills a deep-seated need within their communities. The most enduring and large-scale example of successful cooperative collection development—the Center for Research Libraries—employs the centralized model, which exemplifies to many a loss of local control. The tension endures, and while some suggest the shifting to electronic media may obviate the issue, that seems unlikely.

Bibliographic control, at its core an economic issue, has been a sore spot for CRL from its inception. In the early years, before online catalogs reaching every corner of the globe were even a gleam in the eyes of the most farsighted, CRL policy makers made shortsighted decisions to avoid title-by-title cataloging as a way to amass some of those dollar savings mentioned above. The consequence is a huge collection, with some of its parts growing increasingly invisible because there are insufficient resources available to catalog every title.

Last, but most important, is the overarching issue of finances. At the turn of the century, U.S. not-for-profit organizations are generally undercapitalized and lack the basic resources, if not to pay the daily bills, then to ensure their futures. Libraries, themselves underfunded by their parent institutions, are often reluctant to pay the true cost of cooperative programs. Like its member libraries, CRL has been unable to escape this problem.

DONALD B. SIMPSON

Further Reading

FOCUS on the Center for Research Libraries (April 1989)
Knight, Douglas M., and E. Shepley Nourse, *Libraries at Large: Tradition, Innovation, and the National Interest: The Resource Book Based on the Materials of the National Advisory Commission of Libraries,* New York: Bowker, 1969
Reed-Scott, Jutta, *Scholarship, Research Libraries, and Global Publishing,* Washington, D.C.: Association of Research Libraries, 1996
Simpson, Donald B., "The Center for Research Libraries: Meeting the Opportunity to Fulfill the Promise," *Journal of Academic Librarianship* (November 1983)

Simpson, Donald B., "The Expanded Journals Access Service at The Center for Research Libraries: Its Impact on North American Libraries," in *Proceedings of the Conference on the Impact of Serials on Collection Development*, Binghamton, Oklahoma: Haworth: 1981

Simpson, Donald B., "Improving Access to an International Resource for Research through the Installation of an Automated Library System," in *Proceedings, NIT '93: 6th International Conference New Information Technology for Library and Information Professionals, Educational Media Specialists, and Technologists, November 11–13, 1993, Puerto Rico Convention Center, Puerto Rico*, edited by Ching-chih Chen, West Newton, Massachusetts: MicroUse Information, 1993

Charles University Libraries

Address: Univerzita Karlova Knihovny v Praze
Ovocný trh 5
Praha 1, 116 36
Czech Republic
Telephone: 2-2448-11870, ext. 201 (Central Library)
Fax: 2-244-91629
www.cuni.cz/cuni/knihovny

Founded: 1348

Holdings (1999): Volumes: 4 million.
Current serials: 5,000.

Origins

The library resources of Charles University in Prague, the oldest university in Central Europe (founded in 1348), are currently a very loose network of 238 specialized, independently administered, departmental and research institute libraries. These libraries are administered by 16 faculties and centers including the arts and sciences; law; three separate faculties of medicine, pedagogy, and pharmacy; physical education and sport; social sciences; the Center for Economic Research and Graduate Education; and three separate theological faculties—Catholic, Hussite, and Protestant. In addition, the Center for Scientific Information and Libraries coordinates managerial, cataloging, and reference activities for the Faculty of Arts and Philosophy. The Charles University computer center is responsible for managing the union catalog, and a central library, formed in 1991, contains collections obtained from dissolved Communist-era entities. Despite this degree of decentralization and the difficulty of obtaining a comprehensive view of the university and library today, some of the library's antecedents are relatively clear.

The history of Charles University Library, until approximately 1882, is inextricably linked with that of today's Národní knihovna České republiky (National Library of the Czech Republic). Indeed, the Old Carolinum (established 1362) and New Carolinum (established 1638) collections of Charles University provided a substantial part of the core collections of the Veřejná a univerzitní knihovna (Royal Public University Library) established in 1777. Until 1918 the national library was known as the Královská a univerzitní knihovna (Public University Library).

Following the bifurcation of Charles University into German- and Czech-language entities in 1882, various departmental libraries were formed around fledgling Czech-language faculties, such as the Faculty of Arts and Sciences, paralleling the university collections of the Clementinum. The growth of such collections within the university reflected the loosening of Hapsburg policies on the use of indigenous languages in the Czech lands. Following the creation of the Czechoslovak Republic in 1918, the university maintained its separate German and Czech structure until the Nazi occupation of 1939. The Czech-speaking university was shut down in November 1939, whereas the German-speaking university was elevated in status.

Organizational Structure

In the 14th century, Charles University consisted of four core faculties: theology, law, medicine, and arts. In the course of the 19th and 20th centuries, these were further divided into a system of specialized faculties, each with its own specialized library holdings.

Collections

Information on the history and specific holdings of each of these faculties and their departments is fragmentary at best. The closest entity to a central administration appears to be the Center of Scientific Information and Libraries established in the 1960s. However, it is itself a part of the Faculty of Arts and Sciences, and therefore its work is apparently limited to the holdings of the departments that comprise it. The primary function of the center is to provide centralized cataloging for the departments, as well as providing library information for the faculty, students, and staff of the Faculty of Arts and Sciences.

Unfortunately, gaps in the availability of published information make complete statistics on the distribution of resources throughout the university problematic and elusive. The Faculty of Arts and Philosophy alone accounts for 980,000 volumes, scattered throughout 49 departmental libraries, ranging from the library of logic to the library of the Czech Institute of Ancient Near Eastern Studies. The library of the Faculty of Law is the largest collection of its kind in the Czech Republic, with more than 280,000 volumes. The library of the Catholic Theological Faculty numbers around 90,000 volumes; the Protestant Theological Faculty (established 1919), 190,000 volumes; and the three medical faculty libraries number well over 500,000 volumes.

In addition to these faculty collections, the central library of Charles University, established in 1991, contains approximately 380,000 items. It was assembled from various libraries, such as the Institute of Marxism-Leninism, dissolved after the Velvet Revolution of 1989. The central library maintains an online union catalog that by 2001 covered almost 500,000 titles. In general, after shrugging off decades of Soviet restrictions on collection development areas and accessibility, the university and its libraries have undergone an exciting transformation.

EDWARD KASINEC AND ROBERT H. DAVIS JR.

Further Reading

Cejpek, Jiří, et al., *Dějiny knihoven a knihovnictví v českých zemích a vybrané kapitoly z obecných dějin* (A History of the Library and Books in the Czech Lands and Selected Chapters from General History), Prague: Karolinum, 1996

Dějiny Univerzity Karlovy, 1348–1990 (A History of Charles University, 1348–1990), 4 vols., Prague: Karolinum, 1995

Univerzita Karlova dnes (The Charles University Today), Prague: Karolinum, 1995

Chester Beatty Library

Address: Dublin Castle
Dublin 2
Ireland
Telephone: 1-407-0750
Fax: 1-407-0760
www.cbl.ie

Founded: 1954

Holdings (2000): Volumes: 8,000. Current serials: 15; incunabula: 51; manuscripts: 9,000.

Special Collections: *Areas of Concentration:* Arabic, Persian, and Turkish manuscripts; Biblical studies; fine prints; illuminated manuscripts, printed books, and fine bindings from the 15th through 20th centuries; Oriental art. *Individual Collections:* Early Christian biblical and Manichaean papyri; Islamic collection; Japanese collection.

Origins

The Chester Beatty Library was created by renowned collector, mining engineer, and businessman Sir Alfred Chester Beatty. Born in New York of colonial stock with roots in England, Scotland, and Ireland, he graduated from Columbia University in 1898 in engineering and began his mining career in the Denver, Colorado, area. By 1911 he had become a millionaire and moved to London, where he set himself up as a mining consultant. His collecting passion began when, as a young boy, he started a mineral and stamp collection. In adult life, this broadened into a wide-ranging collection of extraordinary pieces from Chinese snuff bottles, Egyptian and Greek papyri, and Islamic manuscripts to Japanese prints and rare European printings and bindings.

In 1950 Beatty moved from London to Dublin, where he set up his home and installed his collection in a custom-built facility in Shrewsbury Road in the south of the city. In 1954 he opened his library two afternoons a week, and on his death in 1968 he bequeathed his collection to the Irish nation "for the use and enjoyment of the public." These actions earned him recognition during his lifetime, when he became the first person to be made an honorary citizen of Ireland, and on his death, when he was given a state funeral. Although Beatty left his library to the Irish nation, it was not endowed and its care became the responsibility of the government and the trustees. Beatty's philosophy had always been "If you give a man a horse, you don't expect to give him the oats to feed it with as well."

Collections

The collections consist of some 25,000 items and mirror the interests, high standards, eclecticism, and internationalism of Chester Beatty. The collections are wide-ranging and include Babylonian cuneiform tablets; Egyptian, Greek, and Manichaean papyri; Coptic manuscripts and bindings; Hebrew, Ethiopic, Armenian, and Slavonic manuscripts; and Arabic, Persian, and Turkish manuscripts, including some superb copies of the Qur'an. The collections also include Chinese albums, scrolls, jade books, textiles, woodblock prints, and decorative objects; Japanese painted scrolls, woodblock prints, netsuke, and other objets d'art; Western medieval and Renaissance illuminated manuscripts and printed books and fine bindings from the 15th through the 20th centuries; and fine prints from Albrecht Dürer to Henri Matisse.

Beatty took a keen personal interest in his acquisitions while employing scholars and experts such Arthur J. Arberry (expert in the field of Islamic studies) and Eric George Millar (expert in the field of illuminated manuscripts) to seek out and assess potential items. In London he employed a number of librarians to organize and manage his growing collection, including Francis M. Kelly, Joan Kingsford, and James Wilkinson, who were employees of the library before it came to Dublin. It was to Wilkinson that Beatty gave his dictum "Quality, quality, always the quality."

Chief among the library's treasures are the biblical papyri with the earliest known fragments of the New Testament dating from the end of the second century A.D. Another outstanding example from the collection of Qur'ans is that written and illustrated by Ibn-al-Bawwab in A.D. 1001. Despite its relatively small size, the collection attracts international scholars and frequent requests for loan items from important exhibitions around the world.

Crisis and Opportunity

In accordance with Chester Beatty's will, the library is governed by a board of trustees that has absolute discretion in relation to "the proper management, upkeep, and control" of the institution. The library is, and always has been, heavily dependent on the state for its funding and maintenance. During the 1980s, tensions emerged between the board of trustees and the government as a result of mounting annual deficits and a perceived lack of accountability. Under the terms of the will, the trustees were initially appointed by Chester Beatty and given the right to appoint future trustees as the need arose. The president of Ireland and the *Taoiseach* (prime minister) each appointed one member to the board and the director of the National Library of Ireland was appointed in an *ex officio* capacity. In 1989 an independent review of the management practices at the library noted that one of the trustees had been in that position for 21 years and recommended a fixed term appointment of five years for all such nominees. It was not until 1997 that a *cy pres* order was made by the High Court of Ireland, giving the trustees permission to sell the property at Shrewsbury Road and giving the minister for arts, heritage, Gaeltacht, and the Islands the power to appoint three trustees to the board.

In 1991 the international art world and the world of scholarship were rocked by the revelation that the Chester Beatty Library's most senior curator, David James, had been arrested for theft involving more than £1.5 million worth of manuscripts, bindings, and miniatures from the collection. James's position of trust was such that only he was qualified to determine exactly how much was missing from the collections that had been in his care since 1969 and whose catalogs he had altered in order to cover his tracks. He was dismissed from the library and sentenced to five years imprisonment. In the aftermath of the affair, concerns were raised publicly about the cataloging of the collections in the library. In 1992 the government seconded Michael Ryan, keeper of antiquities at the National Museum of Ireland, to the post of director. Following his appointment, strenuous efforts were made to bring catalogs up to standard and to begin a program of computerization and digitization.

The library moved to the Clock Tower Building at Dublin Castle early in the year 2000. It now has two permanent galleries, a short-term exhibition gallery, roof garden, conservation workshop, photographic studio, lecture room, restaurant, shop, dedicated reading rooms, a modern office, and, it is hoped, a bright new future free of the ghosts of its Shrewsbury Road past.

PATRICIA DONLON

Further Reading

Hayes, R.J., "The Chester Beatty Library," *The Book Collector* 7 (Autumn 1958)

Henchy, Patrick, *The Chester Beatty Library, Dublin, and Gallery of Oriental Art,* Dublin: Chester Beatty Library, 1982

Horton, Charles, "The Formation of the Library of A. Chester Beatty: 1910–1932," master's thesis, University of London, 1999

Kennedy, Brian P., *Alfred Chester Beatty and Ireland, 1950–1968: A Study in Cultural Politics,* Dublin: Glendale Press, 1988

Chetham's Library

Address: Chetham's Library
Long Millgate
Manchester M3 1SB
UK
Telephone: 161-834-7961
Fax: 161-839-5797
www.chethams.org.uk

Founded: 1653

Holdings (2000): Volumes: 100,000. Current serial subscriptions: 100; manuscripts: 1,600 linear feet, including 40 medieval manuscripts; pre-1851 books: 60,000.

Special Collections: *Areas of Concentration:* Antiquarian; astrology; genealogy; history and topography of northwest England; social and religious history. *Individual Collections:* John Byrom; James Orchard Halliwell-Phillipps; Manchester collection; Robert Southey; Horace Walpole. *Papers:* Ernest Charles Jones.

The library was founded in 1653 as a result of the will of Humphrey Chetham, a prosperous Manchester textile merchant, banker, and landowner. In his final will of December 1651, Chetham established an educational charity in three parts with a single common purpose: the cure of poverty by the cure of ignorance. To this end his will contained instructions for the founding of a free public library "for the use of schollars and others well affected," instructing the librarian to "require nothing of any man coming into the library," and endowing it with the sum of £1,000 for the purchase of books. Five chained libraries of English puritan theology books were set up in local churches and chapels for the benefit of their congregations. At the same time, Chetham founded a hospital where 40 poor boys from the Manchester region could receive accommodation and education.

In order to house the school and library, Chetham's executors purchased the 15th-century College House, which had formerly provided accommodation for the clergy of the Collegiate Church (now Cathedral), and, following the repair and adaptation of the building, the library was opened to readers in 1656. In 1661 a royal charter of Charles II incorporated the main library and hospital into a single charity, entrusted to a governing body of 24 feoffees, or governors, in accordance with the founder's wishes. In the same year the feoffees invested the residue of Chetham's estate in land to provide income for the purchase of books. By so doing they enabled the library to grow steadily and to adapt itself to changing needs.

The feoffees began by seeking to cover the whole range of knowledge and to build a major collection that would rival the college libraries of Oxford and Cambridge. From the outset the collection was predominantly theological in character. It was not, however, partisan in outlook. Books reflecting both sides of the religious controversies of the age were acquired, as the library fostered an impartial, detached approach to scholarship. By the end of the 17th century, the theology collection amounted to a formidable body of Latinized scholarship that attempted to incorporate a total history of religion dating from the earliest times to the present day. Secular books were not neglected, and the early scientific acquisitions, in particular, were impressive by the standards of any contemporary library. In 1684 the library attempted its first inventory of the collection. In the 30 years or so since the death of the founder, the library had acquired about 3,000 volumes. Theology books accounted for two out of every three books in the library (68 percent), with arts and science at 25 percent, law at 2.5 percent, and medicine at 4.5 percent.

In the 18th century the library's holdings of secular subjects increased at the expense of theology. Thus by 1791, when the library published its first catalog, theology accounted for only some 30 percent of the collection. The printed catalog, which was published initially in two volumes, in Latin, with the books arranged by subject and then in order of size, indicates that the collection comprised some 7,000 titles in perhaps 15,000 volumes. In all areas, the library had significant holdings: Medieval manuscripts included the *Flores historiarum*, partly in the autograph of Matthew Paris; a copy of Gower's *Confessio Amantis*; a 13th-century collection of tracts by Boethius and St. Augustine; and a 14th-century *De situ universorum*. In the sciences, new ideas were covered as well as the classical foundations. Journals included the transactions of the Royal Society and of the academies of St. Petersburg, Paris, and Berlin. Medical theses and tracts from all over Europe stood alongside the works of Nicolo Fabrizi and Gabriele Falloppio, Adrianus Spigelius, Girolamo Mercuriale, and Paolo Zacchia. Natural history included Basilius Besler's *Hortus Eystettensis* (1613) and many of the great color-plate illustrated books, including John Martyn's *Historia Plantarum Rariorum* (1728), Marcus Elieser

Bloch's *Ichthyologie* (1785–97), and J.B. Audebert's *Oiseaux dorés* (1802).

By the middle of the 19th century, it was clear that the library could no longer meet the needs of the rapidly expanding population of Manchester, and following the foundation of the rate (tax) supported public library in 1851, Chetham's was deprived of its unique position as the town's main provider of literary matter. The creation of Owens College, later the university library, and, at the end of the century, the Rylands Library, exacerbated the library's loss of identity. Paradoxically, this crisis coincided with a significant increase in the size of the holdings and the acquisition of many of its greatest collections. In 1850 James Orchard Halliwell donated a collection of 3,100 early proclamations, ballads, and poems, among them many unique items. In 1870 the library was given the collection of the 18th-century Manchester poet and shorthand writer John Byrom. His library of some 3,500 works shows a particular interest in Italian humanism. It includes the library's earliest incunable, the Schweinheim and Pannartz *Lactantius* of 1468, and its earliest English printed book, Aristotle's *Ethica* (1479), printed by Theodoric Rood at Oxford. These were eclipsed by the collection's manuscripts, notably the *Aulus Gellius* written at Florence in 1472 and bound for Matthias Corvinus (King of Hungary) and the collection of the Florentine humanist Coluccio Salutati's works that belonged to Humfrey, Duke of Gloucester, the first patron of Italian humanism in England and founder of the university library of Oxford.

The 20th century saw a decline in the library's fortunes. The original endowment failed to provide enough income and was sold, and in the years after World War II, the feoffees concentrated on the school as a higher priority than the library. In 1969 it was reestablished as a specialist music school and grew to become one of the most important in the country. By comparison, the library suffered. Between 1972 and 1981, important topographical and natural history books were sold to make up its deficit. In the absence of an adequate endowment, the library faced an uncertain future and discussions were held with both the city and the university to consider the future of the library and its collections. In the 1990s the library began to plan for a major financial appeal to secure its independent status as the country's oldest surviving public library and to bring about a transformation in the services it could offer to the academic research community both locally and overseas. The appeal, which was supported by the government's newly established Heritage Lottery Fund, raised more than £2.3 million, sufficient to enable the library to face the future with a degree of confidence it has not had since the early 1800s.

MICHAEL POWELL

Further Reading

Barker, Nicolas, "Chetham's Library: An Appeal," *The Book Collector* 44 (1995)

Bibliothecae Chethamensis, 6 vols., Manchester: Harrop, 1791–1883

Kelly, Thomas, *Early Public Libraries: A History of Public Libraries in Great Britain before 1850*, London: Library Association, 1966

Raines, Francis Robert, and Charles William Sutton, *Life of Humphrey Chetham, Founder of the Chetham Hospital and Library, Manchester*, 2 vols., Manchester: Chetham Society, 1903; reprint, 1974

Smith, H.S.A., "A Manchester Science Library: Chetham's Library in 1658," *Library History* 8 (1989)

Snape, Anne C., "Seventeenth-Century Book Purchasing in Chetham's Library, Manchester," *Bulletin of the John Rylands University Library of Manchester* 67 (1985)

Williams, Moelwyn I., editor, "Chetham's Library," in *A Directory of Rare Book and Special Collections in the United Kingdom and the Republic of Ireland*, London: Library Association, 1985; 2nd edition, edited by Barry Cambray Bloomfield, 1997

Chicago Public Library

Address:	Chicago Public Library
400 S. State Street
Chicago, Illinois 60605
USA
Telephone: 312-747-4090
TTY: 312-747-4066 (Telephone for the hearing impaired)
Fax: 312-747-4968
www.chicagopubliclibrary.org
Founded:	1873
Holdings, Central Library (2000):	Volumes: 5.8 million. Archives and manuscripts: 2,000 linear feet; audio recordings: 200,000; current serials: 14,000; films and videos: 113,000; microforms: 4.8 million; music scores: 133,000.
Special Collections:	*Areas of Concentration:* African American studies; art; blues performers; book arts; Chicago authors; Chicago neighborhoods; gospel artists; history of Chicago theater. *Individual Collections:* Chicago authors and publishing; Chicago neighborhood history; Chicago Public Library archives; Chicago theater; Chicago World's Fairs 1893 and 1933; Vivian G. Harsh research collection of Afro-American history and literature; U.S. Civil War; Mayor Harold Washington collection. *Papers:* Leonidias Berry; Horace R. Cayton; Cyrus Colter; Richard Durham; Langston Hughes; Vernon Jarrett; Marjorie S. Joyner; E. Frederic Morrow; Theodore Charles Stone; Era Bell Thompson.

Origins

By 1871 Chicago had grown from a small prairie settlement on the shore of Lake Michigan to a bustling metropolitan center in less than 40 years. Geographically situated as the hub of transportation and industry between the east and the west, Chicago had a growing population of more than 300,000, making it the fifth largest city in the nation. This rapid expansion, however, was cut short on 8 October 1871, when the Great Chicago Fire swept through the city. The downtown area (and beyond) was almost completely destroyed.

There had been some library activity in Chicago before the fire, the most notable being the Old Chicago Library. Formerly known as the Young Men's Association, this library, founded in 1841, was funded by members' contributions, not by city taxes. Although it was successful throughout most of its duration, dedication to the Old Chicago Library was waning by the time of the fire. All 30,000 volumes, property, and financial documents relating to the library were consumed by the fire, at a time when the enterprise was uninsured.

As news of the fire reached Great Britain, it was believed that the city had lost its public library in the blaze. Thomas Hughes, author of *Tom Brown's School Days* (1857) and a prominent member of Parliament, sent a circular to British writers, publishers, booksellers, private persons, and heads of colleges and learned societies to donate books "as a mark of sympathy now, and a token of that sentiment of kinship which . . . must ever exist between the different branches of the English race." The response was staggering. Individuals who responded to the call and donated books included Queen Victoria, Benjamin Disraeli, Alfred Lord Tennyson, Robert Browning, John Ruskin, and John Stuart Mill. More than 8,000 volumes were collected and sent to Chicago. In addition to the British donation, 1,200 volumes of German literature were assembled and presented by Chicagoans of German descent under the direction of Bernhardt Kihlholz and Julius Dyhrenforth. There were also numerous local donations of books and cash.

This presented the city with a problem. In 1871 neither the state of Illinois nor the city of Chicago had authority to organize and fund a public library. The incoming book donations prompted leading citizens of Chicago to petition Mayor Joseph Medill to call a public meeting to establish a free public library for Chicago. This petition was signed by Marshall Field, Cyrus McCormick, Thomas Hoyne, and other leading citizens. Bills authorizing cities to establish tax-supported libraries in Illinois had been presented in the state legislature before but were unsuccessful. At the time of the Chicago petition, another bill of the same general purport had been introduced by Samuel Caldwell, member of the Illinois House of Representatives from Peoria, with the help of E.S. Wilcox, librarian of the Peoria Public Library. It was this bill, amended to meet Chicago's needs, that became the Illinois Library Act passed on 7 March 1872. Within the month a city ordinance establishing a public library in Chicago was passed by the city council. On 8 April 1872 the first board of directors of the Chicago Public Library (CPL) was appointed, with Thomas Hoyne as its first president.

The Early Mission of the Chicago Public Library

The founders and early leaders of the Chicago Public Library shared the ideals of the national public library movement. They believed that the library was an educational institution that should provide an opportunity for mental improvement to the citizens of Chicago. In the spirit of democracy, the library was all-encompassing, providing books and related reading material for popular education, civic awareness, and scholarly research. In 1896 meetings were held between the head librarians and boards of the three libraries in Chicago serving the public—the Chicago Public Library, the Newberry Library, and the John Crerar Library.

To prevent needless duplication and overlapping collection policies, an agreement was reached that is still in effect today. The Newberry Library resolved to place special emphasis on literature, history, philosophy, and subjects allied to the humanities. The John Crerar Library (now a part of the University of Chicago Library) assumed the natural, physical, and social sciences as its special field. The chief task of CPL was to collect instructional and entertaining books, especially those desired by the public for home use.

The Library's First Home

The library's first home was an abandoned circular water tank measuring 58 feet in diameter. Considered fireproof, the structure was fitted with book shelves and an external stairway connecting to the reading room. At this time, circulating copies of books were not available; all materials had to be consulted within the water tank. Appointed in October 1873, the first librarian was William Frederick Poole, one of the foremost leaders in the library world; on 1 May 1874, under Poole's direction, the library began to circulate books. The first book to be checked out was *Tom Brown's School Days*, and the borrower was Thomas Hoyne, president of the board.

Early Neighborhood Services

Early librarians concentrated on building a significant central library containing a large collection of books for loan purposes, but they also intended to extend service outside the central library directly into the community. The first purpose-built branch library was the Blackstone Library in the Hyde Park neighborhood. Although construction of Blackstone was funded by a private donation, this encouraged the public to call for the city to construct more full-service branch libraries in their own neighborhoods. Throughout the early decades of the 20th century while the central library continued to grow and develop its collections, there was a concurrent drive to provide, extend, and improve library services for Chicago's diverse neighborhoods through delivery stations, deposit stations, branch reading rooms, and ultimately through branch libraries.

A Permanent Home, 1897–1991

The library moved from location to location during its first 24 years of service, including an 11-year stay on the fourth floor of city hall. On 11 October 1897 the central library opened its doors to the public, and the 24-year dream of a permanent home for the Chicago Public Library was realized. The building, located on the grounds of Dearborn Park at Michigan Avenue between Randolph and Washington Streets, cost approximately $2 million to design and build. Designed by Charles Allerton Coolidge, an associate of the firm Shepley, Rutan and Coolidge, the building is a combination of Italian Renaissance, Greek, and neo-Greco architecture that was popular in Chicago following the 1893 World's Columbian Exposition. Much of the interior of the library, including magnificent domes and hanging lamps, was predominantly the work of the Tiffany Glass and Decorating Company of New York. Mindful of the lessons of the Chicago Fire, the building was designed to be virtually incombustible.

Changing Needs of Chicago's Central Library

In 1970, after more than 70 years of continuous operation with only minimal maintenance repairs, the central library building was showing the signs of age and heavy use. Space was inadequate for the large book collection. Some recommended that the building be demolished and the library moved elsewhere. This was averted when the library was placed on the National Register of Historic Places in 1972. In 1974 the board of directors authorized a massive renovation of the aging central library building, a process that took three years and $11 million to complete. In 1976 the library was designated a Chicago landmark.

The renovation of the old central library was only partially successful. There was still a need for more space to hold CPL's growing collections. Opinions varied between adding on to the existing building and constructing an entirely new structure for the central library. After years of debate and discussion among the members of the library board and the Chicago city council, the city determined to develop an entirely new building for the central library.

A New Central Library: The Harold Washington Library Center

On 29 July 1987 the city council authorized a design/build competition and approved a bond issue to finance the project. Under the rules of the competition, architects and builders teamed up to design the new library within the budget set at $144 million. The design/build approach ensured that the city's expense would be limited to the cost of the bond issue. On 20 June 1988 the citizen jury announced to the Library Policy Review Committee that of the five finalists' entries, the vote was nine to two in favor of the proposal made by the SEBUS Group, a consortium of architects, designers, engineers, and contractors.

Named in honor of the late Harold Washington, Chicago's first African American mayor (1983–87), the Harold Washington Library Center (HWLC) opened to the public on 7 October 1991. HWLC houses its collections on more than 70 miles of shelving, and at 756,640 square feet, it is one of the largest public library buildings in the world. In addition to its main collections, the central library maintains a teacher resource center and a talking book center for use by those with a visual or physical disability. It collects materials in 90 foreign languages and houses a variety of special collections. HWLC offers a wide assortment of free exhibitions and public programs, including dance and musical performances, films, author talks, children's programs, and computer workshops.

The Neighborhood Branch Library System: Building for the Future

Today, under the leadership of Mayor Richard M. Daley, the city and library administrations have focused their efforts on significant capital improvements for libraries located in Chicago's neighborhoods. Mayor Daley and the library have overseen the opening of 36 new or renovated Chicago public library buildings citywide, replacing leased storefront libraries and park district reading rooms. In 1996 the Chicago city council approved a request by Mayor Daley and the library board for a new, three-year, $50 million capital improvement plan. Under this plan, the current library commissioner, Mary A. Dempsey, is directing the construction, expansion, and/or renovation of 20 additional library branches in underserved neighborhoods. In 1999 the Chicago city council approved an $800 million bond for more libraries, as well as police and fire stations. These improvements constitute one of the largest library building programs in the world.

The Library's Five-Year Strategic Plan

In addition to the capital improvement plan, CPL embarked upon a five-year strategic plan in 1995. This plan, now successfully concluded, helped to rebuild the library by improving its infrastructure through five major goals: staff development and training; technology; funding; capital planning; and materials acquisition. A new strategic plan began in 2000.

In 1995 the library upgraded its automated public access catalog and circulation system and added online research databases to all public access catalog terminals in all libraries. In the same year, the library established its innovative Internet home page, offering patrons access to the library's catalog, databases, and informational links and serving as a gateway to the Internet. Free computer and Internet access is available at every CPL location.

Special Programming

The Chicago Public Library has created programs to ensure ongoing community support of its neighborhood branch system and its technological improvements. Outreach programs include volunteer tutoring, parenting classes, homework help, computer training, adult book discussion groups in three languages, NatureConnections, the summer reading program, and law at the library. The award-winning Blue Skies for Library Kids project, funded by the Chicago Community Trust through the Chicago Public Library Foundation, created innovative programs for children and families in their communities. The library also works with many of Chicago's museums and cultural institutions in the Check Us Out, Words and Music, Art Access, and Imagination on Loan programs to provide library patrons with free and equal access to Chicago's cultural venues. Other partnerships have included the AT&T Cyber Navigator project to bring additional technological support to neighborhood libraries, and the development of book collections for teenagers through the Andrew Carnegie Foundation of New York.

These significant improvements, along with the city's dedication to neighborhood services, have created a library system that responds to library patrons' rapidly changing needs. Currently, the Chicago Public Library includes the central library, two regional libraries, and 75 neighborhood branch libraries. From its first home in an abandoned water tank to the modern concept of the neighborhood library location and now through the library's aggressive capital improvement plan, the library's services have grown immensely. Although the methods and resources used to serve library patrons may have changed, the goal of the Chicago Public Library remains to support the freedom of all people to read, learn, and discover.

MORAG WALSH

Further Reading

Chicago Public Library, 1873–1923: Proceedings at the Celebration of the Fiftieth Anniversary of the Opening of the Library, January First, Fourth, and Sixth, 1923, Chicago: The Board of Directors [Chicago Public Library], 1923

The Chicago Public Library—Celebrating 125 Years, 1873–1998, Chicago: Chicago Public Library, 1997

Chicago Public Library, Strategic Design Team, 5 Year Strategic Plan, 1995, Chicago: Chicago Public Library Archives, Special Collections & Preservation Division, 1995

Hoyne, Thomas, compiler, *Historical Sketch of the Origin and Foundation of the Chicago Public Library*, Chicago: Beach Barnard, 1877

Memorials of the Old Chicago Library, Formerly Young Men's Association, and the Advent of the New, Chicago: Scully, 1878

Spencer, Gwladys, *The Chicago Public Library: Origins and Backgrounds*, Chicago: The University of Chicago Press, 1943

Chinese University of Hong Kong Library System

Address: Daxue tushuguan xitong, Xianggang Zhongwen Daxue
The Chinese University of Hong Kong
Shatin, New Territories
China
Telephone: 2609-7305
Fax: 2603-6952
www.lib.cuhk.edu.hk

Founded: 1963

Holdings (2001): Volumes: 1.5 million. Audio-visual materials: 25,000; Chinese rare books: 800 titles in 13,000 volumes; current serials: 10,000; microforms: 300,000; oracle bones: 60.

Special Collections: *Areas of Concentration:* Art and drama; business; humanities; medicine; music; religious studies; science; social science. *Individual Collections:* Chinese rare books; William Faulkner; Hong Kong collection; modern Chinese drama collection; *Tripitaka Koreana.*

The University Library System

The university has its origin in three colleges—New Asia College (founded in 1949), Chung Chi College (founded in 1951), and the United College of Hong Kong (founded in 1956). In 1963 the three colleges were amalgamated to form the Chinese University of Hong Kong; Shaw College was added in 1998. The University Library System was founded in 1963 after the merger, and the university library was established in April 1965, initially located in the On Lee Building in Kowloon, where it remained until August 1969. The current building was opened on 15 December 1972 on the Shatin campus and serves as the central library, with a comprehensive collection of books and materials for advanced studies and research. In addition to the university library, the system consists of several other branch libraries: Chung Chi College Elisabeth Luce Moore Library, New Asia College Ch'ien Mu Library, United College Wu Chung Library, Li Ping Medical Library, American Studies Resource Library, Architecture Library, and the Electronic Resources Centre, all located on the Kowloon campus except the medical library, which is in Shatin.

The administration of the university library system is centralized under the university librarian. The founding librarian, Alfred Kaiming Chiu, was appointed in 1966 and contributed to the planning of the university library building. Chi Wang became librarian in 1971, and Lai-bing Kan succeeded him, serving from 1972 to 1983. From 1984 to 1991, Chi Wang, David S. Yen, and Painan R. Wu were in charge of the library system. Frederick Chang followed as acting librarian from 1991 to 1993, and Michael Lee was the university librarian from 1993 to 2000. Colin Storey is the current university librarian, a post he has filled since November 2000.

Collection Highlights

Resources at the university library cover a wide range of subjects and formats. The library houses extensive collections in science, social science, and business administration. Books in Western languages are shelved separately from those in East Asian languages. The university is a depository for publications issued by departments and committees of the Hong Kong government as well as a wide variety of monthly, biannual, and annual reports; statistical analyses; directories; ordinances; and pamphlets in many subject areas. Newspaper material on contemporary China and the genealogical records of the families of the New Territories of Hong Kong are available on microfilm.

The rare book collection consists of more than 13,000 volumes of Chinese classical books in the traditional format of silk-stitched fascicles engraved in China, Japan, and Korea from the Yuan Dynasty (A.D. 1260–1368) to the end of the reign of Qianlong (A.D. 1795) of the Qing Dynasty. During Chiu's tenure as the university librarian, he made a significant effort to gather rare books from private collectors, and five major acquisitions were made including the *Tripitaka Koreana* (a Korean version of the *Tripitaka* totaling 1,341 volumes) believed to be a reprint made from the original wood blocks dated A.D. 1237–48. The library also has a collection of all master's theses and doctoral dissertations by the graduate students of the university since 1967. In the reference collection, works in Western and East Asian languages are intershelved for ready use. Reference librarians maintain a company file that contains more than 30,000 newspaper clippings on more than 638 companies in Hong Kong. The primary sources of the clippings are *Ming Pao, Hsin Pao, Business Post of the South China Morning,* and *Hong Kong Economic Times.* There is also a vertical file of more than 28,000 pamphlets and newspaper clippings of *Ming Pao* and *Business Post of the South China Morning* on more than 270 current topics.

Automation and the Electronic Library

The U.S. Library of Congress classification system has been used since 1969 for Western-language materials and from 1971 for East Asian language materials. The university library used DOBIS (a library automation product offered by Extended Library Access Solutions, or ELIAS) as its integrated library system from 1989 to 1995 but replaced it with INNOPAC (an online computer system of Innovative Interfaces, Inc.) in 1996. The university library now contributes records directly to the online bibliographic service OCLC.

Most electronic resources are networked and can be accessed on the World Wide Web or the library's CD-ROM network (CDLAN) via the campus network. More than 6,000 journals can be accessed via the libraries' website (www.lib.cuhk.edu.hk), as can most of the available full-text collections. Major full-text collections include: EBSCOhost Academic, JSTOR (Journal Storage: an online full-text database of scholarly journals), Lexis-Nexis Academic Universe, OCLC Electronic Collection Online, Ovid Biomedical and Health Care Collections, ProQuest Direct ABI/Inform Global, and ProQuest.

The university library has developed several databases to meet the needs of users, all accessible on the library's homepage and beyond. Five major projects have been completed, including the HKInChiP (Index to Chinese Periodicals of Hong Kong), the Chinese University of Hong Kong (CUHK) Examination Papers Database, the Hong Kong NewsBot, the Database on Chu Bamboo Manuscripts of Guodian, and the Digitization Project.

HKInChiP is an index to Chinese and bilingual journals published in Hong Kong since 1990. It indexes more than 100 titles, of which approximately 50 are the major sources. There were more than 100,000 records in June 1999. The index covers business, social sciences, and humanities topics with emphasis on Hong Kong, Taiwan, China, and Macao.

The CUHK Examination Papers Database contains images of the examination papers of centralized undergraduate course examinations. The papers are based on the hard copies of Course Examinations Question Papers and Examination Papers from 1995 onwards. The database can be accessed in the university library and branch libraries only. All examination papers are copyrighted by the Chinese University of Hong Kong, and users are only permitted to make one copy of each paper for their private study.

The Hong Kong NewsBot is a full-text newspaper retrieval system that searches Hong Kong newspapers available on the web. Users may access the full articles retrieved through the respective newspaper Uniform Resource Locators (URLs) on the World Wide Web until the articles are removed from the Web by the publishers. These newspapers include *Apple Daily, Hong Kong Standard, Ming Pao, Sing Tao Daily, Ta Kung Pao,* and *Wen Wei Po*. Images of selected newspaper clippings of *Hong Kong Standard, Sing Tao Daily, Ta Kung Pao,* and *Wen Wei Po* are also provided and are retained in the system.

The Database on Chu Bamboo Manuscripts of Guodian is jointly developed by the library and the author of *Study on the Chu Bamboo Manuscripts of Guodian*. The publication is on the study of *Guodian Chu mu zhu jian* published in 1998 that describes the bamboo strip fascicles newly excavated in Hubei in 1993. Four collections of manuscripts and works have been digitized and are available through the libraries' website.

Branch Libraries

The branch libraries at the colleges have their own unique features. The Elisabeth Luce Moore Chung Chi College Library, opened in 1951, specializes in music, religious studies, education, sport science, Western literature and languages, Japanese literature and language, philology, and linguistics. The music and religion collections are considered quite significant in Southeast Asia. The instructional materials collection is a special collection of teaching materials for all secondary and primary school subjects in Hong Kong.

The Ch'ien Mu New Asia College Library was founded in 1949. The current building is modeled after the library of Berea College, Kentucky, and houses collections in Chinese literature, fine arts, and philosophy. The stitch-bound books in the closed stack of the library form the largest collection of its kind within the library system.

The Wu Chung United College Library (founded in 1956) has a Hong Kong collection as well as a notable modern Chinese drama collection. In the same building the American Studies Resource Library (founded in 1993) houses the nucleus collection, an interdisciplinary resource donated by the U.S. Information Service library in Hong Kong, and the William Faulkner collection, donated by Professor James Meriwether. A collection of silk-stitched fascicles and a special section on modern Chinese plays published from 1921 to 1945 are kept in closed stacks. Of the 56 pieces of rare oracle bones donated by C.Y. Tang, 45 inscribed pieces are on display in the library, making it the largest collection of its kind in Hong Kong. The description and images of these oracle bones can also be viewed on the libraries' website (www.lib.cuhk.edu.hk/uclib/bones/bones.htm).

The architecture library was established in 1994 to support the core curriculum of the architecture program. Its collection, international in scope with a strong Chinese and regional emphasis, covers subjects in the building industry and environmental sciences. The goal of the architecture library is to achieve coverage in all basic architecture areas of design, technology, construction, architectural practice, history, and theory, as well as in related fields such as housing, interior decoration, environmental design, landscape architecture, computer-aided design, and city planning. One of the major focuses is to develop in-depth coverage of Chinese and Asian architectural and planning topics.

The medical collection is housed in two locations: the preclinical materials in the university library and clinical materials in the Li Ping Medical Library. The Li Ping Medical Library was established in 1980 to serve the information needs of the faculty of medicine. The library subscribes to more than 1,150 biomedical journals and stocks the latest major biomedical books and audiovisual materials. The preclinical, nursing, and pharmacy collection is housed in the university library, whereas medical sciences materials focusing on the curriculum needs of the clinical years form the collection of the medical library, located in the teaching block at the Prince of Wales Hospital. A special collection called the "Medical History of Hong Kong, China, and the Asia Pacific Region" is being developed.

Service and Affiliation

In addition to on-site service, the library also provides library instruction on the Web via its website. The "Ask a Reference Librarian" service through e-mail is currently available to university faculty and students only. Interlibrary loan requests can now be placed online as well, and a 24-hour inquiry service is available by phone in Cantonese, Mandarin, and English. Reference librarians offer fee-based databases and online searching to research students and faculty of the university by appointment only, with charges for this service made on a cost recovery basis.

The library is a member of the Hong Kong Academic and Research Network (HARNET) and the university librarian serves on the Joint University Libraries Advisory Committee (LULAC). Many collaborative projects are under the aegis of the University Grants Committee (UGC). The University Library System is devoted to integrated library automation and implementation of the newest technology. Since the debut and establishment of the Internet in Hong Kong, the library has successfully utilized the Web in many aspects of its operations in order to improve services.

Yu-Lan Chou

Further Reading

Chinese University of Hong Kong, *The First Six Years, 1963–1969: The Vice-Chancellor's Report,* Hong Kong: Chinese University of Hong Kong, 1969

Chinese University of Hong Kong, *University Library System Information Network,* Hong Kong: Chinese University of Hong Kong, 1995

Chinese University of Hong Kong, *Library Handbook: 1999–2000,* Hong Kong: Chinese University of Hong Kong, 1999

"Chinese University of Hong Kong," in *World Guide to Libraries,* 14th edition, edited by Willemina van der Meer, vol. 1, Munich: Saur, 1999

"Chinese University of Hong Kong, University Library System," in *Libraries and Information Centres in Hong Kong,* compiled and edited by Julia L.Y. Chen, Angela S.W. Yan, and Kan Lai-bing, Hong Kong: Hong Kong University Press, 1996

Rydings, H.A., "Libraries in Hong Kong," in *Encyclopedia of Library and Information Science,* edited by Allen Kent et al., vol. 10, New York: Dekker, 1973

Swank, R.C., and Eugene Wu, Central Library of the Chinese University of Hong Kong, a Report, Hong Kong: s.n., 1964

City and University Library of Bern

Address: Stadt- und Universitätsbibliothek Bern
Münstergasse 61
Postfach
3000 Bern 7
Switzerland
Telephone: 31-320-32-11
Fax: 31-320-32-99
www.stub.unibe.ch

Founded: 1528/1535

Holdings (2000): Volumes: 2.2 million. Current serials: 5,400; films and videos: 1,400; incunabula: 460; maps: 42,000; microforms: 57,000; sound recordings: 12,000.

Special Collections: *Areas of Concentration:* Academic literature in all subject areas; Canton of Bern (Bernensia); Eastern Europe; pre-1850 Switzerland (Helvetica). *Individual Collections:* Hedwig Anneler; Kenower Weimar Bash; Jacques Bongars; Wilhelm Fabricius Hildanus; Philipp Emanuel von Fellenberg; Thomas Hollis; Erwin Holzer; Leonhard Hospinian; Gottlieb Ludwig Lauterburg; Margrit Loosli-Usteri; Johann Friedrich von Ryhiner map collection; Hermann Rorschach; Samuel Singer; Fritz Strich; Edouard Tièche; Anna Tumarkin; Paul Richard's Richard Wagner collection; Werner Zesiger.

Origins

A precise date for the foundation of today's municipal and university library, the Stadt- und Universitätsbibliothek Bern (StUB), does not exist. However, its beginnings are linked to the Reformation of 1528, when Bern founded a university for the education of its young theological academics. In this context it is generally assumed that the decision for the foundation of the university library was made between 1528 and 1535. The library of the Chorherrenstift St. Vinzenz on the Münsterplatz (Cathedral Square), first mentioned in archival sources in 1513, and the stock of secularized monasteries formed the core collection of the newly founded university library, situated on the premises of the dissolved Franciscan monastery.

As there was no printer in Bern before the Reformation, the library's 460 incunabula came into its possession from former monastic collections or as donations. In the 16th century it received several donations from renowned scholars, including the 200 volumes that formed the literary remains of Leonhard Hospinian, a humanist from Basel, as well as the donations of Niklaus Pfister (also known as Arthopoeus) and Benedictus Aretius.

The Bongars Library

In 1632 the library received from Jakob Graviseth, as a token of his appreciation for his naturalization, a unique gift: the private library of Jacques Bongars (French diplomat, humanist, and Huguenot). This collection consisted of more than 3,000 printed volumes with more than 6,000 titles and approximately 500 manuscripts. As a result of this donation the stocks of the Bern library were doubled. By 1634 a catalog of the gift was available. Bongars was not a bibliophile collector but a researcher interested in the content of the texts. Therefore his books are not, on the whole, magnificently bound, but have economical contemporary bindings. In 1693 the Bongarsiana as a special collection was dissolved for organizational reasons and integrated into the library's normal shelving sequence. The collection was reassembled in the 1960s as a special stock with a shelf mark of its own. At the same time the volumes were restored, and in 1994 access was facilitated by a newly published catalog.

Extension and Professionalization in the 17th and 18th Centuries

The Bongars donation resulted in a shortage of space that was only resolved at the end of the 17th century. In 1680 the rebuilding of the old university began, lasting several years and resulting in, among other things, a splendid reading room. During the rebuilding, a large number of books were exposed to dust and humidity, so that damage and loss could not be avoided. The new library rooms were the pride of the *Burger* community. A famous painting by Johannes Dünz from 1696 depicts the library commission in the newly constructed reading room.

The rebuilding addressed not only architectural but also functional issues. The old library and the Bongarsiana were united in a new shelving order; in addition, a new catalog was introduced. In order to encourage rich Bern citizens to present the library with books, a donations register was displayed in 1693. The new bylaws of 1698 document the fact that, with the reorganization, the university library had developed into a bourgeois municipal and university library.

In 1726 the first full-time, salaried chief librarian was appointed, an important step toward the library's professionalization. The position was not very lucrative, and therefore it was used repeatedly in the 18th century as a stepping stone to higher positions in public office. Although the Bern government approved funds for book purchases at irregular intervals, the library (as mirrored in the foundation of an independent students' library in 1730 to 1741) could not satisfy all requirements. In 1759 the Ökonomische Gesellschaft (Economic Society) also set up a library of its own, and 1791 saw the beginning of the Bibliothek der Lesegesellschaft (Reading Society Library). Both of these libraries form part of the current Stadt- und Universitätsbibliothek. Moreover, in 1795–96 two special libraries for doctors and preachers were created.

An extension of the premises was planned as early as 1715, but it was only in the years between 1787 and 1794 that a building of the neighboring Münstergasse (Cathedral Street), which had served as a market arcade and granary, could be transformed into a library. During this transformation two magnificent halls were created that have been used as the library's reading rooms (Schultheissensaal, Hallersaal) since that time.

Municipal and University Library Side by Side

The invasion of Switzerland by French troops in 1798 also caused turmoil for the library, but at least it was not carried off to Paris, unlike other city treasures. After being closed for two years, the city's library reopened, and ownership transferred to the municipality of Bern. Since then the municipality, canton (state), and *Burgergemeinde* (*Burger* community) have been financing the library in varying proportions. In 1834 the canton of Bern founded a modern university. With very moderate means the municipal library had to meet the demands of a broader range of university subjects. Donations continued to be of the utmost importance in increasing its holdings. In 1867 the library received the sheet map collection (16,000 items) of the geographer Johann Friedrich von Ryhiner, which today is completely cataloged and searchable online.

In the meantime the university had begun a library policy of its own. From 1859 special libraries (which were not open to the public) were founded by some faculties. In 1887 the university library separated from the municipal library, but owing to financial difficulties and the rapid growth of the university library, they were reunited in 1905. In 1903 the university was transferred from the site of the former Franciscan monastery to a new building north of the train station. Although there was not enough money for a new library building, the most urgent space problems were solved between 1860 and 1863 and between 1904 and 1907 through the addition of two extension wings to the building at the Münstergasse.

The Library in the 20th Century

The spatial separation between library and university contributed to the foundation and extension of many faculty libraries. For this reason the library's management endeavored for decades to establish a new building in the university's vicinity. For various reasons this project could not be realized, and the only solution was to condense and expand the building at the Münstergasse.

Rising student numbers and accelerating book production after 1945 aggravated the spatial difficulties of the library. The alterations and the addition of subterranean stacks between 1967 and 1974, including an additional reading room, created sufficient space again, but it proved inadequate much faster than had been anticipated. The space for books and workstations was completely exhausted by 1995. In 1997 space problems were defused momentarily by the off-site storage of 250,000 rarely used volumes. After 2010 plans will include the creation of subterranean storage stacks in the immediate vicinity of the present location to provide additional space for books and offices.

The increase of the library's holdings is mirrored in staff growth. In 1911 the library employed ten people (a head librarian, two librarians, an auxiliary librarian, two male and female assistants, a caretaker, and a caretaker's assistant). At the beginning of the year 2000 approximately 130 staff members (an equivalent of 80 full-time positions) worked at the library and its branches.

The StUB Foundation of 1951

Like most Swiss university libraries, the StUB has several functions. At one and the same time it is the library of the university, the municipality, and the canton of Bern. The library must provide publications for a wide and heterogeneous public. Students, pupils, and adults each represent one third of its users. Since 1798 three public bodies have been responsible for its finances: the canton of Bern (as representative of the university as a cantonal institution), the *Einwohnergemeinde* (resident's community), and the *Burgergemeinde*. From 1852 to 1951 the *Burgergemeinde* financed most of the costs involved, but after World War II it was no longer prepared to do so. New solutions had to be considered. In 1951 the Stadt- und Universitätsbibliothek Bern foundation was inaugurated and funded by the three foundation bodies according to a new financing arrangement. Since that time the canton of Bern bears the largest part of the costs (80 percent in the year 2000, with the other two parties providing 10 percent each). At the same time, the

Burgerbibliothek (Burger Library) was founded, taking over the manuscripts and graphics section of the former municipal library. Another important element of this reorganization was the foundation in 1948 of the Volksbücherei Bern (popular library), now referred to as Kornhausbibliotheken, which as a general public library, along with its 15 branches, caters to a nonacademic readership.

The Burgerbibliothek Bern

This special library emerged from the Stadt- und Hochschulbibliothek in 1951 and has been an independent institution financed by the *Burgergemeinde* since that time. Its foundation was the manuscript collection consisting of valuable medieval codices, manuscripts, and the bequests of Bern celebrities such as Jeremias Gotthelf and Albrecht von Haller (correspondence). In 1976 the Burgerbibliothek also took over the graphics collection from the StUB. It is one of Switzerland's most important collections of graphic art and photography. In addition the Burgerbibliothek is the archive of Bern's guilds and of the Burgergemeinde. The library is housed in the same building as the StUB. Apart from its archival functions it mainly collects Bern publications (Bernensia) and makes them available to a discerning public in its reference library, which is situated in the baroque Hallersaal.

New Commitments since 1970

At the beginning of the 1970s and after the extension of its building at the Münstergasse, the library turned its attention to numerous new tasks. The alphabetical union catalog of the university's various institutes, which had already been started in 1958, was considerably enlarged. In 1973 the subject librarian system was introduced and a reference collection for the humanities, the social sciences, law, and economics was opened, stocking 25,000 volumes. The textbook collection forms the basis of the open access library extended in 1999, eventually to be increased to at least 100,000 volumes.

Since 1974 an underground stack functioning as a climatized security vault has been provided for valuable old stock. As another measure to preserve its cultural heritage, in 1975–76 the StUB founded a paper and binding restoration studio, thereby playing a pioneer role in Swiss preservation activities (together with other Bern archives and libraries).

The development of the library network at the University of Bern after 1945 was not well coordinated. The number of institute libraries increased without allowing the StUB to influence their acquisitions policies. In 1972 there were, apart from the central library of the University of Bern, 92 additional libraries related to the university. The funds for these decentralized stocks, to which the public had access only with great difficulty, considerably exceeded the funding available to the StUB. In some cases it was possible to create special subject libraries that slowed the trend to fragmentation. Apart from the faculty libraries for theology, veterinary medicine, and the Juristische Bibliothek (law library, in existence since 1926), these subject collections included the Universitätsspitalbibliothek (university hospital library, 1966), the Fachbereichsbibliothek Bühlplatz (science library, 1981) for pre-clinical medicine as well as biosciences and geosciences, the Bibliothek Erziehungswissenschaften (education library, 1988), and the Bibliothek Sozialwissenschaften (social sciences library, 1993).

A further element of a central library service was the creation of the Basisbibliothek Unitobler, opened in 1993 as an open access branch of the StUB providing mainly study literature. This library constitutes the core of a new university center for the humanities and the social sciences in the former Tobler chocolate factory. Furthermore, in 1997 the StUB took over the Schweizerische Osteuropabibliothek (Swiss Library of Eastern Europe, founded in 1948) as a new branch library.

Recent Developments

In 1990, as the last university library in Switzerland to do so, the StUB began its electronic cataloging and participation in the data network of the Universitätsbibliothek Basel. During the 1990s most libraries of the university institutes took the same step. The library's alphabetical catalog was filmed and published in a microfiche edition. The entries from 1965 onward were integrated in two stages into the online catalog Basle-Bern. Since 1993 the circulation system has also been computer based.

In 1994 the StUB was a founding member of the Kommission der Deutschschweizer Hochschulbibliotheken (Commission of Swiss German University Libraries). This commission adopted the newest Automated Library Expandable Program (ALEPH500) library system in 1998 as a data network covering the university libraries of Basel, Bern, Lucerne, St. Gall, and Zürich. In 1999 the migration of the relevant data for the Informationsverbund Deutschschweiz (Data Network of German-Speaking Switzerland) took place, a major step toward a wider range of services.

The StUB continued on its way toward the digital library with the introduction of its website on the Internet in 1995. At the same time it began to build up electronic information channels for its users, including a virtual library featuring its collections for all subject areas and online databases.

Since 1990 the StUB has been in severe financial difficulty, losing one-third of its purchasing power in the area of acquisitions, mainly owing to increasing journal prices. In face of the stagnating allocation of funds, it has proved difficult to continue investing in the area of electronic data processing or to tackle new challenges in the digital library field. Through the use of the ALEPH500 acquisitions module, the coordination of book purchases among the university libraries should be increased, thereby counteracting the loss of substance in the book supply.

CHRISTIAN LÜTHI
TRANSLATED BY ARMANDO E. JANETTA

Further Reading

Bibliotheca Bernensis 1974: Festgabe zur Einweihung des umgebauten und erweiterten Gebäudes der Stadt- und Universitätsbibliothek und der Burgerbibliothek Bern am 29. und 30. August 1974, Bern: Burgergemeinde, 1974

Bloesch, Hans, editor, *Die Stadt- und Hochschulbibliothek Bern: Zur Erinnerung an ihr 400jähriges Bestehen und an die Schenkung der Bongarsiana im Jahr 1632*, Bern: Gustav Grunau, 1932

Eschler, Margaret, *Bongarsiana: The Publications in the Municipal and University Library Bern, Commentary*, Leiden: Inter Documentation, 1994

Michel, Hans A., "Das wissenschaftliche Bibliothekswesen Berns: Vom Mittelalter bis zur Gegenwart," *Berner Zeitschrift für Geschichte und Heimatkunde* 47 (1985)

"Schatzkammern, 200 Jahre Bücher, Handschriften und Sammlungen im Gebäude an der Münstergasse 61–63," *Berner Zeitschrift für Geschichte und Heimatkunde* 56 (1994)

Wo menschliches Wissen lagert . . . : 200 Jahre Stadt- und Universitätsbibliothek, Bern: Pressestelle der Universität Bern, 1994

City and University Library of Frankfurt am Main

Address: Stadt- und Universitätsbibliothek Frankfurt am Main
Bockenheimer Landstrasse 134–138
60325 Frankfurt am Main
Germany
Telephone: 69-212-39-205
Fax: 69-212-39-380
www.stub.uni-frankfurt.de

Founded: 1511

Holdings (2000): Volumes: 4.0 million. Autographs: 36,000; current serials: 13,000; incunabula: 2,702; literary collections: 200; manuscripts: 10,000, including 3,000 medieval manuscripts; microforms: 580,000.

Special Collections: *Areas of Concentration:* Africa; Americana; Asia; 1848 Revolution; Frankfurtiana; German language and literature; Hebraica; history; Judaica; jurisprudence and political science; mathematics; philosophy. *Individual Collections:* Colonial and library archives; Albrecht Dürer; Frankfurt collection; Frankfurt printing; German printed works, 1800–17; incunabula; manuscripts; music and theater collection; philosophical papers; Arthur Schopenhauer. *Papers:* Ludwig Börne; Karl Gutzkow; Max Horkheimer; Engelbert Humperdinck; Leo Löwenthal; Herbert Marcuse; Alexander Mitscherlich; Eduard Rüppell; Arthur Schopenhauer; Friedrich Stoltze.

Origins

Along with the libraries of monasteries and seminaries and the first private book collections, in the last third of the 15th century a small reference library was developed near the Frankfurt Rathaus, consisting primarily of juristic works suited to an increasingly complex city administration. Around 1484 the Frankfurt patron Ludwig of Marburg bequeathed his books to the City Council as a core collection for a future library. Although this initial bequest did not come into the possession of the city until 1527, the city fathers had by 1511 already established the basic requisites for the City Hall Library by the purchase and erection of a building to be used as a library. When the 147 manuscripts and imprints left by Ludwig of Marburg were incorporated, this was already a valuable collection of sources concerning the law, together with related standard commentaries, editions of ancient historians and medieval chronicles, and titles in the areas of grammar, stylistics, and rhetoric. With respect to its practical usefulness for the tasks of the city councilmen, it was already outdated.

In the imperial city of Frankfurt most monasteries and seminars remained untouched by the Reformation, including the monastery of the mendicant Franciscans, which ultimately closed down and was abandoned because of business difficulties in 1529. The Franciscans had a significant book tradition in which, after 1511, the first printed works in Frankfurt came from the proprietary print shop of the monastery. The City Council was able to transform the Franciscans' book collection into a second city library called the Mendicant Library (Bibliothek des ehemaligen Barfüsserklosters), located in the space of the former monastery, and put the library under the financial supervision of the General Eleemosynary Fund, an establishment responsible for the administration of charitable foundations on behalf of needy people. Members of the convent of Protestant-Lutheran preachers took over professional supervision of the library as a subsidiary duty. Annual disbursements were documented for book purchases and bindings, including purchases made at the book fairs. The first catalog of the library was undertaken in 1562 and continued thereafter.

Valuable individual gifts increased in the second half of the 16th century, along with book purchases and regular additions of signed copies from authors. By the end of the century the Mendicant Library had grown to such an extent that increased space and new construction were necessary (1592). Despite that, however, the majority of the books remained together. A third source of access emerged in 1603, when press censorship became in effect a rule of mandatory deposit, which, with the increasing importance of Frankfurt as the center of the book trade, brought regular access for both city libraries.

The 1624 legacy of Frankfurt physician Johann Hartmann Beyer, with its 2,600 titles, exceeded all previous acquisitions. In this library the holdings of Beyer's father, theologian Hartmann Beyer, were combined with those of the physician. Its extent required a new catalog, which was completed in 1641. The library had now grown to more than 4,600 titles, with widespread recognition of its scholarly status.

The United City Library, 1668 to 1884

A resolution of the council in 1668 united both city libraries, a part-time professional leader with secure salary was named, and a regular budget for the acquisition of new publications was stipulated. The mandatory deposit of copies continued to form an important part of the increase in holdings.

Between 1689 and 1690 the council purchased the library of the late Frankfurt patron Johann Maximilian zum Jungen, numbering 7,000 titles, for 3,300 florins. In addition to 900 Italian and 600 French works, the collection of 116 anthologies and 2,768 contemporary pamphlets assembled by Johann Maximilian is of special value. The united library of the mendicant monastery had thereby more than doubled. Johann Martin Waldschmidt became the first full-time librarian in 1691. An official letter regulated all procedures of the library, including stipulations regarding eligible users, control of keys, hours of operation, borrowing privileges and cards, space arrangement, labeling and cataloging of books, binding operations, and the introduction of an access book and a list of desiderata, as well as the formulation of acquisition principles.

During Waldschmidt's tenure, books were newly arranged into ten subject groups, following the practice of the Court Library in Vienna. The previously linked volumes were separated and incorporated into the general arrangement. The first description of the library goes back to the year 1698, in a printed travel report by Wilhelm Ernst Tentzel. In 1706 Achilles Augustus von Lersner, in his *Frankfurt Chronicle* (*Nachgeholte, vermehrte, und continuirte Chronica der weitberühmten freyen Reichs-Wahl- und Handels-Stadt Franckfurt*, 1706–34), devoted a comprehensive section to the library. The most important additions of the era of Waldschmidt were the Oriental collection and the correspondence of scholar Hiob Ludolf. Waldschmidt served until 1706. He was followed by Konrad Weber (1706–17).

The third librarian, Johann Jakob Lucius (1717–31), created the first printed catalog of the City Library, which documents 32,000 titles based on cataloging through 1728. Twice during his tenure he compiled official statistics concerning the entire contents. A third general cataloging was undertaken by the fifth director, Christoph Friedrich Kneusel (who served 1745–68), including titles acquired through 1768. The sixth librarian, Johann Simon Franc von Lichtenstein (1768–94), assembled a catalog of dissertations, another of sermons, and one of incunabula. In the course of the 18th century, the library regularly obtained complete book collections and objets d'art as gifts, inheritances, or through purchase. From the great private library of Zacharias Konrad von Uffenbach, only those Frankfurtiana that were donated were brought into the collection; the council could not decide in favor of the purchase of that entire library. The Barckhausen family legacies (1749 and 1750) provided endowments for the acquisition of new books and an extra subsidy for the librarian. Also from the Barckhausen family came a rich coin collection, later donated to the historical museum of the city.

In 1786 the Franciscan church (Paulskirche) and a dilapidated portion of the monastery were torn down to provide space for the construction of today's (St.) Paul's Church Plaza. The library was dispersed into temporary quarters and suffered under this provision during the following decades. Construction of a new library building was continually postponed. Finally it was undertaken through the legacy, specific in both its objectives and its deadlines, of Johann Karl Brönner. In 1812 he bequeathed to the city 25,000 florins for the construction of a new library, on condition that building would begin no later than ten years after his death. Between the years of 1820 and 1825 the showpiece building at the Schöne Aussicht (Beautiful Vista) was completed. In the decisive years from 1817 to 1830 the council had left the position of librarian vacant, so the library was erected without a librarian's cooperation.

During this hiatus in leadership the book holdings of the Frankfurt monasteries were taken over, following the secularization of church properties in 1803, when their books became the property of the city. The incorporation of more than 20,000 volumes took place in 1822, increasing the size of the City Library by two-thirds. The collection included most of the present incunabula holdings as well as more than 400 medieval manuscripts. As a result, the space provided by the new library building proved to be too small when the move began, so that further interior construction was needed to complete the final move of the books four years later.

The council reacted to the qualitative and quantitative changes in 1827 with a new organizational plan; with two librarians, two assistantships, and a porter as personnel; and with a 2,300-florin annual budget increase, increased again to 3,300 florins in 1859. Johann Friedrich Böhmer (1830–63) earned his appointment to the directorship by his previous service during the years of the provisional arrangement. Once again the task consisted of developing an arrangement and inventory system appropriate to the increased holdings. Böhmer relied for this work on the system of group classifications developed by Martin Schrettinger for the Munich Court Library and thus created a solution that essentially remained in use until the introduction of *numerus currens* in 1930. The building did not yet include a reading room for year-round service. The Hebraica and Judaica collections grew with the legacies of Isaak Markus Jost and Salomon Fuld, and additional gifts brought self-contained collections on gymnastics, statistics, and political science. In 1867 the former library of the German Federal Assembly was given to the City Library, providing something of a counterweight to budget stagnation and the continuous relative decrease in new acquisitions.

Growth and Development, 1884 to 1914

Frankfurt had received better than average benefits from the general economic improvement of Germany following the establishment of the Empire in 1871. For the City Library this positive development was effective after Friedrich Clemens Ebrards took on the directorship in 1884. He succeeded in convincing municipal authorities of necessary measures to make the library a usable modern scholarly institution. A significant increase in the budget and in library personnel, the outfitting of a reading room, and new organization of the collection areas were parts of his program. Taking into consideration the scholarly potential of the other Frankfurt libraries, the City Library concentrated on building up its holdings in history, philosophy, jurisprudence, and political science, and on further developing the collections in its special divisions of Frankfurtiana, Judaica, and Hebraica. It also began new collections in mathematics and Americana. During Ebrards's tenure (1884–1924), the purchase of self-contained collections continued to play an important role. The library obtained Cornill d'Orville's Dürer collection in 1900, newspaper publisher Leopold Sonnemann's pamphlet collection of Gustav Freytag in 1901, the Holzhausen family library in 1923, the Oskar Kling library in 1926, and the aeronautics collection of Louis Liebmann in 1929. The purchase of the Ernst Kelchner library in 1895 was the foundation for the superb collection of bibliophilia and library science, and the 1899 purchase of the Guido Weiss library increased the value of the political science disciplines.

When the Frankfurt Academy of Social and Business Sciences was founded in 1901, the City Library took over the supervision of its educational sites in an agreement with other libraries of the city. The most important partners were the Baron Carl von Rothschild Public Library, an establishment that the Frankfurt Rothschild family had inaugurated in 1887 in line with the Anglo-Saxon model of the public library. In 1902 a contract was made among the City Library, the Rothschild Library, and the City Magistracy, providing for a mutual division of collection development and exchange of materials. Since then the Rothschild Library has received an annual supplement from the City of Frankfurt's budget for the development of its collections in Romance, German, and English studies.

Between 1912 and 1914 the Business Academy of Frankfurt University was completed, and the proven system of a decentralized, external custody of literature was extended to the university. For the first time, plans were made to unify the library resources spatially and to place it in the vicinity of the university. With the outbreak of World War I, however, these plans came to nothing.

World War I and the Postwar Years, 1914 to 1927

The development of the Frankfurt libraries, first hampered by the outbreak of war, was put in still worse straits by the extreme postwar inflation. In hardly any other German city did private foundations play such a major role in the building and maintaining of libraries as they did in Frankfurt. All capital resources, some of which had withstood monetary fluctuations over a period of centuries, lost their entire value in 1923. For the City Library that meant, above all, the loss of the Barckhausen legacy; for the Rothschild Library, its original endowment disappeared. Despite attempts by the London and Paris branches of the Rothschild family to save it, lengthy negotiations between the city and the foundation's board of directors finally resulted in the Rothschild Library's transfer to the City of Frankfurt. Upon Richard Oehler's inauguration as the 13th director of the City Library, the post of Director of the City and University Library of the City of Frankfurt am Main was created for him in 1927 (Oehler would serve until 1945). This centralized position, initially undertaken for organizational reasons, came to include the following five libraries: the City Library, Senckenberg Library, Rothschild Library, Library for Art and Technology, and Library of the City Hospital. Once again plans for the erection of a grand-scale Frankfurt Central Library were openly discussed.

World Economic Crisis, National Socialism, and World War II, 1927 to 1945

All plans for expansion and centralization had to be postponed during the time of the world economic crisis. However, the lack of money actually increased the value of the joint catalog developed by the former director of the Rothschild Library, Christian Wilhelm Berghoeffer, which contributed to the fact that Frankfurt could become a center of borrowing activities, at least in southwest Germany. When the National Socialists grabbed power in Germany in January 1933, their racist and ideological hatred found a target for its attacks in Frankfurt, with its liberal tradition and strong Jewish imprint. One-third of all university professors were forced to leave the university (and later the country), and the same fate befell numerous staff members of the library. The number of students, like the use of the library, fell sharply, and its resources decreased significantly. The scholarly libraries were required to accept books removed from public bookstores and private collections on ideological or racist grounds, and to retain them separately, with no public access.

When the air war reached German cities, there was not enough time for the evacuation of library holdings. The warehousing of the Rothschild Library (renamed the Library for Modern Languages and Music in 1934) was almost completed before bombing began, but more than half of the City Library's holdings were burned in the air attack of December 1943. The Library for Art and Technology was almost totally lost.

Reconstruction Since 1945

With the collapse of the German Empire and Allied occupation of Germany, all members of the National Socialist German Workers Party were removed from library service. Hanns Wilhelm Eppelsheimer (1946–58) became the new leader of the combined City and University Library holdings of the Rothschild Library, the Medical Main Library, and the City Library. The Rothschild Palace, together with disused bunker structures, served as accommodations. The most important tasks were, above all, returning the stored materials to Frankfurt, cataloging them, and readying them for use. From these beginnings Eppelsheimer developed, with the National Bibliographic Registry, the core of the later German Library (Deutsche Bibliothek), in reaction to the division of Germany during the Cold War.

On the basis of the available subject strengths of German libraries in the plan of specialized areas supported by the German Research Association, the Stadt- und Universitätsbibliothek (StUB, or City and University Library) was assigned the areas of Africa South of the Sahara; Oceania; general and comparative linguistics; literature and folklore; Germanistics; German language and literature; scholarship on Judaism; theater, film, and media; general and comparative anthropology; and geography. (Geography was relinquished in 1974; anthropology and radio and television were removed in the 1990s.)

A new version of legal deposit rights and a stronger concentration of West German publishing in Frankfurt after the war brought in a significant regular stream of literature, with its peak reached in the 1960s. The move in 1964 into a newly constructed library building near the university constituted an essential turning point. For the first time all available holdings were located in one building, with easy public access to reading room resources, periodicals, and reference book collections. With the move of the Senckenberg Library's rich holdings in the natural sciences into the same building, the transformation into a modern research institution was complete.

Corresponding to its increased importance for the university and the region were regional tasks that the library gradually assumed. Among these was the development of a Hessian central catalog, as well as the maintenance of a library school. With the introduction of electronic data management, the library assumed leadership for the region in the trial and introduction of borrowing systems; cataloging; development of the Hessian Library and Information System; the introduction and expansion of the Project for Integrated Catalog Automation (PICA); and the introduction of online services. Of importance beyond the region was its leading the collaboration on the *Handbuch der historischen Buchbestände (1985–90)* (Handbook of Historical Book Holdings [1985–1990]) and participation in the *Archiv Deutscher Drucke* (Archive of German Printed Works), for which in 1990 StUB was assigned the period from 1800 to 1970.

Rapidly growing collections and increased use brought with them their own bottlenecks, calling into question some parts of the advances won. Books in storage and longer waiting periods were the consequence. In addition came jurisdictional problems resulting from the transfer in 1967 of the University of Frankfurt from city responsibility to the State of Hessen, but leaving StUB under city administration. The coordination of budgets was problematic because the university and the library received funds from separate sources: the university was funded by the State of Hessen Ministry of Science and Art, whereas the library was funded by the City of Frankfurt (and also a grant from the State of Hessen). This situation is now being resolved by a contract between the City of Frankfurt and the State of Hessen that will, through 2005, oversee the step-by-step transfer of the library to the jurisdiction of the State of Hessen.

JOCHEN STOLLBERG
TRANSLATED BY JAMES H. STAM

Further Reading

Fischer, Franz, "Kontinuität und Neubeginn: Die Entwicklung der Stadt- und Universitätsbibliothek Frankfurt am Main, 1945–1965," in *Die Entwicklung des Bibliothekswesens in Deutschland, 1945–1965*, edited by Peter Vodosek and Joachim-Felix Leonhard, Wiesbaden, Germany: Harrassowitz Verlag, 1993

Kiessling, Edith, *Die Stadt- und Universitätsbibliothek Frankfurt am Main: Blüte, Untergang und Wiederaufbau einer Bibliothek*, Frankfurt: s.n., 1969

Kraft, Alexander, et al., "Stadt- und Universitätsbibliothek, Frankfurt am Main," in *Handbuch der historischen Buchbestände in Deutschland*, vol. 5, *Hessen, A–L*, edited by Bernhard Fabian, Hildesheim, Germany, and New York: Olms, 1992

Lehmann, Klaus-Dieter, "Von der Stiftungsbibliothek zur Forschungsbibliothek: Bibliotheksplatz Frankfurt," in *Literatur in Frankfurt: Ein Lexikon zum Lesen*, edited by Peter Hahn, Frankfurt: Athenäum, 1987

Lehmann, Klaus-Dieter, editor, *Bibliotheca Publica Francofurtensis: Fünfhundert Jahre Stadt- und Universitätsbibliothek Frankfurt am Main*, 2 vols., Frankfurt: Stadt- und Universitätsbibliothek, 1984–86

Ohly, Kurt, and Vera Sack, *Inkunabelkatalog der Stadt- und Universitätsbibliothek und anderer öffentlicher Sammlungen in Frankfurt am Main*, Frankfurt: Klostermann, 1967

Powitz, Gerhardt, *Die datierten Handschriften der Stadt- und Universitätsbibliothek Frankfurt am Main*, Stuttgart, Germany: Hiersemann, 1984

Powitz, Gerhardt, compiler, *Mittelalterliche Handschriftenfragmente der Stadt- und Universitätsbibliothek Frankfurt am Main*, Frankfurt: Klostermann, 1994

Sammlung Elsass und Lothringen: Neuerwerbungen, 1986–1990, Frankfurt: Stadt- und Universitätsbibliothek, 1990

Stollberg, Jochen, editor, *Verzeichnis der Bibliothek der Deutschen Bundesversammlung (1816–1866) im Bestand der Stadt- und Universitätsbibliothek Frankfurt am Main*, Frankfurt: Stadt- und Universitätsbibliothek, 1985

City University of Hong Kong Library

Address: Run Run Shaw Library
Tat Chee Avenue
Kowloon
Hong Kong
Telephone: 3-2788-8846
Fax: 3-2788-9425
www.cityu.edu.hk/lib

Founded: 1984

Holdings (1999): Volumes: 539,000. Current serials: 8,000; films and videos: 18,000; maps: 400; microforms: 547,000; online subscriptions: 9,000; sound recordings: 6,000.

Special Collections: *Areas of Concentration:* Business and management; Chinese culture and civilization; Chinese traditional legal culture; commonwealth legal systems and Anglo-American legal culture in the Asia-Pacific Rim; creative media; English legal history; science and technology. *Individual Collections:* Chinese legal history collection; English law special collection; Pearl River Delta collection.

From Argyle Center to the Kowloon Tong Campus

The origin of the City University of Hong Kong (CityU), formerly known as the City Polytechnic of Hong Kong (CPHK), can be traced to June 1981, when a committee appointed by the Hong Kong government to review postsecondary education in Hong Kong made a recommendation to establish a second polytechnic institute. A planning committee chaired by Sir S.Y. Chung was formed in June 1982. Planning and work proceeded, the City Polytechnic Ordinance was enacted in November 1983, and the City Polytechnic of Hong Kong officially came into existence.

On 22 October 1984 the institution, temporarily located on its interim campus at the Argyle Center Tower II (a 19-story commercial building in downtown Kowloon), was officially opened by the governor of Hong Kong, Sir Edward Youde. It started offering courses while its permanent campus at Kowloon Tong (a district within Kowloon) was still under construction. Despite a modest opening enrollment of 1,200 students, the library had to be set up without delay to support the institution. Occupying the basement and the eighth floor of the Argyle Center Tower II, the library was under great pressure to start operations quickly.

Given the limited number of staff available in the initial period and a tight time frame, the traditional way of ordering and cataloging books was considered impractical, and the shelf-ready system was adopted as an alternative. Vendors were requested to supply precataloged and preprocessed books that could be placed on shelves for use immediately upon delivery to the library. By the end of the first academic year, the library already had a collection of some 19,000 volumes of books and 1,200 titles of periodicals, as well as 1,000 items of media resources materials and a complete set of *British Standards*. Moreover, the library maintained its own press-clipping collection of articles originating in seven leading local newspapers.

In the autumn of 1988, the phase I permanent campus in Kowloon Tong, although only partially completed, was ready for occupancy. The library began moving into the first phase of the new campus, where its initial allotment of space totaled 10,200 square yards (more than 2 acres). During the transitional period the library operated concurrently at both the Argyle Centre and the Kowloon Tong campus. In the summer of 1989 the Argyle Centre years finally ended when the commercial building was handed over to the government to house the Trade and Industry Department as well as the Open Learning Institute.

In 1989 the library no longer relied on the shelf-ready system of acquisition but instead began to do its own cataloging. Its collection grew to 120,000 volumes of books, 17,230 volumes of serials, and 5,200 media resources items by the end of the academic year. The use of technology also increased with the introduction of more and more CD-ROMs and interactive videos. At a ceremony held on 19 March 1990, the library, located on the new campus, was formally named the Run Run Shaw Library in appreciation of Sir Run Run Shaw's generosity in donating HK$10 million to the polytechnic institute.

The library continued to develop and entered a new era when it extended to the phase II campus in 1992, thus increasing its total space from 10,200 square yards (2 acres) to 15,600 square yards (more than 3 acres) with a book stack capacity of about 750,000 volumes and a seating capacity of 2,600, allowing substantial growth in its collections and services ever since.

From a Polytechnic Library to a University Library

On 17 November 1994 the Legislative Council of the Hong Kong government passed the City Polytechnic Amendment Ordinance and sanctioned the use of the title "City University of Hong Kong" effective 23 November 1994. The transition from a polytechnic institute to a university was formally completed on 1 January 1995 with the appointment of a university council. From then on the Run Run Shaw Library was no longer a polytechnic library but a university library. The change in status meant new demands and new challenges. To fit itself into a new role, the library reviewed its own direction of development and formulated its first strategic plan in 1995, covering the period of 1995 to 1998, with the library's vision, mission, goals, and objectives clearly stated. To monitor the success of the action plan, an annual review of progress with respect to the goals and objectives was stipulated.

In September 1998 the library formulated its second strategic plan (for 1998 to 2002) in response to the university's Ambience, Undergraduate education, Research excellence, Outreach, Reward system, and Accountability (AURORA) Strategy. To ensure quality performance, the library's management introduced benchmarking mechanisms in 1996 with target key performance indicators set for each year. Moreover, a set of performance pledges was established in October 1998 and revised again in 1999. Staff appraisal and training are conducted on an annual basis. All of these measures are intended to guarantee that the library continues to offer services of premium quality to the university community.

Technological Development

When the library was first opened in 1984, it used an automation system developed and maintained by the Computing Services Center of the institution. However, as time went by the system proved to be incapable of meeting the needs of the library. After various cost-benefit analyses, the library decided to acquire a commercial turnkey system. INNOPAC, an online computer system from Innovative Interfaces, Inc., was chosen and replaced the old system in October 1996.

In 1986 the library was the first among all tertiary institutional libraries in Hong Kong to install and use CD-ROMs. *Education Resources Information Centre* database (*ERIC*) and Grolier's Electronic Encyclopedia were introduced to users and *Books in Print Plus* and *Bibliofile* were used for acquisition and cataloging purposes.

After 1986 the use of CD-ROMs became increasingly popular, the number of CD-ROM databases available in the library increased, CD-ROMs were networked to facilitate access throughout the university campus, and various full-text image CD-ROM databases such as *Business Periodicals Ondisc, IEEE/IEE Publications Ondisc*, and *Social Sciences Indexes/Full Text* were also acquired. In the late 1990s CD-ROM usage gave way to Internet usage, a trend that included reference and bibliographic databases available on the Web, as well as full-text databases and electronic journals. By 1998, in addition to 260 CD-ROM/Internet electronic databases, the library subscribed to about 140 full-text electronic journals. By 1999 the number of electronic databases grew to 300 and electronic journals increased to more than 3,000. Many of these resources are available for remote access beyond the university campus.

With increasing numbers of electronic and Internet resources available, the library established its Electronic Resources Center in the summer of 1998. As the focal point of electronic resources, the center has provided users with one-stop access to both electronic databases and journals within the library and Internet resources on the Web. The center includes a User Education Room equipped with state-of-the-art facilities and equipment to provide a pleasant venue for conducting library courses and seminars.

The proliferation of electronic and Internet resources, the increasing popularity of the World Wide Web, and improved telecommunication technology led the library closer to the concept of a virtual library. Consequently, the library's website was developed as a gateway to resources and information within and outside the library and also as an integrated platform for accessing various library services.

In its first digitization project, the library has finished digitizing City University examination papers of recent years, from 1996–97 to semester A, 2000–01. Electronic versions of the examination papers are now accessible via the library home page, either on- or off-campus. Without violating the copyright ordinance, other useful library materials will also be digitized.

Special Collections

As a relatively young university, the institution has been able to concentrate its special collections in areas of curricular interest. To promote and support academic study and research activities in Chinese traditional legal culture, the library established the Chinese law special collection in mid-1997. The collection incorporates materials on the Chinese legal system and Chinese philosophy covering the period from ancient China to 1949.

The formation of the English law special collection dates back to the purchase in 1987 of a special collection of 1,371 volumes on English legal history from a private collector, Victor Tunkel (a senior lecturer in law at the Queen Mary and Westfield College of the University of London). The library continues to build and develop Tunkel's collection with the aim of promoting academic interest and scholarly study in English legal history, the commonwealth legal systems, and the Anglo-American legal culture in the Asia-Pacific Rim.

The Pearl River Delta collection was established in mid-1993 with a grant awarded by the Research Grants Council in Hong Kong. The collection was developed with the aim of providing researchers and scholars interested in studying the Pearl River Delta region of China with various materials covering a period from the mid-19th century to the present.

Cooperative Work and Future Development

During the process of building the special collections, the library established close relationships with other universities in mainland China. These relationships facilitate staff training and gift exchange and donation, as well as reciprocal visits. To date the library has organized five rounds of training for librarians from four mainland universities. Moreover, during the past six years more than 6,000 volumes of books have been donated to Peking University, Tsinghua University, China University of Political Science and Law, Fudan University, and Wuhan University. In return the library received 4,000 volumes of books that cannot be acquired through normal channels in Hong Kong. During three acquisition field trips to China in 1993, 1994, and 1998, the library established liaisons with several university libraries and research centers in China and paved the way for further cooperation.

Plans for the library, within the university's Strategic Plan for the Development of Information Technology, include a number of projects dealing with user education, physical renovation, and development of a document/image management system facilitating remote access to Chinese and English materials, all intended to improve services to the university community and beyond.

PAUL W.T. POON

Further Reading

Planning Committee for the City Polytechnic of Hong Kong, *The First Report of the Planning Committee for the Second Polytechnic,* Hong Kong: Hong Kong Polytechnic, 1982

Planning Committee for the City Polytechnic of Hong Kong, *The Second and Final Report of the Planning Committee for the Second Polytechnic,* Hong Kong: Hong Kong Polytechnic, 1983

Poon, Paul W.T., "The Application of Information Technology to Interlibrary Loan: A Case Study," in *Proceedings of the 2nd Pacific Conference: New Information Technology for Library and Information Professionals, Educational Media Specialists, and Technologists, May 29–31, 1989,* edited by Ching-chih Chen and David I. Raitt, West Newton, Massachusetts: MicroUse Information, 1989

Poon, Paul W.T., "Developing a Special Collection on the Pearl River Delta of China: Processes and Strategies," *Asian Libraries* 4, no. 3 (1995)

Quality Education for Professional Excellence: CPHK 10th Anniversary Commemorative Album, Hong Kong: City Polytechnic of Hong Kong, 1994

Columbia University Libraries

Address: Library Information Office
Columbia University
535 West 114th Street
Mail Code 1121
New York, New York 10027
USA
Telephone: 212-854-7309
Fax: 212-854-5082
www.columbia.edu/cu/libraries

Founded: 1784

Holdings (1999): Volumes: 7 million. Archives and manuscripts: 2.9 million items; current serials: 67,000; graphic materials: 625,000; incunabula: 1,100; maps: 130,000; microforms: 5.3 million.

Special Collections: *Areas of Concentration:* Business; East Asian languages and culture; economics; graphic arts; health sciences; history; humanities; international affairs; publishing; social sciences; social work. *Individual Collections:* American Type Founders library; Samuel Avery library collection of architectural books and drawings; Bakhmeteff archive of Russian and East European history and culture; Carnegie Corporation archives; Brander Matthews dramatic museum collection; David Eugene Smith collection of mathematical books and instruments; Starr East Asian library of Chinese, Japanese, and Korean language materials. *Papers:* DeWitt Clinton; Hart Crane; Stephen and Cora Crane; John Jay; Herbert H. Lehman; Gouverneur Morris; Frances Perkins; Lincoln Steffens; Joseph Urban; Tennessee Williams.

King's College, the institution that would later become Columbia University in the City of New York, was granted a charter by King George II of England in 1754. Established primarily in response to the demands of local merchants and businessmen who wished to educate their sons without sending them away, the college was the fifth in the American colonies and the first without a direct religious affiliation. Although its first president, the Reverend Samuel Johnson, was an Anglican clergyman—establishing the close ties to the established church that would mark the first century of the college's existence—the secular origin of the college and its practical mission were reflected in the first gift of books to the new institution. This first gift was from a New York City attorney, Joseph Murray, who bequeathed his library of law books. This donation was followed by a more typical one of theological volumes by the Rector of All Hallows Staining in London and by a gift from Oxford University Press of the 30 books it had published by that time.

The King's College library grew slowly. By the time of the American Revolutionary War, it reportedly comprised no more than 2,000 books, attended to by a professor of mathematics and natural sciences at the college who apparently failed at his appointed charge to create a catalog, as no record of its completion has been found. The books, in any case, were dispersed during the British occupation and the full collection never reassembled.

In the years following its reestablishment as Columbia College in 1784, the school remained a small and essentially local institution, providing a classical education to the sons of New Yorkers. Its library collections were first cataloged in 1818, but they grew slowly in comparison with those of U.S. colleges elsewhere, perhaps reflecting the indifference of a 19th-century commercial community that now pushed its sons in other directions. Students were not encouraged to use the college collections that did exist, and until 1837 when the Reverend Nathaniel Moore was appointed as the first full-time librarian, the books had no regular care.

Moore's manuscript subject catalog of the collections, which by this time had absorbed the law library of James Kent as well as some 300 volumes purchased from the library of Italian Professor (and Mozart librettist) Lorenzo Da Ponte, was compiled in the decade following his appointment and was in use until 1874, surviving the college's move from the downtown area of the city to the more central location of Madison Avenue and 49th Street. Moore also began a systematic catalog of the periodical collection in 1848. He attempted to enlarge the library by soliciting gifts and donations but was unable to compensate for decades of relative neglect. In 1850 the Columbia College Library comprised only 13,000 volumes, in contrast to the 50,000 or more in the collections of Harvard (Cambridge, Massachusetts) and Yale (New Haven, Connecticut). Columbia's absorption of the School of Mines and the School of Law added

7,000 and 4,000 volumes respectively, but in 1864 the School of Mines petitioned to keep its collections separate from those of the college.

The years following the U.S. Civil War were marked by the transformation of the small college and its associated professional schools into what would become the modern university. Slowly, the library collections—essential for research-based scholarship—grew to supply the newly articulated needs of its constituents. After members of the faculty wrote to President Frederick Barnard in 1864, complaining about the administration of the library, a new librarian, Beverly Robinson Betts (1865–83), was appointed. Betts gave the collections their first fully professional attention, replacing Moore's by now seriously outdated catalog with a new printed catalog (1874); however, he failed to develop the collections further. Fortunately, in 1881 New York book collector Stephen Whitney Phoenix, who had graduated from Columbia College some 20 years earlier, added to his $500,000 bequest the first large alumni gift of books: 7,000 volumes from his own library, among them a Shakespeare First Folio, a fine illuminated Book of Hours, and several important U.S. literary manuscripts. In 1883, pushed into an expansion of services and collections by stinging criticism of the library made by the influential poitical science professor John Burgess, President Barnard replaced Betts by the progressive and controversial Melvil Dewey (1883–89).

Dewey's innovations were many: He made great strides in cataloging, hired female librarians for the first time, expanded interlibrary loan practices, and improved reference work. These activities were at first supported by the library committee of the trustees, who allowed him to establish as well a School of Library Economy to train professional librarians. His tenure, however, was short. The relatively vast expenditures required to support his administrative innovations were questioned by the committee, who in their report to the trustees in 1883 were concerned by the possibility that "work is being carried out on a scale unnecessarily large." Moreover, Dewey's sometimes difficult relations with the faculty (who found him arrogant) gradually undermined his position, causing him to leave after only three years. He took his library school with him.

Dewey's successor, George Hall Baker (1889–99), was less controversial but, fortunately, equally capable. He had been in charge of collection development for the library and continued to be interested in providing resources for the various disciplines. His tenure coincided with the growing prosperity of New York City, enabling him to benefit from the competitive philanthropy of Gilded Age alumni through the acquisition of gifts and bequests to the library. When it became clear that the collections had outgrown the new midtown building (completed in 1883) that had been constructed to house them, it was at Baker's urging that a new and more efficient library space was planned for the uptown campus.

The central place that the library occupied in the conception of what had become in 1896 "Columbia University in the City of New York" was symbolized by its new building in Morningside Heights. Designed by the architectural firm of McKim, Mead, and White as the centerpiece of their grand urban plan, Low Library (named after the father of President Seth Low) was the first building completed on the site. A monumental structure that still dominates the campus a century later, it featured a round central reading room overlooked by balconies, lit by arched windows near the roof, and surrounded by storage areas on a number of levels. By the time of Baker's retirement, the library had been expanded to include 275,000 books and would incorporate more than 1 million volumes before the building was abandoned as library space some 30 years later.

Baker was followed by a series of gifted librarians and administrators who, with the support of the new university President Nicholas Murray Butler (1902–45) during his 43-year tenure, rationalized and expanded the collections, streamlined cataloging and administrative practices, and developed the remarkable reference services that would remain for decades the distinguishing characteristic of the Columbia University Libraries. The building of a new home for Avery Library for Architecture and the Allied Arts (1912) and the founding of the East Asian collection, as well as the expansion of subject collections in many areas, reflected the intellectual ferment that permeated the Columbia campus in the last decade of the 19th century and the early years of the 20th. James Hulme Canfield, who had been president of Ohio State University, served as librarian from 1899 to 1909. In 1907 he developed the first undergraduate collection in the country, a library of 10,000 volumes chosen to satisfy the needs of underclassmen. He also introduced printed Library of Congress cards and typewriters to support the bibliographic control department.

Although many of the books in constant use at the university resided in separate departmental libraries, it became clear shortly after the opening of Low that there would not be enough space there for the collections being developed to support the many new graduate schools and disciplines. By 1928 there were 38 separate departmental libraries on the campus. Convinced that small, specialized libraries were duplicative and inefficient despite repeatedly articulated faculty insistence on the importance of local control and autonomy, the trustees of the university, urged by Librarian Charles Williamson (1926–43), concluded that a new building was needed to provide space for consolidation of library operations and future growth. In 1932 South Hall, renamed Butler Library 12 years later, opened. With a 2-million-volume capacity, the building was designed to accommodate graduate and undergraduate research and reference use, as well as the technical services departments and administrative offices. A multistory reading room, with tall windows to the north, echoed the monumental dignity of the abandoned space in the Low Library, which was soon turned over largely to the administrative offices of the university. Five departmental libraries were housed in Butler immediately, and within a few years the special collections library, which had been housed in the Low Library, was moved to the top floors of the building as well.

During the decades following the resignation of President Butler in 1945, the growth of library collections paralleled the expansion of university programs, particularly in the graduate and professional schools. The arrival on campus of a new constituency of veterans and foreign students was accompanied by a national move to acquire resources from areas that had been devastated by World War II or were threatened by the Cold War. Columbia had long been active in developing its international collections and thus welcomed the rapid acquisition of library materials, particularly from Eastern Europe, Russia, Southeast Asia, and the countries of the Pacific Rim. These acquisitions were made possible by Public Law 480, a foreign acquisitions program using foreign currency surpluses administered by the Library of Congress. Within a few years, however, as book and periodicals poured in and approval plans replaced individual selection, it became clear that new spaces would have to be found for the collections. Equally important, some way would have to be found to avoid being swamped by cataloging, binding, and processing backlogs.

The space needs were met, at least temporarily, by a series of internal shifts. Under Librarian Richard Logsdon (1953–69), collections moved from place to place as buildings were constructed uptown and on the perimeters of the Morningside Heights campus to house academic departments and programs. The backlog in cataloging, however, would be a problem for at least 20 more years.

Efforts to provide a collective bargaining unit for the library staff at Columbia had begun in the late 1940s, when a Staff Association was formed. By 1953, however, the Staff Association had fallen apart, a victim both of university resistance to unionization and of a deep divide between the professional and support personnel over philosophy and tactics. By the end of Logsdon's years, however, the tumultuous political climate on the Columbia campus had had its influence on labor relations. In 1969, U.A.W. Local 1199, originally a health and hospital workers union, became the official representative of the library support staff. In the same year, the Representative Committee of Librarians (RCL) was formed to represent the interests of the professional librarians to the library administration and to review promotion, professional development, and ranking procedures. In 1985 a second union, Local 2110, would, after some struggle, become the bargaining unit for technical and office workers at Columbia both inside and outside the library system.

Warren Haas (1970–78), who held the new title Vice President for Information Services and University Librarian, became the first to cope with this newly organized staff. Haas's tenure was in general marked by administrative change, much of it calculated to improve the efficiency of library operations. Following the recommendations of a report issued in 1974 by an outside management consulting firm, Booz, Allen, and Hamilton, and later echoed by the conclusions of a separate faculty-led task force, a new organizational structure was put into place. Subject collections and departmental libraries were organized into three divisions: history and humanities, social science (which includes business), and science. Five distinctive collections—the C.V. Starr East Asian Library, the Avery Architectural and Fine Arts Library, the Law Library, the Rare Book and Manuscript Library, and the Augustus Long Health Sciences Library—remained outside the divisions and reported directly to the university librarian. Although in the late 1970s the law school library came under the jurisdiction of the School of Law, the remaining divisions would maintain their identity until the end of the century. Haas was also responsible for beginning an accurate assessment of the depth and scope of the libraries' collections, as well as the development of the Research Libraries Group (RLG) (Columbia was a founding member) in 1974.

The other major initiative of the Haas period was in the area of library preservation. Activities that he continued and fostered included book conservation and large-scale microfilming operations. He also prepared a major blueprint for the Association of Research Libraries (ARL) on national and international needs in library preservation. After he resigned to become president of the Council on Library Resources in 1978, he continued his work on library preservation, which eventually led to the creation of a national commission on preservation and access.

Significant developments in library technology that would have a profound effect on the libraries were put into place in the Haas period, although it would not be until the tenure of the next vice president and university librarian that their impact would become clear. Under Patricia Battin (1978–86), the sharing with other libraries of bibliographic data (which had been made possible by the refinement of electronic computing technology that allowed institutions to make use of already created records) began to speed up the cataloging process. Columbia librarians were able to catalog directly onto Research Libraries Information Network (RLIN), the RLG information network. This eliminated many backlogs and provided wider access to users at Columbia and throughout the nation. In addition, Battin took a continuing interest in Haas's preservation initiatives before she in turn resigned to become the first president of the Commission on Preservation and Access in 1987. When Battin was succeeded by the new Vice President for Information Services and University Librarian Elaine Sloan (1988–2001), the connection between library services and emerging electronic technologies was made clear by the assignment of responsibility for the Academic Information Systems to the librarian's position. This administrative decision would, in the 1990s, be instrumental in assuring a seamless linkage between computing activities on campus and traditional book delivery and access services, laying the groundwork for the digital innovations of the next decade.

Other changes in the 1980s included the adoption of an effective Online Public Access Catalog (OPAC), Columbia Libraries Information Online (CLIO), and improvements in the cataloging workflow that gradually eliminated the worst of the backlogs in monographic cataloging. An administrative structure was adopted that eliminated the strict division into public and technical services that had persisted even after the earlier reforms. It also established a number of standing committees that crossed subject boundaries, thus at once broadening and flattening library management. Directors of the distinctive libraries and other library units, including preservation and library systems, became part of the new management committee, a body that included the heads of all divisional libraries as well as administrative officers.

The rising costs of monographs and particularly of serials in the later years of the 1980s, underlined by a downswing in the national economy, called attention to the fact that continued expansions in library funding were not guaranteed and that budgets for personnel and operations were vulnerable. A shrinking staff tried with remarkable success to do more with less, devising ways to improve cataloging output and incorporate technological change while maintaining a high level of service to the university community. Inevitably (despite the predictions of a paperless society), book collections continued to expand and the pressure for space became intense. Two library annexes were developed near campus and cooperative collection development, once little more than a wish, became a necessity. Proposals for a new library building were made, but the confined space of the Morningside campus limited the options. In the end, a decision to renovate the 60-year-old Butler Library was announced. New reading rooms, open stacks, and a concentration on services were given high priority. The most dramatic and controversial consequence of this decision was the 1992 demise of the venerable Graduate School of Library Service, which had returned to Columbia in 1928. Its classrooms, stacks, and reference center on the top floors of Butler Library would give way to electronic service units, graduate reading rooms, new stack areas, and offices, as new spaces were opened on the lower levels for undergraduate reading rooms and collections.

Although direct service to the Columbia College population became an increasingly important goal for the libraries as the university began to enlarge its commitment to undergraduate education, electronic technology was the single most important factor in shaping library policy and procedures in the last decade of the 20th century. Professionals in all departments, from reference to acquisitions, struggled to educate themselves and keep up with the changing international marketplace for information. Following trends that had been evident some 30 years before, access rather than ownership became the institutional goal, and the Columbia University Libraries (21 of them by 1999; the title was officially plural) devoted resources to expanding and developing what was now called the digital library. The 21 libraries do not include the Law Library or the separate libraries of Teachers College and Barnard College, institutions that maintain independent library systems. Internally, cooperative programs with ACIS and the Columbia University Press explored new initiatives in providing services to scholars by expanding the horizons of academic publishing and developing centers for teaching and learning. Externally, Columbia joined other research institutions as a partner in the Digital Library Federation (DLF), successfully garnering support for cooperative projects related to the expansion of electronic information sources. Consortial purchasing, rapid interlibrary loan transactions, and the use of commercial document delivery services—all made possible by the speed of information exchange on the World Wide Web—broadened the resource base available to local users.

However, the need to expand library collections to include electronic resources without noticeably diminishing the pace of monograph and periodical acquisitions, combined with the effects of staff reductions some years earlier, placed a strain on the libraries' ability to provide the services required by the campus without compromising the new programs. Following the report of a visiting committee convened by the provost (which praised the libraries but noted the relative paucity of financial resources), the university in 1998 increased the libraries' annual allocation of operating funds. This relieved some of the immediate problems and enabled the administration to develop more effective long-range planning strategies. Much-needed capital projects were initiated or continued with renewed vigor, including the renovation of Butler Library (phased over an eight- to ten-year period) and the construction of a cooperative off-site storage depository in Princeton, New Jersey, shared by the New York Public Library and Princeton University.

Serving the research needs of an international constituency of readers, for more than two centuries the libraries have attempted with some success simultaneously to preserve the resources of the past, provide for the needs of the present, and anticipate the demands and changes in the storage and dissemination of information that lie ahead.

JEAN W. ASHTON

Further Reading

Canfield, J.H., et al., *A History of Columbia University, 1754–1904,* New York: Columbia University Press, and London: Macmillan, 1904

Chernow, Barbara A., *Guide to the Research Collections of the Columbia University Libraries,* New York: Columbia University, 1984

Columbia University Libraries, *Columbia University Libraries: History and Organization,* New York: Columbia University Libraries, 1973

Dewey, Melvil, *Report of the Committee on the Library as to the Organization of the Staff of Service, Presented to the Trustees, June 4, 1883,* New York: Printed for the College, 1883

Dolkart, Andrew S., *Morningside Heights: A History of Its Architecture and Development,* New York: Columbia University Press, 1998

Linderman, Winifred B., "History of the Columbia University Library, 1876–1926," Ph.D. Diss., Columbia University, 1959

Placzek, Adolph S., editor, *Avery's Choice: Five Centuries of Great Architectural Books: One Hundred Years of an Architectural Library, 1890–1990,* New York: G.K. Hall, and London: Prentice Hall International, 1997

Trautman, Ray, *A History of the School of Library Service, Columbia University,* New York: Columbia University Press, 1954

Williamson, Charles, "South Hall, Columbia University, New York," *Columbia University Quarterly* (July 1935)

Complutensian University Library and Madrid's Academic Libraries

Address: Biblioteca de la Universidad Complutense de Madrid
Antiguo Pabellon de Gobierno, Calle Isaac Peral, s/n
Ciudad de Universitaria, 28040, Madrid
Spain
Telephone: 91-3946925/6939
Fax: 91-3946926
www.ucm.es/bucm

Founded: 1499; 1508 at Acalá de Henares

Holdings (2000): Volumes: 2.3 million. Current serials: 15,000; films and videos: 4,000; incunabula: 636; manuscripts: 5,000; maps: 22,000; microforms: 3.7 million; sound recordings: 3,000.

Madrid boasts the Library of the Complutensian University of Madrid (Biblioteca de la Universidad Complutense de Madrid, or BUCM), plus seven city-state provincial universities; two private universities—one international and one Catholic (Jesuit); the national archives; an archeological museum; an art gallery; two palace libraries; and 175 academic, research, and special libraries in research centers, academies, and institutes.

Madrid, an international urban and cultural center of nearly 5 million inhabitants, has eight universities in its metropolitan area, with more than 360,000 students taught by 14,600 faculty, plus 5,500 researchers in various institutes and academies. Like the city itself, the oldest is an early modern creation rather than a medieval foundation, and most of the others are relatively recent developments of the late and post-Franco era. All imitate the historical model of distributed libraries connected with faculties and research centers but are networked into systems. In addition, nearly 200 academies and special libraries are distributed throughout the city. Thus Madrid's academic and research community can access significant resources beyond its university libraries.

The Complutensian University of Madrid (Universidad Complutense de Madrid, or UCM) comes as close to being Spain's national university as possible, with 124,000 students and more than 5,000 faculty plus professional staff; it is situated on a sprawling campus in the suburbs just north of the city. Various offices and institutes are scattered throughout the city and province. Its history is mainly that of a private institution, first ecclesiastical and then royal, before its modern secularization as a state and now a provincial university. UCM is so named because its origins extend into the Middle Ages and predate Madrid's early modern foundation. It was transplanted over several centuries from the ancient cathedral town of Compluto at Acalá de Henares to the east of the present city of Madrid. There, in 1502, Cardinal Gonzalo Ximénez de Cisneros established his famous international school of Biblical and language scholars to compile the famous polyglot Bible, the *Biblio Poliglota Complutense* (printed 1514–17 by Arnau Guillen de Brocar and distributed after 1520). This center dates from 1293, when King Sancho IV of Castile and the Archbishop of Toledo, Gonzalo Garcia Gudiel, founded the first school, the Colegio Mayor de San Ildefonso, based on the nascent universities at Salamanca and Valladolid. (Six such schools were founded by the Spanish Ancién Regime.)

The BUCM grew from the theological nucleus of its medieval founders with support from Toledo, through the collections assembled to support this text-editing and commentary work as part of a general humanistic revival in Spain (codices date from the 12th century, including copies made from Toletan manuscripts, one dated in 1277). Archbishop Cisneros, the protégé of Cardinal Mendoza, armed with the papal decree Inter Caetera from Alexander VI (Rodrigo de Borja), had begun the enlargement of the Colegio Mayor in April 1499 to support law studies, canonical and secular, which evolved by 1513 into the faculty of arts and letters of the Universidad de Alcalá de Henares. Under patronage of the humanist Cisneros, whose power and influence as cardinal and primate of Spain were unparalleled and who maintained widespread connections throughout Europe, books were acquired from new publishing centers and from libraries suffering in the aftermath of the Reformation, resulting in one of the largest collections of incunabula and early imprints on the continent. The resulting library was commonly known therefore as the Biblioteca Cisneriana.

The Colegio Mayor was surrounded by other institutes and study centers supported by various religious orders (Dominicans, Franciscans, Trinitarians, Augustinians, Carmelites, Jesuits, etc.) that developed their own specialties. The Colegio de Madre de Dios (Madrid), for example, was dominated by the theology faculty. The center's interests were not confined to philosophy and theology per se, but as extensions of the new Renaissance humanism collecting spread to all branches of the sciences and, in keeping with pre-Enlightenment tenets, specialized in government as an extension of the older focus on law. So the Colegios de San Eugenio and de San Isidro, where grammarians congregated, became the focal points of arts and letters, including the revival of Greek letters. Lay patrons, including military orders, formed an extensive support system throughout the peninsula during the early modern era.

The Catholic kings were among the library's visitors and patrons, and Felipe II regarded the Universidad de Alcalá as his *real universitaria* (royal university). The Jesuit Colegio de San Pedro y San Pablo in 1603 acquired the status of Colegio Imperial under the protection of Empress Maria, Charles V's daughter and mother of Maximilian II of the Austrian Hapsburg Empire. Felipe V, imitating the French court's buildup of its college in Paris, in 1725 founded within the Colegio Imperial a royal seminar for nobles to gain a proper higher education in fine arts and letters. However, after the era of such great patronage during the late Renaissance and the expansion of the Luso-Hispanic seaborne empire, the institution and its library languished as the fortunes of Spain reversed. Indicative of internal turmoil was the suppression of the Jesuits in 1767, and although restored to their new college of San Isidro in 1770, the old-style house of studies dominated by religious orders was forever changed. This Jesuit institution and all of the colleges became increasingly secularized. After 1845, for example, San Isidro became the center for Estudios Nacionales, a predecessor of the Universidad Literaria de Madrid.

The university's secular revival dates to the reign of Carlos III (1759–88), when the monarchy fostered a modernization movement, especially in general education. The original foundation was augmented by the Royal College of Surgery and Medicine (Real Colegio de Cirugía y Medicina) of San Carlos, with attendant development of a medical library to rival those in Barcelona and Cádiz. By a royal warrant in 1780, this new college was located not in Alcalá but in Madrid. The whole institution began to migrate to the city. The medical school was further augmented when the Real Colegio de Farmacía de San Fernando was founded in 1806, the applied health sciences collections building on older collections in chemistry and biology. The formal transfer of the health science faculties from Alcalá to Madrid was confirmed in 1843. A veterinary school was added in 1857 to the Madrid complex.

Meanwhile the Biblioteca Cisneros was complemented by a public library for general studies in support of the Reales Estudios de San Isidro, and the research library in philosophy, theology, and literature was the beneficiary of transfers from Jesuit colleges after the order's suppression. Their eventual transfer of these collections to Madrid was forecast by the education reforms of the Cortes of Cádiz in 1820. Legislation in 1821 clearly articulated plans for a university in Madrid, the medical colleges were being founded there, and it became just a matter of time before the Universidad de Alcalá would become the Universidad de Madrid. This was ordered by royal decree on 29 October 1836, and the course in arts and sciences commenced during 1839 in various appropriated facilities. The myriad collections and departmental libraries of the old university came together in this formation of the Universidad Central, a fusion of the Universidad de Alcalá, the public school and library, and the allied health establishment. The Biblioteca de la Universidad Complutense (BUC) resulted from the merger of these institutions and was developed into a comprehensive university library system in the fall of 1845 by the Plan de Instrucción Publica of Pedro José Pidal. During the last half of the 19th century, the centralized library administration gave way to departmental libraries with the formation of the Bibliotecas de Jurisprudencía y Teología from the Fondos de Alcalá. The collections of the Reales Estudios de San Isidro became the nucleus of the Biblioteca de Filosofía (arts and humanities), those of the Colegio de San Carlos became the Biblioteca de Medicina, and the Biblioteca de Farmacía was formed from the Colegio de San Fernando.

Conceived as a city unto itself, construction of the new Ciudad Universitaría in the suburbs began in 1911 under Alfonso XIII. The core campus was ready by 1927, and in 1928 the Valdecilla pavilion was opened. The institution's name was changed in 1930 to the Universidad de Madrid as the new campus was being built. The faculty of philosophy and letters moved there in 1932 and 1933 and a library to serve this school was opened in 1935. Influenced by library developments elsewhere, such as the library plans of Maria Moliner, the library system undertook a series of building projects, including reading rooms and a hall of exhibitions, and reconstituted itself with new policies, procedures, and services. Despite costly efforts to enhance Madrid as the Spanish capital with a distinguished university, all progress slowed when Spain plunged into a disastrous civil war in 1936. The Spanish Civil War not only interrupted the move to the new site, but small institute libraries were being amassed for inclusion in the new library. During these moves and ensuing chaos, numerous important codices were lost. True to tradition, the libraries were reassembled after the Civil War in their respective colleges of philosophy and letters, science, law, medicine, pharmacy, and a new veterinary science center.

To distinguish itself from the other university foundations in Madrid, in 1968 the university readopted its historic name of Complutense and the library's designation as the Biblioteca de la Universidad Complutense de Madrid. Thereafter the institution developed its own governance as an autonomous university, and the *Constitucion Española* of 1978 mentioned the library specifically in articles 148.1 and 149.1.28 when establishing the autonomy of Spain's major universities. By the 1980s the BUCM was dedicated to developing a modern library and information system to go far beyond its great historical collections. In keeping with its tradition of distributed libraries under one coordinating or system administration, numerous special institute libraries were created for advanced and highly specialized studies. Beginning with negotiations in 1992 and the concord between the Comunidad Autonomía de Madrid and the Comunidad de Madrid and completed by the Royal Decree of 9 June 1995, the university's material welfare was entrusted to the city and province of Madrid. In 1989 the university library, in accordance with the Sistema Español de Bibliotecas (SEB), Royal Decree 582, article 22, came under a national plan to coordinate academic library development under the leadership of the Biblioteca Nacional (BN). On 11 October 1991 the Statutes of the UCM were approved by Royal Decree 1555, placing the library system under the central services of the university, with a university librarian reporting to the Vice Rector for Research. The organizational charter clearly entrusts to the library system a "functional unity of service" for teaching and research, of all bibliographic collections, documentation, and audiovisual materials of the university, no matter where they are located. Its internal governance was set in the Reglamento of 1979, revised for the new millennium, and a 1992 Reglamento approving the special collections and rare books division to preserve the library's historic collections. An ambitious seven-track, five-year development plan, the *Programa Cisneros*, was adopted for 1997 to 2001, particularly oriented toward networking, use of the Internet, and strategic conversion of select sources into electronic form, developments well illustrated on the current BUCM website.

The BUCM's internal organization is split between a central administrative and technical services division and a campuswide interlibrary bibliographic, documentation, and reference services division housed in the old Pabellon de Gobierno. The public services are situated mainly in the libraries of UMC's 34 teaching and research centers, including 19 departmental libraries for the designated faculties of the university, a secondary school library and six other schools, three institute libraries, a professional center, three documentation centers, and the Fondo Histórico, or rare books and special collections library, in the historic Valdecilla (4,500 manuscripts, 725 incunabula, and 757,000 16th- to 18th-century imprints). The libraries can accommodate 8,400 users at reader stations and circulate nearly one million volumes annually. Collectively they held more than 2 million volumes, 38,000 periodical titles (of which 15,000 are active), plus collections by formats (maps, audiovisuals, and electronic sources—141 databases), most of which are accessible through an Online Public Access Catalog (OPAC) using MAchine-Readable Cataloging (MARC) format standards and Universal Decimal Classification. Of its incunabula and rare books, 900 are now available via the Internet in digital form (350,000 images, e.g., the *Kalendrier des Bergeres* [1499] with its 70 xylographs) via the Dioscorides project, funded by the Glaxo Wellcome and Health Sciences Foundation.

Other University and Research Center Libraries in Madrid

Supplementing the BUCM are many other resources in the city that contribute to the research potential of Spanish scholarship. Madrid is home to both the National Library and National Archives of Spain, plus a host of research libraries in 30 museums and more than 175 other *casas de estudios* (cultural centers), institutes, academies, and government offices. The Biblioteca Nacional, which evolved after 1716 from the Biblioteca Real (1637–), became a national library after 1836 and houses the Museo Bibliográfico Nacional and related institutes for bibliographic control and research. The Archivo Histórico Nacional is a modern creation, but with rich manuscript collections dating back to the tenth century and assembled from all over Spain. The Real Biblioteca del Palacio, dating from 1714 under Felipe V but restarted after the fire of 1734, is largely a 250,000-volume library of highlights, fine bindings, and great exemplars.

In addition to UCM, Madrid has seven other public universities. The newest foundation to offer an alternative to the Complutensian University was built to the north of the city. The Universidad Autónoma de Madrid, with 32,000 students, now has collections of nearly 500,000 (growing at 25,000 books annually), focusing on the contemporary rather than historical, with a strong emphasis on law and politics, the social sciences, and informatics. Others are the Universidad Carlos III de Madrid, mainly a teachers' college that maintains three libraries on its urban campus and another on an outlying campus; the Universidad Nacional de Educación a Distancia, a distributed system that has rapidly built a collection of 250,000 volumes for distance education but relies heavily on online services; the Universidad Politécnica de Madrid; and most recently, the Universidad Rey Juan Carlos. The Jesuits transferred to Madrid in the 1960s a school they founded in 1890 in Santander, which became the Pontifical University of Madrid. The combined holdings of these university libraries, including the Complutensian, is considerably more than 6 million volumes.

More than 100 academy libraries are scattered throughout old Madrid, of which the following are the most important for history and the arts and humanities. The Real Academia Española, founded in 1713, specializing in language and philology, developed a research library after 1737 that was expanded with royal patronage of Felipe IV. It grew to more than 40,000 volumes, including 250 manuscript collections and 38 incunabula. The Real Academia de la Historia, founded by Felipe V in 1738, focused on Spain's history and auxiliary sciences such as epigraphy and paleography, chronology, numismatics, documentary art, and archeology, and has more than 200,000 volumes (mostly pre-19th century), including 167 incunabula, and more than 10,000 manuscript collections. The Real Academia de Bellas Artes de San Fernando, founded in 1752, is dedicated to 18th- and 19th-century studies. The Real Sociedad Geográfica, a late 19th-century foundation, is largely a map library of some 5,200 exemplars, with a working library on cartography. The Sociedad Española de Antropología, Etnografía y Prehistoria, founded in 1921, has more than 8,000 volumes and a major run of series and periodicals (approximately 300 titles). The Real Academia de Ciencias Morales y Políticas, formed by amalgamation of private libraries before the civil war, by the mid-20th century had grown to 32,000 volumes, including 4,200 pre-19th-century volumes and 43 incunabula, plus periodical runs of 1,600 titles. The Real Academia de Jurisprudencia y Legislación is much older than its library, which dates from 1839, and now contains nearly 50,000 volumes and rare book collections of nearly 600 titles in law and political science. There are also special libraries for foreign scholars, such as the Casa Velasquéz for French studies and the U.S. Information Agency library for U.S. studies.

The 95 libraries of the Consejo Superior de Investigaciones Científicas (CSIC), with headquarters in Madrid, are important for research throughout Spain. Although CSIC was founded in 1939, its collections cover a much larger time span, and their scope is defined by disciplines such as theology, philosophy, history, Arabic and Hebraic studies, Latin American studies, philology, local studies, international studies, physics and natural sciences, animal biology and medicine, botany, and engineering and technical studies.

Madrid is in many ways like a gigantic campus with libraries scattered throughout the city and suburbs, but finding them is like exploring a labyrinth. Each academic and research library is focused on its own special interests and traditions. Most are tied to some form of patronage and appear to be private, but most are open (despite irregular schedules) to all scholars with proper identification (a national *tarjeta*, or identification card, for researchers) and an appropriate introduction. Research in Madrid is still somewhat like prospecting, chancy but rewarding. Today modern information technology with OPACs, websites and directories, and networking makes the search easier.

LAWRENCE J. McCRANK

Further Reading

Complutense Treasures: VII Centennial, 1293–1993, the Houghton Library, Harvard University, 4th–26th March, 1993 (exhib. cat.), Madrid: Universidad Complutense de Madrid, 1993

Documentos de trabajo de la BUCM (1993–)

Fernández Fernández, Cecilia, "La Biblioteca de la Universidad Complutense," *Boletín del ANABAD* 46, nos. 3–4 (July–December 1996)

Miguel Alonso, Aurora, "Del plan pidal a la ley moyano: Consolidación de la Biblioteca de la Universidad Central," in *Estudios históricos: Homenaje a los profesores José Maria Jover Zamora y Vicente Palacio Atard*, vol. 2, Madrid: Departamento de Historia Contemporanea, Universidad Complutense, 1990

Ministerio de Educación Nacional, Dirección General de Archivos y Bibliotecas, *Guía de las bibliotecas de Madrid*, Madrid: Dirección General de Archivos y Bibliotecas, Servicio de Publicaciones del Ministerio de Educación Nacional, 1953

Sánchez Mariana, Manuel, "Los fondos históricos de la Biblioteca de la Universidad Complutense de Madrid: Un legado para la ensenanza," in *La Universidad Complutense y las arts: Congreso nacional, celebrado en la facultad de geografía e historia, 30 de noviembre–3 de diciembre de 1993*, Madrid: UCM, 1995

Cornell University Library

Address: Cornell University Library
201 Olin Library
Cornell University
Ithaca, New York 14853
USA
Telephone: 607-255-3393
Fax: 607-255-6788
www.library.cornell.edu

Founded: 1865

Holdings (2000): Volumes: 6.6 million. Archives and manuscripts: 58,000 linear feet; current serials: 62,000; manuscripts: 70,000; maps: 237,000; microforms: 7.6 million; sound recordings: 130,000; videos and films: 5,000.

Special Collections: *Areas of Concentration:* Agriculture; Anglo-American literature; architecture and city planning; 18th-century France and England; labor history; medieval and Renaissance studies; New York state history; Southeast Asian history and cultures; U.S. history; women's studies. *Individual Collections:* Cornell University archives; Dante/Petrarch collections; Fiske Icelandic collection; history of science collection; human sexuality collection; Kheel Center for Labor-Management Documentation and Archives; Samuel May antislavery collection; George Bernard Shaw collection; witchcraft collection; Wordsworth collection. *Papers:* Hans Bethe; Ford Madox Ford; Louis Agassiz Fuertes; James Joyce; Marquis de Lafayette; Antoine-Laurent Lavoisier; Wyndham Lewis; John Nolen; Clarence Stein; E.B. White.

The founders of Cornell University, Ezra Cornell and Andrew Dickson White, inspired the distinctive development of the Cornell University Library. Ezra Cornell, a self-educated and self-made man, cared deeply about education. He established and supported a reading room for the Tompkins County (New York) Agricultural Society, and when his investment in the Western Union Telegraph Company began to pay off, his first major act of philanthropy was to create a public library for Ithaca.

In contrast, Andrew Dickson White's family was prosperous and prominent. From his parents he gained a love and respect for education. Upon graduation from Yale, he traveled in Europe, where he continued his reading, primarily in history, and became an avid book collector. As Cornell's first president, White began developing the university's library both through his own purchases and by encouraging the gifts of others. At its meeting in 1867 the new university's board of trustees appropriated $7,500 for book purchases and increased this sum to $11,000 the next year. Ezra Cornell also provided funds for books and equipment. With Cornell's assistance, White could now influence the creation of a university library. He also persuaded Cornell to purchase, for more than $12,000, its first major collection, the classical literature library of Professor Charles Anthon of Columbia University.

Cornell University opened in October 1868. The library was housed in Morrill Hall, the first university building, and Daniel Willard Fiske, a boyhood friend of White's, was named librarian. Fiske, a linguist and passionate bibliophile, had served as assistant librarian at the Astor Library in New York, the finest endowed reference library of the time (which later became one of the components of the New York Public Library).

In 1872 the library of 15,400 volumes moved to a new building, McGraw Hall, funded by trustee John McGraw. Fiske planned the new library as a noncirculating reference library on the European model, and Cornell may have been the first U.S. university library intended for extensive use by undergraduates as well as by the faculty. At that time most libraries were open only a few hours a day, just long enough for faculty to check out and return books. The Cornell Library was open nine hours a day, longer than any other library in the country.

White and Fiske continued to acquire major scholarly collections, including the Franz Bopp philological library, the library of Goldwin Smith, the William Kelly collection on the history of mathematics, and the Samuel May antislavery collection. In 1872 came the Jared Sparks collection in American history and the 13,000-volume Friedrich Zarncke library of German literature. White's and Fiske's collecting interests aimed to cover the range of human knowledge and provided the nucleus for many of Cornell's most distinguished collections.

White was also responsible for the creation of Cornell's first unit library. As he later reminisced in his 1905 autobiography, "I proposed to the trustees that if they would establish a department of architecture and call a professor to it, I would transfer to it my special library and collections." The trustees approved and appointed Charles Babcock as the first professor of architecture in the United States in 1871. White transferred his personal architecture collection to the library; it contained about 1,200 volumes, including the major journals of the day. In 1882 the library published its first *Library Bulletin,* with notes, articles, and lists of collections and new acquisitions. It promised that "a complete alphabetical author catalogue and a subject catalogue are now in preparation, but their completion will necessarily require a considerable period of time."

When John McGraw died in 1877, he left his substantial estate to his daughter, Jennie, who traveled to Europe three years later to marry Willard Fiske. Shortly after returning to Ithaca in 1881, she died of tuberculosis, leaving the bulk of her estate (approximately $2 million) to Cornell, most of it for the library. Questions immediately arose about the legality of the bequest, as the Cornell Charter restricted the size of the corporation's endowment. Section 5 explicitly stated, "The corporation hereby created may hold real and personal property not exceeding three millions of dollars in the aggregate." Willard Fiske felt betrayed at what he perceived as duplicity on the part of university attorney Douglass Boardman and Henry W. Sage, chairman of the board of trustees; Fiske believed they had influenced the New York State legislature to remove Section 5 from the charter without consulting him. Fiske resigned and joined with other members of the McGraw family to fight the will in a case that lasted for seven years. (Upon his death, Fiske himself left his library and $500,000 to the university.)

After serving as acting librarian, George William Harris was officially appointed librarian in 1886. A faculty-run library council formulated policy, allocated funds, and communicated with the university administration. Cornell was a pioneer in the use of electricity for outdoor lighting, and by 1885 the library became the first in the country to be lighted by electricity, allowing it to be open in the evenings. Library hours were extended to cover the hours from 8:00 A.M. to 9:30 P.M.

Andrew Dickson White resigned as president of Cornell University in 1885 to devote his attention to his family and to study and write. That year Cornell acquired the Merritt King Library, some 4,060 volumes, which became the nucleus of the library for the new law school officially established in 1886. The trustees allocated $1,000 for additional law books. In the law library's first year, Dean Douglass Boardman reported continuous opening during the working days of the year and constant use by the students.

At the same time White also decided to present his personal library to the university. In 1887 he offered about 30,000 volumes on the condition that the university would provide a suitable fireproof room and proper provision for its maintenance and usefulness. Meanwhile the U. S. Supreme Court had ruled against Cornell in the Fiske lawsuit. Promising that "Jennie shall have her library" (as cited in the 1905 autobiography of Andrew Dickson White), Henry Sage agreed to endow a new library building at a cost of more than $500,000.

In 1892 came the dedication of the university library designed by Ithaca architect William Henry Miller, with a bell tower that has become the symbol of Cornell. The building itself was regarded as the finest college library in the country. The stacks were fireproof, and the building provided ample seminar and lecture rooms. Built at a cost of $227,000, it had space for 400,000 books. At the time the Cornell collection claimed 105,000 volumes. As he had promised, Andrew Dickson White presented his historical library of 30,000 volumes, 10,000 pamphlets, and many manuscripts, including his collections on witchcraft, the Protestant Reformation, the French Revolution, and the U.S. Civil War. With the move into the new building, Librarian George William Harris (acting librarian, 1883–90; librarian, 1890–1915) created his own classification system. Based on the British Museum Library system, it was a fixed location device, consisting of shelf numbers that followed a loose systematic arrangement.

Cornell created its third unit library with the establishment of the first state-supported college at Cornell, the New York State College of Veterinary Medicine, in 1894. In 1897 former governor Roswell P. Flower gave $5,000 for a library for the school. Within two years the library was able to add 1,210 books, a number of pamphlets, and 34 periodicals to supplement the 5,000 volumes on veterinary and related subjects formerly in the university library. In 1901 the widow of Governor Flower added a $10,000 endowment for the Flower Library, in his memory.

By 1904 the library contained 286,000 volumes. Willard Fiske died in that year, bequeathing to the library about $500,000 plus his Dante, Petrarch, and Icelandic collections, as well as a library of Rhaeto-Romanic literature, adding to the nucleus of Cornell's outstanding special collections.

The State of New York established the New York State College of Agriculture in 1904. It had a rudimentary library in a room set aside for the purpose, but many departments maintained their own libraries. In 1910 Liberty Hyde Bailey, dean of the college, appropriated $1,250 for the library, to add to the $400 made available annually for the purchase of books. There was no full-time librarian until 1915, when the library moved to Stone Hall.

After a survey of other libraries in 1908, Cornell agreed to allow books to circulate to undergraduates for the first time. Willard Austen (1915–30) succeeded George Harris as librarian in 1915. The next year Andrew Carnegie presented to Cornell a fireproof and burglarproof treasure vault, but within ten years it was full. The Wason collection on China and the Chinese (a collection of works in English relating to China) came in 1918, a bequest of alumnus Charles W. Wason. As the library grew, the Harris classification system became more and more unwieldy. The library attempted to reclassify Spanish and Portuguese language and literature according to a modified version of the Library of Congress (LC) classification system, but a lack of space and funding forced the project to cease in 1930.

In 1924 the library held 710,000 books and was ranked fourth among U.S. university libraries, but it was ninth in the amount spent for books and 12th in the amount spent for library service. Space concerns were increasingly critical, and conditions were even worse in Stone Hall of the College of Agriculture. By 1923 many books had to be put in storage, as the state architect worried about the structural adequacy of Stone Hall to support the weight of the books. (The departmental libraries, financed by department funds, tended to be superior to the central agricultural library.)

Still, additional spectacular gifts mitigated the library's woes. In 1923 the Benno Loewy collection—including law books, rare books, theater books, and manuscripts—and a collection of Masonic literature arrived in three freight cars. In 1925 trustee Victor Emanuel purchased the Wordsworth collection belonging to Cynthia Morgan St. John of Ithaca for the library.

Otto Kinkeldey, a musicologist and librarian from the New York Public Library, became librarian in 1930. Kinkeldey complained bitterly about intolerable crowding in the stacks and reading rooms, insufficient working space, inadequate and underpaid staff, and parsimonious acquisitions funds. The Federal Emergency Relief Agency provided some help by funding student workers for the library. By 1934 a library built for 400,000 books held almost twice that number. As economic conditions in the country worsened, so did the state of the library. In 1928–29 only 10,807 books were bought, and in 1933–34 the number had decreased to 3,484.

Some space relief arrived with the addition in 1937 of a nine-story stack that accommodated an additional 200,000 books. Throughout the 1940s, President Edmund Ezra Day provided annual special grants of $5,000 to the library from the President's Surplus Fund, and in 1941 a library associates group was founded to provide funds for special purchases. Through the efforts of Paul Gates of the History Department and a grant from the Rockefeller Foundation, the Collection of Regional History was founded in 1942 to document everyday life in upstate New York. In 1945 Cornell established the first four-year school of industrial and labor relations in the country, with its own library (now the Catherwood Library); the Business School (now the Johnson School of Management) was founded the following year, also with its own library. The library of the new School of Hotel Administration (formerly a department in Home Economics) opened in 1950.

Stephen McCarthy came from Columbia University to become university librarian in 1946, and with President Day's support the library's fortunes began to improve. McCarthy reorganized the library administration into technical services and public services. The growth of the campus after the war brought renewed resources and vigor. McCarthy hired new people, appropriated rooms for working space, and inspired a new spirit among the staff and users. Purchase funds in 1948 rose to $101,500. College and department libraries were transferred to the university library and brought under one administration. The library board became advisory rather than administrative. Purchasing and acquisitions were centralized and a union catalog established. The library initiated a massive reclassification effort to change from the Harris to the LC system, an effort that would take more than 20 years. As the library was effectively out of stack space, a storage system began. Books thought to be in low demand were transferred to closed storage areas and had to be separately requested.

In 1952 a rare book room was created and the university archives officially established. That fall, the Albert R. Mann Library, named for a former dean of the College of Agriculture, was completed, consolidating the staff, budgets, and collections of the college libraries of Agriculture and Home Economics, plus some departmental libraries.

Cornell University's unique administrative structure includes both state-supported and privately endowed colleges. Unlike most of the other colleges funded by the original Morrill Act, it did not initially receive additional resources from New York State. Over the years, the state has provided support for four of Cornell's colleges: the New York State College of Veterinary Medicine, beginning in 1894; the New York State College of Agriculture in 1904; the New York State College of Home Economics (now Human Ecology) in 1925; and the New York State School of Industrial and Labor Relations (ILR) in 1944. Although all of the colleges report to the university's Board of Trustees and use centralized administrative services, they also retain a large measure of independence. The statutory libraries have separate and distinct budgets developed in the context of their larger college budgets. Although statutory library staff are operationally part of the larger library system, they are considered state employees, with a different salary structure and different benefits. The State University of New York (SUNY) provides central funding through the Statutory Finance Office; supplemental funding comes from the dean's discretionary funds. The endowed libraries, on the other hand, receive most of their appropriations from the university. Although the statutory operating and acquisitions budgets are largely separate, all libraries share in memberships and licensing agreements.

The university received a gift of $3 million in 1957 from trustee John Olin to build a new research library. The planning and construction of the John M. Olin Library was to be one of McCarthy's major achievements. The building was officially dedicated on 10 October 1962, along with the newly remodeled university library, now renamed Uris Library and devoted primarily to undergraduate studies.

The 1960s saw a dramatic expansion of college libraries, including engineering, veterinary, hotel, music, and industrial and labor relations divisions. Fine arts moved into Sibley Hall, management into Malott Hall, and physics and chemistry were combined as the Physical Sciences Library in Clark Hall. The Regional History Collection and university archives grew rapidly, and manuscript acquisition became national in scope. In 1972 the Cornell Program in Oral History was combined with the archival program, and the Department of Manuscripts and University Archives was established. To ensure security (as the libraries were a site of student demonstrations in the late 1960s), the entire card catalog was microfilmed.

As part of a nationwide movement toward library cooperation and resource sharing, the Cornell University Library began contributing records to the online bibliographic tool OCLC in 1973 and joined the Research Libraries Group (RLG) in 1980, during the librarianship of Louis Martin (1979–85). During the 1970s and 1980s, Cornell played a pioneering role in the application of automated techniques for the management of archival holdings. In the 1980s Cornell participated with Yale and Stanford Universities and RLG in developing and implementing the Research Libraries Information Network (RLIN) Archives and Manuscripts Control (AMC) system. Cornell implemented its first online integrated library system in 1986 with the purchase of the Northwestern Online Totally Integrated System (NOTIS) developed by Northwestern University in Evanston, Illinois.

Space continued to be a problem, and the first off-site storage facility was built in 1979. In 1981 Carl A. Kroch endowed the position of Carl A. Kroch University Librarian, one of few such endowed positions in the country. In 1990, under the leadership of University Librarian Alain Seznec (1986–96), Cornell built a new library to house its special collections. The trustees designated space on the Arts Quadrangle but decreed that the library must be underground. The Carl A. Kroch Library opened in 1992. At about the same time, the Olin Research Library, the Uris Undergraduate Library, and the Asia Collections in Kroch Library were reorganized and administered as one unit. The Rare Books Department, the Department of Manuscripts and University Archives, the history of science collections, and the Icelandic collection were combined to form the Division of Rare and Manuscript Collections, a separate administrative unit in Kroch Library.

Sarah E. Thomas was appointed Carl A. Kroch University Librarian in 1996. The library's facilities continued to expand. To meet increasing space needs, funding was approved for a second off-site facility. Two years later the new off-site facility (a high-density warehouse) opened, and books were moved there from campus libraries. The Industrial and Labor Relations Library moved to new quarters in Ives Hall. The State of New York provided funds for an addition to Mann Library (opened in 2000). The management library moved into Sage Hall, which had been completely renovated as the new home of the Johnson Graduate School of Management, and ground was broken for the addition to Lincoln Hall, home of the music library (also opened in 2000).

During the 1990s, Cornell led in the application of digital imaging technologies to library and archival holdings and also in the development of networked access to electronic resources. Although technical innovation has been a hallmark of the program, Cornell has always focused on using new techniques to accomplish basic goals of preservation and access. The Department of Preservation and Conservation, Mann Library, and the Division of Rare and Manuscript Collections led a variety of digital projects, in cooperation with other units and organizations, both on and off campus.

The library conducted pioneering studies in the application of digital imaging technologies and contributed to the use of common standards for document capture, storage, and transmission. The library also played a leadership role in the Digital Access Coalition, a collaborative effort founded in 1992 to foster the use of emerging technologies to improve access to campuswide collections. Its ultimate success was affirmed by the creation of the Cornell Institute for Digital Collections (CIDC) in 1997. With support from the National Science Foundation, the library is also cooperating with the Department of Computer Science to construct digital collections in a manner that enhances access and ensures their longevity. The Library Gateway offers easy and unified access to a rich and expanding suite of electronic databases, and in June of 2000 the library implemented a new library management system, Endeavor's Voyager.

In the 21st century, the 19 units that comprise the Cornell University Library continue to provide outstanding service to the university in support of Cornell's information needs. The library integrates digital information management with traditional resources and services and promotes access to all of its collections through a variety of programs, including instruction, tours, and exhibitions. Thus it continues to play a vital role in the life of the university.

ELAINE D. ENGST

Further Reading

Austen, Willard. "The Story of the Library," in *A Half-Century at Cornell: A Retrospect*, Ithaca, New York: The Cornell Daily Sun, 1930

Becker, Carl, *Cornell University: Founders and the Founding*, Ithaca, New York: Cornell University Press, 1964

Bishop, Morris, *A History of Cornell*, Ithaca, New York: Cornell University Press, 1962

Cornell Library Journal (1966–72)

Dimunation, Mark G., and Elaine D. Engst, *A Legacy of Ideas: Andrew Dickson White and the Founding of the Cornell University Library*, Ithaca, New York: Cornell University Library, 1996

Finch, Herbert, editor, *Andrew Dickson White Papers at Cornell University, 1846–1919 Guide to the Microfilm Collection*, Ithaca, New York: Cornell University Library, 1970

Guerlac, Rita, "Cornell's Library," *The Cornell Library Journal* 2 (1967)

The Library Bulletin of Cornell University (1885–96)

White, Horatio S., *Willard Fiske, Life and Correspondence: A Biographical Study*, New York: Oxford University Press, 1925

Dartmouth College Library

Address: Dartmouth College Library
Dartmouth College
Hanover, New Hampshire 03755
USA
Telephone: 603-646-2236
Fax: 603-646-3702
www.dartmouth.edu/library

Founded: 1769

Holdings (2000): Volumes: 2.3 million. Current serials: 26,000; films and videos: 4,000; manuscripts: 13,000 linear feet; maps: 180,000; microforms: 2.5 million; sound recordings: 29,000.

Special Collections: *Areas of Concentration:* Alumni papers; fine printing; modern British and U.S. literature; New England railroads; New Hampshire history; polar regions. *Individual Collections:* Bryant Spanish collection; Chase-Streeter railroad collection; *Don Quixote*; New Hampshire imprints collection; Hickmott Shakespeare collection; Sine collection of British illustrated books; Spiral Press; Stefansson collection on polar exploration; Stinehour Press; George Ticknor collection. *Papers:* Grenville Clark; Robert Frost; Barry Moser; Maxfield Parrish; Kenneth Roberts; Augustus Saint-Gaudens; Vilhjalmur Stefansson; Genevieve Taggard.

Origins

The library collections of Dartmouth College predate the founding of the institution by nearly five years. In 1764, a group of supporters of Eleazar Wheelock presented him with a quantity of books to be used in the new institution. Thus, when Wheelock received the charter for Dartmouth College in 1769, the institution already possessed a library of nearly 300 volumes, primarily primers, religious tracts, Bibles, and theological works. Most of these titles remain in the library's collections today.

This collection in Hanover, New Hampshire, the home of Dartmouth College, was under the care of Bezaleel Woodward and was maintained in his home. The historian Jeremy Belknap noted in 1774 that, "The College Library is kept at Mr. Woodward's. It is not large, but there are some very good books in it" (Belknap, 1950). Not until the completion of Dartmouth Hall in 1792 was the library housed in a college building. By that time, two literary societies, the United Fraternity and the Social Friends, were present on campus, and each had a library that proved more useful to the students than the college library. The society libraries were not only larger but also provided more access to holdings and had books that were more relevant to undergraduate studies.

The 19th Century

By the first decade of the 19th century, the library numbered 3,000 volumes, including primers, duplicates, and other books of little relevance to the curriculum. Use of the library was limited to one hour per week, with freshmen limited to one book, sophomores and juniors to two, and seniors to three. The first printed catalog of 1809 listed the 3,000 volumes, fully one-third of which were duplicates.

The controversy known as the Dartmouth College Case, *Trustees v. Woodward*, wreaked havoc on both undergraduate education and the library at Dartmouth. In that battle, the State of New Hampshire attempted to change the royal charter and create a Dartmouth University. Students and faculty loyal to Dartmouth College fought through the state and federal courts to gain a judgment from the Supreme Court in 1819 that returned control of the institution and its assets to the college. In the four years of the struggle, however, the library had been moved, confiscated, liberated, and moved again. The resulting loss of books was devastating. In the year the judgment was handed down, Worcester printer Isaiah Thomas, founder of the American Antiquarian Society, presented the college with 470 volumes, a gift that greatly assisted in the rebuilding of the library.

The library was moved to Reed Hall in 1839. Six years later the librarian stated that it would require $10,000 to bring the library to a level comparable to other institutions of higher learning. No funds were made available until George Shattuck presented $2,000 and Roswell Shurtleff presented $1,000 in 1852 for the purchase of books. Both noted, however, that no books purchased with these funds were to be borrowed by undergraduates. Lack of access by undergraduates was exacerbated by

Librarian Oliver Hubbard, who simply closed the library in 1859 to students who did not have a special order from a professor. In 1860 the combined libraries on campus (including the medical school and the society libraries) held 35,000 volumes, only 15,000 of which were in the college library. Hours were less restricted as the college library was open one and one-half hours per day in 1864, and the trustees approved the creation of a newspaper and periodical room.

Librarian Edwin Sanborn noted in 1870 that the library contained no books on U.S. literature—no books by Nathaniel Hawthorne, James Fenimore Cooper, Ralph Waldo Emerson, or Washington Irving—and no materials illustrative of the history of the college. He felt that the history of the college would be lost without immediate action. An appropriation of $1,000 per year was required to bring the collections up to a level required by the curriculum. Four years later, the literary societies agreed to merge their collections with the college library and place them under the administration of a full-time librarian. Other aspects of the agreement included opening the library several hours per day, identifying funds to allow undergraduates to select books, and a uniform fee ($6) collected from all students to support the library.

The first building constructed as a library for the college, Wilson Hall, was completed in 1885 at a cost of $67,000. As the shelving was late in arriving, students were enlisted to move all 60,000 volumes in three days to the new facility, just in time for commencement. After the construction of Wilson Hall, the library and its endowment continued to grow. By 1911 its endowment was valued at $100,000.

Baker Library

Following World War I the college had an enrollment of nearly 2,000 students and a library that was much too small, in both physical size and number of volumes. Rival institutions noted that it was the only college among its peers that had a gymnasium larger that its library. Within a few short months the college was given two gifts that rectified the problem. George Fisher Baker presented the college with a gift of $1 million for a new library, to be named after his uncle Fisher Ames Baker, and Edwin W. Sanborn presented the college with $2 million to endow library support. Baker Library opened in 1928 with 240,000 volumes in the collection and a capacity of 500,000 volumes. The following year Sanborn House (for the English faculty and library) and Carpenter Hall (for the art faculty and library) opened. These two satellite libraries presaged an era of decentralized libraries at Dartmouth.

The white walls of the Reserve Reading Room in Baker Library proved a challenge for José Clemente Orozco when he was artist-in-residence at the college. He requested and received permission to create a series of frescoes entitled *An Epic of American Civilization* from 1932 to 1934. The frescoes, with their harsh Marxist view of the European invasion of the Americas, were immediately controversial on campus as well as internationally. These murals remain a focus for visitors to Baker Library.

Classification

The first system used for classification of books was created at Dartmouth and divided books broadly into categories such as *R* (religion), *F* (fiction), *H* (history), and *G* (geography and travel). In 1901 Cutter numbers were added to further refine the classification. The Dewey Decimal Classification system was introduced in 1920, and no further materials were classified by the old Dartmouth-plus-Cutter scheme. In 1964 the Library of Congress classification was instituted for all new acquisitions. Reclassification of materials from the old Dartmouth scheme and the Dewey scheme continues today.

More Construction

Just 13 years after Baker Library was completed, a stack annex was constructed to hold 500,000 volumes. Inner courtyards in Baker were filled to house stacks and work areas 15 years later. Cook Mathematics Library was opened in 1961. A year later Paddock Music Library was completed in the new Hopkins Center for the Performing Arts and expanded in 1986 to allow for continued growth of the collection. Dartmouth Medical School, the oldest medical school in the United States, finally had its own library when the Dana Biomedical Library was constructed in 1963. Kresge Physical Sciences Library was opened in 1973, and the following year saw the completion of Feldberg Library, housing the collections of the Tuck School of Business Administration and the Thayer School of Engineering.

Two hundred years after its founding, the library celebrated its one-millionth volume with the acquisition of Anne Bradstreet's *The Tenth Muse* (1650) in 1968. Charles N. Haskins, chair of the library building committee, wrote in 1925 that the collections tend to double every 25 years. This equation continues to hold true, as the library celebrated its 2-millionth volume in 1994 with the acquisition of the Edward Sine Collection of British Illustrated Books.

The Otto Years

Margaret Otto became the 16th librarian of the college in 1979. The period following her appointment was an era of great change. In her first year, the library made an initial commitment to produce an online catalog. The initial public version of that catalog was made available in July 1980. Based on the joint efforts of BRS, Inc. (of Scotia, New York), and the library's Automation Department, the online catalog was a very early effort in providing online access to library holdings. By the middle of the decade, the catalog was both stable and robust and was declared a success. Resistance from some users of the library to automation required that the manual catalogs be maintained for several more years. The manual catalog was closed in 1991.

In July of 1988, the library and computing services jointly proposed the creation of the Dartmouth College Information System (DCIS), a navigational tool that would allow users to locate and use catalogs, databases, and other electronic resources quickly and efficiently. After two years of development, DCIS was made public in 1990. As new resources were added to the system and as the system was refined during a decade of use, DCIS has proved to be a remarkable tool for locating and identifying information resources. The addition of a web-based interface in 1998 enhanced the international usefulness of DCIS.

Space for collections, for staff, and for patrons continued to be a problem. A storage facility less than a mile from campus was erected in 1981 and expanded in 1992. That same year, Matthews-Fuller Health Sciences Library was opened in the new hospital complex to serve hospital and clinical staff. Baker Library, with the administrative and technical services staff as well as humanities and social sciences collections and reference staff, remained an issue. The solution to this overcrowding was a generous gift from John Berry, George Berry, the Berry Foundation, and George F. Baker III that permitted the construction of a new facility. Situated adjacent to and connected with Baker Library, the Berry Library was opened in 2000, with renovation scheduled for completion in 2002.

In 1996 Bruce and Diana Rauner provided the resources to renovate Webster Hall, an historic auditorium dating to 1907, into a library for special collections. Rauner Library was opened in the winter of 1998 and dedicated in 1999. The library houses the archives of the college, manuscript collections, photographic collections, and rare books. Centrally located on the College Green, it is a remarkable reuse of a classic building. The strong emphasis placed on the use of primary research materials in undergraduate education makes this library a focus for undergraduate students.

With Otto's retirement in 2000, more than two decades of growth of facilities, development of strong collections, and advances in electronic access to resources came to an end. However, the emphasis on ease of access to materials, strong support of undergraduate education, and strong scholarly collections will continue under future leadership. The library is a member of the online bibliographic service OCLC, the Research Libraries Group (RLG), the Association of Research Libraries (ARL), and the New England Research Libraries.

PHILIP N. CRONENWETT

Further Reading

Belknap, Jeremy, *Journey to Dartmouth in 1774*, edited by Edward C. Lathem, Hanover, New Hampshire: Dartmouth Publications, 1950

Chase, Frederick, *A History of Dartmouth College and the Town of Hanover, New Hampshire*, 2 vols., edited by John King Lord, Cambridge, Massachusetts: Wilson, 1891–1913; 2nd edition, Brattleboro, Vermont: Vermont Printing, 1913–28

Dartmouth College Library, *The Isaiah Thomas Donation, Library of Dartmouth College,* Hanover, New Hampshire: Dartmouth College Library, 1949

Dartmouth College Library Bulletin, 1–5 (1931–53), and new series (1957–)

Morin, Richard W., "Dartmouth College Libraries," in *Encyclopedia of Library and Information Science,* edited by Allen Kent et al., vol. 6, New York: Dekker, 1969

Documentation and Information Center of the Chinese Academy of Sciences

Address: Documentation and Information Center of the Chinese Academy of Sciences
8 Kexueyuan Nanlu, Zhongguancun Road
Beijing 100080
China
Telephone: 10-62566847
Fax: 10-62566846
www.las.ac.cn

Founded: 1951

Holdings (2000): Volumes: 5.6 million. Current serials: 6,000; microforms: 1.1 million; scientific reports: 744,000; stone tablet rubbings: 30,000; thread-bound Chinese classic books: 500,000.

Special Collections: *Areas of Concentration:* Natural sciences, including astronomy, biology, chemistry, geography, mathematics, physics. *Individual Collections:* Chinese classic books from the Ming and Qing dynasties.

History

The Chinese Academy of Sciences (CAS) was established by the government immediately after the People's Republic of China was founded in 1949. In April 1950 a book management division was organized under the general office of CAS to take charge of managing library materials for the whole academy. In February 1951 it was renamed the Library of Academia Sinica (LAS). At that time the Associate Director of the Academy, Meng-he Tao, became the first dean of the library.

The decade of the 1950s was a period of immense growth in Chinese scientific research, highlighted by the "Marching toward Science" call issued by the government in 1956. LAS was no exception, recording remarkable growth in both holdings and personnel and soon possessing one of the most comprehensive scientific collections in the country. After surviving the Cultural Revolution (1966–76) and entering the renaissance of Chinese economics, the First CAS National Conference on Library and Information Work (1978) forged a plan for an integrated library and information system within the CAS. The library enhanced its information services, and in November 1985 it was officially renamed the Documentation and Information Center of the Chinese Academy of Sciences (DICCAS), although it is still commonly referred to as LAS.

As implied by its name, this documentation and information center not only has responsibility for a full range of library duties such as acquisition, circulation, and bibliographic and reference services, but it also provides various information services including online retrieval, database construction, and information analysis. The tasks of the DICCAS were redefined at the Second CAS National Conference on Library and Information Work in 1986 to cover most of the standard features of library organization, including applied research in information and automation studies.

Currently the center has a staff of 370, of which 290 are trained professionals, approximately 60 with senior professional ranking and another 100 with midlevel ranking. The main facility is located at "Science City" in the Zhongguancun area of Beijing. A new library facility is under construction and is expected to open in 2002.

Collections

DICCAS is characterized by its collections in the natural sciences and in advanced technological areas. To serve the research orientation and long-term plans of the CAS, the center collects as comprehensively as possible in the natural sciences, the fields of mathematics, physics, chemistry, astronomy, geography, biology, etc., and in newly emerging disciplines on the frontiers of science and technology.

By the early 1960s, the library had more than 1 million patent documents from 22 countries and 285,000 reels of microfilm, mainly U.S. government publications. Its scientific reports now exceed 744,000 volumes. DICCAS is also responsible for the exchange of scientific and technical publications with more than 60 foreign countries and regions, considerably augmenting its own collections.

In addition to the scientific and technical collections, the center holds significant collections of Chinese classic books such as local chronicles and collected works of the Ming and Qing dynasties. Its approximately 500,000 volumes of thread-bound Chinese classic books form a nationally renowned collection.

Services

Although its first service priority is the needs of its local users, DICCAS also serves external readers. Five basic reading rooms provide access to scientific and technical periodicals, microfilms, rare books, and library and information science materials. Additional rooms are specifically devoted to scientific information retrieval and patent searching. A document supply service handles circulation, reservations, and interlibrary loan requests, with fee-based services available to all users. Document searching and delivery are assisted by other facilities in Beijing and abroad, by Bell and Howell and by the British Library.

DICCAS operates various online bibliographic searching services, including its own Online Public Access Catalog (OPAC) covering its holdings and those of four regional CAS libraries; a union catalog of serials for holdings of CAS and other major academic libraries; and a bibliographical database of dissertations held by the center. Both the OPAC and the union catalog are accessible via the Internet. In 1993 DICCAS initiated a resource-sharing network called APTLIN (a rough acronym for Academy of Sciences, Peking University, and Tsinghua University Library Information Network). Through the National Computing and Networking Facility of China (NCFC; Beijing) and CAS's own telecommunication network, users of CAS in the Zhongguancun area of Beijing have access to the bibliographical databases in DICCAS, the Peking University Library, and the Tsinghua University Library, totaling 3.5 million records. International and domestic online retrieval services are also available at DICCAS and at major CAS institutes and branches. The center recently launched its Mobile Online Service, which gives users yet another means of searching online. Currently the center is developing CAS Internet Portal Sites for various scientific and technical areas. It is also one of the core forces in a digital library project initiated by the APTLIN participants and the National Library of China (Beijing).

Available Publications

In collaboration with related CAS research institutes, DICCAS sponsors the compilation and publication of 13 scientific and technical abstract periodicals, with printed and CD-ROM products produced simultaneously. Abstracting publications cover the fields of mathematics, physics, mechanics, optics, radio electronics, astronomy, geography (two versions), Chinese territorial resources, biology, and paleontology.

Eight of these 13 titles are now online and searchable through the center's Website. A *Chinese Sci-Tech Documents Database* (available since 1983), with entries in English, is also produced from these abstracts and served via Wide Area Information Server (WAIS) software. Among other important databases published by the center are the *Chinese Science Citation Index* (since 1989) and the *CAS Practical Sci-Tech Products Database*, encompassing information on products produced by more than 100 CAS research institutes and 300 companies.

Several well-known comprehensive library and information reference sources and tools compiled by DICCAS have earned their place in Chinese librarianship. These include thesauri of physics and mathematics, a bibliography of Chinese rare books in DICCAS, a CAS textbook of library and information service, and *Précis of the General Bibliography for the Sequel of Si Ku Quan Shu, the Section of Confucian Classics* (1993). The LAC classification system is one of three major classification systems used in China and has been adopted by hundreds of academic and research libraries since its publication in 1958.

The Role of DICCAS in the CAS Library and Information System

DICCAS is involved in the construction of an academy-wide CAS Library and Information System. The system consists of one national center (DICCAS); four regional centers in the cities of Shanghai, Wuhan, Lanzhou, and Chengdu; and 123 library and information service divisions of the CAS institutes distributed all over the country. It has evolved into a system with multiple disciplines, levels, and functions. DICCAS is charged with providing professional guidance to all library and information functions within the entire CAS system. It produced and has been maintaining the classification system, cataloging rules, and manuals used throughout the CAS system.

The CAS Library and Information System holds regular seminars on library and information science. It sponsors various professional training courses and is one of the few institutions in China to offer master and doctoral programs in library and information science.

International Activities

DICCAS is active in international exchanges extending to more than 1,500 institutions in 60 countries and regions. In 1981 it became an institutional member of the International Federation of Library Associations and Institutions (IFLA). It takes an active part in activities sponsored by the Advisory Group of Technical Committee 46 (TC 46) of the International Standards Organization (ISO); TC 46 deals with information and documentation. During the 1990s it began cooperative arrangements with the Research Libraries Group (RLG) in the United States and with Fachinformationszentrum Karlsruhe (FIZKA) in Germany in the areas of library automation and online retrieval. It maintains a librarian exchange program with Seton Hall University Library (South Orange, New Jersey) in the United States. Many of the center's staff members have studied in the United States, Germany, Russia, Great Britain, Canada, Japan, and Australia, and the center regularly welcomes scholars and specialists from many countries and regions.

MARCIA LEI ZENG

Further Reading

The Documentation and Information Center of the Chinese Academy of Sciences (DICCAS), Beijing: DICCAS, 1996

Fang, Josephine Riss, "People's Republic of China, Libraries in," in *Encyclopedia of Library and Information Science*, edited by Allen Kent et al., vol. 22, New York: Dekker, 1977

Lin, Sharon Chien, *Libraries and Librarianship in China*, Westport, Connecticut: Greenwood Press, 1998

Meng, Guang-jun, "Zhongguo Kexueyuan Wenxian Qingbao Zhongxin (Documentation and Information Center of the Chinese Academy of Sciences)," in *Zhongguo da baike quanshu: Tushuguanxue, qingbaoxue, danganxue* (Chinese Encyclopedia: Library Science, Information Science, Archival Science), Beijing: Zhongguo Da Beike Quanshu, 1993

Wu, K.T., "China, Libraries in the People's Republic of," in *Encyclopedia of Library and Information Science,* edited by Allen Kent et al., vol. 4, New York: Dekker, 1970

Duke University Libraries

Address:	William R. Perkins Library Duke University Box 90193 Durham, North Carolina 27708 USA Telephone: 919-660-5800 Fax: 919-660-5923 www.lib.duke.edu
Founded:	1887 as Trinity College Library; 1924 as Duke University Library
Holdings (2000):	Volumes: 5 million. Archives and manuscripts: 27,000 linear feet, including 300 medieval manuscripts; audio recordings: 40,000; current serials: 33,000; films and videos: 11,000; graphic material: 232,000; maps: 132,000; microforms: 4 million; papyri: 1,000.
Special Collections:	*Areas of Concentration:* Advertising history; African and African American studies; ancient, medieval, and Renaissance studies; British history; German studies; history and culture of the U.S. South; history of economic thought; literature in English; religion in the United States and Britain; women's studies. *Individual Collections:* Frank Baker collection of Wesleyana and Methodistica; Harold Jantz collection of German baroque literature and German Americana; Abram and Frances Pascher Kanof collection of Jewish art, archeology, and symbolism; Guido Mazzoni collection of rare Italian imprints; Glenn Negley collection of utopian literature; Trent collection of Walt Whitman manuscripts, imprints, and iconography. *Papers:* Kenneth Arrow; William Watts Ball; Robert Carter; Phyllis Chesler; John Hope Franklin; James Iredell; J. Walter Thompson Company; Carl Menger; Kate Millett; Oskar Morgenstern; Douglass North; Outdoor Advertising Association of America; Don Patinkin;
Special Collections (cont.):	Reynolds Price; William Styron; Anne Tyler; U.S. Socialist Party. Specialized research collections within the library are the John W. Hartman Center for Sales, Advertising and Marketing History; the John Hope Franklin Collection for African and African American Documentation; the Sallie Bingham Center for Women's History and Culture; the Jay B. Hubbell Center for American Literary Historiography.

The Trinity College Era

Duke University began in 1838 as Brown's Schoolhouse, a private subscription school in Randolph County, North Carolina. It shortly became known as Union Institute Academy, named for the society of Methodists and Quakers who sought its state charter in 1841. In 1851 it was rechartered as Normal College and in 1859 renamed Trinity College in affiliation with the Methodist Church.

The history of Duke libraries begins with the debating societies of these schools (the Columbian and the Hesperian Literary Societies), which began collecting books to support their debating programs. Trinity College itself had a small collection, as did the Theological Society of the college in the 1860s. However, it was not until John Franklin Crowell became president in 1887 that these scattered collections were brought together as a college library, estimated at 9,000 volumes. President Crowell was so interested in the organization and strengthening of the library as a resource for learning that he cataloged every book himself. He also began subscriptions to major periodicals and gathered government documents, state publications, surveys, and census reports. In 1892 during Crowell's tenure, Trinity College moved to the "New South" city of Durham, North Carolina, at the urging of two of its leaders: Washington Duke, who gave $85,000 toward the move, and Julian Shakespeare Carr, who provided the site for the new college campus.

Crowell's successor, John Carlisle Kilgo, made the library a priority during his administration, emphasizing in his 1894 inaugural address that the college library, housed in a part of the Washington Duke building, represented a "good beginning" but had growing needs. As a consequence, he appointed the college's first full-time professional librarian, Joseph Penn

Breedlove, who served the college and university for more than 40 years (1898–1939) as head librarian. Breedlove had arrived on campus expecting to keep the library open several hours a day while pursuing graduate studies, but the needs of the library were so great that he was persuaded to make it a career. His enthusiasm was bolstered in part by the announcement that one of Washington Duke's sons, Benjamin Newton Duke, had given Trinity a gift of $50,000, half of which was to be used for library endowment. After studying librarianship at Amherst College, Breedlove introduced the Dewey Decimal System of classification, established an authority source for subject headings, and began keeping accession books. With his own funds he bought a typewriter for producing library cards, college funding for that purchase having been denied.

In 1900 another son of Washington Duke, tobacco magnate James Buchanan Duke, gave the college money to erect a library building, which was completed at the end of 1902. The move to the new library during the winter holidays proved traumatic, as President Kilgo insisted that Breedlove take his holiday while Kilgo superintended the move. The president shortly gave that responsibility over to the groundskeepers, and Breedlove returned to spend the next two months reorganizing the books prior to the official dedication of the new building. Walter Hines Page gave the dedicatory address. In preparation for the event, he asked James B. Duke if he had a message to convey. Duke's reply was, "Tell every man to think for himself," and Page repeated this to the listening crowd. Then he continued, "By that authority, therefore, I dedicate this library to free thought, reverent always, always earnest, but always free. I dedicate it to free thought, not about some subjects only, but about all subjects, the free thought that is the very atmosphere of an ideal democracy" (Breedlove, 1955). This freedom was soon tested on the college campus when Professor John Spencer Bassett, editorializing in the *South Atlantic Quarterly,* dared to praise the life of Booker T. Washington and rank him second only to Robert E. Lee as a Southern leader. There followed angry protests and demands for Bassett's firing, with the faculty, president, and ultimately the board of trustees defending the college's strong stance on the right of intellectual freedom and Bassett's right to express himself.

Among the defenders of the right to free speech was William Preston Few, who served as professor of English, chairman of the library committee, and manager of the library. It was Few who succeeded Kilgo as the next university president (1910–40), and his interest in library affairs remained strong during his presidency. Few urged that the library's collection of materials relating to the history and culture of the southern United States be increased, as he recognized that there were collecting opportunities available that would not continue for long. Funds were raised, donations increased, and the number of books in the library rose from 43,967 to 63,240. Another notable event of the era was that in 1919, women taking classes at the college were given full and equal library privileges, including the right to enter the library during any of its regular hours.

Duke University

In December 1924 the momentous announcement of James B. Duke's creation of a trust fund of $40 million to support educational and charitable purposes in the Carolinas occurred just as the Trinity College Library was outgrowing its stack space. Part of this gift was to be used to build Duke University, named in honor of the family of Washington Duke. The old Trinity College campus became the Woman's College campus (now East Campus) of Duke University, and a new West Campus was built for the men. Both campuses gained new library buildings by 1930. Most of the 235,000 books in the collections went to the General Library on the West Campus, and some specialized collections, supplemented by new purchases, went to the Woman's College Library on the East Campus. Other specialized collections were sent to the law, biology, chemistry, engineering, and hospital libraries. The new university also established a School of Religion Library. President Few named Professor William Kenneth Boyd director of libraries (1930–34) to coordinate their activities and promote their development.

Although the Depression struck soon after the establishment of the new university library system, the university was in the enviable position of having sufficient endowment to continue building a strong research library. In 1931–32 the university allocated more than $240,000 to collection development, an acquisitions expenditure second only to Harvard University's that year. The generous endowment of the Flowers family's George Washington Flowers Memorial Fund and the collecting zeal of history professor Boyd combined to increase the library's documentation of Southern history and culture in particular. Cumulative effects of the Depression did reduce collection development budgets from the peak year of 1931–32, but the library continued to build strong serials collections while allocating less to monographs. The manuscript collections continued to grow through the largess of the Flowers Fund.

After World War II, the university library on the West Campus had outgrown its capacity for books and library services. Parts of the collections had to be packed in boxes and stored off-site, and even new acquisitions went into storage for lack of space to catalog and shelve them. Again a member of the Duke family provided a gift that made an expansion of the library possible. Mary Duke Biddle's gift of $1.5 million resulted in a doubling of the space in the main library by 1949. In that year cataloged holdings numbered more than 960,000 volumes. The library system consisted of the general library, the Woman's College Library, the Divinity School Library, the Law Library, the Hospital Library, and departmental libraries for biology/forestry, chemistry, physics/mathematics, and the College of Engineering. The manuscript collection contained more than one million items. The acquisition of the one-millionth library book was celebrated in September 1950.

Within ten years University Librarian Benjamin E. Powell (1946–75) let the administration know that the library again needed to be expanded. A major planning effort was underway by 1961. Construction began in 1965, and dedication of the expanded library took place in April 1970 with the naming of the library after William R. Perkins, who was general counsel to the founders of the university and author of the Duke Endowment. It was Perkins's son, Thomas L. Perkins, who presented the library with its 2-millionth volume in 1969.

As the production of print materials in the late 20th century continued to accelerate, stretching library budgets to their limits, the Duke Libraries grew swiftly. The acquisition of the 3-millionth volume came in 1979, the 4-millionth in 1992, and the 5-millionth in 2000. The university turned to off-site library facilities to handle the growth of the collections. The first off-site stacks facility opened in 1989 with a capacity of about 650,000 books. With that facility filled, construction for a new modular off-site facility with modern automated retrieval systems got underway in 2000.

Regional Library Cooperation

The first cooperative agreement among libraries in the region began when Duke University and the University of North Carolina established a Joint Committee on Intellectual Cooperation in 1933. The committee's first recommendation concerned libraries and led to liberalized lending agreements. By 1934 through grant funding, each had a copy of the other's author card catalog, which was added to each year thereafter. Regular delivery service for interlibrary loans between Duke and the University of North Carolina began in 1935. In addition to making borrowing between the two institutions easier, in the following years the libraries also sought to end duplication of expensive purchases and pursued grant funding for joint purchases. They agreed on geographic divisions for acquiring state publications and Latin American materials. Attempts at regional cooperation were expanded in 1953 with the Inter-University Committee on Library Cooperation, which included Duke, the University of North Carolina, the State College of Agriculture and Engineering (now North Carolina State University) in Raleigh, and Woman's College in Greensboro. In that effort, agreements were reached on interlibrary loan of books to faculty and graduate students and expanded borrowers' privileges for undergraduate students.

In 1976 University Librarian Connie Dunlap (1975–80), together with the library directors at the University of North Carolina at Chapel Hill and North Carolina State University, began discussion of a long-range plan to broaden cooperative agreements among local libraries. As a result, a major step in regional library cooperation took place in 1977 with the creation of the Triangle Universities Libraries Cooperation Committee, formed to develop a support system for resource sharing in the Durham-Raleigh-Chapel Hill region that had become known as the Research Triangle. This evolved to the Triangle Research Libraries Network (TRLN) in 1980. During the tenure of University Librarian and Director of the Perkins Library System Elvin E. Strowd (interim university librarian, 1981; university librarian, 1982–84), TRLN adopted a memorandum making its primary mission systems development for shared online catalogs and other automated library systems. With participation from Duke University, the University of North Carolina at Chapel Hill, North Carolina State University, and North Carolina Central University, TRLN in 2000 included ten member libraries with holdings approaching 12 million volumes encompassing business, health sciences, law, humanities, engineering, sciences and technology, and the social sciences. Its mission was defined broadly to include cooperative collection development, resource sharing, technical innovation, and collaborative efforts to gain resources to advance information access in the region.

Automation and Strategic Planning

The first automation group in the library was formed in 1968 to bring new efficiency to work flow in the processing of library materials. Duke's Technical Services Database was an early example of libraries' application of automation to record keeping for acquisitions. In 1978 Duke libraries joined the online bibliographic service OCLC to gain access to machine-readable records. Through the efforts of its own library systems department and that of TRLN, Duke unveiled its first public online catalog, known as the Bibliographic Information System (BIS), in July 1986. In 1988 bar coding of materials began and the first computer cluster was installed in the library for general student use. The number of computers in use by library staff steadily grew, and by 1990 the library built a local area network for approximately 90 personal computers. The 1990s also brought electronic access to expanded resources through memberships in the Research Libraries Group (RLG) and the Center for Research Libraries.

Innovation and automation became the focus of activities in many library departments. Electronic resources consumed more of the library budget and staff and users' attention. The Reference Department dedicated a major portion of its instructional classes to automated information access. Staff shared their World Wide Web searching skills with local schoolteachers in collaborative outreach to the local community. Finishing retrospective conversion of the old card catalog was a major priority in the library's Technical Services Department, and the question of whether to convert from the Dewey Decimal System of classification to that of the Library of Congress rose again. Although the debate about conversion goes back to the 1930s on campus, in 2000 Duke remained one of the few U.S. academic research libraries continuing to use the Dewey system. Accelerated document delivery within TRLN was a goal of Interlibrary Loan, and the Public Documents and Maps Department sought to create better online access to its federal and state depository holdings. Website development became a priority for the general library as well as many of the branches. The Rare Book, Manuscript, and Special Collections Library moved ahead with electronic access through its collaboration in the Digital Scriptorium, creating scanned images within expanded information contexts for such varied collections as papyri, photographs, sheet music, African American, women's studies, and advertising.

As Duke University librarians grappled with rapid changes in information technology along with rising expectations of library users in the 1990s, University Librarian Jerry D. Campbell (1985–95) introduced total quality management principles, to challenge traditional thinking and encourage innovation from all levels of staff. Library-wide involvement in strategic planning was a hallmark of his tenure. David S. Ferriero, who became university librarian in 1996, emphasized the library's role as a shared center of the university's intellectual life. More public programming, including readings, lectures, and exhibitions, took place in the library. A second emphasis was on strengthening the library as a center for research and teaching, a goal reflected in the creation of the Center for Instructional Technology within the library. Preservation also became a priority, resulting in the creation of a new permanent position of preservation officer and the securing of funds for a conservation laboratory. Finally, a major fundraising effort aimed at renovation of the library fulfilled the goal of strengthening the library's infrastructure to make it a technologically up-to-date and physically inviting place to work.

Present Organization

The Perkins Library system at Duke University consists of the main library, which also houses the Rare Book, Manuscript, and Special Collections Library; the Lilly Library and Music Library on East Campus; the Vesic Library for Engineering, Mathematics, and Physics; the Biological and Environmental Sciences Library; and the Chemistry Library. In addition, the Pearse Memorial Library is associated with the Marine Laboratory at Beaufort, North Carolina. The University Archives, a separate administrative unit under the office of the president, maintains the permanent records of the university. There are four independent professional school libraries: the Divinity School Library, the Fuqua School of Business Library, the School of Law Library, and the Medical Center Library. All of the Duke libraries emphasize service to their user communities and have a strong history of cooperation in building a union catalog, keeping duplication of materials to a minimum, and sharing electronic resources.

LINDA MCCURDY

Further Reading

Breedlove, Joseph Penn, *Duke University Library, 1840–1940*, Durham, North Carolina: Friends of Duke University Library, 1955

Byrd, Gary D., et al., "Lessons from the History of the Triangle Research Libraries Network . . . The Evolution of a Cooperative Online Network," in *Library Journal* 110 (1985)

Duke University Libraries (1987–)

Durden, Robert F., *The Launching of Duke University, 1924–1949*, Durham, North Carolina: Duke University Press, 1993

Library Notes 1–51/52 (1936–85) (published by Duke University Library)

Powell, Benjamin Edward, "Duke University Library," in *Encyclopedia of Library and Information Science*, edited by Allen Kent et al., vol. 7, New York: Dekker, 1972

Sharpe, John L., III, and Esther Evans, editors, *Gnomon: Essays for the Dedication of the William R. Perkins Library, April 16, 1970*, Durham, North Carolina: Duke University Library, 1970

Durham Dean and Chapter Library

Address: Durham Dean and Chapter Library
The College
Durham, DH1 3EH
UK
Telephone: 191-386-2489
Fax: 191-386-4267
www.durhamcathedral.co.uk

Founded: 995

Holdings (1999): Volumes: 75,000. Incunabula: 60; manuscripts: 2,000, including 360 medieval manuscripts.

Special Collections: *Areas of Concentration:* Early music (primarily 17th century); pre-Reformation manuscripts from the monastic priory. *Individual Collections:* Priory and post-Reformation Dean and Chapter archives. *Papers:* George Allan; Christopher Hunter; Joseph Barber Lightfoot; James Raine; Ian Ramsey; Thomas Randall; Sir Cuthbert Sharp; Robert Surtees.

Early History

Durham Dean and Chapter Library (informally known as Durham Cathedral Library) has a continuous history dating back to before the foundation of the monastic priory by Bishop William of St. Calais in 1083, although its fortunes and purposes have fluctuated over the centuries. The first generation of monks, drawn from existing communities at Wearmouth and Jarrow, brought books with them, including the seventh-century gospel book associated with St. Cuthbert and now known as the Lindisfarne Gospels. St. Calais himself gave 46 books, and the monastic collection grew as the priory developed into one of the major English Benedictine houses of the medieval period. The books were originally cared for by the precentor, but by the end of the 13th century a separate office of *librarius* was recognized. The earliest library lists (from the mid-12th century) are incomplete, but inventories of the 1390s reveal a collection of almost 900 volumes. At that time the collections were largely divided between two locations, the Cloister (for the texts most used for current study) and the Spendement (a secure store where older texts were kept), but between 1414 and 1418 a new purpose-built library room was constructed; it was 60 by 17 feet and located at an upper-floor level off the Cloister. No plan of its layout survives, but manuscript pressmarks show that it contained eight double-sided presses and two single-sided ones. A number of other book cupboards were made during the 15th century.

We do not know exactly how large the library had grown by the time of the dissolution of the monasteries in 1539, but there would have been considerably more than a thousand volumes, both manuscript and printed. The monks began to use printed books at least as early as the 1470s; the earliest acquisitions seem to have come through the dependent cell at Durham College, Oxford, and books were regularly transferred between the two sites. The contents of the library were largely theological, but far from entirely so; like any sizable monastic collection, Durham included classics, law, medicine, chronicles, and other subjects.

In 1539 the priory was refounded as a secular cathedral, governed by a dean and chapter, and a period of transition and uncertainty ensued. The history of the library during the rest of the 16th century is unclear, and many books were dispersed or destroyed. This was a common pattern in all the English cathedrals of that time, although Durham was more fortunate than most in the survival rate of its pre-Reformation books; more than 630 are extant today, of which 330 are still in situ in Durham. There were a few additions to the collection during the later 16th century, but on the whole the evidence suggests that this was a period of decline and neglect, when there was little interest in a communal library and items were easily removed.

The library's rebirth began in 1617, when one of the prebendaries, Francis Bunny, bequeathed £30 to equip a new library. In 1628 a chapter act (a resolution of the Durham Chapter) was passed to create an ongoing purchase fund for books, and a period of rapid activity ensued, with nearly 300 new books acquired during the next few years. John Cosin, later bishop of Durham but then one of the prebendaries, was a driving force behind the initiative. A donors' book was begun and the new post of librarian created, filled by one of the minor canons, Elias Smith, who played a major part in the custody and development of the collection from his appointment in 1633 until his death in 1676. He rearranged the books, cataloged them, and helped to preserve them during the uncertain years of the Civil War and Interregnum (1644–60).

At this time the library remained divided between the old monastic library room and the Spendement. After the Restoration, John Sudbury (dean of Durham from 1662 to 1684) decided to build a new library, using a room that had originally been the monks' refectory and then a hall for the minor canons, which had subsequently fallen into disuse. The work was done at Sudbury's expense and continued after his death in 1684, creating a handsome new library, fitted out with oak shelving according to the traditional stall system of library design. The books were transferred in the late 1690s and the room has remained in use ever since.

Four Centuries of Growth

The library's history has been one of continuous growth since 1628, with a steady stream of acquisitions made possible through a purchase fund augmented by donations. The rate of growth has varied considerably, reflecting fluctuating levels of interest among the members of the chapter. The early 18th century was a period of noteworthy activity, when two sizable gifts were received (500 books from John Bowes in 1722 and 150 books from John Morton in 1723). The library was in the care of Thomas Rud (1711–33), who recataloged the manuscripts. The contents of the library reflected the mixture of theology, classics, history, law, medicine, and other subjects that are typical of many historic collections. Trends in collection development are (again, typically) noticeable, so that an emphasis on continental theology in the early 17th century gives way to a higher concentration of contemporary English theology after the Restoration and a growing interest in county histories, travel books, and atlases. Many of the books purchased during the 17th and 18th centuries were acquired from local booksellers, who also bound them; the survival of these volumes, together with the bills and accounts in the chapter archives, make it possible to study the provincial book trade in Durham in some detail.

During the 1850s the library was again expanded by using space occupied by the monastic dormitory, which had been turned into a prebendal lodging. The house was demolished in 1849, exposing the original beamed ceiling, and the room was fitted out with shelving; the adjacent room, which in turn led into the refectory, became the librarian's office. This arrangement remains in place today, with 19th- and 20th-century printed books housed in the dormitory.

Since the 19th century the library has concentrated on developing a working theological collection, to support the work of the cathedral clergy and to provide a learning and teaching resource for theology students of Durham University. The modern collections are now operated very much as a theology library for students, who are the main users. A formal link has been established with the university, and the library is managed by a professional librarian on the university staff whose time is divided evenly between the university and cathedral libraries. The historic collections constitute a major research resource both for the university and for a wide international range of external users.

Durham is one of the largest of the English cathedral libraries, with its outstanding manuscript collections and a stock of about 20,000 pre-1801 printed books. These include a large and unusual collection of northern European university theses from the late 16th to the early 18th centuries, many of which are very rare. The printed book stock also includes about 60 incunabula, many of which belonged to the last generation of Durham monks. All the pre-1801 printed books were recataloged manually, between 1978 and 1982 with a grant from the British Library (London) administered by Durham University. Copies of the cathedral library records are held in the university library, currently only in manual form, but it is hoped that these will be added to the university's automated catalog during the next few years.

DAVID PEARSON

Further Reading

Crosby, Brian, compiler, *A Catalogue of Durham Cathedral Music Manuscripts,* Oxford and New York: Oxford University Press, 1986

Doyle, A.I., "The Printed Books of the Last Monks of Durham," *The Library* (series 6) 10 (1988)

Hughes, H.D., *A History of Durham Cathedral Library,* Durham: Durham County Advertiser, 1925

Mynors, R.A.B., *Durham Cathedral Manuscripts to the End of the Twelfth Century,* Oxford: Oxford University Press, 1939

Pearson, David, "The Library of John Bowes of Durham," *The Book Collector* 35 (1986)

Pearson, David, "Elias Smith, Durham Cathedral Librarian, 1633–1676," *Library History* 8 (1989)

Piper, Alan J., "The Libraries of the Monks of Durham," in *Medieval Scribes, Manuscripts, and Libraries: Essays Presented to N.R. Ker,* edited by M.B. Parkes and Andrew G. Watson, London: Scolar Press, 1978

Durham University Library

Address: Durham University Library
University of Durham
Stockton Road
Durham DH1 3LY
UK
Telephone: 91-374-3018
Fax: 91-374-7481
www.dur.ac.uk/Library

Founded: 1833

Holdings (2001): Volumes: 1.4 million. Archives and manuscripts: 10,000 linear feet; current serials: 5,000; incunabula: 400; medieval manuscripts: 100; microforms: 150,000; Oriental manuscripts: 100.

Special Collections: *Areas of Concentration:* British history; history of Egypt and the Sudan; local history of northeast England; modern literary manuscripts. *Individual Collections:* Abbott collection; Cosin collection; Mickleton and Spearman medieval manuscripts; miscellaneous collections of autograph letters; Northeast England legal, administrative, and antiquarian manuscripts. *Papers:* Earl Grey (Greys of Howick); Abbas Hilmi II of Egypt; John James Lawson; Malcolm Macdonald; William Plomer; Thomas Wright.

Origins

The founding of the University of Durham by William van Mildert, Bishop of Durham, in association with the Dean and Chapter of Durham Cathedral, was partly a reaction against growing public concern over the income and privileges of the ecclesiastical establishment in Durham, particularly those of its prince bishop. The Act of Parliament by which the university was set up in 1832 created an institution modeled partly on Christ Church, Oxford, with the Dean and Chapter as the governing body and the Bishop as Visitor.

The university library officially began life in January 1833 with a donation of 160 books from van Mildert that were housed in a gallery in Cosin's Library, with which it was associated. The library has since absorbed another significant historical collection (the Bamburgh Library) whose roots lie mainly in the 18th century; thus, the library's historical depth predates the early 19th century. Many of the special collections are housed today in late medieval buildings originally erected as law courts. A board of curators was established to oversee the running of the library.

Cosin's Library

Although the university's book stock was initially small, resources were enhanced by having access to Cosin's Library, which was founded in 1668 as a public library for the Bishopric of Durham. John Cosin graduated from Cambridge in 1614 and was a college fellow there in the early 1620s before becoming a prebendary of Durham Cathedral (1624), master of Peterhouse, Cambridge (1635), and dean of Peterborough (1640). A staunch royalist, he fled during the English Civil War and spent much of the Commonwealth period in Paris as a chaplain to the exiled English court there. In 1660 he returned and was made bishop of Durham.

During the last decade of his life, Cosin devoted much energy to the creation of his library, erecting a new purpose-designed building on the Palace Green, close to Durham Castle and the cathedral. The library is a rectangular room, 52 feet long by 30 feet wide, with a large fireplace and shelving around the walls. It is generally believed to be the first substantial English library designed using wall shelving, rather than the typical 16th- and 17th-century model using presses at right angles to the walls. Cosin was probably influenced by similar designs at the Bibliothèque Mazarine in Paris. Each press is surmounted by portrait roundels, in which the authors depicted represent the subject content beneath. The portraits were painted by Jan Baptist van Eersell using engravings from books in the library as models.

Cosin was a book collector all of his life, and the contents of the library reflect, to some extent, the different stages in his career. It is strong in theological and liturgical texts (he was involved in the 1662 revision of the *Book of Common Prayer*) and includes many rare French Huguenot books and pamphlets acquired during his period in exile. The library was completed shortly before Cosin's death, and his foundation charter of 1669 provided it with a small permanent endowment to provide for a librarian's salary and ongoing maintenance costs. The collection of 5,000 books left by Cosin has survived mostly intact to the present day and has been only slightly increased during the intervening centuries, mostly by small collections of medieval manuscripts from George Davenport, rector of Houghton-le-Spring and chaplain to Cosin, and of printed books by Richard Trevor, bishop of Durham (1752–71). Staff and students of the University of Durham were given access from the beginning, and in 1937 the university became the legal trustee of Cosin's Library.

The University Library in the 19th Century

The university library proper grew slowly during the first few decades of its life, with limited funds for acquisitions. A major transformation came in 1854 when Martin Routh, president of Magdalen College, Oxford, bequeathed his collection to the university. Routh was a theological historian and a great bibliophile who took an interest in the new university at Durham; his library of 15,000 volumes was rich in theology, classics, history, and bibliography (including many of the booksellers' catalogs used in the course of acquiring the collection). Its receipt created the need for new accommodation for the library, and in 1857 it was transferred into the Exchequer Building adjacent to Cosin's Library, which was originally built in 1457 to house the episcopal courts and records of the palatinate. Other smaller gifts received shortly after Routh's bequest included the 2,500-book library of Edward Maltby, bishop of Durham (reduced to 1,600 after a weeding-out exercise in 1929) and the 5,000-book collection of physician Thomas Winterbottom (also reduced by discarding duplicates in the 1920s).

The 19th-century library was neither well stocked nor heavily used. It was staffed by a single librarian and an assistant, had little working space, and was open only a few hours each day. Only graduates were allowed to borrow books from the Routh and Maltby collections until 1885, when undergraduate use was permitted under certain conditions. Librarian Joseph Fowler (1873–1901) is credited with introducing a number of measures to encourage greater use, including cataloging and rearranging of the stock, extension of opening hours, creation of a suggestions book, and introduction of a heating system.

Although a professor of mathematics was included in Durham's establishment from the start, teaching in the university concentrated much more on the arts than the sciences for more than a century, with a particularly strong emphasis on theology. The growth of the library and the development of its collections naturally reflected these subject priorities. The 19th-century curriculum included some provision for lectures in civil engineering and mining, but scientific teaching and research in the northeast came to be centered much more in nearby Newcastle-upon-Tyne, where the School of Medicine was established in 1832 and the College of Physical Science in 1871. Although based in Newcastle, both became formally associated with the University of Durham and awarded Durham degrees.

20th-Century Expansion

Fowler's successor, Edward Stocks (appointed in 1901), continued in this vein, improving the catalog further and creating for the first time a proper reading room for the library. This began a process of expansion that continued throughout the 20th century; in 1929 an adjacent lecture theater was converted to library use, and in 1935 the library was further extended by a mixture of conversion and new building work. Another major extension was built on the site in 1960, and in 1965 a new separate science library building was opened at the university's Stockton Road site, where many of the science departments were based. Continuing growth meant that the Palace Green Library, built around Cosin's Library and the Exchequer Building, eventually became inadequate. A major extension to the Science Library opened in 1984 as the new main university library building; much material was transferred, leaving special collections, law, and music at Palace Green. A separate Oriental section library was created in 1955, but these collections, including an important archive relating to the Sudan, were transferred back to Palace Green after the opening of the new main library.

Reorganization in 1908 created a newly defined federal University of Durham with Durham and Newcastle branches, and in 1937 the medical school and Armstrong College (as the College of Physical Science had been named in 1904) were merged as King's College, Newcastle—still part of the Durham federation but responsible for its own courses and library collections. King's College was split off completely in 1963 to found the University of Newcastle, leaving Durham to expand its scientific activities independently, and several new scientific departments were founded in the 1960s. Increased provision of scientific literature naturally followed from this, and the university library today maintains strong active collections to support teaching and research across many disciplines in both the humanities and the sciences.

In 1958 the Bamburgh Library was transferred to the university library on indefinite loan from Bamburgh Castle in Northumberland. This collection of approximately 8,500 volumes was developed by three successive generations of the Sharp family: John Sharp, Archbishop of York; his sons John and Thomas; and the latter's sons, Thomas and John. It is primarily, therefore, an 18th-century library by formation, but it also includes much material printed before 1700. The collection is wide-ranging in subject; it is strong in theology, classics, literature, and history and has good holdings of early scientific material, particularly in mathematics and natural history.

In 1937 the total book stock was estimated at 55,000 volumes and by the end of the century had increased to approximately 1.3 million, with an estimated annual growth of more than 20,000 volumes a year and 5,400 current periodical subscriptions. The library had a staff of 92 full-time posts, and loan transactions were running at nearly 700,000 per annum. The year 1980 saw the installation of an automated circulation system, and since then much work has been done to transfer all the catalogs (for both the general and the special collections) to an automated platform (work that was still ongoing in 2001).

As a part of the UK higher education system, the University of Durham has both benefited and suffered from the ups and downs of the public funding arrangements that support that sector. A period of major expansion in the 1960s was followed by leaner times in the latter decades of the century, and the fortunes of the library have reflected those trends. The library's managers may look back over those decades and remember a series of financial crises and deferred plans of one sort or another. The new main library of 1984 was itself a scaled-down version of a larger scheme planned in 1974 but canceled for financial reasons. Nevertheless, the library has continued to grow and to cope with ever-increasing demands from greater student numbers and an expanding base of external users interested in the research collections. The holdings of the library proper, coupled with the associated Durham resources of the Cathedral Library and Ushaw College Library (both administered with help from the university library), make Durham an outstanding center for research collections.

DAVID PEARSON

Further Reading

Acomb, Henry Waldo, "The University Library," in *The University of Durham, 1937*, edited by C.E. Whiting, Durham: Durham University, 1937

Doyle, A.I., "Martin Joseph Routh and His Books in Durham University Library," *Durham University Journal* 48 (1955–56)

Doyle, A.I., "Unfamiliar Libraries IV: The Bamburgh Library," *The Book Collector* 8 (1959)

Doyle, A.I., "John Cosin (1594–1672) as a Library Maker," *The Book Collector* 40 (1991)

Fowler, Joseph Thomas, *Durham University: Earlier Foundations and Present Colleges*, London: Robinson, 1904

Whiting, Charles Edwin, *The University of Durham, 1832–1932*, London: Sheldon Press, 1932

Edinburgh University Library

Address: Edinburgh University Library
University of Edinburgh
George Square
Edinburgh EH8 9LJ
Scotland
UK
Telephone: 131-650-3384
Fax: 131-650-3380
www.lib.ed.ac.uk

Founded: 1580

Holdings (2000): Volumes: 2.6 million. Archives and manuscripts: 25,000 linear feet; audiovisual materials: 11,000; incunabula: 377; maps: 110,000; microforms: 267,000; University of Edinburgh dissertations: 29,000.

Special Collections: *Areas of Concentration:* Commonwealth of Nations history; history of medicine and science; law; music; Oriental and medieval manuscripts; Scottish Enlightenment; Shakespeare and Jacobean drama; theology and church history; travel and exploration; 20th-century Scottish and English literature. *Individual Collections:* W.H. Auden collection; Corson Sir Walter Scott collection; Drummond of Hawthornden collection of 17th-century literature; Dugald Stewart collection; Halliwell-Phillipps collections; Keith collection of Sanskrit and Commonwealth law; Arthur Koestler collections of literature and parapsychology; Laing Bequest; Clement Litill Bequest; James Nairn Bequest. *Papers:* John Baillie; James Black; George Mackay Brown; Thomas Chalmers; Christopher Murray Grieve (Hugh MacDiarmid); Arthur Berriedale Keith; Arthur Koestler; Norman MacCaig; Donald Tovey; John Wain.

Origins

Edinburgh University Library (EUL) was founded in 1580 when Clement Litill, an Edinburgh lawyer, died and bequeathed his collection of 276 volumes of theology to the town and church of Edinburgh. Clement and his brother William Litill had campaigned for some years for a college to be founded in Edinburgh. Both were members of the town council, which was granted a letter of *novodamus* by King James VI in 1582 to found a college; this letter confirmed a gift of annuities to the town of Edinburgh in 1567 by the king's mother, Mary Queen of Scots, and extended its scope to include education. A year after the founding in 1583, Clement's books were handed over to the college as the basis for its library. Thus, unlike the three existing universities in Scotland, which were all papal foundations prior to 1500, the University of Edinburgh was a civic foundation (the oldest in the United Kingdom) and was born of the Reformation. The influence of historian George Buchanan was significant in the early years of the college. Buchanan was the finest Reformation scholar of his time in Scotland. He had tutored King James VI as well as his mother, and his nephew Thomas had tutored the first principal of the college, Robert Rollock.

Collections

Donation was the library's normal method of acquiring books in the early years, primarily from students upon graduation. Those who did not graduate were required to give a sum of money that was used for the purchase of books for the library. As relatively few students actually proceeded to graduation, this gradually replaced the donation of actual volumes as the norm. By the end of the 17th century, the library had acquired two significant collections: 700 volumes of English and European literature presented by the poet William Drummond of Hawthornden and 1,800 volumes of theology, philosophy, and history bequeathed by James Nairn, chaplain to King Charles II, that complemented Clement Litill's founding bequest.

The library had grown to become one of the largest in Scotland and was a regular tourist sight for visitors to the City of Edinburgh, who often included brief descriptions of the library in written accounts of their travels. The library's attractions included: George Buchanan's skull, presented by an early-17th-century principal of the college and so thin as to be translucent, and other anatomical oddities, some of which are now in the university's Anatomy Museum; the Bohemian protest against the burning of reformers Jan Hus and Jerome of Prague in 1415; and an illuminated manuscript volume containing Virgil's *Bucolica, Georgics,* and *The Aeneid,* which may have been prepared for King James III, King of Scots, who reigned from 1460 to 1488.

From 1710 to 1837, Edinburgh University Library, like other university libraries, was a library of legal deposit, and as such it was allowed to claim a free copy of every book published in the United Kingdom. This practice was commuted to an annual treasury grant, initially of £575, which was eventually subsumed by the university's annual allocation from the government. The library expanded greatly in size during the later half of the 18th century, largely through the interest and personal efforts of the historian William Robertson, principal of the university from 1762 until his death in 1793. Many of the library's books on philosophy, natural science, and history, which are now primary sources on the Scottish Enlightenment, were acquired upon publication during this period. During the 19th and early 20th centuries, bequests continued to enrich the library's research resources. Its three-volume *Catalogue of Printed Books,* published from 1918 to 1923, is still a useful bibliographical source.

Buildings

For its first 250 years, the library was housed in a series of four buildings within the college precinct on the Kirk o' Field, the area occupied by what is now Old College on South Bridge and, ironically, the site of the collegiate church where Lord Darnley, the father of King James VI of Scotland (James I of England), had been murdered in 1567. In a two-stage move that lasted from the autumn of 1827 until the winter of 1828–29, the books were eventually transferred to the library in the new college building, in which William Playfair's magnificent Upper Library Hall was and still is the pièce de resistance. Now known as the Playfair Library Hall, the upper library is 200 feet in length, with a vaulted roof. There are shelved alcoves with fluted columns at each side on both walls, and a series of portrait busts of 19th-century professors and notable alumni adorn the entrances to the alcoves. No longer part of the university library, it is now used by the university as a function suite.

Separate faculty and department libraries were developed during the 19th and 20th centuries, by the faculties and departments themselves, in other university buildings. Meanwhile, the collections and services housed in Old College became known as the General Library. They expanded to occupy most of the south and west ranges of the Old Quadrangle and required the establishment of additional undergraduate reading rooms in other university buildings. In 1967 the whole of the General Library moved into the present purpose-built main library building on the south side of George Square, a building designed by J. Hardie Glover and Andrew Merrylees (of Sir Basil Spence, Glover and Ferguson, in Edinburgh). The brief for the architects, which has itself become something of a classic among building programs, was completed in 1962, designs were begun in November 1963, and the demolition of the existing buildings began a year later. The main contract was started in March 1965 and completed in June 1967. The building was commissioned and taken over by the university in August, and the library service opened on schedule in September 1967. The cost of the building, including furniture and equipment, was £2.1 million.

Faculty Libraries

During the 1960s the university librarian was given direct responsibility for nearly all the academic libraries in the university, and the library became one of the most decentralized academic library systems in the United Kingdom. Several were libraries of long standing, serving colleges that were incorporated into the university as faculties, with historic and significant research collections of rare books and manuscripts of their own. They include the Royal (Dick) School of Veterinary Medicine Library (founded 1825), the New College Library (founded in 1846 in the Free Church of Scotland theological college), the Reid Music Library (founded circa 1860 and bearing the name of General John Reid, whose bequest founded the chair and the School of Music and purchased many fine books for the university library), and the Moray House Institute of Education Library (founded 1835). Significant new or newly adapted library buildings at the university include the James Clerk Maxwell Library (1972), the Erskine Medical Library (1980), the Darwin Library (1986, extended in 1990 and 1994), the Robertson Engineering and Science Library (1994), and the Drummond Library for geography and archaeology (1996). The proposed Science and Engineering Library, Learning and Information Centre (SELLIC) is much needed on the University's King's Building Science and Engineering campus.

The university library now comprises 23 staffed sites, excluding those collections that are still housed in the class libraries within individual departments, mostly in the faculties of arts and social sciences, who are responsible for their day-to-day management. The library staff numbers 263 individuals (197 full-time employees). The library's annual budget from the university in 1999 was £5 million, of which about 55 percent was spent on staff and 45 percent on books, journals, access to electronic information, and operating costs.

Information Technology

The introduction of computer technology came later to EUL than to many libraries, although in his paper "From Old College to George Square" in Jean R. Guild and Alexander Law's *Edinburgh University Library, 1580–1980* (1982), E.R.S. Fifoot, then university librarian, recalls that in the early 1960s the university attempted to include "a multi-access automatic catalogue with printer" in the brief for the new university library. The University Grants Committee ruled this out as "sounding suspiciously like a computer." Library computing was still in its early stages of development, and each system had to be developed for each institution; off-the-shelf systems were not yet available. A batch-processed ordering system was successfully developed in-house by EUL and the Edinburgh Regional Computing Centre from 1975–76 (it was renamed the Edinburgh

University Computing Service—EUCS—in 1987). But the system had to be discontinued after a few months' operation in the wake of hardware problems. The online bibliographic search service began in 1978, initially in the King's Buildings (science) and Main (arts and social sciences) Libraries, matching the medical information service, which the Faculty of Medicine had funded for itself for some years. The user services departments of EUCS now share the main library building with the university library, and the two services are working even closer together to provide information and information technology services to the students and staff of the university. A new joint Learning Resource Centre opened in 2000.

In 1982 the university approved the library's program, fully endorsed by the Library Committee, for the installation of a wholly integrated online automation system for the library, which was duly inaugurated in 1984. Because of the scattered and decentralized library and university, and because of the highly developed computer network being installed throughout the university by EUCS to meet growing academic demands, EUL actually became one of the first university libraries in the United Kingdom to provide fully networked access to its online catalog.

The library's first computer system was based on a Geac 8000 machine, which was upgraded twice, five and ten years later. In 1999 Geac was replaced by the Web-based Voyager system of Endeavor, Inc.; the same system is shared with the National Library of Scotland (Edinburgh). Extensive (and intensive) programs have made steady progress toward the complete retrospective conversion of the library's catalogs. One was funded by the Manpower Services Commission in the 1980s, and several by the Scottish Higher Education Funding Council in the 1990s. It will, however, be some time before all the books, journals, and manuscripts listed in all the university libraries' catalogs are listed in the online version.

PETER B. FRESHWATER

Further Reading

Borland, Catherine R., *A Descriptive Catalogue of the Western Mediaeval Manuscripts in Edinburgh University Library*, Edinburgh: Constable, 1916

Edinburgh University Library, *Catalogue of the Printed Books in the Library of the University of Edinburgh*, 3 vols., Edinburgh: University Press, 1918

Fifoot, E.R.S., "Edinburgh University Library," in *Encyclopedia of Library and Information Science*, edited by Allen Kent et al., vol. 7, New York: Dekker, 1972

Finlayson, Charles P., *Clement Litill and His Library: The Origins of Edinburgh University Library*, Edinburgh: Edinburgh Bibliographical Society and The Friends of Edinburgh University Library, 1980

Freshwater, Peter B., "Edinburgh University Library, 1967–1992," *University of Edinburgh Journal* 35, no. 3 (June 1992)

Guild, Jean R., and Alexander Law, editors, *Edinburgh University Library, 1580–1980: A Collection of Historical Essays*, Edinburgh: Edinburgh University Library, 1982

Hukk, Mohammed Ashraful, Hermann Ethé, and Edward Robertson, A Descriptive Catalogue of the Arabic and Persian Manuscripts in Edinburgh University Library, Hertford: Austin, 1925

The Piper: Newsletter of the Friends of Edinburgh University Library (1991–)

Treasures of Edinburgh University Library, Edinburgh: University of Edinburgh, 1989

Emory University Libraries

Address: Emory University Libraries
540 Asbury Circle
Atlanta, Georgia 30322
USA
Telephone: 404-727-6861
Fax: 404-727-0805
www.emory.edu/LIB

Founded: 1836

Holdings (2000): Volumes: 2.6 million. Current serials 27,000; films and videos: 11,000; manuscripts: 12,000 linear feet; maps: 26,000; microforms: 3.5 million; sound recordings: 22,000.

Special Collections: *Areas of Concentration:* African American history and culture; American communism; civil rights; Civil War; modern literature, especially Irish, British, and Southern U.S. literature; Southern history, politics, and culture; Southern journalism; women's history. *Individual Collections:* Belfast group poets; Joel Chandler Harris; Seamus Heaney; James Weldon Johnson; René Maran; Keith Read Civil War collection; Flannery O'Connor; Robert Penn Warren; John Wesley and Wesley family collection; W. B. Yeats—Lady Gregory collection. *Papers:* Benny Andrews; "Bricktop" (Ada Smith Ducongé); James Dickey; Ted Hughes; Thomas Kinsella; Michael Longley; Derek Mahon; Ralph McGill; Paul Muldoon; Louise Thompson Patterson.

Origins

Emory University developed from Emory College, a small college for men founded in 1836 by the Georgia Methodist Conference in the new town of Oxford, 40 miles east of Atlanta (so called because John and Charles Wesley had attended Oxford University). The first librarian in college records (dated 1840) was George W. Lane, the professor of ancient languages. The library played little part in the early history of Emory College and was described by Thomas H. English in his *Sesquicentennial Chronicle of the Emory University Library* (1987) as containing "the miscellaneous gatherings of deceased Methodist preachers." The primary collections were in the possession of the college's two literary societies, Phi Gamma and Few, organized by 1839. The two societies owned more than 4,000 volumes between them in 1860, whereas the college library contained fewer than 2,000 volumes. The college was closed during the Civil War, when buildings were used as hospitals, and on its reopening in 1866 the holdings of the small library were found to have been largely scattered and lost.

The first serious attention to the library came under the presidency of Atticus Greene Haygood, a graduate in the class of 1859 and later an agent for the Slater Fund, providing aid to African American education. Through the benefaction of northern philanthropist George Seney, Seney Hall was built (1883) to house college offices, provide classrooms, and give space for the college library. Finally in 1897 the cornerstone was laid for a separate library building, Candler Hall. Shortly after it opened the literary societies transferred their collections to the library, and in 1908 the college received its first book endowment, the John W. Akin fund devoted to English literature, with a gift of $5,000. By 1915, when the Methodist Church, South, at the urging of Bishop Warren Candler, was determined to establish a Methodist university in Atlanta, the college library owned 41,000 volumes, though many were of little value for a research collection.

The Beginnings of the University Library and the Jemison Years

Emory College became the nucleus of the new Methodist university chartered in 1915. Schools of law and theology, the first on the new campus, had separate libraries. The library for the college, which moved from Oxford to the Atlanta campus in 1919, occupied the basement of the theology building.

The development of a university library began with the arrival in 1921 of Margaret Jemison. One of her first decisions was to change the classification system in the library from the Dewey Decimal Classification (DDC) system to that of the Library of Congress (LC). She also began a more systematic development of the collection and worked closely with faculty to secure a separate library building for the new campus. In 1926 the Asa Griggs Candler Library opened its doors. It was named for the founder of the Coca-Cola Company, who had given $1 million, the land to build Emory University in Atlanta, and $400,000 to build the library. Some room in the new building was given over to nonlibrary functions, and it was not until 1955 that the offices of the university president and registrar finally moved to a new administration building, long after the library's conditions had become seriously overcrowded. The Emory Museum, including a collection of mummies and snakes, also resided in the library until the late 1930s. The library school, a new program in the university brought about by Emory's affiliation with the Carnegie Library School of Atlanta, occupied part of one floor in 1930 and remained in Candler Library until the school closed in 1988.

From the late 1920s through the 1950s, the library developed slowly and selectively with a small book budget and two small endowment funds, one for English and one for the social sciences. In 1933 the first foundation support, from the Lewis H. Beck Foundation in Atlanta, brought funds to develop research collections that would allow the growth of graduate programs. The annual gifts from the Beck Foundation were a mainstay of the library during very lean years and remain a source for special purchases.

Building the Collections

Faculty long played a key role in collection building. Beginning with his arrival on campus in 1925, Professor Thomas H. English made the library a major interest and chaired the faculty library committee for 22 years. Over the years faculty representatives from the academic departments had responsibility for selecting materials for purchase, a system that remained in place until the early 1980s, when librarian selectors and bibliographers assumed the major role in collection building. The strength of the book collection in 18th- and 19th-century British literature reflected the common interests of Thomas English and the librarians who managed acquisitions.

Like Emory College itself, the manuscript and rare book collections had their origins in Methodism. In 1911 Bishop Warren Candler (whose brother, Asa, funded the building of the university) purchased from Thursfield Smith of Shrewsbury (England) a sizable collection of letters, unpublished and published materials, mementos, and artifacts of John and Charles Wesley and the Wesley family. Included among this collection is John Wesley's shorthand diary of 1736, kept during his sojourn in Georgia. This acquisition began the library's collection of manuscript and rare book materials.

Collections relating to Southern U.S. history and literature, notably the papers of Joel Chandler Harris of Georgia (author of the Uncle Remus tales) and a large collection of Civil War materials, were added in the late 1920s and 1930s. In 1940 a separate area, known initially as the Treasure Room, was established to bring together the growing collections. Special collections librarians were interested primarily in the Civil War or Georgia history and local literature, and no particular priority was placed on building major contemporary archives of national significance. No aggressive attempt was made, for example, to collect archives documenting the social and political ferment in the South from the 1930s through the 1960s. There was no funding to support such acquisitions in a university with only fledgling graduate programs and no Ph.D. program until 1946. The rare book collection was a high spot collection and as late as the 1980s contained only some 40,000 volumes.

The Lyle Years

When Margaret Jemison retired in 1954, the library held 332,000 volumes largely supporting an undergraduate curriculum, with a total library staff of 29. The next librarian, Guy R. Lyle (author of a standard text, published in 1944, on *The Administration of the College Library*) came with the title of director of libraries, although the organizational structure in the university placed only the central library under his direct management. Lyle oversaw a major renovation of Candler Library and eventually the opening of the Robert W. Woodruff Library in 1969 (named for the head of the Coca-Cola Company and the man who had become the university's greatest benefactor after Asa Griggs Candler). The new building gave the Special Collections Department handsome new quarters on the top floor and alleviated the serious book and staff overcrowding in the Candler Library. At that time the Woodruff Library also incorporated the library of the business school.

In the year that the new building opened, the director of libraries pointed to the lack of adequate funding for building research collections. In 1972 when the Emory libraries celebrated their one-millionth volume (including all libraries of the college and university), director Lyle noted in his annual report that "the library's situation has taken a turn for the worse." With inflation in the price of library materials and no significant increases in the materials budget, the library fell farther behind in the rankings even among its neighboring institutions in the southeast. Lyle retired in 1972, having achieved the construction of a new library building but with a library collection not keeping pace with the growth of the university.

A New Era

The late 1970s began a period of unprecedented growth for Emory libraries. In 1975 the Emory libraries joined the Association of Research Libraries (ARL) and became the first ARL member library to catalog through the automated shared cataloging system of the Southeastern Library and Information Network (SOLINET). Emory was a leading institution in establishing SOLINET and continued to be a leader in automation of library cataloging in the southeast.

One year later the university purchased the library of the Hartford Seminary Foundation, at one stroke more than doubling the size of the theology library and moving it from a ranking of 45th among U.S. theology libraries in the country to number four. Now named the Pitts Library, the theology library currently ranks in the United States as second only to that of Union Theological Seminary (New York). This acquisition was the accomplishment of a masterful entrepreneurial leader who served as dean of the theology school, James T. Laney. It was a surprise to no one when Laney became Emory's 17th president in 1977. Two years later the Emily and Ernest Woodruff Fund of Atlanta, under the direction of Robert Woodruff and his brother, George, made a gift to Emory of the assets of the fund, valued at $107 million dollars, the largest single gift to an educational institution at that time.

The Frye Years

With the Woodruff gift and pressures for wise use of the largesse, President Laney made two decisions that had far-reaching impact on the libraries. In order to bolster Emory's nascent Irish literature collections and with the eminent scholar Richard Ellmann (biographer of Yeats, Joyce, and Wilde) as Woodruff Professor, Laney authorized funds for the library to purchase a major collection of Yeats first editions and manuscripts from the library of his friend and patron, Lady Gregory (née Isabella Augusta Persse). This purchase in 1979 initiated the library's efforts to build a major collection of Irish literature. Laney also brought Billy E. Frye to Emory from the University of Michigan in 1985 to serve as vice president for research, dean of the graduate school, and later as provost. Provost Frye's strong support for libraries and his commitment to library automation and preservation brought to Emory an academic administrator who had a knowledge of research libraries and a significant commitment to their directed growth.

Just prior to Frye's arrival, campus libraries had joined together to build a unified online catalog. With Frye's support, monies were made available for a major retrospective conversion project to assure that all holdings were converted to machine-readable form. Emory also joined the Research Libraries Group (RLG) in 1986 and established a preservation program. When Joan Gotwals arrived from the University of Pennsylvania as director of libraries in 1988, Emory's libraries had, at a critical time, a library director with extensive experience in a major research library.

Recent Trends and Future Developments

Although other research libraries saw retrenchment and stagnant budgets if not outright budget cuts, Emory's libraries received continuing and increasing budget enhancements in the 1990s for materials and staff, in an effort to keep up with the fast-growing university. The library placed priority on electronic resources and services and distinctive special collections in focused areas. A grant from the Luce Foundation in 1993 enabled Emory to undertake a planning project to develop a model for a virtual library. Also in 1993 the library established the Lewis H. Beck Center for Electronic Texts and Services to manage full-text electronic resources and to form collaborative partnerships with faculty in building digital collections. Special Collections has built significant modern literature holdings, particularly Irish and British poetry, along with Southern literature, and (in the last part of the decade) African American collections, with a focus on black print culture and the post-civil rights era. The addition of curators for modern literature and African American materials has had a significant impact on the acquisition of major collections in these areas. The Special Collections Department has placed emphasis on electronic access to special collections materials and on promoting use of the collections by undergraduates.

The Center for Library and Information Technology, an addition to the Woodruff Library dedicated in 1998, emphasized electronic resources and collaboration with the University's Information Technology Division. The integration of libraries and information technology staff and services put Emory at the forefront of library development. The Technology Centers in the new facility brought together multimedia services, the Beck Center for electronic texts, and the Electronic Data Center, created with grant funding in 1996 to aid faculty and staff in the use of numeric electronic data. The addition of the Emory Center for Instruction and Teaching (part of the Center for Library and Information Technology) brought the library into partnership with faculty in developing new methods of teaching. The library has focused on promoting web-based resources and services and on faculty collaboration in building electronic collections. The Billy E. Frye Digital Leadership Institute, a program for educating leaders in managing academic libraries in the electronic age, began at Emory in 2000 under the auspices of the Council on Library and Information Resources with funding from the Woodruff Foundation of Atlanta.

LINDA M. MATTHEWS

Further Reading

English, Thomas H., "Emory University Libraries," in *Encyclopedia of Library and Information Science*, edited by Allen Kent et al., vol. 8, New York: Dekker, 1972

English, Thomas H., *A Sesquicentennial Chronicle of the Emory University Library*, Atlanta, Georgia: Friends of the Emory University Libraries, 1987

Enniss, Stephen, and Schuchard, Ronald, "The Growth of Emory's Modern Irish Collection," *Gazette of the Grolier Club* (new series), no. 50 (1999)

Ex Libris (1971–1985)

Imprint (1986–) (newsletter for Friends of Emory Libraries)

Enoch Pratt Free Library

Address: Enoch Pratt Free Library
400 Cathedral Street
Baltimore, Maryland 21201
USA
Telephone: 410-396-5430
Fax: 410-396-1441
www.pratt.lib.md.us

Founded: 1886

Holdings (2000): Volumes: 2.4 million.

Special Collections: *Areas of Concentration:* Baltimore views; book illustrations to 1900. *Individual Collections:* African American; Baltimore Life Underwriters; Howard Beck memorial philatelic collection; Bevan collection of bookplates; George Cator collection of Baltimore views; gastronomy and wines; greeting cards since 1870; Henry L. Mencken; Edgar Allen Poe; Frederick William Stief collection of cookery; war posters.

Origins

The library "shall be open for all, rich and poor without distinction of race and color, who when properly accredited, can take out the books if they will handle them carefully and return them." So spoke self-made millionaire businessman Enoch Pratt at the 4 January 1886 dedication ceremonies for the four branches and new marble central library building he had just funded for the city of Baltimore. In addition to the building, Pratt provided an endowment that yielded an annual income of $50,000 for the library system, and shortly after it opened, took his place as chairman of a self-perpetuating board of trustees to keep the library out of politics. The Enoch Pratt Free Public was off to an auspicious start.

The Steiner Years, 1886 to 1926

Lewis Steiner was the Pratt's first director. Trained in medicine and with no library experience, Steiner believed the Pratt had three distinctive functions: educational, humanitarian, and recreational. Regarding the latter, he had equally definite ideas. His library, he stated in his 1890 annual report, would house "no books positively injurious to the moral sense" and no printed products of the "sensational press." Understandably, Pratt's clientele was mostly middle class during his tenure and the blue-collar and growing pink-collar classes had little time or inclination to read the "wholesome" literature Steiner was acquiring for their use. When he died in 1892, the Pratt boasted a collection of 106,000 volumes and an annual circulation of 434,000.

Steiner was succeeded by his son Bernard, who was also conservative in his professional outlook. Like his father, Bernard Steiner had no formal library training but had a Ph.D. in history from The Johns Hopkins University. The younger Steiner also thought that the Pratt should be a repository of culture and that it should discourage the reading of popular fiction, which, by the late 1890s, constituted 90 percent of the Pratt's circulation, despite his father's best efforts. Because he and his board believed it was the Pratt's responsibility to serve the needs of what H.L. Mencken would later call the "relatively civilized minority" who made a difference, Bernard Steiner had no reservations about removing works by Horatio Alger and Mrs. E.D.E.N. Southworth for being "too morbid a character for circulation by a library of this kind" (*Baltimore Evening Sun*, 3 September 1897). For the next 30 years, Librarian Steiner exercised tight control over selection and weeding procedures.

Although Andrew Carnegie donated $500,000 in 1906 to erect 20 more free library branches in Baltimore, and the Pratt began a children's story hour in 1917, the Pratt generally remained aloof, not participating in the urban reform movements that enveloped the city between 1900 and 1920. When he died in 1926, Steiner left a collection of 500,000 volumes and circulation of 1 million, but his legacy was also a seriously underfunded and rather lethargic institution compared to other urban public libraries. On 9 November 1927 the *New Republic* described it as "a dreary study in aged clerks, faulty indices and unwise choices" housed in "an architectural fright reminiscent of a Victorian bathroom" where borrowers who actually "used their cards were held slightly suspect." H.L. Mencken was less kind about the architecture. In a 2 February 1925 *Baltimore Evening Sun* column he referred to the building as "so infernally hideous that it ought to be pulled down by the common hangman."

The Wheeler Years, 1926 to 1945

After Steiner's death, the Pratt trustees hired Joseph L. Wheeler away from the Youngstown Public Library in Ohio. Wheeler made quick use of his merchandising skills and opened a collection of 10,000 books that patrons could access directly. He also increased the number of titles they were allowed to check out at one time. At one point in the late 1920s, he even put information advertising library services on the cardboard inserts that local cleaners used for freshly laundered shirts. Wheeler's efforts paid quick dividends. Within three years, the Pratt increased circulation by 100 percent.

In 1928 Wheeler organized a library training class to upgrade staff skills and shortly thereafter began a campaign to erect a new library. In both cases he was successful. When the new building opened in 1933, it housed a collection of 360,000 volumes, supported a staff of 130, and provided seating for 1,100 patrons. Innovations included a separate children's room with a fireplace, a fishpond, and a glass-enclosed amphitheater. Also new were displays in the windows overlooking Cathedral Street, which showcased library materials that focused on local, state, national, and international events of current interest. Under exhibit supervisor Kate Coplan's direction, window displays helped the library win five John Cotton Dana Awards between 1934 and 1963, whereas under children's librarian Margaret Edwards's direction, the Pratt became famous for its pioneering work in young adult services.

Like other urban public libraries during the Great Depression, the Pratt endured increased use and decreased funding. To address perceived community needs evidenced by the large number of unemployed men who frequented the reading rooms, Wheeler focused much attention on "home industries." In 1936 his Business and Economics Department issued a popular pamphlet entitled *Balance Sheet of the New Deal*, which listed 30 titles. His Education, Philosophy, and Religion Department began compiling booklists on self-education, and because these became so widely read, publishers began to send the Pratt review copies for citation in the booklists. In 1934 Wheeler started a Maryland Department that focused on state issues. By that time his 27 branches circulated twice as many books as the central library, and his staff—much more organizationally defined and professionally educated than a decade earlier—had developed a national reputation for service.

The Pratt was also an active participant in World War II, during which two-thirds of the books circulated focused on some aspect of the war. This was supported in part by the distribution of books directly to neighborhoods where war industry workers and their families lived. Books were carried in a horse-drawn wagon preceded by a boy banging on a toy xylophone. Successes in other arenas were mixed. Although Wheeler hired the Pratt's first African American professional librarian in 1936, the Pratt was taken to court six years later for barring an African American from admission to its training class. When Wheeler retired in March 1945, the Pratt held 825,000 volumes, boasted a circulation of 2.6 million, and had nearly triple the number of library cardholders as in 1926.

Consolidating Gains, 1945 to 1959

When Emerson Greenaway of the Worcester Public Library in Massachusetts succeeded Wheeler, he instituted a series of Noon Hour Talks ("Atomic Energy" and "Behind the News" were two of them), initiated a regular bookmobile service (a tractor pulled a trailer through the streets of Baltimore, but without the xylophone preceding it), conducted a successful bond drive to repair or replace several branch libraries in 1947, and added a Film Department in 1949. When he resigned in 1951, the collection totaled 1.1 million volumes. He was succeeded by assistant director Amy Winslow, whose public relations strengths and desire to promote library use and arouse interest in particular types of reading paid immediate dividends. Under her leadership the Pratt averaged some kind of coverage in Baltimore newspapers at least three times per week. After her retirement in 1957, she was succeeded by Arthur Parson, who died suddenly of a heart attack in 1959.

The Castagna Years, 1959 to 1975

Parson was succeeded by Edwin Castagna, former director of the Long Beach Public Library in California. Under his leadership the Enoch Pratt Free Library shifted to meet new circumstances. Like his predecessors, Castagna emphasized community service. He disliked popular fiction, initiated efforts to upgrade the quality of the collection, and aimed the lecture series toward urban development and community action. With the help of federal money, he inaugurated the Metropolitan Maryland Library Service in 1965, extending borrowing privileges to people living in six counties. That same year he began a reclassification project using the Library of Congress (LC) system. He also reorganized the staff by expanding general reference and reducing subject departments from six to three.

A year later the Pratt merged with the Peabody Library, which took responsibility for rare books and genealogy and functioned as a study library for high school and college students. In 1971 the Pratt was designated Maryland's State Library Resources Center (Maryland does not have a state library), and thus began receiving a regular allocation from state coffers. In 1959 Castagna had inherited an institution with a largely white middle-class clientele; when he retired in 1975, the city's demographics (and thus the library's clientele) had changed significantly to a largely working-class African American base. As the Peabody Library's holdings became an increasing burden to the Pratt in the 1970s, lengthy negotiations eventually led to the Peabody's absorption by Johns Hopkins University Library, which now maintains it as part of its Special Collections.

1975 to 2000

Castagna's successor, Ernest Siegel, was director from 1975 until 1980, when he was succeeded by Anne Curry. When the Pratt celebrated its centennial in 1986, it boasted a renovated central building, 31 branches, and two bookmobiles (neither of which had a xylophone), a collection of 1.9 million volumes, and a circulation of 2 million. Half of its budget came from the state, and its Office of Lifelong Learning attempted to address the needs of Baltimore's 200,000 functionally illiterate citizens. Under Curry's leadership, the Pratt formed a working relationship with the Baltimore County Library in Towson and willingly relinquished to it responsibility for circulating popular reading materials.

Carla D. Hayden became Pratt's director in July 1993 and was declared *Library Journal*'s "Librarian of the Year" two years later despite problems including underfunding that forced her to close two branches and reduce hours in the rest. There was also some unfortunate press coverage brought about by the library's attempts to handle issues involving the homeless. In its January 1996 issue, *Library Journal* applauded Hayden for refashioning the Pratt into a new urban institution "designed to deliver information to the right people and places to solve nearly intractable . . . inner city problems." Her contributions included the merging of systems and collections management into an Information Access Division; efforts to construct four new regional library centers (30,000 square feet each) to function as district satellites to the central library; renovation of some branches; and shifts in branch responsibilities to include foreign language and ethnic collections unique to populations in their neighborhoods. Throughout these changes, however, the Pratt maintained a high reputation for outreach and public service that other urban public libraries in the United States have emulated for most of the 20th century.

WAYNE A. WIEGAND

Further Reading

Bluh, Pamela M., "Challenge and Opportunity: Managing the Public Library for a New Century: An Interview with Carla D. Hayden, Director of the Enoch Pratt Free Library," *Library Administration and Management* 13 (1999)

Coplan, Kate M., "Memories of Enoch Pratt Free Library: The PR Director Who Crafted 'The Show Windows of Baltimore' for Three Decades; Reminiscences about Turtles, Tarantulas, and Tearsheets," *American Libraries* 24 (1993)

Kalisch, Philip Arthur, *The Enoch Pratt Free Library: A Social History*, Metuchen, New Jersey: Scarecrow Press, 1969

Nelson, Milo G., "Enoch Pratt Steps into Its Second Century: A Centennial Report," *Wilson Library Bulletin* 60 (1986)

Estense University Library, Modena

Address:	Biblioteca Estense e Universitaria, Modena Piazzetta Sant'Agostino, 337 Modena 41100 Italy Telephone: 59-222248 Fax: 59-230195
Founded:	14th century
Holdings (1999):	Volumes: 600,000. Current serials: 2,000; incunabula: 1,661; manuscripts: 10,000, including 600 medieval manuscripts; music scores: 1,100.
Special Collections:	*Areas of Concentration:* Ancient music; medieval Italian manuscripts; medieval poetry; Renaissance miniatures. *Individual Collections:* Giovan Battista Amici; Giuseppe Bianchi; Giuseppe Campori; Formiggini family.

The Biblioteca Estense originated in the private collection of the house of Este, an ancient feudal family that in 1095 took control of the prosperous city of Ferrara, which they ruled until 1598. In the 13th century, perhaps even in the 12th, the Este possessed books, the oldest extant on chivalrous subjects, as well as books of poems and chronicles. Niccolò II d'Este hosted Petrarch in Ferrara in 1370; Niccolò's brother Alberto founded the Studio Universitario Ferrarese. Niccolò III, his son, invited notable humanists to the court, among them the celebrated Guarino Veronese, to whom he entrusted the education of his own son, Leonello, as well as the formation of a proper library. A literary inventory in 1436 listed 279 manuscripts. Niccolò III commissioned illuminated manuscripts such as a magnificent Bible, now at the Vatican, written in French in 1434 (French being the language of Italian courts of that time). Leonello, on succeeding his father in 1441, surrounded himself with humanists and spared no expense on the growth of the library. He also appointed the first librarian, Biagio Bosoni.

Borso d'Este succeeded his brother Leonello in 1450 and is known for his support of illuminators. He was responsible for the creation of the great Bible, still preserved at the Estense, which bears his name. Ercole I (who succeeded Borso in 1471) continued the great tradition of his house; his wife, Eleonora of Aragon, brought an important library to the court on their marriage. A 1495 inventory of the d'Este royal library lists 512 volumes: 180 in Latin, 113 in vernacular, 45 in French, one in Greek, and one in German.

Ercole's successor, Alfonso I, who came to power in 1505, continued the illustrious tradition, having illuminated the celebrated *Officium Alphonsimum* (1505–10), and his first wife, Anna Sforza, brought a magnificent missal. His second wife, Lucrezia Borgia, also brought many books to the court, which remained splendid and rich in intellectual life. The famous poet Ludovico Ariosto frequented the court in these years. Successors Ercole II and Alfonso II increased the collections. The most important acquisition was owing to the inheritance of the library of Cardinal Rodolfo Pio (1573–), nephew of Alberto Pio, the prince of Carpi who was the protector of the famous printer Aldus Manutius at the end of the 15th century. Rodolfo's library included 155 Greek and 18 Oriental manuscripts, many coming from Albert Pio. Alfonso II, a lover of music, greatly increased the musical collection. Now the Estense preserves one of the best early music collections in Italy.

By the end of the 16th century, the splendor of the Estense Court was sadly nearing its end. Alfonso II had no legitimate children, and Pope Clement VIII took advantage by claiming Ferrara from Alfonso's heir, the illegitimate son Cesare, who in 1598 was forced to exchange Ferrara for Modena and Reggio. After a glorious four-century reign, the house of Este left its historic capital. Cesare was allowed to take with him his private possessions, including the library and archive, but their transportation was disastrous and many precious works were lost. The installation at Modena was even worse, as works were housed in inadequate and humid rooms, without proper supervision. Various moves brought new losses and damage. Finally in 1677 Duke Francesco II assigned an appropriate place for the library in the ducal palace and named as ducal librarian the engineer and poet Giovanni Battista Boccabadati. Since then the succession of librarians has been unbroken (unlike preceding years, when a specific superintendent was not required) and the survival of the library assured. After Boccabadati came Jacopo Cantelli, a geographer, and in 1696, the Benedictine Benedetto Bacchini, Ludovico Muratori's teacher. Bacchini oversaw another move within the same building and then applied himself to compiling a new, up-to-date catalog, in which he entered 934 manuscripts and 20,000 printed works.

In 1700 the new Duke Rinaldo named Ludovico Antonio Muratori, formerly a *dottore* at the Ambrosiana, as librarian.

Thanks to his work in the library and, above all, in the Estensi archives, Muratori became the founder of modern Italian historiography, based on rigorous scientific criteria and careful study of primary resources. At Modena between 1700 and 1750, the year of his death, he prepared several editions of Italian medieval sources that brought about the rediscovery of the Italian Middle Ages.

After Muratori's death in 1750 Duke Francesco III, accepting the ideas of the Enlightenment, opened the library to the public without requiring ducal authorization for use. The mathematician Francesco Vandelli, Muratori's successor, was scarcely fit for the office, and for several years did nothing significant. By contrast Francesco Antonio Zaccaria, Vandelli's successor in 1756, created new catalogs, found new rooms that he decorated and painted, and finally, in 1764, presided over a solemn opening of an expanded library. In 1770 another erudite and illustrious scholar, Girolamo Tiraboschi, became the ducal librarian. Spurred on by the noble ambition of Dukes Francesco III and Ercole III, he effected many acquisitions and other additions from the suppression of the Jesuits. At his death in 1795 there were 100,000 printed books and 3,000 manuscripts in the library.

Napoleon's invasion of Modena in 1795 led to a French dominion that lasted, with a brief interval, until 1814. Although the suppression of various religious institutions enriched the library, it remained closed to the public for financial reasons. In 1814 Francesco IV, Archduke Ferdinand of Austria (the dynasty would from then on be called Austria-Este) procured many important acquisitions, most notably the magnificent collection of Tommaso Obizzi, owner of the Villa of Cataio near Monselice, which included 329 codices in Greek, Hebrew, Arab, Latin, and Italian.

Major events affecting the library, known as the Estense after 1868, included its move to the Palace of the Museums (1880), an unhappy and insufficient location in which it still resides; its union with the university library of Modena; and the acquisition of the Campori collection. Marquis Giuseppe Campori had collected 5,082 codices and 100,000 autographs, which he gave to his city when he died. Numerous acquisitions continued through the 20th century, including the Giulio Bertoni collection of more than 17,000 volumes and booklets on philological subjects, which entered the Estense in 1983.

The Estense Library today is both traditional and innovative. It is open to new technologies, as its website attests. Current projects also include publication of a collection of facsimiles of high quality. The next to appear will be the *Officium Alphonsinum*, the manuscript splendidly illuminated for Alfonso I d'Este between 1505 and 1510 and now partly in Lisbon and partly in Zagreb, Croatia, ideally reconstructed in its unity.

MARINO ZORZI

Further Reading

Fava, Domenico, *La Biblioteca Estense nel suo sviluppo storico, con il catalogo della Mostra permanente e 10 tavole,* Modena: G. T. Vincenzi e Nipoti di D. Cavallotti, 1925

Milano, Ernesto, editor, *Biblioteca Estense, Modena,* Florence: Nardini, 1987

Estonian Academic Library

Address: Eesti Akadeemiline Raamatukogu
10 Rävala Avenue
15042 Tallinn
Estonia
Telephone: 372-665-9401
Fax: 372-665-9400
www.ear.ee

Founded: 1946

Holdings (2000): Volumes: 2.5 million. Current serials: 4,600; electronic documents: 300; graphic arts: 21,000; incunabula, 47; maps: 5,000; manuscripts: 3,000; microforms: 17,000; music scores: 3,000; sound recordings: 200.

Special Collections: *Areas of Concentration*: Publications in Estonian, Estonica, Baltica. *Individual Collections*: Estonian Public Library of the Library of the Estonian Literary Society, including *Bibliotheca Revaliensis ad D. Olai*; Reinhold Grist collection; Mikk Põlde collection; Nicolaus Specht collection; Tallinn Cathedral School Library, the von Pahlen Library; Georg Günther Tunzelmann collection.

Origins

The Estonian Academic of Sciences was first established in 1938, but it was shut down by the Soviet regime in 1940. In its place the regime founded in 1946 the Academy of Sciences of the Estonian Soviet Socialist Republic. The Library of the Academy of Sciences of the Estonian Soviet Socialist Republic was founded on 5 April 1946. As with all the academies of the Soviet Union, the Estonian branch included the central office (the presidium), various research institutes, and a central scientific library. The library was to provide the research institutes with necessary literature and to coordinate the work of branch libraries of the institutes. The Central Library of the Estonian Academy of Sciences (CLAS) opened in January 1947, held 1,800 volumes, employed 13 librarians, and initiated its reading room a year later. By the end of the first year the number of volumes had increased to 7,085, and the number of registered readers was 80.

The collections of the library grew quickly after the library was granted legal deposit rights to all Estonian publications (1947) and deposit copies of all publications of the Soviet Union (1948). The library gave up the latter privilege in 1956, and Russian literature has been acquired only selectively since. Many publications were donated by the Library of the Academy of Sciences of the USSR in Leningrad (now St. Petersburg). In 1947 a special department for restricted use was established for literature prohibited by the Soviet ideological institutions: Such departments existed in four Estonian libraries, and prohibited publications were removed from all other libraries. In 1947 book exchanges with other Soviet republics and foreign research institutions were established to acquire new scientific literature.

Library of the Estonian Literary Society

In 1950 CLAS merged with the Library of the Estonian Literary Society (LELS) (1842 to 1940, formerly belonging to the history museum), and the collection of foreign literature of the liquidated Library of the Learned Estonian Society (1838–1950), which was returned to the society in 1989. The accession of LELS added more than 130,000 volumes, including old and rare books of *Bibliotheca Revaliensis ad D.Olai* founded in 1552. The historical library included many book donations and legacies, and LELS began to collect Baltica in the middle of the 19th century. During the Soviet occupation (1940) the properties of the Estonian Literary Society were nationalized and the treasures of its museum, archive, and library were distributed between newly established national museums. Initially attached to the Estonian History Museum, the library was transferred to CLAS. The department of Baltica and rare books, headed by book historian Voldemar Miller, was founded in 1968 and began to develop the collection of older Estonian literature and to collect postcards, manuscripts, and ex libris by Estonian artists. Today the department holds 300,000 volumes including old books, Estonica, and Baltica.

The Development of the Library, 1960 to 1980s

In 1959 construction of a separate library building by architects Uno Tölpus and Paul Madalik began. The completion of the building opened new prospects for library development. By 1967 all of the collections from different locations in town had been transferred to the new stacks, and seven reading rooms were opened. CLAS held more than 1.5 million volumes, employed 118 librarians, and for the first time all departments had their own workrooms.

The scope of activities expanded when former publisher Felix Kauba was appointed director of the library. In 1962 subject specialization was extended, and the library focused on providing all Estonian scientific research establishments with necessary literature. Collaboration between the libraries of Estonia and other Baltic states became closer, with coordination of acquisitions of foreign literature holding special importance. The main focus of CLAS became the acquisition of literature on the natural sciences. Special attention was paid to reference literature and foreign scientific periodicals. Periodical subscriptions were financed by the Academy of Sciences of the Soviet Union, and for several decades it was the only source of foreign periodicals in Estonia.

At the beginning of the 1970s the importance of bibliographical work grew: The library began to compile the annotated cumulative bibliographies *Estica* and *Finno-Ugric Ethnography and Folklore,* special bibliographies on geological and oil-shale studies, as well as author bibliographies of the members of the Estonian Academic of Sciences. Research concerning the history of the library collections and the history of publishing in Estonia also began at this time. Exhibitions on special subjects and anniversaries became customary.

System of Catalogs

From the very beginning both alphabetical and systematic catalogs have been compiled to make the collections available to readers. The systematic catalog was based on the Universal Decimal Classification (UDC), and the library managed to remain true to this system during the 1970s, when the Soviet Union tried to introduce a new bibliographical classification developed in Russia. At present the systematization is based on the *Universal Decimal Classification, International Medium Edition,* volumes 1 and 2 (1993) and the UDC computer version *UDC Master Reference File* (MRF), *Extensions and Corrections to the UDC.* The library provides access to computer databases via the Internet.

Compilation of the subject catalog began in 1995. In 1999 an integrated subject bibliographical index was completed at the National Library of Estonia (Tallinn), available both in computer and printed versions, and the basis of subject indexing in all the libraries of the Estonian LibraryNet (ELNET) Consortium. Since 1999 all new acquisitions have been cataloged electronically and card catalogs have not been supplemented.

Literature of Estonians in Exile

In 1974 a special collection of publications by exiled Estonian writers (those considered especially dangerous and exiled by the Soviet regime) was added to the department of prohibited literature. This collection could be used only with the permission of the Communist Party of the Estonian Soviet Socialist Republic. Restrictions on exile literature were removed in 1988, and the collection of literature by Estonian exile authors was arranged as a separate department. Information about these publications was entered into all available catalogs, and the compilation of bibliographies about all incoming periodicals was begun. The compilation of the bibliography of Estonian exile literature began in 1995 as part of the Retrospective National Bibliography Program. At present the collection of Estonian Exile Literature holds more than 24,000 volumes, with several author bibliographies of prominent Estonian writers having been published.

Estonian Retrospective National Bibliography

Since 1978 the library has been the center for compiling the Estonian Retrospective National Bibliography (ERNB) under the supervision of Endel Annus. The work was designed as a five-part edition:

Part I: *Estonian Books, 1525–1850* (published in 2000)
Estonian Books, 1851–1900 (vols. 1–2, published in 1995)
Estonian Books, 1901–1917 (vols. 1–2, published in 1993)

Part II: *Books in German, Latin, and Other Languages Published in Estonia, 1632–1800* (vols. 1–3, to be published in 2006)

Part III: *Books in Russian Published in Estonia, 1801–1940* (vols. 1–2, to be published in 2007)

Part IV: *Estonian Periodicals, 1766–1940* (to be published in 2002)

Part V: *Periodicals in German, Russian, and Other Foreign Languages in Estonia, 1675–1940* (published in 1993)

The bibliographies also serve as joint catalogs, registering the availability of publications. Publications in foreign languages published in Estonia have also been registered in Latvian, Russian, Finnish, Swedish, and Danish libraries. They also include data about publications in Estonian and concerning Estonia published in Poland, Germany, Great Britain, Australia, and the United States. The publication of the ERNB has been supported by the government of Estonia, Open Estonian Foundation, Estonian National Culture Foundation, Cultural Endowment of Estonia, the Presidium of the Academy of Sciences of Estonia, and the F. Tuglas Society in Finland.

The Library in Independent Estonia

The first years of independence after liberation from the Soviet regime in 1991 were financially difficult: the old system of the Estonian Academy of Sciences dispersed, and the library became an independent establishment under the Ministry of Culture. Money for the purchase of literature was scarce, and new literature was mostly acquired through donations and gifts. Benefactors included the American Chemical Society, International Science Foundation, the Rectors' Board of Bonn (Germany)

University, and other organizations. Cooperation started with the German firm Lange and Springer to acquire scientific literature. In 1996 the library was renamed the Estonian Academic Library and now is a component of the uniform national information system.

New vistas have opened for international cooperation. Since 1992 EAL has contributed to the *English Short Title Catalogue*, which registers all English publications through the 18th century. The historical collections of EAL are of great interest to German historians, as Estonia has been part of the sphere of German cultural influence for several centuries. At present EAL participates in the project of Osnabrück University to register and microfilm topical publications in the German language published in the 16th to the 18th centuries. EAL is a member of the International Federation of Library Associations and Institutions (IFLA) and participates in the work of Bibliotheca Baltica, an association of Baltic libraries.

Automation

Computer programming started in the early 1980s, when compilation of the ERNB database began. The next stage was the automation of acquisitions, including exchanges. In 1991 a computer network was installed with a server connected to the Internet. In 1996 EAL opened its home page, and seven research libraries (including EAL) launched an integrated information system called ELNET. After an open competition, the INNOPAC system from Innovative Interfaces, Inc., was selected for use by the EAL library system. The U.S.-based Andrew W. Mellon Foundation gave a grant to purchase software and two servers, with installation training beginning in 1997. Bar-coded reader's cards and acquisition modules were introduced in 1999. The main short-term task at the beginning of the 21st century continues to be the conversion of card catalogs and the database of the national bibliography into electronic catalogs.

Recent Trends

EAL promotes the development of an open society with its focus on education. It also supports the integration processes of the Estonian society by the provision of information for research and educational institutions, the preservation and study of the national and world cultural heritage, and the development of library science and information technology. EAL provides library services mainly to undergraduate and postgraduate students, research staff, and faculty members. In addition to the ELNET Consortium, EAL participates in several national programs dealing with the preservation and research of national literature: With support from the United Nations Educational, Scientific, and Cultural Organization (UNESCO), a cooperative project has studied the condition of cultural treasures in the larger libraries of Estonia. The Open Estonian Foundation and Open Society Institute have financed a joint project of libraries and archives to establish a deposit stock of Estonian written cultural heritage. To provide additional resources to its users, the EAL has begun microfilming Estonian newspapers published abroad, and digitizing of library materials is also planned.

TIIU REIMO

Further Reading

Klaassen, Anne, editor, *Eesti Teaduste Akadeemia Raamatukogu 50: Ülevaateid ja mälestusi* (The Library of the Estonian Academy of Sciences), Tallinn: Teaduste Akadeemia Kirjastus, 1996 (with English summaries)

Kraut, Aita, and Tiiu Reimo, *Eesti Teaduste Akadeemia Raamatukogu; Library of the Estonian Academy of Sciences* (bilingual Estonian and English edition), Tallinn: Eesti Teaduste Akadeemia Raamatukogu, 1991

Paas, Marita, "Die historische Kollektionen der Baltica-Abteilung der Bibliothek der Estnischen Akademie der Wissenschaften," *Libri Gedanensis* 13/14 (1997)

Reimo, Tiiu, compiler, "Estnische akademische Bibliothek," in *Handbuch deutscher historischer Buchbestände in Europa*, edited by Bernhard Fabian, vol. 7, part 2, *Finnland, Estland, Lettland, Litauen*, Hildesheim, Germany, and New York: Olms-Weidmann, 1998

Reimo, Tiiu, and Asko Tamme, "The Library of the Estonian Academy of Sciences: A Short Survey of the Present and the Past," *Bibliotheca Baltica* 5 (1997)

Eton College Library

Address: Eton College
Windsor, Berkshire SL4 6DB
UK
Telephone: 1753-671221
Fax: 1753-801507

Founded: 1440

Holdings (2000): Volumes: 85,000. Current serials: 15; incunabula: 206; manuscripts: 1,000.

Special Collections: *Areas of Concentration:* Armenian printed books (1500–1900); English Civil War and early-18th-century English pamphlets; early science; Elizabethan, Jacobean, and Restoration drama; 19th- and 20th-century English literature; 16th- through 18th-century classical writers; 16th-century Italian books. *Individual Collections:* Etoniana collection; Mezzotint collection; Topham drawings and engravings collection. *Papers:* Elizabeth Barrett Browning; Harold Caccia; Lady Diana Cooper; Edward Gordon Craig; Thomas Hardy; Susan Hill; Moelwyn Merchant; L.H. Myers; Anthony Powell; Anne Thackeray Ritchie.

When King Henry VI founded his "College of Our Lady of Eton beside Windsor" near London in 1440, he ordered a building 52 feet long and 24 feet wide in the upper story of the East Cloister to serve as a private reference and borrowing library for the provost and fellows of the college. The king's wishes were put into effect in a desultory fashion. During its first 150 years, the library was moved five times. Its happiest period was in the early 16th century, when Provost Roger Lupton and Fellow William Horman collected 500 books and manuscripts for which they created a handsome library in the present Election Hall. Thirty years later, Thomas Smith, a provost who quarreled with his fellows, decided that the room should become part of his own house and the books dispersed elsewhere. Therefore, it is not surprising that only seven of the 42 manuscripts listed in the 1465 inventory survive and that few of Lupton's and Horman's books are still in the library today.

It is to Henry Savile, provost from 1596 to 1622, that Eton owes the secure establishment of its library. Not only did he set up a printing press to produce his remarkable eight-volume Greek *St. John Chrysostom*, but he also established a bindery where Vincent Williamson worked diligently for the library and school for 20 years. Savile also systematically collected Greek and Latin literature and philosophy, Medieval and Renaissance theology, as well as scientific and medical works. By his death he had more than doubled the number of books in the library, which he moved under the Long Chamber. There the chained books were placed upright on the shelves rather than flat on lecterns or desks as in the past.

Savile himself gave books to the library and actively encouraged others to do so, a practice that has continued to this day. (Eton's Gutenberg Bible; the unique copy of *Ralph Roister-Doister*, the first English comedy; and an early draft of Gray's "Elegy in a Country Churchyard" were all gifts from former Etonians.) In 1639 Provost Henry Wotton, former ambassador to Venice, bequeathed his magnificent collection of early Italian manuscripts, some from Bernardo Bembo's library. Three years later the former head master John Harrison left all of his books to Eton, including 120 important mathematical and scientific works.

By the end of the century and the beginning of Henry Godolphin's provostship, the library had grown so much that there was a lack of space. In 1719 Godolphin unchained the books and commissioned Thomas Rowland to design a new library. The South Gallery of the Cloisters was demolished and the library built there. Completed in 1729, Rowland's new library, laid out in three elegant galleried rooms, was intended to hold 20,000 books. The provost and fellows owned less than a quarter of that number, but the new library, with its welcoming atmosphere, proved an irresistible attraction for new donors. By 1800 it was so full that additional presses were required.

Among the many important 18th-century benefactions, two deserve special mention. In 1736 Richard Topham's famous collection of prints, drawings, and watercolors of classical antiquities (as well as hundreds of books on architecture, archaeology, and numismatics) enlarged the scope of the library and reflected contemporary artistic taste. Antiquarian interest was further enhanced in 1799 when Anthony Storer, aesthete and friend of Horace Walpole, left the library his books: 400 early English plays in quarto, 34 incunabula (including three printed by Caxton), English and Italian literature, Greek and Latin classics, and a number of magnificently extra-illustrated Grangerized volumes. Although some were in their original bindings, others had been sumptuously rebound by the best London binders of the period.

The library ossified for most of the 19th century. The building was full, and a succession of unenterprising provosts saw no reason to develop it further, let alone use it themselves or allow others to use it. The library, which had been opened to limited public access in the 18th century, now shut its doors to the outside world. The boys and masters, who had never been welcome, were also excluded. One of the masters protested strongly to the Public Schools Commission in 1862, but his complaint was suppressed in the report of the commission.

Eventually the growing hostile publicity led to some reluctant action. A book listing the main treasures of the library appeared in 1881, and in 1895 M.R. James published his catalog of the manuscripts. At the same time, Francis Warre-Cornish, the vigorous fellow librarian, started to acquire books. He had no budget, but by selling duplicates (including a Shakespeare quarto), he was able to develop the collection. Among the books he bought were 60 incunabula, including a fine copy of the *Hypnerotomachia*. He also discovered and purchased a manuscript of Higden's *Polychronicon* that had belonged to John Blacman, Henry VI's confessor. (This work has a contemporary drawing of the king attending mass in a marquee erected on the foundations of College Chapel.)

The 20th century saw further progress and expansion. The library no longer remained the preserve of the provost and fellows. Masters, boys, and members of the general public were made welcome, and visiting scholars were encouraged to make use of the library's resources. Head Master Robert Birley examined all the books between 1949 and 1964 and published his findings. During his time, John Hely-Hutchinson presented the library with 50 of his collection of rare bindings, and J.R. Abbey gave his Kelmscott collection. In 1968 Provost Caccia appointed a professional archivist to continue the work done since the 1930s by Noel Blakiston. In the 1980s Provost Charteris ensured that the library had its own budget and a properly trained staff.

In 1968 a 20th-century rare book collection of Old Etonian authors was started in the school library, Eton's main borrowing and reference library. From modest beginnings this collection grew and was extended to include 19th-century authors, including Elizabeth Barrett Browning and Thomas Hardy. Benefactions of complete archives by living authors gave the venture substance and importance, and the entire collection was transferred to the college library. Two floors of the 1517 Lupton's Tower were redesigned and joined to the main library by an internal staircase. At the same time new offices were built. In 1996 the 19th- and 20th-century books and manuscripts were moved to their new home and joined the main collection. Since then more gifts, such as Nicholas Kessler's books on China and Russia, have further enriched the library, which is currently preparing an online catalog of all its holdings.

MICHAEL MEREDITH

Further Reading

Birley, Robert, *The History of Eton College Library*, Eton: Eton College, 1970

Birley, Robert, *One Hundred Books*, Eton: Eton College, 1970

James, Montague Rhodes, *A Descriptive Catalogue of the Manuscripts in the Library of Eton College*, Cambridge: Cambridge University Press, 1895

Meredith, Michael, *One Hundred Books, Manuscripts, and Pictures, 1800–1996, in the Eton College Library*, Eton: Eton College, 1996

Quarrie, Paul, *Treasures of Eton College Library: 550 Years of Collecting*, New York: Pierpont Morgan Library, and Eton: Eton College, 1990

Family History Library

Address:	Family History Library The Church of Jesus Christ of Latter-day Saints 35 North West Temple Street Salt Lake City, Utah 84150-3400 USA Telephone: 801-240-2331; 800-453-3860 x2331 Fax: 801-240-5551; 800-453-3860 x1054 www.familysearch.org
Founded:	1894
Holdings (1999):	Volumes: 300,000. Current serials: 5,000; maps: 3,000; microforms: 2.3 million.
Special Collections:	*Areas of Concentration:* Court records (land, inheritance, naturalization, and citizenship); family histories; local directories and histories; guidebooks; office records (emigration, immigration, military service, taxation, and voting); vital statistics (cemetery, census, church, civil, etc.). *Individual Collections:* Family group records archive.

Library Mission and Development

The library's purpose is to help members of the Church of Jesus Christ of Latter-day Saints to identify their ancestors and link them into families. Although the library serves members of the church, it is open to all researchers.

The church founded the library in 1894 as the library of the Genealogical Society of Utah, a separately incorporated institution. The Genealogical Society of Utah became a department of the church in 1944, but the society's name is still used for the department's microfilming arm; the library is another component of the department. The library was originally known as the Genealogical Library, but in 1987 it was renamed the Family History Library (FHL) in order to eliminate connotations of the word *genealogy* that might lead to the assumption that professional training was needed to research one's ancestry.

The initial collection consisted of 300 books purchased from genealogical enthusiast Franklin D. Richards, a high official of the church. Funded by membership fees and donations, the collection grew slowly. The society was isolated in the intermountain West, far from the locus of genealogical activity along the eastern seaboard.

At the end of its first quarter-century, the library's accomplishments were modest. In 1919 it held 5,027 volumes and tabulated 275 searches, as compared to only 30 ten years earlier. By the end of 1937 the library contained more than 19,200 books, constituting the fifth-largest genealogical collection in the United States at that time.

In 1985 the library moved into the first building constructed specifically to house the collection, at its present location just west of Temple Square in downtown Salt Lake City. In 1964 the society began to establish branches where copies of microfilms could be ordered to be viewed locally, because the central facility in Salt Lake City could not effectively help members of a church growing rapidly in the United States and internationally. These branches were renamed "family history centers" in 1987. Currently there are 3,413 family history centers operating in 65 countries, to which 100,000 microfilm rolls are circulated each month from the FHL.

The Growth of Genealogy

Between 1961 and 1969, the average number of library users increased from 301 per day to more than 600, a large increase over earlier patronage but a small fraction of what would become the case. On its 75th anniversary in 1969 the society sponsored a World Conference on Records. Six thousand participants from around the world came to Salt Lake City to attend more than 230 different sessions on all aspects of genealogy. The society sponsored a second conference in 1980, cementing it and the library as important forces in the international pursuit of identification and preservation of mankind's ancestral heritage.

Despite these efforts, genealogy remained an obscure activity in the eyes of the U.S. public until the January 1977 television broadcast of a miniseries based on Alex Haley's 1976 book *Roots*. News agencies immediately flooded the library with inquiries and requests for interviews. An average of 3,500 people visited the library daily in 1977, up from a peak attendance of 2,000 in the previous year. Even though immediate public attention cooled, genealogy became a major U.S. pastime. In 1999 a daily average of 2,400 visitors came to the library.

Archibald Bennett, secretary of the society and head librarian from 1928 to 1961, made many significant contributions, not only to the library but to the genealogical community as a whole. A prolific author, he wrote 33 instructional texts, including one of the first standard textbooks in the field, *A Guide for Genealogical Research* (1951). He developed the use of the pedigree chart and family group record form used today by nearly all U.S. genealogists. He was elected as a Fellow of the American Society of Genealogists in 1961 and elected to the National Genealogy Hall of Fame in 1994.

Microfilming

Microfilming was a new technology in 1938 when the society began using it as a means of making its collections at remote locations available for research in the library. The society has employed and developed microfilm techniques and procedures for more than 60 years, sharing its expertise with archivists around the world via the International Council on Archives. Society-sponsored microfilming has occurred in more than 100 countries, and there are currently more than 200 cameras acquiring approximately 100 million exposures (about 60,000 new rolls of microfilm) annually for the library collection. Its collection of more than 2.1 million microfilm rolls of genealogical sources from around the world is considered the largest such collection in existence.

Preserving films is as important as creating them. In 1960 excavation of a storage site for film masters began in a granite mountainside located in Little Cottonwood Canyon, south of Salt Lake City. It preserves the microfilm masters under 700 feet of granite, where the temperature and humidity remain constant regardless of outside conditions, providing an ideal venue for preservation in perpetuity.

The Library Today

Since 1984 the church and the Family History Library have strongly promoted the creation of large automated research files. Both church members and volunteers from the genealogical community outside the church have been included in massive indexing efforts. For example, from 1988 to 1996 the church, in cooperation with the Federation of Family History Societies in England, transcribed the 1881 British census, creating a database of 30 million names.

Automated genealogical research currently guides the work of the library and the genealogical program of the church. Information provided by researchers and vital statistics transcribed from original records are available in a number of databases. Two premier databases are: the Ancestral File, which contains approximately 35.6 million names arranged in family groups with ascending and descending pedigrees, and the International Genealogical Index (IGI), which contains approximately 300 million individual names along with dates of birth, christening, and marriage. These and other databases are available at the library's website; they also can be purchased on compact discs.

From an obscure library established during the 19th century, the Family History Library has become a premier repository of genealogical research materials from all areas of the globe.

KAHLILE B. MEHR

Further Reading

Allen, James B., Jessie L. Embry, and Kahlile B. Mehr, *Hearts Turned to the Fathers: A History of the Genealogical Society of Utah, 1894–1994*, Provo, Utah: Brigham Young University Studies, 1995

Cerny, Johni, and Wendy Elliott, editors, *The Library: A Guide to the LDS Family History Library*, Salt Lake City, Utah: Ancestry, 1988

Mehr, Kahlile B., "International Activities and Services of the Genealogical Society of Utah," *Archivum* 37 (1992)

Powell, Ted F., "Saving the Past for the Future: Tales of International Search and Cooperation," *American Archivist* 39 (1976)

Schueler, Donald G., "Our Family Trees Have Roots in Utah's Mountain Vaults," *Smithsonian* 12 (December 1981)

Shoumatoff, Alex, "A Reporter at Large: The Mountain of Names," *New Yorker* 61 (May 1985)

Folger Shakespeare Library

Address: Folger Shakespeare Library
201 East Capitol Street, SE
Washington, D.C. 20003
USA
Telephone: 202-544-4600
Fax: 202-675-0313
www.folger.edu

Founded: 1932

Holdings (2000): Volumes: 280,000. Current serials: 200; graphic materials: 28,000; manuscripts: 55,000; modern books (post-1800): 140,000; playbills: 250,000; promptbooks: 2,000; rare books (pre-1600): 116,000.

Special Collections: *Areas of Concentration:* Art; European imprints; maps; music; photographs; scrapbooks; STC (early English printed books, 1475–1640); theater; Wing imprints (1641–1700). *Individual Collections:* Shakespeare collection. *Papers:* Bacon-Townshend families; Bagot family; Robert Bennett; Cavendish-Talbot families; Augustin Daly; Rich family; state papers of English royalty; Strozzi family.

History

The Folger library was a vision shared by Henry Clay Folger and Emily Jordan Folger. Together they devoted 41 years to building a peerless collection of Shakespeariana, launched with the acquisition of a Fourth Folio in 1889 for $107.50 at the Bangs auction rooms in New York City. Their acquisitions also included the purchase for $10,000 of the unique 1594 quarto of *Titus Andronicus* that had been discovered by accident in Malmö, Sweden, wrapped in sheets of Swedish lottery tickets. But the Folgers will be most remembered as collectors of the First Folio (1623). The couple, as Emily Jordan phrased it, "rather specialized in First Folios," amassing 79 copies and three fragments in the course of their careers, plus 117 copies of the later 17th-century folios. The library, with a collection of more than 90,000 volumes, was dedicated on the anniversary of Shakespeare's birthday, 23 April 1932, with President Hoover presiding.

The building, a landmark structure on the register of historic places, was the work of U.S. architect Paul Philippe Cret. Having decided upon Washington (Mrs. Folger's familiarity with the city may have influenced the final selection of the site as much as Mr. Folger's claim to have picked the nation's capital because "I am an American"), the Folgers quietly acquired a row of townhouses behind the Library of Congress on land ceded by an Act of Congress in 1928. The Folgers' Shakespeare Memorial was an elegant marble building of classical design, embellished with bas reliefs commissioned from John Gregory depicting nine scenes from the plays, with art deco grillwork on the facade, an oak-paneled Tudor long gallery, a reading room with the flavor of an Elizabethan great hall (complete with period furniture and splendid stained glass), and a theater in the spirit of an Elizabethan playhouse. Cret designed the exterior of the building, fortunately talking the Folgers out of a Tudoresque facade while indulging the couple's thoroughly English vision within. Henry Folger never saw the completed building or how the collection was to be housed; he died of heart failure on 11 June 1930, two weeks after the cornerstone was laid. An award-winning modern extension with two levels of underground vault space was opened in 1982.

A marked detour in the development of the collection occurred in 1937, a year after Mrs. Folger's death. It is difficult to say whether she would have approved of the acquisition of the Harmsworth collection—11,000 titles named in the *Short-Title Catalogue of Books Printed in English . . . and of English Books Printed Abroad, 1475–1640* (STC), covering a wide range of subjects—but it was recognized then, as now, to be a major event in the history of the library. Sir Leicester Harmsworth collected in the same period as the Folgers (Tudor-Stuart) but went far beyond Shakespeare in his pursuit. It was the merger of these two great collections in 1937 that made the Folger library a destination for scholars in a wide range of disciplines, lifting the library to a stature it would not have achieved had it remained a bastion exclusively for Shakespeare studies. The arrival of the Harmsworth collection set the precedent for collecting across subject areas from William Caxton to John Dryden, a course still followed.

When the library opened, leadership was shared by Joseph Quincy Adams (a noted Shakespearean from Cornell who was named the library's director of research) and William A. Slade from the Library of Congress. Librarian appointments were made by Mrs. Folger. In 1936 Adams had assumed full administrative responsibility. Following his death in 1946, the Folger was administered briefly by James G. McManaway, who served as acting director from 1946 to 1948, then by Louis B. Wright, who completed the task of organizing the library for scholarly use during the next 20 years. Wright expanded the Folger's horizons significantly, though always giving primacy to the founders' desire that the institution be "first and foremost a library."

O.B. Hardison Jr. became director in 1969 and expanded the library's sphere of activity. A new emphasis was placed on public outreach and cultural programs in the Hardison years, while the library continued to enlarge its role as a research institution. A resident theater company was established and exhibitions and educational initiatives accelerated.

The best treatment of the strains and successes of the growth years appears in *Managing Change in the Non-Profit Sector: Lessons from the Evolution of Five Independent Research Libraries* by Jed Bergman, William Bowen, and Thomas Nygren (1995), a comparative study that takes the Folger into the tenure of Werner Gundersheimer, who became director in 1984, inheriting an institution at financial odds with itself. Gundersheimer faced, for example, the largest deficit yet encountered by the theater. The difficult decision was made to separate the theater from the library. The Folger's Elizabethan Theater is now managed separately and presents a lively range of readings, lectures, early music concerts, and theatrical performances some 180 nights per year, on a scale that both enriches the Folger environment and fulfills the library's mission to provide "interpretive programs for the public" while avoiding fiscal strain of library resources. A Center for Education and Public Programs opened in 2000 across the street from the library.

The library remains under the fiduciary control of the Trustees of Amherst College, as originally provided for by Folger. The 1988 long-range plan concluded that the current governance arrangement "works well and does not require any important alteration." The Folger Library Committee, which has been augmented since 1972 by a majority of non-Amherst trustees, functions quasi-autonomously, although it is officially a subcommittee of the Amherst Board. The arrangement brought some advantages to the Folger, particularly with respect to endowment management.

Collection Strengths

The library's collections focus on English and European literary, cultural, political, religious, and social history from the 15th to 18th centuries, with particular strengths in the 16th and 17th centuries. The Folger has one of the largest collections of STC and Wing imprints (1641–1700) in the world, with approximately 55,000 volumes and broadsides. Early modern continental holdings are strong in Italian, German, French, and Dutch imprints. Performance history in the 18th and 19th centuries is particularly well documented.

At the heart of the library lies the Shakespeare Collection: 186 quartos of the plays and poems of Shakespeare; 79 copies of the First Folio (1623); and a total of 117 copies of the Second (1632), Third (1664), and Fourth (1685) Folios. The collection includes 7,000 other editions of Shakespeare's works, from Nicholas Rowe (1709) to date. Hundreds of editions translate the plays and poems into more than 40 languages. Shakespearean playbills and promptbooks complement print collections.

The library's book collections are supplemented by art works, photographs, maps, early music, non-Shakespearean playbills, theatrical programs and scrapbooks, and films and videos. Thousands of visual resources (etchings, engravings, prints, paintings, photographs) comprise one of the largest collections of 18th- and 19th-century illustrations to Shakespeare, as well as portraits of actors and actresses from that period. Perhaps most notable are the large collection of sketches by Sir George Romney of Shakespearean subjects, paintings and drawings by Henry Fuseli (including a 1579 portrait of Queen Elizabeth I), and an extensive collection of etchings by Wenceslaus Hollar.

Manuscript holdings are rich in early correspondence, commonplace and recipe books, and poetry and plays. Special collections include the Loseley papers of the More family (16th- and 17th-century); papers of the Bacon-Townshend families (16th- and 17th-century); the Cavendish-Talbot families (1548–1607); the Rich family (1485–1820); the Bagot family (1557–1671); the Robert Bennett papers (17th-century); papers of the 19th-century theatrical manager Augustin Daly; 18th-century records of Drury Lane and Covent Garden theaters; more than 200 scrapbooks belonging to the 19th-century antiquary, James Orchard Halliwell-Phillipps; and 200 volumes from the Strozzi family compiled in the 17th and 18th centuries but recording an earlier period.

Microfilm collections include the Cecil papers from Hatfield House; other Loseley papers from the Guildford Muniment Room and Loseley Park; manuscripts from the Tanner and Rawlinson collections at the Bodleian Library and from the Harleian and Lansdowne collections of the British Library; the domestic state papers of Henry VIII, Edward VI, Mary, Elizabeth I, James I, and Charles I; the uncalendared foreign state papers of Elizabeth I; the unpublished state papers of the English Civil War and Interregnum; and the papers of Sir Henry Irving and Ellen Terry from the Shakespeare Centre Library, Stratford-upon-Avon. The library also has the two microfilm sets from University Microfilms International (Bell & Howell/UMI) that best augment print collections for the STC/Wing period: *Early English Books, Series I–II*; and the complete *Thomason Tracts*.

The Library Today

The Folger collection remains its central attraction. In the Harmsworth tradition, the library continues to collect broadly in the STC and Wing periods. Although still the mecca for Shakespeareans, it surprises many that only 25 percent of Folger readers (as users are called there) are working on Shakespeare. Fewer than half work in literary studies. Over the years, major collections have been acquired in such areas as the Reformation, Italian drama, festival books, French and Dutch historical and political pamphlets, herbals, and early maps. From

1475 to 1700 the collection is encyclopedic in range. Beyond the Tudor period, strengths are in drama, promptbooks and performance history, the history of Shakespeare editions, critical/historical literature that elucidates rare book holdings, and modern scholarship on the early modern period.

The Folger awards 30 fellowships a year, and the diverse community of short- and long-term fellows strengthens the Folger environment. A Center for the Study of British Political Thought is based at the library, and the Folger Institute offers a rigorous seminar schedule, stages academic conferences, and hosts regular evening and weekend colloquia on diverse topics. The library also reaches out in other ways, recognizing the importance of its role in the larger world of global scholarship, participation, and exchange.

Technology came late to the Folger but has been integrated successfully. An Integrated Library System (ILS) was implemented in 1996–97, and external access through the library's Website was offered in 2000. Although libraries are fundamentally an environment of print, electronic access is now at the heart of bibliographic control, and newer technologies are evident. Museum shop and ticket sales are now routinely handled through the Folger website as are reference services, orders for images from the collection for scholarly or commercial purposes, exhibition information, advertising, and visitor information. Digitization projects are underway locally and collaboratively through, for example, various commercial ventures, the Research Libraries Information Network's (RLIN's) Archival Resources Service, and in association with the Massachusetts Institute of Technology (Cambridge), which has centered its Shakespeare Electronic Archive at the Folger for both scholarly and educational purposes.

The research agenda is augmented by public and educational programs that bring diverse audiences and enrichment to the library. Interpretive programs for the public are offered by the Folger Consort (the library's resident early music ensemble), through PEN/Faulkner Foundation readings and an acclaimed poetry series, lectures, and numerous theatrical productions. At the center of Folger outreach is the library's education programs that reach younger audiences through initiatives like the Folger Shakespeare Festival, drawing students from 50 to 60 schools per year to the Folger stage to perform scenes from the plays. The Folger is home to the *Shakespeare Quarterly*, *The New Folger Library Shakespeare*, and the *Folger News*, and it actively disseminates information about its collections through scholarly exhibition catalogs.

A balanced budget and endowment support brought welcome stability to the acquisitions, exhibition, fellowship, and public programs during the 1990s and prepared the Folger for its successful entry into the new millennium.

RICHARD J. KUHTA

Further Reading

Bergman, Jed I., William G. Bowen, and Thomas I. Nygren, *Managing Change in the Non-Profit Sector: Lessons from the Evolution of Five Independent Research Libraries*, San Francisco: Jossey-Bass, 1995

Folger News (October, 1969–)

Kane, Betty Ann, *The Widening Circle: The Story of the Folger Shakespeare Library and Its Collections*, Washington, D.C.: The Folger Shakespeare Library, 1976

King, Stanley, *Recollections of the Folger Shakespeare Library*, Ithaca, New York: Cornell University Press, 1950

Pressly, William, *A Catalogue of Paintings in the Folger Shakespeare Library: "As Imagination Bodies Forth,"* New Haven, Connecticut: Yale University Press, 1993

Severy, Merle, "Shakespeare Lives at the Folger," *National Geographic* 171 (February 1987)

Wright, Louis B., "The Harmsworth Collection and the Folger Library," *The Book Collector* 6 (1957)

Wright, Louis B., "A Working Library of Sixteenth- and Seventeenth-Century History," *Libri* 10 (1960)

Free Library of Philadelphia

Address: Free Library of Philadelphia
1901 Vine Street
Philadelphia, Pennsylvania 19103
USA
Telephone: 215-686-5322
Fax: 215-563-3628
www.library.phila.gov

Founded: 1891

Holdings (Central Library, 2000): Volumes: 3 million. Audio recordings: 83,000; clay tablets: 3,000; films and videos: 22,000; graphic images: 1.4 million; incunabula: 900; manuscripts: 18,000; maps: 130,000; microforms: 2 million; sheet music: 620,000.

Special Collections: *Areas of Concentration:* Americana; automotive reference; children's books; common law; cuneiform tablets; European illuminated manuscripts; incunabula; Napoleonica; orchestral and choral music; Oriental manuscripts; Pennsylvania-German imprints, fraktur, and manuscripts; Philadelphia theater; Philadelphia views; prints and printmaking. *Individual Collections:* Charles Dickens; Oliver Goldsmith; Kate Greenaway; Horace; Robert Lawson; Lubin Film Company; Edgar Allan Poe; Beatrix Potter; Howard Pyle; Arthur Rackham.

Origins

Philadelphia businessman George S. Pepper bequeathed approximately $250,000 "to the trustees of such free library which may be established in the city of Philadelphia, east of the Schuylkill River and south of Market Street . . ." when he died in May 1890. The Free Library of Philadelphia was incorporated the following year, largely through the initiative of his nephew William Pepper. Later in 1891 the Philadelphia City Council appropriated $15,000 to the Board of Education, which established the library's first branch at the Wagner Free Institute of Science, a Philadelphia institution committed to popular education. Thus Philadelphia's public library came into existence relatively late in the U.S. public library movement, perhaps due to the numerous subscription and philanthropic libraries that were already available in mid-19th-century Philadelphia. Two of these libraries sought to claim the Pepper bequest. The courts decided in 1893 that the bequest was not intended to go to an existing library, but to a new library that would be open to the general public, and in March 1894 the Free Library opened a main library in three rooms of old City Hall at Fifth and Chestnut Streets. The main and branch libraries were soon consolidated under the management of the trustees of the Free Library.

The year 1899 marked a number of important institutional developments: the establishment of departments of service to the blind and to children, as well as the gift of a collection of 500 incunabula from local industrialist P.A.B. Widener. Widener also presented his Broad Street residence to the city to become a branch of the Free Library. Following the death of his wife in 1905, it was named the H. Josephine Widener Memorial Branch. In 1900 the library opened a department of government documents after having been designated a federal depository library in 1897.

The library's first librarian, John Thomson, moved the main library out of City Hall and into rented space at two other addresses before starting plans for a permanent location in 1911. The major growth during the early years of the 20th century, however, was the construction of branch libraries. In 1900 the library received a gift of $1.5 million from Andrew Carnegie for construction of 30 branch libraries, ten of which were completed between 1906 and 1909. Carnegie stipulated that each branch must have a children's room. The first director of children's work was hired in 1903, a year during which 83 story hours were held for 4,637 children. This marked the beginning of a strong institutional commitment to service for children. Very early in its history, the Free Library also sought to respond to the interests and concerns of the neighborhoods served by the branches, often stocking material in the various languages used within the communities.

The Central Library

The completion of the present central library was a protracted project. The 1911 plan for the new Benjamin Franklin Parkway, designed to connect the city with Fairmount Park, placed the main library midway between the new City Hall and the Philadelphia Museum of Art, the plans for which were also underway. Started by John Thomson, the project was carried out under the direction of the second librarian, John Ashhurst III. Trustee P.A.B. Widener guided the selection of Horace Trumbauer as the architect, but the actual plans were most likely the work of Trumbauer's chief designer, Julian Abele, the first black graduate in architecture from the University of Pennsylvania. From the first design of 1912, the central library resembled buildings on the Place de la Concorde on the Champs Elysées, in keeping with the generally French character of the Parkway design. After many interruptions due to local corruption and larger forces such as World War I, the building opened to the public on 2 June 1927. The total cost of construction was $6.3 million. In the interest of fire safety, the building contained very little wood. Constructed of Indiana limestone with floors of Tennessee marble and terrazzo, its fixtures and furniture were wrought iron or bronze. The art metal manufacturer supplied nearly 3 million pounds of metal, much of it designed and painted to resemble wood.

The plan for the central library included space for Philadelphia attorney Hampton L. Carson's collection on the growth of the common law, which included an extensive collection of manuscripts, printed books, and prints on the subject. Initially placed on deposit with the Free Library in 1927, the Carson collection officially became part of the library on Carson's death in 1929. The Edwin A. Fleisher collection of orchestral music also opened to the public in 1929. Today the Fleisher collection provides loans from its holdings to orchestras worldwide.

In 1930 Mr. and Mrs. John Frederick Lewis Sr. presented a collection of cuneiform tablets to the Free Library. In the years following World War I, Lewis had made numerous trips to Europe to purchase items for his collections. When he died in 1932, his will stipulated that his various collections be given to appropriate local institutions. Subsequently the Free Library received several of these collections from Mrs. Lewis, including books on the history of engraving and the graphic arts, portrait prints (adding to a collection that Lewis had started giving to the library during his lifetime), title pages, European illuminated manuscripts, and Oriental manuscripts (primarily in Arabic and Persian).

The Depression Years through the Mid-20th Century

During the Depression years, the appropriations for new book acquisitions came to a virtual halt, and the *Philadelphia Record* promoted a Give-a-Book Campaign for the Free Library in the late 1930s. Other libraries were also affected by the Depression. In 1943 the Library Company of Philadelphia, a subscription library founded in 1731, entered into an agreement under which the Free Library managed the Library Company's site at Broad and Christian as a branch of the Free Library. The following year the Mercantile Library Company, one of the libraries that had sought money from the Pepper estate in the 1890s, became part of the Free Library. Almost a decade later in 1953, the Free Library opened a separate Mercantile Library for business reference. In all, 11 independent libraries joined with the Free Library. Among these, the Library Company is the only one that resumed independent status.

Franklin Price, the library's third librarian, guided the library through the 1930s and the early 1940s to a period of revitalization following World War II. In 1947 A.S.W. Rosenbach presented his collection of early U.S. children's books to the library. Rosenbach, a local rare book dealer-*cum*-scholar, had been among the first to see the potential for children's books to become a separate area of collecting. In the following years, the library steadily added to its rare and special children's book collections through gifts and purchases, including the purchase from Samuel Castner of his personal collection of 46 scrapbooks containing approximately 8,000 prints, photographs, and clippings related to Philadelphia life, a collection that enriched already sizable holdings in prints and photographs. In 1948 Thomas McKean presented his collection on the automobile, with holdings including technical manuals, sales literature, periodicals, and photographs, as well as secondary literature documenting the history of the automobile from its beginnings to the present.

The most dramatic gift from these years was the Elkins Library, which came as a bequest following the death of William McIntire Elkins in 1947. In addition to Elkins's collections of Oliver Goldsmith, Charles Dickens, and Americana, the library also received the 62-foot-long room (included the paneling, rugs, fireplace, chandeliers, and furniture) in which they had been housed in his private residence. The installation of this room in the central library took two years and prompted the library to create a separate rare book department on the third floor of the central library for Mr. Elkins's and other donors' collections of rare books. The department opened to the public in May 1949. Later gifts to this department included the D. Jacques Benoliel Collection of Dickens Letters, the Moncure Biddle Collection on Horace, the archival collection from the American Sunday-School Union, the H. Bacon Collamore Collection of Beatrix Potter, the Colonel Richard Gimbel Collection on Edgar Allan Poe, and the children's book collections of Frederick R. Gardner. Largely through the Simon Gratz Fund, the Free Library has built a large and significant collection of Pennsylvania-German material, including printed books, fraktur, and manuscripts.

The Greenaway Years, 1951 to 1969

Emerson Greenaway, the library's fourth librarian (later called the director), oversaw innovation and expansion in many areas. Starting in 1958 publishers agreed to send prepublication copies of books so that the library would have them on the shelves when they were published—a system soon known as the Greenaway Plan in the library profession. The following year a new educational films department started loaning 16-millimeter films to groups. During the 1950s numerous branches were renovated and new branches constructed, the central library was reorganized by subject rather than format, and the institution was placed under the jurisdiction of the Civil Service Commission of Philadelphia. The latter resulted in standard qualifying examinations for staff positions.

In 1963 the library opened the Northeast Regional Library, the first of three regional libraries containing holdings as extensive as those of many municipal libraries. State funding that same year led to new responsibilities as a District Library Center for eastern Pennsylvania and as a Regional Resource Library for the entire state. Within a few years the educational films department became the regional film center, expanding its services to eastern Pennsylvania. The library for the blind expanded its program to include service to the physically handicapped of the region. With federal funding the library also created a reader development program to furnish material to combat adult illiteracy. Director Greenaway held leadership positions in the American Library Association, as would future directors Keith Doms and Elliot Shelkrot.

The theater collection began in 1966. Strong in material related to Philadelphia theater, the collection grew to contain holdings on motion pictures, television, radio, and other popular forms of entertainment. Of particular note is the Lubin Film Company Archives, documenting the activities of a Philadelphia-based company in the early years of film history (1911 to 1916). Also in the 1960s, the Drinker Library of Choral Music became the property of the Free Library.

The Doms Years, 1969 to 1987

Under the leadership of Director Keith Doms, later named president and director, the Free Library participated in cooperative cataloging via the OCLC database, beginning in 1974. In 1983 the central library closed its card catalog and committed to an online catalog for bibliographic access as well as circulation records. Following a similar progression, the Computer-Based Information Center opened in 1975, initially to provide access to the *New York Times* Information Bank. Later in the 1970s the library received federal funding to provide access to more databases. As in many other libraries, electronic access to the library's catalog and other computerized resources steadily increased to the point where both services became available through one integrated library system connected to the Internet, by the late 1990s. The 1970s also saw the beginning of the Friends of the Free Library, whose membership included those interested in supporting the libraries' interests through advocacy activities as well as direct support. Friends groups for individual branch libraries were also formed.

The Shelkrot Years, 1987 to Present

Since March 1987 President and Director Elliot L. Shelkrot has enabled the library to bring emerging library technology to all residents of the city of Philadelphia. The Changing Lives campaign (1995–98) increased funding from private foundations and individuals. With that funding in addition to funding from the city of Philadelphia, the library has renovated nearly all of its 55 facilities in neighborhoods throughout the city, equipping them with computers connected to the World Wide Web. This program was particularly designed to further the Free Library's longstanding commitment to provide services to Philadelphia children. With more than 500,000 registered cardholders and annual circulation of 6.3 million in fiscal year 2000, the Free Library upholds its mission to "provide to all segments of Philadelphia's diverse population a comprehensive collection of recorded knowledge, ideas, artistic expression, and information . . . through a variety of means, including current technology." The Free Library is planning major expansion and renovation of the central library to assure preservation of its wealth of resources into the new millennium.

CORNELIA S. KING

Further Reading

Art Metal Construction Co., *Art Metal in The Free Library of Philadelphia,* Jamestown, New York: Art Metal Construction, 1927

Brownlee, David, *Building the City Beautiful: The Benjamin Franklin Parkway and the Philadelphia Museum of Art,* Philadelphia, Pennsylvania: Philadelphia Museum of Art, 1989

Doms, Keith, "Free Library of Philadelphia," in *Encyclopedia of Library and Information Science,* edited by Allen Kent et al., vol. 9, New York: Dekker, 1973

Doms, Keith, "Free Library of Philadelphia," in *Invisible Philadelphia,* edited by Jean Toll and Mildred Gillam, Philadelphia, Pennsylvania: Atwater Kent Museum, 1995

Shaffer, Ellen, "John Frederick Lewis, 1860–1932," *Manuscripts* 15 (1963)

Free University of Amsterdam Library

Address: Universiteitsbibliotheek Vrije Universiteit Amsterdam
De Boelelaan 1105
1081 HV Amsterdam
The Netherlands
Telephone: 20-444-5200
Fax: 20-444-5259
www.ubvu.vu.nl

Founded: 1878

Holdings (2000): Volumes: 2 million. Atlases: 2,800; current serials: 18,000; engraved portraits: 1,000; maps: 60,000.

Special Collections: *Areas of Concentration:* Dutch Protestantism; law; maps; science. *Individual Collections:* Herman Bavinck; biography collection; Henricus Bos; John Bunyan; Jean Calvin; Abraham Kuyper; pre-1800 English printed books; Press Documentation Center.

Origins

The Free University Amsterdam was founded by a group of Dutch Protestants brought together by theologian and Dutch statesman Abraham Kuyper. Kuyper's goal in forming the group was to establish a university that was "free" in the sense that it answered neither to the government nor the church but only to the Bible as God's word. The university opened its doors to students in 1880 and has been in continuous operation since then. Its emphasis is on academic excellence combined with a concern for society, and certain areas of research (such as environmental studies and minority studies) are encouraged. In 1996 the university received the Hoger Onderwijsprijs, a prestigious award from the Dutch government given every two years for academic excellence.

The current Free University Library, the Universiteitsbibliotheek Vrije Universiteit (UBVU), is divided into seven sections: general and special collections; biomedical sciences; economic sciences; library of natural sciences, computer science, and mathematics; arts and religious studies; legal studies; and social sciences. Many of the materials in these areas are located in the main library building or in nearby facilities. The medical library operates as a separate library with a large number of branches for specific medical topics.

In addition to the library, a number of research institutes reflect the collections of UBVU and possess works that complement those at the university. The Institute for Environmental Studies, founded in 1971, focuses chiefly on preserving the environment through research. Other institutes include the Economic and Social Institute; the Interdisciplinary Center for the Study of Science, Society, and Religion; the Institute for Teaching and Educational Practice; the Foundation for Research into World Food Supplies; the Institute for Extramural Medical Research; the Institute of Ethics; and the Radionuclide Center.

Special Collections

The university's original founders devoted much of their time to Dutch Protestantism, and materials related to this subject, along with bibliographies, maps and atlases, international statistics and other information from international organizations, press documentation, and early printed books make up the special collections of UBVU. In addition, the library has established the European Documentation Center, which holds many official European documents as well as official Dutch documents. It acts as an official repository for published materials from the Dutch Central Bureau for Statistics.

Within special collections, the library houses a number of early printed books and manuscripts, mostly on Dutch Protestantism, that are located in the Center for Protestant Literature (CPL). A collection of 60,000 items, the CPL includes material up to 1901, such as 5,200 16th-century items, 1,500 engraved portraits, and materials from the Middle East. During the year 2000, this section of the library published *Protestantism Crossing the Seas*, a short-title catalog of English books printed before 1801 illustrating the spread of Protestant thought and the exchange of ideas between English-speaking countries and the Netherlands. The catalog contains 5,600 volumes, the largest such collection in any non-English-speaking country.

The library also houses a special collection of biographies from around the world, with 75,000 from Africa, 280,000 from North America, 80,000 from the Arab-Islamic world, and 150,000 Jewish biographies. There are also a number of European biographies, including biographical records from the Benelux countries dating back to 1581, from Spain and Portugal to 1602, from Italy to 1646, and from France in the 17th century.

Equally broad in scope is the library's map collection, formed in 1960 as part of the Geographic Institute and based on two collections, the Woods Library (Henricus Bosbibliotheek) and the Seminary Library (Seminariebibliotheek Hoeven). From the former collection came 100 maps, 98 books, and 13 atlases. The Seminary collection added newspapers and pre-1800 atlases and maps, including two 18th-century atlases from Jean Baptiste Bourguignon d'Anville. In 1967 the collection was incorporated into the library and moved in 1970 to the main library. Some access to collections was lost in 1987 when an alliance for additional cartographic support from the Gamma Library was broken. In 1994 the collection was moved to its current location in special collections in the main building. Today it holds approximately 36,000 maps, 25 globes, 2,800 atlases, and numerous other items. An additional 25,000 maps are available in the earth sciences section of the science library.

The Press Documentation Center is among the newer divisions of special collections, with materials reaching back to 1970. The collection holds a number of Dutch, European, African, and Asian periodicals, from *Africa Confidential* and *Le Monde* to *Time* and the *Asian Recorder*. Related to this part of the special collections are the German language periodicals, indexes, and bibliographies, all from the 18th and 19th centuries and recently transferred to microfiche.

Electronic Databases and Computerization

The library has completely embraced the electronic age and has computerized many of its databases, catalogs, and other reference materials. There are a number of electronic databases available at the library, from ABC Political Science and BIOSIS Previews to Attent Research Memoranda and ESB Economie databank. Owing to licensing issues, most of these databases cannot be accessed remotely and require the user to be at a computer terminal on the Free University campus. However, the library staff does provide fee-based services from these databases on request. The library's own catalog is available online for remote use, however, and can be accessed via the UBVU website.

CAROL ANNE CARROLL

Further Reading

Een Vrije Universiteitsbibliotheek: Studies over verleden, bezit en heden van de bibliotheek der Vrije Universiteit, Amsterdam: Van Gorcum, 1980

Fudan University Library

Address: Fudan Daxue Tushu Guan
220 Handan Road
Shanghai 200433
China
Telephone: 21-65643162
Fax: 21-65649814
www.library.fudan.edu.cn

Founded: 1918

Holdings (2000): Volumes: 3.7 million. Audio recordings: 5,000; current serials: 21,000; manuscripts: 60,000; maps: 500; microforms: 500,000.

Special Collections: *Areas of Concentration:* Ancient Chinese books from the Song, Yuan, Ming and Qing dynasties; local chronicles; mathematics; Tanzi and local drama. *Individual Collections:* Ancient Chinese books collection; Min Guo period (1911–49) books collection; Journal of Pure and Applied Mathematics collection.

Origins

The history of the Fudan University can be traced back to Fudan Gongxue, a private college established in 1905 at Wusong, Shanghai. After moving to Li Gong Ci at Xujia Hui in 1912, the college was reorganized in 1917 with the addition of three undergraduate colleges and was named the Private Fudan University. Before students set up a reading room called Wuwu Yueshu She (Wuwu Book Club) in 1918, the university had only a few books on hand. Two years later the university took over the reading room, changed its name to Fudan University Library, and assigned 1918 as the founding date, but allowed the students to continue to manage the library. In addition to the physical facilities, the library received no financial nor personnel support from the university. It was not until 1923, when Du Dingyou, a professional librarian, was appointed as the head, that the library began to function formally.

Library Facilities

After the university relocated to its current address in 1922, the library occupied two rooms in the Yizhu Tang building, and then the entire building in 1926. Library space did not significantly improve until 1929, however, when two wings were added to Yizhu Tang. On 15 January 1930 the enlarged library opened its doors to users and was renamed for Professor Xue Xianzhou, a founding figure of the China Cooperation Movement, as the Xianzhou Library.

Soon after the beginning of the Sino-Japanese War (1937–45), the library left Shanghai with the university, first moving to Lu Shan, Jiangxi Province, then to Chongqing, Sichuan Province, taking only 12,593 volumes with it. The university changed its ownership from private to public in 1941 in order to survive under extremely difficult circumstances. Even with government support, the library budget was still inadequate. When Fudan moved back to Shanghai after the war, the combined library holdings of the Sichuan and Shanghai campuses were only 39,100 volumes, about its size before the war began nine years earlier. After the war, the damaged library building was repaired and reference and periodical rooms were set up in other buildings.

In 1949 Fudan University was taken over by the newly established People's Republic of China. Numbers replaced all the old building names without exception, and the library was no longer called Xianzhou Library. In 1958 a new library building was constructed, and on the night of 18 August 1958 the whole university community was called upon to move 600,000-plus volumes from the old library and other reading rooms to the new library. The task was completed in three hours by 4,500 people, and the new library opened its doors the next morning. Another new library building was erected in 1985 and is twice as large as the old one. Since then, the old library has been used as the science library, and the new one serves as the humanities and social sciences library.

Library Collection

Before being called a library, the collection was only a few thousand volumes, but after receiving donations and acquisitions, the holdings increased to 11,000 volumes in 1926. The library enjoyed rapid growth for seven years after 1930, and holdings reached 39,000 at the end of 1936, including 27,000 in Chinese and Japanese. Most of the schools and departments had their own study rooms to house their special materials, which numbered 13,000 items as of 1933.

The collection resumed growth after the war, and in May 1949 when the Chinese People's Liberation Army took over the university, the library held about 100,000 books. The new government ordered a readjustment and restructuring of the existing colleges and faculties in institutions of higher education throughout China. As one of the consequences, library collections were widely redistributed. In 1951 Fudan University Library received 19,000 volumes from the government and other institutes, and 170,000 volumes more the following year. Meanwhile, 30,000 volumes from its collection were transferred to other institutes. From 1961 to 1964 it lost more than 17,000 volumes, including 322 rare Chinese medical books given to Shanghai Chinese Medicine College in 1964. Nevertheless, the collection continued to grow until it reached 1.2 million volumes by the end of 1965.

The most difficult time in China's modern history, the period of the Cultural Revolution (1966-76), forced the library to close in 1966. It did not resume its normal functions until 1970. Collection development was significantly affected, most severely in serials—1,262 subscriptions (68 percent of 1,858 titles) were cancelled, creating gaps that were hard to fill later. The library transferred 10,000 volumes from its collection in 1968, another 57,000 in 1974, and 50,000 more thereafter, receiving 287,000 volumes from others in 1972 and more than 100,000 volumes from Shanghai Library and other private collections. Among the newly acquired materials were 4,180 volumes of Wang family Ershu Xuan Chinese rare books and 1,608 volumes of Tan Zhengbi's storytelling collection. After the Cultural Revolution, the library budget increased steadily and the collection grew at about 100,000 volumes per year. The holdings were 2.8 million volumes in 1986 and reached 3.5 million at the end of 1998.

The outstanding features of the collection include 360,000 threadbound traditional Chinese books, containing more than 7,000 rare editions, 2,000 manuscripts, more than 400 *tanci* (storytelling to the accompaniment of stringed instruments, in various southern dialects) and local dramas (librettos), 2,000 local chronicles, 7,000 works of literature, and 5,000 journals published before 1949. Two special collections of the Fudan University Library are housed in the Mathematics Department Library and the Foreign Language and Literature Department Library. The former library was established in 1949 and holds 46,000 volumes, 612 journals, with many valuable and complete runs, such as the *Journal für die Reine und angewandte Mathematik* (1826–). The latter library held about 80,000 books, including 10,000 volumes of European and American fiction and more than 400 works by or about Shakespeare.

Classification

In the early years of the library, both Chinese and Western books were classified according to the Dewey Decimal Classification (DDC) system, with a title card catalog, a classified catalog for Chinese, and a dictionary card catalog for Western materials. In 1933 a useful book-form catalog, *Fudan Daxue Tushuguan Tushu Mulu* (Fudan University Library Book Catalog), was compiled. Starting in 1975, all general books were cataloged according to the Zhongguo Tushuguan Tushu Fengle Fa (Chinese Library Classification), whereas a fourfold system was kept for classical Chinese books. The library has also kept its card catalogs for general Chinese and Japanese books (three sets: classification, title, and author), classic Chinese books (two sets: classification and title), Western books (four sets: classification, title, author, and subject), and Russian books (three sets: classification, title, and author). In addition to card catalogs, the library compiled 25 book-form catalogs between 1956 and 1965, such as the *Fudan Daxue Tushuguan Guji Jianmu Chugao* (Fudan University Library Chinese Classic Short Catalog: First Draft), and four more in the 1990s: *Guancang Jiu Pingzhuanshu Mulu* (Library Catalog of the Old Paperbound Books), *Guancang Zhongwen Gongjushu Mulu* (Library Catalog of Chinese Reference Works), *Waiguo Shuxue Jiaocai Mulu: 1979–1988* (Catalog of Foreign Mathematics Textbooks: 1979–1988), and *Zhao Jingshen Zengshu Mulu* (A List of Materials Donated by Professor Zhao Jingshen).

Automation

Fudan was one of the earliest pioneers of academic library automation in China. It first established its Automation Division in 1983, with only a few IBM personal computers. Ten years later, a mainframe K-670 SI/20 Fujitsu was installed. Armed with this advanced equipment, a Chinese catalog database of 350,000 records, a Western catalog database of 50,000 records, and a library collection database of 750,000 records were established, and the acquisition of books and serials, cataloging, and circulation were all computerized. In 1996 the library established its CD-ROM based information searching and retrieval system, providing free services to users on campus via the campus network.

Since 1998 the library has made great technological progress. In addition to a wide range of advanced hardware, Ameritech's Horizon integrated library system was installed with its acquisition, cataloging, circulation, interlibrary loan, serials, and Online Public Access Catalog (OPAC) modules.

Now connected to the campus network, Cernet, and the Internet, Fudan University Library was able to provide access to its Webpac (World Wide Web version of the public access catalog); to electronic databases at Dialog (a commercial database provider) and the Gale Group; to OCLC's First Search via Tsinghua University Library; and to many other commercial databases outside the campus. Some locally developed special databases such as *Fudan Daxue Tushuguan Guji Shuju Ku* (Fudan University Library Ancient Book Database) were also developed and are available to users all over the world.

Organization

Fudan University Library is a system with a two-level structure: the university libraries (the Science Library and the Humanities and Social Sciences Library) and the libraries of schools, departments, and institutes (34 total). The library also contains two centers of the State Commission of Education: the Foreign Textbooks Center and the Documents and Information Center of Humanities. Fudan is an institutional member of the International Federation of Library Associations and Institutions (IFLA) and one of the designated libraries to receive the United Nations Educational, Scientific, and Cultural Organization (UNESCO) publications. It also maintains exchange relations with 310 universities and academic institutes in 36 countries and areas.

GUOQING LI

Further Reading

Fang, Josephine Riss, "People's Republic of China, Libraries in," in *Encyclopedia of Library and Information Science*, edited by Allen Kent et al., vol. 22, New York: Dekker, 1977

Fudan University Library, Shanghai: Fudan University Library, 1998

Lin, Sharon Chien, *Libraries and Librarianship in China*, Westport, Connecticut: Greenwood Press, 1998

Shanghai tushu guan shiye zhi (Annals of Shanghai Libraries), Shanghai: Shanghai Shehui Kexueyuan Chuban She, 1996

Georgian State Public Library

Address: The National Library of the Parliament of Georgia
L. Gudiashvili st. 7
Tbilisi, 380007
Georgia
Telephone: 32-99-80-95
Fax: 32-99-80-95
www.parliament.ge/PARL_99/Library/library.htm

Founded: 1846

Holdings (2000): Volumes: 3.5 million. Other materials: 1.6 million.

Special Collections: *Individual Collections:* Ilya Chavchavadze; David Chubinashvili; David Dadiani; Rapiel Eristavi; George Gekhtman; Jacob Gogebashvili; Peter Umikashvili; Eugene Veidenbaum. *Papers:* Tamar Machavariani; Niko Nikoladze; Akaki Ramishvili; Nicholas Shengelia; Nato Vachnadze.

Background

The National Library of the Parliament of Georgia (NLPG) is a descendant of the public library founded in 1846, formed from the 6,200 printed units inherited from the chancellery of the viceroy. In 1848 the public library received 510 volumes from a private library founded in the beginning of the 1840s by a group of prominent Georgians (Dimitri Kipiani, Zacharia Eristavi, Vakhtang and Grigol Orbeliani, Nikoloz Baratashvili, and Michael Tumanishvili). The Public Library intended to use its limited funds to purchase books concerning the Caucasus.

Initially the library was located in the chancellery of the viceroy, but in 1852 it moved into a new building. By this time the collection had reached 13,000 volumes and used both alphabetic and systematic catalogs. From this early date the library regularly received two copies of every local edition from the Caucasian Censorship Committee, founded in 1848 to maintain censorship of the Russian Imperial authority.

In 1868 the library joined the Caucasian Museum and was named the Caucasian Museum and Tbilisi Public Library. It then began book exchange programs, not only within the Russian Empire but also with European countries. In 1871 both the museum and library moved into a large new building. The first printed catalog appeared in 1861, with continuations published in 1866, 1881, and 1895.

Construction work on the museum closed the library to the public in 1911, but it continued to develop by new purchases and contributions, including 11,000 volumes from the Menshikov family and Eugene Veidenbaum, head of the Archeological Commission. The Tamamshev family donated a large collection of books on theater and drama, and other important collections came from a number of donors, including many books in European languages.

Soviet Period

In 1923 the Georgian State Committee made a decision to found a state public library in Tbilisi, based on the existing Caucasian Museum and public library, which would provide access to Soviet book production. The library was renamed the Karl Marx Georgian State Library in 1952 and renamed the Georgian National Library in the early 1990s. Finally, on 25 December 1996 it was renamed the National Library of the Parliament of Georgia. Today the library is located in four large buildings; the earliest dates from the turn of the century and the latest from 1987. It has been a member of the International Federation of Library Associations and Institutions (IFLA) since 1991.

Directors

At various times the library was directed by prominent people, including Gabriel Tokarev, Adolf Berghe, Paul Meller, Ricard Schmidt, George Gekhtman, I. Nakashidze, Sandro Euli-Kuridze, V. Mgaloblishvili, Pavle Kandelaki, Alexandra Kavkasidze (the first woman director), Akaki Dzidziguri, and Alexander Kartosia. It is currently under the direction of Levan Berdzenishvili.

Historical Collections

The collection of rare volumes includes the first printed Georgian book, the *Georgian-Italian Dictionary*, printed in Italy by the first Georgian printing house founded in 1629 by Nikoloz Cholokashvili. *The Book of Georgian Grammar*, by Francisco Maria Maggio, who visited Georgia between 1637 and 1642, was also printed there in 1670.

The first books printed locally in the Georgian capital of Tbilisi were by printer King Vakhtang VI beginning in 1709. The first 14 printed books from that period are held in the library and include Gospels, Epistles, a Psalter, a Prayer Book and a Book of Hours, and other liturgical books. The library also has *The Knight in the Panther's Skin*, by Shota Rustaveli (the popular Georgian poem from the 12th and 13th centuries) and a 1721 translation by King Vakhtang VI from Farsi of *The Magic of the Stars*. Other books dating from the 18th century were printed in Moscow and Rome. A number of Georgian books were printed in the 19th century in St. Petersburg. Among noteworthy non-Georgian books are the *Essence of Christianity* in Armenian, printed in Amsterdam in 1667, and *The Book of Armenian Grammar* by Iovanes Akopian, printed in Rome in 1675.

Foreign printed editions from the same period include interesting material on Georgia and the Caucasus, such as *Traveling in Kolkheti*, by Italian missionary Archangelo Lamberti (Naples, 1654); *Traveling to Caucasus*, by G. Chardin (London, 1686; Amsterdam, 1711); *Information about Georgia*, by Pietro Delavale (Rome, 1627), and his *Travels* (Paris, 1663); three volumes of *Records of Travels in the East*, by T. Pitton (Lyon, 1717); and six volumes of *Travels in the Caucasus*, by Dubua De Monperet (Paris, 1833 to 1844). The earliest printed book in the library is Seneca's *Tragedies*, published in Florence in 1506. Important manuscripts include a ninth-century liturgical document, "Lectionary from Lagurke," and a 13th-century Gospel translated by Euthymius the Athonite.

Present Times

The library currently consists of six departments: national heritage, development, reader services, information, civic education, and economic management. The general director is supported by two directors who supervise the work of coordinators. The six departments include 26 faculties, six centers, and four working groups. The library has been engaged in computerization of its resources and provides free Internet services for readers. It hosts approximately 14,000 readers every year, using 630 seats in 10 reading halls. In the year 2000 the library claimed 3.5 million volumes and 1.6 million other items.

After cataloging and classification, new acquisitions are housed in four major book stack areas for Georgian, Russian, and European languages and periodicals. Both alphabetical and systematic subject catalogs continue to be maintained, and periodicals also can be found in geographical and chronological catalogs. The library uses a fixed location system: Books are divided by size into six format groups, then each book receives an inventory number according to language and format group. Thus each format group has its own list of inventory numbers.

Among the periodicals there are large collections in Georgian, Russian, Armenian, Azeri, Abkhaz, Osetian, and European languages. The library also possesses a large collection of musical notes/records, audiovisual editions, cartographical works, microfilms, and microfiche.

Research

Since the 1930s the library has been conducting academic research. From 1934 to 1940 it issued five volumes of *The Public Library*, concerning both practical work in the library and issues related to bibliography, librarianship, and the history of printing in Georgia. It has provided a great deal of analytical bibliographical works on Georgian and other periodicals under the supervision of Tamar Machavariani. This work has helped to provide a much clearer understanding of 19th-century Georgian history, as well as identify the pseudonymous and anonymous authors of many Georgian works, including 40 articles now attributed to Ilya Chavchavadze and others attributed to Vazha Pshavela.

In 1954 and 1964 the library published two volumes of the *Catalogue of the Archives of N. Nikoladze*, which reflect rich material about the years between 1829 and 1928. These catalogs are now held in the NLPG.

ETER IMNADZE
TRANSLATED BY TAMARA GRDZELIDZE

German National Library

Die Deutsche Bibliothek

Deutsche Bücherei Leipzig
Address: Deutscher Platz 1
04103 Leipzig
Germany
Telephone: 341-2271-0
Fax: 341-2271-444
www.ddb.de

Founded: 1990

Holdings (2000): Volumes: 9.2 million. Current serials: 51,000; incunabula: 758; maps: 171,000; music scores: 260,000; sound recordings: 183,000.

Special Collections: *Areas of Concentration:* Book history; broadsides; exile; German labor movements; pamphlets; patents; posters; proclamations; socialism. *Individual Collections:* Anne-Frank-Shoah-Bibliothek; Imperial Library (Reichsbibliothek of 1848).

Deutsche Bibliothek Frankfurt am Main
Address: Adickesallee 1
60322 Frankfurt am Main
Germany
Telephone: 69-1525-0
Fax: 69-1525-1010
www.ddb.de

Founded: 1947

Holdings (2000): Volumes: 6.3 million. Autographs: 153,000; current serials: 45,000; maps: 130,000; microforms: 675,000.

Special Collections: *Areas of Concentration:* Exile literature, 1933 to 1945; German-language publications issued abroad.

Deutsches Musikarchiv Berlin
Address: Gärtnerstrasse 25-32
12207 Berlin
Germany
Telephone: 30-77002-0
Fax: 30-77002-299
www.ddb.de

Founded: 1970

Holdings (2000): Volumes: 890,000. Music scores: 336,000; sound recordings: 650,000.

Special Collections: *Areas of Concentration:* Printed music; publications on music; sound recordings.

Germany's current national library system is a result of the *Wende* (turning point) in the German Democratic Republic (GDR, or what was then commonly known as East Germany) in the fall of 1989. Based on the Unification Treaty of 1990, three institutions were combined to form what is known as Die Deutsche Bibliothek: the Deutsche Bücherei in Leipzig (established in 1912), the Deutsche Bibliothek in Frankfurt am Main (established in 1947), and the German Music Archive (Deutsches Musikarchiv) in Berlin (a part of the Deutsche Bibliothek since 1970). Throughout this article, "Die Deutsche Bibliothek" will refer to these three institutions, whereas "the Deutsche Bibliothek" refers to the library in Frankfurt. Die Deutsche Bibliothek, the Deutsche Bibliothek, and the Deutsche Bücherei will remain untranslated in order to avoid confusion with each other, as "German Library" is the translation in each instance.

Die Deutsche Bibliothek is the national library and national bibliographic information center for the Federal Republic of Germany (FRG). It is charged with the complete collection, long-term preservation, and comprehensive documentation of all publications from Germany and German-related publications issued since 1913. Responsibilities include the provision of public access and national bibliographic services with respect to these publications. The Deutsche Bücherei (Leipzig) today collects all publications issued in Germany as well as German-language publications, translations, and literature about Germany published abroad since 1913. It has 450 workstations and 495,000 book requests per year. The primary responsibilities of the Deutsche Bibliothek (Frankfurt) include collecting all German-language publications issued abroad since 1945, and German exile literature from 1933 to 1945. Additionally, the Deutsche Bibliothek develops information and communications technologies. It has 300 workstations and 440,000 book requests per year. The Deutsches Musikarchiv (Berlin) is the central collection for music in Germany. Affiliated with the Deutsches Bibliothek in 1970, it contains the work of the Deutsche Musik-Phonothek (1961 to 1969). It collects printed music, publications on music, and sound recordings, and is responsible for the bibliography of these materials.

The genealogy of Die Deutsche Bibliothek is one of the more interesting chapters in the history of international libraries. Prior to 1990 the realization of a German national library had been a long, unfinished odyssey. The would-be institutions had gone by a dizzying array of names: Deutsche Bibliothek, Deutsche Bücherei, Bavarian State Library (Bayerische Staatsbibliothek), Electoral Library of Cölln on the Spree (Churfürstliche Bibliothek zu Cölln an der Spree), Royal Library (Königliche Bibliothek), Prussian State Library (Preussische Staatsbibliothek), Public Research Library (Öffentliche Wissenschaftliche Bibliothek), State Library of the Prussian Cultural Foundation (Staatsbibliothek Preussischer Kulturbesitz), German State Library (Deutsche Staatsbibliothek), Berlin State Library of the Prussian Cultural Foundation (Staatsbibliothek zu Berlin—Preussischer Kulturbesitz), Hessian Library (Hessische Bibliothek), and West German Library (Westdeutsche Bibliothek), among others. Most telling, perhaps, is that no library had ever before been known explicitly as the German National Library. The development of any of these libraries into a single German national library had always been plagued by something akin to Mephistopheles in Goethe's *Faust*, "the spirit that constantly denies."

As a centuries-long consequence of the fragmentation of the Holy Roman Empire, Germany (in contrast to France and England) had never had a single national library. Between the founding of the Court Library in Munich in 1558 and the German Empire in 1871, Germany had a decentralized library system. The holdings of court and state-based libraries formed a mythical national library. The largest and richest of them today are the Bavarian State Library and the Berlin State Library. The latter benefited by having the empire's capital in Berlin. Then known as the Prussian State Library, it effectively became a national library for all of Germany in the first third of the 20th century. The Third Reich—more exactly, Nazi policy makers—succeeded all too well in obscuring the major inroads that German librarianship had made on the international scene. The trauma brought on by the years from 1933 to 1945 marked subsequent library developments in the two Germanies.

From 1945 to 1990, East German librarianship took its cue from the Soviet Union. It adhered to the Marxist-Leninist principles of the single-rule Socialist Unity Party. Administrative and political structures in the Western-occupied zones led to the creation of pseudo-national libraries in the FRG. Before and after unification in 1990, not every governmental responsibility in the FRG was vested in the federal government. The states (*Länder*), for example, enjoyed great autonomy in cultural affairs, including the administration of their own libraries. Local authorities made up a third key element in the national administrative structure. This separation of powers still significantly affects German libraries today.

Origins to 1912

When Germany was founded in 1871, the idea of a national library was consonant with the drive for German independence. There had been a precedent: Upon hearing of the revolutionary developments in Austria in March 1848, Frederick William IV called a national assembly at the Paulskirche in Frankfurt. On 18 May 1848 the national assembly enthusiastically welcomed the proposal of Heinrich Wilhelm Hahn, publisher of the *Monumenta Germaniae Historica* (1826), to create a national collection. Hahn promised to send every volume of the *Monumenta* to the so-called Imperial Library, and other publishers quickly followed suit. The German revolution, such as it was, was all but over a year later, and with it, the Imperial Library.

The concept of a German national library fueled the aspirations of the new German empire. Emotions in favor of a central collection were jumbled with the presumption of its need. The Imperial Press Law of 1874 allowed the German states to determine their own definition of deposit copies, hindering a centralized collection of German imprints. Prussian libraries collected Prussian titles exhaustively. Other states, such as Saxony, abolished their legal deposit laws altogether. In the early 20th century, German librarians and publishers generally favored the concept of a single national library, at least in theory. In practical terms, however, the idea was less tenable to proponents of the German territories' cultural autonomy. Only after legal questions about deposit copies were resolved could the idea of a national library become more acceptable. The Deutsche Bücherei was founded as a settlement of the issue.

1912 to 1933

The Deutsche Bücherei was an extension of the short-lived Imperial Library. When the non-Prussian states and the German book trade opposed plans to make the Royal Library in Berlin the official German national library, Erich Ehlermann's proposal to erect a new building as an organ of the German book trade met quickly with success. His proposal was brought before a session of the annual booksellers' meeting in Leipzig in 1910. The Deutsche Bücherei was founded by an agreement reached in 1912 between the Association of German Booksellers, the city of Leipzig, and the state of Saxony. The association owned the Deutsche Bücherei; Leipzig and Saxony shared the administrative costs. The Reich later stepped in as a fourth authority, providing financial support during the difficult inflationary period of 1922–23.

Nominally, the Deutsche Bücherei in Leipzig was Germany's library. Yet it was a national library only in certain aspects, and meanwhile the Prussian State Library fulfilled many duties of a national library. The Deutsche Bücherei was difficult to categorize at its inception. It did not correspond to de facto national libraries in Washington, London, and Paris. The primary responsibility of the Deutsche Bücherei was to collect and provide bibliographic data for German imprints and publications relating to Germany printed after 1 January 1913. It was meant to acquire and store an uninterrupted collection of German books published after 1912: Publishers volunteered copies at first, then (from 1935) deposit copies were required. Purchases and voluntary deliveries from abroad were also added. Germanica—that is, German-language literature from abroad, translations of German publications into other languages, and foreign-language publications on Germany—became a primary collecting responsibility in 1941.

Absolute comprehensiveness was unrealistic in the beginning years of the Deutsche Bücherei, as collecting policies were still in the midst of multiple interpretations, but the Deutsche Bücherei did concern itself primarily with the contemporary period. The Deutsche Bücherei was vulnerable to more than the usual growing pains early on. Unprecedented inflation during the interwar years afflicted German libraries, perhaps none more so than the Deutsche Bücherei. Goals in collection building and services had to be curtailed. Whatever the Deutsche Bücherei was (or was not), its inherent utility soon became evident. It was both an archive and a reference library—at once a library for Leipzig and for all Germans.

1933 to 1945

The Third Reich precipitated the material and existential decline of German libraries. A dearth of theory applied to librarianship in Nazi Germany; whatever theory there was related to the championing of Nazi values. Hitler directed his vitriol at the intelligentsia well before he became chancellor in 1933. The following statement in *Mein Kampf* (1925–27) is illustrative: "If our entire intellectual upper crust had not been brought up so exclusively on upper-class etiquette; if instead they had learned boxing thoroughly, a German revolution of pimps, deserters, and such-like rabble would never have been possible." According to the Nazis, intellectuals were omnipresent in the Weimar Republic and therefore especially worthy of blame for Germany's supposed humiliation during and after World War I. German librarianship displayed evident forms of schizophrenia amid the official Nazi cultural policies of coordination (*Gleichschaltung*). Coordination in Nazi Germany subjugated library activities to the interests of the party.

The Deutsche Bücherei was not immune to a bewildering and occasionally inconsistent series of laws implemented by the Nazis. Two general forms of coordination developed at the Deutsche Bücherei. First, the government imposed coordination by hiring politically reliable but unqualified employees. The second instance involved self-imposed coordination by professional librarians in an attempt to mollify the Nazis. In either case, reorganization meant filling vacant positions with party members. The Nazis had implemented most of their directives by 1944, when the Deutsche Bücherei had ceased operations until the end of World War II.

In the first 30 years of its existence, the Deutsche Bücherei had already become the third largest German library, ranking behind only the Prussian State Library and the Bavarian State Library. It flourished thanks to its range of functions. No other German library had such an extensive collection of contemporary German holdings. In addition, the library's high usage figures, interlibrary lending, low-cost reference services, and extensive bibliographies (14 were produced in 1940 alone) were all notable.

1945 to 1990

Deutsche Bücherei

Certain malignant vestiges of state-imposed library coordination in the Third Reich resembled those in the GDR, which was founded in 1949. Coarse rhetoric, an undue reliance on icons and imagery, and totalitarian ideology informed both eras. Both the National Socialists and the Socialist Unity Party of Germany (SED), East Germany's single-rule communist party, mandated that libraries adhere to state ideology. Careerism was linked to party affiliation. Decrepit libraries—buildings destroyed by battle in World War II or those in which necessary renovations were neglected—symbolized the dearth of substance at each state's end. East Germans were told again and again that the GDR was a *Leseland,* or nation for reading, yet what a person could purchase from a bookstore or borrow from a library was, as in Nazi Germany, strictly regulated.

The Deutsche Bücherei in Leipzig and the German State Library in Berlin acted as dual national libraries in the GDR. The Deutsche Bücherei fit very well into the new direction of East German librarianship. The missions of the Deutsche Bücherei and the German State Library were to complement each other. The Deutsche Bücherei was the archival library and the bibliographic center of the GDR, and the German State Library functioned as its research library. The Deutsche Bücherei collected post-1912 German imprints and compiled national bibliographies. The German State Library, as a counterbalance, specialized in foreign literature, pre-1913 German imprints, manuscripts, and incunabula. Although the Deutsche Bücherei had been hit by bombs during World War II (notably on 3–4 December 1943), librarians did not have to worry about the physical reconstruction of the building on the magnitude of the German State Library, which was destroyed by war's end.

A distinctively East German library system was created in two phases. First, the SED integrated the nation's libraries. The government then analyzed the reorganized libraries' achievements, with the intention of attaining even higher standards of efficiency. The Soviet library system served as the model. The Deutsche Bücherei fell under the organization of the Ministry of Higher and Technical Education. There was a conscious effort in the first years of the 1970s to establish a form of cultural demarcation, separating a distinctive GDR identity from a wider German identity that included West Germany.

In the 1974 revision of the GDR constitution, references to "German" were replaced wherever possible by "GDR." The Deutsche Bücherei and the German State Library were significant exceptions. Their stature was thought to transcend boundaries that had been created by occupying powers after World War II—the implication being that they were now, in the mid 1970s, *the* libraries of divided Germany. In theory both libraries were to be inclusive, making all their holdings accessible to all East Germans, scholars, and the general public alike. In reality, however, the government restricted access to selected holdings for selected users. Thus East German libraries may ultimately be remembered more by what they did not provide to library users than by what they did provide. Indeed, much of what East Germans liked to read after the *Wende* was not openly available in GDR libraries prior to the *Wende*.

The achievements of GDR librarianship—such as they were—were dubious. A recent *Wer war wer, DDR: Ein biographisches Lexikon* (Who Was Who, GDR: A Bigraphical Encyclopedia [1992]) is revealing: not a single librarian is listed among the 1,510 entries, not even the general directors of the Deutsche Bücherei or the German State Library. The GDR's deficiencies in research and technology were pronounced; although it ranked among the world's leading nations in gross national product, its libraries and telecommunication networks lay in varying degrees of physical disrepair. Remarkably, for example, only one in seven East German households had a phone as late as 1990. By 1989–90, the Deutsche Bücherei was in need of an overhaul.

Deutsche Bibliothek

Established in 1947, the Deutsche Bibliothek became West Germany's archival and bibliographic center for postwar German and related collections. It collected, stored, cataloged, and made available domestic imprints and Germanica published after 8 May 1945, as well as exile literature from 1933 to 1945. The Deutsche Bibliothek and, since 1970, the German Music Archive, also collected printed music and music recordings. The Deutsche Bibliothek collected GDR literature, just as the Deutsche Bücherei endeavored to collect West German imprints. Both depended on gifts and voluntary deposits by German publishers. Publishers usually supplied two copies of each publication gratis—one to the Deutsche Bibliothek and one to the Deutsche Bücherei. But the Cold War dampened the spirit of voluntary deliveries on at least two occasions. In 1961 West German publishers protested the building of the Berlin Wall by not sending titles to the Deutsche Bücherei. They withheld their publications again in 1968, when East German soldiers marched into Prague. After the deposit law went into effect in West Germany in 1969, West German publishers were obliged to supply their publications to the Deutsche Bibliothek.

The Deutsche Bibliothek collected many kinds of publications: books, maps, periodicals, newspapers, dissertations, microforms, slides, overhead transparencies, sound recordings, and printed music. To be considered eligible for legal deposit, a publication needed to be more than four pages long and to have been produced in at least ten copies. A "publisher" was any disseminator of information. The Deutsche Bibliothek did not retain everything, but what it kept it had to report; what it did not report, it could not keep. Excluded from legal deposit were government publications, daily newspapers as hard copy (only microforms were collected), and audiovisual displays.

Exhaustive collections were theoretically possible after the legal deposit law, but in reality many publications never reached the Deutsche Bibliothek. The onus of provision was on the publishers, so the Deutsche Bibliothek accrued considerable personnel costs in monitoring the arrival (or nonarrival) of materials. Some publishers, nearly all outside the book trade, did not know about their legal obligation to deliver their materials. As a result, 20,000 to 30,000 eligible monographs did not reach the Deutsche Bibliothek annually in the late 1980s. As awareness about the legal deposit system increased, the acquisitions department of the Deutsche Bibliothek increased its cost effectiveness. Searchers reduced expenditures incurred in locating gaps in the collections and in reminding publishers of their obligations.

Developments since 1990

In the early 1990s, as a result of German unification, there was a certain acrimony among major libraries whenever one German library insisted too strongly on its leading role on the national scene. Names, more than anything else, evinced how much was at stake. Many librarians at the Deutsche Bücherei favored the name "German National Library" (Deutsche Nationalbibliothek), whereas their peers in Frankfurt, Berlin, and Munich did not, thinking it to be imprecise and somewhat too nationalistic. Both the Deutsche Bücherei and the Deutsche Bibliothek retained their names under the auspices of Die Deutsche Bibliothek; "national" was not added. The final name chosen in Berlin, the Berlin State Library of the Prussian Cultural Foundation, was a wordy, lackluster compromise. Retaining the name "German State Library" would have irked those who believed the designation to be too profound. On the other hand, another suggestion, "Berlin Library," was thought not to carry sufficient importance (this was just the point, some suggested mischievously). At every step of the way, the Bavarian State Library stood by, ensuring an adequate profile for itself vis-à-vis the other libraries.

The FRG was at some pains in winning over the hearts and minds of millions who genuinely believed in the merits of the GDR. One of the things that may have hindered this was the traumatic process of de-Stasification, which has been likened to de-Nazification in the late 1940s. Stasi agents—the East German secret police—had kept files on millions of East Germans. In the early 1990s, many East German employees of public institutions, including librarians, had to answer two questions: (1) Were you ever a professional, unofficial, or informal employee of the Stasi?

If "Yes," describe the activity and its duration. (2) Did you have a role in the Socialist Unity Party or in other large organizations (including social organizations) before 9 November 1989, or did you have another significant role in the GDR? If "Yes," describe the role and its duration. Employees answering "Yes" to either question were investigated and judged accordingly. Those answering "No" were believed, unless investigators were led to conclude differently, or unless the questionnaire was contradicted by other documents or testimonies. In any case, lying was grounds for automatic dismissal. Investigated librarians fell into three categories: those who were cleared of wrongdoing and allowed to continue in their posts or were promoted; those who were allowed to work at the library in a diminished position because their records were ambiguous; and those who were dismissed. The purges had largely dissipated by the mid-1990s, but their effects are still palpable.

Die Deutsche Bibliothek excels at what it is meant to do. It is renowned for its series of German national bibliographies: the *Deutsche Nationalbibliographie und Bibliographie der im Ausland erschienenen deutschsprachigen Veröffentlichungen* (German National Bibliography and Bibliography of German-Language Works Published Abroad). An overview is as follows:

- Series A: Monographs and periodicals within the book trade; classified by subject; appears weekly.

- Series B: The same types of materials as Series A, but outside the book trade; classified by subject; appears weekly.

- Series C: Maps; classified by author, title, keyword, and publisher; appears quarterly.

- Series D: Cumulation of titles from weekly lists; in two parts: title list, and subject and keyword indices with a systematic overview of subject headings; appears semiannually.

- Series E: Cumulation of Series D; appears every five years.

- Series G: German-language works and works on Germany published abroad; appears quarterly.

- Series H: Dissertations at German universities, as well as published dissertations from abroad; classified by subject, author, title, and keyword; appears monthly.

- Series M: Sheet music; classified alphabetically and by publishers' index, name, title, subject, and keyword; appears monthly.

- Series N: CIP monographs and periodicals; classified by subject, author, title, keyword, and publisher; appears weekly.

- Series T: Audio recordings; classified by subject, company, name, and title; appears monthly.

In addition, the *Deutsche Nationalbibliographie CD-ROM aktuell* (German National Bibliography CD-ROM Up To Date) appears regularly. Access to the bibliographic records of Die Deutsche Bibliothek is also possible via its website and in electronic databases such as the Research Libraries Information Network (RLIN).

The Deutsche Bibliothek is the administrative center of Die Deutsche Bibliothek. The general director of Die Deutsche Bibliothek, Elisabeth Niggemann, is based most of the time in Frankfurt but also spends significant time in Leipzig. Irmgard Spencker and Ute Schwens are the respective deputy directors of the Deutsche Bücherei and the Deutsche Bibliothek. The Deutsche Bibliothek moved to a new building in north Frankfurt in 1997, and renovation at the Deutsche Bücherei continues.

Frankfurt and Leipzig avoid duplication of work by dividing primary responsibilities for collecting monographs from individual German states. The Deutsche Bibliothek oversees imprints from Baden-Württemberg, Bavaria, Bremen, Hesse, Lower Saxony, Hamburg, Schleswig-Holstein, Rhineland-Palatinate, and Saarland; the Deutsche Bücherei those from Brandenburg, Mecklenburg-Western Pomerania, Saxony, Saxony-Anhalt, Thuringia, Berlin, and North Rhine-Westphalia, as well as those from Austria and Switzerland, and Germanica from other nations. The Deutsche Bibliothek produces national bibliographies and monitors norms for international bibliographies. It also maintains the central computer and systems technologies. Regarding exile collections, the Deutsche Bibliothek manages archives and manuscripts, while the Deutsche Bücherei collects printed works. The West German cataloging standard prior to 1990 has been adapted and updated. The Deutsche Bücherei also houses the Deutsches Buch- und Schriftmuseum, and the Anne-Frank-Shoah-Bibliothek.

Under the legal deposit mandate, every German publisher is obliged to send two copies of each new publication to Die Deutsche Bibliothek. German-language publications issued abroad, translations from German, and foreign-language publications about Germany are acquired as complimentary copies or through purchase and exchange. Bibliographic records for these and other titles provide the basis for recording in the *Deutsche Nationalbibliographie* and for other national bibliographic services. Library materials are readily available for use in reading rooms but do not circulate out of the buildings.

In late 1999 Die Deutsche Bibliothek held collections numbering approximately 14.4 million units—9.2 million in Leipzig, 6.3 million in Frankfurt, and approximately 985,000 sound recordings and items of printed music in Berlin. Ironically, the amount of shelf space needed to accommodate these materials is the approximate distance between Frankfurt and Leipzig. Twelve hundred new titles arrive daily to Die Deutsche Bibliothek, and annual accessions amount to some 300,000 units. All three libraries share one website.

Die Deutsche Bibliothek Today: Is It a National Library?

The term *national library* is often a misnomer, as *national* may not be in a library's official name (for example, Library of Congress, British Library, and Bibliothèque de France). Such peer libraries of Die Deutsche Bibliothek commonly have four functions. Each functions as a nation's bibliographic center; the repository for a nation's printed works; a collecting agency for foreign literature as comprehensively as funds allow; and a repository for extensive retrospective collections.

No single German library currently fulfills each of the four functions just mentioned; in fact, none ever has. Die Deutsche Bibliothek fulfills the first two exceedingly well, however, and in its present organization it is as close to a national library as ever in the history of German libraries. Die Deutsche Bibliothek is based on the legal mandate of the federal government, as in the United States the Library of Congress, National Library of Medicine, and National Library of Agriculture are viewed as the national libraries. The international community will unquestionably continue to view Die Deutsche Bibliothek as Germany's national library.

MICHAEL P. OLSON

Further Reading

Gömpel, Renate, *Haus der Bücher—elektronishes Archiv,* Leipzig: Deutsche Bibliothek, 1997; as *House of Books—Digital Archives,* 1997

Jahresbericht (annual; 1990–)

Olson, Michael P., *The Odyssey of a German National Library: A Short History of the Bayerische Staatsbibliothek, the Staatsbibliothek zu Berlin, the Deutsche Bücherei, and the Deutsche Bibliothek,* Wiesbaden, Germany: Harrassowitz, 1996

Rotzsch, Helmut, editor, *Deutsche Bucherei, 1912–1962,* Leipzig: Verlag für Buch- und Bibliothekswesen, 1962

Saevecke, Rolf-Dieter, *Die Deutsche Bibliothek,* Düsseldorf, Germany: Droste, 1980

Glasgow University Library

Address: Glasgow University Library
Hillhead Street
Glasgow G12 8QE
Scotland
UK
Telephone: 141-330-6704
Fax: 141-330-4952
www.lib.gla.ac.uk

Founded: 1475

Holdings (2001): Volumes: 1.5 million. Audiovisual materials: 10,000; current serials: 9,000; incunabula: 1,100; manuscripts: 200,000; maps: 50,000; microforms: 392,000.

Special Collections: *Areas of Concentration:* Alchemy; chapbooks; economic, left-wing, legal, literary, local, medical, musical, political, religious, scientific, and social history; emblem literature; European Union and Council of Europe documentation; fine arts; printed ephemera; Scottish photography, poetry, and theater; Soviet and East European studies; Victorian novels. *Individual Collections:* Ludwig Blau; William Euing; John Ferguson; William Hamilton; William Hunter; William Stirling Maxwell; David Murray; James Dean Ogilvie; Trinity College, Glasgow; Robert Wylie. *Papers:* Henry George Farmer; William Thomson, Baron Kelvin; Ronald David Laing; Dugald Sutherland MacColl; John Blackwood McEwen; James McLagan; Scottish Theatre Archive; Denys Miller Sutton; James Abbott McNeill Whistler; Harold James Lean Wright.

Origins

The founder of the Vatican Library, Pope Nicholas V, issued a bull to establish the University of Glasgow in 1451. Nothing acquired by the university library before 1569 remains, but John Durkan, its historian, has identified many early holdings by using archival records. The university spread beyond the cathedral into High Street, its first library occupying a small closet. James VI granted the university a charter in 1577. His tutor, George Buchanan, subsequently made a donation to the library, and indeed the institution relied almost entirely on outside gifts. A subsidy of £200 from Charles I enabled an acquisitions agent to function in Amsterdam after 1633. In 1641 Thomas Hutcheson, alumnus and local benefactor, gave 2,000 merks (£111) to endow the post of librarian, to be chosen from graduate citizens by the town council and to serve for four years. Few nominees stayed the full term; several also held other posts. Scope for nepotism encouraged friction between the university and town authorities.

New acquisitions had been listed spasmodically, but books were not carefully tended. A thief forfeited his degree and was imprisoned in 1691 when, coincidentally, the first comprehensive catalog was issued. Its 2,000 titles represented some 3,500 volumes. A visitor in 1702 found the library "well digested and the books so ordered, not as at Edinburgh." The theology collection was the largest, followed by philosophy, with small collections of law and medicine. Original manuscripts, even the Book of Pluscarden, an important text about Scottish history before 1436, received little prominence.

Legal Deposit and the Hunter Bequest

In 1709 all four Scottish university libraries were accorded legal deposit status. Acquisitions did not necessarily reflect perceived needs, as only titles entered at the Stationers' Hall in London could be claimed, and transport and binding were added expenses. When the privilege was withdrawn in 1836, calculations to determine compensation showed Glasgow as the heaviest user. Foreign acquisitions at this time were mostly of academy transactions.

Students and staff might read library stock, if relevant to their study and not injurious to faith or morals. The first student class library opened in 1725, but not all were well managed and some later merged into the general library. Professors' personal collections developed into departmental libraries for staff.

A gift in 1720 of £500 from the Duke of Chandos enabled a new library, first discussed in 1726, to be opened in 1744. It accentuated the defects of short-term staffing, but reform was difficult. The town council and the university had alternated in nominating librarians since 1656. At intervals between 1716 and 1736, Professor Gershom Carmichael's four sons, Alexander,

John, Frederick, and Gershom, each acted as librarian, but an attempt to appoint Alexander librarian for life failed. Eventually, the university bought out the city's rights in 1782, and Archibald Arthur, originally appointed in 1774, became the first permanent librarian. His two-volume catalog and shelf list of 20,000 books appeared in 1791, but in 1794 he became professor of moral philosophy, in which he had lectured since 1780. Pluralism and brief tenures continued until a full-time librarian was appointed in 1827.

The anatomist William Hunter's magnificent bequest in 1783 aroused great interest. His will permitted his collections—books, manuscripts, coins, pictures, geological, botanical and anatomical specimens, and ethnographic artifacts—to remain in London until 1807. When they were transferred, the 10,000 printed books, including 530 incunabula, increased collections by 50 percent. The 650 Western and Oriental manuscripts included a superb 12th-century psalter illuminated in northern England. During the next century, the number, size, and quality of collections donated or purchased by public subscription testified to the close relationship developing between the university and the city at the height of its prosperity.

Means to purchase new stock came in 1836 through an annual government grant of £707 to compensate for the loss of legal deposit. Five professors met quarterly in committee to approve new orders, which largely reflected personal interests. Under an 1862 ordinance, the committee regulated the selection, ordering, loan, return, and preservation of books, the approval of books held for reference only, library membership, and an annual stock inspection.

The Dickson Era, 1862 to 1901

The new convenor, Professor William Purdie Dickson, became curator in 1867 to plan a catalog preparing for the transfer of the library's 100,000 volumes. In fact he held office for another 34 years and was the major influence shaping library service well into the next century.

In 1870 the university moved to land overlooking the Kelvin River. The library occupied the west wing of the north part of the building, with two great halls, a gallery, and a basement and capacity for 180,000 volumes. Dickson devised an alphabetical catalog based on rules "by Mr Jewett in his Smithsonian report of 1853," as he wrote in *The Glasgow University Library* (1888). Printed sheets were cut into individual slips, mounted to form guard books. Plans for a subject catalog using a second set of sheets went unfulfilled.

The university took advantage of the commutation of the compensation grant in 1890 to reduce its library's funding. From 1894 £500 in capital and £100 annually from the Bellahouston Trust was intended to improve scientific journal holdings. Dickson continued as curator and chaired a newly constituted committee as one of three members nominated by court, the governing body. In 1888 he had published a pamphlet on the library's history and aims. In 1897, making international comparisons, he issued *The University Library: What It Is, and What It Might Be*. As professor emeritus he was incensed by the university's refusal to meet its library obligations. Rejecting a well-argued case for more shelving, the court recommended a public appeal by the library. Dickson replied that appeals were the court's responsibility and that its suggested target of £60,000 was quite inadequate. He died in 1901, after 39 years dedicated to library interests, leaving the guard book (now available on microfiche) as his enduring monument.

Post-Victorian Prudence

The next chairman, Professor William Hastie, took things more slowly. The shelving issue was shelved, as there was no public appeal. Grants becoming available through a new Carnegie trust lessened pressure. When Hastie died in 1903, the building was full but underfunded. Despite carried-forward balances and £480 from Carnegie, with only £600 available for new purchases, total expenditure (including the Bellahouston £100) came to only £1,450. Annual intake occupied the equivalent of 140 shelves, and 28,000 journal volumes were scattered around the building. After careful investigation, a subcommittee recommended steel stacking, but 20 years passed before Glasgow became the last Scottish university to adopt it. Meanwhile, a manually operated book hoist at £49 was preferred to an electric version costing £180. (An elevator costing £615 was installed in 1919.) Occasionally, technology triumphed more quickly: A telephone, priced at £10, was preferred to a £3 speaking tube, to link the library and the reading room, in which readers were now allowed to study their own books "if essential for their convenience." A 1910 regulation stated: "When a book is taken from the shelf, dust must be blown off the edges before it is opened." In 1914, rather than pay £24 for a vacuum cleaner, approval was given for an extra attendant "to dust the books in a systematic fashion." War mobilization left that post (and several others) unfilled. (In 1917 a machine was bought for £26.)

Another new regulation opened access for approved students to the shelves but only in their own subject area. Other books had to be fetched by library staff. Even so, in 1913 a lengthy petition from the librarian, James Lachlan Galbraith, deplored the damage inflicted on the stock; he quoted an article on insanity in the *Encyclopædia Britannica*: "To overlook the effects will be to earn the reproach of succeeding generations." Neither he nor the committee had a solution. Illness throughout 1915 eventually forced his resignation.

Until 1925 the university was without a librarian. David Murray, a prominent local lawyer and antiquarian, led the committee with zeal, ensuring publication of the catalog of Hunter's library. Shortly before he died in 1928, he donated his own large collection, strong in Scottish local history. The new librarian, William Ross Cunningham (1925–51), previously employed in the Public Record Office, campaigned to increase study space. The steel stacking had extended capacity to 500,000 volumes, but there were scarcely 50 reader places; class libraries had become the main study centers. Plans were caught up in the university's general expansion program, but in 1939 a fashionable, inflexible, circular reading room became the first new university building north of University Avenue. Its gallery incorporated several class libraries, although as many others resisted the invitation to merge.

Having given only tepid support to a national campaign begun in 1926 to lessen the cost of German science journals, Glasgow benefited in 1930 from the resulting general 20 percent reduction in price and size. But in 1932 journal holdings of 1,100 were listed and considered for cancellation. Glasgow's purchases (784) were compared with Edinburgh's (588) to identify scope for further pruning. Later in the 1930s, however, in preparation for the new reading room, book purchase was more generously funded than ever before.

World War II brought early closing, staff shortages, undusted books, and the opening of a suspense account for the eventual purchase of German journal back-runs. With less foresight, in October 1944 a cheap, obsolescent microfilm reader and a camera were acquired; by 1947 necessary replacement parts were unobtainable. In 1946 committee business returned to normal with a resulting clamor for longer opening hours, more generous loan periods, and resolution of conflicts with departmental libraries.

The 1968 Watershed

Growing demands on all services prompted consideration of a new main library building, but discussion took almost 20 years before an 11-story tower opened in 1968 near the circular reading room. The prescient librarian, Robert Ogilvie MacKenna (1951–78), structured reader service around subject librarians. Involved in most functions—book selection, cataloging, classification, reference work, even supervision of binding and interlibrary lending—and based close to the relevant stock, their prime motivation was reader support. An eclectic classification system using in-house notation sought to reflect the institution's academic profile. Uniquely, a commercial firm was invited to manage a bindery on the premises. Plans for a further stage of building were twice modified before completion in the 1980s. They incorporated automated circulation and cataloging systems, investment in which the university had postponed until MacKenna's successor, Henry Heaney, was appointed in 1978. These developed into a total online system in 1993. In 1997 special collections, which had outgrown their ground floor and basement premises, moved to a purpose-built rooftop extension, releasing space for remodeled reference and study space and a new entrance open for more than 90 hours per week to service a user population of 30,000.

These alterations, in part supported by the Wolfson Foundation, were designed to foster dissemination of relevant information, from whatever source. Workstations in a welcoming environment promote networked facilities, particularly via the library's well-designed Web pages. Links and cooperation, locally, nationally, and internationally, are officially encouraged, but the university faces challenges in knowledge management that are more trying than ever before in its history.

[Henry Heaney served as librarian for two decades before his retirement in 1998 and sudden death in 1999, shortly after completing this essay. He was succeeded by Andrew Wale, previously his deputy, who served as director of library services from 1998 to 2001. On his retirement, Christine Bailey was appointed acting director.—Peter Hoare]

HENRY HEANEY

Further Reading

Brown, Jane Hetherington, and Nicholas Pickwood, editors, *The Hunterian Psalter*, Oxford: Oxford Microform, and Glasgow: University of Glasgow, 1983

Dickson, William P., *The Glasgow University Library: Notes on Its History, Arrangements, and Aims*, Glasgow: Maclehose, 1888

Dickson, William P., *The University Library: What It Is, and What It Might Be: A Statement*, Glasgow: Maclehose, 1897

Durkan, John, "The Early History of Glasgow University Library: 1475–1710," *The Bibliotheck* 8 (1977)

Durkan, John, and Anthony Ross, *Early Scottish Libraries*, Glasgow: Burns, 1961

Heaney, Henry, "Subject-Divisional Organisation: The Standard Still Flies," *Library Review* 40 (1991)

Hoare, Peter, "The Librarians of Glasgow University over 350 Years: 1641–1991," *Library Review* 40 (1991)

Hobbs, Timothy, "Research Collections in a Digital Age: The Development of Special Collections in Glasgow, 1977–1997," *Library Review* 47, nos. 5–6 (1998)

Ker, Neil Ripley, *William Hunter as a Collector of Medieval Manuscripts*, Glasgow: University of Glasgow Press, 1983

MacKenna, R.O., "Glasgow: University of Glasgow Library," in *Encyclopedia of Library and Information Science*, edited by Allen Kent et al., vol. 10, New York: Dekker, 1973

MacKenna, R.O., "Subject-Divisional Organization in a Major Scottish Research Library," in *Of One Accord: Essays in Honour of W.B. Paton*, edited by Frank McAdams, Glasgow: Scottish Library Association, 1977

Thorp, Nigel, *The Glory of the Page: Medieval and Renaissance Illuminated Manuscripts from Glasgow University Library*, London: Miller, 1987

Göttingen State and University Library, Lower Saxony

Address:	Niedersächsische Staats- und Universitätsbibliothek Göttingen Platz der Göttinger Sieben 1 37073 Göttingen Germany Telephone: 551-39-5212 Fax: 551-39-5222 www.sub.uni-goettingen.de
Founded:	1734; 1949
Holdings (2000):	Volumes: 4.5 million. Atlases: 5,000; audio recordings: 1,000; autographs: 100,000; current serials: 13,000; graphic material: 10,000; incunabula: 3,100; manuscripts: 13,000, including 440 medieval manuscripts; maps: 211,000; microforms: 1.1 million; music scores: 11,000.
Special Collections:	*Areas of Concentration:* Altaistik and Paleo-Asiatic languages and literature; Anglo-Saxon; Australia and New Zealand; Celtic studies; Estonian language and literature; Finno-Ugritic philology; history of Great Britain and Ireland; history of knowledge (book history, information and library science, law, organization of knowledge and of scholarly institutions); United States; Slavic studies. *Individual Collections:* Brothers Jacob and Wilhelm Grimm; 18th-century church music manuscripts; Carl Friedrich Gauss collection of natural sciences; Gottfried Wilhelm Leibnitz; medieval manuscripts (including the Fulda Sacramentar of 975); Oriental manuscripts (in Aramaic, Coptic, Hebrew, Sanskrit, and Syriac); 16th- to 18th-century law and theology.

The University Library Göttingen was founded as a unit of the Georg August University in 1734. Gerlach Adolph Freiherr von Münchhausen, the founder and first curator, appointed outstanding scholars as the first professors. He persuaded the heirs of Count Joachim Heinrich von Bülow to donate his private library of 8,912 volumes, 40 manuscripts, and 2,000 maps and charts as a foundation of the university library. In addition, 2,154 volumes from the Royal Library of Hanover and 708 volumes from the Gymnasium Library of Göttingen were added. At the same time Johann Mathias Gesner, professor of classical philology, was appointed as *bibliothecarius*, the first librarian. Gesner had been the director of the Thomas School at Leipzig and a friend of Johann Sebastian Bach.

In 1737 the official opening of the library was celebrated with almost 12,000 volumes and a generous budget for acquisitions. Münchhausen still directed the library from Hanover, and his *Leges Biblioteca Buloviana* became the code for the acquisition, classification, and circulation policies of the library. Münchhausen considered the library the noblest part of the university because it provided professors the means to gain fame through their publications and to bestow on the university a reputation that no other German university enjoyed.

Beyond its services to Göttingen and Lower Saxony, the library was intended to serve scholars and students of all countries, for the benefit of the entire civilized world. The libraries of Paris, Bologna, and Salerno were founded on the same principle. Christian Gottlog Heyne later wrote in his 1780 diary "the library is, as it were, the Palladium of the University."

Count Bülow's collection was especially rich in theology, history, law, and politics. It came to the library with an accession catalog organized in four categories—*theologia, jura, historia,* and *miscellanea*—as well as by size (according to the formats of folio, quarto, and octavo). Each of the groups had an alphabetical author catalog to which new titles were added until 1876. Each book was given an assigned location so it could be retrieved easily—not a custom in academic libraries at that time.

In 1740 Gesner appointed a medical student, Georg Matthiae, as assistant (*custos*) to prepare an alphabetical catalog with each title on a separate card. In 1743 a systematic catalog, organized according to the subjects taught at the university, was added and completed in 1755. In addition to currently published acquisitions, major collections were either purchased or donated. Professors were asked to recommend important publications in their fields to be acquired for the library. When Gesner died in 1761, he left a collection of 60,000 volumes to his successor. Thus, in 25 years the library had grown fivefold.

The private library of Johann von Uffenbach, which he had promised to Göttingen as early as 1736, was finally acquired in 1770, a year after his death. It contained about 2,300 volumes in mathematics, technology, and archaeology. From 1771 to 1806, Russian physician Georg Thomas von Asch, who had studied at Göttingen, donated rare early Russian and Oriental manuscripts that became the foundation of Göttingen's outstanding collection of Slavica. Other private collections in law, history, theology, and philosophy were added during the 18th century. Among those gifts, 700 volumes of unique early imprints, the "Monumenta Typographia" of Wilhelm van Duve, became the basis for Göttingen's special collection of incunabula. In 1791 1,150 volumes of German literature from the 16th to the 18th centuries were given to the library by the Deutsche Gesellschaft in Berlin.

Originally in 1737 the university, including the library, was housed in the former monastery of the Pauline Order. The church was still used for religious services. As the library expanded, several rooms that had served as lecture halls were taken over for the book collection. By 1743 books had to be shelved in narrow hallways. When King George II of Hanover visited the university in that year, the auditorium and offices of the medical faculty were used to shelve books. Gradually private homes near the university and another church (that of the Barefoot Friars) were purchased to accommodate the rapidly growing collection. All space was used for book storage and no reading rooms were available during the 18th century. Library assistants handled book circulation from tables in the stacks with limited schedules of eight hours a week until 1761, and from then on for 12 hours a week. After six months, the books had to be returned, even if being renewed.

Johann Wolfgang von Goethe visited the Göttingen University Library in 1810. In a letter he wrote that here one felt in "the presence of a great treasure that quietly gives out incalculable interest." From then until his death in 1832, Goethe was able to borrow books from Göttingen and have them sent to him in Weimar.

During the 19th century, Göttingen became a model for many scholarly libraries. In 1807 Göttingen became part of the Kingdom of Westphalia under the reign of Napoleon's brother Jérôme, and the financial support of the university, and consequently the acquisition budget of the library, were seriously reduced. In 1829 the brothers Jacob and Wilhelm Grimm were appointed as librarians and, soon after that, as professors of literature. However, they were forced to leave the university in 1837 because, along with five other professors, they refused to pledge the oath of personal allegiance to the newly elected king of Hanover. Because the Kingdom of Hanover did not accept a female ruler, the ascension of Queen Victoria disrupted the personal union with England. Thus the queen's cousin, the duke of Cumberland, became king of Hanover, over the objections of the seven professors who refused to submit their personal pledge to the duke (they saw it as a violation of the loyalty oath that, according to the constitution, all professors had pledged to the state). The action of the "Göttingen Seven" became a landmark in German history.

In 1866 the Kingdom of Hanover was annexed by Prussia and became a province of that state. With this change Göttingen lost something of its privileged position, but at the end of the century when other Prussian libraries (Halle, Greifswald, Königsberg, Breslau, Kiel, Marburg, Münster, Bonn, and Berlin) had between 10,000 and 20,000 volumes each, Göttingen had more than 120,000. The Göttingen librarians tried in vain to get state funds for their collections, but they were able to arrange gifts and exchanges with other institutions, including the British Museum Library. In 1883 the library moved to new, enlarged quarters. Three years later, in 1886, Karl Dziatzko, who had been the director of the Breslau University Library, came to Göttingen. In the 17 years of his leadership he initiated major improvements in technical services and introduced interlibrary loans, at first with Marburg and gradually with all Prussian university libraries. He also established the first full professorship in library science (Bibliothekswissenschaften).

Dziatzko's successor, Richard Pietschmann, director from 1903 to 1921, was able to increase the urgently needed government support. He especially developed the Anglo-American collections. During a trip to the United States in 1903, he studied U.S. libraries and established many lasting contacts, including the American banker, J. Pierpont Morgan, who studied mathematics at Göttingen in 1856–57. In 1912 Morgan donated $50,000 to the university library, the interest to be used for the acquisition of Anglo-American literature.

In 1921 the library established subject divisions administered by scholars in their respective fields. Five years after the end of World War I, in 1923, the Deutsche Notgemeinschaft, a government-sponsored foundation to support German scholarship, designated a number of special collection responsibilities for academic libraries. In this early example of national collaboration in shared collection development, Göttingen was assigned and received assistance for acquisitions in Anglo-American natural sciences. In 1933 the library acquired the natural science and technology collection of Carl Friedrich Gauss. During the years of National Socialism, from 1933 to 1945, including World War II, the director, Karl Julius Hartmann (1935–58), tried to protect the library and its staff. In spite of his efforts, three Jewish librarians were forced to leave, among them Alfred Hessel, distinguished scholar and author of publications in the history of librarianship. In 1944 major parts of the library building were destroyed by bombs. Fortunately, books and serials that were stored in the cellar survived. Unfortunately, newspapers and government publications, as well as duplicates that had been transferred to a former potassium mine for protection, were destroyed by an explosion in the fall of 1945. In the same year the ancient handwritten card catalog was discontinued and a new card catalog initiated. For shelf arrangement a new system of "numerus currens" (an arrangement by acquisition number) replaced the former subject arrangement of 1923. In 1956 numerus currens was adopted for the whole collection.

In 1949 the Cultural Ministry of the state government at Hanover announced that Göttingen, which had always served the state, would now officially become the Niedersächsische Staats- und Universitätsbibliothek Göttingen (State and University Library, Lower Saxony). The Deutsche Forschungsgemeinschaft, successor to the Deutsche Notgemeinschaft, designated Göttingen University as the official German repository for natural sciences, Anglo-American literature, Finnish civilization, Altaistik (Central Asian) literature, geophysics, mineralogy, forestry, philosophy of science, scientific journals, and thematic maps. In 1976 the comprehensive collection of textbooks became an added responsibility.

In 1967 electronic data processing was introduced in the cataloging of the journal collection; it was extended to the acquisition of new journals in 1973. This was also the year in which the first branch library opened at the Institute for Chemistry. A medical branch library opened in 1977 at the new campus of University Hospitals. In 1978 the revised Legislation for Higher Education in Lower Saxony confirmed that the library was intended to serve the general public of the state at large and not exclusively the academic and civil service clientele. From 1984 to 1992, in preparation for the move to a new building, the library undertook a major reorganization of departments and services. The first book from the new library was circulated to the president of the university, Professor Norbert Kamp, on 20 August 1992. The official dedication of the new library as the *Niedersächsische Staats- und Universitätsbibliothek* took place on 30 October 1993.

In the 1998 preface to the library's current guide, Director Elmer Mittler describes the new building as a library for the next millennium, combining aesthetics and functionality in unusual perfection. A major portion of the books is housed underground, and all services are flexible. The reading rooms house about 4,500 volumes and are bright, with excellent climate control; their computers have access to all major international databases.

The old library, after major renovations, now houses the rare books, maps, and manuscript collections, as well as equipment for the digitization of older books. To introduce the public to fast-changing developments, a training center for technology is located on the first floor of the old building, thus nicely combining the traditional with the innovative. Göttingen coordinates the European Register of Microform Masters (EROMM), a consortium project that makes reformatted materials available throughout Europe and the United States. As in the early days of Heyne, the Göttingen University Library is again recognized as one of the finest research and public service libraries in Europe.

ANTJE BULTMANN LEMKE

Further Reading

Fabian, Bernhard, "An Eighteenth-Century Research Collection: English Books at Göttingen University Library," *Library*, 6th series (1979)

Gebaute Zukunft: 5 Jahre Neubau der SUB: Neue Dienstleistungen der Niedersächsischen Staats- und Universitätsbibliothek Göttingen, Göttingen, 1998; available at webdoc.sub.gwdg.de/ebook/aw/5jahrsub/deckbl.htm

Hapke, Thomas, "History of Scholarly Information and Communication: A Review of Selected German Literature," *Journal of the American Society for Information Science* 50, no. 3 (1999)

Hartmann, Karl Julius, and Hans Füchsel, editors, *Geschichte der Göttinger Universitäts-Bibliothek*, Göttingen: Vandenhoek and Ruprecht, 1937

Kind-Doerne, Christiane, *Die Niedersächsische Staats- und Universitätsbibliothek Göttingen: Ihre Bestände und Einrichtungen in Geschichte und Gegenwart*, Wiesbaden, Germany: Harrassowitz, 1986

Niedersächsische Staats- und Universitätsbibliothek Göttingen: Dokumentation des Neubaus zur Eröffnung am 30.4.1993, Göttingen: Staatshochbauverwaltung des Landes Niedersachsen, 1993

Schwedt, Georg, *Zur Geschichte der Göttinger Universitätsbibliothek: Zeitgenössische Berichte aus 3 Jahrhunderten*, Göttingen: Göttinger Tageblatt, 1983

Grolier Club Library

Address: Grolier Club Library
47 East 60th Street
New York, New York 10022
USA
Telephone: 212-838-6690
Fax: 212-838-2445
www.grolierclub.org/Library.htm

Founded: 1884

Holdings (2000): Volumes: 100,000. Archives and manuscripts: 1,000 linear feet; bookseller and book auction catalogs: 65,000; current serials: 200; illuminated manuscripts: 12; incunabula: 52; monographs: 35,000.

Special Collections: *Areas of Concentration:* Book arts; bookbinding; book-collecting; graphic design; history of printing; typography. *Individual Collections:* Bibliography; book catalogs; examples of printing and related book arts; the Middle Hill Press. *Papers:* Antiquarian Booksellers' Association of America; Bowyer-Nichols firm of printers; John Fleming; E.P. Goldschmidt; Sol Malkin and AB/Bookman's Weekly; Morgand & Fatout; Emil Offenbacher; Louis Polain; Scribner Rare Book Department; Society of Iconophiles; Sir Thomas Phillipps; Edouard Rahir.

The Grolier Club

The Grolier Club of New York is America's oldest society for those interested in books and prints. Founded in 1884 to promote the "arts pertaining to the production of books," the club's namesake is the great 15th-century French collector Jean Grolier, known for his patronage of Renaissance printers, for the fine bindings he commissioned, and for a generous habit of sharing his books with friends. The Grolier is a unique mix of private club and not-for-profit cultural institution, and its international membership of more than 700 members (collectors, librarians, book designers, and antiquarian book dealers) takes an active role in its mission to promote the book arts through exhibitions, publications, and, most importantly, a research library on the history of books and printing.

The Library

The establishment and maintenance of a research library was not a primary goal of the club's founding members. The aims of the club as set out in its constitution were to be achieved through the occasional publication of finely printed books and through meetings, lectures, and exhibitions. Yet some sort of reference collection (at the very least) must have been in the minds of the founders because the Grolier's first *Yearbook* (1884) lists Librarian Alexander W. Drake among the officers. By the time the club issued its second yearbook in 1887, a library committee had been formed, its purpose being "to gather together for the use of the members all the standard bibliographical works, as well as books relating to the art of printing"—an impossible task today, but not an unreasonable acquisitions policy 100 years ago. In 1887 the club owned 300 volumes, acquired mostly through gift. These threatened to overwhelm the few bookshelves in the club's rented quarters at 64 Madison Avenue, and the accumulation certainly influenced the Grolier's decision in 1890 to construct a building of its own. In that year Richard Hoe Lawrence took over as librarian, and in his 13-year tenure the library grew to more than 5,000 volumes, quickly overflowing the two rooms prepared for it in the club's new headquarters at 29 East 32nd Street. What had started out as a modest cooperative reference library for the club's bibliophile membership had begun to take on the character of a research collection and had become an important focus for member donations.

Reference material predominated, but in the early years of the Grolier Club, before the establishment of rivals such as the Pierpont Morgan Library, the club also routinely reported significant gifts of rare books. Samuel Putnam Avery, collector, print dealer, and founding Grolier member, was from the beginning a major benefactor. Between 1884 and his death in 1903 he ensured that the club had all the newest bibliographies, as well as fine specimens from his own collections of early printing, bindings, and prints. In 1894 the Bruce family of New York typefounders donated a library of several hundred books illustrating (or treating) fine printing and typography, including 94 incunabula.

Faced with maintaining this growing collection, the council appointed for the first time a professional caretaker, Henry Watson Kent, in 1900. He served for three years under Lawrence as assistant librarian, and in 1903 Kent was named librarian. One of his first tasks was to develop a classification scheme for the library. Kent was a member of Melvil Dewey's first class at the newly founded Columbia School of Library Service, and the scheme he developed with Lawrence owes much to the Dewey Decimal Classification system. The Kent-Lawrence system is still used by the club today, and it has been adopted by other similar specialized collections, notably the Saint Bride Printing Library in London.

Ruth Shepard Granniss

The Grolier Club Library owes much to Ruth Shepard Granniss. A graduate of the Pratt Institute Library School, Miss Granniss (as she was universally known) served as Kent's assistant from 1904 until his resignation in 1906, after which time she presided over the library until her retirement in 1944—the longest single tenure of any Grolier Club librarian. The library grew under her care from 8,000 volumes in 1904 to nearly 40,000 volumes in 1944. She oversaw the club's move in 1917 to its current home at 47 East 60th Street, and, once there, she directed the installation of the collections within a grand two-story room designed by architect and club member Bertram Grosvenor Goodhue, which today serves as the library's reading room. She wrote some 20 books and articles on book collecting and bibliography, including *A Descriptive Catalogue of the First Editions in Book Form of the Writings of Percy Bysshe Shelley* (The Grolier Club, 1923). Although modest and retiring (she never allowed herself to be photographed), Miss Granniss was a significant figure in the early-20th-century American book world and deserves more recognition than she has so far received.

Throughout this period (1904-44) important additions to the library continued to come primarily through gift, as founding and early members of the club died. The emphasis remained on examples illustrating the book arts: metal and embroidered bindings (Beverly Chew); early printed books (William Loring Andrews); books designed by Bruce Rogers; representative runs of turn-of-the-century English presses, such as Doves and Ashendene (Charles Williston McAlpin); and an important archive of the work of Frederic W. Goudy (Melbert Cary).

The Catalog Collections

The appointment in 1923 of George Leslie McKay as assistant to Granniss signaled an important shift in focus. McKay was a prolific bibliographer, and he had compiled standard works on popular authors such as John Masefield and H. Rider Haggard. But he is perhaps best known for *American Book Auction Catalogues, 1713-1934* (New York Public Library, 1937), a union list of American auctions created on the model of the 1915 British Museum *List of Catalogues of English Book Sales 1676-1900*. McKay drew heavily on the club's own collection of U.S. catalogs. Since its founding in 1884 the club has solicited and made available to its members the current catalogs of every major European and American antiquarian book dealer and auction house. When these became outdated they were not discarded, as often happens, but carefully filed away as they are today. By the 1920s this core collection, although somewhat haphazardly developed, had begun to be useful to researchers in book history and to attract donations.

Significant additions of rare English and European catalogs from the 17th, 18th, and early 19th centuries were made during George McKay's tenure (curator 1923-44, librarian 1944-57) and under successors Alexander Davidson (librarian 1957-61), J. Terry Bender (librarian 1961-64), and Gabriel Austin (curator 1963-64, librarian 1964-69). Grolier members Waters S. Davis and Lucius Wilmerding were exceptional donors in this area. Together in the 1930s they made dozens of gifts of rare English and French catalogs, the prize being a copy of the very rare first English book auction sale of 1676. The collection of English sales was strengthened in 1961 with a donation by Lionel and Philip Robinson (the London firm of antiquarian booksellers) of 62 17th-century English book auction catalogs, which at a stroke rendered the library's collection the largest in the country. French catalogs of the 18th and 19th centuries were the special interest of Librarian Gabriel Austin, and during his tenure that part of the collection grew to its current size of some 2,500 items—again, the largest group of French catalogs outside France. (A printed catalog of the French catalog collection, funded by the Florence Gould Foundation, is in preparation.) The club today actively continues to collect book catalogs of all kinds. The result is a uniquely valuable archive of the antiquarian book trade and of book collecting, by far the most widely used and best known of the library's resources.

Archives and Collections of Works on Paper

Books and pamphlets predominate in the library, but there are also significant collections of works on paper and archival material. Prints and drawings were, if anything, more interesting than books to early Grolier members (some of the first public exhibitions of Japanese prints in the United States were mounted at the club), and, after a long period of dormancy, interest in the graphic arts is once again reviving among club members. The library's print collections are not large, but there are important holdings in portraits of bookish figures, bookplates, and examples of 19th-century illustration processes. The library holds the papers of the Society of Iconophiles, a New York club of print enthusiasts that met at the Grolier between 1894 and 1935.

The club's largest archival collection is that documenting its own history, but the library selectively acquires the archives of other bookish organizations. The library maintains the archives of the Antiquarian Booksellers Association of America and has recently acquired the papers of Sol Malkin and *AB/Bookman's Weekly*. Individual antiquarian book dealers are another area of strength, represented by papers from the firms of John Fleming, Edouard Rahir, E.P. Goldschmidt, and the Scribner Rare Book Department. One of the club's most important archival collections is a recent gift of member Harrison Horblit, consisting of diaries, scrapbooks, sketchbooks, printed books, and family photographs documenting the life and bibliophile interests of Sir Thomas Phillipps, England's greatest and most eccentric book collector.

Recent Trends

In the last 30 years librarians Robert L. Nikirk (1971–90), Martin Antonetti (1990–97), and Eric Holzenberg (1997–) have brought increased professionalization to staff and services. In 1983 the library hired its first professional cataloger and began to record all of its new acquisitions in the Research Libraries Information Network (RLIN) bibliographic database. Selective small-scale retrospective conversion projects have been carried out in the last five years, notably on the club's collection of French book catalogs, which is now accessible via SCIPIO, a subset of the RLIN database. Increased online cataloging, along with the development of a Grolier Club website, have made the collections more accessible to researchers and greatly increased use of the library. Throughout the period from 1970 to 1990 the Grolier Club Library averaged 170 to 200 visits per year. Between 1990 and the present that figure has risen to more than 600 visits annually.

The Grolier Club Library has benefited greatly from the remarkably consistent generosity of its bibliophile membership, but it no longer thrives solely on donations. Acquisitions funds for the library were voted on an ad hoc basis for most of its existence, and lean periods in the 1940s, 1960s, and 1970s left gaps in the collections, which the library is only now beginning to fill. The library owes its current healthy acquisitions fund (and arguably its very existence) to rare book dealer Lathrop C. Harper. Harper was remarkable among book dealers in that he died a millionaire, and the club is one of nine institutions in New York and elsewhere benefiting from a series of Harper Funds he set up solely for book purchases. His 1957 bequest to the club now makes up a sizable portion of the library's total endowment and ensures that the club can keep up with current books and serials in its specialized field of interest.

Although Grolier Club members visit the library in greater numbers, the collections are used much more intensively by nonmembers, and the library is open by appointment to any qualified researcher. Book sale catalogs are most in demand. Editors of scholarly collections use them to trace letters and manuscripts of important literary and historical figures; researchers find them useful in constructing histories of collections, or particular books within collections; and they are primary source material for the study of literacy, readership, and the development of private and institutional libraries. Although much of the Grolier's reference collection is duplicated elsewhere in New York, the library's accessibility, manageable scale, and tight focus give it distinct advantages. The library's collection of bibliographies is an important resource for the New York book trade, for instance. Designers and typographers consult the club's collections of type specimen books and private press titles. The library's collection of examples illustrating printing, binding, and graphic techniques lends support to a number of local courses each year in bibliography, the book arts, and book history.

The library faces its share of problems: Catalog automation is desperately needed, but the club lacks the funds to undertake a mass retrospective conversion project; the current roster of staff and volunteers is inadequate for the current level of use; the high incidence of brittle 19th-century material in the collection presents daunting conservation problems; the needs of a research collection and a bibliophile society do not always coincide; and, while the library grows daily, the Grolier's beloved clubhouse does not. However, the library (now well into its second century) has also some cause for optimism: a small but dedicated staff, a loyal constituency, a growing reputation, a healthy acquisitions fund, a committed and knowledgeable board, and a generous membership, nearly all of whom are "Friends of the Grolier Club Library" in one sense or another.

ERIC J. HOLZENBERG

Further Reading

Grolier Club, *Transactions of the Grolier Club of the City of New York,* 4 vols., New York: Grolier Club, 1885–1921

Grolier Club, *The Grolier Club 1884–1984,* New York: Grolier Club, 1984

Harvard University Library

Address: Harvard University Library
Cambridge, Massachusetts 02138
USA
Telephone: 617-495-3650
Fax: 617-495-0403
http://lib.harvard.edu/libraries

Founded: 1638

Holdings (2000): Volumes: 14.4 million. Archives and manuscripts: 175,000 linear feet*; cartographic materials*; current serials: 110,000; incunabula: 4,250; microforms: 8.7 million; music scores: 15,000; photographs: 4 million*; sound recordings: 104,000*; video and film: 23,000*. (* indicates holdings exclusive of some distributed collections.)

Special Collections: *Areas of Concentration:* Business; education; Harvard University; history; law; literature; medicine; music; religion; U.S. women.
Individual Collections: Boulay de la Meurthe library on the French Revolution; Daniel Christoph Ebeling collection of Americana; H. Nelson Gay collection of the Italian Risorgimento; Icelandic collection; Amy Lowell's Keats collection; Palha library of Portuguese history and literature; David Bailie Warden library of Americana. *Papers:* American Board of Commissioners for Foreign Missions; American Unitarian Association; Emily Dickinson; R.G. Dun and Company credit ledgers; Ralph Waldo Emerson; Henry Wadsworth Longfellow; Massachusetts General Hospital; Herman Melville.

One basic fact about the Harvard University Library that runs throughout its 200-year history is that, like Harvard University itself, it is decentralized. Each of the Harvard faculties (arts and sciences, business administration, design, divinity, education, government, law, medicine, and public health) is basically responsible for its own financial well-being. The president and the provost, at the head of what is known as the central administration, coordinate the whole system, although they do not manage it. The library system operates within this framework of decentralization, with each faculty basically responsible for its own library, as are the independent research institutions. There is, to be sure, a Harvard University Library (HUL), which consists of employees who are responsible for coordinating the whole complex system and carrying out certain functions. HUL provides the infrastructure for a unified catalog of the collections; it also manages the Harvard Depository (a storage facility), and provides certain preservation services to the library. Most recently, HUL is creating the framework for the Library Digital Initiative and coordinating the creation of digital content by the various libraries.

The decentralization of funding has made possible entrepreneurial library building by various faculties of the university. Decentralization of storage has meant dispersal of the collections so that space, although still an important issue, is not as critical as it would otherwise have been. Decentralization can even be said to have fostered competition. Thus, the very structure of the university has contributed to making HUL the world's largest university library.

The largest of the faculty libraries is the Harvard College Library, itself a group of libraries that serves the faculty of arts and sciences. The Harvard College Library began in 1638 with the bequest of John Harvard, a clergyman in Charlestown, Massachusetts. His library contained some 329 titles in almost 400 volumes. That bequest, which occurred two years after the founding of the unnamed college, was the origin of the Harvard University Library, which is the oldest in the United States. However, age has little to do with the Harvard Library's size, for there were scarcely more than 5,000 books when the building housing the library burned on the night of 14 January 1764. A few books that had been borrowed survived, and the library began again with a few hundred books that had not yet been unpacked and placed on shelves in the library.

The library that burned was not the result of careful selection by the college authorities. Instead, it was mainly the result of gifts, large numbers of them from Great Britain. Indeed, the purpose of printing the catalog of 1723, which recorded about 3,000 volumes, was not to disseminate information to individuals in Cambridge. Rather, it was printed at the request of Thomas Hollis III and his cousin Daniel Neal, English supporters of the library, who felt that they would be in a better position to make useful gifts or to solicit donations from others if they knew what was already at Harvard. The Harvard Corporation sent 100 copies to various agents in England, plus 30 each to Hollis and to Neal. The return to Harvard was not great, but the fact that the catalog was compiled and printed showed high expectations. Historical accounts of Harvard, Yale University (New Haven, Connecticut), and Princeton University (Princton, New Jersey) show that libraries of the colonial colleges eagerly sought donations from England and occasionally received important gifts.

The Harvard Library's most important 18th-century benefactor was the Englishman Thomas Hollis V of Lincoln's Inn. Some of the books still surviving from the 1764 fire came from him, and after the fire, in addition to soliciting gifts from others, he sent between 2,000 and 3,000 volumes of his own to Harvard. Upon his death in 1774, he bequeathed £500 for an endowed fund for books. By commencement in 1766, the 4,350 volumes in the library approached the number in the pre-fire library, thanks largely to gifts from Hollis and others in England and Scotland, as well as from the Province of New Hampshire (700 books) and from John Hancock (1,300 books).

Gifts continued to arrive, sufficient for 9,000 volumes to be recorded in the printed catalog of 1790. Apart from Hollis's gifts, the books were a miscellaneous lot, hardly a systematic effort to form a library. Indeed, a proposal from Benjamin Franklin in 1755, that there be raised a fund for the best new books published each year, was never acted on. For nearly a century afterward, until 1859, the library did not systematically seek to buy newly published books.

The standard procedure was to take advantage of someone's presence abroad to purchase books. An occasional appropriation from general funds was made by the Harvard Corporation, the senior governing body, and some money was raised from the sale of duplicates. Henry Wadsworth Longfellow was one of those who purchased books abroad. By and large, expenditures were very small, with a low point reached in 1806–07, when the list of acquisitions filled only half of a single page.

There were occasional donations of collections. The Beverly, Massachusetts, merchant Israel Thorndike paid for a collection of German theology as well as the important Americana collection of Daniel Christoph Ebeling. A few years later in 1823, Harvard's treasurer, Samuel A. Eliot, personally provided the funds for the Americana library of David Bailie Warden.

To acquire newly published material, in 1816 President John Thornton Kirkland printed as a circular letter an appeal to publishers to send their current publications as well as any other pamphlets or books they were willing to offer. Kirkland seems to have had in mind a voluntary deposit that publishers would make for the "great benefit [which] must accrue to the cause of literature and science and to the particular interests of your profession." The notice was subsequently sent to individuals as well, showing a concern for acquiring current output. This was something new in the thinking of Harvard officials, but the results were insignificant.

Money was clearly needed, and during 1841 and 1842 a major fund-raising effort was undertaken, coinciding with the erection of a new library building, Gore Hall. The amount raised was $17,000, a sum sufficient to ask faculty to draw up lists of desiderata. Much of what was acquired were 18th-century works, but there were also purchases of newly published books. Once those funds were exhausted, there were not sufficient resources to continue such buying. Both President Edward Everett (1846–49) and President James Walker (1853–60) were aware that the creation of a research library was essential if Harvard were to be transformed into an institution truly of higher learning. The quantity of scholarly publications was growing, in the sciences as well as in other fields, and Harvard faculty needed to have access to that literature.

It also became clear in the 1850s that Harvard's library would not necessarily continue to be the largest in the country. In Boston, Massachusetts, the newly formed Boston Public Library was growing rapidly. In New York City, the newly established Astor Library was also overtaking Harvard. In 1851 a fire destroyed most of the collections of the Library of Congress in Washington, D.C., and large sums were spent to rebuild it, sums much larger than anything Harvard had available.

In 1859 William Gray, whose family made many benefactions to Harvard, initiated the process of forming a research library rich in contemporary publications. In a letter to President Walker, he offered $5,000 per year for five years and expressed the wish that in spending these funds "the latest works be preferred to those of earlier date." A faculty library committee allocated the funds ($1,300 of the initial $4,700 allocation going to the sciences), engaged agents in Europe, and began sending orders. Because some funds were held back, the Gray gift lasted longer than five years, but by 1865–66 the budget for books had dropped to $1,134. This sum was not sufficient to enable Harvard to build a research library similar to those of peer institutions. Again, friends of the library came forward. Charles Minot left the library $60,000 by bequest in 1870, specifically for new books. This was an endowed fund in line with the emphasis of President Charles William Eliot (1869–1909) on endowment. By the end of the 1880s, endowed funds for the general purposes of the library had increased to more than $500,000 in principal. Although the scope of the collections would subsequently expand in various ways, the fundamental transformation to a research collection had taken place.

A transformation in cataloging had also taken place. Like collection building, in the 18th century and well into the 19th, cataloging was not an ongoing process but rather an act carried out at a particular time. For the most part, a catalog was created as a library or a collection was purchased, and an individual was paid for producing a catalog. Eighteenth-century catalogs were prepared by buying a blank book and writing the letters of the alphabet at the top of the pages, in preparation for alphabetical entries. If an earlier catalog existed, entries would be copied onto the proper pages, with some space left for new entries. Ultimately, the available space would be inadequate, and entries would be inserted out of order or in a tiny hand. There would follow a supplement, and then the process would begin again. A variation was to print the catalog and then to interleave some copies, the blank leaves providing space for additions.

The difficulty of inserting additions must have hindered ongoing, cumulative effort, despite librarians being instructed to do so. Being up-to-date was only part of the problem with a manuscript book catalog; also significant was that only one person could consult it at a given time, unless multiple copies were made. Printing was required to make multiple copies, and Harvard printed catalogs in 1723 (with supplements in 1725 and 1735), 1773, 1790, and 1830. Printing only solved the problem of multiple user access to a catalog, as each catalog still became out of date within a short time. That problem became particularly evident as books purchased with William Gray's 1859 gift began to arrive.

In 1860 Librarian John Langdon Sibley (assistant librarian, 1841–56; librarian, 1856–77) proposed a card catalog for public use. In doing so, he and Ezra Abbot (the assistant librarian who was the true innovator and creator of the catalog) must have been influenced by the existence of the card catalog that had been proposed in 1840. In that year Thaddeus William Harris (librarian 1831–56) stated in his annual report that a "slip catalogue" would be very useful for the annual inventory as well as for "facilitating the re-arrangement of books in the new library, and would serve for various other useful purposes hereafter."

A card catalog for public use was innovative, and it required the design of cabinets and drawers. As the card catalog meant giving up the printed catalogs that each scholar could have at hand, it is likely that improved subject access was undertaken as a further way of making the change to cards palatable. The new subject catalog was what came to be known as an alphabetico-classed catalog, with headings arranged alphabetically and the headings themselves subdivided, the subdivisions arranged alphabetically under the main heading.

Spending Gray's gift entailed a great deal of work in preparing lists. For example, the desiderata of faculty members had to be made into lists to be sent to the various agents. To do that work, Harvard employed women starting on 11 April 1859, and it was young women who began work on the card catalog in October 1861.

Although the library in Gore Hall (now the basis of the Harvard College Library) was the largest of Harvard's libraries, it was by no means the only one. In the early decades of the 19th century, the faculties of divinity, medicine, and law established their own libraries. For a time, there was also a natural history library, though no records of it exist after 1832. In addition, Harvard student societies had fully functioning libraries. These were substantial in size, having 12,000 volumes in 1849, compared to 56,000 in the college library. Around the middle of the century, various specialized scientific libraries began to be formed. The Lawrence Scientific School, established in 1847, had its own library, and libraries began to be formed at the Observatory (1849), the Museum of Comparative Zoology (1859), the Gray Herbarium (1864), and the Arnold Arboretum (1874). A library devoted to anthropology was begun in 1866.

Sibley, the librarian of the mid-19th century, was an avid collector for the library, and it continued to grow even though funds were very limited throughout much of his tenure. He did not, however, emphasize use of its collections. His successor, Justin Winsor (1877–97), brought with him from the Boston Public Library the public librarian's emphasis on service to users. Indeed, Winsor's pioneering and widely influential emphasis on the library as a "workshop" was highly appropriate for an institution that was becoming a research university. He also brought to the Harvard Library the outlook of an administrator, and his annual reports, although continuing to document acquisitions via narrative accounts, became statistical accounts as well. He tried to run the college library efficiently, and his manuscript "Order no. 1" of 8 December 1877 set forth the "principles of efficient administration," all dealing with the attitudes and conduct he expected of the staff. Winsor was a logical candidate for the presidency of the American Library Association (ALA) and was its first president, serving from 1876 to 1885.

A sign of Winsor's efforts at heightening efficiency was his attempt to centralize library operations. In 1880 the Harvard Corporation ordered that no Harvard library, with the exception of the law school's, should purchase a book except through the librarian of the university (Winsor's title). The order also stated that all books should be sent to the college library for cataloging. However, Winsor's effort at centralizing the libraries failed, perhaps because libraries continued to proliferate. A number of departmental and divisional scientific libraries were established in the 1880s and 1890s, including an architectural library in 1893 that was eventually incorporated in 1936 into the library of the new School of Design.

Winsor's effort at centralization was also hindered by lack of space in which to carry out the work, not to mention lack of space in which to store books. Gore Hall, despite an addition in 1877 (making it the first U.S. library containing tiers of self-supporting stacks), did not long have sufficient space for books and staff. A consequence was that President Eliot proposed storage of "dead books" in his 1900–01 annual report. He envisioned that Harvard and other libraries would store materials in several storage facilities in various parts of the country. Faculty and librarians defeated the proposal, requiring a further addition to Gore Hall in 1907.

Winsor was succeeded in 1898 by William Coolidge Lane, an employee since his graduation in 1881. A few years earlier, Archibald Cary Coolidge, a young instructor in history, had begun to play an increasingly crucial role, beginning with his purchase in 1895 of almost the entire contents of a Harrassowitz catalog of Slavica (1,371 titles). Of the 15,000 total acquisitions that year, Coolidge's gift represented nearly 10 percent, followed by 600 more the next year.

Splendid as those gifts were, they did increase the library's inability to handle satisfactorily the consequences of growth. The library could not keep up with cataloging, nor could it adequately store all of the books; in time it became clear that Lane could not solve the library's problems. He was an inward-looking man, without the connections that would bring in outside resources, and he lacked the standing among the faculty that would have enabled him to rally support for increasing university resources for the library. Coolidge was quite the opposite, and when Abbott Lawrence Lowell became president in 1909, Lane was made the chief staff officer and worked under the direction of Coolidge. At that point Coolidge had the title of chairman of the library council, but to make roles clear Coolidge was given the title of director in 1910, which he held until his death in 1928.

Coolidge immediately set about coping with processing issues. Such a simple matter as adopting a standard-sized catalog card to take advantage of the cooperative movements of that era brought with it the need to copy cards. In addition to a public catalog, it was determined that an official catalog for staff use should be created. For the public catalog, more than 3 million cards were handled and one million new ones prepared. Reclassification was also pushed forward when it became clear in 1912 that soon there would be a new building. Decisions in 1915 to combine the alphabetico-classed catalog with the author catalog, to make the official catalog a union catalog of most Harvard libraries, and to include Library of Congress (LC) cards, set the pattern that was to last until the adoption of the LC classification system in the 1970s and the inauguration of a microfiche Distributable Union Catalog for new acquisitions in 1981.

Much better known is Coolidge's role in transforming the collections. Coolidge saw that the United States was playing an ever-increasing role in the world, and he believed that Harvard should educate those who would be assuming international responsibilities. Through his teaching and through building the Harvard Library, Coolidge internationalized U.S. education, and in so doing exerted great influence upon U.S. education.

Even before becoming director, Coolidge had been instrumental in acquiring more Slavica, the Riant collection on the Crusades, much material on the Ottoman Empire, 10,000 volumes on German history, the von Maurer library of Old Norse law and Scandinavian history and literature, and much more. After becoming director, he brought in several Latin American collections, Western Americana, two extraordinary theatrical libraries, English tracts and local history, numerous author collections (including Amy Lowell's Keats collection), the Palha library of Portuguese history and literature, the Boulay de la Meurthe library on the French Revolution, and more. Coolidge took the steps that resulted in the Harvard-Yenching Library, one of the greatest collections of East Asian materials in the Western world. Coolidge's influence continued after his death in 1928, with the subsequent acquisition of an Icelandic collection of 10,000 volumes and the nearly unrivaled H. Nelson Gay Collection on the history of the Italian Risorgimento.

Coolidge's influence extended beyond the college library. At the law school, a period of growth began after the appointment of Christopher Columbus Langdell as dean in 1870, but it accelerated and widened in scope during the Coolidge years. In fact, Coolidge steered some material to the law school. What was happening in the college and the law school also influenced the business school, established in 1908, to build its library.

In building collections, Coolidge had the advantage of sufficient space. The lowest level of Widener Library, which opened in 1915, was not finished at that time, but temporarily provided adequate space. In only two decades, however, space again became an issue. Keyes D. Metcalf, librarian of Harvard College and director of the Harvard University Library from 1937 to 1955, the first library-school graduate to guide the library system, had to solve the space problem. Indeed, President James Bryant Conant had been particularly impressed by the fact that Metcalf had, at the New York Public Library, pioneered in putting texts on microfilm. Microfilming was, however, only a small part of the solution, applicable primarily to 19th-century newspapers on brittle paper. Metcalf instead found the answer to the space shortage primarily in building new libraries and decentralizing the collections in various ways.

Metcalf built the Houghton Library for rare books, the New England Deposit Library (primarily for storage of material from Widener), and the Lamont Library for undergraduates. In 1956 the Eda Kuhn Loeb Music Library opened, absorbing the music materials from Widener. Materials pertaining to the arts were moved when the Fine Arts Library was established in 1962–63.

At Harvard, separate libraries have tended to mean active collecting, and the Houghton Library, opened in 1942, was no exception. William A. Jackson (1938–64), the first librarian of Houghton, knew that the college library had no tradition of collecting the papers of individuals (the business school had the most extensive holdings of papers), but he also knew that he had an opportunity that, if lost, would never again occur. Jackson emphasized acquisition of the papers of leading authors, particularly those of New England: Thomas Bailey Aldrich, Emily Dickinson, Ralph Waldo Emerson, Thomas Wentworth Higginson, William Dean Howells, members of the James family, Henry Wadsworth Longfellow, James Russell Lowell, and Herman Melville, among others. In the area of printed books, his emphasis on literary texts followed the example set by Coolidge in emphasizing historical texts. Working with Jackson was Philip Hofer, who established the Department of Printing and Graphic Arts, the first such department in a university library. A born collector, Hofer devoted nearly half a century to enlarging, mainly with his own personal funds, the library's holdings of early manuscripts and of well-printed and illustrated books. Hofer's gifts may well be the most valuable ever received by the Harvard Library.

Jackson and Hofer may also be taken as symbols of the personnel revolution brought about by Metcalf. In addition to employing many other librarians who became leaders in the library world (among them Frederick G. Kilgour, founder of OCLC), he also expanded their roles. As early as 1945 he advocated that responsibility for book selection be placed in the hands of librarian specialists, although the first was appointed only toward the end of his tenure, in 1953–54. Paul H. Buck (1955–64), formerly the university's provost, continued Metcalf's revolution in personnel by correcting inequities and improving salaries. In the post-World War II environment, given the expansion of publishing and the existing strength of the library, buying large collections was less important than ongoing acquisition of new publications and filling in gaps through the antiquarian book trade. This kind of growth required a good number of library staff with specialized skills, and Metcalf and Buck made that possible.

Despite the expansion of the collections in types of material and geographic and subject scope, growing internationalization required further expansion. The Center for Middle Eastern

Studies was created in 1954, requiring its own research collection. Five years later a bibliographer was appointed to build one. In the field of Judaica, major collections had been acquired in 1929 and 1951, and in 1957 Lee M. Friedman's gift of his library brought Harvard eminence in the field. In 1962 Friedman also endowed the position of bibliographer in Judaica, assuring ongoing development of Judaica holdings to the point at which the holdings and associated activities (such as cataloging and publishing) would make it a particularly notable resource for the world of scholarship. It should be said, however, that the process is not complete. Although there are instructional courses on Southeast Asia and Africa, the same kind of efforts devoted to collections on other parts of the world have not yet been focused on these areas.

Harvard does not collect all subjects and all types of material. Political papers, for example, are not widely collected because Harvard's newest graduate school, the Kennedy School of Government, has not built its own research library. The holdings in subject areas not represented in the curriculum (such as agriculture) are understandably limited, as Harvard's collections are not universal but are shaped instead by the teaching and research needs of Harvard students and faculty. Occasionally, a library collection is formed in advance of instruction, as when Coolidge began to acquire Slavic materials. And what is now the Schlesinger Library began in 1943 to form a collection devoted to the history of women in the United States.

Although the scope of the Harvard Library is not universal, the Harvard Library in size of collections is comparable to megalibraries such as the Library of Congress, the British Library, the New York Public Library, and the Bibliothèque nationale de France. Total holdings exceed 14 million volumes, exclusive of microforms, manuscripts, visual materials, maps, sound recordings, sheet music, and digital materials. The net increase in the number of volumes of books and periodicals added in a year, according to the 1998–99 annual report, exceeds 287,000.

Large growth has, of course, meant ongoing struggles to store books. Decentralization of the collections into numerous buildings and departments on campus sufficed only for a time. Off-site storage became a necessity, and in 1986 the first module of the Harvard Depository was constructed on land 35 minutes from Harvard Square. Space is available for ten modules, each able to hold approximately 1.7 million volumes. The books are shelved by size in containers that are retrieved via forklift by an attendant who can determine the exact location of a desired volume from its bar code.

For off-site storage to function efficiently, electronic cataloging records have proved a necessity, thus adding impetus to a complete retrospective conversion of the card catalogs of the various libraries. Now HOLLIS, the library's online catalog, is a virtually complete record of printed material held by the library system, and it is the first time since the early 19th century that there has been a unified catalog providing multiple points of access.

That accomplishment and the increased use it fostered, as well as the consciousness of the possibilities of technology, has led to new catalogs and pressures for more information in catalogs.

The Online Archival Search Information System (OASIS) provides information on archival holdings, and Visual Information Access (VIA) covers visual materials. There also exist the searchable files of the Harvard-MIT Data Center. Each of these catalogs requires development of an infrastructure to support it, and the Library Digital Initiative is making possible development of other digital content as well as additional capabilities in the infrastructure. Concern for increasing the capacity to provide access to digital information is also stimulated by the fact that a library whose holdings were largely accessible on open shelves is becoming a library in which a growing percentage of the material is off-site.

As in the mid-19th century, changes in publishing and the intellectual environment (then greater output and greater emphasis on research; now an added means of disseminating information and a growing capacity and desire to use it) are bringing about transformation in the library. In both periods, competition fostered the transformation. Just as those responsible for the Harvard Library 150 years ago wanted it to be a research library comparable to the others being created, so today those responsible for the Harvard Library want it to provide capabilities for access to information that are comparable to those of other institutions.

In the 19th century, each library's success was of benefit to the others, albeit indirectly, through stimulating emulation. Thus, the Astor Library and the Boston Public Library led to an increase in resources devoted to the Harvard Library. Today, the situation is somewhat different, in that one institution's success in developing new digital information (and the capacity for creating it, making it accessible, and preserving it) directly benefits other libraries. There is another way, though, in which the two eras are more directly comparable. For certain kinds of scholarship it has always been necessary to use more than one library. The prefaces of today's publications in the humanities commonly thank librarians at a number of libraries. To be sure, for some kinds of scholarship a researcher's home institution suffices, but for large numbers of scholars no library has ever stood alone. Each library's success in acquiring and making material available has been a blessing for scholarship.

KENNETH E. CARPENTER

Further Reading

Bentinck-Smith, William, *Building a Great Library: The Coolidge Years at Harvard*, Cambridge, Massachusetts: Harvard University Library, 1976

Bond, William Henry, and Hugh Amory, *The Printed Catalogues of the Harvard College Library, 1723–1790*, Boston: Colonial Society of Massachusetts, 1996

Carpenter, Kenneth E., *The First 350 Years of the Harvard University Library*, Cambridge, Massachusetts: Harvard University Library, 1986

"Harvard College Library, 1638–1938," *Harvard Library Notes* 29 (March 1939)

Helsinki University Library/National Library of Finland

Address:	Helsingin yliopiston kirjasto/Helsingfors universitetsbibliotek
	Suomen kansalliskirjasto/Finlands nationalbibliotek
	P. O. Box 15 (Unioninkatu 36)
	University of Helsinki
	FIN-00014 Helsinki
	Finland
	Telephone: 9-191-22709
	Fax: 9-191-22719
	www.lib.helsinki.fi/hyk/hul
Founded:	1640
Holdings (1999):	Volumes: 2.9 million. Current serials: 24,000; incunabula: 400; manuscripts: 10,000 linear feet; microforms: 516,000; maps and posters: 250,000; sound recordings: 200,000.
Special Collections:	*Areas of Concentration:* Finnish literature; foreign research literature in arts and humanities; Russian and Slavonic literature; manuscripts in the field of music and history of learning; maps. *Individual Collections:* American Resource Center; Carl Enckell collection of maps; Frugård archives; Hebraica; medieval fragment collection; Monrepos Library; Nordenskiöld collection of maps; Russica; Jean Sibelius archives; V. Snellman archives; Zachris Topelius archives.

For historical reasons the National Library of Finland is a part of the University of Helsinki, although the library is not a university library in the traditional sense.

Origins to 1827

The library and the university were founded in 1640 in the town of Turku (Abo in Swedish), the regional capital at that time. The collections' nucleus was inherited from the local secondary school, which had been the predecessor of the university. During some periods, the private libraries of professors were of greater importance and were kept more up to date than that of the university.

Finland was a part of Sweden until 1809, and the university held from 1707 the right to a legal deposit copy of everything printed in the country. During the latter half of the 18th century the library grew in importance and developed under Henrik Gabriel Porthan. Porthan was the first to collect all the publications published by Finns or related to Finland. On 14 December 1780 he wrote to Dr. Carl Fredrik Mennander (archbishop of Sweden and the former vice chancellor of the University of Turku): "Every letter published in bygone centuries by our compatriots shall be scrupulously collected." By 1827 the size of the collections had reached the level of 40,000 volumes, which was a remarkable achievement even when considered on a European scale.

In 1809 as a result of the Napoleonic wars, Finland was no longer a part of Sweden and became an autonomous grand duchy directly under the emperor of Russia. The university received a new main building, in which the library received its new premises, and in 1820 the university was granted the legal deposit right to everything printed in the Russian Empire.

From Turku to Helsinki

Due to a great fire in September 1827 that destroyed the whole town of Turku, the university was moved to Helsinki, which had become the capital in 1819. In Helsinki the collections had to be rebuilt and the librarian, Professor Fredrik Wilhelm Pipping, succeeded surprisingly well in recreating the collection of Finnish literature, which can be seen from the bibliography of the Finnish literature that he published in 1856–57.

As a foundation for its new library, the university was given an existing public library (Offentliga biblioteket), which had been established in Helsinki for the needs of civil servants. More important were the donations received from St. Petersburg. In 1829 the Academy of Sciences donated the main part of its collections in theology and law, more than 4,000 volumes. The emperor himself initiated several important book gifts, including the Alexandroff donation consisting of about 24,000 volumes in 1832 and a collection of about 30,000 academic dissertations (many of them unique items) from European universities, which had been accumulated by former general and diplomat Count Peter van Suchtelen.

Additional significant acquisitions included the 1902 purchase of the private library of Adolf Erik Nordenskiöld. This library is still one of the major collections of historical cartography, consisting of about 24,000 maps made before 1800, including an almost complete set of the editions of Ptolemy. A detailed catalog in six volumes has been published, and it is one of the main reference tools in its field. In 1915 a considerable library from the manor Monrepos in the southeastern city of Viborg was transferred to the library. Its 9,000 beautifully bound volumes, in French, German, Latin, and English, represent one of the most important collections of the European Enlightenment.

The legal deposit right to publications printed in the Russian Empire continued to add to the collections. These Russian collections were placed in a separate Russian library in the 1840s, which became a department of the university library in 1924. Internationally it is the library's best known and most used special collection. As a result of the Russian legal deposit, the library now owns remarkable collections of literature published in the Russian Empire in languages such as Armenian, Estonian, German, and Hebrew. The library's collections also contain over 400 incunabula.

During its first years in Helsinki, the library was situated in the great palace of the Senate, the local Finnish government. Construction of a new, separate library building was begun in 1836; the building itself was completed in 1840, and the interior furnishings were completed 1845, the year the library moved in. In 1906 the building was enlarged with an annex called the Rotunda, a well-known piece of Finnish architecture. The building is still one of the library's main assets and continues to be a public attraction.

Toward Modern Times

After World War I, when Finland became independent, the library started to develop into a more modern institution. Its organization was reviewed, its staff resources were strengthened, new training arrangements for librarians were introduced, and the library assumed new tasks. The 1919 Act of Freedom of the Press also reorganized the legal deposit of printed publications. During this period a number of new universities were established, and consequently the number of legal deposit copies was increased. Helsinki University Library was given the task of supervising the delivery of legal deposit copies from the printing houses and distributing the copies to the other deposit libraries. The library started editing a printed union catalog of foreign acquisitions in Finnish research libraries, the first volume of which was published in 1931.

World War II caused a major interruption in the work of the library. Its collections had to be evacuated, and it was impossible to acquire foreign literature. After the war, the U.S. Congress passed Public Law 265 in 1949. This law stipulated that the interest and amortization that the government of Finland was paying to the United States (for a debt granted to it by the U.S. government at the beginning of the 1920s) should be used to support cultural exchange between the countries. During the period of 1950 to 1967, Finnish research libraries received $657,000 for purchasing literature from the United States. Helsinki University Library benefited greatly from this support.

Several improvements in the working conditions of the library were made during the postwar years. In the middle of the 1950s, the library constructed large new underground stacks and a separate storage library was built outside Helsinki. In 1951 microfilming of newspapers started—a major innovation—and currently all Finnish newspapers are microfilmed.

Beginning from the book production of 1944, the library has been responsible for editing and publishing the National Bibliography since 1949. The printed Annual Bibliography was discontinued in 1993 and the monthly list in 1998, as this information is more readily available on the Internet and on two CD-ROM editions. The library is also providing bibliographic information about new Finnish literature.

Automation

In 1972 the library introduced an automated union catalog of periodicals. At the same time the research libraries started to plan a common automated solution. Using an off-line batch mode, the National Bibliography was produced with automated means from 1978 and other catalogs from 1979. The next step was the new online Virginia Tech Library System (VTLS) purchased for use by all university libraries in Finland. The National Bibliography went online in 1990 and the other catalogs a year later. From the beginning the library was responsible for the university's computerized library catalog, which to this day is the only means of connecting the university's numerous libraries. Today the library has almost all of its catalogs, including the entire National Bibliography, available online. From 1989 until 1998, the library ran a separate Center for Retrospective Conversion of Catalogs that was responsible for converting the National Bibliography and selling services to other libraries. A decision was made to purchase a new generation computer system (Voyager of Endeavor Information Systems, Inc.) for all university libraries of the country. An increasing number of other services are being developed using the new networked technology.

The Premises

Recent development has given the library an opportunity to concentrate all of its reader services in the library block in the center of the city. The library has taken over a large adjacent building that has been renovated, and a large underground stack, an addition to the earlier ones, was completed in 2000. In the biggest removal in the history of the library and the university, collections housed outside the library block were moved into the new warehouse. The Slavonic Library has now returned to the same premises as other reader services, and a number of new services have been introduced, such as a new music library and various specialized reading rooms. The library now offers about 450 seats, modern computer facilities, and 450,000 volumes of collections in open access. Unfortunately, however, half of the library—including all technical services, the National Bibliography, and the network services, as well as conservation and microfilming—is still housed elsewhere.

Toward a Clear-Cut National Library

Two decades ago, efforts were made by the Ministry of Education to direct the university toward a better-coordinated library system and to make the university library its main library. Faculties and departments had created libraries of their own. In 1974 when the state took over the Student Union's large library, it became a department of the university library. When the same thing happened with the Library of the Scientific Societies in 1979, it also became a department of the university library. Owing to the development of a new campus for natural sciences, library services were reorganized and the science library separated from the university library in 1995. In 1996 the undergraduate library was also separated from the university library.

These developments were a result of efforts to reorganize the library services of the university. At the same time a need for an efficient National Library grew, and the Ministry of Education started to strengthen the library's role as the National Library. For the first time in 1991, the library's status as the national library was formulated in law, and the library was given new important tasks. In 1990 a new unit for microfilming and conservation was established outside Helsinki, and in 1992 the library was made responsible for national planning and coordination, a task that previously had been carried out in the ministry itself. In 1993 the Automation Unit of Finnish Research Libraries was removed from the ministry to the library, which was made responsible for coordination and further development of the university libraries' joint automation network, LINNEA. The library also is responsible for a number of other common services, including running a number of databases such as the union catalog, LINDA.

Since 1981 a new Legal Deposit Act contains a provision for audiovisual material, and in 1998 the library was given the task of establishing a National Archive for Recorded Sound. The library also has been active in the field of developing methods for collecting legal deposit of electronic publications.

The library has a clear profile as the National Library and is conducting all the duties regarded as core functions of national libraries. Its position as the National Library and its relationship to the university have been clarified after a long-standing debate. Technically the library's budget will remain part of the budget of the university, but the Ministry of Education will make all decisions on funding. In practice the ministry will also directly monitor the library's accomplishments.

Research Activities

The library has a long tradition of conducting research related to its collections. A large project, the Retrospective National Bibliography, started in 1986 and was completed in 2001. In addition to the National Bibliography for 1488 to 1800, a number of other projects have been completed; for example, a large two-volume *Atlas of Finnish Typography* (a reference tool on the history of Finnish typography) was published in 2001. In 1996 the library and the Finnish Sibelius Society launched a major project aiming at publishing a critical edition of the *Complete Works* of Jean Sibelius. This project will require approximately 20 years to complete.

Recent Trends

A new strategy for the National Library was adopted in 1999. It stresses the library's role as a common resource for all research libraries but also emphasizes the library's duties as a significant agent in the field of electronic publishing. Although primary publishing is not regarded as a core function, the library has an important national role in providing services for identification, cataloging, and permanent archiving of electronic publications. These responsibilities will reach far beyond the traditional library quarters. The Legal Deposit Act will soon be revised to include electronic publications.

As the National Library of Finland, the library will be developed as a research library, as the main supplier of networked services to other Finnish libraries and their users, and, finally, as one of the service providers for the whole society in the field of electronic publishing.

ESKO E. HÄKLI

Further Reading

Häkli, Esko, *A.E. Nordenskiöld, a Scientist and His Library*, Helsinki: Helsinki University Library, 1980

Häkli, Esko, "Finland, The National Library of: Helsinki University Library," in *Encyclopedia of Library and Information Science*, edited by Allen Kent et al., vol. 39, New York: Dekker, 1985

Häkli, Esko, "Helsinki University Library—The National Library of Finland," *Alexandria* 2, no. 1 (1990)

Häkli, Esko, "The Slavonic Library at the Helsinki University Library," *European Research Libraries Cooperation (ERLC): The LIBER Quarterly* 2 (1992)

Häkli, Esko, "A Unified Automation System Using VTLS for Academic Libraries in Finland," *Program* 26, no. 3 (1992)

Häkli, Esko, "From Neumes to Network: Music in the Helsinki University Library," *Fontes Artis Musicae* 40, no. 1 (1993)

Häkli, Esko, "The Gift of the St. Petersburg Academy of Sciences, 1829," in *Collections Donated by the Academy of Sciences of St. Petersburg to the Alexander University of Finland in 1829: An Annotated Catalogue*, edited by Sirkka Havu and Irina Lebedeva, Helsinki: Helsinki University Library, 1997

Hasselblatt, Cornelius, "Helsingin yliopiston kirjasto (Helsingfors universitetsbibliotek); Universitätsbibliothek Helsinki," in *Handbuch deutscher historischer Buchbestände in Europa*, edited by Bernhard Fabian, vol. 7, part 2, *Finnland, Estland, Lettland, Litauen*, Hildesheim, Germany, and New York: Olms-Weidmann, 1998

Porthan, Henrik Gabriel, *Dissertatio Historio Bibliothecæ Regiæ Academiæ Aboënsis Exponens* (History of the Library of the Royal Academy of Turku). Turku: s.n, 1771–95

Vallinkoski, J., *The History of the University Library at Turku*, 2 vols., Helsinki: Helsinki University Library, 1948–75

Herzog August Library Wolfenbüttel

Address: Herzog August Bibliothek Wolfenbüttel
Lessingplatz 1
38304 Wolfenbüttel
Germany
Telephone: 5331-8080
Fax: 5331-808-173
www.hab.de

Founded: 1572

Holdings (1999): Volumes: 850,000. Bibles: 3,000; current serials: 1,600; graphic materials: 26,000; incunabula: 4,000; manuscripts: 12,000; maps: 20,000; medieval manuscripts: 3,000; microforms: 180,000; pre-1850 volumes: 411,000; 20th-century artists books: 2,000 titles.

Special Collections: *Areas of Concentration:* European cultural history (medieval and early modern period); 19th- and 20th-century book art. *Individual Collections:* Duke August the Younger of Brunswick–Wolfenbüttel libraries; early music collection; Jürgen Eyssen press book collection; illustrated broadsheets, prints, and engravings collection; Schulenburg family libraries; 17th- and 18th-century princely collections of members of the House of Brunswick or related families; University of Helmstedt libraries (1576–1810); Hermann Zapf typography collection. *Deposit Collections:* Alvensleben family library; Guy Lévis Mano collection: Stolberg funeral sermon collection.

History

The Wolfenbüttel library was founded by the Dukes of Brunswick-Wolfenbüttel and remained in the hands of the Guelf dynasty until 1918, when it became state property. From 1919 to 1926 the library was the State Library of the Free State of Brunswick. In 1927 it was given its present name (Herzog August Bibliothek) and integrated into a Brunswick Museum and Library Foundation, to which it belonged *de jure* until 1970, although the foundation effectively ceased activity after 1945. The library is now a state library chartered to serve the region in which it is located.

The library experienced two periods of massive expansion, one in the 17th century under Duke August and again in the 20th century. Erhart Kästner, librarian from 1950 to 1968, began an extensive reconstruction program aimed at bringing the library and its rich collections back into public awareness. His successor, Paul Raabe, who headed the library until 1992, oversaw the transformation of the library into today's international research center.

The Bibliotheca Augusta

The library takes its name from Duke August, who had amassed one of the largest libraries north of the Alps by the time of his death in 1666. The duke did not inherit a dynastic collection to which he could add his own books. As the youngest son of a minor branch of the Brunswick dynasty, he initially had no prospect of coming to power at all. A series of deaths without issue made it possible for him to accede as Duke of Brunswick-Wolfenbüttel in 1635, when he was already more than 50 years of age. Until that time August had lived the life of a country squire pursuing his intense scholarly interests and laying the foundations for his book collections.

The duke had studied at Rostock and Tübingen and traveled widely as a young man, spending a prolonged period in Italy and visiting France and England. In 1607 he married and settled on his country estate at Hitzacker on the Elbe River. His first marriage gave him a measure of financial independence, and the duke began collecting in earnest. He was not just a collector but also a librarian. Although he devised several systems for cataloging his books, it was not until 1625 that he established the system that has been retained until today. The books are classified in 20 subject groups and shelved according to size. It was August's aim to create a universal library reflecting all aspects of the knowledge of his time. His perspective was that of a North German Lutheran prince educated in a strong humanist tradition and conditioned by the political and theological upheavals through which he lived.

The duke was aided in the construction of his collection by the burgeoning market in books and manuscripts resulting from the Thirty Years' War and by the network of correspondents and book agents throughout Europe that he established over the years. Nuremberg and Augsburg were the most important centers, but the duke had correspondents in The Hague, Paris, London, Rome, and Strasbourg, all of whom were engaged in procuring books and manuscripts for his library. Much of the correspondence with these agents has survived, along with the original catalogs and the complete collection. The collection was virtually closed after the death of the duke and is, to this day, separately shelved, allowing his library to be studied as one man's view of the universal learning of his era.

The University of Helmstedt Library

The University of Helmstedt Library (1576–1810) contains the oldest Wolfenbüttel court library, which accounts for the date of founding generally given by the institution today. In 1572 Duke Heinrich Julius, the first Protestant ruler of the duchy, issued a charter governing the use of the library and appointed a librarian to oversee the collection. In his youth Julius traveled to France and the Low Countries. He retained a love of French language and literature, often buying popular romance novels, among others the first edition of the *Amadis de Gaule* (1500). He also owned the first edition of the saga of *Melusine*, printed by Adam Steinschaber in Geneva in 1478, the first illustrated book to be printed in the French language; today, Julius's is the only surviving complete copy.

Julius also set about requisitioning books and manuscripts from the holdings of the monastic libraries under his jurisdiction. It is surprising that although he founded the University of Helmstedt in 1575 in order to promote the education of the clergy and administrators within his own territories, he does not appear to have given any thought to the development of a university library. He continued to add to his own collection in Wolfenbüttel, however. From 1577 to 1580 he bought a total of 32 manuscripts from the widow of Martin Luther's assistant and editor of Luther's *Table Talk*, Johannes Aurifaber. It was under Julius that the Wolfenbüttel court and its book collections attained European rank.

The Reformation scholar Matthias Flacius Illyricus had put together one of the most important private libraries in Germany while he and his collaborators worked on a vast ecclesiastical history, *The Magdeburg Centuries*. In 1597 Julius bought the collection from Heinrich Petreus, who had married Flacius' widow. It was not until 1614, a year after Julius's death, that the first proper inventory of the Wolfenbüttel library was drawn up. This was the library, comprising 5,000 volumes, that Julius's grandson, Duke Friedrich Ulrich, donated to the university of Helmstedt by charter in 1614, and that was transferred from Wolfenbüttel to Helmstedt four years later.

The only book collections left in Wolfenbüttel were the private "chamber" libraries belonging to the duke and duchess and a number of manuscripts belonging to the family archive. The Helmstedt library was augmented by gifts from succeeding generations of the ducal family and by bequests from the university's professors. By the late 18th century, the university had fallen into decline, and it was closed in 1809–10. In 1815 the valuable manuscript collection was transferred to the ducal library at Wolfenbüttel. Most of the books remained in Helmstedt until 1913, when the larger portion was also sent to Wolfenbüttel. The Wolfenbüttel Helmstedt collection includes not only books from the university library but also 13,000 works printed by the university press, most of them disputations and occasional works connected with academic ceremonies.

The Middle Collection

Whereas the Augusta and Helmstedt collections are separately shelved and have a clearly discernible profile, the Middle Collection is a typical rare book library housing many small collections, or parts of collections, and books acquired for the library over generations. In general it may be said that all books that came into the Wolfenbüttel library after August's death are shelved in the Middle Collection. This includes books belonging to members of the Brunswick dynasty, such as Duchess Philippine Charlotte, sister of Frederick the Great; to institutions such as the Brunswick Collegium *anatomico-chirurgicum* (1887); and to the Brunswick State Theater.

During his period as librarian (1690–1716), the philosopher Gottfried Wilhelm Leibniz made very significant purchases for the library, including (in 1710) the valuable collection of Latin and Greek manuscripts belonging to Marquard Gude. In the latter part of the 18th and throughout the 19th century, the financial resources available to succeeding generations of librarians were extremely restricted. The acquisition of large scholarly collections, often donated or bequeathed to the library, were of vital importance to its continued development. It is estimated that approximately 60,000 books were added to the library in this way.

Post-1950 Holdings

Purchases of modern editions and secondary literature acquired for the library after 1950 are all cataloged and shelved in the stacks according to a *numerus currens* system (i.e., in order of acquisition), unless the books have been selected to form part of the open-shelf reference library, established for users in 1981, which now exceeds 100,000 volumes.

National Archive of 17th-Century Printed Texts

In 1990 the Volkswagen Foundation initiated a project to establish a decentralized national archive of printed texts to compensate for the lack of a single national library in Germany. Wolfenbüttel, with its 17th-century strengths, was selected as the repository for printed texts from the period from 1601 to 1700. In addition to Wolfenbüttel, the chronological division of responsibility is shared among libraries in Munich, Göttingen, Frankfurt, and Berlin. This project is now funded by the federal states in which the contributing libraries are located, allowing the library to complement its holdings by buying originals on the antiquarian book market or microforms of books missing from the collection. Thus far, the library has acquired more than 10,000 printed books and engravings from the 17th century and more than 8,500 microforms. All of these accessions can be retrieved via the library's Online Public Access

Catalog (OPAC) and the Gemeinsamer Bibliotheks-Verbund (GBV) Union Catalog.

Buildings

The first Wolfenbüttel court library under Julius was housed in the vaults of the old Chancellery building, which stood immediately in front of the castle chapel. August transferred his book collection to Wolfenbüttel in 1643. In 1646 he had the upper floors of the stable building on the castle square adapted and expanded to house the library. This is the first library building for which illustrations have survived.

During the librarianship of Leibniz, August's son, Anton Ulrich, commissioned a new library building to be erected on the foundations of the stable building, incorporating its stonework base. The Bibliotheca Rotunda was the first secular library building in Europe since classical antiquity. It was designed as a timber-framed construction and built between 1706 and 1713. The ground floor was still used for stabling horses. From 1705 the books were housed in the Zeughaus (Arsenal), and the new building was not actually put into use until 1723, ten years after its completion. At first the dome (the rotunda by which the building came to be known) was crowned by a celestial globe, but the roof's construction could not support it and it had to be removed. The windows in the dome meant that the main reading room was fed by natural light, providing a model for later library architects such as Antonio Panizzi in his design of the legendary reading room of the British Museum (London). By the mid–19th century, this timber-framed building was too small to house the books and had fallen into a state of grave disrepair. It was demolished in 1887 after a new library building had been built on an adjacent plot of land.

The new building, the Bibliotheca Augusta, is still the central library building and houses the main stacks and a reading room for manuscripts and special collections. It underwent major renovation in the 1960s, when a main hall and exhibition room to display the collections belonging to August were created. In 1981 the Zeughaus, a Renaissance stone building constructed in 1618, was opened to house the library's research facilities. The vaulted hall on the ground floor retains its historic character, whereas the two floors above provide modern library services and a cafeteria.

The open-shelf reference library is located in the Zeughaus, as are the main catalog facilities and the main reading room for all works printed after 1500 except *"rara"*: special collections, large format books, and damaged copies, which must be consulted in the manuscript reading room. From 1981 to 1998 the front half of the Zeughaus hall was used as an exhibition room, but lack of space for books has led to the installation of shelving for the reference library.

The library has museum rooms in the Bibliotheca Augusta (main hall) and in the Lessing House, where the German critic and dramatist Gotthold Ephraim Lessing lived from 1777 to 1781 during his time as librarian in Wolfenbüttel. The house was converted into a literature museum in 1978 and also has housing facilities for guest researchers. From 1981 onward the library quarters went through a steady period of expansion into buildings on the castle square. The library campus now totals eight buildings, including offices for research and administrative staff and facilities for guest researchers and conference participants. The library's Friends society runs two guest houses to accommodate researchers who come to Wolfenbüttel via the fellowship program.

An Independent Research Library

In 1975 the Volkswagen Foundation provided initial financial support for the establishment of a research center at the library. In 1981 the State of Lower Saxony assumed responsibility for providing a permanent budget for this program. In 1990 the Herzog August Bibliothek was given the status of a nonuniversity research institute, with a charter comparable to those of independent research libraries in the United States.

The library research program comprises several distinct areas including an international postgraduate fellowship and conference program to encourage interdisciplinary research linked to library holdings. It runs a publications program in which the results of this research are published, with an annual output comparable to that of a medium-sized publishing house. A program of cultural events makes the library's work accessible to a broader public, both locally and on a national level. The library has its own research staff engaged in projects connected with the holdings. The director is advised by an academic advisory board and by a board of curators. Close links are maintained with similar institutes both at home and abroad. Private initiatives by major benefactors have allowed the library to establish a program of fellowships for doctoral students with dissertation topics that necessitate research in Wolfenbüttel. The institution is aided in fulfilling its charter by Friends societies in both Germany and the United States.

Cataloging and Automation

In the 1970s the library took a great step forward in the cataloging of its hitherto unregistered rare book holdings by establishing various catalogs using cards with title-page copies. To the alphabetical catalog were added catalogs sorted by shelfmark, by place of printing, by language, and by subject. The only systematic catalog to be published for the printed holdings was that for the medical and scientific books (1472 to 1830). The library was a main contributor to the German 16th-century short-title catalog VD16 and produced a short-title catalog of books in German (1600 to 1720) from its own holdings, followed by other special catalogs, such as the catalog of illustrated German broadsheets and the catalog of portrait engravings. The library is a center of manuscript cataloging, not just for the medieval and early modern manuscripts in its own collections but also for those belonging to small libraries and institutions of regional importance.

The library started online cataloging of its modern acquisitions in 1984. These data were fed into the regional database located in the University Library Göttingen. Lower Saxony has adopted the Project for Integrated Catalogue Automation (PICA) cataloging system, and Wolfenbüttel data are now contained in the GBV Union Catalog contributed to by libraries in seven German federal states. The retrospective conversion of catalogs of rare book holdings (1501 to 1850) was undertaken in 1987–98 and was completed in 2001. Approximately 430,000 titles were entered into the Union Catalog. In 1996 the library introduced its own OPAC.

Other automation work has continued with the advent of the Internet and World Wide Web, and the library offers a variety of special bibliographies and catalogs via its website. An online catalog now offers access to the library's collection of 13,000 funeral sermons (1550 to 1750), allowing searches of both bibliographical and biographical information.

By virtue of its role as the national repository for 17th-century printed texts, the library is also one of the main contributors to a project started in 1996 to establish an online German national bibliography of 17th-century imprints (VD17) (www.vd17.de). Cataloging is done with book-in-hand, and the bibliographical information is enhanced by digitized images of key pages appended to catalog records. The database contains some 150,000 records and 450,000 images. The library regards itself as a center of expertise in digitization techniques for old books and manuscripts. In a pilot project, around 350 festival books from the library's 17th-century holdings were digitized and classified to allow researchers to search these resources.

Recent Developments

The library went through a period of rapid expansion in the 20 years from 1970 to 1990. In addition to the positive economic climate of those years, the library's immediate proximity to the East German border meant that it could expect to benefit from special funding accorded to regions near the frontier often threatened by depopulation. Reunification brought an end to special funding in recognition of the needs of the eastern states. The 1990s were a period of retrenchment and economic constraint. Public spending cuts meant that the library was faced with severe personnel cutbacks at all levels. These were partly compensated by strengthening the efficiency of the inner organizational structure.

On the other hand, the library's activities have been steadily expanding and the number of guest researchers visiting the library for extended periods has risen during the past decades. The introduction of automation in all areas of the library, both in library services and in administrative sectors, has meant an increase in efficiency, but staffing cuts have reached a critical point and the institution must regularly reassess its priorities and set mid- to long-term goals.

The most important midterm project is the expansion of the reading room in the Bibliotheca Augusta, thus doing away with damaging transportation of rare book holdings between buildings. In the long term, the library's chronic lack of shelf space renders the renovation of another building on the castle square imperative. The Granary, which was acquired in 1994, was built in 1662 and is the largest timber-framed building in the town. When completed it will house stacks, lecture theaters, seminar rooms, and shelves for another 100,000 volumes on open shelves.

HELWIG R.H. SCHMIDT-GLINTZER

Further Reading

Ausstellungskataloge der Herzog August Bibliothek (1972–)

Burton, Margaret, "Wolfenbüttel," in *Famous Libraries of the World: Their History, Collections, and Administrations*, by Burton, London: Crafton 1937

Esdaile, Arundell J.K., *National Libraries of the World: Their History, Administration, and Public Services*, London: Crafton, 1934; 2nd edition, revised by R.J. Hill, London: Library Association, 1957

Heinemann, Otto von, *Die Herzogliche Bibliothek zu Wolfenbüttel: Ein Beitrag zur Geschichte deutscher Büchersammlungen*, Wolfenbüttel, Germany: Zwissler, 1894; reprint, Amsterdam: s.n., 1979

"Herzog August Bibliothek," in *Handbuch der historischen Buchbestände in Deutschland*, vol. 2, part 2, *Niedersachsen*, edited by Berhard Fabian, Hildesheim, Germany, and New York: Olms-Weidmann, 1992

Raabe, Paul, editor, *Sammler, Fürst, Gelehrter: Herzog August zu Braunschweig und Lüneburg, 1579–1666*, Wolfenbüttel, Germany: Herzog August Bibliothek, 1979

Ruppelt, Georg, and Sabine Solf, editors, *Lexikon zur Geschichte und Gegenwart der Herzog August Bibliothek Wolfenbüttel*, Wiesbaden, Germany: Harrassowitz, 1992

Schmidt-Glintzer, Helwig, et al., editors, *A Treasure House of Books: The Library of Duke August of Brunswick-Wolfenbüttel*, Wiesbaden, Germany: Harrassowitz, 1998

Treasures of the Herzog August Library: Rare Books and Manuscripts; Trésors de la bibliothèque augustéene: Livres et manuscripts précieux (bilingual English and French edition), Wolfenbüttel, Germany: Herzog August Bibliothek, 1984

Wolfenbütteler Beiträge: Aus den Schätzen der Herzog August Bibliothek (1972–)

Historical Society of Pennsylvania

Address:	Historical Society of Pennsylvania 1300 Locust Street Philadelphia, Pennsylvania 19107 USA Telephone: 215-732-6200 Fax: 215-732-2680 www.hsp.org
Founded:	1824
Holdings (2000):	Volumes: 500,000. Current serials: 2,000; genealogies: 10,000 prints and 30,000 manuscripts; graphic materials: 300,000; manuscripts: 15,500 linear feet; maps: 3,000; microforms: 40,000.
Special Collections:	*Areas of Concentration:* African Americana; American Revolutionary history; architectural history; Civil War history; early American maps and newspapers; early American Republic history; early Pennsylvania families; genealogy; Pennsylvania German imprints. *Individual Collections:* Baker collection of Washingtoniana; family papers: Biddle, Cadwalader, Chew, Drinker, Logan, Norris, Pemberton, Penn, Powel, Shippen; first and second drafts of the U.S. Constitution; printer's proof of the Declaration of Independence.

Origins

Founded in 1824 in Philadelphia, the Historical Society of Pennsylvania (HSP) is one of the oldest private membership historical societies in the United States and holds many of the nation's most important historical documents. It was formed in a period of rising national consciousness to which Philadelphia responded in a number of ways: Philadelphian Charles Brockden Brown published the first American historical novel; Revolutionary War hero portraiture boomed in Philadelphia with such artists as Charles Wilson Peale, Edward Savage, and John Trumbull; concern for the preservation of historic buildings was occasioned by the proposed sale of the State House (Independence Hall, home of the Continental Congress) for building lots; and the "triumphal tour" of the Marquis de Lafayette sparked the foundation of historical societies in several former colonies, including Pennsylvania.

The first debates about Pennsylvania's historical society concerned its corporate name and membership restrictions. Some founders proposed calling the new society "Sons of the Soil" and restricting membership to native-born Pennsylvanians, making the "Sons" a hereditary society. The first president, William Rawle Sr., adamantly opposed this idea; he had a vision of a broad membership open to all who felt a strong interest in the mission of the organization—the elucidation of the natural, civil, and literary history of Pennsylvania. Once this vision became the basis of membership, the name was established as the Historical Society of Pennsylvania. Rawle's vision has endured to this day.

The society's constitution established a structure of nine elected officers with an elected council of 13. Purely a voluntary association, the officers and council were responsible for the day-to-day operations of the society, which relied completely upon annual membership dues of $3.00 for funding. Collections came slowly in the beginning—only 60 books in the first 19 years. Still, the society succeeded in publishing three issues of its *Memoirs* by 1827.

From the beginning, the society cultivated the Penn family, colonial proprietors of Pennsylvania. In 1833 Granville Penn, grandson of William Penn, donated the "Armor Portrait," which shows the young William Penn wearing a suit of armor before his conversion to Quaker pacifism. The patronage of the Penn family firmly established the authority and prestige of the society. Soon, other significant gifts of art and artifacts were added to the collection.

The Collections Grow

Under the society's second president, Peter S. Du Ponceau, the core manuscript collection was created when the papers of the Logan family and the Pennsylvania Provincial Council, as well as the diary of Christopher Marshall, were brought to the society. Concurrently, the book collection was enriched in the area of Tudor-Stuart British history. Du Ponceau, in the name of the society, was instrumental in establishing the publication of the *Pennsylvania Colonial Records* and the *Pennsylvania Archives* by the state of Pennsylvania.

In 1846, under the administration of President Thomas Sergeant, the society moved from the American Philosophical

Society to the upper floor of the Athenaeum of Philadelphia's new building. Twelve quarterly issues of the *Bulletin* were published between 1845 and 1848, before publication was suspended. In 1854 the publication fund was established, enabling the society to continue publishing the *Memoirs* until 1895. During this same period a significant book collection of British constitutional history was obtained through the intercession of Louis McLane, U.S. minister to the court of St. James. This collection included published reports of various British agencies such as the Record Commissioners, Calendars of Patent Rolls, Charters in the Tower, Exchequer Calendars, and Fees of Fines. In 1863 the librarian, Townsend Ward, divided the society's collections into four main categories: biographical and genealogical, foreign and American history, ecclesiastical, and miscellaneous.

The Fahnestock bequest of 1869 brought 70,000 pamphlets covering a broad range of Americana. Overwhelmed by this generosity and hard-pressed for space, the society could no longer remain in the rooms at the Athenaeum. In 1872 the society found space to rent in the "Picture House," a two-story building erected by the Pennsylvania Hospital to house the painting "Christ Healing the Sick" by Benjamin West. In 1877 the first issue of the *Pennsylvania Magazine of History and Biography* appeared, and today it remains the oldest continuously published state historical magazine in the nation. Upon reaching its 50th anniversary in 1874, the society had 600 members, a library of 12,000 volumes, a collection of 80,000 pamphlets, a gallery of 65 portraits and 12 historical paintings, and numerous engravings and manuscripts, including the 1870 purchase of the Penn papers.

The Society Matures

In 1882 the society came to its present home at the corner of Locust and 13th Streets. It purchased the Robert Patterson mansion, first remodeled and subsequently rebuilt between 1905 and 1910. By 1890 the collections included 80,000 books and 200,000 pamphlets. Membership stood near 1,600, and the society had enough assets to fund regular acquisition of books and manuscripts.

Between 1884 and 1930, the society established itself as a repository of national significance for manuscript and printed sources of the colonial, revolutionary, and early republic periods. The presentation of the Tilghman, Bradford, Wallace, Franklin, Peters, Pemberton, and Poinsett papers, the Chapman Biddle gift of the letters of George Washington, and the Fatzinger gift of Northampton County papers created the core of this collection, one that was enhanced by the gifts of three autograph collections from Simon Gratz, Ferdinand F. Dreer, and Frank M. Etting. The book collection was augmented by the Charlemagne Tower Collection of Colonial Laws, a gift from Charles R. King of the journals and documents from the U.S. Congress up to 1824, and the acquisition of the library of Benjamin Franklin, including many early American newspapers.

Storage equipment and photographic reproduction services were added in the 1920s and 1930s. During the 1930s the society was assisted by the Federal Works Progress Administration, whose Historical Records Survey compiled the society's first edition of *The Guide to Manuscript Collections of the Historical Society of Pennsylvania*. At the time of its publication in 1940, the manuscript collection had grown to 2.5 million items. In the 1940s the society's library and reading rooms were moved from the first to the second floor. The Assembly Hall was then used as a museum space to display the outstanding collection of American art and artifacts. In 1948 air conditioners were added to preserve the materials stored in the society's four vaults. By the end of the decade, the manuscript collections had swelled to 4 million items, necessitating a new edition of *The Guide*, published in 1949.

The Genealogical Society of Pennsylvania

For many years the society engaged in concerted genealogical activity. Between 1850 and 1860, the society had successfully petitioned the state government to collect vital statistics. From its inception, the *Pennsylvania Magazine of History and Biography* included a genealogical section: "Notes and Queries." Under John Jordan Jr. the society initiated and funded the preservation of baptismal, marriage, and death records. After Jordan's death, the society formally decided in 1892 to organize an auxiliary association known as the Genealogical Society of Pennsylvania (GSP). The charter restricted membership to HSP members, and all materials acquired or created became the property of HSP. The society granted the Genealogical Society space within its building. In 1920 the leaders of the Genealogical Society decided to incorporate separately, although the younger organization physically remained in HSP's building until the 1990s.

The Library Company of Philadelphia

In the late 1950s the Library Company of Philadelphia (LCP) planned to relocate from its Ridgway building on South Broad Street. In 1959 the Historical Society's president, Boyd Lee Spahr, offered Nicholas Wainwright, then president of LCP, the property next to HSP's building. Wainwright accepted, noting cooperative agreements with the society and operational economies could strengthen both institutions. By 1964 the sale had been effected along with an agreement that the society would absorb 10,000 items including LCP's reference books, post-1880 secondary sources, and a large collection of post-1820 newspapers. An inventory at this time found the society's book collection held 120,000 volumes.

Early in 1966 the society welcomed its new neighbor and continued to build cooperation. The working partnership between the two institutions was personified in Wainwright, who during that year was not only the director of the Historical Society, but also the president of LCP's board. With the reciprocal agreement to house LCP's manuscripts at the Historical Society and HSP's rare pre-1820 Americana book collections at the Library Company, the society's collecting focus shifted to manuscripts, graphics, maps, genealogy, and post-1820 Americana, while the LCP committed itself to collecting primarily graphics and rare printed materials.

Between them, the two institutions own a superb collection of African Americana. In 1970 the Ford Foundation awarded a joint-venture grant to the society and the Library Company to further African American studies through the cataloging of their collections. After three years, the 714-page catalog, *Afro-Americana, 1553–1906: Author Catalogue of the Library Company of Philadelphia and the Historical Society of Pennsylvania*, was published by G.K. Hall & Company.

Collections

Today the Historical Society serves the public as one of the nation's best independent, nongovernmental repositories of documentary materials. It holds the largest family history collection in the mid-Atlantic region, has excellent print collections on local and regional history, and offers an impressive manuscript collection renowned for its 17th-, 18th-, and 19th-century holdings. Collections document the political, commercial, and social history of the colonies and the United States in the 17th and 18th centuries; the mid-Atlantic states prior to the Civil War; and the Commonwealth of Pennsylvania and the Philadelphia region from the colonial period to the present. Civil War holdings are comprised of papers; correspondence; diaries; personal accounts; documents on political trends, economic conditions, and social history; and regimental papers and histories. Resources for women's history cross all lines of class, race, and ethnicity from the period of early colonization to the present day, including evidence embedded in letters, diaries, travel journals, account books, family genealogies, organizational and institutional records, graphics, and public data such as census, tax, and property records. Architectural history resources are among the most heavily used research collections. The history of places, houses, and buildings are culled from architectural drawings, real estate documents, fire insurance atlases and surveys, prints, drawings, photographs, watercolors, street panoramas, scrapbook collections, city directories, and newspapers. Art historical resources are also significant, including the papers of the Peale family, Thomas Sully's journal, and sketch and account books of Benjamin West.

Recreating the Society for the 21st Century

In 1974 renovations were being planned to meet the needs of an ever-expanding collection. Changes begun in 1975 included a two-story addition to the back of the building and flooring between the upper and lower levels of Assembly Hall. A modern second elevator was added as well as updates to the electrical wiring, heating and ventilation system, and lighting. In order to accommodate inconvenienced researchers who had to work while construction proceeded around them, the society ceased its tradition of closing for the month of August.

In 1977 work on the third edition of *The Guide to Manuscript Collections of the Historical Society of Pennsylvania* began. Since the 1949 edition, the newly acquired collections had been reported to the *National Union Catalog of Manuscript Collections,* but knowledge of these collections was not widespread. A grant from the National Endowment for the Humanities provided funds for an initial four-year project to survey new acquisitions. In 1986 a grant from the Pew Charitable Trust enabled the society to provide collection-level cataloging on the Research Libraries Information Network (RLIN) bibliographic utility. Finally, in 1991, a new *Guide* was published.

In the 1980s and 1990s the society faced increasing fiscal difficulties. Under Susan Stitt's leadership (1990–98) the society experienced a period of difficult choices, revising operations so that the society could live within its means. In those years it also saw a great transformation of its mission, leading to tensions between the society's leadership and the cultural community of Philadelphia. In 1994 the society recognized that it could not sustain the activities of both a museum and a research library. Faced with this difficult decision, it refocused its mission, determined to find a partner in Philadelphia to take over its museum functions while focusing on its research library role. From 1997 to 1999 the society renovated its building to support this change. The Assembly Hall was restored to its original architectural integrity and became the reading room. Particular attention was given to preservation of collections through repair of the exterior building envelope and installation of a new heating, ventilation, and air-conditioning system. Collection storage was increased through the use of first-floor space and compact storage. The vacated portions of the second floor will eventually house a dedicated graphics reading room and public programs space. Through a cooperative agreement with the Philadelphia Area Consortium of Special Collections Libraries (PACSCL), the society has a Web-based online public catalog that provides access to the records of its nine card catalogs. By 2000, the society had wired its building for computer hookup both at public workstations and in staff offices. The opening of the new facilities has been accompanied by an increase in membership and attendance in the reading rooms. The society ultimately chose the Atwater Kent Museum as the partner for its artifact collection and entered into a leasing agreement. The partnership with Atwater Kent was felt to be the best choice because it kept the collections in Philadelphia, a point of contention within the cultural community. More importantly, the museum's location on Independence Mall would allow a much wider public audience.

PATRICIA KOSCO COSSARD

Further Reading

Carson, Hampton L., *A History of the Historical Society of Pennsylvania,* Philadelphia: Historical Society of Pennsylvania, 1940

"The Formal Opening of the New Fireproof Building of the Historical Society of Pennsylvania, April 6–7, 1910," *The Pennsylvania Magazine of History and Biography* 34, no. 3 (July 1910)

Griffith, Sally, *Serving History in a Changing World: The Historical Society of Pennsylvania in the 20th Century*, Philadelphia: Historical Society of Pennsylvania, 2001

The Society: Its Purposes and Activities, Philadelphia: Historical Society of Pennsylvania, 1943

"Special Anniversary Issue Celebrating 175 Years of the Historical Society of Pennsylvania," *The Pennsylvania Magazine of History and Biography* 124, nos. 1–2 (January/April 2000)

Stitt, Susan, "Pennsylvania," in *Historical Consciousness in the Early Republic: The Origins of State Historical Societies, Museums, and Collections, 1791–1861*, edited by H.G. Jones, Chapel Hill: North Carolinian Society and North Carolina Collection, 1995

Wainwright, Nicholas B., *Philadelphia in the Romantic Age of Lithography*, Philadelphia: Historical Society of Pennsylvania, 1970

Wainwright, Nicholas B., *Notes to Members from the Director, 1965–1974*, Philadelphia: Historical Society of Pennsylvania, 1974

Wainwright, Nicholas B., *One Hundred and Fifty Years of Collecting by the Historical Society of Pennsylvania, 1824–1974*, Philadelphia: Historical Society of Pennsylvania, 1974

Wainwright, Nicholas B., *Paintings and Miniatures at the Historical Society of Pennsylvania*, Philadelphia: Historical Society of Pennsylvania, 1974

Howard University Libraries

Address: Howard University Libraries
500 Howard Place, N.W.
Washington, D.C. 20059
USA
Telephone: 202-806-7234
Fax: 202-806-5903
www.founders.howard.edu

Founded: 1867

Holdings (2001): Volumes: 2.5 million. Audio materials: 16,000; current serials: 14,000; manuscripts: 22,000 linear feet; maps: 180,000; microforms: 3.7 million; video and film: 13,000.

Special Collections: *Areas of Concentration:* African American life and history; art and humanities; behavioral and social sciences; science. *Individual Collections:* Owen Vincent Dodson; Frederick Douglass; W.E.B. Du Bois; Oliver O. Howard; Alain L. Locke; Jesse Edward Moorland; Paul Robeson; Arthur B. Spingarn; Lewis Tappan; Booker T. Washington.

Oliver Otis Howard

The university's name is a memorial to U.S. Civil War general Oliver Otis Howard, a mathematics professor at West Point who was about to become a minister when the Civil War broke out. Despite losing his right arm to wounds suffered at Fair Oaks (Virginia) in 1862, he commanded Northern troops in many of the most important engagements of the war including Chancellorsville (Virginia), Gettysburg (Pennsylvania), and the campaign to take Atlanta (Georgia), and later he commanded the Army of the Tennessee. During his tenure in command, he always insisted that his troops attend prayer and temperance meetings. After the Civil War, Howard was appointed to head the Freedman's Bureau, an organization devoted to protecting and providing assistance to the newly freed slaves. He was fearless and outspoken in his support for black suffrage and made notable efforts to distribute land to African Americans.

Howard's convictions on the equality of man were also seen in his private life. He worked to make his socially elite church in Washington, D.C., racially integrated. In addition, he was one of those responsible for the founding of the all-black college in the District of Columbia that became Howard University; he also served as its third president. The college library received generous support from Howard, who donated books and photographs documenting issues relating to African Americans.

Origins

The library was founded soon after the university opened, when a committee was formed to select books. Several of the founders of the school donated books, pamphlets, and photographic materials to the library. For some years, the growth of the collection remained largely dependent upon donations from individuals. The Reverend Preston Cummings of Leicester, Massachusetts, made the first large-scale contribution when he donated 10,000 volumes in 1868. The school's first librarian, Danforth B. Nichols, a member of the university's original library committee, moved his private library to the school in 1869. Lewis Tappen, a noted abolitionist, presented the library with a substantial gift of materials in 1873. The Tappen collection contained 1,650 items of antislavery books, pamphlets, manuscripts, letters, clippings, pictures, and periodicals.

As with many donations to libraries, much of the materials received by Howard were of little use to an undergraduate population. Although the university did establish an endowment fund in 1870 for the purchase of books, problems persisted in establishing a truly useful collection for the education of the university's students. However, in 1890 the Library of Congress and other departments of the government were authorized by the federal Congress to contribute to the library all books they had in duplicate. This marked the beginning of a useful tool for undergraduates, and with the previously donated collections already on hand, formed the core of one of the first collections of primary source materials illustrating the conditions that led to the founding of the university itself.

In the early years the library was housed in two or three rooms in the main building and was hampered by the lack of trained personnel, limited operating hours, insufficient space, and a collection that was not cataloged. Despite regular requests for trained personnel and a separate facility, it was not until the administration of Librarian Flora L.P. Johnson (1898–1912) that the first cataloger was employed and the Carnegie Library, funded by Andrew Carnegie, was dedicated. The Carnegie Library, however, was quickly outgrown as enrollment at the university rapidly increased.

Moorland Foundation

Owing to the founding principles of the university, there was a need for a separate research collection in the library devoted to materials on black history. To this end, Kelly Miller, a professor and dean of the College of Arts and Sciences at Howard, persuaded the Reverend Jesse Moorland, a trustee, to donate his private library on black history to the university in 1914. Moorland's collection, believed at that time to be the most extensive collection of such materials held by a private individual, was kept separate from the rest of the library holdings and formed the basis for the foundation that bears his name. The 3,000 books, pamphlets, and other materials provided a challenge for the staff, as there was no suitable classification scheme with which to classify the holdings. Several efforts at classification produced a working but rudimentary system, and the library was on its way to providing a powerful research tool for scholars of the African American experience.

Founders Library

In 1929 a new library was funded and named the Founders Library in memory of the 17 founders of Howard University. The building was designed by Albert Irwin Cassell, an African American architect from Towson, Maryland. Dorothy Burnett Porter, a Howard graduate and the first black American woman to be awarded a master's degree in library science from Columbia University (1932), joined the staff in 1930 and helped to plan the new library, which opened in 1939. She also improved the subject classification system for holdings, making scholarly research easier and more efficient and providing access to the broad and varied facets of the African American experience. Individual subjects could be further divided into specific aspects such as time period, geographic location, or social conditions. (For example, researchers could access information on marriage rites on plantations as portrayed in American novels of a specific time.) Porter became the first curator of the Moorland collection and was instrumental in articulating and executing goals for the collection. Perhaps the most important of these was her vision of the collection as a place to accumulate records and preserve materials by and about African Americans. During her tenure of 43 years, she oversaw the library's continued expansion through the addition of other collections, as well as the extension of the scope of its research capabilities; she also helped to guide the library's continuing service to the educational needs of the university's undergraduate community.

The Founders Library now houses the holdings classified in the Library of Congress (LC) classification system and the separate Moorland-Spingarn Research Center, Howard University Museum, and Afro-American Studies Resource Center. The adjoining Undergraduate Library (UGL) opened in 1983. It houses the collection classed in the Dewey Decimal Classification (DDC) system. The Founders Library and UGL house more than half of the books, periodicals, microforms, and other resources held at the university, with comprehensive coverage of disciplines in the behavioral and social sciences, the sciences, and the arts and humanities.

Moorland-Spingarn Collection

In 1946 the university was able to purchase the private library of Arthur Barnette Spingarn, a prominent attorney and advocate for African Americans. While serving in the U.S. Army during World War I, Spingarn was an outspoken critic of the military's treatment of the African Americans in its ranks. He remained a staunch defender of and advocate for African Americans throughout his life, serving as chairman of the Legal Committee of the NAACP and later as its president. Throughout his life he collected works by writers of African descent. His collection, at the time of its purchase by the library, was widely respected for its scope, depth, and quality. The collection was particularly comprehensive in its coverage of Afro-Cuban, Afro-Brazilian, and Haitian writers. Its most famous work was Juan Latino's *Ad Catholicum Pariter et Invictissimum Phillipum Dei Gratia Hispaniarum Regum* (1573). This book of epigrams on the victory of King Philip II (Spain) over the Turks was written by a black slave who, as a professor at the University of Grenada, proved to be one of the most eminent Latinists and humanists of the Spanish Renaissance.

Most noteworthy in the Spingarn collection was the large number of African writers' works. Many of these were and are unknown to the majority of U.S. scholars. The collection features a number of rare and unique volumes and works in various African languages. In the years following the purchase of the collection, Spingarn continued to make additions in an attempt to complete his collecting efforts, and its growth continues today. It remains a prominent jewel in the library's crown and is kept separate from the Moorland Foundation's other collections. A backlog of material needing processing developed owing to the lack of trained personnel, but a Ford Foundation grant was awarded in 1970 that enabled much progress in the management and processing of manuscripts.

Moorland-Spingarn Research Center

In 1973 the Moorland-Spingarn Collection was reorganized as a research center, administratively separate from the other Howard libraries. The center contained the two collections in its title, the Howard University Museum, the Howard University Archives, the Black Press Archives, and the Ralph J. Bunche Oral History collection (formerly the Civil Rights Documentation Project). Later, a separate Manuscript Division was created within the center to aid in its development as a completely modern and professional research organization. This addition allowed the center to produce research as well as to continue with its curatorial and library functions. Since its inception, the Manuscript Division collections have grown rapidly, and plans to divide the Manuscript Division into four departments—manuscript, music, oral history, and prints and photographs—were made during the reorganization. As a result, the Moorland-Spingarn Research Center now represents one of the largest and most diverse depositories of primary research materials on the black experience in the United States.

Howard University Libraries

The Howard University Libraries today consist of a central library group, the Moorland-Spingarn Research Center, the Health Sciences Library, the A.M. Daniel Law Library, the Ralph J. Bunche International Affairs Center Library, and the Afro-American Studies Resource Center. The central library group is comprised of the Founders Library/Undergraduate Library and four branch libraries (architecture, business, divinity, and social work).

Pre-1975 holdings can be accessed using the card catalog, and holdings acquired after 1975 may be accessed in Sterling, the Howard University online public catalog. A new Web-based system, also called Sterling, became available in December 2000. The library's website provides access to bibliographic, full-text, numerical, and multimedia files. Extensive electronic search aids can also be found to help access the manuscript collections.

NANCY R. LEWIS

Further Reading

Arthur B. Spingarn Collection of Negro Authors, Washington, D.C.: Moorland Foundation, Howard University Library, [ca. 1947]

Battle, Thomas C., "Moorland-Spingarn Research Center," *Library Quarterly* 58, no. 2 (1988)

Burkett, Nancy, and Randall K. Burkett, "Dorothy Burnett Porter Wesley," *Proceedings of the American Antiquarian Society* 106, no. 1 (1996)

Culpepper, Betty M., "Genealogical Resources at the Moorland-Spingarn Research Center," *Journal of the Afro-American Historical and Genealogical Society* 2, no. 3 (1981)

Porter, Dorothy B., "A Library on the Negro," *American Scholar* 7 (Winter 1938)

Sims-Wood, Janet, "Researching Black Women's History Resources and Archives at the Moorland-Spingarn Research Center," *Ethnic Forum* 7, no. 1 (1987)

Wilson, Greta S., compiler, *Guide to Processed Collections in the Manuscript Division of the Moorland-Spingarn Research Center,* Washington, D.C.: Moorland-Spingarn Research Center, 1983

Winston, Michael R., "Moorland-Spingarn Research Center: A Past Revisited, a Present Reclaimed," *New Directions* (Summer 1974)

Huntington Library, Art Collections, and Botanical Gardens

Address: Huntington Library, Art Collections, and Botanical Gardens
1151 Oxford Road
San Marino, California 91108
USA
Telephone: 626-405-2100
Fax: 626-449-5720
www.huntington.org

Founded: 1919

Holdings (2001): Volumes: 750,000. Current serials: 600; incunabula: 5,200; manuscripts: 3.5 million; microforms: 250,000; photographs: 600,000; prints and ephemera: 750,000.

Special Collections: *Areas of Concentration*: British and American history and literature; Californiana and western Americana; history of printing; history of science, medicine, and technology. *Branch libraries*: Art reference library; Botanical curatorial library. *Individual collections*: Wilberforce Ames; William K. Bixby; Bridgewater library (Sir Thomas Egerton); Robert A. Brock; Beverly Chew; Elihu Dwight Church; Duke of Devonshire; James Ellsworth; James T. Fields; Grenville Kane; Walter Lewisson; Jack London; John Nicholson; Sir Thomas Phillipps; John Quinn; A.S.W. Rosenbach; George D. Smith; Otto H.F. Vollbehr; Henry R. Wagner. *Papers*: Battle Abbey; Hastings-Huntingdon family; Lord Loudon family; Stowe family.

Henry Edwards Huntington

Henry Edwards Huntington founded the Henry E. Huntington Library and Art Gallery in 1919 as a research library, botanical garden, and art gallery and museum. Huntington was born on 27 February 1850 in Oneonta, New York, the fourth of seven children and the eldest surviving son. Huntington made no efforts to pursue a college education and never obtained a college degree. At age 21, Henry began working with his father as a porter in their family-owned hardware store. He became closely associated with his uncle, Collis Potter Huntington, especially in the Central Pacific Railroad, of which Collis Huntington was president. He inherited large railroad interests from his uncle, providing the necessary wealth for his growing collections. Collis sent him to San Francisco in 1892 as special assistant to the president of the Southern Pacific Railroad. After Collis's death in 1900, Henry became director of the Southern Pacific Company and moved the Southern Pacific offices to Los Angeles, where he influenced the development of the California transportation system through the creation of the Pacific Electric Company (an interurban electric trolley railway system) and the Los Angeles Railway. In 1903 he purchased the J. DeBarth Shorb ranch near Pasadena, part of which became the present Huntington estate.

In 1910 Huntington retired and sold the Pacific Railway System in order to devote the rest of his life to building his art and rare book collections. His Beaux Arts mansion in San Marino (now the art gallery) was completed in that year. On 17 July 1913 he married Arabella Huntington, the widow of his uncle Collis, who became Henry's partner in developing the Huntington residence and art collections until her death in 1924. He himself died in 1927, having acquired more than 200 complete libraries over the 17-year period to form the core of the present-day collections. In 1983 the name of the institution was changed to the Huntington Library, Art Collections, and Botanical Gardens.

Huntington Library Building

Myron Hunt (Huntington's architect) began planning the Huntington residence and library in 1907 with the assistance of Elmer Grey. Huntington originally planned to build his home around the L-shaped library, but eventually he decided to construct a separate library building to house the rapidly growing library collections in New York. The main house was redesigned to accommodate a smaller reading library. The main drawing room would now house a set of Beauvais tapestries purchased for Arabella. The mansion was completed in 1910. In 1919 the library foundation was laid, and the building's exterior was completed by the end of 1920. Special construction techniques were used in response to the 1906 San Francisco earthquake and fire, including specially built bookcases that would sway in tremors without buckling, reinforced concrete flooring, and multiple layers of paint on the walls and ceilings. By 1923 the interior of the library was mostly completed, and the collections and library staff moved from New York. Readers began using the collection after Mrs. Huntington's death in 1924.

Book Collecting

In 1908 Huntington purchased a reference work entitled *Rare Books and Their Prices,* noting in the margins the names of the landmark books and key authors, from the Gutenberg Bible to Thomas Hardy, and using the work as a guide for his collecting career.

In an effort to build his rare book collection in an efficient manner, Huntington considered two options: to purchase titles one at a time on his own or to identify appropriate dealers and hire them as his agents. Huntington chose the latter course and relied on the advice of many experienced bibliographers, librarians, and advisers, including Leslie Bliss, George Watson Cole, Robert O. Schad, Clarence S. Brigham, and Henry R. Wagner, as well as such astute and aggressive agents as Mitchell Kennerley, Henry W. Poor, George D. Smith, A.S.W. Rosenbach, Charles Sessler, Henry Miller, Russell Benedict, Robert Hoe III, Isaac Mendoza, and Joseph Duveen, virtually all of the major book dealers of the period. Although Huntington made all final purchase decisions, his network of advisers played an important role in developing the Huntington Library.

Through his dealers and advisers Huntington purchased not only individual rare book titles but also entire private library collections. For example, Isaac Mendoza purchased the Charles A. Morrogh and John A. Stowe libraries for Huntington in 1904 and 1908, respectively. The Morrogh collection contained more than 1,000 titles (including 57 volumes illustrated by George Cruikshank and 54 Kelmscott Press books printed by William Morris). The Stowe collection contained the complete works of Emily Dickinson, Nathaniel Hawthorne, Henry Wadsworth Longfellow, and Edmund Gibbon. Although his selections of art and architecture demonstrate otherwise, Huntington was not interested in materials he could not read and disposed of such foreign-language materials as quickly as possible. The Huntington remains primarily an English-language collection.

George D. Smith assisted Huntington in purchasing a portion of the Henry W. Poor library in 1908, including important works by Andrew Lang, Oscar Wilde, Robert Burns, and John Greenleaf Whittier. The purchase also included many examples of fine printing from 15th- to 20th-century presses. Smith also helped Huntington to acquire most of the private collection of Robert Hoe III, including a Gutenberg Bible printed on vellum; a collection of William Blake; statutes of Kings Edward III and Edward IV; and first editions of works by Daniel Defoe, Edmund Spenser, Jonathan Steele, John Suckling, and Longfellow. In 1909 Huntington purchased books from dealer Charles Sessler, including works by George Cruikshank, James Gillray, Thomas Rowlandson, Dickinson, John James Audubon, Thomas Hood, William Makepeace Thackeray, and Lord Henry Brougham.

Huntington purchased the Elihu Dwight Church library in 1911. The collection comprised 2,000 titles, including the first printed Latin edition of the Christopher Columbus letter describing his first voyage to the new world (1493), the Bay Psalm Book (*The Whole Booke of Psalmes Faithfully Translated into English Metre* [1640]), a Bible translated into Algonquin by John Eliot, the manuscript of Benjamin Franklin's autobiography, and 12 copies Shakespeare folios and 37 quartos. From his purchase of the Duke of Devonshire's library in 1914, he added four more folio copies and another 57 quartos, as well as 25 books printed by William Caxton.

In 1917 Huntington purchased the Bridgewater library, begun in the 17th century by Sir Thomas Egerton, Baron Ellesmere. The library included 4,400 printed books and more than 14,000 literary manuscripts and letters, the most famous of which is the Ellesmere Chaucer, the most complete manuscript of *The Canterbury Tales,* produced circa 1400. The library also contained a collection of plays amassed by John Larpent, who served as licensing inspector of plays from 1778 to 1824. Huntington regarded the Church, Devonshire, and Bridgewater libraries as the foundation for his collection of British and American literature.

Other Huntington Collections

In addition to the library, the Huntington is comprised of the Botanical Gardens, the Huntington Gallery, the Virginia Steele Scott Gallery, the Arabella Huntington Memorial Collection, and the Art Reference Library.

Huntington hired landscape gardener William Hertrich to develop the Botanical Gardens, begun immediately after the purchase of the estate in 1903. Hertrich developed a number of individual garden venues based on either plant type or geographic location, including lily ponds; a Japanese garden; desert, rose, camellia, palm, subtropical, jungle, herb, and Australian gardens; Zen and bonsai courts; and the succulent conservatory. The Botanical Gardens became one of the main public attractions of the Huntington by the end of the 20th century, in addition to the changing exhibitions in the art galleries and the library.

In 1927, shortly after Henry Huntington's death, the Arabella Huntington memorial collection and the Huntington Gallery were developed. The Arabella collection was displayed in a special wing in the library and emphasized Mrs. Huntington's interests in French furniture, porcelains, and sculpture, as well as renaissance painting. The Huntington Gallery occupied the former Huntington residence and contained collections of British and continental art, primarily from the 18th and 19th centuries, including the famous paintings of Thomas Gainsborough's *Blue Boy,* Thomas Lawrence's *Pinkie,* Joshua Reynolds' *Mrs. Siddons as the Tragic Muse,* and John Constable's *View of the Stour.*

In 1979 the Virginia Steele Scott Foundation presented a collection of 50 American paintings, funds to construct a gallery to display the collection, and an endowment for its professional management. The Virginia Steele Scott Gallery opened in 1984 and included American paintings from the 1730s to the 1930s and collections of American furniture, sculpture, drawings, prints, and photographs. The Scott Gallery houses the archive of American Arts and Crafts architects Charles and Henry Greene, and, since 1982, a permanent exhibition of their furniture and decorative arts, including a reconstruction of the entire dining room from their Robinson house in Pasadena.

Supporting these collections is an art reference library of approximately 30,000 volumes, primarily concerning British and American art, including the Esdaile archives on British sculpture and the C.H. Collins Baker archive of exhibition catalogs and newspaper clippings on British art.

Directors and Libraries

Huntington's first bibliographer and librarian was George Watson Cole, whom he met during the Elihu Dwight Church library purchase. Huntington employed Cole from 1915 to 1924, first as bibliographer and then from 1920 as librarian. Prior to Cole, the catalog consisted of brief notes transcribed on cards by George E. Miles.

During Cole's tenure, book dealer George Smith acquired the Frederick R. Halsey collection of English and American literature for the Huntington, adding more than 20,000 volumes, including the first, third, and fourth Shakespeare folios and first editions of John Milton, Percy Bysshe Shelley, Charles Dickens, Longfellow, Herman Melville, and Edgar Allen Poe. In 1919 Cole published a *Checklist or Brief Catalogue of the Library of Henry E. Huntington: English Literature to 1640*. Cole retired in 1924.

On 24 May 1925 Huntington appointed Leslie Bliss as library director. During Bliss's tenure (1925–58), A.S.W. Rosenbach acquired the libraries of William H. Arnold and Beverly Chew for the Huntington. The Arnold purchase included a group of 146 letters from Hawthorne to his publisher, General Ulysses S. Grant's letter book covering the period of March and April 1865, and the manuscript of Robert Louis Stevenson's *Kidnapped*. Titles in the Beverly Chew library included three parts of Daniel Defoe's *Robinson Crusoe* and William Blake's *Songs of Innocence* and *Songs of Experience*.

John E. Pomfret was appointed the Huntington director in 1951 and served until 1958. Also in 1958, Robert Dougan succeeded Leslie Bliss as librarian, and over the next few years Dougan increased the rare book collection by 80,000 titles and 49,000 reference collection works. In 1966 James Thorpe became Huntington director. Thorpe worked with librarian Daniel Woodward on their concern for developing the library clientele and creating and maintaining a scholarship program for library research. Today, the Huntington is the leading independent research library in the United States for research grants, awarding more than $800,000 annually to approximately 130 research fellows.

For almost all of the 20th century, primary access to Huntington collections was through manual card catalogs. Separate catalogs exist for printed books, manuscripts, photographs, prints, and ephemera, as well as special card files for chronology, place, printers, and bibliographies. In 1986 the Huntington began creating online records in the Research Libraries Information Network (RLIN), a shared library database maintained by the Research Libraries Group (RLG), but card catalogs remain the principal access tools. The library will complete a retrospective conversion of its printed holdings in fall 2001, which will be linked to its website. Other projects are underway to convert manuscript holdings to online access.

Woodward served until 1990, when William A. Moffett became library director. Moffett began the local online catalog, but he is probably best remembered for opening Huntington's photographic archive of the Dead Sea Scrolls to unrestricted access. Moffett received the Librarian of the Year award from the American Library Association's Association of College and Research Libraries, as well as the Immroth Memorial Award for Intellectual Freedom. Moffett also received the Professional Librarian award given by the Special Libraries Association.

Moffett died in 1995 and was succeeded in 1996 by David Zeidberg as Avery Director of the Library, during the presidency of Robert Skotheim. Zeidberg has continued the work of his predecessors in the areas of automation and in the maintenance and preservation of the Huntington collections. He has also strengthened the funding for collection development, established a program of exhibitions with educational components for the general public and school curricula, and has secured funding for a new 90,000-square-foot library wing, which will provide for improved reader facilities, new conservation and photography laboratories, and expanded stack space. The Huntington expects completion of the new library wing late in 2003, the centenary of Henry E. Huntington's original purchase of the estate.

JENNIFER BOONE

Further Reading

Dickinson, Donald C., *Henry E. Huntington's Library of Libraries*, San Marino, California: Huntington Library, 1995

Pomfret, John E., *The Henry E. Huntington Library and Art Gallery: From Its Beginnings to 1969*, San Marino, California: Huntington Library, 1969

Spurgeon, Selena A., *Henry Edwards Huntington: His Life and His Collections: A Docent Guide*, San Marino, California: Huntington Library, 1992

Thorpe, James, *Henry Edwards Huntington: A Biography*, Berkeley, California: University of California Press, 1994

Woodward, Daniel, "Care and Feeding of the Library Researcher," *American Libraries* (March 1987)

Zeidberg, David, S., "The Archival View of Technology: Resources for the Scholar of the Future," *Library Trends* 47, no. 4 (Spring 1999)

Indiana University Libraries

Address: Indiana University Libraries
Indiana University Bloomington
1320 E. 10th Street
Bloomington, Indiana 47405
USA
Telephone: 812-855-0100
Fax: 812-855-1624
www.indiana.edu/~libweb

Founded: 1824

Holdings (2000): Volumes: 6.3 million. Archives and manuscripts: 34,000 linear feet; audio recordings: 151,000; current serials: 32,000; films and videos: 35,000; graphic materials: 3 million; incunabula: 700; maps: 595,000; microforms: 4.4 million.

Special Collections: *Areas of Concentration:* Booksellers; children's literature; early travel literature; film, radio, and television; fine printing; publishers' archives; religion and Bibles. *Individual Collections:* Appleton-Century; Bobbs-Merrill; Calder and Boyars; Cannelton cotton mill; congressional papers; film, radio, and television scripts; Howard shipyards; S. Fischer Verlag. *Papers:* Malcolm Bradbury; Raymond Carver; Athol Fugard; Nadine Gordimer; Emily Hahn; Sylvia Plath; Ezra Pound; Vita Sackville-West; Upton Sinclair; Kurt Vonnegut.

Indiana University

Originally founded on 20 January 1820 as Indiana Seminary and chartered as Indiana College in 1828, Indiana University (IU) was elevated by the board of trustees to the status of university in 1838. The move was made more in the hope of future expansion than in recognition of an enlarged educational philosophy. Although earlier students had access to the private library of the Bayard R. Hall, Andrew Wylie, the seminary's first professor, identified a good library as one of the college's most urgent needs when he was appointed its first president on 5 October 1828. He traveled throughout the East Coast collecting books and raising funds for the new library. In 1836 the institution received a gift of books from the library of William Maclure, a collection that included classic works in French, Greek, and Latin, and that provided a solid foundation upon which to build the collection. Wylie requested a $5,000 annual appropriation for library purchases but ran afoul of the trustees, who questioned the affordability of such an extravagance. Instead, the trustees compiled a list of books to be acquired, provided they could be had cheaply. Fortunately, trustee Robert Dale Owen (son of the Welsh socialist Robert Owen) sought to perpetuate at IU the intellectual tools of books and laboratory equipment that he had collected at his utopian community, New Harmony, Indiana. Through his influence the list included John Smith's *Generall Historie of Virginia*, Thomas Jefferson's *Notes on the State of Virginia*, Edmund Spenser's *Faerie Queene*, David Ricardo's *On the Principles of Political Economy and Taxation*, and the *Arabian Nights*.

Theophilius Wylie, a cousin of Andrew Wylie, is widely regarded as the university's first librarian (1860–79), although Professor James F. Dodds was appointed to that post by the trustees on 27 September 1838. Housed in the College Building, one of the first two buildings erected at Seminary Square, the library may have existed as much for ornamentation as for use. Open only on Saturdays, it contained no tables or chairs, and books could be used only under very restrictive rules.

When the library was destroyed by a fire that consumed the College Building on 11 April 1854, its collection numbered 1,200 volumes. The loss was seen as a calamity for the state. Citizens of Bloomington and Monroe County donated $10,000 toward the immediate construction of a new building, completed in 1855. In 1874 the library moved to the newly constructed Science Building. In 1876 President Lemuel Moss urged the trustees to increase library appropriations to meet his aspirations for a library with the best editions of the best books of the best writers in all departments of thought and knowledge. Such aspirations were again deferred when the library, with 13,000 volumes, was again destroyed by fire on 12 July 1883. The loss of the building was estimated at $33,000 and the lost books valued at $111,000.

Wylie Hall

Following the fire of 1883, President Moss made plans to relocate the campus from Seminary Square to two buildings to be erected in Dunn's Woods, the site of the present campus. Late in January 1885 the library moved from the old campus to the second floor of one of the new buildings, and on 9 January 1886 the *Bloomington Saturday Courier* announced that "all of the books in the library are new and well-selected, $8,000 having been expended on books this year."

In 1887 the trustees adopted rules giving Registrar and Librarian William Spangler (1880–93) official responsibility for the library. The janitor was to help with discipline, and President David Starr Jordan was to advise on matters of book circulation. Regularly enrolled students could use books within the library but could borrow books only with the payment of a one-dollar library fee. The fee entitled a student to borrow one volume at a time for a period not to exceed two weeks.

Maxwell Hall

By 1890 the library had outgrown its location in Wylie Hall and reestablished itself in Library Hall, dedicated on 20 January 1891, 71 years after the founding of Indiana Seminary. Constructed by architects Bunting and Sons in 1890 at a cost of $75,000, the new library building held 14,000 volumes in four rooms (one reading room with a fireplace) with a total capacity for 60,000 volumes. It was renamed Maxwell Hall in 1894. The north half of the reading room was occupied by students' tables and chairs, the other by bookcases housing the collection. The cataloging room, the newspaper reading room, and storage for periodicals and pamphlets were located on the west wing's first floor. The first and second floor of the east wing and the second floor of the west wing contained classrooms. Electric lighting was installed in 1896. As book collections grew, the library gradually acquired nearly all the space in the building. By the early 1900s, the library had again outgrown its building.

Franklin Hall

Maxwell Hall's successor building, Franklin Hall, was designed by architects Patton and Miller of Chicago and completed on 1 January 1908 at a cost of $137,000. President William Lowe Bryan selected the entrance motto from Milton: "A good book is the precious lifeblood of the master spirit." The main reading room had seats for 204 readers and shelving for 6,000 reference works. In 1926 a new wing was added to house the growing collections. Looking toward the future, President Herman B. Wells set his sights on a new university library building in 1948, in anticipation of the time when Franklin Hall would no longer accommodate the needs of a major research university. Additional stacks allowed the library to expand in response to a growing student population and the needs of a research faculty, until a new facility became imperative by the 1960s.

The Main Library

President Elvis J. Stahr had been in office only four months when the faculty library committee made the construction of a new library its highest priority in November 1962. Plans called for an undergraduate library rising from the same foundation as the main graduate library and service divisions. In 1962 cost estimates for this new library were approximately $12.5 million, and in 1964 the Indiana General Assembly appropriated $687,000 to finance preliminary planning. It was not until 1966, however, that specific construction plans were undertaken. In four years the cost had risen to $14.4 million. President Stahr informed the state government that the new building would seat 3,000 undergraduate and 2,000 graduate students; the undergraduate section would house 100,000 volumes, and the general and graduate section would hold 1.5 million volumes, in a building with a protective environment for both people and books.

Construction of the new main library began in 1966. The combined bids for construction totaled $12.3 million, and the structure was to be completed within 1,080 days. Two arson attacks in February and May 1969, with damage estimated at more than $1 million, accelerated completion of the new building, which opened in July and was formally dedicated in October of 1969. Fortunately, the existence of extensive branch libraries was a helpful factor in library continuity until the centralized new building was completed.

Renovation of the main library is now in the planning stage; construction of a new Auxiliary Library Facility, an off-site high-density shelving facility designed to alleviate overcrowded shelves in the main library and the campus libraries, is due to begin in late 2001.

Auxiliary Libraries

Throughout the history of the library, many research collections were housed in laboratories or classrooms, developing over time into departmental collections and then into branch libraries. Today 14 branches are part of the university library, including the Black Culture Center; branches related to chemistry, education, fine arts, geology and geography, health, physical education and recreation, journalism, life sciences, music, optometry, mathematics, and physics; the School of Public and Environmental Affairs libraries; and the Lilly Library. The Law School library, the Kinsey Institute Library, and the Archives of Traditional Music are extrasystem libraries administered outside the university library administration.

In the fall of 1940, the Indiana University Halls of Residence Commission voted to place vending machines in campus dormitories, allocating the profits to students for the purchase of library books and art objects for their residence halls. By 1949 profits from the "coke fund" totaled $10,000 per year, supporting four residence hall libraries, and in 1959 a part-time librarian was appointed to oversee the system. Today, 11 residence hall libraries are supervised by a full-time librarian and staffed with student assistants. The purpose of these libraries is to encourage student participation in book selection.

The Lilly Library

Gifts of the Robert S. Ellison memorial collection of Western Americana, the War of 1812 collection, the Joseph B. Oakleaf collection of Lincolniana, the Augustan collection of British political manuscripts and documents, and the Watkins collection of Wordsworth predate the acquisition of the university's most important gift of rare books and manuscripts, the Josiah Kirby Lilly Jr. collection. This 1956 gift has been characterized as one of the most significant gifts of its kind ever made to a U.S. university. On 19 July 1957, Cecil K. Byrd, associate director of libraries, announced that construction of a special $1.5 million building to house Lilly's collection and other rare collections would begin. The 117-by-122-foot Indiana limestone building was designed by the architectural firm of Egger and Higins to provide stack space for 300,000 volumes and 3 million manuscripts. The building, dedicated on 3 October 1960, currently holds more than 400,000 volumes, 7 million manuscripts, and 150,000 pieces of sheet music, along with an extensive collection of art and artifacts. The Lilly Library's collecting strengths include U.S., British, and European literature and history; the literature of travel and exploration; food and drink; children's literature; music; Indiana history; early printing; illuminated manuscripts; fine bindings; Latin American history; publishers' archives; the U.S. Civil War; and film, radio, and television.

Classification

In 1843 the university published its first catalog of library holdings, categorized and listed under 20 headings. It is not clear whether trustees or faculty did this cataloging. Books were cataloged using the Dewey Decimal Classification system from 1883 to 1918, when conversion to the Library of Congress system began under the direction of Librarian William Jenkins and the supervision of Ida Wolf, with 125,600 books requiring reclassification.

Automation

In 1967 Librarian Robert A. Miller (1942–72) and his staff began to address the issue of library automation. Expensive and unproductive attempts at automation had been made at other universities, and it was clear that library automation required large amounts of random access storage and an adequate central processing unit. All agreed that library automation should receive the highest priority but must be coordinated within a university-wide information system.

From 1973 to 1974, shortly after Miller was succeeded by Dean W. Carl Jackson (1973–80), the library developed a comprehensive statement of the long-term goals and intermediate objectives for library automation. The statement recognized the complex interrelationships among various library processes including acquisitions, cataloging, inventory control, and circulation. In 1975 the library became a member of the online bibliographic service OCLC and thus gained online access to machine-readable cataloging records from hundreds of U.S. libraries. Although participation in OCLC helped to automate acquisitions, cataloging, and inventory control, the goal of an automated circulation system remained years away, pending a significant investment of funds. But without this investment, the library ultimately faced increased labor costs and a substantial deterioration in library operations and services.

In 1986 plans were announced for Information Online (IO), an integrated library information system for the IU libraries, promising the eventual end to the card catalog and automated circulation. In 1990 the library implemented the Northwestern Online Totally Integrated System (NOTIS), opened its Online Public Access Catalog (OPAC), and officially closed the card catalog. Automated circulation was implemented in 1991. After nearly a decade with a catalog split between online records and catalog cards, a massive retrospective conversion project was begun in 1999 to ensure access to all library holdings through the university's new IUCAT system. In 1999 the IU libraries adopted SIRSI, a vendor corporation supplying software and services. SIRSI was implemented in January 2001 and provides Indiana University Libraries with automated library management systems, including a range of functions supporting technical and public services.

LISA M. BROWAR

Further Reading

Carmony, Donald F., *Indiana University: From Seminary Square to Dunn's Woods, 1820–1885*, Bloomington: Indiana University Publications, 1987

Clark, Thomas D., *Indiana University: Midwestern Pioneer*, 4 vols., Bloomington: Indiana University Press, 1970–77

Woodburn, James Albert, D.D. Banta, and Burton Dorr Myers, *History of Indiana University*, 2 vols., Bloomington: Indiana University, 1940–52

International Institute of Social History

Address: Internationaal Instituut voor Sociale
Geschiedenis
Cruquiusweg 31
1019 AT Amsterdam
The Netherlands
Telephone: 20-6685866
Fax: 20-6654181
www.iisg.nl

Founded: 1935

Holdings (2000): Volumes: 1 million. Audiovisual materials: 800,000; current serials: 2,400; digital documents: 3 million; manuscripts: 30,000 linear feet (2,300 archival collections).

Special Collections: *Areas of Concentration:* Dutch and international labor and social history. *Individual Collections:* Amnesty International; Confederación Nacional del Trabajo; Egyptian Communists in Exile; European Trade Union Confederation; Federación Anarquista Ibérica; Freedom Press; Greenpeace International; International Confederation of Free Trade Unions; Russian Party of Socialists-Revolutionaries; Socialist International. *Papers:* Lucien Descaves; Emma Goldman; Leon Kashnor; Karl Kautsky; Ernest Mandel; Karl Marx; Max Nettlau; Sylvia Pankhurst; Kemal Sülker; Lev Trotsky.

Origins

The creation of the International Institute of Social History (IISH) was essentially the work of a single man, Nicolaas W. Posthumus, a socialist who was appointed to the first chair in economic history in the Netherlands in 1913 and was one of the most remarkable scholarly organizers in Dutch history. Apart from IISH, he was instrumental in the foundation of the Netherlands Economic History Archive (NEHA), the Netherlands Institute for War Documentation, and the Faculty of Social Sciences at the University of Amsterdam. At the age of 69 he became the managing director of E. J. Brill's prestigious publishing house and antiquarian bookshop.

The Netherlands Economic History Archive was founded in 1914 with the aim expressed in its charter to collect "primary sources of importance to the economic history of the Netherlands and its colonies in the broadest sense." The emphasis was on the last words; Posthumus never confined his activities to archival records, building a splendid library as well. And he couldn't be bothered by any borders or boundaries, either of economic history or of the Dutch empire. When NEHA eventually transferred part of its holdings to IISH they included, among many other things, some 25 trade union archives and an important collection emanating from the General Yiddish Workers' Union in Lithuania, Poland, and Russia, known as the Bund.

The Central Workers' Life Insurance Bank

Indeed, by the early 1930s NEHA's social-historical section had grown to such an extent that Posthumus made it somewhat more independent and placed it in the care of Annie Adama van Scheltema-Kleefstra, the widow of a well-known socialist poet, who also took up the position of archivist of the Social-Democratic Workers' Party (to supplement her fairly low salary). Her depressing findings on archival practices in the Dutch labor movement may have added to Posthumus' increasing wariness of the aggravating political situation in Europe and influenced his decision to take an even wider approach. In 1935, with the financial backing of the Central Workers' Life Insurance Bank (De Centrale Arbeiders Levensverzekeringsbank), he founded in 1935 the IISH, an entirely independent institution that was, by then, openly international in scope.

The Centrale, as the firm was known for short, had its origins in 1903, the year when the Dutch syndicalist unions lost their most spectacular strike ever and a socialist or modern trade union movement was born out of their defeat. The Centrale was just as modern in that it did not divide any profits among the insureds, as had been usual in workers' insurance companies, but spent them instead on cultural activities related to the movement as a whole. Persuaded by Posthumus, Nehemia de Lieme, the sole pre–World War II director of the Centrale (and a friend of Louis D. Brandeis, with whom he shared a profound interest in Zionism), decided that IISH was a worthy recipient of Centrale profits. From 1935 to 1939, the institute received approximately $4.5 million in today's money, or close to half of the total amount granted for cultural activities by the Centrale before World War II. Admittedly, part of this sum was grudgingly awarded, as Posthumus was prone to making important purchases without consulting anyone.

The Early Years

Whereas NEHA had followed the model of the Cologne-based Economic Archive of Rhineland-Westphalia, IISH was largely modeled on the Marx-Engels Institute founded by David B. Ryazanov in Moscow in 1920. The backbone of its organization consisted of five "cabinets" (so called because the documents were actually stored in the rooms of the curators), each covering a certain geographical area. Foremost among the staff, many of them political refugees, was Boris I. Nikolaevsky, a Russian Menshevik who had long worked with Ryazanov and from 1936 to 1940 headed a subsidiary of IISH in Paris. Scholars and political activists such as Gustav Mayer and Boris Souvarine, the first biographers of Friedrich Engels and Joseph Stalin, respectively, acted as correspondents abroad. Scheltema became the librarian of the institute.

IISH was soon flooded by collections. Some of them were rescued from Germany and Austria under difficult circumstances; others were donated by or purchased from political activists, exiles, and collectors. Part of the institute's success is probably a result of the traditional perception of the Netherlands as a liberal country that threatened no one, a notion that was reinforced by Posthumus' scholarly impartiality toward the bitterly divided world of left-wing politics. Another major factor was the absence of an alternative, the Soviets having turned inward under the pressures of Stalinism. In 1935 approximately half of all European countries were governed by regimes that were authoritarian at best, and their number was rising. For exiled Russians, persecuted Germans, or defeated Spaniards there was scarcely any other place to take their papers than the former high school for girls, prettily situated on one of Amsterdam's central canals, that the city had generously ceded to IISH.

The War and Its Aftermath

In autumn 1938 it was the institute's turn to look for shelter. During the Munich Crisis, Posthumus concluded that a European war was inevitable and would not leave Holland unscathed. In the year preceding the actual outbreak of World War II in 1939, the Institute sent many of its most sensitive collections, including the papers of Marx and Engels, to Harrogate, England. Part of the holdings of the French office were hidden in Amboise, some 100 miles southwest of Paris. (As it turned out, this was to no avail, as they were confiscated by the Nazis.) At the same time, as it was assumed that the United States would remain neutral, Posthumus struck an agreement with Stanford University (California) that provided for a temporary transfer of property rights to the latter in the event of a German invasion of the Netherlands. But when the Nazis did in fact arrive in May 1940, the agreement proved impossible to enforce.

After IISH had been closed by the German Security Service in July, it became the prize in a struggle between the Reich Security Services Headquarters, the German Labor Front, and the Office for the Occupied Territories headed by Alfred Rosenberg. Rosenberg, the notorious author of *Mythus des 20 Jahrhunderts* (1935; *The Myth of the Twentieth Century*), eventually emerged as the winner. The Rosenberg Agency took over the institute's remaining collections, including those confiscated in France, as part of its endeavor to create a central site of national socialist research and education. As a result, IISH holdings were dispersed all over Central Europe in the course of the war.

Today it seems incredible how little was really lost. Largely owing to the efforts of the U.S. Army's Offenbach Archival Depot, all materials that belonged identifiably to IISH were returned from the Western occupation zones in 1946–47. The documents stored in Harrogate (and later transferred to Oxford) also came back in 1946. In 1956 the Polish government returned collections that had ended up in the University of Krakow. In 1958 the institute obtained from a reluctant U.S. Library of Congress the records of the International Working Men's Association that had made it to the United States from France in June 1940.

In 1991 much of what had remained untraceable turned out to have been seized by Soviet security agencies in 1945. These materials were brought together with other archival collections, many of them first stolen by the Nazis, in the top-secret Special Archive constructed in Moscow in 1946 by German prisoners of war. The Soviet government occasionally returned some of the documents to their owners, such as the records of the Spanish Socialist Workers Party deposited with IISH's French branch before the war, but current authorities in Russia see them as trophy archives and tend to dismiss claims of plunder, even from wartime allies. This makes it all the more unlikely that another mystery, the theft of part of Trotsky's papers from the Paris office in 1936 that is widely attributed to Stalin's secret service, will be solved anytime soon.

Two Reconstructions

In impoverished postwar Holland it took IISH the better part of 20 years to reestablish order, and then its efforts were successful only thanks to considerable foreign aid, most notably from the Ford Foundation, which in 1959 offered a grant for sorting and cataloging the huge amounts of manuscripts, books, and serials recovered in indescribably chaotic conditions. The reconstruction came to a symbolic close in 1970–71, when G.K. Hall and Company published the first 12 volumes of a printed alphabetical catalog of the collection of books and pamphlets.

By then the Dutch Ministry of Education, Arts and Sciences had almost entirely taken over the institute's financial burden. After a period of close collaboration with the University of Amsterdam, IISH joined the Royal Netherlands Academy of Arts and Sciences in 1979, although legally its collections remain in the care of the foundation created in 1935. Meanwhile, in 1969 the institute had been housed in a larger building even closer to Amsterdam's city center. Before long this broke down under the increasing physical weight of the collections, which were hastily moved to a suburban warehouse abandoned by the International

Business Machines (IBM) Corporation in 1981. Only in 1989 did IISH move to what would seem to be more permanent premises in Amsterdam's lively Eastern Docks redevelopment area, its first home properly equipped with microclimate control and other amenities.

This journey around the city had been made necessary by the growing numbers of both collections and users. From the mid-1960s on, surging interest in the history of social movements caused reading-room attendance to quadruple in a decade. Books and pamphlets came in at such a rate that by the end of the 1970s the catalog backlog was estimated at 100,000 titles. As more space was clearly not enough, in 1984 the institute decided on a serious reorganization that introduced library automation (1987) and a subsystem for visual documents (1989), among many other things. Collection-level search aids for the archival collections also were first published in 1989.

The Present

Today virtual users outnumber those in the reading room by approximately 100 to 1. The online catalog and other search aids are accessible from a website as well as through the Research Libraries Information Network (RLIN) Archival Resources program of the Research Libraries Group (RLG). Other electronic facilities include Web guides, current bibliographies, discussion lists, and a news service. And although it has been an essential part of the institute's activities from the start, research has become increasingly important. Perhaps its best-known products are the *International Review of Social History* (1936–39; 1956–), published by Cambridge University Press, and the European Social Science History Conference, which every other year brings approximately 1,000 researchers from dozens of countries and many disciplines to the Netherlands.

Although many of the 19th-century Western European collections were complemented through extensive microfilming in Moscow after 1991, the focus of collection development has shifted away from Europe and toward the west, south, and Southeast Asia. As a result, the institute regularly undertakes oral history projects in order to supplement the often meager written resources that are found in the countries concerned. It also created the "Historical Sample of the Netherlands," a meta-source database created from local birth, death, and marriage registers from 1812 to 1922. Postings to selected Internet news groups, some dating as far back as 1990, are being archived on a daily basis. Offices and correspondents in Berlin, Moscow, Ankara, Karachi, Dakha, and Semarang support these new efforts to safeguard an international cultural heritage that still is, too often, in danger of disappearing.

JAAP KLOOSTERMAN

Further Reading

Haag, B. Jaap, and Atie van der Horst, editors, *Guide to the International Archives and Collections at the IISH, Amsterdam,* Amsterdam: International Institute of Social History, 1999

Lucassen, B. Jan, *Tracing the Past: Collections and Research in Social and Economic History: The International Institute of Social History, the Netherlands Economic History Archive, and Related Institutions,* Amsterdam: Stichting Beheer IISG, 1989

Jagiellonian Library

Address: Biblioteka Jagiellońska
al. Mickiewicza 22
30-059 Kraków
Poland
Telephone: 12-633-6377
Fax: 12-633-0903
www.bj.uj.edu.pl

Founded: 1364

Holdings (1999): Volumes: 3.5 million. Current serials: 25,000; *ex libris:* 20,000; incunabula: 3,632; manuscripts: 25,000; maps: 29,000; microforms: 86,000; music scores: 35,000; prints: 47,000.

Special Collections: *Areas of Concentration:* Arts and religious studies; history and theory of literature; linguistics; Polonica; Polish culture and composers. *Individual Collections:* Cartographic collection; graphic art collection; music collection; rare books. *Papers:* Frédéric Chopin; Nicolaus Copernicus; Tadeusz Kościuszko; Adam Mickiewicz; Stanisław Wyspiański.

Structure

The Biblioteka Jagiellońska (Jagiellonian Library) is the main library at Jagiellonian University. In addition, there are two departmental libraries and 46 institute libraries, which are administered independently from the Jagiellonian Library.

History

The history of the Jagiellonian Library is intertwined with the history of the Uniwersytet Jagielloński (Jagiellonian University), which was established on 12 May 1364 by Kazimierz III, King of Poland. It was first known as the Uniwersytet Krakowski (Kraków University), then from the 15th century until 1780 as the Akademia Krakowska (Kraków Academy). The university declined in the mid–14th century under the reign of Louis I, King of Hungary and Poland, and in 1400 Władysław II Jagiełło, King of Poland, using the personal property of his late wife, Queen Jadwiga, refounded the university and introduced wide-ranging organizational reforms.

The library holds three manuscripts dated 1367, 1368, and 1369 that were used for educational purposes at the university. Throughout its early history, the Jagiellonian Library was supported and built through the efforts of professors, students, and alumni. The first major gifts came from Professor Jan Isner, who donated 19 codices in 1410. Other notable donations came from Professor Jan Szczekna, who presented 24 items before 1407. In the mid–15th century, Tomasz of Strzempino (Bishop of Kraków and dean of the Kraków Academy) donated 43 codices, and Jakub Sienieński (Archbishop of Gniezno) donated illuminated manuscripts. In 1462 Professor and Dean Jan of Dąbrówka donated 75 codices, whereas Professor Maciej of Kobylin and Dean Andrzej Grzymała of Poznań donated 30 codices each. The notable Polish historian and chronicler Jan Długosz donated many codices and manuscripts of his own works, including *Banderia Prutenorum* from 1448.

As the university developed, separate libraries at various colleges and dormitories appeared. The largest was the library of the Collegium Maius of the theology and humanities departments, which became the main library of the university. In 1429 a library statute was enacted providing for two honorary curators, elected from among professors, who were authorized to lend books from the collection. After the fire of 1492, the Collegium Maius was rebuilt, and some rooms were designated for the collections. With the development of printing in the second half of the 15th century, the library received many more books. The collections of law, theology, and liberal arts books grew most rapidly. In 1515 professor of theology Tomasz Obiedziński endowed the library, enabling the university to enlarge the Collegium Maius for a new library. These quarters served the library for the next four centuries. In 1538 Bartłomiej of Lipnica endowed a position of curator for himself. The library received an endowment from Benedykt of Koźmin for the acquisition of books in 1559 and was able to buy 261 titles in 384 volumes between 1560 and 1646.

The tradition of book donations to the Jagiellonian Library continued throughout the 15th and 16th centuries. Many notable gifts from professors, students, and bibliophiles were received. In 1586 the library received part of the collection of Sigismund II Augustus, King of Poland. In 1631 professor, dean, mathematician, and astronomer Jan Brożek endowed the library, donating his personal collection of 2,000 volumes. Since the 16th century, the Jagiellonian Library has been renowned for its collections and has been visited by prominent personalities, including many Polish kings. To mark these occasions, a special dedication book was established for visitors, known as the *Księga królewska* (Royal Book). It is estimated that by 1520, the Jagiellonian Library held about 2,000 manuscripts, and that by the middle of the 17th century the library held 10,794 books in over 32,000 volumes.

During that same century, the role of the university declined. The Jesuit order, which had participated actively in education in the past, was dissolved in 1773. The Jagiellonian Library began to organize its collections in a more accessible way, and in 1775 the library hired bibliophile Arsenius Theodorus Fasseau for this task. By the time of his death two years later in 1777, he had organized the manuscript and book collections. Under his direction, two library catalogs were prepared. Professor of classical philology and poet Jacek Przybylski continued this organizational work between 1784 and 1803. In 1807 Anzelm Speiser created a card catalog of the collection, and by 1809 the library held 2,943 manuscripts, 29,994 books and pamphlets, and 2,273 coins.

Between 1777 and 1780 the Komisja Edukacji Narodowej (Commission for National Education), under the leadership of prominent politician and educational reformer Hugo Kołłątaj, supported the Jagiellonian University and the Jagiellonian Library, financially and organizationally. All university libraries were consolidated, and the collections of former Jesuit libraries were incorporated. From 1780 to 1795 the university was named the Szkoła Główna Koronna (Crown Main School), and from 1795 to 1815 it was called the Szkoła Główna Krakowska (Kraków Main School). Since 1815 the institution has been known as Jagiellonian University.

Historian and professor of Slavic languages Jerzy Samuel Bandtkie was director of the library from 1811 to 1835. Under his leadership the Jagiellonian Library doubled the size of its collections. Bandtkie published the first history of the library, *Historya Biblioteki Uniwersytetu Jagiellońskiego w Krakowie* (History of the Library of the Jagiellonian University in Kraków), in 1821. His successor, professor of bibliography Józef Muczkowski (1837–58), continued the expansion and reconstruction of the library. In the 19th century the entire Collegium Maius building was designated for the use of the library. Between 1795 and 1918 Poland was partitioned among Russia, Prussia, and Austria, with Kraków belonging to Austria. In 1862 Viennese authorities granted the Jagiellonian Library the right to receive obligatory legal deposit copies of any publication published in the Austro-Hungarian Empire.

In 1868 the noted Polish bibliographer Karol Józef Teofil Estreicher became director of the library and served until 1905. He had administered the Library of the Main School (today's Warsaw University Library) since 1862. Estreicher appealed to Polish society for help in building a library of national character. At the time of his arrival, the Jagiellonian Library claimed 92,199 books, 5,500 manuscripts, 1,258 maps, 3,889 prints, and about 25,000 volumes of Polonica. During his directorship the library's collections expanded to 274,465 books, 6,440 manuscripts, 2,192 maps, 9,673 prints, and 4,693 musical scores.

The number of Polonica volumes increased to 81,312. In 1888 the library received the personal papers and correspondence of prominent author Józef Ignacy Kraszewski.

Successive directors, professor of history Fryderyk Papée (1905–26) and historian Edward Kuntze (1927–47), modernized and expanded the library. The Jagiellonian Library completed construction of a new building in 1939 and moved its collections to a state-of-the-art building in 1940. During World War II the library functioned as the Staatsbibliothek Krakau (State Library of Kraków) under German administration.

After the war the Jagiellonian Library resumed its functions as a university library, receiving any publications published in Poland as well as materials acquired via purchase and exchange. The library expanded its building in the early 1960s to accommodate growing collections. The library recently opened a new building with state-of-the-art equipment. The Jagiellonian Library constitutes a second national library that collects books and periodicals about Poland and items published in Poland before 1800 and after 1945. In 1979 an intergovernmental decree established the Jagiellonian Library as the II Centralna Biblioteka Nauk Społecznych (Second Central Library of Social Sciences), and it became responsible for collecting research materials in culture, linguistics, history and theory of literature, arts, and religious studies.

Collections

The Oddział Rękopisów (Manuscript Collection) holds 25,689 manuscripts and is the largest collection of early manuscripts in Poland. One of the oldest manuscripts, dating from the late 11th or early 12th century, is *Timaeus Platonis, cum commento Calcidi*. The oldest manuscript written in Kraków is *Ius Magdeburgense*, dated around 1308. *Decretum Gratiani* by Gratian is a valuable collection of 12th-century legal manuscripts. Items related to the history of the Jagiellonian University also constitute an important group of manuscripts. The most important Polish manuscripts are the 13th-century *Bogurodzica* (Mother of God), a religious hymn about Saint Mary, Blessed Virgin; *De revolutionibus* (dated 1520–41), a manuscript handwritten by university alumnus Nicolaus Copernicus; and *Codex picturatus Balthasaris Behem*, named after its chief copyist Baltazar Behem, written and illustrated in Kraków in 1505. *Acta Tomiciana* is an important group of 16th-century manuscripts covering documents, acts, and letters issued during the reign of King Sigismund I. More recent manuscripts contain papers of Polish authors and scholars. The most valuable are the correspondence of Tadeusz Kościuszko, a general during the American Revolution and a leader of the Kościuszko Uprising in 1794; that of Adam Mickiewicz, a national poet; and that of Stanisław Wyspiański, an artist and author from Kraków.

The Odział Starych Druków (Rare Books Collection) comprises incunabula and 16th-century Polish imprints and Polonica. The most valuable items are incunabula from Johann Gutenberg's printing shop in the 1450s and from Kraków's printing presses in the 15th century. The library also holds first editions of works by Polish authors such as Mikołaj Rej, Jan

Kochanowski, Andrzej Frycz Modrzewski, and Marcin Bielski. The collection includes books from libraries of Polish kings Sigismund II Augustus, Sigismund III, and Władysław IV Zygmunt. Polonica from the 17th century constitutes another significant part of this collection.

The Odział Zbiorów Graficznych (Graphic Arts Collection), organized in 1919, includes graphic art by 18th-, 19th-, and 20th-century Polish artists such as Konstanty Brandel, Józef Pankiewicz, and Leon Wyczółkowski. The collection holds about 20,000 Polish bookplates dating from the 16th through 20th centuries and about 300 Italian miniature books from the 13th, 14th, and 15th centuries from the collection of Polish bibliophile Jan Sierakowski. About 40,000 photographs form another large part of this collection.

The Odział Zbiorów Kartograficznych (Cartographic Collection) includes material acquired by the library dating back to the 16th century. The most important items held in this collection are Ptolemy's *Liber geographiae* (1511), *Theatrum orbis terrarum* by Abraham Ortelius (1575), and *Delineatio Specialis et Accurata Ukrainae* by Guillaume Le Vasseur Beauplan (1650).

The Oddział Zbiorów Muzycznych (Music Collection) was formed in 1869 and contains scores and manuscripts of 19th- and 20th-century Polish composers, including Frédéric Chopin.

The largest departmental libraries are the Wydziałowa Biblioteka Prawnicza (Law Library; 142,000 items), the Bilioteka Instytutu Historii (Library of the Institute of History; 136,000 items), and the Biblioteka Instytutu Filologii Polskiej (Library of the Institute of Polish Language, 108,000 items).

Automation

Efforts to automate the Jagiellonian Library began in 1974, when the Krakowski Abonencki Kombinat Informacyjny Użytkowników Stowarzyszonych (KRAKUS) system was introduced to five research libraries in Kraków. In 1975 the library began working on creating a subsystem for its own use. Owing to financial and technical difficulties, work was suspended in 1981, but the library resumed its efforts in 1984. The library purchased its first microcomputer in 1986, and in 1992, with support from the Andrew W. Mellon Foundation, purchased a Virginia Tech Library System (VTLS), an integrated library system. The Jagiellonian Library is a part of the European Academic and Research Network (EARN).

Publications

The Jagiellonian Library has published many works on its history and collections, including multivolume catalogs. Some of the following catalogs are ongoing publications: *Catalogus Codicum Manuscriptorum Medii Aevi Latinorum qui in Bibliotheca Jagellonica Cracoviae Asservantur* (*Katalog łacińskich rękopisów średniowiecznych Biblioteki Jagiellońskiej*; Catalog of Medieval Latin Manuscripts in the Jagiellonian Library, 1980–); *Inwentarz rękopisów Biblioteki Jagiellońskiej* (Inventory of the Manuscripts in the Jagiellonian Library, 1962–); *Katalog czasopism polskich Biblioteki Jagiellońskiej* (Catalog of Polish Periodicals in the Jagiellonian Library, 1974–); *Katalog poloników XVI wieku Biblioteki Jagiellońskiej* (Catalog of Polonica from the 16th Century in the Jagiellonian Library, 1992–95); *Katalog rysunków architektonicznych ze zbiorów Biblioteki Jagiellońskiej w Krakowie* (Catalog of the Architectural Drawings in Collections of the Jagiellonian Library in Kraków, 1989); *Scientific Writings and Astronomical Tables in Cracow* (1984). It also publishes an annual serial *Biuletyn Biblioteki Jagiellońskiej* (Bulletin of the Jagiellonian Library, 1948–).

WOJCIECH SIEMASZKIEWICZ

Further Reading

Bar, Irena, editor, *Przewodnik po Bibliotece Jagiellońskiej* (Guide to the Jagiellonian Library), Kraków: Uniwersytet Jagielloński, 1964

Pirożyński, Jan, "The Jagiellonian Library in Cracow: The Past, the Present, and Prospects for the Future," *Polish Libraries Today* 2 (1993)

Zathey, Jerzy, Anna Lewicka-Kamińska, and Leszek Hajdukiewicz, *Historia Biblioteki Jagiellońskiej* (The History of the Jagiellonian Library), Kraków: Uniwersytet Jagielloński, 1966

Zimmer, Szczepan K., *The Jagellonian University Library in Cracow*, Brooklyn, New York: Czas, 1963

Jewish National and University Library

Address: Bet Ha-Sefarim Ha-Leummi Weha-Universitai
Giv'at Ram
Jerusalem 91341
Israel
Telephone: 2-6584651
Fax: 2-6511771
http://sites.huji.ac.il/jnul

Founded: 1892

Holdings (2000): Volumes: 3 million. Archives: 400; audio recordings: 21,000; current serials: 15,000; films and videos: 500; Hebrew incunabula: 100; Hebrew manuscripts: 10,000, including 2,000 medieval manuscripts; newspaper master negative reels: 15,000; old (pre-1900) maps: 6,000.

Special Collections: *Areas of Concentration:* Arab history and culture; Palestine and Israel; world Jewish history and culture. *Individual Collections:* Cartography of the Holy Land and the Near East; history and philosophy of science and technology; Jewish and general mysticism; manuscripts; microfilms of Hebrew manuscripts; personal archives, autographs, and portraits; sound archives. *Papers:* Joseph Achron; S.Y. Agnon; Paul Ben-Hayim; Walter Benjamin; Hugo Bergmann; Martin Buber; Albert Ehrenstein; Albert Einstein; Ahad Ha'am; Gustav Landauer; Else Lasker-Schüler; Itzik Manger; Joseph Popper-Lynkeus; Mordecai Seter.

Mission

The Jewish National and University Library (JNUL) combines three main functions. As the national library of the State of Israel it collects all Israeli publications, as well as all publications appearing elsewhere in the world that deal with the country. As the national library of the Jewish people, most of whom live outside the State of Israel, it collects all library materials that reflect or represent the history and culture of the Jewish people (mainly published works, manuscripts, personal archives, pictures, and recordings), including all works written in Hebrew script or in Jewish languages (such as Ladino and Yiddish). As a national library and the central library of the Hebrew University, it strives to build research collections in various academic fields, particularly those pertaining to the history of Israel or the Jews (such as Middle Eastern and European history).

The library is entitled by law to receive copies of all works published in Israel, including tangible electronic publications (such as audio and video cassettes and CDs). The library publishes the current national bibliography, *Kiryat Sefer,* a quarterly recording all new Israeli publications as well as worldwide Hebraica and Judaica publications collected by the library; and the *Index of Articles on Jewish Studies,* a semi-annual.

History

The idea of setting up a national library in Jerusalem, where all manuscript and printed books of the Jewish people would be preserved for future generations, was first aired in the January 1872 issue of *Habazeleth,* a Hebrew weekly published in Jerusalem. The response to the call was prompt and effective, and a library intended to fulfill this role was established by 1874. Notwithstanding difficulties that brought the subsequent closure of this library, a successor was opened in 1884. When this failed as well, a third library was established in 1892 by the B'nai B'rith Lodge in Jerusalem, and this one ultimately proved the nucleus from which the present Jewish National and University Library was to grow.

From its beginnings the library has been accessible to all, like a public library, in spite of its predominant national archival aims. Its role as a university library, however, was only assumed in the 1920s, when, under the auspices of the World Zionist Organization, it was integrated into the Hebrew University. The latter, established by the end of World War I, was actually opened on Mount Scopus in 1925, and the library moved over to its new premises there, named after David Wolffsohn, second president of the World Zionist Organization, in 1930.

The inclusion of the library in the structure of the Hebrew University—in 1924 the library was given the name by which it is known to this day—was an important step in its development. Its revised identity gave it a new direction and an academic quality that previously could not have been envisioned. During the first ten years as a university library, the number of volumes in its various collections grew rather impressively, thanks to help offered by many Jewish organizations worldwide, from 30,000 in 1920 to 230,000 in 1930.

The library did not remain on Mount Scopus for very long. Its days there came to an end when the 1948 War of Independence—the first Arab-Israeli war—began. By the end of 1947 Israeli access to Mount Scopus was becoming difficult, and in June 1948 it became nearly impossible. In the intervening months the catalog of the library was moved to the western part of the city, but most of the collections (then numbering some 460,000 volumes, including 180,000 Hebraica and Judaica) remained on Mount Scopus.

The planning and construction of new premises, as well as the creation of replacement collections, took most of the following decade, during which the library was physically scattered in various locations throughout the city. The new Lady Davis (Canada) Building, in the center of the university's new Giv'at Ram campus, eventually opened in 1960.

As in the past, much of the effort to build the new collections fell to individuals and organizations all over the world. A very substantial part of the new collections came, however, from an unexpected source—huge accumulations, in Germany and elsewhere in Europe, of books from Jewish institutional, communal, and private libraries that had been confiscated by German authorities during World War II and intended to constitute, in due course, a comprehensive library for Jewish studies. Some 500,000 volumes whose original owners were no longer there to retrieve them were transferred during the late 1940s and early 1950s to the National Library in Jerusalem, which served as the representative of the Jewish people in this matter. The library retained about half and distributed the rest to other libraries in Israel.

In the 1960s two major special collections were opened. In 1963 the Institute of Microfilms of Hebrew Manuscripts, founded in 1950 on an initiative of Prime Minister David Ben-Gurion, was transferred to the library. The purpose of this collection (now almost complete) is to provide scholars with copies of any Hebrew manuscripts held anywhere in the world. In 1964 the National Sound Archive was founded to collect and preserve recordings of traditional music of the various ethnic groups living in Israel and of Jewish communities abroad, as well as modern Israeli song. The collection presently contains some 250,000 items, most of them original recordings produced by ethnomusicologists, by the library on its own initiative, and by the Israeli radio services.

Another noteworthy change in the history of the library occurred gradually in the wake of another milestone in the history of Israel, the 1967 Six-Day War. Access to Mount Scopus was regained in the course of this war, and the Hebrew University began almost immediately to prepare its return to the old campus there. By 1980 the Faculty of Humanities and the Faculty of Social Sciences, the two main sources of university library users, had moved to the new campus on Mount Scopus, with the result that students and teachers of these faculties have gradually become less frequent users of the library, which remains in Giv'at Ram.

Collections

It is hardly unique to the JNUL, among other national libraries, that the acquisition of its most precious items has been dependent on gifts, rather than its regular budget. Moreover, some of the present special collections were initially private collections, donated or bequeathed to the library by their original creators. Examples include the Abraham Sharon (Schwadron) collection of Jewish autographs and portraits, donated in the 1920s, and two newer collections—the Eran Laor collection of Holy Land maps, itineraries, and descriptions, and the Sidney M. Edelstein collection in the history and philosophy of science and technology—which were given to the library in the 1970s.

Other noteworthy private collections donated to the library include the Max Eitingon collection in psychoanalysis and general humanities; the Harry Friedenwald collection in the history of medicine, with emphasis on the Jewish contribution to medicine; the Jacob Michael collection in Jewish music; the Salman Schocken collection of Hebrew incunabula; the Gershom Scholem collection in Jewish and general mysticism, occultism, and the history of religions; and the A.S. Yahuda collection in history and culture of the Arabs. Among the personal archives of Jewish and Israeli persons of importance, the library holds those of composers such as Joseph Achron, Paul Ben-Hayim, and Mordecai Seter; philosophers such as Hugo Bergmann and Martin Buber; political leaders such as Ahad Ha'am and Gustav Landauer; scholars and scientists such as Walter Benjamin, Albert Einstein, and Joseph Popper-Lynkeus; and writers such as S.Y. Agnon, Albert Ehrenstein, Else Lasker-Schüler, and Itzik Manger.

A National and University Library

The library is an administrative unit of the Hebrew University, and its budget is determined by the president and the rector of the university. Nevertheless, it has always enjoyed the freedom to design its collection development policy independently. Indeed, the successful balancing of national interests with those of a university is difficult, especially when resources are so limited. It may have seemed feasible in circumstances such as those existing in Jerusalem some 90 years ago. At that time, not many of the residents of the city could be regarded as potential library users, and it was only prudent that the young university, regarded as a unique national institution, and the still-embryonic national library would both consider cooperation to be crucial for their chances of survival.

One must bear in mind that building and preserving a comprehensive, nonselective national archival collection almost invariably means preferring national interests over local ones, long-term goals over immediate needs, and security and survival of materials over free access and convenience of use. This is hardly acceptable in a dynamic university community, and considerable care must be taken when reconciliation of such divergencies is required.

Such a combination becomes even more tricky when separate departmental libraries are created, as in the case of the Hebrew

University. Geographical distance between collections, administrative division, and divergent ambitions can all create some unnecessary duplication and a tendency to regard remotely held (and sometimes rather esoteric) collections as an unwelcome burden.

Having said that, and without claiming that the present combination can serve as a perfect model, one is still able to conclude that these conflicts have not seriously affected the library's ability to create a comprehensive national printed archive (books and periodicals, national and local newspapers, maps, music), a large collection of Hebrew manuscripts (mainly codices and legal documents), an almost complete collection of microfilm copies of Hebrew manuscripts, hundreds of personal archives of Jewish creators and leaders, a national sound archive, and even a rich collection of Israeli and Jewish ephemera.

JONATHAN JOEL

Further Reading

The Jewish National and University Library, Jerusalem: Hebrew University of Jerusalem, 1988

Joel, Jonathan, "The Jewish National and University Library, Jerusalem," *Alexandria* 12, no. 2 (2000)

John Carter Brown Library

Address: John Carter Brown Library
Box 1894
Providence, RI 02912
USA
Telephone: 401-863-2725
Fax: 401-863-3477
www.jcbl.org

Founded: 1846

Holdings (1999): Volumes: 55,000; current serials: 13; maps: 1000.

Special Collections: *Area of Concentration:* Colonial history of the Americas (North and South), 1492–1825.

The John Carter Brown Library is an independently funded and administered institution for advanced research in history and the humanities, located in its own building at Brown University since 1904. As a collection of printed materials pertaining to the entire Western Hemisphere during the colonial period (ca. 1492 to ca. 1825), including both European and American imprints, the John Carter Brown Library is generally considered among the most comprehensive.

In certain areas the library has few peers, such as European books about Brazil published before 1822; books printed in Mexico and Peru before 1700; American Revolutionary pamphlets printed in both London and the colonies; works in Native American languages dating from before 1800; German- and French-language titles about the Americas before 1800; and books and maps concerning the discovery of America from 1492 to 1750.

The scholarly value of the library's collection is extraordinary partly because its origins go back to a time when systematic book collecting around a historical theme was a rarity. Although the Brown family had been acquiring books since the early 18th century, the present collection was not fully launched until the mid-19th century, when John Carter Brown began avid pursuit of Americana, an area of interest he termed "the Great Subject." His son, John Nicholas Brown, actively continued this tradition and before his untimely death had conceived the idea of giving the library to the world of historical research as a memorial to his father.

In his will, John Nicholas Brown assigned funds for the construction of an appropriate building and for an endowment to support the library's work. The executors of the bequest, about a year after John Nicholas Brown's death, signed an agreement with the trustees of Brown University to locate the library on the university campus, and the original library building was formally dedicated in 1904. The John Carter Brown Library was apparently the first private research library in the United States to be converted into a charitable public institution endowed in perpetuity for the purpose of serving scholars. In 1990 the library raised the capital to construct a 15,000-square-foot addition to the original structure, designed, like the original, in the classical style and named the Caspersen Building.

When John Carter Brown's private library began to grow substantially in the mid-19th century, he recruited John Russell Bartlett, an experienced bibliophile, to serve informally as his librarian. In 1865 Bartlett published *Bibliotheca Americana. A Catalogue of Books Relating to North and South America in the Library of John Carter Brown of Providence, R. I.*, the first of a series of printed catalogs of the collection, which were published until 1973.

Bartlett was succeeded by George Parker Winship, who served as librarian from 1895 to 1915; Champlin Burrage, 1915 to 1916; Worthington C. Ford, acting librarian from 1916 to 1922; Lawrence C. Wroth, 1923 to 1956; Thomas R. Adams, 1957 to 1982; and currently Norman Fiering, who became librarian in 1983.

NORMAN FIERING

See also Brown University Library

Further Reading

The John Carter Brown Library, *The Dedication of the Library Building May the Seventeenth A.D. MDCCCCIIII, with the Addresses of William Vail Kellen and Frederick Jackson Turner,* Providence, Rhode Island: Merrymont Press, 1905

The John Carter Brown Library, *Opportunities for Research in the John Carter Brown Library,* Providence, Rhode Island: Brown University, 1968

Winship, George Parker, *The John Carter Brown Library: A History,* Providence, Rhode Island, and Boston: Merrymount Press, 1914

Wroth, Lawrence Couselman, *The First Century of the John Carter Brown Library: A History with a Guide to the Collections,* Providence, Rhode Island: Associates of the John Carter Brown Library, 1946

John Rylands University Library of Manchester

Address: Manchester University Main Library
Oxford Road
Manchester M13 9PP
UK
Telephone: 161-275-3751
Fax: 161-273-7488

John Rylands Library
150 Deansgate
Manchester M3 3EH
UK
Telephone: 161-834-5343
Fax: 161-834-5574
www.rylibweb.man.ac.uk

Founded: John Rylands Library, 1900; John Rylands University Library of Manchester, 1972

Holdings (1999): Volumes: 3.7 million. Archives and manuscripts: 8,000 linear feet; audiovisual materials: 15,000; current serials: 9,000; incunabula: 5,000; microforms: 800,000.

Special Collections: *Areas of Concentration:* Aldine Press; antislavery; colonial, commercial, economic, industrial, military, and social history; English and European literature; family muniments (especially Cheshire); history of science, technology, and medicine; incunabula; Jewish and Middle Eastern literature; nonconformist history; Oriental history and literature. *Papers:* Field-Marshal Sir Claude Auchinleck; Carcanet Press; John Dalton; Elizabeth Gaskell; Victor Hugo; William Stanley Jevons; *Manchester Guardian*; Manchester Medical Society; Methodist Church; John Ruskin.

The John Rylands University Library of Manchester (JRULM) is an amalgam of two libraries. Both were founded in the second half of the 19th century, when Manchester was one of the richest and fastest-growing cities in the world.

Owens College

Manchester University's origins lay in the foundation in 1851 of Owens College, created by a bequest from the local textile magnate John Owens. Its library initially relied heavily on benefactions. About 1,200 miscellaneous volumes from Owens's friend James Heywood were followed in 1870 by 7,000 theological and historical works donated by Bishop James Prince Lee. In 1873 the flourishing college moved from makeshift accommodation in the city center to the fine buildings designed by Alfred Waterhouse at the heart of the present campus. In 1880 Manchester became the lead college in the federal institution (to include Liverpool and Leeds) known as the Victoria University. The library expanded to accommodate gifts such as Angus Smith's 4,000 physics and chemistry books in 1885 and Edward Augustus Freeman's 6,500 historical works in 1892. Its greatest benefactor, Richard Copley Christie, not only funded the university's first separate library building (again designed by Waterhouse), which opened in 1898, but also left to the library, at his death in 1902, his outstanding collection of more than 8,000 early printed books. By 1903, the year in which the federal university was disbanded and Owens College became the Victoria University of Manchester, its library housed about 100,000 volumes.

The University of Manchester

Expansion of stock and facilities was sustained during the long librarianship of C.W.E. Leigh (1905–36). By 1930 some 80,000 volumes from the Manchester Medical Society (founded in 1834) had been transferred to the library. Extensions to Christie's building in 1914 and 1927 were followed by the opening in 1936 of a separate Arts and Humanities Library, itself greatly extended in 1956. By 1936 the library, excluding holdings in medical and departmental libraries, housed about 270,000 volumes.

Leigh's similarly long-serving successor, Dr. Moses Tyson, moved from the John Rylands Library to become librarian. He established both bindery and photography departments. By his retirement in 1965 the printed book stock amounted to about 770,000 volumes, of which 100,000 were designated as Special Collections. Departmental libraries (notably those dealing with medicine, social sciences, law, education, and music) became significant in their own right.

The arrival in 1965 of Frederick Ratcliffe as librarian coincided with expansion of British university education backed by generous central funding. Ratcliffe expanded the library by massive purchasing and by actively seeking gifts and deposits of printed and archival collections in private and institutional hands. The archives of the *Manchester Guardian* newspaper were received in 1971. By 1972 the library's printed book stock had passed the 1 million mark. In July of the same year, Ratcliffe achieved his greatest coup when the university library merged with the hitherto independent John Rylands Library.

The John Rylands Library

The Rylands Library was created by Enriqueta Rylands, third wife and widow of the leading Manchester cotton entrepreneur John Rylands. Her monument to her husband was an extravagant neo-Gothic edifice of Cumbrian sandstone and Danzig oak designed by Basil Champneys. Originally conceived as a public library with a bias toward Nonconformist theology, the whole concept was transformed by the purchase in 1892 of 43,000 rare and early printed books, including 3,000 incunabula, from the private library of Earl Spencer. Already an institution of great potential to international scholarship when it opened to the public in 1900, its scope was enhanced in 1901 by the acquisition of the Earl of Crawford's collection of 6,000 Western, Middle Eastern, and Oriental manuscripts featuring exceptional holdings of Latin, Arabic, and Persian material. In 1921 Librarian Henry Guppy, who served from 1899 to 1948, initiated the library's role as an archive repository.

Although Mrs. Rylands had provided endowments that initially made possible an extensive purchasing policy, publication of the *Bulletin* (which still flourishes today) beginning in 1903, and an extension to the library, the endowments' concentration in cotton investments proved disastrous when that industry entered its long decline. By the 1960s doubts were growing as to the library's viability as an independent entity. However, links with Manchester University had always been close, and a policy of modest assistance (from 1949) led eventually to formal amalgamation in 1972 under the title of John Rylands University Library of Manchester (JRULM). The new creation was, after Oxford and Cambridge, by far the largest academic library in Britain.

The John Rylands University Library of Manchester

The late 1970s were dominated by three themes. In-house expertise produced online issuing and ordering systems by 1980. Computerized cataloging followed shortly after. The other two projects—the quest for copyright deposit status and for a solution to the problem of space—were rooted in Ratcliffe's policy of expansion but were also pursued within the context of worsening funding. In 1977 a government committee proposed copyright deposit status similar to that enjoyed by Oxford and Cambridge, but the recommendation was never implemented. As the accommodation crisis became acute, progress toward the construction of a massive extension to the main library proceeded in tandem with a policy of transferring less-used stock to outside storage. Large-scale acquisition, however, continued.

In 1977 the main archives of the Methodist Church were deposited. In the following year the entire library of the Tabley estate in Cheshire was purchased. It contained the collections of many generations of serious book collectors from the early 17th century on.

Ratcliffe's career at Manchester culminated with the completion of a building extension in 1981, bringing together virtually all of the research and teaching collections of the university except the special collections housed in the old John Rylands Library. The opening of the new building coincided with the arrival of a new librarian, Michael Pegg. An unfriendly economic environment did not make his period of office easy, but significant developments took place, partially stimulated by the inability to continue collection building on the same scale as in previous years.

In the 1970s the library was a pioneer in the United Kingdom in the development of computer-based organizational systems and in the new networked information technologies of the Medical Literature Analysis and Retrieval System (MEDLARS). By 1985 the librarian reported that progress was being made "in an information network which will ultimately spread throughout the University and beyond." In 1987 the Consortium of University Research Libraries (CURL) began the creation of a unified database of the holdings of the most important British academic libraries: the JRULM designed and housed the project, now known as COPAC.

Throughout the 1980s the Special Collections Division suffered particularly badly from the harsh financial climate. A growing awareness of the quantity of unlisted and therefore inaccessible material threatened to damage the original Rylands Library's reputation as an important center of scholarship. By the middle of the decade there was serious questioning of the value to the university of an expensive and underused building. From 1986 vigorous efforts to publicize the Rylands's resources and to improve access began with a series of published guides to the collections. In the absence of adequate conventional funding and of any apparent prospect of external benefaction, the library launched the John Rylands Research Institute on the strength of the sale of 90 early printed books in 1988. A national campaign against the sale on the grounds of alleged breach of trust failed. In its aftermath, judicious investment of the £1.5 million proceeds from the book sale financed the cataloging of archives and manuscripts, conservation, and scholarly research, also providing for investment in staff and facilities to upgrade exhibitions and promote the library. Within six years reader usage doubled and general visitors almost tripled.

In 1991 Christopher Hunt was appointed library director. Fundamental changes occurred in the nature of library services, accompanied and stimulated by raised expectations on the part of users of all kinds. By the end of the decade, the JRULM was a hybrid institution: Web-based services were the norm and the larger part of all catalogs were in electronic format. The library was a founding member of an energetic subregional organization, the Consortium of Academic Libraries in Manchester

(CALIM), that encouraged and governed interuse of library and information facilities by members of all four Manchester universities. Similar coordination occurred nationally (within CURL) and internationally (within the Research Library Group, or RLG).

Finally, use of the great printed collections increased substantially. At the beginning of the 1990s, six major catalogs and more than 20 (often very unsatisfactory) lesser ones had to be consulted to discover what was in the old John Rylands Library. By 2000 nearly all of this material was in a single catalog database available, with collection descriptions, on the Web.

PETER MCNIVEN

Further Reading

Field, Clive, "A Literary Paradise Regained: The John Rylands University Library of Manchester," *Bookdealer* 871 (27 October 1988) and 872 (3 November 1988)

Guppy, Henry, *The John Rylands Library, Manchester: 1899–1935*, Manchester: Manchester University Press, 1935

Hodgson, John, editor, *A Guide to Special Collections of the John Rylands University Library of Manchester*, Manchester: John Rylands University Library of Manchester, 1999

Maddison, John, "Basil Champneys and the John Rylands Library," in *Art and Architecture in Victorian Manchester*, edited by John H.G. Archer, Manchester: Manchester University Press, 1985

Ratcliffe, Frederick, "The John Rylands University Library of Manchester," in *Encyclopedia of Library and Information Science*, edited by Allen Kent et al., vol. 17, New York: Dekker, 1969

Taylor, Frank, "The John Rylands Library, 1936–72," *Bulletin of the John Rylands University Library of Manchester* 71 (1989)

Tyson, Moses, *The Manchester University Library*, Manchester: Manchester University Press, 1937

Johns Hopkins University Libraries (Including the George Peabody Library)

Address: Milton S. Eisenhower Library
Johns Hopkins University
3400 N. Charles St.
Baltimore, Maryland 21218
USA
Telephone: 410-516-8335
Fax: 410-516-5080
http://milton.mse.jhu.edu

Founded: 1876; George Peabody Library founded 1866

Holdings (2000): Volumes: 3.4 million. Archives and manuscripts: 14,000 linear feet; audio, video, and film materials: 30,000; current serials: 23,000; incunabula: c. 500; maps: 211,000; microforms: 4 million.

Special Collections: *Areas of Concentration:* Biosciences; cartography; economic and political thought; English literature of the 16th and 17th centuries; German literature; history of medicine, anatomy, surgery, and public health; natural history; Near Eastern and scriptural studies; Romance languages and philology; voyages and exploration. *Individual Collections:* Birney anti-slavery collection; consolidated Bibles collection; Dickey collection of Byron and his contemporaries; Fowler architectural collection; Garrett Americana collection; Hutzler collection of economic classics; Lester S. Levy sheet music collection; Machen, Garrett, and Peabody incunabula collections; Edmund Spenser and his contemporaries; Louis Zukofsky and American modernist poetry. *Papers:* American higher education; W.K. Brooks; Elliott Coleman; D.C. Gilman; Sidney Lanier; Adolf Meyer; Ira Remsen; Benjamin Rowland; William H. Welch; Abel Wolman.

Origins

The evolution of the Johns Hopkins libraries is linked to the special missions of the pioneer university and medical institutions they serve. This history was initially marked by the gifts of two 19th-century philanthropists—Baltimore merchant Johns Hopkins and the Massachusetts-born, London-based financier George Peabody. The former endowed a university and a hospital; the latter had earlier established a library, music conservatory, and lecture lyceum under the terms of his 1857 gift "to raise the culture of Baltimore." Peabody's example inspired Hopkins' gift, but it also made possible the direction that gift would take. Although the Peabody and Hopkins libraries were not completely consolidated until 1982, their histories had been closely interdigitated for more than a century.

In 1869 Hopkins, a Quaker bachelor, incorporated the university and hospital for which he is remembered and to which he left equal shares of his considerable fortune. Although he at that time named the trustees of both institutions, the funding was by testamentary bequest. He died on 24 December 1873; the probated estate amounted to roughly $7 million. The university's half-share of the estate was then the largest single gift ever made to higher education in the United States. This meant the institution started its life handsomely endowed and capable of embodying a concept new to the U. S. scene. Precisely what the donor meant by "university" is, however, far from clear. Charles S. Peirce, an early faculty appointment, referred to the will as "a certain testament, happily free from all definite ideas." The trustees sought a leader who could define these ideas. After a nation-wide consultation with educational leaders, they settled on Daniel Coit Gilman, who was inaugurated as the president of the new university in February 1876.

The Hopkins bequest to the university was free of the usual restrictive stipulations that can hobble educational institutions at their birth. Thus unconstrained by the donor and the trustees, the new university, an engine to "advance" and "diffuse" knowledge, was essentially Gilman's creation. He had studied briefly at Humboldt's University of Berlin, and during his New Haven years, had drawn up plans for the scientific school at Yale University and had endured a rather frustrating experience as Yale librarian. Consequently he had some practical sense of a European model and of U. S. research needs. It was his task and achievement to found what is often styled as the first true university in America.

In addressing this task Gilman had traveled widely and consulted energetically on both sides of the Atlantic. He applied himself to recruiting a cadre of world-class scholars, and, as president, to establishing a scholarly press, encouraging new journals, and introducing new methods in the classrooms and laboratories. But surprisingly, he began his research university without anything like an adequate in-house library. Despite his absolute statement in the *Annual Report for 1878* that "There is no such thing as a strong university apart from a great library," the very modest budgets during the early years hardly seem to bear out this conviction. The administrative equivocation rests on the character and proximity of the Peabody Library—a scholarly reference collection only a few blocks from the original Hopkins campus, which by 1876 contained almost 60,000 carefully chosen volumes in all academic fields except medicine and law.

George Peabody Library

Although it was an important element of Peabody's 1857 gift, his non-circulating scholarly library did not open to the public until 1866, after the Civil War had ended. Originally located in the Renaissance Revival building on Mount Vernon Place housing the Peabody Institute, the rapidly growing collection was moved in 1878 to its present home in the skillfully integrated east wing designed by Edmund G. Lind. Like the original building, this wing is faced with local marble; successive elevation studies by the architect reflect the thought that went into unifying the two structures into a single facade. The glory of the library wing is the main book hall, completely surrounded by stacks that rise, supported on structural and decorative ironwork, six floors to the sky-lighted ceiling. Of additional historical interest, Lind's design is one of the earliest examples of fireproof library construction: French tile blocks were used to insulate the cast- and wrought-iron columns and beams, which, anchored in the masonry walls and foundation, form the structural grid. This is covered with decorative cast-iron in the Néo-Grec style. The great hall was carefully renovated in the 1970s and remains one of Baltimore's noblest interiors.

The Peabody collection (which during the early years of the university was compared favorably as a research resource with the Library of Congress) consists predominantly of 18th- and 19th-century imprints, although there are additional earlier strengths in incunabula, exploration, archaeology, architecture, natural history, and cartography. Over the past two decades strenuous efforts have been expended in preservation and restoration. Also, all titles and the more important archival materials are in the process of conversion to the university's online catalog (a task approximately 95 percent completed).

Early Years at Johns Hopkins: Howard Street

The library of the new university and its subsequent trajectory were thus influenced by the presence of the Peabody and by the emphasis on graduate education and research. For many decades it was a matter of policy not to duplicate the Peabody holdings, and the Hopkins collections have historically been built on a single-copy-per-title principle. (The instructional frustrations as the student population grew have only lately been relieved by technological developments, such as electronic reserves for use in courses.) There was also a pattern extending as late as the 1940s that the librarian would often be concurrently engaged in other academic or administrative pursuits.

The first librarian, charged with installing a general reference collection in time for the October 1876 opening of classes, was Thomas C. Murray (1875–77), a faculty associate in Semitic languages. He inherited a small collection of books that had been assembled for the use of the trustees and immediately set about ordering reference titles and deploying them in a main reading room and suite of five smaller rooms in the recently completed Hopkins Hall. By the end of the academic year he was, however, completely absorbed in his lectures and turned over his post to Arthur W. Tyler, from New York City's Astor Library, who thus brought some professional experience but who tarried only briefly in Baltimore, resigning in 1878. He was succeeded in 1879 (on an interim basis) by one of Gilman's first graduate fellows, A. Duncan Savage, a paleographer.

In October 1879 William Hand Browne assumed the post of librarian at the same time that he joined the faculty in English. He had wide-ranging interests in history and literature and had earlier taken a medical degree although he never practiced medicine. Under his direction the library, which still had but a trifling budget for bound volumes, developed some of the characteristics of a modern research institution, including a broad, international subscription base in serials; an emerging sense of partnership with its peers through interlibrary loans; and the ability to attract significant gifts. Thus by 1889 (after the university's first major financial crisis) the library had more than 1,000 serials under subscription, putting it in a league with the major German universities. In the same year it also received its largest legacy to that date, the library of John W. McCoy of approximately 8,000 choice books. By this time the familiar problem of inadequate space had also emerged, one of the burdens that prompted Browne to resign in 1891 and devote his energies to his faculty appointment.

His successor, Nicholas Murray (1891–1908), had been an assistant to Gilman and as such had been charged with the management of the university's publications, thus becoming the first director of the oldest university press in the nation. Without relinquishing any of his responsibilities to the Publication Agency, as the press was then called, he had also become, in 1883, the assistant librarian. In 1894 he managed the transfer of the library to the newly built McCoy Hall. One floor was devoted to a reference area, general library, and main reading room, but the bulk of the collection was divided among departmental libraries on the other floors. In addition to stacks, each of these included a seminar room with holdings in the specific discipline. This deployment, thought appropriate to the "university idea" of advanced study and research, became a strong tradition at Hopkins that was not significantly altered for 70 years. Most scientific works accordingly were dispersed to the laboratory buildings. Murray's tenure ended sadly with a fire in McCoy Hall on 17 September 1908. Deeply shaken by the substantial damage and losses incurred as a result of the fire, he retired the following week.

He was succeeded by his assistant librarian, M. Llewellyn Raney (1908–27), whose long tenure spanned two campuses and major changes in library management. He supervised the repair of the McCoy Hall facilities and, in the following year, undertook the recataloging and reclassification of the entire library, also appointing a chief cataloger.

Homewood: Gilman Hall

Plans for a "permanent" campus had been underway since early in the Gilman administration but were delayed by several financial crises and the delicate negotiations to acquire sufficient land for growth. By 1902 the university had consolidated its property on North Charles Street, including the Wyman Estate and Homewood House (built in 1801), the split-wing Federal country seat of Charles Carroll Jr. that established the architectural idiom for the new campus. Gilman Hall, a large neo-Colonial structure designed by Parker and Thomas and completed in 1915, was its centerpiece. Traditional on its exterior, the multiuse building, described by its architects as a "pedagogy and research unit," was more innovative in its interior disposition. An outer ring of seminar rooms and faculty offices in the humanities and social sciences surrounded a core of eight floors of stacks and study facilities organized on the departmental basis. When the library (now numbering 196,864 volumes) was installed in 1916, Raney, as recorded in the *Librarian's Report: 1915–16,* spoke of the unique interior arrangements as "the first apartment house among the libraries of the world." Most of the books and journals in the sciences, following the Hopkins tradition of departmentalization (or balkanization), were deployed to the appropriate laboratory buildings as they were constructed. From 1918 to 1921, the university received a major gift from Sir William and Lady Osler establishing, in memory of their son Revere, the Tudor and Stuart Club, an association and collection devoted to the literature and history of the period. The clubrooms and rare books were installed in Gilman Hall. The library and faculty advisers decided to devote a substantial part of the Osler endowment to extending the collection's early editions of Edmund Spenser. This led to the publication, under the general editorship of Edwin Greenlaw, of the monumental *Works of Edmund Spenser: A Variorum Edition* (1932–57).

Raney resigned in 1927 to accept the directorship of the University of Chicago Library. His successor was John C. French (1927–43), called from his post as Collegiate Professor of English. During his tenure he was faced with the severely straitened finances of the Great Depression and the disruptions of the World War II years. This task was somewhat lightened by two events, early and late, that substantially promoted the growth of the library. The first was the organization in 1931 of one of the earliest "Friends of the Library" societies. The founders pledged annual support for acquisitions, lectures, exhibits, a newsletter (*Ex Libris*), and advocacy. The immediate effect on the morale of the faculty and library staff may have been as important as the vital financial support. Over the years the Friends group has grown in size and range of activities, and its purchases have repaired many gaps in the collections. The second event, at the end of French's service, was the bequest in 1942 of the John Work Garrett Library, a collection of exceptional range and quality (more than 30,000 items, from illuminated manuscripts, 140 incunabula, and the four Shakespeare folios to exploration, Americana, and natural history treasures such as Audubon's elephant-folio of *Birds of America*). The repository, Evergreen House, an eclectic Classical Revival mansion at 4545 North Charles Street, passed to the university on Mrs. Garrett's death a decade later. Evergreen, now the university's major rare book center, was extensively renovated from 1986 to 1991, and it also contains the Garretts' collections of art, prints, ethnographic material, and *objets d'art*.

The Welch Medical Library

After years of planning, the Johns Hopkins Hospital opened in 1889; its architect and master planner was John Shaw Billings, also a surgeon and librarian. Billings had fostered the Surgeon-General's Library (since 1956, the National Library of Medicine, Bethesda, Maryland) and created two landmark bibliomedicals, the *Index-Catalogue* (1880–95) and *Index Medicus* (1879– , since 1971 *Medline*); after his Hopkins years, he was the first head of the newly consolidated New York Public Library (1896–1913). In his design Billings made generous accommodations in the main administration building for a library to serve the hospital and, after its opening in 1893, the new medical school. The rapid growth of medical science at Hopkins during the so-called heroic age impelled two of the founding doctors, Osler and William H. Welch (first dean of the medical school), early in the new century to issue calls for a centralized library. Meanwhile departmental libraries, like the medical specialties they served, proliferated. Welch moved on to a second career in 1917 as founder-director of the pioneer School of Hygiene, an experience that strengthened his conviction about the need for a central library facility. He achieved this dream (and his third career) with the joint inauguration in 1929 of the Welch Medical Library and the Institute of the History of Medicine, both housed, then as now, along with the John Singer Sargent portraits of the "Four Doctors" and Mary Garrett, in an imposing Renaissance-style building designed by E.L. Tilton. The library (serving both the university and hospital halves of Hopkins' bequest) and the institute (with its own collection of rare imprints, manuscripts, and instruments) quickly became international centers for historical studies and technological innovation in current information retrieval. Consolidated holdings, including the Lilienfeld Library (public health) and other specialized collections, now total 700,000 volumes. The Chesney Medical Archives, which maintains an active website, currently includes more than 200 collections of personal papers in the fields of medicine, nursing, and public health.

Milton S. Eisenhower Library

The next librarian at the Homewood campus, Homer Halvorson (1943–53), had to cope with the growing stringencies of the Gilman Hall facility, whose contents had tripled in its first half century of use. As early as 1946 he raised the possibility of a repository library for non-circulating material. Although this solution was rejected, holdings at Homewood were by then dispersed between Gilman and seven other buildings. His successor, John Berthel (1954–73), after architectural studies and faculty debates, presided over the planning and construction of a new library building—more accurately, the first central library in the university's history. The decision required a four-year fund-raising effort, but ground was broken in 1962 at the east end of the original quadrangle, facing Gilman Hall. To preserve the scale of Homewood House to the northeast, five of the six floors were constructed below the level of the quadrangle. The Milton S. Eisenhower Library (MSEL) was finally opened in November 1964 with 1.1 million volumes. The original core stacks in Gilman were reserved for storage, while its elegant Hutzler Reading Room became an independent undergraduate study facility.

With the new building came new systems. The expansion in facilities and operations that followed shaped the history of the next 15 years. With the arrival of Berthel's successor, David H. Stam (1973–78), a university library council was formed to coordinate all the libraries of the university's divisions. In 1975 a new computerized circulation system was introduced at the MSEL, replacing an ingenious if labor-intensive punch-card automation, based on a Hopkins Operations Research dissertation, that had allowed daily circulation readouts during the paleohistory of access management. In the same year the library joined the online bibliographic service OCLC, and in 1976 a university bindery and restoration department with a professional training program was opened. In 1976 the library also received the Lester Levy collection of sheet music, a unique record of American popular music and culture from 1780 that now numbers 33,000 items. Recently, as part of a large-scale scanning project, all material out of copyright— approximately 90 percent—has been made available online; under a National Science Foundation grant, a project targeted for completion in 2002 is underway to allow researchers to see and hear the music simultaneously.

When Stam left in 1978 to assume the directorship of research libraries at the New York Public Library, he was succeeded by Susan K. Martin (1978–88), who in the same year directed the library's entry into the Research Libraries Group. Her tenure was marked by significant changes in the university's activities that affected the library: the opening of a new engineering school (1979); the decision by the National Aeronautics and Space Administration (NASA) to locate its Space Telescope Science Institute at Homewood (1981); the complete integration of the Peabody Library (1982); and the opening of the Hopkins-Nanjing Center for Chinese and American Studies (1986). In 1985 MSEL was one of ten research institutions to receive a major National Endowment for the Humanities grant to enter bibliographic material into the Research Libraries Information Network (RLIN). In 1987 the library acquired its 2-millionth volume. Inevitably, space problems were again pressing. Following Martin's departure to Washington, Johanna Hershey (1988–89) was named acting librarian and oversaw the introduction of an online system with remote capabilities (Janus).

Scott Bennett (1989–94) was appointed library director in 1989, the year the university budget topped $1 billion dollars. His tenure saw the development of a book deacidification program, completion of the Evergreen House renovation, and the beginning of a collaboration with the Johns Hopkins University Press (JHUP, founded 1878) in a pioneer Web-based electronic journal-publishing venture (Project Muse), which currently issues 115 titles. After Bennett left to become director of the Yale University libraries, Stephen Nichols (1994–95) took leave from his faculty appointment for a year to serve as interim librarian. In 1995 the library opened an off-campus, high-density shelving facility with an initial transfer of 400,000 titles and annual transfers in equilibrium with acquisitions.

James Neal (1995–2001) took the helm of a library system that was rapidly moving into the digital era. Four divisions—MSEL, the Garrett Library, the Hutzler Reading Room, and the Peabody Library—were consolidated into the Sheridan Libraries, honoring the bibliophile donors whose generosity insured the success of a $50-million campaign—R. Champlin Sheridan (class of 1952), founder of the publishing group that bears his name, and his wife, Debbie. For the first time the rare books and manuscripts in these divisions (which later incorporated the university archives) were brought under a single management. (Major special collections in medicine and public health [Welch Library] and music [Friedheim Library] are still independent library divisions.) In the wake of the apprehension of Gilbert Bland, who had stolen 18th-century maps from the Peabody reading room as well as from other research institutions, one of the first acts of Cynthia Requardt, the Kurrelmeyer Curator of Special Collections under the consolidation, was to institute new security procedures and exchange information with other victimized libraries. During 1997–98, with foundation support, a client/server-based management system (*Horizon*) was installed that finally included all Hopkins libraries in a single, integrated Web-based catalog. The reshaping of the library community by digitalization has been so rapid and various that it must suffice here to summarize from Dean Neal's *Five-Year Report* for the Sheridan Libraries (1999) the focus of the strategic digital library plan on eight key activities, with some examples: (1) expanded access to electronic information resources (from new searchable databases to specific projects such as the Geographic Information Systems and electronic exhibitions of rare books and prints); (2) a more sophisticated management system; (3) application of metadata for the structural searching and analysis of digitized documents (medieval manuscripts project in consortium with Walters Art Gallery [Baltimore] and the Pierpont Morgan Library [New York City]); (4) partnership with faculty in development of electronic courseware; (5) digital conversion of print collections (archives and the Levy collection); (6) collaboration in electronic scholarly publishing initiatives (Project Muse); (7) experimental application of emerging technologies (an on-demand, robotic scanning and retrieval service for the off-campus storage facility); and (8) participation in entrepreneurial enterprises (a consumer-oriented online health service; a virtual library service for other educational institutions). A physical renovation of the three service levels of the

MSEL was completed in 1997, and there are ambitious plans for a renovation of Gilman Hall, including the library's core space.

On the international scene, at the request of the Turkish government the university in 2000 returned to an Istanbul library a significant manuscript, the first 18 sutras of the ninth-century "Gold Koran." The text, in an early Arabic script (*Kufa*), was done entirely in gold leaf, the only intact example of this practice, and had been appraised in 1998 at up to $2.9 million. The manuscript had disappeared from Turkey at some point after an inventory of 1756; it came to the library as part of a 1942 bequest, and Turkey emphasized that Hopkins had in no way acted improperly in its acquisition. Reunited with its other half, it was identified as a national treasure and will be housed in the Nuruosmaniye Library (Istanbul). Among other recent library developments, 2001 marked (1) the establishment (in cooperation with the JHUP) of the Eisenhower Press to publish (both electronically and in hard copy) scholarly conferences and monographs as well as historical materials from the archives; (2) the funding of a virtual showcase for the rich art resources in the Baltimore area, a Web-based project of the Baltimore Art Resource Online Consortium (BAROC); (3) through an award from the Delmas and Kress Foundations, another consortial venture (with the Pierpont Morgan and the Bodleian [Oxford] libraries) expanding the search capabilities of the *Roman de la Rose* website for medieval manuscripts to include "structural" features such as rubrics and miniatures; and, finally (4), the establishment of a new Center for Educational Resources based in the Sheridan Libraries. In many—and often subtle—ways, digital technology and partnerships are thus effecting an *ongoing renovation* of the library's virtual functions, user access, and global capabilities. In July, 2001, after six busy years at Hopkins, James Neal announced his decision to accept an appointment as Vice President for Information Services and University Librarian at Columbia University (New York).

RICHARD MACKSEY

Further Reading

Baer, Elizabeth, *Seventeenth-Century Maryland: A Bibliography*, Baltimore, Maryland: Garrett Library, 1949

Dorsey, John, and James D. Dilts, *A Guide to Baltimore Architecture*, Cambridge, Maryland: Tidewater, 1973; 3rd edition, Centreville, Maryland: Tidewater, 1997

Ex Libris: The Johns Hopkins University Libraries (1931–)

Fowler, Laurence Hall, and Elizabeth Baer, *The Fowler Architectural Collection of the Johns Hopkins University*, Baltimore, Maryland: Evergreen Foundation, 1961

French, John Calvin, *A History of the University Founded by Johns Hopkins*, Baltimore, Maryland: Johns Hopkins Press, 1946

Harvey, A. McGehee, et al., *A Model of Its Kind*, 2 vols., Baltimore, Maryland: Johns Hopkins University Press, 1989

Hawkins, Hugh, *Pioneer: A History of the Johns Hopkins University, 1874–1889*, Ithaca, New York: Cornell University Press, 1960

Macksey, Richard, *A Brief Academic History of The Johns Hopkins University: The Pioneer Century: 1876–1976*, Baltimore, Maryland: Johns Hopkins University, 1976; revised edition, as *The Evolution of an Idea: Hopkins at 125*, 2001

Neal, James, *The Sheridan Libraries: A Five-Year Report*, Baltimore, Maryland: Johns Hopkins University, 1999

Schmidt, John C., *Johns Hopkins: Portrait of a University*, Baltimore, Maryland: Johns Hopkins University, 1986

Warren, Mame, editor, *Johns Hopkins: Knowledge for the World*, Baltimore, Maryland: Johns Hopkins University, 2000

The William H. Welch Medical Library of the Johns Hopkins University, Baltimore, Maryland: Johns Hopkins Hospital, 1930

Kyoto University Library

Address: Kyoto Daigaku Toshokan
Kyoto University
Yoshida Honmachi
Sakyo-ku, Kyoto 606-8501
Japan
Telephone: 75-753-2632; 75-753-2636
Fax: 75-753-2650
www.kulib.kyoto-u.ac.jp

Founded: 1899

Holdings (2000): Volumes: 5.7 million. Current serials: 30,000; microforms: 97,000.

Special Collections: *Areas of Concentration:* Rare books in Chinese, Japanese, and Western histories. *Individual Collections:* Fujikawa Yu; Kawai Hirotami; Konoe family; Nakagami Kazuto; Nakai family; Nakanoin Michinori; Saionji Kinmochi; Seike family; Shimada Bankon; Tanimura Ichitaro.

Origins

The first public university in Japan, the Imperial University of Tokyo, was established in Tokyo in 1877 by the central government with a mission to modernize society and to help Japan catch up with Western civilization at the fastest speed possible. Kyoto Imperial University was founded on 18 June 1897, the second university to be established in Japan. Established in the former capital city, Kyoto, the university's distance from Tokyo authorities allowed it to be more independent of state control, a situation that continues to manifest itself as a tradition of freedom for teachers and students. The benefits of liberty are clear, and the university has produced many outstanding scholars, including four Nobel Prize winners.

On 29 August 1897, immediately after the establishment of the university, the first president (Kinoshita Hiroji, 1897–1907) announced the basic idea of the Kyoto Imperial University Library in the *Osaka Mainichi Shinbun* (Osaka Daily Newspaper):

> Let the doors of the university library be open to the public. In Europe, libraries are the index of the level of the culture. ... But, we have no [academic] library except for one located in Tokyo. ... There must be another library so as to meet the needs of the citizens in the western part of Japan.

Thus the basic principle of the university library is that of the open library. By August 1897 the library had 40,000 volumes, and in July 1898 a two-story library building (the stack room) was finished, and the reading room completed by July 1899. The library was opened on 11 December 1899, a day designated as Foundation Day of the library. Actually, it took much longer to complete the entire structure. The office room was not completed until March 1918, and not until 1925 was the library complete. During a December 1909 visit to the United States, university President Kikuchi Dairoku (1908–12) visited the Library of Congress (LC) and met Librarian Herbert Putnam. As a result of this meeting, LC began to send its catalog cards to the library of Kyoto University.

World War II and the Library

On 21 April 1934 the *Kyoto Teikoku Daigaku Shinbun* (Kyoto Imperial University Newspaper) proudly reported that "the collection of the library has reached one million volumes. Of those, 700,000 volumes have been collected during these 20 years." It added an exaggeration that "the collection is the biggest in Asia." By this time, the shadow of war approached even the library. In July the prefectural police ordered the library not to allow use of certain newspapers and magazines, numbering almost 200 titles. Later, in 1938, the police directed the library to investigate student reading tendencies and preferences.

The collection of the library increased so rapidly before the war that a plan for a new building was proposed as early as 1929. On 24 January 1936 the reading room was destroyed by fire. Fortunately, the fire did not extend to the stack area and almost all materials were saved. Although the fire damaged the library greatly, this situation forced action on the plan for a new building. After much consideration, construction of the building began in 1940 but was soon interrupted by the war, and the new building was not completed until 1948, three years after the war's end.

The December 1941 escalation of the Pacific War brought severe damage to the library, although the city of Kyoto was not bombed. First, the war made it impossible for the library to import foreign books, except those books delivered to the Japanese Embassy in Berlin and sent on to Japan by way of Turkey. Second, the library could not purchase books for student use because research materials for the war were given priority, and paper itself was becoming scarce as the war progressed. Finally, the entire collection was evacuated to two places in a rural part of the city. The evacuation was completed on 14 August 1945, the day before the end of the war.

Democracy and the Library

Following the end of the war, a liberal atmosphere was restored under the guidance of the United States. In March 1947 the School Education Law was enacted, which brought about an extensive reformation in the Japanese education system. The aims of this reform were to affirm the principles of equal opportunity in education and to make these applicable to all levels of education, including higher education. In October 1947 the Kyoto Imperial University Library was renamed Kyoto University Library (KUL), in accordance with the university's name change. In the postwar period many innovations were introduced to the library, including the opening of the new library (1948); the reorganization of its administration and management; the establishment of the chair of library science in the faculty of education (1949); summer schools for training librarians at the request of the education ministry; various programs of exhibits and lectures; and the publication of *Library News* (1950–), which introduced newly acquired books to the academic community.

In 1950 the University of Tokyo and Stanford University (California) opened a seminar on American Studies under the auspices of the Rockefeller Foundation. In the next year, the weeklong Kyoto Seminar on American Studies was held at Kyoto University. In 1959 the library of the Center for American Studies of Kyoto University was established in the library, together with 10,000 volumes transferred from the seminar. This collection immediately became a valuable asset for many scholars. By 1960 library holdings exceeded 2 million volumes. In May 1962, Kyoto University was made the first and only formal Asian member of Human Relations Area Files (HRAF). HRAF serves as both the name of the organization and the name of its collection, which consists of massive anthropological, ethnological, and sociological data on different cultures. Additionally, in 1968 the library received deposit library status for the Organization for Economic Cooperation and Development (OECD) publications.

The importance of services to students was gradually recognized. In December 1963 the library opened its open-stack room with 8,000 volumes, and the reference library was reorganized for convenient use. In the latter 1960s, interest in modernization and the basic role of the library emerged. In October 1964 a special committee on the development of KUL was established, and by 1966 it was raising questions and making suggestions concerning consolidation or decentralization of the libraries, methods of reference and circulation, collection of journals, and the relation of the central library to the 41 campus libraries of the faculties and research institutes. Student unrest erupted at Kyoto University in 1969. A positive effect of this revolt was that it forced consideration of the basic role of the university, a situation from which the library could not remain aloof. The medical library and the libraries of the faculties of economics and letters were entirely closed during the unrest, and library services were at minimal levels in almost all the other libraries. These internal and external factors forced the libraries to reconsider their mission.

New Era of the Library

In 1971 the library held more than 3 million volumes, and the annual increase of books was beyond 100,000. Lack of space, the need for additional services and automation, and the absence of certain facilities and equipment made the existing central library obsolete. To cope with these conditions the advisory council of the university library appointed a special committee, which submitted its final report in March 1971. The report emphasized, among other things, two main points: (1) the need for modernization, automation of every phase of library administration, management, and services; and (2) the need for a clearer functional classification of the library's various roles as a central library, learning library, specialized library, and depository library. Basically, the report regarded libraries of the university as one system of Kyoto University libraries. This direction needed a new central library with strong coordinating power. Although the necessity of such a central library was widely agreed upon, the decision to begin construction was delayed until March 1981, when the advisory committee finally approved the plan for a new university library. It took more than two years to complete the building, which opened in April 1984, a four-story building with two additional subterranean levels.

This central library was expected to achieve the functions of a learning library, research library, depository library, and integrated library. As a learning library for the undergraduate students, the library provides an open-stack area with 80,000 volumes, a reference area with 30,000 volumes, and 800 seats. All students can now freely enter the stacks. Control of the entrance and circulation have been automated.

As a research library, the library maintains extensive reference tools and a rare book collection of approximately 5,000 Japanese and Chinese books, as well as 500 books in Western languages. A climate-controlled rare books room houses rare books collected from various libraries in the university. There are more than 26,000 volumes in several special collections. One is the Seike collection, the former library of the Hunabashi family (a part of the Kiyohara family, of whom Kiyohara Nobukata is famous for his studies of Myogyodo). Considered one of the most important collections on Confucianism in Japan, many of the items in the Seike collection are registered as important national cultural properties. The Nakai collection was assembled by the Nakai family, whose head was a master carpenter and magistrate in the Kinki area during the Edo period. It includes architectural diagrams, notebooks, manuscripts, and maps of Kyoto Imperial Palace, Nijo Castle, and some temples in Kyoto. The Nakanoin Collection includes diaries, poems, and various ancient manuscripts owned by the Nakanoin family, descendants of Nakanoin Michikata. Although libraries of faculties and research institutes have maintained specialized research libraries, the central library further supports these numerous libraries by accumulating extensive reference collections.

As a depository library function, the library has collected back issues of journals and periodicals from libraries of faculties and institutes throughout the university. The capacity of this on-campus storage facility is more than 400,000 volumes. Now Kyoto University Library is planning to establish a large depository library not only for keeping materials, but also for the studies on the preservation of various library materials.

Finally, the integrated library function of the central library, acting officially as Kyoto University Library, has allowed the library to become a strong coordination agency with the numerous libraries of faculties and research institutes. KUL also plays the role of regional academic information center, and through this activity the library contributes to the national academic information system. The central library also promotes international exchange of materials and ideas, as well as interlibrary loans, and offers many exhibits and lectures, many on international topics.

Networking and the Digital Library

All of the university's libraries are connected to the nationwide shared cataloging and information retrieval system of the National Center for Science Information Systems (NACSIS) via the Kyoto University Integrated Information Network System (KUINS), a Local Area Network (LAN). In 1985 the central library began to provide commercial database searches with staff intermediation, and in 1990 it began to provide CD-ROM service (e.g., *Dissertation Abstracts Ondisc*) through stand-alone terminals. Five years later, the library began to offer CD-ROM service (MEDLINE, *Biological Abstracts,* PsycLIT, etc.) via a local network. Since 1988 KUL has provided an Online Public Access Catalog (OPAC) service, which is available on the library's website. In 1998, under the strong leadership of Nagao Makoto (director of the university library, 1995–97, and university president, 1997 to present), the library inaugurated its digital library service via electronic communications. Although this digital library is still in the experimental stage, it offers many precious and important materials (such as Japan's national treasure, the *Konjaku Monogatarisyu: Suzukahon,* one volume of a collection of more than 1,000 short tales anonymously compiled in the early 11th century) to the public worldwide, as well as to the university community.

As the university has grown, new libraries have been established to support academic staff and students; at present there are 64 libraries within the university. Their total holdings comprise approximately 5.7 million volumes. Included is the celebrated nine-volume *Konjaku Monogatarisyu,* which consists of tales about India, China, and Japan, with Buddhist and secular themes, presenting an invaluable picture of Heian society. Another 170 rare volumes are also designated as important national cultural properties. There are approximately 270 library staff members, including 150 full-time staff. The library annually acquires nearly 100,000 volumes and 30,000 current periodical titles. KUL supports 2,500 teaching staff, 7,500 graduate students, 14,000 undergraduate students, and more than 1,000 students abroad, as well as the studies of scholars and students worldwide through various media, including Kyoto University's digital library. Kyoto University Library celebrated its first centennial in 1999.

YOSHITAKA KAWASAKI

Further Reading

Kyoto Daigaku Fuzoku Toshokan (Kyoto University Library), *Kyoto Daigaku Fuzoku Toshokan Rokujunenshi* (A Sixty-Year History of Kyoto University Library), Kyoto: Kyoto Daigaku Fuzoku Toshokan, 1961

Kyoto Daigaku Fuzoku Toshokan Gaiyo (Outline of the Kyoto University Library), 1984– Kyoto: Kyoto Daigaku Fuzoku Toshokan

Kyoto Daigaku Hyakunenshi Hensyu Iinkai (Editorial Committee on the Centennial History of Kyoto University), *Kyoto Daigaku Hyakunenshi: Sousetsu Hen* (A Centennial History of Kyoto Universityn: Outline), Kyoto: Kyoto Daigaku Kouenkai, 1998

Kyoto University Bulletin, 1998/1999 (1998)

Seisyu (Kyoto University Library Bulletin) (1964–)

Welch, Theodore F., *Libraries and Librarianship in Japan,* Westport, Connecticut: Greenwood Press, 1997

Latvian Academic Library

Address: Latvijas Akadēmiskā bibliotēka
Rūpniecības ielā 10
Riga, LV-1235
Latvia
Telephone: 710-6206
Fax: 732-1421
www.acadlib.lv

Founded: 1524

Holdings (2000): Volumes: 1.2 million. Graphic materials: 200,000; manuscripts: 14,000, including 200 pre-1500; incunabula, 210; maps: 1,300; microforms: 15,000.

Special Collections: *Areas of Concentration:* Historical and cultural heritage of Latvia and the Baltic procinces. *Individual Collections:* Joachim Christoph Brotze; August Buchholtz; Kārlis Egle; Uldis Ģērmanis; Wilhelm Ferdinand Hacker; Jakob Michael Reinhold Lenz; Jānis Misiņš; Karl Gottlieb Sonntag; Teodors Zeiferts. *Papers:* Latviešu Nacionālais Fonds; Lettisch-literärische Gesellschaft; Rīgas Latviešu Biedrība.

Mission and Structure

The Latvijas Akadēmiskā bibliotēka (Latvian Academic Library, or LAL) is a comprehensive research library serving the academic and scientific communities of Latvia. Administratively it is the responsibility of the Ministry of Education and Science. The LAL collects materials in all fields and publishes various basic and standard bibliographies of Latvian publications. The holdings of the rare books and manuscripts division deal primarily with the historical and cultural heritage of Latvia and the historic Baltic provinces: Livonia (Livland), Courland (Kurland), and Estonia (Estland). A separate division of the LAL, the Misiņš Library, is the oldest and most complete repository of Latvian cultural heritage. The holdings of the LAL are located in two buildings. The building at Rūpniecības iela 10 houses the Departments of Administration, Acquisitions, Rare Books and Manuscripts, Bibliography, New Information Technologies, and the Misiņš Library. The building at Lielvārdes iela 24 houses the Departments of Readers Services, Book Restoration, and Reproduction Services.

History

The Latvian Academic Library considers 1524 as its birth date, when the Bibliotheca Rigensis (BR, or City Library of Riga) was established. The Bibliotheca Rigensis traces its beginnings to the time when the Reformation established a foothold in Riga and other cities of Livonia (before the middle of the 16th century, the territories of present-day Latvia and Estonia) and the holdings of manuscripts and books of the Roman Catholic monasteries and churches were destroyed or changed owners. In 1524 the City Council of Riga asked Nicolaus Ramm, the pastor of the first Latvian evangelical parish in Riga, to become custodian of a collection of five books from the former Franciscan monastery in Riga, four of which are still at the LAL. The holdings of the library were increased with books from other monastery and church libraries and from private donations.

The first important private donation of books came in 1545 from Hinrick Stulbers. Important donors of books to the library were the Lutheran pastors in Riga: Wenzeslaus Lemchen, Laurentius Lemchen, Gregorius Plinius, Georg Neuner, and Johann von Dahlen. Books published by Manutius in Venice, Italy; Froben and Oporinus in Basle (present-day Basel, Switzerland); Plantin in Antwerp, Belgium; and Etienne in Paris were donated to BR by the poet Daniel Hermann and by the medical doctor Johann Bavarus. In 1664 Hermann Samson Jr., the mayor of Riga (at that time the largest city of imperial Sweden), donated to BR the library of his father Hermann Samson Sr., head of the Livonian Lutheran Church. Since the 17th century the library has regularly received books from the printers of Riga (the first printing press in Riga was established in 1588 in the immediate vicinity of BR) and dissertations from the Cathedral School and the Alexander I Gymnasium (established as Schola Carolina in 1675). The first lists of holdings at BR were prepared at the end of the 16th century, and by the 17th century rules were established regulating the use of the library and the borrowing of books. The oldest inscription in a book at the LAL indicating ownership by BR says: "Liber Bibliothecae Ecclesiae Rigensis 1551." From 1553 to 1891 the library was located in the cloister of the Dom Cathedral.

After the Great Northern War at the beginning of the 18th century, when Livonia and Estonia were incorporated as autonomous provinces of the Russian Empire, Riga became a center from which European cultural mores were transmitted to St. Petersburg and other parts of the Russian Empire. BR assumed an important role in these developments. It also established an exchange agreement with the newly established Russian Academy of Sciences, lasting until 1915. In 1798 the library received about 3,400 books from medical doctor Nicolaus Himsel. Important 18th-century donations to BR came from the Riga publishing house of Johann Hartknoch, the largest in the Baltic provinces in the 18th century. In addition, librarian Johann Gottfried Ageluth established two special collections at BR: Livonica for publications dealing with the present territories of Latvia and Estonia, and Rossica for publications on the Russian Empire. Ageluth's aide at BR from 1765 to 1769 was Johann Gottfried Herder.

Since 1802 BR has received dissertations from the University of Dorpat (Tartu), originally founded in 1632 by Swedish King Gustavus Adolphus in the Estonian part of Livonia and reestablished in 1801 by Russian Czar Alexander I. Among the 500 volumes donated to BR by the legal scholar Johann Christoph Schwarz were important materials for the Livonica collection. In 1832 the library purchased the collection of books and manuscripts of the historian Johann Christoph Brotze. Significant additions to BR were made by acquisition of the libraries of the historian Carl Eduard Napiersky (5,000 volumes) and medical doctor Karl Wilpert (6,000 volumes).

A new cataloging system was introduced by Georg Bergholz, the director from 1861 to 1886. Bergholz also established a special Lettica (or Latvian) section. In 1891 the library was moved to the former Riga city hall, designed by architect Christoph Haberland. From 1904 to 1933 the director of the library was Nikolai Busch, author of many studies on the history and book culture of the Baltic region. His assistant and head of the Lettica Division from 1920 to 1938 was Jānis Misiņš.

Whereas in the middle of the 19th century the holdings of the library consisted of approximately 30,000 volumes, by 1900 there were more than 100,000 volumes. From 1920 to 1940, during the period of Latvian independence, the structure of the library remained unchanged. Since 1920 the library has received obligatory copies of all publications in Latvia. In 1940 the holdings of BR numbered 203,934 volumes, including 31,064 in the Lettica collection, 19,478 in the Baltica collection, and 14,731 in the Rossica collection. In the last days of June 1941, when the advancing German troops battled with Soviet Russian army units in the center of the medieval part of Riga, the library (in the former city hall of Riga) was destroyed and burned. From the 400,000 books and manuscripts at the library, only approximately 46,000 were saved, primarily rare books and manuscripts stored in fireproof vaults. The holdings of BR that survived the ravages of war became the State Historical Library in 1945, and in 1946 these formed the core of the newly established Fundamental Library of the Academy of Sciences of the Latvian Soviet Socialist Republic (SSR). It was the only library in Soviet Latvia that was permitted to keep in its special collections items that for ideological reasons had to be destroyed in other libraries, including Latvian exile publications. After the restoration of Latvian independence, the library was renamed the Academic Library of Latvia in 1992.

From the old and important libraries within the territory of the state of Latvia, only BR, apart from the city library of Liepāja (Libau, established in 1777), continues to exist, though in a diminished size and under a different title and structure. The book collection of the Riga Jesuit College, established under Polish rule (1581 to 1621) and containing unique copies of the earliest Latvian publications, was taken by the Swedes after they conquered Riga in 1621. The library's holdings were deposited at the Uppsala University Library, where most of its holdings are today. The library of the dukes of Courland (more than 3,000 volumes), which was located in Riga when the Russians established their rule in the city in 1710 during the Great Northern War, was sent to St. Petersburg in 1714 by order of Peter the Great, where it formed the core of the library of the newly established Russian Academy of Sciences. The significant and sizable library (more than 42,000 volumes in 1915) of the Academia Petrina in Jelgava (Mitau, established in 1775) was burned in November 1919 by retreating soldiers of the Russian-German corps of General Bermondt-Awaloff, after their defeat by the army of the new Latvian state.

Misiņš Library

The Misiņš Library (ML) contains the oldest and most complete collection of Latvian publications and constitutes a rich repository of publications on Latvia and the historical Baltic provinces in other languages. Now a separate and independent unit within the LAL, it was originally established (1885) as a private library by the bibliophile and bibliographer Jānis Misiņš, and it functioned as such in Riga in the first years after the establishment of Latvian independence. In 1925 Misiņš donated his library to the city of Riga and it was opened to the public in 1928. In 1945 it held approximately 77,000 volumes. On 5 June 1946 the Council of Ministers of the SSR of Latvia placed the ML under the authority of the newly established Academy of Sciences of the SSR of Latvia. In 1954 the ML was merged administratively with the Fundamental Library of the Academy of Sciences and was named the J. Misiņš Division of Latvian Literature at the Fundamental Library of the Academy of Sciences of the SSR of Latvia. Since 1992 its official title has been the Misiņš Library of the Academic Library of Latvia. After the reestablishment of the independence of Latvia in 1991, the ML paid particular attention to the acquisition of Latvian exile publications and archival materials. Today its holdings have reached approximately 1 million items, including books, periodical publications, music scores, postcards, posters, programs, manuscripts, and various ephemera.

Rare Books and Manuscripts

Among the approximately 32,000 volumes in the rare books and manuscripts collections at the LAL, there are 210 incunabula, 800 items printed in the 16th century, approximately 2,000 volumes published in the 17th century, and approximately 3,000 volumes published in the 18th century. The oldest item is a fragment of the *Catholicon* (Mainz, Germany, 1460) by Johannes Balbus. Unique are copies of *Missale Viburgense* (Lübeck, Germany, 1500) and *Plenarium* (Venice, 1496). Among the 16th-century publications, there are many first editions of publications by Martin Luther, including writings addressed to the inhabitants of Riga such as *Der hundertsiebenzvanzigste Psalm, aussgelegt an die Christen zu Riga yn Liffland* (Wittenberg, Germany, 1524), along with writings of Philipp Melanchthon, Ulrich von Hutten, and Andreas Knöpken (one of the leading figures of the Reformation in Riga and Livonia). The LAL's holdings are rich in 16th-century theological literature such as *Brevarium Rigensis* (Amsterdam, the Netherlands, 1513) and historical chronicles such as *Nye Lyfflendiche Chronica* (Rostock, Germany, 1578).

The LAL also owns 80 of the approximately 180 publications of Nicolaus Mollyn, the first printer of Riga, and has a substantial collection of publications in German, Latin, and Latvian by his 17th-century successors Gerhard Schröder, Heinrich Bessemesser, Johann Georg Wilcken, and Georg Matthias Nöller. The 18th-century holdings at the LAL consist primarily of books published in German and Latvian in Riga and Jelgava (Mitau). The LAL owns most of the 580 titles published by Johann Friedrich Hartknoch and his son, the leading 18th-century publishers in the Baltic provinces, including first editions of works by Johann Gottfried Herder, Immanuel Kant, and the multivolume edition of *Topographische Nachrichten von Lief- und Ehstland* (1774 to 1782) by August Wilhelm Hupel. There are also sets of the first Riga newspapers published in German, such as *Rigische Novellen* (c. 1681 to 1710), and of the first Latvian periodical publications. The LAL owns the only complete copy of the first Latvian periodical publication, *Latviešu Ārste* (1768).

The LAL owns approximately 14,000 manuscripts, including many chronicles and documents written since the 13th century and dealing with the history of Riga and the Baltic provinces. There are also 14th- and 15th-century illuminated manuscripts and books of hours such as *Missale Rigense* (14th century). The LAL also holds archives of prominent Baltic German public figures who were born or were active in Riga and the Baltic provinces, such as the archive of Garlieb Merkel, author of *Die Letten* (1797), a work that challenged the existing social and political order in the Latvian parts of the Baltic provinces.

Some of the greatest treasures of the LAL are the 111 volumes of archival materials compiled by Joachim Christoph Brotze, including ten volumes of his "Sammlung verschiedener liefländischer Monumente, Prospecte, Münzen, Wappen...," containing more than 5,000 drawings and watercolors depicting architectural monuments, landscapes, and representatives of all social strata in Riga and the provinces of Livland and Estland. The holdings of the LAL also include manuscripts and archival material dealing with many leading 19th- and 20th-century Latvian scholars and writers, including Ernests Dinsbergs, Kārlis Egle, Anšlavs Eglītis, Pēteris Ērmanis, Uldis Ģērmanis, Matīss Kaudzīte, Reinis Kaudzīte, Atis Kronvalds, and Teodors Zeiferts.

Publications

The LAL has published a number of standard reference works on Latvian publications including *Latviešu periodika, 1768–1945* (Index of Latvian Periodicals [1768–1945], 1977–95); *Latviešu grāmata ārzemēs (1920–1940): Bibliogrāfiskais rādītājs* (Latvian Books Published outside Latvia [1920–1940]: Bibliographic Index, 1998), edited by E. Flīgere and L. Lāce; *Latviešu rakstnieku rokraksti Misiņa bibliotēkā* (Manuscripts of Latvian Authors at the Misiņš Library, 1994), by Līvija Labrence; and its series *Latviešu zinātnieki* (The Scientists of Latvia), about the leading scientists of Latvia.

Automation

The LAL has developed its own strategy for automating its catalogs and electronic, scientific, and technological information. Since 1993 all incoming publications and all rare books are handled in the LAL's integrated automation system, LiberMedia. The LAL is also acquiring basic bibliographic and reference CD-ROM databases as well as offering Internet services to its patrons. The address of the Online Public Access Catalog (OPAC) is www.acadlib.lv/e/katalogs/.

JANIS A. KRESLINS SR.

Further Reading

Arājs, Eduards, editor, *Biblioteke 450: K iubileiu Fundamental'noi biblioteki Akademii nauk Latviiskoi SSR, 1524–1974* (On the 450th Anniversary of the Fundamental Library of the Academy of Sciences of the Latvian SSR, 1524–1974), Riga: Zinātne, 1974 (summaries in Latvian, German, and English)

Arājs, Eduards, editor, *Grāmatas un grāmatnieki: Misiņa bibliotēkas 100. gadadienai, 1885–1985* (Books and Their Keepers: On the Hundredth Anniversary of Misiņš Library, 1885–1985), Riga: Zinātne, 1985

Arājs, Eduards, Kārlis Egle, and Francis Rancāns, *Jānis Misiņš: Izlase* (Jānis Misiņš: Selections of His Writings), Riga: Latvijas PSR Zinātņu Akadēmijas Izdevniecība, 1962

Busch, Nicolaus, *Die Geschichte der Rigaer Stadtbibliothek und deren Bücher*, edited by Leonid Arbusow, Riga: Rigaer Stadtverwaltung, 1937

Kocere, Venta, *Latvian Academic Library*, translated by L. Secenova, Riga: Latvian Academic Library, 1994

Kocere, Venta, *Latvijas Akadēmiskā bibliotēka* (Latvian Academic Library), Riga: Latvijas Akadēmiskā bibliotēka, 1999

Krūmiņa, L., editor, *Latvijas Akadēmiskās bibliotēkas 470 gadu jubilejas zinātniskā konfererence* (Conference Dedicated to the 470-Year Anniversary of Latvian Academic Library), Riga: Latvijas Akadēmiskā bibliotēka, 1994

Labrence, Līvija, *Latviešu rakstnieku rokraksti Misiņa bibliotēkā* (Manuscripts of Latvian Authors at the Misiņš Library), Riga: Latvijas Akadēmiskā bibliotēka, 1994 (summaries in German, English, and Russian)

Lācis, Marija, "Atskats bibliotēkas vēsturē, 1524–1944 (A Survey of the History of the Library, 1524–1944)," in *Rīgas pilsētas bibliotēkas, tagadējās Zinātņu akadēmijas Fundamentālās bibliotēkas vēsture* (The History of the City Library of Riga, the Present Fundamental Library of the Academy of Sciences), Riga: Latvijas PSR Zinātņu Akadēmijas Izdevniecība, 1960

Rancāns, Francis, *Jānis Misiņš un viņa bibliotēka* (Jānis Misiņš and His Library), Riga: Latvijas Valsts Izdevniecība, 1963

Sander, Ojar, "Latvijas Akadēmiskā bibliotēka; Akademische Bibliothek Lettlands," in *Handbuch deutscher historischer Buchbestände in Europa*, edited by Bernhard Fabian, vol. 7, part 2, *Finnland, Estland, Lettland, Litauen*, Hildesheim, Germany, and New York: Olms-Weidmann, 1988

Sander, Ojar, "'Bibliotheca Rigensis' und ihre Bücher, 15. bis 18. Jahrhundert," *Nordost-Archiv* (N.F.) 4, no. 1 (1995)

Šmite, Anna, "Misiņa bibliotēka agrāk un tagad (Misiņš Library in the Past and at the Present)," in *Misiņa bibliotēkas 110 gadu jubilejas zinātniskā konference, Rīgā, 1995. gada 19. septembris* (Misiņš Library Conference Commemorating the 110th Anniversary of Misiņš Library, Riga, 19 September 1995), edited by L. Krūmiņa, Riga: Latvijas Akadēmiskā bibliotēka, 1995

Laurentian Library of the Medici

Address:	Biblioteca Medicea Laurenziana Piazza San Lorenzo 9 50123 Firenze Italy Telephone: 55-214443 or 55-210760 Fax: 55-2302992 www.bml.firenze.sbn.it
Founded:	1571
Holdings (1999):	Volumes: 151,000. Current serials: 200; films: 11,000; incunabula: 540; manuscripts: 13,000; ostraca: 80; papyri: 3,000.
Special Collections:	*Areas of Concentration:* Art history; classics; history; illumination; religious history. *Individual Collections:* Alfieri; Amiatini; Antinori; Ashburnham; Biagi-Passerini; Biscioni; Calci; Carte Concilio; Conventi soppressi; Corali; Da Filicaia; Edili; Ferrucci; Fiesolani; Gaddi (Gaddiani secondi); Giordani; Lodi; Martelli; Mediceo-Palatini; Monastery of San Marco; Mugellani; Niccolini; Norsa; Orientali; Pandette; Pistelli; Plutei; Plutei superiori e Plutei inferiori; Redi; Rinuccini; Rostagno; Santa Croce (Plutei destra e Plutei sinistra); Scioppi; Segni; Strozzi; Tempi; Vitelli.

Origins and Early History

The Laurentian Library of the Medici was begun as a collection of books assembled by Cosimo il Vecchio de' Medici, who also established the political fortune of the Medici family as well as the family's lengthy dominion over Florence. The enormous wealth he accumulated as a banker allowed Cosimo to be quite liberal with his funds, not only with respect to single individuals but also with regard to religious communities and specifically concerning the world of books. Around 1430 Cosimo, together with his brother Lorenzo, completed a vast project concerning the library of the Monastery of San Francesco of the Minorites, located in Bosco ai Frati in Mugello (not far from Florence), where the family originated. In exile in Venice from 1433 to 1434, Cosimo had a library constructed on Michelozzo's design for the Canonici Lateranensi on the island of San Giorgio in Alga (it was demolished in 1614). After his return to Florence, he had two large libraries built within a few years: the city library of the Monastery of San Marco, completed in 1444 (also on Michelozzo's plan), and the library of the Badia Fiesolana of the Canonici Lateranensi, on the surrounding hills under the old town of Fiesole.

As always, the munificence of Cosimo did not stop at the construction of buildings but also included furniture and books. For the San Marco library and the Badia library, Cosimo asked Tommaso Parentucelli (who became Pope Nicolas V in 1447) to make a list, or *canone bibliografico,* of the works that should be contained in it, in order to endow it adequately. Within a few months approximately 200 manuscripts were made by copyists under the direction of the famous bookseller Vespasiano da Bisticci. These were new manuscripts, copied from earlier copies mostly belonging to Niccolò Niccoli.

The influence exercised by this learned man in spreading the *Umanesimo* (humanism) in Florence, although not exclusively cultural, was so great that we may define it as decisive. Thanks to his nearly insatiable desire to collect, Niccoli possessed hundreds of old manuscripts and died in debt. And owing to Niccoli's persuasion of the wealthy class of the city as to the importance of what he had gathered, his wish to perpetuate his own library (*omnibus civibus studiosis*) was realized after his death. Cosimo bought more than 400 manuscripts that had belonged to Niccoli, including the more precious ones, which he endowed to the library to be constituted in the Monastery of San Marco. Following the will of Niccoli, Cosimo ordered that it should be opened to all scholars. The library of San Marco in Florence can thus claim to be the first public library of modern times.

To underline the magnificence of the Medici library at its origin, Angelo Politian—known as Poliziano—some years later called it the "Biblioteca Medicea pubblica." This public library was different from the earlier family or private one, which consisted of a small initial number of manuscripts gathered by Cosimo (today believed to be approximately 80 manuscripts). As it grew larger, it was enriched by the collections of many family members. Among the first to be added were those of the legitimate sons of Cosimo—Piero and Giovanni. To these two sons, at least in part, the history of the book in 15th-century Florence owes its fortune.

The difficulty in obtaining old manuscripts was in part an issue of supply and demand. In Florence the demand was high, leading to a Florentine enterprise, particularly that of Vespasiano da Bisticci, in the copying of manuscripts. Copies were the only way to possess the beloved Latin classics. In order to increase the value of such books, which lacked the authenticity of antiquity, their aesthetic appeal was increased by elaborate and prestigious commissions for bindings decorated with gold leaf and many colors. The beautiful illuminated books of Giovanni and Piero de' Medici did not make for large libraries: Piero's lost inventories of 1464 to 1465 record 128 items, and Giovanni's collection was even smaller. Neither did this family library greatly increase in the first years of the rule of Lorenzo il Magnifico de' Medici (1469–92), who commissioned only a few luxury manuscripts. But we owe to Lorenzo a new politics of the book in the Medici house. Thanks to him, Greek manuscripts appeared in the library for the first time around 1478, when Goro, Priore of Santa Croce sull' Arno, sent him 67 codices. In 1481 there was also the acquisition of manuscripts left by Francesco Filelfo after his death in Florence. Throughout his reign Lorenzo used agents to search for books.

Very probably it was Poliziano who suggested the idea of enlarging the family library, adding to it those texts still lacking from the extraordinary legacy of Greek and Latin antiquity. This was accomplished by imitating what illustrious rulers such as the King of Naples and the Duke of Urbino had recently done (and what the King of Hungary was also preparing to do)—that is, to commission copies of the major works of antiquity. The project was particularly ambitious. In order to get Greek and Byzantine books to copy, Lorenzo sent his agents abroad, twice sending Giano Lascaris to Greece and the Mediterranean islands (1490–92) and once dispatching Poliziano and Pico della Mirandola into the Veneto (1491). For Latin manuscripts he used Florentine copyists. The work was enormous and the results were conspicuous, both for the number of Greek manuscripts they were able to acquire and for the Latin manuscripts produced in Florence, which were characterized by the complex emblems in the illuminated frames of the first page of text. Mattia Corvino's death in 1490 and Lorenzo's death in 1492 interrupted these bibliographical projects. In 1494 Piero's expulsion from Florence was to have even greater consequences for the library.

After the exile of Piero, 17 cases containing the Medici library were deposited by the Signoria of Florence (the ruling government) for safekeeping in the Monastery of San Marco, probably in December 1494. On 19 October 1495 the friars made a loan of 2,000 florins to the Signoria, accepting the books as security. For this occasion an inventory of all of the Medici books, both those already in storage at San Marco and those scattered elsewhere, was made by John Lascaris, Lorenzo's librarian, and Bartolomeo Ciai, the chancellor. Soon after the Signoria, which was unable to repay the 2000 florins, agreed to allow San Marco's Dominican friars to keep the books (up to a value of 3,000 florins) if the friars would pay the Signoria 1,000 florins and dismiss the original loan granted in 1495. On 18 April 1498 an attack was made on San Marco by opponents of Giralamo Savonarola, prior of the monastery, who had denounced corruption in the city. Although leaving the books unharmed, the attack convinced the Signoria to demand that the Medici books be sold to the Palazzo Vecchio. The sale was confirmed on 12 December 1498, and after a temporary stay in the Benedictine Abbey in Florence the books were returned to San Marco in September 1500. The payment of 1,000 florins from the Salviati family on this occasion was very likely one of many measures taken to allow the library to remain intact until the storm had blown over. Finally in 1508 Lorenzo's son Giovanni, Cardinal de' Medici, expressed interest in his father's library. At his request the monastery was paid a substantial sum of more than 2,600 ducats, and by early 1510 the Medici books had already been moved to Giovanni's house in Rome (the Palazzo Madama).

The inventory of 1495 indicates that Lorenzo had increased the family library to some 1,000 manuscripts. A second inventory of the library was made in Rome by Fabio Vigili around 1508. The total number in that inventory, including some books of Piero, is less than 1,000 items, a number confused by the return to the Sassetti family of 67 manuscripts in 1497 and 1498. The library was kept in Rome for some years, but when Pope Leo X died in 1521, his cousin Giuliano (later Pope Clement VII) quickly sent the library to Florence to avoid its confiscation by the Vatican Library. The books were kept in cases for many years. The project of building a new library was commissioned by Clement VII to Michelangelo in 1523–24, but for many reasons (such as lack of financial support and war) it was not finished until 1571, when it was opened to the public. Its completion was the achievement of Cosimo I de' Medici, grand duke of Tuscany.

The first inventory after the library opened, compiled by Giovanni Rondinelli and Baccio Valori in 1589, records approximately 3,000 books, all manuscripts except for some 200 printed books. Cosimo I had succeeded in increasing the library threefold; before its opening he ordered that all the books be stripped of their original covers and bound in purple skin, ordered according to subject, and chained to the 90 benches designed by Michelangelo. His heir, Francesco I, was successful in buying one of the most famous manuscripts in the library, the *Virgilio Laurenziano*. But at that point the library entered a period of inactivity until the 18th century, when the end of the Medici family in 1737 brought into power the Lorenos, princes distinguished for their rigorous reforms.

The 18th Century

With the changed political climate of the Lorenos, the Laurentian Library again became an object of sovereign attention and, as in Cosimo I's time, the intervention of reforming princes left a deep trace, not always in a positive manner. The idea of the Laurentian Library as a library exclusively of manuscripts took root more firmly. A project in 1783 to remove 6,000 manuscripts from the library of Antonio Magliabechi to the Laurentian Library did not succeed, but the plan to remove Medicean printed books to the Maglabechiana, many of them illuminated and embellished, did go forward in the same year, and the books are now part of the Biblioteca Nazionale in Florence.

However, these were also the years in which the Laurentian Library was enriched with entire collections. The acquisition of the Gaddi and Biscioni libraries (in 1755 and 1756) brought 355 and 70 manuscripts respectively. Angelo Maria Bandrini (1757–1803) was appointed librarian in 1757 and over a period of nearly 50 years developed major collections and published an important catalog of those collections. In 1767 other annexations began, and on the order of Pietro Leopoldo the library of Santa Croce was reunited with the Laurentian Library. In 1771, 578 Oriental manuscripts, gathered by Cardinal Ferdinando to furnish models for his Stamperia Orientale in Rome, were also acquired by the Laurentian Library. A decree of 1778 saw the addition to the Laurentian Library of 276 manuscripts from the Duomo, Santa Maria del Fiore, now Fondo Edili. In 1783, the year of the removal of printed books to the Magliabechiana, manuscripts and documents strictly tied to Florentine history were also annexed, including the *Pandette* by Giustiniano and the Greek Gospel Book (Med Pal. 243), which had for centuries been exhibited in the Palazzo Vecchio as symbols of civil and religious authority. The Documents of the Council between the Oriental and Occidental Churches (1439) were annexed as well. However, in this case they were precious *cimeli*, more than manuscripts. Again in 1783, 181 manuscripts from the Badia Fiesolana arrived in the Laurentian Library. Two years later in 1785, 184 Strozziani manuscripts (gathered in the 17th century by Senator Carlo Strozzi) and the very famous Latin Bible from the suppressed Monastery of San Salvatore in Monte Amiata (written between the end of the seventh and the beginning of the eighth century) were added to the Laurentian Library, together with other manuscripts from San Salvatore.

The 19th and 20th Centuries

The Laurentian Library may have fared better in the Napoleonic invasion than other libraries, but the French did take its most celebrated manuscript, the Medici *Virgil*. It was returned in 1816 with the indelible sign of the French captivity: the red stamp of the Bibliothèque nationale and a binding that had, and still has, Napoleon's initial under the imperial crown repeated five times. The suppression of religious orders in Tuscany (1808) marked the sudden end of many monastic libraries. Their dismembered holdings were divided among various public libraries, but in the enormous disorder created by the war, unscrupulous individuals stole or mutilated several manuscripts for their illuminations. Thus in the collection of the *Conventi Soppressi* in the Laurentian Library, manuscripts of the Badia Fiorentina, Santa Maria degli Angeli, Camaldoli, and all of the monasteries of Florence and its province are located next to each other. Only the manuscripts of San Marco were partly preserved intact and in their original order, a reflection of their ancient Medicean patronage. Of great importance was the assignment to the Laurentian Library in 1884 of the Ashburnham collection—almost 2,000 manuscripts, heterogeneous in content and very rich in Italian manuscripts, from one of the first governments after the unification of Italy in 1870. Acquisitions of entire collections (Rinuccini, Scioppi, Calci) or of isolated pieces, bequests (Alfieri, Tempi D' Elci, Da Filicaia, Martelli), and gifts also enriched the library, which now totals more than 13,000 manuscripts.

During World War II the library survived by the storage of manuscripts in the Abbey of Passignano and the *plutei* in the vaults of San Lorenzo. It remains today an incomparable source for classical and humanistic scholars and continues to acquire unique materials within its collecting scope.

The Monumental Building

The monumental building housing the library is the work of Michelangelo and has remained substantially intact since its construction. To Michelangelo we also owe the wooden furniture—the 90 benches called *plutei*. The floor, the ceiling, and the stained glass are the work of artists contemporary with Michelangelo, following his inventions. Only the beautiful staircase leading from the *ricetto*, or vestibule, to the great hall (*libreria*) is considered a spurious element: Finished by Ammannati, it departs from Michelangelo's plan by using stone instead of wood. Michelangelo's project also called for a smaller third space, the "piccola libreria," beyond the great hall, to serve as a small study for the commissioner, the Cardinal Giulio deì Medici, later Pope Clement VII. Two centuries ago the building underwent two great changes. First, five windows were closed and a large door was opened in the western end following construction of a nearby building, the neoclassical Tribuna d' Elci by Pasquale Poccianti, on commission from the Tuscan government (1814–41). This building was destined to house the collection of printed first editions and incunabula given to the Laurentian Library by Angelo Maria d' Elci (15 July 1818). The second change was the completion of the walls of the *ricetto*, patterned on the model of the only one made in the 16th century.

ANGELA DILLON BUSSI

Further Reading

Ames-Lewis, Francis, *The Library and Manuscripts of Piero di Cosimo de' Medici*, New York and London: Garland Press, 1984

De la Mare, Albina Catherine, "Cosimo and His Books," in *Cosimo 'il Vecchio' de' Medici, 1389–1464: Essays in Commemoration of the 600th Anniversary of Cosimo de' Medici's Birth*, edited by Francis Ames-Lewis, Oxford: Clarendon Press 1992

Fryde, Edmund Boleslaw, *Greek Manuscripts in the Private Library of the Medici, 1469–1510*, 2 vols., Aberystwyth: National Library of Wales, 1996

Ullman, Berthold Louis, and Phillip A. Stadter, *The Public Library of Renaissance Florence: Niccolò Niccoli, Cosimo de' Medici, and the Library of San Marco*, Padua: Antenore, 1972

Leeds University Library

Address: Leeds University Library
University of Leeds
Leeds LS2 9JT
UK
Telephone: 113-233-5513
Fax: 113-233-5561
www.leeds.ac.uk/library

Founded: 1874

Holdings (2000): Volumes: 2.6 million. Current serials: 10,000; incunabula: 200; manuscripts: 15,000 linear feet; microforms 320,000.

Special Collections: *Areas of Concentration:* Anglo-French literary relations; cookery; music; science and technology; 17th- and 18th-century English literature. *Individual Collections:* Brotherton collection; Leeds Philosophical and Literary Society library; Leeds Russian archive; Blanche Leigh collection of cookery; Liddle collection; B.T. Melsted Icelandic collection; Novello-Cowden Clarke collection of music; Herbert Read; Harold Whitaker collection of atlases.

General Information

In the early 19th century Leeds grew prodigiously in population and wealth but lacked any traditional institution of higher education. Hence the locally organized and funded Yorkshire College opened in 1874 to provide higher scientific and technological instruction. The college joined the federal Victoria University in 1887 and in 1904 achieved independence as the University of Leeds. Meanwhile, it had developed research interests and extended its subjects of instruction to include the humanities, medicine, law, and social sciences. The library had four chief librarians in its first 100 years: Fanny Passavant (1885–1919), Richard Offor (1919–47), Bertram S. Page (1947–68), and Dennis Cox (1968–86). The next two did not stay until retirement but moved on to other positions: Reg. P. Carr (1986–96) was appointed Bodley's librarian and director of university library services at Oxford in 1996, and his successor, Lynne Brindley (1996–2000), left to become the chief executive of the British Library, London. The present librarian is Jan Wilkinson.

Collections

The initial emphasis was to acquire current literature for undergraduate teaching, but the library did not refuse gifts of other material. During and since Offor's librarianship, it has collected on all fronts by purchase, gift, bequest, and deposit. Much acquisition has been policy-driven, but some research collections have been adventitious, and creditably the library has added to these, creating research foci where none existed before. The book stock exceeded 1 million items in 1970–71.

The most significant single bequest was the private library of Edward Allen, Lord Brotherton, a Leeds industrialist, lord mayor, member of Parliament, and collector. He died in 1930, and his legatees presented his impressive collection to the university in 1936, in accordance with his wishes. This general collection, including some 200 incunabula, is particularly rich in English 17th- and 18th-century literature. Other substantial gifts in the interwar period were scientific and theological books from All Souls' College, Oxford (1926 and 1929); the Icelandic collection of Bogi T. Melsted (1929); the library of the Leeds Philosophical and Literary Society (1937); the Harold Whitaker collection of more than 500 atlases and road books (1939); and the Blanche Leigh collection of some 1,200 cookery books (1939). The library has also developed from its own resources an Anglo-French collection of pre-1800 French translations of English publications, the initiative of Offor and Professor Paul Barbier.

Growth continued after 1945. The Brotherton collection developed a Romany section, received the Novello-Cowden Clarke collection (1954), rich in musical literature, and purchased (1996) the library of critic Herbert Read. The John Preston (1962) and other collections have augmented cookery literature. Lexicography and early French literature have benefited from the Barbier (1947) and Charles A. Buckmaster (1950) bequests. Personal connections facilitated deposit of the Leeds Friends' Old Library (1976) and the Birkbeck Library (1981), bringing several thousand titles of Quaker literature. Gifts from members of faculty include the William B. Thompson collection (1979) of more than 4,000 pedagogic editions of Greek and Latin literature and the Owen Lattimore collection of modern Sinology. The Royal Asiatic Society gave its collection of old Chinese printing (1962–63). In 1961 an anonymous friend purchased Judaica from Cecil Roth's collection for the library, and Ripon Cathedral Library deposited its older books (not exclusively theological) in 1986. Partly from its own resources and partly by bequest (Hans Rosenbusch, 1966), the library developed a collection of German literature, especially 18th-century literary periodicals and early 20th-century first editions.

Apart from individual pieces, including the Anonimalle Chronicle from St. Mary's Abbey, York, the library has many collections of manuscripts and archives. These include business archives relating to the West Riding (Yorkshire) woolen textile industry; education archives (Association of Education Committees, Association for Science Education, and select papers of the Leeds and West Riding Education Authorities); field notebooks of Harold Orton's survey of English dialects; many literary and critical papers (Algernon Swinburne, the Brontë family and Elizabeth Gaskell, Edmund Gosse, G. Wilson Knight, Bonamy Dobrée, Barbara Taylor Bradford, and the *London Magazine*); and papers of some local landed estates. There are also manuscripts in music and fine art (Felix Mendelssohn, Joseph Novello, music critic Herbert Thompson, and artist Jacob Kramer); modern political papers (Lord Boyle, Henry Drummond-Wolff, Louis H. Hayter, Harry Legge-Bourke, and the Glenesk-Bathurst archive mostly relating to *The Morning Post* newspaper); and archives of Quaker meetings in West Yorkshire and of the dean and chapter of Ripon Cathedral.

Other significant acquisitions and collections include Jewish liturgical and other manuscripts collected by Roth; papers of Bishop Ernest J. Tinsley; and scientific and medical material (William Astbury, biomolecular structure; Edmund Stoner, physics; Arthur Smithells, chemistry; Matthew Stewart, pathology; and Charles Scattergood, case books in forensic medicine). The Liddle collection (1988) contains books, manuscripts, and artifacts relating to personal experiences in World War I. The Leeds Russian Archive (1982) holds mainly late 19th- and early 20th-century material, much from émigré sources, including papers of Yury V. Lomonossoff, Ivan A. Bunin, and Leonid Andreyev and their families, and the Zemgor archive, together with papers of some British Russophile academic associations.

The library also cares for some non-book collections. In 1913 it received a very complete collection of British postage stamps, and a coin collection begun after 1918 by the Latin Department transferred to the library in 1977. The department had acquired the Winchester Cabinet of 3,000 coins in 1955, and an additional 11,000 coins were given by Paul Thackeray in the 1990s. The library's collection is strong in Roman and British coins. Besides official portraits, the university has assembled a representative collection of 20th-century art, partly the gift of Michael Sadler in 1923; the collection, its curator, and gallery were transferred to the library in 1992. Furthermore, the university's own administrative archives, which had moved into the library's original accommodation in 1989, became the library's responsibility in 1994. Leeds having been involved with its inception in 1954, the editorial team of the *British Education Index* settled in the library in 1986.

Buildings

A purpose-built library, on the ground floor under the university's Great Hall, opened in 1894. Its design precluded upward expansion, and the site limited it horizontally, so the library spread into other properties and by 1919 occupied approximately 80 separate rooms. A new central library, defrayed by Lord Brotherton and designed by Henry V. Lanchester in an opulently finished classical style, opened in 1936; its mildly symbolic circular plan proved wasteful of space. Increased student numbers and expansion of book stock from the mid-1960s necessitated various temporary expedients to increase capacity. Eventually a second major building, the Edward Boyle Library (1975), provided space for science, technology, and undergraduate course literature. An extension of the Brotherton Library in 1993 provided additional space. Although these measures eased congestion somewhat, closed-access out-storage of less frequently used material has had to continue.

The School of Medicine, established in 1831 and attached to the Leeds General Infirmary, was combined with the Yorkshire College in 1884, and the Medical School with its own library occupied a new building of some architectural distinction in 1894. That facility having become overcrowded and antiquated, most of the school and its library moved to a large new building in 1979. At various times the collections in law, textile science, and education have also been accommodated separately, mainly in undistinguished premises modestly adapted to library purposes.

Management and Staff

Initially professors managed the library, but the work having increased, a full-time, non-graduate librarian, Fanny Passavant, was appointed in 1885. Her job was conceived as clerical but in practice became professional, though she was not invited to attend meetings of the library committee until 1902. Lacking any academic status, she had little role in book selection, which remained a professorial task. Since her successors were graduates and trained librarians, the university had to revise the status and emoluments of the office in the light of practice elsewhere. The matter was delicate, and the university did not admit its librarian, then Offor, to membership in the University Senate until 1934 (ex officio from 1949). The appointment of Lynne Brindley in 1996 as both librarian and dean of information strategy further acknowledged changing circumstances.

Early subordinate staff were non-graduate youths for menial work; capable mature assistants followed, and in 1911 the first graduate assistant was appointed but resigned within a year. Offor inherited two female non-graduate assistants, but introduced a scheme akin to what he had known in London, persuading the university to employ one or more promising youths, who would study part-time for a degree while working in the library. Eventually Offor's "boys" colonized other libraries, notably Geoffrey Woledge, who became librarian of the London School of Economics. Expansion of postgraduate courses in librarianship after

1945 contributed to the demise of the scheme. Offor also successfully opened middle-management posts to graduates with library qualifications and weaned the library committee from individual book selection by focusing on budgetary control in relation to each academic department. Page established the duties of most graduate assistants on a subject basis in 1965, providing both a focus for relationships with teaching departments and scope for utilizing staff interests. Despite some mismatches between supply and demand, this relationship has continued, though recently modified by a team approach to management.

Technical Processes

Originally books were arranged by fixed location with minimal catalog entries handwritten in ledgers and supplemented by loose sheets. Passavant introduced a typewriter and a slip catalog in small loose-leaf binders (this system lasted for some 100 years). Under Offor, catalog rules evolved on an in-house basis, referring to British Museum Library practice in doubtful cases. He introduced a classification scheme suited to a dispersed collection, identifying main classes by their actual names and subdividing by letters and numbers. This process gave more fields at some levels than other schemes and allowed new main classes to be created as required. Development of electronic data processing promised greater efficiency, and from the mid-1970s new systems were phased in, culminating in an online integrated system combining catalog, circulation, and other functions from 1986. The library adopted the *Anglo-American Cataloging Rules*, 2nd edition (AACR 2) in 1974–75 and Library of Congress subject headings in 1991–92, but its own classification system remains. Until computerized, the catalog was principally a name catalog, the subject approach being minimal.

PETER S. MORRISH

Further Reading

Anning, S.T., and W.K.J. Walls, *A History of the Leeds School of Medicine*, Leeds: Leeds University, 1982

Challis, C.E., "Brotherton Library [Coin] Collection," *Coordinating Committee for Numismatics in Britain Newsletter* 24 (2000)

Cox, Dennis, "Leeds University Library," in *Encyclopedia of Library and Information Science*, edited by Allen Kent et al., vol. 14, New York: Dekker, 1975

Gosden, P.H., "The University Archive," *Leeds University Library Readers' Newsletter* 7 (1995)

Gosden, P.H., and A.J. Taylor, *Studies in the History of a University*, Leeds: Leeds University, 1975

Masson, D.I., "The Brotherton Collection of Rare Books and Manuscripts," *University of Leeds Review* 21 (1978)

Morrish, P.S., "The Brotherton Library, Its Judaica, and Cecil Roth," *University of Leeds Review* 23 (1980)

Morrish, P.S., "Dichotomy and Status: Leeds University Librarianship to 1934," *History of Universities* 15 (1997–99)

Morrish, P.S., "Fanny Juliet Passavant (1849–1944): A Leeds Librarian," *Library History* 12 (1996)

Offor, Richard, *A Descriptive Guide to the Libraries of the University of Leeds*, Leeds: Brotherton Library, 1947

Page, Bertram S., and D.I. Masson, "The Brotherton Collection," in *Encyclopedia of Library and Information Science*, edited by Allen Kent et al., vol. 3, New York: Dekker, 1970

Library Company of Philadelphia

Address: Library Company of Philadelphia
1314 Locust Street
Philadelphia, Pennsylvania 19107
USA
Telephone: 215-546-3181
Fax: 215-546-5167
www.librarycompany.org

Founded: 1731

Holdings (1999): Volumes: 500,000. Current serials: 100; graphic materials: 75,000; incunabula: 112; manuscripts: 160,000.

Special Collections: *Areas of Concentration:* 17th- to 19th-century printed and graphic material relating to: African American history; business and economics; German-Americana; history of women; Philadelphia area prints and photographs; philanthropy, education, and reform; popular literature; popular medicine; printing and publishing; science and technology. *Papers:* Anne Hampton Brewster; John Dickinson; Pierre Eugene DuSimitière; Elizabeth Graeme Ferguson; William Henry Fry; John McAllister; Samuel G. Morton; Rittenhouse paper mill; Benjamin and James Rush; John Jay Smith.

Origins

Founded in 1731 by Benjamin Franklin, the Library Company of Philadelphia was the first subscription library in the colonies, and until the 1850s it was the largest public library in the United States. Since the 1950s it has been an independent research library documenting every aspect of U.S. history from the colonial period to roughly 1880. Its origin as a circulating library is the basis of its strength as a research library, as virtually all the books acquired in the 18th and 19th centuries are still on the shelves. It is thus a reasonably accurate reflection of the book culture of British North America, because its core collection is composed of books acquired at the request of its users as they were published. In the colonial period, most books were imported from England, so the Library Company was and still is one of the largest collections of 18th-century English books in North America. It also holds the second largest collection of pre-1801 American imprints (the largest such collection is held by the American Antiquarian Society).

The Library Company was an outgrowth of the Junto, the reading club of young artisans begun by Franklin in 1727. They believed that by reading, conversing, and improving their minds, they would improve their material circumstances, their social position, and ultimately their entire community. After a failed attempt to form a library by pooling the few books they already owned, they decided to go public by forming a chartered corporation, a "company" (in the language of the time) whose members could collectively own a far larger library than any could afford individually. They gathered 50 subscribers willing to purchase shares for 40 shillings each and to pay 10 shillings per year thereafter, to buy books and maintain the library. They signed articles of association on 1 July 1731, and in 1742 a formal charter was obtained from the Penn family. William Penn's secretary, the learned book collector James Logan, gave advice about which books would be best to acquire, and in 1732 the first order of 56 books arrived from London, facilitated by the Quaker merchant and naturalist, Peter Collinson. The first surviving catalog is a 1741 pamphlet printed by Franklin listing 372 titles. Catalogs were printed every 10 to 20 years until 1856, after which they were superseded by a public card catalog.

By the 1740s the library was installed in the west wing of the State House (later known as Independence Hall), and from then until the latter part of the 19th century, it was, in effect, the city's public library. Shareholders could borrow books freely, which had not been the case in earlier public libraries in the colonies. Nonmembers could also borrow books if they left a refundable deposit equal to the value of the book. By the 1770s there were more than 500 members, about a tenth of the households of the city.

In 1773 the library moved to the second floor of Carpenters' Hall, where it served as the Library of the Continental Congress and of the Constitutional Convention. In 1790, just as the new federal government was installing itself in a new complex of buildings near the State House, the Library Company erected a building of its own across the street at Fifth and Chestnut. From then until 1800, when the government moved to Washington, the Library Company served as the de facto Library of Congress. By then almost every town and village in the seaboard states had a subscription or social library modeled on the Library Company.

Throughout the early national and antebellum periods, the library grew not only by acquiring new books as they were published at home and abroad but also by acquiring collections formed by others. In 1785 the Library Company's dynamic new librarian, Zachariah Poulson, was the main buyer at the estate sale of the Swiss-born collector Pierre Eugene DuSimitière. From the 1760s on DuSimitière had been gathering what he saw as the raw materials of history, picking up ephemera from the streets and copying out many documents whose originals are now lost. His collection included hundreds of otherwise unknown imprints relating to the Stamp Act crisis and the Revolutionary War.

In 1792 the 4,000-volume Loganian Library was incorporated into the Library Company. Its nucleus was the 2,600-volume library of James Logan, rich in science, mathematics, and philology, the largest private library in the Pennsylvania at the time of his death in 1751. To this had been added the medical library of his brother, Dr. William Logan of Bristol, England. Thus the Library Company became the largest medical library in the colonies.

The 19th Century

In the early 19th century several more libraries were acquired, the most notable being the 7,000-volume collection of William Mackenzie, a Philadelphia merchant who was among the first Americans to collect books because of their value, rarity, or beauty. He owned such collector's items as Jacobus de Voragine's *Golden Legende* printed by Caxton in 1438 and Jenson's 1476 Italian Pliny on vellum.

In 1869 Dr. James Rush, son of Dr. Benjamin Rush, bequeathed to the Library Company his father's papers and his large medical library, along with nearly $1 million to fund a new building, as the 1790 structure was by then bursting at the seams. The will had stated that the new building was to be near the center of the city, but in a codicil, Rush left the location to the discretion of his executor, who claimed that on his deathbed Rush had changed his mind and whispered that he wanted the building in South Philadelphia instead. This caused a sensation among the shareholders, almost none of whom lived near the proposed site. After several lawsuits contesting the will failed, the bequest was reluctantly accepted, but as soon as the huge new building was finished in 1878, another one almost as large was built about eight blocks away in a more central location.

This fiasco demonstrated how ill equipped was this private institution to supply an essential public service to a large and diverse modern city. Rush's will included other codicils that were further intended to prevent the Library Company from becoming more like the public libraries in other cities. He decreed that the library would collect only books of permanent value that would benefit rather than amuse the public. He banned "every-day novels, mind-tainting reviews, controversial politics," even daily newspapers. Until then the Library Company, supplemented by other smaller specialized subscription libraries, had performed the public library function well enough that Philadelphia's leaders felt that they did not need a tax-supported public library, but the controversy surrounding the Rush bequest showed how untenable the situation was. After years of planning, the Free Library of Philadelphia was chartered in 1891.

The 20th Century and Beyond

In the early 20th century, with its public role diminished, the Library Company became more and more marginal. The Depression wiped out its endowment, and during World War II it was operated as a branch of the Free Library. Some new raison d'être had to be found, or the library would cease to exist. This was provided by the postwar proliferation of graduate programs in U.S. history and a new demand for primary source materials, which opened the eyes of the directors to the value of the books lying unused in their stacks.

The transformation from circulating library to research institution took place under the direction of Edwin Wolf, librarian from 1955 to 1984. Wolf defined the scope of the library's interests as being American history and culture (and its European background) up to about 1880. Another part of this transformation was constructing a new, climate-controlled building, located next door to the Historical Society of Pennsylvania to take advantage of the complementary nature of the two collections. The library's manuscript collection was placed on deposit there, and the Historical Society's early printed books were deposited with the Library Company.

Another crucial part of the transition was the decision not to keep the collections static but to build them up in a way that preserved the focus of the core collection but also made it more responsive to the needs of scholars. Wolf's original plan was to make the library an even more faithful representation of the book culture of the colonial elite, a microcosm of the American Enlightenment. He aggressively collected books owned or annotated by colonial Philadelphians; he reconstructed the private libraries of Benjamin Franklin and William Byrd of Westover; and he published a catalog of James Logan's books. As a result, the Library Company is one of the best places to study early American intellectual history and especially the books that helped to shape the nation from the 1760s through the 1790s.

As the years passed, however, the Library Company began to look at its core collections in new ways. Beginning in 1969 when scholarly interest in African American history was growing, the entire collection was combed and a catalog was published of every imprint relating to that subject, from early European accounts of Africa through the literature of antislavery and abolition to the end of Reconstruction. This collection has since grown considerably and is the library's strongest single subject area. In the early 1970s the same interpretive technique was applied to women's history, including all sorts of books written by, for, or about women.

In the 1980s other special collections were uncovered, and catalogs were published covering pre-1860 U.S. education, philanthropy, agriculture, and natural history. The collection of German-American imprints to 1830 grew to become the largest in existence. Wolf gave his large personal collection of pre-1850 American Judaica. Other strengths were discovered and reinforced in popular fiction, in medical books written for laypersons, and in the broad subject area of business and economics. In the 1970s a separate Print Department was established, which holds a heavily used collection of Philadelphia-area prints and photographs.

The Library Company itself is an object of study. Unfortunately, few borrowing records survive, but the archives include a complete list of shareholders, the minutes of the board meetings, and accession records from 1731 to the present, as well as printed catalogs from 1741 to 1856, and the original card catalog, which survives nearly intact. The books themselves contain annotations, marks of previous ownership, and other features that offer clues about the role they played in the community and the circumstances of their manufacture and dissemination.

The Library Company encourages the scholarly use of its collections by offering fellowships for research on any subject within its scope. An historic townhouse next door has been renovated to house a center for advanced research in early American history. Changing exhibitions of materials from the collections are mounted in the gallery, often accompanied by printed catalogs. From time to time the library sponsors scholarly symposia on subjects related to the collections and publishes the proceedings in book form. Its website includes information on these programs, as well as an online catalog. Its holdings are also accessible in the *English Short Title Catalogue (ESTC)*, the North American Imprints Project (NAIP), and Research Libraries Information Network (RLIN) databases.

JAMES N. GREEN

Further Reading

Library Company of Philadelphia, *"At the Instance of Benjamin Franklin": A Brief History of the Library Company of Philadelphia, 1731–1976*, Philadelphia, Pennsylvania: Library Company of Philadelphia, 1976; revised edition, 1995

Wolf, Edwin, "The First Books and Printed Catalogues of the Library Company of Philadelphia," *Pennsylvania Magazine of History and Biography* 78 (1954)

Wolf, Edwin, "Franklin and His Friends Choose Their Books," *Pennsylvania Magazine of History and Biography* 80 (1956)

Wolf, Edwin, and Marie Elena Korey, editors, *Quarter of a Millennium: The Library Company of Philadelphia, 1731–1981*, Philadelphia, Pennsylvania: Library Company of Philadelphia, 1981

Library of Congress of the United States

Address: Library of Congress of the United States
101 Independence Avenue, S.E.
Washington, D.C. 20540
USA
Telephone: 202-707-5000
Fax: 202-707-1389
www.loc.gov

Founded: 1800

Holdings (2000): Items: 27.8 million print items (including 18.3 million cataloged books). Current serials: 150,000; graphic materials: 13.5 million (including 844,000 films and videos); incunabula: 5,702; manuscripts: 54 million; maps: 4.6 million (including 60,000 atlases); microforms: 13 million; music collection: 4.2 million items; sound recordings: 2.5 million.

Special Collections: *Areas of Concentration:* U.S. history and culture. *Individual Collections:* Martin S. Carson collection of Americana; Charles and Rae Eames collection of design; Farm Security Administration collection of photographs of U.S. life; Hispanic literature on tape archive; Historic American Buildings Survey collection; Dayton C. Miller flute collection; National American Woman Suffrage Association archives; National Association for the Advancement of Colored People (NAACP) archives; Lessing J. Rosenwald collection of early illustrated books; Sanborn collection of fire insurance maps of U.S. cities. *Papers:* Susan B. Anthony; Clara Barton; Alexander Graham Bell; Irving Berlin; Frederick Douglass; George and Ira Gershwin; Bob Hope; papers of ten chief justices of the U.S. Supreme Court; papers of the first 23 U.S. presidents; Walt Whitman.

The Development of a National Institution, 1800 to 1897

The Library of Congress was established as the U.S. Congress prepared to move from Philadelphia, Pennsylvania, to the new capital city of Washington, D.C. On 24 April 1800 President John Adams approved legislation that appropriated $5,000 to purchase "such books as may be necessary for the use of Congress." A congressional committee placed the first order, which arrived from England in May 1801. The 728 books and three maps were stored in the U.S. Capitol, which was to be the library's home until 1897.

On 26 January 1802 President Thomas Jefferson approved the first law defining the role and functions of the new institution. This measure created the post of librarian of Congress and gave Congress the authority to establish the library's rules and regulations. It was clear from the beginning, however, that the institution was to be more than a library solely for the legislature. The 1802 law made the appointment of the librarian of Congress a presidential responsibility and permitted the president and the vice president to borrow books. The privilege was gradually extended to officials in most government agencies.

Jefferson took a keen interest in the library and its collection while he was president of the United States from 1801 to 1809. In 1814 the British invaded Washington and destroyed the U.S. Capitol building and the small Library of Congress within (only one of the library's approximately 3,000 volumes is known to have survived). By then retired to Monticello, Jefferson offered to sell his personal library of more than 6,000 volumes to Congress to "recommence" its library. The purchase was approved in 1815, doubling the library's original size and permanently expanding the scope of its collections. In 1818 Jefferson's library was moved back into the rebuilt Capitol.

Jefferson's library reflected his wide-ranging interests in subjects such as architecture, science, geography, and literature. It also included volumes in French, German, Latin, Greek, and Russian. Anticipating the argument that his collection might be too comprehensive for use by a legislative body, in a letter to the Joint Committee on the Library, dated 12 September 1814, Jefferson stated his view that there was "no subject to which a member of Congress may not have occasion to refer." This Jeffersonian concept of universality is the philosophy and rationale behind the comprehensive collecting policies of today's Library of Congress. Jefferson's library was received and organized at the Library of Congress by George Watterston, the first full-time librarian of Congress.

Between the purchase of Jefferson's library and the 1860s, however, the Library of Congress—or the Congressional Library, as it was known until the end of the 19th century—grew slowly and without distinction. Approximately two-thirds of its 55,000-volume collection, including two-thirds of Jefferson's library, was destroyed in a disastrous fire in the Capitol in 1851. Moreover, the cultural nationalists in Congress, men such as Rufus Choate and George Perkins Marsh, looked to the Smithsonian Institution, established in 1846 in Washington, as the home of a future national library. The head of the Smithsonian, physicist Joseph Henry, adamantly opposed the notion, however, and in 1854 fired his ambitious librarian, Charles Coffin Jewett. Henry instead looked to the Library of Congress, which was rebuilt after the 1851 fire and installed in a handsome fireproof room in the Capitol, as the future national library.

Henry's view was welcomed by Ainsworth Rand Spofford, librarian of Congress from 1864 to 1897, who applied Jefferson's ideas on a grand scale and permanently linked the library's legislative and national functions. Spofford's concept of the Library of Congress as both a library for the U.S. Congress and the national library for the people of the United States has been wholeheartedly accepted by his successors.

Spofford began by obtaining congressional approval for the expansion of the library's room in the Capitol, then promptly filled both new wings with the Smithsonian Institution's library of scientific works (transferred in 1866) and archivist Peter Force's collection of Americana (obtained by purchase in 1867). The Library of Congress suddenly became the largest library in the United States. Spofford's other principal achievements were the centralization in 1870 of all U.S. copyright registration and deposit activities at the library and the construction of a separate building, a 26-year struggle not completed until the monumental new structure (today's Jefferson Building) opened in 1897.

Spofford's view of the proper function of a national library followed the European model, particularly that of the British Museum. For him a national library was primarily a comprehensive collection of a nation's intellectual product. Like Jefferson, Spofford believed that such a wide-ranging collection was needed by Congress if it were to govern a democracy successfully. In an article published in the *International Review* in November 1878, he argued that it was imperative that such a great national collection be shared with all citizens, for the United States was "a Republic which rests upon the popular intelligence."

In 1896, on the eve of the move into the new building, Congress held hearings about the expansion and reorganization of the library. The American Library Association (ALA), involving itself in the affairs of the library for the first time, sent six witnesses, including Melvil Dewey and future librarian of Congress Herbert Putnam. In accordance with the recommendations of Librarian Spofford and the ALA witnesses, the Legislative Appropriations Act of 1897 expanded all phases of the library's activities. This reorganization, effective 1 July 1897, gave the librarian of Congress sole responsibility for making the library's rules and regulations. It also established the Copyright Office as a separate entity within the library and stipulated that the president's appointment of a librarian thereafter be approved by the Senate.

The Jefferson Building

The construction (begun in 1886) and opening, on 1 November 1897, of the library's first separate building was of enormous significance for the institution. Spofford first asked Congress for such a structure in 1871, the year after copyright deposits began flowing into the library's room in the U.S. Capitol. He ran out of shelf space four years later and began filling rooms throughout the Capitol with books, maps, newspapers, and other collections. For Spofford, however, the struggle was worthwhile, for during the 26-year wait he enlisted support for the cause of the Library of Congress as the national library from dozens of congressmen and several presidents. The largest library building in the world when it opened, the imposing new structure, capped by a 23-carat gold-plated dome, was hailed as a national monument to culture and the arts. Its elaborately decorated interior, embellished by works of art from more than 40 U.S. painters and sculptors, linked the United States to classical traditions of learning and simultaneously flexed U.S. cultural and technological muscle.

The enthusiastic reaction to the building from the public, architectural critics, and members of Congress was both gratifying and useful to Librarian Spofford, because it focused attention on the institution and helped it attain its unique national status. However, the most significant aspect of the new building for Spofford was the 326,000 square feet of floor space now available for the national collections that he had been accumulating for three decades. For the first time those collections could be efficiently organized and made available. With ample space for growth, an expanded staff, and support from a well-pleased Congress, the Library of Congress could soon undertake the services expected of a truly national library.

National Service to Libraries and Scholarship, 1897 to 1939

Spofford's successor as librarian of Congress was John Russell Young, a journalist, former diplomat, and skilled administrator who supervised the move into the new building, the reorganization, and the hiring of new staff. Young shared Spofford's view that a national library was an accumulation of a nation's literature.

Herbert Putnam, superintendent of the Boston Public Library (Massachusetts), was named librarian of Congress by President William McKinley in 1899 after Young's untimely death. Putnam extended Spofford's view; to him a national library was much more than a comprehensive collection housed in Washington. He explained, in a December 1901 speech at the annual meeting of the American Historical Association, that it should be a collection "universal in scope" that could be used by the entire country and would serve scholarship both directly and indirectly through interlibrary loans to other libraries. Moreover, *universal* meant research collections representing other cultures, not just the United States, and the librarian began acquiring whole libraries from abroad.

The first experienced librarian to become librarian of Congress, Putnam felt that the national library should reach out from Washington by serving other libraries, and under his decisive leadership the Library of Congress began such service. During his first ten years in office, through the sale and distribution of printed catalog cards (1901), the development of classification schedules and union catalogs, the inauguration of interlibrary loan (1907), and other innovations he nationalized the library's collections and established the patterns of service that exist today.

Under Putnam, who served as librarian of Congress from 1899 to 1939, longer than any other, the Library of Congress began the formidable task of organizing recorded knowledge for public service. The development of its classification scheme and the distribution of cataloging and classification information in a standardized format (the three-by-five-inch catalog card) helped to shape and systematize U.S. scholarship and librarianship. This sharing of the library's bibliographic system propelled the Library of Congress into a position of leadership among the world's libraries.

New Cultural and International Roles, 1939 to 1974

During his brief 18-month tenure as librarian of Congress (1897–99), former diplomat Young sent a circular to U.S. diplomatic outposts soliciting materials from and about other countries. Putnam added major collections from Russia (1907) and Japan (1907) and laid the foundations for the library's collections of Hebraica (1912) and Chinese literature (1928). However, it was poet and writer Archibald MacLeish, librarian of Congress from 1939 to 1944, who articulated the Jeffersonian rationale as it applied to foreign materials. MacLeish's "canons of selection" were put forth in his 1940 annual report as part of a major reorganization that lasted the length of his administration. In the report he asserted that the library should acquire the "written records of those societies and peoples whose experience is of most immediate concern to the people of the United States." The prior year, soon after taking office, Librarian MacLeish had presided over the dedication of the Hispanic Society Room, a new home for the library's Hispanic Division.

MacLeish was a wartime librarian, and there is a sense of urgency in his statements about the importance of libraries, librarians, and especially the Library of Congress, in preserving democracy. In 1941, as U.S. involvement in World War II approached, MacLeish and his colleagues recognized that the library's collections were a national treasure that needed protecting, and items considered irreplaceable were removed from Washington for most of the war. When the Declaration of Independence and the U.S. Constitution were put back on public display in the library's Great Hall in September 1944, the symbolism was implicit: The worst was over and America was close to winning the war.

In 1925, by obtaining major gifts from Elizabeth Sprague Coolidge for the commissioning of music and the construction of a concert hall, Putnam had brought the Library of Congress into the world of classical music. The creation of the American Folk Song project in the Music Division in 1928 was also a pioneering effort. Through his many contacts in politics, arts, and letters, Librarian MacLeish established new public roles for the library in literature and poetry: The rotating consultantship in poetry (today the office of poet laureate consultant in poetry) is one of his legacies. MacLeish also directed the library's collecting efforts toward documenting U.S. culture by reestablishing the motion picture collection and, in the Prints and Photographs Division, emphasizing photography over fine arts.

The major lesson of World War II, according to Luther H. Evans, MacLeish's successor as librarian of Congress, was that "however large our collections may be now, they are pitifully and tragically small in comparison with the demands of the nation." In the same speech, reported in the 2 December 1945 issue of the Washington, D.C., *Sunday Star,* he described the need for larger collections about foreign countries in practical, patriotic terms, noting that during the war, while weather data on the Himalayas from the library's collections helped the U.S. Air Force, "the want of early issues of the *Boelkische Beobachter* prevented the first auguries of Nazism."

Evans, a political scientist, served as librarian of Congress from 1945 to 1953. He looked to a broader national role for the institution but in the end pushed forward its bibliographic, microfilming, and cooperative international activities. The Library of Congress Mission in Europe, organized in 1945 by Evans and his Library of Congress colleague Verner W. Clapp, acquired European publications for the library and other U.S. libraries. The library soon initiated automatic purchase agreements with foreign dealers around the world and greatly expanded its agreements for the international exchange of official publications. In 1945 the library organized a reference library in San Francisco to assist the participants in the meeting that established the United Nations. In 1947 a Library of Congress mission to Japan, headed by Clapp, provided advice for the establishment of the National Diet (parliamentary) Library in Tokyo.

Evans's successor as librarian of Congress was L. Quincy Mumford, who was director of the Cleveland Public Library (Ohio) when nominated by President Dwight D. Eisenhower in 1954. Mumford served until 1974 and, after a relatively slow start, eventually guided the library through its greatest period of rapid national and international expansion. In the 1960s the institution benefited from increased federal funding for education, libraries, and research. Most dramatic was the growth of the foreign acquisitions program, an expansion based at least in part on Evans' earlier initiatives. In 1958 Congress authorized the library to acquire books by using U.S.-owned foreign currency under the terms of the Agriculture Trade Development and Assistance Act of 1954 (Public Law 480). The first appropriation for this purpose was made in 1961, enabling the library to establish acquisition centers in New Delhi (India) and Cairo (Egypt) for the purpose of purchasing publications and distributing them to research libraries throughout the United States.

In 1965 President Lyndon B. Johnson approved the Higher Education Act of 1965. Title IIC of the new law had great significance for the Library of Congress and for academic and research libraries. It authorized the Office of Education to transfer funds to the Library of Congress for the ambitious purpose of acquiring, insofar as possible, all current library materials of value to scholarship published throughout the world and providing cataloging information for these materials promptly after they had been received. This law came closer than any other legislation affecting the Library of Congress to making Jefferson's concept of comprehensiveness part of the library's official mandate. The new effort was christened the National Program for Acquisitions and Cataloging (NPAC). The first NPAC office was opened in London in 1966. A decade later the Library of Congress had ten overseas offices.

The development of international bibliographic standards was now recognized as an important concern. The crucial development took place at the Library of Congress in the mid-1960s: the creation of the Library of Congress MAchine Readable Cataloging format (MARC) for communicating bibliographic data in machine-readable form. This new capability for converting, maintaining, and distributing bibliographic information soon became the standard format for sharing data about books and research materials in other formats and several languages. The possibility of worldwide application was recognized, and the MARC format structure became an official national standard in 1971 and an international standard in 1973.

Librarian Mumford retired in 1974. During the two decades of his librarianship, the library's collections, staff, and appropriation expanded from 33 million to 74 million items; from 1,500 to 4,200 employees; and from $9 million to $96 million. Mumford also initiated the planning and obtained the first appropriation for the library's third major building, the James Madison Memorial Building, which opened its doors to the public in 1980.

Congress and Its Library, 1939 to 1974

Most members of Congress did not pay serious attention to its library until 1896 when, faced with the imminent opening of the new Library of Congress building, the Joint Library Committee held hearings on the library's condition. There was general agreement that the library needed to be expanded and reorganized, and testimony was invited concerning its potential functions and roles. The testimony from leaders of the ALA, who urged a greater national role for the institution, helped to shape its subsequent reorganization. In December 1897 a bill was introduced in Congress providing that the Library of Congress should "be known and styled" as the "National Library." The Joint Committee on the Library recommended approval, but no action was taken. The stage had been set for the tug and pull between the library's legislative and national roles that have become part of its history.

In the 20th century the debate was most visible during the administrations of Librarians of Congress MacLeish, Evans, and Mumford. Members of Congress worried that the legislative support services provided by the library would be overshadowed by the national role advocated by both MacLeish and Evans, particularly through the expansion of the library's cultural role and its services to other libraries. The international role advocated by Evans was another worry. One reaction was the strengthening of the library's Legislative Reference Service (the part of the library that served Congress directly) as part of the 1946 Legislative Reorganization Act.

In addition, the rapid expansion of both the library's national and international roles during the last decade of Mumford's administration was counterbalanced in part by a 1970 law granting increased autonomy for the Legislative Reference Service, which was renamed the Congressional Research Service. Mumford, however, also faced criticism from the other side. In 1962 Senator Claiborne Pell, a member of the joint committee on the library, ignited a controversy when he introduced into the *Congressional Record* a memorandum about the library's various roles that had been prepared at his request by Douglas W. Bryant, associate director of the Harvard University Library (Cambridge, Massachusetts). Bryant's memorandum, reproduced in the library's 1962 annual report, urged further expansion of the library's national role, concluding that

> though it would be desirable, it is not essential to transfer the Library of Congress to the Executive; but it is essential that legislation recognize officially what the library is and what it ought to do, and that a National Advisory Board (if not a National Research Library Foundation) be established in the Executive Branch.

Mumford's response, also printed in the 1962 report, strongly defended the library's location in the legislative branch of government. He also pointed out that "the Library of Congress today performs more national library functions than any other national library in the world."

The Boorstin and Billington Eras, 1975 to the Present

A new public role for the Library of Congress emerged under the leadership of historian Daniel J. Boorstin, who was nominated by President Gerald R. Ford and served as librarian of Congress from 1975 to 1987. Boorstin was sworn in on 12 November 1975 in the library's Great Hall in a ceremony that signaled the new librarian's sense of symbolism and tradition. The oath of office, taken on a Bible from the Jefferson collection, was administered by Carl Albert, the Speaker of the House of Representatives, with President Ford and Vice President Nelson A. Rockefeller participating in the ceremony.

Boorstin immediately faced two major challenges: the need to review the library's organization and functions and the lack of space for both collections and staff. His response to the first was the creation of a task force on goals, organization, and planning, a staff group that conducted, with help from eight outside advisory groups, a one-year review of the library and its various roles. Many of the task force's recommendations were incorporated into a subsequent administrative reorganization. The move into the library's James Madison Memorial Building, which began in

1980 and was completed in 1982 (after two decades of planning and construction), relieved administrative as well as physical pressures and enabled Boorstin to focus on what he deemed most important: the strengthening of the library's ties with Congress and the development of new relationships between the library and scholars, authors, publishers, cultural leaders, and the business community.

The Library of Congress grew steadily during Boorstin's administration, with its annual appropriation increasing from $116 million to more than $250 million. Like MacLeish, Boorstin relied heavily on his professional staff in technical areas such as cataloging, automation, and the preservation of the library's collections. However, he took a keen personal interest in collection development (particularly the strengthening of the library's foreign-language collections), in copyright, in the symbolic role of the Library of Congress in life in the United States, and, as he noted in his introduction to the *Guide to the Library of Congress* (1962), "the world's greatest Multi-Media Encyclopedia." Boorstin's style and accomplishments increased the visibility of the institution to the point that, in an article in the 6 January 1987 issue of the *New York Times,* reporter Irvin Molotsky called the post of librarian of Congress "perhaps the leading intellectual public position in the nation."

Boorstin's successor, historian James H. Billington, was nominated by President Ronald Reagan and took the oath of office on 14 September 1987. Billington immediately took personal charge of the library, instituting his own major review (by the management and planning committee) and subsequent reorganization. Convinced that the Library of Congress needed to share its resources more widely and to increase its public visibility and level of support dramatically, he aggressively pursued a new educational role for the institution. In 1990 he established a development office with congressional approval, as well as the James Madison Council, a private-sector support and advisory board consisting mostly of business leaders.

The library's National Digital Library is the centerpiece of Billington's efforts. Funded by private sector donations and congressional appropriations, the goal of the National Digital Library program is to digitize millions of the library's unique U.S. history collections and make them freely available to teachers, students, and the general public via the Internet. By late 1999 more than 2 million items from more than 60 collections had been digitized. In September 1999 the library opened a National Digital Library Learning Center, a facility for training teachers about classroom uses of the digitized U.S. history collections. In December 2000, at the end of its bicentennial year, the library met its bicentennial goal of mounting 5 million images on its American Memory website.

As the 20th century drew to a close, once again the ever-expanding Library of Congress had run out of space in its buildings on Capitol Hill, but new spaces had been obtained. In 1998, with support from the private sector, the library began developing a National Audiovisual Conservation Center on a 41-acre tract in Culpepper, Virginia. More than 5.3 million items from its motion picture, radio, television, and recorded sound collections will be stored there, and a state-of-the-art preservation laboratory is being built. In the fall of 1999 construction began on the library's major new storage facility, a series of buildings on a 100-acre site at Fort Meade, Maryland, 20 miles north of Capitol Hill.

The Library of Congress Today

The Library of Congress, probably the world's largest and most comprehensive library, occupies a unique place in U.S. civilization. Established as a legislative library, it grew into a national public institution in the 19th century, a product of U.S. cultural nationalism. Since World War II, it has become an international resource of unparalleled dimension. Today the library provides direct service to users through 21 reading rooms located in its three massive structures on Capitol Hill: the Thomas Jefferson Building (1897), the John Adams Building (1939), and the James Madison Memorial Building (1980).

The library's status since 1870 as the official copyright agency of the United States has enabled it to develop unique collection strengths, especially in motion pictures, maps and atlases, music, and U.S. public documents, as well as U.S. history, politics, and literature. In addition to materials received through the copyright registration process, materials are acquired through gifts and purchases and from other government agencies (state, local, and federal), the Cataloging in Publication program (a prepublication arrangement with publishers), and exchange with libraries in the United States and abroad. In all, the library receives approximately 22,000 items each working day and adds approximately 10,000 items to its collections daily.

Since 1962 the library has maintained offices abroad to acquire, catalog, and preserve library and research materials where such materials are essentially unavailable through conventional acquisition methods. Overseas offices in Rio de Janeiro (Brazil), Cairo (Egypt), New Delhi (India), Jakarta (Indonesia), Nairobi (Kenya), and Islamabad (Pakistan) collectively acquire materials from more than 60 countries. Nearly two-thirds of the library's book and serial collections are in languages other than English. More than 450 languages are represented in the collections. Many of the foreign-language collections are exceptionally strong, particularly those in Arabic, Chinese, Japanese, Korean, Portuguese, Russian, Spanish, and Tibetan. The foreign newspaper and foreign law collections also are noteworthy in size and scope.

Using private funds and congressional appropriations, the library has made its bibliographic records and selected items from its Americana collections available electronically since 1994. The subsequent rapid development of its website—through which it now freely shares selected collections, bibliographic data, and information about current legislation, copyright, and its collections, services, and programs—has made the Library of Congress an increasingly important educational force. In 2000 the Library of Congress' website received more than 1 billion hits, making it one of the most frequently used institutional websites in the world.

A complicated government agency firmly embedded in the legislative branch of the U.S. government, the Library of Congress never has been officially recognized as a national library. Nevertheless, it performs most of the functions expected of a national library. Its mission, determined by its chief operating officers and executive committee, is to make its remarkable collections and resources, many of them unique and irreplaceable, "available and useful to the Congress and the American people and to sustain and preserve a universal collection of knowledge and creativity for future generations."

The story of the Library of Congress is the story of the accumulation of diverse functions and collections. As noted in the 1962 memorandum (now part of the *Congressional Record*) from Harvard University's Associate Librarian Bryant, "the major functions of the Library of Congress might have been assigned to three or four separate agencies ... an explanation of why they have been combined would call for a study of history rather than of administrative logic."

The positive side of the library's diverse mix of functions is that it brings together the concerns of government, learning, and librarianship—an uncommon combination, but one that has greatly benefited U.S. politics, scholarship, and culture. The difficult side is twofold. First, its sheer size is a problem for users and administrators alike. Second, the differences inherent in the library's varied functions, particularly its dual role as a legislative library and as a national (and international) institution, frequently lead to criticism and conflict, both outside and inside the institution.

The diversity of the Library of Congress is startling. Simultaneously it serves as a legislative library, the major research arm of the U.S. Congress; the copyright agency of the United States; a center for scholarship that collects research materials in most subjects and media and in more than 450 languages; a public, tax-supported institution that is open to everyone over the age of 18 and to all Americans through its popular website and serves readers in 21 reading rooms; a government library that is heavily used by agencies in all three branches of government; the national library for the blind and physically handicapped, with regional branches throughout the country; the world's largest law library; one of the world's largest providers of bibliographic data and products; a center for the commissioning and performance of chamber music; the home of the nation's poet laureate; the sponsor of exhibitions and of musical, literary, and cultural programs that reach across the country and the world; a research center and laboratory for the preservation of research materials, particularly books, maps, prints, manuscripts, and motion pictures; a major center for digitizing documents, motion pictures, manuscripts, photographs, and sound recordings and making these collections available via the Internet; and, in all likelihood, the world's largest repository of maps, atlases, printed and recorded music, motion pictures, and television programs.

As it marked its bicentennial in the year 2000 with the theme "Libraries-Creativity-Liberty," the Library of Congress was still guided by Thomas Jefferson's belief that democracy is knowledge-based and depends on the free, unhampered pursuit of truth by an informed and involved citizenry.

JOHN Y. COLE

Further Reading

Bisbort, Alan, and Linda Barrett Osborne, *The Nation's Library: The Library of Congress, Washington, D.C.*, Washington, D.C., Library of Congress, 2000

Cole, John Y., editor, *The Library of Congress in Perspective: A Volume Based on the Reports of the 1976 Librarian's Task Force and Advisory Groups*, New York: Bowker, 1978

Cole, John Y., *For Congress and the Nation: A Chronological History of the Library of Congress*, Washington, D.C.: Library of Congress, 1979

Cole, John Y., and Henry Hope Reed, editors, *The Library of Congress: The Art and Architecture of the Thomas Jefferson Building*, New York: Norton, 1997

Conaway, James, *America's Library: The Story of the Library of Congress, 1800–2000*, New Haven, Connecticut: Yale University Press, 2000

Day, Sara, editor, *Gathering History: The Marian S. Carson Collection of Americana*, Washington, D.C.: Library of Congress, 1999

Johnston, William Dawson, *History of the Library of Congress, 1800–1864*, Washington, D.C.: Government Printing Office, 1904; reprint, New York: Kraus Reprint, 1967

Melville, Annette, compiler, *Special Collections of the Library of Congress*, Washington, D.C.: Library of Congress, 1980

Rosenberg, Jane A., "Foundation for Service: The 1896 Hearings on the Library of Congress," *The Journal of Library History* 21 (1986)

Rosenberg, Jane A., *The Nation's Great Library: Herbert Putnam and the Library of Congress, 1899–1939*, Urbana: University of Illinois Press, 1993

Virga, Vincent, et al., *Eyes of the Nation: A Visual History of the United States*, New York: Knopf, 1997

Wagner, Margaret E., editor, *American Treasures of the Library of Congress: Memory, Reason, Imagination*, New York: Abrams, 1997

Library of the Royal Palace, Spain

Address: Real Biblioteca
c/Bailén, s/n
E-28071 Madrid
Spain
Telephone: 91-454-8733
Fax: 91-454-8867

Founded: ca. 1700

Holdings (1999): Volumes: 250,000. Graphic materials: 16,000; incunabula: 260; manuscripts: 5,000; maps and atlases: 4,000; musical scores: 8,000.

Special Collections: *Areas of Concentration:* Bibles; bookbinding; history of books and printing; illustrated books and periodicals; prints, engravings, and drawings (Old Master through 18th century); rare atlases; Romantic period publications; Spanish and colonial Spanish American historical and literary manuscripts. *Individual Collections:* Books of hours collection; Cervantes collection; Ignatius Loyola; Celestino Mutis archives; Valladolid's *Librería del Sol* papers; Emperor Charles V.

Early Years

1760 is frequently cited as the year in which the Library of the Royal Palace in Madrid was founded. However, the little direct evidence that exists suggests that this actually occurred somewhat later, during the early years of Charles IV's monarchy (1788–1808). It was then that the library took on a truly official character, gained its own set of rooms within the palace, and began to have its holdings organized and classified in systematic fashion by a head librarian employed expressly to oversee it.

Nevertheless, whatever the actual date of its founding, the library's origins lie in the early part of the 18th century, when the Spanish monarchs—through gifts, bequests, purchases, and donations—began to accumulate a significant private library of books, manuscripts, drawings, and prints. The size of the library at the end of the 18th century is difficult to estimate, but it probably contained in excess of 10,000 printed books and bound volumes of manuscripts, in addition to a large number of maps, atlases, prints, and drawings. Ferdinand VII, who ascended to the throne in 1808 and after the Napoleonic interregnum reigned from 1814 to 1833, maintained a strong interest in the welfare of the library. Under his patronage its holdings grew substantially. Ferdinand was also enamored of fine bindings and arranged to have many volumes expertly and beautifully bound. For nearly a century after his death, few large collections were added to the library. Although the holdings remained relatively static throughout this period, the royal family recognized the singular value of its library, both as a bibliographic and historical treasure in its own right and as a resource for specialized study and investigation.

During the latter part of the 19th century and into the early years of the 20th, a number of improvements were made in the library's internal operations and organization. Two of the library's directors were especially effective in this regard, Manuel Remón Zarco del Valle and Juan Gualberto López Valdemoro. Under their administration the staff was increased, a modern classification scheme was implemented, the first printed catalogs of the library's holdings were published, and use of the library (requiring special permission, as it still does today) was made available to a wider, less select audience.

The Post-1931 Years

The founding of the Spanish Republic in 1931 brought several changes to the library. Preeminent among these was a change in its name, from Royal Library (Biblioteca Real) to Palace Library (Biblioteca de Palacio). Further improvements were made in its cataloging operations and in the published descriptions of its collections.

It was in this period that the library began to organize exhibitions of its rare books and other specialized materials. In 1937, during the second year of the Spanish Civil War (1936–39), the library was removed from the royal palace and stored in the Prado Museum. It was returned to the palace in 1939. In 1940 the royal library was declared to be part of the country's national patrimony (*patrimonio nacional*), a designation affording it special protection and supervision. It continues to be administered by agencies of the national patrimony while simultaneously retaining its character as a private library of the royal family. Since 1952 the library has been open for tours by visitors to the palace. In recent decades, it has also organized numerous exhibitions, many of which have been accompanied by published catalogs. At present the library occupies some 25 rooms on two floors within the palace. The use of its materials is restricted to qualified individuals demonstrating a specific research need.

Major Holdings of the Library

The collections of the palace library are organized into the following divisions: printed books, manuscripts, fine arts (prints, drawings, music, and photographs), maps, and periodicals. In addition, the library houses a museum of coins and commemorative medals. Over its nearly 300 years of history, the library has gathered these materials from various sources. Initially many of the books and manuscripts came from suppressed convents and monasteries and from offices and departments of the royal administration. Even more important, especially during the 18th century, were a series of private libraries acquired by the royal family, some through purchase, others through a donation or bequest made by the owner. Among the more notable private libraries thus acquired were those of Gregorio Mayáns y Siscar, historian Juan Bautista Muñóz, government official José Manuel de Ayala, churchman Joaquin Ibáñez, the count of Gondomar, and the great naturalist and Enlightenment figure José Celestino Mutis.

Printed Books

The book collection of the palace library, while today numbering more than 250,000 volumes, is perhaps best understood as a series of special collections, each independent of the other, but also linked in certain ways, both topically and chronologically. The core of the book collection, figuratively speaking, is its incunabula. While these are relatively few in number (approximately 260), they are distinguished by their rarity and, in many cases, uniqueness. This collection is complemented by a large body of 16th-century imprints, representing work done by all of the major European publishers as well as publishers operating in the centers of the Spanish colonial world. Standing out among the 16th-century books are the library's collections of Holy Bibles and of early scientific works, exceptional for their typographical elements and engraved illustrations. These same features distinguish many of the library's 18th- and 19th-century imprints, which include special strengths in European (especially French) Romanticism and in book design and illustration (fine bindings and books containing lithographs or steel, copper, or wood engravings). Of special note is the library's *colección cervantina*—a comprehensive, world-wide collection of books in all editions and formats by and about the celebrated author of *Don Quijote*, Miguel Cervantes de Saavedra.

Manuscripts

The manuscript section of the palace library constitutes a pastiche of documents—letters, political and scientific reports, poetry and books in manuscript form, royal decrees and diplomatic instructions, the writings of ecclesiastical and church officials—both in the original and in copied form and dating from the late Middle Ages to the end of the 19th century. This mass of material was first organized into a formal collection in the early 19th century, although a partial listing of the library's manuscripts had been compiled in the middle of the 18th century. The work of inventorying and cataloging the holdings of the section continues to the present day. All of the library's cataloged manuscripts are mounted in bound volumes, which currently number more than 3,000. Among official crown documents found in the collection are decrees and ordinances issued by Alfonso XI, Henry II, and the Catholic monarchs, as well as letters written by Emperor Charles V. The religious documents include autograph letters of Ignatius Loyola and other officials of the Jesuit Order. Among the richest parts of the collection are those dealing with colonial Spanish America, as the library contains the original manuscript copies of several classic works documenting and illustrating the physical and human geography of Spanish America in the 17th and 18th centuries.

The section also contains medieval codexes and illuminated manuscripts as well as a book of hours collection, the latter being particularly strong in its holdings of 15th-century Flemish, Italian, and French copies (including the personal copy of Queen Isabel).

Prints and Drawings

The palace library also holds a select and highly representative collection of prints and drawings containing the work of prominent Spanish and other European artists and engravers from the 16th through the 19th centuries. The majority of this collection originally belonged to the family of Charles III and was thus transferred to the library some two hundred years ago. A substantial number of the library's older prints were, following the practice of the time, trimmed at the edges and pasted into albums (approximately 200 prints per album). This treatment, while unfortunate in certain respects, has nonetheless allowed the collection to remain in nearly pristine physical condition. Artists represented in the print collection include Albrecht Dürer, Phillip Galle, Peter van der Heyden, Frans Hals, Van Dyck, Robert Nanteuil, Giambattista Piranesi, Nicolo Boldrini, and—from Spain—José de Ribera and Francisco de Goya. The drawings collection is of equal importance, historically and artistically.

Spanning the same chronological period and containing both sketches and formal compositions, the collection's subject matter is typical of the genre, and thus includes portraits, landscapes, views of cities and monuments, architectural plans, and depictions of birds, flowers, mountains, and other animals and objects of nature. Considered as the centerpiece of the drawings collection is a series of perspectives and plans completed in the 16th century by Juan de Herrera for King Philip II's proposed palace and monastery of the Escorial. In addition to prints and drawings, the fine arts section contains a minor collection of photographs. This collection, which numbers some 12,000 items, is primarily of historical and documentary value and concentrates on views and images of the royal family in the context of official events and ceremonies.

Music, Maps, and Periodicals

The holdings of the palace library are rounded out by its music, map, and periodical collections. All three are important but of modest scope and size. The music section contains approximately 8,000 scores, covering religious, symphonic, chamber, and vocal compositions primarily of the 18th and 19th centuries. Some earlier pieces, including 15th- and 16th-century musical scores used for court performances, are also included. Notable segments of the music collection are 18th-century operatic scores in manuscript form and published music of the Romantic period, prized as much for its chromolithographed covers as for its musical content.

The map collection contains a variety of cartographic material, including atlases, gazeteers, navigational charts, city plans, and maps of varying topical emphasis in both published and manuscript form from the 16th century to the present. The total number of pieces in the collection exceeds 4,000 and includes some of the principal European atlases of the Age of Discovery, such as those by Mercator, Lafreri, Ortelio, and Braun.

The periodical collection is distinguished primarily for its holdings of 19th-century materials such as almanacs, calendars, guidebooks, newspapers, and illustrated magazines published in Spain and, to a lesser extent, France, England, and other European countries. These publications were donated to the library (often in rather scattered runs) by members or associates of the royal family who subscribed to particular titles out of personal interest or for reasons of state. In recent years the palace library has placed a greater emphasis on building its periodical collection more systematically. Subscriptions and standing orders have been added to the traditional reliance upon gift and exchange.

RUSS T. DAVIDSON

Further Reading

Carrión, Manuel, "Spain, Libraries in," in *Encyclopedia of Library and Information Science,* edited by Allen Kent et al., vol. 28, New York: Dekker, 1980

López Serrano, Matilde, "La biblioteca y sus museos," in *El Palacio Real de Madrid,* edited by López Serrano, Madrid: Editorial Patrimonio Nacional, 1975

Santiago Páez, Elena, "La Biblioteca de Palacio," *Reales Sitios* 1 (1964)

Santiago Páez, Elena, "Las bibliotecas del Alcázar en tiempos de los Austrias," in *El Real Alcázar de Madrid: Dos siglos de arquitectura y coleccionismo en la corte de los reyes de España,* edited by Fernando Checa Cremades, Madrid: Nerea, 1994

London Library

Address: London Library
14 St. James's Square
London SW1Y 4LG
England
UK
Telephone: 20-7930-7705
Fax: 20-7766-4766
www.londonlibrary.co.uk

Founded: 1841

Holdings (2001): Volumes: 1 million.
Current serials: 500.

Special Collections: *Areas of Concentration:* Art; architecture; humanities; philosophy; religion; social history; topography; travel. *Individual Collections:* Art collection of European art forms; classics collection; German collection; Higginson collection of fox hunting; Iberian collection; Scandinavian collection.

The London Library was opened on 3 May 1841 as the result of a short but successful campaign by a group of prominent London literary and cultural personages, led by Thomas Carlyle, whom the library reverences as its founder. His campaign of public speaking and pamphleteering was actuated by his dissatisfaction with the accessibility and facilities of the then British Museum Department of Printed Books. He and his collaborators also recognized that London lacked a lending library of serious literature such as were available in the main provincial cities of England. Their agitation led to the establishment of a collection that within a year of opening contained more than 13,000 volumes and justified the printing of the first *Catalogue* in spring 1842. Government of the new institution was vested (and still is) in a committee of 24 together with a president (originally the fourth earl of Clarendon, a statesman of much literary cultivation) and vice presidents. By 1848 the library had 882 members: a far cry from today's 8,500, but a very promising start.

As far as is practicable the library still remains true to Carlyle's ideal of browsing and borrowing, with the books arranged on open stacks in broad subject divisions and a liberal borrowing policy that included a postal loan service from the start. Book selection has always been in line with the founders' intentions and is informed by a sense of the enduring value of volumes selected. Carlyle's intellectual purposefulness has helped to shape a stock that now runs to more than a million volumes, originally "in every department of literature and philosophy," but now broadly in the humanities, including works in many foreign languages.

The library initially rented premises in Pall Mall but soon outgrew them and from 1845 leased a run-down townhouse in the northwest corner of St. James's Square, and in 1879 bought its freehold. It has thus been on its present site for over a century and a half, well placed now as then, between Piccadilly and Pall Mall, near learned societies, art galleries, and social clubs. The original house was demolished in the 1890s, and the present building took its place on a site that has been added to by purchases of adjacent land. The issue hall, reading room, and stacks with cast-iron grid floors are still serviceable after a hundred years, and there have been several extensions to the buildings in the 1920s, 1930s, and 1990s. Convenience of location, concentration of backstock, and a conservative appreciation of the library's special facility for associative browsing have combined to make it specially esteemed by the literary community both of London and Great Britain.

Its first librarian (and administrative secretary) was an unsuccessful bookseller, John George Cochrane (1841–52), the second a literary man-about-town, W. Bodham Donne (1852–57). Donne was succeeded by Robert Harrison (1857–93), a professional who had worked previously at the Leeds Library. Harrison had also traveled in Russia, and his Slavonic interests are reflected in the library's Russian collection, unusually strong for its period. This interest was continued by Harrison's long-serving successor Sir Charles Hagberg Wright (1893–1940). Wright was only 31 when appointed, with only a few years at the National Library of Ireland by way of previous experience, but he proved to be determined and industrious, seeing that the library was well set-up in its new building and devoting himself to the catalog with great industry and determination. His deputy, Christopher Jones Purnell (1940–50), succeeded him, to be followed all too briefly by the bibliographer and man of letters Simon Nowell-Smith (1950–56). Since then the librarians have been Stanley Gillam (1956–80), Douglas Matthews (1980–93), and Alan Bell (1993–).

From the start the London Library has enjoyed not just the support of the literary world but its active participation. Carlyle himself (1870–81), Alfred, Lord Tennyson (1885–93), Sir Leslie

Stephen (1893–1904), Arthur Jones Balfour (1904–29), and T.S. Eliot (1952–65) have been among its presidents, and the committee roll over the years contains a great many names prominent in authorship and publishing. Constitutionally the library was incorporated by royal charter in 1933 (with a supplemental charter in 1968), and it has long been a registered charity, thus securing it a number of fiscal benefits. The committee meets quarterly, with subcommittees for book selection policy, investments, general purposes (including buildings), and pension matters (the library has its own superannuation fund), all meeting at similar intervals to manage an institution that now has about 8,500 members, over 50 staff, more than a million volumes, and an investment portfolio valued at about £15 million.

The library is self-financing and remains independent of government support. Its original annual subscription was £2, with an entrance fee of £6. Today, income from the library's investments meets the loss on the subscription account, thus fulfilling the founders' intentions that its facilities should be available "on terms rendering it generally accessible." The current subscription of £150 per annum entitles London members to ten volumes at a time, and those living out of the London region up to 15. Loans are renewable but subject to recall should the books be required by another member.

It is difficult to characterize the membership as a whole, especially when so many applicants are reluctant to identify themselves as belonging to that welcome category of "reader"—those who need the library for recreational reading rather than organized academic study or in connection with creative writing. It serves a literary community in the broadest sense—including publishers, reviewers, journalists, biographers, critics, and picture-researchers—as well as a scholarly one, and has a wide range of institutional members. This last group includes both houses of Parliament, for which the London Library is a major source of non-senatorial literature; the central and faculty libraries of a number of universities; and several heavy users in the public library sector. It also participates, much more as a lending than a borrowing institution, in the British Library's interlibrary loan network, thus achieving a national outreach that belies the metropolitan emphasis of its name.

The book stock grew rapidly from the time of the foundation, when Cochrane was able to make substantial purchases of older continental books then available inexpensively in the London trade. From the start members were generous, and the general stock of the library often surprises, with donor labels recording gifts from Victorian luminaries such as John Stuart Mill. By 1913 the stock was over 250,000; by 1928, over 400,000; by 1950, over 500,000. The growth rate in recent times, including both purchases and donations, averages 7,000 volumes a year. There are few special collections, the major one being the Higginson collection (received in 1961) of books on the history of English fox hunting, and other large-scale acquisitions have been distributed among the general collections rather than retained intact as discrete collections. The Allen Library, a religious collection strong in Bibles and Reformation history purchased *en bloc* in 1920, is an example of a usefully dispersed acquisition. The Allen books included some incunabula, sold in 1966 with other pre-1500 books at what then seemed good prices, to relieve overstretched finances. Such a disposal was unusual, and the library has not repeated the experiment. Some minor 19th-century fiction was thinned out in the 1920s, losing books that would nowadays be of considerable interest. The policy of not discarding from the cumulated stock obviously influences purchasing. At the outset the new institution distanced itself from the fiction-for-hire circulating libraries; nowadays its acquisitions, in fiction as much as in scholarship, are considered in the light of probable durability.

Hagberg Wright's major contribution, apart from rebuilding and extending the premises, lay in the catalog. The 1842 foundation catalog had been continued by annual printed accession lists, but after 50 years, a completely new catalog was urgently necessary. Wright set to work with immense industry, and in 1903 a catalog of 1,626 pages was published; it was revised to include the contents of eight annual supplements to make two volumes published in 1913–14. Supplementary volumes came out in 1920, 1929, and 1953. These six hefty volumes of the author catalog bound in maroon buckram are a monument to Wright and his deputy Purnell. They are complemented by four volumes of *Subject Index* (1909, 1923, 1938, 1955), bound in blue buckram; the first volume is prefaced by an interesting methodological essay by Hagberg Wright. The whole set, familiar on the reference shelves of many British libraries and some abroad, constitutes a very useful database *avant la lettre*. They long proved their worth as general bibliographical guides. Wright's care over the identification of anonyma and pseudonyma was professionally valuable in the author catalog, and the analysis of the contents of composite works gave the subject index a special cachet.

For use in the library, the author catalog has been cut up and pasted on album sheets in 38 folio volumes. Since 1953 it has been supplemented by card catalogs (author and subject), which became too large for printing to be practicable. A retrospective conversion program is now in hand, which in the first instance is concentrating on converting records in the card catalog to machine-readable material for online access.

In anticipation of its 150th anniversary in 1991, the library mounted an appeal for extending its buildings on the limited free space still available on its constricted but cherished inner city site, and for the accelerated computerization of its catalogs. Complementing these aims, Mrs. Drue Heinz's trust established a literary fund for book purchasing. The building project was assisted by a substantial donation by the family trust of a single member, Ian Anstruther, which enabled the library to redevelop a small café at the west end of its site. Especially useful was the airspace above the leased-out catering premises for a tall, slim, high density, closed-access storage area for the rare book collections. This Anstruther Wing also includes an adaptable workroom, used at present for a "first-aid" conservation project on the library's earlier books. The anniversary appeal financed a useful extension to the main book stacks and provided the reading room with an area adapted for the use of library IT equipment and personal computers. In spite of this alteration, overall book storage space remains badly overcrowded, and office accommodation inadequate for current administrative needs. The possibility of off-site storage of part of the book stock is now under investigation, not least to allow shunting space that would enable antique but now sordid storage areas to be renovated. This will undoubtedly be an expensive exercise, and funding will be needed beyond the library's existing resources.

The 1991 appeal also has enabled the library to make financial provision over an extended period for the retrospective conversion of its printed and card catalogs. Catalog automation started in 1984, when periodic cumulations were bound up to produce volumes devoted mainly to recent acquisitions; their book format helped to reconcile a then highly conservative membership to a radical change that was not fully apparent until a substantial part of the public catalog appeared on screens instead of as a printout. The next stage, converting the 1950–83 card catalog, is now fully under way using the online bibliographic service OCLC. The growing resource of the online catalog is posted on the library's website, which allows the library to bring up to date its long-standing tradition of serving the needs of its "country" members, often based far from London. The retrospective conversion program will, like accommodation needs for books, members, and staff, remain a substantial element in the library's curatorial and financial planning for many years to come.

The London Library is an institution where changes have to be introduced so tactfully as to be almost imperceptible. The adjustments of recent years are far-reaching but leave its late Victorian ambience seemingly undisturbed. The services it offers its members extend well beyond mere lending, and with the help of new technology they are capable of much further development.

ALAN BELL

Further Reading

Bell, Alan, "The London Library," *Alexandria* 11, no. 3 (1999)

Grindea, Miron, editor, *The London Library*, Ipswich, Suffolk: Boydell Press, 1978

London Library, *Founders and Followers: Literary Lectures Given on the Occasion of the 150th Anniversary of the Founding of the London Library*, London: Sinclair-Stevenson, 1992

Mockert, Barbara, "The London Library," in *German Studies: British Resources*, edited by David Paisey, London: British Library, 1986

Wells, John, *Rude Words: A Discursive History of the London Library*, London: Macmillan, 1991

Los Angeles Public Library

Address: Central Library
630 West Fifth Street
Los Angeles, California 90071
USA
Telephone: 213-228-7000
Fax: 213-228-7069
www.lapl.org

Founded: 1872

Holdings (Central Library, 2000): Volumes: 2.2 million. Books on tape: 82,000; CDs: 45,000; current serials: 15,000; films and videos: 160,000; maps: 90,000; photographs: 3.5 million.

Special Collections: *Areas of Concentration:* Automobile repair manuals; California cookbooks, fiction, and history; fairy tales; genealogy; Los Angeles city directories; maps; Mexicana; Mother Goose editions. *Individual Collections: Los Angeles Herald Examiner* newspaper photo morgue; Security Pacific Los Angeles collection; George Smith Biblioteca Taurina bullfight collection; southern California menus collection; southern California unpublished plays collection; Turnabout Theatre collection.

Origins

The City of Los Angeles, with 444 square miles and a population of 3.7 million according to the 2000 U.S. Census, grew from a small pueblo. Even before La Ciudad de Nuestra Senora La Reina de Los Angeles incorporated in 1850, its citizens planted the seeds for the Los Angeles Public Library. In 1844, 1856, and 1859, Los Amigos del Pais (the Friends of the Country) furnished reading rooms with donated books for members' use. Although these attempts did not last, they led to the successful organization of the Los Angeles Library Association.

On 7 December 1872, 200 distinguished citizens in the city's population of 6,000 met to establish the Los Angeles Library Association. They created a board of trustees, rented four rooms in the Downey Block on Temple Street, set membership fees, and appointed journalist and scholar John Littlefield as the first librarian.

Legislation to Establish a Public Library

The reading rooms were so popular that the library association urged the California State Legislature to pass an act providing for the establishment of a public library in Los Angeles. The Enabling Act passed in 1874, a municipal ordinance in 1878, and the city council then took possession from the Los Angeles Library Association of library books and furnishings. In 1889 with the first home rule Los Angeles City Charter, the public library became a city department headed by a five-person board of library commissioners appointed by the mayor and approved by the city council. The commission had control of the operations and funds of the public library, appointed the city librarian, determined salaries, and established quarters for the library. For many years the city librarian was a political appointee. There were 11 city librarians between 1872 and 1911.

Into the 20th Century

Mary Foy (1880–84) was 18 years old when she succeeded Littlefield as city librarian in 1880. In four years she tripled the collection to 3,000 volumes, started the card catalog system, and began collecting books in foreign languages. Tessa L. Kelso, an advocate of women's rights who smoked, cut her hair short, and refused to wear a hat, was appointed city librarian in 1889. Ms. Kelso introduced dynamic changes to the library: free access to open shelves, the elimination of subscription fees, a local history collection, and a collection of sheet music and orchestral scores. She started a training system for librarians leading to the Los Angeles Library School. She devised a classification system for government documents that became the basis for the classification system used by the U.S. superintendent of documents. In six years the collection grew from 6,000 to 42,000 volumes, and the Los Angeles Public Library (LAPL) moved to City Hall.

In 1900 Mary L. Jones took over a crowded library in a growing city. She expanded library services in Los Angeles by starting the branch library system. The first extension of library services was the Boyle Heights Delivery Station, which became the Benjamin Franklin Branch. Within four years eight branch libraries were opened. Charles Fletcher Lummis, journalist and raconteur, walked across America from Cincinnati to Los Angeles to become city editor of the *Los Angeles Times*, editor of *Land of Sunshine: A Southern California Magazine* (1894–1901), author of *The Land of Poco Tiempo* (1928), and founder of the Southwest Museum. From 1905 to 1910, he was also city librarian of the LAPL. Clad in cowboy attire, corduroy pants, jacket, sash, and moccasins, Lummis branded books with the inscription *L.A. PUB LIBRARY* to discourage stealing. He moved the 123,000-volume collection of the central library into the Hamburger Department Store.

The 1920s: The First Building Program Era

The colorful iconoclasts of the early decades moved the library five times from rented space to larger rented space, but the job of creating a permanent home for the central library and for expanding the LAPL infrastructure to 46 library facilities was achieved by the perseverance, stability, and leadership of City Librarian Everett Robbins Perry (1911–33). Perry began by reorganizing the central library into subject departments and moved the library one more time into rented space in the Metropolitan Office Building. In the 1920s he led three successful campaigns to pass building bonds to fund the construction of a central library and 25 branch libraries.

Los Angeles was the largest and fastest growing city on the Pacific Coast. In 1920 its population was 576,673; in 1930 it was 1.2 million. The "Yes" campaign urged: "Grow Up, Los Angeles! Own Your Own Public Library and Take Your Place with Progressive Cities." And they did.

Bertram Grosvenor Goodhue, architect of the 1915 Panama-California Exposition in San Diego and of the 1920 Nebraska State Capitol, was selected to design the library on more than five acres of the Normal Hill site at Fifth, Flower, Grand, and Hope Streets. Like the city of Los Angeles itself, Goodhue's design was dynamic and eclectic, a mixture of Byzantine, Egyptian, Spanish Colonial, and modern architecture. The torch atop the library's mosaic pyramid symbolizing the light of learning is reflected in the friezes, quotations, sculpture, carved stone reliefs, murals, the rotunda's "solar system" chandelier, and the fountains and gardens of the library's west lawn. Work by artists Lee Lawrie, Julian Garnsey, Albert Herter, Dean Cornwall, and Harley Burr Alexander became integral parts of the building.

The three-story, 260,000-square-foot building, built at a cost of $2.3 million, opened on 6 July 1926. The Central Library housed 250,000 volumes, provided library services in 15 reading rooms through its departments, and had sufficient space for administrative and technical services. Its architecture and art established the Central Library as a landmark building in Los Angeles.

The development of the branch system, like the founding of the library, was a grassroots effort. As neighborhoods grew, community people petitioned the library commission for libraries. The commission established a matching challenge: If the communities would provide facilities, the library would provide books and staff for a probationary one-year period. If successful, full operation would be assumed by the LAPL. And when smaller cities were annexed to Los Angeles, their public libraries became part of the library system. A handful of branches were in permanent buildings funded by Carnegie grants. Twenty-five branch buildings were constructed between 1923 and 1928, and more than 5 million books circulated annually.

Depression and War

City Librarian Althea Warren (1933–47) led the LAPL during difficult times. Library usage skyrocketed to 13.3 million circulation (typical of Depression-era library use) at the same time that the budget decreased; hours and staff salaries were reduced. The per capita book circulation in Los Angeles was the highest in the country at 10.7, higher than that of New York (3.7) and Chicago (3.8).

Postwar Boom

As freeways multiplied and the automobile culture expanded the city, there soon were 62 branch libraries and four bookmobiles throughout the city. Harold Hamill, the city librarian (1947–70), oversaw the introduction of a new lending system based on microphotography and electronic tabulation, the construction of 28 new branch library facilities funded by a 1957 bond issue, and the automation of circulation records.

The downside to the growth of the branch library collections and staffing was the condition of the Central Library. The central collection had grown from 250,000 volumes in 1926 to 1.3 million volumes in 1966, and the building was overcrowded, poorly maintained, and unsafe. It had no air conditioning, not enough electrical outlets, and (literally) rats in the basement and bats in the tower. Plans to replace the Central Library failed due to lack of funding, but eventual recognition of the Central Library as an historic and cultural monument changed the plans for a new library into plans for renovation and expansion of the historic library.

Disasters

Between 1986 and 1994 the Los Angeles Public Library suffered several major disasters. City Librarians Wyman Jones (1970–90), Elizabeth Martinez (1990–94), and other library staff faced intense challenges in continuing to provide library services. Fire, water, and earthquakes devastated buildings and collections.

On 29 April 1986 the fire alarm at the Central Library sounded. Staff and patrons, accustomed to frequent false alarms, calmly filed out of the building, but this was not a false alarm. The fire, a result of arson, destroyed 375,000 books and periodicals. The fire department saved the building, and there were no injuries, but the water that suppressed the flames threatened the rest of the 2 million books. Staff and volunteers from throughout Southern California came together in a massive three-day, around-the-clock rescue effort to pack the wet books for freeze-dry preservation. A second arson fire devastated an additional 25,000 books.

In October 1987 the Whittier Earthquake closed three historic, unreinforced masonry branch library buildings with significant structural damage. On 29 April 1992 a jury decision reached in the Rodney King beating trial led to rampage in Los Angeles. Twenty-nine people were killed in the riots and hundreds of buildings were destroyed and damaged, including two branch libraries located in rental space in mini-malls.

And then on 18 January 1994 the Northridge Earthquake (6.7 on the Richter scale) shook the southland. Of the 17 branch libraries in the valley, 16 were closed owing to damage, as were a dozen more in the city.

The Second Building Program Era

The disasters of the 1980s and 1990s brought overwhelming public and political support for public library services as people fought back to restore the resources and services of the library. A creative financing plan partnering the public and private sectors provided $213.9 million to renovate and expand the Central Library from 260,000 to 540,000 square feet. Mayor Tom Bradley and ARCO CEO Lodrick Cook led a successful "Save the Books" campaign to raise $10 million to replace the books destroyed in the 1986 Central Library fires. A bond issue to renovate, expand, and build 27 branch libraries was approved in 1989 for a $96.7-million building program. Eleven historic libraries were renovated and expanded. Sixteen new libraries were built. And the Library Foundation of Los Angeles, a nonprofit development organization, was formed in 1992 to raise funds to enhance the programs and services of the Los Angeles Public Library. The foundation has raised $3 million annually for the library since 1992. The funds have been used for innovative pilot projects in technology, cultural enhancements, and library services to children and teenagers.

The LAPL operating budget, approved by the city council and the mayor, increased from $55 million in 1990 to $86 million in 2000. In 1998, 73 percent of Los Angeles voters approved a construction bond issue of $178.3 million for 32 new branch libraries. The funds to build these libraries completed the master plan for branch library facilities adopted by the library commission in 1988.

Leadership for the 21st Century

After five years of temporary library services in a building five blocks from the historic library, 80,000 people waited in lines to enter the Central Library at its grand reopening on 3 October 1993. The integrity of the historic building had been regained and the west lawn gardens and fountains had been restored as the result of a design by Lawrence Halprin. The new eight-story east wing, designed by Hardy Holzman Pfeiffer Associates, includes a dramatic atrium with cascading escalators and columns. The focal point in a revitalized downtown, the library is an educational, recreational, and cultural center with nine subject departments, an auditorium for 235, meeting rooms, collection space for 3.75 million books, a children's storytelling theater, a library store, a café, exhibit galleries, 1,500 readers seats, and more than 300 computers.

Under the leadership of City Librarian Susan Kent since 1995, the Los Angeles Public Library has made great strides in the areas of virtual library development and digitization of unique library resources in public libraries. The Central Library and all 67 branches are electronically connected to each other and the Internet with more than 2,000 computer stations. Every personal computer provides access to the library's website, the online library catalog, hundreds of information databases, and the Internet. The digitization of the library's extensive photo collection began in 1997 with 20,000 photos available on the website; the collection has continued to grow. In March 2000 the digitization of the library's California indexes, documents, and photos through the Electronic Neighborhood project became available on the website as Regional History Resources. The library continues to expand services to the people of Los Angeles with the Central Library and the regional library now open seven days and four nights per week and the community branches open six days and two to four nights per week. Between 1990 and 2005, 90 percent of the infrastructure of the Los Angeles Public Library will have been replaced with new, state-of-the-art library facilities, tripling the amount of public library space in the Central Library and 71 branch libraries.

FONTAYNE HOLMES

Further Reading

Bruckman, John D., "Los Angeles Public Library," in *Encyclopedia of Library and Information Science*, edited by Allen Kent et al., vol. 16, New York: Dekker, 1975

Cao, Jerry Finley, "The Los Angeles Public Library: Origins and Development, 1872–1910," Ph.D. diss., University of Southern California, 1977

Fine, Jud, and Harry Reese, *Spine: An Account of the Jud Fine Art Plan at the Maguire Gardens, Central Library, Los Angeles*, Los Angeles: Los Angeles Library Association, 1993

Hyers, Faith Holmes, compiler, *Hand Book of the Central Building Los Angeles Public Library*, Los Angeles: Los Angeles Public Library, 1927

Hyers, Faith Holmes, compiler, *Hand Book of the Branch Libraries, Los Angeles Public Library, 1928*, Los Angeles: Phillips Printing Company, 1928

Los Angeles Public Library, *Forty-eight Annual Report Includes: Brief History of the Los Angeles Public Library*, Los Angeles: s.n., 1936

Soter, Bernadette Dominique, *The Light of Learning: An Illustrated History of the Los Angeles Public Library*, Los Angeles: Library Foundation of Los Angeles, 1993

Luis Angel Arango Library

Address: Biblioteca Luis Angel Arango
Calle 11 #4-14
Bogotá
Colombia
Telephone: 571-3431212
Fax: 571-2863551
www.banrep.gov.co/blaa/home.htm

Founded: 1932

Holdings (1999): Volumes: 950,000. Current serials: 15,000; films and videos: 3,000; incunabula: 34; manuscripts: 9,000; maps: 14,000; microforms: 3,000; slides: 61,000; sound recordings: 14,000.

Special Collections: *Areas of Concentration:* Banking; business; Colombian imprints from 1738 to 1810; finance; historical collections of Colombian and Latin American economics; law; 19th-century Colombian pamphlets, newspapers, and illustrated periodicals; Spanish New World chroniclers; travelogues of 19th-century European travelers to the New World. *Individual Collections:* Darío Achury y Valenzuela; Luis Augusto Cuervo; Donaldo Bossa Herazo; Darío Echandía; Laureano García Ortiz; Jorge Ortega Torres; Alfonso Patiño Roselli; Alvaro Restrepo Vélez; Howard Rochester; Enrique Uribe White. *Papers:* Julio Arboleda; Tomás Cipriano de Mosquera; José Joaquín Pérez; Alberto Lleras Camargo; Carlos Lleras Restrep; Rafael Núñez; Eduardo Santos; Guillermo Uribe Holguín.

The Biblioteca Luis Angel Arango (BLAA) is the foremost research library in Colombia and a nationally recognized leader in setting library standards, including bibliographic control and cooperation on a national level. By its own reckoning, it ranks as the third largest in bibliographic holdings in Latin America and serves an average of 9,300 users each day. In a region where libraries have traditionally suffered from chronic underfunding and inefficient planning and have tended toward custodial rather than service-oriented functions, the BLAA stands among a handful of Latin American libraries as a model of focused, sustained growth and public service. Its success is largely due to the fact that it has been funded and managed by the Banco de la República (BR), the Colombian central bank. An administratively and legally semiautonomous entity, the BR has avoided the bureaucratic and financial vagaries that have plagued most government-sponsored institutions in the region, including the Biblioteca Nacional de Colombia (National Library of Colombia, also in Bogotá), whose substantial historical collections have long been accessible only for on-site specialized research and whose bibliographic, collecting, and information functions have been partially superseded by the BLAA.

With regional branches and documentation centers in 24 cities around the country, the BLAA forms part of the BR's larger cultural program that includes the Gold Museum of pre-Columbian artifacts and regional branches. Also included are a Numismatic Museum; a Philatelic Museum; a permanent art collection and exhibition halls with substantial holdings of Colombian, Latin American, and modern European art, averaging 30 exhibitions yearly; a historic collection of musical instruments; and a concert hall hosting an average of 90 concerts per year. The bank's publishing house produces several journals; working paper series; and monographs on economics, banking, finance, political economy, history, library-related issues, archaeology, and the arts. The BR also funds and manages several foundations that promote archaeological, scientific, and technological research as well as the fine arts. The BLAA and its regional branches also regularly sponsor academic and library-oriented seminars, conferences, and workshops.

The future the BLAA had modest origins as a small documentation center within the BR at its founding in 1923. The collection consisted largely of government documents such as compilations of laws and annual reports issued by the Finance Ministry, financial and economic materials, and other internal documents the BR had inherited from its predecessor institution, the recently defunct Monetary Conversion Board. Although originally designed to meet the research and information needs of the BR staff, the collection gradually acquired a local reputation among university students and researchers at other institutions, who consulted the material on an informal basis. The collection grew slowly but steadily as selected monographs and journals supporting research were collected and as new official publications were added along with the BR's own publications, particularly the monthly *Revista del Banco de la República,* beginning in 1923.

During the decade of the 1930s the BR undertook two initiatives that would prove decisive with respect to its future role in the cultural arena. In point of fact, these initiatives stemmed from a legal stipulation requiring the bank to allocate a portion of its revenue to cultural activities with public access. However, the specific shape and national relevance these projects gradually acquired were determined by a series of factors ranging from philanthropically minded leadership within the bank, public demand, and chance circumstances.

The first of these events was the official opening of the library to the public in 1932. At this point a separate administrative division to manage the library was created within the bank, and the first full-time librarian, Blanca Barberi Lezcano, was hired. In 1932 an advertisement posted in the *Revista* announced the opening of the library with the expressed purpose of fostering the study of economics and related disciplines. Housed within the BR's old headquarters in the Pedro A. López Building, the library officially opened its doors on Sunday 3 July 1932 to students and other members of the public interested in it holdings, offering daily services from 2:00 to 4:30 in the afternoons, except Saturdays and holidays. The other event was the establishment of the Gold Museum in 1939, which developed from similarly inauspicious beginnings. Following a recent law protecting archaeological sites and their contents as national patrimony, the bank's vaults became de facto repositories for a sizable number of pre-Columbian gold artifacts turned over by private donors. Initially established to preserve the valuables, the museum was open only to special visitors and later (in 1959) to the general public.

Little is known about the library's acquisitions policy or its personnel in the early days. According to one source, the reading room could accommodate fewer than 25 people, although by the following year the collection had expanded to an estimated 4,000 titles. Its primary focus remained on economics, finance, banking and related legislation, political economy, and business.

The decade from the mid-1940s to the mid-1950s marked a turning point. The library expanded rapidly through the purchase of a number of private collections, changing its orientation from a narrowly specialized concentration to a more general focus. Once again the future presented itself in the form of a chance occurrence. In 1944 the private collection of Colombian historian Laureano García Ortiz, with 25,000 titles, was offered for sale to the library. The opportunity came just as the library was considering expanding the scope of its holdings. Consisting mostly of Colombian history and literature, with several thousand 19th-century pamphlets and newspaper and journal titles as well as the personal papers of several 19th-century Colombian statesmen, the collection is still considered the core of the library's Colombian historic holdings.

In that same year, the reading room was expanded, and between 1945 and 1949 the library began a major classification project. Under its new director, Luis Alberto Camargo, and with the help of historian Enrique Otero Munoz, the Dewey Decimal Classification (DDC) system was adopted. In 1949–50 the library published its first printed catalog, in two volumes, containing approximately 8,000 entries. (A new printed catalog, in 33 volumes, would be published between 1961 and 1983.) In the wake of the Laureano García Ortiz collection purchase, the library embarked on a more aggressive acquisitions policy. By 1958 the personal libraries of numerous Colombian statesmen had been added, most notably those of Jorge Soto del Corral, Carlos Lozano y Lozano, Luis Rueda Concha, Carlos Cuervo Márquez, Leopoldo Borda Roldán, and Luis Augusto Cuervo. By 1959 library holdings were estimated at more than 70,000 titles.

The library's growth and the bank's increasing involvement in cultural ventures during these years was in no small measure due to the active support of the BR's director, Luis Angel Arango. A prominent banker and lawyer from Medellín, Arango was also an avid connoisseur of literature and the arts who steered the institution toward a more active role in existing cultural ventures and the establishment of new ones. During his term as bank director (1947–57), the bank engaged in projects such as the Numismatic Museum, the restoration of the Church of San Diego and other religious buildings in the city, the Center for Social Action for Children, and the expansion of the Gold Museum for public access.

It was Arango's vision to establish the library on a more independent footing as the center of the BR's cultural programs. Under his leadership, in the late 1940s plans were drawn to move the library to a separate location. The time was ripe for change. The BR itself was relocating its headquarters, spurred in large part by security concerns in the wake of the infamous 9 April 1948 riots known as the *bogotazo*. Furthermore, the library's current facilities were inadequate to house a growing collection and increased user demand.

In 1956 the architectural firm of Esguerra, Sáenz, and Samper began designs for the new library building at its present location in the historic neighborhood of La Candelaria. Arango died the year before the new building was completed, and so on 28 February 1958 Jaime Duarte French, the new library director, inaugurated the building that bore Arango's name.

The new facility reflected the library's expanded public service orientation and its new role as a cultural center for the plastic and performing arts. Its main feature was an expansive reading room with a seating capacity of 250, crowned by an imposing half-dome. Adorned with sculptures and an interior garden, the building also included a children's reading room, a music listening room, a conference room, and an art exhibition hall. Stack capacity allowed for four times its holdings of 70,000 volumes. In addition to the unique purchases mentioned above, the collection had acquired other noteworthy items, including 18 European incunabula, the diary of founding father General Francisco de Paula Santander, a large number of religious tracts, including the first text printed in Colombia, *Septenario al corazón doloroso de María Santíssima* (1738); the only extant copy of *Cristo paciente* (1787), the first full-length book published in the colony; and the manuscripts of 17th-century mystic, Mother Josefa del Castillo. That same year, the library launched its official journal, *Boletín cultural y bibliográfico*, featuring bibliographic information, book reviews, literary criticism, historical essays, and cultural information.

During the 1960s and 1970s the BLAA assumed its role as a leading research library in the country. One telling statistic of public reception of the library's expanded services and facilities is that user frequency almost tripled, from 118 to almost 300 visitors per day, within a year after the new building opened. By 1963 that number had grown to 1,000.

In 1965 the first of several expansions of the library's facilities was undertaken. It doubled the capacity of the reading room, installed private carrels for researchers, and added two new reading halls that were also service points—the Colombian Room and the Map Room. Book stack capacity was also doubled to 560,000, and administrative and technical work areas were expanded and improved. Perhaps the most aesthetically prominent feature of this first expansion was the 367-seat prizewinning wood-paneled concert hall, also designed by Esguerra, Sáenz, and Samper. A new exhibit gallery was also constructed for the library's growing art collection.

By 1975 the BR had purchased the entire block and properties adjacent to the BLAA, and four years later a second expansion of the library was completed. On 18 January 1979 the new Hemeroteca Luis López de Mesa (a newspaper and periodicals room) was inaugurated as a separate department. An informal reading room opened on the first floor along with a bookstore selling the BR's publications, among other things. The Museum of Religious Art began operating across the street.

The decade of the 1980s ushered in an era of decentralization of the BR's activities, including those in the cultural arena, reflecting broader political trends within the country. Under the BR directors Rafael Gama Camacho and Hugo Palacios Mejía, branch libraries were opened around the country: Manizales (1981), Cartagena (1981), Girardot (1981), Riohacha (1981), Pasto (1981), Pereira (1983), Tunja (1983), Ipiales (1984), Ibagué (1984), Armenia (1986), Leticia (1986), Quibdó (1987), and Honda (1998). Managed by a regional head librarian, the branches reflect publishing output and special collections from their respective regions but depend on the BLAA for all aspects of their functioning, including technical services, acquisitions, and service-oriented policies.

In 1979 the BR had created a new administrative division to oversee all aspects of the institution's cultural activities. Until 1984 the library director was also the head of the cultural affairs division. In 1983 Duarte French retired after 30 years of service as director of the BLAA. He was succeeded as head of the cultural affairs division by Juan Manuel Ospina, during whose three-year tenure the library's journal, *Boletín cultural,* was substantially improved. Changes included reformatting the design and greater quality control under a permanent editorial board composed of prominent Colombian intellectuals. A new expansion of the library was also planned, in response to expanding collections and user demand for services.

In 1984 the first professionally trained librarian, Lina Espitaleta, was appointed library director. In conjunction with the new head of the BR's cultural division since 1985, poet and literary critic Darío Jaramillo Agudelo, Espitaleta oversaw the library's largest physical expansion (carried out between 1988 and 1990). The project was undertaken by the firm of Alvaro Rivera Realpe, who based its design on surveys of local user information needs and major world libraries. Greatly expanded to occupy the entire city block, the library reopened on 5 May 1990 with a user capacity of 1,950 and stacks that could accommodate 1.5 million volumes.

In a parallel program, the BLAA decided to follow international bibliographic standards. In 1986, the library purchased the integrated online cataloging system, Northwestern Online Totally Integrated System (NOTIS) and subsequently adopted the MAchine-Readable Cataloging (MARC) format. In 1989 the library began retrospective conversion of its catalog to electronic form. By 1990 some 250,000 online records were accessible to the public within the library. Finally, the periodicals room was again incorporated within the library, which was now divided into four administrative units: Technical Services (which includes Cataloging, Acquisitions, and Maintenance), Public Services, Serials, and Branches. In 1990 the management of the branches was transferred to the bank's cultural subdivision, although the BLAA continues to provide the basic services of acquisitions, cataloging, training, and formulation of public service policies. Collection development since then has been coordinated by an outside committee chaired by the library director, whose members include representatives from various fields of knowledge. Today the BLAA houses specialized departments handling music, geography, social sciences, arts and humanities, audiovisual, constitution and law, rare books and manuscripts, science and technology, newspapers and periodicals, maps, general room, and reference.

But the BLAA's new facilities, which could now accommodate up to 6,000 readers, were soon stretched to the limit. In Latin America, libraries with public functions such as the BLAA's generally service the needs of school-age users due to the chronically limited resources of academic libraries. This is the main reason that user frequency tends to be so high in public libraries around the region. Because of its substantial resources and its tradition of attention to user needs, the BLAA has perhaps felt even more acutely the need to negotiate priorities and resolve the tension between its own stated mission as an advanced research library and a national library vis-à-vis its desire to continue fulfilling a wider public library role.

Under historian Jorge Orlando Melo, who succeeded Espitaleta as library director in 1994, attention to university-level and advanced researchers (who account for 75 percent of users today) has been made a priority, whereas attention to K–12 needs is being phased out. To further relieve physical use of library facilities, lending services began in 1996, with loans totaling 200,000 in 1999. Since 1997 the online catalog has been accessible via the Web, and high-demand items from the collection as well as basic reference materials geared to primary and secondary school needs have been digitized and made available through the library's website. In addition, the BLAA has acted as consultant and active participant in a $50 million local government-funded project to improve public and academic libraries in Bogotá. Early in the new millennium ten new libraries opened, with a combined user capacity of 4,000, an automated union catalog connected to the BLAA, and interlibrary loan services.

Today, the BR's library system headed by the BLAA includes the major public libraries of 19 cities in Colombia, with a combined average of 5.5 million users yearly. Although national bibliographic responsibilities have traditionally been carried out by the government-sponsored Instituto Caro y Cuervo, the BLAA performs such functions as setting cataloging standards within the country and providing cataloging services for publishers. In combination with its regional branches, the Biblioteca Luis Angel Arango system also offers the most complete coverage of publishing output in the country.

HORTENSIA CALVO

Further Reading

Boletín cultural y bibliográfico (1958–)
Duarte French, Jaime, "La Biblioteca Luis Angel Arango," *Revista del Banco de la República* (May 1959)
Hatty, Ivonne, *La misión cultural del Banco de la República*, Santafé de Bogotá: Banco de la República, 1999

Lund University Library

Address: Lunds Universitetsbibliotek
Helgonabacken
P.O. Box 3
221 00 Lund
Sweden
Telephone: 222-00-00
Fax: 222-42-42
www.lub.lu.se

Founded: 1671

Holdings (1998): Volumes: 3.2 million. Current serials: 12,000; films: 50,000; incunabula: 275; manuscripts: 132,000; microforms: 92,000.

Special Collections: *Areas of Concentration:* Arts and sciences; Danish history; ecology; law; medicine; newspapers; Swedish literature and imprints; technology; theology. *Individual Collections:* Sten Broman collection of Elseviers; De la Gardie collection; Necrologium Lundense; Otto Taussigs collection of Franz Schubert originals. *Papers:* Vilhelm Ekelund; Carl F. Hill; Esaias Tegnér; Ernst Wigforss.

Lund is one of the oldest cities in Sweden, with roots from the end of the tenth century. In the middle of the 11th century, Lund, then a part of Denmark, became a bishopsite and, at the beginning of the 12th century, an archbishopsite of Denmark. A cathedral was erected along with a small library. Several other churches and four monasteries were subsequently established in Lund, making it the center for literary culture in Denmark. After the Reformation in 1536, many churches were torn down, and Lund rapidly declined. Nearly all books from the cathedral library were transferred to Copenhagen, later to be incorporated into the collections of the Royal Library.

In the 17th century Sweden extended its boundaries through warfare, and the territories of Scania, Halland, and Blekinge became incorporated after the peace agreement between Sweden and Denmark was signed in Roskilde in 1658. Lund University was founded in 1666 in an effort to provide a source of higher education within Sweden and to encourage Swedes to pursue their education at home rather than at Copenhagen University. The Lund University Library (Lunds universitetsbibliotek), or LUB, was established in 1671 when the university obtained the remains of the cathedral library, consisting of 370 printed books and 15 manuscripts. The country's peace, however, was an insecure one, and in 1676 the most devastating battle in Scandinavian history (fought in Lund) claimed the lives of 8,000 Swedes and Danes and destroyed the fledgling university. University Librarian Christopher Rostius fled to nearby Malmö and never returned to Lund.

In 1684, after the university's restoration, the library received its most important acquisition when King Karl XI donated the 6,000 volume collection of Emund Griepenhielm, which consisted almost entirely of spoils of the Thirty Years War (1618–48). During these years, the university also claimed that University Librarian Rostius had, for some period of time, been paid without properly executing his duties. The dispute was resolved through an agreement providing that Rostius' private library of approximately 500 titles be incorporated into the university library's collections. As Rostius had been a doctor of medicine and a professor at several German universities before he came to Lund, his library was an important scientific addition to the university library.

Since 1698 the library has had the right of legal deposit of all Swedish imprints. Although the growth of the library during its first 150 years was slow and sporadic, library holdings reached 20,000 volumes by the beginning of the 19th century. An international book exchange system established in 1819, together with an organized acquisitions policy, increased the library's holdings substantially in the following years.

In the 1850s an alphabetical card catalog covering the library's holdings was initiated under University Librarian Edward Berling. One of the young assistants working on this project was Elof Tegnér. Although Tegnér moved to the Royal Library in Stockholm after several years in Lund, he eventually returned to assume the position of university librarian after Berling's death in the early 1880s. Recognized as one of the outstanding librarians in Sweden, Tegnér initiated a national union catalog of acquisitions (published annually by the Royal Library in Stockholm), and in Lund he physically rearranged the library collections and created a subject-based card catalog inspired by Antonio Panizzi's system inaugurated at London's British Museum Library in 1839. Tegnér's cataloging system took 15 years to complete and was continued until the end of 1957, when the stacks were organized according to the Sveriges Allmänna Bibliotek (Swedish Public Libraries), or SAB, classification system.

During Tegnér's tenure, space became a significant problem. The library had acquired a good deal of space when the university vacated its original building in 1880, leaving it entirely to the library, but acquisitions had grown so rapidly that plans for a new building were necessary. Tegnér favored an annex close to the existing building, but others preferred a totally new building on All Saints Hill on the outskirts of town, at the site of the pre-Reformation monasteries. Tegnér died in 1900 and the new library was built on All Saints Hill, opening during the summer of 1907. The All Saints building has remained the university library's main site since that time, with the addition of a freestanding book tower built in the 1930s and a large building constructed in the 1950s that surrounds the tower and links it permanently to the old main building, now known as Universitets Bibliotek 1 (UB1).

The explosive growth of Lund University in the late 1960s and early 1970s led to a new separate building (UB2), opened in 1977 on the Technical University Campus, a half mile from All Saints Hill. This building is devoted to collections in medicine and the natural sciences. In 1965 a separate textbook library, the first of its kind in Sweden, was established, receiving the name UB3 in 1978; a special library (UB4) for newspapers was also founded. The library receives paper deposit copies of all daily editions of every newspaper in the country, totaling up to eight editions of each paper per day, all retained in paper copies. As a result, the newspaper collection grows by approximately 109 shelf yards annually. The old main library (UB1) became the main library for the humanities, theology, social sciences, and law, as well as continuing to house the library director and administrative functions.

In the early 1900s University Librarian Carl af Petersens applied to the Swedish Parliament for funds, hoping to increase the library staff and build an organization capable of managing its services. His vision included (in addition to the director) five staff members to handle circulation and three full-time staff members and one half-time staff member to manage book exchange activities and the foreign and Swedish collections. In 1915 the library's organization included four departments: the Swedish Department, the Foreign Department, the Manuscript Department, and a department overseeing the reading rooms and circulation. This organization stood for some 70 years, with the addition of a Cataloging Department in 1958.

Not only did Lund University grow in the 1970s, the library staff expanded tremendously as well. In 1986 there was a radical faculty-based reorganization that divided the library into four subject-based sections—humanities/theology, social sciences/law, medicine/odontology, and natural sciences/techniques—in order to make library services more efficient and cost effective. Although this organization was not ideal, after several iterations the library settled (in the 1990s) upon a discipline-based organization supported by a consortium of libraries within the university (institutional and faculty libraries) in order to make all collections accessible to faculty members and students.

In the mid-1970s an online catalog was established in Sweden by several research libraries within the national Library Information System (LIBRIS). In 1988 LUB had already cataloged or linked its holdings to 500,000 LIBRIS entries when a local library automation system, Lund OnLine I Tjänst Alltid (In Service Always), or LOLITA, was installed in Lund, and copies of all Lund-related entries were transferred to LOLITA. After ten years, the LOLITA system contained more than one million entries, all of which could also be found in the LIBRIS union catalog.

Online database reference services developed into CD-ROM-based article reference databases in a local network by the end of the 1980s. In 1992 the Lund University Electronic Library was established at UB2 as a project to create network-based information services on the Internet with Wide Area Information Server (WAIS), gopher, and World Wide Web capabilities. The library's first web Uniform Resource Locator (URL), www.ub2.lu.se, was the first web server in Sweden. The Lund University Electronic Library (now called NetLab) has become a pioneer in the digital library world and has carried out some distinguished projects involving electronic library and information services, financed primarily by external bodies such as the Nordic Council for Scientific Information (NORDINFO) and the European Union.

The LUB's total holdings are estimated at 3.2 million volumes. The most special and rare volume in the library is the *Necrologium Lundense* from the 1120s, the oldest manuscript written in Scandinavia. Among other holdings in the library's Manuscript Department are the archives of Magnus Gabriel De la Gardie and 800 special archives, many of them personal archives of authors from the southern parts of Sweden.

The largest special collection is, however, the Swedish imprint collection, which is more complete than those held in other Swedish libraries, with the exception of the Royal Library in Stockholm. In addition to copies of all Swedish printed books and journals, the LUB has an extensive collection of "small-prints," ephemera of all kinds, flyers, announcements, commercial magazines, staff and personnel magazines, and other uncataloged material, which is organized into subject-based archives, growing annually by some 175 shelf yards.

In 1946 Lund University Library started a publication series, *Skrifter utgivna av Lunds universitetsbibliotek*, in which 11 Lund University Library–related monographs have been published covering special printed collections in the library or based on archives in the Manuscript Department.

STEINGRÍMUR JÓNSSON

Further Reading

Blomberg, Barbro, *Lund University Library*, Lund: Lund University Library, 1993

Gerle, Eva, *Lunds universitetsbiblioteks historia fram till år 1968*, Stockholm: Almqvist and Wiksell International, 1984

Sjöberg, Sven G., *Christopher Rostius, 1620–1687: Läkare, polyhoster, professor i Lund och Bibliotheca Rostiana, ett rekonstruktionsförsök*, Lund: Lund University Press, 1997

Malatestiana Library, Cesena

Address:	Biblioteca Comunale Malatestiana, Cesena Piazza Bufalini 1 47023 Cesena Italy Telephone: 547-610892 Fax: 547-21237 www.delfo.forli-cesena.it/coce/Malatestiana/malatestiana/fs-Homepage.html
Founded:	1452
Holdings (2000):	Volumes: 404,000. Current serials: 600; codices: 200; incunabula: 286; manuscripts: 2,000; 16th-century editions: 3,200.
Special Collections:	*Areas of Concentration:* Greek and Hebrew codices; works of the church fathers. *Individual Collections:* Codices copied by Andrea Catrinello, Matteo Contuggi, Jacopo Macario, and Jacopo da Pergola.

The Biblioteca Malatestiana in Cesena enjoys the distinction of being the oldest working library in the world still housed in its original building and still using its original fittings. Undoubtedly inspired by the enviable example set in Florence by Cosimo de' Medici, Prince Novello Malatesta (Lord of Rimini and heir to a dynasty that for 250 years ruled a rural region south of Ravenna on either side of the Rubicon River, where the Apennine Mountains meet the Adriatic Sea) was moved to glorify his family name by creating a great library of his own. He had his chance in 1445 when a group of Franciscan monks received permission from Pope Eugenius IV to expand a small school it operated at its Cesena friary into a college by adding on a book repository.

Although a papal bull (decree) authorized the expansion, it did not provide money for the construction, and it was at this point that Novello Malatesta—described as a sensitive man with a deep love of books and literature—stepped in and assumed responsibility for the project. He would later record in a papal bull his intention to provide a specific sum of money to build the permanent collections as well. In 1447 he commissioned a design from the architect Matteo Nutti, who paid careful attention to the elegant plans prepared just seven years earlier by Michelozzo di Bartolommeo for the library at the Monastery of San Marco in Florence, the original repository for the Medici family collections. That graceful building still stands, but the books it contained were moved to the Biblioteca Laurenziana (Florence), designed by Michelangelo, in the 16th century.

Construction of the Malatestiana was begun on the second floor of a new wing at the Franciscan friary and completed in 1452, with another two years spent on installing the decorations and crafting the furniture. A dormitory and refectory for the use of the friars occupied the ground floor. The library accommodations include two aisles of parallel desks arranged so they can be entered from the outside of each row by the exterior walls, and also from a wide corridor that runs down the center of the long rectangular room. There are 29 lecterns in each aisle, for a total of 58. Illumination comes through the numerous arched windows that line the side walls and from a circular window at the front. The soft natural light is evenly distributed by a vaulted ceiling that is supported in the center aisle by two rows of white columns, each bearing a different capital, and by a floor of brownish-red reflective tiles. On a pediment above the double wooden door at the entrance is the Malatesta family device, a carving of an elephant inscribed with the curious motto, *"Elephas Indicus culices non timet"* (the Indian elephant does not fear mosquitoes). Another inscription on the pediment, also in Latin, translates: "Novello Malatesta, son of Pandolfo, gave this work." Inside, all the fittings and pear wood furnishings are original, including the wrought-iron chains that are still used to attach Novello Malatesta's manuscripts to the desks.

Always a bit off the beaten path from the major metropolitan centers of Florence, Venice, and Milan, Cesena never enjoyed ready access to the producers and purveyors of manuscripts, a circumstance of geography that persuaded Novello to set up his own in-house scriptorium to make copies of books he was unable to buy on the open market but could borrow from other collections. A bindery was established nearby to service his needs as well. For material outside of Italy, Novello engaged the services of agents such as Francesco Filelfo and Giovanni Aurispa. The content generally followed the canonical list drawn up in 1439 and 1440 for Cosimo de' Medici by Tommaso Parentucelli, later Pope Nicholas V, the bibliophile pontiff credited with creating the Vatican Library as a true reflection of Renaissance thought and for establishing the University of Glasgow in Scotland.

Most of the Malatestiana books are works of the church fathers—St. Augustine, St. Jerome, St. Gregory, and St. Ambrose alone account for 31 volumes—although there are some notable exceptions. Fourteen codices are Greek, including copies of Homer's *Odyssey* and the *Republic* and *Dialogues* of Plato, which may have been bought from a dealer in one lot. A small collection of Hebrew codices was acquired from the Cesena City Council. No fewer than 15 codices were written in the graceful italic script of Jacopo da Pergola, most of them dated and signed, including exquisitely illuminated copies of Pliny's *Natural History* and Plutarch's *Lives*. Other copyists known to have worked at the scriptorium were Jacopo Macario of Venice, Andrea Catrinello of Genoa, and Matteo Contuggi of Volterra.

In addition to Italian copyists, Novello engaged the services of a number of talented foreigners, including the French notary Jean d'Epinal, who married a local woman in Cesena and changed his name to Johannes de Spinalo. One of his manuscripts, a copy of St. Augustine's *Commentary on the Gospel of St. John,* was illuminated in Ferrara by the noted miniaturist Taddeo Crivelli, who decorated a number of other books for the Cesena library. Indeed, almost all of the 200 codices produced in the scriptorium were illuminated, 30 of them embellished by an artist who signed himself as "F.Z.," believed to be Frater Zuane. For many of the manuscripts, the ornamentation consists simply of the Malatesta family crest, with the initials *NM* on the first page. The court binder favored brown goatskin, with metal bosses, clasps, and chains for security. Novello's library gained appreciative notice quickly; the humanist Flavio Biondo judged it as being in league with the best repositories in Italy.

When Novello died in 1465 at the age of 47, the systematic program of collection development he had set in place ended abruptly, and his early death probably explains why humanistic literature and poetry are not represented in any great depth among the holdings. The scriptorium was closed forthwith, and outside of a major donation of 119 manuscripts in 1474 from Giovanni di Marco of Rimini (Novello's physician), the inventory was basically complete. One reason cited for the library's long record of survival in situ is that it was subsequently enclosed within a larger building that today maintains three separate collections, providing a shield to outside elements. More consequential, however, was the perceptive decision of Novello to give the citizens of Cesena joint custody of the Biblioteca Malatestiana along with the Franciscan friars in residence, an arrangement that proved critical during the periods of dispersal and abolition that swept through Italy many years later. What endures is a beautiful Renaissance library of uncommon significance, one that demands a place on any bibliophilic tour of Italy.

NICHOLAS A. BASBANES

Further Reading

Chiaramonti, Scipione, *Caesenae historia,* Cesena: De Neris, 1640; reprint, Bologna, Italy: Forni, 1967

Hobson, Anthony, *Great Libraries,* London: Weidenfeld and Nicolson, and New York: Putnam, 1970

Muccioli, Guiseppi M., *Catalogus codicum manuscriptum Malatestianae caesenatis bibliothecae fratrum minorum conventualium,* 2 vols., Cesena: Blasini, 1780–84

Staikos, Konstantinos Sp., *The Great Libraries: From Antiquity to the Renaissance (3000 B.C. to A.D. 1600),* New Castle, Delaware: Oak Knoll Books, and London: British Library, 2000

Manchester Public Libraries

Address: Manchester Central Library
St. Peter's Square
Manchester M2 5PD
UK
Telephone: 161-234-1900
Fax: 161-234-1963
www.manchester.gov.uk/libraries/index.htm

Founded: 1852

Holdings (1999): Volumes: 2.1 million. Current serials: 2,000; manuscripts: 10,000 linear feet; maps: 32,000; music scores: 300,000.

Special Collections: *Areas of Concentration:* Art; commerce; family history; Manchester history; music; theater. *Individual Collections:* Broadside ballads; Samuel Taylor Coleridge collection; Thomas De Quincey collection; Elizabeth Gaskell collection; Gleave collection of Brontë; Alexander Ireland collection; Local Studies Unit and Archives; 19th-century tracts; oral history recordings; theater collection. *Papers:* Margaret Ashton; Millicent Garrett Fawcett; James L. Hodson.

Origins

The Manchester Public Libraries were begun under the Free Libraries Act of 1850. Soon after the act was passed, Mayor John Potter immediately began raising money for the establishment of a library and appointed a library committee. The committee is now the Manchester City Council Libraries and Theatre Department. Potter's drive and dedication were responsible for the creation of the libraries.

The library committee appointed Edward Edwards as chief librarian to develop the collection with James Crossley, president of the Chetham Society. Edwards is an important figure in the history of librarianship in England. He contributed to the Free Libraries Act of 1850 and published articles on library statistics in the Athenaeum. He not only established Manchester's cataloging practices but was actively part of the team that developed the British Museum's new catalog for the printed book department, and later in life he cataloged the library at Queen's College, Oxford. He published several important works on library history. These include *Memoirs of Libraries*, 1859; *Libraries and Founders of Libraries*, 1865; and the "Library" article in the *Encyclopædia Britannica*, 1869.

Edwards and Crossley purchased 18,000 volumes and received an additional 3,300 donated titles, bringing the base collection to 21,300 titles, from which they decided to create two special collections. The first, involving commerce, trade, and manufacturing, began with 7,000 volumes and is still a department of the central library now known as the Commercial Library. The second collection was on local history and consisted of 500 volumes printed in Manchester or by natives of the city. This has developed into the Local Studies Unit and Archives of the central library.

In January 1851 the Hall of Science in the Campfield section of the city was purchased and converted into library space. Its inauguration as the Manchester Free Library on 2 September 1852 was attended by noted dignitaries and literary figures, including John Bright (member of Parliament for Manchester), Charles Dickens, Sir Edward Bulwer Lytton, and William Makepeace Thackeray. Four days later the library was open to the public, and more than 138,000 volumes were circulated during its first year.

Relocation of the Central Library

The central library was relocated several times before finding its current home in St. Peter's Square. It was moved from Campfield in 1877 when the floors began to give way under the weight of the collection, necessitating its closure and the removal of the collection. Although newly vacated space in Old Town Hall on King Stuart Street was altered into a reference library allowing reopening in February 1878, the building was too small to be used as a central library. In 1912 the collection migrated to a building in Piccadilly. Despite building additions in 1916 and in 1919, this building also proved inadequate, although the library was forced to remain there for several more years.

In 1930 a new central library building began construction in St. Peter's Square. The passing of the Manchester Corporation Act in 1920 provided the driving force for the purchase of the St. Peter's Square site for the construction of the library and a Town Hall extension. In 1928 E. Vincent Harris was selected to design the St. Peter's Square structure after a two-year search and competition. The building is circular in shape with a large Corinthian portico that serves as its main entrance from the square. Prime Minister Ramsay MacDonald laid its foundation stone. The building was completed in 1934 and was inaugurated by King George V. At the time it was the largest public library in Britain.

The Departments and Collections

The Central Library is made up of many departments and is currently automating its holdings. In the library's basement is the Library Theatre. It is the longest established creative theater company in Manchester. The General Readers Library contains most of the library's popular titles and covers a broad range of subjects. The subject departments are the Commercial Library, the European Information Unit, the Social Sciences Library, the Technical Library (which covers science and technology), and the Chinese Library. Other departments serve very specific needs and house special collections.

In addition to the founding collection, there are several other specialized library units. The Local Studies Unit and Archives contains 145,000 photographs and illustrations related to Manchester, now in the process of being digitized. The Visually Impaired People's Unit provides full access to information using modern technology including a Kurzweil Reading Machine, Talking Teletext, the Electronic Newspaper, and computers with speech synthesis, large printing, and Braille output. Transcription services and personal readings are also available. The Arts Library contains 10,000 books and 150 videos available for loan, and a reference collection of 80,000 titles. The collection houses the theater collection, an archive of local theater history from the 1700s to the present day. It includes thousands of programs and reviews of dramatic performances. The Art Library, in addition to fine and applied arts and performing arts, also provides coverage of sports and games.

Special Collections

Dr. Henry Watson was a prominent local musician, teacher, a professor at the Royal Manchester College of Music (now the Royal Northern College of Music), and the music librarian at the central library. The Henry Watson Music Library (HWML) was founded in 1902 and became part of the central library in 1949. The collection now contains 600,000 books and individual pieces of music and 16,000 LP recordings on vinyl discs, most available for loan. The HWML also includes two important manuscript collections: the Aylesford collection, which includes Georg Friedrich Handel manuscripts; and violin sonatas and a set of "The Four Seasons" part-books from Antonio L. Vivaldi.

The Languages and Literature Library opened on the fourth floor of the current Manchester Central Library in 1963 in a space previously used for storage. In addition to standard circulating materials, the department houses the majority of the library's special collections. Several came from the Moss Side library, an independent library whose building was demolished in the 1960s when the collection became part of the Manchester Public Libraries. These include the Gaskell collection, the De Quincey collection, and the Gleave Brontë collection.

The Gaskell collection centers on Elizabeth Gaskell, who came to Manchester in 1832 as the wife of a local minister. The collection contains manuscripts, including a short story, music books, and letters; personal items from her library; and autographed editions of her works. There are more than 230 editions of her novels and more than 700 biographical and critical items, as well as her husband's sermons, hymns, and newspaper clippings. The De Quincey collection focuses on author Thomas De Quincey, who was born in Manchester. It contains six boxes of magazine articles; 150 first or early editions of his works, including U.S. editions; books about and belonging to De Quincey; and some manuscript fragments.

The Gleave Brontë collection contains early editions of the Brontë sisters' books, the books and pamphlets relating to them, and newspaper clippings. The Coleridge collection belonged to James Albert Green, first librarian of the Moss Side Library, and was purchased by the library after his death. The collection contains more than 740 volumes, including first editions of Samuel Taylor Coleridge's works, books about Coleridge, 50 editions of "The Rime of the Ancient Mariner," early editions of other works, newspaper clippings, and a large collection of portraits. Other significant collections include the archives of local novelist and editor James L. Hodson, the Chinese collection assembled by Thomas Bellot, broadside ballads from the 16th to 19th centuries, and many editions of Robert Louis Stevenson's *Treasure Island*.

Circulating Branches

In addition to the central library, the Manchester Public Library maintains 22 branch libraries serving regions of traditionally high unemployment. Five new branches were opened in 1979–80 as part of an inner-city program designed to provide better service for that community.

Aims and Services

The libraries' mission statement includes the provision of universal access to information, works that stimulate and engage the imagination, published works to support people in their lifelong learning, a wide range of materials to improve opportunities for self-development and enhance quality of life, and works to enhance the enjoyment and general quality of life.

Services added in recent years include a mobile library service for those unable to reach a branch library; it visits 33 sites each week. A Sheltered Housing Scheme begun in September 1996 visits 80 sites every three weeks. Monthly home visits are provided to 1,100 residents who live either in their own homes or in 60 homes for the elderly. A postal cassette service for the visually impaired is available for those registered as partially sighted or blind. Other civil libraries serve the city architect's office, the city solicitor's department, and the Strangeways jail.

PAOLINA TAGLIENTI

Further Reading

Credland, W.R., compiler, *Handbook, Historical and Descriptive,* 2nd edition, Manchester: Manchester Public Libraries, 1907

Godwin, T.M., "Developments in Manchester's Public Libraries as a Result of the Inner City Programme," *Journal of Librarianship* 13, no. 3 (1981)

Jackson, A., and P. Martin, "Non-use of Manchester's Library Service: An Investigation," *Public Library Journal* 6, no. 4 (1991)

Manchester Public Libraries, *Manchester Central Library: An Illustrated Record,* Manchester: Libraries Committee, 1934

Mazarine Library

Address: Bibliothèque Mazarine
Institut de France
23 quai de Conti
75006 Paris
France
Telephone: 1-44-41-4406
Fax: 1-44-41-44-07
www.bibliotheque-mazarine.fr

Founded: 1643

Holdings (1999): Volumes: 500,000. Current serials: 700; incunabula: 2,380; manuscripts: 4,600; microforms: 10,000.

Special Collections: *Areas of Concentration:* French history and theology; 16th- to 18th-century scholarship. *Individual Collections:* Demangeon-Perpillou geography collection; Faralicq collection of bibliophilia; Faugère collection of Jansenist materials.

Origins

Established in 1642 as the first public library in France by the first minister of Louis XIV, Cardinal Jules Mazarin (Giulio Mazzarini), the Mazarine Library today stands as one of the principal research libraries in Paris. Thanks largely to the efforts of his indefatigable librarian Gabriel Naudé, Cardinal Mazarin was able to establish one of the largest collections in Europe in the mid-17th century.

The Library of a Cardinal-Minister

Naudé was author of the 1627 *Advis pour dresser une bibliothèque* (Advice for Establishing a Library), an early manual of library economy. With almost unlimited funds and the aid of a long ministerial arm, Naudé assembled the foundation collection of the Mazarine Library from three principal sources: purchase of well-established libraries (beginning with that of Jean Descordes, which numbered more than 6,000 titles and was purchased for 22,000 livres in 1643); bulk purchases from Parisian booksellers; and donations, including books falling into the hands of the French army abroad. Within 15 months, Naudé amassed some 10,000 titles for Mazarin. He then set out on an ambitious buying tour, traveling to Italy, Germany, the Low Countries, and England. By the end of the decade, the library counted some 40,000 books on its shelves. This made it one of the largest in Europe at the time, probably second in size only to the ducal library at Wolfenbüttel. Even while the library was still in its early stages of formation, it was open to the public all day every Thursday and was touted in the contemporary Parisian press as a veritable academy.

Amid the wealth of private and institutional libraries in 17th-century Paris, the Mazarine stood in direct competition with both the Bibliothèque du Roi (Royal Library) and the well-established libraries of the Parisian parliamentary elite. The rich collections of the latter—such as those of Henri de Mesmes and Jacques Auguste de Thou—combined humanist and historical interests with the legal and political concerns of their owners to establish a unique model of a working professional library. As collections of family archives, legal documents, and working papers, such libraries functioned as very real sources of political power. In Rome, Mazarin already had amassed a sizable collection of some 5,000 volumes. Through Naudé, who had already served as the de Mesmes librarian in the 1620s and was well versed in the Parisian parliamentary library tradition, Mazarin set out to adapt the model of Cardinal Francesco Barberini's new library in Rome to new ends in Paris. He approached Barberini for a copy of the architectural plans of his library—again through the offices of Naudé, who had served briefly in Italy as librarian to Cardinal Antonio Barberini, brother to Francesco—but the request was rebuffed. Although Cardinal Richelieu's substantial library offered a distinct precedent, it was Mazarin who firmly established the model of the encyclopedic ministerial library as an instrument of prestige and policy alike. This model would be followed by Nicolas Fouquet, Jean-Baptiste Colbert, and others.

The status of the Mazarine Library as an icon of the first minister's power became apparent during the Fronde of 1651. During this brief period of civil war, Mazarin was forced to flee France. His palace and goods were seized and ordered to be sold by the Parisian parliament. The library was first on the auction block—with the caveat that it was not to be sold intact. Naudé fled to Stockholm, where he became librarian to Queen Christina of Sweden, one of the prime beneficiaries of the Mazarine sale. After

Mazarin's return to power, books were quietly returned to the cardinal. These amounted to only a fraction of the library's original holdings, and the library did not soon regain its former glory. Built above the stables of Mazarin's palace on what is now the flank of rue Richelieu, the original Mazarine library building was later taken over for the Royal Library by Colbert.

The Death of Mazarin (1661) to the Revolution (1789)

In his will Mazarin left substantial funds for the foundation of a college in Paris, to which his library was to be attached. In 1668 Colbert arranged for an exchange of duplicates between the Mazarine and the Royal Library; the Mazarine received some 2,341 books for the 3,678 it sent to the crown. Further, Colbert effected a forced purchase for the Royal Library of all 2,156 of the library's manuscripts. The buildings for the college, erected opposite the Louvre across the Seine, were complete by 1674, but arrangements for the installation of the library were not finalized until 1691. The library furnishings from the Palais Mazarin were moved to the college and used within the new library. It was thus that the cardinal's library was incorporated into the Collège des Quatre Nations. In its new incarnation the library was furnished with a librarian, a sublibrarian, and two servants, and it was to be open to the public twice a week. The Mazarine played a relatively uneventful role serving its new constituency of students and professors, and its prized collections continued to draw visitors from both Paris and abroad. It was valued by scholars for its encyclopedic holdings and the relative ease with which admission was gained and books consulted. It was thus no ordinary college library. Readers complained of noise made by students; professors of the college, for their part, complained that it was almost impossible to use the library as they were occupied with teaching during its hours of opening and did not enjoy borrowing privileges.

The Revolution of 1789 was kind, even munificent, to the library. In contrast to other libraries with ecclesiastical foundations, the status of the Mazarine as a public library ensured that its collections were not subject to confiscation. Together with the Sainte-Geneviève and Arsenal libraries, the Mazarine was thus one of the few Parisian libraries besides the Royal Library to survive the Revolution intact. The great study libraries of the Parisian religious houses, to the contrary, were nationalized and their collections placed in *dépôts littéraires* (the warehouses where books nationalized during the Revolution were kept pending allocation elsewhere). Those libraries that survived helped themselves liberally to the spoils. By this method the Mazarine acquired some 50,000 volumes of printed books and 4,000 manuscripts, as well as a considerable number of artworks from the *dépôts littéraires* of Paris and Versailles.

19th and 20th Centuries

In 1790–91 the library was under the administration of the Commissaires de l'Instruction publique. By 1795 the Collège des Quatre Nations had become one of five *écoles centrales* for the Department of the Seine, and the library was incorporated within the new institution. The *écoles centrales* were dissolved in 1802 and replaced by the *lycées*, and the Mazarine at that point severed all ties with the French secondary education system. Until 1831 the library remained under the jurisdiction of the Ministry of the Interior. In 1831 it was briefly overseen by the Ministry of Commerce and Industry and from 1832 by the Ministry of Public Education. Various schemes, most notably in 1812 and again in 1815, to unite the Mazarine with the library of the Institut de France (home of the five great national learned societies, including the Académie française and the Académie des inscriptions et belles-lettres), with which it shared premises, were unsuccessful; from 1820, however, the two libraries were placed under the same administrative umbrella. With a staff of 13, the administration of the library during this period was top-heavy, with few funds remaining for conservation and acquisitions. The library opened to the public only a few hours a day. A damning report of 1831 levied charges of nonattendance to duties and general lassitude against all three of the major Parisian libraries, the Mazarine included.

The year 1839 witnessed the reorganization of libraries in France on a national scale, and the administration of the Mazarine was brought into conformity with the norms of the Bibliothèque Nationale de France (National Library). Librarians were to be chosen from among members of the university, established writers and scholars, and pupils of the national school of library and archive administration, the École des Chartes. A purchasing committee was established, and the library was to be open to the public from nine in the morning to four in the afternoon. Yet there remained considerable limits to the professionalization of the library in the 19th century. Until 1875 librarians were required to serve in the library only one day a week, expanded to two in 1875 and to three in 1877. Only in 1887 were universal requirements of university or professional qualifications instituted and an examination and system of grades and promotions established.

Numbering some 45,000 volumes of printed books in 1760, by 1848 the library held some 135,000 printed books, 1,300 incunabula, and 3,039 manuscripts. Funds for acquisitions were few, and growth of the collection was slow throughout most of the 19th century; between 1847 and 1863, for example, the library purchased only 676 titles and received another 2,744 by donation. In 1877 the collection of printed books stood at 155,410; by 1902 it had grown to 200,000.

Throughout its modern history the Mazarine has catered to a public of scholars and advanced students. It remains an excellent resource for the study of French history, theology, and scholarship of the 16th to 18th centuries. Since 1926 the Mazarine has been a deposit library for local publications across France, rendering the library a unique center for the consultation of periodical and ephemeral publications of local scholarly societies and provincial presses.

Catalogs

During the tenure of Naudé and until the death of Mazarin it appears that no catalogs of the collection were made. In 1668

Colbert ordered a catalog of duplicates of printed books and of manuscripts to be drawn up for the purpose of the exchange with the Royal Library. An inventory from 1690 was signed by Librarian Louis Piques as he took charge of the collection; a shelf list, this served as the only entirely autonomous catalog of the library for almost a century. In place of an independent author index, the library used a copy of Thomas Hyde's 1674 printed alphabetical author catalog of the Bodleian Library (Oxford, UK), with Mazarine pressmarks entered in the margins and Mazarine additions entered on interleaved blank sheets.

Pierre Desmarais, appointed librarian in 1722, undertook to catalog the entire collection in 1750; he died in 1760 leaving the catalog to be taken over by his assistant Gaspard Michel (called Leblond). It was completed in 1785. The alphabetical author catalog drawn up by Desmarais and Leblond was an enormous undertaking and finally produced a catalog of some 38 folio volumes. A separate subject catalog was also in use, divided into three format categories: folio, quarto, and smaller formats. Books on the shelves followed this subject arrangement. Both catalogs continued in service until 1870, with entries added for new acquisitions. Only the folios were recataloged, in 1845.

This rather confusing state of affairs was compounded by the fact that the confiscations of the revolutionary period were not entered into either of the existing catalogs. They were instead cataloged independently, divided by subject (theology, law, literature, philosophy, and history) and alphabetically by author within each subject class. The system was abandoned in 1870 in favor of a straightforward accession system, with a separate alphabetical author catalog established for post-1870 accessions. Although closed to new accessions, the old catalogs remained in use; no retrospective cataloging was undertaken. As a result, many uncataloged items continue to greet the reader even now when consulting collectively bound imprints. In 1884 a new catalog for the entire collection was begun and completed in 1900–01 with 509 volumes. In 1901 a card catalog system was instituted. The library currently enjoys alphabetical author and title card catalogs and subject card catalogs. Particularly useful for researchers interested in the first centuries of print is a chronological imprint catalog that indexes the library's holdings by place of publication. A catalog of the library's manuscripts was published from 1885 to 1892; a catalog of incunabula appeared in 1893.

PAUL NELLES

Further Reading

Art et Metiers du Livre 222 (January/February 2001) (special issue devoted to the Mazarine Library)

Charmasson, Thérèse, and Catherine Gaziello, "Les grandes bibliothèques d'étude à Paris," in *Histoire des bibliothèques françaises,* vol. 3, edited by André Vernet, Paris: Promodis–Éditions du Cercle du Librairie, 1991

Franklin, Alfred, *Histoire de la Bibliothèque Mazarine depuis sa fondation jusqu'à nos jours,* Paris: Aubry, 1860

Gasnault, Pierre, "De la bibliothèque de Mazarin à la bibliothèque Mazarine," in *Histoire des bibliothèques françaises,* vol. 2, edited by André Vernet, Paris: Promodis-Éditions du Cercle du Librairie, 1988–92

Péligry, Christian, "Bibliothèque Mazarine," in *Patrimoine des bibliothèques de France: Un guide des régions,* vol. 1, edited by Anne-Marie Reder, Paris: Payot, 1995

Queyroux, Fabienne, "Recherches sur Gabriel Naudé (1600–1653), érudit et bibliothécaire du premier XVIIe siècle," thesis, École des Chartes, 1990

McGill University Libraries

Address: McLennan Library Building
3459 McTavish Street
McGill University
Montreal, Quebec H3A 1Y1
Canada
Telephone: 514-398-4677
Fax: 514-398-7356
www.library.mcgill.ca

Founded: 1821

Holdings (2000): Volumes: 3.2 million. Current serials: 16,000; films and videos: 29,000; incunabula: 130; manuscripts: 3,000 linear feet; maps: 239,000; microforms: 1.5 million; sound recordings: 42,000.

Special Collections: *Areas of Concentration:* Architecture and art; book history; British history; Canadiana; Islamic studies; legal history; maps; medical history; ornithology and zoology; philosophy. *Individual Collections:* William Blake; William Colgate printing; David Hume; Søren Kierkegaard; Lawrence M. Lande Canadiana; Napoleon; Arthur Rackham; Redpath tracts; Wainwright civil law. *Papers:* Murray Ballantyne; Leon Edel; Henry Viscount Hardinge; Stephen Leacock; Hugh MacLennan; Sir William Osler; Wilder Penfield; Christopher Sandford; Casey Wood.

Established by Royal Charters from King George IV in 1821 and Queen Victoria in 1852, McGill University was founded by James McGill, a Scottish-born merchant whose will left £10,000 and his country estate for an institution of higher learning. Teaching began only in 1829 when the Montreal Medical Institution (founded in 1823) became the university's Faculty of Medicine. Despite the opening of the Faculty of Arts and its building in 1843, McGill languished until the appointment of William Dawson as principal in 1855. Dawson, who was the leading Canadian scientist of the day and subsequently knighted, laid the foundations for McGill's emergence as a leading national and international university. McGill continues to be characterized by visionary administrators, creative faculty and staff, and generous benefactors. The university's main campus is situated on the slopes of Mount Royal in the center of downtown Montreal; the Macdonald College campus (Faculty of Agriculture and Environmental Sciences) is situated 25 miles to the west in Sainte Anne de Bellevue.

Origins to 1893

The McGill library system began with the medical library, whose origins date from 1823. Its collection numbered 904 volumes in 1845, had increased to 2,101 titles in 1870, and numbered 15,000 volumes in 1898, making it possibly the largest academic medical library in either Canada or the United States at the time. Otherwise, there are only vestigial remains of libraries at McGill, before the 1850s.

Upon his arrival at McGill in 1855, Dawson established a college library in his office with himself as librarian. Charles Markgraf ran the library, with only student assistance, from 1857 to 1882, in addition to being a professor of German. After moving into separate quarters in the newly constructed west wing of the Arts Building, in 1862, the library was open weekdays from 10:00 A.M. to 4:00 P.M. and Saturdays from 10:00 A.M. to 1:00 P.M. Despite averaging less than four percent of the university's budget, the library grew steadily during this period, thanks partly to benefactors such as Peter and Grace Redpath, Canada's first great library benefactors, who over many decades gave books, money, and a library building. Their most famous collection is the Redpath tracts, now grown to more than 20,000 British polemical pamphlets from the 17th to the 19th centuries.

The library's printed catalog of 1876 described a collection with 5,201 titles (including 103 journals) and 11,021 volumes. The subject distribution of the collection (excluding the medical library) was roughly as follows: history, 28 percent; literature, philosophy, and religion, 22 percent; science, 18 percent; classical literature, 10 percent; architecture and fine arts, 2 percent; books of reference (including such things as laws and sermons in addition to bibliographical and factual sources), 18 percent.

The Gould/Lomer Era, 1893 to 1947

In addition to their institutional achievements, the first two university librarians developed outstanding national and international reputations. Accomplishments of Charles Gould's tenure (1892–1919) included hosting the American Library Association's annual conference in Montreal, 1900; becoming the first

Canadian president of the ALA, 1908 to 1909; serving as president of the Bibliographical Society of America, 1912 to 1913; helping to found the Ontario Library Association, 1901; supervising Canadian contributions to the *Catalogue of Scientific Literature*, 1902 to 1921; and chairing the ALA committee that produced the first interlibrary code, 1916. Achievements during Gerhard Lomer's tenure (1920–47) included editing the first Canadian union list of serials, 1924; founding the Quebec Library Association, 1932; carrying out the study that led to the establishment of regional libraries in the province of Prince Edward Island, 1932; and hosting the ALA conference in Montreal, 1934. In addition, Lomer had to cope with the Great Depression of the 1930s and also World War II, with their accompanying financial disruptions.

In 1893 the 35,000-volume main collection moved into Redpath Library, the first specifically designed library building in the Province of Quebec. Built in a Romanesque style, it featured a monumental reading room and a separate stack wing. Thanks to university support and private benefactions, McGill enjoyed Canada's largest academic library collection during the first half of the 20th century; it grew to approximately 550,000 volumes by 1950. As these collections could not be contained within Redpath Library despite stack extensions in 1901 and 1920, a number of campus libraries developed. In addition to the medical library, other prominent libraries included those dedicated to agriculture; art and architecture; commerce; education; engineering; law; the physical sciences; and zoology and ornithology. These libraries reflected McGill's growing range of graduate and professional programs. The most famous campus library of this era was undoubtedly the Osler Library of the History of Medicine, which opened in 1929 with Sir William Osler's collection as its nucleus. Many other important rare book collections developed during this period, particularly the Canadiana collections. A great disappointment was the relocation of the Gest Chinese collection to Princeton University in 1936, after it had been on deposit at McGill for ten years.

One of the greatest accomplishments of this era was Canada's first library education program, established by Gould as a summer school in 1904. With the assistance of Carnegie Corporation grants, it was converted by Lomer, first into a sessional program in 1927, and then into a graduate program in 1930. Other accomplishments of these years were the McLennan Traveling Library (which brought culture to countless Canadians) and the McGill University Publications, a reprint series that was a progenitor of Canadian academic publishing.

Expansion and Adjustment, 1948 to 1974

Richard Pennington (1947–64) was the third and last university librarian. His tenure began with a number of notable accomplishments, the most significant being the 1954 wing of Redpath Library, which increased its capacity severalfold so that the original stack wing became an annex to the new structure. The new wing contained Canada's first undergraduate library. A number of new research collections were developed, particularly the Napoleon collection and the William Colgate printing collection. Pennington also did much to encourage the bibliophilic interests of Lawrence M. Lande; most of Lande's Canadiana collections and all of his Blake collection now reside at McGill. It was unfortunate, therefore, that Pennington seemed unable to provide the administrative and budgetary support needed for the 1960s. Two library reports, one national (1962) and the other institutional (1963), were highly critical of the library's management and plans for the future. The truth was, however, that McGill was devoting only 3 percent of its operating budget to the library, a relatively small amount by Canadian standards.

In 1964 the post of Director of Libraries was created with its first incumbents being John Archer (1964–67), Keith Crouch (1967–72), and Richard Farley (1972–74). They transformed the McGill libraries into a system with a centralized administration and budget, demanding approximately 8 percent of the university budget in a period sometimes referred to as the golden age of Canadian higher education. The university library commission's recommendation in 1971 to organize McGill's 30 or so libraries into a federated area library system was accomplished in 1972 to 1974. At the same time, professional librarians were granted the status of non-teaching academic staff. During the 1960s and 1970s, the library system was largely relocated in new facilities, the most notable example being a new main library complex, with the opening of the McLennan Library (1969) and the gutting and rebuilding of the adjoining Redpath Library (1970). A manifestation of the expanding role of research was the promotion to departmental status of the main library's government document and rare book collections, in 1962 and 1965, respectively.

Like their predecessors, the library directors had national and international profiles. Archer became president of the Canadian Library Association (1966–67) and president of the University of Regina (Saskatchewan) (1974–76). Richard Farley became the head of the U.S. National Agricultural Library (1974–83).

Contraction and Readjustment, 1974 to Present

Optimism that university support for the library would continue indefinitely was overturned by a combination of political, economic, and technological factors. Nationally, the Canadian economy suffered from a combination of stagnation and inflation, leading to large government deficits during the 1970s and 1980s. This was followed in the 1990s by severe government spending cutbacks in the public sector, including funds for universities. Provincially, a separatist government was elected to power in Quebec in 1976. The resulting political and linguistic instability led to economic decline in the province that only began to recover at the century's end. Institutionally, McGill faced uncertainty about its role as an English-language institution in a predominantly francophone environment. Private giving and endowments were able to compensate only partially for provincial and federal cutbacks in funding. Although McGill was committed to maintaining the quality of the teaching faculties at international levels, its commitment to maintaining the libraries was only at a national level. Newly emerging information technologies were used to justify decreased financial support of the libraries.

Declining support for the McGill University libraries can be seen by comparing figures for 1974 and 1999: The number of libraries dropped from 25 to 16; the staff from 400 (90 librarians) to 221 (62 librarians); and the libraries' share of the university budget declined from approximately 8 to 5 percent (about $16 million out of operating budget expenditures of approximately $300 million). There was a corresponding decline in McGill's statistical ranking within the Canadian Association of Research Libraries and the U.S. Association of Research Libraries. The relative decline of McGill University in a national magazine's ranking of Canadian universities was largely owing to lowered support for the library. Following a McGill Cyclical Review report in 1992, the area library system was dismantled. The closing and merging of campus libraries in the 1980s and 1990s was accompanied by much controversy. Growing concern over the state of the libraries resulted in the creation of a Task Force on Scholarly Communication and Libraries, chaired by two vice principals (January 2000).

Even so, the McGill libraries can point to many positive developments during this period. A number of new library facilities were built, notably agriculture (1978), physical sciences and engineering (1982), and law (1998). Several other libraries had their physical facilities significantly upgraded. In recognition of its research prominence, the McLennan Library's Department of Rare Books and Special Collections was relocated in larger and more accessible quarters (1997) and reconstituted as a division reporting to the director of libraries (1998). Information technology was introduced over the past 30 years as follows: online searching, 1972 to 1973; computer-assisted cataloging University of Toronto Library Automation Systems (UTLAS), 1974; a computer-output-microfiche (COM) catalog, 1982; Northwestern Online Totally Integrated System (NOTIS) integrated library system, 1985; an online catalog, 1987; a retrospective conversion project (RECON), 1988; a geographic information system, 1994; full-text databases, including journals, 1995; an in-house digital publishing project, 1996; subsidized unmediated desktop document ordering and delivery (replacing some interlibrary loans), 1996; a numeric electronic data resource service, 1997; and the Ex Libris Automated Library Expandable Program (ALEPH 500) library management system, 2000.

Following in the footsteps of their predecessors, the library directors of this period set the tone for the library: Marianne Scott (1975–84), Hans Möller (acting director, 1984–86), Eric Ormsby (1986–96), and Frances Groen (1996–). Marianne Scott became president of the Canadian Library Association (1981–82) and the first woman and graduate librarian to serve as national librarian of Canada (1984–99). Following a decade as director, Ormsby resumed his teaching of Islamic studies. Frances Groen served as president of the Medical Library Association (1989–90) and of the Canadian Association of Research Libraries (1999–2001).

PETER F. McNALLY

Further Reading

Frost, Stanley Brice, *McGill University for the Advancement of Learning,* 2 vols., Montreal, Quebec: McGill-Queen's University Press, 1980–84

McNally, Peter F., "The McGill University Libraries," in *Encyclopedia of Library and Information Science,* edited by Allen Kent et al., vol. 17, New York: Dekker, 1976

McNally, Peter F., "Scholar Librarians: Gould, Lomer, and Pennington," *Fontanus: From the Collections of McGill University* 1 (1988)

McNally, Peter F., "Dignified and Picturesque: Redpath Library in 1893," *Fontanus: From the Collections of McGill University* 6 (1993)

McNally, Peter F., "Fanfares and Celebrations: Anniversaries in Canadian Graduate Education for Library and Information Studies," *The Canadian Journal of Information and Library Science; Revue canadienne des sciences de l'information et de bibliothéconomie* 18, no. 1 (April 1993)

McNally, Peter F., "McLennan Library: Twenty-Fifth Anniversary," *Fontanus: From the Collections of McGill University* 7 (1994)

McNally, Peter F., "Charles Henry Gould," in *Dictionary of Canadian Biography,* vol. 14, Toronto, Ontario, and Buffalo, New York: University of Toronto Press, 1998

McNally, Peter F., and Kevin Gunn, "The McGill University Library Catalogue of 1876: A Preliminary Statistical Analysis," *Fontanus: From the Collections of McGill University* 9 (1996)

Mitchell Library

Address: Mitchell Library
North Street
Glasgow, Scotland G3 7DN
UK
Telephone: 141-287-2999
www.mitchelllibrary.org

Founded: 1877

Holdings (1998): Volumes: 1.2 million. Current serials: 2,000; manuscripts: 1,000 linear feet; maps: 30,000; music scores: 44,000.

Special Collections: *Areas of Concentration:* Angling; architecture; art; family history; Glasgow history; historic scientific journals; maps; music. *Individual Collections:* William Adam collection; Robert Burns collection; Langmuir collection; Sir Thomas Lipton Medlrum collection; North British locomotive collection; Reid memorial angling collection; Royal Glasgow Institute of Fine Arts; Scottish poetry collection; Scottish Women's Hospital collection; Wotherspoon collection. *Papers:* Bedlay of Chryston; Bogle family papers; Brisbane of Largs; Scottish Licensed Trade Veto Defence Fund; individual Scottish trade unions; Shawfield papers.

Origins

Following his death in 1874, Stephen Mitchell (a tobacco manufacturer) left £66,998 to Glasgow for the establishment of a public library. His instructions were for it to be left to earn interest until the sum reached £70,000, which it did in 1876. The library's first controversy centered on the type of institution it would become, a central reference library or a system of branch libraries scattered around the city.

Since its founding in 1877, the Mitchell Library has had a complex relationship with the city of Glasgow. The city established a library committee to direct the establishment of the library, the majority favoring a central reference library. A second committee was later appointed to manage its growth under the Glasgow Corporation Act. Throughout the library's history there have been space and money problems, as well as controversy surrounding its mission, organization, leadership, and design. However, collection scope was never restricted, and a diverse collection of rare books, manuscripts, music, and reference materials has evolved.

The library committee requested the town clerk, Dr. Warwick, to compile a report detailing the library's mission. Warwick's vision, as detailed in that report, was of a classless institution that would promote free access, and his vision has continued to be the library's mission.

In 1876 Francis Thorton Barrett was hired as the first head librarian. He began the library's collection with purchases from three private collections, including the entire library of Scottish historian Professor Cosmo Innes, part of the Reverend William Stevenson's collection on church history, and part of William Ewing's rare book collection. A total of 17,000 volumes became the base of the Mitchell's collection. The volumes were stored in a room of the city chambers, as no physical library space existed. In July 1877 space was rented, and the library was formally opened on the first of November, only to experience continuous space problems for the next 100 years. Barrett's decisions to catalog the library into broad subjects rather than a specific classification scheme and to maintain the collection in closed stacks (available only through paging) would prove shortsighted and problematic.

Space Problems

By the mid-1880s overcrowding in the stacks required a new location for the library. The city Water Commissioner's offices on Miller Street were converted into a new library, providing space for up to 150,000 volumes and 400 seats. However, the renovation fell about 18 months behind schedule, and during that period the library was forced to close, with only a magazine room open to patrons.

The Marquis of Bute officially opened the new building on 7 October 1891. At a cost of £22,000, the new facilities severely diminished the library's endowment. The library quickly outgrew the building and by 1894 again reported a lack of space for both patrons and materials. Left with little funding, no solution was possible until the Glasgow Corporation Act, allowing for additional public funding, was passed in 1899.

In 1904 a site on North Street was purchased for a new building. The second controversy in the library's history surrounded the selection of an architect. A design competition was held, but the library committee and the new Glasgow Corporation disagreed on the final selection. After much debate and amendment to his plan, William B. Whitie was named architect, and building began in 1907. From June 1910 to October 1911 the library was again reduced to a magazine room, but on 16 October 1911 the new library was opened by the Earl of Roseberg.

By 1935 the collection was at 400,000 volumes and the Mitchell Library again experienced growth pains. An extension begun in 1939 was stopped by the war, but ten years later construction resumed. The extension was completed in 1953 and opened by another Earl of Roseberg (the son of the earl noted above). This new building began an experiment of departmentalization with a separate music room followed by a Glasgow Room in 1950, beginning a complete transformation of the library's entire arrangement.

In 1962 a fire in the adjoining St. Andrew Hall gave the library an opportunity to expand, allowing further departmentalization and a complete reclassification of the collection. Construction began on the current building in 1972 but was not completed until 1981. Princess Alice, Duchess of Gloucester, opened the building on 3 November 1982. It has stack space for 3 million volumes and 700 seats, and it now contains the following departments: science and technology; philosophy and religion; rare books and manuscripts; social sciences; Glasgow Collection; music; arts and recreation; history and topography; and language and literature, as well as a central main reading room.

Special Collections

The Mitchell Library has many separate collections in its holdings. The Manuscript and Rare Books Department is largely the result of donations and includes a collection of 4,000 rare volumes on ornithology from the Robert Jeffrey collection and a Private Press collection of 2,000 volumes. The Language and Literature department contains the Poets Corner, which is based on the Scottish poetry collection that was begun by the first head librarian, Francis Barrett. Barrett also began the Glasgow collection, which contains a variety of materials concerning the city.

PAOLINA TAGLIENTI

Further Reading

Alison, W.A.G., "Glasgow's Extended Mitchell Library," *SLA News* 156 (1980)

Garrett, Wilma, "The Creation of a Specialist Subject Department at the Mitchell Library, Glasgow," *Art Libraries Journal* 10, no. 2 (1985)

Gillespie, R.A. and M. Wallace, "The Mitchell Library and GRIN," *REFER* 2, no. 1 (1982)

Gillespie, Roy A., "The Mitchell Library, 1877–1977," *SLA News* 141 (1977)

Mitchell Library, *The Mitchell Library, Glasgow, 1877–1977*, Glasgow: Glasgow District Libraries, 1977

The Mitchell Library, Glasgow: Glasgow District Libraries, 1982

Moscow M.V. Lomonosov State University A.M. Gor'kii Scientific Library

Address: Nauchnaia biblioteka im. A.M. Gor'kogo
Moskovskogo gosudarstvennogo universiteta
im. M.V. Lomonosova
119899 Moscow University Prospekt
Russia
Telephone: 939-22-41
Fax: 202-94-04
www.lib.msu.su/

Founded: 1756

Holdings (1999): Volumes: 8.5 million. Archives and manuscripts: 200,000; audio cassettes: 1,500; current serials: 3,300; incunabula: 124; microforms: 40,000.

Special Collections: *Areas of Concentration:* Cyrillic printed books; European printed books; leaflets and posters; Oriental manuscripts; Slavonic manuscripts. *Individual Collections:* Konstantin Vasil'evich Bazilevich; Fedor Ivanovich Buslaev; Aleksei Petrovich Ermolov; Timofei Nikolaevich Granovskii; Fedor Evgen'evich Korsh; Prince Nikolai Vasil'evich Repnin; Sergei Mikhailovich Solov'ev; Decembrist Nikolai Turgenev; Vasilii L'vovich Velichko. *Papers:* Nicholas Bugaev; Zakhar G. Chernyshov; Ivan Ivanovich Ianzhul; Fedor E. Korsh, P.N. and M.N. Krechetnikovs; Nicholas V. Repnin; Alexander A. Viazemskii.

History

The Maxim Gorky Research Library of the Moscow State University (MGU) was named in honor of Mikhail Vasil'evich Lomonosov, to whom the organization of the university and its library traces its origins. In his "Drafts Concerning the Establishment of a University in Moscow," Lomonosov laid out the structure of the entire university. Founded in 1756, the library opened to readers on 3 July 1756, becoming the first public library in the city of Moscow. During this time, serious attention on the part of the Scholarly Council of the university was concentrated on enhancing the library's holdings. The first staff member of the library was Sublibrarian Danilo V. Savich (1756–61), who compiled the first catalog of the library. Among the directors (and librarians) were Anton Antonovich Teils (1757–61), Ioghan-Gotfrid Reikhel (1761–78), Khariton Andreevich Chebotarev (1778–89), Ivan Andreevich Geim (1809–21), the well-known A.I. Kalishevskii (1908–25), and the historian and bibliographer Petr Andreevich Zaionchkovskii (1904–83).

By the beginning of the 19th century, MGU held approximately 20,000 volumes and had access to more than 10,000 additional volumes held by various scholarly, society, and smaller institutional libraries in Moscow. For example, the library of the Society for Russian History and Antiquities held some 2,700 printed books and manuscripts. By the time of the Napoleonic invasion of the Russian Empire in 1812, the library contained more than 20,000 bound items, among them collections that had been donated by figures such as the grandee and bibliophile Pavel Grigor'evich Demidov, who donated some 3,000 valuable printed and manuscript books (along with a printed catalog) to the university's Museum of Natural History in 1803; more than 4,000 volumes given by Professor M. Shaden in 1807; and in 1808, materials given by the president of the Imperial Academy of Sciences (1783–96) and confidante of Catherine II, Princess Ekaterina Romanovna Dashkova.

The Moscow Fire of 1812 destroyed virtually all of the university's book collections, as well as the personal libraries of many professors. Only some 51 collections and 12 manuscripts (which had all been evacuated to Nizhnii Novgorod) were saved. On 12 July 1813 an appeal "To All Lovers of Societal Enlightenment" was published in *Moskovskie vedomosti* concerning the losses suffered in the fire. One of the most significant gifts made as a result of this appeal was some 2,500 volumes from the Imperial Academy of Sciences, including Western European publications of the 16th through 18th centuries. The "Lovers of Societal Enlightenment," on the basis of donated collections, spearheaded efforts toward the reconstitution of the library. Under Ferdinand Fedorovich Reiss (1822–32), a systematic catalog of the library's collection was created and published in 1826.

Despite damage from Nazi bombardment, the library never closed to readers during World War II, and bibliographic publications continued to be issued. The library's employees took measures to safeguard the collections and catalogs, including the relocation of some 5,000 of the rarest items—such as Slavonic manuscripts and early printed books—to storage sites in provincial districts farther from the front. Unique materials were evacuated to Khvalinsk in the fall of 1941 and later to Kustanai in Kazakhstan, where they were kept safely. The majority of volumes from the collections of professors and Russian cultural figures was stored in the university's cellars.

Already in 1944 renovations on the library began, and the Department of Rare Books was established on the basis of MGU's own holdings, supplemented by duplicates from the Lenin State Library and collections from libraries whose physical plants were destroyed during the war.

In December 1945 the library was designated a legal depository library for works printed throughout the USSR. Three years later, work began on the construction of a new campus for MGU on the Lenin (Sparrow) Hills above the city. Many of the specialized departmental libraries, at that time containing around 1 million of the 5 million volumes then in the university's collections, moved to the new campus.

During the 1960s, 1970s, and 1980s the library became an important bibliothecal research center. Staff investigated a variety of subjects relating to the classification and description of library materials, the preparation of thematic bibliographies and indexes for the use of the university's students, as well as readership studies. The further development of rare book and manuscript collections and the conservation and restoration of library materials were also major preoccupations of these decades. The 1980s also saw the preparation of descriptive bibliographies of rare books in the library, as well as the issue of facsimile editions of unique and rare items in the collection.

The period since the collapse of the USSR has witnessed the implementation and expansion of computerization of library work, according to international standards. Although greater emphasis is now placed on automation, the library continues to produce catalogs focusing on its unique holdings.

Collections and Buildings

The library contains a number of personal collections, the first of which was purchased by the library in 1821—the collection of Professor Ivan Andreevich Geim, containing some 1,090 volumes of history, geography, classical authors, and Russian and Western European literature. In 1844 the library received a donation of 3,603 volumes of philosophical and historical works from the libraries of Mikhail Nikitich Muravev (writer, statesman, and trustee of the university) and A.M. Muravev.

During its first 50 years, the library occupied quarters in the main university building near the Resurrection Gate opposite the Mint (Monetnyi dvor, the site of today's Historical Museum). By the 1770s the library was housed in two chambers, one of which contained several special windows for better illumination.

Since 1901 the Central (Fundamental) Library of the University has been located in the Central Building on Mokhovaia Street in the heart of Moscow, just blocks from both the Kremlin complex and the Russian State Library. Based on the plans of K.M. Bykovskyi, the new library was built with funds provided by various donors. It contains book stacks, reading rooms, an interlibrary loan service, and the Division of Rare Books and Manuscripts (founded in 1947). In addition to this building, the collections are distributed through more than 15 buildings of Moscow University, with 60 reading rooms and 16 loan points circulating more than 4 million books and serving some 1.8 million users each year. Today the collection of scholarly and pedagogical literature contains more than 8.5 million volumes, with approximately 2.5 million in foreign languages, as well as 1,500 cassettes and 40,000 microforms. There are several catalogs of the collection—general, alphabetical, subject—and periodicals in Russian and foreign languages. Since 1990 all new acquisitions have been cataloged in U.S. MAchine-Readable Cataloging (USMARC) format in the electronic catalog, which as of 2001 included more than 230,000 entries. The university library is a methodological center for libraries of institutions of higher learning in the Russian Republic.

Division of Rare Books and Manuscripts

The Rare Books and Manuscripts Collections include more than 200,000 volumes, with particularly strong holdings of Slavic, Greek (10th to 11th centuries), Latin (13th century), and Oriental manuscripts. Holdings of Western European materials are also strong and include the manuscript Gospels of 1072, with beautiful miniatures, prepared at the order of the Byzantine Emperor Michael VII Ducas and brought to Moscow by Sophia (Zoe) Paleologos. The library also claims one of the rarest and most valuable monuments to printing history found in Russia: a fragment of Gutenberg's *Ars grammatica* of Aelius Donatus, printed before 1450. Numerous examples of the imprints of Aldo Manuzio, Johann Froben, and other noted presses such as Etienne, Elzevir, and Plantin are also held by the library, along with hundreds of rare French, English, Italian, Dutch, German, and Spanish imprints of the 18th and 19th centuries found in many of the private libraries donated as collections to the MGU.

The territorial collections of Slavonic and Russian manuscripts and old printed books of the 14th to 20th centuries are among the most valuable collections and came to the library in part as a result of the annual expeditions of the history faculty and the archaeographical laboratory and the university, organized and headed by Irina Vasil'evna Pozdeeva. These expeditions began in 1966 and have gathered some 3,500 monuments of Cyrillic book culture, including more than 1,500 from the 15th century through the first half of the 17th century, documenting the living religious and cultural traditions of Russia's often geographically remote communities of Orthodox Old Believers that have largely remained isolated since Russia's Middle Ages.

The collection includes more than 15,000 books in European languages, among them 124 incunabula and 700 paleotypes (books printed between 1501 and 1550), archival materials, and first editions of the works of the national poet, Aleksandr Sergeevich Pushkin (29 of 37 editions), as well as collections of engravings and drawings. The autographs of major figures in Russian culture are found in hundreds of autographed copies of printed books. Since 1920 the library has received obligatory deposit copies from Russian publishers and conducts an international book exchange with almost 1,000 libraries in 63 countries.

EDWARD KASINEC AND ROBERT H. DAVIS JR.

Further Reading

Iz fonda redkikh knig i rukopisei nauchnoi biblioteki Moskovskogo universiteta (From the Collections of Rare Books and Manuscripts of the Research Library of Moscow), Moscow: Izd-vo Moskovskogo Universiteta, 1993

Lesokhina, E.I. and A.M. Kharkova, *Istoriia biblioteki Moskovskogo universiteta, 1917–1949* (History of the Moscow State University Library, 1917–1949), Moscow: Isd-vo Moskovskogo Universiteta, 1981

Opyt raboty nauchnoi biblioteki MGU (Results of the Work of the Research Library of MGU), Moscow: Moskovskii gos. Universitet, 1988

Sorokin, Viktor Vasilevich, *Istoriia biblioteki Moskovskogo universiteta, 1800–1917* (History of the Moscow State University Library, 1800–1917), Moscow: Izd-vo Moskovskogo Universiteta, 1980

Stepanova-Gerasimova, E.G., and E.I. IAtsunok, *Fondy redkikh i tsennykh izdannii (knizhnykh pamiatnikov) v bibliotekakh RSFSR: Ukazatel'* (Index of the Rare and Precious Printed Book [Book Monument] Collections in the Libraries of the Russian Soviet Federal Socialist Republic), Moscow: Gos. Biblioteka SSSR im V.I. Lenina, 1990

Mount Athos Monasteries Libraries

Address: Akte Hagion Oros
Chalkidiki
Greece
Telephone: 377-22586
Fax: 377-23766
www.athosfriends.org

Founded: 963

Holdings (2000): Volumes: 204,000.
Manuscripts: 15,000.

Special Collections: *Areas of Concentration:* Byzantine manuscripts; Gregorian chants; illuminated manuscripts; theological manuscripts.

Named for Athos, a mythical Thracian giant who is said to have been buried beneath an immense pile of rock in a cosmic dual with the god Poseidon, the promontory on the upper seaboard of Greece known as Mount Athos is home to 20 Orthodox Christian monasteries and a dozen smaller dependencies. Together, these monasteries and dependencies contain a collection of treasures that include 15,000 manuscripts, many of them brilliantly illuminated parchments. Among Byzantine materials from the ninth to 15th centuries still extant, the Athonite collections are regarded as preeminent. It has been estimated that this trove represents approximately one-quarter of all the Greek manuscripts in the world, exceeding the combined totals of the collections at the Vatican Library and the Bibliothèque nationale in Paris, which together number slightly less than 10,000 codices. Nearly 3,000 of the manuscripts on Mount Athos are musical and represent approximately one-third of all the known primary material on the Byzantine chant; of these, some 1,500 have been cataloged in an ongoing project that is projected to encompass seven volumes.

A semi-autonomous state, Mount Athos is self-governed under an administrator appointed by the Greek government. Its special status was reaffirmed by the Greek Constitution of 1927 and later by a vote of the European Union. The 223-square-mile monastic republic occupies the easternmost of three promontories attached to the Chalcidice Peninsula, poking its slender mass 35 miles into the Aegean Sea on a line pointing toward Asia Minor and the island of Lemnos. Although connected to the Greek mainland by a narrow isthmus, there is no direct access to the territory by road, and visitors must travel two hours by ferry from the port city of Ouranoupolis to get there.

The all-male theocracy of 2,000 Orthodox Christian monks continues a tradition that began in A.D. 963 with the arrival of St. Athanasius, a one-time schoolteacher who chose a rocky outcrop at the base of the mountain on the promontory's outer tip to establish the Great Lavra monastery. With funds provided initially by Byzantine Emperor Nicephorus Phocas, Lavra has enjoyed the backing of affluent patrons through much of its existence, even during the years of the Ottoman occupation (1424–1912), when it received support from Eastern Orthodox countries in the Danube basin and from the czars of Russia. The other 19 monasteries were established in the years that followed.

The artwork and manuscripts that have been safeguarded on the holy mountain over the centuries were produced by craftsmen, scribes, and illuminators to express their deepest devotion and to perpetuate a heritage that was threatened with what seemed to be certain extinction in the 15th century. With the fall of Constantinople to the Turks in 1453, what had been the longest-surviving political entity in Europe, the Byzantine Empire, came to an abrupt end.

Although the Byzantine state was lost forever, its ideals were kept alive on Mount Athos, some 300 miles west of the fallen capital. Many monks fled there in haste, taking along whatever icons and manuscripts they could gather and adding them to the treasures already assembled over the previous 500 years. Painters and artisans followed as well and produced an eclectic body of work that became stylistically distinctive in its own right. Many other manuscripts have made their way to Mount Athos as gifts from a variety of sources, ranging from wealthy lords and mighty emperors to unpretentious monks and grateful pilgrims. In addition to the books and manuscripts, an unrivaled inventory of wood-carvings, medallions, pectoral pendants, votive lamps, liturgical fans, candlesticks, crosses, and jewel-encrusted boxes (all of them icons in one fashion or another) remain safely locked in sacristies, treasure rooms, and libraries. Inside the churches and refectories, which are architectural triumphs in their own right, frescoes depicting narrative scenes from the life of Christ cover 25 acres of total wall surface.

As many as 20,000 monks lived on the holy mountain at its height, but there have been decided lulls, such as the one in 1971 when the numbers dipped to a nadir of 1,145. A resurgence in young men's interest in the monastic life followed thereafter, and the numbers have almost doubled since that time. Recent census figures also show that the new residents are younger (with an average age now under 40) and better educated than ever before. Only three men, or 2.8 percent of the total, who moved to Mount Athos between 1960 and 1964 had attended college, whereas 27 percent of those who have arrived since then—343 monks—have university degrees.

These figures are particularly important because one explanation often given to justify the removal of artifacts from monasteries has been the presumed incompetence of those charged with their safekeeping. As recently as 1965, Leo Deuel, a Swiss-born writer and teacher of history at City College in New York, expressed irritated dismay at the reluctance of the fathers to share their manuscripts. "Like some negligent but perversely possessive parent, they could not tolerate an outsider's attention to their abused children," he wrote in *Testaments of Time*, a popular history of the worldwide search for ancient documents. "At one point these half-literate monks would be entirely oblivious of the hoary, rotting manuscripts, and at the next, when the foreign visitor expressed the slightest interest, they declared them to be of extravagant value." Deuel was delighted to relate how such 19th-century opportunists as the Englishman Robert Curzon, the 14th baron of Zouche, were able to "outwit the monks and clergy" and return home with many exciting finds.

In his 1849 memoir, *Visits to Monasteries in the Levant*, Curzon recalled the travels he made to Egypt, the Holy Land, Syria, and Greece in the early 1800s with the express purpose of finding the "literary treasures" that he later deposited in the British Museum Library. Describing his first visit to the Great Lavra, Curzon wrote that before he was allowed to enter the monastic library, he had been required to join the abbot in a breakfast of garlic cloves "pounded down, with a certain quantity of sugar" into a white paste mixed with shreds of cheese. "Who could have expected so dreadful a martyrdom as this?" he asked. "I made every endeavor to escape this honour." But if Curzon wanted to see the books, he had to eat the concoction, and eat it he did, even though "the taste of that ladleful stuck to me for days." Given the key to the library and left alone to poke around at will for hours, he was overwhelmed by what he saw and decided to bide his time: "I did not attempt to purchase anything, as it was not advisable to excite the curiosity of the monks upon the subject; nor did I wish that the report should be circulated in other convents that I was come to Mount Athos for the purpose of rifling their libraries."

Curzon was by no means alone in his relentless zeal for acquisitions, with the result that the Athonite monks exercise great caution today in deciding who may be allowed to see their books. This is also why at least one of their brethren is always in attendance when manuscripts are being consulted. Researchers are required to explain the nature of their work before they are granted access to the libraries.

Male visitors of all faiths are welcome on the holy mountain, but only 110 residence permits are issued each day by patristic officials in Ouranoupolis. Of these, only ten are allotted to non-Orthodox applicants, which means that arrangements to visit are best made well in advance. Every approved visitor is entitled to four days of full hospitality at any of the monasteries, although scholars can make arrangements for longer stays. Specific information on arranging visits is available through the Friends of Mount Athos, a nonprofit group based in England. A website is maintained by the North American secretary, Robert W. Allison, professor of philosophy and religion at Bates College in Lewiston, Maine, and a Byzantine scholar who has been traveling to Mount Athos since 1977 under the sponsorship of the Patriarchal Institute for Patristic Studies in Thessaloniki. He is supervising a project to microfilm all 400 manuscripts maintained at Philotheou, one of the smaller monasteries, and to prepare a descriptive catalog of its contents, which have suffered no major depredations or destruction in more than 800 years.

Because each monastery is, in essence, a sovereign state, decidedly distinctive collections of books and manuscripts have evolved over the centuries, each worthy of close scholarly attention. The oldest monastery, the Great Lavra, also has the largest library, reporting 2,242 manuscripts among its holdings, including 100 that are Slavonic. Lavra suffered its most severe losses between the 16th and 19th centuries; the materials that remain on-site include a number of geographical, medical, legal, and classical texts. One of its most spectacular pieces is the Codex Euthalianus, or Codex H, of the Epistles of St. Paul, which contains eight leaves written in the sixth-century majuscule known as *biblique*.

Vatopedi, established in the tenth century above a small inlet on the northeast side of the promontory, is the second oldest monastery. It maintains two separate libraries, one consisting of books printed after 1900 in a variety of European languages. Continuing a Vatopedi tradition of education that reached its height in the 18th century with establishment of the Athonite Academy, it also maintained a college that in its few decades of existence turned out some of the most important Greek scholars of the period. The majestic ruins, with an arched stone aqueduct still intact, overlook the monastery from a nearby hill. The second library is maintained in the Tower of Our Lady, an imposing stone bulwark built on the northeast corner of the monastic precinct in the 16th century to defend against pirate attacks. Since 1867 the tower has been a repository of rare books, prints, engravings, and manuscripts. The 2,058 manuscripts, many of them brilliantly illuminated on parchment with gold and lapis lazuli, are kept on the top floor. One of the monastery's best-known possessions is a 13th-century manuscript of the geographers Ptolemy and Strabo.

Iveron, now a Greek monastery, was founded by a Georgian in the tenth century and includes in its magnificent library of 20,000 printed books and 2,000 manuscripts approximately 100 important texts on parchment in the Georgian language, the largest collection of its kind outside of the nation of Georgia.

Among Iveron's high spots are several imperial and patriarchal documents. St. Panteleimon, the only Russian Orthodox monastery on Mount Athos, maintains a library of 20,000 printed books and 1,920 manuscripts that is especially rich in Slavonic material. During the years of the Soviet Union, its collection was regarded as one of the best resources in the world for primary research in this field. Similar circumstances apply at Zographou, the Bulgarian monastery, and Chelandari, a Serbian enclave; there also are several Romanian *sketae,* or hermitages.

Celebrated principally for their manuscripts, the Athonite libraries also have many printed books, including some important incunabula, several of which were displayed at the landmark "Treasures of Mount Athos" exhibition held in 1997 in Thessaloniki, Greece's second-largest city. This event marked the first time in their 1,000-year history that the monks had allowed any of their extraordinary artworks to leave the holy mountain. The catalog of the exhibition, edited by Athanasios A. Karakatsanis and published in Greek and English editions, includes numerous authoritative essays, including several on the libraries and their holdings.

NICHOLAS A. BASBANES

Further Reading

Basbanes, Nicholas A., *Patience and Fortitude: A Roving Chronicle of Book People, Book Places, and Book Culture,* New York: HarperCollins, 2001

Curzon, Robert, *Visits to Monasteries in the Levant,* London and New York, 1849; reprint, Ithaca, New York: Cornell University Press, and London: Barker, 1955

Deuel, Leo, *Testaments of Time: The Search for Lost Manuscripts and Records,* New York: Knopf, 1965; London: Secker and Warburg, 1966

Hasluck, F.W., *Athos and Its Monasteries,* London: Paul Trench Trubner, and New York: Dutton, 1924

The Holy and Great Monastery Vatopaidi: Tradition, History, Art, 2 vols., Mount Athos: Hiera Megiste Mone Vatopaidiou, 1998

Kadas, Sotiris, *Mount Athos: An Illustrated Guide to the Monasteries and Their History,* 7th edition, Athens: Ekdotike Athenon, 1998

Karakatsanis, Athanasios A., editor, *Treasures of Mount Athos,* Thessaloniki, Greece: Ministry of Culture, 1997

Norwich, John Julius, and Reresby Sitwell, *Mount Athos,* New York: Harper and Row, and London: Hutchinson, 1966

Municipal Library of Lyons

Address: Bibliothèque municipale de Lyon
30 Boulevard Vivier-Merle, Part-Dieu
69431 Lyon CEDEX 03
France
Telephone: 4-78-62-18-00
Fax: 4-78-62-19-49
www.bm-lyon.fr

Founded: 1565; 1765

Holdings (2000): Volumes: 2 million. Current serials: 6,000; films and videos: 13,000; graphic materials: 116,000; incunabula: 1,048; manuscripts: 12,000, including 500 medieval manuscripts; maps: 2,000; microfilms: 2,000; sound recordings: 125,000.

Special Collections: *Areas of Concentration:* Bindings; China; esoterica; history of the book; Lyon and the Rhône-Alpes region; occult studies; theology; World War I. *Individual Collections:* Charavay collection; Chinese collection; Coste collection of Lyon history; esotericism and Freemasonry; Lacassagne collection of criminal anthropology; Lyon Press; Morin-Pons collection of Lyon genealogy; photograph collection; sound and music collection; World War I. *Papers:* Claude Farrière; Stanislas Rodanski.

Fifteen libraries and three bookmobiles make up the Bibliothèque municipale de Lyon (BML), whose central library is at Part-Dieu. Currently the library serves the general public as a resource for materials of all genres and in all subjects. The library also works in partnership with the educational and cultural communities of Lyon. In addition, the BML has important manuscript and archival collections relating to the history of the book and to the region. It is a legal depository, with the mission of collecting and preserving materials deposited by printers in the eight departments making up the Rhône-Alpes region. It balances its responsibilities to the general public with responsibilities to researchers and to posterity.

Collections

The earliest basis of the library's collection comes from the Collège de la Trinité founded in 1527 and run by the Jesuits after 1565. It was not until the 17th century that the books held there were brought together to form a library. The collection continued to grow, thanks to gifts from the Consulate and Jesuits. In 1693, 5,000 books and manuscripts from the library of the archbishop of Lyon were deeded to the library. The collections of the first public library, then housed in the Hôtel de Fléchère, date from 1731. The collections were formed primarily of law books given by prominent lawyers and statesmen. In 1765, after the expulsion of the Jesuits, the Consulate decided to bring the two libraries together into one that would be open to the public: the Bibliothèque de la Ville de Lyon. Nonetheless, some of the books in the Jesuit library were sold in 1777 by bookseller François de Los Rios. Following the Revolution, which closed the library from 1795 until 1803, the municipality was ordered to maintain the library and appointed the first librarian, Antoine Delandine, in 1812. The effect of the Revolution on the collections was both positive (as they grew through confiscations) and negative (as they shrank due to items sent elsewhere or damaged during the turmoil, not to mention the siege of the city when the library itself was a seat of defense). The defeat of the city cost the library 28 manuscripts, 94 incunabula, and more than 11,000 medals. In 1825 the Académie de Lyon reclaimed its previously confiscated collection, impoverishing the municipal library. The first card catalog was begun in 1827, after the costs of printing a catalog (even though the majority of them were paid for by the city for many years) became prohibitive.

In 1831 Gabriel Prunelle, the mayor of Lyon, established a second municipal library dedicated to the arts and sciences, the Bibliothèque du Palais des Arts, whereas the original library maintained collections in theology, law, history, and belles-lettres. Eventually, the library at the Palais des Arts also contained the collections of the Académie and other scientific societies; it held 20,500 volumes in 1844. Despite a large number of thefts, the foundations of the fine collection of prints were also laid in the late 1840s. As in many other French public libraries, limited financial resources and low acquisitions budgets marked the 19th and early 20th centuries. In 1911 the two libraries were brought together into the Palais Saint-Jean. Enriched by gifts (most notably that from magistrate Jean-Antoine-Louis Coste of materials relating to the region) and thanks to the establishment of a local legal depository law in 1943, the regional collections are extensive. They include images, photographs, and valuable ephemera. In 1997 the library became the primary recipient of the legal deposit for all materials published in the region, a responsibility previously held by the centralized national library system.

Other collections relating to local industries include items formerly held by the École de tissage (the school of weaving, founded in 1865), which were given to the library in 1985. Lyon has long been a publishing center, and an important collection on the history of the book was begun in 1970 by Henri-Jean Martin (conservator of the BML from 1964 to 1970). In association with the Bibliothèque nationale de France (BNF), the Museum of Printing in Lyon, and the national library school—the École nationale supérieure des sciences de l'information et des bibliothèques (ENSSIB)—the BML is responsible for collecting materials on the history of the book. In 1994, in partnership with the printing museum and ENSSIB, the BML became an associate institution of the BNF. In this role, it collects in the history of the book and printing, as well as in information science, and has also offered courses on the history of the book and manuscripts.

An important collection of World War I materials was begun in 1915, by order of Mayor Edouard Herriot. Thanks to a Franco-Chinese institute hosted in Lyon from 1921 to 1946, collections from the Jesuit missions in China, and generous donations from the People's Republic of China and Taiwan, the Chinese collection is one of the richest in France. In 1993 the BML received the collections of Louis and Auguste Lumière, inventors and cinematographic pioneers, and the National Foundation for Photography, which was created in 1976.

Conservation

The library has put considerable effort into conservation activities. The 17-story, climate-controlled Part-Dieu building contains more than one million items, many of them rare books and manuscripts. The newly acquired collections of the Jesuit library at Chantilly will take up nearly all of the remaining space. The Music Department is also responsible for the preservation of more than 85,000 vinyl records and other historic recordings. Since 1997 the library has been responsible for the collection and conservation of regional publications and other materials; the BNF provides it with the fourth copy of legally deposited works printed in the region. This collection includes far more than books (for example, prints, postcards, and posters, as well as other ephemera), which gives it a great richness and depth. In 1997 the library received more than 7,000 books and 2,500 periodical subscriptions (some 73,000 issues) through this program.

The library has also been active in making its collections, particularly those of regional interest, accessible through modern technologies. The BML holds more than 14,000 items and 200,000 articles relating to the region. Since 1993 journal articles have been scanned and indexed for viewing at the multimedia stations of the Part-Dieu library. The library has placed more than 43,000 images from prints, photographs, postcards, and posters of old Lyon on the *Vidéodisque des collections ethnographiques en Rhône-Alpes* (VIDERALP) laserdisc. Furthermore, 80,000 references to books, journal articles, and videos are cataloged and available through the collective catalog of regional documentation: *Mémoire et actualité de la region Rhône-Alpes* (1995–).

Public Service

While the library was associated with the Jesuit academy, it was in principle reserved for those professors associated with the school. It would, however, often welcome outside users. The public library established in 1731 was open only Monday and Thursday, for four hours each day, and was a noncirculating collection. The Revolutionary era emphasized free and complete public access to education and libraries, but the means were often lacking and the collections too damaged and disarranged to be of great use. In 1911 the city responded to the pressure of burgeoning collections and from patrons who desired a single location by acquiring a building large enough to house both the Bibliothèque de la Ville de Lyon and the Bibliothèque du Palais des Arts. After 1959 the network of libraries and programs grew rapidly. Each of the nine administrative districts of Lyons is served by its own library.

The Part-Dieu building is divided into seven thematic departments: youth, arts and crafts, languages and literature, music, culture, society, and sciences. The building was constructed between 1969 and 1972, partially in response to the creation of a new civic center, and at the time was remarkable for its size. The 14 branch libraries serving the nine districts and the main library share a catalog, brought online in 1986. In the 1990s the library underwent a considerable process of both physical and administrative reorganization, in order to divide the library by topic. Each department was asked to support all media and all services at all levels (general and research). The Bibliothèque municipale continues to look to the future and upgrade its systems and services. In 1999 the catalog migrated to a new platform and Internet access is now available in all 15 libraries.

In 1999 the library counted 80,072 active users, with many (37 percent for Part-Dieu and 49 percent for the branches) visiting more than once a week. Younger readers make up a large percentage of the user population; the library has a strong youth focus and works with education students. The branch libraries work closely with the communities they serve to present programs and offer services tailored to those users. In addition, the library has established a program in conjunction with the Semi-Freedom Center of Lyon to develop prison libraries. In response to new technologies and increasing patron demand, the library offers a team of instructors to provide, free of charge, instruction in everything from the basics of computing to online research.

Cooperation

Like so many libraries, the BML is heavily involved in cooperative exchanges and agreements. These range from regional commitments to universities and institutions in Lyon to the centralized Catalogue Collectif de France, and internationally to the Research Libraries Group (RLG). Through these agreements, the library serves as editor and publisher of indices relating to the locale, as well as contributing to European and international efforts. For example, it participates in the *Illustrated Incunabula Short-Title Catalogue* (1997–); a version of the ISTC on CD-ROM, it contains illustrations of key pages of the items. In addition, the library works closely with the École nationale supérieure des sciences de l'information et des bibliothèques (ENSSIB) and has welcomed more than 85 interns from the school.

The Bibliothèque municipale maintains its place at the center of collections of regional materials, and it also participates in building national and international networks. The library continues to respect its traditions and historical mission, as well as paying close attention to the needs of its current and future patrons.

SARAH G. WENZEL

Further Reading

Collet, Anne-Christine, "La réorganisation en departments thématiques," *Bulletin d'informations des bibliothécaires français* 170 (1996)

Niepce, Léopold, *Les bibliothèques anciennes et modèrnes de Lyon*, Lyon: Georg, 1876

Vernet, André, editor, *Histoire des bibliothèques françaises*, 4 vols., Paris: Promodis–Éditions du Cercle de la Librairie, 1988–92; see especially vol. 3, *Les bibliothèques de la Révolution et du XIXe siècle, 1789–1914* (1991), and vol. 4, *Les bibliothèques au XXe siècle, 1914–1990* (1992)

National Agricultural Library of the United States

Address: National Agricultural Library
10301 Baltimore Avenue
Beltsville, Maryland 20705
USA
Telephone: 301-504-5755
Fax: 301-504-6927
www.nal.usda.gov

Founded: 1862

Holdings (2000): Volumes: 2.3 million. Archives and manuscripts: 32,000 linear feet; audio materials: 542,000; cartographic materials: 422,000; current serials: 21,000; graphic materials: 4.2 million; microforms: 5.4 million.

Special Collections: *Areas of Concentration:* Agriculture and agricultural history; botany; entomology; horticulture; natural history; poultry sciences. *Individual Collections:* Forest Service historical photograph collection; Thomas Jefferson correspondence collection; nursery and seed trade catalog collection; poster collection; rare book collection; screwworm eradication collection; USDA history collection; USDA pomological watercolor collection.

Mission

The National Agricultural Library (NAL) serves as a national library of the United States and as the library of the U.S. Department of Agriculture (USDA) as part of the Agricultural Research Service (ARS). NAL, with a primary focus on research, serves USDA employees and groups of users from both the private and public sectors: scientists, professors, government officials, farmers, business leaders, and students nationally and internationally. It seeks to acquire, manage, preserve, disseminate, and provide access to information, as well as to provide quality stewardship of its unique collection.

NAL's collection development policy is strongly tied to the information needs of the USDA. The NAL, the Library of Congress, and the National Library of Medicine participate in a collaborative collection development plan that assists in providing comprehensive resources to the users of these libraries.

Origins

Long before Abraham Lincoln signed the Organic Act of 1862, legislation facilitating the creation of a departmental library for the USDA, George Washington visualized a U.S. repository for agricultural information. In 1859, when Lincoln spoke before the Wisconsin State Agricultural Society in Milwaukee, he similarly expressed his belief in the importance of print resources by linking reading and information to the solving of problems.

In 1862 President Lincoln charged the USDA with acquiring and disseminating useful agricultural information to the people of the United States. Acting on Lincoln's directive, the first U.S. Commissioner of Agriculture, Isaac Newton, established "an agricultural library" within the new USDA, with Aaron Burt Grosh (1867–69) as its first librarian. Grosh was a clergyman and one of the founders of the National Grange. He was succeeded by Stuart Eldridge (1869–71), who was a professor of anatomy at Georgetown University.

The first collection was garnered from 1,000 volumes transferred to the Department of Agriculture Library from the Agricultural Division of the Patent Office (established in 1839). In 1864 the Department of Agriculture allocated a portion of its budget to pay the salary of a librarian. In 1868 when the Department of Agriculture building was completed, a library was created, and in 1872 the collection totaled 8,000 volumes.

As part of its collection development plan, exchanges with agricultural associations in the U.S. and in foreign countries greatly enhanced the library's holdings. In 1880 the library expanded its collection efforts to include the subjects of agricultural and home economics, animal husbandry, pure food and drug administration, and soil conservation. By 1892 the library staff had grown to 39 employees, and the collection included 122,000 books and pamphlets and 2,000 periodicals on a wide variety of agricultural topics.

Reorganization Years

Although librarian Ernestine H. Stevens (1877–93) set the stage for the physical and intellectual development of the library by moving the museum (which was created with the library) out of the library to provide additional space for library resources, it was William Parker Cutter (1893–1901) who carried the expansion concept much farther. He introduced a formal catalog, increased access to the collection by implementing a classification system, methodically increased collections in needed areas, and set up several bureau libraries. In 1896 Congress gave first authority to the Department of Agriculture Library to purchase relevant materials and work toward developing a comprehensive collection of agriculture-related sources. In 1904 the library began to print and distribute cards for the materials it collected.

Librarian Claribel R. Barnett (1907–40) continued the tradition of greater access to more resources by recognizing the needs of researchers for access to materials in many fields. She was also responsible for reorganizing library functions. Establishment of a plan to guide acquisition and service greatly enhanced the productivity of the Department of Agriculture Library. Through Barnett's efforts and the cooperation of the American Documentation Institute, the library became the experimental site for supplying interlibrary loan materials through microfilm and photocopy in 1934.

During the 1940s, the need to consolidate and centralize widespread library services gained favor. Because of the library's decentralized organizational structure, inherent inefficiencies in service delivery, collection efforts, and administration were evident. The bureau libraries reported to the individual bureaus (e.g., agriculture, animal industry, and chemistry and soils), not the head librarian. Although the main library was ultimately responsible for their operations, this decentralized structure prevented successful coordination of effort and efficient utilization of financial resources. Through the implementation of two edicts, the centralized library system came into existence. The first, the Office of the Secretary Memorandum No. 808 (1940), decreed centralization of five basic library responsibilities, including acquisition, supervision, and evaluation.

World War II

During and immediately after World War II, the library continued to reorganize. On 1 January 1942 the Secretary of Agriculture issued another memorandum, No. 973, stating the need for further centralization resulting from President Roosevelt's wartime decision to move bureaus out of Washington, D.C. Concerned that further dispersion of bureaus would thwart access to bureau materials and cause further deterioration of operational systems, the secretary petitioned the president for an executive order to place all library service units under the immediate control of the agriculture library. This move was accomplished on 23 February 1942 by Executive Order No. 9069. A supplement to order No. 973 enacted on 2 February 1942 allowed the president to call upon Department Librarian Ralph R. Shaw (1940–54) to manage the administration of all library facilities and services.

The bureau libraries, however, did not wish to relinquish control of the individual collections they managed and resisted the staff reassignments following this reorganization. Eventually the collections and staff were centralized, and Shaw took the opportunity to streamline technical services operations, as well as institute several innovative programs, including the establishment of satellite centers at universities around the country that provided library services on a contract basis. He was also widely regarded as an innovator in library automation.

Global Era

NAL became a national library in 1962 during the administration of Librarian Foster E. Mohrhadt (1954–68). It was also at this time that NAL took a more active role in the global information arena. In 1967, through the joint efforts of the Library of Congress, the National Library of Medicine, and the National Agricultural Library, a plan was developed for coordinated library automation.

Until 1969 NAL was located at USDA Headquarters in Washington, D.C. In 1969, under the leadership of John Sherrod (1968–73), the library moved to its current home in Beltsville, Maryland, on the grounds of the USDA's Beltsville Agricultural Research Center. NAL has been at its current location, a 14-story brown brick building, ever since. Richard A. Farley succeeded Sherrod as NAL librarian in 1974.

Electronic Era

The 1990 Farm Bill designated NAL as the primary agricultural information resource of the United States. This bill formally recognized NAL's responsibility to the public, private, and international agricultural information communities, as well as to the USDA. With this responsibility in mind, NAL Director Joseph Howard (1982–93) created the Electronic Information Initiative in December 1992 to research, plan, and implement a systematic program of managing data in electronic form. The Electronic Information Initiative Statement acknowledged the changing nature of information management and the shortcomings of a paper-based information delivery system. Since then, production of digitized information, telecommunications innovations, and the Internet have become essential in allowing NAL to develop an electronic library for meeting the needs of users in the 21st century. On 1 January 1995, the National Agricultural Library designated electronic information the "preferred medium." With the advent of computer technology and its inherent capabilities, the NAL looked forward to a time of expanded service to an unlimited pool of users located throughout the world.

On 1 December 1994 NAL merged with the U.S. Agricultural Research Services (ARS) under a total reorganization of the U.S. Department of Agriculture. Although the NAL director now reported to the ARS administrator, the national library status and organizational identity remained the same as before the merger. Downsizing and restructuring were part of the reorganization and resulted in staff reductions of 7 percent.

As NAL, considered the leading agricultural library in the world, continues to move toward comprehensive electronic accessibility, it also must meet the challenges engendered by budget constraints. Cancellation of subscriptions to serials as well as slower growth of print materials in general are direct results of diminished financial support and new electronic requirements.

Primary Services

In addition to the main library in Beltsville, NAL maintains a reference center in Washington, D.C., at USDA headquarters. Eleven specialized information centers within the main library provide information services in areas of particular concern to world agriculture. Subjects covered include agricultural trade and marketing, alternative farming systems, animal welfare, and aquaculture. NAL and a nationwide network of state land grant universities as well as USDA libraries form a document delivery service that allows interlibrary loan of agricultural materials nationwide to USDA personnel.

NAL's Government Printing Office (GPO) collection has been enhanced over the years (since 1895) by thousands of federal agency publications sent by GPO to the collection. The documents collected support the missions of USDA and the NAL itself. By participating in the program, NAL is obligated to provide on-site users with free access to the depository publications in the collection.

Since the early 1990s NAL has put forth a major effort to capitalize on the use of Web-based services and to realign staff and budget to support customer demand. NAL has completed phase one of a project to move all NAL master negative microfilm to offsite storage in Boyers, Pennsylvania. This was a major step toward NAL's goal of becoming a "library without walls," of using the burgeoning electronic information technology to make its collection and expertise as widely available throughout the world as possible. To that end, NAL maintains and supports several online databases, catalogs, and directories. They include AGRICOLA (AGRICultural OnLine Access), NAL's bibliographic database of 3.5 million citations for materials pertaining to all aspects of agriculture and related subjects, available at www.usda.gov/ag98. Other online resources include AgDB (Agriculture Databases), available at www.agnic.org/agdb, and AGNIC (Agricultural Network Information Center) at www.agnic.org.

Over 170 journals in agricultural, biological, and social sciences are available online at NAL through Web-based access to the International Digital Electronic Access Library. NAL's Electronic Media Center (EMC) allows library users to gather information from NAL's electronic resources.

In 1998 the Public Services Division launched an initiative to create a new reference service model that includes support of electronic reference interactions and delivery of information. NAL continues to encourage its patrons to send requests and receive materials electronically. Electronically submitted requests are the primary type of document delivery requests NAL receives. Electronic delivery of materials to patrons increased by 60 percent over 1997 and is expected to continue to rise.

Recent Developments

In 1994, in a reorganization of the Economic Research Service (ERS), the Agricultural and Rural History Section was eliminated. Following discussion of numerous options, USDA Deputy Secretary Richard Rominger decided to transfer the historical collection from the USDA to the NAL. The collection, which includes extensive archival materials on secretaries of agriculture beginning with Secretary of Agriculture Henry Agard Wallace (1933–40), was also transferred to the NAL in 1996.

In 1996 Public Law 104-127 (FAIR Act) mandated that the secretary of agriculture develop and maintain a system to monitor and evaluate agricultural research and extension activities conducted or supported by the Department of Agriculture. This system will enable the secretary to measure the impact and effectiveness of research, extension, and education programs according to priorities, goals, and mandates established by law.

On 14 November 1994 Pamela Andre was appointed director of NAL. She had previously been appointed associate director for automation at NAL in 1984, after being employed in various positions at the Library of Congress.

In 1998 NAL began a major renovation of its building under the leadership of NAL Deputy Director Keith Russell. NAL undertook the renovation because of a severe shortage of storage space for the collection, a desire for even more customer-friendly areas for users, and the need to upgrade the 30-year-old building's infrastructure to facilitate electronic delivery of services and materials. Construction caused NAL to temporarily move some services and close certain areas of the building. Renovations will be complete in the early part of the 21st century.

LYNNE C. CHASE

Further Reading

Adkinson, Burton W., *Two Centuries of Federal Information*, Stroudsberg, Pennsylvania: Dowden Hutchinson and Ross, 1978

Carabelli, Angelina Jacqueline, *Abraham Lincoln: His Legacy to American Agriculture*, Beltsville, Maryland: Associates of the National Agriculture Library, 1972

Clapp, Verner W., and Scott Adams, editors, *Current Trends in Libraries of the U.S. Government,* Urbana: University of Illinois Library School, 1953

Lacy, Mary G., "The Library of the U.S. Department of Agriculture," *Library Journal* 46 (1921)

Morhardt, Foster E., "The Library of the United States Department of Agriculture," *The Library Quarterly* 27, no. 2 (April 1957)

National and University Library of Bosnia and Hercegovina

Address: Nacionalna i univerzitetska biblioteka Bosne i Hercegovine
Zmaja od Bosne 8B
71000 Sarajevo
Bosnia-Hercegovina
Telephone: 33-275-301
Fax: 33-533-204

Founded: 1945

Holdings (1999): Volumes: 300,000. Archives and manuscripts: 3,000; CD-ROMs: 500 Oriental manuscripts; incunabula: 2.

Special Collections: *Areas of Concentration:* Bosnian literary figures; Bosnian recorded music; official publications of Bosnia-Hercegovina. *Papers:* Mehmed-beg Kapetanović Ljubušak.

1945 to 1992

Following its establishment after World War II, the future National and University Library of Bosnia and Hercegovina was granted the right of legal deposit for all materials produced in the territory of Bosnia-Hercegovina. As the national library for the country, it also served as the repository for many manuscript and printed book rarities, photographs, ephemera, and archives of prominent personalities. In 1951 a Department of Special Collections was established to inventory, collect, and care for such materials properly. These collections mirrored the ethnic and cultural diversity of Bosnia-Hercegovina, with materials drawn from all of the religious and ethnic groups comprising the former Yugoslavia—particularly Muslim, Catholic, Jewish, and Eastern Orthodox—as well as numerous examples relevant to the histories and cultures of Western, Eastern, and Southern Europe. Among the significant collections were more than 500 manuscripts on Islamic subjects from the 15th through 19th centuries; 250 items written in Bosnian script from the 16th and 17th centuries; the personal archives of lexicographer Mehmed-beg Kapetanović-Ljubušak, the literary figure Jovan Kršić, and the poet Silvije Strahimir Kranjčević; and the archives of various cultural societies and foreign diplomatic missions from the 19th century.

As a national library, the library carried on extensive contacts with other library institutions throughout the former Yugoslavia as well as internationally. The initiation of online cataloging in the early 1990s held the promise of even greater collaboration with like institutions. The library was also a regional center for library science education and the national bibliography, attempting to document the record of printing in Bosnia-Hercegovina. Today the departments devoted to the bibliographic registration of Bosnia's publishing output, including the assigning of international standard bibliographic numbers (ISBNs) and international standard serial numbers (ISSNs), have been reestablished. After 1951 the library also became the university library and broadened the range of academic disciplines collected.

The National and University Library of Bosnia and Hercegovina contained approximately 2 million volumes prior to a sustained mortar and artillery attack by Bosnian Serbs in August 1992. Approximately 85 percent of the collection—including some 150,000 rare books and manuscripts—was lost, along with the library's catalog of holdings. Currently the library has a total collection of approximately 300,000 volumes, including donations from a host of international organizations and institutions.

August 1992 to the Present

During the four years of war in Bosnia-Hercegovina (May 1992 to November 1995), thousands of architectural, religious, artistic, and cultural monuments and institutions were destroyed, of which the National and University Library of Bosnia and Hercegovina was one of the most visible in both a metaphoric and real sense. Its targeting and destruction was but one of a series of such systematic attacks on institutions containing the documentation of Bosnia's multiethnic past.

Recognizing the intense competition for resources in rebuilding war-torn Bosnia-Hercegovina, the National University Library has established modest short-term goals aimed primarily at the creation of a new collection devoted to the information needs of Bosnia's citizens. In addition, some 6,000 students and faculty continue to rely on the library for their research needs. Therefore the provision of current materials in all media has been a foremost concern, including subscriptions to leading Western medical and economic journals. Remarkably, in 2000 the library achieved a modicum of normality, focusing on the tasks of acquisitions, national bibliographic registration, and reference services to the nation's citizens.

Many of the items lost in the destruction of the National University Library were irreplaceable. Similarly, Bosnia's Oriental Institute, once a rich trove of Islamic manuscripts, was specifically targeted and destroyed by Bosnian Serb shells on 17 May 1992. Nevertheless, a high priority is to reconstitute holdings of Bosniaca (defined as materials in any format produced on or pertaining to Bosnia-Hercegovina over the centuries) as fully as possible from libraries and individuals abroad. There are more than 20 active programs throughout the world aimed at assisting Bosnian libraries. Among the first institutions to offer support were the national libraries of the former Yugoslav republics of Croatia and Slovenia. Two major long-term efforts to renew collections include the Bosnian Library Project (which solicits donations of new academic works from university presses, libraries, and individual donors) and the Bosnian Manuscript Ingathering Project (which seeks to locate copies or detailed notes of Islamic manuscripts lost in the destruction of the Oriental Institute). To date these projects have brought more than 30,000 volumes to Bosnian libraries, including some 500 copies of Oriental Institute manuscripts transferred to CD-ROM format. The involvement of the Sabre Foundation (Cambridge, Massachusetts) has provided for shipment of more than 22 tons of donated books to Bosnia since the mid-1990s.

Perhaps the biggest obstacle to reconstituting the printed collections of Bosniaca is the fact that the National and University Library's union catalogs—the most complete record of Bosnian publishing extant—were destroyed along with its collections. Beginning in 1995 the online bibliographic service OCLC, in coordination with representatives from the Harvard University (Cambridge, Massachusetts), Yale University (New Haven, Connecticut), and University of Michigan (Ann Arbor) libraries, began the Bosniaca Bibliographic Database Project. Search methodologies were developed for identifying relevant records, yielding some 104,000 OCLC records as of 1996.

A priority of the new National and University Library of Bosnia and Hercegovina is the digitization of those portions of its collections devoted to documentation of the country's history and culture of tolerance, making them accessible to readers throughout the world. Before the war the library had a staff of some 108 professional librarians; this number has dropped significantly, to 69 as of 2001. Staff recruitment and training has therefore been a high priority since the end of the war.

Facilities

From 1951 to 25 August 1992, the library occupied the former City Hall (the Vijecnica), completed in a Moorish Revival style in 1896. Although gutted by the fires set by exploding mortar rounds, the walls of the building survived, and the structure is today under restoration, albeit slowly, with funds provided by Austria and the European Union. Today the library occupies a floor in a 21,500-square-foot former military barracks.

It is hoped that someday the old library will be renovated (to date, only the roof has been repaired) and will serve once again as the home of the remaining rare books, manuscripts, and archives in the National and University Library of Bosnia and Hercegovina's care.

EDWARD KASINEC AND ROBERT H. DAVIS JR.

Further Reading

Bašović, Ljubinka, *Biblioteke i bibliotekarstvo u Bosni i Hercegovini, 1918–1945* (Libraries and Librarianship in Bosnia and Hercegovina, 1918–1945), Sarajevo: Veselin Masleša, 1986

Bašović, Ljubinka, *Biblioteke i bibliotekarstvo u Bosni i Hercegovini, 1945–1975* (Libraries and Librarianship in Bosnia and Hercegovina, 1945–75), Sarajevo: Svjetlost, 1977

Bašović, Ljubinka, *Vodič kroz naučne i stručne biblioteke u Bosni i Hercegovini* (Guide to Academic and Oflicial Libraries in Bosnia and Hercegovina), Sarajevo: Narodna biblioteka SR BiH, 1970

Hadžiosmanović, Lamija, *Biblioteke u Bosni i Hercegovini za vrijeme austrougarske vladavine* (Libraries of Bosnia and Hercegovina at the Time of the Austro-Hungarian Empire), Sarajevo: IRO "Veselin Masleša," OO Izdavačka Djelatnost, 1980

Kujundzic, Enes, Nada Milicevic, and Amra Rešidbegoric, *Prilog bibliografiji—Bibliografija Bosne i Hercegovine* (Contributions towards Bibliography: A Bibliography of Bosnia and Hercegovina), Sarajevo: Narodna i Univerzitetska Biblioteka Bosne i Hercegovine, 1994

Mowat, Ian, "Surviving in Sarajevo: The Continuity of Academic Life in a War Zone," *Learned Publishing* 8, no. 4 (1995)

Pejanović, Đorde, *Istorija biblioteka u Bosni i Hercegovini, od početka do danas* (The History of the Library of Bosnia-Hercegovina, from Its Foundation to the Present), Sarajevo: "Veselin Masleša," 1960

Pistalo, Borivoje, "Foundation for the Restoration of Library Holdings and Information Infrastructure of the National and University Library of Bosnia and Herzegovina at the Institute of Information Science in Maribor, Slovenia," *European Research Libraries Cooperation* 3, no. 2 (1993)

Riedlmayer, Andras, "Libraries Are Not for Burning: International Librarianship and the Recovery of the Destroyed Heritage of Bosnia and Herzegovina," *INSPEL* 30, no. 1 (1996)

Zeco, Munerva, "Research Notes: The National and University Library of Bosnia and Herzegovina during the Current War," *Library Quarterly* 66 (1996)

National and University Library of Croatia

Address: Nacionalna i sveučilišna knjižnica
Hrvatske bratske zajednice bb
10000 Zagreb
Croatia
Telephone: 1-616-41-11
Fax: 1-616-41-86
www.nsk.hr

Founded: 1606

Holdings (1999): Volumes: 2.5 million. Audio recordings: 31,000; incunabula: 187; current serials: 14,000; dissertations and theses: 21,000; graphic materials: 166,000; manuscripts: 136,000 items; maps: 27,000; printed music: 17,000.

Special Collections: *Areas of Concentration:* Croatian Protestant books; Croatica; émigré publications; 15th- and 16th-century Croatian writers; maps; music; prints and drawings. *Individual Collections:* Bibliotheca Metropolitana; Glagolitic and Cyrillic manuscripts; Glagolitic incunabula (including the Croatian *editio princeps*, 1483 Missal); International Permanent Exhibition of Publications (ISIP); pre-1835 Croatica rare books and manuscripts; 16th-century Glagolitic books; typographic works of Croatian printers Andrija Paltašić (Andreas de Paltasichis Catterensis) and Dobruško Dobrić (Bonino Boninis). *Papers:* Ivana Brlić-Mažuranić; Ljudevit Gaj; Vatroslav Jagić; Miroslav Krleža; Eugen Kvaternik; Pavao Ritter-Vitezović; Nikola Tommaseo.

Historical Overview

A medieval kingdom with the name Croatia existed from the eighth century. Initially part of the Frankish and Byzantine dynastic realms, it achieved sovereign status under Duke Branimir in 879. The Croatian written record dates from this period, primarily in the form of registers and codices from the monastic libraries, the earliest of which are from the 11th century. In 1102 Croatia entered into a personal union with Hungary under King Koloman, which lasted until 1526, when Croatian nobles called upon the Hapsburgs for protection against the Ottomans. The political formation thus created by contractual and legal association with the Hapsburgs lasted until the dissolution of the Hapsburg Empire in 1918. From 1867 Croatian lands were divided between the two constitutionally autonomous parts of the Dual Monarchy of Austria-Hungary. Croatia was a constituent part of the Kingdom of Serbs, Croats, and Slovenes from 1918 until 1941. From 1945 to 1991, Croatia was a republic of the Yugoslav Federation. Since 1991 it has been an independent country.

The Nacionalna i sveučilišna knjižnica (National and University Library) was not affected in the Wars of the Yugoslav Secession (1991–94), although its collection of rare books and manuscripts was temporarily closed.

The Library

The beginning of the National and University Library in 1606 is tied to the arrival of Jesuits in Croatia. The library supported the Zagreb Collegium Societatis Iesu (Jesuit Grammar School), the Academia Zagrabiensis (Zagreb Academy) college from 1612, and Regia Scientiarium Academia (Academy of Sciences) from 1669. After the dissolution of the Jesuit order in 1773, the library was transferred to the Academy of Science. The collection was opened to the public in 1818 and became part of the newly established Pravoslavna akademija (Academy of Law) in 1850. In 1874 the library became part of a newly founded university, one of ten university libraries in the Hapsburg Monarchy.

These formative years determined the dual mission of the library—to collect the written record of Croatian culture, research, and science, and to be a primary research library supporting Sveučilište u Zagrebu (Zagreb University) curricula. From 1874 to 1943, both the state and the university had authority over library administration. The library was separated from the university in 1943.

The library was moved several times in its history. From 1776 it was housed in the Jesuit Collegium and then in the Academy of Science and from 1883 in the building of the University of Zagreb. The building specifically constructed for the library, Sezessionist palace on Marulić Square, housed the collection from 1913. Proposals for expansion date from 1947 and plans for building a new library from the early 1960s. The present library building (designed for 4.5 million volumes) was opened in 1995.

Jesuit Collegium, 1606 to 1773

Extant records show that the library of the Jesuit Collegium collection was developed in areas of the school curriculum, with steady annual growth of approximately 50 volumes from 1645 to 1773. The earliest gifts to the library were collections of Nikola Istvanffy, Franjo Pacota, Ursula Thonhausen, Petar Petretić, and Juraj Plemić. At the time of its secularization in 1773, the library had 6,000 volumes. The individuals in charge of the library included Pavao Cyriani, Ladislav Despotović, Juraj Patačić, Franjo Plemić, Franjo Zdelar, Ivan Galjuf, Nikola Lovrenčić, Franjo Ksaver Pejačević, and Nikola Plantić.

The National Library: Academy of Sciences Library, 1773 to 1874

The Academy's library was run by a succession of librarians. They were Matija Kirinić (1776–80; 1796–1805), Josip Mikoczy (1780–96), Franjo Klohammer (1805–14), Ladislav Žužić (1815–34), who was instrumental in opening the library for the public and transforming it into an institution of national prominence, and Matija Smodek (1841–75), who contributed to its systematic arrangement and development of the catalogs. During most of its existence, the library was without a regular budget. It suffered losses to its collection when the Faculty of Theology separated from the Academy of Science in 1784. This move resulted in the transfer of a substantial part of its collection to Budapest, diminishing it by half and robbing it of its most valuable books. The gift of a library of historian Baltazar Adam Krčelić in 1777 (the most significant single donation in the library's history) and those of Eleonora Patačić and Maximilian Vrhovac reflected the movement to build a publicly accessible national collection. By 1819 the library grew to 10,000 books and manuscripts. An imperial decree of 1856 conferred the status of the national institution of learning on the academy, which brought a permanent annual budget to the library. Its collection, primarily works in Latin, German, French, and Italian and a negligible number of Croatian books, lacked an essential ingredient of a national library—books in the national vernacular. This was a combined effect of the Croatian multilingual environment (with Latin, German, and Italian constituting the languages of official communication), the reading habits of the educated elites, and a limited market for books in the native language. Establishment of legal deposit in 1816 meant that the library received a copy of each title printed by the University Press in Budapest. From 1837 to 1919, the library developed its collection through legal deposit copies of imprints from Croatia and Slavonia. The books published in Istria and Dalmatia were not included until 1875, creating serious gaps in the collection.

The University Library: Sveučilišna knjižnica, 1874 to 1943

The library had 47,000 volumes when it became part of the University of Zagreb in 1874. Ivan Kostrenčić was the first professionally trained librarian (1875–1911) appointed as its head. He developed the library statute modeled on the Austrian rules for university libraries (1876) and the interlibrary loan program. He also began the systematic collection of contemporary scholarship and materials of national importance. Acquisition of the library of the Nardoni muzej (National Museum) in 1875 brought many rare books and manuscripts. In 1901 the library acquired the right to store and use the Bibliotheca Metropolitana (Metropolitan Library) for a period of 50 years. Its 50,000 volumes reflect the history of the Zagreb Archdiocese from the 11th century. Other acquisitions included the collection of Ban Tomašić (15,000 volumes primarily in law and history) and the libraries of 17th-century Croatian nobleman Nikola Šubić Zrinski and 19th-century reformer Ljudevit Gaj (16,000 volumes and more than 700 manuscripts). These are pivotal for research of the Illyrianist Movement and early Croatian literature. Through systematic development the library built a collection of national importance, despite gaps in Istrian and Dalmatian imprints (especially newspapers) and early Croatian literature. The collection grew to 145,630 volumes by 1918 and doubled in six years, owing to legal deposit copies from the territory of the former Yugoslavia after 1919. By 1940 it had grown to 350,000 volumes. Significant additions were the collections of linguist Vatroslav Jagić (1924), Vladimir Lunaček (1927), the Statistical Office in Zagreb (1934), Ivan Bach (1935), and the Masonic Lodge (1940). After Kostrenčić the library heads included Velimir Deželić (1911–19), Franjo Fancev (1919–26), and Mate Tentor (1927–43).

The National and University Library: Nacionalna i sveučilišna knjižnica, 1943 to the Present

For the last 50 years the library has been separate from the university, with emphasis given to its national function. In 1960 it was officially named Nacionalna i sveučilišna biblioteka (Nacionalna i sveučilišna knjižnica in the 1990s). Library directors in this period were Marko Orešković (1943–45), Matko Rojnić (1945–76), Veseljko Velčić, Petar Piskač, Ivan Mihel (1990–96), and Josip Stipanov (1996–). In 1948 the library had 400,000 volumes and by 1972 more than 1 million. These increases were owing to federal copyright deposit laws (1945, 1953, and 1965). In contrast, acquisition of material published abroad was difficult because access to hard currency involved approval by relevant ministries. Exchange of publications with institutions abroad was inadequate to fill gaps in foreign-language materials. With the collapse of communism in the late 1980s and the dissolution of Yugoslavia in 1991, legal deposit from the former Yugoslav republics stopped. Simultaneously, the collection was strengthened in two important areas—government-suppressed publications and those issued by Croatians outside Croatia. The Library Act of 1997 regulated legal deposit for printed, audiovisual, and electronic publications in Croatia.

Classification and Catalogs

An alphabetic inventory already existed in 1610. The library has an alphabetical catalog covering the years 1646 to 1684, and the 1773 inventory lists books in 13 groups that reflect shelf location. Immediately after incorporation with the Academy of Science library, the library was not ordered and had no catalog. Subsequently, the collection was arranged in seven classes, with classified and alphabetical catalogs. The systematic work on the catalogs began in 1842. In the eight years following 1858, several catalogs were developed: a card catalog; a topographic catalog in book form; the alphabetical catalog of books, manuscripts, and maps; and a systematic catalog. Kostrenčić started an alphabetical catalog based on the Vienna instructions and drafted a scheme for a systematic catalog in 1899. Introduction of the typewriter in 1911 facilitated the production of the alphabetic and classified card catalogs, which were completed and opened to the public in 1918. The shelf arrangement by fixed location gave way to a *numerus currens* system with the move of the library to the new building in 1913. Reorganization of the classified catalog according to the Prussian model from the 1930s determined its shape for the next 40 years.

The library's mainframe computer has been used to support its cataloging function since 1981. Descriptive cataloging according to International Standard Bibliographic Description (ISBD) and rules for access points following those developed by Eva Verona were introduced in 1976. Classification according to Universal Decimal Classification (UDC) occurred in the 1980s, and use of a locally developed controlled vocabulary began in 1997 (preceded by the use of descriptors without hierarchical relationships from 1990 to 1997). The library's online catalog, Crolist (600,000 bibliographic records), includes cataloging from 1980 and all works of Croatian history and literature. The latest interface allows searching by 12 access points, including subject access (by UDC number and topical headings). The card catalogs retained in the library include an alphabetic author-title catalog (split into two files, for works before 1975 and those from 1975 to 1980), classified catalogs arranged according to a locally developed system and by UDC, a union catalog of foreign imprints (1956 to 1964 for all of former Yugoslavia, and 1964 to 1980 for Croatia only), and several union catalogs for periodicals.

Automation

The Croatian library network was developed concurrent with library automation. Significant development has occurred since the early 1990s with the systematic computerization of library functions. This prompted shared cataloging that is used by more than 20 regional and research libraries in Croatia, with the number of member libraries (primarily municipal and university libraries) increasing daily. Crolist is the integrated library system, with modules for acquisitions, cataloging, serials control, circulation, and searching (the DOS version is used by more than 150 libraries in Croatia). The library has had a website since 1996 and has been represented in the European Internet gateway to European national libraries (Gabriel) since 1999.

Recent Trends

The major event in the last decade was the library's move to a new building, which provided impetus for reorganization of library services. An open stacks policy for a substantial part of its collection, user-oriented reference, and focus on bibliographic instruction strengthened the library's function as a central university library after many years of subordination to its national function. Management of electronic resources presents a new challenge for the library. In response to a 1997 law mandating legal deposit of these materials, the library started cataloging remotely available resources using International Standard Bibliographic Description for Electronic Resources (ISBD [ER]). The development of policies for archiving and deposit of electronic books, bibliographic control of 150 electronic journals currently published in Croatia, adaptation of standards (the Dublin Core, aimed to improve resource discovery), and reformatting of paperbound materials to electronic formats including systematic work on digitization of newspapers (started in 1993) are underway. Migrating historical collections into a distributed electronic environment is likely to involve collaboration with other libraries, archives, and museums, as well as the application of metadata standards emerging in the cultural heritage community.

MARIJA J. DALBELLO

Further Reading

Fancev, Franjo, *Kr. sveučilišna knjižnica u Zagrebu* (The Royal University Library in Zagreb), Zagreb: Narodne Novine, 1925

Horvat, Jesenko, et al., "Nacionalna i sveučilišna biblioteka u Zagrebu (The National and University Library in Zagreb)," *Arhitektura* 49 (1996)

Magić, Vladimir, and Olga Maruševski, "Metropolitana," *Arhitektura* 49 (1996)

Petrović, Stevo, *Hrvatska kr. sveučilišna biblioteka* (The Croatian Royal University Library), Zagreb: Tisak Kr. Zemaljske Tiskare, 1913

Rojnić, Matko, *Nacionalna i sveučilišna biblioteka* (The National and University Library), Zagreb: Hrvatsko Bibliotekarsko Društvo, 1974

Sečić, Dora, "Kraljevska sveučilišna knjižnica u Zagrebu, 1874.–1918.: Prinosi proučavanju i vrednovanju razvoja srednjoeuropske knjižnice s dvojnom funkcijom (The Royal University Library in Zagreb, 1874–1918: A Contribution to the Study and Evaluation of the Development of a Central European Library with a Dual Function)," Ph.D. diss., University of Zagreb, 1996

Stipanov, Josip, "Nova zgrada Nacionalne i sveučilišne knjižnice (The New Building of the National and University Library)," *Vjesnik bibliotekara Hrvatske* 38 (1995)

Stipčević, Aleksandar, editor, *Libraries in Croatia,* translated by Aleksandra Horvat and Danica Ladan, Zagreb: Croatian Library Association, 1975

Verona, Eva, "Prinosi povijesti Sveučilišne knjižnice u Zagrebu i njena uređenja (1773.–1814.) (A Contribution to the History of the University Library in Zagreb and Its Arrangement [1773–1814])," *Vjesnik bibliotekara Hrvatske* (1955–57)

Verona, Eva, *Prinosi povijesti Akademijine knjižnice (sadašnje Nacionalne i sveučilišne biblioteke) u Zagrebu, 1814.–1874.* (A Contribution to the History of the Academy Library [Presently the National and University Library] in Zagreb, 1814–1874), Zagreb: Hrvatsko Bibliotekarsko Društvo, 1987

National and University Library of Strasbourg

Address: Bibliothèque Nationale et Universitaire
de Strasbourg
6 place de la Republique
Boite Postale 1029/F
Strasbourg 67070
France
Telephone: 3-88-25-2800
Fax: 3-88-25-2803
www-bnus.u-strasbg.fr

Founded: 1871

Holdings (1999): Volumes: 3 million. Coins and medals: 40,000; current serials: 6,000; incunabula: 2,018; manuscripts: 6,000; maps: 45,000; microforms: 90,000; ostraca: 4,000; papyri and clay tablets: 10,000.

Special Collections: *Areas of Concentration:* Alsace; cuneiform; European studies; German culture; ostraca; papyrus; religion. *Individual Collections:* Don Bentheim monastery collection; Böcking collection; Czarnowsky architecture collection; Haller von Hallerstein archeology collection; Hermann collection of natural sciences; Michaelis archeology collection; Max Müller Sanskrit collection; numismatic collection; Jean de Pange collection of history and literature; Witte collection on Dante. *Papers:* S. de Dietrich; Marie Jaell; Albert and Adolphe Matthis.

The Bibliothèque Nationale et Universitaire de Strasbourg (BNUS, or National and University Library of Strasbourg) is unique among French libraries in that it has a dual function and its own legal identity. It is both a national library focusing on Alsace and equally an academic library connected to the university system of Strasbourg. This status was declared on 19 June 1872 and confirmed by imperial decree on 29 July 1891. The library obtained autonomous legal status and was administratively and financially separate from the Kaiser Wilhelm Universität. Administrative duties were handled by a commission consisting of the mayor of Strasbourg, a university professor, and a representative from the Catholic seminary. The law of 1926 changed the library's charter from "academic and regional" to "national and academic." The institution retained, however, a separate legal status and financial autonomy. After 1926 the library was led by a director and a 20-member administrative council.

In 1962, when French academic libraries were given the mission of serving their universities instead of forming more comprehensive research collections, the BNUS was exempted from these restrictions. A law passed on 27 March 1973 ordered the BNUS to reorganize in conformity with educational reforms, while at the same time preserving its independent status as a national library. Following the law of 1992, the BNUS, although still autonomous, reports to the Ministère de l'enseignement supérieur, from which it receives funding. The university presidents and representatives of local authorities form the BNUS administrative council, led by the chancellor of Strasbourg. The library receives the legal deposit of materials published in the eastern departments: Bas-Rhin, Haut-Rhin, and the Territoire de Belfort.

From the Ashes

From its beginning, the library was shaped by the struggle between France and Germany for political, linguistic, and cultural dominance in Alsace-Lorraine. During the night of 24–25 August 1870, the Bibliothèque de la Ville at Temple Neuf, housing the collections of the city library and of the Protestant seminary, at that time the second-largest library in France, was destroyed by German artillery. Nothing had been placed in safekeeping, and 300,000 volumes, irreplaceable manuscripts, and incunabula were lost. In 1871, with Alsace part of Germany, the new Bibliothèque universitaire et regionale was founded. The German regime reinvented the University of Strasbourg after the German model of specialized research institutes. The new Kaiser Wilhelm Universität was established on 28 April 1872, two months before the official establishment of the library.

Spearheading the call for the new library was Karl August Barack (director, 1870–1900). In October 1870 he launched a campaign for material and financial support, and by 2 June 1875 2,750 institutions and individuals (primarily German) had contributed either books or funds. These joined a small collection from the Académie—the university founded by Napoléon I—and the departments of law, literature, medicine, and sciences. The library was installed on two floors of the Château des Rohan, which it shared with the rest of the university. Public services were located on the ground floor, and the second floor held rare books and exhibition space.

The civil commissioner Friedrich Christian Hubert von Külwetter and two professors, von Möller and von Sybel, were charged with determining the scope and function of the library: academic, regional, or municipal. They decided that the library would be organized along the lines of German libraries and would be both academic and regional: the Kaiserliche Universitäts- und Landesbibliothek. They also decided to focus on the acquisition of Alsatian material, in keeping with the mission of the regional library, as well as on literature generally.

The city received 600,000 francs and the Protestant seminary 160,000 francs toward the purchase of books for the new university library. By the inauguration on 9 August 1871, the library held 200,000 volumes. It had a large staff compared to others of its era, including Barack and three librarians. Initially, their budget was the equivalent of half of the budget for the Parisian Bibliothèque nationale.

The collection continued to grow rapidly. In March 1879 the library held 386,073 volumes and ranked fourth among German libraries. By 1876 there were already plans in place for a new building. The provincial diet ceded to the library the Kaiserplatz, which is today the Place de la République. Architects August Hertel and Skjold Neckelman designed the Italian Renaissance-style edifice, which was finished in 1895 at a cost of 1.4 million francs. The new building was inaugurated on 29 November 1895.

Julius Euting, an orientalist, succeeded Barack in November 1900. He arranged for the library to join a German cartel to acquire papyri and other Middle Eastern material. His policies also emphasized that the library was not an imperial library (*Reichsbibliothek*) but a regional library responsible to the region. The next director, Georg Wolfram (1909–18), was able to obtain more money and more staff. Under Wolfram, the library became the largest academic library in the world, holding more than 1 million volumes.

World War I

Strasbourg, still in German control, was near the front lines of World War I, and the library took precautions and placed manuscripts in safe areas. It also sought to reclaim those books on loan to German libraries. Many members of the library staff were mobilized; the library's main hall became a storehouse and the exhibition area a workshop, and an effort was made to lend books to soldiers. In addition, an important collection of material relating to the war was begun. After the German defeat, Wolfram was forced to flee Strasbourg, and 21 out of 33 employees, all German, were fired.

When Strasbourg returned to French control in 1919, the French hoped to use the university and library as tools to turn Alsatians into Frenchmen and also as a beacon of French culture to Eastern Europe. Under the German administration, it had been difficult for Alsatians to become librarians in the Kaiserliche Universitäts- und Landesbibliothek. Ernest Wickersheimer (1920–50) was the first Alsatian to hold the position of library director, although he had to relinquish it during part of World War II.

World War II

During World War II and the occupation, the university and the library divided into two groups, one remaining in Strasbourg and the other seeking refuge in Clermont-Ferrand. The collection was also divided, but following the armistice the Germans returned the majority of books to Strasbourg. In Strasbourg the library administration continued to be composed of Alsatians until 1941, when Karl Julius Hartmann (1941–44) became head of an all-German staff, replacing Wickersheimer as director. Hartmann oversaw the evacuation of some library materials, which was fortunate as the building was bombarded three times in four years. On 28 November 1944 the medical section and post-1914 French theses were almost completely destroyed. Losses included at least one librarian deported to Buchenwald, approximately 300,000 volumes destroyed, and damage to the reading rooms.

Following the liberation of Strasbourg in 1944, the BNUS again became a French library. Wickersheimer returned and spent the last years of his tenure reconstituting the library. Gifts from the United Kingdom, the United States, Denmark, the Institut catholique de Paris, and the Strasbourg Faculté de médecine aided in the reestablishment of the collections. Wickersheimer also oversaw the reintegration of the Clermont collection and the return from Germany to Strasbourg of the card catalogs, items confiscated by the Third Reich, and books bought by the Germans from 1941 to 1944. In repairing the damage done to the building, improvements were made to gain space and the decor was redone in a contemporary style. In 1950 the BNUS was again second only to the Bibliothèque nationale among French libraries, and it remains the second-largest library in France.

The university's evolution from 1945 to 1968 was marked by an enormous increase in the student body, numerous construction projects, the hiring of many new professors, the creation of research institutes (including the Institut des hautes etudes alsaciennes) and a renewed international focus. The library, under the leadership of Maurice Picard (1950–53), Georges Collon (1953–58), and Norbert Schuller (1959–74), devoted itself to restoring and expanding the collections and the building. The medical library was created in 1962 and a science library in 1968. However, the branch libraries as well as the humanities library that remained in the original building were under a single administration. Substantial reparations paid to the library in the 1960s permitted replacement of damaged materials and new acquisitions.

After 1968

As a result of the profound changes in the French university system following the political and social upheavals of 1968, the University of Strasbourg became both administratively and physically a different place. Three unités de Formation et de Recherches were formed, replacing one academic entity: Université Louis Pasteur (Strasbourg-I), Université Marc Bloc (Strasbourg-II), and Université Robert Schumann (Strasbourg-III). The law of 27 March 1973 ordered the reorganization of the BNUS. In 1976, during the administration of Jean Sansen (1975–77), the administrative offices, law, and Alsatian sections moved into a building on rue du Maréchal Joffre. Director Lily Grenier (1978–88) oversaw the opening of an Annexe de Pharmacie in 1979 and a new medical library in 1984.

In 1992 the government imposed a new organization for academic libraries. The BNUS became a general research and reference library for all of the Strasbourg universities, with responsibility for coordinating interlibrary loans. Five departments were created, one technical and four subject specific. The science, pharmaceutical, and medical libraries came under the jurisdiction of the Université Louis Pasteur. In 1993 the interior of the building was restructured to give readers more space.

Cataloging and Access

Items were cataloged according to the Prussian system from the library's founding until 1918, when Alsace rejoined France. Books were organized into 12 sections, each one the responsibility of a chief librarian. The library maintained two catalogs: a classed catalog and an alphabetical main-entry catalog. Readers were not permitted to use the card catalogs. Professors and *privatdozenten* (lecturers) were given access to the stacks, although most students were not. However, lending rules were comparatively generous, and readers could take home up to 12 volumes at a time. After 1918 items were shelved by size in one of 13 general subjects. This switch involved the enormous effort of giving each item a new call number. Card catalogs became accessible to patrons, and students gained access to the library. Finally, the classed catalog was eliminated in favor of an alphabetical subject catalog. Currently, the catalog of books and journals holds approximately 1.8 million records, 300,000 of which are in the online catalog. A large conversion process, which includes the holdings of the Alsatian collection, continues today.

Present and Future

The Franco-German conflict has been resolved over the past 50 years by the integration of Alsace into France and the rise of international cooperation. Within France, in general, regionalism has become more marked, evidenced in Alsace through greater attention to things Alsatian and an interest in bilingualism. At the same time, there is more attention paid to Franco-German relations and the European Union. Projects the BNUS has undertaken include microfilming the output of Alsatian presses from 1870 to 1918 and the creation of an Alsatian bibliographic database. The library continues to welcome the public, consonant with the mission of a national library; 31 percent of cardholders in 1992 were not affiliated with the university. The BNUS is the Centre d'acquisition et de diffusion de l'information scientifique et technique (CADIST) for religion (one of the first initiated in 1980), European issues, Germanic and Slavic cultures, and Alsatian studies. As such, it has an obligation to collect in the field, to be active in preservation, and to serve as a resource for other libraries. The BNUS, as well as being associated with the universities of the upper Rhine, is one of four European *pôles* (centers) and since 1994 is an associate *pôle* of the Bibliothèque Nationale de France. In the latter role, it seeks to increase collections in the CADIST areas and as a legal depository. In 1995–96 the BNUS began an exchange program with central and Eastern European countries, reinforcing its collections in these areas. A new building is planned to house the growing collections of this great academic and national library with a distinct European perspective.

SARAH G. WENZEL

Further Reading

Burton, Margaret, *Famous Libraries of the World: Their History, Collections, and Administrations*, London: Grafton, 1937

Dubled, Henri, *Histoire de la Bibliothèque nationale et universitaire de Strasbourg*, Strasbourg: Press de l'Université, 1964; 2nd edition, Strasbourg: Société Savante d'Alsace et des Régions de l'Est, 1975

Geiss, Étienne, "Bibliothèque nationale et universitaire de Strasbourg: Quelques aspects de ses amenagements et de ses extensions de 1945 à nos jours," *LIBER-Bulletin* 16 (1981)

Grenier, Lily, "Bibliothèque nationale et universitaire de Strasbourg: Esquisse historique," *LIBER-Bulletin* 16 (1981)

Kratz, Isabelle, "Au fil du Rhin: Politiques documentaires dans la confederation des Universités du Haut-Rhin," *Bulletin des bibliothèques de France* 35, no. 4 (1990)

Sansen, Jean, "Les transformations de la Bibliothèque nationale et universitaire de Strasbourg," *Bulletin des bibliothèques de France* 22, no. 1 (1977)

National Art Library, Victoria and Albert Museum

Address: National Art Library, Victoria and Albert Museum
Cromwell Road
South Kensington
London SW7 2RL
UK
Telephone: 207-9422-400
Fax: 207-942-2394
www.nal.vam.ac.uk

Founded: 1837

Holdings (1999): Volumes: 1 million. Current serials: 2,100 titles; exhibition catalogs: 60,000; medieval manuscripts: 300.

Special Collections: *Areas of Concentration:* Architecture; artists' books; decorative arts; Far Eastern, Indian, and Southeast Asian art and design; history of the art, craft, and design of the book; literary manuscripts; penmanship and calligraphy. *Individual Collections:* Art and design archives, including archives of Biba, the Crafts Council, and Heal and Son; Clements collection of armorial bookbindings; Alexander Dyce collection; James Forster collection; Linder archive of Beatrix Potter; Eduardo Paolozzi's Krazy Kat Arkive of 20th-century popular culture; Victoria and Albert Museum archive. *Papers:* Ford Madox Brown; Charles Dickens; David Garrick; Jonathan Swift; Leonardo da Vinci notebooks.

Origins

The roots of the National Art Library (NAL) go back to the School of Design in London, set up under British government sponsorship in 1837. This establishment was a response to a Select Committee report of 1835–36 expressing concern that goods made in Britain generally suffered from a lack of good design principles, in contrast to the more elegant products of continental competitors. The school began life in Somerset House in the Strand, with a mission to train artisans in the rudiments of design. The underlying philosophy was akin to the thinking that motivated the Great Exhibition of 1851, when manufactured goods from all over the world were brought together in the Crystal Palace in the interests of improving public taste. Items purchased after the close of the exhibition formed the nucleus of a new Museum of Ornamental Art, to which the library of the School of Design was added; it was originally based in Marlborough House but moved to the present site in South Kensington in 1857.

The library, which began to be formed in the 1830s, was a small collection of basic texts on practical art that were thought suitable for teaching craftsmen the fundamental principles of ornament. Money for book purchase was available from the start, and by the time of the move to the new museum in 1852 there were approximately 1,500 volumes in all, divided between a lending collection of approximately 1,000 and a reference library of 500. The books were apparently in poor condition, as a contemporary report on the library states that the lending-library books were almost worn out through constant use, and the reference materials had been largely cut up to provide examples for drawing classes. However, under the enthusiastic leadership of Henry Cole (in charge of the museum from its foundation until his retirement in 1873), the library quickly grew.

Cole, who introduced the title "National Art Library" in 1868, had a grand vision for the collection and saw it as a truly national resource. He devised a plan for the creation of a comprehensive and international bibliography of books on art, drawn not only from the holdings of NAL but also from other major libraries of the world. The resulting list would form a combined catalog and desiderata list for NAL itself, on the assumption that books not already held would be added in due course. According to Cole, the British government would no longer have to catalog all foreign works contained in the library, since their titles would be contributed by foreign nations. In practice the scheme became a little less wide ranging, and during the 1860s an editorial team led by J.H. Pollen worked through various catalogs and bibliographical sources, extracting titles and checking the books when possible against the holdings of NAL and the British Museum Library in London. The first edition of the resulting *Universal Catalogue of Books on Art* was issued in 1870, containing nearly 15,000 entries, and a supplementary volume was issued in 1877. After this work, the momentum for such an ambitious undertaking ebbed, but a copy of the *Universal Catalogue* was cut up and used as NAL's working catalog. Although a new card cataloging system was introduced in the 1890s, parts of the *Universal Catalogue* remained in use in this way until the 1990s.

When the library moved to Marlborough House in 1852, it opened its doors to the general public, who were admitted for sixpence a week or ten shillings a year; these subscription arrangements remained in place until 1865, when access became free. In 1853 there were 170 subscribers, but by 1880 the number of readers was nearly 30,000 per annum, and the library contained approximately 60,000 books and 65,000 prints and drawings. Between 1870 and 1871 the entire collection was rearranged and reclassified with a subject classification approach. Books arrived both by purchase and by gift, and the period around 1870 saw the addition of two major bequests: the libraries of Alexander Dyce and James Forster, each containing approximately 15,000 volumes. Dyce was a literary scholar who published numerous editions of the works of the English poets and dramatists. His library was wide ranging in subject but particularly rich in classics, English literature, Italian poems and plays, and theology. Forster was a close contemporary of Dyce who is best known today as a literary historian, although he had a varied career as a journalist and public servant. He was a close friend and the first biographer of Charles Dickens and inherited many of Dickens' original manuscripts. Forster's collection included numerous other manuscript highlights, such as the letters of David Garrick, papers relating to Jonathan Swift, and three notebooks of Leonardo da Vinci. The Dyce and Forster bequests brought a great deal of rare and interesting literary material to the library, ensuring that the collection remains an important resource for a broad scholarly community, beyond the specific bounds of art history.

The fine and decorative arts do, however, form the library's main focus, and it is within these areas that the development of the collection has concentrated since the end of the 19th century. The subjects covered reflect the broad mission of the museum itself (rechristened the Victoria and Albert Museum in 1899) and include architecture, furniture, ceramics, woodwork, textiles, jewelry, sculpture, and many other practical and theoretical aspects of art history. Literature on paintings and drawings is also a major feature, although the prints and drawings themselves were transferred to the museum's Department of Prints, Drawings, and Paintings in 1905.

The library also comprises the museum's curatorial department for the art of the book, a tradition that goes back to its beginnings. A separate museum gallery for books and manuscripts, administered by the library, was opened in 1909 but was converted to other use in 1978, since which time the library has not had a proper gallery of its own. Book bindings were being acquired as art objects in the late 1850s, and continuous development in this area has ensured that the library has an important collection of fine and interesting bindings of all periods. This activity has been fostered by several librarians with an interest in the field, including James Weale, one of the great pioneers of bookbinding history and keeper of the library between 1890 and 1897. More recently, John Harthan (librarian, 1962–76) ensured that the library built up good holdings of modern designer bindings of the middle and latter 20th century. The library has also maintained its collections of modern private press books, and Jan van der Wateren (librarian, 1987–2000) created within the library a unique collection of late-20th-century book art, building upon a long tradition of acquiring *livres d'artistes*. The Archive of Art and Design was established in 1978 to collect and conserve the papers of individuals, associations, and companies involved in art and design processes, with a particular emphasis on 20th-century British design.

The library serves both as the working library of the museum and its curatorial staff and as a wider public resource, and the relative importance assigned to these two roles has varied over the years. In 1899 the head of the Department of Science and Art (the government department responsible for the museum), giving evidence to a government commission on the work of the museum, declared that the library was "simply an accessory branch of the Museum, primarily for the use of the Art Museum and the Art students," and this philosophy tended to dominate the library's development during the first half of the 20th century. During the second half of the century, the emphasis gradually changed, fueled partly by an expansion in higher education and an increase in the number of students and others interested in art history. The title "National Art Library" was discontinued in 1900 but was revived in the 1980s. By the end of the 20th century, the library's role was defined in its leaflets and literature as "threefold: it is a curatorial department in its own right; a research and reference library; and the library of the Museum and its staff."

The library has never been a national library in the copyright receipt sense and has had to rely on government funding (filtered through the museum and its administration) in order to acquire stock. But it is certainly a collection of national importance, considering the comprehensiveness of its coverage of the art and design field and the depth of its special collections. Its importance in this context was recognized in the 1972 *Report of the National Libraries Committee* (the Dainton Report) that led to the establishment of the British Library. The report suggested that "benefits to users and economies might result if the British Library of Art [as NAL was then called] were fully integrated within a national libraries organisation." The issue was not pursued further at the time—a missed opportunity—and the library has continued to develop its mission independent of any formal national coordination. Maintaining the currency of the holdings and promoting wider public awareness of the library have both been important themes in recent decades, and much effort has gone into an extensive program of retroconversion of a confusing legacy of manual catalogs into automated form. The library continues to operate in two handsome late-19th-century reading rooms and associated accommodations within the main museum building, but space constraints became a major concern toward the end of the 20th century. Plans for a possible relocation did not materialize, but this is an issue that may feature in the library's future.

DAVID PEARSON

Further Reading

Barontini, Chiara, "From the Library of the School of Design to the National Art Library: 150 Years of Art Librarianship," Master's Thesis, University College, School of Library, Archive, and Information Studies (London), 1993

Cocks, Anna Somers, *The Victoria and Albert Museum: The Making of the Collection,* Leicester, Leicestershire: Windward, 1980

Physick, John, *The Victoria and Albert Museum: The History of Its Building,* London: Victoria and Albert Museum, 1982

Wateren, Jan van der, "The National Art Library into the 1990s," *Art Libraries Journal* 15, no. 4 (1990)

Wheen, A.W., "The Library of the Victoria and Albert Museum," in *The Libraries of London,* edited by Raymond Irwin, London: The Library Association, 1949

White, Eva, *From the School of Design to the Department of Practical Art: The First Years of the National Art Library, 1837–1853,* London: Victoria and Albert Museum, 1994

National Central Library (Republic of China)

Address: Kuo-li chung-yang t'u-shu-kuan
20 Chung Shan South Road
Taipei
Taiwan 10040
Republic of China
Telephone: 2-23619132
Fax: 21489
www.ncl.edu.tw or infolib.ncl.edu.tw

Founded: 1933

Holdings (1999): Volumes: 1.7 million, including 922,000 in Chinese, 441,000 in Western languages, and 138,000 in Japanese and Korean. Current serials: 25,000; films and videos: 7,000; Han bamboo inscriptions: 30; ink rubbings: 14,000; maps: 12,000; microforms: 644,000.

History

The National Central Library (NCL) of the Republic of China (ROC) on Taiwan was founded in 1933 in Nanjing. At that time there were two national libraries in China: the National Library in Beijing founded in 1909 and the NCL, established after the government of the Republic of China opened its capital in Nanjing. Chiang Fu-tsung, a distinguished librarian and scholar, was appointed director to plan for the new national library. Through his efforts a sizable collection of Qing Dynasty archives and 46,000 books held in Beijing by the Ministry of Education were moved to Nanjing to become the founding collection of the new library. He also purchased a fine collection of stone rubbings from a private collector in Tianjin.

By 1937 the collection surpassed 180,000 volumes. During the Sino-Japanese War (1937–45), the library relocated to Chungking (the wartime capital), but only a small portion of the total collection could be evacuated. To protect the rare books from Japanese air raids, the library was moved to Peisha Town across the Yangtze River from Chungking. In the early 1940s, risking his life and using assumed names, Chiang covertly visited Japanese-occupied Shanghai, Guangzhou, and Hong Kong to acquire valuable rare Chinese books for the library. Many of these books were from private collectors who were no longer able to keep their collections owing to wartime hardship. After the war, Chiang was responsible for moving the library back to Nanjing. Through his persistent efforts, many missing collections were located and successfully recovered from Japan.

When the ROC government moved to Taiwan in 1949, the library followed. It was reestablished in Taipei in 1954 within the Botanical Garden. The rare book collection of the library was strengthened by the return of a large rare book collection by the Library of Congress (LC) in 1965. These 30,000 books, including publications and manuscripts of the Song (960–1279), Yuan (1271–1368), and Ming (1368–1644) dynasties, had been sent from the National Beijing Library to the United States for safekeeping during the Sino-Japanese War. In September 1986 the nine-floor library, with its greatly expanded collections, moved to its new site at the current location near the National Theater, the National Music Hall, and the Chiang K'ai-shek Memorial Hall. Professor Wang Chen-ku, library director from 1977 to 1989, was largely responsible for the planning and construction of the new library building.

Mission and Organization

In carrying out its mission to preserve the national culture, foster scholarship and research, promote cultural and education activities, and advance the development of library and information services for the whole country, the library's main responsibilities are: (1) collecting and preserving the nation's publications and documents; (2) acquiring important publications and documents of other countries; (3) compiling bibliographic indexes; (4) providing reference, circulation, and information services; (5) handling the international exchange of publications; (6) strengthening international contacts and cooperation between domestic and foreign libraries; and (7) undertaking research and consulting for the development of the library profession. In addition, the library operates the Center for Chinese Studies to enrich the research resources for Sinological studies, to provide support services, and to promote interaction among researchers and scholars.

According to the Regulations on the Organization of the NCL issued by presidential proclamation on 30 January 1996, the library—which is directly under the jurisdiction of the Ministry of Education—has been formally recognized as the national library. It has a director with deputy directors in charge of the following departments: acquisitions, cataloging, reader services, reference, special collections, information services, training and counseling, and research and development. Their responsibilities also include the Bureau of International Exchange of Publications, the Center for Chinese Studies, the International Standard Bibliographic Number (ISBN) Center, the Bibliographic Information Center, the general affairs office, and the accounting and personnel offices. The library may appoint advisers and establish advisory committees. Currently, the following committees have been established: collection development, subject analysis, reader services, automation and networking, and cooperation and extension.

Collections

Because of the frequent moves, the collections consisted of only 120,000 volumes in 1954, mostly from the salvage of wars. However, many of these were ancient wooden tablets, ink rubbings, manuscripts, and rare books dating back more than 2,000 years. They are considered true national treasures. As of June 1998 the total collections had grown to 2,236,462 items. All of the materials from the ancient time to the present are important resources for Chinese studies.

Reader and Information Services

Serving as both the national library and a research library, a wide range of reader and information services is provided. In addition to general and special reading rooms for various collections (which can seat 2,000), there are also 66 individual studies for researchers. Reference services are provided on-site or by letter, by telephone, or via one of the online networks. The library's online catalog, electronic databases, government information, and full-text digital collections can also be accessed remotely.

Among the items housed in specialized reading rooms are recent Chinese publications, Chinese journals and newspapers, foreign journals and newspapers, rare books, audiovisual collections, law publications, government documents, the Mainland China collection, Chinese studies collection, fine art collection, and Japanese and Korean collections. A separate Technical Information Library is located in the Science and Technology Building in Ho-ping East Road.

Automation and Networking

Library automation at the NCL began in 1981, and since then nearly all library operations have been computerized. A national bibliographic database (which includes new books, rare books, periodicals, periodical articles, theses and dissertations, and government publications) has been created to provide easy online access to the bibliographic information of library collections in Taiwan. In recent years, full-text imaging and distribution of many of the digitized databases on CD-ROM has been implemented. Furthermore, beginning in February 1998 the Internet has been used to promote its Remote Electronic Access/Delivery of National Central Library (READncl System) for full-text access (www.read.net.tw). Online cooperative cataloging among Taiwan's academic and public libraries through National Books and Information Network (NBINet) has also made significant progress under the leadership of the NCL.

The library is also responsible for the assignment of ISBN and ISSN numbers in Taiwan and the maintenance of the records thereof. Its work with CIP (cataloging in publication) has been a service welcomed by libraries, publishers, and readers.

International Cooperation and Exchange

Promoting international contacts and cooperation has always been one of the major goals of the NCL. Through its Bureau of International Exchange of Publications, the library has established exchanges with more than 1,200 libraries and academic organizations in more than 110 nations and areas. The NCL is an active participant in many international library, information, and scholarly organizations. It has sent staff members to attend major conferences and to take part in book exhibitions and fairs around the world. Moreover, it has organized many international conferences in Taiwan on library and information science. Its Center for Chinese Studies also hosts yearly meetings on Chinese studies. Since the founding of the center in 1981, approximately 200 scholars from 30 countries have received grants to conduct research at the center. These popular grants cover both travel and living expenses for three months to one year.

Research and Counseling

Domestically, the library has undertaken many research projects, conducted numerous conferences and workshops for librarians, and produced a variety of publications. Among its significant publications are: the *Bulletin of the National Central Library*, the *National Central Library Newsletter* (in English and available on the NCL website), the *National Central Library News Bulletin*, the *Catalog of Research Dissertations on Chinese Culture*, the *Yearbook of R.O.C. Libraries*, *Chinese Machine-Readable Cataloging Formats*, and the *Bibliography of the National Central Library's Rare Book Collection*. In addition, the Center for Chinese Studies publishes *Chinese Studies*, the *Newsletter for Research in Chinese Studies*, and the *Current Contents of Foreign Periodicals in Chinese Studies*, as well as special-topic bibliographies.

Since the institution became the National Central Library in 1996, its responsibility for assisting and coordinating the planning and development of the nation's libraries has been formalized and increasingly emphasized. To facilitate overall development of library and information services on Taiwan, the library works closely with the Ministry of Education and the Library Association of China (Taiwan) in the development of library programs and standards; it also advocated for adoption of the Library Law finally approved by the government in 2000. Library staff members on an as-needed basis often offer consulting services to other libraries.

HWA-WEI LEE

Further Reading

Fung, Margaret Chang, "The Evolving Social Mission of the National Central Library in China, 1928–1966," Ph.D. diss., Indiana University, 1983

Fung, Margaret Chang, "Dr. Chiang Fu-tsung, a Giant in the Preservation and Dissemination of Chinese Culture," in *Collection of Essays in Honor of Mr. Chiang Fu-tsung on His Ninetieth Birthday,* edited by Yen Wen-yu et al., Taipei: Library Association of China, 1987

Guojia tushuguan guankan (National Central Library News Bulletin) (1967–)

Guoli zhongyang tushuguan guankan (National Central Library Bulletin) (1967–)

Guoli zhongyang tushuguan jianguan jinian tekan (Special Memorial Publication for the New Library Building of the National Central Library), Taipei: National Central Library, 1986

National Central Library, Taipei: National Central Library, 1998

National Central Library Newsletter (1969–)

Sung Chien-cheng, et al., "Guojia tushuguan (National Central Library)," Disanci zhonghua minguo tushuguan nianjian (The Third Yearbook of the Libraries of the Republic of China), edited by the National Central Library, Taipei: National Central Library, 1999

Yen Wen-You, *Zhongguo tushuguan fazhan shi* (The History of Library Development in China), Taipei: Library Association of China, 1983

National Diet Library of Japan

Address: Kokuritsu Kokkai Toshokam
1-1-10 Nagata-cho, Chiyoda-ku
Tokyo 100
Japan
Telephone: 3-358-12331
Fax: 3-359-79104
www.ndl.go.jp

Founded: 1948

Holdings (2000): Volumes: 7.3 million. Audiovisual materials: 44,000; current serials: 60,000; maps: 452,000; microforms: 6.8 million; sound recordings: 455,000.

Special Collections: *Areas of Concentration:* Japanese history, politics, and culture. *Individual Collections:* Allied occupation of Japan; Japanese modern political history documents; Tokugawa Shogunate government succession documents. *Papers:* Ito Bunko; Shirai Bunko; Fuken Komiyama; Nanryo Komiyama; Shiki Masaoka; Wenceslau de Moraes; Shigeki Nishimura; Tetsuro Watsuji.

Establishment of the National Diet Library

The National Diet Library (NDL) was established under the National Diet Library Law enacted in February 1948 by the Japanese Diet (Parliament). The preamble of the law declares, "The National Diet Library is hereby established as a result of the firm conviction that truth makes us free and with the object of contributing to international peace and the democratization of Japan as promised in our Constitution."

The character of the Japanese Diet had gone through a radical transformation after World War II to adjust itself to the democratic principles expounded in the new Japanese Constitution. This led to the realization that the establishment of a parliamentary library with an effective research function was of paramount importance for the deliberation of state affairs by Diet members. The Diet Law promulgated in April 1947 ordained that "A Diet Library shall be attached to the Diet in order to help members of the Diet conduct their investigations and researches."

In December 1947, in response to a request made by the Japanese Diet, the U.S. Library Mission, consisting of Verner W. Clapp, assistant librarian of the Library of Congress, and Charles H. Brown, chairman of the Oriental committee of the American Library Association, came to Japan to offer advice on the establishment of a Diet library, in close collaboration with the Committees for Library Management of both Houses of the Diet and other Japanese organs. In the course of the discussions, in addition to the library's function of assisting the Diet, its role as the national central library was greatly enhanced. On the basis of the U.S. Library Mission's recommendations, the newly drafted National Diet Library Law was promulgated in February 1948 and the National Diet Library was established.

Thus the NDL has the functions of both a parliamentary library and a national central library. The library was expected to play a role in contributing to the democratization of the country after World War II. Tokujiro Kanamori, who had worked to establish the Constitution of Japan, was appointed the first librarian, and Masakazu Nakai was named deputy librarian.

Buildings and Organization

The history of the NDL can be divided into roughly three periods. The first turning point after its foundation in 1948 was the series of reorganizations in 1959, 1961, and 1963, which completely unified the library in the Nagata-cho building. The second was the completion of the Annex Building in 1986. The third is just beginning with the establishment of two new divisions: the International Library of Children's Literature in 2000 and the Kansai-kan projected in 2002. At each turning point the library structure has been reorganized, new facilities constructed, and the concept of the library changed. These three periods overlap to some extent, as it takes some time before a changed concept is reflected in actual work and services.

Akasaka, Miyakezaka, and Ueno, 1948 to 1959

The NDL was opened in June 1948 with the Akasaka Detached Palace as its base. Whereas the Imperial Library before World War II had collected admission fees, the new library offered free services to the general public. A branch office was set up at Miyakezaka near the Diet, where the staff dealt with services for Diet members.

In 1949 the former Imperial Library, located at Ueno in Tokyo before the NDL was founded, was merged with the NDL and became the Ueno Branch Library. However, none of the facilities at any of the three disparate locations was suitable for library work, and a new building for the NDL was greatly desired.

Unification in the Nagata-cho Building, 1959, 1961, and 1963 to 1986

The proposals of the U.S. Library Mission predicted that in 25 years (by 1973) the NDL would have 10 million volumes, 3,500 readers, and 1,500 staff members. From these numbers, it was estimated that 99,000 square yards for stacks and 26,000 square yards for other facilities were necessary, and the library planned to construct a building of this size in two stages. For the design of the building, a public competition was held, the first for a public facility after World War II.

Before the end of the first stage of construction the NDL was reorganized in 1959, again in 1961, and yet again in 1963, with all facilities to be united at the Nagata-cho building. Not until 1968, the 20th anniversary of the library, was the second stage of construction completed.

Completion of the Annex Building

The NDL began to plan construction of an annex building at Nagata-cho in 1975 to remedy the shortage of stack space and other problems. The completion of the Annex Building in 1986 was accompanied by further library reorganization. It shifted its emphasis to remote services, recommending that readers use their community or university libraries when appropriate but also fostering mutual cooperation among libraries and within the community. The library now offers interlibrary loan or photocopying services for items not available at those libraries, offering the best possible services to visitors who can satisfy their needs only at the NDL. The library now sees itself as the last resort in a complex web of information access.

Kansai-kan

The NDL is now building a new facility provisionally called Kansai-kan, with ample storage space for ever-increasing library materials and electronic library functions in the Kansai Science City, which lies in the Keihanna Hills area of Kyoto, Nara, and Osaka Prefectures.

The Kansai region is located about 300 miles west of Tokyo and is the second biggest economic and cultural area after the metropolitan area. The plan to construct the Kansai-kan originated from a local request in the Kansai region about 20 years ago; the NDL deliberated on this request, drafting a basic plan twice. The plan shifted to the stage of implementation when the National Diet Library Building Commission submitted a recommendation to the Diet in December 1994 that a new facility of the NDL should be constructed in stages in Kansai Science City. The budget for construction of the Kansai-kan has been appropriated since fiscal year 1995. An international design competition was held from 1995 to 1996. Based on the winning prize design, Kansai-kan is scheduled for completion in March 2002.

International Library of Children's Literature

Services for children at the NDL have evolved since its inception. From July 1948 to March 1950 there was a reading room for children aged 10 to 14 years old. After that period, persons 20 years of age or older were permitted to use all library materials. However, as publications deposited with the NDL included children's literature, there has been a steady demand for the comprehensive acquisition, preservation, and supply of children's literature published in Japan. One early plan called for the Ueno Branch Library to be placed under the control of the Tokyo Metropolitan Government, but a later plan called for a library of children's literature for the site. The concern that Japanese children had come to spend less and less time reading led to wide support for the creation of the International Library of Children's Literature (ILCL). The Ueno building is being remodeled for its new purpose in two stages. Phase I was completed in May 2000 and opened one-third of the facility to the public. The entire renovation is scheduled to be completed in 2002, at which point the ILCL will provide full service as the national center of children's literature and related materials.

Collections

The NDL's collection process can be classified into three categories of materials. First, when the Imperial Library became the Ueno Branch Library, the NDL inherited its rich collection, in addition to the holdings of the libraries of the House of Representatives and the House of Peers. The Imperial Library held a collection of Japanese publications and documents creating during and before the Edo period, as well as from the Meiji, Taisho, and early Showa periods.

Second, as a parliamentary library the NDL collects materials necessary for debates in the Diet, as well as collections to assist in lawmaking. The Research and Legislative Reference Bureau and the Detached Library in the Diet of the NDL provide legislative research and library service to Diet members. The bureau also maintains the website "Chosa no mado" (Windows on Research Services) to provide Diet members and their staff with its publications, research reports, the full-text database of the minutes of the Diet, and other information.

Third, as a national library the NDL's functions include operation of the legal deposit system and compilation of the national bibliography. The modern legal deposit system, which aims at the preservation of and access to the Japanese cultural heritage, was started in 1947 when the Diet Law stipulated official publications as objects of legal deposit. The system was already known in the early Meiji period as part of efforts to establish the modern Japanese education system. However, it was the National Diet Library Law enforcement beginning in 1948 that established the system both in name and reality. The scope of acquisition covered all publications including books, periodicals, pamphlets, maps, printed music, phonographic records, and motion pictures. Motion pictures have since been excluded from the legal deposit system because of problems in preservation, use, and budget. In 1990 CD-ROMs were added to the NDL's collection for the first time. The Legal Deposit System Research Council was established in 1997 to consider the effects of new formats on a new and revised legal deposit system. Their report of July 1999 added packaged electronic publications such as CD-ROMs to the law, and their acquisition by the NDL began in October 2000.

As for special collections, the NDL inherited a collection of Japanese doctoral dissertations from the Imperial Library and has been collecting these materials extensively through direct deposit from universities since 1974. In addition the NDL possesses scientific research reports produced under grants from the Ministry of Education and also comprehensive collections of Japanese parliamentary documents.

Japanese official publications collected under the deposit system are one of the distinctive collections of the library. To judge from inquiries into some of the main publication catalogs and acquisition lists, however, only 50 percent of official publications are deposited in the NDL. The NDL has tried to collect these publications more comprehensively through its network of branch libraries in the executive and judicial agencies. This branch library system, unique in the library world, was created to offer the library's services to the whole of the legislative, judicial, and administrative agencies of Japan. The branch libraries are internal organizations of the NDL, and through them the NDL offers library services such as reference service and loan service to the Japanese government and judicial agencies.

Technical Services and the Japanese National Bibliography

Following the U.S. Library Mission in 1948, Robert B. Downs, director of the library of the University of Illinois at Urbana, came to Japan and made separate recommendations on library technical processes, tools and standards to be used, and a model structure for bibliographic processing.

The Japanese national bibliography started as a list of deposited materials, separate from the list of domestic publications and the NDL catalog. These were consolidated in 1981 under the title *Nihon zenkoku shosi shu-kanban* (Weekly Japanese National Bibliography) using new data processing techniques. Computers were introduced in 1971 to process bibliographic information automatically. From the beginning the goal was to process the Japanese language, including Chinese characters. Data input was begun in 1977 using a system developed to compile catalogs of Japanese books, which led eventually to JAPAN/MARC. In 1980 data on Japanese books began to be available online within the library. General distribution of the data in JAPAN/MARC format was started in 1981. J-BISC (Japan Biblio Disc), a CD-ROM version of JAPAN/MARC, was created and began distribution in 1988, marking the eventual demise of the library's printed card catalog distribution service. The NDL is now preparing to provide the current Japanese national bibliography through the internet on the NDL website.

International Cooperation Services

The international cooperation services of the NDL fall into three basic categories: exchange of publications, provision of library services, and staff exchanges and visits. In 1949 the NDL was designated by the United Nations Educational, Scientific, and Cultural Organization (UNESCO) as the international exchange center in Japan. The system was completed when the Japanese Government ratified the UNESCO conventions concerning the international exchange of publications in 1984. The NDL sends official publications to some 1,000 overseas institutions and receives materials on the basis of equivalent volume. The NDL also exchanges non-official publications with other national libraries in order to acquire materials on Japan published in other countries.

The NDL began international library loan services when it joined the International Federation of Library Associations and Institutions (IFLA) program for international lending in 1960. International photo duplication service began in 1953. At first it served primarily as a substitute for the loan service when the library could not lend requested materials, and the main part of the service was microfilm copy. However, with the spread of photocopiers the photo duplication service replaced the loan service as the main method of international lending. Although the NDL has accepted reference inquiries from abroad since its opening, it was in 1959, when the Division for Interlibrary Services took this service under its charge, that the international reference service became one of the NDL's international services. In 1987 the library established rules concerning international use of library materials in the NDL in which the three international services of loan, photo duplication, and reference were treated equally.

There had been a need for the provision of academic information by the NDL since its establishment. The Division of International Affairs, organized in 1948, offered international exchange service and produced several English bibliographies of Japanese academic publications. By the reorganization in 1959, the work of the division was divided and bibliographies in English discontinued or combined with others. However, English translations continue in the major bibliographies of the NDL, and lists of books on Japan in Western languages have been issued since 1961, first as a part of the English newsletter of the library, then as an independent journal. The NDL has given a high priority to the acquisition of overseas materials on Japan. The NDL also serves as the Japanese national center for the ISSN (International Standard Serial Number) network and carries out international registration for each serial published in Japan.

To promote interlibrary cooperation and strengthen mutual understanding, the NDL has maintained the mutual visit programs with the National Library of China since 1981, with the

Russian State Library since 1990, and with the National Library of Korea since 1997. The training program for Japanese librarian studies abroad started in 1997 in cooperation with the Japan Foundation and other Japanese organs. This five-year program has invited a total of 64 librarians from 25 countries. As the Asia regional center for the IFLA PAC (Preservation and Conservation) core program, the NDL has sent its staff abroad as consultants and has received trainees from other Asian countries.

Library Networks in Japan and the Role of the NDL

The concept and activities associated with a library network had existed in Japan even before the term came into use. One of the activities was the publication of union catalogs containing location information for library materials in multiple libraries. In 1949, shortly after its foundation, the NDL started to compile a union catalog of its branch libraries and had published several volumes by 1959. *A Union Catalog of Foreign Books,* which contained bibliographic records of newly acquired foreign books in major libraries in Japan, was published annually by the NDL from 1954 to 1983 and discontinued with the 1987 cumulative edition. The NDL also published its *Union List of Serial Publications in Public Libraries in Japan* from 1963 to 1968; it has not been revised.

In the late 1980s the National Center for Science Information Systems (today called the National Institute of Informatics) developed the science information network of academic libraries in Japan; the NDL started the national union catalog network of major public libraries in Japan in 1998. The purpose of the networks is not to cooperate in cataloging but to support interlibrary loans nationwide by request via email on the system.

The NDL launched its website in 1996 and since 1998 has been developing an infrastructure system to make its databases and digitized materials available on the Web. It will come into use as the Electronic Library Infrastructure System in 2002.

MIYUKI KISHI

Further Reading

Chiyo, M., "National Diet Library in the 21st Century: The Construction Plan of the Kansaikan," *IFLA Journal* 23, no. 2 (1997)

Kado, Akira, and Nanae Otsuka, "Japanese Government Documents: The NDL's Perspective," *Journal of East Asian Libraries* 117 (February 1999)

Maruyama, Shojiro, "Japanese Bibliographic Information—Its Control and Standardization," *Electronic Library* 5, no. 1 (February 1987)

Miyasaka, Itsuro, "Recent Developments of the Japanese National Bibliography," *International Cataloguing* 10, no. 1 (1981/1/3)

National Diet Library Newsletter (1963–)

"Report of the United States Library Mission to Advise on the Establishment of the National Diet Library of Japan," and "Report on Technical Processes, Bibliographical Services, and General Organization," in *Kokuritsu Kokkai Toshokan sanjunen shi,* Tokyo: Kokuritsu Kokkai Toshokan, 1980

National Libraries of Italy

National Central Library Vittorio Emanuele II, Rome
Address: Biblioteca Nazionale Centrale Vittorio
Emanuele II
Viale Castro Pretorio 105
00185 Roma
Italy
Telephone: 649891
Fax : 64457635
www.bncrm.libraribeniculturali.it

Founded: 1876

Holdings (2000): Volumes: 6 million. Autographs: 40,000; current serials: 10.000; films: 93,000; incunabula: 1,935; manuscripts: 8,000; maps: 26,000; pamphlets: 1.3 million.

Special Collections: *Areas of Concentration*: Abbey of Santa Maria, Farfa; dueling; Italian 20th-century literature; Jesuit collections; Oriental books; Roman topography. *Individual Collections*: Gabriele D'Annunzio; Anthanasias Kircher; Sessorian collection

National Central Library, Florence
Address: Biblioteca Nazionale Centrale, Firenze
Piazza dei Cavalleggeri 1 B
50122 Firenze
Italy
Telephone: 55-24919-1
Fax: 55-2342-482
www.bncf.firenze.sbn.it

Founded: 1737; 1861 as National Central Library.

Holdings (2000): Volumes: 5.4 million. Autographs: 1 million; current serials: 15,000; incunabula: 3,711; manuscripts: 25,000.

Special Collections: *Area of Concentration*: History of science; Italian history and literature; Reformation. *Individual Collections*: Antonio Cocchi; Ugo Foscolo; Galileo Galilei; Francesco Guicciardini; individual writings of

National Central Library, Florence (cont.)
Special Collections (cont.): Michelangelo Buonarroti; Antoine Lafrery collections; Giacomo Leopardi; Lorenzo de' Medici; Torquato Tasso.

National Library of Naples
Address: Biblioteca Nazionale Vittorio Emanuele III
Piazza del Plebiscito, 1
Palazzo Reale
80132 Napoli
Italy
Telephone: 81-427717
Fax: 81-403820
www.adnet.it/bnn

Founded: 1804

Holdings (1999): Volumes: 1.8 million. Current serials: 4,000; incunabula: 4,563; manuscripts: 34,000; maps: 3,000; papyri: 2,000.

Special Collections: *Areas of Concentration*: Incunabula; Neapolitan history and literature; papyri; theater history. *Individual Collections*: Herculaneum papyri; Nicholas Lapegna; Giacomo Leopardi; Gherardo Marone; Riccardo Ricciardi; Taccone library.

Marciana National Library, Venice
Address: Biblioteca Nazionale Marciana
Piazzetta San Marco 7
30124 Venezia
Italy
Telephone: 41-208788
Fax: 41-5238803
marciana.venezia.sbn.it

Founded: 1468

Holdings (2000): Volumes: 1 million. Current serials: 1,000; incunabula: 2,884; manuscripts: 13,000; maps: 400; music scores: 6,000.

Marciana National Library, Venice (cont.)

Special Collections:	*Areas of Concentration:* Greek manuscripts; Oriental collections; Venetian history. *Individual Collections:* Bessarion library; Marino Sanudo.

National University Library of Turin

Address:	Biblioteca Nazionale Universitaria Torino Piazza Carlo Alberto 3 10123 Torino Italy Telephone: 11-889737 Fax: 11-8178778
Founded:	1720
Holdings (1999):	Volumes: 980,000. Current serials: 11,000; incunabula: 1,602; manuscripts: 4,000; prints and drawings: 12,000.

Royal Library of Turin

Address:	Biblioteca Reale Piazza Castello 191 10100 Turino Italy Telephone: 11-545305 Fax: 11-543855
Founded:	1831
Holdings (1999):	Volumes: 186,000. Current serials: 1,000; incunabula: 187; manuscripts: 4,000; parchments: 1,000.
Special Collections:	*Areas of Concentration:* Heraldry; military affairs; the Risorgimento; Sardinian states. *Individual Collections:* House of Savoy library.

Introduction

The Italian library system is very complex, a reflection of the complexity of the history of Italy, a country once comprised of various independent states that were not unified until the 19th century. Today the major libraries are national property, whereas certain collections of exceptional importance belong to religious institutions, and other libraries worthy of note are the property of various municipalities or of private institutions.

During the *ancien régime* the oldest, most precious libraries, as well as those most important for the dimensions of their collections, belonged to monasteries and convents. With the suppression of religious orders in the Napoleonic Age, many of these libraries were dispersed or destroyed; only a few were preserved.

For instance, of the 30 or more great religious libraries existing in Venice at the fall of the Venetian Republic in 1797, only one remains: that of St. Lazarus of the Armenians. Napoleon respected this library because the Armenian monks, by an irony of fate, declared themselves subjects of the Ottoman Empire. By the end of Napoleonic rule, all the others had disappeared. At Padua, the 13th-century Antoniana Library was saved, even though it was an institution of the Order of the Minor Conventual Brothers; it was, and is still today, annexed to the Basilica of St. Anthony of Padua and was thus spared. The Malatestiana Library of Cesena was preserved as property of the community, even though it was operated by the Franciscans.

The number of libraries belonging to the Italian state today is roughly 35, though the number varies, often depending on political factors. The university libraries of Palermo, Catania, and Messina have passed to the region of Sicily; probably those of Padua and Bologna will pass to their respective universities. To these 35 libraries must be added the 11 libraries annexed to the national monuments, namely those of certain ancient monasteries. The state has assumed administration of these libraries, even when such monasteries maintain complete autonomy. The monasteries (such as Montecassino, Praglia, and Cava dei Tirreni) are illustrious, but the libraries are much less memorable, as they were totally reconstructed after the suppressions of the 19th century.

All state libraries depend on the Ministry of Culture and Environment (Ministerio dei beni culturali ed ambientali, established in 1975) and in particular upon its General Direction (Direzione Generale) in Rome (formerly the Central Office, but renamed in 2001). The General Direction furnishes financial support to libraries for their activity and coordination, while preserving their autonomy. State libraries are part of one national organization, the general lines of which are defined by the General Direction, aided by two technical organizations: the Central Institute for the Pathology of the Book (Istituto Centrale per la patologia del libro, ICPL), which gives instruction and guidance in matters of conservation and restoration; and the National Center for the Union Catalog (Istituto Centrale per il Catalogo Unico, ICCU), which provides direction in matters of cataloging.

All libraries have their own catalogs, often in ancient forms of manuscript, print, or cards, but now moving toward electronic form and unification. A national library service, the National Library Service (Servizio Bibliotecario Nazionale, or SBN), was created by ICCU in 1992 (www.iccu.sbn.it), aiming to have accessible in a single database all titles acquired since that date. SBN includes libraries not run by the state and other organizations, a total of approximately 1,000 institutions, all moving in the direction of a single national catalog (database creation began in 1996). Some libraries are adding pre-1990 holdings to SBN's database; some have added individual collections; and others, such as the Biblioteca Marciana, are working toward complete conversion of their holdings.

A campaign directed by the General Direction of the Ministry of Culture has reproduced on microfilm a good part of the manuscript patrimony of Italian libraries, with a working copy in the appropriate library and another security copy kept in Rome.

The General Direction also promotes electronic reproduction of special collections and is providing funds both for digitization and for appropriate security measures in individual libraries. The cultural politics of each library are generally free from central interference except for participation in big initiatives, such as exhibitions for the Millennial Jubilee in 2000.

Among the state libraries, two are called "national central" libraries: that of Florence, the first capital of a united Italy in 1861, and that of Rome, which became the second and definitive capital in 1870. These two libraries must document Italian cultural publications received through legal deposit of every book printed in Italy; another copy of each book is deposited in the state library of the province where the book is printed.

Another seven have the title of "national library," but this is simply a name to which no particular legal jurisdiction is attached. In some cases these are ancient and illustrious libraries; in others, the name has been given for motives of political opportunity and does not correspond to any particular national characteristic.

The origins of the state libraries are diverse. Some were the original private libraries of ancient reigning dynasties that have become open public collections. This is the case of the Estense Library of Modena and of the Medicea Laurenziana Library, once collections of the courts of the houses of Este and of the Medici (each is described elsewhere in these volumes). The Reale (Royal) Library of Turin is the private library of the house of Savoy, formed in the 1700s and early 1800s. The ancient collections of the royal house of Savoy had been given in 1723 by King Vittorio Amedeo II to the University Library of Turin.

An important group of state libraries includes public libraries of the ancient states of Italy. The oldest is the Biblioteca Nazionale Marciana, established in 1468 as the library of the Venetian republic. The Biblioteca Nazionale Centrale Firenze in Florence was opened to the public in 1747 by the grand duke of Tuscany; the Biblioteca Palatina of Parma in 1761 by the duke of Parma and Piacenza; the Biblioteca Statale of Lucca in 1780 by the republic of Lucca; and the Biblioteca Nazionale Vittorio Emanuele III in Naples by Ferdinand IV of the House of Bourbon in 1804. Pope Benedict XIV (Prospero Lambertini) ordered the public opening of the University Library of Bologna in 1755. By the wish of Maria Theresa of Austria, the Biblioteca Nazionale Braidense in Milan was opened in 1770 and the Biblioteca Statale in Cremona in 1780. Her son, Francis I, founded the library, known today as the Biblioteca Statale Isontina e Civica in Gorizia, in 1825.

Another group of state libraries called *universitarie* (university libraries) consists of libraries annexed to ancient universities; more recently many have added decentralized departmental or faculty libraries for use in particular disciplines. Today these old university libraries are open to all, not reserved to students and university professors; they are, therefore, similar to other state libraries except for some residual ties with the university of the city. The university libraries of Padua (founded by Venice in 1629), Sassari (1556), Genoa (1773), Pavia (1778), and Pisa (1742), and the 19th-century university library of Naples (1816),

are all good examples, containing extensive resources of international importance.

All the libraries mentioned above took advantage of the 18th- and 19th-century suppression of religious institutions to build their collections. The Society of Jesus (Jesuits) was the first victim when it was expelled from Portugal (1759), and then from France (1767), Spain (1767), and Naples (1768); in the end the suppression was accepted in 1773 by Pope Clement XIV (then reestablished in 1814). These developments had great consequences in the European world of culture, where the powerful Jesuits had set aside great resources for education, including their libraries, which passed from the Jesuits to the respective states, often along with buildings and furnishings. Instruction, until that time dominated by the Jesuits, became the duty of the state, and to the state also passed the relevant instruments of education—above all, the books. Other suppressions of lesser entities came about after 1780 in the Venetian republic and in Austria and its territories.

Of a very different gravity were the suppressions effected after the French invasion of Italy began in 1796. These suppressions, at first massive but selective, became more widespread in 1810. No religious order was spared, and magnificent libraries were devastated and dismembered. The dispersal of the Library of the Convent of San Marco at Florence, created by Cosimo de' Medici with the manuscripts of Niccolò Niccoli and Coluccio Salutati in 1441; and the sacking of the magnificent Venetian libraries of St. Michael and St. George and of Santa Maria della Salute are notable examples of the devastation. All three disappeared. There were immense losses of books and precious furnishings, even though public libraries did receive part of the collections taken from religious libraries.

New suppressions took place after Italian unification in 1870. The Piedmontese law, anticlerical in inspiration, was extended to provinces annexed to the house of Savoy, so that the religious entities saved from previous suppressions, or later reconstituted, were struck again. Particularly notable was the case of Rome. After Italian annexation of the city, 16th-century Roman library (the Biblioteca Vallicelliana, 1581), and three later libraries (the Biblioteca Angelica, 1614, the Biblioteca Alessandrina, and the Biblioteca Casanatense, 1701) passed, fortunately intact, to the state, which continued their successful public operations. Collectively they hold thousands of incunabula and significant manuscripts. Meanwhile, the Biblioteca Nazionale Centrale in Rome was formed in 1876, using the spoils of other Roman monastic libraries and convents.

The two state libraries of Florence that passed to the state and became public were special cases: the Biblioteca Riccardiana (17th century) and the Biblioteca Marucelliana (1752), whose original collections were the private libraries of two rich and cultured families, the Riccardis and the Marucellis. The first became the property of the municipality of Florence in 1813, was then returned to the grand duke, and finally acquired by the Italian state. The second was acquired in 1783 by the grand duke of Tuscany and then also acquired by the state. Of more recent formation are the libraries of Bari (1877), Trieste (1956),

Cosenza (1978), and Macerata (1990), as well as four Roman libraries: the libraries of Modern and Contemporary History (1906), of Archeology and the History of Art (1922), of Medicine (1925), and of Antonio Baldini (1962: named for the Roman humorist and editor).

As various as the libraries themselves is the diversity of works kept in them. Some are extremely rich in ancient and precious manuscripts and early books; others have none. Some have immense collections (more than 5 million books at the National Library of Florence, 6 million at the National Library of Rome, and 1.5 million at the National Library of Naples); others have only a few thousand volumes. Each attempts to document the culture of its city or territory, or alternatively a particular subject (such as the Roman libraries mentioned above). Most tend to keep ancient and precious documents relative to the cultural history of their region, along with works of wider interest.

This essay will emphasize those libraries with collections of more than regional interest, to provide a useful orientation to potential users. It is obvious that the scholar interested in the history of Milan would turn first to the National Braidense Library in Milan. Others may not know that the Reale Library of Turin keeps precious drawings by Leonardo da Vinci; or that for 18th-century Venetian music, the collections of the National Library of Turin are even more useful than those, albeit rich, of the Marciana Library of Venice. Particular attention will be paid, therefore, to the two National Central Libraries of Rome and of Florence, to the National Library of Naples, to the Marciana Library of Venice, and to the National and the Royal libraries of Turin, with the caveat that rich cultural resources exist far beyond these few institutions. Additional articles on the Ambrosiana Library, the Capitular Library of Verona, the Malatestina Library in Cesena; the Estense Library and University of Modena; and the Laurentian Library of the Medici, all of which are in some measure the property of the state, are found elsewhere in these volumes.

National Central Library Vittorio Emanuele II, Rome

In 1870 the armed forces of the Kingdom of Italy, proclaimed only nine years earlier, entered Rome through the open walls of Porta Pia, a site guarded by only a few pontifical police. With this action, the newly born kingdom completed the unity of the peninsula and procured for itself a capital of immense prestige, the city of the Caesars and of the popes. Ruggerio Bonghi, a scholar, man of politics, and minister of public instruction, soon employed his energies in creating in the capital a great library designed to match the national libraries of the greatest European countries, in particular that of the British Museum in London. In reality, men and means were lacking for such a purpose. To Bonghi's aid came the law of 19 June 1873 that decreed the suppression of Roman religious bodies, permitting monastery and convent libraries to pass to the Italian state. An impressive patrimony of books was thus made available for the new library. Four religious libraries were left intact, and thus passed as they were to the state; another 69 were confiscated and transported to the building chosen as the seat of the national library. Even the building itself was the fruit of expropriation from a religious order, a vast 17th-century edifice of the Jesuits' Roman College in the center of Rome.

The libraries taken from the religious institutions were often magnificent, but the legitimate owners, knowing what awaited them, had hastily removed as much as they could, so that many precious works never arrived at the national library. The beginning was very difficult. The material amassed was enormous, the personnel inadequate, and the ministerial pressure to open the library relentless. On 14 March 1876, approximately 250,000 works remained uncataloged when Minister Bonghi personally took on direction of the library. Despite his daily visits to check on the work, the colossal undertaking was too much for him and his helpers.

Soon the administration of Prime Minister Marco Minghetti, of which Bonghi was a part, collapsed, and Bonghi resigned as minister and director of the library. Carlo Castellani, the librarian who had carried out the function of prefect under Bonghi, became the actual director in the same year of 1876. On 1 September 1877 Bonghi left Rome to direct the Biblioteca Medicea Laurenziana in Florence. A few years later, after his Roman successor's resignation, he was recalled to the national library in Rome on 1 April 1879.

This marked the most difficult time for the library. In addition to insufficient personnel and funds, the indifference of the government, and the lack of catalogs and inventories (many had been concealed by the religious orders before the expropriation), there was the hostility Castellani inspired owing to his difficult and haughty personality. In August 1879 a commission was named by the Ministry of Public Instruction for the compilation of the catalog, which later became a commission of inquest. Castellani, accused of ineptitude for selling valuable works by weight, was removed, and the library closed. Although Castellani was fully absolved two years later, a new director, Luigi Cremona, had begun to reorganize and gradually overcome its initial difficulties. Nonetheless, the decentralization of some of the collections and the donation of the Chiciana collection to the Vatican of Pope Pius IX for a time diminished the importance of the library.

Little of note occurred during the next several decades. In 1917 a great exhibition was devoted to the formation of the Italian state (the *Risorgimento*). Large collections of books, periodicals, and newspapers attracted wide readership. The influx of Italian printed books resulting from legal deposit laws created serious space issues that were unsuccessfully addressed by building projects of 1912 and again in 1929. Finally they led to construction of a new building near the Castro Pretorio area, not far from the university. The work began in 1964 and was finished ten years later. On 31 January 1975 the new center was inaugurated and was immediately criticized on both aesthetic and functional grounds. The edifice is formed of three separate sections: a book warehouse with a 6-million-volume capacity, an administrative office block, and a third section providing reading rooms for 1,188 users and an auditorium for congresses and conferences with space for 350.

The major and most ancient collections are those from the Jesuits. The library confiscated from the Casa Professa del Gesù numbered 20,000 volumes and the library of the Roman College approximately 80,000 volumes; both are now combined in the national library. The printed books date mostly from 1600 to 1800. There are a total of 1,752 manuscripts from the same period; those of the celebrated scientist Athanasius Kircher are of great interest.

The Sessorian collection from the church and monastery of the Holy Cross of Jerusalem in Rome, close to the fourth-century imperial palace called the Sessorium, is equally important. The collection includes 558 manuscripts, including approximately 40 of the most ancient from the old monastery of Nonantola. Among the minor sources worthy of note are those from the abbey of Santa Maria of Farfa whose scriptorium, founded in the eighth century and flourishing in the 11th century, accounts for 22 parchment manuscripts in the collections.

Of particular interest is the Chinese and Japanese collection, mostly from the library of the Jesuits of the Roman College. The Jesuits, as is well known, managed to win the trust of the Ming emperors thanks to the extraordinary astronomical, cartographical, and mathematical competence of Father Matteo Ricci, who entered the Heavenly City of Beijing in 1582, and of his successors, Johann Adam von Schall and Ferdinand Verbiest. The library of the Roman College contained many rare works in Chinese aimed at the diffusion of the Catholic faith (e.g. editions of religious texts, lives of saints, and prayer books) as well as scientific works and a great number of Chinese classics. Later the national library received 6,039 scrolls (with 419 works) from Beijing, from the Summer Palace of the Emperor, and from the house of a dignitary. These were the spoils of war for Italian troops from the international expedition against the Boxer Uprising (1901). Another 2,641 volumes (282 titles) originated from the Italian Legation in Beijing, having been saved by Baron Guido Amedeo Vitale from the pillage of Beijing in 1901. More modern acquisitions include a collection of books on dueling and the archives of various Italian writers including Gabriele Ł'Annunzio.

National Central Library, Florence

The National Library in Florence began from the private collection of Antonio Magliabechi. Trained by his father as a goldsmith, Magliabechi, born in 1633, soon understood that his true vocation was that of a scholar. Cardinal Leopold de' Medici facilitated his studies to the extent that Magliabechi became immensely erudite, was in correspondence with the learned throughout the world, and developed a collection of more than 30,000 books accumulated in striking disorder in his house. There one walked on books, sat on them, used them as chairs; it is said that the bizarre collector read unceasingly, slept in his clothes in order not to waste time, and never changed his suit or wig. He reportedly had a series of disgusting habits, including the use of little salted fish as bookmarks.

Nevertheless, his erudition was such that well-read Europeans venerated him, and Cosimo III, grand duke of Tuscany, in 1673 named Magliabechi librarian of the Palatine Library, located on the third floor of the Pitti Palace, in which the sovereign had collected many books previously dispersed in various residences of the Medici. Magliabechi designated the city of Florence as heir to his own library and also left funds for additions to the collections. He entrusted the collection to his learned friend Anton Francesco Marmi, who in turn in 1736 willed that his personal books join those left by Magliabechi. In 1737 grand duke Gian Gastone, the successor of Cosimo III, ordered that the Magliabechi and Marmi collections should form the public library of Florence. A year earlier he decreed that all Florentine printers deposit in the Magliabechi library a copy of every book they printed. Gastone died in 1737, the last of the Medicean dynasty.

The grand duke had also provided suitable premises in the Uffizi Palace, and in 1747 the Magliabechiana Library opened to the public. After a year library visitors numbered 50 per day. In addition to various donations, its major expansion came by merger with the private library of the grand duchy. Peter Leopold of Lorraine donated his library to the Magliabechiana in 1771 (approximately 10,000 volumes belonging to the Medici and many others brought by Francis of Lorraine when he became successor to the Medici).

Cultured princes, kindly lovers of books and study, represented the Lorraine dynasty (later Hapsburg-Lorraine). In 1814 Ferdinand III, after his long Napoleonic exile, reconstituted his court library, the New Palatine, with 40,000 volumes brought from Vienna. To these were added various acquisitions overseen by the grand duke, Ferdinand III. Even his son and successor, Leopold II, devoted great care to the Palatine Library until he abandoned his states following the Piedmontese invasion in 1859. In 1861 under the newly united Italian government, the two libraries of the New Palatine and the Magliabechiana were merged to constitute a library of 150,000 volumes, of which 80,000 printed books and 3,100 manuscripts derived from the New Palatine Library.

In 1861 the Magliabechiana changed its name to the Biblioteca Nazionale (the only one at that time) before Florence became the capital of the newly united kingdom of Italy. After the subsequent annexation of Rome as capitol in 1870, the national need for a Roman library presence led to the establishment in 1875 of the Biblioteca Nazionale Vittorio Emanuele II, as a second other important national library (see above). In 1877 the Florence library acquired Francesco Guicciardini's famous Reformation collection. The 1885 Regulations for Public State Libraries granted mandatory rights of deposit for printed books to both libraries and also added the word Central to their titles.

The next five decades constituted a difficult period for the library, with delays in everything from bibliographic publications to new construction. A new building, designed by Cesare Bazzani, was started in 1911 but not completed until 1935. Although the final move was rapid and efficient, the construction was architecturally mediocre, and the building quickly proved insufficient. Unanticipated growth led to construction of an additional wing, completed in 1962.

The most dramatic event in the library's history was the disastrous flood of 4 November 1996. On the same day that the sea struck Venice so hard as to cause fear of the city's destruction, the river Arno invaded the city of Florence, bringing along tons of mud and naphtha. The library was badly hit, particularly in its basement, where works of great importance (folios, maps, engravings, catalogs, and card files) were completely overrun by water and mud. It was a disaster of biblical proportions: 1.2 million volumes seemed lost forever, but the library found unexpected emergency relief as hundreds of volunteers arrived from all over the world to help in limiting the damage. By the end of the millennium restoration work was not yet finished, but it is fair to say that the Florence flood compelled far greater attention to the problems of library preservation, not only in Italy but also throughout the library world.

From 1958 to 1993 the library published the *Bibliografia nazionale italiana* (the National Italian Bibliography), cataloging printed works received on copyright deposit. From 1886 to 1957 it also published the monthly *Il bollettino delle publicazioni italiane ricevute per diretto di stampa*, which since 1886 has listed Italian publications received on copyright deposit. In 1994 the national bibliography was divided into three sections: monographs; periodicals; and theses and dissertations, with only the last of these produced in Florence, the others in Rome. The bibliography has had electronic support since 1995.

In recent years the library has placed itself in the Italian avant garde of automation services to the public and in cataloging. Public access, book requests, and book reshelving are all regulated by an electronic system called Utenti on line (UOL). A new digital area was inaugurated on 15 December 1999, a room with 48 workstations and computers for online catalog consultation. Here one can consult more than 85 bibliographical databases, as well as various works digitized by the library for online access (1.6 million images from manuscripts, ancient books, and periodicals).

The library now holds 5.4 million books, 25,000 manuscripts, and 15,000 current periodicals. Among the most important collections is the Galilean collection, which contains many scientific manuscripts, including the collection of medical doctor Antonio Cocchi acquired from the grand duke in 1774; the Guicciardini collection already mentioned; and the Antonio Lafrery (a 16th-century Roman printer) collection of geographical charts and prints, mostly from the 1500s, many known only from these unique examples. There are also approximately 1 million letters and autographs, including writings by Niccolo Machiavelli, Angelo Poliziano, Lorenzo de' Medici, Torquato Tasso, Ugo Foscolo, and Giacomo Leopardi.

National Library of Naples

The first nucleus of this great library was the collection of Cardinal Alessandro Farnese (later Pope Paul III, the pope of the Council of Trent best known from his magnificent portrait by Titian). He began to collect books around 1493 and by 1495 had started construction of the famous Roman palace (now the French embassy) in which the library was housed. In the 16th century, the librarian was the celebrated scholar, collector, and antiquarian Fulvio Orsini. The library escaped the sack of Rome in 1527 but endured two fires in the early 17th century. It was also the victim of serious robberies by followers of Queen Christina of Sweden, a guest of the Farnese family in Rome in 1654–55; her servants, not having been paid, tried to steal with they could. In 1653 the Farnese, having become dukes of Parma and Piacenza, had the library moved to Parma and the books entirely rebound in leather with golden lilies on the back, a style that makes them easily recognizable today.

Antonio Farnese, the last of the dynasty, died in 1731 without direct heirs. Based on the Treaty of London of 1718, the succession passed to the children of Elisabeth Farnese, wife of Philip V of Spain and mother of Don Carlos of Bourbon, crown prince of Spain. Carlos spent two years in Parma before becoming king of Naples as Charles IV. He entered Naples with great pomp on 10 May 1734. For Parma it was a disaster, as the ducal palaces were stripped of their most precious furnishings, and the Farnese Library was transferred to Naples, where Carlos reigned as an independent sovereign. Among his projects for the capital was the creation of a great public library, an idea shared by the Spanish viceroy, Pedro Fernandez, Count de Lemos, whose collection of books for the Palace of Royal Studies became the nucleus of the University Library of Naples.

Carlos also had thought of the Palace of Royal Studies (a 1615 building, now the Museo Archeologico Nazionale Napoli) as a site for his public library, but the collections were temporarily housed in the Palace of Capodimonte, since the former required restoration. At the death of his father (Ferdinand VI) in 1759, Carlos went to Madrid to assume the Spanish crown, leaving Naples and the Kingdom of the Two Sicilies to his son, Ferdinand I. Nonetheless, the Farnesian nucleus of the library was augmented by the newly confiscated library of the Neapolitan convent of the Society of Jesus, together with the library of the Prince of Tarsia.

The French invasion in 1799 obliged Ferdinand III to flee Naples when the Partenopea Republic was installed in the city, inspired by the principles of the French Revolution. One of the most important religious libraries confiscated was that of the Augustinians of St. John of Carbonara, of great interest as it contained the library of humanist Aulo Giano Parrasio. His books, as well as those of brothers Antonio and Girolamo Sirapando, were then gathered into the Royal Library of Naples, now finally located in the Palace of Royal Studies. On 13 January 1804 the solemn official opening of the library was held in its new location. Publication of the printed catalog of the collections had already begun in 1801.

When in 1806 Napoleon returned and Bonaparte's brother-in-law Joachim Murat assumed the throne of Naples, Ferdinand IV repaired to Sicily. The confiscation of religious properties resumed, with the Charterhouse of Padula alone providing thousands of books and codices. Murat also saw to the acquisition of an almost complete collection of books edited by the famous printer Giambattista Bodoni, and the library of the Marquis Francesco Antonio Taccone (which had been designated for the university library in Naples but to which the Bourbons had the right of choice).

After the Napoleonic system collapsed in 1815 and Ferdinand IV repossessed his kingdom as Ferdinand I, the library took the name Royal Bourbon Library (Reale Biblioteca Borbonica). In 1818 the king bought the collection of incunabula of the politician and historian Melchiorre Delfico. In 1860 the house of Bourbon definitively lost the kingdom of Naples, conquered by the volunteer army of Guiseppe Garibaldi and the troops of the Savoy. The direction of the library was then entrusted to the philosopher Vito Fornari, who remained at his post for 40 years. The suppression of monasteries and convents began yet again, and in 1875 the library of St. Giacomo was annexed to the library, as were the books of the Palatine Library (the private library of the king) and the private library of the heroic Queen Maria Carolina, wife of Francesco II, who had fought to the last in defense of the dynasty.

Other important acquisitions were the result of wills and gifts. In 1882 Antonio Ranieri, friend of Giacomo Leopardi, left to the library his Leopardi autographs and correspondence (legal controversies delayed the acquisition until 1907). In 1888 Count Eduardo Lucchesi Palli gave his collection: 61,000 volumes and 1,500 autographs largely dealing with theater history. The 20th century was no less important for the growth of the library, notably through the receipt by the national library of the papyrus manuscripts belonging to the *Officina dei Papiri Ercolanesi* (see below), and the physical transfer in 1923 of the library to the Royal Palace, which King Victor Emanuel III decided to cede to the Italian state. Many thought that the Royal Palace of the Bourbons was the ideal seat for the library, including Benedetto Croce, whose high prestige, both intellectual and moral, had great weight within the government. The transfer was decreed on 2 August 1922, and the move was carried out between 1923 and 1927. On 17 May 1927 the new center was inaugurated, taking the name of the reigning sovereign, Vittorio Emanuele III.

Other significant additions in the early 20th century included the Brancacciana Library (the oldest library in Naples open to the public) and the Provinciale Library, a collection of approximately 30,000 volumes on scientific subjects, geographic maps, and rare travel books. When Italy entered World War II in 1940, there was serious danger to the library with its facade facing the port; in fact, bombs hit the Royal Palace in 1943, causing heavy damage. Manuscripts and rare books had previously been sent for safekeeping inland, and the losses involved only the furniture and decorations of the palace.

Among the ancient riches of the library, the collection of the Herculaneum papyri (received in 1910) is of exceptional importance. Excavations carried out in Herculaneum (buried by the eruption of Vesuvius in 79 B.C.) between 1752 and 1754 revealed some burned material, which were discovered by Camillo Paderni to be the papyri of an ancient library. The Officina dei Papiri was founded to carry out the unfolding of the papyri and to make them legible. After several failed attempts, it was Father Antonio Piaggio who succeeded in 1756 to build a machine that could unroll the burned papyri sufficiently to make them legible. Once unrolled, the papyri were entrusted to designers, whose work was to reproduce whatever they were able to see of the ancient writing. Copper plates for printing were made from the designs. But many difficulties remained. In 1820 Humphry Davy, a British scientist, tried new techniques, and other experiments followed. Recently a new method has been used, called *Osloensis* after the Norwegian team of Professors Brynjhulf Fosse and Knut Kleve, using a mixture of gelatin and acetic acid. The national library maintains the entire collection of 1,816 papyri from Herculaneum; 496 are entirely unrolled, 185 are partially unrolled, and much work remains to be done. These documents include works by Epicurus and Philodemus, once preserved in the villa of the Pisoni.

In 1947 Duchess Elena d'Aosta, member of the Royal family, donated her private library, rich in materials and memoirs about Africa. In 1957 a hall was dedicated to the famous philosopher, Benedetto Croce, whose books and papers are preserved in the library. The library's Americana collection was dedicated to John Fitzgerald Kennedy in 1964. An earthquake in 1980 caused some damage, but the constant activity of exhibitions, conferences, and lectures continues to make the library an important center of culture in Southern Italy.

Marciana National Library, Venice

Venice might have had a library as early as the 14th century, the property of the state and open to the public. The idea had come to Petrarch to give his library to the republic, out of admiration for the beauty of the city and its political stability. It contained a collection of great importance; as the first library with a humanist plan, it was quite different from medieval libraries. The republic solemnly accepted Petrarch's gift in September 1362 and granted him the use of a beautiful house on the Riva degli Schiavoni, into which Petrarch moved, together with his books. But after a period of time, his restless spirit felt attracted to a different sort of life. Francesco da Carrara, the *signore* of Padua, offered him a canonry and a house in that city, where he moved in 1367, taking his books with him. With his move the dream of a public library, the first after those of ancient Rome, disappeared.

The dream was taken up a century later by the cardinal, politician, and scholar, the Greek Bessarion. After the fall of Constantinople to Ottoman forces in 1453, Bassarion devoted himself to saving the written testimony of Greek civilization, which he feared would completely disappear under the destructive advance of the Turks; he believed that wherever their invasion arrived, wars and pillage caused entire libraries to disappear. He feared that Greek thought, unlike religious works already widely diffused, might vanish altogether. His chief worry was the manuscripts containing works produced by the ancient world. Therefore he acquired manuscript after manuscript, looking for them in Greece and elsewhere, buying them or having them copied by his amanuenses, or copying them himself. He succeeded in building a library that contained all or almost all the works then extant from ancient Greek civilization. There were the philosophical works, particularly Plato, as well as the surviving works of mathematicians, astronomers, geographers, physicians, tragedians, and the poets of antiquity. Some of his codices were of extraordinary rarity and importance, including a 10th-century codex of the entire *Iliad* of Homer with interlinear glosses and marginalia summarizing the greatest works of ancient criticism about the poem, otherwise lost works that survive only in these parchment pages. Other works were handed down in other codices, but those collected by Cardinal Bessarion are among the best and most complete: a 10th-century Hippocrates, fundamental for Greek medicine; the Photius of the same century, summarizing the content of many ancient works now lost; and codices containing Demosthenes, Dio Cassius, and Aristotle's *Organon*, all of the tenth century.

In 1468 Bessarion gave his collection to the Venetian republic for reasons he described in a famous letter accompanying the gift. There was no safer place, he said, owing to the justice that inspired the government of the city and the harmony that reigned there. He saw no city more suitable for the Greeks, who had gone there in great numbers over the centuries and now were found there in exile after the loss of their homeland. To these, Venice seemed a second Byzantium. In Venice Bessarion had always been received with warmth and affection and found it his true homeland. It was also the only European power, other than Hungary, to fight against the Turks.

Venice solemnly accepted the gift of 1,000 codices, approximately half in Greek, and placed the collection in the ducal palace in 1530. The next year they were transferred to a room on the upper floor of the church of St. Mark, which could be reached from the porch of the church, and finally in 1560 located in a separate building, strategically placed directly across the Piazzetta from the palace. The new building, the present-day Marciana Library, is a noble, classical, and richly ornamented palace designed by the state architect, Jacopo Sansovino. The library of Cardinal Bessarion thus became the property of Venice. It was named for St. Mark, the protector and symbol of the Venetian state.

The library was entrusted by Bessarion to the procurators of San Marco (high magistrates who administered the church and its properties, second in honor only to the doge, or chief magistrate), who had since 1480 been responsible for the palace library, holding the title *Bibliothecarius Sancti Marci*. The first was the patrician Marco Barbarigo, then succeeded by his brother Agostino. They were both powerful politicians and their charge was mainly honorary. Then after 1486, a proper librarian was appointed, the historian Marc'Antonio Sabellico, who died in 1506. After a long hiatus, the poet and diplomat Andrea Navagero was appointed in his place in 1515. He in turn was replaced in 1529 by the scholar, poet, and future cardinal Pietro Bembo. The other noblemen and scholars were elected by the Senate, but without continuity until 1626. In that year a senate decree provided that the office should be entrusted to a patrician elected by the senate itself, and that a Greek scholar (to be known as the *custos*) should work with the *bibliothecarius*.

Learned and illustrious patricians were often named librarian at the end of their careers. Several became doges (Marco Barbarigo and his brother Agostino, already mentioned, in the 15th century, Silvestro Valier in the 17th, and Marco Foscarini and Alvise Mocenigo IV in the 18th century). Two 18th-century custodians, Anton Maria Zanetti and Jacopo Morelli, were particularly famous. Zanetti compiled an inventory of Venetian public statues, elegantly illustrated by his own hand. He also compiled a two-volume catalog of the library's manuscripts (with the Greek scholar Antonio Bongiovanni) published in 1740–41, as well as a catalog of public paintings (those conserved in state palaces and Venetian churches).

The learned priest Jacopo Morelli directed the library in the turbulent and tragic period of the fall of the republic (1797) and during the successive French, Austrian, and French regimes. It was his sad lot to accommodate Napoleon's wish to use the library building as part of the royal palace and to transfer the library itself back to the Ducal Palace. There it remained until 1905, when it was moved to the Zecca (the Mint). In 1920 King Victor Emmanuel III restored the library building to its ancient purpose but permitted the library to keep the Zecca. Today the library occupies both the Sansovino buildings (Zecca and library) and also a part of the adjacent Procuratie.

The Zecca today houses most of the books and offices. It is a severe building of classical style, erected by Sansovino and finished in 1547. The great reading room is in s former courtyard, once open but now covered by a glass and wood roof. The two most beautiful rooms are in the library built by Sansovino between 1537 and 1553, one that once housed Bessarion's library, and the adjoining Antisala (vestibule). The walls of the first are decorated with 11 imaginary portraits of ancient philosophers (six by Tintoretto) and the ceiling with 21 roundels, three by Paolo Veronese. The Antisala once housed the Statuary Museum of the Republic, approximately 200 pieces of ancient sculpture mostly donated in 1587 by the Patriarch of Aquileia, Giovanni Grimani. Today 71 have been restored to their original locations; the others are at the Archeological Museum. In the center of the ceiling is a canvas by Titian representing Wisdom (*La Sapienza*). The two rooms today belong to a unified museum itinerary that includes the Museum of Archeology and the Correr Museum.

The initial collection of the Marciana, formed by the codices of Bessarion, was gradually enriched with bequests and gifts and, beginning in the 18th century, with acquisitions. In 1603 a law established the obligation of Venetian printers to deposit in the library a copy of every imprint, the first example of legal deposit in Italy. The Greek part of the library was enhanced in 1622 by Giacomo Gallicio, who gave 20 Greek codices to obtain the freedom of a prisoner dear to him. These included a magnificently illustrated commentary on the Book of Job dated A.D. 905. In 1796 patrician Giacomo Nani, commander of the fleet in the Levant, gave 300 Greek codices. Among Venetian historical manuscripts in the library are the testament of Marco Polo (1321), the diaries of Marino Sanudo (53 volumes from 1496 to 1533 covering the most significant political, cultural, and civil events of the time), and many ancient chronicles. The Oriental collection, with its 100 codices also by Nani, is important as well. In the 20th century, gifts from glottologist Emilio Teza (on Oriental civilizations and on African and South American dialects) and from Angiolo Tursi (works of foreign travelers in Italy) have also enriched the library.

Many projects are now under way to foster the study and use of the collections. Much of the catalog of post-1990 printed books is available on the library's Online Public Access Catalog (marciana.venezia.sbn.it/opac) as are many printed catalogs of particular subjects, and other bibliographic tools. Similar access is planned for the entire works of the great Venetian mathematician and cartographer Vincenzo Coronelli, editor of voluminous collections of views, guides, and almanacs. Another project deals with music of the 18th century, as noted below.

The Marciana Library has published its journal *Miscellanea Marciana* since 1986, as well a newsletter; both appear irregularly as needed. Its initiatives are also sustained by the American Friends of the Marciana Library, whose newsletter can be found on the Marciana website (marciana.venezia.sbn.it).

National University Library of Turin

The National University Library of Turin was opened in 1720 as the library of the Royal University of Sciences (Regia Università delle Scienze), located in the palace recently finished by architect Filippo Juvarra. In 1723 King Vittorio Amedeo II united the collection with 10,000 volumes of the Royal Library of the house of Savoy and 4,000 volumes of the Civic Library. Enriched with donations and the spoils of suppressed convents, it was severely damaged by fire in 1904 and by an air raid in 1942. In 1972 it was transferred to its present premises.

Among surviving manuscripts are five remarkable Coptic papyri of the sixth through eighth centuries, 110 Hebrew manuscripts, and 289 Greek manuscripts, some from the ninth and tenth centuries. There are 71 codices from the illustrious monastery of Bobbio, approximately 100 antique French manuscripts, and many Latin codices written in France, the oldest being a Rabanus Maurus of the 9th-century.

The musical collections are of extraordinary interest, including an early-15th-century codex acquired in 1991 that contains 23 compositions previously unknown. Another French-Cypriot codex, dating from 1414 to 1420, contains 228 Latin or French compositions collected in Cyprus at the court of the Lusignan; no other copies are known. Two collections are named in honor of the children of donors Mauro Foà (1927) and Renzo Giordano (1930). These complementary collections contain the music of Count Giacomo Durazzo, an 18th-century Genoese nobleman who was appointed *Generalmusikdirector* at the court of Vienna in the time of Christoph Willibald Gluck. Among the 465 volumes in these collections are works by Antonio Vivaldi and Alessandro Stradella, 19 volumes of arias of Venetian operas, and 2,800 compositions of organ *intavolatura*. The best part of the collection comes from the magnificent 18th-century library of the Venetian patrician Giacomo Soranzo.

Planned around these collections is a project financed by the Ministry of Culture called the Digital Archive of Venetian Music, a partnership of the National Library of Turin, the Marciana, and the Discoteca di Stato (the Italian archives of recorded sound in Rome). Its aims are to reproduce digitally the entire body of Venetian music kept in the two libraries and making the music electronically accessible.

Royal Library of Turin

When King Vittorio Amedeo II gave the best of his collection to the library of Turin University in 1723, some books remained at the court; after 1831 this small collection was notably enriched by the family collection of King Carlo Alberto. In 1946 these collections passed to the Italian state. Among the most precious items is a small codex dated 1467, containing the scholastic exercises of the 15-year-old Ludovico Sforza, future duke of Milan, ornate with exquisite miniatures. The young Ludovico is portrayed along with his preceptor, the celebrated humanist Francesco Filelfo.

Another collection contains approximately 2,000 drawings by masters of the 15th to 18th centuries, among them Michelangelo, Raphael, Leonardo da Vinci (a magnificent self-portrait), Lodovico Carracci, Nicolas Poussin, Rembrandt Harmenszoon van Rijn, Giovanni Battista Tiepolo, and Giovanni Batista Piazzetta. In 1893 the Russian collector Teodoro Sabachnicov, perhaps fascinated (as were many others) by the regal beauty of King Umberto I's wife, Margherita, donated to the sovereign a codex of Leonardo da Vinci's notes on the flight of birds, as well as ink sketches and sanguine drawings. In 1920 another collector, Henri Fatio of Geneva, gave three missing leaves of this codex to the library. In 1972 Marina Bersano Begey donated the archive of her family, rich in documents about Polish history. Now the library, open to scholars and a more general public, mainly acquires material concerning the history of its city. The library is also involved in the publication of facsimiles of some of its important manuscripts.

Municipal Libraries

In addition to religious and state libraries, many important libraries belong to municipalities or *comuni*. These are institutions that have nothing to do with the ancient city-states (the medieval municipalities that opposed the Roman-Germanic Empire in the 12th and 13th centuries and helped form the greatness of medieval Italy). Rather, these present-day *comuni* are administrative jurisdictions that oversee many important municipal libraries developed from a variety of sources, including inheritance or donation. The Trivulziana Library (Biblioteca Trivulziana) in Milan and the Malatestiana Public Library (Biblioteca Communale Malatestiana) in Cesena are among the most important. (The latter is discussed in a separate essay in this dictionary.)

The Trivulziana Library is joined with the library of the Archivio Storico Civico (Civic Historic Archives). It was formed in the second half of the 16th century by Marquis Alessandro Teodoro Trivulzio and his brother, Don Carlo. It possesses many antique codices, including one from the 8th century containing the *Epitome Juliani* (a juridical work of the later Roman period), and various manuscripts illuminated for the princely families of the Estes and Sforzas. There is also an autograph codex by Leonardo da Vinci. In 1935 the descendants of the Trivulzio family sold the library to the municipality of Milan. The catalog is partially available electronically through SBN (www.sbn.it).

Libraries Belonging to Private Institutions

Some private institutions possess important libraries, and two examples are included here. The Library of the Querini Stampalia Foundation of Venice (Fondazione Scientifica "Querini Stampalia" Biblioteca) was formed through the farsightedness of a Venetian patrician, Giovanni Querini. In 1864 he bequeathed his palazzo, his picture gallery, his library, and his patrimony of furnishings to a foundation he created in the name of his family. According to his will, the library was required to be open during afternoons and evenings, when other institutions were closed—a wise and useful arrangement still appreciated by scholars and students today who use the comfortable reading rooms until 11:30 P.M. The library is that of a cultivated family of Venetian patricians, and it is kept up to date in historical and literary fields. The original collection has grown with the continued acquisition of modern books; adjacent buildings have recently been added to the Querini palace to provide additional space for both library and programs. The holdings of the Querini Stampalia Foundation include 300,000 volumes, 1,200 manuscripts, 97 incunabula, and 1,600 16th-century editions.

The Giorgio Cini Foundation of Venice (Fondazione Giorgio Cini) is the fruit of the generous design of a great financier, Count Vittorio Cini, senator of the kingdom of Italy, who wished to honor the memory of his son, Giorgio, who was tragically killed in an airplane accident in April 1949. To this end, in 1951 he created the foundation bearing Giorgio's name and restored the entire island of St. Giorgio, once the seat of an important monastery with buildings by Palladio and Longhena.

During the Napoleonic years, the island was destined for military use and sustained considerable damage. Today the island and its monuments are perfectly restored, and the cultural institution of great prestige that Count Cini created is housed there. Cini gave to the foundation his collection of art (by Sandro Botticelli, Piero della Francesca, Bernardino Luini, and others), and also his collection of ancient books from the 15th and 16th centuries. Many of these illustrated books, often unique, come from the celebrated collection of the Prince of Essling, a great 19th-century bibliophile and scholar. Among these books, for instance, is one missal according to the rite of the Church of Sarum (Salisbury), printed in Venice in 1492 by German typographer Johann Hamman for two Dutch investors, sufficient proof of the international links of the ancient Venetian printing industry. The Cini Foundation has acquired other important collections, among which the Oriental collections are of great interest (Chinese and Indian, with unique ancient Indian music). The collection of art books is probably the best in Italy (100,000 volumes). The holdings of the Giorgio Cini Foundation include 150,000 volumes, 2,000 incunabula and 16th-century editions, 300 manuscripts and miniatures, and extensive photographic collections (see www.cini.it).

MARINO ZORZI

See also Ambrosiana Library; Capitular Library of Verona; Estense Library and University of Modena; Laurentian Library of the Medic; Malatestiana Library, Cesena

Further Reading

Annuario delle biblioteche italiane, 5 vols., Rome: Palombi, 1969–81 (with an extensive bibliography for every library described)

Arduim, Franca, "The Two National Central Libraries of Florence and Rome," *Libraries & Culture* 25 (1990)

Aschero, Antonia Ida Fontana, "The Biblioteca Nazionale Centrale of Florence: Tradition and Innovation in Support of the Information Society," *Alexandria* 12, no. 3 (2000)

Biblioteca Nazionale Centrale, Firenze, Florence: Nardini, 1989

Biblioteca Nazionale Centrale, Roma: I fondi, le procedure, le storie: Raccolta di studi della Biblioteca, Rome: Tipografia della Biblioteca Nazionale Centrale, 1993

Bibliografia Nazionale Italiana, Rome, 1958-

Bottasso, Enzo, *Storia della biblioteca in Italia*, Milan: Editrice Bibliografica, 1984

De Gregorio, Vincenzo, *La Biblioteca casanatense di Roma*, Naples: Edizioni Scientifiche Italiane, 1993

Giacobello Bernard, Giovanna, editor, *Leonardo e le meraviglie della Biblioteca Reale di Torino*, Milan: Electa, and Turin: Biblioteca Reale, 1998

Guerrieri, Guerriera, *La Biblioteca nazionale Vittorio Emanuele III di Napoli*, Milan-Naples: Ricciardi, 1974

Hobson, Anthony, *Great Libraries,* London: Weidenfeld and Nicolson, and New York: Putnam, 1970

Manelli Goggioli, Maria, *La Biblioteca Magliabechiana*, Florence: Olshki, 2000

Merola, Giovanna, and Claudia Parmeggiani, "Improving the Italian Library Network: The Servizio Bibliotecario Nazionale," *Alexandria* 12, no. 3 (2000)

Ministero per i Beni e le Attività Culturali, *Biblioteche d'Italia: Le biblioteche pubbliche statali*, Milan and Rome: Centro Tibaldi, 1991; 3rd edition, 1996 (on the state libraries)

Romano, Fiorella, editor, *Biblioteca Nazionale Vittorio Emanuele III, Napoli,* Florence: Nardini, 1993

Staikos, Konstantinos Sp, *The Great Libraries: From Antiquity to the Renaissance (3000 B.C. to A.D. 1600)*, New Castle, Delaware: Oak Knoll Books; London: British Library, 2000

Zorzi, Marino, *La Libreria di San Marco*, Milan: Mondadori, 1987

Zorzi, Marino, editor, *Biblioteca Marciana, Venezia,* Florence: Nardini, 1988

National Libraries of Korea

National Library of Korea

Address: Gungnip Jungang Doseogwan
San 60-1, Banpo Dong, Seocho Gu
Seoul, 137-702
Republic of Korea
Telephone: 2-590-0544
Fax: 2-590-0546
www.nl.go.kr

Founded: 1945

Holdings (2000): Volumes: 3.6 million. Archives: 7,000; current serials: 26,000; films and videos: 82,000; manuscripts: 234,000; maps: 4,000; microforms: 231,000; sound recordings: 126,000.

Special Collections: *Areas of Concentration:* Art and sport; audiovisual materials; digital information resources; geography; government publications; Korean cultural and intellectual heritage; library and information science; philosophy and religion; social sciences. *Individual Collections:* Government-designated national treasures; rare and old books; Seoul municipal treasures. *Papers:* Hong Cheon Ahn; Han Mo Chung; Chong Doo Kim; Sung Whan Kim; Dong Ho Lee; Young Rae Lee; Chang Jae Lim; Seo Chang Oh; Jae Soo Seo; Soon Hyung Yoo.

National Assembly Library

Address: Gukhoe Doseogwan
1 Yoido-dong, Yongdeungpo-gu
Seoul 150-703
Republic of Korea
Telephone: 2-788-4143
    (general information in English)
Fax: 2-788-4402
www.nanet.go.kr

Founded: 1952

Holdings (2001): Volumes: 1.5 million. Current serials: 15,000; films and videos: 9,000; incunabula: 112; manuscripts: 15,000; maps: 2,000; microfilm: 50,000.

National Assembly Library (cont.)

Special Collections: *Areas of Concentration:* Business administration and industry; environment; government publications; international organization publications; Korean studies; law; linguistics; North Korean publications; parliamentary papers. *Individual Collections:* Government-designated national treasures; rare and old books; Seoul municipal treasures. *Papers:* Young Whan Cho; Chin Bae Kim; Dong Gil Kim; Se Il Sohn; Chi Hyung Yoon.

Introduction

Unlike the United States, where the Library of Congress functions as a quasi-national library, the Republic of Korea (South Korea) has two national libraries. One of these is the National Central Library (since 1996 known in English as the National Library of Korea, or NLK) and the other is the National Assembly Library (NAL). The system of two national libraries developed because each was designated to receive two legal deposit copies of all publications issued in Korea and both serve as national information clearinghouses.

In its earliest years, the National Central Library in Seoul, under the Ministry of Education, was relatively small and underdeveloped. It has since grown, however, to the point that it is now fully deserving of the name "national library." The NAL, under the National Assembly of Korea, also functions as a national library but with special attention to legislative materials and materials supporting legislative activities. Both are qualitatively different from libraries such as the Korea Institute of Industry and Technology Information Center (KINITI), under the Ministry of Industry and Resources, which functions partially as an independent national library but primarily for the fields of industry and technology. Therefore, when speaking of a national library in Korea, it is both the National Library of Korea and the National Assembly Library that must be examined.

Although this essay focuses primarily on the two National Libraries of South Korea, mention must be made of North Korea, officially the Democratic People's Republic of Korea. North Korea also has a national library, which came into being in 1946 when the Pyongyang Public Library was designated as the national library of North Korea, subsequently changing its name to the National Central Library. The library was temporarily closed during the Korean War (1950–53), but after the cease-fire it reopened in a three-story building. Its major functions include publishing reference materials, organizing exhibitions, conducting seminars on Communism and the works of Kim Il Sung, and controlling provincial libraries. In 1964 the collection of the National Central Library was approximately 1,500,000 volumes. This increased to about 2,300,000 volumes by 1971. Since then, officially reliable data about the National Central Library have not been reported.

North Korea also has a quasi-national library, the People's Great Learning Center, founded in 1982 to celebrate the 70th birthday of Kim Il Sung. It is the largest library in North Korea, equipped with a variety of modern features such as computer and telecommunication facilities. The center claims to be staffed by 800 librarians and 200 translators, to have a collection of 20,000,000 volumes, and to contain numerous reading rooms and audio-visual facilities. While nominally a library, the center functions primarily as a national information and educational facility designed to infuse and propagate Communism and to praise Kim Il Sung and his son, Kim Jeong Il.

There is little communication or exchange of material between North and South Korea. However, given the fact that both Koreas share a common origin, history, culture, and language, dialogue between them has progressed rapidly, and the outline of future cooperation is already visible.

This essay attempts to update and expand two earlier English-language essays on the two Korean national libraries in South Korea (Koh, 1980; Lee and Um, 1994). Readers interested in the general development of libraries in Korea from ancient times to the present, particularly developments related to early paper making and printing technology and to the creation of the Korean alphabet (Hangul), should refer to the Koh article as well as other sources suggested under the Further Reading section.

Historical Background

Established in October 1945, immediately after the liberation of Korea from almost four decades of Japanese colonial rule (1910–45), the NLK was the successor to the Chosun Government General Library established in 1923 by the Japanese colonial government. Under Japanese rule public libraries and school libraries were virtually nonexistent and did not include Korean-language materials. Although the Chosun Government General Library contained the largest collection in Korea at that time, it too had limited collections and, like the few other libraries that were in operation, was restricted in its users. It should also be noted that the collection of Kyujanggak, the Royal Household Library (technically the national library of the country prior to the Japanese occupation in 1910) is housed in the Seoul National University Library, not in either of the national libraries.

The NLK commenced operations as a new central library in October 1945, two months after the country gained its independence in August 1945. It was not until 1949, however, that the legal foundation for a national library was first established by a presidential ordinance regarding the "Organization of the National Library." Unfortunately, the Korean War brought destruction to the country, including its nascent libraries. During the time when Seoul was occupied by North Korean forces, both the director and associate director of the NLK in Seoul refused to evacuate the library, choosing to remain and defend the collection.

In the 1960s Korea commenced economic reconstruction by initiating a series of five-year economic development plans. It was the 1963 Library Law that established a firm and comprehensive foundation for the operation of a national library by legally designating a title, the National Central Library. However, the same law, paradoxically, required all publishers, including government agencies, to deposit two copies of all publications with both the NLK and the NAL.

Beginning in the 1960s, when the national government viewed the role of libraries as educational institutions, the National Central Library fell under the jurisdiction of the Ministry of Education. The 1991 Library Promotion Law, however, expanded and enhanced the role of the library as a cultural institution and transferred jurisdiction from the Ministry of Education to the Ministry of Culture. There have been several subsequent administrative reorganizations, and as of 1998 the library is under the Ministry of Culture and Tourism. In 1988 the NLK moved to its current location in the southern part of the capital city, Seoul.

The NAL was founded on 20 February 1952 in Pusan, the provisional capital of the nation during the Korean War. At the end of the war, the library moved to Seoul along with the National Assembly. The NAL began with an initial collection of 3,604 volumes, one reading room, and a staff of four.

The NAL primarily serves National Assembly members, parliamentary committees, and legislative staffs. The first comprehensive legal foundation for this library was the passage of the National Assembly Library Act on 17 December 1963. This act designated the library as one of the two official deposit libraries, and from 1964 onward it began its role as a national deposit library. In 1988, following the implementation of democratic reforms, the National Assembly Library Act was reenacted, and the library became a fully independent organization under the National Assembly.

The present NAL building was completed in October 1987 as one of the three main buildings in the National Assembly Compound in the heart of downtown Seoul.

Organizational Structure

The 1994 Library and Reading Promotion Law stipulates that the NLK be "responsible for the acquisition, processing, analysis, accumulation, and preservation of books, other types of documents, and audiovisual materials, as well as making them readily available to the public." The library is organized, under its director, into two sections, the Library Management and Library Service Departments, with six divisions and one office under them. It has relationships with many institutions and libraries in Korea and with 291 institutions in 92 countries. The NLK also operates one branch library to support public services. As of 1999 there were 216 people employed in the library, including 117 professionals and 31 administrators. In the same year, the budget was approximately 20 billion won (approximately $20 million); of this total, facilities improvement received about 33 percent while salaries received 29 percent.

As a legal deposit library, the NLK receives original materials including books, government agency publications, periodicals, recordings, audiovisual materials, maps, slides, computer software, and micromaterials. Approximately 60 percent of the total collection is legal deposit copies. The rest of the collection is acquired through purchase, exchange, donation, and so forth.

A number of classification systems and cataloging rules were formerly in use for collections housed in the National Library. Since 1945, however, Western books are classified according to the Dewey Decimal Classification (DDC) system while the Korean Decimal Classification (KDC) system is employed for oriental books and nonbook materials as well as for old and rare books.

Although the primary function of the NAL is to serve the National Assembly, it is also open to government ministries and agencies, scholars, teachers, advanced students, members of the press, and the staff of foreign embassies. Under the chief librarian, there are two offices (planning, budget, and auditing; legislative information and digital library management), two bureaus (acquisition and processing; reference services), and one division (general services). Under these there are two counselors and ten divisions. The NAL maintains relationships with about 3,000 domestic institutions and about 300 institutions worldwide. As of 1999 there were 251 employees including 173 professionals and 68 technical workers. In the same year, the budget was about 14.5 billion won (approximately $14.5 million), of which salaries were about 50 percent and digitalization and facilities improvement about 32 percent. Acquisition accounts for approximately 7 to 8 percent of the total budget.

The National Assembly Library concentrates its collection in the areas of the social sciences and humanities. Most foreign materials are purchased except those that are acquired through exchange programs. The collections of the NAL are classified according to the DDC system but are cataloged under Korean Cataloging Rules (KCR).

Automation and the Digital Library Project

The two national libraries began automation in the early 1980s. The NLK opened its first library automation office in 1982 and subsequently expanded its efforts in response to the rapid development of information technologies. It led in the automation of bibliographic controls and standardization by developing, in 1984, the Korean Machine Readable Cataloging (KOMARC) system. Through its Total System Service, the NLK offered an integrated library information system from the acquisition of materials to the provision of public service.

A comprehensive computerized library service became available to the public in 1996 when the digital library system was launched. In 1991 the effort to adapt the NLK to a digital environment culminated in the Korean Library Information Service Network (KOLIS-NET), which links the library with other libraries and institutions throughout the nation. The KOLIS-NET includes organizations such as the Korea Education and Research Information Institution, the Korean Institute of Science and Technology (KIST) Research and Development Information Center, and regional center libraries as well as unit libraries throughout the nation.

Although the NAL began an aggressive automation project in the early 1980s with the construction of online bibliographic and legislative databases, it shared a computer mainframe located in the Korea Institute for Economy and Technology (KIET) until 1989. As the project rapidly developed, the NAL built and expanded its full-text databases for legislative information. For example, full-text databases have been completed for the entire National Assembly Records and its index, the National Assembly's Inspection of State Affairs, and government reports submitted to the National Assembly for the purposes of state inspection. The automation of the NAL intensified with the opening in 1994 of the Multimedia Resources Center, where digital information resources and other audiovisual and nonprint materials such as CD-ROMs are utilized. Concurrently, the NAL was connected via intranet with an extensive local area network (LAN) infrastructure linking the offices of assembly members, parliamentary committees, political party groups, the secretariat, and the library.

A full-fledged online legislative information service began with the introduction of a NAL website in March 1996; a menu system for easy access to National Assembly materials was developed, entitled the National Assembly Total Information Online Network (NATION). Under the auspices of the Economic Planning Board, the NAL, in cooperation with the NLK and the Ministry of Education, developed a national digital library plan in 1997. In the first phase, from 1998 to 1999, the NAL selected government publications, social science dissertations, and selected image databases for inclusion. The second phase, beginning in 1999, digitizes materials related to Korea that were collected from overseas as well as selected materials from Korean academic journals, Korean doctoral dissertations, and master's theses.

Current Library Services

The NLK is the largest public library in the country. All materials in the NLK are classified according to subject areas such as humanities, and by types of materials such as serials. The collection is housed in 20 different reading rooms and in six stacks and is accessed through card catalogs and book catalogs, online public access catalogs, CD-ROM net, and via telecommunication networks and the Internet. The multimedia resources room is well equipped with audiovisual and other multimedia materials and is popular with researchers and the public.

As the general administrative center of the National Information System and the National Library Cooperative Network, the NLK is charged by law with providing instruction and support to other libraries, supervising the management of documents and information, and promoting library cooperation through the computer network infrastructure. This last task has included establishing a cooperative nationwide library network, coordinating interlibrary loans, developing and supplying the KOMARC system, and providing a national bibliography database. Internationally, the NLK provides Korean studies materials to overseas libraries and universities and participates in international forums and other cooperative and exchange activities. Among other publications, the NLK has produced the *Korean National Bibliography* since 1963.

The NLK also offers in-service training courses for civil servant librarians to improve their knowledge and skills and to enhance career opportunities. Begun in 1983, this program annually trains more than 1,400 librarians. In addition to educational programs, the library regularly holds exhibitions and cultural events, promotes reading and lifelong learning programs, and encourages local libraries to develop similar programs.

The NAL collections are housed in 15 rooms divided into closed and open stacks. Monographs and old and rare books are housed in closed stacks; the NAL maintains open stack reading rooms for master's and doctoral theses, parliamentary documents, laws and legal documents, United Nations documents, general reference materials, nonbook materials, and periodicals. The NAL is fully automated and is equipped with an online public access catalog (OPAC) for its collections. In recent years, the NAL has issued an increasing number of regular membership cards and temporary permission notes to the public in an effort to promote further utilization of the library. Among other publications, the NAL has published the *Index to National Assembly Databases*, the *Index to Periodical Articles* (1964–), and the *Index to Master's and Doctoral Degree Theses* (1945–).

The NAL provides specialized reference services to its members. For instance, the legislative information research and analysis is provided to the members of the assembly to help with legislative activities. Also, the translation and interpretation duties by professionals with area specialties is a unique NAL service. The NAL is a participating member of the Global Legal Information Network (GLIN) hosted by the U.S. Library of Congress Law Library.

MYOUNG CHUNG WILSON AND CHANSIK CHO

Further Reading

Cho, Chansik, "Development of Librarianship in South Korea, 1945–1992: A Historical Study," Ph.D. diss., Rutgers University, 1995

Guide to the National Assembly Library, Seoul: The National Assembly Library, 1997

Han, Sang-Wan, "Nambukhan munwha kyorurul euihan doseogwankwa haksuljungbo kyoru hyupruk bangan (A Suggestion on the Exchange of Library and Scholarly Information as Part of Cultural Exchange between South and North Korea)," *Kukhoe doseogwan bo* (National Assembly Library Review) 37, no. 5 (2000)

Koh, Gertrude L., "Korea, Libraries in the Republic of," in *Encyclopedia of Library and Information Science*, edited by Allen Kent et al., vol. 13, New York: Dekker, 1980

Lee, Pongsoon, and Young Ai Um, "National Libraries," in *Libraries and Librarianship in Korea*, by Lee, Westport, Connecticut: Greenwood Press, 1994

Nam, Tae-Woo, "Bukhaneu kunchoongdoseogwanyong doseoboonlupyo yungu (A Study on the Library Classification System of North Korea)," *Hankuk munheonjungbo hakheoji* (Journal of the Korean Society for Libray and Information Sienece) 34, no. 1 (2000)

The National Library of Korea, *Gungnip Jungang Doseogwan/The National Library of Korea, 1988/99*, Seoul: The National Library of Korea, 1999 (in Korean and English)

National Library of Australia

Address: National Library of Australia
Parkes Place
Canberra, Australian Capital Territory 2600
Australia
Telephone: 2-6262-1111
Fax: 2-6257-1703
www.nla.gov.au

Founded: 1901; officially named National Library of Australia, 1961

Holdings (2000): Volumes: 2.7 million. Aerial photographs 838,000; audio (oral history) recordings: 61,000; current serials: 43,000; films and videos: 16,000; graphic materials: 611,000; manuscripts: 3,000 linear feet; maps: 585,000; music scores: 175,000.

Special Collections: *Areas of Concentration:* Australian history, literature, politics, and public administration; naval exploration; New Zealand; the Pacific; Papua New Guinea. *Individual Collections:* Captain James Cook; John Alexander Ferguson; Rex Nan Kivell; Gregory M. Mathews; Edward Augustus Petherick.

Origins

The genesis of the National Library of Australia (NLA) may be found in the establishment of the Parliament of the Commonwealth of Australia in Melbourne during 1901. From the first it was understood that this parliament would eventually move to a location in a new capital city and would require its own library. Among the joint standing committees formed in that year was a library committee to inquire into the development of a library for Parliament.

There is some evidence that federal parliamentarians of the time favored a library that would do more than just provide services to members of Parliament. Ideas were expressed of a national library modeled on the U.S. Library of Congress (Washington, D.C.) with its impressive building, its reference and legislative services, its availability to the public, and the development of its collection through copyright legislation. The library committee echoed a number of these ideas, most notably in its report of 1907:

> ... the Library Committee is keeping before it the ideal of building up, for the time when Parliament shall be established in the Federal Capital, a great Public Library on the lines of the world-famed Library of Congress at Washington; such a Library, indeed, as shall be worthy of the Australian Nation; the home of the literature, not of a State, or of a period, but of the world, and of all time . . . .

The ideals were high, but in reality the Commonwealth Parliamentary Library (Melbourne), under its librarian Arthur Wadsworth, was small and modestly funded. The library's budget ranged from £500 in 1901–02 to £1,800 in 1908–09, but in many years the full amount was not spent. By 1909 the number of volumes in the library had surpassed 22,000. Although the staff included seven members in 1910, criticism of the library's disorganized state prompted the addition of a cataloger in 1911. Much of the library's activity at this time was directed toward the needs of Parliament, and the national character of the collection was slow to materialize.

Melbourne

Several events in the next few years assisted the library in developing a more national role. The first was the acquisition (by act of Parliament in 1911) of the collection of Edward Augustus Petherick, bibliographer and book collector. This brought 10,000 volumes and 6,500 pamphlets, maps, and pictures relating to Australia, New Zealand, and the Pacific into the library's collection. The second was the passage of the Copyright Act, 1912, which directed that a copy of every book published in Australia be delivered to the librarian of the parliament. The Copyright Act was immensely useful in building the collection of the future national library, but its usefulness was somewhat tempered by Wadsworth's practice of discarding many deposited publications that he considered unworthy of retention. Another significant event was the library's publication of important source material relating to the early history and settlement of Australia. A landmark in Australian historical research, *Historical Records of Australia*, first appeared in 1912 with a total of 34 volumes published by 1926. The 1923 purchase of a collection of manuscripts by

Captain James Cook gave the future national library one of its greatest treasures.

Canberra

Canberra became Australia's capital and seat of government in 1927. Government departments and agencies, including the library, were slowly transferred to the new capital. A continuing preoccupation for new librarian Kenneth Binns, who succeeded Wadsworth in 1927, was storage for the library's growing collections. In 1935 the library occupied a building designated as the national library, but its collections remained dispersed in a number of locations around the city. A positive outcome of moving to Canberra was the operation of a public library service to the residents and students of the new city, who were permitted to borrow books from the national collection.

A milestone was reached in 1936 when the library began the publication of the *Annual Catalogue of Australian Publications*, forerunner of the national bibliography. During the war years, the library's growing importance to government was evidenced by the establishment of liaison offices: in Melbourne, 1942 to 1946; London, 1944; and New York, 1945.

Growth, 1948 to 1968

In 1947 Harold White succeeded Binns as librarian, and the library embarked on an unparalleled era of growth and expansion in its collecting. Purchasing power had risen after World War II, and the library began to buy material from all over the world. White maintained an extensive correspondence with people and institutions everywhere, set up exchange arrangements, and solicited gifts and donations. The library was fortunate in securing a number of fine private collections that increased its holdings, transforming it from a gentleman's library into a truly national institution.

The most outstanding collection was that of Sir John Ferguson, judge of the New South Wales Industrial Commission. An avid bibliographer and collector, he had long been associated with the library, particularly during the compilation of his great *Bibliography of Australia* (1941–69). In 1946 he began the transfer of more than 34,000 books, pictures, and manuscripts, a process that ended in 1969 with the purchase of the remainder of his collection from his trustees. The collection remains the foundation of the library's Australiana collections and contains significant material on New Zealand and the Pacific. Previously Gregory Macalister Mathews had presented a collection of books, pictures, and manuscripts on Australian ornithology. In 1959 the library obtained the first part of the collection of Sir Rex Nan Kivell, a rich assemblage of material including books, maps, manuscripts, and photographs and pictures on the early history of Australia, New Zealand, and the Pacific.

World War II had revealed certain fundamental weaknesses in the library's holdings relating to East and Southeast Asia. This was corrected in the postwar period, laying the foundation for the library's present collections of vernacular materials from that part of the world, which are significant. Material from Indonesia began to be collected from the early 1950s and eventually resulted in the establishment of a permanent cooperative acquisition scheme operated on behalf of a number of Australian libraries and the establishment of an acquisition office in Jakarta in 1970. Chinese language materials were collected from the mid-1950s and strengthened with a number of private collections. The development of the Japanese collection dates from the war years when the library took over a collection of books left behind by the departing Japanese embassy at the outbreak of war. Other collections were subsequently bought to augment the material. The collection of Korean material dates from the early 1950s and the library's Thai collections from 1957.

National Library Act

From 1935 the library had been granted an annual sum from the prime minister's department to support its extra-parliamentary or national functions. Beginning with £2,500 in 1935–36, the sum steadily rose thereafter. It was an unsatisfactory arrangement, giving control of expenses to a department not responsible for the library. In 1956 Parliament appointed a committee chaired by Sir George Paton, vice-chancellor of the University of Melbourne, to "examine the whole question of the National Library and its functions and advise whether any change in the present form of control is desirable, and, if so, the changes which should be made." The report was presented the following year and recommended the separation of the Parliamentary Library, the National Library, and the Government Archives. The National Library was to be placed under the control of a board responsible to a minister. In 1960 legislation was passed establishing the National Library on a statutory basis and outlining its functions.

The Paton report had also strongly recommended the provision of a new building to alleviate the crowded conditions in Parliament House and the overflow into ten buildings, huts, and basements scattered about Canberra. In 1964 work began on a functional semiclassical building that was opened in August 1968.

Services to the Nation

Allan Fleming became national librarian in 1970. During his time the question of establishing a national scientific and technological information authority was examined. In 1974–75 the library was funded to manage a program of consultation and planning for an Australian library-based information system. George Chandler succeeded Fleming (as director-general, rather than national librarian) in 1974. He reorganized the library and cooperated with other libraries in an attempt to bring about some of the recommendations on science and technology and a library-based information system. Due to a period of severe financial restraint in government, the subject-based services he set up in science and technology, the social sciences, and the humanities could not be maintained.

More successful was the library's increasing use of technology. It pioneered the introduction of computer-based information services in Australia and identified the need for resource-sharing networks, specifically a national online cataloging network. In 1979 the library identified the Washington (D.C.) Library Network (WLN) as suitable for its needs and began using its system. Harrison Bryan, who became director-general in 1980, sought and won acceptance from the Australian library community for the introduction of a national shared cataloging system known as the Australian Bibliographic Network (ABN). This service provided Australia with a truly national online cataloging system and union catalog.

Increasing its involvement in the international scene, the library established the Australian International Standard Bibliographic Number (ISBN) agency in 1967, followed by the International Standard Serial Number (ISSN) agency in 1983. The *Australian National Bibliography* was redesigned along the lines of the *British National Bibliography* and automated in 1971. The library participated in committees and groups working to develop or revise bibliographic standards. It issued addenda volumes to Ferguson's *Bibliography of Australia,* and in 1988 the long-awaited *Australian National Bibliography, 1901–1950,* was published.

During the 1980s the operation of the public library system was transferred to local government and the film and sound collections to the newly established National Film and Sound Archive. But the library was active in developing other national and international activities. Coordination of preservation and conservation work, library services for people with disabilities, and assistance to libraries in the developing world, especially those of Asia and Oceania, became important new areas of work.

Access to Information

Under Warren Horton, director-general from 1985 to 1999, the NLA reassessed its role. It reaffirmed its core function, that of building the Australian collection and operating a national library infrastructure. The educational, publishing, and public relations roles of the library were strengthened. A new collection development policy was issued in 1991, and the library began to reduce its collecting from some overseas countries (principally Europe) on the grounds that other Australian libraries collected this material. The change recognized that the vision of the founding fathers for a large universal library had never materialized; economic restraints, combined with the urgent need to address other forms of Australiana such as electronic publications, made the decision inevitable.

The final years of the 20th century saw the library increasingly involved with technologies to enhance access to its collections. The library's large card catalogs were converted (1988 to 1992), and a computer catalog, together with an integrated library management system, was introduced. In 1995 the library began to offer services from its website. An archive for preserving Australian online publications, Preserving and Accessing Networked Documentary Resources of Australia (PANDORA), was pioneered. An attempt to develop a futuristic new national network in conjunction with the National Library of New Zealand did not come to fruition, and in 1999 the library replaced ABN with a system named Kinetica, based on the Canadian AMICUS system. Following the completion of Horton's second seven-year term (1999), Deputy Director-General Jan Fullerton was appointed director-general of NLA. Digitization of collection items commenced, and the library took steps to integrate access to its own collections and the growing number of electronic resources available, providing a solid foundation for unmediated access to documentary resources in Australia and throughout the world.

JAN FULLERTON

Further Reading

Biskup, Peter, and Margaret Henty, editors, *Library for the Nation,* Belconne, Capital Territory: Australian Academic and Research Libraries, and Canberra National Library of Australia, 1991

Burmester, C.A., *National Library of Australia: Guide to the Collections,* 4 vols., Canberra: National Library of Australia, 1974–82

Kenny, Janice, *National Library of Australia: History and Collections,* Canberra: National Library of Australia, 1984

Osborn, Andrew, and Margaret Osborn, *The Commonwealth Parliamentary Library, 1901–27, and the Origins of the National Library of Australia,* Canberra: Department of the Parliamentary Library, 1989

National Library of Brazil

Address: Fundaçáo Biblioteca Nacional
Avenida Rio Branco, 219
Rio de Janeiro, RJ, 20040-008
Brazil
Telephone: 21-262-8255
Fax: 21-220-4173
www.bn.br

Founded: 1810

Holdings (1999): Volumes: 1.45 million. Current serials: 20,000; engravings: 37,000; graphic materials: 200,000; incunabula: 216; manuscripts: 800,000, including 200 medieval manuscripts; maps: 26,000; microforms: 20,000; music scores: 150,000; sound recordings: 29,000.

Special Collections: *Areas of Concentration:* Agriculture; botany; Braziliana; Brazilian history; chemistry; Latin American music; mathematics; medicine; physics; social sciences; zoology. *Individual Collections:* Rare books; Royal Library collection.

The National Library of Brazil began its existence as the Royal Library of Portugal, refounded in the Ajuda Palace after the 1 November 1755 Lisbon earthquake and resultant conflagration had destroyed the royal library in the Ribeira Palace. Thanks to the gold and diamond mines in Brazil, the Portuguese crown was wealthy enough to reconstruct a worthy substitute within a few years, complete with a respectable number of incunabula and other rarities. The basis of the new collection was the library of the bibliophile and historian Nicolau Francisco Xavier da Silva, who had died on 17 August 1754 and left his books to the king of Portugal. The following collections were added: the "magnificent" library of Tomé de Sousa Coutino Castelo Branco, 11th Count of O Redondo, bequeathed by his second wife Margarida de Velhena in 1757; the library of José Freire Montarroio Mascarenhas, the widely traveled "father of Portuguese journalism"; and the 5,764 books given by the bibliophile-bibliographer Diogo Barbosa Machado from 1770 to 1773. The repressive measures of the king's all-powerful minister Sebastião José de Carvalho e Melo, marquis of Pombal, added books from the victims of his purge of the old aristocracy and expulsion of the Society of Jesus from 1758 to 1760. Notable among these were the library of Leonor Tomásia, marchioness of Távora (decapitated in January 1759); the library of José de Mascarenhas, eighth duke of Aveiro (broken on the wheel the same day); the library of the Jesuit Colegio de Todos os Santos on the Azores; and the collections of the "children of Palhavã" (the royal bastards Antonio and José, exiled in 1760). The library received a copy of everything printed by the government press from its establishment by Pombal in 1768, and its accessions were further enhanced by the 12 September 1805 enactment of a copyright deposit law (reinforced by later Brazilian legislation in 1822, 1847, 1853, 1865, and 1907).

In 1807 Napoleon attacked Portugal, and the court and government accepted the offer of naval escort to safety in Rio de Janeiro from Portugal's old ally and economically dominant partner, Great Britain. The royal library followed, in three consignments, in July 1810 and in March and November 1811. The collection was ordered housed on the upper floor of Rio's Carmelite monastery in what is now Rua Primeiro de Maio, and its installation there on 29 October 1810 is now regarded as its official foundation date. The following year it became available for consultation by scholars as an act of royal grace, but it was not open to the general public until 1814. When it arrived in Brazil it was, by far, the largest national library in Latin America and one of the world's major book collections, but the library did not formally pass into Brazilian ownership until Pedro I, the new emperor of an independent Brazil, made the retention of almost the entire library a condition of the peace treaty of 29 August 1825. In 1822, the year of independence, the library acquired the 6,300-volume library of former chief minister António de Araújo e Azevedo, first count of Barca, whose diplomatic career had taken him to The Hague, Paris, Rome, and St. Petersburg. The library also acquired 5,000 volumes from the "Patriarch of Brazilian Independence," José Bonifácio the elder, in 1838.

However much Portugal and Brazil were tied to Britain economically, culturally they were to remain, for the next century and a half, in thrall to France. Even the word *livraria* came to be understood as *librarie* and was supplanted by *biblioteca* in its original sense. After Waterloo, João VI had given the job of librarian to one of the many Bonapartist exiles in Brazil (under supervision of Bishop Gregório José Viegas), and he was followed in the 1840s by Camille Cléau, illegitimate grandson of the last Bourbon king. French methods and attitudes were to dominate in the library (as in the book trade) until the 1930s.

In 1858 the library was moved to the Rua do Passeio, into what is now the Music School of the University of Rio de Janeiro. In 1876 it held 120,000 volumes and 3,000 current periodicals, and its annual budget was almost trebled, from 25 contos (almost $50,000) to 68 contos ($135,000), which had permitted the launch of its regular *Anais* (annals). In 1878 it was renamed, *a la française*, the Biblioteca Nacional. In 1889, when Brazil became a republic, the library held 170,000 volumes plus the Coleção Teresa Cristina Maria of 50,000 volumes left by the last emperor, Pedro II, prior to going into exile. Construction of the present building, designed for 400,000 volumes, was begun on 15 August 1905 on the then newly built Avenida Rio Branco in the heart of downtown Rio, and the new building opened on 29 October 1910 (between 1922 and 1926 it temporarily housed the House of Deputies). The library has suffered since the 1950s from inadequate funding for maintenance, acquisitions, and staffing, although cooperation with the U.S. Library of Congress led to an ambitious microfilming project intended to cover (among other things) all Brazilian newspapers and 19th-century government documents. The decision not to transfer the library with other federal agencies to Brasília in 1960 was perhaps justified by the greater demand for its services in Rio but left the new capital without a public library.

The library was reformed when Rubem Ludwig, probably the most energetic minister of education and culture under the military regime of 1964 to 1985, undertook between 1982 and 1983 the most drastic overhaul of the building and its services since the move into the new building in 1910. He persuaded librarian Célia Ribeiro Zaher to return from her post with the United Nations Educational, Scientific, and Cultural Organization (UNESCO) to oversee the changes, and Ludwig improved the institution's finances by placing them under the Fundação Pro Memória. The building's serious lack of storage space at the time was somewhat alleviated in 1984 when an annex was acquired in nearby Palacio Gustavo Capanema, 16 rua da Imprensa.

By 1990 the staff consisted of 71 librarians (154 established posts) and 250 clerical workers (352 established posts), but 192 positions were cut in June 1990 by President Fernando Collor, who combined a general anti-intellectual outlook with an extreme dedication to free market principles and hostility to all government-run enterprises. The library suffered in consequence, but fortunately Collor was successfully impeached for corruption in 1992. His successor as president of the republic, Itamar Franco, permitted another reform of the library in 1994, mainly achieved through the use of outside funding, when the library became a *fundação* (a type of semiautonomous state agency) in its own right. One important result was a program to digitize much of the more valuable holdings, particularly maps and music.

The library has offered training courses in library science since 1911, although these have long since lost their original unique nature and importance (Brazil now has some 30 library schools in as many universities). Its function as an official register of copyright is less important under UNESCO's international copyright agreement (only 3,537 authors used it in 1986, when Brazil's output of new monograph titles was close to 10,000), but the library has acquired a special importance as the nation's International Standard Bibliographic Number (ISBN) agency.

LAURENCE HALLEWELL

Further Reading

Bates, Margaret J., "Libraries in Rio de Janeiro," *ALA Bulletin* 36 (1942)

"Biblioteca Nacional, 180 anos," *COFI* 126 (September/October 1990)

Biblioteca Nacional (Brazil): Relatório da Diretora-Geral, 1986, Rio de Janeiro: Biblioteca Nacional, 1987

"A Biblioteca Nacional do Brasil," *CBL informa* 85, no. 7 (April 1990)

"Bibliotecas," in *Grande enciclopédia portuguesa e brasileira*, vol. 4, Lisbon and Rio de Janeiro: Editorial Enciclopédia, 1935

"Bibliotecas," in *Grande enciclopédia portuguesa e brasileira: 2. parte: Brasil*, vol. 1, Lisbon: Editorial Enciclopédia, 1967

"Brazil, Libraries in," in *Encyclopedia of Library and Information Science*, edited by Allen Kent et al., vol. 4, New York: Dekker, 1970

Cardozo, Manoel S., "The National Library of Brazil," *Hispanic American Historical Review* 26 (1949)

Doyle, Plinio, *Biblioteca Nacional, 1810–1910–1980*, Rio de Janeiro: Biblioteca Nacional, 1980

Guia da Biblioteca Nacional, Rio de Janeiro: Biblioteca Nacional, 1960

Herkenhoff, Paulo, *Biblioteca Nacional: A história de uma coleção*, Rio de Janeiro: Salamandra, 1996

Maia, Alicia Barros, *Biblioteca Nacional*, Rio de Janeiro: Biblioteca Nacional, 1984

Monte-Mor, Janice, "Reforma da Biblioteca Nacional," *Ciência da informação* 1, no. 1 (1972)

"National and Special," in *Developing Libraries in Brazil, with a Chapter on Paraguay*, by Cavan M. McCarthy, Metuchen, New Jersey: Scarecrow Press, 1975

Santos, Hamilton dos, "Fundação pode salvar a Biblioteca Nacional," *Estado de São Paulo* (18 July 1990)

Santos, Hamilton dos, "Poeta na Biblioteca Nacional," *Estado de São Paulo* (27 November 1990)

REF Z 721 .I57 2001 v.1

International dictionary of
library histories

DISCARDED
URI LIBRARY